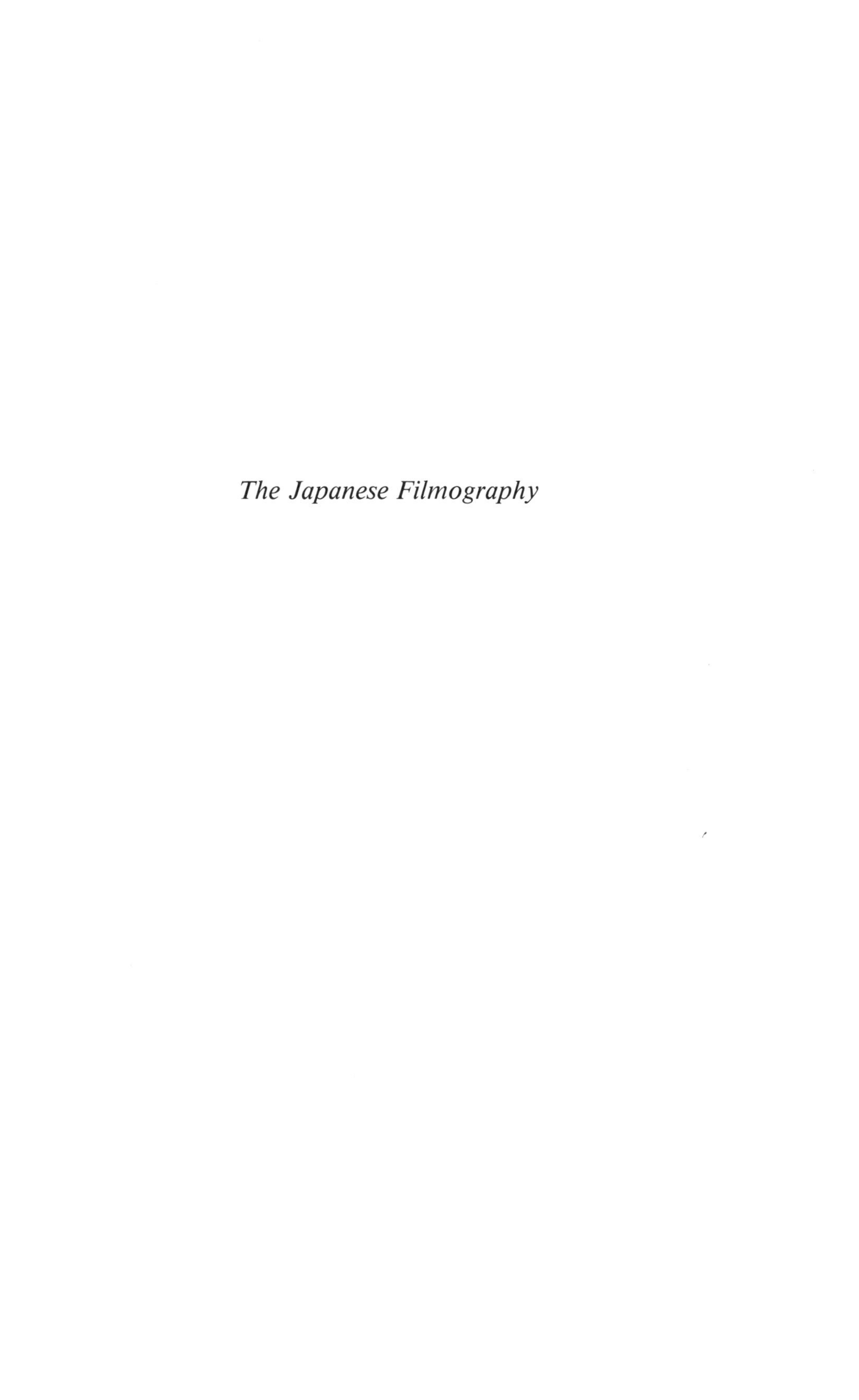

The Japanese Filmography

ALSO BY STUART GALBRAITH IV

Japanese Science Fiction,
Fantasy and Horror Films
(McFarland, 1994)

Motor City Marquees
(McFarland, 1994)

The Japanese Filmography

A Complete Reference to 209 Filmmakers and the Over 1250 Films Released in the United States, 1900 through 1994

by Stuart Galbraith IV

McFarland & Company, Inc., Publishers
Jefferson, North Carolina, and London

British Library Cataloguing-in-Publication data are available

Library of Congress Cataloguing-in-Publication Data

Galbraith, Stuart, 1965–
The Japanese filmography : a complete reference to 209 filmmakers and the over 1250 films released in the United States, 1900 through 1994 / by Stuart Galbraith IV.
p. cm.
Includes bibliographical references and index.
ISBN 0-7864-0032-3 (lib. bdg. : 50# alk. paper)
1. Motion pictures – Japan – Catalogs. 2. Motion pictures – Japan – Biography – Dictionaries. I. Title.
PN1993.5.J3G35 1996
016.79143'0952 – dc20 95-23421
CIP

Manufactured in the United States of America

McFarland & Company, Inc., Publishers
Box 611, Jefferson, North Carolina 28640

Respectfully dedicated to
Akira Kurosawa
and
Toshiro Mifune

and to the memory of
Takashi Shimura

Acknowledgments

My deepest gratitude to the following individuals and organizations without whom this book would not exist: Tony Sol, who was lucky enough to live in Los Angeles during the glory days of the Toho La Brea, the Kokusai, and Linda Lea, and offered tremendous insight to films that have not been seen in the United States in far too many years; credits expert Michael Hayes (where does he get this stuff?); *kaiju eiga* fan extraordinaire Guy Tucker, who took time out from his own book on Japanese sci-fi pictures to help point out the sizable contributions of such luminous Toho bit players as Senkichi Omura and Kenzo Tabu; David Milner, who graciously made himself available at all hours to answer questions and offer sage advice; Chris D, whose expertise in Daiei and Toei action films was most appreciated; Steve Hanson and Ned Comstock at the Cinema-Television Library at the University of Southern California; Rick Jewell, Drew Casper and Darrell Davis for their suggestions and support; and Anne Sharp Galbraith, whose kindness and generosity helped make this book possible.

Also: Norihiko Asao, Cinema Collectors, Mike Copner and *Cult Movies*, Yukari Fujii, Stuart (III) and Mary Galbraith, Kimi and Ryuji Honda, Akira Ifukube, Koichi Kawakita, the staff of the Margaret Herrick Library, Osamu Kishikawa, Takashi Nakao, Minoru Nakano, Ted Okuda and *Filmfax*, August Ragone, Steve Ryfle, Masaru Sato, Kenpachiro Satsuma, Clarence and Edie Sharp, Yoshiko Shibata, Yasutaka Shioda, Yoshio Tsuchiya, Moto Yokoyama, and Yuko Yoshikawa.

Table of Contents

Acknowledgments vii
Introduction 1
How to Use This Book 5

Personnel 7
Studios 87
Feature Films 91

Appendices
Appendix I. A Chronology 463
Appendix II. Japanese Home Market Statistics 467
Appendix III. Awards 473
Appendix IV. Animated Features 487

Selected Bibliography 489
Index of Titles and Alternate Titles 491

Introduction

With the release of Akira Kurosawa's *Rashomon* (1950), Western audiences became enamored of Japanese cinema. It was the first Japanese feature to receive anything like a wide release in the United States, and by a major distributor, RKO. Within just a few years, American audiences were introduced to Mizoguchi's *Ugetsu* and Kinugasa's *Gate of Hell*, among others, and the critical and relative commercial boom was strong enough to support, if only in the largest cities, movie theaters which exhibited *exclusively* Japanese films. These theaters catered not only to the Japanese-Americans of our Little Tokyos and Japantowns, but to filmgoers of all ethnicities who simply enjoyed good movies.

Sadly, the rise of the cable and video industries in the late 1970s, combined with maddening distribution restrictions enacted by certain Japanese film companies, put such theaters out of business. Los Angeles boasted a half-dozen Japanese-language theaters in the 1960s; there is not one in 1995. The Japanese film industry itself is but a shadow of its glorious past; gone are its days as the most prolific feature film-producer in the world (producing a record 547 features and featurettes in 1959 alone, out-producing even India). Precious little of its product is released in the United States. Even Kurosawa appears to have lost much of his stateside audience (at least in the minds of potential theatrical and home video distributors). His brilliant, underrated 1991 film *Rhapsody in August* was barely released in the United States, and his 1993 *Madadayo* has, as this book went to press, yet to be shown beyond the festival circuit. Even Juzo Itami, the actor-turned-director whose *Tampopo* seemed to revitalize the American market for Japanese features, is facing similar distribution difficulties.

Even in the realm of video cassettes a great many classics—films by Mizoguchi, Ozu, Oshima, Kurosawa, Kinoshita, Toyoda, etc.—are presently unavailable, to say nothing of the exciting genre work of Yamada, Honda, Fukuda, Misumi, and Fukasaku. Many appreciators of these films have gone so far as to purchase *Japanese* videotapes and laserdiscs of these movies; the dialogue may not be understandable but it is the only way many in the West can see them.

Many of the Japanese films that *are* available on videotape present problems of their own. One of the biggest—and the main reason this book was written—is in crediting the key individuals in front of and behind the camera. American versions of Japanese films, both dubbed and subtitled, often list only the director and a few actors in their credits, leaving out all the others, and defeating the aims of serious criticism and scholarship. It has heretofore been difficult to know if the guy who played the kidnapper in this film is the same guy who played the truck driver in that film.

While much admirable work has been done in the area of theory-oriented writing on Japanese cinema—from the indispensable Donald Richie to Noël Burch—a good deal of very basic reference work needs to be done. It is surprising that something as fundamental as an English-language book on actor Toshiro Mifune—Japan's biggest star and one of the cinema's greatest actors—has yet to be published.

The purpose of this work is to provide the reader with a detailed reference to 1,300 or so of the most important and or interesting Japanese features that were once, are presently, or might someday soon become available for viewing in the United States. Of course this is a tricky issue—some of the films listed were shown on an extremely limited basis (generally limited to Japanese American neighborhood venues, or as part of a festival or retrospective), and have not been heard from in many years. I have been somewhat selective in those films not yet released in the United States or whose distribution is uncertain. I have tried to include every Japanese feature presently available on videotape or laserdisc, as well as those which are reasonably accessible for distribution in 16 and 35mm. I have included several dozen lost films from important directors (notably Ozu and Mizoguchi) because of their standing in world cinema, as well as notable (and often surprising) international coproductions and American films shot in Japan using funds tied up there.

Perhaps most importantly, I have tried to sort out the many familiar, popular and important actors and actresses, directors, screenwriters, composers and cameramen so that one might learn that the actor who played the kidnapper in *High and Low* is indeed the same guy who played the truck driver-noodle expert in *Tampopo*.

A few words of caution: Research has confirmed what many have long believed: The line between the high art of Ozu, Oshima, and Teshigahara, and the much-maligned Japanese genre film—Yakuza thrillers, monster movies, karate films—is much thinner than one might expect. The nature of the studio system in Japan and its prolific output was such that actors and technicians scurried from film to film with some rather surprising results. For instance, Eiji Okada, star of *Hiroshima mon amour* and *The Woman in the Dunes*, once battled a giant reptilian chicken in *The X from Outer Space*. Actors the caliber of Toshiro Mifune and Chishu Ryu (Ozu's favorite patriarchal figure) appeared in Tora-san comedies. Ken Uehara, star of the acclaimed *The Story of Tank Commander Nishizumi*, was a semiregular in Toho's "Young Guy" series. These are not films to be denigrated. They were polished, sometimes even lavish productions, created by a studio system rivaled only by Hollywood (though Japan's lasted considerably longer).

Japanese films can and should be more accessible in the United States. With this book, the reader may, at long last, sort through what has made it to these shores thus far.

STUART GALBRAITH IV
August 1995

How to Use This Book

Personnel entries are listed as follows

Name Birth date. Education. Death date (where appropriate). Capsule biography.
Filmography.

Names are written in the Hepburn system (favored in international business, literature, the press, and films), and are listed in the Western order: individual name first, family name last (i.e., Kenji Mizoguchi as opposed to Mizoguchi Kenji), although they are of course alphabetized by family name.

As Japanese names are often difficult for even the Japanese to read, they have, in the past, often been mistransliterated. Whenever possible, they have been corrected or standardized for this book. For example, one of the most familiar character actors in Japanese movies is almost always misbilled as "Akira Nishimura." His real name is Ko Nishimura, and that is how his name is listed throughout the book. Common mistranslated forms of names are cross-referenced.

Names in boldface within the capsule biography (e.g., "she was a favorite of **Kenji Mizoguchi**. . .") indicate that the subject has or had a particularly strong tie to that person or film series. The reader is advised to refer to that entry for additional data.

Studio entries are listed as follows

Studio Capsule history.

Names in boldface within the capsule history indicate a particularly strong tie to that person or film series. The reader is advised to refer to that entry for additional information.

Film entries are listed as follows

> ***U.S. Release Title / Japanese Release Title*** ("Translation of Japanese Title"). Production credits, including, where known, producer(s), director, screenwriter(s), director of photography, et al.
>
> CAST: actors (and their roles).
>
> Production company. Japanese distributor (if different). Sound format (when known). Black and white or color. Screen shape (e.g., Academy ratio, ToeiScope, Panavision, etc.). Running time of Japanese version. Release date in Japan.
>
> U.S. VERSION: U.S. distributor. English subtitles or English-dubbed. Production credits for U.S. version (subtitles, etc.). Running time of American version. MPAA rating (if any). Release date of American version.

Note: Animated features, documentaries, short film compilations and the like are listed in boldface in brackets (e.g., **[Animated]**) following the translation of the Japanese title, and prior to the production credits.

The filmography portion lists films alphabetically by the *original* theatrical or home video release title, which is why *Seven Samurai* is listed under "M" for *The Magnificent Seven*, and *Ugetsu* under "T" for *Tales of Ugetsu*.

Frequently used alternate titles are cross-referenced (such as *Alone in the Pacific* for *My Enemy the Sea*), but the more obscure and unconfirmed ones (such as *Macbeth* for *Throne of Blood*) are noted in the film entry only.

Personnel

Nick Adams Actor. *b.* Nicholas Adamshock, July 10, 1931, Nanticoke, Pennsylvania. *d.* 1968. *ed.* St. Peter's Coll. A rising American film star during the 1950s and early 1960s, Adams appeared in such films as *Mister Roberts, Picnic, Rebel Without a Cause* (all 1955), *No Time for Sergeants, Teacher's Pet* (1958), *The Interns* (1962), and *Twilight of Honor* (1963). For the latter he was nominated for an Academy Award, but virtually overnight his fortunes tumbled and the actor aged noticeably. He was brought to Japan by producer Henry G. Saperstein as part of a co-production deal with Toho, where Adams earned the respect of the Japanese crew. He remains the only professional Hollywood actor to gain stardom in Japanese films. He had an affair with actress **Kumi Mizuno**, and made two more films, but the following year Adams died of a drug overdose.

Films Include: Frankenstein Conquers the World [Jap/US], Monster Zero [Jap/US] (1965); The Killing Bottle (1967).

Yasushi Akutagawa Composer. *b.* July 12, 1925. *ed.* Tokyo College of Music. *d.* 198?. Prolific film composer from 1949 most associated with director **Kon Ichikawa**.

Films Include: Young People (1952); Gate of Hell (1953); The Heart (1955); The Pit (1957); Odd Obsession, Fires on the Plain (1959); Her Brother, A Woman's Testament, Bonchi (1960); Ten Dark Women, Eternity of Love (1961); Being Two Isn't Easy, The Outcast (1962); An Actor's Revenge, My Enemy the Sea (1963); The Scarlet Camellia (1964); Portrait of Hell (1969); The Shadow Within (1970); The Castle of Sand (1974); Mt. Hakkoda, The Demon, Village of Eight Gravestones (1977); The Incident (1978); Nichiren (1979).

Eisei Amamoto Actor. *b.* January 2, 1926. *ed.* Tokyo University. Gaunt, even bony eccentric character actor specializing in wildly theatrical villains. In films since 1954, Amamoto remains a cult figure in Japan. He is best remembered in the West as the husband in Kinoshita's *Twenty-Four Eyes* (his debut), the evil megalomaniac "Dr. Who" in Toho's sci-fi fantasy *King Kong Escapes* (1967), and the kindly toymaker in *Godzilla's Revenge* (1969).

Films Include: Twenty-Four Eyes (1954); Samurai Saga, The Three Treasures (1959); The Secret of the Telegian (1960); Daredevil in the Castle, Yojimbo (1961); Gorath (1962); Attack of the Mushroom People, The Lost World of Sinbad, Atragon (1963); The Weed of Crime, Dagora the Space Monster, Ghidrah—The Three-Headed Monster (1964); What's Up Tiger Lily? [US production incorporating Japanese footage], The Sword of Doom, Ebirah Horror of the Deep (1966); King Kong Escapes [Jap/US], The Age of Assassins, Kojiro, The Killing Bottle, The Emperor and the General (1967); Mighty Jack [made for TV], Kill (1968); Godzilla's Revenge, Portrait of Hell (1969); The Battle of Okinawa (1971); Message from Space (1978).

Ichiro Arishima Actor. *b.* Tadao Oshima, March 3, 1916, in Nagoya. *d.* 1987. Beloved comedy star, mainly at Toho, and a regular of that studio's "Young Guy" and "Company President" film series. Orphaned as a teenager, he turned to the theater in the mid-1930s, and entered films at Shochiku in 1947. He moved to Toho in 1955, where he became one of Japan's most familiar supporting players. Active in films, theater, and television until his death.

Films Include: Wakai no chi wa moete (1947); The Princess of Badger Palace, Romance and Rhythm, The Rickshaw Man (1958); The Three Treasures (1959); My Friend Death, Weaker Sex, The Dangerous Kiss (1960); The Diplomat's Mansion, Oban's Dipping Contest (1961); Bull of the Campus, Pride of the Campus, Tatsu, Chushingura, King Kong vs. Godzilla (1962); The Lost World of Sinbad (1963); The Rabble, The Sandal Keeper (1964); Ironfinger (1965); Campus A-Go-Go, It Started in the Alps, Come Marry Me (1966); Judo Champion, Las Vegas Free-for-All, Swindler Meets Swindler (1967); Young Guy Graduates, Young Guy on Mt. Cook (1969); Bravo Young Guy, The Ambush—Incident at Blood Pass (1970).

Yoshitaka Asama Screenwriter, director. *b.* 1940, in Miyagi. A screenwriter closely associated with **Yoji Yamada**; together they have written all of

Yamada's "Tora-san" films from *Tora-san, the Good Samaritan* (1971). In 1979, Asama turned to directing as well, with mixed success.

FILMS INCLUDE **[as screenwriter or co-screenwriter]**: Tora-san the Good Samaritan, Tora-san's Love Call (1971); Tora-san's Dear Old Home, Tora-san's Dream-Come-True (1972); Tora-san's Forget Me Not, Tora-san Loves an Artist (1973); Tora-san's Lovesick, Tora-san's Lullaby (1974); Tora-san's Rise and Fall, The Village, Tora-san the Intellectual (1975); Tora-san's Sunrise and Sunset, Tora's Pure Love (1976); Tora-san Meets His Lordship, The Yellow Handkerchief, Tora-san Plays Cupid (1977); Stage-Struck Tora-san, Branch School Diary, Talk of the Town Tora-san (1978); Tora-san the Matchmaker, Tora-san's Dream of Spring (1979); Tora-san's Tropical Fever, A Distant Cry from Spring, Foster Daddy Tora! (1980); Tora-san's Love in Osaka, Tora-san's Promise (1981); Hearts and Flowers for Tora-san, Tora-san the Expert (1982); Tora-san's Song of Love, Tora-san Goes Religious? (1983); Tora-san's Forbidden Love (1984); Tora-san the Go-Between, Tora-san's Island Encounter (1985); Final Take, Tora-san's Bluebird Fantasy (1986); Tora-san Goes North, Tora-san Plays Daddy (1987); Hope and Pain, Tora-san's Salad-Day Memorial (1988); Tora-san Goes to Vienna, Tora-san My Uncle (1989); Tora-san Takes a Vacation (1990); Tora-san Confesses, My Sons (1991); Tora-san Makes Excuses (1992); Tora-san's Matchmaker (1993); **[as director]**: Wonderful World of Music (1979); A Long Way 'Round (1980); Story of Him and Me (1981); Extra (1982); Story of an Exciting Beach (1987); Children on the Island (1987).

Kiyoshi Atsumi Actor. *b.* 1928, in Tokyo. Much-loved character actor, in films from 1948, and best known for his starring role in Yoji Yamada's **"Tora-san"** film series, all of which have starred Atsumi.

FILMS INCLUDE: Attack Squadron! (1963); Bwana Toshi (1965); The Man Without a Map, The Sexploiters (1968); Am I Trying, Tora-san Part 2 (1969); Tora-san His Tender Love, Tora-san's Grand Scheme, Tora-san's Runaway (1970); Tora-san's Shattered Romance, Tora-san the Good Samaritan, Tora-san's Love Call (1971); Tora-san's Dear Old Home, Tora-san's Dream-Come-True (1972); Tora-san's Forget Me Not, Tora-san Loves an Artist (1973); Tora-san's Lovesick, Tora-san's Lullaby (1974); The Village, Tora-san's Rise and Fall, Tora-san the Intellectual (1975); Tora-san's Sunrise and Sunset, Tora's Pure Love (1976); Village of Eight Gravestones, Tora-san Meets His Lordship, Tora-san Plays Cupid (1977); Stage-Struck Tora-san, Talk of the Town Tora-san (1978); Tora-san the Matchmaker, Tora-san's Dream of Spring (1979); Tora's Tropical Fever, Foster Daddy Tora! (1980); Tora-san's Love in Osaka, Tora-san's Promise (1981); Hearts and Flowers for Tora-san, Tora-san the Expert (1982); Tora-san's Song of Love, Tora-san Goes Religious? (1983); Marriage Counselor Tora-san, Tora-san's Forbidden Love (1984); Tora-san the Go-Between, Tora-san's Island Encounter (1985); Tora-san's Bluebird Fantasy, Final Take (1986); Tora-san Goes North, Children on the Island, Tora-san Plays Daddy (1987); Hope and Pain, Tora-san's Salad-Day Memorial (1988); Tora-san Goes to Vienna, Tora-san My Uncle (1989); Tora-san Takes a Vacation (1990); Tora-san Confesses (1991); Tora-san Makes Excuses (1992); Tora-san's Matchmaker (1993).

Chieko Baisho Actress. *b.* 1941, in Tokyo. Petite character actress in films from 1961. Best known as **Tora-san**'s long-suffering sister; she has appeared in all of the entries. Her younger sister, Mitsuko Baisho (b. 1946), is also an actress.

FILMS INCLUDE (see above for Baisho's *Tora-san* credits): Where Spring Comes Late (1970); The Village (1975); Two Iida (1976); A Distant Cry from Spring (1980); Station (1981); Final Take, Lost in the Wilderness (1986).

Minoru Chiaki Actor. *b.* July 30, 1917, in Hokkaido. Popular character actor in films from 1949, and best remembered for his work in **Akira Kurosawa**'s films of the 1950s. Chiaki was the cheerful woodcutter in *Seven Samurai* (1954), and the dopey peasant paired with **Kamatari Fujiwara** in *The Hidden Fortress* (1958), the latter character the basis for "C-3PO" in *Star Wars* (1977). His film work tapered off dramatically beginning in the late 1960s, but he received a Japanese Academy Award for his work in *Grey Sunset* (1985).

FILMS INCLUDE: Stray Dog (1949); Rashomon (1950); The Idiot (1951); Seven Samurai, The Story of Shunkin (1954), Gigantis the Fire Monster, I Live in Fear (1955); Throne of Blood, The Lower Depths, The Men of Tohoku (1957); The Hidden Fortress, The Flower (1958); Saga of the Vagabonds, The Human Condition II (1959); The Youth and His Amulet (1961); The Inheritance, The Body (1962); High and Low [cameo] (1963); The Face of Another (1966); Innocent Sinner (1970); Grey Sunset (1985).

Shinichi "Sonny" Chiba Actor, stunt coordinator. *b.* Sadao Maeda, January 23, 1939, in Fukuoka. The son of a test pilot, Shinichi and his four siblings moved to a Chiba military base during World War II. Brought to Toei as part of that studio's 1960 New Face Contest, Chiba was quickly signed to two teleseries that same year: "Rainbow Week" and "Messenger of Allah." He eventually starred in more than two dozen TV shows, including "Darkness: 5th Degree" and "JNR Conductor 36." At the same time, films such as *Key Hunter* (1968) bolstered his theatrical film career, and by the early 1970s Chiba had achieved an international following with his wildly popular "Street Fighter" karate film series. His brother, Jiro Yabuki [Chiba] is also a film star.

FILMS INCLUDE: The Drifting Detective [debut], Invasion of the Neptune Men (1961); Terror Beneath the Sea, The Golden Bat (1966); Key Hunter (1968); Memoir of Japanese Assassins (1969); The Street Fighter (1975); The Executioner, The Return of the Street Fighter, Sister Street Fighter [cameo], The Bodyguard (1976); Champion of Death (1977); Message from Space (1978); The Street Fighter's Last Revenge, Hunter in the Dark (1979); Time Slip, Virus (1980); Samurai Reincarnation, The Bloody Bushido Blade, Karate Killer, Time Slip (1981); Legend of the Eight Samurai, Shogun's Ninja (1983); Sure Death 4 (1987); Tetsuro Tamba's Spirit World, The School [also prod.], Shogun's Shadow (1989); Yellow Fang [also dir.] (1990); Aces: Iron Eagle III [US] (1992).

Yasuki Chiba Director. *b.* 1910. Toho genre director specializing in genre comedies and co-productions with Hong Kong.

FILMS INCLUDE: Downtown (1955); Different Sons, A Night in Hong Kong (1961); Born in Sin, Star of Hong Kong (1962); Honolulu–Tokyo–Hong Kong (1963); Night in Bangkok, The Daphne (1966).

Harold S. Conway Actor. *b.* 1910 (?). Very amateur supporting player cast in Western roles, often as a government official in Toho fantasy and war films. Not to be confused with **Andrew Hughes** and **George Furness**, who essayed similar roles in these pictures.

FILMS INCLUDE: The Mysterians (1957); The Last Death of the Devil, Battle in Outer Space (1959); Mothra, The Last War (1961); King Kong vs. Godzilla (1962); Godzilla vs. the Thing (1964); Las Vegas Free-for-All (1967); Goke–Bodysnatcher from Hell, Genocide (1968), Battle of the Japan Sea (1969).

Ikuma Dan Composer. *b.* April 7, 1924. *ed.* Tokyo College of Music. Toho film composer, primarily of *jidai-geki*, often for **Hiroshi Inagaki**.

FILMS INCLUDE: Sword for Hire (1952); A Billionaire, Samurai I (1954); Samurai II (1955); Madame White Snake, Samurai III (1956); Saga of the Vagabonds (1959); I Bombed Pearl Harbor, Life of a Country Doctor (1960); The Angry Sea, The Last War (1961); Love Me Love Me (1962); Attack Squadron! (1963); The Japanese Are Here (1968).

Mike Daning Actor. *b.* 1922 (?). Beefy, steely-eyed amateur supporting player in genre films for Shochiku and Toei. Best remembered as "Dr. Stein" in *The X from Outer Space* (1967).

FILMS INCLUDE: Rodan [bit] (1956); Ironfinger (1965); Terror Beneath the Sea (1966); The X from Outer Space, Monster from a Prehistoric Planet (1967), Genocide (1968).

Robert Dunham Actor, stunt coordinator. *b.* 1933 (?), in the United States. In Japanese films following service in the Korean War, from 1956 through 1974, both as a supporting player and stunt driver. Unlike many Western actors in Japanese films, Dunham spoke excellent Japanese, and this earned him larger roles than most, including a hilarious co-starring turn in *Dagora the Space Monster* (1964).

FILMS INCLUDE: Mothra, The Flesh Is Hot [bit] (1961); Dagora the Space Monster, Flight from Ashiya [US/Jap] (1964); The Green Slime [Jap/US/It] (1968); Mastermind [US/Jap] (1969); Godzilla vs. Megalon (1973); ESPY (1974).

Yu Fujiki Actor. *b.* March 2, 1931, in Tokyo. A mostly comical performer in Toho programmers, Fujiki nonetheless appeared in heavy drama and melodramas at the studio going back to the mid–1950s. By the early 1960s, however, Fujiki found his niche in comedies, where he was frequently teamed with Toho star **Tadao Takashima**. Best known to American audiences as the egg-loving reporter in *Godzilla vs. the Thing* (1964), and as one of Toshiro Mifune's opponents in *Samurai II* (1955).

FILMS INCLUDE: There Was a Man, Samurai II (1955); The Lower Depths, Throne of Blood (1957); The Hidden Fortress (1958); The Three Treasures (1959); This Greedy Old Skin, When a Woman Ascends the Stairs, The Gambling Samurai (1960); Daredevil in the Castle, A Night in Hong Kong (1961); King Kong vs. Godzilla, Different Sons, Chushingura, Star of Hong Kong (1962); Atragon (1963); Godzilla vs. the Thing, The Sandal Keeper (1964); White Rose of Hong Kong (1965); Sensation Seekers (1966); Las Vegas Free-for-All, Tenamonya—Ghost Journey (1967); Admiral Yamamoto, Fancy Paradise (1968); Yog—Monster from Space (1970).

Susumu Fujita Actor. *b.* January 8, 1912, in Fukuoka. *d.* 1991. Beefy, macho, stern-looking star of **Akira Kurosawa**'s first film as director, *Sanshiro Sugata* (1943), and its sequel. The actor might well have continued playing leading roles for the director if not for Fujita's role in the "Flag of Ten" incident of 1947, when ten of Toho's top stars left the studio to protest poor labor relations. The group formed Shintoho, and Fujita had several good roles in Ichikawa films of the early 1950s, but mismanagement there and Fujita's fading popularity brought him back to Toho and elsewhere in memorable character roles. He was Toshiro Mifune's old rival in *The Hidden Fortress* (1958), the cowardly yet wise ex-yojimbo in *Yojimbo* (1961)—and stoic generals in countless Toho fantasies.

FILMS INCLUDE: Sanshiro Sugata (1943); Sanshiro Sugata Part II, Those Who Tread on the Tiger's Tail (1945); No Regrets for Our Youth (1946); 1001 Nights with Toho (1947); A Flower Blooms (1948); Sanshiro of Ginza, Heat and Mud (1950); River Solo Flows (1951); Escapade in Japan [US], The Mysterians (1957); The Hidden Fortress (1958); The Human Condition II, I Want to Be a Shellfish (1959); The Bad Sleep Well, The Gambling Samurai (1960); Daredevil in the Castle, Yojimbo (1961); Chushingura (1962); High and Low, Attack Squadron!, Siege of Fort Bismarck, Atragon (1963); Godzilla vs. the Thing [includes footage of Fujita shot specifically for the American edition], Dagora the Space Monster (1964); Samurai Assassin, Frankenstein Conquers the World [Jap/US] (1965); The Emperor and the General, Kojiro (1967); Admiral Yamamoto (1968); Battle of the Japan Sea (1969); Tora! Tora! Tora! [US/Jap] (1970); Imperial Navy (1981).

Kamatari Fujiwara Actor. *b.* January 15, 1905, in Tokyo. *d.* 1985. In films from 1933, Fujiwara specialized in weak salaryman-types and suspicious peasants, especially for **Akira Kurosawa**. Unforgettable as the "dead" accountant "Wada" in Kurosawa's *The Bad Sleep Well* (1960), the suspicious "Manzo" in *Seven Samurai* (1954), and as Minoru Chiaki's diminutive companion in *The Hidden Fortress* (1958), the latter the basis for "R2-D2" in *Star Wars*. He also appeared in at least one non–Japanese production: Arthur Penn's *Mickey One* (1965).

FILMS INCLUDE: Wife! Be Like a Rose (1935); Horse (1941); Ikiru, Man Who Went to Sea (1952); Mr. Pu (1953); Seven Samurai, The Invisble Man (1954); I Live in Fear (1955); The Men of Toho-ku, The

Lower Depths (1957); The Hidden Fortress (1958); Samurai Saga, Girl in the Mist, I Want to Be a Shellfish (1959); The Bad Sleep Well (1960); Happiness of Us Alone, Yojimbo (1961); Different Sons, Ayako, Sanjuro, Chushingura (1962); High and Low (1963); Three Outlaw Samurai (1964); Mickey One [US], Red Beard (1965); The Sword of Doom (1966); Eyes the Sea and a Ball (1967); The Day the Sun Rose (1968); Double Suicide (1969); Dodes'ka-den (1970); The Battle of Okinawa (1971); Kagemusha (1980); The Funeral (1984).

Kinji Fukasaku. Director. *b.* 1930. *ed.* Nippon University. Inventive director of fast-paced genre films, mainly at Toei. He began his career one year after graduating from Nippon University in the fine arts department, in 1953. He worked as an assistant director at the newly formed Toei under Tsuneo Kobayashi and Masamitsu Igayama. He directed his first feature, *The Wandering Detective,* in 1961, and his enormous output has barely slowed since, specializing in lean action films set in the past, present, and future.

FILMS INCLUDE: The Wandering Detective (1961); Jakoman and Tetsu, Human Wolves (1964); The Kamikaze Guy (1966); Black Lizard, Blackmail Is My Life, The Green Slime [Jap/US/It] (1968); The Boss, Black Rose (1969); Tora! Tora! Tora! [co-dir.; US/Jap], Our Dear Buddies, Bloody Gambles (1970); Gamblers in Okinawa, Kamikaze Guy (1971); Yakuza Papers (1973); Message from Space (1978); Virus (1980); Samurai Reincarnation, The Gate of Youth [co-dir.] (1981); Legend of the Eight Samurai (1983); Shanghai Rhapsody (1984); House on Fire (1986); The Rage of Love (1988).

Jun Fukuda Director. *b.* February 17, 1923, in Matsuyama. Second-string director at Toho from the late 1950s through the mid-1970s, specializing in gangster films and comedies. However, he is best known in the West for his science fiction output, which includes five Godzilla movies. He joined the studio in 1946, and worked as an assistant director to Hiroshi Inagaki before directing his first film, *The Terrible Crime/Playing with Fire*, in 1959.

FILMS INCLUDE: The Terrible Crime (1959); The Secret of the Telegian (1960); The Merciless Trap, Counterstroke (1961); Witness Killed (1962); Operation Mad Dog, Young Guy in Hawaii (1963); The Weed of Crime (1964); White Rose of Hong Kong, Ironfinger (1965); Sensation Seekers, Ebirah Horror of the Deep (1966); Son of Godzilla (1967); Booted Babe Busted Boss (1968); Great Space Adventure, Young Guy Graduates, Young Guy on Mt. Cook (1969); City of Beasts (1970); Godzilla on Monster Island (1972); Godzilla vs. Megalon [also co-scr.] (1973); Godzilla vs. the Cosmic Monster [also co-scr.], ESPY (1974); The War in Space (1977).

Eiji Funakoshi Actor. *b.* 1923, in Tokyo. Durable star at Daiei who portrayed a wide range of roles in virtually every genre. In films from 1947, he worked frequently with Kon Ichikawa, and was especially memorable in *Fires on the Plain* (1959) and as the father in *Being Two Isn't Easy* (1962).

FILMS INCLUDE: The Golden Demon (1953); Bridge of Japan (1956); A Woman of Osaka, The Story of Shunkin, I Married a Prize Fighter, The Pit, Chorus Girls, Warm Current (1957); Tainted Flowers (1958); Goodbye Hello, Fires on the Plain, Jirocho Fuji, It's You I Love (1959); Kao, Patterns of Love, Afraid to Die, The Woman Who Touched the Legs, A Woman's Testament, Bonchi (1960); A Design for Dying, Marriageable Age, All

for Love, Ten Dark Women, Ghost Story of Kakui Street (1961); The Smell of Poison, The Outcast, Being Two Isn't Easy, Her Hidden Past (1962); When Women Lie, Red Water (1963); The Money Dance, Super-Express, Passion (1964); Gammera the Invincible (1965); The Ghostly Trap, The Night Before Pearl Harbor (1968); Attack of the Monsters, The Blind Beast, Thousand Cranes (1969); Tora-san's Rise and Fall (1975).

George Furness Actor. *b.* 1898, in New York. Gravelly voiced, British-accented supporting player in Japanese films, as well as non-Japanese productions filmed in Japan, usually in roles of authority. Furness' *other* job was as an American lawyer; he had, in fact, defended former Foreign Minister Mamoru Shigemitsu in the International Military Tribunal for the Far East.

FILMS INCLUDE: The Mysterians (1957); The Last Voyage [US] (1960); Gorath, My Geisha [US] (1962); Las Vegas Free-for-All (1967).

Hideo Gosha Director. *b.* 1929, in Tokyo. *d.* 1992. Director of rugged, violent *jidai-geki*, and likened by some writers to Anthony Mann or Robert Aldrich. Beginning in 1980, he moved away from samurai films and into more contemporary settings.

FILMS INCLUDE: Three Outlaw Samurai (1964); Sword of the Beast (1965); Secret of the Urn, Samurai Wolf (1966); Samurai Wolf—Hell Cut (1967); Tenchu!, Goyokin (1969); The Wolves (1971); Violent Street (1974); Bandit vs. Samurai Squad (1978); Hunter in the Dark (1979); The Geisha (1983); Fireflies of the North (1984); Death Shadows, Kai, Tracked (1985); Four Days of Snow and Blood (1989); Carmen 1945 (1988); Spider Web (1991).

Heinosuke Gosho Director, screenwriter. *b.* February 1, 1902, in Tokyo. *d.* May 1, 1981. Director of *shomin-geki* (common people dramas) who helmed Japan's first talkie, *The Neighbor's Wife and Mine* (1931). Criticized early in his career for his fondness for flawed leading characters, his humanistic work has since been reevaluated, and these early films are now considered classics. He started at Shochiku as an assistant to Yasujiro Shimazu, and later worked at Toho and later still as one of the founders of "Studio Eight," a production company affiliated with Shintoho. He served as president of the Japanese Association of Film Directors (1964-75), and won the International Peace Prize at the Berlin Film Festival for *Where Chimneys Are Seen* (1953). Eleven of his films have placed in *Kinema Jumpo* 's annual Ten Best List, and he won the Mainichi Film Prize for *One More Time* (1947).

FILMS INCLUDE: Spring in Southern Islands/ Spring of Southern Island, No Clouds in the Sky, Man's Heart, Youth, A Casket for Living (1925); Town People, First Love, A Rapid Stream, Mother's Love/Mother I Miss You, Daughter, My Beloved Child, Girl Friend (1926); The Lonely Roughneck, Intimate Dream, Tricky Girl, Death of a Maiden, Moon-faced, The Village Bride (1927); If You Like It, Debauchery Is Wrong, Road to God, A New Kind of Woman (1928); One Night of Passion (1929); Bachelors Beware, A Corner of Great Tokyo, A Smiling Character, The Girl Nyuyo, Woman Don't Make Your Name Dirty, Big Forest, Story of Kinuyo, Story of Night, Sad Story of a Barmaid (1930); Island of Naked Scandal, The Neighbor's Wife and Mine, Memories of Young Days (1931); My Stupid Brother, Willows of Ginza, A Studio Romance, Cuckoo, Love in Tokyo (1932); The Bride Talks in Her Sleep, Dancing Girls of Izu, Heaven Linked with Love, The 19th Spring, Goodbye My Girl, Caress (1933); Now That I Was Born Woman, Everything That Lives, A Bridegroom Talks in His Sleep (1934); Yearning, Burden of Life (1935); A Married Lady Borrows Money, Woman of a Pale Night, The New Road I, The New Road II (1936); Song of a Flower Basket (1937); Wooden Head (1940); New Snow (1942); The Five-Storied Pagoda (1944); The Girls of Izu (1945); Once More (1947); Image (1948); Dispersing Clouds (1951); Morning Conflicts (1952); Where Chimneys Are Seen/Four Chimneys (1953); An Inn at Osaka, The Valley Between Love and Death, The Cock Crows Again (1954); Growing Up (1955); Twice on a Certain Night (1956); Behold Thy Son/

Setsuko Hara and Ken Uehara in *Sounds from the Mountains* (1959). (Photo courtesy Darrell Davis.)

Yellow Crow, Elegy of the North (1957); Firefly Light, Avarice, Maria of the Ant Village (1958); Journal of Orange Flower (1959); When a Woman Loves, White Fangs (1960); Hunting Rifle, As the Clouds Scatter (1961); Get Married Mother (1962); A Million Girls (1963); An Innocent Witch (1965); Our Wonderful Years (1966); Rebellion of Japan (1967); Woman and Bean Soup, Seasons of Meiji (1968).

Mie Hama Actress. *b.* November 20, 1943, in Tokyo. Petite, sexy star of dozens of Toho programmers. A former model, best remembered in the West as "Kissy Suzuki," 007's love interest in *You Only Live Twice*, and as "Madame X" in *King Kong Escapes* (both 1967), released that same year. Today Hama remains a popular television personality.

Films Include: A Night in Hong Kong, Wanton Journey, The Youth and His Amulet (1961); King Kong vs. Godzilla, Different Sons (1962); The Lost World of Sinbad, Siege of Fort Bismarck, Crazy Free-for-All—Die You Good-for-Nothing!,

Hong Kong Free-for-All, Attack Squadron! (1963); The Weed of Crime, The Gay Braggart, The Sandal Keeper, The Beautiful Swindlers [Fr/Dutch/Jap/It], You Can Succeed Too (1964); Adventures of Takla Makan, Ironfinger (1965); What's Up Tiger Lily? [US production incorporating Japanese footage], The Mad Atlantic, The Boss of Pick-Pocket Bay (1966); Sensation Seekers, King Kong Escapes [Jap/US], You Only Live Twice [Brit/US/S. Afr], Las Vegas Free-for-All (1967); Monsieur Zivaco, Stormy Era, The Night of the Seagull, Mexican Free-for-All (1968); The Cleanup (1969); Hang in There Young Guy (1975); Kitchen (1989).

Hajime Hana Actor. *b.* 1930, in Tokyo. *d.* 1993. Member of the popular comedy troupe "The Crazy Cats," who starred in the 14-feature "Crazy" film series (1963-70; itself preceded by a 1962 warm-up feature and followed by an unofficial reunion film, *Memories of You*), and many of the ten "Man of Japan" films. Hana typically played boastful and vain men of minor authority opposite Hitoshi Ueki and Kei Tani (the other members of the troupe, usually cast in supporting roles, were Hiroshi Inuzuka, Senri Sakurai, Shin Yasuda, and Eitaro Ishibashi). In later years Hana eased into a wide range of character roles.

FILMS INCLUDE: The Woman Who Touched the Legs (1960); Young Season, The Crazy Bride and Her Seven Friends (1962); Crazy Free-for-All—Don't Procrastinate, Crazy Free-for-All—Die You Good for Nothing, Hong Kong Free-for-All (1963); Don't Call Me a Con Man (1965); The Boss of Pick-Pocket Bay, It's Crazy—I Can't Explain It Way Out There, Great Crazy Free-for-All (1966); Industrial Spy Free-for-All, Las Vegas Free-for-All, Monsieur Zivaco (1967); Mexican Free-for-All (1968); Computer Free-for-All, The Crazy's Great Explosion (1969); Taking a Crazy Punch at Shimizu Harbor (1970); Preparations for the Festival (1975); Hunter in the Dark (1979); A Distant Cry from Spring (1980); Karate Cop 3 (1984); Kai (1985); Memories of You (1988); Haru Kuru Oni (1989); Tekken, Donmai (1990); Private Lesson (1993).

Susumu Hani Director. *b.* October 19, 1926, in Tokyo. Initially a still photographer, Hani gradually moved into documentaries before directing narrative features which have retained his documentarian sensibilities, and which frequently deal with the problems of youth and the emergence of women. He won several international film prizes for his short *Children Who Draw* (1955), and for the feature *Children Hand in Hand* (1965). In 1981 he directed James Stewart's last starring film, the bizarre *The Green Horizon* (1981). Married to actress **Sachiko Hidari**, with whom he frequently works.

FILMS INCLUDE: **[Documentary Shorts]:** Water in Our Life (1952); Snow Festival, Drains in the City (1953); Your Beer, Children in the Classroom (1954); Children Who Draw (1955); Group Guidance, Twin Sisters (1956); Zoo Diary (1957); Horyuji Temple, The Living Sea (1958); Dances in Japan (1960). **[Features]:** Bad Boys (1961); A Full Life, Children Hand in Hand (1962); She and He (1963); Bwana Toshi (1965); Bride of the Andes (1966); Inferno of First Love (1968); Aido—Slave of Love (1969); Mio (1970); Timetable/Morning Schedule (1972); A Tale of Africa/The Green Horizon (1981).

Setsuko Hara Actress. *b.* Masae Aida in 1920, in Yokohama. Hara joined Nikkatsu in 1935, and shot to popularity in the Japanese/German co-production *The New Earth* (1937). An idealized, wholesome star, Hara was nicknamed "the eternal virgin" as a testament to her onscreen purity. Although she worked for a variety of directors, she is best remembered for her six films with **Yasujiro Ozu**—*Late Spring, Early Summer, Tokyo Story, Tokyo Twilight, Late Autumn*, and *Early Autumn*—always in the role of a strong, postwar woman. She was especially memorable as the kindly middle-aged widow who graciously cares for her dead husband's parents—after their own children reject them—in *Tokyo Story* (1953). Following Ozu's death, Hara suddenly retired, and since has lived the life of a recluse in Kamakura.

FILMS INCLUDE: The New Earth [Jap/Ger] (1937); Pastoral Symphony (1938); The Suicide Troops of the Watchtower (1942); Toward the Decisive Battle in the

Sky, Hot Wind (1943); Light and Shadow, The Girl I Loved, Green Native Country, No Regrets for Our Youth, A Beauty (1946); A Ball at the Anjo House, Ladies of the Night (1947); Temptation (1948); Late Spring, Here's to the Girls, Blue Mountains (1949); The Idiot, Early Summer, Repast (1951); Tokyo Story, Hakugyo (1953); Sounds from the Mountains (1954); Sudden Rain/ Shower (1956); The Chieko Story, Tokyo Twilight, Women in Prison (1957); Women Unveiled, Holiday in Tokyo (1958); Woman's Heart, A Woman's Secret (1959); The Wayside Pebble, Hope of Blue Sky, Daughters Wives and a Mother, Late Autumn, Life of a Country Doctor (1960); Love and Fascination, Early Autumn (1961); Chushingura (1962).

Kazuo Hasegawa Actor. *b.* February 27, 1908, in Kyoto. *ed.* elementary school. *d.* April 6, 1984, of brain cancer. On the stage at the age of five and trained in the art of Kabuki, Hasegawa joined the film industry at Shochiku in 1927, under the name Chojiro Hayashi. He was a huge and prolific star, a veteran of more than 120 features by the time he moved to Toho in 1937. During Hasegawa's departure he was attacked by a thug—allegedly hired by his former studio—and permanently scarred on his cheek. However, the much-publicized attack only increased his popularity, and the actor began appearing under his own name at this time. He was part of the mass exodus from Toho to Shintoho in 1947, but was lured, in turn, by Daiei in 1949, where he later doubled as an executive officer. He gained international acclaim starring in the Academy Award-winning *Gate of Hell* (1953), and was most associated with that picture's director, **Teinosuke Kinugasa**. However, he also worked with such artists as Daisuke Ito, Kenji Misumi, and Kon Ichikawa (memorably in *An Actor's Revenge*) and with Kenji Mizoguchi in *A Story from Chikamatsu* (1954). By the time he retired from the industry in 1963 to concentrate on his stage work, Hasegawa had appeared in more than 300 films. Three of his children, Narutoshi Hayashi, Toshiko Hasegawa, and Kiyo Hasegawa, are actors.

FILMS INCLUDE: Childish Sword Master [debut] (1927); Tales from a Country by the Sea (1928); Blizzard Pass (1929); Before Dawn (1931); The Surviving Shinsengumi, The Loyal Forty-Seven Ronin/ Chushingura (1932); Two Stone Lanterns (1933); A Sword and the Sumo Ring (1934) Yukinojo's Disguise I, Yukinojo's Disguise II (1935); Yukinojo's Disguise III (1936); The Summer Battle of Osaka (1937); Song of the White Orchid (1939); Vow in the Desert, The Man Who Disappeared Yesterday (1941); Lord for a Night, Bonbon (1946); The Devil of Edo (1947); Firebird (1948); A Tale of Genji (1951); Saga of the Great Buddha (1952); Lion's Dance, Rise of Kodokan, Gate of Hell (1953); A Story from Chikamatsu (1954); Guinji with the Seven Faces, Tojura's Love (1955); Three Women Around Yoshinaka, Zangiku monogatari (1956); A Fantastic Tale of Naruto, Migratory Birds of the Snow, Ukifune (1957); Eight Brides, Shogun's Holiday, Chushingura, A Man Who Stakes His Life, Whistles of Migratory Birds, Will o' the Wisp, Nichiren—A Man of Many Miracles, Ambush at Iga Pass (1958); The Footmark of a Snow Fairy, Halo of Heat Haze, The Woman and the Pirates, Jirocho Fuji, The Gaijin, Yotsuya Ghost Story, Utamaro Painter of Women, A Gambler as I Am (1959); The Ogre of Mount Oe, The Purloined Man, The Sword and the Sumo Ring, Spring Rain Umbrella, Three Brothers and the Underworld, The Last Betrayal (1960); Happiness of Us Alone, Smoke of Night, Cherry Tree Gate, Across the Lock Gate to the Sea, Clear Weather (1961); The Great Wall (1962); An Actor's Revenge (1963).

Shinobu Hashimoto Screenwriter. *b.* 1917, in Hyogo. A Toho screenwriter from 1950, he co-wrote most of Kurosawa best films, including *Rashomon* (1950), *Ikiru* (1952), and *Seven Samurai* (1954).

FILMS INCLUDE [as screenwriter or co-screenwriter]: Rashomon (1950); Ikiru (1952); Eagle of the Pacific (1953); Farewell Rabaul, Seven Samurai (1954); I Live in Fear (1955); Throne of Blood, I Married a Prize Fighter **[story]** (1957); The Hidden Fortress, Summer Clouds (1958); A Whistle in My Heart, I Want to Be a Shellfish [also dir.] (1959); The Bad Sleep Well (1960); Harakiri (1962); Pressure of Guilt (1963); Samurai Assassin (1965); The Sword of Doom (1966); Rebellion, The Emperor and the General (1967); Tenchu!, Under the Banner of Samurai (1969); Dodes'ka-den, The Shadow Within (1970); Submersion of Japan (1973); The Castle of Sand [also co-prod.] (1974); Mt. Hakkoda [also prod.] (1977); Kagemusha [adviser only] (1980)

Fumio Hayasaka Composer. *b.* August 19, 1914. *d.* October 15, 1955, of tuberculosis. Though primarily a concert composer, Hayasaka nevertheless wrote some of the most important film scores of the early postwar period. He was most associated with **Akira Kurosawa**, for whom he wrote the music to *Rashomon* (1950) and *Seven Samurai* (1954), and **Kenji Mizoguchi**, for whom he wrote the scores to *Ugetsu* (1953) and *Sansho the Bailiff* (1954).

FILMS INCLUDE: A Flower Blooms, Drunken Angel (1948); Stray Dog (1949); Portrait of Madame Yuki, Scandal, Rashomon (1950); Miss Oyu, The Idiot, Lady Musashino (1951); Ikiru (1952); Seven Samurai, A Story from Chikamatsu (1954); Princess Yang Kwei-Fei, New Tales of the Taira Clan [score completed by Masaru Sato], I Live in Fear [completed by Masaru Sato] (1955).

Bokuzen Hidari Actor. *b.* February 20, 1894, in Saitama. *d.* 1971. Sad-faced character actor who specialized playing older, peasant-type roles. Memorable as the pathetic peasant Toshiro Mifune tries to whip into shape in *Seven Samurai* (1954), and as the priest in *The Lower Depths* (1957).

FILMS INCLUDE: Scandal (1950); The Idiot (1951); Man Who Went to Sea (1952); The Life of Oharu, Ikiru (1952); Seven Samurai (1954); I Live in Fear, Love Makeup (1955); The Lower Depths (1957); An Echo Calls You (1959); The Human Vapor (1960); The Youth and His Amulet (1961); Pride of the Campus (1962); Siege of Fort Bismarck (1963); Zatoichi's Flashing Sword (1964); Gammera the Invincible, Red Beard (1965); Sex and Life, Along with Ghosts (1969); The Little Hero (1970); Oh My Comrade! (1971).

Sachiko Hidari Actress. *b.* 1930, in Toyama. In films beginning 1952, Hidari's career was boosted when she was discovered by director **Heinosuke Gosho**, and later with her director-husband **Susumu Hani**. Memorable in the latter's film, *He and She*, and Shohei Imamura's *The Insect Woman* (both 1963). Still active in films.

FILMS INCLUDE: Faults of Youth (1952); The Battle of the Flowers and the Stupid Father, Tenacious Santa, Half Virgin (1953); An Inn at Osaka, The Cock Crows Again, A Billionaire (1954); The Maid's Kid (1955); Darkness at Noon (1956); The Crime of Shiro Kamisaka, Temptation, Condemned (1957); The Story of a Nun, A Man in the Fog, The Boy Who Came Back, Journey of Youth (1958); Cast-off, The Condition of a Fountain, The Cliff of a Girl-Ghost (1959); Dear Emperor, The Insect Woman, She and He, Escape from Hell (1963); Hunger Straits (1964); Bride of the Andes, Our Wonderful Years (1966); Une Vie (1967); Mishima—A Life in Four Chapters [US/Jap] (1985); Song of the Spring Horse (1986).

Akihiko Hirata Actor. *b.* Akihiko Onoda, December 26, 1927, in Kyojo. *ed.* Tokyo University of Interior Design. *d.* July 25, 1984, of cancer. Following a stint as a still photographer and assistant director under elder brother Yoshiki Onoda at Shintoho, Hirata joined Toho in 1953. His long face, intense features led to his casting as "Dr. Serizawa," the tormented scientist and inventor of the oxygen destroyer in *Godzilla, King of the Monsters!* (1954). Playing everything from snarling villains to easy-going corporate executives, Hirata became a genre star with a genuine cult following, though the unprecedented success of the first Godzilla film also typecast him. He was a favorite of director **Ishiro Honda**, and was popular with his fellow actors as well, described by one as a "mother hen" who looked after his co-stars. Beginning in the mid-1960s, Hirata began turning up in sci-fi teleseries as well, including "Ultra Seven," "Fireman," "Rainbowman," and "Giant Ironman 17." His association with the genre continued right up until his death; he helped announce the production of *Godzilla 1985* , but was too ill to appear in the film and his role was ultimately played by Yosuke Natsuki.

FILMS INCLUDE: Embrace [debut], Even the Mighty Shed Tears (1953); Farewell Rabaul, Godzilla King of the Monsters!, Samurai I (1954); Samurai II (1955); Rodan (1956); A Tea-Picker's Song of Goodbye, A Rainbow Plays in My Heart I-II, A Farewell to the Woman Called My Sister, Secret Scrolls I, The Mysterians (1957); Secret Scrolls II, Varan the Unbelievable, The H-Man (1958); Saga of the Vagabonds, Samurai Saga, The Three Treasures (1959); Get 'Em All, Man Against Man, I Bombed Pearl Harbor, Westward Desperado, The Secret of the Telegian (1960); The Merciless Trap, Kill the Killer!, Big Shots Die at Dawn, Daredevil in the Castle, Mothra (1961); Structure of Hate, Girl of Dark, Operation Enemy Fort, Gorath, Chushingura, Young Generation, King Kong vs. Godzilla, Sanjuro (1962); Attack Squadron!, Siege of Fort Bismarck, Atragon (1963); Whirlwind, The Weed of Crime, Ghidrah—The Three-Headed Monster (1964); Ironfinger (1965); The Boss of Pick-Pocket Bay, Ebirah Horror of the Deep (1966); Son of Godzilla, The Emperor and the General, Kojiro, The Killing Bottle (1967); Admiral Yamamoto (1968); Latitude Zero [Jap/US], The Crazy's Great Explosion, Battle of the Japan Sea (1969); Prophecies of Nostradamus, Godzilla vs. the Cosmic Monster (1974); Terror of Mechagodzilla (1975); The War in Space (1977); Fugitive Alien [made for TV] (1978); Sayonara Jupiter (1984).

Ishiro Honda Director. *b.* May 7, 1911, in Yamagata. *ed.* Nippon University. *d.* February 28, 1993, of respiratory failure. Japan's greatest and most prolific *kaiju eiga* (monster movie) director joined Toho's predecessor, PCL, in 1933, where he soon began a lifelong friendship with **Akira Kurosawa**. The two worked as assistant directors, mostly for Kajiro Yamamoto, until 1938, when Honda was drafted into service. He returned to assistant direction after the war, including second unit shooting on Kurosawa's *Stray Dog* (1949). He directed his first film that same year, and his *Eagle of the Pacific* (1953) was a critical and commercial hit. The following year he directed *Godzilla, King of the Monsters!* (1954); its international success helped open the export market, and begat an entire subgenre of science fiction cinema. Honda himself directed six more **Godzilla** films, and most of Toho's other fantasy output through the early 1970s. In stark contrast to the vast majority of directors of American science fiction films during this period, Honda's films displayed a surprising degree of sophistication—intelligent use of color and props as structuring metaphors, sly character placement, etc.—though most of his films, like the original *Godzilla*, were altered to a greater or lesser degree for U.S. release. He continued to direct non-genre films though the late 1950s, but almost exclusively sci-fi films after 1960, despite the success of his last non-genre effort, *Come Marry Me* (1966). And while Honda was, arguably, Toho's biggest money earner, by 1970 he was considered a has-been, and he moved, reluctantly, into sci-fi television. However, his old friend Kurosawa brought him back into features as an associate director on Kurosawa's recent features. In this position, Honda collaborated with Kurosawa on the screenplays and directed some footage, notably the battle sequences of *Kagemusha* and *Ran* (1985), "The Tunnel" segment of *Akira Kurosawa's Dreams* (1990), and the Buddhist ceremony in *Rhapsody in August* (1991). The director, often mis-billed as *Inoshiro* Honda, was preparing an environmental science fiction feature when he died at the age of 81.

FILMS INCLUDE: **[as director]**: Stray Dog [asst. dir. only], A Story of a Co-op [documentary] (1949); Ise Island [documentary] (1950); The Blue Pearl (1951); The Skin of the South, The Man Who Went to Sea/The Man Who Came to the Bay (1952); Adolescence Part II, Eagle of the Pacific (1953); Farewell Rabaul, Godzilla King of the Monsters! (1954); Love Tide/Love Make-up, Mother and Son/O-en-san, Half Human—The Story of the Abominable Snowman (1955); Young Tree, Night School, Goodbye People of Tokyo, Rodan (1956); Good Luck to These Two, A Tea-Picker's Song of Goodbye, A Rainbow Plays in My Heart I-II, A Farewell to the Woman Called My Sister, The Mysterians (1957); Song of a Bride, The H-Man, Varan the Unbelievable (1958); An Echo Calls You, Inao—The

Story of an Iron Arm, Seniors Juniors Co-workers, Battle in Outer Space (1959); Sanbo—The Magic Water Wheel [USSR; dubbing dir. only], The Human Vapor (1960); Mothra, The Man in Red (1961); Gorath, King Kong vs. Godzilla (1962); Attack of the Mushroom People, Atragon (1963); Godzilla vs. the Thing, Dagora the Space Monster, Ghidrah—The Three-Headed Monster (1964); Frankenstein Conquers the World [Jap/US], Monster Zero [Jap/US] (1965); War of the Gargantuas [Jap/US], Come Marry Me (1966); King Kong Escapes [Jap/US] (1967); Destroy All Monsters (1968); Godzilla's Revenge, Latitude Zero [Jap/US] (1969); Yog—Monster from Space (1970); Terror of Mechagodzilla (1975). **[as associate director and uncredited co-director and co-screenplay]**: Kagemusha (1980); Ran (1985); Come Back Hero [cameo only] (1987); Akira Kurosawa's Dreams (1990); Rhapsody in August (1991); Kids [cameo only], Madadayo/Not Yet (1993).

Kojiro Hongo Actor. *b.* February 15, 1938, in Okayama. Handsome leading man at Daiei during the 1960s, usually cast as a stalwart hero; best known in this country as Siddartha in *Buddha* (1961), and as the star of several Gamera movies.

Films Include: Etajima the Navy Academy, The Doomed Bride, Jirocho Fuji (1959); The Kamikaze Special Attack Corps, The Two Musashis, Princess Sen of Edo, Jirocho the Chivalrous, The Ogre of Mt. Oe (1960); Buddha (1961); The Whale God, The Great Wall (1962); Japan's Number One Judo-Man (1963); Return of the Giant Majin, War of the Monsters (1966); The Return of the Giant Monsters, The Woman Gambler (1967); The Two Bodyguards, Destroy All Planets, Kaidan botandoro (1968); Broken Swords, The Falcon Fighters, Gateway to Glory, The Magoichi Saga, Along with Ghosts, The Haunted Castle (1969); Mission Iron Castle (1970); Zero Fighters (1975); Gamera—The Guardian of the Universe (1995).

Hiromichi Horikawa Director. *b.* 1916, in Kyoto. He joined Toho after graduating from Tokyo University, and worked as an assistant director under Kurosawa before making his directorial debut in 1955. Specializes in crime films.

Films Include: Seven Samurai [asst. dir. only] (1954); The Story of the Fast-Growing Weeds (1955); The Summer the Sun Was Lost (1956); Throne of Blood [asst. dir. only] (1957); The Prodigal Son, The Naked General (1958); The Path Under the Plane-Trees (1959); The Black Book, The Blue Beast (1960); Eternity of Love, Ca[illegible] Dried Bonito (1961); My Daughter an[illegible] (1962); Pressure of Guilt, Black and White (1963); Brand of Evil, Les Plus Belles Escroqueries du Monde (1964); Last Judgment, You Can if You Try (1965); Goodbye Moscow, Sun Above Death Below (1968); The Militarists (1970); The Alaska Story (1977); Have Wings on Your Heart (1978); Mutchan (1985); War and Flowers (1989).

Yuriko Hoshi Actress. *b.* December 6, 1943, in Tokyo. Hugely popular star at Toho beginning in 1959, Hoshi has appeared in a wide range of films, from dramas to comedies, *jidai-geki* thrillers to musicals. Still active in films and on television.

Films Include: The Dangerous Kiss, Man Against Man (1960); Daredevil in the Castle, The Man from the East, Poignant Story, The Last War, The Last Challenge, Counterstroke (1961); Bull of the Campus, Pride of the Campus, Till Tomorrow Comes, The Wiser Age, Born in Sin, Chushingura, My Daughter and I, Operation Enemy Fort, Witness Killed (1962); Honolulu-Tokyo-Hong Kong, Long Way to Okinawa, Warring Clans, Attack Squadron!, A Woman's Life (1963); Godzilla vs. the Thing, Tiger Flight, The Rabble, Whirlwind, Ghidrah—The Three-Headed Monster (1964); Campus A-Go-Go, It Started in the Alps, Night in Bangkok, Rise Against the Sword, The Daphne, Green Light to Joy, River of Forever, It's Crazy—I Can't Explain It Way Out There (1966); Kojiro, Let's Go Young Guy!, Judo Champion, Pomegranate Time, Devils'-in-Law (1967); Kill, Cry of the Mountains (1968); Gone with Love Come with Memory (1969); Band of Assassins (1970); Karate Cop 3 (1984).

Andrew Hughes Actor. *b.* 1908 (?). Distinguished Australian businessman and member of the Tokyo Amateur Dramatic Club, Hughes appeared in numerous

Kojiro Hongo (right) and director Kenji Misumi on the set of *Buddha* (1961).

Western roles in Japanese films, usually as a government official or businessman.

FILMS INCLUDE: The Last Voyage [US] (1960); Flight from Ashiya [US/Jap] (1963); The Golden Bat, Terror Beneath the Sea [Jap/US/It] (1966); Las Vegas Free-for-All, King Kong Escapes [Jap/US], Monsieur Zivaco (1967); Destroy All Monsters, Booted Babe Busted Boss (1968); Battle of the Japan Sea (1969); Submersion of Japan (1973).

Kon Ichikawa Director. *b.* Uji Yamada on November 20, 1915, in Mie. Japan's most consistently commercially successful postwar director, Ichikawa has worked in every genre, from satirical comedies to heavy drama to documentaries to horror-laced mysteries. He joined the animation department of J.O. Studios in 1933, and transferred to Tokyo when the company merged with Toho in the early 1940s. He won great accolades for the war dramas *The Burmese Harp* (1956) and *Fires on the Plain* (1959), the recently restored documentary *Tokyo Olympiad* (1965), and his adaptation of Junichiro Tanizaki's *The Makioka Sisters* (1983). In 1976 he directed the wildly popular *The Inugami Family*, which spawned several sequels also directed by Ichikawa. Most of his films are laced with a wry, critical, generally pessimistic commentary on Japanese society, and he is a master in his use of anamorphic wide screen. Married to screenwriter **Natto Wada** until her death in 1983; she wrote or co-wrote the plurality of his films, often with Ichikawa. The director himself frequently wrote under the pseudonym "Kuri Shitei," a reference to Agatha Christie. He won the San Giorgio Prize at the Venice Film Festival for *The Burmese Harp*, which Ichikawa remade with nearly equal acclaim in 1985.

FILMS INCLUDE: A Girl at Dojo Temple [banned] (1945–6); A Thousand and One Nights at Toho [co-dir.] (1947); A Flower Blooms, 365 Nights I, 365 Nights II (1948); Human Patterns, Passion Without End (1949); Sanshiro of Ginza, Heat and

Mud, Pursuit at Dawn (1950); Nightshade Flower, The Lover, The Man Without Nationality, Stolen Love, River Solo Flows, Wedding March (1951); Mr. Lucky, Young People, The Woman Who Touched the Legs, This Way That Way (1952); Mr. Pu, The Blue Revolution, The Youth of Heiji Senigata, The Lover (1953); All of Myself, A Billionaire, Twelve Chapters on Women (1954); Ghost Story of Youth, The Heart (1955); The Burmese Harp, Punishment Room, Bridge of Japan/Nihombashi (1956); The Crowded Streetcar, The Hole/ The Pit, The Men of Tohoku (1957); Conflagration, Money and Three Bad Men (1958); Goodbye Good Day, The Key/ Odd Obsession, Fires on the Plain, Police and Small Gangsters (1959); A Ginza Veteran, Bonchi, A Woman's Testament [co-dir.], The Women Who Touched the Legs [scr. only], Her Brother (1960); Ten Dark Women, The Sin (1961); Being Two Isn't Easy (1962); An Actor's Revenge, Along on the Pacific (1963); The Money Dance (1964); Tokyo Olympiad (1965); Topo Gigio and the Missile War [It] (1967); Youth, Tournament, Kyoto (1968); Japan and the Japanese, Dodes'ka-den [co-prod. only] (1970); To Love Again (1972); The Wanderers, Visions of Eight [co-dir.] (1973); I Am a Cat (1975); Between Women and Wives, The Inugami Family (1976); The Devil's Bouncing Ball, Island of Horrors (1977); Queen Bee (1978); Hinotori, House of Hanging (1979) Ancient City (1980); Lonely Heart (1981); The Makioka Sisters, Fine Snow (1983); Ohan (1984); The Burmese Harp (1985); The Adventures of Milo and Otis [assoc. dir. only] (1986); Actress, Princess of the Moon (1987); Tsuru (1988); The Noh Mask Murders (1991).

Raizo Ichikawa Actor. *b.* August 29, 1931, in Kyoto. *d.* 1969. In films from 1954, this Daiei star is best known for his starring turn in that studio's violent "Kyoshiro Nemuri" sword film series, which was cut short by the actor's untimely death.

FILMS INCLUDE: New Tales of the Taira Clan (1955); Ukifune, Osaka Story, Love of a Princess (1957); The 7th Secret Courier for Edo, Chushingura (1958); His Lordship the Brigand, Love of a Princess, Samurai Vendetta, Jirocho Fuji, Stop the Old Fox (1959); Bonchi, Enchanted Princess, The Ogre of Mt. Oe, The Two Musashis, Jirocho the Chivalrous (1960); Buddha, The Radiant Prince, The Missing Leaf, All for Love (1961); The Outcast, The Great Wall, Her Hidden Past, It Happened on the Road to Edo, The One and Only Girl I Ever Loved (1962); An Actor's Revenge, Book of Death, The Third Shadow (1963); Adventures of Kyoshiro Nemuri, Exploits of Kyoshiro Nemuri, Kiyoshi Nemuri at Bay (1964); Flaming Sword of Kiyoshi Nemuri, Mysterious Sword of Kiyoshi Nemuri (1965); The Princess' Mask, Villain Sword (1966); Trail of Traps, The Wife of Seishu Hanaoka (1967).

Akira Ifukube Composer. *b.* March 31, 1914, in Kushiro, Hokkaido. Following his formal training as a violinist at Hokkaido University, Ifukube was drafted into the military, where he and his brother contracted radiation poisoning; his brother died and Ifukube was disabled for several months. Persuaded by college classmate Fumio Hayasaka to join him at Toho's music department, Ifukube began scoring features in 1947, concurrent with a teaching position at Gei-Dai University. Heavily influenced by both Russian symphonic and Ainu folk music (he was raised on the Tokatsu Plain), Ifukube's ominous, deeply felt and psychologically charged style was well-suited to epic genre films, as were his stirring nationalistic marches. He is best remembered for his score to *Godzilla, King of the Monsters!* (1954; he also created the monster's roar) and nearly two dozen other effects-oriented spectacles produced at Toho and Daiei. He wrote scores for many "Zatoichi" films, the entire "Majin" trilogy, and Tomu Uchida's six "Musashi Miyamoto" pictures. The composer worked regularly with **Daisuke Ito**, **Kon Ichikawa** (memorably in *The Burmese Harp*), and **Hiroshi Inagaki**. His film worked tapered off beginning in the 1970s, but he continued to teach and was persuaded to return to the **"Godzilla"** series for several films in the early 1990s.

FILMS INCLUDE: Snow Trail, Invitation to Happiness (1947); Second Life Danshichi on the Black Horse, The Woman in the Typhoon Area, The Living Portrait, The President and the Shopgirl (1948); A Public

Prosecutor and a Gaoleress, A Quiet Duel, Senta Was Cut, Beautiful Punishment, Confession at Midnight, Jakoman and Tetsu, The Rainbow Man, A Signal Fire of Love, Growing Village, Have a Song on Your Lips (1949); I Am a Bodyguard, Shudder, A Sexy Ceremony of Women, Street of Anger, A White Beast, Listen to the Voice of the Sea, Confusion, Beyond the War, A Warship Has Already Had Smoke, Les Miserables I-II (1950); Beyond Love and Hate, Pretended Full Dress, Devilish Judge, Reeds Quivering with a Breeze, The Man with No Nationality, A Free School, Who Judges Me?, Unlimited Passion, Stolen Love, Swearing by the Flag, The Genji Story, A True Story – Goemon Ishikawa (1951); Oath of the Plain, The Final Boss, The Avalanche, Sister of Nishijin, Escaping the Street of Death, Mad Woman with Furisode, The Violence, A Generation of Horse Masters, Children of Hiroshima, The Violent Stream (1952); A Thousand Cranes, Ostracism, A Reduced Drawing, A Half-Blood, About Love, Desire, The Saga of Anatahan, An Alligator in Genkai, White Fish, The Crab-Canning Ship, Before Dawn, A Fascinated Soul, The Outlaw, Life of Woman, Hiroshima, Cello Player Gorshe (1953); A Samurai's Love, Ashizuri Cape, The Story of Koto in Springtime, A Drain, Fellows of Green, Life Theatre – Nostalgia, Muddy Adolescence, Godzilla King of the Monsters!, Young Men, The Story of Shunkin, A Whirlpool in Springtime (1954); The Glow of the Firefly/Auld Lang Syne, A Life of a Woman in Meiji, A Rush of Fire, A Way to the Fountain, A Woman in Ginza, The Tokyo Mafia, The Maidservant, A Wolf, Three Faces, The Eye of the Typhoon, A Generation of the King, Beauty and the Beast, Kidnapper, Blueba, The Police Diary II, The Bullet-Marked Street (1955); Kodokan with Roses, The Burmese Harp, Black Belt – Sangokushi, Silver Suicide, A Crime of Kamisaka, Darkness of Daylight, Wandering About the Shore, Will-o'-the-Wisp, Sound of Youth, A Married Couple of Desirable Persons, Don't Fall in Love with Yanpachi, Sound of Fog, Rodan (1956); A Story of a Girl, Actresses, Osaka Story, Secret Scrolls I, Hateful Things, A Flower in Hell, Who Murdered?, Fellows at Sea, The Last Escape, Whir and the Earth, Downtown, The Ground, The Mysterians (1957); Secret Scrolls II, Only Women Have Sorrow, The Bridge of Only Two Persons, The Disaster, The Ice Wall, The Adulterous, Yukichi Fukuzawa's Boyhood, Over the Seasonal Wind, Varan the Unbelievable (1958); The Big Boss, A Whistle in My Heart, A Lady and a Pirate, Samurai Saga, Crush the Wall, A Murdered Stewardess, The Three Treasures, Battle in Outer Space (1959); Shinran I, Injured Thousand Ryo, Shinran II, Throne of Flames, Sir Tadano's Travels (1960); Daredevil in the Castle, Musashi Miyamoto I – Untamed Fury/Zen and Sword, A Bad Reputation, Buddha, Two Sons (1961); Her Hidden Past, The Life and Opinion of Zatoichi, Chisakobe, Conspirator, The Whale God, King Kong vs. Godzilla, The King of Shin, Chushingura, The King, Musashi Miyamoto II – Duel Without End, Musashi Miyamoto III – The Worthless Duel (1962); Zatoichi Enters Again, The Little Prince and the Eight-Headed Dragon, This Neck – Ten Thousand Goku, Execution, Zatoichi the Fugitive, Wizard Priest, Zatoichi on the Road, Thirteen Assassins, Atragon (1963); The Teigin Affair – A Condemned Criminal, Godzilla vs. the Thing, Band of Assassins, Dagora the Space Monster, Woman Running Along by the Waterslide, A Gambler in Suruga, Zatoichi – A Bloody Journey, The Boss of Beggars, Musashi Miyamoto IV – Duel at Ichijoji Temple, Ghidrah – The Three-Headed Monster (1964); Ieyasu Tokugawa, Zatoichi – The Blind Swordsman's Revenge, The Japanese Islands [Birth of the Japanese Islands?], The Wild One, Frankenstein Conquers the World [Jap/US], Musashi Miyamoto V – The Last Duel, Monster Zero [Jap/US], Zatoichi and the Chess Expert (1965); The Princess' Mask, Majin, Adventures of Takla Makan, Zatoichi – The Blind Swordsman's Vengeance, The Mixed Fight, War of the Gargantuas [Jap/US], The Return of the Giant Majin, 13,000 Suspects, Sword of the Ruffian, Majin Strikes Again, Eleven Samurai (1966); King Kong Escapes [Jap/US], Zatoichi Challenged (1967); The Snow Woman, Madmen in Kawachi, Destroy All Monsters, Young Men – Challenge! (1968); Sky Scraper!,

The Devil's Temple, Latitude Zero [Jap/US] (1969); Zatoichi Meets Yojimbo, Yog—Monster from Space, Will to Conquer, Swords of Death (1970); Godzilla on Monster Island [stock music from *Birth of the Japanese Islands* only] (1972); Zatoichi's Conspiracy, The Human Revolution (1973); Wolf—Chop the Setting Sun, Sandakan 8 (1974); Terror of Mechagodzilla, The Door Has Opened (1975); A Great Elm (1976); Love and Faith (1978); Godzilla vs. Biollante [themes only] (1989); Godzilla vs. King Ghidorah (1991); Godzilla vs. Mothra (1992); Godzilla vs. Mechagodzilla (1993); Godzilla vs. Space Godzilla [themes only] (1994); Godzilla vs. Destroyer (1995).

Hisashi Igawa Actor. *b.* November 17, 1936, in Hoten, Manchuria. Important character player, often cast as grumpy fathers or corrupt executives, and closely associated with the recent films of Kurosawa. He was the greedy father in *Rhapsody in August* (1991), an ex-student in *Madadayo* (1993), and the patriarch who makes his dying wife cook one last meal in *Tampopo* (1985).

FILMS INCLUDE: Harakiri (1962); The Face of Another, Zatoichi—The Blind Swordsman's Pilgrimage (1966); When Spring Comes Late, Dodes'ka-den, Tora-san's Runaway (1970); The Village, Kaseki (1975); Double Suicide at Sonezaki (1977); Demon Pond (1980); Tampopo (1985); Hachi-Ko (1987); Akira Kurosawa's Dreams (1990); Rhapsody in August, Hikarigoke, Kamigata Kugaizoshi, War and Youth (1991); Madadayo (1993).

Ryo Ikebe Actor. *b.* February 11, 1918, in Tokyo. Entering Toho's story department to learn the art of screenwriting, Ikebe was discovered by director Yasujiro Shimazu, and quickly became popular with younger audiences, especially women. He was notoriously uncomfortable in period films, and often rather unexpressive. He appeared in many of **Kon Ichikawa** and **Shiro Toyoda**'s films, but is probably best remembered as the white collar worker in Ozu's *Early Spring* (1956), and for his later appearances in Toho fantasy films, including *Battle in Outer Space* (1959) and *Gorath* (1962). His performances became increasingly wooden in later years, but his popularity was renewed in the Yakuza genre at Toei during the 1960s, particularly opposite **Ken Takakura** in that studio's "Arajishi jinki" series.

FILMS INCLUDE: Fighting Fish (1941); War and Peace, Four Love Stories (1947); Apostasy (1948); Blue Mountains (1949); Pursuit at Dawn, Conduct Report of Professor Ishinaka, Street of Violence (1950); The Lover, River Solo Flows, The Blue Pearl (1951); Postwar Japanese/The Moderns, Young Generation, The Woman Who Touched the Legs, Morning Conflicts (1953); All of Myself, Geisha Konatsu, With All My Heart, Bride in a Bathing Suit, The Second Kiss (1954); Love Tide, Brotherly Love, No Response from Car 33, The Lone Journey, The Immortal Pitcher, The Rookie Manager (1955); The Maiden Courtesan, Early Spring, Madame White Snake, Ambition, The College Hero (1956); Snow Country, Evening Calm, The Decoy (1957); The Happy Pilgrimage, The Princess of Angor Wat, The Post as Director, Theatre of Life (1958); Submarine E-57, Never Surrenders!, Police and Small Gangsters, Pilgrimage at Night, Three Dolls Go to Hong Kong, Battle in Outer Space (1959); Kao, Man Against Man, I Bombed Pearl Harbor (1960); Gorath, Chushingura, Structure of Hate (1962); Attack Squadron!, Siege of Fort Bismarck (1963); Twilight Path, Pale Flower (1964); Beast Alley (1965); Burning Clouds (1967); Sky Scraper! (1969); The Battle of Okinawa (1971); Someday Somewhere (1975); The War in Space (1977); Before Spring (1980); Station (1981); Mishima—A Life in Four Chapters [US/Jap] (1985); Lost in the Wilderness (1986); See You (1988).

Saburo Iketani Actor. *b.* 1922 (?). Character actor at Toho who seems to have spent his entire career playing news readers and the like in genre films.

FILMS INCLUDE: Godzilla King of the Monsters! (1954); Rodan (1956); Battle in Outer Space (1959); Mothra, The Last War (1961); Gorath (1962); Monster Zero [Jap/US] (1965); Destroy All Monsters (1968).

Tadashi Imai Director. *b.* January 8, 1912, in Tokyo. *ed.* Imperial University. Marxist filmmaker who began his career as an assistant at J.O. Studios in 1935. Though attacked by the right, his *Green Mountains* (1949) was a tremendous commercial success, thanks largely to his keen story-telling ability. His subsequent work openly criticized and analyzed the social injustices of Japanese society, particularly under the wartime leadership, and was heavily influenced by Italian neorealism. His 1960s work was only slightly more commercially minded; he moved into Huston-esque literary adaptations. His *Bushido—Samurai Saga* won the Grand Prize at the Berlin Film Festival, and Imai has even directed an animated feature, *The Snow Fairy* (1981).

FILMS INCLUDE: Namazu Military Academy, Our Instructor (1939); The Village of Tajinko, Women's Town, The General (1940); Married Life (1941); The Suicide Troops of the Watchtower (1943); The Angry Sea (1944); An Enemy of the People, Life Is Like a Somersault (1946); 24 Hours of a Secret Life [co-dir.] (1947); Blue Mountains, Woman's Face (1949); Till We Meet Again (1950); And Yet We Live (1951); Echo School, Pictures of the Atom Bomb (1952); The Tower of Lilies, Muddy Waters (1953); Here Is a Spring, Yukiko, Because I Love [co-dir.] (1955); Darkness at Noon (1956); Rice, A Story of Pure Love (1957); The Adulterous/Night Drum (1958); Kiku and Isamu (1959); The Cliff (1960); Pan Chopali (1961); The Old Woman of Japan (1962); Bushido—Samurai Saga (1963); A Story from Echigo, The Revenge (1964); When the Cookie Crumbles (1967); The Time of Reckoning (1968); River Without a Bridge (1969); River Without a Bridge II (1970); A Woman Named Oen (1971); Ah! My Friends Without Voice/My Voiceless Friends, Special Boy Soldiers of the Navy, Eternal Cause (1972); The Life of a Communist Writer (1974); Brother and Sister, Yoba (1976); Rika (1978); The Snow Fairy (1981); Himeyuri Lily Tower (1982); War and Youth (1991).

Shohei Imamura Director, screenwriter. *b.* 1926, in Tokyo. *ed.* Waseda University. He joined Shochiku as an assistant director under Ozu, but moved to Nikkatsu three years later, in 1954, as an assistant and screenwriter to Yuzo Kawashima, and made his directorial debut with *Stolen Desire* (1958). From 1970 to 1978, Imamura worked exclusively in television, where he directed several highly lauded documentaries. In 1979 he returned to theatrical features—and was "discovered" by Western critics—with *Vengeance Is Mine*, a critical and commercial success. In 1988 he directed *Black Rain*, a moving study of Hiroshima A-Bomb survivors, which was released in the United States at the same time as the Ridley Scott/Michael Douglas thriller *Black Rain*, which created much confusion for moviegoers. Imamura's blunt, in-your-face style goes against the grain of what most Western audiences expect from Japanese films, and the director has a Kubrick-like passion for preproduction research and planning. *The Flesh Is Hot* won the Best Film Award by the Japan Newspaper Film Critics Association, *The Insect Woman* received the Silver Bear at the Berlin Film Festival, and he won the Palm d'Or at Cannes in 1983 for his remake of *The Ballad of Narayama*.

FILMS INCLUDE: Early Summer [asst. dir. only] (1951); Tea and Rice [asst. dir. only] (1952); Tokyo Story [asst. dir. only] (1953); The Balloon [co-scr. only] (1956); Turning to Hell [co-scr. only], Saheiji Finds a Way/ Sun Legend of the Shogunate's Last Days [co-scr. only], Stolen Desire, Lights of Night/Nishi Ginza Station, Endless Desire (1958); Turning to Hell [co-scr. only], My Second Brother/The Diary of Sueko (1959); The Flesh Is Hot/Pigs and Battleships (1961); Cupola Where the Furnaces Glow [scr. only] (1962); Son of a Samurai/The Young Samurai [co-scr. only], The Insect Woman (1963); Unholy Desire (1964); The Amorists/The Pornographers (1966); A Man Vanishes, Neon Jungle [co-scr. only] (1967); East China Sea [story and co-scr. only], Kuragejima—Tales from a Southern Island (1968); History of Postwar Japan as Told by a Bar Hostess (1970); Vengeance Is Mine (1979); Eijanaika (1980); The Ballad of Narayama (1983); The Pimp, Zegan (1987); Black Rain (1988).

Hiroshi Inagaki Director. *b.* December 30, 1905, in Tokyo. *d.* 1980. Originally an actor (in films from 1915), Inagaki turned to directing in the late

1920s. His tremendous output (several hundred films) go against his careful compositions and staging. He is best remembered for his historical spectacles, often told in several parts, such as his magnificent and visually spectacular Musashi Miyamoto trilogy, general known as *Samurai I-III* (1954–56), and his epic telling of the Loyal Forty-Seven Ronin, the all-star *Chushingura* (1962). From the early 1950s he frequently worked with star **Toshiro Mifune**. Their collaborations on *Samurai I* and *The Rickshaw Man* (1958) earned Inagaki the Academy Award for Best Foreign Film (1956), and Golden Lion at the Venice Film Festival (1958), respectively.

FILMS INCLUDE: Peace of the World, The Wandering Gambler (1928); Elegy of Hell II [co-dir.], Elegy of Hell III, Duck Journey Diary, The Great Palisade, A Swordsman's Picture-Book (1929); Three Jesting Ronin (1930); The Image of a Mother, A Sword and the Sumo Ring (1931); Yataro's Sedge Hat, Travels Under the Blue Sky, Instruction Period (1932); Bad Luck I (1933); Bad Luck II, Journey of Eight Children (1934); White Snow of Fuji, The Great Bodhisattva Pass I, White Hood I (1935); The Great Bodhisattva Pass II, Journey of a Thousand and One Nights (1936); Spirit of Wilderness, Matchless Sword (1937); A Great Power Rising in the World, Shadow of Darkness, Hell of Mushi (1938); Mazo I, Mazo II, Kesa and Morito [co-dir.] (1939); Musashi Miyamoto I, Musashi Miyamoto II, Musashi Miyamoto III (1940); Festival Across the Sea, The Last Days of Edo, Duel at Ichijoji Temple (1941); One-eyed Dragon (1942); The Life of Matsu the Untamed (1943); Signal Fires in Shanghai (1944); Last Abdication (1945); Children Hand in Hand (1947); Boy with the Black Horse (1948); Forgotten Children (1949); Kojiro Sasaki I (1950); Kojiro Sasaki II, Kojiro Sasaki III, Pirates (1951); Lightning Advance, Sword for Hire, The Lady from Shanghai (1952); Traveling with a Breeze (1953); Samurai/Samurai I—Musashi Miyamoto (1954); Samurai II—Duel at Ichijoji Temple, The Lone Journey (1955); Samurai III—Duel at Ganryu Island, Rebels on the High Sea, The Storm (1956); Secret Scrolls I, A Geisha in the Old City (1957); Ninjutsu/Secret Scrolls II, Rat Kid on Journey, The Rickshaw Man (1958); Samurai Saga, The Three Treasures (1959); Life of a Country Doctor (1960); Daredevil in the Castle, The Youth and His Amulet, Bandits on the Wind (1961); Tatsu, Chushingura (1962); Young Swordsman (1963); Whirlwind, The Rabble (1964); Rise Against the Sword (1966); Kojiro (1967); Under the Banner of Samurai (1969).

Yujiro Ishihara Actor. *b.* 1934, in Kobe. *d.* 1987, of lung cancer. When his brother, novelist Shintaro Ishihara, sold the rights to his bestseller, *Season in the Sun,* to Nikkatsu, it was with the condition that Yujiro play the lead. After this auspicious debut, Ishihara remained a huge star through the late 1960s. He made a come-back of sorts, producing and starring in the popular TV cop show "Seibu keisatsu" in the 1980s. Best remembered in the West as one of the contestants in *Those Magnificent Men in Their Flying Machines* (1965).

FILMS INCLUDE: Season in the Sun, Crazed Fruit/Juvenile Passion, The Baby Carriage, Human Torpedoes (1956); Jazz-Girl Tanjo, The Champion, Pleasure of Life, Saheiji Finds a Way, Harbor Rats, The Eagle and the Hawk, I'll Be Waiting, The Stormy Man (1957); Fangs of the Nights, The Rusty Knife, Street in the Sun, Tomorrow Is Another Day, That Wonderful Guy, The Man Who Rode the Typhoon, The Left Hand of Jiro, Showdown in the Storm, Crimson Wings (1958); The Stream of Youth, We Live Today, Explosion Came, The Echo of Love, Love and Death, Dream Young Man's Dream, The Wild Reporter, The Sky Is Mine, When a Man Risks His Life (1959); The Cards Will Tell, Duel on the Silver Peak, Blossoms of Love, The Day of Youth, The White-Collar Dreamer, The Tough Guy, The Reformer, Wait for Tomorrow, The Man at the Bullfight (1960); For This We Fight, That Guy and I, Toying with Life, Storm Over Arabia (1961); The City of Men, Love in Ginza, The Seat of Youth, Facing the Clouds, I Hate but Love, The Zero Fighter, Fresh Leaves, Rainbow Over the Kinmen, A Man with a Dragon Tatoo (1962); My Enemy the Sea, I Fly for Kicks, Escape into Terror, Foggy Night Blues, Alone on the Pacific (1963); Red Handkerchief, Sunset Hill, Gambler's Blood, Rub Out the Killers, The Eternal Life, Black Channel (1964); Those Magnificent Men in Their Flying Machines or How I Flew from London to Paris in 25 Hours and 11 Minutes [US/Brit], Moved to Tears, The Duel at Red Valley (1965); A Couple of the World, Youth President, Outline of Violence, Kill the Night Rose, Harbor of No Return, Challenge for Glory, The Last Escape (1966); A Warm Misty Night, The Storm Came and Went, Lone Hawk of the Waterfront, The Golden Mob (1967); Tunnel to the Sun, The Sword Gamblers, Sun Over Kurobe Gorge, Man of a Stormy Era (1968); Under the Banner of Samurai, Eiko's 5000 kilograms, Tenchu!, The Cleanup (1969); The Ambush: Incident at Blood Pass, Men and War (1970).

Ichizo Itami *see* **Juzo Itami**

Juzo Itami Actor, director, screenwriter. *b.* 1933, in Kyoto. *ed.* high school. Son of director Mansaku Itami, Juzo worked as an amateur boxer and commercial designer before turning to film acting in 1960. He worked steadily in films, sometimes billed as Ichizo Itami, throughout the 1960s and 1970s, before turning to directing and screenwriting in 1984. These ensemble comedies—all of which star his actress wife, **Nobuko Miyamoto**—are by far the most popular, critically acclaimed satires ever to come out of Japan, and have consistently won over Japanese critics as well. The quality and popularity of his work has in fact drawn many of his former co-stars back into the spotlight in roles ranging from leads to tiny walk-ons. His frequent target is the Yakuza (Japanese Mafia), and their apparent lack of humor led to a brutal attack on the director by several thugs who slashed his throat. This only served to further the director's resolve on the subject, however, as reflected in his latest works. A man of many talents, Itami has also hosted a talk show, worked as a translator, a chef, and as the editor of a magazine on psychoanalysis.

Films Include: **[as actor]**—Dislike, The Phony University Student, Her Brother (1960); The Ten Dark Women (1961); 55 Days at Peking [US] (1963); Lord Jim [US] (1964); A Man's Face Is His History (1966); A Treatise on Japanese Bawdy Songs (1967); The Concubines, Tokyo 196X (1968); Heat Wave Island (1969); My Sister My Love (1974); I Am a Cat (1975); Labyrinth in the Field (1980); The Makioka Sisters (1983); The Family Game (1983); Sweet Home [also prod.] (1989). **[as director, co-producer and screenwriter]**—The Funeral (1984); Tampopo (1985); A Taxing Woman (1987); A Taxing Woman's Return (1988); A-Ge-Man—Tales of a Golden Geisha (1990); Minbo—or the Gentle Art of Japanese Extortion (1992); The Seriously Ill (1993).

Daisuke Ito Director, screenwriter. *b.* 1898, in Ehime. *d.* 1981. Director specializing in violent period films, first at Shochiku and Nikkatsu, and later at Daiei.

Films Include: Smoke (1925); Panic and Calm, The Sun, First Shrine (1926); A Diary of Chuji's Travels I, A Diary of Chuji's Travels II, Evil Spirit, Wandering, The Servant, Changeful Revenge (1927); A Diary of Chuji's Travels III, Ooka's Trial I, Ooka's Trial II, Ooka's Trial III, Yotsuya Ghost Story New Edition (1928); Man-Slashing Horse-Piercing Sword (1929); Ooka's Trial Continued, The Rise and Fall of Shinsengumi I, The Rise and Fall of Shinsengumi II (1930); Samurai Japan I, Samurai Japan II, Ooka's Trial Continued II (1931); The First Year of the Meiji Era, Messenger to Satsuma (1932); The Loyal Forty-Seven Ronin I, The Loyal Forty-Seven Ronin II (1934); People's Building (1935); Pass of Morning Mist, The Forty-Eighth Comrade (1936); Swordsman Mataemon Araki, Sad Tune (1938); Pass of Eagle's Tail (1941); Kurama Tengu Appears in Yokohama (1942); The Duel at Hannya-zaka (1943); International Smuggling Gang (1944); The King of Chess (1948); The Motherland Far Far Away, Les Miserables (1950); The Mysterious Palanquin, Five Men of Edo (1951); Lion's Dance (1953); Samurai's Love, The Story of Shunkin (1954); The Life of a Woman in the Meiji Era, The Servant's Neck, The Life of a Chess Player,

Genroku's Handsome Youth (1955); Flowers of Hell (1957); The Gay Masquerade (1958); The Woman and the Pirates (1959); The Conspirator (1961); The King of Chess (1962); An Actor's Revenge [co-scr. only].

Hisaya Ito Actor. *b.* August 7, 1938, in Kobe. Tall, Western-looking actor who made his debut as a teenager, in Tadashi Imai's *Tower of Lilies* (1953). He joined Toho in 1957 and was groomed for stardom but never quite caught on. However, he continued to appear in a wide range of roles in films and series television. Best known in the West as the assassin in *Ghidrah – The Three-Headed Monster* (1964).

FILMS INCLUDE: Tower of Lilies [debut] (1953); Seven Samurai [bit] (1954); The Mysterians (1957); The H-Man, Varan the Unbelievable, Rat Kid on Journey (1958); Battle in Outer Space, The Three Treasures (1959); I Bombed Peal Harbor, The Human Vapor, Six Suspects (1960); Death on the Mountain (1961); Chushingura (1962); Atragon (1963); Ghidrah – The Three-Headed Monster (1964); Frankenstein Conquers the World (1965); War of the Gargantuas [Jap/US], Ebirah Horror of the Deep (1966); Destroy All Monsters, Admiral Yamamoto (1968).

Jerry Ito Actor. *b.* July 12, 1927, in New York. The son of Kisaku Ito and an American model, Ito excelled in bilingual roles, often cast as a villain (notably in Ishiro Honda's *Mothra*), though he played the title role in the comedy *Wall-Eyed Nippon* (1964), about a *gaijin* (foreigner) who marries a Japanese woman. Frequently mis-billed as Jelly Ito.

FILMS INCLUDE: Mothra, The Manster [US/Jap], The Last War (1961); Interpol Code 8 (1963); Wall-Eyed Nippon (1964); Mighty Jack [made for TV] (1968).

Shima Iwashita Actress. *b.* January 3, 1941, in Tokyo, to actors Koyoshi Nonomura and Miyoko Yamagishi. *ed.* Seijo University. In 1960, two years after making her television debut, Iwashita joined Shochiku, the studio with whom she is most associated. Her popularity was such that with her husband, director **Masashiro Shinoda**, father, and producer Masayuki Nakajima, formed Hyogen-sha Film Co., Ltd. Memorable in Ozu's *Late Autumn* (1960) and *An Autumn Afternoon* (1962), Masaki Kobayashi's *Harakiri* (1962), and later in her husband's *Double Suicide* (1969), she was in constant demand throughout the decade in dramatic roles. In 1977, she received the Japanese Academy Award, for *The Ballad of Orin*.

FILMS INCLUDE: Youth in Fury, The River Fuefuki, Lesson for Widows, Late Autumn, Country in My Arms (1960); Killers on Parade, Far Beyond the Waves, Epitaph to My Love, A Pearl in the Waves, A Thief and Culture Order, Enraptured (1961); Her Last Pearl, Harakiri, An Autumn Afternoon (1962); The Hidden Profile, A Legend or Was It?, Twin Sisters of Kyoto [dual role] (1963); Destroyer Yukikaze, The Assassin, Mr. Radish and Mr. Carrot, Samurai from Nowhere, Twilight Path (1964); Snow Country, Samurai Gold Seekers, The Scarlet Camellia (1965); The Kii River, Springtime, Miss Ohanahan, Punishment Island (1966); Rebellion in Japan, Portrait of Chieko, Clouds at Sunset, Une Vie (1968); Gion Matsuri/The Day the Sun Rose (1968); Double Suicide, Red Lion, Through Days and Months, The Song in My Heart (1969); The Scandalous Adventures of Buraikan, Forbidden Affair, The Shadow Within (1970); Shadow of Deception (1971); Himiko (1974); Under the Blossoming Cherry Trees (1975); The Demon, Melody in Gray, The Ballad of Orin/Banished (1977); Bandit vs. Samurai Squad (1978); MacArthur's Children, Fireflies of the North (1984); No More Love No More God, House Without a Dining Table (1985); Gonza the Spearman (1986); Takeshi – Childhood Days (1990).

Kyoko Kagawa Actress. *b.* Kyoko Ikebe, December 5, 1931, In Ibaragi. *ed.* high school. In films from 1949, Kagawa has worked with several of Japan's greatest directors, including Ozu (in *Tokyo Story*), Mizoguchi (*Sansho the Bailiff, The Story of Chikamatsu*), Ishiro Honda (*Mothra*), and Hiroshi Inagaki (*The Three Treasures, The Secret Scrolls*). However, she is best known in the West

The great Daisuke Kato (right) with Masako Tsutsumi in *The Abe Clan* (1938). (Photo courtesy Darrell Davis.)

for her association with **Akira Kurosawa**. She played Toshiro Mifune's wife in both *The Bad Sleep Well* (1960) and *High and Low* (1963), his love interest in *The Lower Depths* (1957), and the mad woman in *Red Beard* (1965). She has appeared infrequently in films since her 1963 marriage to writer Takuji Makino (together they lived in New York during the mid-1960s), but was reunited with director Kurosawa for *Madadayo/Not Yet* in 1993.

Films Include: Jump Out the Window [debut] (1950); Tokyo Story (1953); Sansho the Bailiff, The Story of Chikamatsu (1954); The Cat Shozo and the Two Women, Dancer and the Warrior (1956); The Man in the Storm, Osaka Story, Secret Scrolls I, The Lower Depths, The Prodigal Son, Earth (1957); Secret Scrolls II, The Child Writers (1958); The Three Treasures (1959); My Friend Death, The Bad Sleep Well (1960); Daredevil in the Castle, Death on the Mountain, Mothra (1961); Girl of Dark (1962); High and Low (1963); Red Beard (1965); The Family (1974); Have Wings on Your Heart (1978); Tora-san's Dream of Spring (1979); Mt. Aso's Passion (1990); Madadayo (1993).

Daisuke Kato Actor. *b.* February 18, 1911, in Tokyo. *d.* 1975. Portly, moon-faced actor and one of the *Seven Samurai* (1954). In films beginning in 1933, Kato's career as a character performer took off when he went free-lance in 1954, and the actor was in constant demand through the early 1970s. He is perhaps best remembered as the dopey "Inokichi" in *Yojimbo* (1961), Hideko Takemine's shy suitor in Mikio Naruse's *When a Woman Ascends the Stairs* (1960), and as the nostalgic ex-sailor in Ozu's *An Autumn Afternoon* (1962).

Films Include: The Abe Clan (1938); The Loyal Forty-Seven Ronin I (1941); The Loyal Forty-Seven Ronin II (1942); Rashomon (1950); Ikiru, The Life of Oharu, Mother (1952); The Blue Revolution (1953); Late Chrysanthemums, Seven Samurai, Samurai I (1954); Samurai II, Floating Clouds, Tojura's Love (1955); Street of Shame, Early Spring (1956); The Naked General, The Happy Pilgrimage (1958); Seniors Juniors Coworkers, I Want to Be a Shellfish (1959); I Bombed Pearl Harbor, Wonton Journey, The Gambling Samurai, When a Woman Ascends the Stairs (1960); A Night in

Hong Kong, Early Autumn, Snow in the South Seas [also story based on his autobiography], Yojimbo (1961); Star of Hong Kong, The Wiser Age, Born in Sin, Lonely Lane, An Autumn Afternoon, Chushingura (1962); Crazy Free-for-All – Don't Procrastinate, An Actor's Revenge [co-scr. only] (1963); Twilight Path, Super-Express (1964); Five Gents' Trick Book, Judo Saga, We Will Remember (1965); The Daphne, The Thin Line, Once a Rainy Afternoon, Moment of Terror, 5 Gents on the Spot (1966); The Emperor and the General, Two in the Shadow, Our Silent Love (1967); The Night Before Pearl Harbor, Admiral Yamamoto (1968).

Haruya Kato Actor. *b.* June 22, 1928, in Tokyo. Memorable bit player at Toho, whose boyish, Bud Cort–like features belied his years, and which suited him to a variety of roles (e.g., a would-be firefighter in *The Mysterians*, a reporter in *Ghidrah – The Three Headed Monster*, etc.). He was a regular on the Tsuburaya teleseries "Ultra Q," and more recently appeared in Nobuhiko Kobayashi's *Tenkose* (1982).

FILMS INCLUDE: Portrait of Madame Yuki [debut] (1950); The Mysterians (1957); The H-Man (1958); The Angry Sea (1960); Moonlight in the Rain, Mothra (1961); King Kong vs. Godzilla (1962); Dagora the Space Monster, Ghidrah – the Three-Headed Monster (1964); Frankenstein Conquers the World [Jap/US] (1965); Come Marry Me (1966); Monsieur Zivaco (1967); Exchange Students (1982); Rhapsody in August (1991).

Shintaro Katsu Actor. *b.* November 29, 1931, in Tokyo. Popular, beefy Daiei star who shot to stardom as the blind swordsman **"Zatoichi"** in the long-running film series. Katsu had been playing doomed heroes and psychotic heavies when he landed the role for which he is most associated. Beginning in 1962, Katsu starred in several Zatoichi films per year. By the end of the decade, he had assumed producer reigns on most of his pictures as well, and even directed a few. He also starred in Daiei's 16-film "Tough Guy" series (1961–74) and produced the long-running "Lone Wolf and Cub" film and (later) television series, which starred his brother, **Tomisaburo Wakayama**. Meanwhile, Katsu's own series survived Daiei's bankruptcy in the early 1970s, and moved to Toho before it was successfully adapted for television, also with Katsu. He was cast in the dual, title role of Kurosawa's *Kagemusha* (1980), but his ego clashed with the director's during the first week of filming, and Katsu was replaced by Tatsuya Nakadai. Later in the decade, Katsu was arrested on a drug possession charge, and later still his son accidentally but fatally injured a crew member with a sword on the set of one of his father's films. However, Katsu's popularity remains unabated, and he revived his most famous character in 1989, the 26th feature in the Zatoichi saga.

FILMS INCLUDE: Ghost-Cat of Goju-san Tsugi, Three Sisters of Gion, Dancer and the Warrior (1956); Necromancy, Osaka Story (1957); Ghost-Cat Wall of Hatred, Chushingura, The Jovial Rascals of Edo (1958); Ghost from the Pond, Samurai Vendetta, Jirocho Fuji, It's You I Love, The Doomed Bride (1959); The Ogre of Mt. Oe, Enchanted Princess, Jirocho the Chivalrous, The Two Musashis, The Buried Treasure, Secrets of a Court Masseur (1960); Buddha, Blind Devotion, Three Young Samurai (1961); The Great Wall, The Whale God, The Life and Opinion of Zatoichi, The Return of Zatoichi, The Beast Within (1962); Zatoichi Enters Again, Zatoichi the Fugitive, Zatoichi, Nothing But Guts, I Can Get Away with Anything, Rabble Tactics (1963); Zatoichi and the Chest of Gold, Zatoichi's Flashing Sword, Fight Zatoichi Fight, The Money Dance (1964); Adventures of a Blind Man, The Blind Swordsman's Revenge, Zatoichi and the Doomed Men, Hoodlum Soldier, Showdown for Zatoichi, The Wild One (1965); Zatoichi – The Blind Swordsman's Vengeance, Zatoichi – The Blind Swordsman's Pilgrimage (1966); Zatoichi – The Blind Swordsman's Cane Sword, Zatoichi – The Blind Swordsman's Rescue, The Hoodlum Priest (1967); Zatoichi – The Blind Swordsman and the Fugitives, Zatoichi – The Blind Swordsman Samaritan, The Man Without a Map, The Funeral Racket (1968); Devil's Temple, The Hoodlum Priest, The Magoichi Saga, Tenchu!, Tough Guy, Lone Avenger (1969); The Ambush: Incident at Blood Pass, Zatoichi Meets Yojimbo, The Blind Swordsman's

Fire Festival (1970); The Blind Swordsman Meets His Equal [Jap/HK], Inn of Evil (1971); Zatoichi at Large, Zatoichi in Desperation [also pro./dir.] (1972); Zatoichi's Conspiracy [also pro.] (1973); Zatoichi [also dir.] (1989).

Koichi Kawakita Director of Special Effects. *b.* December 2, 1942, in Tokyo. Special effects director at Toho since the late 1980s, succeeding Eiji Tsuburaya and Teruyoshi Nakano. He joined Toho in 1962, and directed the effects work for several science fiction teleseries prior to moving into features.

Films Include: Samurai of the Big Sky (1976); Sayonara Jupiter (1983); Zero (1984); Nineteen (1987); Gunhed, Godzilla vs. Biollante (1989); Godzilla vs. King Ghidorah (1991); Godzilla vs. Mothra (1992); Monster Planet Godzilla [3-D short], Godzilla vs. Mechagodzilla (1993); Yamato Takeru, Godzilla vs. Space Godzilla (1994); Godzilla vs. Destroyer (1995).

Seizaburo Kawazu Actor. *b.* August 31, 1908, in Tokyo. *d.* 1983. Popular Shochiku star of the 1930s, who later became a familiar character performer, often cast as gang leaders and government officials.

Films Include: The Straits of Love and Hate (1937); The Song of the Camp, Ah My Home Town (1938); The Loyal Forty-Seven Ronin I (1941); The Loyal Forty-Seven Ronin I (1942); Gion Festival Music (1953); The 7th Secret Courier for Edo (1958); Stop the Old Fox, Utamaru, Painter of Women (1959); I Bombed Pearl Harbor (1960); Mothra, The Last War (1961); Chushingura (1962); Attack Squadron! (1963); Dagora the Space Monster (1964); A Boss with the Samurai Spirit (1971).

Yuzo Kayama Actor. *b.* April 11, 1937, in Kanagawa. Popular singer and star of the 18-film "Young Guy" film series (1961–71), including a revival feature made in 1981. In films since 1960, he has worked infrequently in films since the early 1970s. The son of actor **Ken Uehara** (who appeared opposite him in several features), Kayama is best known in the West as the leader of the inept samurai (opposite Toshiro Mifune) in *Sanjuro* (1962), and for his starring performance as the young doctor with much to learn in *Red Beard* (1965).

Films Include: Man Against Man, Westward Desperado (1960); Big Shots Die at Dawn, The Man from the East, Lovers of Ginza, Happiness of Us Alone (1961); Bull of the Campus, Different Sons, Pride of the Campus, Born in Sin, Chushingura, Operation X, Sanjuro (1962); Honolulu-Tokyo-Hong Kong, Warring Clans, Siege of Fort Bismarck, Attack Squadron!, Young Guy in Hawaii (1963); Yearning (1964); Judo Saga, Campus A-Go-Go, We Will Remember, Red Beard (1965); It Started in the Alps, Night in Bangkok, The Sword of Doom, Come Marry Me (1966); Let's Go Young Guy!, The Emperor and the General, Two in the Shadow, Judo Champion, Too Many Moon, Las Vegas Free-for-All (1967); Goodbye Moscow, Sun Above Death Below, Admiral Yamamoto, Young Guy in Rio (1968); Young Guy Graduates, Young Guy on Mt. Cook, Battle of the Japan Sea, Bullet Wound (1969); Bravo Young Guy, The Creature Called Man, Duel at Ezo, The Militarists (1970); The Battle of Okinawa (1971); ESPY (1974); Wonderful World of Music [music only] (1979).

Ed Keane Actor. *b.* 1911 (?). American businessman in Japan and part-owner of the Kokusai Agency, which provided Western-looking actors for Japanese films, including himself (e.g., the mayor of Newkirk City in *Mothra*).

Films Include: The Barbarian and the Geisha [US] (1958); Battle in Outer Space (1959); The Last War, Mothra, The Human Condition III (1961); Gorath (1962).

Ryuzo Kikushima Screenwriter. *b.* 1914, in Yamanashi. *d.* 1989. Screenwriter closely associated with the films of **Akira Kurosawa**; he co-wrote such classics as *Throne of Blood* (1957), *Yojimbo* (1961), and *High and Low* (1963).

Films Include **[as screenwriter or co-screenwriter]:** Stray Dog (1949); Scandal (1950); Throne of Blood (1957); The Hidden Fortress (1958); The Three Treasures (1959); When a Woman Ascends the Stairs, Life of a Country Doctor, The Bad Sleep Well, Afraid to Die (1960); Yojimbo (1961); Sanjuro (1962); High and Low, She Came for Love (1963); The Magoichi Saga, Gone with Love Come with Memory (1969); Tora! Tora! Tora! [US/Jap] (1970); Willful Murder (1981); Princess from the Moon (1987).

Isao Kimura Actor. *b.* June 22, 1923, in Hiroshima. *d.* 1981. The youngest member of the *Seven Samurai* (1954), Kimura, billed as Ko Kimura early in his career, had been in films as early as 1942. He won much acclaim as the criminal in Kurosawa's *Stray Dog* (1949), and as Takashi Shimura's disciple in *Seven Samurai*. Kimura also demonstrated a keen sense of comedy appearing opposite drag queen Akihiro Maruyama in the campy *Black Lizard* (1968), and as the lead in Ichikawa's darkly humorous *A Billionaire* (1954).

FILMS INCLUDE: Stray Dog (1949); Ikiru, Vacuum Zone (1952); A Billionaire, Seven Samurai (1954); Throne of Blood (1957); Summer Clouds (1958); Zen and Sword (1960); Temple of the Wild Geese (1962); High and Low (1963); The Assassin (1964); Conquest, Snow Country (1965); The Secret of the Urn (1966); The Affair (1967); Black Lizard (1968); Secret Information (1969); Will to Conquer (1970).

Takeshi Kimura Screenwriter. *b.* February 4, 1911. *d.* January 1988, of asphyxiation caused by a throat obstruction. Toho screenwriter specializing in dark, sci-fi features. From 1964 he wrote under the pseudonym Kaoru Mabuchi.

FILMS INCLUDE **[as screenwriter or co-screenwriter]:** Red Senkichi (1952); Farewell Rabaul (1954); Rodan (1956); The Mysterians, Secret Scrolls II (1957); The H-Man (1958); The Human Vapor (1960); The Last War, Daredevil in the Castle (1961); Gorath (1962); The Lost World of Sinbad, Attack of the Mushroom People (1963); Whirlwind (1964); Frankenstein Conquers the World [Jap/US], Adventures of Takla Makan, War of the Gargantuas [Jap/US] (1966); King Kong Escapes (1967); Destroy All Monsters (1968); Godzilla vs. the Smog Monster (1971).

Keisuke Kinoshita Director. *b.* December 5, 1912, in Hamamatsu. Lyrical, sometimes sentimental Shochiku director of contemporary melodramas and breezy comedies (primarily geared for female audiences), and perhaps best represented by his lovely *Twenty-Four Eyes* (1954). Though he left the studio for television work in the mid-1960s, he continued to direct features, albeit infrequently, through the late 1980s. Two of his works were awarded the Kinema Jumpo Prize for Best Film: *Twenty-Four Eyes* and *The Ballad of Narayama* (1958), which was subsequently remade by Shohei Imamura. Kinoshita also directed the first Japanese all-color feature, *Carmen Comes Home* (1951), and many of his films were scored by his prolific composer-brother, Chuji Kinoshita.

FILMS INCLUDE: The Blossoming Port, Magoroku Is Still Alive (1943); Army, Jubilation Street (1944); A Morning with the Osone Family, The Girl I Loved (1946); Marriage, Phoenix (1947); Woman, A Portrait, Apostasy (1948); Here's to the Girls, The Yotsuya Ghost Story I, The Yotsuya Ghost Story II, The Broken Drum (1949); Engagement Ring (1950); Carmen Comes Home, The Good Fairy, Youth, Sea of Fireworks (1951); Carmen's Pure Love (1952); A Japanese Tragedy (1953); The Eternal Generation, Twenty-Four Eyes (1954); Distant Clouds, She Was Like a Wild Chrysanthemum (1955); Clouds at Twilight, The Rose on His Arm (1956); The Lighthouse/Times of Joy and Sorrow, Candle in the Wind (1957); The Ballad of Narayama, The Eternal Rainbow (1958); Snow Flurry, Sekishun-cho, Thus Another Day (1959); Spring Dreams, The River Fuefuki (1960); Immortal Love (1961); New Year's Love, Ballad of a Workman (1962); Sing Young People, A Legend or Was It? (1963); The Scent of Incense (1964); Eyes the Sea and a Ball (1967); Dodes'ka-den [prod. only] (1970); Love and Separation in Sri Lanka (1976); My Son/My Son! My Son! (1979); Children of Nagasaki (1983); Times of Joy and Sorrow/Big Joys Small Sorrows (1986); Children on the Island (1987); Father (1988).

Teinosuke Kinugasa Director, screenwriter. *b.* January 1, 1896, in Mie. *d.* 1982. The director of the Oscar-winning *Gate of Hell* (1953) began his career as an actor, an *oyama*, playing female roles at the Nikkatsu Mukojima studio in 1918. (He later led a walkout of actors who protested the move, in the mid-1920s, to hire female actors to play female roles.) He directed his first feature three years later, and soon began a long association with actor **Kazuo Hasegawa**, and followed him to Toho in 1939, and to Daiei ten years later.

Kinugasa visited the Soviet Union in the late 1920s, and his sometimes expressionistic work appears to have been greatly influenced by his education under Eisenstein. Kinugasa's *Crossroads* (1928) had played limited engagements in New York and Europe (as *The Slums of Tokyo*), but it was his *Gate of Hell* that earned him an international reputation. His use of color in that film was influential in the West (far more than the film itself, a rather ordinary work), and director John Huston hired Kinugasa as a consultant on *The Barbarian and the Geisha* (1958), a film Huston made largely because of Kinugasa's film.

FILMS INCLUDE: Two Little Birds, Spark (1922); The Golden Demon, The Spirit of the Pond, Beyond Decay (1923); She Has Lived Her Destiny I, She Has Lived Her Destiny II, Secret of a Wife, Love, Fog and Rain, Lonely Village, Dance Training, A Woman's Heresy (1924), Love and a Warrior, The Sun (1925); A Page of Madness, Shining Sun Becomes Clouded I, Shining Sun Becomes Clouded II, Shining Sun Becomes Clouded III (1926); Cassowary, Epoch of Loyalty, Star of Married Couples, The Palanquin, A Brave Soldier at Dawn, Moonlight Madness (1927); Gay Masquerade, Tales from a Country by the Sea, Female Demon, The Slums of Tokyo/Crossways/Crossroads, Before Dawn (1931); The Surviving Shinsengumi, The Loyal Forty-Seven Ronin (1932); Two Stone Lanterns, Gimpei from Koina (1933); A Sword and the Sumo Ring (1934); Yukinojo's Disguise I, Yukinojo's Disguise II (1935); Yukinojo's Disguise III (1936); The Summer Battle of Osaka (1937); Miss Snake Princess I, Miss Snake Princess II (1940); The Battle of Kawanakajima (1941); Forward Flag of Independence (1943); Rose of the Sea (1945); Lord for a Night (1946); Four Love Stories – Circus of Love, Actress (1947); Koga Mansion (1949); The Face of a Murderer (1950); Migratory Birds under the Moon, Lantern Under a Full Moon (1951); Saga of the Great Buddha (1952); Gate of Hell (1953); The Duel of a Snowy Night, End of a Prolonged Journey (1954); It Happened in Tokyo, A Girl Isn't Allowed to Love, The Romance of Yushima (1955); Three Women Around Yoshinaka, Spark (1956); Ukifune, A Fantastic Tale of Naruto (1957); A Spring Banquet, A Woman of Osaka, The Snow Heron, The Barbarian and the Geisha [US; script consultant only] (1958); It's You I Love, Stop the Old Fox (1959); The Lantern (1960); Blind Devotion, Otoko and Sasuke (1961); When Women Lie [co-dir.], The Sorcerer (1966); The Little Runaway [co-dir.; Jap/ USSR] (1967).

Nadao Kirino Actor. *b.* November 24, 1937, in Matsuyama. Often mis-billed as "Hiroo Kirino," this character actor specialized in military roles and henchmen. Memorable as Kumi Mizuno's husband in *Gorath* (1962).

FILMS INCLUDE: The H-Man, Varan the Unbelievable (1958); Battle in Outer Space (1959); The Secret of the Telegian, I Bombed Pearl Harbor (1960); The Last War (1961); Gorath, Chushingura, King Kong vs. Godzilla (1962); The Lost World of Sinbad, Attack Squadron!, Atragon (1963); Dagora the Space Monster, The Weed of Crime (1964); Monster Zero [Jap/US] (1965); War of the Gargantuas [Jap/US] (1966); Las Vegas Free-for-All, King Kong Escapes [Jap/US] (1967); Destroy All Monsters (1968).

Kyoko Kishida Actress. *b.* 1930, in Tokyo. *ed.* Actors' Institute of Bungaku-za. Hard-working actress best remembered as *The Woman in the Dunes* (1964). Still active in films.

FILMS INCLUDE: Muddy Waters [debut] (1953); Get 'Em All (1960); The Diplomat's Mansion, The Human Condition III (1961); An Autumn Afternoon, Love at the Foggy Harbor, Being Two Isn't Easy (1962); Bushido (1963); Brand of Evil, Love and Greed, Passion, Woman in the Dunes (1964); School of Love, Conquest (1965); The Face of Another, A Tale of Genji (1966); The Shogun and His Mistress, Who Is Gomez? (1967); The Time of Reckoning (1968); Vixen (1969); Inn of Evil (1971); Jigoku, Nichiren (1979); Rikyu (1989).

Shin Kishida Actor. *b.* October 17, 1939, in Tokyo. *d.* December 28, 1982, of lung cancer. In films as early as 1961, and often mis-billed in the West as "Mori Kishida," the late actor specialized playing weird villains, often assassin types, though he played comical roles as well. He frequently appeared on Japanese television, and even worked as a television writer for a time. Best remembered as "Dracula" in Toho's *Lake of Dracula* (1971).

FILMS INCLUDE: Zatoichi Meets Yojimbo (1970); Lake of Dracula (1971); Shogun Assassin (1972); Godzilla vs. the Cosmic Monster (1974); Evil of Dracula (1975); Utamaru's World (1977); Antarctica (1983).

Keiju Kobayashi Actor. *b.* November 23, 1923, in Gunma. Popular actor began his career at Nikkatsu, but became a star at Toho as the second lead (to **Hisaya Morishige**) in that studio's long-running "Company President" series, which ran an incredible 40 features, from 1956 to 1971. Kobayashi also starred in the NHK television version of "Red Beard," and while Kobayashi did not appear in Kurosawa's film version, he was memorable as the samurai kept in the closet in *Sanjuro* (1962). During the 1970s, the actor generally eased out of comedies and into dour statesman roles, playing the Prime Minister in both *Submersion of Japan* (1973) and *Godzilla 1985* (1984). He also gave a memorable performance as Tojo in *The Militarists* (1970), and received the Purple Riband from the Japanese government.

FILMS INCLUDE: Repast (1951); Mr. Lucky (1952); Adolescence II, Eagle of the Pacific (1953); Night School (1956); The Naked General, Summer Clouds, The Happy Pilgrimage, Holiday in Tokyo (1958); The Three Treasures (1959); Perils of Bangaku, Wanton Journey, Playboy President, My Hobo, I Bombed Pearl Harbor, The Master Fencer Sees the World (1960); Eternity of Love, Early Autumn, Happiness of Us Alone (1961); The Wiser Age, Chushingura, Lonely Lane, Sanjuro (1962); Pressure of Guilt (1963); Could I But Live (1964); Five Gents' Trick Book, Samurai Assassin, Beast Alley, We Will Remember, Dark the Mountain Snow (1965); The Daphne, Five Gents at Sunrise, The Thin Line, Five Gents on the Spot (1966); The Emperor and the General, Our Silent Love, Discover Japan with the Five Gents (1967); Five Gents and a Chinese Merchant (1968); Five Gents Fly to Kyushu (1969); Five Gents Fly to Taiwan, Five Gents and a Kuniang, The Ambitious, Band of Assassins, The Militarists (1970); The Battle of Okinawa (1971); Submersion of Japan/Tidal Wave (1973); Tora-san the Intellectual (1975); Imperial Navy (1981); Godzilla 1985 (1984); A Taxing Woman (1987).

Masaki Kobayashi Director. *b.* February 4, 1916, in Hokkaido. Kobayashi joined Shochiku in 1941, but soon was drafted, captured and became a prisoner of war. He first found success with *Room With Thick Walls* (1956), but it was his *The Human Condition* trilogy (1959–61), based, in part, on his own experiences in the military, which first brought him international acclaim. The first film won the Silver Prize of San Giorgio at the Venice Film Festival; this was followed by a special Jury Prize at Cannes three years later for *Harakiri* (1962). *Kwaidan* (1964), his best-known work in the United States, was a critical success in this country, but initially despised in Japan as pandering to the international market. A meticulous filmmaker, famous for his long shooting schedules, Kobayashi has worked sporadically since the late 1960s.

FILMS INCLUDE: My Son's Youth (1952); Sincere Heart (1953); Three Loves, Somewhere Beneath the Wide Sky (1954); Beautiful Days (1955); Room with Thick Walls, The Fountainhead, I'll Buy You (1956); Black River (1957); The Human Condition I—No Greater Love, The Human Condition II—Road to Eternity (1959); The Human Condition III—A Soldier's Prayer (1961); The Inheritance, Harakiri (1962); Kwaidan (1964); Rebellion (1967); Hymn to a Tired Man (1968); Dodes'ka-den [prod. only] (1970); Inn of Evil (1971); Kaseki [orig. made for TV] (1975); International Military Tribunal for the Far East—The Tokyo Trial (1983); House Without a Dining Table (1985).

Setsuo Kobayashi Director of Photography. *b.* 1920, in Shizuoka. Superb DP who joined Daiei after seven years of military service. He worked regularly with **Kon Ichikawa** and later, **Yasuzo Masamura**. His more notable work includes *Fires on the Plain* (1959), *The Whale God* (1962), *An Actor's Revenge* (1963), and *The Burmese Harp* (1985)

FILMS INCLUDE: The Hole (1957); Goodbye Good Day, Fires on the Plain (1959); The Last Betrayal, The Woman's Testament [co-dp] (1960); Les Mesdemoiselles, Wife's Confession, Just for Kicks, Ten Dark Women (1961); The Whale God, Stolen Pleasure, Being Two Isn't Easy (1962); An Actor's Revenge, Red Water (1963); Passion, A Public Benefactor/Tycoon, Super-Express, The Dedicated Gunman (1964); Hoodlum Soldier (1965); The School of Spies, Horn and Car, The Red Angel (1966); The Shroud of Snow, The Bogus Policeman, An Idiot in Love, The Wife of Seishu Hanaoka (1967); Evil Trio, Time of Reckoning, The House of Wooden Blocks (1968); The Blind Beast, Thousand Cranes, Vixen (1969); Just for You (1971); The Wanderers (1973); The Skies of Haruo (1977); Double Suicide at Sonezaki (1978); Nogumi Pass (1979); The Burmese Harp (1985); Princess of the Moon (1987).

Yukiko Kobayashi Actress. *b.* October 6, 1946, in Tokyo. Exotic-looking though fairly wooden actress. Later a staple of Japanese television.

FILMS INCLUDE: Come Marry Me (1966); Destroy All Monsters (1968); The Vampire Doll, Yog—Monster from Space (1970).

Momoko Kochi Actress. *b.* March 7, 1932, in Tokyo. A former dancer recruited in Toho's New Face Contest of 1953, and within one year appeared as the ingenue in that studio's biggest production of 1954—*Godzilla, King of the Monsters!* However, her star quickly faded, though she continued to work steadily in television commercials.

FILMS INCLUDE: Godzilla King of the Monsters! (1954); Half Human (1955); A Rainbow Plays in My Heart, The Mysterians (1957); Happiness of Us Alone (1962); Husty (1983).

Kokuten Kodo Actor. *b.* January 29, 1887. *d.* 1969 (?). Almost always mis-billed as "Kuninori Kodo," this busy character actor appeared in a variety of roles, from the bitter father-in-law in Kurosawa's *No Regrets for Our Youth* (1946), to the native island chief in *Godzilla, King of the Monsters!* (1954).

FILMS INCLUDE: Sanshiro Sugata (1943); No Regrets for Our Youth (1946); Snow Trail (1947); Stray Dog, The Quiet Duel (1949); Scandal (1950); The Blue Pearl, The Idiot (1951); Seven Samurai, Sword for Hire (1952); Godzilla King of the Monsters! (1954); Half Human, Samurai II, I Live in Fear (1955); Throne of Blood (1957); The Hidden Fortress (1958).

Hiroshi Koizumi Actor. *b.* August 12, 1926. A popular leading man of the 1950s and early 1960s, Koizumi began his career as a radio announcer at NHK. A New Face find of 1951, Koizumi made his first film at Toho the following year. As his star began to fade, the actor eased into television, where he hosted a popular game show, "Quiz Grand Prix." Though he continues to act occasionally, Koizumi in recent years has found great financial success as a landowner and restaurateur.

FILMS INCLUDE: Mr. Lucky (1952); Twelve Chapters About Women (1954); Gigantis the Fire Monster (1955); Holiday in Tokyo (1958); Girl in the Mist (1959); Perils of Bangaku, I Bombed Pearl Harbor (1960); Lovers of Ginza, A Night in Hong Kong, Mothra (1961); Different Sons, Star of Hong Kong, Chushingura (1962); Atragon, Attack of the Mushroom People (1963); Godzilla vs. the Thing, Dagora the Space Monster, Ghidrah—The Three-Headed Monster (1964); The Daphne (1966); Battle of the Japan Sea (1969); Prophecies of Nostradamus, Godzilla vs. the Cosmic Monster (1974); Godzilla 1985 [cameo] (1984); Tetsuo II Body Hammer [prod. only; participation unconfirmed] (1992).

Yoshio Kosugi Actor. *b.* September 15, 1903, in Tochigi. *d.* March 12, 1968. Toho character actor in almost constant demand throughout his career, playing coarse men of authority. His deeply etched, stern features and piercing eyes brought him numerous working class roles for Kurosawa, and South Seas native chiefs in several Toho fantasies.

FILMS INCLUDE: Horse (1941); Sanshiro Sugata (1943); Those Who Tread on the Tiger's Tail (1945); Snow Trail (1947); Eagle of the Pacific (1953); Seven Samurai (1954); Half Human (1955); The Mysterians

(1957); The Hidden Fortress (1958); Saga of the Vagabonds, The Three Treasures (1959); The Human Vapor, The Gambling Samurai, I Bombed Pearl Harbor (1960); The Youth and His Amulet, Mothra, Daredevil in the Castle (1961); Tatsu, King Kong vs. Godzilla (1962); Attack Squadron!, The Lost World of Sinbad (1963); Godzilla vs. the Thing, Whirlwind, Ghidrah—The Three-Headed Monster (1964); Frankenstein Conquers the World [Jap/US] (1965); The Emperor and the General (1967).

Akira Kubo Actor. *b.* December 1, 1936, in Tokyo. A child actor in industrial and educational shorts, including one by director Seiji Maruyama, who remembered him when casting the lead in Senkichi Taniguchi's *The Surf* (1954). Popular in war and fantasy films, he is best remembered as the stalwart hero of *Destroy All Monsters* (1968), the doomed college professor in *Attack of the Mushroom People* (1963), and as the nerdy inventor in *Monster Zero* (1965). After 1970 he worked primarily on the stage, and played the villain in the "Mitokoman" teleseries of the late 1970s.

FILMS INCLUDE: Kaneo naru Oka [debut] (1948); Adolescence II (1953); The Surf/The Sound of the Waves, Farewell Rabaul (1954); A Bridge for Us Alone (1956); Throne of Blood (1957); The College Hero, The Young Beast (1958); A Whistle in My Heart, Three Dolls in the College, The Three Treasures (1959); Three Dolls from Hong Kong, Westward Desperado (1960); Sanjuro, Gorath (1962); Attack of the Mushroom People, Le Fee Diabolique (1963); Whirlwind (1964); We Will Remember, Monster Zero [Jap/US] (1965); Son of Godzilla (1967); Kill, Admiral Yamamoto, Destroy All Monsters (1968); Battle of the Japan Sea (1969); Yog—Monster from Space (1970); Rikyu (1989); Gamera—Guardian of the Universe [cameo] (1995).

Koreyoshi Kurahara Director. *b.* 1927. *ed.* Nippon University. After a stint as an assistant director at Nikkatsu, Kurahara moved to Shochiku and, three years later, made his directorial debut. Among his better-known works is *The Black Sun* (1964), about a black AWOL soldier who befriends a Japanese jazz fan.

FILMS INCLUDE: I'll Be Waiting (1957); A Man in the Fog, The Man Who Rode the Typhoon, Showdown in the Storm (1958); The Third Assassin, Dynamite, Women from the Bottom of the Sea, A Turning to Hell, Our Own Age (1959); Blackmail, The Warped Ones (1960); Desperation, That Youth May Be Eternal, Gambler in the Sea, Breaking the Storm Barrier (1961); The Call of Mexico, Love in Ginza, I Hate But Love, Like a Wild Beast (1962); I Fly for Kicks (1963); The Black Sun, The Flame of Devotion (1964); The Awakening (1965); The Heart of Hiroshima (1966); Longing for Love (1967); Eiko's 5000 kilograms (1969); Kitakitsune Story (1978); The Gate of Youth [co-dir.] (1981); Antarctica (1983); Road/Hopeless Cause (1986); See You (1988); Strawberry Road (1991).

Susumu Kurobe Actor. *b.* October 22, 1939. Supporting player at Toho with an unremarkable feature career, often cast as a thug or foreign spy. He won lasting fame, however, when he played the title character in the Tsuburaya-produced teleseries "Ultraman" in 1966-67.

FILMS INCLUDE: Ghidrah—the Three-Headed Monster (1964); Beast Alley, None But the Brave [US/Jap], Ironfinger (1965); What's Up Tiger Lily? [US production incorporating Japanese footage] (1966); Ultraman [feature derived from teleseries], King Kong Escapes [Jap/US], Son of Godzilla (1967); Destroy All Monsters, Admiral Yamamoto (1968); Latitude Zero [Jap/US] (1969).

Akira Kurosawa Director, screenwriter. *b.* March 23, 1910, in Tokyo. Japan's greatest and most recognizable filmmaker, Akira Kurosawa first gained international attention with his examination of the relative nature of truth: *Rashomon* (1950). He had joined P.C.L.'s assistant director program shortly before the studio evolved into Toho, where he worked for more than 30 years. Kurosawa and fellow A.D. (and lifelong friend) **Ishiro Honda** worked under **Kajiro Yamamoto**. As an assistant director, Kurosawa not only prepared budgets and schedules and filmed second unit, but also wrote screenplays and edited film (notably in Yamamoto's *Horse*). He directed his first feature, *Sanshiro Sugata*, in 1943, and it was a commercial and critical hit. More films followed (under the watchful eye of the Japanese military, followed by the Occupation Forces), but it wasn't until the late 1940s, when the combative, rebellious director teamed with the equally rebellious **Toshiro Mifune** that his work evolved from the merely excellent to master works of cinema. *Rashomon* was soon followed by *Ikiru* and *Seven Samurai*, ranking 10th, 34th and 24th in John Kobal's international poll of film critics of the greatest films of all-time. *Rashomon* itself won a special Oscar, following its surprise Grand Prize win at the Venice Film Festival. The director's humanist masterpieces continued one after another through the mid-1960s, with adaptations of *Macbeth* (as *Throne of Blood*) and *The Lower Depths* (both 1957); the thrilling *High and Low* (1963) and *The Hidden Fortress* (1958); his *Hamlet*-esque *The Bad Sleep Well* (1960); and violent *jidai-geki* masterpiece *Yojimbo* (1961). Following the success of *Red Beard* (1965), Kurosawa was signed to direct two American films: the first an action-adventure piece for Joseph E. Levine about a trio of escaped convicts who take over a *Runaway Train*, the other the Japanese half of the ambitious *Tora! Tora! Tora!*. The latter soon ran into trouble at Twentieth Century–Fox when, depending on who's story is to be believed, Kurosawa left either because he had been falsely led to assume that David Lean was directing the Western half and became disillusioned with the project in general, or that the director's eccentricities had become intolerable and that he had been fired. In any event, Kurosawa returned to Japan to direct the interesting but atypical *Dodes'ka-den* (1970), his first flop in many years. Suddenly regarded as a has-been, *Dodes'ka-den* 's failure, combined with an undetected ulcer, compelled the director to attempt suicide as his elder brother had before him. Unlike his elder brother, his attempt failed, though his recovery was a slow one indeed. Ostracized from the mainstream film industry, he went to the Soviet Union for his next film, the magnificent *Dersu Uzala* (1975), which won the Academy Award for Best Foreign Film, but did little to bolster his reputation in Japan. It took the support and resources of George Lucas and Francis Ford Coppola to get his next film made: *Kagemusha* (1980). It was the director's first commercial smash in Japan in 15 years, and seen in the West as a tremendous come-back film (winning the Palme d'Or at Cannes to boot). This come-back continued with *Ran* (1985), a French/Japanese co-production generally regarded as the best film of the director's autumn years. Critics were kind to the then-80-year-old filmmaker's *Dreams*; peculiarly less so with his deeply moving *Rhapsody in August* (1991). The death of longtime friend and indispensable collaborator Ishiro Honda (in 1993) affected Kurosawa's recent output, but as this book went to press, Japan's greatest filmmaker was preparing a new *jidai-geki*, some 52 years after his directing debut. His son, Hisao Kurosawa, has co-produced his father's recent work. The elder Kurosawa's *Something Like an Autobiography* (1982) covers his personal and professional years through the production of *Rashomon*.

FILMS INCLUDE: **[as screenwriter or co-screenwriter]**: Horse (1941); Currents of Youth, A Triumph of Wings (1942); Wrestling Ring Festival (1944); Bravo Tasuke Isshin (1945); Four Love Stories [Shiro Toyoda episode], Snow Trail (1947); A Portrait (1948); The Lady from Hell, Jakoman and Tetsu (1949); Escape at Dawn, Tetsu Jiruba, Fencing Master (1950); Beyond Love and Hate, The Den of Beasts, The Duel at the Key-Maker's Corner (1951); Sword for Hire (1952); Blow Spring Breeze (1953); A Troop Has Disappeared, Sanshiro Sugata, The Story of Fast-Growing Weeds (1955); Three Hundred Miles Through Enemy Lines (1957); Saga of the Vagabonds (1959); The Magnificent Seven [US; story only] (1960); Jakoman and Tetsu, The Outrage [US; story only] Fistful of Dollars [It; uncredited story basis only] (1964); Judo Saga [also ed.] (1965); Battle Beyond the Stars [US; uncredited story basis only] (1980); Runaway Train [US; story only] (1985); Ah Ying/Ming Ghost [Thai; uncredited story basis only] (1992). **[as director/co-screenwriter]**: Sanshiro Sugata (1943); The Most Beautiful (1944); Sanshiro Sugata II,

They Who Step on the Tiger's Tail (1945); Those Who Make Tomorrow [co-dir.], No Regrets for Our Youth (1946); One Wonderful Sunday (1947); Drunken Angel (1948); The Quiet Duel, Stray Dog (1949); Scandal, Rashomon (1950); The Idiot (1951); Ikiru (1952); Seven Samurai (1954); I Live in Fear (1955); Throne of Blood, The Lower Depths (1957); The Hidden Fortress (1958); The Bad Sleep Well (1960); Yojimbo (1961); Sanjuro (1962); High and Low (1963); Red Beard (1965); Dodes'kaden (1970); Dersu Uzala [USSR/Jap] (1975); Kagemusha [Jap/US] (1980); Ran [Jap/Fr] (1985); Akira Kurosawa's Dreams [Jap/US] (1990); Rhapsody in August (1991); Madadayo/Not Yet (1993).

Toshio Kurosawa Actor. *b.* February 4, 1944, in Yokohama. Signed during Toho's New Talent search of 1964, Kurosawa (no relation to Akira) starred in the teleseries "Hangman" before graduating to feature stardom beginning in the late 1960s.

FILMS INCLUDE: Big Wind from Tokyo, Moment of Terror, Come Marry Me (1966); Discover Japan with the Five Gents, The Izu Dancer, Pomegranate Time, Seventeen, The Emperor and the General (1967); Hymn to a Tired Man, Two Hearts in the Rain, Admiral Yamamoto, Goodbye Moscow (1968); Resurrection of the Beast, Battle of the Japan Sea (1969); Duel at Ezo (1970); Submersion of Japan/Tidal Wave (1973); Prophecies of Nostradamus (1974); Evil of Dracula (1975); Horror of the Great Vortex (1978).

Machiko Kyo Actress. *b.* Motoko Yano, on March 25, 1924, in Osaka. Hard-working, beautiful actress—one of Japan's greatest—most associated with Kenji Mizoguchi, Kyo had been on the stage since 1936, and had initially found success as a dancer. She made her film debut in 1944, and joined Daiei five years later. Kyo was superb as the ghostly Lady Wakasa in Mizoguchi's *Ugetsu* (1953), and appeared in most of his later works. However, she was equally memorable as the wife in Kurosawa's *Rashomon* (1950), and as the aristocratic spouse in Kinugasa's *Gate of Hell* (1953). The international success of all three pictures brought Kyo to the United States, where she appeared opposite Marlon Brando in *Teahouse of the August Moon* (1957). Later still she did fine work in Ichikawa's *Odd Obsession*, Ozu's *Floating Weeds* (both 1959), Teshigahara's *The Face of Another* (1966), and in Toyoda's *Sweet Sweat* (1964), the latter winning her the Kinema Jumpo Award for Best Actress.

FILMS INCLUDE: Tengo-daoshi [debut], Three Generations of Danjuro (1944); Final Laughter (1949); The Snake Princess [two parts], The Motherland Far Far Away, Song of Asuka, Resurrection, Rashomon (1950); Clothes of Deception/Under Silk Garments, School of Freedom, Pier of Passion, The Enchantress, Tale of Genji, Life of a Horse-Trader (1951); Red Group of Asakusa, I'll Never Forget, The Song of Nagasaki, White Thread of the Cascades, Beauty and the Bandits, Saga of the Great Buddha, Her Scoop, Ugetsu, Spies, Older Brother Younger Sister, Gate of Hell (1953); A Certain Woman, The Doctor and the Nurse, The Story of Shunkin, The Princess Sen, Bazoku Geisha, Whirlpool of Spring (1954); A Girl Isn't Allowed to Love, Princess Yang Kwei-Fei, Tojuro's Love, New Woman's Dialogue (1955); Three Women Around Yashinaka, Street of Shame (1956); The Teahouse of the August Moon [US], The Hole/The Pit, Chorus Girls, A Woman's Skin/Skin of a Woman, Flowers of Hell, Night Butterflies (1957); Chance Meeting, Only Women Have Trouble, Chushingura, A Woman of Osaka, Tainted Flowers, The Ladder of Success/The Naked Face of Night, The Perfect Mate (1958); Goodbye Hello, The Makioka Sisters, The Woman and the Pirates, Paper Pigeon, Odd Obsession, Fighting Fishes of the Night, Floating Weeds, Jirocho Fuji, A Woman's Testament (1959); A Wandering Princess, The Last Betrayal, The Woman Who Touched the Legs, A Face, Assault from Hell (1960); Marriageable Age, Fantastico, A Design for Dying, Samurai's Daughter, Buddha (1961); The Great Wall, A Woman's Life (1962); The Third Wall, Sweet Sweat (1964); The Face of Another, The Daphne (1966); Thousand Cranes (1969); The Family (1974); Tora's Pure Love (1976); Make Up (1985).

Akihiro Maruyama Actor. *b.* 1935, in Nagasaki. Campy drag star—the Japanese equivalent of Divine—who starred in the cult classic *Black Lizard* (1968) and its less successful follow-up. The actor began his career as a French chansons vocalist at age 17. He became a popular entertainer, this despite the fact that by this time he wore heavy make-up and unisex-style clothes. In 1967, he began a hugely successful series of shows in Tokyo's underground theater with poet Shuji Terayama. Maruyama met Yukio Mishima, and the two became friends. When Mishima adapted *Black Lizard* for the stage, the writer recommended Maruyama for the title role, an outrageously glamourous jewel thief. After Mishima's suicide, Maruyama changed his name to Akihiro Miwa, and began writing an Ann Landers-style advice column. The multifaceted actor-singer-writer still appears frequently on television and on the stage.

FILMS INCLUDE: Black Lizard (1968); Black Rose/The Black Rose Inn (1969).

Yasuzo Masumura Director. *b.* 1924, in Kofu. *ed.* Tokyo University. *d.* 1986. After graduating from the law department at Tokyo University, Masumura joined Daiei in 1948 as an assistant director. He went to Italy to study the neorealists and worked under Mizoguchi and Ichikawa before directing his first feature in 1957. By the mid-1960s he had earned the reputation as something of a sensationalistic director of violent and sexually charged works which bordered on the obscene.

FILMS INCLUDE: Kisses, A Cheerful Girl, Warm Current (1957); The Precipice, The Build-Up, The Lowest Man, Disobedience (1958); The Most Valuable Madam, The Cast-Off, So Beautiful It's a Sin, Across Darkness (1959); A Woman's Testament [co-dir.], Afraid to Die, The Woman Who Touched the Legs, The False Student (1960); Love and Life, All for Love, Wife's Confession, Just for Kicks (1961); Stolen Pleasure, The Black Test Car, A Woman's Life (1962); Black Report, When Women Lie [co-dir.], Delinquents of Pure Heart (1963); Love and Greed, Passion, Super-Express (1964); Hoodlum Soldier, The Wife of Seisaku (1965); Spider Girl, The School of Spies, The Red Angel (1966); Two Wives, An Idiot in Love, The Wife of Seishu Hanaoka (1967); Evil Trio, The Sex Check, The House of Wooden Blocks, One Day at Summer's End (1968); The Blind Beast, Vixen (1969); The Hot Little Girl (1970); Lullaby of the Good Earth (1976); Double Suicide at Sonezaki (1978).

Shue Matsubayashi Director. *b.* July 7, 1920, in Shimane. Toho's master of war movies (and an Imperial Navy veteran), Matsubayashi graduated from Nippon University and joined the studio immediately after. He directed many entries of the studio's "Company President" films, but is best remembered for his action-packed war movies of the 1960s, made in collaboration with special effects artist **Eiji Tsuburaya**, including the apocalyptic *The Last War* (1961).

FILMS INCLUDE: The Blue Mountains (1957); The College Hero (1958); Submarine E-57 Never Surrender! (1959); The Master Fencer Sees the World, Storm Over the Pacific, I Bombed Pearl Harbor (1960); The Last War (1961); Kamikaze! (1963); Five Gents' Trick Book (1965); Five Gents on the Spot (1966); Discover Japan with the Five Gents, Five Gents Prefer Geisha (1967); Five Gents and a Chinese Merchant (1968); Five Gents Fly to Kyushu (1969); Five Gents Fly to Taiwan, Five Gents and Kuniang (1970); Imperial Navy (1981).

Hiroki Matsukata Actor. *b.* 1942, in Tokyo. Toei leading man in films since 1960. Despite an engaging screen presence and appearances in scores of films, the actor is virtually unknown in the West, and best remembered as the hero in Toei's costume fantasy *The Magic Serpent* (1966). In the 1970s he was one of the top stars of the Yakuza genre, memorably in Toei's "War Without Code" film series. A favorite of directors **Kinji Fukasaku** and Sadao Nakajima. Though his feature career slowed somewhat beginning in the early 1980s, he continues to appear in features.

FILMS INCLUDE: The Magic Serpent (1966); Broken Swords, The Full Moon Swordsman, Fylfot Swordplay (1969); Mission Iron Castle (1970); The Shogun

Assassins (1979); The School (1989); The Great Shogunate Battle (1991).

Zenzo Matsuyama Screenwriter, director. *b.* 1925, in Kobe. Humanist director-screenwriter, married to actress **Hideko Takamine**. A student of Kinoshita, Matsuyama won acclaim as the screenwriter of **Masaki Kobayashi**'s *The Human Condition*, but his work as director has been spotty.

FILMS INCLUDE: **[as screenwriter or co-screenwriter]**: Beautiful Days, Distant Clouds (1955); The Fountainhead, Printemps a Nagasaki [Fr/Jap?], I'll Buy You (1956); Black River (1957); The Human Condition I-II, Girl in the Mist (1959); Flowing Night, Goodbye to Glory, Daughters Wives and a Mother (1960); The Human Condition III, A Thief and Culture Order, Eternity of Love (1961); Differnent Sons, Tokyo Bay (1962); The Rats among the Cats, The Injured Boy, Honolulu-Tokyo-Hong Kong (1963); Yearning (1964); Come Marry Me (1966); River of Forever (1967); Long Journey Into Love (1973). **[as director/screenwriter]**: My Hobo (1960); Happiness of Us Alone (1961); Mother Country (1962); Could I But Live (1964); We Will Remember, Dark the Mountain Snow (1965); Our Silent Love, O Luna My Pony! (1967); Father and Son (1968); Two Iida (1976); This Is Noriko (1981); Mother (1988); Rainbow Bridge (1993).

Toshiro Mifune Actor. *b.* April 1, 1920, in Tsingtao, China, to Japanese parents. Japan's greatest film actor, and arguably the only one to achieve true international stardom. Following service during the war and a brief stint studying aerial photography, Mifune entered Toho's "New Face" contest and received two small film roles. He quickly became known as a rebellious, difficult performer. However, **Akira Kurosawa** cast him in the landmark *Drunken Angel* (1948), and Mifune quickly shot to stardom. With his intense eyes and emotionally naked performances, Mifune created singularly unforgettable characters in every film made with the director, especially *Rashomon* (1950), *Seven Samurai* (1954), *The Bad Sleep Well* (1960), *Yojimbo* (1961), and *High and Low* (1963). With one exception, Mifune appeared in all of Kurosawa's features through 1965, with the actor frequently reflecting Kurosawa's own psyche, much as Alfred Hitchcock had done with Cary Grant and especially James Stewart during this same period. Concurrently, Mifune starred in other directors' films, notably Hiroshi Inagaki's *Samurai* trilogy (1954–56) between more routine assignments. Mifune's star status was such at Toho that he was able to form his own production company in the early 1960s, and he even directed one film, *The Legacy of the Five Hundred Thousand* (1963). At the same time, however, his relationship with Kurosawa was beginning to sour. Real-life whiskers grown for the lengthy production of *Red Beard* prevented the actor from accepting other roles, just as his international marketability was reaching its apex. Mifune had appeared in a little-seen Mexican film in 1961, but it was the epic *Grand Prix* (1966) that launched a second career in international productions, this despite the fact that the actor is almost always dubbed in the United States. Mifune's willingness to appear in these mostly bloated overseas productions further strained his relationship with Kurosawa, and following the director's attempted suicide in 1971, Mifune and Kurosawa parted ways for good. By the early 1970s, Mifune sadly became little more than an actor-for-hire, appearing in mostly undistinguished productions rarely up to his incredible talents. His many honors include two Best Actor Awards at the Venice Film Festival (for *Yojimbo* and *Red Beard*), and similar accolades from *Kinema Jumpo* in 1961 and 1968.

FILMS INCLUDE: These Foolish Times (1946); Snow Trail (1947); Drunken Angel (1948); Jakoman and Tetsu, The Quiet Duel, Stray Dog (1949); Scandal, Engagement Ring, Conduct Report on Professor Ishinaka, Escape from Prison, Rashomon (1950); Pirates, Beyond Love and Hate, Elegy, The Idiot, Life of a Horse-Trader, Kojiro Sasaki III, Who Knows a Woman's Heart?, The Meeting of the Ghost of Apres Guerre (1951); Tokyo Sweetheart, Sword for Hire, The Life of Oharu, Vendetta of Samurai, Fog Horn, A Swift Current, The Man Who Came to the Port,

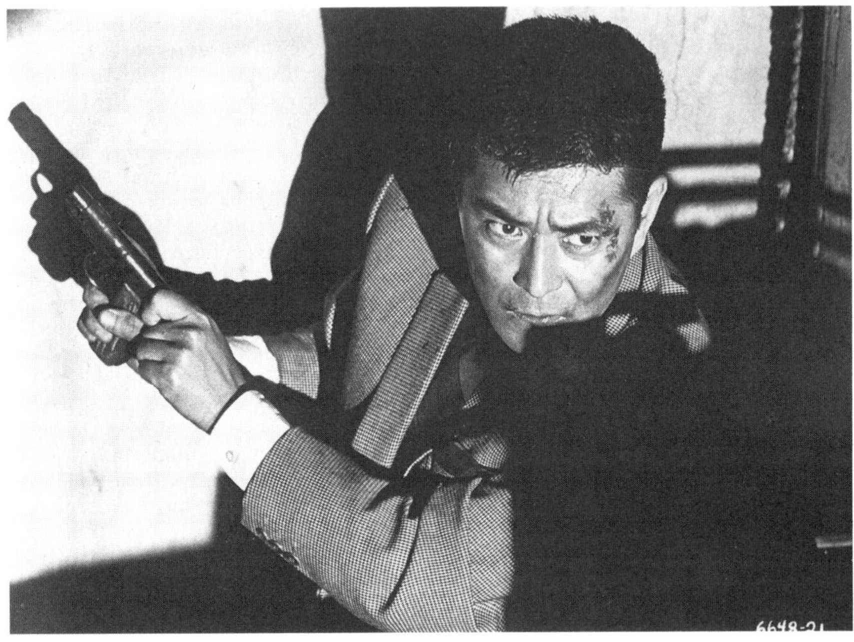

Tatsuya Mihashi in *What's Up, Tiger Lily?* (1966).

Sunflower Girl (1952); Eagle of the Pacific, My Wonderful Yellow Car, The Last Embrace (1953); Seven Samurai, The Black Fury, Samurai I, The Surf (1954); A Man Among Men, I Live in Fear, Peace of the World [two parts], No Time for Tears, Samurai II, All Is Well (1955); Rainy Night Duel, The Underworld, Settlement of Love, A Wife's Heart, Scoundrel, Rebels on the High Sea, Samurai III (1956); Throne of Blood, Downtown Girl, The Lower Depths, The Man in the Storm, Secret Scrolls I, Be Happy These Two Lovers, Dangerous Hero (1957); The Rickshaw Man, Secret Scrolls II, Holiday in Tokyo, Theatre of Life, The Happy Pilgrimage, The Hidden Fortress (1958); The Big Boss, Samurai Saga, Saga of the Vagabonds, The Three Treasures, Desperado Outpost (1959); The Last Gunfighter, The Gambling Samurai, Man Against Man, I Bombed Pearl Harbor, The Bad Sleep Well (1960); Animas Trujano/The Important Man [Mex], Daredevil in the Castle, Yojimbo, The Youth and His Amulet (1961); Sanjuro, Tatsu, Chushingura (1962); Attack Squadron!, High and Low, The Legacy of the Five Hundred Thousand [also dir.], The Lost World of Sinbad (1963); Whirlwind (1964); Samurai Assassin [also co-prod.], Red Beard, Judo Saga, The Retreat from Kiska, Fort Graveyard (1965); Rise Against the Sword, The Sword of Doom, Adventures of Takla Makan, The Mad Atlantic, Grand Prix [US] (1966); Rebellion, The Emperor and the General (1967); Tunnel to the Sun [also co-prod.], Admiral Yamamoto, Gion Matsuri/The Day the Sun Rose (1968); Hell in the Pacific [US/Jap], Under the Banner of Samurai [also co-prod.], Battle of the Japan Sea, Red Lion [also co-prod.], Band of Assassins, Safari 5000 (1969); The Ambitious, The Ambush—Incident at Blood Pass, The Militarists, Zatoichi Meets Yojimbo (1970); Soleil Rouge/Red Sun [It/Fr/Sp] (1971); Paper Tiger [Brit] (1975); Midway [US] (1976); Proof of the Man (1977); Love and Faith/Lady Ogin (1978); The Bushido Blade, 1941 [US], Winter Kills [US] (1979); Port Arthur, Shogun [US-produced teleseries released as a feature in Japan], Inchon [US/Kor; release delayed until 1982] (1980); The Challenge [US] (1982); The Miracle of Joe the Petrel, Sanga Moyu (1984); No More God No More Love (1985); Princess of the Moon (1987); Tora-san Goes North (1988); The Death of a Tea Master, Haru kuru oni (1989); Journey of Honor [US] (1990; released delayed until 1992); Agaguk/Shadow of the Wolf [Fr/Can] (1990; release delayed until 1993); Strawberry Road (1991); Picture Bride [US] (1994).

Tatsuya Mihashi Actor. *b.* November 2, 1923, in Tokyo. Suave leading man at Toho during the 1960s whose specialties were the melodrama and thriller genres. Best remembered in the West as Toshiro Mifune's brother-in-law in *The Bad Sleep Well* (1960), his executive secretary in *High and Low* (1963), and, ironically, as "Phil Moscowicz" in Woody Allen's *What's Up, Tiger Lily?* (1966), in which Mihashi's lines were comically re-dubbed by another actor, using footage from several spy films. In the late 1960s Mihashi turned to television, starring in such Toho-produced teleseries as "S.S.P. Combat Team" and "Palm Reader Samurai."

Films Include: Twelve Chapters About Women, The Heart (1955); The Burmese Harp (1956); Temptation in Glamour Island (1958); Six Suspects, Soft Touch of Night, Wanton Journey, The Wayside Pebble, I Bombed Pearl Harbor, The Bad Sleep Well, The Human Vapor (1960); Lovers of Ginza, Challenge to Live, Snow in the South Seas, Kill the Killer!, Procurers of Hell (1961); Witness Killed, Tatsu, The Wiser Age, Chushingura (1962); Operation Mad Dog, Interpol Code 8, The Legacy of the Five Hundred Thousand, Outpost of Hell, High and Low (1963); Tiger Fight, The Weed of Crime (1964); Adventure on Takla Makan, None but the Brave [US/Jap], International Secret Police—Key of Keys (1965); The Mad Atlantic, The Thin Line, What's Up Tiger Lily? [US production incorporating Japanese footage] (1966); The Killing Bottle, Kojiro (1967); Resurrection of the Beast (1969); Tora! Tora! Tora! [US/Jap], The Militarists (1970); Imperial Navy (1981).

Norihei Miki Actor. *b.* 1925, in Tokyo. Popular character actor in films since 1950, and star of several film series. Still active in films.

Films Include: Sun-Wu King (1959); Wanton Journey, My Hobo (1960); Chushingura (1962); Five Gents' Trick Book, Zatoichi—The Blind Swordsman's Revenge (1965); Hotsprings Holiday (1968); The Song from My Heart (1969); Weird Trip (1972); Demon Pond (1980); The Ballad of Narayama (1983); Himatsuri (1985); Black Rain (1988).

Rentaro Mikuni Actor. *b.* January 20, 1923, in Tottori. In films since 1951, first at Shochiku, this highly respected actor is best known in the United States as the platoon leader of **Kon Ichikawa**'s *The Burmese Harp* (1956), Toshiro Mifune's boyhood friend in *Samurai I*, and the husband in "The Black Hair" episode of *Kwaidan* (1964). Besides Ichikawa, the actor is also associated with *Kwaidan* director **Masaki Kobayashi** He was born Masao Sato, and worked under that name until his first great success, in Kinoshita's *The Good Fairy* (1951), when he adopted the name of his character. Still active in films.

Films Include: The Good Fairy, Youth, Sea of Fireworks (1951); Doctor's Day Off, The Lady from Shanghai, Roars of Spring, Sword for Hire (1952); The Blue Revolution, Husband and Wife, Flight Zone, The Lover, Wife, Eagle of the Pacific, Red Light District, A Reunion (1953); A Fine Son-in-Law, Youth Covered with Mud, Samurai I (1954); Police Diary, Everything That Lives, Bodyguard of Hell, Each Within His Shell (1955); The Burmese Harp (1956); The Eagle and the Hawk, Flesh Is Weak (1957); Night Drum/The Adulteress, A Face at Midnight, The Undefeated Woman, Wind Woman and Wanderer, Avarice, Outsiders (1958); The Song of the Cart, A Dead Drifter, The Murderer Must Die, Kiku and Isamu (1959); This Life I Love, The Chase After Opium Dealers, The Outcast, The Last Japanese Soldier, The Devotion on the Railway (1960); Our Town, Untamed Fury, Like Fire Is My Life, Run Genta Run, The Catch (1961); Harakiri, The Hell's Kitchen, Duel Without End, Tokyo Untouchable,

Lucianna Paluzzi (foreground), Linda Miller (with head bandage), and Cathy Horlan in *The Green Slime* (M-G-M).

Osho I (1962); The Life of a Rickshaw Man, A Story of Army Cruelty, Escape, The Horseman, Osho II, Escape from Hell, The Rat Among the Cats, The Worthless Duel (1963); Kwaidan, A Story from Echigo, Human Wolves, Hunger Straits (1964); The Burglar Story, The Last Duel (1965); Threat, The Grapes of Passion, Punishment Island, Typhoon [also dir.] (1966); Zatoichi – The Blind Swordsman's Rescue (1967); Kuragejima – Legends from a Southern Island (1968); Band of Assassins, Duel at Ezo, City of Beasts, Men and War, Swords of Death (1970); Shadow of Deception, Zatoichi at Large (1972); The Tattered Banner, Himiko (1974); The Inugami Family, Yoba (1976); Mt. Hakkoda (1977); Vengeance Is Mine (1979); The Promise (1986); River of Fireflies (1987); Free and Easy, A Taxing Woman's Return (1988); Free and Easy 2, Rikyu (1989); Shinran – The Path to Purity [also dir., co-scr. and story], Free and Easy 3 (1990); Free and Easy 4, Hikarigoke, My Sons (1991); Free and Easy 5 (1992); The Seriously Ill (1993).

Linda Miller Actress. *b.* 1945 (?). American actress living in Tokyo and the daughter of Jackie Gleason; she essayed the Fay Wray-esque role in *King Kong Escapes* (1967).

FILMS INCLUDE: Strange Rampage [US] (1966); King Kong Escapes [Jap/US] (1967); The Green Slime [bit; Jap/US/It.] (1968).

Kenji Misumi Director. *b.* 1921, in Kyoto. *d.* 1975, of a heart attack. Misumi joined Nikkatsu in 1941, but soon moved to Daiei, where he spent the bulk of his career. Working primarily at the Daiei-Kyoto studios (where nearly all of the studio's period films are made), Misumi excelled at *jidai-geki*, including many *Zatoichi* films, as well as a *The Wild One*, an adaptation of *The Rickshaw Man* starring Zatoichi himself, Shintaro Katsu. Misumi also directed Japan's first 70mm production, *Buddha* (1961). His lean, mean, but visually sumptuous style places him alongside Ishiro Honda in the uppermost rank of genre directors.

Films Include: Basket of Lichen (1954); Free Lance Samurai (1957); Halo of Heat Haze, A Thousand Flying Cranes, The Yotsuya Ghost Story, Iron Button (1959); Princess Sen in Edo, The Purloined Map, Patterns of Love, What Price Love, Satan's Sword I, Satan's Sword II (1960); Buddha (1961); Her Hidden Past, The Life and Opinion of Zatoichi, Destiny's Son (1962); New Class Management, The Third Wall (1963); The Sword, Adventures of Kyoshiro Nemuri (1964); Sword Devil, Zatoichi – The Blind Swordsman and the Chess Expert, The Wild One (1965); The Virgin Waitress, Lone Wanderer, Dynamite Doctor, The Return of Majin (1966); The Shroud of Snow, The Sisters and I, The Homely Sisters, Zatoichi Challenged (1967); Zatoichi – The Blind Swordsman Samaritan, The Funeral Racket, The Two Bodyguards (1968); Devil's Temple, The Magoichi Saga (1969); The Angry Sword, Zatoichi Fire Festival (1970); The Woman Gambler's Iron Rule (1971); Hanzo the Blade, Sword of Vengeance, Lone Wolf and Child – Baby Cart at the River Styx, Lightning Swords of Death, Lone Wolf and Child – Heart of a Father Heart of a Child (1972); Lone Wolf and Child – Path Between Heaven and Hell (1973); The Last Samurai (1974).

Kazuo Miyagawa Director of Photography. *b.* January 23, 1908, in Kyoto. A legend in Japan, Miyagawa worked under directors Akira Kurosawa, Kon Ichikawa, Kenji Misumi, and Kenji Mizoguchi, among others, to become an international force in the field of cinematography. The Voyager Collection's laserdisc of *Ugetsu* features an interview with the cameraman, whose work includes such landmark films as *Rashomon* (1950), *Sansho the Bailiff* (1954), *Yojimbo* (1961), *Tokyo Olympiad* (1965), and numerous "Zatoichi" films. A master of both color and black and white, of standard and wide screen. In films from 1926.

Films Include: Choice Silver (1935); First Class Teaching, Paradise of Nineteen Brides (1936); Matchless Sword (1937); A Great Power Rising in the World (1938); Mazo I, Mazo II, Kesa and Morito (1939); Musashi Miyamoto I, Musashi Miyamoto II, Musashi Miyamoto III (1940); Powerful Sea Clan (1942); The Life of Matsu the Untamed (1943); Wrestling Festival, Woman Using a Short Sword, Thus Blows the Divine Wind (1944); Last Abdication (1945); A Woman Opens the Door, A Woman Takes Off Her Gloves (1946); The Devil's Defeat (1947); Children Hand in Hand, Man Judging Woman, That Kind of Adventure (1948); Divine Council, Ghost Train (1949); Third Floor Love, Rashomon (1950); Brilliant Murder, Miss Oyu (1951); The Sisters of Nishijin, White Threads of the Cascades, Cage for Husbands, A Tale of Genji (1952); Thousand Cranes, Tales of Ugetsu, Desires, Gion Music, Sansho the Bailiff, The Woman in the Rumor, A Tale of Chikamatsu (1954); New Tales of the Taira Clan (1955); Street of Shame, Dancer and the Warrior, Undercurrent (1956); Love of a Princess, Night Butterflies, Underworld Boss (1957); Treasure Huntress, Conflagration, The Gay Masquerade (1958); The Woman and the Pirates, The Key/Odd Obsession, Floating Weeds (1959); The Woman's Testament [co-dp], Bonchi/Basin, Her Brother (1960); Marriageable Age, Tough Guy I, Tough Guy II, Yojimbo (1961); The Sin (1962); Tough Guy III, The Third Wall, Rabble Tactics, The Bamboo Doll (1963); Zatoichi – Masseur Ichi and a Chest of Gold, Money Talks, Engaged in Pleasures (1964); Two Notorious Men Strike Again, Tokyo Olympiad [supervisor and co-phot.] (1965); Spider Tattoo, Zatoichi – The Blind Swordsman's Vengeance (1966); A Certain Killer, Zatoichi – The Blind Swordsman's Rescue (1967); Zatoichi – The Blind Swordsman and the Fugitives, The Funeral Racket (1968); Devil's Temple (1969); Zatoichi Meets Yojimbo, Zatoichi – The Blind Swordsman's Fire Festival (1970); Silence (1971); Melody in Gray (1977); Kagemusha (1980); The Love Suicides at Sonezaki (1981); MacArthur's Children (1984); Gonza the Spearman (1986); The Dancer (1989).

Mariko Miyagi Director. *b.* 1927, in Tokyo. A former singer/dancer who, in 1968, established the Nemunoki Institute for handicapped children. In 1974, she produced, directed, wrote and even composed the music for *The Silk Tree Ballad*, a documentary feature about the Institute.

Since then she has made several films about her work and, more importantly, the children.

Films Include: The Silk Tree Ballad (1974); Children Chasing Rainbows (1975); Mariko–Mother (1976); Hello Kids! (1986).

Seiji Miyaguchi Actor. *b.* 1913, in Tokyo. *d.* 1985. A gaunt, horse-faced actor in films from 1945, specializing in thugs and stoic executive roles. Memorable as the expert swordsman in *Seven Samurai* (and the basis for the Robert Vaughn role in *The Magnificent Seven*).

Films Include: Ikiru (1952); Seven Samurai (1954); Throne of Blood (1957); Ballad of Naruyama (1958); It's You I Love, The Human Condition I (1959); Get 'Em All, The Bad Sleep Well (1960); Twin Sisters of Kyoto, Attack Squadron!, High and Low (1963); Kwaidan, Samurai from Nowhere, The Crest of Man (1964); The Emperor and the General (1967); Admiral Yamamoto (1968); To Love Again (1972); Shogun [US teleseries released as a feature in Japan] (1980); The Challenge [US] (1982).

Nobuko Miyamoto Actress. *b.* 1945, in Hokkaido. Although in films since 1967, Miyamoto's career really took off in the mid-1980s when she starred in several comedies directed by her husband (from 1969), **Juzo Itami**. The success of *Tampopo* and *A Taxing Woman* in particular made her, arguably, the best-known Japanese actress outside Japan during the 1980s.

Films Include: Tora-san's Shattered Romance (1971); The Funeral (1984); Tampopo (1985); The Karate Kid Part II [shamisen and kouta advisor only] (1986); A Taxing Woman (1987); A Taxing Woman's Return (1988); Sweet Home (1989); A-Ge-Man–Tales of a Golden Geisha (1990); Minbo–or The Gentle Art of Japanese Extortion (1992); The Seriously Ill (1993).

Kenji Mizoguchi Director. *b.* May 16, 1898, in Tokyo. *d.* August 24, 1956, of leukemia. Born to a poor family, the young Mizoguchi saw his older sister given up for adoption where, at the age of 14, she was sold into prostitution. Fortunately, the sister married a wealthy patron, but the experience left Mizoguchi with an emotional scar later reflected in his work. He studied painting and first worked as an illustrator for a Kobe newspaper before joining the Mukojima Studio of Nikkatsu in 1922. He worked as an assistant director under Osamu Wakayama and made his film debut the following year when several older directors when on strike. His films generally focus on long-suffering but determined women and the abusive men in their lives. Famous for his leisurely dolly shots, obsession with multiple screenplay drafts and painterly eye, he reemerged at Daiei in the 1950s with the strong support from producer Masaichi Nagata. *Osaka Elegy, Sisters of the Gion* (both 1937) and *The Loyal Forty-Seven Ronin I-II* (1941-42) are generally regarded as the high-water marks of his early career, with *The Life of Oharu* (1952), *Ugetsu* (1953), and *Sansho the Bailiff* (1954) the peak of his later years. He was closely associated with **Yoshikata Yoda**, who wrote or co-wrote virtually all of the director's films from 1936; his most frequent onscreen heroine (and offscreen

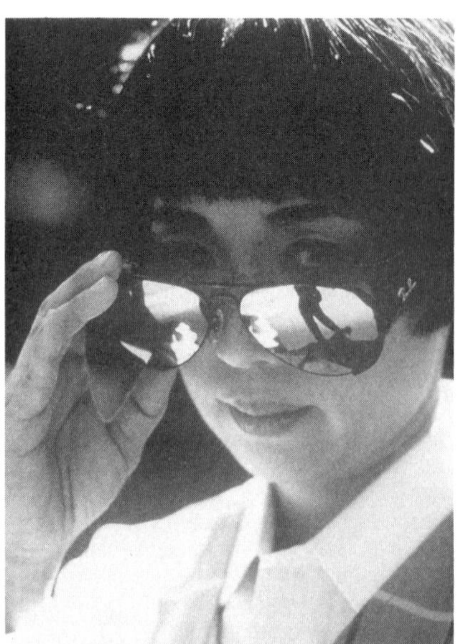

Nobuko Miyamoto in *A Taxing Woman*.

lover) **Kinuyo Tanaka**, beginning 1940; and cinematographer **Kazuo Miyagawa** during the final period of the director's work. He died of leukemia just as he was beginning to earn international recognition, and some ten years before he was singularly embraced by the French New Wave as one of the screen's greatest directors. Awards: the International Prize at the Venice Film Festival, for *The Life of Oharu* (1952). His work was examined in *Kenji Mizoguchi: The Life of a Film Director* (1975), and his relationship with Kinuyo Tanaka was dramatized in *Actress* (1987).

FILMS INCLUDE: The Resurrection of Love, Hometown, The Dream of Youth, City of Desire, Failure's Song Is Sad, 813: The Adventures of Arsene; Foggy Harbor, Blood and Soul, The Night, In the Ruins (1923); The Song of the Mountain Pass, The Sad Idiot, The Queen of Modern Times, Women Are Strong, This Dusty World, Turkeys in a Row, A Chronicle of May Rain, No Money No Fight, A Woman of Pleasure, Death at Dawn (1924); Queen of the Circus, Out of College, The White Lily Laments, The Earth Smiles, Shining in the Red Sunset, The Song of Home, The Human Being, Street Sketches (1925); General Nogi and Kuma-san, The Copper Coin King, A Paper Doll's Whisper of Spring, My Fault New Version, The Passion of a Woman Teacher, The Boy of the Sea, Money (1926); The Imperial Grace, The Cuckoo (1927); A Man's Life (1928); Nihombashi, Tokyo March, The Morning Sun Shines, Metropolitan Symphony (1929); Home Town, Mistress of a Foreigner (1930); And Yet They Go (1931); The Man of the Moment, The Dawn of Manchukuo and Mongolia (1932); Taki no Shiraito the Water Magician/The Water Magician, Gion Festival, The Jimpu Group (1933); The Mountain Pass of Love and Hate, The Downfall of Osen (1934); Oyuki the Madonna, Poppy (1935); Osaka Elegy, Sisters of the Gion (1937); The Straits of Love and Hate (1937); Ah My Home Town, The Song of the Camp (1938); The Story of the Last Chrysanthemum (1939); The Woman of Osaka (1940); The Life of an Actor, The Loyal 47 Ronin I (1941); The Loyal 47 Ronin II (1942); Three Generations of Danjuro, Musashi Miyamoto (1944); The Famous Sword Bijomaru, Victory Song (1945); The Victory of Women, Utamaro and His Five Women (1946); The Love of Sumako the Actress (1947); Women of the Night (1948); My Love Burns (1949); Portrait of Madame Yuki (1950); Miss Oyu, Lady Musashino (1951); The Life of Oharu (1952); Tales of Ugetsu, Gion Festival Music (1953); Sansho the Bailiff, The Woman of the Rumor, A Story from Chikamatsu (1954); The Princess Yang Kwei-fei [Jap/HK], New Tales of the Taira Clan (1955); Street of Shame (1956); Osaka Story [story only] (1957).

Kumi Mizuno Actress. *b.* Maya Igarashi January 1, 1937, in Niigata. Sexy Toho star of the late 1950s through the late 1960s, best known in the West for her roles in Toho fantasy films. She was especially memorable in the horror-allegory *Attack of the Mushroom People* (1963), and opposite **Nick Adams** (with whom she had an affair) in *Frankenstein Conquers the World* and *Monster Zero* (both 1965). Since the late 1960s she has worked primarily on the stage and in television.

FILMS INCLUDE: A Bridge for Us Alone (1956); A Whistle in My Heart, I Want to Be a Shellfish, The Three Treasures (1959); Westward Desperado, The Gambling Samurai (1960); The Merciless Trap, Challenge to Live, Poignant Story, The Last Challenge, Counterstroke, Big Shots Die at Dawn, Kill the Killer! (1961); Till Tomorrow Comes, Chushingura, Witness Killed, Operation X, Operation Enemy Fort, Gorath (1962); Attack of the Mushroom People, Interpol Code 8, The Lost World of Sinbad (1963); The Weed of Crime, Whirlwind (1964); Frankenstein Conquers the World [Jap/US], White Rose of Hong Kong, Monster Zero [Jap/US](1965); What's Up Tiger Lily? [US production incorporating Japanese footage], War of the Gargantuas [Jap/US], Ebirah Horror of the Deep (1966); The Killing Bottle (1967); Swirling Butterflies (1970); Thieving Ruby (1988).

Kazuo Mori Director. *b.* 1911, in Ehime. *d.* 1989. Prolific Daiei director whose work includes Chambara, Yakuza, and mainstream features. Best known as the director of numerous "Zatoichi" features, including many episodes of the teleseries that followed. Often billed as *Issei* Mori.

FILMS INCLUDE: Tojura's Love (1955); Love of a Princess (1957); The 7th Courier for Edo (1958); His Lordship the Brigand (1959); The Secrets of a Court Masseur, Jirocho the Chivalrous (1960); The Young Samurai, The Radiant Prince (1961); The Return of Zatoichi, The Beast Within (1962); I Can Get Away with Anything (1963); Zatoichi and the Doomed Men (1965); Majin Strikes Again (1966); The Curse of the Ghosts (1969); Kodokan Judo (1971); Zatoichi at Large (1972).

Masayuki Mori Actor. *b.* Yukimitsu Arishima, January 13, 1911, in Sapporo City, Hokkaido, the son of writer Takeo Arishima. *ed.* Imperial University, Kyoto. *d.* October 7, 1973, of cancer. In the theater from 1929, and in films 13 years later, Mori is one of the most important actors in Japanese cinema, though in recent years his status appears to have fallen somewhat in Japan. A chameleon of a performer, he was most associated with tormented upper-class types, but also played working class heroes and doomed lovers. He is best remembered for his work with **Akira Kurosawa, Kenji Mizoguchi and Mikio Naruse**. For Kurosawa he played the proud husband in *Rashomon* (1950) and the ruthless company executive in *The Bad Sleep Well* (1960). In 1951, he starred opposite Setsuko Hara in Kurosawa's *The Idiot*, with Mori essaying the role of Dostoyevsky's title character. For Mizoguchi, Mori starred as the potter who leaves his loving wife in *Ugetsu* (1953), and for Naruse he was Hideko Takamine's wealthy lover in *When a Woman Ascends the Stairs* (1960). Under Naruse's direction, Mori won the *Kinema Jumpo* Award for Best Actor for his performance in *Floating Clouds* (1955).

FILMS INCLUDE: A Mother's Card [debut] (1942); Sanshiro Sugata II, Those Who Tread on the Tiger's Tail (1945); Those Who Make Tomorrow (1946); A Ball at the Anjo House (1947); The Day Our Lives Shine, Apostasy (1948); A Fool's Love, The Broken Drum (1949); Rashomon (1950); Stolen Love, The Idiot, Woman of Musashino/Lady Musashino (1951); This Way That Way (1952); Older Brother Younger Sister, Tales of Ugetsu, Thousand Cranes, A Reunion (1953); The Heart, A Certain Woman, Temptation of Pleasure (1954); Human Torpedoes, Floating Clouds, The Princess Yang Kwei-fei [Jap/HK] (1955); Elegy of the North, Untamed Woman (1957); Woman Unveiled, Budding Love, Night Drum/The Adulteress (1958); The Path Under the Platanes, Woman's Heart, A Whistle in My Heart, The Setting Sun (1959); When a Woman Ascends the Stairs, Daughters Wives and a Mother, This Greedy Old Skin, Her Brother, The Bad Sleep Well (1960); Nocturne of a Woman, Poignant Story, Challenge to Live, A Design for Dying, Refresher Course for Wives, Love Old and New (1961); Bushido, My Enemy the Sea (1963); Homecoming (1964); Retirement for Mr. Napoleon (1965); Scattered Clouds (1967); Admiral Yamamoto, Sun Above Death Below (1968); Through Days and Months, Gateway to Glory (1969); Zatoichi – The Blind Swordsman's Fire Festival (1970); Ken to hana (1972).

Hisaya Morishige Actor. *b.* May 4, 1913, in Osaka. Character actor in films since 1947, and star of two Toho film series: the 40-film "Company President" (1956–71) series, of which Morishige starred in all but the last two; and the 24-film "Train Station" (1958-69). Still active in films.

FILMS INCLUDE: River Solo Flows (1951); Snow Country (1957); Panda and the Magic Serpent [voice only], Temptation in Glamour Island, The Child Writers (1958); The Angry Sea, Life of a Country Doctor, This Greedy Old Skin, Wanton Journey, Playboy President, The Wayside Pebble (1960); The Diplomat's Mansion, Early Autumn, An Urban Affair, Snow in the South Seas (1961); Chushingura, This Madding Crowd (1962); Madame Aki, The Maid Story (1963); Ghost Story of a Funny Act in Front of Train Station (1964); Five Gents' Trick Book, Tale of a Carpenter, We Will Remember (1965); Five Gents at Sunrise, 5 Gents on the Spot (1966); Big Wind at the Spa, How to Win a Race, Discover Japan with the Five Gents, Rat Race at the School, Tokyo Century Plaza, The Way-Out Shrine (1967); Five Gents and a Chinese Merchant (1968); Five Gents Fly to Kyushu (1969); Five Gents Fly to Taiwan, Five Gents and a Kuniang (1970); Tora-san's Shattered Romance (1971); Zatoichi at Large (1972); Theater of Life (1973); The Voyage of the Canoe "Che-Che-Meni" [narrator only] (1977); Imperial Navy (1981); Sayonara Jupiter (1984); Senbon Matsubara [voice only] (1991).

Yoshimitsu Morita Director. *b.* 1950, in Chigasaki. A self-taught filmmaker, the director of *The Family Game* produced dozens of films in 8mm while studying broadcasting at Nippon University. Largely working with his own funds, he produced his first feature in 1978, and three years later his *No – Yonamona* won much acclaim. A self-described "child of radio and TV," Morita works very fast, often shooting his pictures in less than a week.

FILMS INCLUDE: No – Yonamona (1981); Boys and Girls, Maruhon Uwasano Stripper (1982); Pink Cut, The Family Game (1983); Last Christmas (1992).

Shiro Moritani Director. *b.* September 28, 1931, in Tokyo. *ed.* Waseda University. *d.* 1984. Moritani joined Toho as an assistant director in 1950 (where he often worked under Akira Kurosawa), making his debut with *Zero Fighter* in 1966. He has directed several of Toho's biggest films of the late 1960s/early 1970s, notably the epic *Submersion of Japan* (1973).

FILMS INCLUDE: Zero Fighter (1966); Too Many Moons, Seventeen (1967); Kubi, Judge and Jeopardy (1968); Love Revisited, Bullet Wound (1969); Take Care Red Riding Hood (1970); The Surf (1971); Shadow of Love (1972); Submersion of Japan/Tidal Wave (1973); Mt. Hakkoda (1977); Abandoned (1981).

Shinji Murayama Director. *b.* 1921, in Nagano. Prolific Toei director of the 1950s and 1960s who worked in almost every genre. Allied with the studio since 1949, after an education in an industrial high school and at the *Asahi* Newspaper. He works primarily in the Yakuza genre, though he directed the studio's take on *The Rickshaw Man* story in 1963.

FILMS INCLUDE: Boyhood of an Agriculture Pioneer, Appleyard Romance, Mother Goes Sightseeing (1957); Tokyo Patrol – Seven Detectives, Tokyo Patrol – The Taxi Driver Murders, Trumpet of Victory (1958); Dismembered Corpse, The Third Woman, Challenger at Midnight, Police Murderer, Lost Articles, The Murderer Must Die (1959); Secret Passage, The Chase After Opium Dealers (1960); Love at the Foggy Harbor, Tokyo Untouchable (1962); The Life of a Rickshaw Man, The Navy (1963); The Gorgeous Geisha (1964); Night Hunter (1965); Cheating Love (1966); Yanagase Blues, Journey (1967); Night Guy, The Young Eagles of the Kamikaze, Secret Turkish Bath, Isezakichi Blues (1968).

Masaichi Nagata Producer, executive. *b.* January 21, 1906. *d.* October 24, 1985, of pneumonia. **Daiei** producer/executive generally credited with bringing Japanese films to the attention of Western audiences in the early 1950s with the unexpected international success of Kurosawa's *Rashomon* (1950), and later his heavy promotion of his studio's films abroad, particularly the later works of **Kenji Mizoguchi**. He joined Nikkatsu in 1924, and helped form Daiei in 1942. He succeeded Ken Kikuchi as president in 1947, and remained with the company until its bankruptcy, and later made four independently produced features. His first son, Hidemasa Nagata (b. 1925) is also a producer.

FILMS INCLUDE: Rashomon (1950); Gate of Hell, The Golden Demon, Tales of Ugetsu (1953); Sansho the Bailiff (1954); The Phantom Horse (1955); Floating Weeds, Fires on the Plain (1959); Buddha (1961); The Great Wall (1962); Gammera the Invincible (1965); Majin (1966); Nichiren (1979).

Hiroyuki Nagato Actor. *b.* January 10, 1934, in Kyoto. Nikkatsu actor, originally a child star, seen to good advantage as the two-bit gangster in Shohei Imamura's *The Flesh Is Hot/Pigs and Battleships* (1961), and other high-end efforts by house directors. In films from 1940.

FILMS INCLUDE: The Flesh Is Hot/Pigs and Battleships (1961); The Outcast (1962); Appointment with Danger (1970); Things That Teachers Can Do (1981).

Tatsuya Nakadai Actor. *b.* 1932, in Tokyo. Important actor in Japanese cinema, in films from 1953. With his malleable but intense features and saucer-like eyes, Nakadai, like Masayuki Mori and Tsutomu Yamazaki, became something of a chameleon in Japanese films. He was unforgettable as the idealist Kaji in **Masaki Kobayashi**'s *Human Condition* trilogy (1959-61), and is strongly associated with that director, appearing also in *Harakiri* (1962) and *Kwaidan* (1964). And seven years after appearing as an extra in **Akira Kurosawa**'s *Seven Samurai* (1954), Nakadai essayed strong supporting roles in *Yojimbo* (1961, as the pistol-packin' heavy), *Sanjuro* (1962), and *High and Low* (1963, as the chief detective). After Kurosawa's falling out with Toshiro Mifune and an aborted collaboration with Shintaro Katsu, Nakadai starred in the director's comeback features, *Kagemusha* (1980) and *Ran* (1985), for which Nakadai received excellent notices. He frequently works with **Kon Ichikawa** and **Kihachi Okamoto**, and, in recent years, scored a tremendous commercial success in the sentimental weepy *Hachi-ko* (1987).

Films Include: Room with Thick Walls (1953); Seven Samurai [extra] (1954); Untamed Woman, Black River (1957); A Toast to Marriage, Go and Get It, Conflagration, A Boy and Three Mothers, The Naked Sun (1958); The Human Condition I, Beast Shall Die, Odd Obsession, The Human Condition II (1959); Love Under the Crucifix, Get 'Em All, When a Woman Ascends the Stairs, The Blue Beast, Daughters Wives and a Mother (1960); Poignant Story The Human Condition III, Yojimbo, As the Clouds Scatter, The Bitter Spirit/Immortal Love (1961); Sanjuro, The Inheritance, Harakiri (1962); High and Low, The Legacy of the Five Hundred Thousand, White and Black, Pressure of Guilt, A Woman's Life (1963); Kwaidan, Onibaba (1964); Illusion of Blood, Fort Graveyard (1965); The Sword of Doom, Cash Calls Hell, The Face of Another, The Daphne (1966); The Age of Assassins, Kojiro, Who Is Gomez?, Rebellion, Journey (1967); Kill, Admiral Yamamoto [narrator only], Today It's Me—Tomorrow You [It] (1968); Goyokin, Battle of the Japan Sea, Portrait of Hell, Tenchu! (1969); The Ambitious, Duel at Ezo, The Scandalous Adventures of Buraikin, Zatoichi—The Blind Swordsman's Fire Festival, Will to Conquer (1970); Inn of Evil, The Battle of Okinawa (1971); Rise Fair Sun (1973); I Am a Cat (1975); Queen Bee, Bandit vs. Samurai Squad, Blue Christmas (1978); Hinotori, Hunter in the Dark (1979); Kagemusha [dual role], Port Arthur (1980); Willful Murder (1981); Fireflies of the North (1984); House Without a Dining Table, Ran (1985); Road/Hopeless Love (1986); Hachi-ko (1987); Oracion (1988); Four Days of Snow and Blood (1989); Faraway Sunset (1992).

Ko Nakahira Director. *b.* 1926, in Tokyo. *ed.* Tokyo University. *d.* 1978. Nakahira studied art but joined Shochiku (at their Ofuna Studio) at the age of 22 as an assistant director under Yuzo Kawashima and Minoru Shibuya. He moved to Nikkatsu in 1954, and was promoted to director two years later. Because so little of the studio's library has been released in the United States, Nakahira's work, tough yet sensitive social problem and action films, remains largely unknown in this country.

Films Include: Crazed Fruit/Juvenile Passion, A Man Spied Upon, Summer Storm, (1956); Who Is the Murderer, Temptation, Flesh Is Weak (1957); The Four Seasons of Love, Crimson Wings (1958); The Talented Woman, Let Us Destroy This Wall, A Secret Rendezvous (1959); The Girls and the Students, Jungle Block, Wait for Tomorrow (1960); That Guy and I, Storm Over Arabia (1961); Captain by Chance, These Young People Bad and Terrible, Danger Pays (1962); When the Snows Tell, I Have the Sun in My Back, Bright Sea (1963); Yuka from Monday, The Hunter's Diary, Jungle Interlude, Whirlpool of Flesh (1964), The Moral of Modern Hooligans, The Black Gambler, Marriage Consultation, The Black Challenger (1965); The Devil's Left Hand, A Red Glass (1966); The Free Island, Taro's Youth (1967); Spiders a Go-Go (1968).

Haruo Nakajima Actor. *b.* January 1, 1929, in Yamagata. Minor player at Toho who became the man inside Godzilla and a host of other giant monsters through the early 1970s. Nakajima shared the role of Godzilla in the first film, but

Tatsuya Nakadai stars as Lord Hidetora, the powerful 16th century warlord whose passage from authority destroys his family and his kingdom in *Ran* (1985).

usually played the part solo from 1955. Nakajima also played giant monsters on Japanese television. After the death of effects master Eiji Tsuburaya, Nakajima grew weary of playing monsters, and retired in 1972.

FILMS INCLUDE: [Nakajima's monster roles are noted in brackets.] Sword for Hire (1952); Eagle of the Pacific (1953); Seven Samurai, Godzilla King of the Monsters! [as Godzilla, and in a bit role] (1954); Gigantis the Fire Monster [as Godzilla] (1955); Rodan [as Rodan] (1956); The Mysterians [as Mogera] (1957); The H-Man, The Hidden Fortress, Varan the Unbelievable [as Varan] (1958); Mothra [as Mothra] (1961); Gorath [as Magma the Giant Walrus], King Kong vs. Godzilla [as Godzilla] (1962); Attack of the Mushroom People [as a mushroom man] (1963); Godzilla vs. the Thing [as Godzilla], Ghidrah—The Three-Headed Monster [as Godzilla] (1964); Frankenstein Conquers the World [as Baragon], Monster Zero [as Godzilla] (1965); War of the Gargantuas [as Gairah, the Green Gargantua], Ebirah Horror of the Deep [as Godzilla] (1966); King Kong Escapes [as King Kong], Son of Godzilla [as Godzilla] (1967); Destroy All Monsters [as Godzilla] (1968); Latitude Zero [as a giant, winged-lion] (1969); Yog—Monster from Space [as Gezora the Giant Squid] (1970); Godzilla vs. the Smog Monster [as Godzilla] (1971); Godzilla on Monster Island [as Godzilla] (1972).

Ganjiro Nakamura Actor. *b.* 1902, in Osaka. Older character actor best known for his performance as the aging actor in Yasujiro Ozu's *Floating Weeds*, and as the aging husband in Ichikawa's *The Key/Odd Obsession* (both 1959). In films from 1941.

FILMS INCLUDE: Dancer and the Warrior (1956); Ukifune, Osaka Story (1957); Conflagration, The Prodigal Son, Summer Clouds (1958); Odd Obsession/The Key, Floating Weeds, The Three Treasures (1959); A Woman's Testament, Kaidan kasanagafuchi, When a Woman Ascends the Stairs, Princess Sen in Edo, The Two Musashis (1960); Late Autumn, Buddha, All for Love (1961); Ghost Story of Stone Lanterns, The Great Wall, The Outcast, It Happened on the Road to Edo, Temple of the Wild Geese (1962); An Actor's Revenge, The Bamboo Doll, The Third Wall (1963); Kwaidan (1964); Kenji Mizoguchi: The Life of a Film Director (1975).

Kanzaburo Nakamura *see* **Kinnosuke Nakamura**

Kinnosuke Nakamura Actor. *b.* 1932, in Tokyo. Following in the footsteps of his Kabuki actor-father, Nakamura made his stage debut at four, and entered films at age 20 at the newly founded Toei. He made well over 100 films there, mostly *jidai-geki*, or period films, with Nakamura usually cast as the handsome leading man. Still active in films.

FILMS INCLUDE: Whistling Boy, The Last of the Samurai (1954); A Fugitive Hero, The Red Peacock, Peaceful Sea (1955); Ghost Ship [two parts], Breeze of Love (1957); Bullseye for Love, The Swords of Mystery, Wind Woman and Wanderer, A Ghost Story in Passage, Sword and Love, Destiny of a Credential Agent, Hero of the Town, Thunder Kid, The Gay Revengers (1958); Lords and Pirates, The Forbidden Castle, The Actor Detective, The Great Bodhisatva Pass III, The Hawk of the North, Their Own World, Shogun Travels Incognito, The Young Fury, The Bravest Fishmonger (1959); The Samurai Vagabonds, Yataro's Sedge Hat, Shinran [two parts], Collapse of a Boss (1960); The Shogun and the Fishmonger, Untamed Fury, The Conspirator (1961); A Carpenter and Children, Duel Without End (1962); Bushido/Bushido – Samurai Saga, Sasuke and His Comedians, The Worthless Duel, Samurai and Orphans (1963); The Duel at Ichijoji Temple, The Sharks, The Revenge (1964); The Last Duel, Shadow of the Waves, Illusion of Blood (1965); The Secret of the Urn (1966); The Day the Sun Rose, Gion Matsuri (1968); The Song from My Heart, Under the Banner of Samurai, Goyokin, Portrait of Hell, The Magoichi Saga (1969); The Ambitious, The Ambush – Incident at Blood Pass (1970).

Noboru Nakamura Director. *b.* 1913, in Sendai. *ed.* Tokyo University. *d.* 1981. A master of classical drama, Nakamura rose up through the ranks of assistant directors at Shochiku and directed his first feature in 1941. His *Twin Sisters of Kyoto* (1963) won the Golden Harvest Award at the 10th Film Festival in Asia. Other important works by the director include *The Mask and Destiny* (1955) and *The Estuary* (1961). Not to be confused with the actor Nobuo Nakamura (q.v.).

FILMS INCLUDE: Song of a Flower Basket, Pioneer Love (1946); Counterattack of Girls (1947); Travelling Suit, Scarlet Rose (1948); Love Trio (1949); Road to Rise and Fall, Spring Tide (1950); Love Letter Trial (1951); The Waves (1952); Spring Drum, Natsuko's Venture, The Cliff, The Journey (1953); Family Conference, The Sun Never Sets, Edo Sunset (1954); A Woman's Life, The Mask and Destiny, Yearning (1955); Beautiful Feeling, White Devil-Fish, Midnight Visitor (1956); Cloudburst, Payoff with Love (1957); Triple Betrayal, Country Boss (1958); Waiting for Spring, Love Letters, Vagabond Lovers, Marry a Millionaire (1959); My Love, Of Men and Money, Trapped in Love (1960); Women of Tokyo, A Lonely Geisha, The Estuary (1961); Flower in a Storm I-II (1962); Twin Sisters of Kyoto, Whirlwind, Marriage Ceremony (1963); Our Happiness Alone, The Beautiful People (1964); Absolute Majority (1965); Springtime, The Kii River (1966), Three Faces of Love, Portrait of Chieko (1967); Spring Breeze, My Destiny (1968); Through Days and Months, Marriage Japanese Style (1969); Journey of Love (1970); Love and Death (1971); Love Stopped the Runaway Train, Three Old Women (1974); Nichiren (1979).

Nobuo Nakamura Actor. *b.* September 14, 1908. *d.* 1990. Familiar character actor, a favorite of both Kurosawa and Ozu, usually cast as government officials or corporate executives. Occasionally, the actor donned old-age make-up as well – until he finally grew into those roles late in life. Best remembered in this country as the deputy mayor in *Ikiru* (1952), the old scientist in *Dagora, the Space Monster* (1964) and *War of the Gargantuas* (1966), and as the sly old man who out-cons the con-man in *Tampopo* (1985). Not to be confused with the director Noboru Nakamura (q.v.).

FILMS INCLUDE: Ikiru (1952); Tokyo Story (1953); I Live in Fear, Half Human (1955); Early Spring (1956); Tokyo Twilight, Throne of Blood (1957); Equinox Flower (1958); The Human Condition I (1959); The Bad Sleep Well, Late Autumn (1960); The Diplomat's Mansion, The Last

War, Blind Devotion (1961); An Autumn Afternoon (1962); High and Low (1963); Dagora the Space Monster (1964); Frankenstein Conquers the World [Jap/US] (1965); Longing for Love, War of the Gargantuas [Jap/US] (1966); The Emperor and the General (1967); The Creature Called Man (1970); Submersion of Japan/Tidal Wave (1973); The Devil's Bouncing Ball Song (1977); Tampopo (1985).

Satoshi Nakamura *see* **Tetsu Nakamura**

Tetsu Nakamura Actor. *b.* September 19, 1908, in Canada, to Japanese and Canadian parents. *d* 1992 (?). Often mis-billed as "Satoshi Nakamura," this bilingual actor played roles in English-language productions shot in Japan, as well as in Japanese films, where he was often cast in non-Japanese Asian roles. Best remembered as the scientist who creates *The Manster* (1961).

Films Include: Tokyo File 212 [US/Jap] (1950); The Mysterians (1957); The H-Man (1958); The Human Vapor, I Bombed Pearl Harbor (1960); The Manster, Mothra, A Night in Hong Kong (1961); The Big Wave [US/Jap] (1962); The Lost World of Sinbad, Atragon (1963); None But the Brave [US/Jap] (1965); The Killing Bottle (1967); Latitude Zero [Jap/US] (1969); Yog—Monster from Space (1970); Marco [US/Jap] (1973); The Last Dinosaur [US/Jap] (1977).

Teruyoshi Nakano Director of Special Effects. *b.* October 1935. An assistant director under **Eiji Tsuburaya** from 1962, Nakano followed him as the head of Toho's special effects department following the former's death in 1970. Nakano's work was hampered by low budgets and a reliance upon stock footage from previous efforts (mainly due to the decline of the industry at large), but he did fine work in several expensive disaster films, especially the hit *Submersion of Japan* (1973). **Koichi Kawakita** took over the department in the late 1980s, and today Nakano creates effects-oriented amusement park rides.

Films Include: The Battle of Okinawa, Godzilla vs. the Smog Monster, Lake of Dracula (1971); Godzilla on Monster Island (1972); Godzilla vs. Megalon, Submersion of Japan/Tidal Wave (1973); Godzilla vs. the Cosmic Monster, Prophecies of Nostradamus (1974); ESPY, The Terror of Godzilla, Evil of Dracula (1975); The War in Space (1977); Deathquake (1980); The Imperial Navy (1982); Godzilla 1985 (1984); Princess from the Moon, Tokyo Blackout (1987).

Mikio Naruse Director, screenwriter. *b.* 1905, in Tokyo. *d.* 1969. Director of *Late Chrysanthemums* (1954), *Floating Clouds* (1955), *When a Woman Ascends the Stairs* (1960) and *Lonely Lane* (1962), and *shomin-geki* ("common people drama") master. He studied under Heinosuke Gosho, and from him he learned a keen sense of pathos and lyricism. He directed his first film in 1930, but it was his postwar work which is best remembered today. Though primarily a comedy director early in his career, he eventually moved into pessimistic dramas, often centered around lonely, struggling women, and usually played by **Hideko Takamine**. However, as David Shipman noted, "His best films are suffused with a melancholy, with a desire for what might have been, which becomes, as art, warming and enlightening—and despairing rather than depressing."

Films Include: Mr. and Mrs. Swordplay, Pure Love, Record of Newlyweds, Depression Period, Strength of Love (1930); Now Don't Get Excited, Hardworking Clerk, Fickleness Gets on the Train, Beard of Strength, Weeping Blue Sky (1931); Erroneous Practice, Lost Spring, Stepchild, Apart from You (1932); Everynight Dreams, Careless (1933); Three Sisters with Maiden Hearts, The Actress and the Poet, Wife Be Like a Rose!, The Girl in the Rumor (1935); On the Way to Spider Gate, Dawn in the Boulevard (1936); New Grief, Avalanche (1937); Tsuruhachi and Tsurujiro (1938); The Whole Family Works, Sincerity (1939); An Itinerant Actor (1940); A Dearly Loved Face, The Moon Over Shanghai (1941); Song of a Lantern (1943); Theatre (1944); Victory in the Sun, Toshiya Story (1945); The Descendants of Taro Urashima

(1946); Four Love Stories [co-dir.], Spring Awakening (1947); The Bad Girl (1949); White Beast, Conduct Report on Professor Ishinaka, Town of Anger (1950); Dancing Princess, Repast (1951); Mother, Lightning (1952); Husband and Wife, Wife, Older Brother Younger Sister (1953); Sounds from the Mountains, Late Chrysanthemums (1954); Floating Clouds, The First Kiss [co-dir.] (1955); Sudden Rain, Wife's Heart, Flowing (1956); Untamed Woman (1957); Summer Clouds (1958); A Whistle in My Heart (1959); When a Woman Ascends the Stairs, Daughters Wives and a Mother, Flowing Night, The Approach of Autumn (1960); As a Wife As a Woman (1961); A Woman's Place, Lonely Lane (1962); Woman's Life (1963); Yearning (1964); The Thin Line, Moment of Terror (1966); Two in the Shadow/Scattered Clouds (1967).

Yosuke Natsuki Actor. *b.* February 27, 1936, in Tokyo. Leading man at Toho during the 1960s, usually in adventure films. He was the young man who leaves home at the beginning of *Yojimbo* (1961), and later starred in *Dagora, The Space Monster* and *Ghidrah—The Three-Headed Monster* (1964). However, he is probably best remembered in Japan for his leading roles in war movies. He replaced the ailing Akihiko Hirata in *Godzilla 1985* (1984).

FILMS INCLUDE: The H-Man [bit] (1958); Three Dolls in the College (1959); I Bombed Pearl Harbor, Life of a Country Doctor, The Gambling Samurai (1960); Yojimbo, Daredevil in the Castle, The Last Challenge, Kill the Killer!, Counterstroke, Bandits on the Wind (1961); Girl of Dark, The Wiser Age, Chushingura, Operation Enemy Fort (1962); Operation Mad Dog, Interpol Code 8, Attack Squadron!, Outpost of Hell, Siege of Fort Bismarck (1963); Whirlwind, The Weed of Crime, Tiger Flight, Dagora the Space Monster, Ghidrah—The Three-Headed Monster (1964); The Daphne (1966); Goal for the Young, The Eyes the Sea and a Ball (1967); Shogun [US teleseries released as a feature elsewhere] (1980); Godzilla 1985 (1984).

Peggy Neal Actress. *b.* 1947. Amateur performer living in Japan who played the ingenue in Toei's *Terror Beneath the Sea* (1966) and Shochiku's *The X from Outer Space* (1967). Other credits include *Las Vegas Free-for-All* (also 1967).

Toshiyuki Nishida Actor. *b.* 1940, in Fukushima. Wide-mouthed star of Shochiku's "Free and Easy" film series. In films from 1970, he is best known in the West as the star of the epic *The Silk Road* (1988).

FILMS INCLUDE: The Tattered Banner (1974); Edo Porn (1981); Karate Cop (1982); Heaven Station (1984); Lost in the Wilderness (1986); Free and Easy, The Silk Road (1988); Free and Easy 2 (1989); Free and Easy 3 (1990); Free and Easy 4 (1991); A Class to Remember, Free and Easy 5 (1992).

Akira Nishimura *see* **Ko Nishimura**

Ko Nishimura Actor. *b.* January 25, 1923, in Sapporo. Gaunt actor—almost always mis-billed as "Akira Nishimura"—with deeply etched features, and in constant demand from the late 1950s. A kind of younger Seiji Miyaguchi, he played "Shirai," the company executive Toshiro Mifune nearly pushes out of a window in *The Bad Sleep Well* (1960). The actor, who later starred in the teleseries "Mito Komon," has appeared in several hundred features since his film debut in 1951.

FILMS INCLUDE: The Burmese Harp (1956); The Bad Sleep Well, The Angry Sea (1960); Yojimbo, Blind Devotion, The Man in Red, The Flesh Is Hot/Pigs and Battleships (1961); Gorath, Temple of the Wild Geese (1962); Pressure of Guilt, Attack Squadron! (1963); Unholy Desire (1964); House of Terrors, The Scarlet Camellia, Ghost of a One-Eyed Man, Red Beard (1965); The Sword of Doom (1966); Zatoichi—The Blind Swordsman's Rescue, Whispering Joe (1967); Black Lizard, Kaidan botandoro, Samurai Wolf II, Fear of the Snake Woman, Zatoichi—The Blind Swordsman Samaritan, The Sexploiters (1968); Black Rose, Lone Avenger (1969); Mondo Grottesco [narrator only], Quick-Draw Okatsu, The Wild Sea (1969); Waterfront Blues, Play It Cool (1970);

Under the Blossoming Cherry Trees (1975); Love and Faith/Lady Ogin (1978).

Kogo Noda Screenwriter. *b.* November 19, 1893, in Hokkaido. *d.* 1968. Screenwriter associated almost exclusively with **Yasujiro Ozu**.

FILMS INCLUDE **[as screenwriter or co-screenwriter]:** Fighting Friends—Japanese Style, The Life of an Office Worker, A Straightforward Boy (1929); An Introduction to Marriage, That Night's Wife, The Revengeful Spirit of Eros, Lost Luck (1930); Tokyo Chorus (1931); Where Now Are the Dreams of Youth, Until the Day We Meet Again (1932); Woman of Tokyo (1933); An Innocent Maid (1935); The Story of Tank Commander Nishizumi (1940); Victory of Women (1946); Late Spring (1949); The Munekata Sisters (1950); Early Summer (1951); The Flavor of Green Tea Over Rice (1952); Tokyo Story (1953); Early Spring (1956); Tokyo Twilight (1957); Equinox Flower (1958); Good Morning/Ohayo, Floating Weeds (1959); Late Autumn (1960); The End of Summer (1961); An Autumn Afternoon (1962).

Ken Ogata Actor. *b.* 1937, in Tokyo. Important leading player, in films from 1960, though he first attained stardom some fifteen years later. Best known as the lead in *Vengeance Is Mine* (1979), and in the title role of *Mishima—A Life in Four Chapters* (1985).

FILMS INCLUDE: The House of Wooden Blocks, The Sex Check (1968); Farewell My Beloved, The Song from My Heart (1969); The Castle of Sand, The Last Samurai (1974); The Demon (1977); Vengeance Is Mine (1979); Virus [Jap/US] (1980); Samurai Reincarnation, Edo Porn (1981); The Ballad of Narayama, The Geisha, The Big Catch (1983); Okinawan Boys (1983); Mishima—A Life in Four Chapters [US/Jap], Tracked, Kai (1985); House on Fire (1986); Zegan (1987); Oracion (1988); Company Executives, Shogun's Shadow, Zatoichi (1989); Goodbye Mama, The Great Kidnapping/Rainbow Kids (1991).

Eiji Okada Actor. *b.* June 13, 1920, in Chiba. *ed.* Keio University, in economics. Entering films in 1949—four years after his stage debut—Okada achieved international acclaim as the star of *Hiroshima mon amour* (1959), and in other existentialist roles, including the man trapped by the *Woman in the Dunes* (1964) Okada is also familiar to American audiences as the project leader battling *The X from Outer Space* (1967). Recently he gave a moving performance—without uttering a word—as the grandfather in *Traffic Jam* (1991). Not to be confused with the actor Masumi Okada (q.v.), also in films during this same period.

FILMS INCLUDE: Hana no sugao [debut] (1949); Till We Meet Again, Sentimental Journalist (1950); Twenty Years in a Storm, Reeds that Rustle in the Wind (1951); Vacuum Zone, Mother, Dawn—Fifteenth of August (1952); The Tower of Lilies, Hiroshima (1953); A Billionaire, Forsaken (1954); Christ in Bronze, Here Is a Spring (1955); A Story of Pure Love (1957); Fearless Opposition (1958); Hiroshima mon amour [Fr/Jap], The Hawk of the North (1959); Outlaws in the Skies, The Pirates (1960); The Ugly American [US] (1962); He and She (1963); Woman in the Dunes, The Assassin, The Scent of Incense (1964); Judo Saga, The Scarlet Camellia, Samurai Spy (1965); The Face of Another (1966); Portrait of Chieko,

Ken Ogata stars as Yukio Mishima, the most internationally famous and controversial Japanese writer of the postwar era in *Mishima—A Life in Four Chapters* (1985).

The X from Outer Space, Rebellion of Japan (1967); Tattooed Temptress, Stormy Era, Secret Information, Tunnel to the Sun (1968); Vixen, Bullet Wound, Secret Information (1969); This Transient Life (1970); Zatoichi's Conspiracy (1973); ESPY (1974); The Alaska Story (1977); Love and Faith/Lady Ogin (1978); Deathquake (1980); Antarctica (1983): The Sea and Poison (1986); The Death of a Tea Master (1989); Hikarigoke, Traffic Jam (1991).

Mariko Okada Actress. *b.* January 11, 1933, in Tokyo. In films since 1951, first at Toho and later at Shochiku, Okada specialized in period films, frequently cast as a less-than-pure temptress or bossy wife to the more pure characterizations typified by Kaoru Yachigusa and Kyoko Kagawa. Memorable in Inagaki's *Samurai* trilogy (1954-56). In recent years she has worked, memorably, in several Itami comedies (e.g., the etiquette teacher in *Tampopo*).

FILMS INCLUDE: The Lover (1953); Samurai I (1954); Samurai II, Floating Clouds (1955); Samurai III (1956); Secret Scrolls I (1957); Secret Scrolls II (1958); Late Autumn (1960); An Autumn Afternoon (1962); Kwaidan, Twilight Path (1964); Illusion of Blood (1965); The Lake (1966); The Smell of Poison, The Affair (1967); Waterfront Blues (1970); I Am a Cat (1975); Appassionata (1984); Tampopo (1985); A Taxing Woman (1987).

Masumi Okada Actor. *b.* September 22, 1940 in France, the son of Japanese and Danish parents. Bilingual actor brought to Japan at the age of four, and not to be confused with Eiji Okada (q.v.), though, like the star of *Hiroshima mon amour*, he is often cast in Western roles, and has even played Frenchmen.

FILMS INCLUDE: Six Suspects (1960); The Return of the Filthy Seven (1967); Living Skeleton, Blazing Continent (1968); Latitude Zero [Jap/US] (1969); Marco [US/Jap] (1973); Shogun [US teleseries released as a feature in Japan] (1980); Sayonara Jupiter (1984).

Kihachi Okamoto Director, screenwriter. *b.* 1924, in Tottori. *ed.* Meiji University. Joining Toho immediately after graduating from college, Okamoto made his first feature in 1958. Best known for violent *jidai-geki*, including *The Sword of Doom* and *Samurai Assassin*.

FILMS INCLUDE: All About Marriage/Marriage in General (1958); The Big Boss, Desperado Outpost, The Last Gunfight (1959); Westward Desperado (1960); Big Shots Die at Dawn, Procurers of Hell (1961); Warring Clans (1963); Samurai Assassin, Fort Graveyard, Blood and Sand, Ironfinger [scr. only] (1965); The Sword of Doom (1966); The Emperor and the General (1967); Human Bullets, Kill! (1968); Red Lion (1969); Zatoichi meets Yojimbo (1970); The Battle of Okinawa (1971); Sanshiro Sugata (1977); Noisy Dynamite, Blood Type—Blue (1978); The Last Game (1979); At This Late Date the Charleston (1981); Dixieland Daimyo (1986); Rainbow Kids/The Great Kidnapping (1991).

Kozo Okazaki Director of Photography. *b.* 1919, in Tokyo. Award-winning cinematographer who frequently has worked in Hollywood productions filmed in Japan.

FILMS INCLUDE: Anniversary for Lovers (1939); The Saga of Anatahan (1953); The Princess of Badger Palace (1958); This Madding Crowd (1962); Sweet Sweat (1964); Dark the Mountain Snow (1965); Our Silent Love, River of Forever (1967); Hymn to a Tired Man (1968); Goyokin (1969); The Scandalous Adventures of Buraikan (1970); Rise Fair Sun (1973); The Family, The Silk Tree Ballad (1974); I Am a Cat, Kaseki, The Yakuza [US], Children Chasing Rainbows (1975); Mariko—Mother, The Alaska Story (1977); Love and Faith/Lady Ogin, The Bad News Bears Go to Japan [US] (1978); My Son! My Son! (1979); Abandoned (1981); The Challenge [US] (1982); House Without a Dining Table (1985); Big Joys Small Sorrows, Hello Kids! (1986); Father (1988); Tetsuro Tamba's Great Spirit World (1989); War and Youth (1991).

Kazuki Omori Director, screenwriter. *b.* March 3, 1952, in Osaka. Regarded as one of the more interesting talents to come out of Japan in recent years, despite a tendency to replicate American genre cliches in his work. He began making films as a teenager, first in Regular-8, then 16mm. One of his shorts won the Kido Prize for screenplay writing, and Omori abandoned his premed schooling to join Toho. In recent years, Omori has written and/or directed several "Godzilla" films for the studio.

FILMS INCLUDE: Orange Road Express (1978); Disciples of Hippocrates (1980); Young Girls in Love, Modern Time (1986); A Goodbye to the Girls/Women Who Say Goodbye (1987); Godzilla vs. Biollante (1989); Mr. Moonlight, Godzilla vs. King Ghidorah (1991); Godzilla vs. Mothra [scr. only] (1992); Godzilla vs. Destroyer [scr. only] (1995).

Senkichi Omura Actor. *b.* April 27, 1923, in Tokyo. Bit player at Toho, a favorite of director **Ishiro Honda**, who specialized playing working class go-getters. He was the translator in *King Kong vs. Godzilla* (1962), and the man who retrieves the hat in *Ghidrah—The Three-Headed Monster* (1964).

FILMS INCLUDE: The Man Who Went to Sea (1952); Seven Samurai (1954); Half Human, Gigantis the Fire Monster, I Live in Fear (1955); The Mysterians, Throne of Blood (1957); The Rickshaw Man, The Hidden Fortress, Varan the Unbelievable, The H-Man (1958); The Three Treasures (1959); The Gambling Samurai, The Secret of the Telegian, The Angry Sea, I Bombed Pearl Harbor (1960); Daredevil in the Castle, Mothra (1961); King Kong vs. Godzilla, Chushingura (1962); The Lost World of Sinbad, Attack Squadron!, High and Low (1963); Godzilla vs. the Thing (1964); Frankenstein Conquers the World [US/Jap] (1965); Come Marry Me (1966); Kagemusha (1980).

Nagisa Oshima Director. *b.* March 31, 1932, in Kyoto. *ed.* Kyoto University. The leader of the Japanese New Wave, Oshima studied political history before entering films as an assistant director at the Shochiku-Ofuna Studios in 1954, and, two years later, published the film magazine *Eiga hihyo* ("Film Comment"). He made his feature debut in 1958, but left Shochiku the following year when his *A Foggy Night in Japan* was suddenly pulled from circulation just three days into its release. He formed his own production company (Sozosha, and later Oshima Productions) as a result. *Death by Hanging* (1968) caught the eye of Western critics, who lauded his criticism of Japanese racism (against Koreans, a taboo subject to be sure), and especially his experimental cutting, use of hand-held shots, and utter rejection of the Classical style. In 1976 he directed the notorious *In the Realm of the Senses*, for which he was charged with obscenity but not convicted. The darling of many Western film theorists, he is regarded as "the Godard of the East," though more generally viewed as a daring but pretentious formalist by mainstream critics.

FILMS INCLUDE: A Town of Love and Hope (1959); Naked Youth, The Sun's Burial, A Foggy Night in Japan/Night and Fog in Japan (1960); The Catch (1961); A Small Adventure (1963); The Pleasures of the Flesh, Yunbogi's Diary (1965); Violence at High Noon (1966); Sing a Song of Sex, Ninja Bugeicho, Night of the Killer (1967); Death by Hanging, A Sinner of Paradise (1968); Diary of a Shinjuku Thief, Boy (1969); He Died After the War/The Man Who Left His Will on Film (1970); The Ceremony (1971); Summer Sister (1972); In the Realm of the Senses [Jap/Fr] (1976); Empire of Passion (1978); Merry Christmas Mr. Lawrence [Jap/UK] (1983); Max mon amour [Jap/Fr] (1986).

Hideji Otaki *see* **Shuji Otaki**

Shuji Otaki Actor. *b.* 1925, in Tokyo. Often mis-billed as "Hideji Otaki" and "Hideo Otaka," this important, prolific actor has recently been associated with the work of Itami. Originally a stage director, he turned to acting in 1955.

FILMS INCLUDE: City of Beasts (1970); Lake of Dracula (1971); The Village, Tora-san the Intellectual (1975); Older Brother Younger Sister (1976); The War in Space (1977); Hunter in the Dark, Deathquake, Kagemusha (1980); Station (1981); The Funeral (1984); Tampopo (1985); A Taxing Woman, Tokyo Blackout (1987); Black Rain (1988); Minbo—Or the Gentle Art of Japanese Extortion (1992).

Nobuko Otowa Actress. *b.* October 1, 1925, in Tottori. *ed.* Takarazuka

Girls Opera School. Initially a singer with something of a prima donna reputation, Otowa joined Daiei in 1950. Later associated with Kindai Eiga Kyokai and directors **Kaneto Shindo** and **Kozaburo Yoshimura** (and married the former), she won a gold medal at the Moscow Film Festival for her work in *The Island* (1961). She was also excellent as the bitter, jealous old woman in *Onibaba* (1964). Still active in films.

Films Include: Shojo bachi [debut] (1950); Migratory Birds Under the Moon, Story of a Beloved Wife, A Tale of Genji, Lantern Under a Full Moon, Miss Oyu (1951); Red Group of Asakusa, Avalanche, The Song of Matchless Moonlight, Children of Hiroshima (1952); Thousand Cranes, Castle Called Woman, Eighty Percent of the Village, Epitome, Desires, Before Dawn, A Woman's Life, Hiroshima (1953); Kimpei from Koina, A Beautiful Person, Gutter, An Inn at Osaka, The Valley Between Life and Death, Youth Covered with Mud, People of Young Character (1954); The Beauty and the Dragon, Wolves (1955); Twice on a Certain Night, Morning Dawn (1956); Ukifune, Skin Color of the Moon, A Geisha in the Old City (1957); Avarice, The Happy Pilgrimage, Only Women Have Trouble, The Child Writers, Stray Cat, Secret Scrolls II (1958); The Lucky Dragon No. 5, The Three Treasures, Account of My Beloved Wife (1959); When a Woman Loves, The Twilight Story, Some Pumpkin (1960); The Island, The Shrikes, The Last War, Immortal Love, Tokyo Detective Story, The Diplomat's Mansion, The Youth and His Amulet (1961); Till Tomorrow Comes, Long Way to Okinawa, This Madding Crowd (1962); The Maid Story,When Women Lie (1963); Twilight Path, The Scent of Incense, Onibaba (1964); Shadow of Waves, Conquest (1965); Rise Against the Sword, Lost Sex, Once a Rainy Day (1966); The Izu Dancer, Libido (1967); Kuroneko, Operation Negligee (1968); Odd Affinity, Red Lion, Heat Wave Island (1969); Live Today Die Tomorrow! (1970); My Way (1974); Kenji Mizoguchi: The Life of a Film Director (1975); The Life of Chikuzan—Tsugaru Shamisen Player (1977); A Nurse's Husband Fights On (1980); The Horizon (1984); Tree Without Leaves (1986); Sakuratai 8.6 (1988); The Strange Tale of Oyuki (1992).

Eitaro Ozawa Actor. *b.* March 27, 1909, in Tokyo. *d.* 1988. Familiar character actor in films as early as 1934, and active until his death 54 years later. Often cast as detectives or local government officials. Memorable as the would-be samurai in *Ugetsu* (1953). Billed as "Sakae Ozawa" in some of his earlier work.

Films Include: My Love Has Been Burning (1949); Scandal (1950); Tales of Ugetsu (1953); A Story from Chikamatsu (1954); Tojura's Love (1955); Undercurrent (1956); Go and Get It, The H-Man (1958); The Human Condition I (1959); When a Woman Ascends the Stairs (1960); Romance Express, Wife's Confession (1961); Ayako, Gorath, A Woman's Life (1962); Lips of Ruin, The Assassin (1964); Beast Alley, Illusion of Blood (1965); Moment of Terror (1966); Zatoichi Challenged (1967); The Day the Sun Rose, A Ronin Called Nemuri (1968); Vixen, Black Rose (1969); Sandakan 8, Kenji Mizoguchi: The Life of a Film Director (1975); The Inugami Family (1976); House of Hanging (1979); Imperial Navy (1981); Godzilla 1985 (1984); A Taxing Woman (1987).

Sakae Ozawa *see* **Eitaro Ozawa**

Yasujiro Ozu Director. *b.* December 12, 1903, in Tokyo. *d.* December 12, 1963. Along with Kenji Mizoguchi and Akira Kurosawa, Ozu is widely regarded as Japan's greatest filmmaker, even though his art would not be fully recognized in the West until some ten years after his death. Considered the most "Japanese" of Japanese filmmakers (as opposed to the Western-influenced Kurosawa), Ozu's work, particularly that of his later years, is astonishingly consistent. His famous and almost constant use of waist-high camera angles (more accurately subject-level, in the sitting position), character parallelism, 360-degree cutting—and, for the most part, a rejection of camera movement, dissolves and fades, have made him a true original—a wholly unpretentious, economical formalist who quietly thrived under the Japanese studio system. His best films usually followed the everyday lives of lower- and middle-class families, particularly how the younger and older generations sadly but inevitably drifted apart. He worked as a teacher before joining Shochiku as an assistant cameraman in 1923, and directed his first film four years later. After several dozen genre films, mostly comedies, Ozu's vision began to emerge. He allied himself with screenwriter **Kogo Noda**, actor **Chishu Ryu**, and actress **Setsuko Hara** in the late 1930s—the first great period of his work. His career was interrupted by military service, and Ozu spent six months as a British P.O.W. His career resumed in the late 1940s, again at Shochiku, with a renewed vigor. His many important works include *Late Spring* (1949), *Tokyo Story* (1953), *Equinox Flower* (1958), *Floating Weeds* (1959), and *An Autumn Afternoon* (1962). He died of cancer on his 60th birthday.

FILMS INCLUDE: Sword of Penitence (1927); Dreams of Youth, Wife Lost, Pumpkin, A Couple on the Move, Body Beautiful (1928); Treasure Mountain, Days of Youth, Fighting Friends, I Graduated but... (1929); Life of an Office Worker, A Straightforward Boy, Introduction to Marriage, Walk Cheerfully, I Flunked but..., That Night's Wife, The Revengeful Spirit of Eros, Luck Touch My Legs, Young Miss, The Lady and Her Favorites (1930); The Beauty's Sorrows, The Chorus of Tokyo (1931); Spring Comes from the Ladies, I Was Born but..., Where Are the Dreams of Youth?, Until the Day We Meet Again (1932); Woman of Tokyo, Women on the Firing Line, Passing Fancy (1933); A Mother Ought to Be Loved, A Story of Floating Weeds (1934); The Young Virgin, Tokyo Is a Nice Place, An Inn in Tokyo (1935); College Is a Nice Place, The Only Son (1936); What Did the Lady Forget? (1937); The Toda Brothers (1941); There Is a Father (1942); Record of a Tenement Gentleman, A Hen in the Wind (1948); Late Spring (1949); The Munakata Sisters (1950); Early Summer (1951); The Flavor of Green Tea Over Rice (1952); Tokyo Story (1953); Early Spring (1956); Tokyo Twilight (1957); Equinox Flower (1958); Good Morning, Floating Weeds (1959); Late Autumn (1960); Early Autumn (1961); An Autumn Afternoon (1962).

The Peanuts (Emi and Yumi Ito) Singers, actresses. Twin sisters born in 1941. Popular singing stars who embarked on a film career at Toho in the early 1960s. Memorable as the twin fairies in three fantasies: *Mothra* (1961), *Godzilla vs. the Thing* and *Ghidrah—The Three Headed Monster* (both 1964). The characters were revived in 1966, 1992 and 1994, but by then the Itos had relinquished their roles. They still perform occasionally, and remain popular.

FILMS INCLUDE: Mothra (1961); Me and Me (1962); Double Trouble (1963); Godzilla vs. the Thing, Ghidrah—The Three-Headed Monster (1964); Don't Call Me a Con Man (1965); Las Vegas Free-for-All (1967).

Chishu Ryu Actor. *b.* May 13, 1906 [1904, according to one source], in Kumamoto. *d.* 1993. A longtime friend and associate of director **Yasujiro Ozu**, Ryu was Ozu's mirror, and was to the director what Takashi Shimura was to Akira Kurosawa (or, as writer Robin Wood puts it, was a Fernando Rey to Ozu's Bunuel), and appeared in all of the director's films with but two exceptions: *The Beauty's Sorrow* (1931) and *What Did the Lady Forget?* (1937). In films for an incredible 66 years, he was especially memorable as the father in Ozu's *Late Spring* (1949), *Tokyo Story* (1953), and *An Autumn Afternoon* (1962). In later years, he appeared regularly as the temple priest in Yoji Yamada's "Tora-san" series. One of his last roles was another gem—the 103-year-old man in *Akira Kurosawa's Dreams* (1990). Winner of the Tokyo Blue Ribbon Prize for Best Supporting Actor (for *Early Summer*, 1951), and recipient of the Best Actor Awards at the Mainichi Film Concourse, in 1948, 1951, and 1970.

FILMS INCLUDE: Sword of Penitence (1927); Dreams of Youth, Wife Lost, Pumpkin, A Couple on the Move, Body Beautiful (1928); Treasure Mountain, Days of Youth, Fighting Friends, I Graduated but... (1929); Life of an Office Worker, A Straightforward Boy, Introduction to Marriage, Walk Cheerfully, I Flunked but..., That Night's Wife, The Revengeful Spirit of Eros, Luck Touched My Legs, Young Miss, The Lady and Her

Favorites (1930); The Chorus of Tokyo (1931); Spring Comes from the Ladies, I Was Born but. . . , Where Are the Dreams of Youth?, Until the Day We Meet Again (1932); Woman of Tokyo, Women on the Firing Line, Passing Fancy (1933); A Mother Ought to Be Loved, A Story of Floating Weeds (1934); The Young Virgin, Tokyo Is a Nice Place, An Inn in Tokyo (1935); College Is a Nice Place, The Only Son (1936); The Light of Asakusa (1937); The Toda Brothers/The Brothers and Sisters of the Toda Family (1941); There Is a Father/There Was a Father, South Wind (1942); The Blossoming Port (1943); The Fellows Who Ate the Elephant, Children Hand in Hand (1947); Record of a Tenement Gentleman, A Hen in the Wind (1948); Late Spring, Forgotten Children (1949); The Munakata Sisters (1950); Early Summer, Carmen Comes Home (1951); The Flavor of Green Tea over Rice (1952); Tokyo Story, The Journey (1953); What Is Your Name, Twenty-Four Eyes (1954); The Immortal Pitcher, Stray Sheep, She Was Like a Wild Chrysanthemum, The First Kiss (1955); The Storm, Early Spring (1956); Tokyo Twilight/Twilight in To kyo, The Crowded Streetcar (1957); Equinox Flower, The Rickshaw Man (1958); Good Morning, I Want to Be a Shellfish, Floating Weeds, The Path Under the Platanes (1959); Late Autumn, Salary-Man Menjiro Sanpei—Wife's Honor, Salary-Man Menjiro Sanpei—Husband's Sigh, The Bad Sleep Well, Internees of Kampili (1960); Storm on the Silvery Peaks, Bandits on the Wind, A Thief and Culture Order, The Last War, The Youth and His Amulet, The Human Condition III, Early Autumn (1961); The Wiser Age, An Autumn Afternoon, Flower in a Storm (1962); The Rat Among the Cats, Tange Sazen (1963); A Marilyn in Tokyo, Gazing at Love and Death (1964); Twilight Path, The Soundless Cry, Red Beard (1965); The Four Loves (1966); The Emperor and the General, Local Line Love (1967); Battle of the Japan Sea, Am I Trying, Fight for the Glory (1969); Tora-san's Grand Scheme, Where Spring Comes Late, Tora-san's Runaway (1970); Tora-san's Shattered Romance, High-School Outcasts, Tora-san's Love Call (1971); Tora-san's Dream-Come-True (1972); Tora-san's Forget-Me-Not (1973); Tora-san's Lullaby (1974); Tora-san the Intellectual (1975); Tora-san Meets His Lordship (1977); Talk of the Town Tora-san (1978); Tora-san the Matchmaker, Tora-san's Dream of Spring (1979); Tora-san's Sunrise and Sunset (1976); Foster Daddy Tora! (1980); Tora-san's Love in Osaka, Tora-san's Promise (1981); Tora-san the Expert (1982); Tora-san's Song of Love, When We Are Old, Tora-san Goes Religious (1983); I Lived But..., The Funeral, Tora-san's Forbidden Love (1984); Tora-san's Island Encounter, Tokyo-ga (1985); Final Take—The Golden Age of Movies, Tora-san's Bluebird Fantasy (1986); Tora-san Goes North (1987); Tora-san's Salad-Day Memorial, Tora-san Goes to Vienna (1988); Tora-san Goes to Vienna, Tora-san My Uncle (1989); Tora-san Takes a Vacation (1990); Akira Kurosawa's Dreams (1990); Tora-san Confesses (1991); Hikarigoke (1991); Tora-san Makes Excuses (1992).

Shin Saburi Actor, director. *b.* February 12, 1909, in Hokkaido. *d.* 1982. Important character actor, often cast in patriarchal roles, and as government officials. Memorable as the father in Ozu's *Equinox Flower* (1957), and as the father dying of cancer in Kobayashi's *Kaseki* (1975).

Films Include: [as actor] The Story of Tank Commander Nishizumi (1940); The Brothers and Sisters of the Toda Family (1941); There Was a Father (1942); The Flavor of Green Tea over Rice (1952); Earth (1957); Thirst for Love, Equinox Flower (1958); Late Autumn (1960); The Family, The Castle of Sand (1974); Kaseki (1975); Island of Horrors (1977); The Incident (1978); The Three Undelivered Letters (1979); Deathquake (1980).

Keiji Sada Actor. *b.* 1926, in Kyoto. *ed.* Waseda University *d.* 1964. Popular star of both light romances and heavy drama (in films beginning 1947) whose life and career ended abruptly in an auto accident. He was discovered by Kinoshita, though is best remembered in the West as Tatsuya Nakadai's friend in *The Human Condition I* (1959), and as Chishu Ryu's married son obsessed with a set of golf clubs in Ozu's *An Autumn Afternoon* (1962).

FILMS INCLUDE: Phoenix, Red Lips (1947); Here's to the Girls (1949); Carmen Comes Home, School of Freedom (1951); Sad Speech, The Boy Director, Stormy Waters, The First Step of Married Life (1952); Spring Drum, A Japanese Tragedy, The Journey (1953); Somewhere Beneath the Wide Sky, Diary of Fallen Leaves, A Young Lady as President, A Medal, Family Conference, What Is Your Name? (1954); College for Men, The Sun Never Sets, You and Your Friend, The Refugee, Beautiful Days, New Every Day, Distant Clouds (1955); The White Bridge, Look for Your Bride, Tokyo-Hong Kong Honeymoon, The Fountainhead, Footprints of a Woman (1956); The Sound of Youth, I'll Buy You, Tears, A Case of Honor, The Embraced Bride, Monkey Business, The Lighthouse/Times of Joy and Sorrow, Payoff with Love, Candle in the Wind (1957); True Love, Triple Betrayal, The Country Boss, Equinox Flower, The Invisible Wall (1958); Waiting for Spring, The Human Condition I, Good Morning, Eighteen, Map of the Ocean, The Human Condition II, Tokyo Omnibus, Showdown at Dawn, Fine Fellow (1959); The Scarlet Flower, Hot Corner Murder, White Pigeon, Of Men and Money, Women of Kyoto, Wild Trio, Study, Late Autumn, The Grave Tells All, Dry Earth (1960); Hunting Rifle, Uzu, Blue Current, Enraptured, As the Clouds Scatter, Immortal Love, Tokyo Detective Saga (1961); Flower in a Storm, Ballad of a Workman, An Autumn Afternoon, Mama I Need You (1962); Escape from Hell, The Hidden Profile (1963); A Marilyn in Tokyo, The Assassin, Brand of Evil, Sweet Sweat (1964).

Yutaka Sada Actor. *b.* March 30, 1911, in Tokyo. A prolific bit player at Toho, memorable as the the chauffeur whose son is kidnapped in Kurosawa's *High and Low* (1963).

FILMS INCLUDE: The Invisible Man (1954); I Live in Fear (1955); The Mysterians, Throne of Blood (1957); The Hidden Fortress (1958); The Three Treasures (1959); Man Against Man, I Bombed Pearl Harbor, The Secret of the Telegian, The Bad Sleep Well (1960); The Youth and His Amulet, The Last War (1961); High and Low, Siege of Fort Bismark (1963); Godzilla vs. the Thing (1964); Frankenstein Conquers the World [Jap/US], Red Beard (1965); Moment of Terror, Ebirah Horror of the Deep (1966); Las Vegas Free-for-All (1967); Fancy Paradise, Destroy All Monsters (1968); Battle of the Japan Sea, Godzilla's Revenge (1969); The Battle of Okinawa (1971).

Kenji Sahara Actor. *b.* July 5, 1932. Two years after joining Toho, Sahara [not to be confused with Kenji Kasahara or Kenji Sawada] starred in the studio's first *kaiju eiga* in color, *Rodan* (1956), and the first in wide screen, *The Mysterians* (1957). His association with the genre was solidified with his starring role in the Tsuburaya teleseries "Ultra Q," an anthology program not unlike "The Outer Limits," and which immediately preceded "Ultra Man." He has remained a fixture in Japanese sci-fi, appearing in more Japanese sci-fi features than any other major player, though since the mid-1960s his participation in features has been limited to supporting roles. Memorable as the villain in *Godzilla vs. the Thing* (1964).

FILMS INCLUDE: Godzilla, King of the Monsters! [extra] (1954); Flame in the Snow (1955); Rodan (1956); The Mysterians (1957); The H-Man, The Princess of Badger Palace (1958); Man from the East (1960); Snow in the South Seas, Moonlight in the Rain, Mothra [cameo] (1961); Gorath, King Kong vs. Godzilla, Chushingura, Young Generation (1962); Atragon, Attack of the Mushroom People (1963); Godzilla vs. the Thing, Ghidrah—The Three-Headed Monster [cameo] (1964); None But the Brave [US/Jap], Frankenstein Conquers the World [Jap/US] (1965); War of the Gargantuas [Jap/US] (1966); Son of Godzilla (1967); Destroy All Monsters, Admiral Yamamoto (1968); Godzilla's Revenge, Battle of the Japan Sea (1969); Yog—Monster from Space (1970); Godzilla vs. the Cosmic Monster [cameo] (1974); The Terror of Godzilla (1975); Godzilla vs. King Ghidorah (1991); Godzilla vs. Mechagodzilla (1993); Godzilla vs. Space Godzilla (1994).

Takashi Shimura, Kyoko Kagawa and Frankie Sakai (right) lead the fine cast of *Mothra* (1961).

Frankie Sakai Actor. *b.* February 13, 1929, in Kagoshima. Beefy comic actor, also adept at drama, and best known in the West for his strong supporting role in the miniseries *Shogun* (1980), as the resourceful reporter "Bulldog" in Ishiro Honda's *Mothra* (1961), and as the patriarch facing Armageddon in *The Last War* (also 1961). However, Sakai is best known in Japan for lighter roles, especially in two long-running series, "Boss Man" and "Train Station."

FILMS INCLUDE: A Boy and Three Mothers, Go and Get It, Temptation in Glamour Island, Romance and Rhythm (1958); Ishimatsu Travels with Ghosts, I Want to Be a Shellfish (1959); My Friend Death, Weaker Sex, Westward Desperado, Soft Touch of Night (1960); Snow in the South Seas, This Madding Crowd, Mothra, Romance Express, Dark the Mountain Snow, The Last War, A Geisha's Diary, The Diplomat's Mansion (1961); Chushingura (1962); You Can Succeed Too, Ghost Story of a Funny Act in Front of Train Station (1964); Five Gents' Trick Book (1965); Five Gents at Sunrise, 5 Gents on the Spot (1966); Big Wind at the Spa, How to Win a Race, Discover Japan with the Five Gents, Tokyo Century Plaza, Topsy-Turvy Journey, Yosakai Journey (1969); Oh My Comrade! (1970); Weird Trip (1972); Blood (1974); Mastermind [US; filmed in 1969] (1976); Have Wings on Your Heart (1978); Shogun [US teleseries released as a feature in Japan] (1980); Waiting for the Flood (1991); Uneasy Encounters [cameo] (1994).

Sachio Sakai Actor. *b.* February 13, 1929, in Tokyo. Character actor whose character was more or less replaced by Raymond Burr in the American version of *Godzilla, King of the Monsters!* (1954). The actor, who bears a strong if peculiar resemblence to comic Shemp Howard of the Three Stooges, is still active in films. Memorable as Matahachi Honiden in *Samurai II* and *III*, and as one of the bank robbers in *Godzilla's Revenge* (1969).

FILMS INCLUDE: One Wonderful Sunday (1947); Drunken Angel (1948); Eagle of the Pacific (1953); Godzilla King of the Monsters! (1954); Half Human, Samurai II

(1955); Samurai III (1956); Throne of Blood (1957); The Hidden Fortress (1958); Saga of the Vagabonds (1959); I Bombed Pearl Harbor, The Dangerous Kiss, Secret of the Telegian, Westward Desperado (1960); Romance Express, Daredevil in the Castle (1961); Gorath, Chushingura, King Kong vs. Godzilla, Tatsu (1962); Whirlwind, The Weed of Crime (1964); Ironfinger (1965); What's Up Tiger Lily? [US production incorporating Japanese footage] (1966); The Killing Bottle, King Kong Escapes [Jap/US] (1967); Godzilla's Revenge (1969); Yog—Monster from Space, The Vampire Doll (1970); The Battle of Okinawa (1971); Marco [Jap/US] (1973); Akira Kurosawa's Dreams (1990); Rhapsody in August [bit] (1991).

Hiroyuki "Henry" Sanada Actor. *b.* 1960, in Tokyo. Action star associated with Toei, often in fast-paced *jidaigeki* or sci-fi thrillers.

Films Include: Swords of the Space Ark [made for TV], Message from Space (1978); Samurai Reincarnation (1981); Ninja Wars (1982); Legend of the Eight Samurai, Shogun's Ninja (1983); The Street of Desire, Mah-Jong (1984); Thieving Ruby (1988); Yellow Fang (1990); We Are Not Alone (1993); Uneasy Encounters (1994).

Katsuhiko Sasaki Actor. *b.* December 24, 1944, in Tokyo. Shortly after making his film debut in 1971, Sasaki starred in a number of genre films at Toho, where he remains a fixture. Also active in television.

Films Include: The Battle of Okinawa (1971); Godzilla vs. Megalon (1973); Evil of Dracula, The Terror of Godzilla (1975); Godzilla vs. Biollante (1989); Godzilla vs. King Ghidorah (1991).

Kei Sato Actor. *b.* 1928, in Fukuoka. Leading player of the 1960s. Memorable as the outsider who visits the mother and daughter in *Onibaba* (1964).

Films Include: Onibaba, Kwaidan (1964); The Sword of Doom, Spider Tattoo, Zatoichi—The Blind Swordsman's Vengeance (1966); Kuroneko, Hymn to a Tired Man (1968); Diary of a Shijuku Thief (1969); Live Today Die Tomorrow! (1970); The Ceremony, Inn of Evil (1971); Zatoichi's Conspiracy (1973); Imperial Navy (1981); International Military Tribunal for the Far East—The Tokyo Trial [narrator only] (1983); Godzilla 1985 (1984); I Want to Live Once More (1985).

Makoto Sato Actor. *b.* March 18, 1934, in Saga. Intense, manic-looking actor who became a star in war and crime films despite his rather peculiar looks. He joined Toho in 1956, and starred in that studio's "Three Guys" film series. He later appeared in Japanese television opposite frequent co-star Tatsuya Mihashi, in "S.S.P. Combat Team." Best known in the West as the Black Pirate in *The Lost World of Sinbad* (1963), and as the gangster who nearly eludes *The H-Man* (1958). Often mis-billed as *Mitsuru* Sato.

Films Include: The Hidden Fortress, The H-Man (1958); I Bombed Pearl Harbor, Man from the East, Westward Desperado (1960); Bandits on the Wind, The Merciless Trap, The Man in Red, Blood on the Sea, The Last Challenge, Counterstroke (1961); Operation Enemy Fort, Operation X, Witness Killed, Chushingura (1962); Siege of Fort Bismark, The Lost World of Sinbad, Warring Clans, Outpost of Hell, Attack Squadron!, Interpol Code 8, Operation Mad Dog (1963); Tiger Flight, Whirlwind, The Weed of Crime (1964); Fort Graveyard, Adventures of Takla Makan (1965); Rise Against the Sword, The Mad Atlantic, The Daphne, What's Up Tiger Lily? [US production incorporating Japanese footage] (1966); The Emperor and the General, The Killing Bottle (1967); Admiral Yamamoto, Booted Babe Busted Boss, I the Executioner, Zatoichi—The Blind Swordsman Samaritan (1968);The Falcon Fighters, Battle of the Japan Sea (1969); Tattooed Swordsman (1970); Message from Space (1978); Imperial Navy (1981); Exchange Students (1982); Shogun's Ninja (1983).

Masaru Sato Composer. *b.* May 29, 1928. If Akira Ifukube is the Bernard Herrmann of the East, than Masaru Sato must surely be its Henri Mancini. The jazz-influenced composer took over the scoring reigns of **Akira Kurosawa**'s *I Live in Fear* and Mizoguchi's *New Tales of the Taira Clan* (both 1955) when mentor

Fumio Hayasaka died suddenly. Sato then scored all of Kurosawa's films through *Red Beard* (1965), and nearly 300 other movies in the years since. In recent years he scored several films for the late **Hideo Gosha**. His best work includes *The Bad Sleep Well* (1960), *Yojimbo* (1961) and, strangely enough, *Ebirah Horror of the Deep* (1966) and *Son of Godzilla* (1967).

Films Include: Seven Samurai [asst. comp. only] (1954); I Live in Fear [co-score], New Tales of the Taira Clan [co-score], Gigantis the Fire Monster, Half Human—The Story of the Abominable Snowman (1955); Throne of Blood, The Lower Depths (1957); The H-Man, The Hidden Fortress (1958); I Want to Be a Shellfish (1959); The Bad Sleep Well (1960); Procurers of Hell, Yojimbo, Challenge to Live (1961); Operation X, Operation Enemy Fort, Sanjuro (1962); High and Low, The Lost World of Sinbad, The Legacy of the 500,000 (1963); Samurai from Nowhere, Could I But Live (1964); Samurai Assassin, Ironfinger, Dark the Mountain Snow, Fort Graveyard, Red Beard (1965); The Mad Atlantic, River of Forever, Ebirah Horror of the Deep, The Sword of Doom, Moment of Terror (1966); The Emperor and the General, The Age of Assassins, Portrait of Chieko, Son of Godzilla (1967); Kill, Admiral Yamamoto, Booted Babe Busted Boss (1968); Forward Ever Forward, Goyokin, Red Lion, Under the Banner of Samurai, Live Your Own Way, The Magoichi Saga (1969); City of Beasts, Men and War, Where Spring Comes Late, The Scandalous Adventure of Buraikan, The Song from My Heart, Tenchu!, The Ambitious, The Ambush, Men and War (1970); Men and War II, The Battle of Okinawa (1971); Submersion of Japan/Tidal Wave, Men and War III, Long Journey Into Love (1973); Godzilla vs. the Cosmic Monster (1974); The Yellow Handkerchief, The Alaska Story (1977); Blue Christmas, Branch School Diary (1978); The Shogun Assassins, The Last Game, Nogumi Pass, Hunter in the Dark (1979); A Distant Cry from Spring (1980); Willful Murder, There Was a War When I Was a Child, At This Late Date the Charleston (1981); The Geisha (1983); Fireflies of the North (1984); Kai, Tracked (1985); Rainbow City Tokyo, The Forest of the Little Bear (1987); The Silk Road (1988); Haru Kuru Oni, Shogun's Shadow (1989); The Great Kidnapping/Rainbow Kids (1991).

Yasuko Sawaguchi Actress. *b.* 1965, in Osaka. Pop star recruited by Toho in 1984. Despite mostly wooden performances she remains one of the leading players in contemporary films. Also popular on the NHK television network.

Films Include: Karate Cop 3—Song of the Sea, Godzilla 1985 (1984); Sisters' Slope, The Crying-Deer Mansion (1986); Actress, Princess of the Moon (1987); Godzilla vs. Biollante [cameo] (1989); Yamato Takeru (1994).

Ikio Sawamura Actor. *b.* September 4, 1905, in Tochigi. *d.* 1975, of cancer. Short, round-faced little old man with a high-pitched voice and one of the most familiar supporting players in Japanese films of the 1950s and 1960s. Sawamura was a popular star of the musical stage during the 1940s and 1950s who joined Toho in 1954. His features and especially his voice were superbly suited to sly, working class types. Though his roles were often mere walk-ons, Sawamura was a guaranteed scene-stealer and always memorable. He was the corrupt officer/bell ringer in *Yojimbo* (1961), and was a favorite of both Akira Kurosawa and Ishiro Honda.

Films Include: Throne of Blood (1957); The Hidden Fortress (1958); Battle in Outer Space, The Three Treasures (1959); The Bad Sleep Well, Perils of Bangaku, The Secret of the Telegian (1960); Yojimbo, The Youth and His Amulet, Daredevil in the Castle, Eternity of Love (1961); Gorath, King Kong vs. Godzilla (1962); High and Low, Atragon (1963); Godzilla vs. the Thing, Ghidrah—The Three-Headed Monster (1964); Frankenstein Conquers the World [Jap/US], Red Beard (1965); Ebirah Horror of the Deep, Come Marry Me, War of the Gargantuas [Jap/US] (1966); King Kong Escapes [Jap/US], Las Vegas Free-for-All, Tenamonya—Ghost Journey, The Age of Assassins (1967); Fancy Paradise, Destroy All Monsters (1968); Portrait of Hell, Godzilla's Revenge (1969); Marco [US/Jap] (1973); The Terror of Godzilla (1975).

Hideo Sekigawa Director. *b.* 1908, in Niigata. Leftist filmmaker at Toho from 1936, initially a documentarian, famous as the one of the directors of the 1946 *Those Who Make Tomorrow* (with Akira Kurosawa and Kajiro Yamamoto), and for his anti-American work *Hiroshima* (1953).

FILMS INCLUDE: Those Who Make Tomorrow [co-dir.] (1946); Twenty-Four Hours of a Secret Life [co-dir.] (1947); A Second Life (1948); Listen to the Roar of the Ocean, Warships Without Smoke (1950); My Crime While at the First Higher School, Life of a Railway Worker (1951); Dawn 15th of August, Mixed-Blood, Children (1952); Hiroshima (1953); Orgy (1954); The Boyhood of Dr. Noguchi (1956); Sound of Youth, Roar and Earth (1957); Gunfight on Seventh Street, Beyond the Seasonal Wind, Horrible Midnight, Mother and Gun (1958); Beast's Passage, A Dead Drifter, The Silent Murder (1959); This Life I Love, Devil's Banknotes, Drifting Boys, The Devotion on the Railway (1960); Like Fire Is My Life, Detective Morgan and a Man of Mystery (1961); The Procurer, Fancy Man, The Dupe (1965); Tattooed Temptress, Devil in My Flesh (1968); The Skyscraper Story (1969).

Shinichi Sekizawa Screenwriter. *b.* June 2, 1920, in Kyoto. *d.* 1993. Toho genre screenwriter, specializing in live-action science fiction fantasies. In contrast to fellow scriptwriter **Takeshi Kimura**, Sekizawa's scripts were generally lighter, though often more political, even leftist in content.

FILMS INCLUDE **[as screenwriter or co-screenwriter]**: Fearful Invasion of the Flying Saucers [also dir.] (1955); Varan the Unbelievable (1958); Battle in Outer Space, The Big Boss (1959); The Secret of the Telegian, Westward Desperado (1960); Mothra (1961); King Kong vs. Godzilla, Operation Enemy Fort (1962); Atragon, The Lost World of Sinbad (1963); Dagora the Space Monster, Godzilla vs. the Thing, Ghidrah—The Three-Headed Monster (1964); Gulliver's Travels Beyond the Moon, Monster Zero [Jap/US] (1965); The Mad Atlantic, Ebirah Horror of the Deep (1966); Ultraman, Jack and the Witch/Jack and the Beanstalk, Son of Godzilla (1967); Latitude Zero [Jap/US], Godzilla's Revenge (1969); Godzilla on Monster Island (1972); Godzilla vs. Megalon [story only] (1973); Godzilla vs. the Cosmic Monster [story only] (1974).

Koreya Senda Actor. *b.* September 15, 1904, in Kanagawa. Gray-haired supporting player, memorable in the leading role of the professor in Ichikawa's *The Blue Revolution* (1953), and as Prince Fumimaro Konoye in *Tora! Tora! Tora!* (1970).

FILMS INCLUDE: The Love of Sumako the Actress (1947); The Lover (1951); The Blue Revolution, Gate of Hell, Eagle of the Pacific (1953); The Phantom Horse (1955); Dancer and the Warrior (1956); The H-Man, Image Wife [also scr.], Varan the Unbelievable (1958); Battle in Outer Space (1959); The Blue Beast (1960); The Radiant Prince, Buddha (1961); Her Hidden Past (1962); Pressure of Guilt (1963); Tora! Tora! Tora! (1970).

Noriko Sengoku Actress. *b.* April 29, 1922 or 1924 [sources vary], in Tokyo. Actress associated with the works of **Akira Kurosawa** from the late 1940s through the mid-1950s. She was the bar girl in love with Toshiro Mifune in *Drunken Angel* (1948), the woman arrested for pistol-selling in *Stray Dog* (1949), a nurse in *The Quiet Duel* (also 1949), and the wife of one of the sons in *I Live in Fear* (1955).

FILMS INCLUDE: Drunken Angel (1948); The Quiet Duel, Stray Dog (1949); Scandal (1950); The Life of Oharu (1952); Seven Samurai (1954); I Live in Fear (1955); The Big Wave [US/Jap] (1962); Kwaidan (1964); Monster Zero [Jap/US] (1965); The Blind Beast (1969); Okage (1992).

Minoru Shibuya Director. *b.* 1907, in Tokyo. *d.* 1980. Journeyman Shochiku director from 1937, originally an assistant to Gosho, best known as the director of *Twilight Path* (1964), a project begun by Ozu and Kogo Noda, but filmed by Shibuya owing to Ozu's untimely death.

FILMS INCLUDE: Madame Shall Not Know, Mother's Marriage Proposal (1937); A Humming Girl, Mother and Child, Mother Stay at Home (1938); South Wind, The New Family, The Fox (1939); A Woman's Resolution (1940); Tokyo Customs, Ten

Day's Life, Cherry Country (1941); A Family, A Certain Woman (1942); The Angry Ghost, Uncle (1943); Passion Fire (1947); Devotion Now Vanished, Face of a Flower (1949); First Love Questions and Answers, Crazy Uproar (1950); School of Freedom (1951); Doctor's Day Off, Postwar Japanese/The Moderns (1952); Topsy Turvy (1953); A Medal (1954); Christ in Bronze (1955); Footprints of a Woman (1956); A Case of Honor, The Unbalanced Wheel (1957); Days of Evil Women (1958); Affair in the Mist (1959); Bananas (1960); The Shrikes, A Thief and Culture Order (1961); Heaven for a Drunkard (1962); The Rat Among the Cats (1963); A Marilyn of Tokyo, Twilight Path (1964); Ode to an Old Teacher (1966).

Yoko Shimada Actress. *b.* 1953, in Kumamoto. Star, opposite Richard Chamberlain, of the epic American miniseries *Shogun* (1980), even though Shimada, cast as a translator, spoke no English and had to learn her lines phonetically. In films from 1972, one year after her Japanese television debut.

FILMS INCLUDE: The Castle of Sand (1974); I Am a Cat (1975); The Inugami Family (1976); Shogun [US teleseries released as a feature elsewhere] (1980); My Champion (1981); The Man Who Assassinated Ryoma (1987); Labyrinth Romanesque (1988).

Takashi Shimura Actor. *b.* Shoji Shimazaki March 12, 1905, in Hyogo. ed. English at Kansai U. *d.* February 11, 1982, of emphysema. Important character actor, possibly Japan's finest, who gave brilliant performances as the dying government worker in *Ikiru* (1952) and as the leader of the *Seven Samurai* (1954). Shimura formed an amateur theater group at the age of 24, before turning professional the following year. He joined Shinko Kinema in 1934, and made his film debut in 1935. He worked for a variety of studios throughout his career—Nikkatsu, Shochiku, Daiei—but was most associated with Toho, for whom he worked almost constantly beginning in 1941. He was in war pictures, melodramas, period films. However, he is best known in the West for his collaborations with **Akira Kurosawa**; he appeared in 22 films for the director, from *Sanshiro Sugata* (1943) through *Kagemusha* (1980, role cut for US version). Shimura also appeared in countless fantasy films—he was a priest in Kobayashi's *Kwaidan* (1964), the paleontologist Dr. Yamane in *Godzilla, King of the Monsters!* (1954) and its sequel, and in similar roles in more than a dozen other films, including *The Mysterians* (1957), *Gorath* (1962), and *Frankenstein Conquers the World* (1965).

FILMS INCLUDE: Osaka Elegy (1936); The Last Days of Edo (1941); Sanshiro Sugata (1943); The Most Beautiful (1944); Those Who Tread on the Tiger's Tail (1945); Those Who Make Tomorrow, No Regrets for Our Youth (1946); Snow Trail (1947); Drunken Angel (1948); The Quiet Duel, Stray Dog (1949); Scandal, Rashomon, Sanshiro at Ginza (1950); The Blue Pearl, The Idiot, Stolen Love, The Life of a Horse-Trader (1951); Ikiru, The Life of Oharu, Sword for Hire (1952); Eagle of the Pacific (1953); Geisha Konatsu, Mother's First Love, Seven Samurai, Godzilla King of the Monsters! (1954); Last Embrace, No Response from Car 33, The Tears of Geisha Konatsu, No Time for Tears, I Live in Fear, The Grass Whistle, Gigantis the Fire Monster, There Was a Man (1955); I Saw a Killer, Samurai III (1956); The Lord Takes a Bride, Throne of Blood, The Mysterians (1957); Chushingura, The Dead End, The Hidden Fortress (1958); Inao—The Story of an Iron Arm, The High-Flying Bride, Samurai Saga, Saga of the Vagabonds, A Whistle in My Heart, Stop the Old Fox, The Three Treasures (1959); Perils of Bangaku, Afraid to Die, Princess Sen in Edo, I Bombed Pearl Harbor, The Bad Sleep Well, Man Against Man (1960); Yojimbo, Daredevil in the Castle, Challenge to Live, Mothra (1961); Sanjuro, Chushingura, Different Sons, Gorath, The Whale God (1962); Attack Squadron!, The Lost World of Sinbad, High and Low (1963); Kwaidan, Ghidrah—The Three-Headed Monster (1964); Samurai Assassin, The Soundless Cry, The Retreat from Kiska, Red Beard, Frankenstein Conquers the World [Jap/US], Night in Bangkok (1965); The Harbor of No Return (1966); The Emperor and the General, When the Cookie Crumbles (1967); Industrial Spy, Kaidan botandoro, Admiral Yamamoto, Zatoichi—The Blind Swordsman and the Fugitives, The Day the Sun Rose (1968); Am I Trying, Under the Banner of Samurai (1969); Tora-san's Love Call (1971); Zatoichi's Conspiracy (1973); Prophecies of Nostradamus (1974); Love and Faith/Lady Ogin, Talk of the Town Tora-san (1978); Kagemusha [role cut for US version] (1980).

Eitaro Shindo Actor. *b.* Tatsugoro Shindo on November 10, 1899, in Fukuoka. *ed.* high school. *d.* February 18, 1977. Prolific character actor who specialized playing villains, especially for **Kenji Mizoguchi,** for whom he essayed the title role in *Sansho the Bailiff* (1954). According to one source, Shindo appeared almost exclusively in *jidai-geki* after Mizoguchi's death.

FILMS INCLUDE: Osaka Elegy, Sisters of the Gion (1936); The War at Sea from Hawaii to Malaysia (1942); Drunken Angel, Jakoman and Tetsu (1948); Tale of Genji, Miss Oyu, The Lady from Masashino, Repast (1951); The Life of Oharu (1952); A Geisha (1953); Sansho the Bailiff, A Woman of Rumor, A Story of Chikamatsu, The Story of Shunkin (1954); Tojuro's Love, Princess Yang Kwei-fei [Jap/HK] (1955); New Tales of the Taira Clan, Three Sisters of Gion, Dancer and the Warrior, Street of Shame (1956); Chushingura (1958); The Body (1962); Kenji Mizoguchi: The Life of a Film Director (1975).

Kaneto Shindo Director, screenwriter. *b.* April 28, 1912, in Hiroshima. He joined Shinko-Kinema Tokyo Studio in 1928, in the art department. Eleven years later he moved to Koa Films as a screenwriter, and when that company was absorbed by Shochiku, he worked under Kosaburo Yoshimura and Kenji Mizoguchi, from whom he adopted a similarly progressive depiction of women. (In 1975, Shindo made the documentary *Kenji Mizoguchi—Life of a Film Director.*) With producer Hisao Itoya, director Tengo Yamada, and actor Taiji Tonoyama, Shindo formed an independent production company, Kindai Eiga Kyokai, and directed his first film there the following year. Born in Hiroshima, Shindo's films and characters often address issues of the atomic bomb. His third wife is actress **Nobuko Otowa**, who has appeared in the majority of his films, memorably in *Onibaba* (1964), *Kuroneko* (1968), among many others. Award: Grand Prize, Moscow Film Festival, for *The Island* (1960)

FILMS INCLUDE: **[as screenwriter]**: A Ball at the Anjo House (1947); Flame of My Love, Here's to the Girls (1949); Pursuit at Dawn (1950); Clothes of Deception, A Tale of Genji (1951); Violence (1952); A Woman Walking Alone on the Earth, Thousand Cranes, Desires, Before Dawn (1953); The Beauty and the Dragon (1955); On This Earth, Forbidden Lips (1957); The Precipice, The Adulteress, The Lowest Man, The Naked Sun, The Ladder of Success (1958); The Devotee, This Life I Love, The Wayside Pebble, The Gambling Samurai, Women of Kyoto (1960); Challenge to Live, A Design for Dying, Her Devotion (1961); Their Legacy, Stolen Pleasure, Destiny's Son, The Whale God (1962); Elegant Beast, When Women Lie [co-scr.] (1963); A Public Benefactor/Tycoon, Passion, The Gorgeous Geisha (1964); The Wife of Seisaku (1965); Fighting Elegy, The Spider Girl, Dynamite Doctor (1966); Two Wives, A Fallen Woman, The Wife of Seishi Hanaoka (1967); The House of the Sleeping Virgins (1968); Thousand Cranes, Devil's Temple (1969); Odd Affinity (1970); The Battle of Okinawa (1971); Under the Military Flag (1972); The Perinnial Weed (1975); The Incident (1978); The Three Undelivered Letters (1979); Deathquake (1980); Domino (1983); Hachi-ko, Actress (1987). **[as director/screenwriter]**: The Story of a Beloved Wife (1951); Avalanche, Children of Hiroshima (1952); Epitome/A Geisha Girl Ginko, A Woman's Life (1953); Gutter (1954); Wolves (1955); Harbor Rats (1957); Only Women Have Trouble (1958); The Lucky Dragon No. 5, The Bride from Japan (1959); The Island (1960); The Man (1962); Mother (1963); Onibaba (1963); The Conquest (1965); Lost Sex (1966); Libido (1967); Kuroneko, Operation Negligee (1968); Odd Affinity, Heat Wave Island/Heat Haze (1969); Tentacles, Naked Nineteen-Year-Old, Live Today Die Tomorrow! (1970); Sanka, Iron Ring, A Paean (1972); Heart, Kokoro/Love Betrayed (1973); My Way/Going My Way

(1974); Kenji Mizoguchi—Life of a Film Director (1975); The Life of Chikuzan—Tsugaru Shamisen Player (1977); The Strangling (1979); Edo Porn (1981); Hokusai Ukiyoe Master (1982); The Horizon (1984); Tree Without Leaves (1986); Sakuratai 8.6 (1988); The Strange Tale of Oyuki (1992).

Masahiro Shinoda Director. *b.* March 9, 1931, in Gifu. *ed.* Waseda University. With Yoshida and Oshima, Shinoda ushered in the Japanese New Wave. Sensual, visually adept, but often indulgent, his best works include *Assassination* (1964), *Double Suicide* (1969), *Demon Pond* (1980), and *MacArthur's Children* (1984). Initially an assistant director at Shochiku under Noboru Nakamura (at the Ofuna Studios), he began directing youth films in 1960. He left the studio five years later to formed his own production company, Hyogen-sha ("Expression Company"), and released his first indie production in 1967. Married to actress **Shima Iwashita**, who has appeared in many of his films.

Films Include: One Way Ticket for Love, Youth in Fury (1960); Killers on Parade, Epitaph to My Love, Love Old and New (1961); Our Marriage, Glory on the Summit, Tears on the Lion's Mane (1962); Pale Flower, The Assassin (1964); With Beauty and Sorrow, Samurai Spy (1965); Punishment Island (1966); Clouds at Sunset (1967); Double Suicide (1969); The Scandalous Adventures of Buraikan (1970); Silence (1971); Sapporo Winter Olympic Games (1972); The Petrified Forest (1973); Himiko (1974); Under the Blossoming Cherry Trees/The Blossoming Cherries (1975); Nihon-maru, Sado's Ondeko-za (1976); The Ballad of Orin (1977); Melody in Gray (1978); Demon Pond (1979); Devil's Island (1980); MacArthur's Children (1984); Gonza the Spearman (1986); The Dancer (1989); Takeshi (1990).

Yumi Shirakawa Actress. *b.* October 21, 1936, in Tokyo. Leading lady at Toho from 1956 through the early 1960s. Her feature film output slowed following her marriage in 1964, though in recent years she is frequently on Japanese television.

Films Include: Rodan (1956); The Mysterians (1957); The Princess of Badger Palace, The H-Man (1958); The Big Boss (1959); Inao—The Story of an Iron Arm, Six Suspects, Man Against Man, The Secret of the Telegian (1960); Early Autumn, Challenge to Live, Romance Express, The Man in Red, The Last War (1961); Gorath, Different Sons, Chushingura (1962); Wall-Eyed Nippon (1964); Adventures of Takla Makan (1966); Devils-in-Law (1967).

Kin Sugai Actress. *b.* February 28, 1926, in Tokyo. Character actress who specialized playing highly emotional working-class mothers. She was the leader of the group of women petitioning for a children's playground in *Ikiru* (1952), and the widow in Itami's *The Funeral* (1984).

Films Include: Ikiru (1952); Godzilla King of the Monsters! (1954); The Bad Sleep Well (1960); Eternity of Love, The Youth and His Amulet (1961); Could I But Live, Kwaidan (1964); Red Beard (1965); An Innocent Witch (1966); Dodes'ka-den, I the Executioner (1970); The Funeral (1984); Himatsuri (1985).

Kazuo Suzuki Actor. *b.* January 18, 1937, in Tokyo. Supporting player at Toho, almost always in henchmen roles possibly due to the actor's striking resemblance to Peter Lorre.

Films Include: Godzilla vs. the Thing, Ghidrah—The Three-Headed Monster, The Weed of Crime (1964); We Will Remember, Monster Zero [Jap/US] (1965); Come Marry Me, Ebirah Horror of the Deep (1966); King Kong Escapes [Jap/US], Las Vegas Free-for-All, Son of Godzilla (1967); Destroy All Monsters (1968); Battle of the Japan Sea, Portrait of Hell (1969); The Terror of Godzilla (1975).

Seijun Suzuki Director. *b.* Seitaro Suzuki on May 24, 1923, in Nihonbayashi, Tokyo. Following military service and a mixed college career, Suzuki joined Shochiku's Ofuna Studio in October 1948. He worked as an assistant to Noboru Nakamura and Minoru Shibuya, among others, before moving to Nikkatsu (which was then re-entering production) in 1954. He worked under So Yamamura and others, and wrote screenplays before his directorial debut two years later. His early films were B-pictures designed to fill out a double-bill, but his artistry attracted the attention of film students and movie buffs, and his *Gate of Flesh* (1964) won much praise. However, Suzuki's films became more controversial by the mid-1960s, and he was fired by Nikkatsu in that studio's attempt to find a scapegoat for the company's financial woes. Suzuki sued, and while he eventually won the case, he was blacklisted by the majors for some ten years, though he returned to prominence with *Zigeunerwisen* in the 1980s.

FILMS INCLUDE: Harber Toast—Victory Is in Our Grasp, Pure Emotions of the Sea, Satan's Town (1956); Inn of Floating Weeds, Eight Hours of Terror, The Nude and the Gun (1957); Beauty of the Underworld, Spring Never Came, Young Breasts, Voice Without a Shadow (1958); Love Letter, Passport to Darkness, Age of Nudity (1959); Take Aim at the Police Van, Sleep of the Beast, Clandestine Zero Line, Everything Goes Wrong, Fighting Delinquents (1960); Tokyo Knights, The Big Boss Who Needs No Gun, The Man with the Scatter-gun, The Wind-of-Youth Group Crosses the Mountain Pass, Blood-Red Water in the Channel, Million Dollar Smash-and-Grab (1961); High-Teen Yakuza, The Guys Who Bet on Me (1962); Detective Bureau 2-3—Go to Hell Bastards!, Youth of the Beast, The Bastard, Kanto Waderer (1963); The Flower and Angry Waves, Gate of Flesh, Our Blood Won't Allow It (1964); Story of a Prostitute, Stories of Bastards—Born Under a Bad Star, One Generation of Tattoos (1965); Carmen from Kawachi, Tokyo Drifter, Fighting Elegy (1966); Branded to Kill (1967); A Tale of Sorrow and Sadness (1977); Zigeunerweisen (1980); Heat-Haze Theatre (1981); Capone's Flood of Tears, Lupin III—The Golden Legend of Babylon [animated; co-dir.] (1985); Yumeji (1991).

Yoshifumi Tajima Actor. *b.* August 4, 1918, in Kobe. Also billed as Yoshibumi Tajima, this prolific character player essayed a wide range of roles, from detectives to soldiers to henchmen. He was a favorite of **Ishiro Honda**, and his finest screen role was in Honda's *Godzilla vs. the Thing* (1964), in which Tajima played the comically tragic Kumayama.

FILMS INCLUDE: Night School, Rodan (1956); The H-Man, Varan the Unbelievable (1958); Saga of the Vagabonds, The Three Treasures (1959); When a Woman Ascends the Stairs, I Bombed Pearl Harbor, The Secret of the Telegian, The Bad Sleep Well, The Human Vapor (1960); Mothra (1961); King Kong vs. Godzilla [role cut for US version] (1962); Atragon, High and Low (1963); Godzilla vs. the Thing, Dagora the Space Monster, Ghidrah—The Three-Headed Monster (1964); Frankenstein Conquers the World [Jap/US], Monster Zero [Jap/US] (1965); War of the Gargantuas [Jap/US] (1966); King Kong Escapes [Jap/US] (1967); Destroy All Monsters, Admiral Yamamoto (1968); Godzilla's Revenge, Battle of the Japan Sea (1969); Godzilla 1985 [cameo] (1984).

Ken Takakura Actor. *b.* 1931, in Fukuoka. *ed.* Meiji University. Japan's biggest star of the 1970s and 1980s, though precious little of his film work has been seen in this country. He starred opposite Michael Douglas in Ridley Scott's *Black Rain* (1989). In films from 1956, he starred in several long-running film series: the 11-film "Nippon kyoukakuden" film series (1964-71), as well as "Abashiri bangaichi" and "Showa-zankyoden."

FILMS INCLUDE: Denko Karate-uchi [debut] (1955), Drifting Avenger (1968); Memoir of Japanese Assassins (1969); Too Late the Hero [US] (1970); The Yakuza [US] (1975); The Yellow Handkerchief, Mt. Hakkoda (1977); A Flower in Winter (1978); A Distant Cry from Spring (1980); Station (1981); Love, Antarctica (1983); Yasha (1985); See You (1988); Buddies, Black Rain [US] (1989)

Hideko Takamine Actress. *b.* Hideko Hirayama on March 27, 1924, in Hakodate. *ed.* high school. One of the most popular and important stars of the Japanese cinema from the late 1930s (following a successful career as a child actor) through the mid-1960s. With her high cheekbones, beautiful eyes, and bird-like grace, Takamine resembled Claudette Colbert, and appeared in vaguely similar roles, that of a strong, determined woman who perseveres through a combination of resourcefulness and gentle sincerity. She was at Toho until the "Flag of Ten" strike, when she moved to Shin-Toho as that studio's leading actress, before going independent in 1951. She is strongly associated with director **Mikio Naruse**, for whom she did a dozen films, following her discovery by Kajiro Yamamoto and prior to a series of collaborations with her director-husband (from 1955), **Zenzo Matsuyama**. For Naruse she starred in *Floating Clouds* (1955), for which she received the Kinema Jumpo and Japan Mainichi Eiga Concourse awards for Best Actress. She was also memorable in Yamamoto's *Horse* (1941) and Kinoshita's *Twenty-Four Eyes* (1954), and many others. Although she has essentially retired from films—her last was in 1979—she continues to work as a painter, and is the author of nine books.

Films Include: Mother [debut] (1929); A Great Corner of Tokyo (1930); Tokyo's Chorus, The Neighbor's Wife and Mine (1931); A Cuckoo (1932); Song of the Flower Basket (1937); Composition Class (1938); Chushingura, Our Teacher/Our Instructor (1939); Horse, Hideko the Bus Conductor (1941); The Descendants of Taro Urashima, Lord for a Night (1946); The Devil of Edo, Invitation to Happiness, 1001 Nights with Toho (1947); A Flower Blooms, 365 Nights in Tokyo, 365 Nights in Osaka (1948); Goodbye, Spring Flirtation (1949); The Munekata Sisters (1950); Carmen Comes Home (1951); Carmen's Pure Love, Trouble in the Morning/Morning Conflicts, Lightning (1952); Castle Called Woman, Wild Geese, Four Chimneys/Where Chimneys Are Seen (1953); The Garden of Women, Twenty-Four Eyes (1954); Eternal Generation, The Second Kiss, Somewhere Beneath the Wide Sky, The First Kiss, New Tales of the Taira Clan, Because I Love, Floating Clouds, Distant Clouds (1955); Three Women Around Yoshinaka, A Wife's Heart, Flowing, Children's Eyes, Street of Wandering Pigeons (1956) Untamed, The Lighthouse/Times of Joy and Sorrow, A Candle in the Wind/Danger Stalks Near (1957); Chase, The Rickshaw Man (1958); The Journey of a President and His Secretary (1959); When a Woman Ascends the Stairs, Daughters Wives and a Mother, Woman Altogether, The River Fuefuki (1960); Happiness of Us Alone, The Human Condition III—A Soldier's Prayer, As a Wife/As a Woman/The Other Woman, The Bitter Spirit/Immortal Love (1961); A Woman's Place, Mother Country, Ballad of a Workman, The Wiser Age, The Seasons We Walked Together, Lonely Lane, My Hobo (1962); A Woman's Life (1963); Yearning (1964); Could I But Live, Dark the Mountain Snow (1965); Moment of Terror (1966); The Wife of Seishu Hanaoka, Our Silent Love (1967); Devil's Temple (1969); Love and Separation in Sri Lanka (1976); My Son! My Son! (1979).

Akira Takarada Actor. *b.* April 24, 1935. Shortly after joining Toho at the age of nineteen, Takarada landed the starring role (opposite Momoko Kochi) in *Godzilla, King of the Monsters!* (1954). He has been associated with the genre ever since, with leading roles in nearly a dozen fantasy features. During the 1960s, the popular, handsome actor also appeared in numerous romantic melodramas and musicals, and in the 1990s made a feature film comeback starring in Juzo Itami's *A-Ge-Man: Tales of a Golden Geisha* (1990), and especially as the hotel manager in Juzo Itami's *Minbo—Or the Gentle Art of Japanese Extortion* (1992).

Films Include: Godzilla King of the Monsters! (1954); Half Human (1955); Holiday in Tokyo, Romance and Rhythm, The College Hero, The Flower (1958); The Big Boss, Samurai Saga, A Whistle in My Heart, Three Dolls in the College, The Three Treasures (1959); Six Suspects, I Bombed Pearl Harbor, The Dangerous Kiss (1960); The Poem of the Blue Star, A Night in Hong Kong, Early Autumn, Lovers of Ginza, The Last War (1961); Star of Hong Kong, Long Way to Okinawa, The Wiser Age, Lonely Lane, Different Sons, Chushingura, Women of Design (1962); Honolulu-Tokyo-Hong Kong, A Woman's Life (1963); Godzilla vs. the Thing, Wall-Eyed Nippon, Chorus at Dawn (1964); Ironfinger, Monster Zero [Jap/US], White Rose of Hong Kong (1965); Big Wind from Tokyo, The Daphne, Ebirah Horror of the Deep (1966); King Kong Escapes [Jap/US], Let's Go Young Guy

(1967); Fancy Paradise, Booted Babe Busted Boss (1968); Latitude Zero [Jap/US] (1969); A-Ge-Man—Tales of a Golden Geisha (1990); Minbo—Or the Gentle Art of Japanese Extortion, Godzilla vs. Mothra (1992).

Tadao Takashima Actor. *b.* July 27, 1930, in Kobe. Popular comic actor who was a member of a jazz band prior to his film debut at Toho in 1951. Like Akira Takarada, Takashima is best known in the West for his fantasy film work rather than his comedies, though his work within the genre has generally been in lighter, even comic roles. He was the man put in charge of bringing King Kong to Japan in *King Kong vs. Godzilla* (1962), and starred opposite Nick Adams and Kumi Mizuno in *Frankenstein Conquers the World* (1965). His sons, **Masahiro Takashima** (*b.* 1965) and **Masanobu Takashima** (*b.* 1966), have been genre stars since the late 1980s, also at Toho.

FILMS INCLUDE: Fearful Invasion of the Flying Saucers (1955); This Greedy Old Skin (1960); Eternity of Love, Moonlight in the Rain, The Poem of the Blue Star (1961); King Kong vs. Godzilla, Chushingura, Love Me Love Me (1962); Atragon (1963); You Can Succeed Too (1964); Frankenstein Conquers the World [Jap/US] (1965); The Daphne (1966); Swindler meets Swindler, Sensation Seekers, Son of Godzilla (1967); Four Crazy Soldiers (1971); Godzilla vs. Mechagodzilla (1993).

Toru Takemitsu *b.* October 8, 1930, in Tokyo. Film composer who emerged from the ranks of the Japanese New Wave. Most associated with **Masaki Kobayashi** and **Masahiro Shinoda**.

FILMS INCLUDE: The Inheritance (1961); Harakiri (1962); Woman in the Dunes, Kwaidan (1964); Rebellion (1967); Hymn to a Tired Man, The Man Without a Map, Two Hearts in the Rain (1968); Dodes'kaden (1970); The Ceremony (1971); Himiko (1974); Under the Blossoming Cherry Trees, Kaseki (1975); Melody in Gray (1977); Empire of Passion (1978); An Ocean to Cross (1980); International Military Tribunal for the Far East—The Tokyo Trial (1983); House Without a Dining Table, Himatsuri, Ran (1985); Gonza the Spearman (1986); Onimaru (1988); Rikyu (1989).

Tetsuro Tamba Actor. *b.* July 17, 1922, in Tokyo. Burly star of gangster movies and melodramas, in films from 1952, and best known in the West as "Tiger" Tanaka, head of the Japanese Secret Service in the James Bond film *You Only Live Twice* (1967). However, Tamba (sometimes billed as Tetsuro *Tanba*), appeared in many other features released in the U.S. and elsewhere, including Masaki Kobayashi's *Harakiri* (1962) and *Kwaidan* (1964).

FILMS INCLUDE: The Depths (1957); Bridge to the Sun, Get 'Em All (1960); The Diplomat's Mansion, Daredevil in the Castle, The Flesh Is Hot/Pigs and Battleships, Bridge to the Sun [US/Fr] (1961); Harakiri (1962); Tange-Sazen (1963); The Assassin, Samurai from Nowhere, Three Outlaw Samurai, The 7th Dawn [Brit], Kwaidan (1964); The Birth of Judo, The Treasure of Death Castle [also dir.], (1965); The Secret of the Urn (1966); Portrait of Chieko, You Only Live Twice [US/Brit/SA] (1967); Diamond of the Andes, Black Lizard, Fear of the Snake Woman (1968); The Private Police, Orgies of Edo, Goyokin (1969); Crimson Bat Oichi—Wanted Dead or Alive, The Underground Syndicate, The Five Man Army, The Scandalous Adventures of Buraikan (1970); The Wolves, The Battle of Okinawa (1971); Submersion of Japan/Tidal Wave (1973); The Castle of Sand, Prophecies of Nostradamus (1974); The Alaska Story (1977); Bandit vs. Samurai Squad, Message from Space (1978); Hunter in the Dark, The Shogun Assassins (1979); Samurai Reincarnation, Imperial Navy (1981); Shogun's Ninja (1983); Heaven Station (1984); Poisson d'avril, Be Free! (1986); A Taxing Woman's Return, Tokyo Pop [US] (1988); Tetsuro Tamba's Great Spirit World [also prod., dir.], The Political Game, Shogun's Shadow (1989); Tetsuro Tamba's Great Spirit World 2 (1990).

Kinuyo Tanaka Actress, director. *b.* December 29, 1909, in Shinomoseki. *d.* March 21, 1977, of a brain tumor. Superlative, round-faced heroine of numerous **Kenji Mizoguchi** features, beginning with *Osaka Elegy* in 1936, and ending with *The Woman of Rumor* in 1954. She did appear in other directors' work—notably **Hiroshi Shimizu**, with whom she was briefly married; Mikio Naruse (*Mother*); Ozu (*Equinox Flower*); Kinoshita (especially as the old woman in The *Ballad of Narayama*); Kurosawa (*Red Beard*); and Heinosuke Gosho (*Four Chimneys*)—before directing several films of her own—the first Japanese woman to do so—beginning in 1953. Still, it was her long professional—and personal—association with Mizoguchi that earned the actress the best roles of her career. She was unforgettable as the mother in *Sansho the Bailiff* (1954) and as Oharu in *The Life of Oharu* (1952). Her career began as a biwa player in the Biwa Shojo Kageki Girls Revue. She made her film debut in 1924, and the following year joined Shochiku's Kamata Studio, where she soon became their biggest star. She won the *Kinema Jumpo* Prize as Best Actress for her work in *The Ballad of Narayama* (1958) and *Sandakan 8* (1974). The latter film also earned her the Berlin Festival Best Actress Award. She discussed her personal and professional relationship with Mizoguchi in Kaneto Shindo's *Kenji Mizoguchi: Life of a Film Director* (1975), and her life was dramatized by Shindo in *Actress* (1987). Not to be confused with the actor **Kunie Tanaka**.

Films Include: A Woman from the Genroku Era [debut] (1924); Killer of 100 Men in Ichinji Temple (1925); People in the Town/Town People, A Torrent, She/Girlfriend (1926); Shameful Dream/Intimate Dream, Tales from a Country by the Sea, Mother Do Not Shame Your Name, The Village Bride (1928); The Situation of the Human World/Man's Worldly Appearance, He and Life, I Graduated But. . . , A Happy Song (1929); A Smiling Life, Young Miss, The Great Metropolis—Chapter on Labor, Story of Kinuyo (1930); I Flunked But. . . , The Neighbor's Wife and Mine (1931); Chushingura/The Loyal Forty-Seven Ronin, You Are Stupid/My Stupid Brother, Willows of Ginza/A Willow Tree in the Ginza, Where Now Are the Dreams of Youth? (1932); Sleeping Words of the Bride/The Bride Talks in Her Sleep, A Tokyo Woman/Woman of Tokyo, Dancing Girls of Izu, Dragnet Girl (1933); An Innocent Maid, Burden of Life, Okoto and Sasuke (1935); Osaka Elegy, New Way, Song of the Flower Basket (1936); The Tree of Love (1937); Woman of Osaka (1940); Duel at Ichijoji Temple, Flower (1941); A Certain Woman (1942); Enemy Air Attack (1943); Three Generations of Danjuro, Army/The Army, A Tale of Archery at the Sanjusangendo, Musashi Miyamoto (1944) Women's Victory/The Victory of Women, Utamaro and His Five Women (1946); Marriage, Love of Sumako/The Love of Actress Sumako, Phoenix (1947); A Hen in the Wind, Women of the Night (1948); My Love Has Been Burning/ Flame of My Love, The Yotsuya Ghost Story, Waltz at Noon (1949); Engagement Ring, The Munakata Sisters (1950); Ginza Cosmetics, Miss Oyu, Lady Musashino/Woman of Musashino (1951); Sisters of Ninshijin, Mother, The Life of Oharu (1952); Love Letter [also dir.], Her Secret, Four Chimneys, Tales of Ugetsu, Lion's Dance (1953); Five Sisters, Sansho the Bailiff, The Woman of Rumor/The Woman in the Rumor (1954); The Moon Rises [also dir.], Umbrella in Moonlight, Floating Clouds, The Life of a Chessplayer (1955); Street of Wandering Pigeons, Extreme Sadness, Flowing, The Storm, Mixed Family (1956); On This Earth, Women in Prison, A Geisha in the Old City, Yellow Crow/Behold thy Son (1957); The Ballad of Narayama, Only Women Have Trouble/Sorrow Is Only for Women, Equinox Flower (1958); Mother and Her Children, These Wonderful Girls, The Three Treasures, Their Own World (1959); Her Brother, A Wandering Princess [also dir.], Love Under the Crucifix [dir. only] (1960); Eternity of Love (1961); Lonely Lane, Girl of Dark [dir. only], Mama I Need You (1962); A Legend or Was It?, My Enemy the Sea (1963); The Scent of Incense (1964); Red Beard (1965); Tora-san's Dream-Come-True (1972); Three Old Women, Sandakan 8 (1974); Let's Go Grand' Ma!, Kenji Mizoguchi: Life of a Film Director (1975); Lullaby of the Good Earth (1976).

Kunie Tanaka Actor. *b.* 1932, in Gifu. Character performer in films from 1957. His Robert Mitchum-esque features often led to his casting as underworld types, often hitmen, though he frequently appears in comedies as well. Memorable as the dopey samurai who opposes Toshiro Mifune in *Sanjuro* (1962), and as the tragic drunken yakuza in Gosha's *The Wolves* (1971). He also played second banana to Yuzo Kayama in Toho's "Young Guy" series.

FILMS INCLUDE: The Bad Sleep Well (1960); Sanjuro, Bull of the Campus (1962); Young Guy in Hawaii, Kwaidan (1964); Campus-A-Go-Go (1965); The Face of Another, Zatoichi – The Blind Swordsman's Pilgrimage, It Started in the Alps (1966); Let's Go Young Guy, Judo Champion, River of Forever, Sensation Seekers (1967); Young Guy in Rio (1968); Goyokin, Young Guy Graduates, Young Guy on Mt. Cook, Forward Ever Forward (1969); Bravo Young Guy!, Dodes'ka-den, Sex Phobia (1970); The Wolves, Young Guy the Ace Rider, Tora-san the Good Samaritan (1971); Evil of Dracula (1975); Station (1981); The House of Wedlock (1986); Tomorrow (1988); Tasmania Story (1990); Hikarigoke (1991); A Class to Remember (1993).

Tokuzo Tanaka Director. *b.* 1921 or 1925 [sources vary], in Osaka. *ed.* Kansai University. *Jidai-geki* director at Daiei's Kyoto Studio from 1958, 11 years after joining the company. He often worked with Daiei star **Shintaro Katsu**, directing numerous **"Zatoichi"** and "Tough Guy" movies. Not to be confused with Daiei director Shigeo Tanaka.

FILMS INCLUDE: The Jovial Rascals of Edo (1958); The Naughty Rogue, The Lord and the Gambler, The Princess Says No (1959); The Ogre of Mount Oe (1960); Fantastico, Silver Medal of Love, Tough Guy I, Tough Guy II (1961); The Whale God (1962); Zatoichi Enters Again, Zatoichi the Fugitive, Tough Guy III (1963); I Stand Alone, Engaged in Pleasure, Twilight Fog (1964); Two Notorious Men Strike Again, The Private and the C.O. (1965); The Hoodlum Soldier Deserts Again, Zatoichi – The Blind Swordsman's Vengeance (1966); Assignment Dragon No. 3, Night Flight, The Hoodlum Flag Bearer, The Last Gallantry (1967); The Ronin Called Nemuri, Yukionna, The Hoodlum Soldier and the $100,000 (1968); Secrets of a Women's Temple, Handcuffs, Girl with Bamboo Leaves (1969).

Tomoyuki Tanaka Producer. *b.* April 26, 1910. *ed.* University of Kansai. Toho executive whose films have been seen by more people in the West than any other Japanese producer. He brought Toho international attention with his Japanese take on *King Kong* and *The Beast from 20,000 Fathoms: Godzilla, King of the Monsters!* (1954). He went on to produce nearly all the studio's science fiction/fantasy film output, as well as most of its war movies, and other features directed by the studio's top house directors, including **Akira Kurosawa** and **Hiroshi Inagaki**. Though frail in recent years, he is still associated with his most famous star – **Godzilla** – and has produced all 22 films to date. His wife is the character actress Chieko Nakakita (*b.* 1925), best known for her co-starring role in Kurosawa's *One Wonderful Sunday* (1947).

FILMS INCLUDE: Pursuit at Dawn (1950); Sword for Hire (1952); Eagle of the Pacific (1953); Godzilla King of the Montsters! [also co-scr.] (1954); Gigantis the Fire Monster, I Live in Fear, Half Human (1955); Rodan, Madame White Snake (1956); The Lower Depths, Secret Scrolls [also co-scr.], Throne of Blood, The Mysterians (1957); The H-Man, The Hidden Fortress, Varan the Unbelievable, The Rickshaw Man, Secret Scrolls II [also co-scr.] (1958); Desperado Outpost, Saga of the Vagabonds, The Three Treasures, Battle in Outer Space (1959); The Secret of the Telegian, The Human Vapor, I Bombed Pearl Harbor, The Bad Sleep Well, Westward Desperado (1960); Yojimbo, The Last War, Mothra, Daredevil in the Castle (1961); Gorath, King Kong vs. Godzilla, Sanjuro, Chushingura (1962); Outpost of Hell, High and Low, Atragon, Attack of the Mushroom People, Attack Squadron!, The Lost World of Sinbad, Siege of Fort Bismarck (1963); Godzilla vs. the Thing, The Rabble, Tiger Flight, Whirlwind, Dagora the Space Monster, Ghidrah – The Three-Headed Monster (1964); Judo Saga, Frankenstein Conquers the World [Jap/US], Red Beard, Monster Zero [Jap/US] (1965); The Adventure of Takla Makan, What's Up Tiger Lily? [US production incorporating Japanese footage], War of the Gargantuas [Jap/US], Ebirah Horror of the Deep (1966); Rebellion, King Kong Escapes [Jap/US], The Age of Assassins, The Killing Bottle, The Emperor and a

General, Son of Godzilla (1967); Kill!, Destroy All Monsters, Admiral Yamamoto (1968); Portrait of Hell, Latitude Zero [Jap/US], Godzilla's Revenge, Battle of the Japan Sea (1969); The Vampire Doll, Yog—Monster from Space (1970); Godzilla vs. the Smog Monster (1971); Godzilla on Monster Island (1972); Godzilla vs. Megalon, Submersion of Japan/Tidal Wave (1973); Prophecies of Nostradamus, Godzilla vs. the Cosmic Monster, ESPY (1974); The Terror of Godzilla (1975); House, The Alaska Story, Mt. Hakkoda, The War in Space (1977); Deathquake, Kagemusha (1980); The Makioka Sisters (1983); Sayonara Jupiter, Godzilla 1985 (1984); Gunhed, Godzilla vs. Biollante (1989); Godzilla vs. King Ghidorah (1991); Godzilla vs. Mothra (1992); Godzilla vs. Mechagodzilla (1993); Godzilla vs. Space Godzilla (1994); Godzilla vs. Destroyer (1995).

Tetsuro Tanba *see* **Tetsuro Tamba**

Kei Tani Actor. *b.* 1932, in Tokyo. Or "Tani Kei" (a stage name based on Danny Kaye) as the Japanese would say. Popular, round-faced comedian and leading patsy of the Crazy Cats who starred in "Toho's Crazy Series" and most of the "People of Japan" entries. Tani was usually cast as an unlucky schlemiel or lovelorn underdog, just the opposite of Hitoshi Ueki's manic, scheming con man. In recent years Tani has appeared in the popular "Free and Easy" film series. Not to be confused with another Toho supporting player, Akira Tani (*b.* 1910).

Films Include: Young Season, The Crazy Bride and Her Seven Friends (1962); Crazy Free-for-All—Don't Proscrastinate, Crazy Free-for-All—Die You Good for Nothing, Hong Kong Free-for-All (1963); The Gay Braggart (1964); Don't Call Me a Con Man (1965); The Boss of Pick-Pocket Bay, It's Crazy—I Can't Explain It Way Out There, Great Crazy Free-for-All (1966); Industrial Spy Free-for-All, Las Vegas Free-for-All, Monsieur Zivaco (1967); Mexican Free-for-All, Five Gents and a Chinese Merchant, Fancy Paradise (1968); Computer Free-for-All, The Crazy Cat's Great Explosion, Who Am I? (1969); Taking a Crazy Punch at Shimizu Harbor (1970); Lonely Heart (1981); Memories of You (1988); Free and Easy (1988); Free and Easy 2 (1989); Free and Easy 3 (1990); Taro! Tokyo, Free and Easy 4 (1991); Free and Easy 5 (1992).

Senkichi Taniguchi Director. *b.* February 19, 1912, in Tokyo. Journeyman Toho director from 1947 through the late 1960s, with no particular style, but associated with lower-end A-pictures. His spy film *Kagi no Kagi* ("Key of Keys") relooped by Woody Allen into the comedy *What's Up, Tiger Lily?* (1966). Married to actress **Kaoru Yachigusa**.

Films Include: Snow Trail (1947); The Surf/The Sound of the Waves (1954); I Married a Prize Fighter [scr. only] (1957); The Gambling Samurai, Man Against Man (1960); Blood on the Sea (1961); Operation Enemy Fort (1962); Outpost of Hell, The Lost World of Sinbad (1963); What's Up Tiger Lily? [US production incorporating Japanese footage] (1966); The Killing Bottle (1967); The Bamboozlers (1968).

Tomotaka Tasaka Director. *b.* 1902, in Hiroshima. *d.* 1974. Nikkatsu director of family and war films from 1926, four years after joining their Kyoto Studio. In Hiroshima when the atomic bomb was dropped, Tasaka was hospitalized for several years, and unable to resume his career until 1949. Unfortunately, precious little of this interesting director's work has been seen in the United States.

Films Include: Rise and Fall of Love, Railway Train (1926); Soldier's Justice, Black Hawk, Soap Girl, Double Marriage I (1927); Reckless Period, Spinning Earth, Street of Love, Recollections of a Sailor, Village of the Shining Sun (1928); She and I, Banquet, Nikkatsu Parade—Labor Volume, Guardians of Love, Throne of Clouds (1929); Behold This Mother, Spring Wind (1930); Heart of Reality (1931); Spring and a Girl (1932); The Life of a Woman in the Meiji Era (1935); Memory of a Rose I-II (1936); Five Scouts, A Pebble by the Wayside, Air Raid [co-dir.] (1938); Airplane Drone, Mud and Soldiers I-II (1939); You and I (1941); Mother-and-Child Grass (1942); Navy (1943); Tatsu the Drunkard [co-dir.] (1949); I'll Never Forget the Song of Nagasaki (1952); The Maid's Kid (1955); Baby Carriage (1956); Pleasure of Life

Hiroshi Teshigahara

(1957); Street in the Sun (1958); The Stream of Youth (1959); Run Genta Run (1961); A Carpenter and Children I-II (1962); The Sharks (1964); Osan I-III (1965); Koto—The Lake of Tears (1966); A House of Shame [completed in 1963] (1967); Scrap Collectors Ltd. (1968).

Jun Tazaki Actor. *b.* Minoru Tanaka, August 28, 1910, in Aomori. *d.* 1985. Popular character actor, often cast as gruff men of authority, especially in Toho science-fiction fantasies and war movies of the 1960s, and later in similar roles on Japanese television. Best remembered for his riveting performance as the doomed spaceship commander in *Gorath* (1962), and especially as the fiercely nationalistic, Captain Nemo–like hero of *Atragon* (1963), both for director **Ishiro Honda**.

FILMS INCLUDE: Tokyo File 212 [US/Jap], Pursuit at Dawn (1950); Gate of Hell (1953); Seven Samurai (1954); The Man in the Storm, Dancing Mistress (1957); The Three Treasures (1959); Soft Touch of Night, The Blue Beast, Man Against Man, The Two Musashis, I Bombed Pearl Harbor (1960); Daredevil in the Castle, Blood on the Sun, The Last Challenge, Big Shots Die at Dawn, Procurers of Hell, Counterstroke (1961); Tatsu, Gorath, Operation Enemy Fort, Chushingura, King Kong vs. Godzilla (1962); Attack Squadron!, The Lost World of Sinbad, Atragon, Siege of Fort Bismarck, High and Low (1963); Godzilla vs. the Thing, Dagora the Space Monster, Kwaidan, The Weed of Crime (1964); Frankenstein Conquers the World [Jap/US], Monster Zero [Jap/US] (1965); War of the Gargantuas [Jap/US], The Boss of Pick-Pocket Bay, Ebirah Horror of the Deep (1966); The Killing Bottle, The Emperor and the General (1967); Fancy Paradise, Destroy All Monsters (1968); Battle of the Japan Sea (1969); Crimson Bat Oichi—Wanted Dead or Alive (1970); Imperial Navy (1982); Ran (1985).

Hiroshi Teshigahara Director. *b.* 1927, in Hiroshima. *ed.* Tokyo Art Institute. Brilliant, indulgent avant-garde director of *Woman in the Dunes* (1964). His father was a famous flower arranger, and Teshigahara himself had been a painter early in his career. He worked as an assistant on several shorts about A-bomb survivors before forming his own production company in 1961. Despite the international acclaim of his second film, the director has worked only sporadically since the mid-1960s.

FILMS INCLUDE: The Pitfall (1962); Woman in the Dunes (1964); La Fleur de l'Age [co-dir.] (1965); The Face of Another (1966); The Man Without a Map (1968); Rikyu (1989); Gouhime (1992).

Eijiro Tono Actor. *b.* September 17, 1907, in Gunma. In films from 1938, the popular coarse-faced character actor has appeared in a wide range of roles for a variety of studios. He was memorable as the pathetic ex-teacher in Ozu's *An Autumn Afternoon* (1962), and as the sake-seller in Kurosawa's *Yojimbo* (1961). Tono was also a regular in Toho's "Company President" film series, and originated the role of "Mito Komon" in the Japanese teleseries of the same name, from 1969-1979.

FILMS INCLUDE: The Love of Sumako the Actress (1947); A Hen in the Wind (1948); Stray Dog (1949); Heat and Mud (1950); River Solo Flows (1951); Tokyo Story, Wild Geese (1953); Samurai I, Seven Samurai (1954); Samurai II, I Live in Fear (1955); Samurai III, Undercurrent, Early Spring (1956); The Lower Depths, The Secret Scrolls I (1957); The Young Beast, Ohayo, The Three Treasures (1959); Twilight Story, The Gambling Samurai (1960); Yojimbo, Buddha, The Flesh Is Hot, Immortal Love, The Last War (1961); The Great Wall, This Madding Crowd, An Autumn Afternoon (1962); High and

Low (1963); Sword of the Beast, The Wild One, The Spy, Red Beard (1965); Lost Sex (1966); The Naked General, Zatoichi – The Blind Swordsman's Cane Sword, Monsieur Zivaco (1967); Kill, The Saga of Tanegashima (1968); Tora-san Pt. 2 (1969); Tora! Tora! Tora! [US/Jap], Will to Conquer (1970); The Battle of Okinawa (1971); Island of Horrors (1977); Hunter in the Dark (1979).

Shiro Toyoda Director. *b.* 1905, in Kyoto. *d.* 1977. An actors' director whose films are usually based on strong literary sources, Toyoda himself was an aspiring playwright when he joined the industry in 1925, at Shochiku. He moved to Tokyo Hassei Eiga in 1936, and moved again, for good, to Toho in 1942. His films, generally *jidai-geki*, often deal with the rights of the individual in a conformist society, and are often darkly humorous in nature.

FILMS INCLUDE: Painted Lips, Collapse of a Swimming Woman (1929); Friendship Marriage, The Heart of a Proud Woman (1930); Three Women (1935); Tokyo Osaka Scoop, Harbor of Fickle Winds (1936); Public Disgrace [co-dir.], Young People (1937); Crybaby Apprentice, Winter Inn, Nightingale (1938); Crossfire [co-dir.] (1939); Spring on Lepers' Island, Ohinata Village (1940); A Record of My Love (1941); Young Figure (1943); Cypress Boards (1946); Four Love Stories [co-dir.] (1947); My Love on the Other Side of the Mountain (1948); The Four Seasons of Woman (1950); Eriko and Tomoni I-II, Wagtail Tune (1951); Wind Once More, Whisper of Spring (1952); Wild Geese (1953); A Certain Woman (1954); Grass Whistle, Marital Relations (1955); Madame White Snake, Shozo a Cat and Two Women (1956); Snow Country, Evening Calm (1957); Hotelman's Holiday (1958); Bringing Up Husbands, Pilgrimage at Night (1959); The Curio Master, The Twilight Story (1960); The Diplomat's Mansion (1961); Till Tomorrow Comes, Under What Star (1962); Madame Aki, Kitchen Place, New Marital Relations (1963); Sweet Sweat (1964); Shadow of the Waves, Illusion of Blood, Tale of a Carpenter (1965); River of Forever, Tokyo Century Plaza (1967); Portrait of Hell (1969).

Eiji Tsuburaya Director of Special Effects. *b.* July 7, 1901, in Fukushima. *d.* January 25, 1970. Japan's undisputed master of special effects was educated as an engineer, but was so intrigued with motion picture photography that, at Nikkatsu in 1919, he became a cameraman instead. During this period he saw *King Kong* (1933), and for many years wanted to do something similar. He joined Toho studios and quickly gained fame for his intricate special effects photography in war movies, in which elaborate miniatures were combined with optical effects. In 1954, he refined this technique in the elaborate *Godzilla, King of the Monsters!*, in which a man in a rubber costume, elaborate puppets, and a very limited amount of stop-motion animation were added. The huge success of that film led to a boom in fantasy film production, concurrent with the durable war film genre. His sci-fi output ingeniously combined incredibly detailed recreations of urban landscapes with the singularly unrealness of his monsters and mechanical contrivances. In the West, in recent years, his work has come to be regarded as fakey, but in fact his artistry was widely regarded both in Japan and abroad as state-of-the-art until shortly before his death. In the mid-1960s, he formed his own production company, Tsuburaya Enterprises, which produced an endless stream of popular sci-fi teleseries, including "Ultra Q," and "Ultraman."

FILMS INCLUDE: A Page of Madness [co-dir. of phot. only] (1926); New Earth (1937); Navy Bombers, Burning Sky (1940); War at Sea from Hawaii to Malaya (1942); Colonel Kato's Falcon Squad (1944); The Transparent Man (1949); The Saga of Anatahan [also prod. design], Eagle of the Pacific (1953); Farewell Rabaul, The Invisible Man, Godzilla King of the Monsters! (1954); Gigantis the Fire Monster, Half Human – The Story of the Abominable Snowman (1955); Rodan, Madame White Snake (1956); The Mysterians (1957); The H-Man, Varan the Unbelievable (1958); Battle in Outer Space, The Three Treasures (1959); The Last War, The Secret of the Telegian, The Human Vapor, I Bombed Pearl Harbor (1960); Mothra, The Last War (1961); Gorath, King Kong vs. Godzilla, Chushingura (1962); Attack of the Mushroom

People, Attack Squadron!, The Lost World of Sinbad, Atragon (1963); Godzilla vs. the Thing, Dagora the Space Monster, Ghidrah – The Three-Headed Monster (1964); None But the Brave [US/Jap], Frankenstein Conquers the World [Jap/US], Don't Call Me a Con Man, Monster Zero [Jap/US] (1965); Zero Fighter, War of the Gargantuas [Jap/US], It's Crazy – I Can't Explain It Way Out There, Ebirah Horror of the Deep/Godzilla vs. the Sea Monster (1966); Ultraman [also ex. prod.], King Kong Escapes [Jap/US], Son of Godzilla [sup. only] (1967); Destroy All Monsters [sup. only], Admiral Yamamoto (1968); Battle of the Japan Sea, Latitude Zero [Jap/US], Godzilla's Revenge [sup. only] (1969).

Yoshio Tsuchiya Actor. *b.* May 18, 1927, in Yamanashi. Intense supporting player for **Akira Kurosawa** and especially in genre films directed by **Ishiro Honda**, usually cast as a ready-to-crack-up team member or eccentric villain. He starred in the title role of Honda's *The Human Vapor* (1960), six years after his debut as the equally tragic farmer whose wife was kidnapped in *Seven Samurai* (1954). He was groomed as a leading man in the mid-1950s, but preferred the more bizarre supporting parts; he played evil aliens in *The Mysterians* (1957) and *Monster Zero* (1965), even though his face was almost completely obscured, and claims to have actually seen a UFO. He more or less reprised his *Seven Samurai* role in *Yojimbo*, and played men possessed by aliens or driven mad by monsters in a dozen films; he was especially memorable in the unfortunately named *Attack of the Mushroom People* (1963). He continues to act, mostly on the stage, and made a memorable return to genre films as as the platoon leader-turned-corporate executive in *Godzilla vs. King Ghidorah* (1991).

FILMS INCLUDE: Seven Samurai [debut], The Invisible Man (1954); Gigantis the Fire Monster, I Live in Fear [bit] (1955); The Mysterians, Throne of Blood (1957); The H-Man, Varan the Unbelievable, The Hidden Fortress (1958); Battle in Outer Space (1959); The Secret of the Telegian, The Bad Sleep Well, I Bombed Pearl Harbor, The Human Vapor (1960); Yojimbo, Death on the Mountain (1961); Tatsu, Chushingura, Sanjuro (1962); High and Low, Attack of the Mushroom People (1963); Frankenstein Conquers the World [US/Jap], Red Beard, Monster Zero [US/Jap] (1965); Kojiro, The Emperor and the General, The Killing Bottle, Two in the Shadow, Son of Godzilla (1967); Admiral Yamamoto, Kill, Destroy All Monsters, Death by Hanging, Booted Babe Busted Boss (1968); Battle of the Japan Sea (1969); Yog – Monster from Space, The Ambush – Incident at Blood Pass, Funeral Parade of Roses (1970); Godzilla vs. King Ghidorah (1991).

Yoko Tsukasa Actress. *b.* Yoko Shoji, on August 20, 1934, in Sakai-minato. *ed.* Kyoritsu Women's Junior College. Tsukasa had worked as a secretary at the New Japan Broadcast Company and as a model before joining Toho in 1953, where she soon became their biggest female star. Tsukasa appeared in melodramas, comedies, period and modern films, and later frequently starred in various Japanese teleseries. Memorable as the daughter in two of Ozu's later works, *The End of Summer* (1961) and *Late Autumn* (1960); as the heroine of Nakamura's *The River Kii* (1966), for which she received awards from *Kinema Jumpo* and others; as a regular in Toho's "Boss Man" series; and for her collaborations with **Mikio Naruse**.

FILMS INCLUDE: Forever Be Mine (1954); No Response from Car 33, The Immortal Pitcher, The President's Boss, Mother and Son, The First Kiss, Marital Relations, Three Brides for Three Sons (1955); Brother and Sister, Three Young Men and a Dream Girl, The Summer the Sun Was Lost, Ambition (1956); Forsaken Pedals I, Forsaken Pedals II, The Night Holds a Secret, Schooldays, The Blue Mountains I, The Blue Mountains II (1957); City of Love, The Flower, Summer Clouds, Owl Lecture, Holiday in Tokyo (1958); The Path Under the Plane-Trees, Account of My Beloved Wife, Samurai Saga, The College Ruggers, Saga of the Vagabonds, Girl in the Mist, The Young Lovers, Three Dolls in College, The Three Treasures (1959); The Last Gunfight, The Forbidden Scoop, The Blue Beast, Flowing Night, Late Autumn, The Angry Sea, The Masterless Forty-Seven I (1960); The Masterless Forty-Seven

II, Eternity of Love, Challenge to Live, A Night in Hong Kong, Yojimbo, Early Autumn (1961); The Wiser Age, Chushingura, Lonely Lane, Women of Design (1962); Twilight Path, The Beast Called Man, Five Gents' Trick Book (1965); Five Gents at Sunrise, Moment of Terror, Five Gents on the Spot, The Daphne, The Kii River/The River Kii (1966); Devils-in-Law, Kojiro, Two in the Shadow, Five Gents Prefer Geisha, Rebellion (1967); Admiral Yamamoto (1968); Battle of the Japan Sea, Goyokin (1969); Band of Assassins (1970); Prophecies of Nostradamus (1974); Island of Horrors (1977); Queen Bee (1978).

Koji Tsuruta Actor. *b.* December 6, 1924, in Shizuoka. *d.* 1987. Effeminate yet tough-looking star at Toho in period and war films, and later at Toei in Yakuza thrillers. Like many Toho/Toei stars, Tsurata was a popular singer before turning to films in 1946. Memorable as Kojiro Sasaki in Hiroshi Inagaki's *Samarai* series.

FILMS INCLUDE: The Flavor of Green Tea Over Rice (1952); Samurai II, The Romance of Yushima (1955); Samurai III (1956); Secret Scrolls I (1957); The Happy Pigrimage, The Spell of the Hidden Gold, Rat Kid on Journey, Secret Scrolls II (1958); The Big Boss, Saga of the Vagabonds, The Three Treasures (1959); I Bombed Pearl Harbor, The Secret of the Telegian (1960); Attack Squadron!/Kamikaze (1963); Killer's Mission, Memoir of Japanese Assassins (1969); Gamblers in Okinawa (1970); Imperial Navy (1981).

Tomu Uchida Director. *b.* April 26, 1898, in Okayama. *d.* 1970. Originally an actor, Uchida joined Nikkatsu as an assistant director under Minoru Murata and Kenji Mizoguchi. His early films were primarily comedies, but shortly before the war he turned to realistic *shomin-geki*. He lived in Manchuria during and after the war, only to return to Japan in 1954 where he joined Toei. There he made the memorable, five-part "Musashi Miyamoto" series (1961-65).

FILMS INCLUDE: Pain, Rising in the World, Idler, Cannon Smoke and Rain of Shells (1927); Spinning Earth II, A Ray, Wind of This World (1928); A Living Doll, Nikkatsu Parade—Sports Volume, The Sea-Loving Son Sails Away, Sweat (1929); Successive Victories, Return to Heaven (1930); Jean Valjean I-II, Miss Nippon, Stories of Human Interest, The Revenge Champion (1931); Mother Earth Rises (1932); Asia Calling (1933); Hot Wind (1934); Throne of the White Man (1935); Theatre of Life (1936); The Naked Town, Unending Advance (1937); A Thousand and One Nights in Tokyo (1938); The Earth (1939); History (1940); A Bloody Spear on Mount Fuji, Twilight Beer Hall, Each Within His Shell (1955); Disorder by the Kuroda Clan (1956); The Great Badhisattva Pass I, The Eleventh Hour (1957); The Thief Is Shogun's Kin, The Great Badhisattva Pass II, Outsiders (1958); The Great Badhisattva Pass III, Their Own World (1959); Wine Woman and a Lance, Murder in Yoshiwara (1960); Musashi Miyamoto—Untamed Fury (1961); Love Not Again, Musashi Miyamoto II—Duel Without End (1962); Musashi Miyamoto III—The Worthless Duel (1963); Musashi Miyamoto IV—The Duel at Ichijoji Temple, Hunger Straits/A Fugitive from the Past (1964); Musashi Miyamoto V—The Last Duel (1965); Kaku and Tsune (1968); Swords of Death (1971).

Ken Uehara Actor. *b.* November 7, 1909, in Tokyo. *d.* 1991. Distinguished actor in films for some 55 years, from his debut in 1935 until one year before his death. Memorable in the title role of *The Story of Tank Commander Nishizumi* (1940). Later, he appeared in several films for **Kon Ichikawa**, and later still several Toho fantasies. Father of actor **Yuzo Kayama**.

FILMS INCLUDE: The Story of Tank Commander Nishizumi (1940); A Flower Blooms, 365 Nights (1948); Human Patterns, New Version of the Ghost of Yotsuya I-II (1949); Portrait of Madame Yuki, The Munekata Sisters (1950); Repast, Wedding March, Nightshade Flower, The Man Without a Nationality (1951); When Chimneys Are Seen, A Japanese Tragedy (1953); Late Chrysanthemums, All of Myself, Twelve Chapters on Women (1954); Undercurrent, Dancer and the Warrior (1956); Holiday in Tokyo (1958); I Bombed Pearl Harbor (1960); Mothra, A Night in Hong Kong, Nocturne of a Woman (1961); Gorath, Bull of the

Campus, Pride of the Campus, Honolulu-Tokyo-Hong Kong (1962); Atragon (1963).

Misa Uehara Actress. *b.* 1938 (?). Toho star whose career appears to have lasted but a few years, from about 1958 to 1960. She was given a huge build-up in Akira Kurosawa's *The Hidden Fortress* (1958), where she played the role that served as the basis for Princess Leia in *Star Wars* (1977), and for which she dominated the Japanese print ads, even over star Toshiro Mifune. Apparently no relation to Ken Uehara.

FILMS INCLUDE: The Hidden Fortress (1958); Saga of the Vagabonds, The Three Treasures (1959); I Bombed Pearl Harbor (1960).

Hitoshi Ueki Actor. *b.* February 25, 1927, in Mie. Popular singing star of Toho's "Crazy Cats" film series and other musical comedies from 1958. In recent years Ueki has found success in character roles.

FILMS INCLUDE: The Age of Irresponsibility in Japan, Young Generation, The Crazy Bride and Her Seven Friends (1962); Crazy Free-for-All—Don't Procrastinate, Crazy Free-for-All—Die You Good for Nothing, Hong Kong Free-for-All (1963); Don't Call Me a Con Man (1965); Industrial Spy Free-for-All, Las Vegas free-for-All, Monsieur Zivaco (1967); Mexican Free-for-All (1968); Computer Free-for-All, The Crazy Cats' Great Explosion (1969); Taking a Crazy Punch at Shimizu Harbor (1970); Tattoo (1982); The Crazy Family (1984); Ran, Congratulatory Speech (1985); Big Joys Small Sorrows (1986); The Story of a Company (1988).

Kirio Urayama Director. *b.* 1930, in Hyogo. *ed.* Nagoya University. *d.* 1985. Seven years after joining Nikkatsu as an assistant director, Urayama directed his first feature. His next film, *Each Day I Cry*, won much acclaim, including the Golden Prize at the 3rd International Film Festival (1963), but he appears to have worked only sporadically thereafter.

FILMS INCLUDE: Cupola Where the Furnaces Glow (1962); Each Day I Cry (1963); The Girl I Abandoned (1969).

Ken Utsui Actor. *b.* October 24, 1931, in Tokyo. Beefy actor in films since 1953, best-known in the West as "Starman," a Superman-type superhero (originally named "Supergiant") in Shintoho's nine-film series (1957-59), which were re-edited into four campy features which have been a staple of U.S. Saturday afternoon television since the mid-1960s.

FILMS INCLUDE: Atomic Rulers, Invaders from Space (1957); Attack from Space, Evil Brain from Outer Space (1958); The Great Wall (1962); When Women Lie (1963); The Black Trump Card (1969); The Wild One (1965); The Falcon Fighters, Gateway to Glory (1969); The Little Hero (1970).

Natto Wada Screenwriter. *b.* 1920, in Hyogo. *d.* 1983. Wife of director **Kon Ichikawa**, Wada collaborated with the director on most of his postwar films, from about the time of their marriage in 1948.

FILMS INCLUDE **[as screenwriter or co-screenwriter]**: Human Patterns, Passion Without End (1949); The Lover, Stolen Love, River Solo Flows, Wedding March (1951); This Way That Way, The Woman Who Touched the Legs, Young People (1952); The Youth of Heiji Zenigata, Mr. Pu, The Lover [different from 1951 film] (1953); A Billionaire, Twelve Chapters About Women (1954); Ghost Story of Youth (1955); Bridge of Japan, Punishment Room, The Burmese Harp (1956); The

Ken Utsui

Crowded Streetcar (1957); Conflagration (1958); Odd Obsession/The Key, Fires on the Plain (1959); Ten Dark Women, Bonchi, The Woman Who Touched the Legs [remake] (1960); Being Two Isn't Easy, The Outcast (1962); An Actor's Revenge, My Enemy the Sea (1963); Tokyo Olympiad (1965); The Burmese Harp (1985); Tsuru (1988).

Akiko Wakabayashi Actress. *b.* December 13, 1939, in Tokyo. Exotic sex symbol of the 1960s, best remembered as the Japanese spy who assists James Bond in the first half of *You Only Live Twice* (1967), and as the Princess/Martian in *Ghidrah – The Three Headed Monster* (1964).

FILMS INCLUDE: Song for a Bride (1958); Bandits on the Wind (1961); King Kong vs. Godzilla (1962); The Lost World of Sinbad (1963); Wall-Eyed Nippon, Dagora the Space Monster, The Weed of Crime, Ghidrah – The Three-Headed Monster (1964); The Thin Line, It Started in the Alps, What's Up Tiger Lily? [US production incorporating Japanese footage], Sensation Seekers (1966); You Only Live Twice [Brit/US/S. Afr.] (1967).

Ayako Wakao Actress. *b.* November 6, 1933, in Tokyo. Daiei star typically cast ordinary but resilient young women. Best remembered in this country as the business-minded prostitute in Kenji Mizoguchi's *Street of Shame* (1956), and as Lady Namiji in Ichikawa's *An Actor's Revenge* (1962). After Daiei's bankruptcy, Wakao appeared in a "Tora-san" film, then essentially retired from films until she appeared opposite Toshiro Mifune in Ichikawa's fantasy *Princess of the Moon* (1987).

FILMS INCLUDE: I'll Never Forget the Song of Nagasaki, Escape from the Dead Street (1952); Teenager's Sex Manual, Gion Music, Her Secret, Dangerous Age, Tomorrow Will Be a Sunday (1953); The Messenger from the Moon, Temptation of Teenagers, A Certain Woman, The Girl Who Distributed Happiness, A Girl Isn't Allowed to Love (1954); The Phantom Horse, Farewell to Innocence (1955); Punishment Room, Bridge of Japan, Street of Shame (1956); Tears, The Betrothed, Love of the Princess, I Married a Prize Fighter, Evening Calm, A Cheerful Girl (1957); Eye Pupils of Tokyo, Amusement of Seven Married Couples, Truth About Youth, Whistles of Migratory Birds, My Son's Revolt, The Judo Champ, Chushingura, A Grain of Wheat, The Naked Face of Night/The Ladder of Success (1958); Goodbye Good Day, The Most Valuable Madam, Time of Roses and Blossoming Flowers, The Cast-Off, Various Flowers, Floating Weeds, So Beautiful It's a Sin, The Gaijin/The Foreigner, Ripe and Marriageable, Enchanted Princess (1959); A Woman's Testament, The Rockabilly Lady, Afraid to Die, Bonchi, Victory or Defeat, The Priest and the Beauty, The False Student, So Like the Flowers (1960); The Three Ginza Boys, The Radiant Prince, Les Mesdemoiselles, Wife's Confession, A Design for Dying, All for Love, A Geisha's Diary, Marriageable Age (1961); Their Legacy, The Temple of the Wild Geese, The Third Wall, Stolen Pleasure, A Night to Remember/Hiroshima Heartache, Diary of a Mad Old Man, The Great Wall, Elegant Beast (1962); An Actor's Revenge, The Bamboo Doll, She Came for Love (1963); Passion, Love and Greed, The Night of the Honeymoon, The Forest of No Escape, A Public Benefactor/Tycoon (1964); I'll Cry Alone, Strange Triangle, The Wife of Seisaku, While Yet a Wife, Shadow of Waves (1965); Spider Tattoo, The Freezing Point, The Virgin Witness, The Red Angel (1966); When the Cookie Crumbles, Two Wives, The Wife of Seishu Hanaoka, The Dark Trap, The Shroud of Snow (1967); The Saga of Tanegashima (1968); Thousand Cranes (1969); Zatoichi Meets Yojimbo (1970); Tora-san's Shattered Romance (1971); Kenji Mizoguchi: The Life of a Film Director (1975); Princess of the Moon (1987).

Tomisaburo Wakayama Actor. *b.* September 1, 1929, in Tokyo. *d.* 1992. Late brother of actor **Shintaro Katsu**, Wakayama made his film debut in 1955, one year after that of his younger sibling. Best known in this country as the star of the six-film "Lone Wolf/Baby Cart" film series (1972–74), two of which were dubbed and widely released in the United States:

Tomisaburo Wakayama (left) and Akihiro Tomikawa in *Shogun Assassin* (1972).

Shogun Assassin (1972; US release: 1980) and *Lightning Swords of Death* (1972; US release: 1983).

FILMS INCLUDE: Life and Opinion of Zatoichi, Ghost of Oiwa (1961); Zatoichi and a Chest of Gold (1964); Memoir of Japanese Assassins, The Fort of Death, Killer Mission, The Priest Killer (1969); Ballad of Death, The Priest Killer Comes Back, The Underground Syndicate (1970); Gamblers in Okinawa, A Boss with the Samurai Spirit (1971); Sword of Vengeance/ Lightning Swords of Death, Shogun Assassin [US version contains 10–20 minutes from Sword of Vengeance] (1972); ESPY (1974); Under the Blossoming Cherry Trees (1975); The Devil's Bouncing Ball (1977); Hinotori, The Bad News Bears

Go to Japan [US/Jap] (1978); My Son! My Son! (1979); Samurai Reincarnation, Flames of Blood (1981); Tetsuro Tamba's Great Spirit World, Black Rain [US] (1989); Oh-te (1991).

Kaoru Yachigusa Actress. *b.* January 6, 1931, in Osaka. Virginal star of Toho *jidai-geki* films of the 1950s and early 1960s; she starred opposite Toshiro Mifune in Inagaki's *Samurai* trilogy. Married to director **Senkichi Taniguchi**.

FILMS INCLUDE: Samurai I (1954); Samurai II, Madame Butterfly (1955); Samurai III, Madame White Snake (1956); Snow Country (1957); Rat Kid on Journey, Temptation in Glamour Island, Holiday in Tokyo (1958); Ishimatsu Travels with Ghosts (1959); The Human Vapor (1960); The Song from My Heart (1969); Tora-san's Dream-Come-True (1972); Hachi-ko (1987).

Isuzu Yamada Actress. *b.* Mitsu Yamada on February 5, 1917, in Osaka. Though best known today for her memorable work in three of **Akira Kurosawa**'s films, Yamada first impressed audiences 20 years earlier in several films for **Kenji Mizoguchi**, notably *Osaka Elegy* and *Sisters of Gion* (both 1936). The daughter of actor Kusuo Yamada, she made her film debut in 1930. Later in her career she appeared in several films for Kurosawa: she was the Lady Macbeth character in *Throne of Blood* (1957), and the grotesque, domineering wife in *Yojimbo* (1961). Soon thereafter, she largely retired from films to concentrate on her leftist stage work. She has been married five times: to actors Ichiro Tsukida, Shotaro Hanayagi, and Yoshi Kato; producer Kazuo Takimura; and director **Teinosuke Kinugasa**, with whom she made several films. Her daughter, Michiko Saga, is also an actress.

FILMS INCLUDE: Tsurugi o koete [debut], Great Cushingura (1930); The Revenge Champion (1931); Peerless Patriot, The Life of Bangoku (1932); The Pass of Love and Hate, Paper Cranes of Osen, People's Building (1934); Oyuki the Madonna (1935); Osaka Elegy, Sisters of the Gion (1936); The Summer Battle of Osaka, Yoshida Palace (1937); Tsuruhachi and Tsurujiro, Silent Mutual Election (1938); Chushingura II (1939); The Snake Princess/Miss Snake Princess (1940); Shanghai Moon, The Battle of Kawanakajima, The Man Who Disappeared Yesterday (1941); Song of a Lantern/The Song Lantern (1943); The Way of Drama (1944); Bijomaru Sword (1945); Cypress Boards, Lord for a Night (1946); 1001 Nights With Toho, Actress (1947); Koga Mansion, Fencing Master (1950); The Mysterious Palanquin, Storm Clouds Over Hakone (1951); Postwar Japan/The Moderns, Because of Mother Because of Woman (1952); Woman Walking Alone on the Earth, Epitome/A Geisha Girl Ginko, Hiroshima (1953); A Billionaire, The Loyal Forty-Seven Ronin (1954); Christ in Bronze, Because I Love, Stone Battle, Growing Up/Comparison of Heights/Daughters of Yoshiwara (1955); Bundle of Love, Shozo a Cat and Two Women, Flowing, Clouds at Twilight, The Statue of Mother and Child, How Sorrowful (1956); Throne of Blood, Tokyo Twilight, A Matter of Valor, Black River, The Girl in the Shade, The Lower Depths, Downtown (1957); A Boy and Three Mothers, The Four Seasons of Love, Days of Evil Women (1958); Third Class Chief, Son Hear My Cry, A Gambler as I Am (1959); Wandering, Princess Sen in Edo, Flowing Night, Goodbye to Glory, Country in My Arms (1960); Daredevil in the Castle, The Shrikes, Buddha, Yojimbo (1961); The Body, The Great Wall (1962); The Shogun and Her Mistress (1967); Kenji Mizoguchi – The Life of a Film Director (1975); Shogun's Samurai (1978); Sure Death (1984); Sure Death 2 – Stop the Conspiracy (1985).

Yoji Yamada Director, screenwriter. *b.* September 13, 1931, in Osaka. *ed.* Tokyo University. Shochiku director-screenwriter, and creator of the long-running **"Tora-san"** film series, for which he has written all 47 features to date, and has directed all but two. He joined the studio in 1954, and made his directorial debut with *A Young Tenant* in 1961. Though he directs other films concurrent with the Tora-san features, it is that gentle, funny series for which he is best known.

FILMS INCLUDE: A Young Tenant/The Strangers Upstairs (1961); Downtown Sunshine/The Sunshine Girl (1963); The Honest Fool, Honest Fool Sequel, The

Director Yoji Yamada (right) and his longtime cinematographer, Tetsuo Takaba, on the set of *Hope and Pain* (1988).

Donkey Comes on a Tank (1964); The Trap (1965); Gambler's Luck, The Lovable Tramp (1966); Let's Have a Dream, Song of Love, The Greatest Challenge of All (1967); The Million Dollar Pursuit, The Shy Deceiver (1968); Vagabond Schemer, Am I Trying/ Tora-san Our Lovable Tramp, Tora-san Pt. 2 (1969); Tora-san His Tender Love [scr. and story only], Tora-san's Grand Scheme [scr. and story only], Tora-san's Runaway, Where Spring Comes Late (1970); Tora-san's Shattered Romance, Tora-san the Good Samaritan, Tora-san's Love Call (1971); Tora-san's Dear Old Home, Home from the Sea, Tora-san's Dream-Come-True (1972); Tora-san's Forget-Me-Not, Tora-san Loves an Artist (1973); Tora-san's Lovesick, The Castle of Sand [co-scr. only], Tora-san's Lullaby (1974); Tora-san's Rise and Fall, The Village, Tora-san the Intellectual (1975); Tora-san's Sunrise and Sunset, Tora's Pure Love, Two Iida [co-scr. only] (1976); Tora-san Meets His Lordship, The Yellow Handkerchief, Tora-san Plays Cupid (1977); Stage-Struck Tora-san, Talk of the Town Tora-san (1978); Tora-san the Matchmaker, Branch School Diary [co-scr. only], Tora-san's Dream of Spring (1979); A Distant Cry from Spring, Tora's Tropical Fever, Foster Daddy Tora! (1980); Tora-san's Love in Osaka, Tora-san's Promise (1981); Hearts and Flowers for Tora-san, Tora-san the Expert (1982); Tora-san's Song of Love, Tora-san Goes Religious? (1983); Marriage Counselor Tora-san, Tora-san's Forbidden Love (1984); Tora-san the Go-Between, Tora-san's Island Encounter (1985); Final Take, Tora-san's Bluebird Fantasy (1986); Tora-san Goes North, Tora-san Plays Daddy (1987); Tora-san's Salad-Day Memorial, Hope and Pain, Free and Easy [co-scr. only] (1988); Tora-san Goes to Vienna, Tora-san My Uncle (1989); Tora-san Takes a Vacation (1990); Tora-san Confesses, My Sons (1991); Tora-san Makes Excuses (1992); A Class to Remember, Tora-san's Matchmaker (1993).

Kajiro Yamamoto Director. *b.* May 12, 1902, in Tokyo. *d.* 1974. Best remembered in the West as the mentor to **Akira Kurosawa** and **Ishiro Honda**, Yamamoto nevertheless had a long and fruitful career as a director working in many genres. He did many films with Japan's great prewar comedian, Kenichi Enomoto (better known as "Enoken," and whom Kurosawa cast as the porter in *Those Who Tread on the Tiger's Tail*), as well as the influential *Horse* (1941).

FILMS INCLUDE: Bomb Hour (1925); New Strategy, Ordeal, Smiling Nikkatsu (1932); Gate to the Blue Sky, Conquest of a Wife, Love Crisis (1933); Public Activity, Alpine Victory (1934); Violet Girl, Tricks of an Errand Boy (1935); I Am a Cat, Enoken's Millionaire I-II (1936); A Husband's Chastity I-II, Beautiful Hawk, Enoken's Pickpocket (1937); The Loves of a Kabuki Actor, Composition Class, Enoken Is Surprised at Life (1938); Easy Alley, The Loyal Forty-Seven Ronin (1939); Enoken Has His Hair Cropped (1940); Horse (1941); The Hope of Youth, The War at Sea from Hawaii to Malaya (1942); Colonel Kato's Falcoln Squadron, Torpedo Squadrons Move Out (1944); Misfortunes of Love (1945); Those Who Make Tomorrow [co-dir.] (1946); Four Love Stories [co-dir.] (1947); Wind of Honor, Spring Flirtation (1949); Escape from Prison (1950); Elegy, Hopu-san, Who Knows a Woman's Heart (1951); Rainbow-Colored Street (1952); Girls Among the Flowers (1953); Mr. Valiant, Mr. Valiant Rides Again, An Angel of Saturday (1954); A Man Among Men, The History of Love (1955); The Underworld, A Young Lady on Her Way (1956); An Elephant (1957); Rise and Fall of a Jazz Girl, A Holiday in Tokyo (1958); Adventures of Sun Wu Kung (1959); Ginza Tomboy, Woman Altogether (1960); Love Me Love Me [prod. only], Samurai Joker, Thief on the Run (1965); Swindler Meets Swindler (1967).

Satsuo Yamamoto Director. *b.* July 15, 1910, in Kagoshima. *d.* 1983. Leftist filmmaker originally allied with Mikio Naruse at Shochiku, who followed the director to Toho until that studio fired him for his leftist views. He made *Vacuum Zone* (1952), a scathing anti-military feature, no doubt inspired, in part, by his wartime service on the front lines in China. In later years, he turned to violent genre films.

FILMS INCLUDE: Young Miss (1937); La Symphonie Pastorale, Family Diary I-II (1938); Beautiful Start, Street (1939); End of Engagement (1940); Triumphal Wings (1942); Hot Wind (1943); War and Peace [co-dir.] (1947); Street of Violence (1950); Storm Clouds Over Hakone (1951); Vacuum Zone (1952); To the End of the Sun, The Street Without Sun (1954); Because I Love [co-dir.], Duckweed Story (1955); Avalanche, Typhoon No. 13 (1956); His Scarlet Cloak (1958); The Song of the Cart, The Human Wall (1959); The Battle Without Arms, Matsukawa Derailment Incident (1960); A Band of Assassins I (1962); Red Water, A Band of Assassins II (1963); A Public Benefactor/Tycoon (1964); The Witness Seat, The Burglar Story, The Spy (1965); Freezing Point, The Great White Tower (1966); The Bogus Policeman, Zatoichi—The Blind Swordsman's Rescue (1967); The Bride from Hades (1968); Vietnam (1969); Men and War I (1970); Men and War II (1971); Men and War III (1973); The Family (1974); Nomugi Pass (1979).

So Yamamura Actor, director. *b.* Yoshida Koga on February 24, 1910, in Tenri. *ed.* Imperial University. Understated

So Yamamura in *Tora! Tora! Tora!* (1970).

performer in films from 1946, often in distinguished roles, particularly late in life, where he his often cast as statesmen. Best remembered as the neglectful doctor-son in Ozu's *Tokyo Story* (1953), as the dying businessman in Kobayashi's *The Inheritance* (1962), and as Admiral Isoroku Yamamoto in *Tora! Tora! Tora!* (1970).

FILMS INCLUDE: **[as actor]**: For Life (1946); Actress, The Love of Actress Sumako (1947); Return to the Capitol, Portrait of Madame Yuki, The Munekata Sisters (1950); Dancing Princess, The Good Fairy, Woman of Musashino, Miki the Swordsman, School of Freedom (1951); Repast, Postwar Japan/The Moderns, The Woman Who Touched the Legs (1952); Muddy Waters, Tokyo Story (1953); Sounds from the Mountains, Immortal Japan, Gutter (1954); He Who Lived Judo, Autumn Interlude, Princess Yang Kwei-Fei [Jap/HK], Ghost Story of the Youth (1955); The Summer the Sun Was Lost, Early Spring, Darkness at Noon, 48-Year-Old Rebel/Protest at 48 Years Old (1956); Tokyo Twilight, Night Butterflies, The Pit/The Hole, The Chieko Story, Story of First Love, Roar and Earth (1957); His Hell Revolver, Chushingura, The Barbarian and the Geisha [US] (1958); The Human Condition I, The Cast of Night, Fatal Arms, Across Darkness (1959); Life of a Country Doctor, The Doctors Condemned (1960); Last-Ditch Glory, The Last War, The Estuary, Record of Love, That Is the Port Light, A Geisha's Diary (1961); My Daughter and I, Star of Hong Kong, Glory on the Summit/Burning Youth, Tears on the Lion's Mane, Born in Sin, The Inheritance, If It Were a Dream, Their Legacy, The Pacific War and the Himeyuri Corps (1962); Return of Ninja, Diary of a Mad Old Man (1963); A Public Benefactor/Tycoon (1964); School for Sex, With Beauty and Sorrow, The Retreat from Kiska (1965); The Emperor and the General (1967); Tora! Tora! Tora! [US/Jap], The Militarists (1970); Prophecies of Nostradamus (1974); Deathquake (1980); Godzilla vs. King Ghidorah (1991). **[as director]**: The Crab-Canning Ship (1953); Black Tide [also act.] (1954); Maidens of Kashima Sea, Mother and Her Children [also act.] (1959); The Song of Fukagawa (1960).

Tsutomu Yamazaki Actor. *b.* 1936, in Chiba. Chameleon actor who first won raves as the kidnapper in Kurosawa's *High and Low* (1963), and later in several **Juzo Itami** films, especially *Tampopo* (1985), where he played the burly truck driver/noodle expert. In films from 1960.

FILMS INCLUDE: The University Scamps [debut], The Angry Sea (1960); The Diplomat's Mansion (1961); Till Tomorrow Comes, Women of Design (1962); The Legacy of the 500,000, A Woman's Life, High and Low (1963); Brand of Evil (1964); White Rose of Hong Kong, Red Beard, School of Love (1965); Tora-San Pt. 2 (1969); Village of Eight Gravestones (1977); Kagemusha, Demon Pond, Deathquake (1980); Farewell to the Ark (1982); The Funeral (1984); Tampopo (1985); A Taxing Woman (1987); Rikyu, Sweet Home (1989); We Are Not Alone (1993).

Kimyoshi Yasuda Director. *b.* February 15, 1911, in Tokyo. *d.* 1983. Chambara director at Daiei who dabbled in many other genres as well, including mysteries, horror and Yakuza films.

FILMS INCLUDE: The Jovial Rascals of Edo (1958); When I Became a Champion Sumo Wrestler (1960); The Lord and the Amazon (1961); Kumoemon and His Wife (1962); Zatoichi (1963); The Mysterious Sword of Kyoshiro Nemuri (1965); The Exploits of Kyoshiro Nemuri, Majin (1966); Zatoichi's Cane Sword, The Tokyo Gambler (1967); 100 Monsters, Zatoichi – The Blind Swordsman and the Fugitives, The Human Tarantula (1968); Along with Ghosts (1969); The Masseur's Curse (1970); Zatoichi Meets His Equal [Jap/HK] (1971); Zatoichi's Conspiracy (1973).

Yoshishige Yoshida Director. *b.* 1933, in Fukui. New Wave director, and part of the movement that also included Oshima and Shinoda, though Yoshida's impact was considerably less felt. He joined Shochiku in 1955 as an assistant to Kinoshita. Still active in films.

FILMS INCLUDE: Good-for-Nothing, Dry Earth (1960); Bitter End of a Sweet Night (1961); An Affair at Akitsu (1962); Eighteen Roughs (1963); Nippon Escape (1964); Forbidden Love (1965); Woman of the Lake (1966); The Affair, Impasse

Tsutomu Yamazaki in *A Taxing Woman* (1987).

(1967); Affair in the Snow, Farewell to Summer Light (1968); A Promise (1986); Onimaru (1988).

Kozaburo Yoshimura Director. *b*. September 9, 1911, in Shiga. Also billed as "Kimisaburo Yoshimura," he began his career as an assistant to Yasujiro Shimizu at Shochiku. He was drafted into the military, but upon his return made his feature debut, *Sneaking*, in 1934. He continued to work as an AD through the end of the decade, where he learned his craft from luminaries such as Gosho and Naruse. He returned to the service during most of the war, then began collaborating with **Kaneto Shindo**, which included the formation of a production company, Kindai Eiga Kyokai. His films include the humanist war film *The Story of Tank Commander Nishizumi* (1940) and *A Tale of Genji* (1951).

FILMS INCLUDE: Sneaking (1934); Lively Alley, Tomorrow's Dancers, Five Brothers and Sisters, Warm Current (1939); The Story of Tank Commander Nishizumi (1940); Blossom (1941); The Spy Isn't Dead Yet, South Wind (1942); On the Eve of War (1943); Decisive Battle [co-dir.] (1944); The Fellows Who Ate the Elephant, A Ball at the Anjo House (1947); Temptation, The Day Our Lives Shine (1948); Jealously, Ishimatsu of the Forest, Waltz at Noon (1949); Spring Snow, End of War Disasters, About Twenty-Years-Old (1950); Clothes of Deception/Under Silk Garments, School of Freedom, A Tale of Genji (1951); The Sisters of Nishijin, Violence (1952); Thousand Cranes, Desires, Before Dawn (1953); Cape Ashizuri, People of Young Character (1954); Because I Love [co-dir.], Women of Ginza, The Beauty and the Dragon (1955); Date for Marriage, Undercurrent (1956); Osaka Story, Night Butterflies, On This Earth (1957); A Grain of Wheat, The Naked Face of Night/The Ladder of Success (1958); A Telephone Ring in the Evening (1959); A Woman's Testament [co-dir.], Women of Kyoto (1960); Marriageble Age, A Design for Dying (1961); Their Legacy, A Night to Remember/Hiroshima Heartache (1962); When Women Lie [co-dir.], The Bamboo Doll (1963); The Heart of the Mountains (1966); A Fallen Woman (1967); The House of the Sleeping Virgins, A Hot Night (1968); Sweet Secret (1971); Rika the Mixed-Blood Girl, Lullaby of Hamagure (1973); The Tattered Banner/Ragged Flag (1974).

Noriaki Yuasa Director and special effects director. *b.* 1933, in Tokyo. Daiei filmmaker associated with the studio's big effects pictures, especially the **"Gamera"** series, of which he has helmed most of the entries.

FILMS INCLUDE **[as director and special effects director]**: Gammera the Invincible (1965); War of the Monsters [spfx dir. only] (1966); The Return of the Giant Monsters (1967); War of the Planets, The Snake Girl and the Silver-Haired Witch (1968); Attack of the Monsters, Girl of Your Type (1969); Gamera vs. Monster X, The Little Hero, The Dream Girl (1970); Awakening, Gamera vs. Zigra, Snow Country Elegy (1971); Gamera Super Monster (1980).

Osman Yusef Actor. *b.* 1921 (?). *d.* 1985 (?). Turkish-born actor cast in Western roles during the 1960s and 1970s. Best remembered as Jerry Ito's henchman in *Mothra*, and the American who buys the house on the hill in Shohei Imamura's *The Flesh Is Hot/Pigs and Battleships* (both 1961). Also known as Johnny Yuseph and Osman Yuseph.

FILMS INCLUDE: Battle in Outer Space, The Last Death of the Devil (1959); Mothra, Daredevil in the Castle, The Last War, The Flesh Is Hot/Pigs and Battleships (1961); Gorath (1962); Son of Godzilla, Monsieur Zivaco, (1967); The Street Fighter (1973); Prophecies of Nostradamus (1974).

Studios

Daiei Motion Picture Co., Ltd. Literally "big picture," Daiei was one of Japan's six majors (the others being **Nikkatsu**, **Shintoho**, **Shochiku**, **Toei** and **Toho**), a fully integrated motion picture company that produced, distributed exhibited its product. During World War II the major studios were merged into two large companies. Producer **Masaichi Nagata** convinced the government to create a third studio, Dai-Nippon Eiga ("Great Japan Film") in 1942. Nagata's move was highly controversial; he was accused of bribery and arrested. However, the studio, now called Daiei, lived on and soon secured the talent of directors the calliber of **Kon Ichikawa, Kenji Mizoguchi** and **Teinosuke Kinugasa**, as well as superb craftsman the likes of **Kenji Misumi** and others. Daiei specialized in *jidai-geki*, or historical films, particularly in Chambara thrillers often starring **Shintaro Katsu** or his brother, **Tomisaburo Wakayama**. Katsu starred in several of the studio's most popular film series, including the long-running **"Zatoichi"** saga. Another popular series at Daiei was their answer to Toho's Godzilla, **"Gamera,"** a giant flying turtle. That series, like "Zatoichi," outlived Daiei itself, which went bankrupt in the early 1970s. The company was reorganized minus its distribution/exhibition arms, and its much smaller output is usually released by other distributors, usually Shochiku or Toho.

Nikkatsu Corp The oldest of the integrated studios, precious little of Nikkatsu's output has been seen in this country; unlike Toho, Daiei and Shochiku, Nikkatsu never established a strong distribution system in the United States. The studio began as the Japan Cinematograph Company in 1912, and dominated the exhibition market, operating nearly 70 percent of Japan's film theaters, and, for a time, was rivaled only by Shochiku in terms of production. The transition to sound (and Nikkatsu's difficulties therein), combined with the wartime reoganization (in which much of Nikkatsu's production facilities were absorbed by Daiei) led the studio to abandon production altogether during the 1940s, though it resumed with a renewed vigor by the mid-1950s. The industry fall-out during the early 1970s led Nikkatsu to distribute soft-core pornographic features ("Roman Porn"), but the company survived and continues operating to this day.

Shintoho Co., Ltd. Ambitious but ultimately unsuccessful attempt by dissatisfied actors and artists at Toho to form a thriving, artistically challenging production company. Formed in 1947 following a series of bitter, violent strikes at Toho, Shintoho ("New Toho") began with 10 top stars and directors. By the early 1950s the company was in serious financial trouble. Soon, it began producing films for the masses, especially period thrillers (often laced with then-daring nudity), war movies and kiddie serials. The company went bankrupt in 1961.

Shochiku Co., Ltd. An entertainment conglomerate nearly 100 years old, Shochiku's empire includes not only the fully integrated film company but also extensive legitimate theater holdings, video stores, and other entertainment industries. It is the studio of **Yasujiro Ozu, Nagisa Oshima, Yoji Yamada** and **"Tora-san,"** and, until the 1950s, **Kenji Mizoguchi**. It is the largest and most consistantly successful of the majors, and rivaled only by Toho. The company began producing films in 1920, 24 years after its founding as a Kabuki show producer by twin brothers Matsujiro Shirai and Takejiro Otani. (The company takes its name from "Matsu" and "Take," which can also be read "Sho" and "Chiku," and meaning, literally, "bamboo and pine," the corporate logo.) Unlike the other majors, which kept studios in Tokyo and Kyoto, Shochiku operated its production company out of Kamata until 1936, when it moved its operations to Ofuna. Shochiku has long imported Western-made films, first under a subsidiary, Fuji Pictures Corp., which merged with the production arm to become Shochiku-Fuji in 1983.

Toei Co., Ltd. Studio best-known in this country for its highly-charged action films and teleseries, including the action sequences in TV's "Mighty Morphin' Power Rangers." Formed in 1953, Toei quickly established itself as a reliable producer of "B" movies designed to fill out double- and triple-bills. By the end of the decade it began producing animated features as well and, until the 1980s, dominated the field much like Disney in the United States. Action directors and stars began to emerge by the late 1960s, notably directors **Tomu Uchida** and **Kinji Fukasaku** and actor **Shinichi "Sonny" Chiba**, whose "Street Fighter" karate movies were big box office in the U.S. during the mid-1970s.

Toho Co., Ltd. The studio of **Akira Kurosawa, Toshiro Mifune** and **"Godzilla,"** Toho was formed when P.C.L., Photo Chemical Laboratories, entered production in 1933. The company thrived during the war, but bitter labor strikes followed, and, in 1947, several top stars and other talent left to form **Shintoho Co., Ltd.** in what is known as the "Flag of Ten" incident. Still, Toho retained the talents of directors Kurosawa, **Mikio Naruse, Hiroshi Inagaki, Ishiro Honda** and others and was wildly successful during the 1950s and 1960s. They also succeeded in capturing an American audience more than any other studio by selling its most exploitable product (monster movies, Kurosawa films, war films, etc.) to American distributors while exhibiting its less commercial fare in American movie houses it owned and operated, such as the Toho LaBrea in Los Angeles. Like Shochiku, Toho is today an entertainment giant; its production arm is now just a small piece in its massive conglomerate pie.

Feature Films

A.K. / Kurosawa Akira ("Akira Kurosawa") [**documentary**]. Producer, Serge Silberman; Associate Producer, Masato Hara; Director/Screenplay/Editor, Chris Marker; Director of Photography, Frans-Yves Marescot; Music, Toru Takemitsu, performed by the Tokyo String Quartet; Assistant Photographers, Tsutomu Ishizuka and Hiroshi Ishida; General Production Manager, Ully Pickardt; Production Manager, Takashi Ohashi; Coordination, Hisao Kurosawa; Special Effects, Patrick Duroux; Sound Editor, Catherine Adda; Sound Recording, Junichi Shima; Sound Rerecording, Claude Villand; Special Thanks, Catherine Cadou; Japanese Eye, Yuko Fukusaki; Calligraphy, Teishu Murata.

WITH: Akira Kurosawa, Tatsuya Nakadai, and the cast and crew of *Ran*.

A Greenwich Film Production/Herald Nippon/Herald Ace Production. A French/Japanese co-production in French and Japanese, filmed in conjunction with the production of *Ran* (1985, q.v.). Color. 75 minutes. Released 1985.

U.S. VERSION: Released by Orion Classics. English subtitles, Cinetitres. Includes footage from *Horse* (1941), *Rashomon* (1950), *Seven Samurai* (1954), *Throne of Blood* (1957), and *Kagemusha* (1980). Dedicated to the memory of Fumio Yanoguchi, Kurosawa's longtime sound recordist, who died during the postproduction of *Ran* (1985). Released February 1986.

Abandoned / Hyoryu ("Aimless"). Producer, Shunji Oki; Director, Shiro Moritani; Screenplay, Sakae Hirosawa and Shiro Moritani, based on an original story by Akira Yoshimura; Director of Photography, Kozo Okazaki; Art Director, Nobuo Kurihara; Music, YAMANA (i.e., Genichi Kawakami).

CAST: Kinya Kitaoji, Tsunehiko Watase, Yoshiko Mita.

A Tokyo Eiga Co., Ltd. Production. Color. Panavision (?). 151 minutes. Released 1981.

U.S. VERSION: Distributor, if any, is undetermined.

About Love, Tokyo / Ai ni Tsuite, Tokyo ("About Love, Tokyo"). Producers, Masaru Koibuchi and Mitsuo Yanagimachi; Director/Screenplay, Mitsuo Yanagimachi; Director of Photography, Shohei Ando; Art Director, Takeo Kimura; Music, Hajime Mizoguchi.

CAST: Xiao Tong (Ho Jun), Asuka Okasaka, Hiroshi Fujioka, Qian Po, Gu Xiao Tong, Zeng Chun Hui.

An About-Love-Tokyo Production Committee Production. Color. Spherical wide screen (?). 110 minutes. Released 1992.

U.S. VERSION: Released by the Shibata Organization. English subtitles. 110 minutes. No MPAA rating. Released May 7, 1993.

Actress / Eiga joyu ("Film Actress"). Producers, Tomoyuki Tanaka and Kon Ichikawa; Director, Kon Ichikawa; Screenplay, Kaneto Shindo, Shinya Hidaka, and Kon Ichikawa, based on the life of Kinuyo Tanaka; Director of Photography, Yukio Isohata; Art Director, Shinobu Muraki; Editor, Chizuko Osada; Music, Kensaku Tanigawa; Sound Recording, Tetsuya Ohashi.

CAST: Sayuri Yoshinaga (Kinuyo Tanaka), Mitsuko Mori (mother), Bunta Sugawara (Kenji Mizoguchi), Koji Ishizaka (Shiro Kido), Kiichi Nakai (Heinosuke Gosho), Yasuko Sawaguchi (Seiko).

A Toho Co., Ltd. Production. Color. Spherical wide screen. 130 minutes. Released 1987.

U.S. VERSION: Released by Toho International Co., Ltd. English subtitles. 130 minutes. No MPAA rating. Released June 20, 1987.

Admiral Yamamoto / Rengo Kantai Shireicho-kan Yamamoto Isoroku ("Combined Fleet Admiral Isoroku Yamamoto"). Executive Producer, Tomoyuki Tanaka; Director, Seiji Maruyama; Screenplay, Katsuya Suzaki and Seiji Maruyama; Director of Photography, Kazuo Yamada; Music, Masaru Sato; Art Director, Takeo Kita; Editor, Ryohei Fujii; Sound Recording, Yoshio Nishikawa; Sound Effects, Toho Sound Effects Group; Sound, Toho Recording Centre. *Special Effects Unit:* Director, Eiji Tsuburaya; Photography, Teisho Arikawa;

Optical Photography, Yukio Manoda and Sadao Iizuda; Art Director, Akira Watanabe; Lighting, Kuichiro Kishida; Assistant Director, Teruyoshi Nakano.

CAST: Toshiro Mifune (Admiral Isoroku Yamamoto), Yuzo Kayama (1st Lt. Ijuin), Toshio Kurosawa (1st Lt. Kimura), Makoto Sato (Genda), Koshiro Matsumoto (Minister Yoneuchi), Masayuki Mori (Prime Minister Konoe), Daisuke Kato (Chief of Press Section), Yoko Tsukasa (Sumie Kimura), Wakako Sakai (Tomoko Yakuki), Kenjiro Ishiyama (Commander Momotake), Eijiro Yanagi (Nagano), Seiji Miyaguchi (Ito), Susumu Fujita (Kurita), Fuyuki Murakami (Air Force Commander Iwakeini), Kazuo Nakaya (Staff Officer Tsuji), Ryutaro Tatsumi (Boatman Kitaro), Yoshio Inaba (Chief of Staff Ugaki), Yoshio Tsuchiya (Staff Officer Kuroshima), Akihiko Hirata (Staff Officer Watanabe), Masaaki Tachibana (Staff Officer Arima), Yu Fujiki (Staff Officer Fujii), Kenji Sahara (Staff Officer of Infomation Section), Yoshifumi Tajima (Air Force Officer), Jun-ichiro Mukoi (Fukutome), Tadashi Okabe (Tomioka), Ryuji Kita (Minister of the Navy Oikawa), Masao Imafuku (Minister of the Army Hata), Toru Abe (Chief of Staff Soka), Hisaya Ito (Staff Officer of Navigation), Naoya Kusakawa (Staff Officer of Machines), Rinsaku Ogata (Capt. Hayakawa), Hideo Mineshima (Maj. General Yamaguchi), Akira Kubo (1st Lt. Takano), Ryo Tamura (Sub-Lt. Mikami), Tatsuji Ehara (Sub-Lt. Morisaki), Shinsuke Awaji (Ohmori), Hiroyuki Ohta (Nogami), Toru Ibuki (First Army Staff Officer), Susumu Kurobe (Second Army Staff Officer), Tatsuya Nakadai (narrator).

A Toho Co., Ltd. Production. Eastman Color. Toho Scope. Westrex Recording System. Filmed at Toho Studios, Ltd. (Tokyo). 128 minutes. Released August 14, 1968.

U.S. VERSION: Released by Toho International Co., Ltd. English subtitles. Footage was later incorporated into *Midway* (Universal, 1976). Japanese title also given as *Yamamoto Isoroku.* 131 minutes. Released December 1968.

The Adolescent. Director, Osamu Yamaskich.

CAST: Reiko Tsumlira, Aki Fujikama Kazuya Taguchi.

Production company undetermined. Black and white.

U.S. VERSION: Released by Olympic International Films. English subtitles? Director, James E. McLarty. The cast names are utterly absurd, but that's how they are given in all available sources. 66 minutes. No MPAA rating. Released December 20, 1967.

The Adventures of an American Rabbit **[animated]**. Producers, Masaharu Eto, Masahisa Saeki, and John G. Marshall; Director, Fred Wolf and Nobutaka Nishizawa; Screenplay, Norm Lenzer, based on characters created by Stewart Mokowitz; Music/Lyrics, Mark Volman, Howard Kayland, and John Hoier; Animation, Shingo Araki, Kenji Yokoyama, Yukiyoshi Hane, Yoshitaka Yashima, Shigeo Matoba, Hirohide Shikishima, Ikuo Fudanuki, Katsuyoshi Nakatsuru, and Takashi Nashizawa.

Voice Characterizations (US Version): Bob Arbogast (Theo), Pat Freley (Tini Meeny), Barry Gordon (Rob Rabbit/American Rabbit), Bob Holt (Rodney), Lew Horn (Dip/various characters), Norm Lenzer (Bruno), Kenneth Mars (Vultor/Buzzard), John Mayer (Too Loose), Maitzi Morgan (Lady Pig), Lorenzo Music (Ping Pong), Lauri O'Brien (Bunny O'Hare), Hal Smith (Mentor), Russi Taylor (Mother), Fred Wolf (Fred Red).

A Toei Animation Production Co., Ltd. Production, in association with Clubhouse Pictures (?). A Japanese/U.S. co-production. Color. Wide screen. 85 minutes. Released 1986 (?).

U.S. VERSION: Released by Clubhouse Pictures, Inc. English-dubbed. 85 minutes. MPAA rating: G (?). Released 1986.

The Adventures of Little Samurai / Shonen sarutobi sasuke ("Boy Sasuke Sarutobi") **[animated]**. Director, Akira Daikubara; Screenplay, Michihei Muramatsu; Directors of Photography, Seigo Otsuka and Mitsuaki Ishikawa; Animation, Chikao Tera, Kazuko Nakamura, Shuji Konno, Masatake Kita, Daikichiro Kusube, Taku Sugiyama, and Reiko Okuyama.

VOICE CHARACTERIZATIONS: (undetermined).

A Toei Animation Studio Co., Ltd. Production. A Toei Co., Ltd. Release. Eastman Color. ToeiScope. 83 minutes. Released 1959.

U.S. VERSION: Distributor, if any, is undetermined.

The Adventures of Milo and Otis / Koneko monogatari ("Kitten Story"). Executive Producer, Haruo Shikanai; Executive in Charge of Production/Production Supervisor, Hisashi Hieda; Producers, Masaru Kakutani and Satoru Ogata; Director/Screenplay, Masanori Hata; Poem, Shuntaro Tanigawa; Production Coordinators, Shoichiro Ishimaru and Sumikazu Okazaki; Associate Director, Kon Ichikawa; Directors of Photography, Hideo Fujii and Shinji Tomita; Editor, Chizuko Osada; Art Director, Takeharu Sakaguchi; Special Effects, Yoshio Kojima; Assistant Director, Takashi Ueno; Sound Recording, Minoru Nobuoka and Tetsuya Ohashi; Animal Supervisor, Mieko Hata; Animal Trainers, Toshiaki Ishikawa, Hiroko Ishikawa, Chikao Nakata, Mieko Hata, Yuji Fujimoto, Yuko Yamazaki, Etsuko Nakabayashi, Michitaka Komiyama, Takayuki Komiyama, Isao Hiraga, Takeshi Tsuyama, Kazuya Yamamoto, Yoichi Saijo, Keiko Saijo, Masae Onishi, Manabu Mashita, Akiko Yoshikawa, Konomi Hiraoka.

VOICE CHARACTERIZATIONS: (undetermined).

A Fuji Television Network Production. Dolby Stereo. Eastman Color. Panavision. 95 minutes. Released 1986.

U.S. VERSION: Released by Columbia Pictures. English narration. Narrator, Dudley Moore; Screenplay, Mark Saltsman; Editors, Peter Verity and Walt Mulconery; Music, Michael Boddicker; Orchestrations, Thomas Pasatieri; Music, Editors, Nancy Fogerty and Bill Bernstein; Song: "Walk Outside," by Dick Tarrier and performed by Dan Crow; Titles/Opticals, Cinema Research Corp. International Title: *The Adventures of Chatran*. U.S. prints by DeLuxe. 75 minutes. MPAA rating: "G." Released August 1989.

Adventures of Takla Makan / Kiganjo no boken ("Adventures in Kigan Castle"). Executive Producer, Tomoyuki Tanaka; Director, Senkichi Taniguchi; Screenplay, Kaoru Mabuchi (Takeshi Kimura); Director of Photography, Kazuo Yamada; Music, Akira Ifukube; Sound, Toho Recording Centre; Sound Effects, Toho Sound Effects Group.

CAST: Toshiro Mifune, Mie Hama, Tadao Nakamaru, Yumi Shirakawa, Tatsuya Mihashi, Makoto Sato.

A Toho Co., Ltd. Production. Black and white (processed by Tokyo Laboratory, Ltd.). Toho Scope. Western Electric Mirrophonic recording. Filmed in Iran near Isfahan, and at Toho Studios, Ltd. (Tokyo). 105 minutes. Released April 1966.

U.S. VERSION: Released by Toho International Co., Ltd. English subtitles. Alternate titles: *Adventure of the Strange Stone Castle, Adventure in the Strange Castle* and *Adventure in Taklamakan*. 100 minutes. No MPAA rating. Released February 14, 1968.

Adventures of the Polar Cubs / Hokkyoku no Mushika Mishika ("Mushika and Mishika of the North Pole") [**animated**]. Producers, Satoshi Ito and Takeo Nishigaki; Director, Chikao Katsui; Animation Director, Hatsuo Sugime; Art Director, Kiyoshi Miyamoto.

VOICE CHARACTERIZATIONS: (undetermined).

A Nikkatsu Children's Films, Inc./ Mushi Production Co., Ltd. Production. Color. Wide screen (?). 78 minutes. Released 1979.

U.S. VERSION: Release undetermined. 78 minutes. No MPAA rating.

Aesop's Fables / Manga Isoppu monogatari ("Aesop's Comic Book of Stories") [**animated**]. Producer, Chiaki Imada; Director, Norio Hikone; Screenplay, Hirohisa Soda; Music, Akihiko Komori.

VOICE CHARACTERIZATIONS: (undetermined).

A Toei Co., Ltd. Production. Color. ToeiScope (?). 61 minutes. Released 1983.

U.S. VERSION: Distributor, if any, is undetermined.

The Affair / Joen ("Flaming Desire"). Director, Yoshishige Yoshida; Screenplay, Yoshishige Yoshida and Takeshi Tamura; Director of Photography, Mitsuji Kanau; Art Director, Chiyo Umeda; Music, Shigeru Ikeno.

CAST: Mariko Okada (Oriko), Yoshie Minami (her mother), Tadahiko Sugano (Furuhata), Shigako Shimegi (his sister), Isao Kimura (Mitsuharu), Etsushi Takahashi (laborer).

A Gendai Eiga Co., Ltd. Production. A Shochiku Co., Ltd. Release. Black and white. Shochiku GrandScope. 101 minutes. Released May 1967.

U.S. VERSION: Released by Shochiku Films of America. English subtitles. 97 minutes. No MPAA rating. Released 1967 (?).

The Age of Assassins / Satsujin kyo jidai ("The Age of Assassins"). Producers, Tomoyuki Tanaka and Kenichiro Kakuta; Director, Kihachi Okamoto; Screenplay, Ei Ogawa, Tadashi Yamazaki and Kihachi Okamoto, based on the novel *Ueta isan* by Michio Tsuzuki; Art Director, Iwao Akune; Director of Photography, Rokuro Nishigaki; Editor, Yoshitami Kuroiwa; Music, Masaru Sato; Sound Recording, Noboru Tokei; Sound, Toho Recording Centre; Sound Effects, Toho Sound Effects Group.

CAST: Tatsuya Nakadai (Shinji Kikyo), Reiko Dan (Keiko Tsurumaki), Hideo Sunazuka (Bill Otomo), Eisei Amamoto (Shogo Mizorogi), Keiichi Taki (Ikeno), Misako Tominaga (woman with artificial eye), Seishiro Hisano (man with crutch), Yasuzo Ogawa (Mabuchi), Tatsuya Ehara (Aochi), Atsuko Kawaguchio (Yumie Komatsu), Wataru Omae (Oba-Q), Toru Ibuki (Atom), Hiroshi Hasegawa (Solan), Masanari Nibe (Pappy), Tsutomu Okeura (Hide), Masaji Oki (Yasu), Bruno Luske (Bruckmayer), Ikio Sawamura (old murderer), Terumi Oka (little woman), Satoko Fukai (big woman), Naoya Kusakawa (chief editor), Koji Uno (man with long neck), Yutaka Nakamura (laughing mad man), Tamami Urayama (barking mad man), Yaeko Izumo (Hokke mad woman), Tomoaki Tsuchiya (mad man with Haori).

A Toho Co., Ltd. Production. Westrex recording system. Black and white (processed by Tokyo Laboratory Ltd.) Toho Scope. 99 minutes. Released March 1967.

U.S. VERSION: Released by Toho International Co., Ltd. English subtitles. International title: *Epoch of Murder Madness*. Apparently reissued in Japan at 69 minutes, which is the only version currently available. No MPAA rating 99 minutes. Released 1967.

Ah, My Home Town / Aa Kokyo ("Ah, My Home Town"). Director, Kenji Mizoguchi; Screenplay, Yoshikata Yoda, based on an idea by Hideo Koide; Director of Photography, Junichiro Aojima.

CAST: Fumiko Yamaji (Omiyo), Masao Shimizu (Kazuo Sakamoto), Seiichi Kato (Omiyo's father), Seizaburo Kawazu (Shinkichi Takino), Isamu Yamaguchi (Hanada), Mari Mihato (Hanada's daughter), Kumeko Urabe, Koichi Toribashi.

A Shinko Kinema Oizumi Co., Ltd. Production. Filmed at Shinko Kinema Oizumi Studios (Tokyo), and on location in Yamagata. Black and white. Academy ratio. Running time undetermined. Released September 22, 1938.

U.S. VERSION: Distributor, if any, is undetermined.

AIDO—Slave of Love / Aido ("Aido"). Director, Susumu Hani; Screenplay, Susumu Hani and Isamu Kurita, based on a story by Isamu Kurita; Director of Photography, Yuji Okumura; Art Director, Itsuro Hirata; Music, Teizo Muramatsu, Akio Yashiro, Naotada Odaka, and Saori Yuki.

CAST: Yuri Suemasa (Aido), Kenzo Kawarazaki (Shusei), Kimiko Nukamura (Madame Enjoji), Ruriko Tanuma (Yoko), Kenzaburo Shirai (professor), Takamitsu masuda (Yamamoto), Jusaburo Tsujima (Detective Iwashita).

A Hani Production. A Shochiku Co., Ltd. Release. Eastman Color. Spherical wide screen (1.85:1). 105 minutes. Released May 24, 1969.

U.S. VERSION: Released by Shochiku Films of America, Inc. English subtitles. No MPAA rating. Released 1970 (?).

AKIKO—Portrait of a Dancer / Akiko aru dansa no shozo

("Akiko—Portrait of a Dancer") [**documentary**]. Producer, Mitsuru Kudo; Director, Sumiko Haneda; Director of Photography, Kikumatsu Soda.

WITH: Akiko Kanda, and the Akiko Kanda Dance Company.

A Jiyu Kobo, Inc. Production. Color. Academy ratio (?). 107 minutes. Released 1985.

U.S. VERSION: Distributor, if any, is undetermined.

Akira / Akira [**animated**]. Executive Producer, Sawako Noma; Producers, Ryohei Suzuki and Shunzo Kato; Associate Producer, Yoshimasa Mizuo; Director, Katsuhiro Otomo; Screenplay, Katsuhiro Otomo and Izo Hashimoto, based on the graphic novel by Katsuhiro Otomo; Director of Photography, Katsuji Misawa; Editor, Takeshi Seyama; Art Design, Kazuo Ebisawa, Yuji Ikehata, Koji Ono; Assistant Director, Toshiharu Mizutani; Special Effects Artist, Takashi Maekawa; Special Effects Backgrounds, Noriko Takaya; Music, Shoji Yamashiro, performed by Geino Yamashirogumi; Music, Editor, Haruhiko Ono; Sound Architect, Keiji Urata; Sound Recording Director, Susumu Aketagawa; Sound Recording Producer, Tokuya Shimada; Sound Recording Production Manager, Kozo Ogata; Sound Recording Supervisor, Tetsuo Segawa; Sound Recording, Keiji Muraki, Shiro Sasaki, Heizo Yoda, Hideo Takada, Keiichiro Yoshioka; Dolby Stereo Consultant, Mikio Mori; Sound Effects Supervisor, Shizuo Kurahashi; Sound Effects Foley, Kenji Shibasaki, Toyo Onkyo; Production Assistant, Keiko Nobumoto; Production Coordinator, Ken Tsunoda; Production Managers, Yoichi Ikeda, Takahisa Yokomizo; Animation Photography (*Asahi Production*) Atsushi Okui, Akio Saito, Kazuta Furubayashi, Shuichi Ito, Hideko Takahashi, Tetsu Keibu, Kazunobu Okeda, Yoichi Hasegawa, Yuki Asaine, Toshiyuki Umeda, Youji Toki, Hiroyuki Matsuzawa, Yukinori Sakai. (*Toms Photo*) Hajime Hasegawa, Kenichi Kobayashi, Takashi Nomura, Hiroshi Kanai, Moriyuki Terashita, Hitoshi Nishiyama, Hitoshi Shirao, Takahisa Ogawa, Hironori Yoshino, Kiyoshi Kobayashi, Atsushi Yoshino, Kazunari Ichinozuka, Mika Saki, Atsuko Ito, Kyoko Osaki, Rie Takeuchi, Koji Asai. *Computer Graphics*: (*High-Tech Lab*) Ryoichiro Debuchi, Yuriko Amemiya, Chie Furubayashi, Yukiko Katsuya, Naoko Motoyoshi. Animation (chief) Takashi Nakamura, (director) Yoshio Takeuchi, Hiroaki Sato (key), Atsuko Fukushima, Toshiyuki Inoue, Tomihiko Okubo, Masuji Kigami, Yoshiyuki Okiura, Sadahiko Sakamaki, Satoshi Hirayama, Seiji Muta, Satoru Utsunomiya, Kazuyoshi Takeuchi, Toyoaki Emura, Masatomo Sudo, Shinichi Suzuki, Hitoshi Ueda, Kuni Tomita, Ayumi Tomobuki, Chiharu Sato, Yasuhiro Seo, Yoshinori Tokiya, Hideki Nimura, Hiroyuki Kitakubo, Satoshi Urushibara, Hideko Yamauchi, Yasuomi Umetsu, Akinobu Takahashi, Shinichi Terasawa, Toshiaki Hontani, Tatsuo Ryuno, Shoichi Masuo, Shuichi Obara, Yoshinori Kaneda, Toshio Kawaguchi, Masaaki Endo, Kyoko Matsubara, Shinji Otsuka, Tatsuyuki Tanaka, Kazuyoshi Yaginuma, Jiro Kanai, Hiroyuki Takagi, Makiko Futaki, Shinji Hashimoto. (*Telecom Animation Film Co.*) Koichi Maruyama, Yoshinobu Michihata, Masanori Ono, Kenji Yazaki, Hiroaki Noguchi, Toshihiko Masuda, Yuichiro Yano, Yuko Kusamoto, Hiroyuki Aoyama, Seiichi Takiguchi, Hirokazu Suenaga, Toshiya Washida, Keiko Tomizawa; Animation Checkers, Mitsunori Murata, Hisahiko Komiya, Hitomi Tateno; Layout Artists, Takashi Watabe, Kiyomi Tanaka; Background Artists, (*Studio Fuga*) Tsutomu Uchida, Asako Kodaira, Satoshi Kuroda, Miyuki Kudo, Kenji Kamiyama, Katsufumi Haryu, Mariko Kobayashi, Noboru Tatsuike, Hajime Soga, Tatsuya Kushida, Sanae Ichioka, Toru Hishiyama, Tokuhiro Hiraki, Masatoshi Kai. (*Studio Uni*) Jiro Kawano, Kaori Yamasaki, Tatehiko Uchida, Akira Furuya, Akiyoshi Iijima, Takashi Nakamura (*Baku Production*) Mitsuharu Miyamae, Hirofumi Hagimiwa, Kazuhiro Sato, Osamu Honda, Tatsuo Imamura (*Ishigaki Production*) Yukihiro Shibuya, Mamoru Konno, Hiroyuki Mitsumoto, Kenichi Takahashi, Hiroyuki Ogura, Kazutoshi Shimizu, Kazuhiro Kinoshita, Yoji Nakaza, Yukiko Iijima, Eiko Sudo, Yoshie Kanajima,

Kaoru Honma, Fukiko Hashizume. (*Kobayashi Production*) Shinji Kimura, Nobuhiro Otsuka, Takumi Nagayasu; In-Betweeners, (*Nakamura Production*) Hisao Yamazaki, Takashi Noto, Takayuki Ishizuka, Shusaku Chiba, Shinichi Sasaki, Takuro Shinpo, Koichi Taguchi, Masayuki Yanase, Setsuya Tanabe, Koichi Hatsumi, Kazuyuki Iizuka, Noriyuki Nakajima, Tatsuya Uetsu, Teiji Hiramatsu, Yoshiyuki Fukuda (*Dragon Production*) Junko Isaka, Midori Nagaoka, Tomoko Takei, Chieko Shiobara, Masami Takebuchi, Katsumoto Ehara, Kenji Yamamoto, Yuichi Miura, Yoshiaki Wakaki, Takayuki Shimura, Akiko Nakamura, Mariko Takekuchi, Kaori Miyagawa, Yoshiko Kuriihara, Daihachi Okajima, Kenichi Katsui, Mariko Araki, Akiko Yoshii, Miyuki Murai (*Telecom Animation Film Co.*) Shunsuke Harada, Yoko Sakurai, Junko Saito, Masako Hayashi, Akiko Kawauchi, Noboru Sasaki, Norio Saito, Kayoko Nakafuji, Hisao Yokohori, Yoko Nagashima, Toshie Nkagome, Yasuhiro Takema, Yoyoi Toki, Takashi Kawaguchi, Takuo Tominaga, Takashi Umeda, Hiroko Yoshizawa, Junko Uenoyama, Masayuki Osawa, Shojiro Nishimi, Masato Mukai, Takeshi Konakawa, Emiko Hirama, Yuji Nakamura, Hiroko Takatani, Yukari Fujii, Yumi Yanagawa, Masayoshi Shimura, Natsuko Takahashi, Nobuo Kamaki, Hiroshi Sato, Seiko Azuma, Akira Tsukada, Keiko Yozawa, Yoshiko Fujita, Miyuki Aoki, Tatsushi Narita, Mayumi Suzuki, Hinako Komatsu, Sachiko Kobayashi, Koji Kawasaki, Yoshiaki Matsuo, Eiichiro Nishiyama, Hiroko Watanabe, Rie Niidome, Takuya Iinuma, Yasuyuki Shimizu, Emiko Nishiyama; Ink and Paint (*Yuminsha*) Shihoko Nakayama, Naoko Kawakami, Mika Tsuda, Minoru Ueno, Atsushi Sano, Minako Mori, Hideyuki Yagisawa, Tomoka Mitsui, Yukihiko Michimoto, Yumiko Kawaguchi, Junichi Uehara, Harumi Yatsu, Atsushi Fujitsuka, Hiromi Shirouchi, Mayumi Kimura Miho Uchiyama; Checkers, Noriko Shiotani, Noriko Ogawa, Yuriko Kashiwakura, Teruyo Tateyama; Color Keys, Kimie Yamana, Michiko Ikeuchi, Setsuko Tanaka.

Voice Characterizations: Mitsuo Iwata, Nozomu Sasaki, Mami Koyama, Tetsusho Genda, Hiroshi Otake, Koichi Kitamura, Michihiro Ikemizu, Yuriko Fuchizaki, Masaaki Okura, Taro Arakawa, Takeshi Kusao, Kazumi Tanaka, Masayuki Kato, Yosuke Akimoto, Masato Hirano, Yukimasa Kishino, Kazuhiro Kando, Tatsuhiko Nakamura, Sachie Ito, Issei Futamata, Kozo Shioya, Michitaka Kobayashi, Hideyuki Umezu, Satoru Inagaki, Kayoko Fujii, Masami Toyoshima, Yuka Ono, Taro Ishida, Mizuho Suzuki.

An Akira Committee Co., Ltd. Production. Dolby Stereo. Color. Spherical wide screen. 124 minutes. Released July 1988.

U.S. VERSION: Released by Streamline Pictures. English-dubbed. An English-subtitled version is also available. Laserdisc version is matted. Running time of Japanese version also given at 100 minutes. 124 minutes. No MPAA rating. Released December 1989.

Akira Kurosawa's Dreams / Yume ("Dreams"). Producers, Hisao Kurosawa, Mike Y. Inoue; Director, Akira Kurosawa; Screenplay, Akira Kurosawa and [uncredited] Ishiro Honda; Creative Consultant and Uncredited Co-Director; Ishiro Honda; Directors of Photography, Takao Saito, Masaharu Ueda; Photography Collaborator, Kazutami Hara; Art Directors, Yoshiro Muraki, Akira Sakuragi; Music, Shinichiro Ikebe; Sound, Kenichi Benitani; Costume Designer, Emi Wada; Assistant Director, Takashi Koizumi; Production Manager, Teruyo Nogami; Production Coordinator, Izuhiko Suehiro; Associate Producers, Allan H. Liebert, Siekichi Iizumi; Technical Cooperation, Sony; Sound Effects, Ichiro Minawa, Masatoshi Saito; Set Decorator, Koichi Hamamura; Casting Assistant, Yasunori Suzuki; Unit Managers, Kunio Niwa, Masahiko Kumada; Choreographer, Michiyo Hata; Piano Player, Ikudo Endo; Assistant Directors, Okihiro Yoneda, Naohito Sakai, Tsuyoshi Sugino, Kiyoharu Hayano, Toru Tanaka, Vitorio Dalle Ore; Assistant Cameramen, Yoshinori Sekiguchi, Toshio Wattanabe, Hidehiro Igarashi, Hiroyuki Kitazawa, Hiroshi Ishida, Kazushi Watanabe, Shigeo Suzuki, Kosuke Matsushima, Mitsu Kondo,

Hiroshi Hattori; Lighting Technicians; Yukio Choya, Tadatoshi Kitagawa, Makoto Sano, Tetsuo Sawada, Miyanobu Inori, Hisanori Furukawa, Isao Yasui, Hideho Ioka, Hiromasa Yonahara; Lighting Rigging, Kenzo Masuda, Yukio Tanaka; Sound Assistants, Soichi Inoue, Masahito Yano, Noriaki Minami; Grips, Isanu Miwano, Satoshi Tsuyuki, Sadanu Takahara, Yuichi Horita; Art Assistants, Kyoko Heya, Nariyuki Kondo, Yasuyoshi Ototake; Set Construction, Ichio Utsuki, Kazuharu Tsuboi; Props, Satoshi Ota, Yuzuru Sakai, Nami Ishida, Yoshiaki Kawai; Wardrobe, Kazuko Kurosawa, Akira Fukuda, Yoko Nagano, Mitsuru Otsuka; Assistant Editors, Rysuke Otsubo, Hideto Aga, Yosuke Yafune; Negative Cutters, Tome Minami, Noriko Meharu; Make-up Artists, Shoshichiro Ueda, Tameyuki Aimi, Norio Sano; Hairdressers, Sakai Nakao, Yumiko Fujii; Still Photographer, Daizaburo Harada; Production Publicity, Yasuhiko Higashi; Mountain Climbing Adviser, Tadao Kanzeki; Dance Instructor, Tokiko Mochizuki; Transportation, Takashi Takei, Kimihiko Tsurugaya, Toru Ikegaki, Keisuke Utsumi, Yasuhisa Serizawa, Masaharu Komatsuki; In Charge of Location Site (Gotemba), Magosaku Osada, Shizuo Osada; Production Accountants, Shuji Matsumoto, Hiroko Idetsu; Production Assistants, Shushin Hosoya, Satoshi Shimozawa, Kazutoshi Wadakura; Recording Studio, Toho Recording Centre; Raw Stock, Kodak Japan; Art Department, Toho E-B; Props, Takatsu Soshoku Bijutsu; Explosives, Ohira Special Effects; Hair Styles and Wigs, Yauada Katsura; Wardrobe, Tokyo Isho; Sound Effects, Toyo Onkyo Kauove; Music Production, Tokyo Concert; Sound Equipment, Tisman Service; Camera Equipment, Sanwa Cine-Equipment Rental Co., Ltd.; Lighting Equipment, Lee Colortran International; Vehicles, Nippon Shomei, Film Link International; Background Music, Ippolitov-Ivanov "In The Village," from Caucasian Sketches Suite for Orchestra Op. 10; Conducting Moscow Radio Symphony Orchestra, Vladimir Fedoseev; Hi-Definition TV Technology, Sony PCL; Photo-Composite Process, Akio Suzuki, Mikio Inoue, Mutsuhiro Harada, Yoshiya Takahashi; EBR Process, Tonio Onata, Takaya Takizawa; HDTV Coordinator, Tetsuji Maezawa; Composite Technology, Den-Film-Effects; Special Effects Unit (Japan) Visual Effects, Minoru Nakano; Technical Editor, Michihisa Miyashige; Optical Photography, Takashi Kobayashi, Takashi Kawabata; Optical Camera Operators, Makoto Negishi, Takabuni Hirata; Matte Painting, Taksuhiro Miyaguchi. Visual Effects (U.S.), Industrial Light & Magic, a Division of LucasArts Entertainment Company. *ILM Visual Effects Unit:* Supervisors, Ken Ralston, Mark Sullivan; Producer, Peter Takeuchi; Art Director, Claudia Mullaly; Model Supervisor, Barbara Affonso; Optical Supervisor, Bruce Veccitto; Editor, Michael Gleason; Coordinator, Jil Sheree Bergin; Camera Operators, Terry Chostner, Selwyn Eddy III; Assistant Camera Operators, Randy Johnson, John Gazdik, Robert Hill; Matte Camera Operators, Jo Carson, Wade Childress, Paul Huston, Charles Canfield; Assistant Matte Camera Operator, Nancy Morita; Matte Painters, Yusei Useugi, Caroleen Green; Matte Assistant, Jonathan Crowe; Modelmakers, Brian Gernand, E'ven Stromquist, Randy Ottenberg, Wesley Seeds, Marge McMahon; Optical Lineup, Peggy Hunter, Dave Karpman, Lori Nelson, Thomas Tosseter; Optical Camera Operators, Jon Alexander, Jeff Doran; Postproduction Coordinator, Susan Adele Colletta; Rotoscope Artist, Barbara Brennan; Stage Supervisor, Brad Jerrell; Head Electrician, Tim Morgan; Electrician, David Murphy; Chief Pyro Technician, Charles Ray; Pyro Technician, Reuben Goldberg; Cloud Tank, Craig Mohegan.

CAST: *Sunshine Through the Rain:* Mitsuko Baisho (Mother of "I"), Toshihiko Nakano ("I" as a Young Child). *The Peach Orchard:* Mitsunori Isaki ("I" as a Boy), Mie Suzuki ("I's" Sister). *The Blizzard:* Akira Terao ("I"), Mieko Harada (The Snow Fairy), Masayuki Yui, Shu Nakajima, Sakae Kimura (Members of the Climbing Team). *The Tunnel:* Akira Terao ("I"), Yoshitaka Zushi (Private Noguchi). CROWS: Akira Terao ("I"), Martin Scorsese (Vincent Van Gogh). *Mt. Fuji in Red:* Akira Terao ("I"), Toshie

Negishi (Child-Carrying Mother), Hisashi Igawa (Power Station Worker). *The Weeping Demon:* Akira Terao ("I"), Chosuke Ikariya (The Demon). *Village of the Watermills:* Akira Terao ("I"), Chishu Ryu (103-year-old Man).

Also: Mugita Endo, Ryujiro Oki, Masaru Sakurai, Masaaki Sasaki, Keiki Takenouchi, Kento Toriki, Shu Nakajima, Tokuju Nasuda, Masuo Amada, Sakae Kimura, Shogo Tomomori, Ryo Nagasawa, Akisato Yamada, Tetsu Watanabe, Ken Takemura, Yasuhiro Kajimoto.

Makoto Hasegawa, Nagamitsu Satake, Satoshi Hara, Yasushige Turuoka, Shigeru Edaki, Hideharu Takeda, Katsumi Naito, Masaaki Enomoto, Norio Takei, Eiji Iida, Koji Kanda, Hideto Aota, Kazue Nakanishi, Rika Miyazawa, Mika Edaki, Mayumi Kamimura, Sayuri Yoshioka, Teruko Nakayama, Sachicko Nakayama.

Toshiya Ito, Takashi Ito, Motoyuki Higashimura, Yasuhito Yamanaka, Haruka Sugata, Noriko Hayami, Ayaka Takahashi, Yuko Ishiwa, Sachiko Oguri.

Masayo Mochida, Miki Kado, Ikeya Sakiko Yamamoto, Mayumi Ono Yumiko Miyata, Aya Ikaida, Megumi Hata, Asako Hirano, Chika Nishio, Yuko Harada, Tomomi Yoshizawa, Kunido Ishizuka, Maumi Yoda, Hatsue Nishi, Michiko Kawada, Machiko Ichihashi, Yumi Ezaki, Chika Yanabe, Mayuko Akashi.

Fujio Tokita, Michio Hino, Michio Kida, Ayako Honua, Haruko Togo, Reiko Nanao.

Shin Tonomura, Junpei Natsuki, Shigeo Kato, Saburo Kadowaki, Goichi Nagatani, Shizuko Azuma, Yoshie Kihira, Yukie Shimura, Setsuko Kawaguchi, Kemeko Otowa.

Machiko Terada, Umiko Takahashi, Harumi Fuji, Hiroko Okuno, Mon Ota, Akitoku Inaba, Ko Ishikawa, Tatsunori Takuhashi.

Yoshiko Maki, Hiroko Maki, Ryoko Kawai, Miyako Kawana, Miyuki Egawa, Megumi Sakai, Yoko Hayashi, Yuko Matsumura, Takashi Odajima, Mitsuru Shibuya, Koichi Imamura, Wasuke Izumi.

Sachio Sakai, Torauemon Utazawa, Yukimasa Natori, Tadashi Okumura, Kenzo Shirahana, Masato Goto, Sumimaro Yochini, Juichi Kubozono, Masami Ozeki, Yasuyuki Iwanaga, Akira Tashiro, Koichi Kase, Kenji Fujita, Hiroto Tamura, Osamu Yayama, Yuji Sawayana, Mitsuji Tsuwako, Masatoshi Miya.

Maiko Okamoto, Nana Yanakawa, Yuka Kojima, Shizuka Isami, Mai Watanabe, Sayuri Kobayashi.

Hayakawa Productions, Himawani Theatre Group, Inc., Motoko Inagawa Office, Tanbe Dojo, Kokugakuin University Mizutamakai.

An Akira Kurosawa USA, Inc. Production. A Japanese/U.S. co-production. Released by Toho Co., Ltd. (?). Dolby Stereo. Eastman Color (processed by Inagica). Prints by Technicolor. Spherical Panavision. Thanks to the Akira Kurosawa Film Society. Filmed at Kurosawa Film Studio and Toho Studios, Ltd (Tokyo). 120 minutes. Released 1990.

U.S. VERSION: Released by Warner Bros., Inc. English Subtitles, Donald Richie, Tadashi Shishido. In Japanese and English with English Subtitles. Actors whose roles are not specified are grouped on screen as above. Japanese title also given as *Konna yume wo mita* ("I Had This Dream"). 120 minutes. MPAA Rating: "PG." Released August 24, 1990.

Alakazam the Great / Saiyu-ki

("The Journey to the West") **[animated]**. Producer, Hiroshi Okawa; Director, Teiji Yabushita, Osamu Tezuka, and Daisaku Shirakawa; Screenplay, Osamu Tezuka; Screenplay, Keinosuke Uekusa; Original Adaptation, Hideyuki Takahashi and Goro Kontaibo; Original Drawings, Yasuji Mori and Akira Daikubara; Animation, Koichi Mori, Yasuo Otsuka, Masao Kumagawa, Akira Daikubara, and Hideo Furusawa; Art Work and Color, Masaaki Yano, Hajime Numai, and Koichi Maeba; Background, Eiko Sugimoto, Kimiko Saito, Kazuko Ozawa, Mataji Urata, and Saburo Yokoi; Photography, Seigo Otsuka, Harusato Otsuka, Komei Ishikawa, and Kenji Sugiyama.

Voice characterizations: (undetermined). A Toei Animation Studio Co., Ltd. Production. A Toei Co., Ltd. Release. Eastman Color. ToeiScope. 88 minutes. Released 1960.

U.S. VERSION: Released by American

A scene from *Alakazam the Great* (1960), one of Japan's earliest animated features.

International Pictures. A James H. Nicholson and Samuel Z. Arkoff Presentation. Producer, Lou Rusoff; Director, Lee Kresel [Kressel]; Screenplay, Lou Rusoff and Lee Kresel [Kressel]; Editor, Salvatore Billitteri and Laurette Odney; Music, Les Baxter; Music Coordinator, Al Simms; Orchestra (Conductor?), Albert Harris. Songs: "Ali the Great," "Bluebird in the Cherry Tree," "Under the Waterfall," "Aliki-Aliko-Alakazam," by Les Baxter; Sound, Titra Sound Corp; Sound Editor, Kay Rose; Music Editors, Eve Newman and George Brand. Prints by Pathe. Wide screen process advertised as Magiscope. International title: *The Enchanted Monkey*. Copyright July 14, 1961 by Alta Vista Productions. 84 minutes. No MPAA rating. Released July 14, 1961.

Voices for U.S. Version: Frankie Avalon (Alakazam), Dodie Stevens (De De), Jonathan Winters (Sir Quigley Broken Bottom), Arnold Stang (Lulipopo), Sterling Holloway (narrator).

The Alaska Story / Arusuka monogatari ("Alaska Story"). Producers, Tomoyuki Tanaka and Hiroaki Fujii; Director, Hiromichi Horikawa; Screenplay, Masato Ide, based on a story by Jiro Nitta; Director of Photography, Kozo Okazaki; Art Director, Kazuo Satsuya; Music, Masaru Sato.

Cast: Kinya Kitaoji (the cabin boy), Kyoko Mitsubayashi (his Eskimo wife), Eiji Okada (her father), Tetsuro Tamba (tribal chief), Don Kenny, William Ross.

A Tokyo Eiga Co., Ltd. Production, in association with Toho Co., Ltd. A Toho Co., Ltd. Release. Color. Spherical wide screen. 141 minutes. Released 1977.

U.S. Version: Released by Toho International Co., Ltd. in subtitled format. No MPAA rating. Released April 7, 1978.

All of Myself / Watashi no subete o ("All of Myself"). Producer, Kazuo Takimura; Director, Kon Ichikawa; Screenplay, Haruo Umeda, Tatsuo Asano, and Kon Ichikawa, based on a story by Kazuo Kikuta; Director of Photography, Mitsuo Miura; Music, Ryoichi Hattori; Art Director, Gen Akune; Lighting, Ichiro Inohara; Sound, Ariaki Hosaka.

CAST: Ryo Ikebe (Saburo Seki), Ineko Arima (Rui Kenjo), Kinuko Ito (Michiko Kitamura), Ken Uehara (Atsushi Kazama), Sumiko Hidaka (Otoshi).

A Toho Co., Ltd. Production. Black and white. Academy ratio. Running time undetermined. Released May 12, 1954.

U.S. VERSION: Distributor, if any, is undetermined, though likely Toho International Co., Ltd.

The All-Out Game / Botate Asobi (title undetermined). Director, Akira Okazaki; Screenplay, Katsuya Suzaki; Director of Photography, Kyuji Yokote; Art Director, Tomohisa Yano; Music, Harumi Ibe.

CAST: Kimisaburo Onogawa (Daisaku Hotta), Saburo Shindo (Rikiya Kudo), Kei Wakakura (Shiro Usami), Eiko Yanami (Mitsuyo Aikawa), Yoko Namikawa (Kyoko Imai), Junko Yashiro.

A Daiei Motion Picture Co., Ltd. Production. Fujicolor. DaieiScope. 82 minutes. Released September 12, 1970.

U.S. VERSION: Released by Daiei International Films. English subtitles. 82 minutes. No MPAA rating. Released April, 21, 1971.

All Under the Moon / Tsuki wa dochi ni dete iru ("Where Is the Moon Up?"). Producer, Bong-ou Lee; Director, Yoichi Sai; Screenplay, Ui-shin Chong and Yoichi Sai, based on the novel by Sogil Yan; Director of Photography, Junichi Fujisawa; Music, Masahide Sakuma.

CAST: Goro Kishitani, Ruby Moreno, Moeko Ezawa.

A Cine Qua Non Release. Color. Spherical wide screen (?). 109 minutes. Released 1993.

U.S. VERSION: Released by Cine Qua Non. English subtitles. One source gives the running time of the Japanese version as 95 minutes. 109 minutes. No MPAA rating. Released 1994.

Alladin and the Wonderful Lamp [sic] / Arajin to maho no ranpu ("Aladdin and the Wonderful Lamp") [**animated**]. Producer, Chiaki Imada; Director, Yoshikatsu Kasai; Screenplay, Akira Miyazaki, based on *The Arabian Nights*; Art Director, Fumihiro Uchikawa; Music, Katsuhiro Tsuboyoshi.

VOICE CHARACTERIZATIONS: (undetermined).

A Toei Animation Co., Ltd. Production. Color. Wide screen. 65 minutes. Released 1981.

U.S. VERSION: Distributor, if any, is undetermined. 65 minutes. No MPAA rating.

Along with Ghosts / Tokaido abaketo chu ("Ghost Journey Along Tokaido Road"). Producer, Masaichi Nagata; Director, Kimiyoshi Yasuda; Screenplay, Tetsuro Yoshida; Director of Photography, Hiroshi Imai; Music, Hiroshi Watanabe; Sound, Daiei Recording Studio; Special Effects, Daiei Special Effects Department.

CAST: Kojiro Hongo (Hyakutaro), Pepe Hozumi (Shinta), Masami Rurukido (Miyo), Mutsuhiro (Tora Saikichi), Yoshio Yamaji (Higuruma), Bokuzen Hidari (Jinbei).

A Daiei Motion Picture Co., Ltd. Production. A Masaichi Nagata Presentation. Westrex Recording System. Daieicolor. DaieiScope. 78 minutes. Released March 21, 1969.

U.S. VERSION: Released by Daiei International Films, Inc. English subtitles. Shown in Los Angeles, other playdates undetermined. Also known as *Journey Along Tokaido Road*. A sequel (?) to *100 Monsters* (Daiei, 1968). No MPAA rating. 78 minutes. Released 1969.

Am I Trying / Otoko wa tsuraiyo ("It's Tough to Be a Man"). Director, Yoji Yamada; Screenplay, Azuma Morisaki and Yoji Yamada, based on the teleseries created by Yoji Yamada; Director of Photography, Tetsuo Takaba; Art Director, Chiyo Umeda; Music, Naozumi Yamamoto.

CAST: Kiyoshi Atsumi (Torajiro "Tora-san" Kuruma), Chieko Baisho (Sakura Kuruma, his sister), Sachiko Mitsumoto (Fuyuko), Shin Morikawa (Ryuzo Kuruma, *Tora's uncle*), Chieko Misaki (Tsune Kuruma, *Tora's aunt*), Gin Maeda (Hiroshi Suwa, *Sakura's fiancé*), Chishu Ryu (Gozen-sama, *the temple priest*), Takashi Shimura (Professor Suwa, *Hiroshi's father*).

Japanese ad art for *Along with Ghosts* (1969). That's Kojiro Hongo holding the sword.

A Shochiku Co., Ltd. Production. Eastman Color. Shochiku GrandScope. 91 minutes. Released August 27, 1969.

U.S. VERSION: Released by Shochiku Films of America, Inc. English subtitles. The 1st "Tora-san" feature. Reissue title: *Tora-san, Our Lovable Tramp.* Followed by *Tora-san Pt. 2* (1969). No MPAA rating. Released July 18, 1974.

The Ambitious / Bakumatsu ("Bakumatsu"). Director/Screenplay, Daisuke Ito; Director of Photography, Kazuo Yamada; Art Director, Juichi Yamada; Music, Masaru Sato.

CAST: Kinnosuke Nakamura (Ryoma Sakamoto), Tatsuya Nakadai, Sayuri Yoshinaga, Noboru Nakaya, Katsuo Nakamura, Eitaro Matsuyama, Shigeru Kamiyama, Shinsuke Mikimoto, Keiju Kobayashi, Toshiro Mifune.

A Nakamura Productions, Ltd. Production. A Toho Co., Ltd. Release. Eastman Color. Panavision. 121 minutes. Released February 1970.

U.S. VERSION: Released by Toho International Co., Ltd. English subtitles. 120 minutes. No MPAA rating. Released August 26, 1970.

The Ambush: Incident at Blood Pass / Machi-buse ("Ambush"). Executive Producers, Toshiro Mifune and Yoshio Nishikawa; Director, Hiroshi Inagaki; Screenplay, Kyu Fujiki, Hideo Oguni, Hajime Takaiwa, and Ichiro Miyakawa; Director of Photography, Kazuo Yamada; Music, Masaru Sato.

CAST: Toshiro Mifune (Yojimbo), Shintaro Katsu (Gentetsu), Kinnosuke Nakamura, Ruriko Asaoka (Okuni), Yujiro Ishihara (Yataro), Mika Kitagawa (Oyuki), Ichiro Arishima (Tokubei), Yoshio Tsuchiya, Ryunosuke Yamazaki (Tatsu), Jotaro Togami (Gonji), Chusha Ichikawa (samurai).

A Mifune Productions, Ltd. Production. A Toho Co., Ltd. Release. Eastman Color. Panavision. 118 minutes. Released April 29, 1970.

U.S. VERSION: Released by Toho International Co., Ltd. English subtitles. Also known as *The Ambush.* Note: 115 minutes. No MPAA rating. Released December 18, 1970. Reissued in 1971 as *Machibuse.*

The Amorists / Jinruigaku nyumon ("An Introduction to Anthropology"). Producer, Jiro Romoda; Director, Shohei Imamura; Screenplay, Koji Numata and Shohei Imamura, based on the novel by Akiyuki Nozaka; Director of Photography, Shinsako Himeda; Art Directors, Ichiro Takada and Hiromi Shiozawi; Editor, Mutsuo Tanji; Music, Toshiro Kusunoki; Sound Recording, Shinichi Beniya.

CAST: Shoichi Ozawa (Yoshimoto "Subu" Ogata), Sumiko Sakamoto (Haru Masuda), Masaomi Kondo (Koichi), Keiko Sagawa (Keiko), Ganjiro Nakamura (elderly client), Chocho Miyako, Haruo Tanaka, Shinichi Nakano, Ko Nishimura, Ichiro Sugai.

An Imamura Production. A Nikkatsu Corp. Release. Black and white. NikkatsuScope. 128 minutes. Released March 1966.

U.S. VERSION: Released by Toho International Co., Ltd. English subtitles. 128 minutes. Released August 1966. Reissued by East/West Classics in 1989 as *The Pornographers: An Introduction to Anthropology.* Subtitles, Audie Bock. Video version letterboxed.

Ancient City / Koto ("Koto"). Producers, Takeo Hori and Hideo Sasai; Director, Kon Ichikawa; Screenplay, Shinya Hidaka and Kon Ichikawa, based on the novel by Yasunari Kawabata; Director of Photography, Kiyoshi Hasegawa; Art Director, Gakugen Sakaguchi; Music, Shinichi Tanabe.

CAST: Momoe Yamaguchi, Tomokazu Miura, Keiko Kishi.

A Horikaku Production Co., Ltd. Production. A Pony Release. Color. Panavision (?). 125 minutes. Released 1980.

U.S. VERSION: Distributor, if any, is undetermined.

The Angry Sea / Chi no hate ni ikuru mono ("People Who Live at the End of the Earth"). Producer, Kazuo Takimura; Director, Seiji Hisamatsu; Screenplay, Mutsuaki Saegusa and Seiji Hisamatsu; Director of Photography, Seiichi Endo; Art Director, Takeo Kita; Music, Ikuma Dan.

CAST: Hisaya Morishige (fisherman), Mitsuko Kusabue, Jun Funato, Yoko

Tsukasa, Masao Oda, Tsutomu Yamazaki, Ryutaro Nagai, Hiroyuki Ota, Jun Hamamura, Toru Yuri, Zeko Nakamura, Haruya Kato, Senkichi Omura, Hikaru Tashioka, Ko Nishimura.

A Toho Co., Ltd./Morishige Productions, Ltd. Production. A Toho Co., Ltd. Release. Eastman Color. Toho Scope. 125 minutes. Released October 16, 1960.

U.S. VERSION: Released by Toho International Co., Ltd. English subtitles. 93 minutes. No MPAA rating. Released February 1961.

Antarctica / Nankyoku monogatari ("South Pole Story"). Executive Producers, Hiroshi Furuoka, Haruo Shikami, and Koreyoshi Kurahara; Producers, Masaru Kakutami and Koretsudu Kuruhara; Director, Koreyoshi Kuruhara; Production Supervisors, Hisashi Hieda; Chief Producers, Tomohiro Kaiyama and Juichi Tanaka; Assistant Producers, Tsuneyoshi Morishima and Koretaugu Kurahara; Screenplay, Tatsuo Mogami, Kan Saji Toshiro Ishido and Koreyoshi Kurahara; Music, Vangelis; Director of Photography, Akira Shiizuka; 2nd Unit Director of Photography, Masahiro Tanaka; Lighting, Haruo Kawashima; Sound Recording, Kenichi Benitani; Art Director, Hiroshi Tokuda; Editors, Akira Suzuki and Koreyoshi Kurahara; Dog Trainer, Tadomi Miya; Aurora Directors of Photography, Masanao Sato and Kazuo Higuchi; General Adviser, Masayoshi Murayama.

CAST: Ken Takakura (Uchiuda), Tsurehiko Watase (Ochi), Masako Natsume, Keiko Oginome, Eiji Okada, Takeshi Kusaka, Shigeru Koyama, Shin Kishida, Takashi Obayashi.

A Fuji Telecasting Co., Ltd./Gakken Co., Ltd./Kurahara Productions Production. A Nippon Herald Films, Inc. Release. Dolby Stereo. Spherical; wide screen (?). 143 minutes. Released July 23, 1983.

U.S. VERSION: Released by TLC, a division of the 20th Century-Fox Film Corporation. English subtitles. 112 minutes. MPAA rating: "G." Released March 1984. Reissued at 143 minutes in 1985.

Anything Goes Three Dolls' Way / One chan wa tsuiteruze ("The Ladies Are in Luck"). Director, Masanori Kakei.

CAST: Reiko Dan (Punch), Noriko Shigeyama (Senti), Sonomi Nakajima (Pinch).

A Toho Co., Ltd. Production. Eastman Color. Toho Scope. 87 minutes. Released November 20, 1960.

U.S. VERSION: Distributor, if any, is undetermined, though almost certainly Toho International Co., Ltd. with English subtitles. The 6th "Three Dolls" feature. 87 minutes. No MPAA rating.

Appointment with Danger / Onna no keisatsu, Kokusaisen Machiaishitsu ("Women's Cop, International Airport Terminal"). Director, Yuji Tanno; Screenplay, Ryuzo Nakanishi and Michio Sato, based on the story by Toshiyuki Kajiyama; Director of Photography, Yoshihiro Yamazaki; Art Director, Tomozo Kawahara; Music, Taichiro Kosugi.

CAST: Akira Kobayashi (Kagari), Kunio Kaga (Tabuchi), Tokie Hidari Sawako), Yuko Tobe (Yuko), Mina Aoe (Mina), Hiroyuki Nagato (Takijima), Jiro Okazaki, Hisashi Kawaguchi.

A Nikkatsu Corp. Production. Fujicolor. NikkatsuScope. 84 minutes. Released February 7, 1970.

U.S. VERSION: Released undetermined. English subtitles. No MPAA rating.

Aru mittsu "Bi to shu" ("Beauty and Ugliness"). Director/Screenplay, Kan Mukoi. "Shikimu" ("Love Dream"): Director/Screenplay, Shinya Yamamoto. "Kuchibeni" ("Lipstick") Director, Koji Wakamatsu; Screenplay, Jiku Yamatoya.

CAST: *Bi to shu:* Mitsugu Gujii (old man), Takako Uchida (young girl). *Shikimu:* Michiyo Mako (the beauty), Yuichi Minato (the man). *Kuchibeni:* Hiroshi Nikaido (newlywed husband), Yoshiko Okada (newlywed wife), Masayoshi Nogami (fisherman).

A Nihon Cinema Production. Black and white. Academy ratio. 73 minutes. Released 1967.

U.S. VERSION: Distributor, if any, is undetermined. International title: *A Certain Adultery*.

Asiapol Secret Service / Ajia himitsu keisatsu ("Asian Secret

American ad art for Ishiro Honda's *Atragon* (1963).

Police"). Director, Akinori Matsuo; Screenplay, Iwao Yamazaki; Director of Photography, Kazumi Iwasa; Art Director, Kimihiko Nakamura; Music, Toshiro Mayuzumi.

CAST: Hideaki Nitani (Ryutaro Saeki), Joe Shishido (Georgie Eaton), Ruriko Asaoka (Kyoko Misaki), Fang Ying (Yang Ming Hua), Wang Hsieh (Lai Yu Tien).

A Nikkatsu Corporation Production. Eastman Color. NikkatsuScope. Released 1966.

U.S. VERSION: Released by Toho International Co., Ltd. English subtitles. 97 minutes. No MPAA rating. Released February 1969.

The Assassin / Ansatsu ("Assassination"). Director, Masahiro Shinoda; Screenplay, Nobuo Yamada; Story, Ryotaro Shiba; Director of Photography, Masao Kosugi; Music, Toru Takemitsu.

CAST: Tetsuro Tamba (Hachiro Kiyokawa), Shima Iwashita, Isao Kimura, Eitaro Ozawa, Eiji Okada, Keiji Sada.

A Shochiku Co., Ltd. Production. Black and white. Shochiku GrandScope. Released 1964.

U.S. VERSION: Released by Shochiku Films of America, Inc. English subtitles. 104 minutes. No MPAA rating. Released October 30, 1964.

At This Late Date, the Charleston / Chikagoro naze ka Charusuton ("At This Late Date, the Charleston"). Producers, Kihachi Okamoto and Shiro Sasaki; Director, Kihachi Okamoto; Screenplay, Kihachi Okamoto and Go Riju; Director of Photography, Katsuhiro Kato; Art Director, Kazuo Ogata; Music, Masaru Sato.

CAST: Go Riju, Yuki Kodate, Ichiro Zaitsu.

A Kihachi Productions/Art Theater Guild of Japan Co., Ltd. (ATG) Production. Black and white. Panavision (?). 116 minutes. Released 1981.

U.S. VERSION: Distributor, if any, is undetermined.

Atragon / Kaitei gunkan ("Undersea Battleship"). Producer, Tomoyuki Tanaka; Director, Ishiro Honda; Screenplay, Shinichi Sekizawa, based on the novels *Kaitei gunkan*, by Shunro Oshikawa, and *Kaitei okoku*

("The Undersea Kingdom") by Shigeru Komatsuzaki; Director of Photography, Hajime Koizumi; Music, Akira Ifukube; Production Designer, Takeo Kita; Sound, Toho Recording Centre; Sound Effects, Toho Sound Effects Group. *Special Effects Unit*: Director, Eiji Tsuburaya; Photography, Teisho Arikawa, Mototaka Tomioka; Matte Photography, Hiroshi Mukoyama; Set Decoration, Akira Watanabe; Lighting, Kuichiro Kishida; Assistant to Tsuburaya, Teruyoshi Nakano.

CAST: Jun Tazaki (Captain Jinguji), Tadao Takashima (Commercial Photographer Susumu Hatanaka), Yoko Fujiyama (Makoto Jinguchi, *the Captain's daughter*), Yu Fujiki (Yoshio Nishibe), Ken Uehara (Retired Admiral Kosumi), Tetsuko Kobayashi (Empress of Mu), Susumu Fujita (defense commander), Akihiko Hirata (Mu Agent #23), Kenji Sahara (journalist/Mu agent), Yoshifumi Tajima (Amano), Hiroshi Koizumi (professor), Eisei Amamoto (High Priest of Mu), Hisaya Ito (kidnapping victim), Ikio Sawamura, Akemi Kita, Nadao Kirino.

A Toho Co., Ltd. Production. Eastman Color (processed by Tokyo Laboratories Ltd.). Toho Scope. 96 minutes. Released December 22, 1963.

U.S. VERSION: Released by American International Pictures. English-dubbed. A James H. Nicholson and Samuel Z. Arkoff Presentation. Rerecording, Titra Sound Studios; prints by Pathe. Wide screen process billed as Colorscope in the United States. International title: *Atoragon the Flying Supersub*. Copyrighted at 90 minutes, December 23, 1964, by AIP. Actual running time of U.S. version: 79 minutes. No MPAA Rating. Released March 11, 1965.

Attack of the Monsters / Gamera tai daiakuju Giron ("Gamera Against the Giant Evil Beast Giron"). Executive Producer, Masaichi Nagata; Producer, Hidemasa Nagata; Director, Noriaki Yuasa; Planning, Kazumasa Nakano; Screenplay, Fumi Takahashi; Music, Shunsuke Kikuchi; Director of Photography, Akira Kitazaki; Sound, Daiei Recording Studio; Special Effects Director, Kazufumi Fujii; Special Effects, Daiei Special Effects Department; Monster Design, Ryosaku Takayama.

CAST: Nobuhiro Kajima (Akio), Christopher Murphy (Tom), Miyuki Akiyama (Tomoko), Yuko Hamada (Koniko), Eiji Funakoshi (Dr. Shiga), Kon Omura (Kondo), Edith Hanson (Tom's mother).

A Daiei Motion Picture Co., Ltd. Production. Westrex recording system. Eastman Color (processed by Daiei Laboratory). DaieiScope. 82 minutes. Released March 21, 1969.

U.S. VERSION: Never released theatrically in the United States. Released directly to television by American International Television (AIP-TV) in 1969. English-dubbed. A James H. Nicholson & Samuel Z. Arkoff Presentation. Prints by Perfect. The 5th "Gamera" feature. Followed by *Gamera vs. Monster X* (1970). Reissued to television and released to home video as *Gamera vs. Guiron*, with new credits and dubbing, and featuring footage deleted from the AIP-TV version. Reissue version released by King Features Entertainment, Inc., a subsidiary of the Hearst Corp., and as a Sandy Frank Syndication, Inc. Presentation. Copyright 1969 by Daiei International Films, Inc. No MPAA Rating. 82 minutes.

Attack of the Mushroom People / Matango ("Matango"). Producer, Tomoyuki Tanaka; Director, Ishiro Honda; Screenplay, Takeshi Kimura, loosely based on W.H. Hodgson's short story, "The Voice of the Night," and a treatment by Shinichi Hoshi and Masami Fukushima; Director of Photography, Hajime Koizumi; Editor, Reiko Kaneko; Music, Sadao Bekku; Sound, Toho Recording Centre; Sound Effects, Toho Sound Effects Group; *Toho Special Effects Group*: Director, Eiji Tsuburaya; Photography, Teisho Arikawa.

CAST: Akira Kubo (Professor Kenji Murai), Kenji Sahara (Koyama), Yoshio Tsuchiya (Fumio Kasai), Hiroshi Koizumi (Sakeda), Miki Yashiro (Akiko Soma), Kumi Mizuno (Mami Sekeguchi), Hiroshi Tachikawa (Etsuro Yoshida), Eisei Amamoto (mutated sailor), Yutaka Oka (doctor), Haruo Nakajima (mushroom man).

A Toho Co. Ltd. Production. Eastman Color (processed by Tokyo Laboratory Ltd.). Toho Scope. 90 minutes. Released August 11, 1963.

U.S. VERSION: Never released theatrically in the United States. Released directly to television by American International Television (AIP-TV) in 1965. English-dubbed. A James H. Nicholson and Samuel Z. Arkoff Presentation; Rerecording, Titra Sound Studios; prints by Pathe. International Title: *Matango, Fungus of Terror*. 88 minutes. No MPAA Rating.

Attack of the Super Monsters **[part-animated]**. Executive Producer, Noboru Tsuburaya; Series Creator, Ifumi Uchiyama; Director, Toru Sotoyama; Teleplay, Masaki Tsuji; Music, Seiji Yokoyama.

VOICE CHARACTERIZATIONS: Tetsuya Onishi.

A Tsuburaya Enterprises Production. A Japanese teleseries re-edited to feature length for American television, and never released theatrically in the United States. 16mm. Color. Academy ratio.

U.S. VERSION: Never released theatrically in the United States. Derived from "Kyoryu sentai Koseidon" ("Dinosaur Fighting Team Koseidon"), which ran 52 episodes on the TV Tokyo network during the 1978-79 television season. 83 minutes. No MPAA rating.

Attack Squadron! / Taiheiyo no tsubasa ("The Wing in the Pacific Ocean"). Producer, Tomoyuki Tanaka; Director, Shue Matsubayashi; Screenplay, Katsuya Suzaki; Art Director, Takeo Kimura; Editor, Yoshitami Kuroiwa; Assistant Director, Koji Kajita; Music, Ikuma Dan. *Toho Special Effects Group*: Director, Eiji Tsuburaya; Photography, Teisho Arikawa, Mototaka Tomioka; Art Director, Akira Watanabe.

CAST: Toshiro Mifune (Commander Senda), Yuzo Kayama (Squadron Commander), Yosuke Natsuki (Captain Nobuo Adaka), Susumu Fujita (*Yamato* Commander Ito), Takashi Shimura (admiral), Jun Tazaki (commander), Akihiko Hirata (Senda's aide), Yoshifumi Tajima (sailor), Yoshio Kosugi (destroyer captain), Senkichi Omura (transport pilot), Hideo Sunazanka (squadron pilot), Makoto Sato, Yuriko Hoshi, Ryo Ikebe, Mie Hama, Kiyoshi Atsumi, Ko Nishimura, Ichiro Nakaya, Seiji Miyaguchi, Tadao Nakamaru, Seizaburo Kawazu, Masao Shimizu, Nadao Kirino, Ren Yamamoto, Yutaka Nakayama, Ko Mishima, Katsumi Tezuka, Kozo Nomura, Akira Wakamatsu, Shoichi Hirose, Wataru Omae, William Schoolinger, Jack Davis.

A Toho Co., Ltd. Production. Eastman Color. Toho Scope. 101 minutes. Released 1963.

U.S. VERSION: Released by Toho International Co., Ltd. English subtitles. Released to home video by Combat Video/Video City Distributing in 1988 as *Kamikaze*. English-dubbed. 101 minutes. No MPAA rating.

Aurora / Aurora no shitade ("Under the Aurora"). Producers, Shigeru Okada and Kikuo Tashiro; Director, Toshio Goto; Screenplay, Atsushi Yamatoya, based on an original story by Yukio Togawa; Director of Photography, Yuji Okumura; Music, Reijiro Koroku.

CAST: Koji Yakusho, Andrei Boltnev, Nikita Mikhalkov.

A Toei Co., Ltd. Production. A Japanese-Russo co-production in Japanese and Russian. Color. Anamorphic wide screen (?). 127 minutes. Released 1990. U.S. version: Distributor, if any, is undetermined.

An Autumn Afternoon / Samma no aji ("Taste of Mackerel Pike"). Producer, Shizuo Yamanouchi; Director, Yasujiro Ozu; Screenplay, Yasujiro Ozu and Kogo Noda; Director of Photography, Yushun Atsuta; Art Directors, Tatsuo Hamada and Shigeo Ogiwara; Editor, Yoshiyasu Hamamura; Music, Takanori Saito; Sound Recording, Yoshisaburo Seno.

CAST: Chishu Ryu (Shuhei Hirayama), Shima Iwashita (Machiko Hirayama, *his daughter*), Shinichiro Mikami (Kazuo Hirayama, *his younger son*), Keiji Sada (Koichi Hirayama, *his older son*), Mariko Okada (Akiko Hirayama, *Koichi's wife*), Nobuo Nakamura (Shuzo Kawai), Kuniko Miyake (Nobuko Kawai), Ryuji Kita (Susumu Horie), Eijiro Tono (Sakuma, *the "Gourd"*), Teruo Yoshida (Miura), Daisuke Kato (the ex-sailor), Michiyo Tamaki, Haruko Sugimura, Kyoko Kishida, Toyo Takahashi.

A Shochiku Co., Ltd. Production.

Filmed at Shochiku-Ofuna Studios. Agfacolor. Academy ratio. 133 minutes. Released November 18, 1962.

U.S. VERSION: Released by Shochiku Films of America, Inc. English Subtitles. Alternate title: *The Widower*. 113 minutes. No MPAA rating. Released 1964. Reissued by New Yorker Films at 133 minutes.

Ayako / Aru Osaka no onna ("A Woman in Osaka"). Executive Producers, Sanezumi Fujimoto and Masakatsu Kaneko; Director, Eizo Sugawa; Screenplay, Yoshikata Yoda; Director of Photography, Seiichi Endo; Music, Seiji Hiraoka.

CAST: Reiko Dan (Ayako), Keizo Kawasaki, Kamatari Fujiwara, Kyu Sazanka, Chisako Hara, Hikaru Mayuzumi, Eitaro Ozawa, Homare Suguro.

A Toho Co., Ltd. Production. Eastman Color. Toho Scope. 90 minutes. Released 1962.

U.S. VERSION: Released by Toho International Co., Ltd. English subtitles. 90 minutes. No MPAA rating. Released April 1964.

Bad Boys / Furyo Shonen ("Bad Boys"). Director, Susumu Hani; Screenplay, Susumu Hani, based on the book *Pinioned Wings*; Director of Photography, Mitsuji Kanau; Music, Toru Takemitsu.

CAST: Yukio Yamada, Hirokazu Yoshitake, Koichiro Yamazaki, Yasuo Kurokawa, Masayuki Ito.

Production Company undetermined. Black and white. Academy ratio (?). 89 minutes. Released 1961.

U.S. VERSION: Released by Brandon Films. English subtitles. 89 minutes. No MPAA rating. Released 1966 (?).

The Bad News Bears Go to Japan. Producer, Michael Ritchie; Associate Producer, Hisashi Yabe; Director, John Berry; Co-Producer, Bill Lancaster; Directors of Photography, Gene Polito (US), Kozo Okazaki (Japan); Production Design, Walter Scott Herndon; Editor, Richard H. Harris; Associate Producer, Terry Carr; Music, Paul Chihara; Themes from "The Mikado," Music and Lyrics by W.S. Gilbert and Sir Arthur Sullivan; Songs: "Birdman's Flying High" and "Mean Bones," Music and Lyrics by Paul Chihara; Song Arranger, Mike Melvoin; Set Decorator, Cheryl Kearney; Makeup, Robert Mills; Wardrobe, Tommy Welsh and Nancy Martinelli; Japan Location Liason, Charlotte Dreiman; Property Master, Mike Minor; Unit Production Manager, Terry Carr; Assistant Director, Jerry Ziesmer; 2nd Assistant Director, Alan Brimfield; Editor, Dennis Virkler; Sound Mixer, Gene Cantamesa; Rerecording Mixer, John K. Wilkinson; Music Editor, Robert Krueger; Sound Effects Editor, Bill Andrews and Henry Asman; Assistant Film Editor, Carolyn H. Abe; Key Grip, Marlin Hall. *Japanese Crew*: Production Services, Toei Co., Ltd.; Dialogue Coach, Shinichiro Sawai; Unit Manager, William "Bill" Ross; Interpreter, Michie Ross; Baseball Advisor, Takashi Arakawa; Hair Stylist, Hisako Hanazawa. Promotional Material, Champion Spark Plugs, Denny's, Japan Air Lines, Rawlings, Keio Plaza Hotel, Sony; Animation, Group Tac; Titles, Pacific Title.

CAST: Tony Curtis (Marvin Lazar), Jackie Earle Haley (Kelly Leak), Tomisaburo Wakayama (Coach Shimizu), Antonio Inoki (himself), Hatsune Ishihara (Arika), George Wyner (network director), Lonny Chapman (Louis the Gambler), Matthew Douglas Anton (E.R.W. Tillyard III), Erin Blunt (Ahmad Rahim), George Gonzales (Miguel Agilar), Brett Marx (Jimmy Feldman), David Pollack (Rudy Stein), Jeffrey Louis Starr (Mike Engleberg), Scoody Thornton (Mustapha Rahim), Abraham Unger (Abe Bernstein), Dick Button (himself), Regis Philbin (Harry Hahn), Kinichi Hagimoto (game show host), Hugh Gillin (Pennywall), Robert Sorrells (Locke), Clarence Barnes (Mean Bones Beaudine), Michael Yama (usher), James Staley (network man #4), Dick McGarvin (network man #5), Tak Kubota (referee), Jerry Ziesmer (Eddie of Network), Gene LeBell (Mean Bones' manager), Victor Toyota (interpreter), Yangi Kitadani (fight announcer), Marjorie Jackson (waitress), Jerry Maren (page boy), Tim P. Sullivan (network man #2), Bob Kino (moderator), Dennis Freeman (network man #5), Kyoko Fuji (madam), Ginger Martin (director's aide), Daniel Sasaki (band leader), Don Waters (network man #1), Hector Guerrero (stunt double).

A Michael Ritchie Production, in association with Toei Co., Ltd. A Paramount Pictures Release. A U.S./Japanese co-production in English and Japanese. Color (prints by Movielab). Spherical Panavision. 91 minutes. MPAA rating: "PG." Released 1978.

The Bad Sleep Well / Warui yatsu hodo yoku nemuru ("The Worse You Are the Better You Sleep"). Producers, Tomoyuki Tanaka and Akira Kurosawa; Director/Editor, Akira Kurosawa; Screenplay, Shinobu Hashimoto, Hideo Oguni, Ryuzo Kikushima, Eijiro Hisaita, and Akira Kurosawa; Production Supervisor, Hiroshi Nezu; Director of Photography, Yuzuru Aizawa; Art Director, Yoshiro Muraki; Lighting, Ichiro Inohara; Sound Recording, Fumio Yanoguchi and Hisashi Shimonaga; Music, Masaru Sato; Sound, Toho Dubbing Theatre; Sound Effects, Toho Sound Effects Group.

CAST: Toshiro Mifune (Koichi Nishi), Takeshi Kato (Itakura), Masayuki Mori (Company President Iwabuchi), Takashi Shimura (Administrative Officer Moriyama), Ko Nishimura (Contract Officer Shirai), Kamatari Fujiwara (Accountant Wada), Gen Shimizu (Accountant Miura), Kyoko Kagawa (Keiko Nishi), Tatsuya Mihashi (Tatsuo Iwabuchi), Kyu Sazanka (Kaneko), Chishu Ryu (Public Prosecutor Nonaka), Seiji Miyaguchi (Okakura), Nobuo Nakamura (lawyer), Susumu Fujita (commisioner), Koji Mitsui, Yoshifumi Tajima, and Hisashi Yokomori (journalists), Somesho Matsumoto (Hatano), Kin Sugai (Tomoko Wada), Toshiko Higuchi (Masako Wada), Koji Nanbara (Horiuchi), Yoshio Tsuchiya (A.D.A. secretary), Kunie Tanaka (hit man), Hiromi Mineoka (maid), Natsuko Kahara (Furuya's wife), Yutaka Sada (receptionist), Ikio Sawamura (driver), Ken Mitsuda (Arimura).

A Kurosawa Films/Toho Co., Ltd. Production. A Toho Co., Ltd. Release. Black and white. Toho Scope. Western Electric Mirrophonic recording (encoded with Perspecta Stereophonic Sound). Filmed at Toho Studios, Ltd. (Tokyo). 151 minutes. Released September 4, 1960.

U.S. VERSION: Released by Toho International Co., Ltd. English subtitles. 135 minutes. No MPAA rating. Released January 22, 1963. Reissued by Janus Films. Reissue and home video version restored. Home video version letterboxed. Alternate titles: *The Worse You Are the Better You Sleep* and *The Rose in the Mud.*

Ballad of Death / Hitokiri Kannon-uta ("Kannon's Song of Murder"). Director, Takashi Harada; Screenplay, Koji Takada; Director of Photography, Toshio Masuda; Art Director, Yoshimitsu Amamori; Music, Takeo Yamashita.

CAST: Bunta Sugawara (Priest Ryotatsu), Tomisaburo Wakayama (Dr. Mitamura), Akiko Kudo (Maya), Minoru Oki (Banri), Norihiko Umeji (Rintaro).

A Toei Co., Ltd. Production. Eastman Color. ToeiScope. 88 minutes. Released November 11, 1970.

U.S. VERSION: Release undetermined. English subtitles. No MPAA rating.

Ballad of Narayama / Narayama bushi-ko ("Study on the Ballad of Narayama"). Producers, Ryuzo Otani and Masaharu Kokaji; Director, Keisuke Kinoshita; Screenplay Keisuke Kinoshita, based on the story *Narayama bushi-ko*, by Shichiro Fukuzawa; Director of Photography, Hiroyuki Kusuda; Art Directors, Kisaku Ito and Chiyoo Umeda; Editor, Yoshi Sugihara; Sound Recording, Hisao Ono; Music, Chuji Kinoshita; Ballads: "Nagauta" by Rokuzaemon Kineya, "Joruri" by Matsunosuke Nozawa.

CAST: Kinuyo Tanaka (Orin), Teiji Takahashi (Tatsuhei), Yuko Mochizuki (Tama-yan), Danko Ichikawa (Kesakichi), Keiko Ogasawara (Matsu-yan), Seiji Miyaguchi (Mata-yan), Yunosuke Ito (Matayan's son), Ken Mitsuda (Teru-yan).

A Shochiku Co., Ltd. Production. Fuji Color. Shochiku GrandScope. 98 minutes. Released 1958.

U.S. VERSION: Released by Films Around the World, Inc. English subtitles. Remade in 1983. 98 minutes. No MPAA rating. Released June 19, 1961.

The Ballad of Narayama / Narayama bushi-ko ("Study on the Ballad of Narayama"). Producers, Goro Kusakabe and Jiro Tomoda; Director, Shohei Imamura; Screenplay, Shohei Imamura, based on the stories *Narayama bushi-ko* and *Men of Tohoku*, by Shichiro Fukuzawa; Director of Photography, Masao Tochizawa; Art Director, Tadataka Yoshino; Lighting, Yasuo Iwaki; Music, Shinichiro Ikebe, performed by the Tokyo Concert Orchestra. Songs: "Song of Risuke" by Hitoshi Machida, theme song performed by Sumiko Sakamoto; Costumes, Kyoto Isho; Makeup, Seiko Igawa; Titles, Hideo Suzuki; Sound Recording, Yoshiichi Beniya; Hawk Trainer, Uichiro Takeda; Editor, Hajime Okayasu; Production Controller, Shinji Komiya; Production Manager, Kanji Aoi; Assistant Director, Kunio Takeshige.

CAST: Ken Ogata (Tatsuhei), Sumiko Sakamoto (Orin, *his mother*), Takejo Aki (Tamayan, *his wife*), Tonpei Hidari (Risuke, aka "Smelly," *his brother*), Seiji Kurasaki (Kesakichi, *his eldest son*), Kaoru Shimamori (Tomekichi, *his youngest son*), Ryutaro Tatsumi (Matayan, *the old neighbor*), Junko Takada (Matsu), Nijiko Kyokawa (Okane), Mitsuko Baisho (Oei), Shoichi Ozawa (Shozo), Mitsuaki Fukamizu (Tadayan), Norihei Miki (Shioya, *the old salt dealer*), Akio Yokoyama (Amaya), Sachie Shimura (Amaya's wife), Masami Okamoto (Amaya's son), Fujio Tsuneda (Jisaku), Taiji Tonoyama (Teruyan, *chief village elder*), Keishi Takamine (Arayashiki), Nijiko Kiyokawa (Okane), Tsutomu Miura, Nanshi Kobayashi, Akio Yokoyama, Kaoru Shimamori, Yukie Shimura, Masami Okamoto, Kan Eto, Fusako Iwasaki, Hideo Hasegawa, Kenji Murase, Sayuka Nakamaru, Azumi Tanba, Kosei Sato.

A Toei Co., Ltd. Production. Color. Spherical wide screen. 131 minutes. Released 1983.

U.S. VERSION: Released by Kino International. English subtitles. Previously filmed in 1958. 128 minutes. No MPAA rating. Released April 9, 1984.

Band of Assassins / Shinsengumi ("Shinsen Group"). Producers, Toshiro Mifune, Yoshio Nishikawa, and Hiroshi Inagaki; Director, Tadashi Sawashima; Screenplay, Kenro Matsura; Director of Photography, Kazuo Yamada; Art Director, Hiroshi Ueda; Music, Masaru Sato.

CAST: Toshiro Mifune (Isami Kondo), Keiju Kobayashi (Hijikata), Kinya Kitaoji (Okita), Rentaro Mikuni (Kamo Serizawa), Ganemon Nakamura, Katsuo Nakamura, Umenosuke Nakamura, Yoko Tsukasa, Junko Ikeuchi, Yuriko Hoshi, Yumiko Nogawa.

A Mifune Productions, Ltd. Production. A Toho Co., Ltd. Release. Eastman Color. Panavision. 122 minutes. Released January 1970.

U.S. VERSION: Released by Toho International Co., Ltd. English subtitles. 122 minutes. No MPAA rating. Released April 15, 1970.

Bandits on the Wind / Yato kaze no naka o hashiru ("Bandits Run in the Wind"). Executive Producer, Tomoyuki Tanaka; Director, Hiroshi Inagaki; Screenplay, Masato Ide and Hiroshi Inagaki; Director of Photography, Kazuo Yamada; Music, Kan Ishii.

CAST: Yosuke Natsuki (Taro), Makoto Sato (Gale), Somegoro Ichikawa (Gen), Izumi Yukimura (Kayo), Chishu Ryu (village priest), Akiko Wakabayshi (Sawa), Mannosuke Nakamura, Jun Tatara, Tadao Nakamaru, Koshiro Matsumoto, Chusha Ichikawa.

A Toho Co., Ltd. Production. Black and white. Toho Scope. 111 minutes. Released 1961.

U.S. VERSION: Released by Toho International Co., Ltd. English subtitles. 111 minutes. No MPAA rating. Released September 14, 1962.

Bang! / Asobi no Jikan wa Owaranai ("Playtime Isn't Over"). Producers, Masahiko Yoshida, Yoshinori Sakamoto, Yasuki Tarumi; Director, Sadaaki Haginiwa; Screenplay, Hiroshi Saito; Director of Photography, Hiroshi Takase; Music, Kan Takagi.

Opposite: **(Left to right) Takeshi Kato, Kamatari Fujiwara and Toshiro Mifune in *The Bad Sleep Well* (1960).**

CAST: Masahiro Motoki, Tadashi Nishikawa, Mami Ito.

A Nikkatsu Visual Link/Suntory/NTV Production. Color. Spherical wide screen (?). 111 minutes. Released 1991.

U.S. VERSION: Distributor, if any, is undetermined.

The Barbarian and the Geisha. Executive Producer, Darryl F. Zanuck; Producer, Eugene Frenke; Director, John Huston; Screenplay, Charles Grayson, Alfred Hayes, and Nigel Balchin; Story, Ellis St. Joseph; Director of Photography, Charles Galloway Clarke; Color Consultant, Leonard Doss; Art Directors, Lyle Reynolds Wheeler and Jack Martin Smith; Editor, Stuart Gilmore; Music, Hugo Friedhofer; Technical Supervisor, Mitsuo Hirotsu; Technical Art Adviser, Kisaku Ito; Japanese Technical Adviser, Kampo Yoshikawa; Assistant to the producer, Paul Nakaoka; Assistant to the director, Gladys Hill; Camera Operator, Til Gabbini; Assistant Cameraman; Scotty McEwin; Sound Supervisor, Carlton W. Faulkner; Sound, William Donald Flick and Warren B. Delaplain; Supervising Sound Editor, Walter A. Rossi; Assistant Director, Joseph E. Rickards; Set Decorations, Walter M. Scott and Don C. Greenwood; Executive Wardrobe Designer, Charles LeMaire; Makeup Supervision, Ben Nye, Sr.; Makeup, Webster Overlander; Hair Styling Supervisor, Helen Turpin; Dialog Director, Minoru Inuzaka; Supervising Music Editor, George Adams; Musical Director, Lionel Newman; CinemaScope Lenses, Bausch & Lomb.

CAST: John Wayne (Townsend Harris), Eiko Ando (Okichi), Sam Jaffe (Henry Heusken), So Yamamura (Baron Tamura), Norman Thomson (Captain Edmunds), James Robbins (Lt. Fisher), Morita [no other name given] (Prime Minister), Kodaya Ichikawa (Daimyo), Hiroshi Yamato (Shogun), Tokujiro Iketaniguchi (Harusha), Fuji Kasai (Lord Hotta), Takeshi Kumagai (Chamberlain), Charles "Bad Chuck" Roberson (stunts), Ed Keane.

A Twentieth Century-Fox Film Corporation Production. A Twentieth Century-Fox Film Corp. Release. English language. Filmed at Eiga Film (sic!?) Studios (Kyoto), and on location in Japan, and completed at Twentieth Century-Fox Studios (Century City, California). Eastman Color (prints by De Luxe). CinemaScope. Westrex Recording System. Stereophonic Sound. Working titles: *The Townsend Harris Story* and *The Barbarian*. Partly financed with funds locked up in Japan. 105 minutes. No MPAA rating. Released September 30, 1958.

Barefoot Gen / Hadashi no Gen ("Barefoot Gen") **[animated]**. Producer/Screenplay, Keiji Nakazawa; Director, Mori Masaki; Director of Photography, Kinichi Ishikawa; Music, Kentaro Haneda.

VOICE CHARACTERIZATIONS: (undetermined).

A Gen Production. A Herald Enterprises, Inc. Release. Color. Wide screen. 85 minutes. Released 1983.

U.S. VERSION: Released by Tara Releasing. 80 minutes. No MPAA rating. Released June 13, 1992.

The Bastard / Akutaro ("The Bastard"). Producer, Masayuki Takagi; Director, Seijun Suzuki; Screenplay, Ryozo Kasahara, based on the novel by Toko Kon; Director of Photography, Shigeyoshi Mine; Art Director, Takeo Kimura; Music, Hajime Okumura; Assistant Director, Saburo Endo.

CAST: Ken Yamanouchi (Togo Konno), Masako Zumi (Emiko Okumura), Midori Ashiro (Yoshi Okano), Hiharu Kuri (Ponta, *a geisha*), Ninsuke Ashida (Principal Kondo), Hamime Sugiyama (Marui, *a student*), Keisuke Noro (Suzumura, *a student*), Isao Sano (Dr. Okamura), Rieko Takamine (Takako, *Togo's mother*), Iko Azuma (Masae, *Yoshie's mother*).

A Nikkatsu Corp. Production. Black and white. NikkatsuScope. 95 minutes. Released 1963.

U.S. VERSION: Released by Nikkatsu Corp. English subtitles. Alternate titles: *The Young Rebel* and *The Incorrigible One*. 95 minutes. No MPPA rating. Released 1993.

Battle in Outer Space / Uchu Daisenso ("Great War in Space"). Pro-

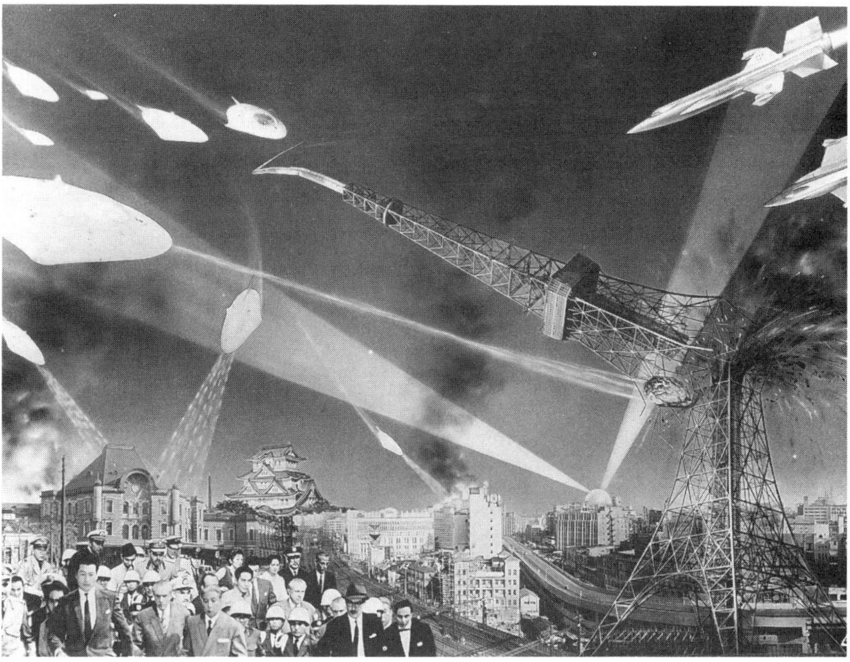

Colorful still from *Battle in Outer Space* (1959). Look closely and you will find three Harold S. Conways among the fleeing citizens.

ducer, Tomoyuki Tanaka; Director, Ishiro Honda; Screenplay, Shinichi Sekizawa; Story, Jotaro Okami; Art Director, Teruaki Abe; Director of Photography, Hajime Koizumi; Editor, Ichiji Taira; Music, Akira Ifukube; Sound Recording, Choshichiro Mikami; Production Manager, Yasuaki Sakamoto; Assistant Director, Koji Kajita; Lighting, Rokuro Ishikawa; Sound, Toho Dubbing Theatre; Sound Effects, Toho Sound Effects Group. *Toho Special Effects Group*: Director, Eiji Tsuburaya; Art Director, Akira Watanabe; Photography, Teisho Arikawa; Lighting, Kuichiro Kishida; Matte Work; Hiroshi Mukoyama; Optical Photography, Kinsaburo Araki.

CAST: Ryo Ikebe (Major Ichiro Katsumiya), Kyoko Anzai (Etsuko Shiraishi), Minoru Takada (Dr. Adachi), Koreya Senda (defense commander), Len Stanford (Dr. Roger Richardson), Harold S. Conway (Dr. Immerman), Elise Richter (Sylvia), Hisaya Ito (Koguri), Yoshio Tsuchiya (Iwamura), Kozo Nomura (rocket commander), Fuyuki Murakami (Inspector Ariaki of the International Police), George Whyman, Nadao Kirino, Ikio Sawamura, Osman Yusef, Jiro Kimagawa, Katsumi Tezuka, Mitsuo Isuda, Tadashi Okabe, Yasuhisa Tsutumi, Kisao Hatamochi, Koichi Sato, Tatsuo Araki, Rinsaku Ogata, Keisumi Yamada, Malcom Pearce, Leonard Walsh, Heinz Bodmer, Dona Carlson, Yokikose Kamimera, Yutaka Oka, Shigeo Kato, Saburo Kadowaki, Yushihiko Goxoo, Shinjiro Hirota.

A Toho Co., Ltd. Production. A Western Electric Mirrophonic recording (encoded Perspecta Stereophonic Sound). Eastman Color (processed by Far West Laboratories, Ltd.). Toho Scope. 93 minutes. Released December 26, 1959.

U.S. VERSION: Released by Columbia Pictures Corporation. English-dubbed. English Language Version Production, Bellucci Productions; Dialogue, Joseph Bellucci; prints by Pathé. Copyright June 1,

1960 by Columbia Pictures Corp. Double-billed with *12 to the Moon* (Columbia, 1960). 90 minutes. No MPAA rating. Released May/June 1960.

The Battle of Okinawa / Gekido no showashi – Okinawa ketsusen ("Strong, Ominous Movement – Battle of Okinawa"). Producers, Sanezumi Fujimoto and Hiroshi Haryu; Director, Kihachi Ikamoto; Screenplay, Kaneto Shindo; Director of Photography, Hiroshi Murai; Art Director, Yoshiro Murakai; Music, Masaru Sato; Asst. Director, Kensho Yamashita. *Toho Special Effects Group:* Director, Teruyoshi Nakano.

CAST: Keiju Kobayashi, Yuzo Kayama, Tetsuro Tamba, Tatsuya Nakadai, Mayumi Ozora, Katsuhiko Sasaki, Kenji Sahara, Eisei Amamoto, Ryo Ikebe, Ichiro Nakaya, Goro Mutsumi, Kamatari Fujiwara, Takamaru Sasaki, Akira Yamauchi, Eijiro Tono, Sachio Sakai, Ren Yamamoto, Seishiro Kuno, Chotaro Togin, Wataru Omae, Shoichi Hirose, Yutaka Sada, Kazuo Suzuki, Yutaka Nakayama, Akira Nishikawa.

A Toho Co., Ltd. Production. Color. Panavision. 149 minutes. Released 1971.

U.S. VERSION: Released by Min-On of America, Inc. English subtitles. 149 minutes. No MPAA rating. Released September 11, 1973.

Battle of the Japan Sea / Nihonkai Daikaisen ("Great Battle of the Japan Sea"). Executive Producer, Tomoyuki Tanaka; Director, Seiji Maruyama; Screenplay, Toshio Yasumi; Director of Photography, Hiroshi Murai; Art Director Takeo Kita; Music, Masaru Sato. *Toho Special Effects Group*: Director, Eiji Tsuburaya; Photography, Mototaka Tomioka and Yoichi Manoda; Art Director, Noriyoshi Inoue; Wire Manipulation, Fumio Nakadai; Assistant Director, Teruyoshi Nakano.

CAST: Toshiro Mifune (Admiral Togo), Tatsuya Nakadai (Colonel Akashi), Yuzo Kayama (Commander Hirose), Chishu Ryu (General Nogi), Mitsuko Kusabue (Mrs. Togo), Ryutaro Tatsumi (General Yamamoto), Koshiro Matsumoto (Emperor Meiji), Toshio Kurosawa (Pvt. 1st Class Maeyama), Susumu Fujita, Yoko Tsukasa, Akira Kubo, Makoto Sato, Susumu Fujita, Akihiko Hirata, Yoshio Tsuchiya, Kenji Sahara, Yoshifumi Tajima, Hiroshi Koizumi, Jun Tazaki, Takeshi Kato, Yutaka Sada, Kazuo Suzuki, Wataru Omae, Chotaro Togin, Seishiro Kuno, Yutaka Oka, Fumiko Homma, Ted Gunther, Jacob Shapiro, Harold S. Conway, Hans Horneff, Osman Yusef, Peter Williamson, Andrew Hughes.

A Toho Co., Ltd. Production. Eastman Color. Toho Scope. 128 minutes. Released August 13, 1969.

U.S. VERSION: Released by Toho International Co., Ltd. English subtitles. 128 minutes. MPAA rating: "G." Released October 28, 1970.

Beast Alley / Kemonomichi ("Animal Trail"). Executive Producers, Sanezumi Fujimoto and Masakatsu Kaneko; Director, Eizo Sugawa; Screenplay, Yoshiro Shirasaka and Eizo Sugawa; Director of Photography, Yasumichi Fukuzawa; Music, Toru Takemitsu.

CAST: Junko Ikeuchi (Tamiko), Keiju Kobayashi, Ryo Ikebe, Yunosuke Ito, Eitaro Ozawa, Susumu Kurobe.

A Toho Co., Ltd. Production. Eastman Color. Toho Scope. 150 minutes. Released 1965.

U.S. VERSION: Released by Toho International Co., Ltd. English subtitles. Possibly released in the United States in black and white. 142 minutes. No MPAA rating. Released July 1966.

The Beast and the Magic Sword. Executive Producer, Sigueiro Amachi; Producer-Director-Screenplay, Jocinto Molina (Alvarez); Director of Photography, Julio Burgos.

CAST: Paul Naschy [Jocinto Molina Alvarez] (Count Waldemar Daninsky), Julia Saly, Beatriz Escudero, Sigueiro Amachi, Junko Asahina, Violeta Cela, Yoko Fuji, Gerard Tichy, Conrado San Martin.

An Aconito Film (Madrid)/Amachi Films (Tokyo) Production. A Japanese-Spanish co-production. Eastman Color. Wide screen (1.66:1). Running time undetermined. Released 1983.

U.S. VERSION: Never released theatrically in the United States (?). Sold directly to television (?). Released in Spain in 1983 as *La Bestia y la Espada Magica* ("The Beast and the Magic Sword"), running 118 minutes. Working title: "La Bestia y los samurais" ("The Beast and the Samurais"). Last of the Spanish-made "Count Daninsky the Werewolf" series, preceded, in order, by *Frankenstein's Bloody Terror* (U.S. release, 1972), *Night of the Werewolf* (U.S. release, 1968), *Assignment Terror* (U.S. release, 1970), *The Werewolf and the Vampire Woman* (U.S. release, 1975), *The Fury of the Wolfman* (U.S. release, 1971) *Doctor Jekyll and the Werewolf* (U.S. release, 1974), *Curse of the Devil* (U.S. release, 1977), *Horror of the Werewolf* (U.S. release, 1976), and *Return of the Wolfman* (U.S. release, 1980). 100 minutes. No MPAA rating.

The Beasts' Carnival. Producer-Director-Screenplay, Jocinto Molina (Alvarez); Director of Photography, Alejandro Ulloa.

CAST: Paul Naschy [Jocinto Molina Alvarez] (The Spainard), Eiko Nagashima (Mieko), Lautaro Murua, Silvia Aguilar, Azucena Hernandez, Julia Saly, Kogi Maritugu, Mieko Gustanave.

A Dalmata Films (Madrid)/Hori Kikaku Co., Ltd. (Tokyo) Production. A Japanese-Spanish co-production. Filmed in Japan, Thailand, and Spain. Eastman Color. Wide screen (1.66:1). Running time undetermined. Released 1980.

U.S. VERSION: Distributor, if any, is undetermined. Released in Spain in 1980 as *El Carnaval de los bestias*

Beat '71 / Boso shudan '71. ("Fast, Irresponsible Group"). Director, Toshiya Fujita; Screenplay, Shuichi Nagahara and Tatsuya Asai; Director of Photography, Kenji Hagiwara; Art Director, Kazuhiko Chiba; Music, Hiroki Tamaki.

CAST: Meiko Kaji (Furiko), Takeo Chii (Takaaki), Yoshio Inaba (Yoshitaro Araki), Yoshio Harada, Tatsuya Fuji, Bunjaku Han, Michiko Tsukasa.

A Nikkatsu Corp. Production. Fujicolor. NikkatsuScope. 87 minutes. Released January 3, 1971.

U.S. VERSION: Release undetermined. English subtitles. No MPAA rating.

The Beautiful Swindlers. Producer, Pierre Roustang. *Amsterdam:* Director, Roman Polanski; Screenplay, Roman Polanski and Gerard Brach; Director of Photography, Jerzy Lipman; Editor, Rita von Royen; Music, Krzysztof. *Naples:* Director, Ugo Gregoretti; Director of Photography, Tonino Delli Colli; Music, Piero Umiliani. *Paris:* Director, Claude Chabrol; Director of Photography, Jean Rabier; Editor, Jacques Gaillard; Music, Pierre Jansen. *Tokyo:* Director, Hiromichi Horikawa; Director of Photography, Asakazu Nakai; Music, Keitaro Miho.

CAST: *Amsterdam:* Nicole Karen, Jan Teulings, Arnold Gelderman. *Naples:* Gabriella Giorgelli, Beppe Mannaiuolo, Guido Giuseppone. *Paris:* Jean-Pierre Cassel, Catherine Deneuve, Francis Blanche, Sacha Briquet, Jean-Louis Maury. *Tokyo:* Mie Hama, Ken Mitsuda.

A Ulysse Productions/Primex Films/ Lux Films/Vides/Toho Co., Ltd./Caesar Films Production. A French-Dutch-Japanese-Italian co-production in French, Dutch, Japanese, and Italian with appropriate subtitles. Eastman Color. Franscope and Toho Scope. 90 minutes. Released 1964 (?).

U.S. VERSION: Released by Ellis Films and Continental Distributing, Inc. English subtitles. Released in France in August 1964 as *Les plus belles escroqueries du monde*, and in Italy in 1964 as *Le truffe piu belle del mondo.* A fifth segment, directed by Jean-Luc Godard and featuring Jean Seberg, Charles Denner, and Laszlo Szabo, was excised and released as *Le grand escroc*, a short subject. Released in black and white in the United States. Announced as *World's Greatest Swindlers.* 90 minutes. No MPAA rating. Released September 12, 1967.

Beauty's Sorrows / Bijin aishu ("Beauty's Sorrows"). Director, Yasujiro Ozu; Screenplay, Tadao Ikeda, based on a story by Henri de Regnier; Director of Photography, Hideo Shigehara.

CAST: Tatsuo Saito, Tokihiko Okada, Yukiko Inoue, Sotaro Okada, Mitsuko Yoshikawa.

A Shochiku Co., Ltd. Production. Filmed at Shochiku-Kamata Studios.

Twenty-two-month-old Hiro Suzuki (wearing hat) in Kon Ichikawa's *Being Two Isn't Easy* (1962).

Silent with benshi. Black and white. Academy ratio. 158 minutes. Released May 29, 1931.

U.S. VERSION: Never released in the United States. A lost film.

Before Dawn / Yoake mae ("Before Dawn"). Director, Kozaburo Yoshimura; Screenplay, Kaneto Shindo; Director of Photography, Yoshio Miyajima; Music, Akira Ifukube.

CAST: Osamu Takizawa (Hanzo Aoyama), Nobuko Otawa (his daughter), Shin Date (his father), Chikako Hosokawa (his mother), Fukuko Sayo (his wife), Akira Yamanouchi (his son), Masao Shimizu (Juheiji), Jukichi Uno (Kanekichi), Taiji Tonoyama (ox-cart driver).

A Kindai Eiga Kyokai-Mingei Theatrical Troupe Production. A Toho Co., Ltd. Release. Black and white. 142 minutes. Released 1953.

U.S. VERSION: Released by Toho International Co., Ltd. English subtitles. 142 minutes (possibly cut to 120 minutes). No MPAA rating. Released November 4, 1966.

Being Two Isn't Easy / Watashi wa nisai ("I Am Two Years Old"). Producers, Hidemasa Nagata and Kon Ichikawa; Planning, Hiroaki Fujii; Director, Kon Ichikawa; Screenplay, Natto Wada, based on a story by Michio Matsuda; Director of Photography, Setsuo Kobayashi; Art Director, Takashi Senda; Lighting, Yukio Ito; Editor, Tatsuji Nakashizu; Sound Recording, Kimio Hida; Music, Yasushi Akutagawa; Animation, Ryuichi Yokoyama.

CAST: Hiro Suzuki (Taro, *the baby*), Eiji Funakoshi (Goro, *his father*), Fujiko Yamamoto (Chiyo, *his mother*), Kumeko Urabe (his grandmother), Misako Watanabe (his aunt), Mantaro Ushio (laundryman), Kyoko Kishida (Chiyo's friend), Masako Kyosuka (older sister of the mother), Shiro Otsuji (the young doctor), Mayumi Kurata (next-door neighbor), Jun Hamamura (middle-aged doctor), Akira Natsuki (doctor at hospital), Yoko Hizakura, Hiroko Hanai.

A Daiei Motion Picture Co., Ltd. Production. Agfacolor. Academy Ratio. 88 minutes. Released November 18, 1962.

U.S. VERSION: Released directly to the non-theatrical market by Janus Films. Alternate title: *I Am Two Years Old.* English subtitles. No MPAA rating. Released 1971.

The Bell / Kane ("The Bell"). Producer/Director/Screenplay, Yukio Aoshima; Director of Photography, Tadashi Sato, Mitsuo Nakagawa, and Tomomi Kamata; Music, Yukio Aoshima and Keitaro Miho.

CAST: Keitaro Miho, Keisuke Ishizu, Katsuhiko Matsunami, Yukio Aoshima. Production company undetermined. 16mm? Black and white. 61 minutes. Released 1967. *Note:* There is no dialog, just music and sound effects.

The Bermuda Depths / Bamyuda no nazo ("Mystery of Bermuda"). Producers, Arthur Rankin, Jr., Jules Bass; Associate Producer, Benni Korzen; Director, Tom Kotani; Screenplay, William Overgard; Story, Arthur Rankin, Jr.; Director of Photography, Jeri Sopanen; Music, Maury Laws; Editor, Barry Walter; Song "Jennie," Music by Maury Laws, Lyrics by Jules Bass, vocals by Claude Carmichael; Director of Underwater Photography, Stanton Waterman; Assistant Underwater Photography, George Waterman; Diving Consultant, Teddy Tucker; Location Manager, J.A.D. Froud; Sound, Francis Daniels; Boom Man, Keith Gardner; Sound Mixer, Richard Elder; Music Recording, John Richards; Gaffer, Michael Lesser; Best Boy, Jonathan Lumiere; Key Grip, Dustin Smith; Makeup, Fern Buchner; Propman, Peter Polotanoff; Production Supervisor, Barbara Hilsey; Production Assistants, Thomas Bush, Todd Rankin, Linda Wilkinson; Assistant to the Director, Nobuko Oganasofa; 1st Assistant Cameraman, Douglas Hart; 2nd Assistant Cameraman, Thomas Weston; Still Photographer, Peter Moran; Special Props, Gary Zeller, Jean Vickery, Beverly Welch, Donald Berry; Costumes, Emma Randolph; Sound Effects Editing, Peter Stass; Assistant Editors, Jill Savic, Wendy Warner, Jim Tatum, Jr.; Casting Consultant, Shirley Rich. *Special Effects Unit* (Tsuburaya Enterprises, Inc.): Associate Producers, Kinshiro Okube, Masaki Iizuki; Director, Mark Segawa; Assistant Director, Akihiko Takahasi; Optical Effects, Minoru Nakano.

CAST: Leigh McCloskey (Magnus Dens), Carl Weathers (Eric), Connie Selleca (Jennie Haniver), Julie Woodson (Doshan), Ruth Attaway (Delia), Burl Ives (Dr. Paulis), Eilse Frick, Nicholas Ingham, Kevin Petty, Nicole Marsh, George Richards, John Instone, Jonathan Ingham, Patricia Rego, Doris Riley, Tracy Anne Sadler.

A Rankin/Bass Productions, Inc. Production, in association with Tsuburaya Enterprises, Inc. An Arthur Rankin, Jr./ Jules Bass Film. Distributed by JAD Films International, Inc. A Japanese/U.S. coproduction in English. The producers gratefully acknowledge the valuable cooperation of the Government of Bermuda and its Ministries and the Bermuda Biological Station. Filmed on location in Bermuda, and at Tsuburaya Enterprises, Inc. Studios (Tokyo). Color by Movielab. Spherical Panavision. 90 minutes. July 20, 1979.

U.S. VERSION: Never released theatrically in the United States. Broadcast on the American Broadcasting Companies, Inc. (ABC) network January 27, 1978. Syndicated by JAD TV. 95 minutes.

Between Women and Wives / Tsuma to onna no aida ("Between Women and Wives"). Producers, Ichiro Sato, Kiichi Ichikawa, and Osamu Tanaka; Directors, Kon Ichikawa and Shiro Toyoda; Screenplay, Toshio Yazumi, based on a novel by Harumi Setouchi; Directors of Photography, Kozo Okazaki and Kiyoshi Hasegawa; Art Director, Shinobu Muraki; Music, Masaru Sato; Sound Recording, Eishiro Hayashi and Fumio Yanoguchi; Lighting, Shinji Kojima and Kiyohisa Hirano.

CAST: Yoshiko Mita (Azumi), Mayumi Ozora (Yuko), Wakako Sakai (Noriko), Akiko Nishina (Yoko), Meiko Kaji (Eiko Maeda), Takahiro Tamura (Masayuki, *Yuko's husband*), Saburo Shinoda (Kenichi), Yusuke Okada (Taku, *Noriko's husband*).

A Geiensha Production, in association with Toho Co., Ltd. A Toho Co., Ltd. Release. Color. Panavision (?). 111 minutes. Released January 17, 1976.

U.S. VERSION: Released by Toho International Co., Ltd. (?). English subtitles. 111 minutes. No MPAA rating. Released May 21, 1976.

BGS of Ginza / Yoru no nettaigyo ("Tropical Fish in the Night"). Director, Umeji Inoue; Screenplay, Umeji Inoue and Akira Saiga; Director of Photography, Keiji Maruyama; Art Director, Gohei Morita; Music, Kenjiro Hirose.

CAST: Yoshiko Kayama (Miwa), Yumiko Nogawa (Yuka), Kikko Matsuoka (Hideko), Etsuko Nami (Kiriko), Bontaro Miake (Nonomiya), Yasunori Irikawa (Shunichi), Takuya Fujioka (Gondo), Sentaro Tatsuya (Oki), Rumi Koyama, Saroi Yuki, Taiichiro Hirokawa, Yasushi Nagata, Jun Kajima, Chikako Kaga, Hiroshi Aoyama, Noboru Nakada, Kentaro Imai, Ryusuke Kita, Kenji Nagisa, Daisuke Nakano, Kosaku Yamayoshi, Shuichi Oki, Akiye Kokubu, Rutaro Hanai.

A Shochiku Co., Ltd. Production. Color. Released May 1965.

U.S. VERSION: Released by Shochiku Films of America, Inc. English subtitles. Running time undetermined. No MPAA rating. Released April 20, 1970.

The Big Boss / Ankokugai no Kaoyaku ("Beard of the Dark City"). Producer, Tomoyuki Tanaka; Director, Kihachi Okamoto; Screenplay, Motosada Nishigame and Shinichi Sekizawa; Director of Photography, Asaichi Nakai; Art Director, Iwao Akune; Music, Akira Ifukube.

CAST: Koji Tsuruta (Ryuta Komatsu), Akira Takarada (Mineo Komatsu, *his brother*), Toshiro Mifune (Kashimura), Mitsuko Kusabue (Rie), Yumi Shirakawa (Junko), Keiko Yanagawa (Yoko).

A Toho Co., Ltd. Production. Fuji Color. Toho Scope. 100 minutes. Released January 15, 1959.

U.S. VERSION: Release undetermined, possibly by Toho International Co., Ltd. in subtitled format. No MPAA rating.

Big Joys, Small Sorrows / Shin Yorokobimo Kanashimimo Ikutoshitsuki ("New Times of Joy and Sorrow"). Producers, Nobuyoshi Otani, Soya Hikida, Kazuo Watanabe, and Masatake Wakita; Director/Screenplay, Keisuke Kinoshita; Director of Photography, Kozo Okazaki; Music, Chuji Kinoshita.

CAST: Go Kato, Hitoshi Ueki, Reiko Ohara, Yoko Shinoyama, Hayao Okamoto, Kunio Konishi, Misako Konno, Kiichi Nakai.

A Shochiku Co., Ltd. Production. Color. Panavision (?). 130 minutes. Released 1986.

U.S. VERSION: Released by Shochiku Films of America, Inc. in subtitled format. 130 minutes. No MPAA rating. Released July 1986.

Big Shots Die at Dawn / Kaoyaku akatsukini shisu ("The Beard Died at Dawn"). Executive Producers, Reiji Miwa and Tomoyuki Tanaka; Director, Kihachi Okamoto; Screenplay, Ichiro Ikeda and Ei Ogawa; Director of Photography, Yukio Ota; Music, Sei Ikeno.

CAST: Yuzo Kayama (Jiro), Jun Tazaki, Yukiko Shimazaki, Akihiko Hirata, Kumi Mizuno, Mickey Curtis, Tadao Nakamaru.

A Toho Co., Ltd. Production. Eastman Color. Toho Scope. 97 minutes. Released 1961.

U.S. VERSION: Release undetermined, likely Toho International Co., Ltd. in subtitled format. 97 minutes. No MPAA rating.

The Big Wave. Executive Producer, Pearl S. Buck; Producer/Director, Tad Danielewski; Screenplay, Pearl S. Buck and Tad Danielewski, based on the

A heavily made up Sessue Hayakawa in *The Big Wave* (1961).

1948 novel *The Big Wave* by Pearl S. Buck; Director of Photography, Ichio Yamazeki; Editor, Akikazu Kono; Music, Toshiro Mayuzumi, conducted by Hiroshi Yoshizawa; Song "Be Ready at Dawn," Music by Toshiro Mayuzumi, Lyrics by Tad Danielewski; Production Supervisor, Masayuki Nakajima; Production Manager, Clark Playlow; Assistant Director, Joseph E. Markarof; Dialogue Coach, Sylvia Danielewski; Script Supervisor, Noriko Maebatake; Art Director, Itsuro Hirata; Property Master, Satoru Sango; Special Effects, Kenji Inagawa; Wardrobe, Yoshiaki Murata and Iku Tsuda; Makeup, Haruhiko Yamada; Gaffer, Yokichi Hishinuma; Sound Recording, Hidejiro Yotsie; Sound Mixing, Michio Okazaki; Sound Effects, Toho Sound Effects Group; Sound, Toho Recording Centre.

CAST: Sessue Hayakawa (The Old Gentleman), Ichizo Itami (Toru), Mickey Curtis (Yukio), Kiji Shitara (Toru as a boy), Hiroyuki Ota (Yukio as a boy), Rumiko Sasa (Setsu), Judy Ongg (Setsu as a girl), Reiko Higa (Haruko), Sachiko Atami (Haruko as a girl), Heihachiro "Henry" Okawa (Yukio's father), Cheiko Murata (Yukio's mother), Tetsu Nakamura (Toru's father), Frank Tokunaga (Toru's grandfather), Shigeru Nihonmatsu (old servant), Noriko Sengoku (Toru's mother).

A Stratton Productions, Inc. Production, in cooperation with Toho Co., Ltd. A Japanese/U.S. co-production in English. Western Electric Mirrophonic Recording. Black and white (processed by Tokyo Laboratory, Ltd.). Wide screen. 98 minutes (?). Released 1961 (?).

U.S. VERSION: Released by Allied Artists Pictures Corporation. Prints by De Luxe. 73 minutes. No MPAA rating. Released April 2, 1962.

Big Wind from Tokyo / Ishinaka sensei gyojoki ("Conduct Report of Professor Ishinaka"). Director, Seiji Maruyama.

CAST: Akira Takarada, Toshio Kurosawa, Keiko Sawai, Megumi Matsumoto.

A Toho Co., Ltd. Production. Color. Toho Scope. 90 minutes. Released December 1966.

U.S. VERSION: Released by Toho International Co., Ltd. English subtitles. Previously filmed as *Conduct Report of Professor Ishinaka* (1950). 90 minutes. No MPAA rating. Released October 1967.

A Billionaire / Okuman Choja ("A Billionaire"). Planning, Enzaburo Honda; Director, Kon Ichikawa; Screenplay, Kon Ichikawa, Natto Wada, Kobo Abe, Taizo Yokoyama, and Keiji Hasebe; Director of Photography, Takeo Ito; Lighting, Koji Hirata; Music, Ikuma Dan; Art Director, Totetsu Kirakawa; Sound Recording, Shigeto Yasue.

CAST: Isao Kimura (Koroku Tate), Yoshiko Kuga (Sute Kagami), Isuzu Yamada (Hanakuma, *the middle-aged geisha*), Yunosuke Ito (Ebizo Dan, *the politician*), Kinzo Shin (Juji Gan, *the unemployed*), Toyoko Takahashi (Han Gan, *his wife*), Eiji Okada (Monta, *their eldest son*), Yoshi Kato (Sanpeita Den, *the superintendent of the tax office*), Sachiko Hidari (Asako, *his daughter*).

A Seinen-Haiyu Club Production. A Shintoho Co., Ltd. Release. Black and white. Academy ratio. 83 minutes. Released November 22, 1954.

U.S. VERSION: Distributor undetermined. English subtitles. 83 minutes. No MPAA rating.

The Birth of Judo / Yawara sempu ("Judo Cyclone"). Director/Screenplay, Kunio Watanabe; Story, Tsuneo Tomita; Director of Photography, Takeo Kawarazaki; Art Director, Seiichi Toriizuka; Music, Eiichi Yamada.

CAST: Soichi Hirai (Shogoro Yano), Yoko Matsuyama (Suga Yano), Shintaro Kuraoka (Yujiro Toda), Ryohei Uchida (Gennosuke Egaki), Tetsuro Tamba (Shuzo Izawa).

A Shochiku Co., Ltd. Production. Color. Shochiku GrandScope (?). Released March 1965.

U.S. VERSION: Released by Shochiku Films of America, Inc. English subtitles. Running time undetermined. No MPAA rating. Released July 9, 1965.

The Bite. Director, Kan Mukai.

CAST: (not available).

Production company undetermined.

Black and white. Release date undetermined.

U.S. VERSION: Released by Olympic International Films. 62 minutes. No MPAA rating. Released 1965.

Black Cat Mansion / Borei kaibyo yashiki ("Mansion of the Monstrous Ghost-Cat"). Producer, Mitsugu Okura; Director, Nobuo Nakagawa; Screenplay, Jiro Fujishima and Yoshihiro Ishikawa; Director of Photography, Tadashi Nishimoto.

CAST: Toshio Hosokawa, Midori Chikuma, Fuji Satsuki, Shin Shibata, Keinosuke Wada, Ryuzaburo Nakamura, Fumiko Migata.

A Shintoho Co., Ltd. Production. Western Electric Mirrophonic recording. Black and white. Shintoho Scope. 69 minutes. Released 1958.

U.S. VERSION: Distributor, if any, is undetermined. No MPAA rating.

Black Lizard / Kurotokage ("Black Lizard"). Producer, Akira Oda; Director, Kinji Fukasaku; Screenplay, Masashige Narusawa and Kinji Fukasaku, based on the play by Yukio Mishima (itself based on the novel by Rampo Edogawa); Director of Photography, Hiroshi Dowaki; Editor, Keiichi Uraoka; Production Manager, Tatsuo Hagiwara; Art Director, Kyohei Morita; Music, Isao Tomita; Song Performance, Akihiro Maruyama; Assistant Director, Hideo Oe; Set Decoration, Keinosuke Ishiwatari; Costumes, Masako Watanabe; Sound, Toshio Tanaka; Sound Effects, Hirobumi Sato.

CAST: Akihiro Maruyama (Midorigawa, *aka Kurotokage, the Black Lizard*), Isao Kimura (Detective Kogoro Akechi), Keiko Matsuoka (Sanae Iwasa/Yoko Sakurayama), Junya Usami (Shobei Iwasa), Yusuke Kawazu (Junichi Amamiya), Ko Nishimura (Keiji Matoba), Toshiko Kobayashi (Hina), Sonosuke Oda (Harada), Kinji Hattori (Toyama), Kyoichi Sato (Ohkawa), Jun Kato (Sakai), Ryuji Funakoshi (Kizu), Mitsuko Takera (show dancer), Tetsuro Tamba (Kuroki, *Akechi's friend*), Yukio Mishima (living doll).

A Shochiku Co., Ltd. Production. Fujicolor (processed by Shochiku Laboratory), Shochiku GrandScope. 86 minutes. Released August 1968.

U.S. VERSION: Released by Shochiku Films of America, Inc. English subtitles. 86 minutes. No MPAA rating. Released July 1969. Reissued by Cinevista with English subtitles in February 1985 and running 83 minutes. *Credits for reissue version*: A Rene Fuentes-Chao & John R. Tilley Presentation. Subtitles, Cinetype, Inc. (Hollywood); Subtitles Editor, H. Eisenman. The AFI Catalog credits Eastman Color. Not widely distributed until the late 1980s/early 1990s. Followed by *Black Rose* (1969).

Black Rain / Kuroi ame ("Black Rain"). Executive Producer/Director, Shohei Imamura; Producer, Hisa Iino; Screenplay, Shohei Imamura and Toshiro Ishido, based on the novel by Masuji Ibuse; Director of Photography, Takashi Kawamata; Cameramen, Masashi Chikamori, Masakazu Oka, and Junichi Watanabe; Lighting, Yasuo Iwaki; Editor, Hajime Okayasu; Art Director, Hisao Inagaki; Set Decorator, Akira Kanda; Special Effects, Masatoshi Saito; Music, Toru Takemitsu, performed by Tokyo Concerts; Makeup, Shigeko Igawa; Special Makeup Effects, Isao Haruyama; Title Calligraphy, Hirohide Watanabe; Sound Recording, Kenichi Benitani; Dialect Adviser, Shigeko Ohara; Yuichi's Stone Carvings, Yoichi Shimizu; Production Supervisor, Yasushi Matsuda; Production Manager, Kunihide Hiramasu; Assistant Directors, Kitaka Tsukino, Tadashi Miike, Nobuaki Ito.

CAST: Yoshiko Tanaka (Yasuko), Kazuo Kitamura (Shigematsu Shizuma), Etsuko Ichihara (Shigeko Shizuma), Shoichi Ozawa (Shokichi), Norihei Miki (Kotaro), Keisuke Ishida (Yuichi), Hisako Hara (Kin), Masa Yamada (Tatsu), Tamaki Sawa (middle-aged woman in Ikemoto-ya), Shoji Kobayashi (Katayama), Kazuko Shirakawa (old woman with white flag), Kenjiro Ishimaru (Aono), Mayumi Tateichi (Fumiko of Ikemoto-ya), Taiji Tonoyama (old priest), Fujio Tsuneda (40-year-old man with burns), Toshie Kusunoki (Kane), Reiko Nanao (Rui), Satoshi Iinuma (Takamaru), Toshi-

Ken Takakura and Michael Douglas in Ridley Scott's *Black Rain* (1989), not to be confused with Shohei Imamura's 1988 film of the same name.

hiko Miki (Factory Foreman Fujita), Yohachi Fuji (cab driver), Sabu Kawahara (Kanemaru), Mitsunori Fukamizu (Nojima), Noboru Mitani (post office clerk), Shuji Otaki (Dr. Fujita), Isayoshi Yamazaki (young Yakuza), Mari Kamei (nurse), Tatsuya Irie (young man), Kazue Minami (1st village woman), Takaomi Miura (boy), Hiromi Yasui (2nd village woman), Toru Iwasaki (Nojima's stepfather), Nobuko Tani (Nojima's stepmother), Shinichi Hibino (Dr. Ando), Tessui Tada (Buddhist monk), Toshiko Yokota (woman throwing roof tiles), Yoshiro Hori (wood seller), Hitomi Ishihara, Junko Hori (women of the Nojima family), Tetsuhiko Miyoshi (Takeo Takamaru), Kazuko Kawakami (Takamaru's 2nd wife), Junko Takahashi (middle-aged woman at station).

An Imamura Productions/Hayashibara Group/Tohokushinsha Film Co., Ltd. Production. A Toei Co., Ltd. Release. Black and white. Spherical wide screen. 123 minutes. Released 1988.

U.S. VERSION: Released by Angelika Films. English subtitles. 117 minutes. No MPAA rating. Released September 27, 1989.

Black Rain. Executive Producers, Craig Bolotin and Julie Kirkham; Associate Producer, Alan Poul; Producers, Stanley R. Jaffe and Sherry Lansing; Director, Ridley Scott; Screenplay, Craig Bolotin and Warren Lewis; Director of Photography, Jan De Bont; Art Director, Norris Spencer; Editor, Tom Rolf; Costume Designer, Ellen Mirojnick; Music, Hans Zimmer; Casting, Dianne Crittenden.

CAST: Michael Douglas (Nick), Andy Garcia (Charlie Vincent), Ken Takakura (Masahiro Matsumoto), Kate Capshaw (Joyce Kingsley), Yusaku Matsuda (Sato), Shigeru Koyama (Ohashi), John Spencer (Oliver), Tomisaburo Wakayama (Sugai), Yuya Uchida (Nashida).

A Jaffe/Lansing Production, in association with Michael Douglas. A Paramount Pictures Release. A U.S. production in English and filmed, in part, in Japan. Dolby Stereo. 125 minutes. MPAA rating: "R." Released September 22, 1989.

Black Rose / Kurobara no yakata ("The Mansion of Black Rose"). Producer, Akira Oda; Director, Kinji Fukasaku; Screenplay, Hiro Matsuda and Kinji Fukasaku, based on the play *Kurobara no yakata* by Yukio Mishima; Director of Photography, Ko Kawamata; Art Director, Masao Kumagi; Music, Hajime Kaburagi.

CAST: Akihiko Maruyama (Ryuko), Eitaro Ozawa (Kyohei), Masakazu Tamura (Wataru), Ayako Hosho (Kyohei's wife), Ko Nishimura.

A Shochiku Co., Ltd. Production. Eastman Color. Shochiku GrandScope. 91 minutes. Released January 25, 1969.

U.S. VERSION: Released by Shochiku Films of America, Inc. English subtitles (?). 90 minutes. No MPAA rating. Released July 30, 1969.

Blazing Continent / Moeru tairiku ("Blazing Continent"). Director, Shogoro Nishimura; Screenplay, Ei Ogawa and Michio Sotake, based on a story by Haruo Ikushima; Director of Photography, Shohei Ando; Art Director, Yoshinaga Yoko; Music, Keitaro Miho.

CAST: Tetsuya Watari (Keiichi), Chieko Matsubara (Saeko), Masumi Okada (Kenneth), Miyoko Akaza, Ken Sanders, Akira Yamauchi.

A Nikkatsu Corp. Production. Fujicolor. NikkatsuScope. 90 minutes. Released December 14, 1968.

U.S. VERSION: Release undetermined. English subtitles. No MPAA rating.

The Blind Beast / Moju ("The Blind Beast"). Executive Producer, Masaichi Nagata; Producer, Kazumasa Nakano; Director, Yasuzo Masamura; Screenplay, Yoshio Shirasoka, based on the story "Moju," by Rampo Edogawa; Director of Photography, Setsuo Kobayashi; Art Director, Shigeo Mano; Sound Recording Supervisor, Takeo Sudo; Sound, Daiei Recording Studio; Music, Hikaru Hayashi.

CAST: Eiji Funakoshi (Michio Sofu), Mako Midori (Aki Shima), Noriko Sengoku (Shino, *Michio's mother*).

A Daiei Motion Picture Co., Ltd. Production. A Masaichi Nagata Presentation. Westrex recording system. Daieicolor. DaieiScope. 86 minutes. Released January 1969.

U.S. VERSION: Released by Daiei International Films, Inc. English subtitles. Reissued by Roninfilm as *Warehouse*, and running 86 minutes, in February 1974. Running time between 84-90 minutes, sources vary. No MPAA Rating. Released April 1969.

Blood / Oreno chi wa tanin no chi ("My Blood Is the Stranger's Blood"). Executive Producer, Kiyoshi Higuchi; Director, Toshio Senda; Screenplay, Toshio Senda, based on the novel by Yasutaka Tsutsui; Director of Photography, Keiji Maruyama; Editor, Yoshi Sugiwara; Assistant Director, Hidewo Oe; Art Director, Shigemori Shigeta; Sets, Katsuo Kojima; Set Decorator, Takeshi Machida; Costumes, Shochiku Isho Co., Ltd.; Lighting, Lei Miura; Music, Hiroshi Takada; Sound Recording, Kan Nakamura; Sound Mixing, Kogyo Kowo; Fighting Instructor, Takamitsu Watanabe; Production Manager, Tadashi Shibata; Assistant Production Manager, Junichi Mine.

CAST: Shohei Kano (Ryosuke Kinugawa), Frankie Sakai (Rokusuke Sawamura), Etsuko Nami (Fusako), Wataru Nachi (Ranko), Ichiro Nakaya (Itami), Toru Abe (Toraichiro Yamaga), Isao Hashimoto (Samonji), Yoshiwo Aoki (Ohashi), Kuniyasu Atsumi (Adachi), Kazuo Kato (Fukuda), Takanobu Hozumi (Fori), Housei Komatsu (Chief of Police), Hatsuo Yamatani (Ito), Kin Omae (Hauda).

A Shochiku Co., Ltd. Production, in cooperation with Yokohama Dreamland.

Color (processed by Shochiku Laboratory). Panavision (?). 94 minutes. Released October 12, 1974.

U.S. VERSION: Distributor, if any, is undetermined. Alternate title (?): *My Blood Belongs to Someone Else.*

Blood on the Sea / Kurenai no Umi ("Sea of Deep Red"). Director, Senkichi Taniguchi; Screenplay, Takeo Kunihara; Director of Photography, Kazuo Yamada.

CAST: Yuzo Kayama, Yosuke Natsuki, Makoto Sato, Yuriko Hoshi, Kumi Mizuno, Akemi Kita.

A Toho Co., Ltd. Production. Eastman Color. Toho Scope. 89 minutes. Released 1961.

U.S. VERSION: Released by Toho International Co., Ltd. English subtitles. 89 minutes. No MPAA rating. Released March 23, 1962.

The Bloody Sword of the 99th Virgin / Kyuju-kyuhonme no kimusume ("The 99th Virgin"). Producer, Mitsugu Okura; Director, Shinpei Magatani; Screenplay, Susumu Takahira and Jiro Fujishima; Director of Photography, Kagai Okado.

CAST: Bunta Sugawara, Namiji Matsura.

A Shintoho Co., Ltd. Production. Western Electric Mirrophonic recording. Black and white. Shintoho-Scope. 82 minutes. Released September 12, 1959.

U.S. VERSION: Distributor, if any, is undetermined. Also known as *Blood Sword of the 99th Virgin.* No MPAA rating.

Bloom in the Moonlight / Waga ai no uta—Taki Rentaro monogatari ("My Love Song—Story of Rentaro Taki"). Producers, Tan Takaiwa and Seiji Urushido; Director, Shinichiro Sawai; Screenplay, Akira Miyazaki, Ryoji Ito and Shinichiro Sawai; Director of Photography, Daisaku Kimura; Music, Masaru Sato.

CAST: Toru Kazama, Isako Washio, Go Kato.

A Toei Co., Ltd./Nippon TV Corp. Production. Color. Spherical wide screen (?). 125 minutes. Released 1993.

U.S. VERSION: Unreleased in the United States as this book went to press.

The Blue Beast / Aoi Yaju ("The Blue Beast"). Producers, Sanezumi Fujimoto and Masakatsu Kaneko; Director, Hiromichi Horikawa; Screenplay, Yoshio Shirasaka; Director of Photography, Asakazu Nakai; Music, Sei Ikeno.

CAST: Tatsuya Nakadai (Yasuhiko Kuroki), Yoko Tsukasa (Ayako Eto), Koreya Senda (Ayako's father), Ichiro Nakaya (Goda), Jun Tazaki (Ogawa), Keiko Awaji (Yoshie).

A Toho Co., Ltd. Production. Black and white. Toho Scope. 95 minutes. Released 1960.

U.S. VERSION: Released by Toho International Co., Ltd. English subtitles. 95 minutes. No MPAA rating. Released January 29, 1965.

The Blue Revolution / Aoiro kakumei ("The Blue Revolution"). Producer, Masumi Fujimoto; Director, Kon Ichikawa; Screenplay, Masato Inomata, based on a story by Tatsuzo Ishikawa; Director of Photography, Masao Tamai; Music, Toshiro Mayuzumi; Art Director, Shinobu Muraki; Lighting, Choshiro Ishii; Sound Recording, Nao Shimonaga.

CAST: Koreya Senda (Tatsukichi Koizumi), Sadako Sawamura (Tsuneko Koizumi, *his wife*), Yoichi Tachikawa (Junpei, *their oldest son*), Tatsuji Ehara (Atsushi, *their second son*), Asami Kuji (Miyoko Namiki), Rentaro Mikuni (Fukuzawa), Yunosuke Ito (Assistant Professor Kamoi), Daisuke Kato (Takegoro Inugai), Yuriko Tashiro (Harue).

A Toho Co., Ltd. Production. Black and white. Academy ratio. Running time undetermined. Released June 10, 1953.

U.S. VERSION: Distributor, if any, is undetermined, though most likely Toho International Co., Ltd.

The Body / Ratai ("Naked Body"). Executive Producers, Masao Shirai and Shigeru Wakatsuki; Director, Masashige Narusawa; Screenplay, Masashige Narusawa, based on the 1954 novel *Ratai* by Kafu Nagai; Director of Photography, Ko Kawamata; Art Director, Koji

Uno; Music, Toru Takemitsu and Joji Iwata.

CAST: Machiko Saga (Sakiko Okamu), Ichiro Sugai (her father), Kumeko Urabe (her mother), Kazuko Matsuo (Kimiko), Mitsuko Takara (Marie Angel), Minoru Chiaki (Sasaki), Yusuke Kawazu (Sota), Hiroyuki Nagato (Takasugi), Eitaro Shindo (Hyodo), Isuzu Yamada (proprietess of sex club), Chieko Naniwa (Naka), Isao Sasaki (the handsome boy).

A Shochiku Co., Ltd. Production. Eastman Color. Shochiku GrandScope. 98 minutes. Released 1962.

U.S. VERSION: Released by Shochiku Films of America, Inc. English subtitles. 85 minutes. No MPAA rating. Released February 24, 1964.

Body Beautiful / Nikutaibi ("Beauty of the Body"). Director, Yasujiro Ozu; Screenplay, Yasujiro Ozu and Akira Fushimi; Director of Photography, Hideo Shigehara.

CAST: Tatsuo Saito,, Choko Iida, Mitsuko Yoshikawa, Chishu Ryu.

A Shochiku Co., Ltd. Production. Filmed at Shochiku-Kamata Studio. Silent with benshi. Black and white. Academy ratio. 60 minutes. Released December 1, 1928.

U.S. VERSION: Never released theatrically in the United States. A lost film.

The Bodyguard. Executive Producer, Terry Levene; Director of Photography, Joel Shapiro; Editor, Victor Zimet; Music, Maurice Sarli.

CAST: Shinichi "Sonny" Chiba, Judy Lee, Aaron Banks, Bill Louie. A Nippon-American Productions Presentation. A U.S./Japanese co-production.

U.S. VERSION: Released by Aquarius Releasing. English-dubbed. Postproduction, August Films (New York); Director, Simon Nuchtern; Dialogue Director, Joseph Ellison. 87 minutes. Released 1978.

Bonchi / Bonchi ("Bonchi"). Producer, Masaichi Nagata; Planning, Hisaichi Tsuji; Director, Kon Ichikawa; Screenplay, Natto Wada and Kon Ichikawa, based on the novel by Toyoko Yamazaki; Director of Photography, Kazuo Miyagawa; Art Director, Yoshinobu Nishioka; Music, Yasushi Akutagawa; Lighting, Kenichi Okamoto; Sound Recording, Masao Osumi; Editor, Shigeo Nishida.

CAST: Raizo Ichikawa (Kikuji), Tamao Nakamura (Hiroko, *his wife*), Mitsuko Kusabue (Ikuko), Machiko Kyo (Ofuku), Ayako Wakao (Ponta), Fubuki Koshiji (Hisako), Kikue Mori (Kino, *Kikuji's grandmother*), Isuzu Yamada (Sei, *Kikuji's mother*), Eiji Funakoshi (Kihei, *Kikuji's father*).

A Daiei Motion Picture Co., Ltd. Production. Eastman Color. DaieiScope. 105 minutes. Released April 14, 1960.

U.S. VERSION: Distributor undetermined, likely Daiei International Films, Inc. English subtitles. 105 minutes. No MPAA rating. Released April 1981 (?).

Booted Babe, Busted Boss / Ogon no me ("Golden Eye"). Executive Producers, Tomoyuki Tanaka and Tomohiro Kaiyama; Director, Jun Fukuda; Screenplay, Michio Tsuzuki, Ei Ogawa, and Jun Fukuda; Director of Photography, Kazuo Yamada; Art Director, Shigekazu Ikuno; Music, Masaru Sato.

CAST: Akira Takarada (Andrew Hoshino), Bibari "Beverly" Maeda (Ruby), Tomomi Sawa (Mitsuko), Andrew Hughes (Stonefeller), Makoto Sato (Tezuka), Yoshio Tsuchiya (Kurokawa).

A Toho Co., Ltd. Production. Eastman Color. Toho Scope. 80 minutes. Released March 16, 1968.

U.S. VERSION: Released by Toho International Co., Ltd. English subtitles. English-dubbed version also available. A sequel to *Ironfinger* (1965). 80 minutes. No MPAA rating. Released 1967 (?).

Born in Sin / Kawano hotoride ("By the River"). Executive Producers, Sanezumi Fujimoto and Masakatsu Kaneko; Director, Yasuki Chiba; Screenplay, Toshiro Ide; Story, Yojiro Ishizaka; Director of Photography, Rokuro Nishigaki; Music, Toshiro Mayuzumi.

CAST: Yuzo Kayama, Yuriko Hoshi, So Yamamura, Mitsuko Kusabue, Daisuke Kato, Chikage Awashima.

A Toho Co., Ltd. Production. Eastman Color. Toho Scope. Released 1962.

U.S. VERSION: Released by Toho International Co., Ltd. English subtitles. 116 minutes. No MPAA rating. Released May 24, 1963.

The Boss of Pick-Pocket Bay / Crazy no musekinin shimizu minato ("Irresponsible Crazys at Shimizu Harbor"). Executive Producer, Shin Watanabe; Director, Takashi Tsuboshima; Director of Photography, Fukuzo Koizumi; Music, Yasushi Miyagawa and Tessho Hagiwara.

CAST: The Crazy Cats (Hitoshi Ueki, Kei Tani, Hajime Hana, Hiroshi Inuzuka, Senri Sakurai, Shin Yasuda, and Eitaro Ishibashi), Reiko Dan, Mie Hama, Noriko Takahashi, Akihiko Hirata, Yutaka Nakayama, Jun Tazaki.

A Watanabe Productions/Toho Co., Ltd. Production. A Toho Co., Ltd. Release. Eastman Color. Toho Scope. 94 minutes. Released 1966.

U.S. VERSION: Released by Toho International Co., Ltd. English subtitles. The 5th "Crazy" feature. Followed by *It's Crazy: I Can't Explain It Way Out There* (1966). 94 minutes. No MPAA rating. Released 1966.

A Boss with the Samurai Spirit / Kapone no Shatei, Yamato Damashi ("The Boss's Inner Circle with the Samurai Spirit"). Director, Takashi Harada; Screenplay, Tatsuo Nogami; Director of Photography, Toshio Masuda; Art Director, Yoshimitsu Amamori; Music, Takeo Yamashita.

CAST: Tomisaburo Wakayama (Capone), Minoru Oki (Kokichi), Willy Dorsey (Sandy), Seizaburo Kawazu (President Ato), Ryosuke Kagawa (Boss Izumasa), Kikue Mori (Grandmother Yoshino), Tomoko Mayama, Toru Yuri.

A Toei Co., Ltd. Production. Eastman Color. ToeiScope. 90 minutes. Released January 23, 1971.

U.S. VERSION: Release undetermined. English subtitles. No MPAA rating.

Botandoro ("Botandoro"). Director, Akira Nobuchi.

CAST: Chiyonosuke Azuma, Yuriko Tashiro.

A Toei Co., Ltd. Production. Black and white. Academy ratio. Running time undetermined. Released 1955.

U.S. VERSION: Distributor, if any, is undetermined. International title: *Peonies and Stone Lanterns.*

Boy / Shonen ("Boy"). Producers, Masayuki Nakajima and Takuji Yamaguchi; Director, Nagisa Oshima; Screenplay, Tsutomu Tamura; Directors of Photography, Yasuhiro Yoshioka and Seizo Sengen; Art Director, Jusho Toda; Editor, Sueko Shiraishi; Music, Hikaru Hayashi; Sound Recording, Hideo Nishizaki; Sound Effects, Akira Suzuki; Assistant Directors, Kiyoshi Ogasawara, Yun-do Yun, and Daiji Ozeki; Production Manager, Toshimi Kinoshita.

CAST: Tetsuo Abe (Toshio), Fumio Watanabe (father), Akiko Koyama (stepmother), Tsuyoshi Kinoshita (little brother).

A Sozo-sha/A.T.G. Production. Eastman Color, with black and white sequences. Anamorphic wide screen. 105 minutes (?). Released 1961 (?).

U.S. VERSION: Released by Grove Press. English subtitles. Wide screen process billed as CinemaScope in the United States. 97 minutes. No MPAA rating. Released April 9, 1970.

A Boy and Three Mothers / Haha sannin ("Three Mothers"). Producer, Kazuo Takimura; Director, Seiji Hisamatsu; Screenplay, Toshiro Ide; Director of Photography, Masahisa Himeda; Music, Ichiro Saito.

CAST: Isuzu Yamada (Natsu, *the foster-mother*), Michiyo Kogure (Keiko, *the mother-in-law*), Michiyo Aratama (Kazuko, *the real mother*), Frankie Sakai (Seiji, *the father*), Tatsuya Nakadai (Kawakami, *the engineer*), Makoto Niki (the boy).

A Tokyo Eiga Co., Ltd. Production, in association with Toho Co., Ltd. A Toho Co., Ltd. Release. Black and white. Toho Scope. 102 minutes. Released 1958.

U.S. VERSION: Release undetermined, possibly by Toho International Co., Ltd. in subtitled format. No MPAA rating.

Brand of Evil / Aku no monsho ("Crest of Evil"). Producers, Sanezumi Fujimoto and Reiji Miwa; Director, Hiromichi Horikawa; Screenplay, Shinobu Hashimoto and Sakae Hirosawa; Director of Photography, Yuzuru Aizawa; Music, Toshiro Mayuzumi.

CAST: Tsutomu Yamazaki (Detective Kikuchi), Michiyo Aratama, Kyoko Kishida, Keiji Sada, Eijiro Yanagi, Shiro Osaka.

A Takarazuka Motion Picture Co., Ltd. Production. A Toho Co., Ltd. Release. Black and white. Toho Scope. Released 1964.

U.S. VERSION: Released by Toho International Co., Ltd. English subtitles. 133 minutes. No MPAA rating. Released February 12, 1965.

Branded to Kill / Koroshi no rakuin ("Branded to Kill"). Producer, Kaneo Iwai; Director, Seijun Suzuki; Screenplay, Hachiro Guryu; Director of Photography, Kazue Nagatsuka; Editor, Mutsuo Tanji; Art Director, Sukezo Kawahara; Music, Naozumi Yamamoto; Aassistant Director, Masami Kuzu.

CAST: Jo Shishido (Goro Hanada, *the Number Three Killer*), Mariko Ogawa (Mami Hanada, *his wife*), Annu Mari (Misako Nakajo), Koji Nanbara (Number One Killer), Isao Tamagawa (Michihiko Yabuhara), Hiroshi Minami (Gihei Kasuga).

A Nikkatsu Corp. Production. Black and white. NikkatsuScope. 91 minutes. Released 1967.

U.S. VERSION: Released by Nikkatsu Corp. English subtitles. 91 minutes. No MPAA rating. Released 1993.

Bravo, Young Guy / Burabo! yangu gai ("Bravo, Young Guy"). Producer, Sanezumi Fujimoto; Director, Katsumi Iwauchi; Screenplay, Yasuo Tanami; Music, Kenjiro Hirose.

CAST: Yuzo Kayama (Yuichi), Wakako Sakai, Kunie Tanaka, Ichiro Arishima.

A Toho Co., Ltd. Production. Eastman Color. Panavision. 89 minutes. Released January 1970.

U.S. VERSION: Released by Toho International Co., Ltd. English subtitles. The 15th "Young Guy" feature. 89 minutes. No MPAA rating. Released May 27, 1970.

Bride of the Andes / Andesu no hanayome ("Bride of the Andes"). Director/Screenplay, Susumu Hani; Director of Photography, Juichi Nagano; Music, Hikaru Hayashi.

CAST: Sachiko Hidari (Tamiko), Ancermo Fukuda (Taro), Koji Takahashi (Sasaki), Don Mateo (Quiquis), Takeshi Hika (Takeshi).

A Tokyo Eiga Co., Ltd./Hani Productions, Ltd. Production. A Toho Co., Ltd. Release. Eastman Color. Toho Scope. Filmed on location in Peru and Bolivia. 103 minutes. Released 1966.

U.S. VERSION: Released by Toho International Co., Ltd. English subtitles. 103 minutes. No MPAA rating. Released May 1967.

The Bridge Between / Sanga ari ("There Is a Mountain and River"). Producer, Sennosuke Tsukimori; Planning, Keisuke Kinoshita; Director, Zenzo Matsuyama; Screenplay, Zenzo Matsuyama and Eijiro Hisaita; Director of Photography, Hiroyuki Kusuda; Art Director, Shigemasa Toda; Music, Chuji Kinoshita.

CAST: Takahiro Tamura (Yoshio Inoue), Hideko Takamine (Kishimo Inoue, *his wife*), Tamotsu Hayakawa (Haruo, *their eldest son*), Mickey Curtis (Akira, *their second son*), Keiju Kobayashi (Kyuhei Goda), Yoshiko Kuga (Sumi Goda, *his wife*), Akira Ishihama (Ichiro, *their son*), Miyuki Kuwano (Sakura, *their daughter*).

A Shochiku Co., Ltd. Production. Eastman Color (?). Shochiku GrandScope (?). Running time and release date undetermined.

U.S. VERSION: Released by Shochiku Films of America, Inc. English subtitles. No MPAA rating. Release date undetermined.

Bridge of Japan / Nihonbashi ("Nihonbashi"). Producer, Masaichi Nagata; Director, Kon Ichikawa; Screenplay, Natto Wada, based on a story by Kyoka Izumi; Director of Photography, Kimio Watanabe; Music, Koji Taku; Art Director, Atsuji Shibata; Lighting, Tsunekichi Shibata; Sound Recording, Mitsuo Hasekawa; Color Consultant, Sentaro Iwata.

CAST: Chikage Awashima (Otaka Inaba), Fujiko Yamamoto (Kiyoha Takinoya), Ayako Wakao (Ochiyo), Ryuji Shinagawa (Shinso Kuzuki), Eijiro Yanagi (Denkichi Igarashi), Eiji Funakoshi (Shinpachiro Kasahara), Eiichi Takamura (Kiyoha's husband).

A Daiei Motion Picture Co., Ltd. Production. Eastman Color. Academy ratio. 112 minutes. Released October 1, 1956.

U.S. VERSION: Distributor, if any, is undetermined. Alternate title: *Nihombashi*. No MPAA rating.

Bridge to the Sun. Producer, Jacques Bar; Director, Etienne Perier; Screenplay, Charles Kauffman, based on the 1957 autobiography by Gwendolyn Terasaki; Directors of Photography, Marcel Weise and Seiichi Kizuka; Editors, Robert and Monique Isnardon; Art Director, Hiroshi Mizutani; Music, Georges Auric; Assistant Directors, Jacques Roufflo, Oliver Gerard, and Takashi Fugie; Special Effects, Koji Inagawa.

CAST: Carroll Baker (Gwen Terasaki), James Shigeta (Hidenari Terasaki), James Yagi (Hara), Tetsuro Tamba (Jiro), Hiroshi Tomono (Ishi), Nori Elisabeth Hermann and Emi Florence Hirsch (Maki Terasaki), Sean Garrison (Fred Tyson), Ruth Masters (Aunt Peggy).

A Jacques Bar/Metro-Goldwyn-Mayer Production. A Loews Company Release. A French/U.S. co-production in English and filmed in Japan, Washington, D.C., and Paris. Black and white. Spherical wide screen. 113 minutes. No MPAA rating. Released 1961.

Broken Swords / Hiken yaburi ("Challenge to Secret Swords"). Executive Producer, Masaichi Nagata; Director, Kazuo Ikehiro; Screenplay, Daisuke Ito; Story, Kosuke Gomi; Director of Photography, Chishi Makiura; Art Director, Shigenori Shimoishizaka; Music, Takeo Watanabe.

CAST: Hiroki Matsukata (Tenzen Tange), Kojiro Hongo (Yasubei Nakayama), Tomomi Iwai (Chiharu), Shigeru Tsuyuguchi (Ryunoshin Nagao), Yoshi Kato, Tatsuo Matsumura.

A Daiei Motion Picture Co., Ltd. Production. Fujicolor. DaieiScope. 90 minutes. Released May 1969.

U.S. VERSION: Released by Daiei International Films, Inc. English subtitles. 90 minutes. No MPAA rating. Released November 1969.

Brother and Sister / Ani Imoto ("Older Brother, Younger Sister"). Producers, Hideyuki Shiino and Masakatsu Kaneko; Director, Tadashi Imai; Screenplay, Yoko Mizuki; Director of Photography, Kazutami Hara; Art Director, Kazuo Takenaka; Music, Takeshi Shibuya.

CAST: Kumiko Akiyoshi, Masao Kusakari, Kimiko Ikegami, Shoji Otaki, Natsuko Kahara, Atomu Shimojo.

A Toho Co., Ltd. Production. Color. Panavision. 98 minutes. Released 1976.

U.S. VERSION: Released by Toho International Co., Ltd. English subtitles. Alternate title: *Older Brother, Younger Sister*. No MPAA rating. Released July 1, 1977.

The Brothers and Sisters of the Toda Family / Toda-ke no kyodai ("The Brothers and Sisters of the Toda Family"). Director, Yasujiro Ozu; Screenplay, Yasujiro Ozu and Tadao Ikeda; Director of Photography, Yushun Atsuta.

CAST: Hideko Takamine, Shin Saburi, Hideo Fujino, Fumiko Katsuragi, Mitsuko Yoshikawa, Masao Hayama, Tatsuo Saito, Kuniko Miyake, Yoshiko Tsubouchi, Michiko Kuwano, Chishu Ryu.

A Shochiku Co., Ltd. Production. Filmed at Shochiku-Ofuna Studios. Black and white. Academy ratio. 105 minutes. Released March 1, 1941.

U.S. VERSION: Distributor undetermined, likely Shochiku Films of America, Inc. English subtitles. 105 minutes. No MPAA rating. Released May 11, 1982.

Buddha / Shaka ("Buddha"). Producer, Masaichi Nagata; Associate Producer, Akinari Suzuki; Director, Kenji Misumi; Screenplay, Fuji Yahiro; Production Manager, Masatsugu Hashimoto; Assistant Directors, Akira Inoue, Yoshiyuki Kuroda; Director of Photography, Hiroshi Imai; Lighting, Kenichi Okamoto; Music, Akira Ifukube, performed by the Tokyo Symphony Orchestra, Conducted by Jin Ueda; Editor, Kanji Suganuma; Color Consultant, Yoshiaki Kiura; Technical Advisers, Gakuro Nakamura Takio

Scene from Japan's first 70 mm feature, Kenji Misumi's *Buddha* (1961).

Nakamura; Choreography, Kiitsu Sakakibara; Art Director, Kisaku Ito; Art, Akira Naito; Set Decorator Teruo Kajitani; Decoration Consultant, Toshiharu Takatsu; Costume Designer, Hachiro Nakajima; Costume Consultant, Yoshio Ueno; Animation, Tomio Sagisu; Drawings, Yoshio Watanabe; Sound Recording Supervisor, Masao Osumi; Sound, Daiei Recording Studio; Special Effects, Tatsuyuki Yokota, Soichi Aisaka; Special Photographic Effects, Toru Matoba, Chishi Makiura, Daiei Special Effects Department.

CAST: Kojiro Hongo (Prince Siddhartha), Charito Solis (Princess Yashodhara), Shintaro Katsu (Devadatta), Machiko Kyo (Nandabala), Raizo Ichikawa (Kunala), Fujiko Yamamoto (Usha), Hiroshi Kawaguchi (Ajatashatru), Katsuhiko Kobayashi (Ananda), Tamao Nakamura (Auttami), Junko Kano (Matangi), Mieko Kondo (Amana), Tokiko Mita (Sari), Hiromi Ichida (Naccha), Michiko Ai (Kilika), Matasaburo Niwa (Sonna), Keizo Kawasaki (Upali), Reiko Fujiwara (child's mother), Gen Mitamura (Shariputra), Ryuzo Shimada (Bhutika), Joji Tsurumi (Arama), Shiro Otsuji (Kalodayi), Yoshiro Kitahara (Kaundinya), Jun Negami (Mahakashyapa), Ganjiro Nakamura (Ashoka), Toshio Chiba (Graha), Ryuichi Ishii (Bandhu), Yoichi Funaki (Maudgaliputra), Sanemon Arashi (Rayana), Osamu Maryuama (Jivaka), Gen Shimizu (Kisaka), Isuzu Yamada (Kalidevi), Yumeji Tsukioka (Takshakara), Tanie Kitabayashi (Sumi), Chikako Hosokawa (Maya), Haruko Sugimura (Vaidehi), Koreya Senda (Shuddhodana), Eijiro Tono (Suratha), Bontaro Miyake (Channa), Asamu Takizawa (Ajita), Jukai Ichikawa (Bimbisara), Koichi Katsuragi (Suprabuddha), Ryyonosuke Azuma (Bashpa), Shintaro Nanjyo (Mahanaman), Kinya Ichikawa (Chunda), Seishiro Hara (Bhadrika), Saburo Date (Ashvajit), Reiko Kongo (Sabhaya), Kimiko Tachibana (Amita).

A Daiei Motion Picture Co., Ltd. Production. A Masaichi Nagata Presentation. Filmed at Daiei-Kyoto Studios. Westrex Recording System. Stereophonic Sound. Eastman Color (processed by Daiei Laboratory). Super Technirama 70. 156 minutes. Released November 1, 1961.

U.S. VERSION: Released by Lopert Pictures. English subtitles (?). A Lopert Pictures Corporation Release. Prints by Technicolor. Released in Super 70 Technirama. *Note:* Contains some footage filmed in Daieiscope and converted to 70mm. Japan's first 70mm release. 139 minutes (later edited to 135 minutes and released dubbed). No MPAA rating. Released July 2, 1963. Reissued January 25, 1967.

Bull of the Campus / Daigaku no wakadaisho ("Young Boss of the University"). Executive Producer, Sanezumi Fujimoto; Director, Toshio Sugie; Screenplay, Ryozo Kasahara and Yasuo Tanami; Director of Photography, Takeshi Suzuki; Music, Kenjiro Hirose.

CAST: Yuzo Kayama (Yuichi), Yuriko Hoshi, Reiko Dan, Ken Uehara, Yoko Fujiyama, Akemi Kita, Machiko Naka, Tatsuyoshi Ebara, Asami Kuzi, Ichiro Arishima, Choko Iida.

A Toho Co., Ltd. Production. Eastman Color. Toho Scope. 83 minutes. Released July 8, 1961.

U.S. VERSION: Released by Toho International Co., Ltd. English subtitles. First feature in the 18-film "Young Guy" series (1961–81). Followed by *Pride of the Campus* (1962). International title: *Sir Galahad in Campus* [sic!]. 94 minutes. No MPAA rating. Released May 1962.

Bullet Wound / Dankon ("Bullet Wound"). Executive Producer, Tomohiro Kaiyama; Director, Shiro Moritani; Screenplay, Hidekazu Nagahara; Director of Photography, Takao Saito; Art Director, Yoshiro Muraki; Music, Toru Takemitsu.

CAST: Yuzo Kayama (Takimura), Kiwako Taichi (Saori), Kei Sato, Eiji Okada.

A Toho Co., Ltd. Production. Eastman Color. Panavision. 94 minutes. Released September 1969.

U.S. VERSION: Released by Toho International Co., Ltd. English subtitles. 94 minutes. No MPAA rating. Released March 28, 1970.

The Burmese Harp / Biruma no tategoto ("The Burmese Harp"). Producer, Masayuki Takaki; Director, Kon Ichikawa; Screenplay, Natto Wada, based on the 1946 novel by Michio Takeyama; Director of Photography, Minoru Yokoyama; Art Director, Takashi Matsuyama; Editor, Masanori Tsujii; Lighting, Ko Fujibayashi; Music, Akira Ifukube; Sound Recording, Masakazu Kamiya.

CAST: Shoji Yasui (Corporal Yasuhiko Mizushima), Rentaro Mikuni (Captain Inoue), Tatsuya Mihashi (defense commander), Tanie Kitabayashi (old woman), Yunosuke Ito (village head), Takeo Naito (Kobayashi), Jun Hamamura (Ito), Shunji Kasuga (Maki), Ko Nishimura (Baba), Hiroshi Tsuchikata, Sanpei Mine, Yoshiaki Koto.

A Nikkatsu Corporation Production. Black and white. Academy ratio. 143 minutes. Released 1956.

U.S. VERSION: Distributor undetermined, but apparently received some limited play (as *Harp of Burma*) to qualify for the 1956 Academy Awards. English subtitles. Reissued by Brandon Films with English subtitles. Remade in 1985. 116 minutes. No MPAA rating. Released April 28, 1967.

The Burmese Harp / Biruma no tategoto ("The Burmese Harp"). Executive Producers, Haruo Shikanai, Atsushi Okumoto, and Matsuo Takahashi; Producers, Hiroaki Fujii, Masaru Kakutani, and Masaya Araki; Planning, Hisashi Hieda and Matsuo Takahashi; Director, Kon Ichikawa; Screenplay, Natto Wada, based on the 1946 novel by Michio Takeyama, and the 1956 film; Director of Photography, Setsuo Kobayashi; Art Director, Iwao Akone; Lighting, Teiichi Saito; Editor, Chizuru Osada; Sound Recording, Tetsuya Ohashi; Music, Naozumi Yamamoto.

CAST: Koji Ishizaka (Commander Inoue), Kiichi Nakai (Private Mizushima), Takuzo Kawatani (Sgt. Ito), Atsushi Watanabe (Pvt. Kobayashi), Fujio Tokita (old man), Tanie Kitabayashi (old woman), Bunta Sugawara (platoon commander).

A Fuji Television Network, Inc./ Hakuhodo, Inc./Kinema Tokyo Co., Ltd. Production. A Toho Co., Ltd. release. Color. Panavision (?). 133 minutes. Released 1985.

U.S. VERSION: Release undetermined. Previously filmed in 1956. No MPAA rating.

Buru kurisumasu ("Blue Christmas"). Director, Kihachi Okamoto; Director of Photography, Daisaku Kimura; Music, Masaru Sato; Sound, Toho Recording Centre; Sound Effects, Toho Sound Effects Group.

CAST: Tatsuya Nakadai.

A Toho Co., Ltd. Production. Color (processed by Tokyo Laboratory Ltd.). Panavision (?). 134 minutes. Released 1978.

U.S. VERSION: Distributor, if any, is undetermined. International title: *Blood Type: Blue*.

Bushido / Bushido zankoku monogatari ("Cruel Story of Bushido"). Producer, Hiroshi Okawa; Director, Tadashi Imai; Screenplay, Naoyuki Suzuki, based on an original story by Norio Nanjo; Director of Photography, Makoto Tsuboi; Music, Toshiro Mayuzumi.

CAST: Kinnosuke Nakamura (Iikura), Masayuki Mori (Lord Hori), Kyoko Kishida (Lady Hagi), Yoshiko Mita (Kyoko), Ineko Arima, Shinjiro Ebara.

A Toei Co., Ltd. Production. Black and white. ToeiScope. 122 minutes. Released 1963.

U.S. VERSION: Released by Toei International (?). English subtitles. 122 minutes. No MPAA rating. Released September 12, 1964.

Bwana Toshi / Buwana Toshi no uta ("Song of Bwana Toshi"). Producer, Nobuyo Horiba; Director, Susumu Hani; Screenplay, Susumu Hani and Kunio Shimizu; Directors of Photography, Manji Kanau and Mitsuji Kaneko; Music, Toru Takemitsu.

CAST: Kiyoshi Atsumi (Toshi), Hamisi Salehe (Toshi's assistant), Tsutomu Shimomoto (Onishi), Bibi Agnes, Haide Gitaposta, Gilba Haide.

A Toho Co., Ltd./Hani Productions, Ltd. Production. Eastman Color. Toho Scope. Filmed on location in Africa. 115 minutes. Released 1965.

U.S. VERSION: Released by Brandon Films. English subtitles. 98 minutes. No MPAA rating. Released June 1967.

The Call of Flesh / Jotai ("A Woman's Body"). Executive Producer, Hisao Ichikawa; Director/Screenplay, Hideo Onichi; Director of Photography, Masaharu Utsumi; Music, Toru Takemitsu.

CAST: Reiko Dan, Koji Nambara, Yuko Kusunoki, S. Sakamoto.

A Toho Co., Ltd. Production. Black and white. Toho Scope. Released 1964.

U.S. VERSION: Released by Gold Star Pictures. English subtitles (?). 97 minutes. No MPAA rating. Released August 1966.

Campus A-Go-Go / Ereki no wakadaisho ("Young Boss of the Electric Guitar"). Producer, Sanezumi Fujimoto; Director, Katsumi Iwauchi; Screenplay, Yasuo Tanami; Director of Photography, Rokoru Nishigaki; Music, Kenjiro Hirose.

CAST: Yuzo Kayama, Yuriko Hoshi, Choko Iida, Kunie Tanaka, Ichiro Arishima, Masaya Nihei, Toshio Kurosawa, Ken Uehara.

A Toho Co., Ltd. Production. Color. Toho Scope. 94 minutes. Released 1965.

U.S. VERSION: Released by Toho International Co., Ltd. English subtitles. The 6th "Young Guy" feature. Followed by *It Started in the Alps* (1966). 94 minutes. No MPAA rating. Released September 2, 1966.

Carmen Comes Home / Karumen kokiyo ni kaeru ("Carmen Returns Home"). Director/Screenplay, Keisuke Kinoshita; Director of Photography, Hiroyuki Kusuda.

CAST: Hideko Takamine (Okin, *aka Carmen*), Toshiko Kobayashi (Akemi), Takeshi Sakamoto (Shoichi), Shuji Sano (Taguchi), Chishu Ryu (principal), Yuko Mochizuki (Carmen's sister).

A Shochiku Co., Ltd. Production. Eastman Color. Academy ratio. 86 minutes. Released 1951.

U.S. VERSION: Released by Brandon Films, Inc. English subtitles. The first Japanese color feature. Sequel: *Carmen's*

Pure Love (1952). 86 minutes. No MPAA rating. Released December 22, 1959.

Carmen from Kawachi / Kawachi Karumen ("Kawachi Carmen"). Producer, Shizuo Sakagami; Director, Seijun Suzuki; Screenplay, Katsumi Miki, based on the novel by Toko Kon; Director of Photography, Shigeyoshi Mine; Editor, Akira Suzuki; Art Director, Takeo Kimura; Music, Taichiro Kosugi; Assistant Director, Masami Kuzu.

CAST: Yumiko Nogawa (Tsuyuko Takeda), Ruriko Ito (Senko Takeda, *her sister*), Chikaco Miyagi (Kiku, *their mother*), Michio Hino (Yukichi, *their father*), Shoichi Kuwayama (Ryoganbo, *the yamabushi*), Koji Wada (Akira Sakata), Asao Sano (Kanzo), Tamio Kawachi (Seiji Takano), Zenpei Saga (Chobei Saito), Masako Kusunoki (Yoko Kashima), Kayo Matsuo (Yukie).

A Nikkatsu Corp. Production. Black and white. NikkatsuScope. 89 minutes. Released 1966.

U.S. VERSION: Released by Nikkatsu Corp. English subtitles. 89 minutes. No MPAA rating. Released 1993.

Carmen 1945 / Nikutai no mon ("Body at the Gate"). Producer, Shigeru Okada; Director, Hideo Gosha; Screenplay, Kazuo Kasahara, based on an original story by Taijiro Tamura; Director of Photography, Fujio Morita; Music, Moshifumi Izumimori.

CAST: Rino Katase, Yuko Natori, Tsunehiko Watase.

A Toei Co., Ltd. Production. Color. Panavision (?). 119 minutes. Released 1988.

U.S. VERSION: Distributor, if any, is undetermined.

Carmen's Pure Love / Karumen junjosu ("Carmen's Pure Love"). Director/Screenplay, Keisuke Kinoshita; Director of Photography, Hiroyuki Kusuda.

CAST: Hideko Takamine (Okin, *aka Carmen*), Toshiko Kobayashi (Akemi).

A Shochiku Co., Ltd. Production. Black and white. Academy ratio. 103 minutes. Released 1952.

U.S. VERSION: Distributor, if any, is undetermined. A sequel to *Carmen Comes Home* (1951).

The Castle of Cagliostro / Kariosutoro no shiro ("Castle of Cagliostro") **[animated]**. Producer, Yutaka Fujioka; Director, Hayao Miyazaki; Screenplay, Hayao Miyazaki and Haruya Yamazaki, based on the story by Monkey Punch; Animation Director, Yasuo Otsuka; Editor, Mototoshi Tsurubuchi; Music, Yuji Ono.

VOICE CHARACTERIZATIONS: (undetermined).

A TMS Co., Ltd. Production. Color. Wide screen (?). 110 minutes. Released 1991.

U.S. VERSION: Released by Streamline Pictures. English subtitles. 100 minutes. No MPAA rating. Released April 1991. Reissued English-dubbed in 1994. Producer, Carl Macek, in association with Jerry Beck, Fred Patten and Robin Leyden.

The Castle of Sand / Suna no utsuwa ("Containers of Sand"). Producers, Yoshiharu Mishima and Shinobu Hashimoto; Director, Yoshitaro Nomura; Screenplay, Yoshitaro Nomura, Shinobu Hashimoto, and Yoji Yamada, based on the novel by Seicho Matsumoto; Director of Photography, Ko Kawamata; Music Director, Yasushi Akutagawa; Music, Kosuke Sugano.

CAST: Tetsuro Tamba (Detective Imanishi), Go Kato (Eiryo Waga), Kensaku Morita (Detective Yoshimura), Yoko Shimada (Reiko, *Waga's sweetheart*), Karin Yamaguchi (Sachiko, *Waga's fiancée*), Ken Ogata (Miki), Seiji Matsuyama (Miki's son), Yoshi Kato (Waga's father).

A Shochiku Co., Ltd. Production. Color. Panavision (?). 143 minutes. Released November 1974.

U.S. VERSION: Released by Shochiku Films of America, Inc. English subtitles. 143 minutes. No MPAA rating. Released October 10, 1975.

The Ceremony / Gishiki ("Ceremony"). Director, Nagisa Oshima;

Screenplay, Tsutomu Tamura, Momoru Sasaki, and Nagisa Oshima; Director of Photography, Toichiro Narushima; Editor, Keiichi Uraoka; Music, Toru Takemitsu.

CAST: Kenzo Kawarazaki (Masuo), Atsuko Kaku (Ritsuko), Atsuo Nakamura (Terumichi), Aiko Koyama (Satsuko), Kei Sato (Kazuomi), Kiyoshi Tsuchiya (Tadashi).

A Sozosha/Art Theatre Guild Production. Color. Spherical wide screen (?). 123 minutes. Released 1971.

U.S. VERSION: Released by New Yorker Films. English subtitles. 123 minutes. No MPAA rating. Released February 7, 1974.

The Challenge. Executive Producer, Lyle S. Poncher; Producers, Robert L. Rosen and Ron Beckman; Director, John Frankenheimer; Screenplay, Richard Maxwell and John Sayles, based on their story; Director of Photography, Kozo Okazaki; Editor, John "Jack" W. Wheeler; Production Design, Yoshiyuki Ishida; Music, Jerry Goldsmith; Sound, John Glassock; Art Director, Yoshiyuki Ishida; Unit Production Managers, Alan Levine (US) and Kijuro Ota (Japan); 1st Assistant Directors, Mike Abe and Hisao Nabeshima; 2nd Assistant Directors, Masaichi Shirao, Toshinori Hirayanagi, and Etsu Totoku; Casting, Patrick Mook (US), Hisao Nabeshima (Japan); Camera Operator, Michael A. Benson; 1st Asst. Cameraman, Richard Meinardus; Assistant to John Frankenheimer, Max Whitehouse; Production Advisor, Wai Hung; Script Supervisor, June Samson; Special Effects, Roger Hanson; Makeup, Bob Dawn and Yukio Ueda; Hair Stylist, Masato Abe; Set Decorator, Koichi Hamamura; Property Master, Kyoji Sasaki; Sword and Stunt Coordinator, Hiroyoshi Yamaguchi; Gaffer, Kazuo Shimomura; Key Grip, Koichi Haruta; Unit Publicist, Lou Dyer; Still Photographer, Don Smetzer; Wardrobe Design, Etsuko Yagyu; Men's Costumer, Hiroshi Hamazaki; Women's Costumer, Masatoshi Utsumi; Location Auditor, Robert Monosmith; Location Manager, Toshiro Suzuki; Postproduction Sound, Compact Sound Services; Rerecording Mixers, John T. Reitz, David E. Campbell, and Joe D. Citarella; Sound Mixer, John Glassock; Music Editor, Bob Takagi; Supervising Sound Editor, Robert Henderson; Sound Editor, Alan Murray; Looping Editor, Jack A. Finlay; Asst. Editor, Steve Polivka; Main Titles/Special Visual Effects, Private Stock Effects, Inc.; Special Thanks, Mifune Productions, Kyoto International Convention Center.

CAST: Scott Glenn (Rick), Toshiro Mifune (Toshio Yoshida), Donna Kei Benz (Akiko), Atsuo Nakamura (Hideo, *Yoshida's brother*), Calvin Jung (Ando), Clyde Kusatsu (Go), Sab Shimoto (Toshio), Kyioaki Nagai (Kubo), Kenta Fukasaku (Jiro), Shogo Shimada (Yoshida's father), Yoshio Inaba (instructor), Seiji Miyaguchi (old man), Miiko Taka (Yoshida's wife), Akio Kameda (boxer), Hisashi Osaka (knifeman), Yuko Okamoto (TV monitor girl #1), Tae Matsuda (TV monitor girl #2), Pat McNamara (fight promoter), Pamela Bowman (girl in gym), Roy Andrews (hanger-on), Henry Celis (Jorge), Kazunaga Tsuji (Hashimoto), Kusuo Kita (thug), Naoto Fujita (Tanaka), Masao Hisanori (Oshima), Ryuji Yamashita (Toshio Yoshida as a child), Toshio Chiba (customs officer), Minoru Sanada (porter), Shigehiro Kino (van's driver), Katsutoshi Nakayama (taxi driver), Masatoshi Ishikawa (thug's driver), Eriko Sugita (con person #1 in bar), Munehisa Fujita (con person #2 in bar), Sanaye Nakahara (cashier), Kanata Uyeno (waitress), Katsumi Shirono, Noboru Ishihara, Masaru Sakurai, Toshio Matsushima, Takashi Totsuka, Kazuo Arai, Mitsuyuki Oshima, Yoshio Otake, Hiroyuki Yuasa, Kanichi Hayashi, Akiyoshi Arima, Masuji Fujiwara, Roku Yoshinaka, Tsuneo Ito, Haruo Matsuoka, Michio Harada, Kenji Ono, Takafumi Tanaka, Hiroshi Oike, Yuichi Yoneda, Seiji Nishino, Yoshifumi Tsuboike, Yoshikazu Yoshimoto, Kazunori Asano, Akira Kato, Takashi Okamura, Shigeji Aoki (stunts).

A Poncher/Rosen/Beckman Production for the CBS Theatrical Films Corp. An Embassy Pictures Release A U.S./ Japanese co-production in English and Japanese. Eastman Color. Spherical wide screen. Working title: *The Equals*. 112 minutes (running time also given at 106 minutes). MPAA rating: "R." Released 1982.

Challenge to Live / Ai to honoho to ("Love and Flame"). Executive Producer, Sanezumi Fujimoto; Producer, Masumi Fujimoto; Director, Eizo Sugawa; Screenplay, Kaneto Shindo, based on the 1960 story *Chosen* by Shintaro Ishihara; Director of Photography, Fukuzo Koizumi; Art Director, Iwao Akune; Music, Masaru Sato; Sound Recording, Masanao Uehara.

CAST: Tatsuya Mihashi (Izaki), Yoko Tsukasa (Saeko Sawada), Yumi Shirakawa (Keiko Takamine), Masayuki Mori (Sawada resident), V.S. Shes (Prime Minister Mesacin), Chanty Zebery (Effran), Schuan [no other name given] (Maft), Kumi Mizuno, Takashi Shimura.

A Toho Co., Ltd. Production. Eastman Color. Toho Scope. 99 minutes. Released June 17, 1961.

U.S. VERSION: Released by Toho International Co., Ltd. English subtitles. 99 minutes. No MPAA rating. Released March 1962.

The Challenging Ghost / Gekko kamen – yurei to no gyakushu ("Moonlight Mask – Counterattack of the Ghost Party"). Director, Shoichi Shimazu.

CAST: Fumitake Omura.

A Toei Co., Ltd. Production. Black and white (processed by Toei Chemistry Co., Ltd.). ToeiScope. 61 minutes. Released July 28, 1959.

U.S. VERSION: Distributor, if any, is undetermined. The 5th "Moonlight Mask" feature. Followed by *The Last Death of the Devil* (1959).

Cherry Blossoms in the Air – The Suicide Raiders – Oh, Buddies! / Hana no tokkotai – Aa, senyuyo! ("The Flower Fighting Force – Oh, War Buddies!"). Director, Kenjiro Morinaga; Screenplay, Ryuzo Nakanishi, based on an original story by Yasunori Kawauchi; Director of Photography, Yoshihiro Yamazaki; Art Director, Bugen Sakaguchi; Music, Masayoshi Ikeda.

CAST: Ryotaro Sugi (Shinkichi), Tatsuya Fuji (X), Akio Hasegawa (Y), Mitsuo Hamada (Z), Masako Izumi (Miho), Koji Nambara (Commander Akiyama).

A Nikkatsu Corp. Production. Fujicolor. NikkatsuScope. 95 minutes. Released May 16, 1970.

U.S. VERSION: Release undetermined. English subtitles. No MPAA rating.

The Cherry Orchard / Sakura no sono ("The Cherry Orchard"). Producers, Yutaka Okada and Kosaburo Sasaoka; Director, Jun Nakahara; Screenplay, Hiroaki Jinno, based on an original story by Akimi Yoshida; Director of Photography, Junichi Fujisawa; Music, Federico Mompou.

CAST: Hiroko Nakajima, Miho Tsumiki, Yasuyo Shiratori, Aki Kajiwara.

An Argo Project, Inc. Production. Color. Spherical wide screen (?). 96 minutes. Released February 2, 1991.

U.S. VERSION: Distributor, if any, is undetermined.

The Child Writers / Tsuzurikata kyodai ("Teaching Them How to Write"). Producer, Kazuo Takimura; Director, Seiji Hisamatsu; Screenplay, Tyshio Yasumi, based on the compositions of Tanji, Yoko, and Fusao Nogami; Director of Photography, Michio Takahashi; Art Directors, Takeo Kita and Teruaki Abe; Music, Ichiro Saito.

CAST: Takao Zushi (Fumio), Yuko Mochizuki (mother), Masao Oda (father), Hisaya Morishige (Kawahira, *the tinker*), Kyoko Kagawa (Fumio's teacher), Nobuko Otowa (aunt).

A Toho Co., Ltd. Production. Black and white. Toho Scope. 100 minutes. Released September 9, 1958.

U.S. VERSION: Released by Toho International Co., Ltd. in subtitled format. No MPAA rating. Released August 29, 1971.

Children Drawing Rainbows / Niji o kakeru Kodomo-tachi ("Children Running Across the Rainbow") [**documentary**]. Producer/Director/Screenplay/ Art Director, Mariko Miyagi; Director of Photography, Kozo Okazaki; Music, Mitsuhiko Sato.

WITH: Mariko Miyagi, Christopher Eschenbach, and the Children of the Nemuoki School.

A Mariko Miyagi Production. Color. Academy ratio. 86 minutes. Released 1975 (?).

U.S. VERSION: Distributor, if any, is undetermined.

Children of Nagasaki / Konoko o Nokoshite ("Leaving This Child"). Producers, Hideo Sasai, Akira Tojo, Hiroshi Kanazawa, and Moritsune Saito; Director, Keisuke Kinoshita; Screenplay, Taichi Yamada, Kazuo Yoshida, and Keisuke Kinoshita, based on an original story by Takashi Nagai; Director of Photography, Kozo Okazaki; Music, Chuji Kinoshita.

CAST: Go Kato, Yukio Toake, Chikage Awashima, Masatomo Nakabayashi.

A Shochiku Co., Ltd./Hori Productions Production. A Shochiku Co., Ltd. Release. Color. Panavision (?). 128 minutes. Released 1983.

U.S. VERSION: Released by Shochiku Films of America. English subtitles. No MPAA rating. Released December 1983.

Children on the Island / Nijushi no hitomi ("24 Eyes"). Executive Producers, Shizuo Yamanouchi, Shinji Nakagawa, Yoichi Hattori, and Yozo Isozaki; Producers, Takeshi Motomura, Toru Najima, and Toshihiro Iijima; Director, Yoshitaka Asama; Screenplay, Keisuke Kinoshita, based on the novel by Sakae Tsuboi; Director of Photography, Mitsufumi Hanada; Music, Shigeaki Saegusa.

CAST: Yuko Tanaka (Hisako Oishi), Tetsuya Takeda (her husband), Sumie Sasaki (her mother), Misako Konno (Masuno), Taro Kawano (Isokichi), Naoko Nozawa (Sanae), Miho Takagi (Matsue), Tatsuo Matsumura (principal), Kiyoshi Atsumi (narrator).

A Shochiku Co., Ltd. Production. Color. Spherical Wide screen. 129 minutes. Released 1987.

U.S. VERSION: Release undetermined, possibly by Shochiku Films of America, Inc., with English subtitles. No MPAA rating.

Chizuko's Younger Sister / Futari ("Two People"). Producers, Kuniyoshi Kawashima, Kyoko Obayashi, and Shuji Tanuma; Director, Nobuhiko Obayashi; Screenplay, Chiho Katsura, based on the novel by Jiro Akagawa; Director of Photography, Juichi Nagano; Music, Joe Hisaishi.

CAST: Hikari Ishida, Tomoko Nakajima, Toshinori Omi, Sumiko Fuji, Ittoku Kishibe.

A PSC Co., Ltd. Production. Color. Spherical wide screen (?). 150 minutes. Released 1991.

U.S. VERSION: Distributor undetermined. 120 minutes. No MPAA rating. Released October 18, 1991.

Chushingura ("Chushingura"). Executive Producers, Sanezumi Fujimoto, Tomoyuki Tanaka, and Hiroshi Inagaki; Director, Hiroshi Inagaki; Screenplay, Toshio Yasumi, based on the 1748 Kabuki play-cycle *Kanadehon Chushingura* by Izumo Takeda, Senryu Namiki, and Shoraku Miyoshi; Director of Photography, Kazuo Yamada; Art Director, Kisaku Ito; Lighting, Masashiichi Kojima; Music, Akira Ifukube; Sound Recording, Yoshi Nishikawa; Choreography, Kiyokata Seruwaka; Assistant Director, Teruo Maru. *Toho Special Effects Group:* Director, Eiji Tsuburaya.

CAST: Koshiro Matsumoto (Chamberlain Kuranosuke Oishi), Yuzo Kayama (Takuminokami Asano), Chusha Ichikawa (Kozukenosuke Kira), Toshiro Mifune (Genba Tawaraboshi), Yoko Tsukasa (Aguri Asano), Setsuko Hara (Riku Oichi, *the chamberlain's wife*), Tatsuya Mihashi (Yasubei Horibe), Yosuke Natsuki (Kinemon Okano), Ichiro Arishima (Lord Denpachiro Tamura), Norihei Miki (Gayboy Geisha), Frankie Sakai (Carpenter Goro), Keiju Kobayashi (Awajinokami Wakisake), Yuriko Hoshi (Otsuya), Makoto Sato (Kazuemon Fuwa), Ryo Ikebe (Chikara Tsuchiya, *Kira's next-door neighbor*), Hisaya Morishige (Hanbei), Daisuke Kato (Kichiemon Terasaka), Yumi Shirakawa (Ume), Kumi Mizuno

***Opposite:* Yosuke Natsuki and Yuriko Hoshi in *Chushingura* (1962). Note Eiji Tsuburaya's forced-perspective set and the young girls playing adult women in the background.**

(Saho, *a spy*), Akira Takarada (Gunpei Takada), Takashi Shimura (Hyobe Chishaka), Hiroshi Koizumi (Gengo Otaka), Akira Kubo (Lord Date), Jun Tazaki (Kiken Murakami), Seizaburo Kawazu (Asano official), Yu Fujiki (Takebayashi), Yoshio Kosugi (Yasubei's tough father), Akihiko Hirata, Tadao Takashima, Yoshio Tsuchiya, Nadao Kirino, Hisaya Ito, Ren Yamamoto, Kenji Sahara (Asano samurai), Reiko Dan (Okaru), Sachio Sakai (spy), Kamatari Fujiwara (innkeeper), Ikio Sawamura (mat-maker), Mie Hama (woman refugee), Senkichi Omura (concerned citizen at collapsed bridge), Michiyo Aratama, Somegoro Ichikawa, Mannosuke Nakamura, Keiko Awaji, Mitsuko Kusabue, Sadako Sawamura, Chieko Nakakita, Susumu Fujita.

A Toho Co., Ltd. Production. Eastman Color. Toho Scope. 206 minutes. Released 1962.

U.S. VERSION: Released by Toho International Co., Ltd. English subtitles. 108 minutes. No MPAA rating. Released October 3, 1963. Reissued by Berkely Cinema Guild in 1966 running 204 minutes. Subtitles, Herman G. Weinberg. Also known as *Chushingura: 47 Samurai*. Reissued by East-West Classics subtitled and running 208 minutes. The otherwise excellent letterboxed video version is missing ent'racte, and possible overture, intermission and exit music as well. Subtitles, Steve Barger; Subtitles Editor, Audie Bock.

City of Beasts / Yaju toshi ("City of Beasts"). Director, Jun Fukuda; Screenplay, Yoshihiro Ishimatsu, based on a story by Haruhiko Oyabu; Director of Photography, Yuzuru Aizawa; Art Director, Juichi Ikuno; Music, Masaru Sato.

CAST: Toshio Kurosawa (Arima), Rentaro Mikuni (Ishihama), Noriko Takahashi (Mitsuko Ishihama, *his daughter*), Hosei Komatsu (Iwano), Shuji Otaki (Hanaya), Ryuji Kita (Kanamori), Kaai Okada.

A Toho Co., Ltd. Production. Eastman Color. Panavision (?). 88 minutes. May 23, 1970.

U.S. VERSION: Release undetermined, possibly by Toho International Co., Ltd. English subtitles. No MPAA rating.

A Class to Remember / Gakko ("School"). Producer, Shigehiro Nakagawa; Director, Yoji Yamada; Screenplay, Yoji Yamada and Yoshitaka Asama, based on an original story by Yoji Yamada; Directors of Photography, Tetsuo Takaba and Mutsuo Naganuma; Music, Isao Tomita.

CAST: Toshiyuki Nishida, Keiko Takeshita, Kunie Tanaka, Kiyoshi Atsumi.

A Shochiku Co., Ltd./Nippon Television Network Production. Dolby Stereo. Color. Spherical wide screen (1.85 × 1). 128 minutes. Released 1993.

U.S. VERSION: Released by Shochiku Co., Ltd. English subtitles. 128 minutes. No MPAA rating. Released July 6, 1994.

The Claws of Satan / Gekko kamen – Satan no tsume ("Moonlight Mask – Nail of Satan"). Director, Eijiro Wakabayashi.

CAST: Fumitake Omura, Tomoko Matsushima.

A Toei Co., Ltd. Production. Black and white (processed by Toei Chemsitry Co., Ltd.). ToeiScope. 62 minutes. Released December 17, 1958.

U.S. VERSION: Reportedly released in the United States, distributor undetermined. The 3rd "Moonlight Mask" feature. Followed by *The Monster Gorilla* (1959).

The Cleanup / Arashi no Yushatachi ("Encouraging People of the Storm"). Director, Toshio Masuda; Screenplay, Shuichi Nagahara; Director of Photography, Yoshihiro Yamazaki; Art Director, Takeo Kimura; Music, Harumi Ibe.

CAST: Yujiro Ishihara (Shimaji), Mie Hama (Akiko Shima), Tetsuya Watari (Karasawa), Sayuri Yoshinaga, Hideaki Nitani, Yoko Yamamoto.

A Nikkatsu Corp. Production. Fujicolor. NikkatsuScope. 100 minutes. Released December 31, 1969.

U.S. VERSION: Release undetermined. English subtitles. No MPAA rating.

The College Hero / Daigaku no ninkimono ("The College Hero"). Producers, Masumi Fujimoto and Hisao

Ichikawa; Director, Shue Matsubayashi; Screenplay, Katsuya Suzaki; Director of Photography, Taiichi Kankura; Art Director, Shinobu Muraki; Music, Koji Taku.

CAST: Akira Takarada (Kageyama), Fubuki Koshiji (his sister), Reiko Dan (Junko), Akira Kubo (Taki), Izumi Yukimura (his sweetheart), Ryo Ikebe (Coach Urano).

A Toho Co., Ltd. Production. Eastman Color. Toho Scope. 104 minutes. Released September 30, 1958.

U.S. VERSION: Release undetermined, possibly by Toho International Co., Ltd. in subtitled format.

College Is a Nice Place / Daigaku yoi toko ("College Is a Nice Place"). Director, Yasujiro Ozu; Screenplay, Masao Arata, based on an idea by James Maki [Yasujiro Ozu]; Director of Photography, Hideo Shigehara.

CAST: Toshiaki Konoe, Chishu Ryu, Sanae Takasugi, Tatsuo Saito, Kenji Oyama, Choko Iida.

A Shochiku Co., Ltd. Production. Filmed at Shochiku-Kamata Studios. Silent. Black and white. Academy ratio. Running time undetermined. Released March 19, 1936.

U.S. VERSION: Never released theatrically in the United States. A lost film.

Come Marry Me / Oyome ni oide ("Come Marry Me"). Producer, Sanezumi Fujimoto; Director, Ishiro Honda; Screenplay, Zenzo Matsuyama; Director of Photography, Shinsaku Uno; Music, Kenjiro Hirose.

CAST: Yuzo Kayama, Yoko Naito, Keiko Sawai, Ichiro Arishima, Yukiko Kobayashi, Toshio Kurosawa, Yutaka Wakayama, Kenzo Tabu, Kazuo Suzuki, Senkichi Omura, Haruya Kato, Ikio Sawamura, Chishu Ryu.

A Toho Co., Ltd. Production. Color. Toho Scope. 84 minutes. Released 1966.

U.S. VERSION: Released by Toho International Co., Ltd. English subtitles. 84 minutes. No MPAA rating. Released September 20, 1967.

Comic Magazine / Komikku zasshi nanika irani ("I Don't Want Comic Magazine"). Producer, Yutaka Okada; Director, Yojiro Takita; Screenplay, Yuya Uchida and Isao Takagi, based on the comic magazine headlines of 1985; Director of Photography, Yoichi Shiga; Art Director, Minoru Oshiwa; Lighting, Masao Kanazawa; Editor, Masatsugi Sakai; Music, Katsuo Ono; Sound Recording, Takashi Sugisaki; Assistant Director, Heikichi Fujiwara.

CAST: Yuya Uchida (Toshiaki Kinameri), Yumi Aso (girlfriend), Beat Takeshi [aka Takeshi Kitano] (Yakuza killer), Hiromi Go (George), Rikiya Yasuoka (man at drinking bar), Tsurutaro Kataoka (gigolo), Kazuyoshi Miura (himself), Seiko Matsuda (herself), Pussycat Club.

An M & R Film Production. Color. Spherical wide screen. 120 minutes. Released 1986.

U.S. VERSION: Released by Cinecom. English subtitles. No MPAA rating. Released March 24, 1986.

Company Executives / Shacho ("Company President"). Producer, Shigeru Okada; Director, Toshio Masuda; Screenplay, Hiro Masuda; Director of Photography, Kiyoshi Kitasaka; Music, Ryudo Uzaki.

CAST: Ken Ogata, Yukiyo Toake, Toru Emori.

A Toei Co., Ltd. Production. Color. ToeiScope (?). 129 minutes. Released 1989.

U.S. VERSION: Distributor, if any, is undetermined.

Computer Free-for-All / Buchamukure daihakken ("Buchamukure Great Discovery"). Executive Producer, Tomoyuki Tanaka; Director, Kengo Furusawa; Screenplay, Yasuo Tanami; Director of Photography, Senkichi Nagai; Art Director, Kazuo Ogawa; Music, Naozumi Yamamoto; Sound, Toho Recording Centre; Sound Effects, Toho Sound Effects Group.

CAST: Hajime Hana (Hanakawado), Kei Tani (Tanii), Hitoshi Ueki (Uemura), Hiroshi Inuzuka, Senri Sakurai, Eitaro Ishibashi, Shin Yasuda, Masumi Kagawa, Sami Nabeo.

A Watanabe/Toho Co., Ltd. Production. Westrex Recording system. Eastman

Color. Academy ratio (?). 84 minutes. Released January 1, 1969.

U.S. VERSION: Released by Toho International Co., Ltd. English subtitles. The 12th "Crazy" feature. Followed by *The Crazy Cats' Great Explosion* (1969). 84 minutes. No MPAA rating. Released April 30, 1969.

The Concubines / Chin-P'ing-Mei ("Plum Flowers in the Golden Vase"). Producer, Kiyoshi Ogasawara; Assistant Producer, Hideo Tomohisa; Director, Koji Takamatsu; Screenplay, Jiku Yamatoya, based on the 16th-century novel *Chin P'ing Mei* (presumably) by Shin-chen Wang; Director of Photography, Hideo Ito; Lighting, Hajime Isomi; Art Director, Shukei Hirataka; Set Design, Ogawa Kogei; Editor, Tadashi Tsuji; Music, Masao Yagi; Sound Recording, Takashi Sugizaki; Assistant Directors, Michio Akiyama and Isao Okijima; Production Manager, Masayuki Yamana; Costumes, Tokyo Costumes Co., Ltd.

CAST: Tomoko Mayama (Pan Chin Lien), Shikyoku Takashima (Wu Sing), Juzo Itami (Hsi Men Ching), Ruriko Asari (Li Ping-Brh), Riko Kurenai (Chun Mei), Hatsuo Yamatani (Wu Ta), Ko Hei Tsusaki (Ying), Yuzo Yachikawa (Hau Yung).

A Unicorn Productions, Ltd. Production. Distributor undetermined. Eastman Color. Anamorphic wide screen. Released 1968 (?).

U.S. VERSION: Released by Box Office International Pictures, Inc. A Harry Novak Presentation. English subtitles (?). English version (i.e. subtitles?), James E. McClarty. Alternate title: *The Notorious Concubines*. Wide screen process billed as CinemaScope in the United States. 90 minutes. No MPAA rating. Released July 1969.

Conflagration / Enjo ("Conflagration"). Producer, Masaichi Nagata; Director, Kon Ichikawa; Screenplay, Natto Wada and Keiji Hasebe, based on a story by Yukio Mishima; Director of Photography, Kazuo Miyagawa; Music, Toshiro Mayuzumi; Art Director, Yoshinobu Nishioka; Lighting, Kenichi Okamoto; Sound Recording, Masao Okada; Editor, Shigeo Nishida.

CAST: Raizo Ichikawa (Goichi Mizoguchi), Tatsuya Nakadai (Kashiwagi), Ganjiro Nakamura (Tayamadosen), Yoichi Funaki (Tsurukawa), Yae Kitabayashi (Aki, *Goichi's mother*), Jun Hamamura (Shodo, *Goichi's father*).

A Daiei Motion Picture Co., Ltd. Production. Black and white. DaieiScope. 96 minutes. Released August 19, 1958.

U.S. VERSION: Distributor undetermined, though likely Daiei International Films, Inc. English subtitles. 96 minutes. No MPAA rating. Released September 1964.

Conquest / Akuto ("Villain"). Director/Screenplay, Kaneto Shindo; Original Story, Junichiro Tanizaki, based on the prologue and first act of the 1748 Kabuki play-cycle *Kanadehon Chushingura* by Izumo Takeda, Senryu Namiki, and Shoraku Miyoshi; Director of Photography, Kiyoshi [Kiyomi] Kuroda; Music, Hikaru Hayashi.

CAST: Kyoko Kishida (Kaoyo), Eitaro Ozawa, Nobuko Otawa, Ko Kimura, Taiji Tonoyama.

A Kindai Eiga Kyokai Co., Ltd. Production. A Toho Co., Ltd. Release. Black and white. Toho Scope. 119 minutes. Released 1965.

U.S. VERSION: Released by Toho International Co., Ltd. English subtitles. 119 minutes. No MPAA rating. Released September 1966.

Could I But Live / Ware hitotsubu no mugi naredo ("I Am a Grain of Barley, but..."). Executive Producers, Ichiro Sato and Hideyuki Shino; Director/Screenplay, Zenzo Matsuyama; Director of Photography, Hiroshi Murai; Music, Masaru Sato.

CAST: Keiju Kobayashi (Sakata), Hideko Takamine (mistress), Yoshie Mizutani, Kon Omura, Shiro Otsuji, Kin Sugai, Kikue Mori.

A Tokyo Eiga Co., Ltd. Production. A Toho Co., Ltd. Release. Black and white. Toho Scope. 108 minutes. Released 1964.

U.S. VERSION: Released by Toho International Co., Ltd. English subtitles. 108 minutes. No MPAA rating. Released January 19, 1965.

Counterstroke / Hoero Datsugokushu ("Barking Order to the Escaped Convict"). Executive Producers, Tomoyuki Tanaka and Reiji Miwa; Director, Jun Fukuda; Screenplay, Katsuya Suzaki; Director of Photography, Shoji Uchiumi; Music, Kenjiro Hirose.

CAST: Makoto Sato, Yosuke Natsuki, Yuriko Hoshi, Jun Tazaki, Kumi Mizuno.

A Toho Co., Ltd. Production. Black and white. Toho Scope. 75 minutes. Released 1961.

U.S. VERSION: Release undetermined, possibly by Toho International Co., Ltd. in subtitled format. No MPAA rating. Release date, if any, is undetermined.

A Couple on the Move / Hikkoshi fufu ("A Couple on the Move"). Director, Yasujiro Ozu; Screenplay, Akira Fushimi, based on an idea by Ippei Kikuchi; Director of Photography, Hideo Shigehara.

CAST: Atsushi Watanabe, Mitsuko Yoshikawa, Kenji Oyama, Tomoko Naniwa, Ichiro Ogushi, Chishu Ryu.

A Shochiku Co., Ltd. Production. Filmed at Shochiku-Kamata Studios. Silent with benshi. Black and white. Academy ratio. 60 minutes. Released September 28, 1928.

U.S. VERSION: Never released in the United States. A lost film.

The Crab-Canning Ship / Kanikosen ("The Crab-Canning Ship"). Producer, Tengo Yamada; Director, So Yamamura; Screenplay, So Yamamura, based on the novel by Takiji Kobayashi; Director of Photography, Yoshio Miyajima; Art Director, Motoshi Kijima; Music, Akira Ifukube.

CAST: So Yamamura (Matsuki), Masayuki Mori (the doctor), Akitake Kono (Shibaura), Ko Mihashi (Asakawa), Akira Tani (Suda), Mikizo Hirata (foreman), Rosaki Kawarazaki (boy), Shin Morikawa (Kurasa), Sumiko Hidaka (whore), Sanae Nakahara (Natsu), Harue Wakahara (dancer), Shisue Yamagishi (mother), Yasushi Mizura (young man).

A Gendai Productions Production. Black and white. Academy ratio. 112 minutes. Released 1953.

U.S. VERSION: Distributor undetermined. English subtitles. 112 minutes. No MPAA rating. Release date undetermined.

The Crazy Family / Gyakufunsha kazoku ("Retro-Firing Family"). Executive Producers, Kazuhiko Hasegawa, Toyoji Yamane, and Shiro Sasaki; Producer, Banmei Takahashi; Planning, Susumu Miyasaka and Shosuke Taga; Director, Sogo Ishii; Screenplay, Yoshinori Kobayashi, Fumio Konami, and Sogo Ishii, based on an idea by Yoshinori Kobayashi; Director of Photography, Masaki Tamura; Art Director, Terumi Hosoishi; Set Decorator, Yoshikazu Furuya; Lighting, Yuzuru Sato; Music, 1984; Song Performers, Hitoshi Ueki and Katsuya Kobayashi; Costumes, Kyoto Costumes; Makeup, Midori Konuma; Sound Recording, Shin Fukuda (Fukushima Onkyo Co., Ltd.); Editor, Junichi Kikuchi; Production Manager, Toshihiro Osato; Assistant Director, Hideyuki Yonehara; Special Effects, Takashi Ito; Special Modeling Art, Hiroshi Hayashida; Suspension Effects, Liberty House, Yukimitsu Sugano, and Kame Ogasawara; Fight Director, Yoshijiro Nishimoto; Stunts, Japan Action Club; Dialect Instructor, Reiko Katsura.

CAST: Katsuya Kobayashi (Katsuhiko Kobayashi, *the father*), Mitsuko Baisho (Saeko Kobayashi, *the mother*), Yoshiki Arizono (Masaki Kobayashi, *the son*), Yuki Kudo (Erika Kobayashi, *the daughter*), Hitoshi Ueki (Yasukuni Kobayashi, *the grandfather*), Kazuhiko Kishino, Toyoko Koumi, Akira Ogata, Iwao Hayazaki, Nobuhiro Gomori, Yoshinori Inoue, Hirona Takahashi, Kunihiro Ide, Alex Ablamov.

A Director's Company/Art Theatre Guild/Kokusai Hoei Production. Color. Spherical Wide screen. 107 minutes. Released 1984.

U.S. VERSION: Released by New Yorker Films. English subtitles. 107 minutes. No MPAA rating. Released February 1986. Alternate title: *Black-Jet Family*.

The Creature Called Man / Jaga wa hashitta ("Jaguar Run"). Executive Producer, Yorihiko Yamada;

Director, Kiyoshi Nishimura; Screenplay, Hiroshi Nagano and Yoshihiro Ishimatsu; Director of Photography, Kazutami Hara; Art Director, Shinobu Muraki; Music, Masahiko Sato.

CAST: Yuzo Kayama (Toda), Jiro Tamiya (Kujo), Mariko Kaga (Toda's assistant), Nancy Sommers (Kujo's girl friend), Nobuo Nakamura (Head of N-Bussan), Shigeru Koyama.

A Toho Co., Ltd. Production. Eastman Color. Panavision. Released April 1970.

U.S. VERSION: Released by Toho International Co., Ltd. English subtitles. 93 minutes. No MPAA rating. Released October 7, 1970.

The Crescent Moon / Yumiharizuki ("The Crescent Moon"). [production credits unavailable].

CAST: Chiyonsuki Azuma, Yumika Hasezawa, K. Yashioji.

A Toei Co., Ltd. Production. Black and white (processed by Toei Chemistry Co., Ltd.). Academy ratio. 55 minutes. Released 1955.

U.S. VERSION: Distributor, if any, is undetermined. Part two of a trilogy (?).

The Crest of Man [production credits unavailable].

CAST: Sayuri Yoshinaga, Mitsuo Hamada, Seiji Miyaguchi, Tanie Kitabayashi.

A Nikkatsu Corporation Production. Released 1964 (?).

U.S. VERSION: Released by Toho International Co., Ltd. English subtitles. Running time undetermined. No MPAA rating. Released October 1965.

Crimson Bat Oichi: Wanted, Dead or Alive / Mekura no Oichi Inochi Moraimasu ("Blind Oichi, I Will Have Your Life"). Director, Hirokazu Ichimura; Screenplay, Teruo Tanaka, based on a story by Koji Takada; Director of Photography, Masao Kosugi; Art Director, Chiyoo Umeda; Music, Takeo Watanabe.

CAST: Yoko Matsuyama (Oichi), Yuki Meguro (Sankuro), Shinji Hotta (Jinbei), Hitoshi Omae (Jokai), Jun Tazaki (Boss Nadaman), Meicho Soganoya (Kamecho), Reiko Oshida (Ohan), Tetsuro Tamba (Hyoe).

A Shochiku Co., Ltd. Production. Eastman Color. Shochiku GrandScope. 86 minutes. Released April 8, 1970.

U.S. VERSION: Released by Shochiku Films of America, Inc. English-dubbed and subtitled versions available. The 4th and final "Crimson Bat" feature. No MPAA rating. Released October 5, 1973.

Crimson Bat, the Blind Swordswoman / Makka na Nagaredori ("Wandering Red Bird"). Director, Teiji Matsuda; Screenplay, Ikuro Suzuki; Director of Photography, Shintaro Kawasaki; Art Director, Toshitaka Kurahashi; Music, Hajime Kaburagi.

CAST: Yoko Matsuyama (Oichi, *the Crimson Bat*), Isamu Nagato (Jubei), Akitake Kono (Yasuke), Jun Tatara (Nihei), Satoshi Amatsu (Denzo), Chizuko Arai (Obun).

A Shochiku Co., Ltd. Production. Eastman Color. Shochiku GrandScope. 88 minutes. Released March 15, 1969.

U.S. VERSION: Released by Shochiku Films of America, Inc. English subtitles. The 1st feature in the 4-film "Crimson Bat" series (1969–70). Followed by *Trapped, the Crimson Bat* (1969). No MPAA rating. Released July 30, 1969.

The Crowded Streetcar / Manin densha ("The Crowded Streetcar"). Producer, Hidemasa Nagata; Director, Kon Ichikawa; Screenplay, Natto Wada and Kon Ichikawa; Director of Photography, Hiroshi Murai; Music, Koji Taku; Art Director, Tomo Shimogawara; Lighting, Isamu Yoneyama; Sound Recording, Toshikazu Watanabe.

CAST: Hiroshi Kawaguchi (Tamio Moroi), Chishu Ryu (Genroku, *his father*), Haruko Sugimura (Otome, *his mother*), Michiko Ono (Runa Iki), Keizo Kawasaki (Taro Washiba).

A Daiei Motion Picture Co., Ltd. Production. Black and white. Academy ratio. 100 minutes. Released March 29, 1957.

U.S. VERSION: Distributor, if any, is undetermined, though likely Daiei International Films in subtitled format.

Cry for Happy. Producer, William Goetz; Director, George Marshall; Screenplay, Irving Beecher, based on the novel by George Campbell; Director of Photography, Burnett Guffey; Editor, Chester W. Schaeffer; Art Director, Walter Holscher; Music, George Duning; "Cry for Happy," Music and Lyrics by George Duning and Stanley Styne, sung by Miyoshi Umeki; Sound Recording, Lambert Day; Assistant Director, George Marshall, Jr.

CAST: Glenn Ford (Andy Cyphers), Donald O'Connor (Murray Prince), Miiko Taka (Chiyoko), James Shigeta (Suzuki), Miyoshi Umeki (Harue), Howard St. John (Admiral Bennett), Joe Flynn (Mcintosh), Chet Douglas (Lank), Tsuruko Kobayashi (Koyuki), Harriet E. MacGibbon (Mrs. Bennett), Robert Kino (Eudo), Bob Okazaki (Izumi), Harlan Warde (Chaplain), Nancy Kovack (Miss Cameron), Ted Knight (Lt. Glick), Bill Quinn (Lyman), Chiyo Nakasone (Keiko).

A William Goetz Production. A Columbia Pictures Corp. Release. A U.S. production in English and filmed, in part, in Japan. Stereophonic sound. Eastman Color. CinemaScope. 110 minutes. Released January 1961.

Cry of the Mountain / Kitahodaka zessho ("Superb Song of Kitahodaka"). Director, Tadashi Sawashima.

CAST: Yuriko Hoshi, Kinya Kitaoji.

A Toho Co., Ltd. Production. Released September 1968.

U.S. VERSION: Released by Toho International Co., Ltd. English subtitles (?). 93 minutes. No MPAA rating. Released October 1969.

Curse of the Blood / Kaidan zankoku monogatari ("Cruel Ghost Legend"). Producer, Tsuneo Kosumi; Director, Kazuo Hase; Screenplay, Masahige Narusawa, based on the novel, *Kaidan ruigafuchi* by Renzaburo Shibata; Director of Photography, Kenji Maruyama; Production Manager, Hisamune Tamau; Assistant Director, Hideo Ohe; Art Director, Kyohei Morita; Set Decoration, Shinei Bijutsu Kozei; Editor, Kazuo Ota; Sound Effects, Takashi Matsumoto; Music, Hajime Kaburagi.

CAST: Matsuhiro Tomura (Shinzaemon Fukaya), Nobuo Kaneko (Shojun Yasukawa), Masakazu Tamura (Shinichiro), Yusuke Kawazu (Shinzo), Hiroko Sakurai (Ohisa), Saeda Kazaguchi (Toyosuga), Masumi Harukawa (Okuma), Yukie Kagawa (Hana), Eizo Kitamura (Sobe Shimofusaya), Genshu Hanayagi (Toyo).

A Shochiku Co., Ltd. Production. Fujicolor (processed by Shochiku Laboratory). Shochiku GrandScope. 88 minutes. Released March 31, 1968.

U.S. VERSION: Released by Shochiku Films of America, Inc. English subtitles. Alternate title: *Cruel Ghost Legend. Note:* Released in the United States in black and white. 88 minutes. No MPAA rating. Released 1969 (?).

The Curse of the Ghost / Oiwa no borei ("The Ghost of Oiwa"). Executive Producer, Hiroshi Ozawa; Producer, Masaichi Nagata; Director, Issei Mori; Screenplay, Kinya Naoi, based on the play *Yotsuya kaidan* by Nanboku Tsuruya; Director of Photography, Senkichiro Takeda; Art Director, Seiichi Ota; Music, Ichiro Saito; Sound Recording, Iwao Otani; Lighting, Shinichi Ito; Editor, Toshio Taniguchi; Assistant Director, Hitoshi Obuchi; Special Effects, Daiei Special Effects Department.

CAST: Kei Sato (Iyemon), Yoshihiko Aoyama (Yomoshichi, *a samurai*), Shoji Kobayashi (Naosuke), Jun Hamamura (Oiwa's father), Gen Kimura (Okuda), Kazuko Ineno (Oiwa), Kyoko Mikage (Osode), Sonosuke Sawamura (Takuetsu), Yasuhiro Mizukami (Kohei), Chikako Masago (Oume), Ikuno Mori, Shozo Nanbu, Tatsuo Hanabu, Tokio Oki, Teruko Omi.

A Daiei Motion Picture Co., Ltd. Production. A Masaichi Nagata Presentation. Westrex recording system. Fujicolor. DaieiScope. 94 minutes. Released 1969.

U.S. VERSION: Released by Daiei International Films, Inc. English subtitles. Other versions include *Shinchaku kaidan* (1949), *Tokaido Yotsuya kaidan* (1959), *Yotsuya kaidan* (1959), and *Yotsuya kaidan* (1965). 94 minutes. No MPAA Rating. Released 1969.

Cyborg 009 / Saiborg 009 ("Cyborg 009") [**animated**]. Director, Yugo Serikawa; Screenplay, Takashi Iijima and Yugo Serikawa; Chief Animator, Keiichiro Kimura.

VOICE CHARACTERIZATIONS: (undetermined).

A Toei Animation Studio Co., Ltd. Production. A Toei Co., Ltd. Release. Eastman Color. ToeiScope. 64 minutes. Released 1966.

U.S. VERSION: Distributor, if any, is undetermined. No MPAA rating. Sequel: *Cyborg 009—Underground Duel* (1967).

Cyborg 009—Underground Duel / Saiborg 009—kaiju senso ("Cyborg 009—Monster War") [**animated**]. Director, Yugo Serikawa; Screenplay, Kei Iijima, Yugo Serikawa, and Daisaku Shirakawa; Director of Photography, Shigeyoshi Ikeda.

VOICE CHARACTERIZATIONS: (undetermined).

A Toei Animation Studio Co., Ltd. Production. A Toei Co., Ltd. Release. Eastman Color. ToeiScope. 60 minutes. Released 1967.

U.S. VERSION: Distributor, if any, is undetermined. Available with English subtitles. Followed by a sequel in 1980.

Dagora, the Space Monster / Uchu daikaiju Dogora ("Giant Space Monster Dogora"). Executive Producer, Tomoyuki Tanaka; Director, Ishiro Honda; Screenplay, Shinichi Sekizawa, based on Jojiro Okami's story "Space Mons"; Director of Photography, Hajime Koizumi; Art Director, Takeo Kita; Editor, Ryohei Fujii; Music, Akira Ifukube; Sound Recording, Fumio Yanoguchi; Sound, Toho Recording Centre; Sound Effects, Hishashi Shimonaga, Toho Sound Effects Group; Assistant Director, Ken Sano. *Toho Special Effects Group*: Director, Eiji Tsuburaya; Cameramen, Teisho Arikawa and Mototaka Tomioka; Art Director, Akira Watanabe; Lighting, Kuichiro Kishida; Optical Photography, Yukio Manoda, Yoshiyuki Tokumasa and Sadao Iizuka; Assistant to Tsuburaya, Teruyoshi Nakano; Wire Manipulation, Fumio Nakadai; Matte Process, Hiroshi Mukoyama.

CAST: Yosuke Natsuki (Inspector), Robert Dunham (Mark Jackson), Hiroshi Koizumi (Kirino), Yoko Fujiyama (Musiyo), Jun Tazaki (chief inspector), Yoshifumi Tajima (Tada the Gangster), Eisei Amamoto (safecracker), Susumu Fujita (General Iwasa), Akiko Wakabayashi (moll), Seizaburo Kawazu (bearded diamond thief), Nobuo Nakamura (scientist), Haruya Kato (Sabu), Nadao Kirino (thief), Jun Funato (inspector's partner), Akira Wakamatsu, Chotaro Togin.

A Toho Co., Ltd. Production. Eastman Color (processed by Tokyo Laboratory Ltd.). Toho Scope. 81 minutes. Released August 11, 1964.

U.S. VERSION: Reviewed by *Variety* at the Trieste Sci-Fi Film Festival, but information on its U.S. theatrical release, if any, is undetermined. Possibly released by Toho International, either dubbed or in subtitled format in July 1965. International title: *Space Monster Dogora*. Released to television by American International Television (AIP-TV). English-dubbed. A James H. Nicholson & Samuel Z. Arkoff Presentation. Executive Producers, James H. Nicholson and Samuel Z. Arkoff; Postproduction Supervisor, Salvatore Billitteri; Rerecording, Titra Sound Studios; Prints by Pathé. Copyright 1965 by American International Productions. Although the above English-language title is correct, the monster is referred to throughout the film as "Dogora," and not "Dagora," which may explain the confusion over the monster's name. No MPAA Rating. 80 minutes.

Daijou, mai furendo ("Don't Worry, My Friend"). Producer, Hidenori Taga; Director/Screenplay, Ryu Murakami; Director of Photography, Kozo Okazaki; Lighting, Kazuo Shimamura; Assistant to the Director, Ryoichi Nakajima; Art Director, Osamu Yamaguchi; Sound Recordist, Hideo Nishizaki; Sound, Toho Recording Centre; Sound Effects, Toho Sound Effects Group; Editor, Sachiko Yamaji; Music Direction, Kazuhiko Kato.

CAST: Peter Fonda (Gonzy Traumerai),

Jinpachi Nezu (Doctor), Reana Hirota (Mimimi), Hirayuki Watanabe (Hachi), Yahiyuki No (Manika), Kumi Aiochi (Reiko).

A Toho Co., Ltd. Production. A Kitty Films, Inc. Picture. Color (processed by Tokyo Laboratory, Ltd.). Panavision. 119 minutes. Released April 15, 1983.

U.S. VERSION: Apparently unreleased in the United States. International Title: *All Right, My Friend.* Available through Toho International Co., Ltd.

The Dancer / Maihime ("The Dancer"). Producers, Masato Hara and Manfred Durniok; Director, Masahiro Shinoda; Screenplay, Hans Borgelt, Tsutomu Tamura and Masahiro Shinoda, based on an original story by Ogai Mori; Directors of Photography, Jurgen Jurges and Kazuo Miyagawa; Music, Cong Su.

CAST: Hiromi Go, Lisa Wolf, Brigitte Grothum, Haruko Kato, Mareiko Carriere.

A Herald Ace, Inc./Manfred Durniok Produktion Production. A Japanese/German co-production. Color. Panavision (?). 123 minutes. Released 1989.

U.S. VERSION: Distributor is undetermined. 123 minutes. No MPAA rating. Released April 20, 1991.

Dancing Mistress / Kaidan Iro-Zange-Kyoren onna shisho. Producer, Akira Koito; Director, Ryosuke Kurahashi; Screenplay, Shinichi Yanagawa; Director of Photography, Mikio Hattori.

CAST: Hiroshi Nawa, Yataro Kitagami, Jun Tazaki, Achako Hanabishi, Machiko Mizukara, Michio Saga.

A Shochiku Co., Ltd. Production. Black and white (processed by Shochiku Laboratory). Academy ratio. Running time undetermined. Released 1957.

U.S. VERSION: Distributor, if any, is undetermined.

The Dangerous Kiss. Director, Yuzo Kawashima; Screenplay, Zenzo Matsuyama; Music, Toshiro Mayuzumi.

CAST: Akira Takarada, Michiyo Aratama, Reiko Dan, Mitsuko Kusabue, Akemi Kita, Ichiro Nakatani, Seizaburo Kawazu, Haruko Togo, Takao Zushi, Kichijiro Ueda, Shintaro Ishihara, Sachio Sakai, Ichiro Arishima, Yuriko Hoshi, Sadako Sawamura.

A Toho Co., Ltd. Production. Eastman Color. Toho Scope. 83 minutes. Released 1960.

U.S. VERSION: Released by Toho International Co., Ltd. English subtitles. 83 minutes. No MPAA rating. Released February 24, 1961.

The Daphne / Jinchoge ("The Daphne"). Producer, Masumi Fujimoto; Director, Yasuki Chiba; Screenplay, Zenzo Matsuyama; Director of Photography, Asakazu Nakai; Music, Toshiro Mayuzumi.

CAST: Machiko Kyo (1st daughter), Haruko Sugimura (Daphne), Reiko Dan (3rd daughter), Yuriko Hoshi (4th daughter), Yoko Tsukasa (2nd daughter), Yosuke Natsuki (4th daughter's husband), Daisuke Kato, Akira Takarada, Makoto Sato, Tadao Takashima, Hiroshi Koizumi, Keiju Kobayashi, Tatsuya Nakadai.

A Toho Co., Ltd. Production. Eastman Color. Toho Scope. Released 1966.

U.S. VERSION: Released by Toho International Co., Ltd. English subtitles. 106 minutes. No MPAA rating. Released August 1967.

Daredevil in the Castle / Osaka-jo monogatari ("Story of Osaka Castle"). Producer, Tomoyuki Tanaka; Director, Hiroshi Inagaki; Screenplay, Hiroshi Inagaki and Takeshi Kimura; Original Story, Genzo Murakami; Director of Photography, Kazuo Yamada; Music, Akira Ifukube; Sound, Toho Recording Centre; Sound Effects, Toho Sound Effects Group. *Toho Special Effects Group*: Director, Eiji Tsuburaya; Photography, Teisho Arikawa and Mototaka Tomioka; Art Director, Akira Watanabe; Lighting, Kuichiro Kishida; Matte Process, Hiroshi Mukoyama; Optical Photography, Taka Yuki, Yukio Manoda.

CAST: Toshiro Mifune (Mohei), Kyoko Kagawa (Ai), Yuriko Hoshi (Senhime), Akihiko Hirata (Hayatonosho [Hayato] Susukida), Isuzu Yamada (Yodogami), Yoshiko Kuga (Kobue), Takashi Shimura, Hanchiro Iwai, Seizaburo Kawazu, Yu

Fujiki, Jun Tazaki, Danko Ichikawa, Yosuke Natsuki, Susumu Fujita, Tetsuro Tamba, Tadao Nakamaru, Sachio Sakai, Yoshio Kosugi, Kichijiro Ueda, Chieko Nakakita, Ren Yamamoto, Shin Otomo, Eisei Amamoto, Senkichi Omura, Akira Tani, Ikio Sawamura, Koji Uno, Yasuhisa Tsutsumi, Haruo Nakajima, Hans Horneff, Bill Bassman, Toshiko Nakano, Osman Yusef.

A Toho Co., Ltd. Production. Western Electric Mirrophonic recording (encoded with Perspecta Stereophonic Sound). Eastman Color (processed by Tokyo Laboratory Ltd.). Toho Scope. 95 minutes. Released January 3, 1961.

U.S. VERSION: Released by Frank Lee International, Inc. English subtitles. Alternate title (?): *Devil in the Castle.* 95 minutes. No MPAA rating. Released June 6, 1961.

The Daring Nun / Ama-kuzure ("Destructive Nun"). Director, Kazuo Ikehiro; Screenplay, Kazuo Funabashi and Tetsuo Yoshida, based on an original story by Toko Kon; Director of Photography, Senkichiro Takeda; Art Director, Shigenori Shimoishizaka; Music, Takeo Watanabe.

CAST: Michiyo Yasuda (Sister Shunko), Kayo Mikimoto (Ikuko), Ichiro Nakatani (Goro), Kuniko Miyake (Mother Superior), Naomi Kobayashi, Shigako Shimegi.

A Daiei Motion Picture Co., Ltd. Production. Black and white. DaieiScope. 83 minutes. Released October 5, 1968.

U.S. VERSION: Distributor, if any, is undetermined. English subtitled version available. No MPAA rating.

Dark the Mountain Snow / Rokujo Yukiyama Tsumugi ("Making Yarn at the Falling Castle on Snow Mountain"?). Executive Producers, Ichiro Sato and Hideyuki Shiino; Director/Screenplay, Zenzo Matsuyama; Director of Photography, Kozo Okazaki; Music, Masaru Sato.

CAST: Hideko Takamine (Ine Rokujo), Frankie Sakai (Jiro), Keiju Kobayashi (Kyuemon's brother), Mayumi Ozora (Jiro's fiancée), Kikue Mori (Kyuemon's mother), Shigeru Shamiyama (Kyuemon Rokujo).

A Toho Co., Ltd. Production. Black and white. Toho Scope. 106 minutes. Released 1965.

U.S. VERSION: Released by Toho International Co. Ltd. English subtitles (?). 106 minutes. No MPAA rating. Released September 1966.

Dawn of Judo / Sugata Sanshiro ("Sanshiro Sugata"). Director, Kunio Watanabe; Screenplay, Kunio Watanabe, based on an original story by Tsuneo Tomita; Director of Photography, Hiroshi Nishimae; Art Director, Koken Kimura; Music, Yutaka Makino.

CAST: Muga Takewaki (Sanshiro Sugata), Koji Takahashi (Shogoro Yano), Nan Ozaki (Saotome), Yuji Hori (Murai), Joji Takagi (Higaki), Meicho Soganoya.

A Shochiku Co., Ltd. Production. Eastman Color. Shochiku GrandScope. 87 minutes. Released July 25, 1970.

U.S. VERSION: Released by Shochiku Films of America, Inc. English subtitles. Previously filmed by Akira Kurosawa as *Sanshiro Sugata* (1943), and later by Kihachi Okamoto (also as *Sanshiro Sugata*) in 1977. Not to be confused with director Watanabe's *The Birth of Judo* (1965). 87 minutes. No MPAA rating. Released February 17, 1971.

Day-Dream / Hakujitsumu ("Day-Dream"). Producer, Toyojiro Nagashima; Director, Tetsuji Takechi; Screenplay, Tetsuji Takechi, based on the short story "Hakujitsumu yume," originally presented in the September 1926 issue of *Chuo Koron*; Director of Photography, Masayoshi Kayanuma; Editor, Hanjiro Kaneko; Music Compilation, Sukehisa Shiba.

CAST: Kanako Michi (Cheiko), Akira Ishihama (Kurahashi), Chojuro Hanakawa (the dentist), Yasuko Matsui (the nurse).

A Daisan Productions, Ltd./Shochiku Co., Ltd. Production. Black and white with color sequences. Shochiku GrandScope. Released 1964.

U.S. VERSION: Released by Joseph Green Pictures, Inc. English subtitles (?). 92 minutes. No MPAA rating. Released December 4, 1964. Reissued 1966 with additional footage shot in the United States. Reissue Credits: Producer/Director,

Joseph Green; Director of Photography, Victor Peters; Assistant Camerman, Glen Tracy; Art Director/Masks Created by Anne George; Editor, Nat Greene.

The Day the Sun Rose / Gion matsuri ("Gion Festival"). Director, Tetsuya Yamanouchi; Screenplay, Hisayuki Suzuki and Kunio Shimizu, based on the story *Gionmatsuri* (1968) by Katsumi Nishiguchi; Planning, Daisuke Ito; Cooperation, Kyoto Prefecture, Kyoto City.

CAST: Kinnosuke Nakamura (Shinkichi), Toshiro Mifune (Kuma), Shima Iwashita (Ayame), Yunosuke Ito (Akamatsu), Takahiro Tamura (Sukematsu), Takashi Shimura (Tsuneemon), Eitaro Ozawa (Kadokura), Kamatari Fujiwara.

A Nihon Eiga Fukko Kyokai Production. A Shochiku Co., Ltd. Release. Color. Shochiku GrandScope (?). 168 minutes. Released 1968.

U.S. VERSION: Released by Shochiku Films of America, Inc. English subtitles. 168 minutes. No MPAA rating. Released February 12, 1969.

Days of Youth / Wakai hi ("Days of Youth"). Director, Yasujiro Ozu; Screenplay, Yasujiro Ozu and Akira Fushimi; Director of Photography, Hideo Shigehara.

CAST: Ichiro Yuki, Tatsuo Saito, Junko Matsui, Shinichi Himori, Chishu Ryu.

A Shochiku Co., Ltd. Production. Filmed at Shochiku-Kamata Studios. Silent with benshi. Black and white. Academy ratio. 60 minutes. Released April 13, 1929.

U.S. VERSION: Released by Shochiku Films of America, Inc. 60 minutes. No MPAA rating. Released 1972 (?).

Death by Hanging / Koshikei ("Death by Hanging"). Producers, Masayuki Nakajima, Tatsuji Yamaguchi, Nagisa Oshima; Director, Nagisa Oshima; Screenplay, Tsutomu Tamura, Mamoru Sasaki, Minichiro [Michinori] Fukao, and Nagisa Oshima; Supervisor, Teruyoshi Mukae; Assistant Director, Kiyioshi Ogakawara; Art Director, Jusho Toda; Director of Photography, Yasuhiro Yoshioka; Editor, Sueko Shiraishi; Music, Hikaru Hayashi; Sound Recording, Hideo Nishizaki; Sound Effects, Akira Suzuki.

CAST: Kei Sato (head of execution guard), Fumio Watanabe (education officer), Toshio Ishido (chaplain), Masao Adachi (security officer), Mutsuhiro Toura (doctor), Hosei Komatsu (prosecutor), Masao Matsuda (prosecution official), Akiko Koyama (girl), Yun-do Yun (R), Yoshio Tsuchiya (Rikichi), Kuninori Kodo (Gisaku), Nagisa Oshima (commentator).

A Sozosha (Creative Company)/Art Theatre Guild Production. Black and white. Spherical wide screen. 117 minutes. Released 1968.

U.S. VERSION: Released by Grove Press. English subtitles. 117 minutes. No MPAA rating. Released December 8, 1971.

Death of a Tea Master / Sen no Rikyu – Hongakubo Ibun ("Sen no Rikyu – Hongakubo's Student Writings"). Producer, Kazunobu Yamaguchi; Director, Kei Kumai; Screenplay, Yoshitaka Yoda, based on the novel *Hongakubo ibun* by Yasushi Inoue; Director of Photography, Masao Tochizawa; Music, Teizo Matsumura; Art Director, Takeo Kimura.

CAST: Eiji Okada (Honkakubo), Toshiro Mifune (Rikyu), Kinnosuke Yorozuya, Go Kato, Shinsuke Ashida, Eijiro Tono.

A The Seiyu, Ltd. Production. Color. Spherical wide screen (?). 107 minutes. Released 1989.

U.S. VERSION: Distributor undetermined. 107 minutes. No MPAA rating. Released June 1990.

Death on the Mountain / Aru sonan ("An Accident"). Executive Producer, Ichiro Nagashima; Director, Toshio Sugie; Screenplay, Teruo Ishii; Story, Seicho Matsumoto; Director of Photography, Tokuzo Kuroda; Music, Yoshiyuki Kozu.

CAST: Hisaya Ito, Takashi Wada, Kiyoshi Kodama, Kyoko Kagawa, Yoshio Tsuchiya.

A Tokyo Eiga Co., Ltd. Production. A Toho Co., Ltd. release. Black and white. Toho Scope. 87 minutes. Released June 17, 1961.

U.S. VERSION: Released by Toho International Co., Ltd. English subtitles. 87 minutes. No MPAA rating. Released November 1961.

Deathquake / Jishin retto ("Earthquake Islands"). Executive Producer, Tomoyuki Tanaka; Director, Kenjiro Omori; Screenplay, Kaneto Shindo; Director of Photography, Rokuro Nishigaki; Music, Toshiaki Tsushima; Art Director, Iwao Akune; Sound Recording, Kenshiro Hayashi; Gaffer, Shinji Kojima; Assistant Producer, Hideyuki Takai; Assistant Director, Masahiro Nara; Editor, Nobuo Ogawa; Sound Effects, Toho Sound Effects Group; Production Manager, Kishu Morichi. *Toho Special Effects Group:* Director, Teruyoshi Nakano; Directors of Photography, Takeshi Yamamoto and Mitsuhiro Hasegawa; Lighting, Masakuni Morimoto; Art Director, Yasuyuki Inoue; Assistant Director, Eiichi Asada; Optical Photography, Takeshi Miyanishi; Optical Effects, Tadaaki Watanabe; Production Manager, Keisuke Shinoda.

CAST: Hiroshi Katsuno, Toshiyuki Nagashima, Yumi Takigawa, Kayo Matsuo, Shuji Otaki, Eiji Okada, Shin Saburi, Norihei Miki, Tsutomu Yamazaki.

A Toho Co., Ltd. Production. Color (processed by Tokyo Laboratory Ltd.). Spherical wide screen. 127 minutes. Released August 30, 1980.

U.S. VERSION: Released by Shochiko Films of America. English subtitles (?). No MPAA rating. Released February 5, 1982. Released directly to television by UPA Productions of America (?), and to home video by MNTEX Entertainment, Inc. English-dubbed. 102 minutes. No MPAA rating. Running time also given at 94 minutes. Director's name is not given on the English-language version, while Shindo's name was withheld for the Japanese release. Alternate title: *Magnitude 7.9.*

Deer Friend / Kojika monogatari ("A Young Deer Story"). Producer, Yoshihiro Yuki; Director, Yukihiro Sawada; Screenplay, Takahisa Katsume and Yukihiro Sawada; Director of Photography, Akira Shizuka; Music, Joe Hisaishi.

CAST: Tomokazu Miura, Midori Kanazawa, Teppei Yamada.

A Nikkatsu Studios Production. Color. Spherical wide screen (?). 116 minutes. Released 1991.

U.S. VERSION: Distributor, if any, is undetermined.

The Demon / Kichiku. Producers, Yoshitaro Nomura and Yoshiki Nomura; Director, Yoshitaro Nomura; Screenplay, Masato Ide; Director of Photography, Takashi Kawamata; Art Director, Kyohei Morita; Music, Yasushi Akutagawa.

CAST: Shima Iwashita, Ken Ogata, Mayumi Ogawa.

A Shochiku Co., Ltd. Production. Color. Panavision (?). 110 minutes. Released 1977.

U.S. VERSION: Released by Shochiku Films of America in subtitled format. No MPAA rating. 110 minutes. Released June 22, 1979.

Demon Pond / Yashagaike ("Demon Pond"). Executive Producers, Shigemi Sugisaki, Yukio Tomizawa, Kanji Nakagawa; Director, Masahiro Shinoda; Screenplay, Takeshi Tamura and Haruhiko Minura, based on the play, *Yashanga ike* Kyoka Izumi; Assistant Producer, Seikichi Iizumi; Director of Photography, Masao Kosugi; Assistant Director, Isao Kumagai; Second Unit Director, Noritaka Sakamoto; Art Directors, Kiyoshi Awazu, Setsu Asakura, Yutaka Yokoyama; Music, Isao Tomita; Editors, Zen Ikeda, Sachiko Yamachi; Choreography, Rui Takemura; Special Effects Director, Nobuo Yajima.

CAST: Tamasaburo Bando (Yuri/Princess Shirayuki), Go Kato (Akira Hagiwara), Tsutomu Yamazaki (Gaukuen Yamasawa), Koji Nanbara (Priest Shikami), Yatsuko Tanami (nurse), Hisashi Igawa (the carp), Norihei Miki (catfish messenger), Juro Kara (Denkichi), Ryunosuke Kaneda (Diet member), Fujio Tokita (the crab), Jun Hamamura (the shadow/Yatabei, *the Bellkeeper*), Megumi Ishii (the camellia), Tadashi Furuta (the mackerel), Kazuo Sato (tiger priest), Kai Ato (the bone), Hatsuo Yamatani (Yoju, the villager), Maki Takayama (Yoju's Wife), Yumi Nishigami (Yoju's daughter), Toru Abe (leader of village assembly), Shigeru Yazaki (village teacher), Dai Kanai (village headman), Toshie Kobayashi (village woman), Hitoshi Omae (Furosude Kotori), Fudeko Tanaka (old woman).

A Shochiku Co., Ltd. Production. Shochikucolor. Spherical wide screen. Stereophonic sound (MagOptical?). 123 minutes. October 20, 1979.

Yuri Solomin and Maxim Munzuk in Akira Kurosawa's moving *Dersu Uzala* (1975).

U.S. VERSION: Released by Shochiku Films of America, Inc. English subtitles. Reissued by Kino International in 1982, also in subtitled format, as a Myron Bresnick Presentation from Grange Communications, Inc. 123 minutes. No MPAA rating. Released 1980.

Demons / Shura ("Demons"). Director, Toshio Matsumoto; Screenplay, Toshio Matsumoto, based on the Kabuki play by Nanboku Tsuruya; Director of Photography, Tatsuo Suzuki.

CAST: Katsuo Nakamura (Gengo), Yasuko Sanjo (Koman), Juro Kara (Sango), Masao Imafuku (Hachiemon).

A Matsumoto Productions/Art Theatre Guild Production. Color. Spherical wide screen (?). 135 minutes. Released 1971.

U.S. VERSION: Released by Film Images. English subtitles. 135 minutes. No MPAA rating. Released January 1974.

The Depths / Kaidan kasanegafuchi ("Ghost Story: Death of Kasane"). Producer, Mitsugu Okura; Director, Nobuo Nakagawa; Screenplay, Yasunori Kawauchi, based on the story "Shinkei Kasanegufuchi," by Encho Sanyutei; Director of Photography, Yoshimi Hirano.

CAST: Katsuko Wakasugi, Takashi Wada, Tetsuro Tamba, Noriko Kitazawa, Kikuko Hanaoka.

A Shintoho Co., Ltd. Production. Western Electric Mirrophonic recording. Eastman Color. Shintoho-Scope. 57 minutes. Released 1957.

U.S. VERSION: U.S. distributor undetermined. Also known as *The Ghost of Kasane* and *Ghost Story—The Kanane Swamp.* Remade by Daiei in 1960 and 1970 as *Kaidan Kasanegafuchi.* No MPAA rating.

Dersu Uzala / Derusu Uzara ("Dersu Uzala"). Producers, Nikolai Sizov and Yoichi Matsue; Director, Akira Kurosawa; Screenplay, Akira Kurosawa and Yuri Nagibin, based on the book *Dersu, okhotnik* by Vladimir K. Arsenieva; Associate Directors, Teruyo Nogami and Vladimir Vasiliev; Camera Operators, Asakazu Nakai, Yuri Gantman, and

Fyodor Dobronravov; Artist, Yuri Raksha; Music, Isaak Shvarts; Production Manager, Karlen Korshikov; Sound Operator, O. Burkova; Interpreter, Lev Korshikov.

CAST: Maxim Munzuk (Dersu Uzala), Yuri Solomin (Captain Vladimir K. Arsenieva), Svetlana Danilichenko (Mrs. Arsenieva), Dima Kortishev (Vova Arsenieva), Schemeikl Chokmorov (Yan Rao), Vladimir Kremena (Turtwigin), A. Pyatkov, M. Bichkov, B. Khorulev.

A Mosfilm/Atelie-41 Production. A Herald Eiga Release. A Soviet/Japanese co-production in Russian. Filmed at Mosfilm Studios (Moscow), and on location in Siberia, R.S.F.S.R. Six-track magnetic stereophonic sound. Sovcolor. Sovscope 70. 141 minutes (see below). Released August 2, 1975.

U.S. VERSION: Released by Sovexport Film. English subtitles. No MPAA rating. Released 1975. Reissued by New World Pictures, in association with Sovexportfilm, on October 5, 1976, also subtitled. A Roger Corman Presentation. Released in the Soviet Union as *Dersu Uzala* in 1976 running 181 minutes plus intermission (Part One: 90 minutes; Part Two: 91 minutes). Awards: Academy Award, Best Foreign Language Film (1975); Gold Medal, Moscow Film Festival (1975). Home video reissue version is letterboxed.

Desperado Outpost / Dokuritsu Gurentai ("Independent Gangsters"). Producer, Tomoyuki Tanaka; Director/Screenplay, Kihachi Okamoto; Director of Photography, Yuzuru Aizawa; Music, Masaru Sato.

CAST: Makoto Sato, Toshiro Mifune, Izumi Yukimura, Misa Uehara, Koji Tsuruta, Tadao Nakamaru.

A Toho Co., Ltd. Production. Black and white. Toho Scope. 109 minutes. Released October 6, 1959.

U.S. VERSION: Distributor, if any, is undetermined, though almost certainly Toho International Co., Ltd. with English subtitles. First feature in a 6-film series (1959-64), all starring Sato. Followed by *Westward Desperado* (1960). No MPAA rating.

Destroy All Monsters / Kaiju soshingeki ("All Monsters Attack"). Producer, Tomoyuki Tanaka; Director, Ishiro Honda; Screenplay, Kaoru Mabuchi (Takeshi Kimura) and Ishiro Honda; Director of Photography, Taiichi Kankura; Music, Akira Ifukube; Editor, Ryohei Fujii; Art Director, Takeo Kita; Sound Recording, Shoichi Yoshizawa; Sound, Toho Recording Centre; Sound Effects, Hisashi Shimonaga, Toho Sound Effects Group; Assistant Director, Seiji Tani. *Toho Special Effects Group*: Director, Eiji Tsuburaya; Special Photography, Teisho Arikawa; Optical Photography, Yukio Manoda, Sadao Iizuda; Art Director, Akira Watanabe; Lighting, Kyuighiro Kishida; Scene Manipulation, Fumio Nakadai.

CAST: Akira Kubo (SY-3 Flight Captain Katsuo Yamabe), Jun Tazaki (Dr. Yoshida), Yoshio Tsuchiya (Dr. Otani), Kyoko Ai (Queen of the Kilaaks), Yukiko Kobayashi (Kyoto Manabe), Kenji Sahara (Nishikawa), Andrew Hughes (Dr. Stevenson), Chotaro Togin (Okada), Yoshifumi Tajima (General Sugiyama), Hisaya Ito (Tada), Yoshio Katsude (young scientist), Henry Okawa (engineer), Kenichiro Maruyama (2nd engineer), Ikio Sawamura (old farmer who finds Kilaak transmitter), Yutaka Sada (policeman), Hiroshi Okada (doctor at hospital), Hideo Shibuya (1st reporter), Yutaka Oka (2nd reporter), Ken Echigo, Yasuhiko Saijo, Seishiro Hisano, Wataru Omae (SY-3 Engineers), Nadao Kirino, Kamayuki Tsubono, Naoya Kusakawa (detectives), Rinsaku Ogata (1st Officer), Haruya Sakamoto (2nd Officer), Susumu Kurobe, Kazuo Suzuki, Minoru Ito, Toru Ibuki (Control Center staff), Yukihiko Gondo (Soldier), Keiko Miyauchi, Atsuko Takahashi, Ari Sagawa, Yoshio Miyata, Kyoko Mori, Midori Uchiyama, Wakako Tanabe, Michiko Ishii (Kilaaks), Saburo Iketani (news reader), Haruo Nakajima (Godzilla *and* government official), Little Man Machan (Minya), Hiroshi Sekita (Angilas), Susumu Utsumi (King Ghidorah). (*Note:* Emi & Yumi Ito do not appear in the film as is reported in some sources).

Opposite: **Chotaro Togin, Akira Kubo, and Hisaya Ito battle evil aliens (including Kyoko Ai, third alien woman from the left) in *Destroy All Monsters* (1968).**

A Toho Co., Ltd. Production. Eastman Color (processed by Tokyo Laboratory, Ltd.). Toho Scope. Doubled-billed with a reissue of *Atragon* (Toho, 1963). 88 minutes. Released August 1, 1968.

U.S. VERSION: Released by American International Pictures. English-dubbed. A James H. Nicholson & Samuel Z. Arkoff Presentation. Postproduction Supervisor, Salvatore Billitteri; prints by Berkey-Pathé. Wide screen processed billed as ColorScope in the United States. Voice characterization for Akira Kubo, Hal Linden. Includes brief stock footage from *Ghidrah – The Three-Headed Monster* (1964). Released in the United Kingdom as *Operation Monsterland*. International titles (?): *March of the Monsters, Attack of the Marching Monsters.* Reissued in Japan in 1972 (re-edited by Ishiro Honda to 74 minutes) as *Gojira dengeki taisakusen* ("Godzilla Electric Battle Masterpiece"). The 9th "Godzilla" feature. Followed by *Godzilla's Revenge* (1969). 86 minutes. MPAA Rating: "G." Released May 23, 1969.

Destroy All Planets / Gamera tai uchu kaiju Bairasu ("Gamera Against the Space Monster Bairusu"). Executive Producer, Masaichi Nagata; Producer, Hidemasa Nagata; Director, Noriyaki Yuasa; Screenplay, Nizo Takahashi; Director of Photography, Akira Kitazaki; Music, Kenjiro Hirose; Editor, Shoji Sekiguchi; Sound Recording Supervisor, Kimio Hida; Sound, Daiei Recording Studio; Special Effects Directors, Kazufumi Fujii, Yuzo Kaneko; Monster Design, Ryosaku Takayama; Special Effects, Daiei Special Effects Department.

CAST: Kojiro Hongo (Nobuhiko Shimada), Toru Takatsuka (Masao Nakaya), Peter Williams (Dr. Dobie), Carl Clay [Carl Crane] (Jim Morgan), Michiko Yaegaki (Mariko Nakaya), Mari Atsumi (Junko Aoki), Junko Yashiro (Masako Shibata), Koji Fujiyama (Commander of Jietat), Genzo Wakayama (boss' voice), Chikara Hashimoto, Kenichiro Yamane, Kenji Go, Akira Natsuki, Ken Nakehara (men like the doctor [?!]), Mary Morris [Merry Murus].

A Daiei Motion Picture Co., Ltd. Production. A Masaichi Nagata Presentation. Westrex recording system. Eastman Color (processed by Daiei Laboratory). DaieiScope. Filmed at Daiei-Tokyo Studios. 81 minutes. Released March 20, 1968.

U.S. VERSION: Never released theatrically in the United States. Released directly to television by American International Television (AIP-TV) in 1969. English-dubbed. A James H. Nicholson & Samuel Z. Arkoff Presentation; Postproduction supervisor, Salvatore Billitteri; Director, Bret Morrison; Editors, Eli Haviv, Emil Haviv; Prints by Perfect. International title: *Gamera vs. Viras*. Also known as (U.K. title?) *Gamera vs. the Outer Space Monster Virus*. The film is often listed at 72–75 minutes, which may have been a reissue running time. The 4th "Gamera" feature. Followed by *Attack of the Monsters* (1969). Includes extensive stock footage from *Gammera the Invincible* (1965), *War of the Monsters* (1966) and *The Return of the Giant Monsters* (1967). 81 minutes. No MPAA rating.

Detective Bureau 2-3: Go to Hell, Bastards! / Tantei jimusho 2-3: Kutabare akutodomo ("Detective Bureau 2-3: Wicked Alliance Destroyed"). Producer, Shozo Ashida; Director, Seijun Suzuki; Screenplay, Iwao Yamazaki, based on the novel by Haruhiko Oyabu; Director of Photography, Shigeyoshi Mine; Art Director, Takeharu Sakaguchi; Music, Haruo Ibe; Assistant Director, Hiromi Higuchi.

CAST: Jo Shishido (Hideo Tajima), Reiko Masamori (Chiaki), Kawachi (Manabe), Asao Sano (Tajima's father), Kotoe Hatsui (Irie), Kinzo (Hatano), Naomi Hoshi, Koichi Uenoyama, Masako Kusunoki (Misa, *Manabe's girlfriend*).

A Nikkatsu Corp. Production. Color. NikkatsuScope. 89 minutes. Released 1963.

U.S. VERSION: Released by Nikkatsu Corp. English subtitles. 89 minutes. No MPAA rating. Released 1993.

The Devil's Bouncing Ball Song / Akuma no Temari-uta ("The Devil's Bouncing Ball Song"). Producers,

Kon Ichikawa and Osamu Tanaka; Planning, Haruki Kadokawa; Director, Kon Ichikawa; Screenplay, Kon Ichikawa, based on a story by Seishi Yokomizo; Director of Photography, Kiyoshi Hasegawa; Music, Kunihiko Murai; Art Director, Shinobu Muraki; Sound Recording, Nobuyuki Tanaka; Lighting, Kojiro Sato.

CAST: Koji Ishizaka (Kosuke Kindaichi), Keiko Kishi (Rika Aoike), Koji Kita (Kanao Aoike, *Rika's son*), Eiko Nagashima (Satoko Aoike, *Rika's daughter*), Misako Watanabe (Harue Bessho), Akiko Nishina (Chie Bessho, *Harue's daughter*), Mitsuko Kusabue (Atsuko Yura), Takao Zushi (Toshiro Yura, *Atsuko's son*), Yoko Takahashi (Yasuko Yura, *Atsuko's daughter*), Hisako Hara (Yuriko Yura, *the grandmother*), Ryutaro Tatsumi (Kahei Nire), Goro Oba (Naota Nire, *Kahei's son*), Tetsuya Ushio (Ryuji Nire), Yukiko Nagano (Ayako Nire, *Kahei's daughter*), Nobuo Nakamura (Hoan Tatara), Takeshi Kato (Police Inspector Todoroki).

A Toho Co., Ltd. Production. Color. Spherical wide screen. 144 minutes. Released April 2, 1977.

U.S. VERSION: Distributor, if any, is undetermined, though likely Toho International Co., Ltd. English subtitles. 144 minutes. No MPAA rating.

Devil's Temple / Oni no sumu yakata ("Mansion Where the Devil Lives"). Director, Kenji Misumi; Screenplay, Kaneto Shindo; Story, Junichiro Tanizaki; Director of Photography, Kazuo Miyagawa; Art Director, Akira Naito; Music, Akira Ifukube.

CAST: Shintaro Katsu (Mumyo Taro), Hideko Takamine (Kaede), Michiyo Aratama (Aizen), Kei Sato (high priest).

A Daiei Motion Picture Co., Ltd. Production. Eastman Color. DaieiScope. 76 minutes. Released May 1969.

U.S. VERSION: Released by Daiei International Films, Inc. English subtitles. 76 minutes. No MPAA rating. Released November 1969.

Diamonds of the Andes / Sekido o kakeru otoko ("Hanging Man at the Equator"). Director, Buichi Saito; Screenplay, Akira Saiga and Buichi Saito; Director of Photography, Yoshihiro Yamazaki; Art Director, Akiyoshi Satani; Music, Naozumi Yamamoto.

CAST: Akira Kobayashi (Jiro Ibuki, alias Goro Yajima), Akiko Wakabayashi (Reiko), Tetsuro Tamba (Munakata), Ryohei Uchida (Masa), Nobuo Kaneko (Kishida), Eiji Go (Saeki), Celia Paul (Maria).

An Arrow Enterprises Production. A Nikkatsu Corp. Release. Fujicolor. NikkatsuScope. 103 minutes. Released April 28, 1968.

U.S. VERSION: Distributor, if any, is undetermined. English subtitled version available. No MPAA rating.

Diary of a Shinjuku Thief / Shinjuku dorobo nikki ("Diary of a Shinjuku Thief"). Director, Nagisa Oshima; Screenplay, Tsutomu Tamura, Mamoru Sasaki, Masao Adachi, and Nagisa Oshima; Directors of Photography, Yasuhiro Yoshioka and Seizo Sengen.

CAST: Tadanori Yoko (Birdey), Juro Kara (singer), Rie Yokoyama (Umeko), Tetsu Takahashi, Kei Sato, Fumio Watanabe (themselves), Moichi Tanabe, the Situation Players.

A Sozosha/Art Theatre Guild Co., Ltd. Production. Color and Black and white, with Eastman Color inserts. Academy ratio. 94 minutes. Released 1969.

U.S. VERSION: Released by Grove Press. English subtitles. Alternate title: *Diary of a Shinjuko Burglar*. 94 minutes. No MPAA rating. Released July 1973.

Different Sons / Futari no musako ("Two Sons"). Executive Producer, Sanezumi Fujimoto; Director, Yasuki Chiba; Screenplay, Zenzo Matsuyama; Director of Photography, Masao Tamai; Music, Akira Ifukube.

CAST: Akira Takarada (Kensuke), Yuzo Kayama (Shoji), Kamatari Fujiwara (father), Yuko Mochizuki (mother), Yumi Shirakawa (Kensuke's wife), Yoko Fujiyama (daughter), Mie Hama, Chisako Hara, Hiroshi Koizumi, Masami Taura, Yu Fujiki, Takashi Shimura.

A Toho Co., Ltd. Production. Eastman Color. Toho Scope. 95 minutes. Released 1962.

U.S. VERSION: Released by Toho International Co., Ltd. English subtitles. 95 minutes. No MPAA rating. Released October 19, 1962.

The Diplomat's Mansion / Tokyo yawa ("Night Story of Tokyo"). Director, Shiro Toyoda.

CAST: Reiko Dan (bar girl), Hiroshi Akutagawa (diplomat), Tsutomu Yamazaki (his son), Chikage Awashima (madam), Nobuko Otawa, Kyoko Kishida, Tetsuro Tamba, Nobuo Nakamura, Chisako Hara, Masao Oda, Frankie Sakai, Ichiro Arishima, Hisaya Morishige.

A Tokyo Eiga Co., Ltd. Production. A Toho Co., Ltd. Release. Color (?). Toho Scope (?). 108 minutes. Released May 16, 1961.

U.S. VERSION: Released by Toho International Co., Ltd. English subtitles. 109 minutes. No MPAA rating. Released October 27, 1961.

Disciples of Hippocrates / Hipokuratesu-tachi ("We of Hippocrates"). Producer, Shiro Sasaki; Director/Screenplay, Kazuki Omori; Director of Photography, Yasuhiro Hotta; Art Director, Kazumasa Otani; Music, Shuichi Chino.

CAST: Masato Furuoya, Ran Ito, Akira Emoto, Magahiro Mitsuta, Hajime Nishizuka.

A Cinemahaute Co., Ltd./Art Theatre Guild of Japan Co., Ltd. Production. Color. Spherical wide screen (?). 126 minutes. Released 1980.

U.S. VERSION: Distributor undetermined. English subtitles. 126 minutes. No MPAA rating. Released September 16, 1984.

Dismembered Ghost / Kaidan barabara yurei ("Dismembered Ghost Story"). Director, Kinya Ogawa.

CAST: Rieko Akikawa (Masako), Setsu Shimizu (Masako's Stepmother), Miki Hayashi (Surmiko), Kenichiro Masayama (Tsukagoshi), Hiroshi Nikaido (Shinjiro).

An Okura Eiga Production. Black and white. Academy ratio. 71 minutes. Released 1968.

U.S. VERSION: Distributor undetermined. International title: *A Ghost Story—Barabara Phantom*. Released 1968 (?).

A Distant Cry from Spring / Harukanaru Yama no Yobigoe ("A Distant Cry"). Producer, Kiyoshi Shimazu; Director, Yoji Yamada; Screenplay, Yoji Yamada and Yoshitaka Asama, based on an original story by Yoji Yamada; Director of Photography, Tetsuo Takaba; Art Director, Mitsuo Degawa; Music, Masaru Sato.

CAST: Ken Takakura (Kosaku Tajima), Chieko Baisho (Tamiko Kazami), Hidetaka Yoshioka (Takeshi Kazami), Hajime Hana, Mizuho Suzuki.

A Shochiku Co., Ltd. Production. Color. Panavision (?). 124 minutes. Released 1980.

U.S. VERSION: Released by Shochiku Films of America, Inc. in subtitled format. 124 minutes. No MPAA rating. Released October 17, 1980.

Dixieland Daimyo / Jazz Daimyo ("Jazz Feudal Lord"). Producers, Yo Yamamoto and Masao Kobayashi; Director, Kihachi Okamoto; Screenplay, Toshio Ishida and Kihachi Okamoto, based on an original story by Yasutaka Tsusui; Director of Photography, Yudai Kato; Music, Yasutaka Tsutsui and Yosuke Yamashita.

CAST: Ikko Furuya, Ai Kanzaki, Pharez Whitted, Lenny Marsh.

A Daiei Co., Ltd. Production. Color. Panavision (?). 85 minutes. Released 1986.

U.S. VERSION: Distributor, if any, is undetermined.

Dodes'ka-den / Dodesukaden ("Dodes'ka-den"). Executive Producers, Akira Kurosawa, Yoichi Matsue; Producers, Keisuke Kinoshita, Kon Ichikawa, Masaki Kobayashi; Director, Akira Kurosawa; Screenplay, Akira Kurosawa, Hideo Oguni and Shinobu Hashimoto, based on the novel as *The Town Without Seasons* by Shugoro Yamamoto; Editor, Reiko Kaneko; Music, Toru Takemitsu; Production Supervisor, Hiroshi Nezu; Assistant Director, Kenjiro Omori; Art Directors, Yoshiro Muraki and Shinobu Muraki; Directors of Photography, Takao Saito and Yasumichi Fukuzawa; Still Photographer, Naomi Hashiyama; Recording, Fumio Yanoguchi and Hiromitsu Mori; Sound, Toho Recording

Centre; Sound Effects, Toho Sound Effects Group.

CAST: Yoshitaka Zushi (Rokuchan), Kin Sugai (Okuni-san), Kazuo Kato (roadside painter), Junzaburo Ban (Yukichi Shima), Kiyoko Tange (Shima's wife), Michio Hino (Okawa), Tatsuhei Shimokawa (Nomoto), Keiji Furuyama (Matsui), Hisashi Igawa (Masuo Masuda), Hideko Okiyama (Tatsu Masuda), Kunie Tanaka (Hatsuan Kawaguchi), Jitsuko Yoshimura (Yoshie Kawaguchi), Koji Mitsui (tavern proprietor), Shinsuke Minami (Ryotaro Sawagami), Yuko Kusunoki (Misao Sawagami), Toshiyuki Tonomura (Taro Sawagami), Satoshi Hasegawa (Jiro Sawagami), Kumiko Ono (Hanako Sawagami), Tatsuhiko Yanashisa (Shiro Sawagami), Mika Oshida (Umeko Sawagami), Tatsuo Matsumura (Kyota Watanaba), Mari Tsuji (Otane Watanaba), Tomoko Yamazaki (Katsuko Watanaba), Masahiko Kametani (Okabe), Minoru Takashima (policeman), Keiji Sakakida (sake shop proprietor), Noboru Mitani (beggar), Hiroyuki Kawase (beggar's son), Hiroshi Kiyama (sushi shop proprietor), Michiko Araki (Japanese restaurant proprietess), Shoichi Kuwayama (Western style restaurant cook), Toki Shiozawa (waitress), Hiroshi Akutagawa (Mr. Hei), Atsushi Watanabe (Mr. Tamba), Kamatari Fujiwara (old man), Masahiko Tanimura (Mr. So), Kiyotaka Ishii (Kumanbachi's first child), Mihoko Kaizuka (Kumanbachi's second child), Hideaki Ezumi (detective), Sanji Kojima (thief), Akemi Negishi (attractive wife), Reiko Niimura (1st Wife), Yoshiko Maki (2nd Wife), Toshiko Sakurai (3rd Wife), Matsue Ono (4th Wife), Toriko Takahara (5th Wife), Akira Hitoma (1st man calling out to Misao), Kanji Ebata (2nd man calling out to Misao), Masahiko Ichimura (3rd man calling out to Misao), Masaya Nihei (4th man calling out to Misao), Shin Ibuki (5th man calling out to Misao), Tsuji Imura (Mrs. Watanaka), Jerry Fujio (Kumamba), Michiko Araki (bad girl).

A Yonki no Kai/Toho Co., Ltd. Production. Westrex recording system. Eastman Color (processed by Tokyo Laboratory Ltd.) Academy ratio. 244 minutes (later edited to 140 minutes). Released October 1970.

U.S. VERSION: Released by Toho International Co., Ltd. English subtitles. 140 minutes. No MPAA rating. Released October 5, 1971. Reissued by Janus Films in November 1974.

Doggie March / Wanwan Chushingura ("Bow-Wow Chushingura") [**animated**]. Director, Daisaku Shirakawa; Screenplay, Kei Iijima and Daisaku Shirakawa; Directors of Photography, Kenji Sugiyama and Jiro Yoshimura.

VOICE CHARACTERIZATIONS: (undetermined).

A Toei Animation Studio Co., Ltd. Production. A Toei Co., Ltd. Release. Eastman Color. ToeiScope. 82 minutes. Released 1963.

U.S. VERSION: Distributor, if any, is undetermined. Loosely based on *The Loyal Forty-Seven Ronin*.

Don't Call Me a Con Man / Daiboken ("Big Adventure"). Executive Producer, Tomoyuki Tanaka; Director, Kengo Furusawa; Screenplay, Ryozo Kasahara and Yasuo Tanami; Director of Photography, Tadashi Iimura; Sound, Toho Recording Centre; Sound Effects, Toho Sound Effects Group.

CAST: Hitoshi Ueki (reporter), Reiko Dan, Fubuki Koshiji, Kei Tani, Hajime Hana, Emi and Yumi Ito [The Peanuts], Hiroshi Inuzuka, Senri Sakurai, Eitaro Ishibashi, Shin Yasuda, Andrew Hughes, Harold S. Conway, Nadao Kirino, Hisaya Ito.

A Toho Co., Ltd. Production. Eastman Color (processed by Tokyo Laboratory Ltd.). Toho Scope. 106 minutes. Released October 31, 1965.

U.S. VERSION: Released by Toho International Co., Ltd. English subtitles. International title: *Crazy Adventure*. The 4th "Crazy" feature. Followed by *The Boss of Pick-Pocket Bay* (1966). 109 minutes. No MPAA rating. Released December 21, 1966. Reissued June 1, 1993, as *Don't Call Me a Crime Man*.

Double Suicide / Shinju ten no Amijima ("Double Suicide: Heaven's

Amijima"). Producers, Masayuki Nakajima and Masahiro Shinoda; Director, Masahiro Shinoda; Screenplay, Taeko Tomioka, Masahiro Shinoda and Toru Takemitsu, based on the puppet play *Shinju ten no Amijima* ("The Love and Suicide at Amijima," 1720) by Monzaemon Chikamatsu; (Additional?) Dialog, Taeko Tomioka; Director of Photography, Toichiro Narushima; Art Director, Kiyoshi Awazu; Music, Toru Takemitsu.

CAST: Kichiemon Nakamura (Jihei), Shima Iwashita (Koharu/Osan), Hosei Komatsu (Tahei), Yusuke Takita (Magoemon), Kamatari Fujiwara (Yamatoya owner), Yoshi Kato (Gosaemon), Shizue Kawarazaki (Osan's mother), Tokie Hidari (Osugi).

A Hyogensha/Art Theatre Guild Production. A Toho Co., Ltd. Release. Black and white. Academy ratio (?). 103 minutes. Released 1969.

U.S. VERSION: Released by Toho International Co., Ltd. English subtitles. 103 minutes. No MPAA rating. Released February 11, 1970.

Double Suicide at Sonezaki / Sonezaki shinju ("Double Suicide at Sonezaki"). Producers, Hiroaki Fujii, Motoyasu Kimura, Ryohei Nishimura; Director, Yasuzo Masamura; Screenplay, Yoshio Shirasaka and Yasuzo Masamura, based on the play by Monzaemon Chikamatsu; Director of Photography, Setsuo Kobayashi; Art Director, Shigeo Mano; Music, Ryudo Uzaki.

CAST: Meiko Kaji, Ryudo Uzaki, Hisashi Igawa.

A Kodasha Co., Ltd./Kimura Productions/Art Theatre Guild of Japan Co., Ltd. Production. Color. Spherical wide screen (?). 112 minutes. Released 1978.

U.S. VERSION: Released by Toho International Co., Ltd. English subtitles. 112 minutes. No MPAA rating. Released August 24, 1979.

Double Trouble (production credits unavailable).

CAST: Yumi Ito and Emi Ito [The Peanuts], Keisuke Sonoi.

A Toho Co., Ltd. Production. Color (?). Toho Scope (?). Released 1963 (?).

U.S. VERSION: Released by Toho International Co., Ltd. English subtitles. Running time undetermined. No MPAA rating. Released November 13, 1964.

The Downfall of Osen / Orizuru Osen ("Osen of the Paper Cranes"). Director, Kenji Mizoguchi; Screenplay, Tatsunosuke Takashima, based on the short story "Baishoku Kamonanban" by Kyoka Izumi; Director of Photography, Minoru Miki.

CAST: Isuzu Yamada (Osen), Daijiro Natsukawa (Sokichi Hata), Mitsusaburo Ramon (Ukiki), Genichi Fujii (Matsuda), Ichiro Yoshizawa (Uwaki), Shin Shibata (Kumazawa), Mitsuru Tojo (Amadani), Junichi Kitamura (Sakazuki no Heishiro), Shizuko Takizawa (Osode), Sue Ito (Sokichi's grandmother), Susei Matsui (benshi/narrator).

A Daiichi Eiga Co., Ltd. Production. Filmed at Daiichi-Sagano Studios (Kyoto). Silent. Black and white. Academy ratio. 90 minutes. Released January 20, 1935.

U.S. VERSION: Distributor undetermined. English subtitles. 78 minutes. Released May 20, 1981.

Downtown / Shitamachi ("Downtown"). Director, Yasuki Chiba; Screenplay, Fumiko Hayashi; Director of Photography, Rokuro Nishigaki; Music, Akira Ifukube.

CAST: Toshiro Mifune, Isuzu Yamada, Keiko Awaji, Harunori Kametani.

A Toho Co., Ltd. Production. Black and white. Academy ratio. 59 minutes. Released 1955.

U.S. VERSION: Released by Brandon Films, Inc. English subtitles. No MPAA rating. Released 1966 (?).

Dragnet Girl / Hijosen no onna ("Dragnet Woman"). Director, Yasujiro Ozu; Screenplay, Tadao Ikeda, based on an idea by James Maki [Yasujiro Ozu]; Director of Photography, Hideo Shigehara.

CAST: Joji Oka, Kinuyo Tanaka, Hideo Mitsui, Sumiko Mizukubo, Chishu Ryu.

A Shochiku Co., Ltd. Production. Filmed at Shochiku-Kamata Studios. Silent. Academy ratio. Black and white. 60 minutes. Released April 27, 1933.

U.S. VERSION: Released by Shochiku Films of America, Inc. English intertitles. Released 1972 (?).

The Dragon's Fangs. Director, Tan Iida.
CAST: Hideki Takahashi, Yumiko Nogawa, Shinsuke Ashida, Jun Negami.
A Nikkatsu Corporation Production. Color (?). NikkatsuScope (?). Released 1966 (?).
U.S. VERSION: Released by Toho International Co., Ltd.
English subtitles (?). Running time undetermined. No MPAA rating. Released May 13, 1967.

Dream of Love (production credits unavailable).
CAST: Wakako Sakai.
A Toho Co., Ltd. Production. Color. Panavision (?). Released 1969 (?).
U.S. VERSION: Released by Toho International Co., Ltd. English subtitles (?). Running time undetermined. No MPAA rating. Released June 17, 1970.

The Dreams of Youth / Wakoundo no yume ("The Dreams of Youth"). Director/Screenplay, Yasujiro Ozu; Director of Photography, Hideo Shigehara.
CAST: Tatsuo Saito, Nobuko Wabaka, Hisao Yoshitani, Junko Matsui, Takeshi Sakamoto, Kenji Oyama, Chishu Ryu.
A Shochiku Co., Ltd. Production. Filmed at Shochiku-Kamata Studios. Silent with benshi. Black and white. Academy ratio. 50 minutes. Released April 29, 1928.
U.S. VERSION: Never released in the United States. A lost film.

Drifting Avenger / Koya no toseinin. Director, Junya Sato; Screenplay, Yoshihiro Ishimatsu; Director of Photography, Ichiro Hoshijima; Art Director, Shinichi Eno; Music, Masao Yagi.
CAST: Ken Takakura (Ken Kato), Kenneth Goodred (Marvin), Judith Roberts (Rosa).
A Toei Co., Ltd. Production. Filmed in Australia. Eastman Color. ToeiScope. 107 minutes. Released June 15, 1968.
U.S. VERSION: Distributor, if any, is undetermined. No MPAA rating.

Drunken Angel / Yoidore tenshi ("Drunken Angel"). Producer, Sojiro Motoki; Director/Editor, Akira Kurosawa; Screenplay, Keinosuke Uegusa and Akira Kurosawa; Director of Photography, Takeo Ito; Art Director, So Matsuyama; Lighting, Kinzo Yoshizawa; Music, Fumio Hayasaka; Still Photographer, Masao Soeda; Sound Recording, Wataru Konuma; Sound, Toho Dubbing Theatre.
CAST: Takashi Shimura (Dr. Sanada), Toshiro Mifune (Matsunaga), Reisaburo Yamamoto (Okada, *the gang-boss*), Chieko Nakakita (Nurse Miyo), Michiyo Kogure (Nanae, *Matsunaga's mistress*), Noriko Sengoku (Gin, *the bar girl*), Eitaro Shindo (Takahama), Choko Iida (old servant), Taiji Tonoyama (shop proprietor), Katao Kawasaki (flower shop proprietor), Sachio Sakai (young hoodlum), Yoshike Kuga (girl), Shizuko Kasagi (singer), Masao Shimizu (boss), Sumire Shiroki (Anego).
A Toho Co., Ltd. Production. Western Electric Mirrophonic recording. Black and white (processed by Kinuta Laboratories Ltd.; prints by Tokyo Laboratory Ltd.). Academy ratio. 98 minutes. Released April 27, 1948.
U.S. VERSION: Released by Brandon Films, Inc. English subtitles. A version running 150 minutes was prepared but never released; the original negatives and all existing prints are of the cut version. Alternate title: *A Drunken Angel*. 98 minutes. No MPAA rating. Released December 1959.

Duel at Ezo / Ezo yakata no ketto ("Duel at Ezo Mansion"). Executive Producers, Sanezumi Fujimoto and Yorihiko Yamada; Director, Kengo Furusawa; Screenplay, Ryozo Kasahara; Story, Renzaburo Shibata; Director of Photography, Hiroshi Murai; Art Director, Motoji Kojima; Music, Kenjiro Hirose.

CAST: Yuzo Kayama (Saburota Edo), Rentaro Mikuni (Shimbei Usa), Shogo Shimada (Jirozaemon Ezo), Mitsuko Baisho (Aka Shu), Kunie Tanaka (Kurobei), Toru Abe (ronin), Toshio Kurosawa (Kyuma), Tatsuya Nakadai (Daizennokami).

A Tokyo Eiga Co., Ltd. Production. A Toho Co., Ltd. Release. Eastman Color. Panavision. Released February 7, 1970.

U.S. VERSION: Released by Toho International Co., Ltd. English subtitles. Alternate title: *Fort Ezo*. 131 minutes. No MPAA rating. Released July 1, 1970.

Duel in the Storm/Arashi no Hatashiji ("Fatal Duel in the Storm"). Director, Akinori Matsuo; Screenplay, Seiji Hoshikawa; Director of Photography, Kazumi Iwasa; Art Director, Kimihiko Nakamura; Music, Taichiro Kosugi.

CAST: Akira Kobayashi (Seijiro Nakamura), Hideki Takahashi (Naoaki Yagiri), Ryotaro Sugi (Sakichi Kawanaya), Yumiko Nogawa (Okyo Kawanaya), Tamaki Sawa (Choko), Yoko Yamamoto (Koyuki).

A Nikkatsu Corp. Production. Fujicolor. NikkatsuScope. 94 minutes. Released August 1, 1968.

U.S. VERSION: Distributor, if any, is undetermined. English subtitled version available. No MPAA rating.

Dying at a Hospital / Byoin de Shinu to iu Koto ("Dying at a Hospital"). Producer, Toshio Tsukamoto; Director, Jun Ichikawa; Screenplay, Jun Ichikawa, based on the book by Fumio Yamazaki; Director of Photography, Tatsuhiko Kobayashi; Music, Bun Itakura.

CAST: Ittoku Kishibe, Masayuki Shinoya, Akira Yamanouchi.

An OPT Communications, Inc. Production. Color. Spherical wide screen. 100 minutes. Released 1993.

U.S. VERSION: Unreleased in the United States as this book went to press.

Eagle of the Pacific / Taiheiyo no washi ("Eagle of the Pacific"). Producer, Sojiro Motoki; Director, Ishiro Honda; Screenplay, Shinobu Hashimoto; Director of Photography, Kazuo Yamada; Art Director, Takeo Kita; Music, Yuji Koseki; Associate Director (?), Motoyoshi Oda; Special Effects, Eiji Tsuburaya, Akira Watanabe, and Hiroshi Mukoyama.

CAST: Denjiro Okochi, Toshiro Mifune, Rentaro Mikuni, Keiju Kobayashi, Minoru Takada, Toranosuke Ogawa, Minosuke Yamada, Fuyuki Murakami, Heihachiro "Henry" Okawa, Takashi Shimura, Yoshio Kosugi, Koreya Senda, Sachio Sakai, Takamaru Sasaki.

A Toho Co., Ltd. Production. Black and white. Academy ratio. 119 minutes. Released October 21, 1953.

U.S. VERSION: Distributor, if any, is undetermined. No MPAA rating.

Early Autumn / Kobayakawa-ke no aki ("Fall of the Kobayakawa Family"). Producers, Sanezumi Fujimoto, Masakatsu Kaneko, and Tadahiro Teramoto; Director, Yasujiro Ozu; Screenplay, Kogo Noda and Yasujiro Ozu; Director of Photography, Asakazu Nakai; Art Director, Tomo Shimogawara; Music, Toshiro Mayuzumi; Sound Recording, Koichi Nakagawa.

CAST: Ganjiro Nakamura (Manbei), Setsuko Hara (Akiko), Yoko Tsukasa (Noriko), Michiyo Aratama (Fumiko), Yumi Shirakawa (Takako), Reiko Dan (Yuriko), Keiju Kobayashi (Hisao), Akira Takarada (Noriko's boyfriend), Daisuke Kato (Yanosuke), Chieko Naniwa (Tsune Sasaki), Haruko Togo (Teruko), Haruko Sugimura, Hisaya Morishige, Chishu Ryu, Yuko Mochizuki.

A Toho Co., Ltd. Production. Agfacolor. Toho Scope. 103 minutes. Released October 29, 1961.

U.S. VERSION: Released by Toho International Co., Ltd. English subtitles. 103 minutes. No MPAA rating. Released February 1962. Reissued by New Yorker Films on November 30, 1970 as *The End of Summer*. Alternate title: *The Last of Summer*.

Early Spring / Soshun ("Early Spring"). Director, Yasujiro Ozu; Screenplay, Yasujiro Ozu and Kogo Noda; Director of Photography, Yushun Atsuta.

CAST: Ryo Ikebe, Chikage Awashima, Keiko Kishi, Chishu Ryu, Daisuke Kato, Teiji Takahashi, Kumeko Urabe, Haruko Sugimura, So Yamamura, Kuniko Miyake, Eijiro Tono, Chieko Nakagita, Nobuo Nakamura.

A Shochiku Co., Ltd. Production. Filmed at Shochiku-Ofuna Studios. Black and white. Academy ratio. 144 minutes. Released January 29, 1956.

U.S. VERSION: Released by New Yorker Films. English subtitles. 144 minutes. No MPAA rating. Released September 1974.

Early Summer / Bakushu ("Early Summer"). Producer, Takeshi Yamamoto; Director, Yasujiro Ozu; Screenplay, Kogo Noda and Yasujiro Ozu; Director of Photography, Yuharu Atsuta; Music, Senji Ito; Editor, Yoshiaki Hamamura; Assistant Director, Shohei Imamura.

CAST: Setsuko Hara (Noriko), Chishu Ryu (Koichi), Kuniko Miyake (Fumiko), Chikage Awashima (Ayako), Chieko Higashiyama (grandmother), Ichiro Sugai (grandfather), Haruko Sugimura (Mrs. Yabe), Kan Nihonyanagi (Kenichi Yabe), Shuji Sano (Mariko), Kuniko Igawa (Takako).

A Shochiku Co., Ltd. Production. Filmed at Shochiku-Ofuna Studios. Black and white. Academy ratio. 135 minutes. Released October 3, 1951.

U.S. VERSION: Released by New Yorker Films. English subtitles. 135 minutes. No MPAA rating. Released August 2, 1972.

Earth / Tsuchi ("Earth"). Director, Tomu Uchida; Screenplay, Ryuchiro Yagi and Tsutomu Kitamura, based on the novel by Takashi Nagatsuka; Director of Photography, Michiio Midorikawa; Music, Akihiro Norimatsu.

CAST: Isamu Kogugi (Kanji), Akiko Kazami (Itsugi, *his daughter*), Donguriboya [no other name given] (Yokichi, *his son*), Kaichi Yamamoto (Ukichi), Buntaro Miake (Heizo), Reisaburo Yamamoto (Kane, *a horse dealer*), Sanemon Suzuki (Gen-san), Masako Fujimura (Tami), Chieko Murata (landowner's wife), Mieshi Bando (Katsu), Mari Ko (Ohume), Kyosuke Sawa (Hikozo), Chie Mitsui (Yoshie), Miyoko Sakura (Aki), Isamu Yonekura (Kumakichi), Toshinosuke Nagao (village policeman).

A Nikkatsu Corp. Production. Black and white. Academy ratio. 92 minutes. Released 1939.

U.S. VERSION: Distributor undetermined. English subtitles. 92 minutes. No MPAA rating. Release date undetermined.

The Earth / Aasu ("Tomorrow"). Producer, Teruo Yamakawa; Director, Soo-Kil Kim; Screenplay, Soo-Kil Kim, based on an original story by Yoshiko Nishida; Director of Photography, Dok-Chol Kim; Music, Junnosuke Yamamoto.

CAST: Masahiro Sakaguchi, Yoichi Honda, Saburo Shinoda.

The Earth Production Committee Production. Color. Spherical wide screen (?). 83 minutes. Released 1991.

U.S. VERSION: Distributor, if any, is undetermined.

East China Sea / Higashi Shinakai ("East China Sea"). Director, Tadahiko Isomi; Screenplay, Shohei Imamura and Tadahiko Isomi; Story, Shohei Imamura; Director of Photography, Masahisa Himeda; Music, Hajime Kaburagi.

CAST: Masakazu Tamura (Rokuro), Seizaburo Kawazu (Ganaha), Yukie Kagawa (Kana), Ryohei Uchida, Kin Omae, Toshinari Yamano, Takanobu Hoizumi, Haruko Kato, Akemi Nara, Taiji Tonoyama, Nakajiro Tomida, Shoichi Kuwayama, Hirayoshi Aono, Shuntaro Tamamura, Yoshiyuki Nemoto, Michie Mori, Takumi Shinjo, Kanjuro Arashi, Tetsuya Watari.

An Imamura Productions Production. A Nikkatsu Corporation Release. Fujicolor. NikkatsuScope. Released October 1968.

U.S. VERSION: Distributor undetermined. The AFI Catalog credits Nikkatsu Corp. but this seems unlikely. English subtitles (?). 105 minutes. No MPAA rating. Released April 1969.

Ebirah, Horror of the Deep / Gojira, Ebirah, Mosura: Nankai no dai ketto ("Godzilla, Ebirah, Mothra:

Big Duel in the South Seas"). Executive Producer, Tomoyuki Tanaka; Director, Jun Fukuda; Screenplay, Shinichi Sekizawa; Director of Photography, Kazuo Yamada; Editor, Ryohei Fujii; Lighting, Kiichi Onda; Assistant Director, Ken Sano; Music, Masaru Sato; Sound Recording, Shoichi Yoshizawa; Sound, Toho Recording Centre; Sound Effects, Toho Sound Effects Group; Art Director, Takeo Kita. *Toho Special Effects Group*: Director, Eiji Tsuburaya; Photography, Teisho Arikawa, Motonari Tomioka and Taka Yuki; Optical Photography, Yukio Manoda, Sadao Iizuda; Matte Process, Hiroshi Mukoyama; Art Director, Akira Watanabe; Lighting, Kyuighiro Kishida; Scene Manipulation, Fumio Nakadai; Assistant Director, Teruyoshi Nakano.

CAST: Akira Takarada (Yashi), Kumi Mizuno (Daiyo), Akihiko Hirata (Red Bamboo captain), Jun Tazaki (base commander), Hideo Sunazuka (Mita), Chotaro Togin (Ichiro), Toru Watanabe (Ruta), Toru Ibuki (Yata), Eisei Amamoto (Red Bamboo naval officer), Ikio Sawamura (elderly slave), Hisaya Ito (scientist), Chieko Nakakita (Yata's mother), Haruo Nakajima (Godzilla), Hiroshi Sekida (Ebirah), the Bambi Pair (Mothra's priestesses), Shigeki Ishida (newspaper editor), Kazuo Suzuki (native on dock), Yutaka Sada (man with hat visiting Yata's mother), Fumiko Homma (medium), Studio No. 1 Dancers (Infant Island natives), Wataru Omae, Kenichiro Maruyama.

A Toho Co., Ltd., Production. Eastman Color (processed by Tokyo Laboratory, Ltd.). Toho Scope. 87 minutes. Released December 17, 1966.

U.S. VERSION: Released to U.S. television by AIP-TV (American International Pictures Television) in 1968. English-dubbed. Title later changed to *Godzilla versus the Sea Monster*, which is what is on current TV and video prints. Continental Distributing, Inc. may have released the film theatrically (as a Walter Reade, Jr. Presentation), but this has not been confirmed. Prints by Movielab. Voice characterization for Akira Takarada, Hal Linden. The original script pitted King Kong, not Godzilla, against a giant octopus. Ishida's role was cut from the AIP-TV version. International title: *Big Duel in the North Sea. Note:* Most U.S. prints are missing all cast and credit lists save title. Character names and spelling thereof is approximate. Reissued in Japan in 1972 (re-edited by Ishiro Honda to 74 minutes). 82 minutes. No MPAA Rating.

Edo Porn / Hokusai manga ("Hokusai Comic"). Producers, Manabu Akashi and Hiroyuki Chujo; Director/Screenplay, Kaneto Shindo; Director of Photography, Keiji Maruyama; Art Director, Shigemori Shigeta; Music, Hikaru Hayashi.

CAST: Ken Ogata, Toshiyuki Nishida, Yuko Tanaka, Kanako Higuchi.

A Shochiku Co., Ltd. Color. Panavision. 119 minutes. Released 1981.

U.S. VERSION: Released by Shochiku Films of America, Inc. in subtitled format. No MPAA rating. Released July 1982.

Eijanaika ("That's All Right, Isn't It?"). Producers, Shoichi Ozawa and Jiro Tomoda, Shohei Imamura, and Shigemi Sugizaki; Director, Shohei Imamura; Screenplay, Shohei Imamura and Ken Miyamoto, based on an original story by Shohei Imamura; Director of Photography, Masahisa Himeda; Art Director, Akiyoshi Satani; Music, Shinichiro Ikebe.

CAST: Kaori Momoi, Shigeru Izumiya, and Masao Kusakari.

A Shochiku Co., Ltd./Imamura Productions Production. Color. Panavision (?). 151 minutes. Released 1981.

U.S. VERSION: Released by Shochiku Films of America, Inc. English subtitles. 151 minutes. No MPAA rating. Released January 8, 1981.

The Emperor and a General / Nippon no ichiban nagai hi ("The Longest Day of Japan"). Executive Producers, Sanezumi Fujimoto and Tomoyuki Tanaka; Director, Kihachi Okamoto; Screenplay, Shinobu Hashimoto, based on the story *Nippon no ichiban nagai hi* (1965) by Soichi Oya; Director of Photography, Hiroshi Murai; Lighting, Tsuruzo

Nishikawa; Art Director, Iwao Akune; Music, Masaru Sato; Sound Recording, Shin Tokai.

CAST: Toshiro Mifune (War Minister Anami), So Yamamura (Navy Minister), Chishu Ryu (Prime Minister), Seiji Miyaguchi (Foreign Minister), Takashi Shimura (Information Chief), Toshio Kurosawa (Major Hatanaka), Sho Shimada (Imperial Commander Mori), Susumu Fujita (Colonel Haga), Yunosuke Ito (Major General Nonaka), Daisuke Kato (Yabe of NHK), Jun Tazaki (Colonel Kosono), Michiyo Aratama (Yuriko Hara), Nobuo Nakamura (Lord Kido), Kenjiro Ishiyama (General Tanaka), Keiju Kobayashi (Chamberlain Tokugawa), Yuzo Kayama (Tateno of NHK), Koshiro Matsumoto (Emperor Hirohito), Rokko Toura, Yoshio Kosugi, Ushio Akashi, Takeshi Kato, Akihiko Hirata, Tadao Nakamura, Ryuji Kita, Eisei Amamoto, Makoto Sato, Ichiro Nakaya, Koji Mitsui, Yoshio Tsuchiya.

A Toho Co., Ltd. Production. Black and white. Toho Scope. 157 minutes. Released September 1967.

U.S. VERSION: Released by Toho International Co., Ltd. English subtitles. Alternate title: *Japan's Longest Day*. 157 minutes. No MPAA rating. Released March 1968.

The Emperor's Naked Army Marches On / Yuki Yukite Shingun

("The Emperor's Army Marches On") [**documentary**]. Producer, Sachiko Kobayashi; Associate Producers, Shohei Imamura, Yasuko Tokunaga and Yunoshin Moiyoshi; Director/Director of Photography, Kazuo Hara; Screenplay, Kazuo Hara, based on an idea by Shohei Imamura; Assistant Director, Takuji Yasuoka and Koichi Omiya; Assistant Cameramen, Toshiaki Takamura and Satoru Hirasawa; Editor, Jun Nbeshima; Sound Recording, Toyohiko Kuribayashi.

WITH: Kenzo Okuzaki, Shizumi Okuzaki, Kichitaro Yamada, Iseko Shimamoto, Minoru Takami, Yukio Seo, Toshiya Nomura, Rinko Sakimoto, Toshio Hara, Masaichi Hamaguchi, Taro Maruyama, Shichiro Kojima, Masao Koshimizu, Riichi Aikawa, Eizaburo Oshima, Kichitaro Yamada.

A Shisso Productions Production, in association with Imamura Prductions and Zanzou-sha. 16mm. Color. 123 minutes. Released 1987.

U.S. VERSION: Released by Kino International. English subtitles. 123 minutes. No MPAA rating. Released March 15, 1988.

Empire of Passion / Ai no Borei

("Ghost of Love"). Producer/Director, Nagisa Oshima; Screenplay, Nagisa Oshima, based on the novel by Itoko Nakamura; Production Coordinators, Shibata Organization, Inc.; Director of Photography, Yoshio Miyajima; Art Director, Jusho Toda; Editor, Keiichi Uraoka; Music, Toru Takemitsu; World Sales, Argos Films.

CAST: Kazuko Yoshiyuki (Seki), Tatsuya Fuji (Toyoji), Takahiro Tamura (Gisaburo), Takuzo Kawatani (Hotta), Akiko Koyama (boss), Taiji Tonoyama (Toichiro), Sumie Sasaki, Eizo Kitamura, Masami Hasegawa, Kenzo Kawarazaki, Takaaki, Sugiura.

An Oshima Productions, Ltd./Argos Films, S.A. Production. An Oshima Release. A Japanese/French co-production. Eastman Color. Academy ratio. 108 minutes. Released 1978.

U.S. VERSION: Released by BCR Ltd. Group 1. English subtitles. Released internationally by Argos in May 1978. Released in France is *Fantom amour* (?). Home video title: *In the Realm of Passion*. 106 minutes. MPAA rating: "R." Released March 26, 1979.

The Empty Table / Shokutaku no nai ie

("The House with No Dining Table"). Executive Producer, Genjiro Kawamoto; Producers, Ginichi Kishimoto and Kyoko Oshima; Director, Masaki Kobayashi; Screenplay, Masaki Kobayashi, based on an original story by Fumiko Enji; Director of Photography, Kozo Okazaki; Lighting, Kazuo Shimomura; Editor, Nobuo Ogawa; Art Director, Shigemasa Toda; Set Decorator, Shoichi Yasuda; Music, Toru Takemitsu, performed by Tokyo Concerts; Sound Recording, Hideo Nishizaki; Sound Effects, Akira Honma; Planning, Masayuki Sato, Masato Hara; Production Manager, Masahiro Oba; Assistant Director, Yoshitomi Tomoya.

CAST: Tatsuya Nakadai (Nobuyuki Kidoji), Mayumi Ogawa (Yumiko Kidoji), Kie Nakai (Tamae Kidoji), Kiichi Nakai (Otohiko Kidoji), Takeyuki Takemoto (Osamu Kidoji), Shima Iwashita (Kiwa Nakahara), Mikijiro Hira (Kawabe), Azusa Mano (Kanae Sawaki), Shinobu Otake, Daisuke Ryu, Takayuki Takemoto, Toru Masouka, Asao Sano, Toyoshi Fukuda, Shoji Kobayashi, Torahiko Hamada, Tokuko Sugiyama, Tetsuo Kobayashi, Natsuyo Kawakami, Katsue Niida, Yoshiko Maki, Satoko Akiyama, Ko Hashimoto, Tsuyoshi Yano, Kiyoshi Yamamoto, Jun Takeuchi, Hiroshi Kamiyama, Takeshi Endo, Shinji Ogawa.

A Marugen Building Group/Haiyu-za Film Production/Herald Ace Production. Color. Spherical wide screen (?). 142 minutes. Released 1985.

U.S. VERSION: Release undetermined. English subtitled version available. Subtitles, S.J. Walton, Wordsmiths (Tokyo). Alternate title: *House with No Dining Table*. 142 minutes. No MPAA rating.

Enchanted Princess / Hatsuharu tanuki goten ("Early Spring at Racoon Dog Palace"). Executive Producer, Masaishi Nagata; Director/ Screenplay, Keigo Kimura; Director of Photography, Hiroshi Imai; Sound, Daiei Recording Studio.

CAST: Raizo Ichikawa, Ayako Wakao, Shintaro Katsu, Tamao Nakamura, Atsuko Kindaichi, Yoshie Mizutani.

A Daiei Motion Picture Co., Ltd. Production. A Masaichi Nagata Presentation. Western Electric Mirrophonic recording. Daieicolor. Academy Ratio. 85 minutes. Released 1960.

U.S. VERSION: U.S. distributor, if any, is undetermined.

The Enchantment / Yuwakusha ("Seducer"). Coordinating Producer, Kazuo Oshiba; Planning, Koichi Murakami and Juichi Horiguchi; Producers, Toshiro Kamata, Kei Sasaki, and Shinya Kawai; Director, Shunichi Nagasaki; Screenplay, Goro Nakajima; Story, Shunichi Nagasaki and Tomoko Ogawa; Director of Photography, Makoto Watanabe; Lighting, Akio Watanabe; Editor, Yoshiyuki Okuhara; Production Designer, Katsumi Kaneda; Music, Satoshi Kadokura; Wardrobe, Hajime Tozuka; Sound Recording, Hitoshi Yamada; Sound Effects, Yukio Hokari; Assistant Producer, Hirosuke Kato; Production Manager, Toshihisa Watai; Assistant Directors, Masatsugu Takeyasu and Hirohisa Sasaki.

CAST: Kumiko Akiyoshi (Miyako Shinohara), Masao Kusakari (Kazuhiko Sotomura), Kiwako Harada (Harumi Yoshii), Takeshi Naito (Dr. Shinbori), Tsutomu Isobe (Hirayama), Meika Seri (Nurse Kubo), Tomoko Onuki (girl biker), Akio Kaneda (Noda), Issei Kai (taxi driver), Taro Suwa (cop), Hyoe Enoki (security guard at Ecole de Paris), Junkichi Orimoto (car park attendant), Kiyoshi Kurosawa (librarian), Renji Ishibashi (Kaburagi), Kaori Tachioka, Miho Hirata, Yoko Amemiya, Kaori Oguri, Noriyo Kimura, Mayumi Morisaki, Mari Asazato, Junko Kondo, Mutsuko Oya, Fusae Umagami, Akihito Osuga, Takeshi Yamada, Shimon Kumai.

A Fuji Television/Cinemahout/Black Box Production. Eastman Color. Spherical wide screen. 109 minutes. Released 1989.

U.S. VERSION: Released by Fuji Television. English subtitles. Subtitles, Jeanette Amano. 109 minutes. No MPAA rating. Released April 27, 1990.

Equinox Flower / Higanbana ("Equinox Flower"). Director, Yasujiro Ozu; Screenplay, Yasujiro Ozu and Kogo Noda, based on the novel by Ton Satomi; Director of Photography, Yuharu Atsuta.

CAST: Shin Saburi (Wataru Hirayama), Kinuyo Tanaka (Kyoko Hirayama), Ineko Arima (Setsuko), Keiji Sada (Masahiko), Chieko Naniwa, Fujiko Yamamoto, Chishu Ryu, Nobuo Nakamura, Teiji Takahashi, Fumio Watanabe, Yoshiko Kuga, Miyuki Kuwano.

A Shochiku Co., Ltd. Filmed at Shochiku-Kamata Studios. Eastman Color. Academy ratio. 118 minutes. Released September 7, 1958.

U.S. VERSION: Released by New Yorker Films. English subtitles. 118 minutes. No MPAA rating. Released June 1977.

Eriko / Otoko Tomodachi ("Male Friends"). Producers, Toru Aizawa and Takeo Sayama; Director, Takumi Yamaguchi; Screenplay, Yukiko Takayama, based on an original story by Noriko Minobe; Director of Photography, Kozo Okazaki; Music, Kiyoaki Takanashi.

CAST: Mariko Tsutsui (Eriko), Toshiya Nagasawa, Shingo Tsurumi, Maiko Kawakami.

A Film Crescent Co., Ltd. Production. Color. Spherical wide screen. 100 minutes. Released 1993.

U.S. VERSION: Unreleased in the United States as this book went to press.

Erogami no onryo ("The Revengeful Spirit of Eros"). Director, Yasujiro Ozu; Screenplay, Kogo Noda; Story, Seizaburo Ishihara; Director of Photography, Hideo Mohara.

CAST: Tatsuo Saito (Kentaro Yumaji), Hikaru Hoshi (Daikuro Ishikawa), Satoko Date (Yumeko), Ichiro Tsukida (Yumeko's boyfriend).

A Shochiku Kamata Production. Silent. Black and white. Academy ratio. 41 minutes. Released July 27, 1930.

U.S. VERSION: Distributor, if any, is undetermined. International title: *The Revengeful Spirit of Eros.*

Escapade in Japan. Producer/Director, Arthur Lubin; Screenplay, Winston Miller; Director of Photography, William Snyder; Editor, Otto Ludwig; Art Directors, George W. Davis and Walter Holscher; Music, Max Steiner.

CAST: Teresa Wright (Mary Saunders), Cameron Mitchell (Dick Saunders), Jon Provost (Tony Saunders), Roger Nakagawa (Hiko), Philip Ober (Lt. Colonel Hargrave), Kuniko Miyake (Michiko), Susumu Fujita (Kei Tanaka), Katsuhigo Haida (Captain Hibino), Tatsuo Saito (Mr. Fushimi), Hideko Koshikawa (Dekko-san), Ureo Egawa (Chief of Kyoto Police), Frank Tokunaga (farmer), Ayako Hidaka (farmer's wife), Henry Okawa (police officer).

An Arthur Lubin Production. A Universal-International Presentation. A Universal Pictures Co., Inc. Release. A U.S. production in English and filmed in Kyoto, Tokyo, and Nara (Japan). Stereophonic sound (?). Eastman Color (prints by Technicolor). Technirama. 90 minutes. Released September 1957.

ESPY / Esupai ("Espy"). Executive Producer, Tomoyuki Tanaka; Producer, Fumio Tanaka; Director, Jun Fukuda; Screenplay, Ei Ogawa; Story, Sakyo Komatsu; Art Director, Shinobu Muraki; Director of Photography, Masaharu Ueda; Editor, Michiko Ikeda; Music, Masaaki Hirao; Recording Mixer, Toshiya Ban; Sound Toho Recording Centre; Sound Effects, Toho Sound Effects Group. *Toho Special Effects Group*: Director, Teruyoshi Nakano.

CAST: Hiroshi Fujioka (Yoshio Tamura), Kaoru Yumi (Maria Harada), Masao Kusakari (Jiro Miki), Yuzo Kayama (Hojo), Tomisaburo Wakayama (Ulrov), Katsumasa Uchida (Goro Tatsumi), Steve Green (Baltonian Prime Minister), Eiji Okada (Salabad), Robert Dunham (pilot), Goro Mutsumi.

A Toho-Eizo Production. A Toho Co., Ltd. Release. Westrex recording system. Color (processed by Tokyo Laboratory Ltd.). Panavision. Filmed on location in Switzerland, and at Toho Studios (Tokyo). 94 minutes. Released December 28, 1974.

U.S. VERSION: Released by Toho International Co., Ltd. English subtitles. 94 minutes. No MPAA rating. Released 1975. Released to home video as *E.S.P./SPY* (though jackets retain *ESPY* title). English-dubbed. A UPA Productions of America Release. A UPA/Henry G. Saperstein Presentation. 86 minutes.

Eternal Love / Zansetsu ("Leftover Snow"). Director, Katsumi Nishikawa; Screenplay, Yoshio Chito and Masayasu Daikubara; Director of Photography, Kenji Hagiwara; Art Director, Bugen Sakaguchi; Music, Masayoshi Ikeda.

CAST: Kazuo Funaki (Takahiko Shinjo), Chieko Matsubara (Akiko Imamura), Isao Yamagata (Kenichiro, *Takahiko's father*), Yatsuko Tanami (Mitsuyo, *Takahiko's stepmother*), Reiko Kobayashi (Yuriko, *Takahiko's sister*).

A Nikkatsu Corp. Production. Fujicolor. NikkatsuScope. 94 minutes. Released March 30, 1968.

U.S. VERSION: Distributor, if any, is undetermined. English subtitled version available. No MPAA rating.

Eternity of Love / Wakarete ikiru toki mo ("When We Live Separately"). Executive Producers, Sanezumi Fujimoto and Hidehisa Ide; Director, Hiromichi Horikawa; Screenplay, Zenzo Matsuyama, Toshiro Ide, and Hiromichi Horikawa; Director of Photography, Asakazu Nakai; Music, Yasushi Akutagawa.

CAST: Yoko Tsukasa (Michi), Tadao Takashima, Kiyoshi Kodama, Keiju Kobyashi, Hiroshi Akutagawa, Seizaburo Kawazu, Kinuyo Tanaka, Ikio Sawamura, Kenzo Tabu, Kin Sugai, Asao Koike, Chikako Hosokawa.

A Takarazuka Motion Picture Co., Ltd. Production. A Toho Co., Ltd. Release. Eastman Color. Toho Scope. Released April 4, 1961.

U.S. VERSION: Released by Toho International Co., Ltd. English subtitles. 100 minutes. No MPAA rating. Released November 1961.

Evil of Dracula / Chio o suu bara ("The Bloodsucking Rose"). Executive Producer, Fumio Tanaka; Director, Michio Yamamoto; Screenplay, Ei Ogawa and Masaru Takasue, based on a character created by Bram Stoker; Director of Photography, Kazutami Hara; Art Director, Kazuo Satsuya; Music, Riichiro Manabe; Editor, Michiko Ikeda; Sound, Toho Recording Centre; Sound Effects, Toho Sound Effects Group; Special Effects Director, Teruyoshi Nakano; Special Effects, Toho Special Effects Group.

CAST: Toshio Kurosawa (Professor Shiraki), Kunie Tanaka (the doctor), Mariko Mochizuki (Kumi?), Katsuhiko Sasaki (Professor Yoshi), Shin Kishida (the principal), Mio Ohta, Mika Katsuragi, Keiko Aramaki, Yunosuke Ito.

A Toho-Eizo Co., Ltd. Production. Color (processed by Tokyo Laboratory, Ltd.). Panavision. 87 minutes. Released July 20, 1974.

U.S. VERSION: Released by Toho International Co., Ltd. English subtitles. 81 minutes. No MPAA rating. Released April 2, 1975. Released to television by United Productions of America in 1980 (?). English-dubbed. A UPA Productions of America Presentation. Executive Producer, Henry G. Saperstein. International Title: *The Bloodthirsty Roses*.

Eyes, the Sea and a Ball / Natsukashiki fueya taiko ("Dear Flute and Drum"). Executive Producers, Sanezumi Fujimoto, Keisuke Kinoshita, and Masakatsu Kaneko; Director/Screenplay, Keisuke Kinoshita; Director of Photography, Hiroyuki Kusuda; Music, Chuji Kinoshita.

CAST: Yosuke Natsuki, Mayumi Ozora, Kumeko Urabe, Kamatari Fujiwara, Yoichiro Takahashi.

A Takarazuka Motion Picture Co., Ltd./Kinoshita Productions, Ltd. Production. A Toho Co., Ltd. Release. Color. Toho Scope. 114 minutes. Released 1967.

U.S. VERSION: Released by Toho International Co., Ltd. English subtitles (?). 114 minutes. No MPAA rating. Released June 1968.

Fables from Hans Christian Andersen / Andersen monogatari ("Andersen Stories") [**animated**]. Director, Kimio Yabuki; Screenplay, Hiroshi Inoue and Morihisa Yamamoto, based on the writings of Hans Christian Andersen; Art Director, Tadashi Koyama; Music, Seichiro Uno.

VOICE CHARACTERIZATIONS: (undetermined).

A Toei Animation Studio Co., Ltd. Production. A Toei Co., Ltd. Release. Eastman Color. ToeiScope. 80 minutes. Released March 19, 1968.

U.S. VERSION: Release undetermined. Available with English subtitles. No MPAA rating.

The Face of Another / Tanin no kao ("The Face of a Stranger"). Executive Producers, Nobuyo Horiba, Kiichi Ichikawa and Tadashi Ohono; Producer/Director, Hiroshi Teshigahara; Screenplay, Kobo Abe, based on his novel (English translation by E. Dale Saunders and published by Knopf); Director of Photography, Hiroshi Segawa; Music, Toru Takemitsu; Editor, Fusako Shuzui; Production Supervisor, Hiroshi Kawazoc; Production Manager, Iwao Yashida; Lighting, Mitsuo Kume; Sound, Keiji Mori; Design, Kiyoshi Awazu; Still Photography, Yasuhiro Yoshioka; Art, Shin Isozaki.

CAST: Tatsuya Nakadai (Mr. Okuyama), Machiko Kyo (Mrs. Okuyama), Kyoko Kishida (his nurse), Mikijiro Hira (his doctor), Eiji Okada (the director), Bibari "Beverly" Maeda ("Mrs."), Miki Irie (girl), Kunie Tanaka, Minoru Chiaki, Etsuko Ichihara, Hideka Muranatsu, Yoshie Minami, Shinobu Itomi, Hisashi Igawa.

A Teshigahara Production Picture, in association with Tokyo Eiga Co., Ltd. A Toho Co., Ltd. Release. Westrex Recording System. Black and white. Academy ratio (one sequence presented in cropped wide screen). 122 minutes. Released July 10, 1966.

U.S. VERSION: Released by Toho International Co., Ltd. English subtitles. 122 minutes. No MPAA rating. Released June 9, 1967. Reissued in May 1975 by Rising Sun as a Toho Co., Ltd. Presentation. Home video version subtitled.

The Face of War **[documentary]**. Producer/Director, Tore Sjoberg; Screenplay, Erik Holm, Cordella Lewis, C.D.B. Bryan, and C.D. Brandt; Editor, Ingmar Ejve, Music, Georg Riedel.

A Nippon Eiga Shinsha/Minerva International Films Production. A Swedish/Japanese co-production. Black and white. Academy ratio. 105 minutes. Released 1963 (?).

U.S. VERSION: Released by Janus Films. English narration. Narrator, Bryant Halliday. Released in Sweden in 1963 as *Krigets vanvett*. Japanese title undetermined. Alternate title: *Krigets ansikte*. 105 minutes. No MPAA rating. Released October 31, 1963.

The Falcon Fighters / Aa rikugun hayabusa sentotai ("Ah, Army Falcon Combat Unit"). Director, Mitsuo Murayama; Screenplay, Katsuya Suzaki; Director of Photography, Kimio Watanabe; Art Director, Koichi Takahashi; Music, Seitaro Omori; Special Effects Director, Noriaki Yuasa.

CAST: Makoto Sato (Lt. Takeo Kato), Shiho Fujimura (his wife), Sei Hiraizumi (2nd Lt. Kihara), Kojiro Hongo (2nd Lt. Ando), Jun Fujimaki (Cho Eishun), Yoko Namikawa (Keiko), Akio Hasegawa, Ken Utsui.

A Daiei Motion Picture Co., Ltd. Production. Fujicolor. DaieiScope. Released 1969.

U.S. VERSION: Released by Daiei International Films, Inc. English subtitles. 100 minutes. No MPAA rating. Released May 1970.

The Family Game / Kazoku geemu ("The Family Game"). Producers, Shiro Sasaki and Yu Okada; Director, Yoshimitsu Morita; Screenplay, Yoshinori Kobayashi and Yoshimitsu Morita, based on a novel by Yohei Homma; Director of Photography, Yonezo Maeda; Art Director, Katsumi Nakazawa; Lighting, Kazuo Yabe; Sound Recording, Osamu Onodera; Editor, Akimasa Kawashima; Assistant Director, Shusuke Kaneko.

CAST: Yusaku Matsuda (Yoshimoto, *the tutor*), Juzo Itami (Mr. Numata, *the father*), Saori Yuki (Mrs. Numata, *the mother*), Ichirota Miyagawa (Shigeyuki, *the younger brother*), Junichi Tsujita (Shinichi, *the older brother*).

An Art Theatre Guild/New Century Producers/Nikkatsu Studio Production. A Nikkatsu Corp. Release. Academy ratio. 107 minutes. Released 1983.

U.S. VERSION: Released by Circle Releasing Corp. A Ben Barenholtz Presentation. English subtitles. 107 minutes. No MPAA rating. Released March 31, 1984.

The Famous Sword / Meito Bijomaru ("The Famous Sword of Bijomaru"). Director, Kenji Mizoguchi; Screenplay, Matsutaro Kawaguchi, based on the tale of Masamune Yotsuya, a famous Edo swordsmith; Director of Photography, Shigeto Miki and Haruo Takeno; Art Authenticity, Kusune Kainosho.

Juzo Itami, Saori Yuki, Yusaku Matsuda, Ichirota Miyagawa and Junichi Tsujita in *The Family Game* (1983).

CAST: Shotaro Hanayagi (Kiyone Sakurai, *the swordsmith*), Isuzu Yamada (Sasae Onoda), Ichijiro Oya (Kozaemon Onoda, *her father*), Eijiro Yanagi (Kiyohide Yamatomori), Hiroshi Ishii (Seiji Kiyosugu).

A Shochiku Co., Ltd. Production. Filmed at Shochiku-Kyoto Studios. Black and white. Academy ratio. 65 minutes. Released February 8, 1945.

U.S. VERSION: Distributor undetermined. English subtitles. Title also given as *The Famous Sword Bijomaru*. 66 minutes. No MPAA rating. Released 1981 (?).

Faraway Sunset / Toki Rakujitsu ("Faraway Sunset"). Producers, Kazuyoshi Okuyama and Kyuemon Oda; Director, Seijiro Koyama; Screenplay, Kaneto Shindo, based on a story by Kaneto Shindo and Junichi Watanabe; Director of Photography, Masahiko Iimura; Music, Tetsuji Hayashi.

CAST: Yoshiko Mita, Hiroshi Mikami, Tatsuya Nakadai, Riho Makise, Hiroyuki Nagato, Takahiro Tamura, Shingo Yamashiro, Julie Dreyfess.

An Asahi National Broadcasting Co., Ltd./Tokyu Agency, Inc./Shochiku Co., Ltd. Production. Color. Panavision (?). 119 minutes. Released 1992.

U.S. VERSION: Released by Shochiku Films of America, Inc. English subtitles. 119 minutes. No MPAA rating. Released November 11, 1993. Alternate title: *The Distant Setting Sun*.

Farewell, My Beloved / Wakare ("Separation"). Director, Hideo Oba; Screenplay/Original Story, Genyo Takahashi; Director of Photography, Hiroyuki Nagaoka; Art Director, Tadakata Yoshino; Music, Chuji Kinoshita.

CAST: Kazuo Funaki (Makito), Mayumi Ozora (Yuko), Ken Ogata (Tadayuki), Nana Ozaki (Yumiko).

A Shochiku Co., Ltd. Production. Eastman Color. Shochiku GrandScope. Released February 1969.

U.S. VERSION: Released by Shochiku Films of America, Inc. English subtitles (?). 93 minutes. No MPAA rating. Released October 1969.

Farewell to the Ark / Saraba Hakobune. Producers, Fujio Sunaoka, Kyoko Kujo, and Shiro Sasaki; Director,

Shuji Terayama; Screenplay, Shuji Terayama and Rio Kishida; Director of Photography, Tatsuo Suzuki; Music, J.A. Seaser.

CAST: Mayumi Ogawa, Tsutomu Yamazaki, Yoshio Harada.

A Himawari Theater Group, Inc./Jinriki Hikoki-sha/Art Theatre Guild of Japan Co., Ltd. Production. Eastman Color. Spherical wide screen (?). 127 minutes. Released 1983.

U.S. VERSION: Distributor, if any, is undetermined. No MPAA rating.

Father / Chichi ("Father"). Producers, Nobuyoshi Otani, Junji Shizuma, and Matsuo Takahashi; Director/Screenplay, Keisuke Kinoshita; Director of Photography, Kozo Okazaki; Music, Chuji Kinoshita.

CAST: Eiji Bando, Kiwako Taiji, Makoto Nonomura.

A Shochiku Co., Ltd./Big Bang Co., Ltd./Kinema Tokyo Co., Ltd. Production. Color. Panavision (?). 75 minutes. Released 1988.

U.S. VERSION: Distributor, if any, is undetermined, possibly by Shochiku Films of America, Inc. in subtitled format. No MPAA rating.

La Fée Diabolique / Subarashii akujo ("Wonderful Bad Woman"). Executive Producer, Shin Morita; Director, Hideo Onchi; Music, Toru Takemitsu.

CAST: Reiko Dan, Akira Kubo, Nami Tamura.

A Toho Co., Ltd. Production. Black and white. Toho Scope. 89 minutes. Released 1963.

U.S. VERSION: Distributor undetermined, likely Toho International Co., Ltd. in subtitled format.

Fight for the Glory / Eiko eno kurohyo ("Black Panther for the Glory"). Producer, Kiyoshi Higuchi; Director, Hirokazu Ichimura; Screenplay, Shiro Ishimori; Director of Photography, Masao Kosugi; Art Director, Chiyo Umedal Editor, Shizu Ozaka; Music, Hiroki Ogawa; Songs Sung by Kensaku Morita, Yuki Meguro, and Mikiko Hirota.

CAST: Kensaku Morita (Goro Matsunaga), Miyoko Akaza (Misa), Yuki Meguro (Yuji Komiwama), Chishu Ryu (Yonoshin), Shuji Sano (Professor Kanzaki), Etsuko Ikuta (Yukiko), Yuko Enatsu (Naomi), Akuko Motoyama, Yoshiyuki Hosokawa, Taro Nanshu, Zaizu Ichiro, Akemi Kita, Mitsuko Takahashi, Miyoshi Kaneko, Jun Kashima, Nana Ozaki, Etsuko Nami, Mikiko Hirota.

A Shochiku Co., Ltd. Production. Eastman Color. Shochiku GrandScope. Released December 1969.

U.S. VERSION: Released by Shochiku Films of America, Inc. English subtitles. 85 minutes. No MPAA rating. Released April 1970.

Fighting Elegy / Kenka ereji ("Fighting Elegy"). Producer, Kazu Otsuka; Director, Seijun Suzuki; Screenplay, Kaneto Shindo, based on the novel by Takashi Suzuki; Director of Photography, Kenji Hagiwara; Editor, Mutsuo Tanji; Art Director, Takeo Kimura; Music, Naozumi Yamamoto; Assistant Director, Masami Kuzu.

CAST: Hideaki Takahashi (Kiroku Nanbu), Junko Asano (Michiko), Mitsuo Kataoka (Takuan), Yusuke Kawazu (Suppon, *"Turtle"*), Seijiro Onda (Kiroku's father), Chikako Miyagi (Yoshino, *Michiko's mother*), Isao Tamagawa (Principal of Kitakata Junior High School), Keisuke Noro (Kaneda), Hiroshi Midorigawa (Ikki Kita).

A Nikkatsu Corp. Production. Black and white. NikkatsuScope. 86 minutes. Released 1966.

U.S. VERSION: Released by Nikkatsu Corp. English subtitles. Alternate titles: *Elegy for a Quarrel, Scuffle Elegy, Elegy to Violence* and *The Born Fighter*. 86 minutes. No MPAA rating. Released 1993.

Fighting Friends—Japanese Style / Wasei kenda tomodachi ("Fighting Friends—Japanese Style"). Director, Yasujiro Ozu; Screenplay, Kogo Noda; Director of Photography, Hideo Shigehara.

CAST: Atsushi Watanabe, Ichiro Yuki, Tomoko Naniwa, Hisao Yoshitani, Ichiro Takamotsu, Chishu Ryu.

A Shochiku Co., Ltd. Production. Filmed at Shochiku-Kamata Studios. Silent with benshi. Black and white. Academy ratio. 100 minutes. Released July 5, 1929.

U.S. VERSION: Never released in the United States. A lost film.

Final Take / Kinema no Tenchi ("Heavenly Film World"). Producer, Toru Okuyama; Director, Yoji Yamada; Screenplay, Yoji Yamada, Hisashi Inoue, Yoshitaka Asama, and Taichi Yamada; Director of Photography, Tetsuo Takaba; Music, Naozumi Yamamoto.

CAST: Narimi Arimori, Kiyoshi Atsumi, Chieko Baisho, Kiichi Nakai, Chishu Ryu, Keiko Matsuzaka, Ken Tanaka, Masami Shimojo, Chieko Misaki, Hidetaka Yoshioka, Gin Maeda, Hajime Hana, Senri Sakurai, Koshiro Matsumoto.

A Shochiku Co., Ltd. Production. Color. Spherical panavision. 135 minutes. Released 1986.

U.S. VERSION: Released by Shochiku Films of America, Inc. English subtitles. 117 minutes. No MPAA rating. Released August 2, 1986.

The Final War / Daisanji sekai taisen — yonju-ichi jikan no kyofu ("World War III: 41 Hours of Fear"). Director, Shigeaki Hidaka; Screenplay, Hisataka Kai; Director of Photography, Tadashi Aramaki [Arakami].

CAST: Tatsuo Umemiya (Shigero), Yoshio [Yoshiko] Mita, Yayoi Furusato, Noribumi Fujishima, Yukiko Nikaido, Michiko Hoshi.

A New Toei Co., Ltd. Production. Black and white (processed by Toei Chemistry Co., Ltd.). ToeiScope. 77 minutes. Released October 19, 1960.

U.S. VERSION: Released by Sam Lake Enterprises. English-dubbed (?) Also known as *World War III Breaks Out* and *41 jikan no kyofu*. 77 minutes (?). No MPAA Rating. Released December 3, 1962.

Fireflies in the North/Kita no Hotaru ("Fireflies in the North"). Producer, Shigeru Okada; Director, Hideo Gosha; Screenplay, Koji Takada; Director of Photography, Fujio Morita; Music, Masaru Sato.

CAST: Tatsuya Nakadai, Shima Iwashita, Mari Natsuki.

A Toei Co., Ltd./Shigeto Co., Ltd. Production. Color. Panavision (?). 125 minutes. Released 1984.

U.S. VERSION: Distributor, if any, is undetermined. No MPAA rating.

Fires on the Plain / Nobi ("Fires on the Plain"). Producer, Masaichi Nagata; Director, Kon Ichikawa; Screenplay, Natto Wada, based on a story by Shohei Oka; Director of Photography, Setsuo Kobayashi; Art Director, Atsuji Shibata; Lighting, Isamu Yoneyama; Sound Recording, Kenichi Nishii; Editors, Hiroaki Fujii and Kon Ichikawa; Music, Yasushi Akutagawa.

CAST: Eiji Funakoshi (Tamura), Osamu Takizawa (Yasuda), Mickey Curtis (Nagamatsu), Mantaro Ushio (sergeant), Kyu Sazanka (army surgeon), Yoshihiro Hamaguchi (non-commisioned officer), Asao Sano, Maoya Tsukita , Hikaru Hoshi (soldiers).

A Daiei Motion Picture Co., Ltd. Production. Black and white. DaieiScope. 105 minutes. Released November 3, 1959.

U.S. VERSION: Released by Harrison Pictures. English subtitles. An Edward Harrison Presentation. 105 minutes. No MPAA rating. Released July 25, 1962.

Fist of the North Star **[animated]**. Director, Toyo Ashida; Screenplay, Susumu Takahisa, based on the comic book by Tetsuo Hara; Director of Photography, Tamiyo Hasada; Music, Katsuhisa Hattori.

VOICE CHARACTERIZATIONS: (undetermined).

A Toei Animation Co., Ltd. Production. Color. Spherical wide screen (?). 100 minutes (?). Released 1986.

U.S. VERSION: Released by Streamline Pictures. English-dubbed. Producer/Adapter, Carl Macek; Dialogue Director/Screenplay, Tom Wyner. 100 minutes. No MPAA rating. Released December 1991. Voice Characterizations for U.S. Version: John Vickery (Ken), Melodie Spivack (Julia), Michael McConnohie

(Shin), Wally Burr (Raoh), Holly Sidell (Lynn).

5 Gents on the Spot / Zoku shacho gyojiki ("President's Conduct Report, Part II"). Director, Shue Matsubayashi; Screenplay, Ryozo Kasahara; Director of Photography, Takeshi Suzuki.

CAST: Hisaya Morishige (Hisataro Iwato), Frankie Sakai (Tsuyoshi Kebanai), Keiju Kobayashi (Takashi Ishikawa), Michiyo Aratama (Sumiko), Yoko Tsukasa (Kyoko Ishikawa), Daisuke Kato (Tyuzo Togashi), Norihei Miki (Benjiro Mameda).

A Toho Co., Ltd. Production. Color. Toho Scope. Released 1966.

U.S. VERSION: Released by Toho International Co., Ltd. English subtitles. The 30th feature in the 40-film "Company President" series (1956-1971). 90 minutes. No MPAA rating. Released January 11, 1967.

Five Gents' Trick Book / Shacho ninpocho ("Five Gents Secret Scroll"). Producer, Masumi Fujimoto; Director, Shue Matsubayashi; Screenplay, Ryozo Kasahara; Director of Photography, Takeshi Suzuki; Music, Yoshiyuki Kozu.

CAST: Hisaya Morishige (Hisataro Iwato), Asami Kuji (Toyoko Iwato), Keiju Kobayashi (Takashi Ishikawa), Daisuke Kato (Tyuzo Togashi), Norihei Miki (Benjiro Mameda), Yoko Tsukasa (Kyoko Ishikawa), Frankie Sakai (Tsuyoshi Kebanai), Junko Ikeuchi (Chiyo Suza), Michiyo Aratama (Sumiko), Reiko Dan (Yuriko).

A Toho Co., Ltd. Production. Eastman Color. Toho Scope. 95 minutes. Released January 3, 1965.

U.S. VERSION: Released by Toho International Co., Ltd. English subtitles. The 27th "Company President" feature. 95 minutes. No MPAA rating. Released December 21, 1965.

Five Scouts / Gonin no Sekkohei ("Five Scouts"). Director, Tomotaka Tasaka; Screenplay, Yoshio Aramaki, based on an original story by Yashiro Takashige (Tomotaka Tasaka); Director of Photography, Saburo Isayama; Art Director, Takashi Matsuyama.

CAST: Isamu Kosugi (Platoon Leader Okada), Bontaro Miake (Sergeant Fujimoto), Ichiro Izawa (Private Koguchi), Shiro Izome (Corporal Nakamura).

A Nikkatsu Corp. Black and white. Academy ratio. 73 minutes. Released 1938.

U.S. VERSION: Distributor undetermined. English subtitles. 73 minutes. No MPAA rating. Released 1970.

The Flesh Is Hot / Buta to gunkan ("Pigs and Battleships"). Director, Shohei Imamura; Screenplay, Hisashi Yamanouchi; Director of Photography, Shinsaku Himeda; Art Director, Kimihiko Nakamura; Music, Toshiro Mayuzumi.

CAST: Hiroyuki Nagato, Jitsuko Yoshimura, Shiro Osaka, Shoichi Ozawa, Yoko Minamida, Sanae Nakahara, Masao Mishima, Tetsuro Tamba, Takeshi Kato, Mitzi Mori, Akira Yamauchi.

A Nikkatsu Corporation Production. Black and white. NikkatsuScope. 108 minutes. Released January 1961.

U.S. VERSION: Released by European Producers International. English subtitles. A Gaston Hakim Presentation. 77 minutes. No MPAA rating. Released September 13, 1963. Reissued as *The Dirty Girls,* running 66 minutes, and as *Pigs and Battleships*, running 108 minutes.

Flight from Ashiya / Ashiya Kara no Hiko ("Flight from Ashiya"). Executive Producer, Masaichi Nagata; Producer, Harold Hecht; Director, Michael Anderson, Sr.; Screenplay, Elliott Arnold and Waldo Salt, based on the 1959 novel *Flight from Ashiya* by Elliott Arnold; Music, Frank Cordell; Directors of Photography, Joseph MacDonald and Burnett Guffey; Production Designer/Special Effects Sequences Director, Eugene Lourie; Editor, Gordon Pilkington; Assistant Director, Milton Feldman; Production Manager, Gilbert Kurland; Technical Adviser, Maj. Eugene C. Watkins, USAF; Art Director, Tomo Shimogawara; Sound, Masao Osumi; Makeup, Daniel J. Striepeke and Eric Allwright; Lighting Technician, Gengon Nakaoka; Assistant Art

Director, Bruno Avesani; Set Decorators, Abe-san (no other name available), Giorgio Giovanini; Chief of Construction, Alberto (no other name), Unit Production Manager, Doc Merman; Translator, Markarov (no other name) Special Photographic Effects, Daiei Special Effects Department.

CAST: Yul Brynner (Sgt. Mike Takashima), Richard Widmark (Col. Glenn Stevenson), George Chakiris (Lt. John Gregg), Suzy Parker (Lucille Carroll), Shirley Knight (Caroline Gordon), Eiko Taki (Tomiko), Joseph di Reda (Sgt. Randy Smith), Mitsuhiro Sugiyama (Japanese boy Charlie), E.S. Ince (Capt. Walter Mound), Andrew Hughes (Dr. Horton), Danielle Gaubert (Leila), Paul Frees (voice characterizations).

A Harold Hecht Films/Daiei Motion Picture Co., Ltd. Production. A Harold Hecht Presentation. A Daiei Motion Picture Co., Ltd. Release. A Japanese/U.S. co-production in English. Filmed at Daiei Studios (Kyoto), Studio Cinecitta S.p.A. (Rome), and on location in Tokyo, Kyoto, Osaka, and Tachikawa, Japan. Eastman Color. Panavision. Westrex Recording System. Released 1963.

U.S. VERSION: Released by United Artists Corporation. Prints by De Luxe. 100 minutes. No MPAA rating. Released March 25, 1964.

Floating Clouds / Ukigumo

("Floating Clouds"). Director, Mikio Naruse; Screenplay, Yoko Mizuki, based on the novel *Ukigumo* by Fumiko Hayoshi; Assistant Director, Kihachi Okamoto; Art Director, Satoshi Chuko; Director of Photography, Masao Tamai; Music, Ichiro Saito; Sound, Toho Dubbing Theatre; Sound Effects, Toho Sound Effects Group.

CAST: Hideko Takemine (Yukiko Koda), Masayuki Mori (Kengo Tomioka), Daisuke Kato (Senkichi Mukai), Mariko Okada (Osei Mukai, *Senkichi's wife*), Cheiko Nakakita (Kuniko Tomioka, *Kengo's wife*), Isao Yamagata (Sugio Iba), Akira Sera (Kinsaku Ohta), Roy H. James (American soldier), Mayuri Mokusho (bar girl).

A Toho Co., Ltd. Production. Black and white. Academy ratio. Filmed at Toho Studios, Ltd. (Tokyo). 123 minutes. Released 1955.

U.S. VERSION: Released by Corinth Films. English subtitles. Advertised as "An Akira Kurosawa Film" (sic!). 123 minutes. No MPAA rating. Released June 1980.

Floating Weeds / Ukikusa

("Floating Weeds"). Producer, Masaichi Nagata; Director, Yasujiro Ozu; Screenplay, Kogo Noda and Yasujiro Ozu; Story, Yasujiro Ozu, based on the screenplay for the film *Ukikusa monogatari* (1934) by Tadao Ikeda; Director of Photography, Kazuo Miyagawa; Art Director, Tomo Shimogawara; Music, Takanobu Saito.

CAST: Ganjiro Nakamura (Komajuro Arashi), Haruko Sugimura (Oyoshi), Hiroshi Kawaguchi (Kiyoshi), Machiko Kyo (Sumiko), Ayako Wakao (Kayo), Koji Mitsui (Kikinosuke), Mantaro Ushio (Sentaro), Haruo Tanaka (Yatazo), Chishu Ryu (theater owner), Tadashi Date (Sensho), Mutsuko Sakura, Hitomi Nozoe.

A Daiei Motion Picture Co., Ltd. Production. Daiei Color. Academy ratio. Filmed on location on the Kii Peninsula, Shijima. 119 minutes. Released November 17, 1959.

U.S. VERSION: Released by Altura Films International. English subtitles. Previously filmed by Ozu as *A Story of Floating Weeds* (1934). 119 minutes. No MPAA rating. Released November 24, 1970.

The Flower / Hana no bojo

("The Yearning Flower"). Producer, Eizaburo Adachi; Director, Hideo Suzuki; Screenplay, Tadao Ikemoto, Akira Sugimoto, and Tsutomu Sawamura, based on an original story by Nobuko Yoshiya; Director of Photography, Tadashi Iimura; Art Director, Yasuhide Kato; Music, Yasushi Akutagawa.

CAST: Yoko Tsukasa (Kozue Domoto), Haruko Sugimura (her mother-in-law), Akira Takarada (Tsuda), Mina Mitsui (his sister), Mitsuko Kusabue (Tsuzuki), Minoru Chiaki (Yanami).

A Toho Co., Ltd. Production. Agfacolor. Toho Scope. Running time undetermined. Released 1958.

U.S. VERSION: Release undetermined, possibly Toho International Co., Ltd. in subtitled format. No MPAA rating.

A Flower Blooms / Hana hiraku ("A Flower Blooms"). Producer, Yutaka Abe; Director, Kon Ichikawa; Screenplay, Toshio Yasumi, based on a story by Yaeko Nogami; Director of Photography, Joji Ohara; Music, Fumio Hayasaka; Sound Recording, Masakazu Kamiya; Art Director, Takashi Kono; Lighting, Ko Fujimura.

CAST: Hideko Takamine (Machiko Sone), Michiko Yoshikawa (Machiko's mother), Susumu Fujita (Teruhiko's Kawai), Ken Uehara (Saburo Seki), Hideko Mimura (Yoneko Oba).

A Shintoho Co., Ltd. Production. Black and white. Academy ratio. Running time undetermined. Released April 13, 1948.

U.S. VERSION: Distributor, if any, is undetermined.

Flying Phantom Ship / Soratobu yureisen ("Flying Phantom Ship") [**animated**]. Director, Hiroshi Ikeda; Screenplay, Masaki Tsuji, based on an original story by Shotaro Ishimori; Chief Animator, Yoichi Otabe; Art Director, Isamu Tsuchida; Music, Kosuke Onozaki.

VOICE CHARACTERIZATIONS: (undetermined).

A Toei Animation Studio Co., Ltd. Production. A Toei Co., Ltd. Release. Eastman Color. ToeiScope. 60 minutes. Released July 20, 1969.

U.S. VERSION: Distributor, if any, is undetermined. No MPAA rating.

Forbidden Affair / Sono hito wa jokyoshi ("He's a Minor Professor"). Director, Masanobu Deme; Screenplay, Fukiko Miyauchi; Director of Photography, Tokuzo Kuroda; Art Director, Motoji Kojima; Music, Sei Ikeno.

CAST: Shima Iwashita (Maki Hayami), Shiro Mifune (Ryo Takeuchi), Takashi Kanda, Rokko Toura.

A Tokyo Eiga Co., Ltd. Production. Fujicolor. Toho Scope. 93 minutes. Released August 29, 1970.

U.S. VERSION: Released by Toho International Co., Ltd. English subtitles. 93 minutes. No MPAA rating. Released September 23, 1971.

The Forbidden Fruit / Shin kokosei burusu ("New High School Student Blues"). Director, Michihiko Obimori; Screenplay, Masayoshi Imako, based on an original story by Seijin Shibata; Director of Photography, Ko Kitasaki; Art Director, Akira Yamaguchi; Music, Harumi Ibe.

CAST: Keiko Sekine (Kyoko), Yoshiro Uchida (Kenji), Naoyuki Sugano, Yutaka Mizutani.

A Daiei Motion Picture Co., Ltd. Production. Fujicolor. DaieiScope. 83 minutes. Released December 25, 1970.

U.S. VERSION: Released undetermined, possibly by Daiei International Films. English subtitled version available.

Fort Graveyard / Chi to suna ("Blood and Sand"). Executive Producer, Tomoyuki Tanaka; Director, Kihachi Okamoto; Screenplay, Kihachi Okamoto and Kan Saji; Director of Photography, Rokuro Nishigaki; Music, Masaru Sato.

CAST: Toshiro Mifune (Sergeant Kosugi), Tatsuya Nakadai, Yunosuke Ito, Reiko Dan, Makoto Sato.

A Toho Co., Ltd. Production. Black and white. Toho Scope. 132 minutes. Released 1965.

U.S. VERSION: Released by Toho International Co., Ltd. English subtitles. The 7th and final film in a series. 132 minutes. No MPAA rating. Released May 1966.

The Fort of Death / Gonin no Shokin Kasegi ("Five People Making Money"). Director, Eiichi Kudo; Screenplay, Koji Takada; Director of Photography, Juhei Suzuki; Art Director, Yoshimitsu Amamori; Music, Toshiaki Tsushima.

CAST: Tomisaburo Wakayama (Ichibei Shikoro), Minoru Oki (Yataro Mochizuki), Tomoko Mayama (Kagero), Eizo Kitamura (Hayato Onizuka), Kenji Ushio (Kunai Aoto), Ichiro Nakatani (Mondo Shibaike), Kajuro Arashi (Tazaemon), Asao Koike (Lord Ozeki), Goro Ibuki.

A Toei Co., Ltd. Production. Eastman

Color. ToeiScope. 97 minutes. Released December 13, 1969.

U.S. VERSION: Distributor, if any, is undetermined. English subtitled version available. No MPAA rating.

Forward, Ever Forward / Wakamono wa yuku ("Young People Learning"). Director, Tokihisa Morikawa; Screenplay, Hisashi Yamanouchi; Director of Photography, Yoshio Miyajima; Art Director, Hiroshi Yamashita; Music, Masaru Sato.

CAST: Kunie Tanaka (Taro), Isao Hashimoto (Jiro), Kei Yamamoto (Saburo), Orie Sato (Orie), Shoji Matsuyama, Natsue Kimura.

A Shochiku Co., Ltd. Production. Black and white. Shochiku GrandScope. 99 minutes. Released May 10, 1969.

U.S. VERSION: Release undetermined, likely by Shochiku Films of America, Inc. English subtitles. No MPAA rating.

Foster Daddy, Tora! / Otoko wa tsuraiyo – Torajiro kamone uta ("It's Tough to Be a Man: Torajiro's Song of the Seagull"). Producer, Kiyoshi Shimazu; Director, Yoji Yamada; Screenplay, Yoji Yamada and Yoshitaka Asama, based on characters created by Yoji Yamada; Director of Photography, Tetsuo Takaba; Art Director, Mitsuo Idegawa; Music, Naozumi Yamamoto.

CAST: Kiyoshi Atsumi (Torajiro "Tora-san" Kuruma), Ran Ito (Sumire), Chieko Baisho (Sakura Suwa, *Tora-san's sister*), Gin Maeda (Hiroshi Suwa, *her husband*), Masami Shimojo (Tora's uncle), Chieko Misaki (Tsune, *Tora's aunt*), Hisao Dazai (president), Chishu Ryu (Gozen-sama, *the temple priest*), Tatsuo Matsumura (Teacher Hayashi).

A Shochiku Co., Ltd. Production. Color. Panavision (?). 96 minutes. Released 1980.

U.S. VERSION: Released by Shochiku Films of America, Inc. English subtitles. The 26th "Tora-san" feature. Followed by *Tora-san's Love in Osaka* (1981). 96 minutes. No MPAA rating. Released 1980.

Four Days of Snow and Blood / Ni-ni-roku ("226"). Producer, Kazuyoshi Okuyama; Director, Hideo Gosha; Screenplay, Kazuo Kasahara; Director of Photography, Fujio Morita; Music, Akira Senju.

CAST: Kenichi Hagiwara, Tomokazu Miura, Tatsuya Nakadai, Masahiro Motoki, Naoto Takenata.

A Shochiku-Fuji Co., Ltd. Production. Fujicolor. Panavision (?). 114 minutes. Released 1989.

U.S. VERSION: Released by Shochiku Films of America, Inc. in subtitled format. Alternate title: *226*. No MPAA rating. Released November 1989.

The Fox with Nine Tails / Kyubi no kitsune to Tobimaru ("The Fox with Nine Tails and Tobimaru") [**animated**]. Executive Producer, Takashi Senda; Producer, Gentaro Nakajima; Director, Shinichi Yagi; Screenplay, Michio Yoshioka; Story, Kido Okamoto; Animation, Taku Sugiyama; Director of Photography, Masayoshi Kishimoto; Art Director, Isamu Kageyama; Music, Shigeru Ikeno.

VOICE CHARACTERIZATIONS: (unavailable).

A Japan Animated Film Co., Ltd. Production. A Daiei Motion Picture Co., Ltd. Release. Fujicolor. DaieiScope (?). Released 1969 (?).

U.S. VERSION: Released by Daiei International Films, Inc. English subtitles. 81 minutes. No MPAA rating. Released October 1969.

Frankenstein Conquers the World / Furankenshutain tai chitei kaiju Baragon ("Frankenstein Against the Subterranian Monster Baragon"). Producer, Tomoyuki Tanaka; Director, Ishiro Honda; Screenplay, Kaoru Mabuchi (Takeshi Kimura), from a synopsis (i.e. adaption) by Jerry Sohl, based on a story by Reuben Bercovitch, and suggested by characters from Mary Wollstonecraft Shelley's novel, *Frankenstein*; Director of Photography, Hajime Koizumi; Color

Opposite: **The cast of *Frankenstein Conquers the World* (1965) – Yoshio Kosugi (soldier with mustache), Nick Adams, Tadao Takashima, Kumi Mizuno, Kozo Nomura (with camera) and Tadashi Okabe (far right).**

Director (?), Kiyashi Tsurusaki; Music, Akira Ifukube; Editor, Ryohei Fujii; Art Director, Takeo Kita; Makeup, Rika Konna; Casting Assistant, Ai Maeda; Sound Effects, Hisashi Shimonaga, Toho Sound Effects Group; Sound, Toho Recording Centre; Transportation, Yashitomi Transportation. *Toho Special Effects Group*: Director, Eiji Tsuburaya; Photography, Teisho Arikawa, Mototaka Tomioka; Lighting, Kuichiro Kishida; Art Director, Akira Watanabe; Assistant to Tsuburaya,Teruyoshi Nakano; Optical Photography, Yukio Manoda and Sadao Iizuka; Scene Manipulation, Fumio Nakadai.

CAST: Nick Adams (Dr. James Bowen), Tadao Takashima (scientist), Kumi Mizuno (Dr. Sueko Togami), Yoshio Tsuchiya (1st Officer Kawai, *the sailor who delivers the heart*), Kenji Sahara (soldier), Jun Tazaki (military advisor), Susumu Fujita (Osaka police chief), Nobuo Nakamura (scientist at museum), Takashi Shimura (Hiroshima doctor), Yoshifumi Tajima (submarine commander), Yoshio Kosugi, Nadao Kirino (soldiers), Peter Mann (German scientist), Hisaya Ito (policeman), Koji Furuhata (Frankenstein monster as an adult), Haruo Nakajima (Baragon), Haruya Kato, Senkichi Omura (doomed TV crew), Kenzo Tabu (newspaper editor), Kozo Nomura, Tadashi Okabe (reporters), Keiko Sawai (dying girl), Ikio Sawamura (dog owner), Yutaka Sada (hospital manager), Kenchiro Kawaji.

A Toho Co., Ltd. Production, in association with Henry G. Saperstein Enterprises. Eastman Color (processed by Tokyo Laboratory Limited). Toho Scope. 95 minutes. Released August 8, 1965.

U.S. VERSION: Released by American International Pictures. English-dubbed. A James H. Nicholson and Samuel Z. Arkoff Presentation from UPA Productions of America. Executive Producers, Henry G. Saperstein and Reuben Bercovitch; Re-recording Supervisor, Salvatore Billitteri; Prints by Pathé. AIP and UPA Productions of America given on actual prints; current television edition is minus all AIP credits. Double-billed with *Tarzan and the Valley of Gold* (AIP, 1966). The Japanese laserdisc edition includes an alternate ending shot but not used. Initially conceived as a match-up between the Frankenstein monster and Godzilla. 87 minutes. No MPAA rating. Released July 8, 1966.

Free and Easy / Tsuri baka Nisshi ("Diary of a Fishing Fool"). Producer, Shizuo Yamanouchi; Director, Tomio Kuriyama; Screenplay, Yoji Yamada and Akira Momoi; Director of Photography, Kosuke Yasuda; Music, Bingo Miki.

CAST: Toshiyuki Nishida, Eri Ishida, Rentaro Mikuni, Kei Tani.

A Shochiku Co., Ltd. Production. Color. Panavision (?). 93 minutes. Released 1988.

U.S. VERSION: Release undetermined, possibly by Shochiku Films of America, Inc. in subtitled format. The first "Free and Easy" feature (1988-present). Followed by *Free and Easy II* (1989). No MPAA rating.

Free and Easy II / Tsuribaka Nisshi: 2 ("Diary of a Fishing Fool 2"). Producer, Makoto Naito; Director, Tomio Kuriyama; Screenplay, Yoji Yamada and Takashi Horimoto; Director of Photography, Kosuke Yasuda; Music, Joe Hisaishi.

CAST: Toshiyuki Nishida, Rentaro Mikuni, Mieko Harada, Kei Tani.

A Shochiku Co., Ltd. Production. Color. Panavision (?). 92 minutes. Released 1989.

U.S. VERSION: Distributor, if any, is undetermined, possibly by Shochiku Films of America, Inc. in subtitled format. The 2nd "Free and Easy" feature. Followed by *Free and Easy 3* (1990). No MPAA rating.

The Friendly Killer / Noboryu tekkahada ("Rising Dragon"). Director/Screenplay, Teruo Ishii; Director of Photography, Sei Kitaizumi; Art Director, Takeo Kimura; Music, Masao Yagi.

CAST: Hiroko Ogi (Katsumi), Akira Kobayashi (Masa), Toru Abe (Yasukawa), Tatsuya Fuji, Kokan Katsura, Yoko Yamamoto, Tomo Koike, Shoki Fukae, Eiji Go, Hideki Takahashi, Kiyoko Tange, Setsuko Minami, Tomoko Aki, Hatsue Tonoka, Toru Yuri, Shunji Sayama.

A Nikkatsu Corporation Production. Fujicolor. NikkatsuScope. Released March 28, 1969.

U.S. VERSION: Distributor undetermined. English subtitles (?). 90 minutes. No MPAA rating. Released March 18, 1970.

Fugitive Alien. Producers, Noboru Tsuburaya, Jushichi Sano, and Akira Tsuburaya; Directors, Kiyosumi Kukazawa and Minoru Kanaya; Teleplay, Keiichi Abe, Bunko Wakatsuki, Yoshihisa Araki, Hiroyasu Yamamura, Hideyoshi Nagasaka, Toyohiro Ando; Music, Norio Maeda; Special Effects, Tsuburaya Enterprises.

CAST: Tatsuya Azuma, Miyuki Tanigawa, Jo Shishido, Choei Takahashi, Tsutomu Yukawa, Hiro Tateyama, Akihiko Hirata.

A Japanese teleseries re-edited to feature length for American television and never released theatrically in Japan. A Tsuburaya Productions, Ltd. Production. 16mm. Color.

U.S. VERSION: Never released theatrically in the United States. Released directly to television in 1988 by King Features Entertainment, a subsidiary of the Hearst Corp. English-dubbed. A Sandy Frank Enterprises Presentation. Feature Concept/Editor, William L. Cooper, Jr.; Creative Consultant, Jessie Vogel, Cinemedia, Ltd. Copyright 1986 by Tsuburaya Productions, Ltd. Followed by *Star Force: Fugitive Alien II.* Derived from the teleseries "Suta-urufu" ("Star Wolf"), which aired in Japan in 1978. 102 minutes. No MPAA rating.

The Funeral / Ososhiki ("The Funeral"). Executive Producers, Yasushi Tamaoki and Yutaka Okada; Producer, Seigo Hosogoe; Associate Producer/Director/Screenplay, Juzo Itami; Director of Photography, Yonezo Maeda; Black and white photography, Shinpei Asai; Lighting, Shosaku Kato; Graphics, Kenichi Samura; Editor, Akira Suzuki; Art Director, Hiroshi Tokuda; Music, Joji Yuasa; Costumes, Fumio Iwasaki; Makeup, Midori Konuma; Sound Recording, Minoru Nobuoka; Sound Transfers, Kyoji Kawano; Sound Effects, Yoshio Kojima; Production Assistants, Masahiro Ito; Jiyoki Sato; Casting, Kosaburo Sasaoka; Assistant Directors, Hideyuki Hirayama, Mamoru Taira, Masara Kamiyama.

CAST: Tsutomu Yamazaki (Wabisuke Inoue), Nobuko Miyamoto (Chizuko Amamiya), Kin Sugai (Kikue Amamiya), Shuji Otaki (Shokichi Amamiya), Ichiro Zaitsu (Satomi), Nekohachi Edoya (Ebihara), Koen Okumura (Shinkichi Amamiya), Chikako Yuri (Ayako), Masahiko Tsugawa (Dr. Kimura), Kaoru Kobayashi (Inose), Haruna Takase (Yoshiko Saito), Chishu Ryu (priest), Isao Bido (Shigeru), Ittoku Kishibe (Akira), Takashi Tsumura (Aoki), Michiyo Yokoyama (Mrs. Kimura), Hikaru Nishikawa (Mrs. Hanamura), Midori Ebina (Kiyo), Hiroko Futaba (Shokichi's wife), Hiroko Seki (teacher in videotape), Mitsuko Yoshikawa (Mrs. Iwakiri), Kamatari Fujiwara (little old man and Old People's Club member), Haruo Tanaka (2nd old man and Old People's Club member), Ryosuke Kagawa (Old People's Club chairman), Asao Sasano (Kurosaki), Koji Okayama (Okumura), Sauda Ippei (Sakakibara), Yoshiharo Kato, Saoyoshi Satogi (Ebihara's assistants), Akio Kaneda (Fuku), Go Riju (man who climbs tree), Mariko Nakamura (hospital caller), Hideo Fukuhara (TV studio guard), Atsuyoshi Matsukidaira (hanamura), Koji Tanaka (Taro), Manpei Ikeuchi (Jiro), Hideo Nagai (Osamu), Keiichiro Nakada (Tet-Chan), Matsue Matsumoto, Eriko Ohashi, Kazuyo Kawamura, Reiko Shinjo (nurses), Yosai Inoue (telegram deliverer), Go Toneatsu (young man), Shizuo Sato (father), Hirayuki Tsuchiyama (priest), Yoshiharu Tojukai, Mitsuko Yoshikawa (members of the Old People's Club), Kiyoshi Kurosawa (assistant director), Noboru Nakayama (Sakuma), Tetstaro Tsuruno (man from agency), Noriyuki Osagai (makeup man), Michihiro Tokuno (cameraman), Masahiro Irie, Hiroyuki Yamada, Shiho Matsunami (VTR operators), Sakihiro Sakai (funeral guest), Ichiro Oba (dead man), Hidekazu Nagae.

An Itami Productions/New Century Producers Production. A Toho Co., Ltd. Release. Fujicolor with black and white insert. Spherical wide screen. 124 minutes. Released 1985.

U.S. VERSION: Released by New Yorker Films. English subtitles. Subtitles, Teiko Seiki, Dynaword, Inc. Alternate title: Death Japanese Style. 124 minutes. No MPAA rating. Released March 16, 1987.

Funeral Parade of Roses / Bara no soretsu ("Funeral Parade of Roses"). Producer, Mitsuru Kudo; Director/Screenplay, Toshio Matsumoto; Director of Photography, Tatsuo Suzuki; Art Director, Setsu Asakura; Editor, Toshie Iwasa; Music, Joji Yuasa; Sound Recording, Mikio Katsuyama.

CAST: Peter (Eddie), Osamu Ogasawara (Leda), Toyosaburo Uchiyama (Guevara), Don Madrid (Tony), Emiko Azuma (Eddie's mother), Yoshio Tsuchiya (Gonda).

A Matsumoto Productions Co., Ltd. Production. Black and white. Academy ratio (?). Released 1970 (?).

U.S. VERSION: Distributor undetermined. 105 minutes. No MPAA rating. Released October 29, 1970.

Gambler's Code (production credits unavailable).

CAST: Hideki Takahashi, Kazuko Izumi.

Production company undetermined. Black and white. Released 1966 (?).

U.S. VERSION: Distributor undetermined. Running time undetermined. No MPAA rating. Released December 14, 1966.

Gamblers in Okinawa / Bakuto gaijin butai ("Fighting Foreigner Gamblers"). Director, Kinji Fukasaku; Screenplay, Norio Konami, Hiro Matsuda, and Kinji Fukasaku; Director of Photography, Hanjiro Nakazawa; Art Director, Hiroshi Kitagawa; Music, Takeo Yamashita.

CAST: Koji Tsuruta (Masuo Gunji), Noboru Ando (Kudo), Tomisaburo Wakayama (Yanabara), Kenjiro Morokado (Gushiken), Kenji Imai (Mad Dog Jiro), Rinichi Yamamoto (Haderuma), Akiko Kudo.

A Toei Co., Ltd. Production. Eastman Color. ToeiScope. 93 minutes. Released January 12, 1971.

U.S. VERSION: Distributor, if any, is undetermined. English subtitled version available. No MPAA rating.

The Gambling Samurai / Kunisada Chuji ("Chuji Kunisada"). Producer, Masumi Fujimoto; Director, Senkichi Taniguchi; Screenplay, Kaneto Shindo; Director of Photography, Rokuro Nishigaki; Art Director, Takeo Kita; Music, Masaru Sato.

CAST: Toshiro Mifune (Chuji Kunisada), Michiyo Aratama (Toku), Kumi Mizuno (Kiku), Daisuke Kato (Enzo), Yosuke Natsuki (Asataro), Eijiro Tono (Chief Kansuke), Yu Fujiki (Gantetsu), Susumu Fujita (Magistrate Jubei Matsui), Senkichi Omura (detective at barbershop), Yoshio Kosugi (detective), Kankuro Nakamura.

A Toho Co., Ltd. Production. Agfacolor. Toho Scope. Western Electric Mirrophonic Recording (encoded with Perpecta Stereophonic Sound). 101 minutes. Released 1960.

U.S. VERSION: Released by Toho International Co., Ltd. English subtitles. *Note:* Mifune's character is not a samurai, despite the title. 93 minutes. No MPAA rating. Released September 27, 1960.

***Gamera* Series** Popular Daiei film series about a giant fire-breathing monster turtle. Unlike Toho's Godzilla series (q.v.), the Gamera pictures were singularly marketed for children, and creatively the series was vastly inferior, with cheaper effects and a painful reliance on stock footage from earlier entries. The second "m" in the monster's name was dropped after the first feature, which was also the only one in black and white. After a long absence, a new, surprisingly accomplished Gamera film was released in 1995.

FILMS INCLUDE: Gammera the Invincible/Gamera (1965); War of the Monsters /Gamera vs. Barugon (1966); The Return of the Giant Monsters/Gamera vs. Gaos (1967); Destroy All Planets (1968); Attack of the Monsters/Gamera vs. Guiron (1969); Gamera vs. Monster X (1970); Gamera vs. Zigra (1971); Super Monster/ Gamera Super Monster (1980); Gamera – The Guardian of the Universe (1995).

Gamera – The Guardian of the Universe / Gamera – daikaiju kuchu kessen ("Gamera – Decisive Air Battle"). Executive Producer, Yasuyoshi Tokuma, Hiroyoki Kato, Seiji Urushido, and Shigeru Ono; Producer, Tsutomu Tsuchikawa; Director, Shusuke Kaneko; Screenplay, Kazunori Ito; Director of Photography, Junichi Tozawa; Music, Ko Otani; Special Effects Director, Shinji Higuchi; Asst. SFX Director, Makoto Kamiya; Effects Photography, Hiroshi Kidokoro; Lighting, Hokoku Hayashi; Art Director, Toshio Miike; Monster Suits, Tomo Haraguchi; Visual Effects Supervisor, Hajime Matsumoto; Digital Effects, Takashi Kawabata; Computer Graphics, Atsunori Sato; Computer Graphic Images, Yoshishige Matsuno; Script Girl, Junko Kawashima; Mechanical Effects, Izumi Negishi; Assistant Directors, Shozo Katashima and Makoto Kamiya.

CAST: Tsuyoshi Ihara (Yoshinari Yonemori), Akira Onodera (Naoya Kusanagi), Ayako Fujitani (Asagi Kusanagi), Shinobu Nakayama (Mayumi Nagamine), Yukijiro Hotaru (Police Detective Osako), Kojiro Hongo, Akira Kubo (ships' captains), Takateru Manabe (Gamera), Yumi Kameyama (Gyaos), Hatsunori Hasegawa, Hirotaro Honda.

A Daiei Co., Ltd./Nippon Television Network/Hakuhodo Co., Ltd. Production. A Toho Co., Ltd. Release. Dolby Stereo. Color. Spherical wide screen. 95 minutes. Released March 1995.

U.S. VERSION: Released by Daiei Co., Ltd. English subtitles. 95 minutes. No MPAA rating. Released May 19, 1995. Subtitles, Jeanette Amano. The 9th feature in the "Gamera" film series. A sequel has been announced.

Gamera vs. Monster X / Gamera tai maju Jaiga ("Gamera Against the Demon Beast Jaiga"). Executive Producer, Masaichi Nagata; Producer, Hidemasa Nagata; Director, Noriyaki Yuasa; Screenplay, Nizo Takahashi; Director of Photography, Akira Kitazaki; Sound, Daiei Recording Studio; Music, Shunsuke Kikuchi Special Effects Director, Kazufumi Fujii; Special Effects, Daiei Special Effects Department; Monster Design, Ryosaku Takayama.

CAST: Tsutomu Takakuwa, Cary Barris, Katherine Murphy, Kon Omura, Junko Yashiro.

A Daiei Motion Picture Co., Ltd. Production. A Masaichi Nagata Presentation. Westrex recording system. Eastman Color (processed by Daiei Laboratory). DaieiScope. 83 minutes. Released March 21, 1970.

U.S. VERSION: Never released theatrically in the United States. Released directly to television by American International Television (AIP-TV) in 1970. English-dubbed. A James H. Nicholson & Samuel Z. Arkoff Presentation. American Version by Titra Productions, Inc. Postproduction supervisor, Salvatore Billitteri; Director, Bret Morrison; Editors, Eli Haviv, Emil Haviv. Prints by Perfect. The 6th "Gamera" feature. Followed by *Gamera vs. Zigra* (1971). U.K. Title (?): *Monsters Invade Expo 70*. Includes stock footage from *War of the Monsters* (1966), *Return of the Giant Monsters* (1967), *Destroy All Planets* (1968), and *Attack of the Monsters* (1969). No MPAA rating. 83 minutes.

Gamera vs. Zigra / Gamera tai shinkai kaiju Jigura ("Gamera against the Deep Sea Monster Jigura"). Executive Producer, Hidemasa Nagata; Producers, Yoshihiko Manabe; Director, Noriyaki Yuasa; Screenplay, Nizo Takahashi; Director of Photography, Akira Uehara; Art Director, Tomohisa Yano; Lighting, Heihachi Kuboe; Editor, Zenko [Yoshiyuki] Miyazaki; Assistant Director, Masami Akise; Music, Shunsuke Kikuchi; Sound Recording, Hideo Okuyama; Sound, Daiei Recording Studio. *Daiei Special Effects Department*: Director, Kazufumi Fujii; Monster Design, Ryosaku Takayama.

CAST: Eiko Yanami (Woman X/Chikako Sugawara), ReikoKasahara (Kiyoko Ishikawa), Mikiko Tsubouchi (Mrs. Ishikawa, *Kenichi's mother*), Koji Fujiyama (Dr. Tom Wallace), Isamu Saeiki (Dr. Yosuke Ishikawa), Yasushi Sakagami (Kenichi Ishikawa), Arlene Zoellner (Margie Wallace), Gloria Zoellner (Helen Wallace), Shin Minatsu, Yoshio Yoshida, Akira Natsuki, Goro Kudan, Daihachi Kita, Daigo Inoue.

A Daiei Motion Picture Co., Ltd. Production. DaieiColor. DaieiScope. 87 minutes. Released July 17, 1971.

JAPAN AIR LINES

U.S. VERSION: Never released theatrically in the United States. Released directly to television by King Features Entertainment, a subsidiary of The Hearst Corporation, in 1987. English-dubbed. A Sandy Frank Film Syndication, Inc. Presentation. The 7th "Gamera" feature. Followed by *Super Monster* (1980). No MPAA rating. 87 minutes.

Gammera the Invincible / Daikaiju Gamera ("Giant Monster Gamera"). Executive Producer, Masaichi Nagata; Producer, Hidemasa Nagata; Director, Noriaki Yuasa; Planner (i.e. Production Manager?), Yonejiro Saito; Screenplay, Nizo Takahashi, based on an idea by Yonejiro Saito; Director of Photography, Nobuo Munekawa; Editor, Tatsuji Nakashizu; Sound Recording Supervisor, Masao Osumi; Sound, Daiei Recording Studio; Special Effects Director, Yonesaburo Tsukiji, Daiei Special Effects Department; Monster Design, Ryosaku Takayama.

CAST: Eiji Funakoshi (Dr. Hidaka), Harumi Kiritachi (Kyoko), Junichiro Yamashiko (Aoyaki), Yoshiro Uchida (Toshio), Michiko Sugata (Nobuyo), Yoshiro Kitahara (Sakurai), Jun Hamamura (Dr. Murase), George Hirose (Japanese Ambassador), Bokuzen Hidari.

A Daiei Motion Picture Co., Ltd. Production. Black and white (processed by Daiei Laboratory). DaieiScope. 78 minutes. Released November 27, 1965.

U.S. VERSION: Released by World Entertainment Corp. A Harris Associates Presentation. English-dubbed. Executive Producer, Ken Barnett; Director, Sandy Howard; Additional Dialog, Richard Kraft; Director of Photography, Julian Townsend; Editing, Ross-Gaffney, Inc.; Art Director, Hank Aldrich; Assistant Director, Sidney Cooperschmidt; Theme Song, Wes Farrell (performed by The Moons); Additional scenes filmed in Totalscope. International Title (?): *The Monster Gamera.*The 1st "Gamera" feature. Followed by *War of the Monsters* (1966). Home Video and television reissue version title: *Gamera.* Distributed by King Features Entertainment, a subsidiary of Hearst Corp; A Sandy Frank Film Syndication, Inc. Presentation. Reissued to television and home video in 1987 in the original 78-minute Japanese version (minus the added footage) and the entire film is redubbed. Cast names Anglicized for television and home video version. 86 minutes. No MPAA rating. Released December 15, 1966.

Additional Cast for U.S. VERSION: Brian Donlevy (General Terry Arnold), Albert Dekker (Secretary of Defense), Diane Findlay (Sergeant Susan Embers), John Baragrey (Captain Lovell), Dick O'Neill (General O'Neill), Mort Marshall (Jules Manning), Alan Oppenheimer (Dr. Emeric Contrare), Stephen Zacharias (Senator Billings), Bob Caraway (Lieutenant Simson), Gene Nua (Lieutenant Clark), John McCurry (Airman First Class Hopkins), Walter Arnold (American Ambassador), Louis Zorich (Russian Ambassador), Robin Craven (British Ambassador), Marvin Miller, Jack Grimes (dubbing cast).

The Gangster VIP / Daikanbu ("Bosses of Gangsters"). Director, Toshio Masuda; Screenplay, Kaneo Ikegami and Reiji Kubota; Story, Goro Fujita; Director of Photography, Kurataro Takamura; Art Director, Takeo Kimura; Music, Naozumi Yamamoto.

CAST: Tetsuya Watari (Goro Fujikawa), Chieko Matsubara (Yukiko Hashimoto), Mitsuo Hamada (Takeo Tsujikawa), Tamio Kawaji (Isamu Tsujikawa), Kyosuke Machida (Katsuhiko Sugiyama), Kayo Matsuo (Yumeko).

A Nikkatsu Corporation Production. Fujicolor. NikkatsuScope. Released January 1968.

U.S. VERSION: Released by Toho International Co., Ltd. English subtitles. 94 minutes. No MPAA rating. Released May 1968.

Gate of Flesh / Nikutai no mon ("Gate of Flesh"). Producer, Kaneo Iwai; Director, Seijun Suzuki; Screenplay, Goro Tanada, based on the 1947 novel by Taijiro

Opposite: **Eiji Funakoshi (wearing tie) in *Gammera the Invincible* (1965). Note the Kanji characters crudely blacked out for this American still.**

Tamura; Director of Photography, Shigeyoshi Mine; Art Director, Takeo Kimura; Music, Naozumi Yamamoto; Assistant Director, Masami Kuzu.

CAST: Jo Shishido (Shintaro Ibuki), Satoko Kasai (Sen Komasa), Yumiko Nogawa (Maya Borneo), Kayo Matsuo (O-Miyo, *"the Jeep"*), Tomiko Ishii (Otoku, *"the Idiot"*), Misako Tominaga (Machiko), Koji Wada (Abe), Keisuke Noro (Ishii), Isao Tamagawa (Cho), Chico Rolando (black pastor).

A Nikkatsu Corporation Production. Color. NikkatsuScope. 90 minutes. Released 1964.

U.S. VERSION: Released by Toho International Co., Ltd. English subtitles. Previously filmed in 1948, by Masahiro Makino. 90 minutes. No MPAA rating. Released December 11, 1964. Reissued by Nikkatsu Corp. in 1993.

Gate of Hell / Jigokumon ("Gate of Hell"). Producer, Masaichi Nagata; Director, Teinosuke Kinugasa; Screenplay, Teinosuke Kinugasa, based on the play *Kesa's Husband*, by Kan Kikuchi; Director of Photography, Kohei Sugiyama; Art Director, Kisaku Ito; Lighting, Shonojo Kato; Editor, Nishida Shigeo; Costume Design, Sanzo Wada; Assistant Director, KenjiMisumi; Technical Consultant, Michio Midorikawa; Music, Yasushi Akutagawa; Sound Recording, Yukio Kaibara.

CAST: Kazuo Hasegawa (Morito), Machiko Kyo (Lady Kesa), Isao Yamagata (Wataru Watanabe), Yataro Kurokawa (Shigemori), Kotaro Bando (Rokuro), Jun Tazaki (Kogenda), Koreya Senda (Kiyomori), Tatsuya Ishiguro (Yachuta), Kenjiro Uemura (Masanaka), Gen Shimzu (Saburosuke), Kikue Mohri (Sawa), Masao Shimizu (Nobuyori), Michiko Araki (Mano), Yoshie Minami (Tone), Ryosuke Kagawa (Yasutada).

A Daiei Motion Picture Co., Ltd. Production. Filmed at Daiei-Kyoto Studios. Eastman Color. Academy ratio. 88 minutes. Released October 31, 1953.

U.S. VERSION: Released by Edward Harrison. English subtitles. Alternate title: *Hell's Gate*. 88 minutes. No MPAA rating. Released December 25, 1954.

The Gate of Youth / Seishun no mon ("Gate of Youth"). Producers, Sanezumi Fujimoto and Hiroshi Hairyu; Director, Kiriro Urayama; Screenplay, Gyo Hayasaka and Kiriro Urayama, based on an original story by Hiroyuki Itsuki; Director of Photography, Hiroshi Muraki; Music, Riichiro Manabe.

CAST: Ken Tanaka, Shinobu Otake, Shoichi Ozawa, Akira Kobayashi, Sayuri Yoshida, Yukei Tanabe, Ken Matsuda, Haruhiko Urayama.

A Toho Co., Ltd. Production. Color. Panavision. 188 minutes. Released 1975.

U.S. VERSION: Released by Toho International Co., Ltd. in subtitled format. Followed by *The Gate of Youth—Part II* (1977). 188 minutes. No MPAA rating. Released January 1, 1976.

The Gate of Youth / Seishun no mon ("Gate of Youth"). Producer, Shigeru Okada; Directors, Kinji Fukasaku and Koreyoshi Kurahara; Screenplay, Tatsuo Nogami, based on an original story by Hiroyuki Itsuki; Director of Photography, Hanjiro Nakazawa; Art Director, Tokumichi Igawa; Music, Hako Yamazaki.

CAST: Bunta Sugawara, Keiko Matsuzaka, Koichi Sato.

A Toei Co., Ltd. Production. Color. ToeiScope (?). 188 minutes. Released 1981.

U.S. VERSION: Released by Shochiku Films of America, Inc. English subtitled version available. Previously filmed as *The Gate of Youth* (1975) and *The Gate of Youth—Part II* (1977). 145 minutes. No MPAA rating. Released April 2, 1982.

The Gate of Youth—Part II / Seishun no mon—jiritsuhen ("Independent Gate of Youth"). Producers, Sanezumi Fujimoto and Hiroshi Hairyu; Director, Kiriro Urayama; Screenplay, Gyo Hayasaka and Kiriro Urayama; Director of Photography, Hiroshi Muraki; Art Director, Yoshiro Muraki; Music, Riichiro Manabe.

CAST: Ken Tanaka, Shinobu Otake, Ayumi Ishida.

A Toho Co., Ltd. Production. Color. Panavision. 161 minutes. Released 1977.

U.S. VERSION: Release undetermined, possibly by Toho International Co., Ltd. in subtitled format. No MPAA rating.

Kazuo Hasegawa and Machiko Kyo in *Gate of Hell* (1953).

Gateway to Glory / Aa, Kaigun ("Ah, Navy"). Director, Mitsuo Murayama; Screenplay, Ryuzo Kikushima and Yoshihiro Ishimatsu; Director of Photography, Akira Uehara; Art Director, Koichi Takahashi; Music, Seitaro Omori.

CAST: Kichiemon Nakamura (Ichiro Hirata), Shogo Shimada (Admiral Yamamoto), Ryunosuke Minegishi, Masayuki Mori, Sachiko Murase, Eiko Azusa, Ken Utsui, Kojiro Hongo, Jun Fujimaki.

A Daiei Motion Picture Co., Ltd. Production. Eastman Color. DaieiScope. Released July 1969.

U.S. VERSION: Released by Daiei International Films, Inc. English subtitles. 122

minutes. No MPAA rating. Released January 1970.

The Gay Braggart / Nippon ichino horafuki otoko ("The Number One Braggart in Japan"). Director, Kengo Furusawa.

CAST: Hitoshi Ueki, Mie Hama, Mitsuko Kusabue, Kei Tani.

A Toho Co., Ltd. Production. Color. Toho Scope. 93 minutes. Released 1964.

U.S. VERSION: Released by Toho International Co., Ltd. English subtitles. The 2nd of ten "Number One Man in Japan" features (1963-71). 94 minutes. No MPAA rating. Released January 29, 1965.

A Geisha / Gion bayashi ("Gion Festival Music"). Producer, Hisakazu Tsuji; Director, Kenji Mizoguchi; Screenplay, Yoshikata Yoda, based on an original magazine story by Matsutaro Kawaguchi; Director of Photography, Kazuo Yamada; Art Director, Kazumi Koike; Music, Ichiro Saito; Sound Recording, Iwao Otani.

CAST: Michiyo Kogure (Miyoharu), Ayako Wakao (Eiko), Seizaburo Kawazu (Kusuda), Chieko Naniwa (Okimi), Eitaro Shindo (Sawamoto), Mikio Koshiba (Kanzaki), Ichiro Sugai (Saeki), Kanji Kobayashi (Kanzaki), Sumao Ishiura (Kokichi), Saburo Date (Imanishi), Haruo Tanaka (Ogawa), Kikue Mori (teacher of domestic arts), Midori Komatsu (Oume), Emiko Yanagi (Kaname).

A Daiei Motion Picture Co., Ltd. Production. Filmed at Daiei-Kyoto Studios. Black and white. Academy ratio. 87 minutes. Released August 12, 1953.

U.S. VERSION: Distributor undetermined. English subtitles. 87 minutes. No MPAA rating. Release date undetermined.

The Geisha / Yokiro ("Yokiro"). Producer, Shigeru Okada; Director, Hideo Gosha; Screenplay, Koji Takada, based on an original story by Tomiko Miyao; Director of Photography, Fujio Morita; Music, Masaru Sato.

CAST: Ken Ogata, Kimiko Ikegami, Atsuko Asano.

A Toei Co., Ltd. Production. Color. ToeiScope (?). 144 minutes. Released 1983.

U.S. VERSION: Distributor, if any, is undetermined. No MPAA rating.

Genocide / Konchu daisenso ("War of the Insects"). Producer, Tsuneo Kosumi; Director, Kazui Nihomatsu; Screenplay, Susumu Takahisa, based on the story "Konchu dai senso" by Kingen Amada; Director of Photography, Shizu Hirase; Editor, Akimitsu Terada; Music, Syunsuke Kikuchi; Assistant Director, Keiji Shiraki; Art Director, Tadatake Yoshino; Set Decoration, Yoshizo Nakamura; Special Photographic Effects, Keiji Kawakami and Shun Suganuma; Sound, Hiroshi Nakamura; Sound Effects, Takashi Matsumoto.

CAST: Keisuke Sonoi (Yoshito Nagumo), Yusuke Kawazu (Jozi Akiyama), Emi Shindo (Yukari Akiyama), Reiko Hitomi (Junko Komura), Cathy Horlan (Annabelle), Ralph Jesser (Gordon), Toshiyuki Ichimura (Seborey Kudo), Tadayuki Ueda (Tsuneo Matsunaga), Hiroshi Aoyama (Toru Fujii), Chico Roland (Charlie), Eriko Sono (Nagumo's Assistant), Worflum Begichas (adjutant), Franz Gruber (doctor), William Douyuak (correspondent) Mike Daning (aircraft captain), Raina Gessman (subpilot), Harold S. Conway (commander), Happie Barman (crewman), Saburo Aonuma (detective).

A Shochiku Co., Ltd. Production. Eastman color (processed by Shochiku Laboratory). Shochiku GrandScope. 84 minutes. Released November 9, 1968.

U.S. VERSION: Released by Shochiku Films of America, Inc. English-dubbed version available. Advertised as *War of the Insects*. No MPAA rating. 84 minutes. Released 1969.

The Gentle Twelve / Juninin no yasashii Nihonjin ("Twelve Gentle Japanese"). Producer, Yutaka Okada; Director, Shun Nakahara; Screenplay, Koki Mitami; Director of Photography, Kenji Takama; Music, Kozaburo Matsumoto.

CAST: Michiko Hayashi, Koichi Ueda, Sansei Shiomi.

A New Century Producers Production. Color. Spherical wide screen (?). 116 minutes. Released 1991.

U.S. VERSION: Released by Argo Pictures. English subtitles. Running time of

Japanese version also given as 106 minutes. 106 minutes. No MPAA rating. Released 1994.

Get 'Em All / Kenju yo saraba ("Farewell the Gun"). Director, Eizo Sugawa.

CAST: Hiroshi Mizuhara, Akihiko Hirata, Yukiko Shimazaki, Akemi Kita, Tatsuya Nakadai, Kenzo Tabu, Seiji Miyaguchi, Tetsuro Tamba, Kyoko Kishida, Chieko Nakakita, Jerry Fujio.

A Toho Co., Ltd. Production. Black and white. Toho Scope. 87 minutes. Released November 27, 1960.

U.S. VERSION: Released by Toho International Co., Ltd. English subtitles (?). 87 minutes. Released November 17, 1961.

Getting Old with a Sense of Security / Anshinshite oiru tameni ("Getting Old with a Sense of Security") [**documentary**]. Producer, Mitsuru Kudo; Director, Sumiko Haneda; Director of Photography, Kiyoshi Nishio.

A Jiyu Kobo Co., Ltd. Production. Filmed in Gifu. 16mm (?). Color. Academy ratio (?). 151 minutes. Release 1991 (?).

U.S. VERSION: Distributor, if any, is undetermined.

Ghidrah – The Three-Headed Monster / San daikaiju chikyu saidai no kessen ("The Greatest Three Giant Monsters Battle on Earth"). Executive Producer, Tomoyuki Tanaka; Director, Ishiro Honda; Screenplay, Shinichi Sekizawa; Director of Photography, Hajime Koizumi; Music, Akira Ifukube; Song: "Call Happiness," Music, Hiroshi Miyagawa, Lyrics, Tokiko Iwatani; Editor, Ryohei Fujii; Art Director, Takeo Kita; Lighting Supervisor, Shoshichi Kojima; Sound Recording, Fumio Yanoguchi; Sound Effects, Hishashi Shimonaga, Toho Sound Effects Group; Sound, Toho Recording Centre; Production Manager, Shigeru Nakamura; Assistant to the Director, Ken Sano; Sound Technician, Osamu Chiku; Assistant Manager, Tadashi Koibe. *Toho Special Effects Group:* Director, Eiji Tsuburaya; Photographers, Teisho Arikawa, Mototaka Tomioka; Matte Photography, Yukio Manoda, Taka Yuki; Matte Process Work, Hiroshi Mukoyama; Set Decoration and Suit Design, Akira Watanabe; Lighting, Kuichiro Kishida; Assistant Director, Teruyoshi Nakano.

CAST: Yosuke Natsuki (Detective Shindo), Yuriko Hoshi (Naoko Shindo), Hiroshi Koizumi (Professor Murai), Takashi Shimura (Dr. Tsukamoto), Emi Ito and Yumi Ito [The Peanuts] (Mothra's priestesses), Akiko Wakabayashi (Mas Dorina Salno [Princess Selina Salno]), Hisaya Ito (Malmess), Akihiko Hirata (Chief Detective Okita), Kenji Sahara (Chief Editor Kanamaki), Ikio Sawamura (fisherman), Yoshifumi Tajima (ship's captain), Eisei Amamoto (Woo, *the princess' aide*), Yoshio Kosugi (native chief), Haruya Kato (reporter), Senkichi Omura (man who offers to retrieve hat), Toru Ibuki, Kazuo Suzuki, Susumu Kurobe (would-be assassins), Kozo Nomura (geologist), Somesho Matsumoto (UFO expert who explains princess' fall), Haruo Nakajima (Godzilla), Shoichi "Solomon" Hirose (Ghidrah [King Ghidorah]), Minoru Takada, Yuriko Hanabusa, Nakatiro Tomita, Shigeki Ishida, Shin Otomo, Yukaka Nakayama, Senya Aozora, Ichiya Aozora, Heichiro "Henry" Okawa, Junichiro Mukai, Yoshiniko Furuta, Shoji Ikeoa, Hideo Shibuya, Kenchiro Katsumoto, Katsumi Tezuka, Koji Uno, Daisuke Inoue, Oshio Miura, Tamami Urayama, Tokuzo Komaga, Mitsuo Isuda, Yoshio Hattori, Kenji Tsubono, Kazo Imai, Suburo Kadowaki, Kenzo Echigo, Toku Ihara, Bin Furuya, Jun Kuroki, Yutaka Oka, Koji Uraga, Haruya Sakamoto.

A Toho Co., Ltd. Production. Eastman Color (processed by Tokyo Laboratory, Ltd.). Toho Scope. 92 minutes. Released December 20, 1964.

U.S. VERSION: Released by Continental Distributing, Inc. English-dubbed. A Walter Reade-Sterling, Inc. Presentation. Americanization by Bellucci Productions; English Dialogue/Dubbing Director, Joseph Bellucci; Additional Music and Sound Effects, Filmsounds, Inc.; Post-Production Consultant, Ray Angus; Additional Optical Photography, Film

Cinematics, Inc.; Prints by Movielab. The 5th "Godzilla" feature. Followed by *Monster Zero* (1965). 81 minutes. No MPAA rating. Released September 1965. Reissued in Japan in 1971 (re-edited by Ishiro Honda to 73 minutes) as *Gojira Mosura Kingughidorah: Chikyu saidai no kessen* ("Godzilla, Mothra, King Ghidorah: The Greatest Battle on Earth").

Ghost of Otamaga-Ike / Kaibyo Otamaga-Ike ("Monstrous Cat of Otamaga Pond"). Producer, Mitsugu Okura; Director, Yoshihiro Ishikawa; Screenplay, Jiro Fujishima and Yoshihiro Ishikawa; Director of Photography, Kikuzo Kawasaki.

CAST: Shozaburo Date, Noriko Kitazawa, Yoichi Numata, Namiji Matsura.

A Shintoho Co., Ltd. Production. Western Electric Mirrophonic recording. Eastman Color. Shintoho-Scope. 75 minutes. Released July 2, 1960.

U.S. VERSION: U.S. distributor, if any, is undetermined. International title: *The Ghost Cat of Otam-ag-Ike.* No MPAA rating.

Ghost of the One-Eyed Man / Kaidan katame no otoko ("Ghost Story—The One-Eyed Man"). Producer, Hiroshi Okawa; Director, Tsuneo Kobayashi; Screenplay, Hajime Takaiwa and Ichiro Miyagawa; Director of Photography, Noboru Takanashi.

CAST: Ko Nishimura (Koichiro), Sanae Nakahara, Kikuko Hojo, Masao Mishima, Yusuke Kawazu.

A Toei Co., Ltd. Production. Black and white (processed by Toei Chemistry Co., Ltd.). ToeiScope. 84 minutes. Released 1965.

U.S. VERSION: U.S. distributor, if any, is undetermined. Also known as *Curse of the One-Eyed Corpse.*

The Ghost of Yotsuya / Tokaido Yotsuya kaidan ("Ghost Story of Yotsuya in Tokaido"). Producer, Mitsugu Okura; Director, Nobuo Nakagawa; Screenplay, Masayoshi Onuki and Yoshihiro Ishikawa, based on the Kabuki play, *Tokaido Yotsuya kaidan* by Nanboku Tsuruya; Director of Photography, Tadashi Nishimoto; Art Director, Haruyasu Kurosawa.

CAST: Shigeru Amachi (Iuemon Tamiya), Noriko Kitazawa (Osode Samon), Kazuko Wakasugi (Oiwa Samon), Shuntaro Emi (Naosuke), Junko Ikeuchi (Ume Ito), Ryozaburo Nakamura (Yomoshichi Hikobei), Jun Otomo (Takuetsu).

A Shintoho Co., Ltd. Production. Western Electric Mirrophonic recording. Eastman Color. Shintoho-Scope. 76 minutes. Released July 11, 1959.

U.S. VERSION: Released by Shimoto Enterprises. English subtitles. Also known as *Ghost Story of Yotsuda in Tokaido.* Some prints have mistransliterated the women's names. Oiwa became Iwa, Osode became Sode, for example. No MPAA rating. Release date undetermined.

Ghost Ship / Yurei-sen ("Ghost Ship"). Director, Teija Matsuda; Screenplay, Katsuya Suzaki, based on the novel *Yurei-sen* by Jiro Osaragi; Director of Photography, Shintaro Kawasaki.

CAST: Kinnosuke Nakamura, Ryutaro Otomo, Ryunosuke Tsukigata, Denjiro Okochi, Yumiko Hasegawa, Hiroko Sakuramachi.

A Toei Co., Ltd. Production. Toeicolor. ToeiScope. Running time undetermined. Released 1957.

U.S. VERSION: Distributor, if any, is undetermined.

Ghost Story of Youth / Seishun kaidan ("Ghost Story of Youth"). Producers, Takeshi Yamamoto and Masayuki Takagi; Director, Kon Ichikawa; Screenplay, Natto Wada, based on a story by Bunroku Shishi; Director of Photography, Shigeyoshi Mine; Music, Toshiro Mayuzumi; Art Director, Kimihiko Nakamura; Lighting, Ko Fujibayashi; Sound Recording, Masakazu Kamiya.

CAST: Mie Kitahara (Chiharu Okumura), So Yamamura (Tetsuya, *her father*), Tatsuya Mihashi (Shinichi Utsunomiya), Yukiko Todoroki (Choko, *his mother*), Hisako Yamane (Tomi Funakoshi), Michiko Soga (Fudegoma), Izumi Ashikawa (Shinko Fujitani).

A Nikkatsu Corp. Production. Black and white. Academy ratio. Running time undetermined. Released April 19, 1955.

U.S. VERSION: Distributor, if any, is undetermined.

The Ghostly Trap / Kaidan otoshiana ("Ghost Story Trap"). Producer, Kazuo Tsukaguchi; Executive Producer, Masaichi Nagata; Director, Koji Shima; Screenplay, Kazuo Funabashi; Art Director, Atsuji Shibata; Director of Photography, Joji Ohara; Editor, Toyo Suzuki; Music, Seitaro Omori; Sound Recording Supervisor, Tsuchitaro Hayashi; Sound, Daiei Recording Studio.

CAST: Mikio Narita (Haruo Kuramoto), Eiji Funakoshi (Fumio Nishino), Mayumi Nagisa (Etsuko Nishino), Mako Sanjo (Midori Yukawa), Bontaro Miake (President Yukawa), Kiyoko Hirai (Michiko Yukawa), Mitsuko Tanaka (Natsuko Fukuhara), Mariko Fukuhara (Hanako), Yukiko Tsuyama (Namiko), Yuzo Hayakawa (Sakabe), Chikara Hashimoto (Udegawa), Isamu Saeki (Fujioka), Kenichi Tani (Chief of Satomi Section), Yasuhei Endo (head of department), Kenji Oyama (managing director), Nobuo Namikata (executive director), Mari Atsumi (usher), Akira Natsuki (doctor), Shinsuke Kijima (first official), Naomasa Kawashima (second official), Ken Nakahara (Ikegami).

A Daiei Motion Picture Co., Ltd. Production. A Masaichi Nagata Presentation. Filmed at Daiei-Kyoto Studios. Westrex recording system. Black and white (processed by Daiei Laboratory). DaieiScope. 78 minutes. Released 1968.

U.S. VERSION: Released by Daiei International Films, Inc. English subtitles. Also known as *Ghost Story of Booby Trap*. International title: *The Pit of Death*. 78 minutes. No MPAA rating. Released 1968.

Ghosts on Parade / Yokai daisenso ("Great War of Monsters"). Executive Producer, Akihiko Murai; Producer, Yamato Yashiro; Director, Yoshiyuki Kuroda; Screenplay, Tetsuro Yoshida; Director of Photography, Hiroshi Imai; Art Directors, Seiichi Ota, Shigeru Kato; Lighting, Hiroshi Mima; Editor, Toshio Taniguchi; Assistant Director, Toshiaki Kunihiro; Music, Shigeru Ikeno; Sound Recording Supervisor, Tsuchitaro Hayashi; Sound, Daiei Recording Studio; Special Sound Effects, Yo Kurashima; Special Effects, Daiei Special Effects Department; Martial Arts Director, Eiichi Kusumoto.

CAST: Yoshihiko Aoyama (Shinhachiro [Shimpachiro] Mayama), Akane Kawasaki (Chie), Osamu Okawa (Iori Odate), Tomo Uchida (Dainichibo), Gen Kimura (Saheiji Kawano), Takashi Kanda (Hyogo Isobe), Hanji Wakai, Kenji Wakai (guards), Hinode Nishikawa (lower officer), Ikuko Mori (long-necked monster), Chikara [Tsutomu] Hashimoto (Daimon), Gen Kuroki (Kappa, *the River Monster*), Hideki Hanamura (Nebula Monster), Keiko Yukitomo (two-faced woman), Tokio Oki (Yasuzo), Hiromi Inoue (Shinobu), Yukiyasu Watanabe (Moichi), Mari Kanda (Osaki), Kisao Ashida.

A Daiei Motion Picture Co., Ltd. Production. A Masaichi Nagata Presentation. Westrex recording system. Fujicolor (processed by Daiei Laboratory). DaieiScope. Filmed at Daiei-Kyoto Studios. 79 minutes. Released December 14, 1968.

U.S. VERSION: Released by Daiei International Films, Inc. English subtitles. International title (?): *Spook Warfare*. No MPAA rating. 79 minutes. Released 1968.

Gigantis the Fire Monster / Gojira no Gyakushu ("Godzilla's Counterattack"). Producer, Tomoyuki Tanaka; Director, Motoyoshi Oda; Screenplay, Takeo Murata and Shigeaki Hidaka; Story, Shigeru Kayama; Art Director, Takeo Kita; Assistant Art Director, Teruaki Abe; Director of Photography, Seiichi Endo; Music, Masaru Sato; Sound, Masanobu Miyazaki; Recording, Toho Dubbing Theatre; Sound Effects, Toho Sound Effects Group; Lighting, Masaki [Masayoshi] Onuma; *Toho Special Effects Group*: Director, Eiji Tsuburaya; Art Director, Akira Watanabe; Lighting, Masao Shirota; Optical Photography, Hiroshi Mukoyama.

CAST: Hiroshi Koizumi (Shoichi Tsukioka), Minoru Chiaki (Koji Kobayashi), Setsuko Wakayama (Hidemi Yamaji), Yokio [Yukio] Kasama (Kohei Yamaji, *president of the fishery*), Mayuri Mokusho (Radio Operator Yasuko Inoue),

Angilas (Katsumi Tezuka) battles Gigantis (Haruo Nakajima) – or is that Godzilla? – in *Gigantis the Fire Monster* (1959).

Sonosuke Sawamura (Hokkaido Branch Manager Shingo Shibeki), Masao Shimizu (Zoologist Dr. Tadokoro), Takeo Oikawa (Osaka Municipal Police Commisioner), Seijiro Onda (Captain Terasawa of Osaka Defense Corps), Yoshio Tsuchiya (Tajima, *member of Osaka Defense Corps*), Minosuke Yamada (Commander of Osaka Defense Corps), Ren Yamamoto (commander of landing craft), Takashi Shimura (Dr. Kyohei Yamane), Senkichi Omura and Junpei Natsuki (convicts), Haruo Nakajima (Godzilla), Katsumi Tezuka (Angilas).

A Toho Co., Ltd. Production. Black and white (processed by Kinuta Laboratories Ltd.). Academy ratio. Western Electric Mirrophonic soundtrack. 82 minutes. Released April 24, 1955.

U.S. Version: Released by Warner Brothers Pictures, Inc. English-dubbed. A Paul Schreibman Presentation. Producer, Paul Schreibman; Executive Producer, Harry B. Swerdlon; Associate Producer, Edmund Goldman; Director of Dubbing and Editing, Hugo Grimaldi; Sound Effects Editor, Alvin Sarno; Music Editor, Rex Lipton; Voice Characterizations, Paul Frees, George Takei, Keye Luke, Marvin Miller, others unidentified; Prologue Narrator, Marvin Miller; Sound, Ryder Sound Services, Inc. (Westrex recording system); Additional Music, Paul Sawtell, Bert Shefter, including stock music from *Kronos* (20th Century-Fox, 1957); prints by Technicolor. Copyright June 13, 1959 by Harry B. Swerdlon; renewed 1987 by Toho Co., Ltd. Includes footage from *Unknown Island* (Film Classics, 1948). Identity of additional stock footage, possibly outtakes from *The Lost Continent* (Lippert, 1951), the Mexican-made *Adventuras en la Centro del la Tiera* (?) and *One Million B.C.* (United Artists, 1940) is unconfirmed. Spherical wide screen. Double-billed with *Teenagers from Outer Space* (Warner Bros., 1959). 78 minutes. No MPAA rating. Released May 21, 1959. *Note:* Released to Japanese-speaking theaters in the United States prior to its dubbed-release as *Godzilla Raids Again*, which is also the title of syndicated television and on home video version (though video version credits still read "Gigantis the Fire Monster"). The 2nd "Godzilla" feature. Followed by *King Kong vs. Godzilla* (1962).

Girl Diver of Spook Mansion / Ama no bakemono yashiki ("Spook Mansion of Girl Diver"). Producer, Mitsugu Okura; Director, Morihei Magatani; Screenplay, Akira Sugimoto and Nao Akatsukasa; Director of Photography, Kagai Okado.

CAST: Yoko Mihara (Yumi), Bunta Sugawara, Reiko Sato, Masayo Banri, Yoichi Numata.

A Shintoho Co., Ltd. Production. Western Electric Mirrophonic recording. Black and white. Shintoho-Scope. 82 minutes. Released 1959.

U.S. VERSION: Distributor, if any, is undetermined. Advertised as *The Haunted Cave*. Sequel: *Ghost of the Girl Diver* (1960). No MPAA rating.

The Girl I Abandoned / Watashi ga suteta onna ("The Girl I Abondoned"). Director, Kirio Urayama; Screenplay, Hisashi Yamanouchi, based on the novel by Shusaku Endo; Director of Photography, Shohei Ando; Art Director, Yoshinaga Yoko; Music, Toshiro Mayuzumi.

CAST: Choichiro Kawarazaki (Tsutomu Yoshioka), Toshie Kobayashi (Mitsu), Ruriko Asaoka (Mariko), Chikako Natsumi (Shimako), Haruko Kato, Shoichi Ozawa, Takeshi Kato, Teruko Kishi, Hideaki Ezumi, Toru Emori, Hisataka Yamane, Ryotaro Tatsumi, Kunie Origa, Hideharu Otaki, Fumie Kitahara, Tadao Nakamura, Minako Sakaguchi, Hiroshi Shimada, Shoichi Ozawa, Sumie Sasaki, Toshio Hayano, Asao Sano, Junko Kuroda, Shigeru Tsuyuguchi, Shusaku Endo.

A Nikkatsu Corporation Production. Fujicolor. NikkatsuScope. Released September 3, 1969.

U.S. VERSION: Distributor undetermined, possibly Toho International Co., Ltd. English subtitles (?). 116 minutes. No MPAA rating. Released December 11, 1970.

Girl in the Mist. Director, Hideo Suzuki; Screenplay, Zenzo Matsuyama, based on an original story by Yojiro Ishikaza.

CAST: Yoko Tsukasa (Yoshiko), Hitomi Nakahara (Taeko), Hiroshi Koizumi (Uemura), Takashi Ito (Shinji), Choko Iida (grandmother), Kamatari Fujiwara, Nijiko Kiyakawa (parents).

A Toho Co., Ltd. Production. Black and white (?). Toho Scope (?). Running time and release date undetermined.

U.S. VERSION: Released by Brandon Films, Inc. English subtitles. 44 minutes. No MPAA rating. Released December 22, 1959.

Girl of Dark / Onna bakari no yoru ("Only Women at Night"). Executive Producer, Ichiro Nagashima; Director, Kinuyo Tanaka; Screenplay, Sumie Tanaka, based on a story by Masako Yana; Music, Hikaru Hayashi.

CAST: Chisako Hara, Yosuke Natsuki, Chikage Awashima, Akihiko Hirata, Kyoko Kagawa.

A Toho Co., Ltd. Production. Black and white. Toho Scope. 75 minutes. Released 1962.

U.S. VERSION: Release undetermined, possibly released by Toho International Co., Ltd. in subtitled format. 75 minutes. No MPAA rating.

Girl with Bamboo Leaves / Sasabue Omon ("Bamboo Leaf Whistle Oman"). Executive Producer, Akihiko Murai; Producer, Masaichi Nagata; Director, Tokuzo Tanaka; Screenplay, Tetsuro Yoshida, based on an original story by Teruo Tanashita; Director of Photography, Chishi Makimura; Art Director, Akira Naito; Lighting, Reijiro Yamashita; Editor, Hiroshi Yamada; Assistant Director, Rikio Endo; Music, Hiroaki Watanabe; Sound Recording, Masahiro Okumura; Sound, Daiei Recording Studio; Special Effects, Daiei Special Effects Department.

CAST: Michiyo Yasuda (Omon), Ryohei Uchida (Senjuro Kurosaka), Manami Fuji (Oen), Akane Kawasaki (Osayo), Fujio Suga (Gonzo), Asao Uchida (Shokichi), Ryutaro Gomi (Jirokichi), Manabu

Morita (Matahachi), Gen Kimura (Tatsukichi), Ichiro Yamamoto (Benji), Tokio Oki (Fujisaku), Ryuji Kita (Giju), Takeshi Date (Chokichi), Ryuji Kamikata, Ryuta Kamikata.

A Daiei Motion Picture Co., Ltd. Production. A Masaichi Nagata Presentation. Westrex Recording system. Fujicolor. DaieiScope. 75 minutes. Released 1969.

U.S. Version: Released by Daiei International Films, Inc. English subtitles. No MPAA rating. Released 1969.

Go and Get It / Buttuke honban ("Action Without Rehearsal"). Producers, Ichiro Sato and Nobuteru Yamasaki; Director, Kozo Saeki; Screenplay, Kyozo Kasahara, based on the book by Hajime Mizuno and Moto Ogasawara; Director of Photography, Seiichi Endo; Art Director, Tatsuo [Takeo?] Kita; Music, Yoshiyuki Kozu.

Cast: Frankie Sakai (Tetsuo Matsumoto), Keiko Awaji (Mrs. Matsumoto, *his wife*), Tatsuya Nakadai (his assistant), Eitro Ozawa (Yamada), Shuji Sano (Kobayashi).

A Tokyo Eiga Co., Ltd. Production. A Toho Co., Ltd. Release. Black and white. Academy ratio. 98 minutes. Released 1958.

U.S. Version: Distributor, if any, is undetermined, possibly Toho International Co., Ltd. in subtitled format.

The Go Masters / Mikan no Taikyoku ("Imperfect Go Masters"). Executive Producers, Yasuyoshi Tokuma and Wang Yang; Producers, Masahiro Sato and Wang Zhi-min; Directors, Junya Sato and Duan Ji-Shun; Screenplay, Li Hong-Zhou, Ge Kang-Tong, Fumio Konami, Yasuko Ono and Tetsuro Abe; Directors of Photography, Shohei Ando and Luo De-An; Lighting, Hideo Komagai and Xu He-Qing; Art Directors, Takeo Kimura and Xiao Bin; Sound Recording, Fumio Hashimoto and Lu Xian-Chang; Music, Hikaru Hayashi and Jiang Ding-Xian.

Cast: Rentaro Mikuni, Sun Dao-Lin, Misako Konno, Shen Guan-Chu, Tsukasa Ito, Shen Dan-Ping, Mayumi Ogawa, Huang Zong-Ying, Keiko Matsuzaka, Du Peng, Nobuko Otowa, Yu Shao-Kang, Yoshiko Mita.

A Mikan no Taikyoku Production Committee/Toko Tokuma Co., Ltd./ Beijing Film Studios Production, in association with Daiei Co., Ltd. and China Film Co-Production Corp. A Japanese/Chinese co-production in Mandarin and Japanese, and filmed in China. Color. Academy ratio. 133 minutes. Released 1982.

U.S. Version: Released by Circle Releasing Corporation. English subtitles. A Ben Barenholtz Presentation. Subtitles, Tadashi Shishido. 133 minutes. No MPAA rating. Released April 20, 1984.

***Godzilla* Series** Enduring Toho film series, begun in 1954 in response to the American film *The Beast from 20,000 Fathoms* (1953), itself inspired by the 1952 reissue of *King Kong*. Initially the character—a mutant dinosaur turned radioactive fire-breather—symbolized Japan's postwar and Cold War fears. However, Godzilla was gradually humanized and eventually evolved into a likable, even heroic creature, warding off even more outlandish monsters than itself. The first film, produced by **Tomoyuki Tanaka**, directed by **Ishiro Honda**, with music by **Akira Ifukube** and special effects directed by **Eiji Tsuburaya**, was a huge international success; it was the first Japanese film to be widely released in the United States in mainstream movie theaters. It was and is highly regarded in Japan, but marketed as an exploitation film and heavily altered in the U.S., setting a negative precedent for the often ambitious Japanese fantasy films that immediately followed. The series hit a creative and commercial slump throughout the 1970s (during which time the series was geared almost exclusively for children), but returned with a renewed vigor in 1984 following a nine-year absence. **Haruo Nakajima** played Godzilla through 1972; since 1984 the role has been essayed by Kenpachiro Satsuma.

Films: Godzilla, King of the Monsters! (1954); Gigantis the Fire Monster/Godzilla Raids Again (1955); King Kong vs. Godzilla (1962); Godzilla vs. the Thing/ Godzilla vs. Mothra; Ghidrah—The

Three-Headed Monster (1964); Monster Zero/Godzilla vs. Monster Zero [Jap/US] (1965); Ebirah Horror of the Deep/Godzilla versus the Sea Monster (1966); Son of Godzilla (1967); Destroy All Monsters (1968); Godzilla's Revenge (1969); Godzilla vs. the Smog Monster (1971); Godzilla on Monster Island/Godzilla vs. Gigan (1972); Godzilla vs. Megalon (1973); Godzilla vs. the Cosmic Monster/Godzilla vs. Mechagodzilla (1974); The Terror of Godzilla/Terror of Mechagodzilla (1975); Godzilla 1985 (1984); Godzilla vs. Biollante (1989); Godzilla vs. King Ghidorah (1991); Godzilla vs. Mothra (1992); Monster Planet Godzilla [3-D short], Godzilla vs. Mechagodzilla (1993); Godzilla vs. Space Godzilla (1994); Godzilla vs. Destroyer (1995).

Godzilla, King of the Monsters! / Gojira ("Godzilla"). Producer, Tomoyuki Tanaka; Director, Ishiro Honda; Screenplay, Takeo Murata, Ishiro Honda, based on a story by Shigeru Kayama; Director of Photography, Masao Tamai; Art Directors, Takeo Kita and Satoshi Chuko; Lighting, Choshiro Ishii; Editor, Yasunobu [Hidenobu] Taira; Sound Recording, Hisashi Shimonaga; Sound, Toho Dubbing Theatre; Sound Effects, Ichiro Mikame, Toho Sound Effects Group; Music, Akira Ifukube; Production Manager, Teruo Maki; Assistant Director, Koji Kajita. *Toho Special Effects Group*: Director, Eiji Tsuburaya; Art Director, Akira Wanatabe; Optical Photography, Hiroshi Mukoyama; Lighting, Kuichiro Kishida; Co-Godzilla Design, Ryosaku Takayama and Iwao Mori.

CAST: Takashi Shimura (Professor Kyohei Yamane), Momoko Kochi (Emiko Yamane), Akira Takarada (Hideto Ogata), Akihiko Hirata (Dr. Daisuke Serizawa), Sachio Sakai (Hagiwara), Fuyuki Murakami (Dr. Tanabe), Ren Yamamoto (Masaji Sieji), Toranosuke Ogawa (president of shipping company), Ren Imaizumi (chief of shipping company's radio section), Miki Hayashi (chairman of Diet committee), Seijiro Oda (Member of Parliment Oyama), Kin Sugai (Member of Parliment Ozawa), Takeo Oikawa (head of defense forces), Keiji Sakakida (Mayor Inada), Toshiaki Suzuki (Shinkichi), Tsuruko Mano (Shinkichi's mother), Kokuten Kodo (old fisherman), Tadashi Okabe (Dr. Tanabe's assistant), Shizuko Higashi (partygoer), Kiyoshi Kamota (partygoer's escort), Katsumi Tezuka (newspaper deskman), Haruo Nakajima (power substation engineer), Tamae Sengo (mother), Kenji Sahara (young lover on ship), Haruo Nakajima, Katsumi Tezuka, and Ryosaku Takasugi (Godzilla), Masaaki Hashi, Ichiro Tai, Yasuhisa Tsutumi, Jiro Suzukawa, Saburo Iketani.

A Toho Co., Ltd. Production. Black and white (processed by Kinuta Laboratories, Ltd.). Academy ratio. Western Electric Mirrophonic recording. 98 minutes. Released November 3, 1954.

U.S. VERSION: Released by Godzilla Releasing Company (i.e. Embassy Pictures Corp.). English-dubbed. A Jewell Enterprises/TransWorld Presentation. Executive Producers, Terry Turner, Joseph E. Levine; Producers, Richard Kay, Harry Rybnick, Edward B. Barison; Director/Editor, Terrell O. Morse, Sr. [Terry Morse]; Director of Photography, Guy Roe. Academy ratio. Originally announced by TransWorld as *Godzilla—The Sea Beast*. Double-billed with *Prehistoric Women* (reissue; Eagle-Lion, 1950). Dubbed version originally credited Honda, Morse and Burr, and title was over black background, not water. 81 minutes. No MPAA rating. Released April 1956. *Note:* Original version released to Japanese-speaking theaters, possibly with English subtitles, in the United States in 1955 as *Gojira*. Reissued minus dubbing and plus subtitles by Toho International Co., Ltd. in June 1982. Interestingly, the U.S. version was converted to anamorphic wide screen and released theatrically in Japan, as *Kaiju o Godzilla* ("Monster King Godzilla"), on May 29, 1957, though it's also known under the U.S. title. Home video and television reissue version credited as A UPA/Henry G. Saperstein Presentation. Current video and television versions are missing all screen credits save title. Some Japanese reissue prints run 90 minutes. First feature in Toho's 22-film (through 1995) "Godzilla" series. Followed by *Gigantis the Fire Monster* (1955). Additional

Cast for U.S. Version: Raymond Burr (Steve Martin), Frank Iwanaga (Security Officer Tomo Iwanaga), James Yagi (voice characterization for Akira Takarada).

Godzilla 1985 / Gojira ("Godzilla"). Executive Producer,Tomoyuki Tanaka; Associate Producer, Fumio Tanaka; Director, Koji Hashimoto; Screenplay, Shuichi Nagahara, based on the original story, "The Resurrection of Godzilla," by Tomoyuki Tanaka; Director of Photography, Kazutami Hara; Production Designer/Art Director, Akira Sakuragi; Music, Reijiro Koroku, performed by the Tokyo Symphony Orchestra; Tokyo Symphony Orchestra conductor, Katsuaki Nakaya; Sound, Toho Eizo Sound Studio; Recording Mixer, Noboyuki Tanaka; Sound Effects, Toho Sound Effects Group; Dolby Stereo Consultant, Mikio Mori, Continental Far East Inc., Tokyo; Lighting, Shoji Kojima; Editor, Yoshitami Kuroiwa; Still Photographer, Yoshinori Ishizuki; Assistant Director, Takao Okawara; Production Manager, Takehide Morichi; Songs: "Goodbye My Love," Lyrics by Toyohisa Araki, Music by Takashi Miki, and Sung by Yasuko Sawaguchi (Fanhouse Records); and "Godzilla," Lyrics by Linda Henrick, Music by Reijiro Koroku, and Sung by The Star Sisters (Warner/Pioneer); Soundtrack available on King Records (K28G-7226); Associate Music Producer, Toho Music Publishing Co., Produced by Tadahiko Maeda; Computer Graphics, Yutaka [Hiroshi] Tsuchiya; Visual Consultant, Toshifumi Sakata; Assistants to the Director, Takashi Wakiya, Takehisa Takarada; Assistant Sound Technician, Noboru Ikeda; Assistant Lighting, Akira Oba; Lighting Grip, Shunji Yokota; Continuity, Hiroko Kajiyama; Make-Up, Fumiko Umezawa; Maintenance, Kazuo Suzuki; Set Construction, Yoshiki Kasahara, Toho Art Co., Ltd.; Set Decoration, Akio Tashiru, Toho Art Co., Ltd.; Electrician, Hideo Inangaki; Special Engineering, Toyo Tanaka; Assistant Editors, Sae Higashijima, Junko Shirato; Negative Cutter, Fusako Takahashi; Costumes, Kenji Kawasaki, Kyoto Costume Co., Ltd.; Casting Director, Tadao Tanaka; Assistant Producers, Kiyomi Kanazawa, Morio Hayashi; Special Advisors, Hitoshi Takeuchi (Professor Emeritus, Tokyo University), Hideo Aoki (Military Consultant), Yorihiko Osaki (Doctor of Engineering), Klein Uberstein (Science Fiction Writer); Cooperation, Mitsubishi Motor Cars, Hattoro Seiko Co., Ltd., Mitsubishi Rayon Co., Ltd., Mitsui Oak Line, Bandal, Inc., International Container Terminal, Ltd., Ogawa Modelling, Inc., Computer Graphic Laboratory, Inc., Tomy Corp., Soishiro Tahara (Journalist). *Toho Special Effects Group*: Director, Teruyoshi Nakano; Photography, Takeshi Yamamoto and Toshimitsu Oneda; Production Designer/Art Director, Yasuyuki Inoue; Lighting, Kohei Mikami; Pyrotechniques, Tadaaki Watanabe, Mamoru Kume, Mitsuo Mikakawa; Prosthetics (Suit Construction), Nobuyuki Yasumaru; Wire Works, Koji Matsumoto, Mitsuo Miyakawa; Matte Photography, Takeaki Tsukuda and Yoshio Ishii; Optical Photography, Takeshi Miyanishi and Yoshikazu Manoda; Pyrotechnician, Takeshi Miyanishi; Still Photographer, Takashi Nakao; 2nd Unit Director, Eiichi Asada; Production Manager, Masayuki Ikeda; Cybot Manufacturer, Shunichi Mizuno; Assistant Director, Kyotaka Matsumoto; Assistant Photographer, Toshio Yamaga; Assistant Art Director, Gen Komura; Lighting Assistant, Katsuji Watanabe; Lighting Grip, Tadaaki Ohide; Mantainence, Yoshio Takenaka; Film Editor, Midori Kobayashi; Producer, Shigeo Matsubichi.

CAST: Keiju Kobayashi (Prime Minister Mitamura), Ken Tanaka (Goro Maki), Yasuko Sawaguchi (Naoko Okumura), Shin Takuma (Hiroshi [Ken] Okumura), Yosuke Natsuki (Professor Hayashida), Taketoshi Naito (Chief Cabinet Secretary Takegami), Tetsuya Takeda (street bum), Eitaro Ozawa (Finance Minister Kanezaki), Mizuho Suzuki (Foreign Minister Emori), Junkichi Orimoto (Defense Agency Secretary Mori), Shinsuke Mikimoto (Chief of Staff Kakurai), Mikita Mori (Internal Affairs Secretary Okochi), Nobuo Kaneko (Home Affairs Minister Isomura), Kiyoshi Yamamoto (Science and Technology Agency Director Kajita),

Takeshi Kato (Internal Trade and Industry Minister Kasaoka), Yoshifumi Tajima (Environmental Director-General Hidaka), Yasuhiko Kono (Maritime Forces Chief of Staff Kishimoto), Eiji Kanai (Ground Forces Chief of Staff Imafuji), Isao Hirano (Air Force Chief of Staff Kiyohara), Kunio Murai (Secretary Henmi), Kenichi Urata (Secretary Ishimaru), Hiroshi Koizumi (Geologist Minami), Kei Sato (Chief Editor Godo), Takenori Emoto (Desk Editor Kitagawa), Takeo Morimoto (newscaster), Takashi Ebata (No. 5 Yahata Maru captain), Shigeo Kato, Sennosuke Tahara (Yahata Maru crew), Shinpei Hayashiya (Cameraman Kamijo), Sho Hashimoto (Super X Commander Hagiyama), Kenji Fukuda (Super X lieutenant), Shin Kazenaka (Uno), Yumiko Tanaka (Akemi), Tetsuya Ushio, Kensui Watanabe (operators), Walter Nichols (Ambassador Chevsky), Luke Johnston (Captain Kathren), Dennis Falt (Soviet submarine captain), Nigel Reed (Soviet sub lieutenant), Terry Sonberg (Parasebo crew member), Koji Ishizaka (nuclear power plant technician), Hiroshi Kamayatsu (Shinkansen passenger), Kenpachiro Satsuma (Godzilla).

A Toho Co., Ltd. Production, in association with Toho Eizo Co., Ltd. Dolby Stereo and TKL-Stereo. Color (processed by Tokyo Laboratory Ltd.). Spherical wide screen. 103 minutes. Released December 15, 1984.

U.S. VERSION: Released by New World Pictures in August 1985. English-dubbed. English-language version produced by New World Pictures in association with Toho Co., Ltd. Director, R.J. Kizer; Producer, Anthony Randel; Screenplay, Lisa Tomei; Director of Photography, Steve Dubin; Editor, Michael Spence; Associate Producer, Andrea Barshov Stern; Assistant Director, Lee S. Berger; Camera Assistant, Samuel Buddy Fries; Gaffer, Amy C. Halpern; Best Boy, Lewis A. Weinberg; Key Grip, Tracy Heftzger; Best Boy Grip, Paul S. Isiki; Swingman (i.e. electrician/grip), Richard Kuhn; Sound Mixer, Mark Sheret; Sound Boom Operator, Glenn Berkovitz; Script Supervisor, Veronica Flynn; Hair/Make-Up, Mary Michael George; Art Director and Stylist (i.e. Wardrobe Supervisor), Carol Christine Clements; Assistant Art Director, Greg Lacy; Set Decorator, Pam Moffat; Assistant Wardrobe, Kathryn Sparks; Postproduction Coordinator, James Melkonian; Assistant Editor, Kevin Sewelson; Second Assistant Editor, Mehran Ty Salamati; Production Assistant, Lisa M. Dannenbaum; Production Assistant/Driver, Christopher Ward Trott; Sets, Design Setters; Casting, Danny Goldman; Production Secretary, Anne Marie Trulove; Main Title Design, Ernest D. Farino, Jr.; Computer Readout Animation. Bert Mixon; Sound Design, Biggert Production Services; Supervising Sound Editor, Bob Briggert; ADR (Automatic Dialog Replacement) Mixer; Richard Rogers; Postproduction Sound Services, Ryder Sound, Inc.; Sound Director, Leo Chaloukian; Rerecording Mixers; John Keene "Doc" Wilkinson, Charles "Bud" Grenzbach, Joseph Citarella; Additional Music, Chris Young (copyright New World Pictures; Administraters, Chilly D. Music, WB Music Corp. ASCAP); Additional Optical Effects, Ray Mercer & Company; Negative Cutter, Diane Jackson; Special Thanks, The Dr Pepper Bottling Company, Robert Hamlin, David Millheiser, Cynthia T. Clark and Kef Music Publishing, Elliot Chiprut, Stewart Levin, Jill Elliot; processing and prints by Technicolor. Copyright 1985 by Toho Co., Ltd. U.S. footage financed, in part, by Dr Pepper. The U.S. version contains additional music by Christopher Young from *Def-Con 4* (New World, 1985). U.S. credits wrongly bill Takehide Morichi as Prime Minister. Preceded by the animated short subject, *Bambi Meets Godzilla* (Marv Newland, 1969). The 16th "Godzilla" feature. Followed by *Godzilla vs. Biollante* (1989). Note: The extremely poor stereo separations on the U.S. version in no way reflect the excellent use of stereo in the Japanese edition. Features stock footage from *Submersion of Japan* (1973) and *The Last Days of Planet Earth* (1974). International Title: *The Return of Godzilla.* 91 minutes. MPAA rating: "PG." Released August 1985. Additional Cast for U.S. Version: Raymond Burr (Mr. [Steve] Martin), Warren Kemmerling (General Goodhue), James Hess (Colonel

Godzilla (Haruo Nakajima) battles Gigan (Kenpachiro Satsuma, right) while King Ghidorah (Kanta Ina, top left) and Angilas (Yukietsu Omiya, bottom left) look on in *Godzilla on Monster Island* (1972). The film is considerably less exciting than this still would suggest. (Photo courtesy Ted Okuda.)

Rascher), Travis Swords (Major McDonough), Crawford Binion (Lietenant), Justin Gocke (Kyle), Bobby Brown, Patrick Feren, Mark Simon, Shepard Stern, Alan D. Waserman (Extras).

Godzilla on Monster Island / Chiku kogeki meirei: Gojira tai Gaigan ("Earth Destruction Directive: Godzilla against Gaigan"). Executive Producer, Tomoyuki Tanaka; Director, Jun Fukuda; Screenplay, Shinichi Sekizawa; Director of Photography, Kiyoshi Hasegawa; Art Director, Yoshifumi Honda; Music, Akira Ifukube; Theme Song, Toho Records; Songs by Susumu Ishikawa; "Godzilla's March," Lyrics by Shinichi Sekizawa and Jun Fukuda, Music by Kunio Miyauchi; Assistant Director, Fumikatsu Okada; Film Editor, Yoshio Tamura; Lighting, Kojiro Sato; Mechanical Effects, Takesaburo Watanabe; Sound Recording, Fumio Yanoguchi; Sound, Toho Recording Centre; Production Manager, Takehide Morichi. *Toho Special Effects Group*: Director, Teruyoshi Nakano; Art Director, Yasuyuki Inoue; Photography, Mototaka Tomioka; Miniature Set Operation, Fumio Nakadai; Optical Printing, Toshiyuki Tokumasa; Sets, Toshiro Aoki; Matte Processing, Saburo Doi.

CAST: Hiroshi Ishikawa (Gengo Kotaka), Yuriko Hishimi (Tomoko Tomoe), Tomoko Umeda (Machiko Shima), Minoru Takashima (Shosaku Takasugi), Kunio Murai (Takashi Shima), Zan Fujita (World's Children Land chairman (see below)), Toshiaki Nishizawa (Secretary Kubota), Wataru Omae (employee), Kuniko Ashiwara (middle-aged woman), Kureyoshi Nakamura (priest), Akio Muto (editor of *Comics Magazine*), Gen Shimizu (commander of the defense forces), Haruo Nakajima (Godzilla), Yukietsu

Omiya (Angilis), Kanta Ina (King Ghidorah), Kenpachiro Satsuma (Gaigan).

A Toho-Eizo Co., Ltd. Production. A Toho Co., Ltd. Release. Fujicolor (processed by Tokyo Laboratory Ltd.). Panavision. 89 minutes. Released March 12, 1972.

U.S. VERSION: Released by Downtown Distributing Co., Inc. (i.e., Cinema Shares International). English-dubbed. U.K. title: *War of the Monsters*. Television and home video title: *Godzilla vs. Gigan*. Includes extensive stock footage from *Ghidrah – The Three-Headed Monster* (1964), *Monster Zero* (1965), *War of the Gargantuas* (1966), *Son of Godzilla* (1967), *Destroy All Monsters* (1968) and *Godzilla vs. the Smog Monster* (1971). The 12th "Godzilla" feature. Followed by *Godzilla vs. Megalon* (1973). Nakajima's last film as Godzilla. Satsuma is billed as "Kengo Nakayama." Ifukube's music consists entirely of stock themes from *Birth of the Japanese Islands*, and other Toho releases. 89 minutes. MPAA Rating: "G." Released August 1977.

Godzilla vs. Biollante / Gojira vs. Biorante ("Godzilla vs. Biollante"). Executive Producer, Tomoyuki Tanaka; Associate Producer, Shogo Tomiyama; Director/Screenplay, Kazuki Omori, based on an original story, "Gojira tai Biorante" by Shinichiro Kobayashi; Assistant Director, Hideyuki Inoue; Assistant Directors, Yutaka Kubo, Kazuhiko Fukami and Isao Kaneko; Director of Photography, Yudai Kato; Camera Operators, Takashi Wakiya, Motonobu Kiyohisa and Hideyuki Yamaguchi; Lighting, Takaeshi Awakibara; Lighting Assistants, Kohei Mikami, Yasuo Watanabe, Kazumi Kawagoe, Shohei Iriguchi, Hiroyuki Futami, Kenya Kato, Takamasa Nakatani; Recording Mixer, Kazuo Miyauchi; Sound Recordists; Sadakazu Saito, Tatsuaki Watanabe, Osamu Kageyama; Special Mechanical Effects, Mitsuo Miyagawa, Kazuo Kayama; Production Design, Shigekazu Ikuno; Art Department, Juichi Ikuno, Osami Tonjo, Fumiko Osada, Hiroto Niigaki; Set Decoration, Akio Tashiro, Osamu Minamizawa, Yuichiro Endo, Masataka Kawara, Toho Art Co., Ltd.; Electrical Set Decoration, Hideo Inagaki, Yoshinao Tanaka; Construction, Eiji Suzuki, Yoshiki Kasahara, Toho Art Co., Ltd.; Still Photographer, Yoshinori Ishizuki; Hair and Make-Up, Harumi Ueno; Costumes, Kenji Kawasaki, Kyoto Costume Co., Ltd.; Continuity, Yukiko Eguchi; Casting, Tadeo Tanaka; Editor, Michiko Ikeda; Assistant Editors, Miho Shiga, Mitsuko Saito, Masami Ohashi; Sound Effects, Shinichi Ito; Music Composer, Koichi Sugiyama; Music Arranger and Conductor, David Howell; "Godzilla Themes" by Akira Ifukube; Dolby Stereo Consultant, Mikio Mori, Continental Far East, Inc., Tokyo; Production Manager, Kishu Morichi; Production Runners, Takaya Fukuya, Satoshi Fukushima, Yasuo Kobayashi, Sho Matsue; Publicity Director, Masao Daimon; Publicists, Yuichiro Nakanishi, Minami Ichikawa; Cooperation, New MGC, Reebok, others undetermined. "Thanks to the Defense Agency for their cooperation in the making of this motion picture." *Toho Special Effects Group*: Director, Koichi Kawakita; Assistant Director, Kyotaka Matsumoto; Assistants to Kawakita, Hideki Chiba, Makoto Kamiya, Yuichi Abe; Director of Photography, Kenichi Eguchi; Miniature Photography, Yoshio Nozawa, Hiroshi Kidokoro, Masashi Sasaki, Katsumi Arita, Takahide Majio; Lighting, Kaoru Saito; Lighting Assistants, Nobuyuki Seo, Hoya Hayashi, Takhiro Sekino, Masaaki Yokomichi, Shigeru Izumiya, Tsuneo Tanaami; Production Designer, Tetsuzo Osawa; Special Art Department, Takashi Naganuma, Yuji Tsukuba, Isao Takahashi, Masato Matsumura; Prosthetics, Nobuyuki Yasumaru, Tomoki Kobayashi, Yoko Nagata; Wire Works, Koji Matsumoto; Wire Works Assistants, Koshu Katori, Masahiko Shiraishi; Miniature Pyrotechniques, Tadaaki Watanabe, Mamoru Kume; Pyrotechnicians, Yasushi Iwata, Toshitaka Watanabe, Katsumi Nakajo; Miniature Sets, Yasuo Nomura, Sadao Ogasawara; Still Photographer, Takashi Nakao; Editing, Yukari Yaginuma; Continuity, Yoshiko Hori; Production Runners, Taro Kojima, Masaya Kowakura, Isamu Suzuki; Biollante Design, Atsuhiko Sugita, Noritaka Suzuki, Shinji Nishikawa; Mechanical Designs, Kou Yokoyama. Special *Optical Effects Unit*: Optical Effects; Yoshiyuki

Kishimoto, Horiaki Hojo; Motion Control, Ryoji Kinoshita, Kenichi Abe; Video Effects, Kenji Kagiwara; Timing, Maruo Iwata; Effects Animation Michiaki Hashimoto, Hajime Matsumoto, Masakazu Saito; Animation, Kazuaki Mori, Aki Yamagata, Ryuichi Akahori; Computer Graphics, Tetsuo Obi, Hisashi Kameya, Satoshi Mizuhata; Matte Paintings, Kazunobu Sanbe; Matte Painter, Yoshio Ishii; Coordinators, Toshihiro Ogawa, Masaharu Misawa; Producers, Takashi Yamabe, Mitsuhara Umano.

CAST: Kunihiko Mitamura (Kazuhito Kirishima), Yoshiko Tanaka (Asuka Okochi), Masanobu Takashima (Major Sho Kuroki), Megumi Odaka (Miki Saegusa), Toru Minegishi (Lieutenant Goro Gondo), Ryunosuke Kaneda (Seido Okouchi), Koji Takahashi (Dr. Genichiro Shiragami), Yasuko Sawaguchi (Erika Shiragami), Toshiyuki Nagashima (Director of Technical Division Seiichi Yamamoto), Yoshiko Kuga (Chief Cabinet Secretary Keiko Owada), Manjhat Beti (SSS9), Koichi Ueda (Self Defense Agency Chairman Yamaji), Isao Toyohara and Kyoka Suzuki (Super X2 operators), Kenji Hunt (John Lee), Derrick Holmes (Michael Low), Hirohisa Nakata (Director General of the Defense Agency), Katsuhiko Sasaki (Director of Science Technology Takeda), Kenzo Hagiwara (ground forces staff officer), Kazuyuki Senba (Maritime staff officer), Koji Yamanaka (Air Force staff officer), Iden Yamanrahl (Abdul Saulman), Hiroshi Inoue Kazuma Matsubara, Ryota Yoshimitsu, Tetsu Kawai, Yasunori Yumiya (Self Defense Forces officials), Shin Tatsuma (Director of Giant Plant Observation Akiyama), Abdullah Herahl (researcher), Curtis Kramer, Brian Wool, Robert Conner (commandos), Beth Blatt (CCN Newscaster Susan Horn), Makiyo Kuroiwa (nurse), Haruko Sagara (TVC-TV reporter), Hiromi Matsukawa (newscaster), Demon Kogure (himself), Isao Takeno (Chief of Super X2 repair crew), Kenpachiro Satsuma, Shigeru Shibazaki, and Yoshitaka Kimura (Godzilla), Masao Takegami (Biollante).

A Toho Co., Ltd. Production, in association with Toho-Eizo Co. Dolby Stereo/ TKL-Stereo. Color (processed by Tokyo Laboratory Ltd.). Spherical wide screen. 104 minutes. Released December 16, 1989.

U.S. VERSION: Never released theatrically in the United States. Released directly to home video and cable television. English-dubbed. Home video version is matted but with mono sound. Features brief stock footage from *Submersion of Japan* (1973). From this point forward the Japanese began using "vs." instead of "tai" in their written titles, even though they are still pronounced "tai" in Japan. The 17th "Godzilla" feature. Followed by *Godzilla vs. King Ghidorah* (1991). 104 minutes. MPAA rating: "PG."

Godzilla vs. King Ghidorah / Gojira vs. Kingughidorah ("Godzilla vs. King Ghidorah"). Executive Producer, Tomoyuki Tanaka; Producer, Shogo Tomiyama; Associate Producer, Tomiya Ban; Director/Screenplay, Kazuki Omori; Director of Photography, Yoshinoru Sakiguchi; Art Director, Ken Sakai; Sound Recording, Katsuo Miyauchi; Lighting Director, Tsuyoshi Awakihara; Editor, Michiko Ikeda; Music, Akira Ifukube, conducted by Satoshi Imai; Sound, Toho Recording Centre; Sound Effects, Toho Sound Effects Group; Dolby Stereo Consultant, Mikio Mori, Continental Far East, Inc., Tokyo. *Toho Special Effects Group*: Director, Koichi Kawakita; Photography, Kenichi Eguchi and Toshimitsu Oneda; Art Director, Tetsuzo Osawa; Lighting, Kaoru Saito; Pyrotechniques; Tadashi Watanabe; Wire Works, Koji Matsumoto; Sculpting, Tomoki Kobayashi; Assistant Director, Kenji Suzuki.

CAST: Anna Nakagawa (Emmy Kano), Megumi Odaka (Miki Saegusa), Kosuke Toyohara (Kenichiro Terasawa), Kiwako Harada (Chiaki Morimura), Tokuma Nishioka (Takehito Fujio), Shoji Kobayashi (Security Chief Ruzo Dobashi), Yoshio Tsuchiya (Yasuaki Shindo), Richard Berger (Grenchiko), Chuck Wilson (Wilson), Kenji Sahara (prime minister), Robert Scottfield (M11), Koichi Ueda (Ikehata, *the mad veteran*), Kenpachiro Satsuma (Godzilla).

A Toho Pictures Production. Dolby Stereo/TKL-Stereo. Color (processed by

Tokyo Laboratory, Ltd.). Spherical wide screen. Released December 14, 1991.

U.S. VERSION: Unreleased in the United States as of this writing. The 18th "Godzilla" feature. Followed by *Godzilla vs. Mothra* (1992).

Godzilla vs. Mechagodzilla / Gojira vs. Mekagojira ("Godzilla vs. Mechagodzilla"). Executive Producer, Tomoyuki Tanaka; Producer, Shogo Tomiyama; Director, Takao Okawara; Screenplay, Wataru Mimura; Director of Photography, Yoshinori Sekiguchi; Art Director, Ken Sakai; Lighting, Hideki Mochizuki; Music, Akira Ifukube, conducted by Satoshi Imai; Sound Recording, Kazuo Miyauchi. *Toho Special Effects Group*: Director, Koichi Kawakita; Photography, Kenichi Eguchi; Still Photographer, Takashi Nakao.

CAST: Masahiro Takashima (Kazuma Aoki), Ryoko Sano (Azusa Gojo), Daijiro Harada (Takuya Sasaki), Megumi Odaka (Miki Saegusa), Ichirota Miyagawa (Jun Sonezaki), Kenji Sahara (Director Segawa), Tadao Takashima (Director Hosono), Akira Nakao (General Aso), Yusuke Kawazu (Professor Omae), Lasale Ishii (Kunio Katsuragi), Sherry Sweeny (Katherine Burger), Leo Mengetti (Doctor Asimov), Keiko Imamura and Sayaka Osawa (teachers who speak in unison), Kenpachiro Satsuma (Godzilla), Wataru Fukuda (Mechagodzilla), Hariken Ryu (Baby Godzilla).

A Toho Co., Ltd. Production, in association with Toho-Eizo Co., Ltd. Color. Spherical wide screen. Six-track Dolby Stereo Digital and four-track Dolby stereo. 108 minutes. Released December 11, 1993.

U.S. VERSION: Unreleased in the United States as this book went to press. Announced as *Gojira 5: Gojira vs. Mekagojira*. Not to be confused with, nor is it a remake of *Godzilla vs. Mechagodzilla* (original U.S. title: *Godzilla vs. the Cosmic Monster*, 1974) The 20th "Godzilla" feature. Followed by *Godzilla vs. Space Godzilla* (1994).

Godzilla vs. Megalon / Gojira tai Megaro ("Godzilla Against Megalon"). Producer Tomoyuki Tanaka; Director, Jun Fukuda; Screenplay, Jun Fukuda, based on an original story by Shinichi Sekizawa; Director of Photography, Yuzuru Aizawa; Editor, Michiko Ikeda; Music, Riichiro Manabe; Sound, Toho Recording Centre; Sound Effects, Toho Sound Effects Group. *Toho Special Effects Group*: Director, Teruyoshi Nakano; Mechanical Effects, Takesaburo Watanabe; Optical Effects, Yukio Manoda; Art Director, Yasuyuki Inoue.

CAST: Katsuhiko Sasaki (Goro), Hiroyuki Kawase (Rokuro "Rolluchan," *Goro's kid brother*), Robert Dunham (Antonio, *the Seatopian leader*), Yutaka Hayashi, Kotaro Tomita, Shin Mikita.

A Toho-Eizo Co., Ltd. Production. A Toho Co., Ltd. Release. Fujicolor (processed by Tokyo Laboratory, Ltd.). Panavision. 81 minutes. Released March 17, 1973.

U.S. VERSION: Released by Cinema Shares International Distribution Co., Inc. English-dubbed. Features stock footage from *Ghidrah – The Three-Headed Monster* (1964), *Ebirah, Horror of the Deep* (1966), *War of the Gargantuas* (1966) *Destroy All Monsters* (1968) and *Godzilla on Monster Island* (1972). Cut to 50 minutes for U.S. television network presentation. An R-rated version exists, but apparently never released as such. The 13th "Godzilla" feature. Followed by *Godzilla vs. the Cosmic Monster* (1974). 74 minutes. MPAA rating: "G." Released April 1976.

Godzilla vs. Mothra / Gojira vs. Mosura ("Godzilla vs. Mothra"). Executive Producer, Tomoyuki Tanaka; Producer, Shogo Tomiyama; Director, Takao Okawara; Screenplay, Kazuki Omori; Original Music, Akira Ifukube, conducted by Satoshi Imai; "Godzilla/Mothra Themes," Akira Ifukube, Yuji Koseki and Hiroshi Miyagawa; *Toho Special Effects Group*: Director, Koichi Kawakita; Photography, Kenichi Eguchi; Still Photographer, Takashi Nakao.

CAST: Tetsuya Bessho (Takuya Fujita),

Satomi Kobayashi (Masako Tezuka), Akira Takarada (Environmental Planning Board Chief Joji Minamino), Keiko Imamura and Sayaka Osawa (The Cosmos), Shoji Kobayashi (Security Chief Ruzo Dobashi), Takehiro Murata (Marutomo Corporation Executive Ando), Makoto Otake (Marutomo Corporation CEO Takeshi Tomokane), Megumi Odaka (Miki Saegusa), Kenji Sahara (Takayuki Segawa), Kenpachiro Satsuma (Godzilla).

A Toho Co., Ltd. Production. Dolby Stereo. Color (processed by Tokyo Laboratory, Ltd.). Spherical wide screen. 104 minutes. Released December 12, 1992.

U.S. Version: Unreleased in the United States as of this writing. A quasi-remake of *Mothra* (1961) and *Godzilla vs. the Thing* (1964). The 19th "Godzilla" feature. Followed by *Godzilla vs. Mechagodzilla* (1993).

Godzilla vs. Space Godzilla / Gojira vs. Supesu Gojira ("Godzilla vs. Space Godzilla"). Executive Producer, Tomoyuki Tanaka; Producer, Shogo Tomiyama; Director, Kensho Yamashita; Screenplay, Hiroshi Kashiwabara; Director of Photography, Masahiro Kishimoto; Music, Takayuki Hattori; Godzilla Themes, Akira Ifukube; Songs: "Echos of Love," performed by Date of Birth, "Groove It – Yourself" performed by Katsu [no other name given]. *Toho Special Effects Group*: Director, Koichi Kawakita; Director of Photography, Kenichi Eguchi; Still Photographer, Takashi Nakao.

Cast: Jun Hashizume (Koji Shinjo), Megumi Odaka (Miki Saegusa), Senkichi Yoneyama (Kiyoshi Sato), Towako Yoshikawa (Chinatsu Gondo), Akira Emoto (Akira Yuki), Yosuke Saito (Susumu Okubo), Keiko Imamura and Sayaka Osawa (The Cosmos), Kenji Sahara (Takayuki Segawa, *director of UNGCC*), Akira Nakao (Takaaki Aso), Koichi Ueda (Iwao Hyodo), Kenpachiro Satsuma (Godzilla), Ryo Hariya (Space Godzilla), Wataru Fukuda (MOGERA), Little Frankie (Little Godzilla).

A Toho Co., Ltd. Production. Dolby Stereo. Color (processed by Tokyo Laboratory, Ltd.). Spherical wide screen. 105 minutes. Released December 10, 1994.

U.S. Version: Unreleased in the United States as this book went to press. The 21st "Godzilla" feature. Followed by *Godzilla vs. Destroyer* (1995). Ifukube's music is stock from earlier films.

Godzilla vs. the Cosmic Monster / Gojira tai Mekagojira ("Godzilla against Mechagodzilla"). Executive Producer, Tomoyuki Tanaka; Director, Jun Fukuda; Screenplay, Hiroyasu Yamamura and Jun Fukuda, based on an original story by Shinichi Sekizawa and Masami Fukushima; Director of Photography, Yuzuru Aizawa; Art Director, Kazuo Satsuya; Editor, Michiko Ikeda; Sound Recording, Fumio Yanoguchi; Music, Masaru Sato; Sound, Toho Recording Centre; Sound Effects, Toho Sound Effects Group. *Toho Special Effects Group*: Director, Teruyoshi Nakano; Photography, Mototaka Tomioka, Takeshi Yamamoto; Optical Photography, Yukio Manoda; Mechanical Effects, Takesaburo Watanabe; Art Director, Yasuyuki Inoue.

Cast: Masaaki Daimon (Keisuke Shimizu), Kazuya Aoyama (Masahiko Shimizu), Akihiko Hirata (Professor Hideto Miyajima), Hiroshi Koizumi (Professor Wagura), Reiko Tajima (Saeko Kaneshiro), Hiromi Matsushita (Iko Miyajima), Masao Imafuku (Azumi priest), Beru-Bera Lin [aka Barbara Lynn] (Azumi Princess Nami Kunizu), Shin Kishida (Interpol Agent Namura), Takayasu Torii (Interpol Agent Tamura), Goro Mutsu (commander of the alien attack force), Daigo Kusano (Kawa Yanagi), Kenji Sahara (ship's captain), Yasuzo Ogawa (construction workshop supervisor).

A Toho-Eizo Co., Ltd. Production. A Toho Co., Ltd. Release. Fujicolor (processed by Tokyo Laboratory, Ltd.). Panavision. 84 minutes. Released March 21, 1974.

U.S. Version: Released by Downtown Distribution Co., Inc. (i.e. Cinema Shares). English-dubbed. Title changed

Akira Takarada, Yuriko Hoshi, Yu Fujiki, and Hiroshi Koizumi eye Mothra's priestesses (The Peanuts) in *Godzilla vs. the Thing* (1964).

from *Godzilla vs. the Bionic Monster* after Universal Pictures, the production company behind "The Six Million Dollar Man" and "The Bionic Woman," threatened legal action because of the film's title. Television and home video title: *Godzilla vs Mechagodzilla*. Not to be confused with *Godzilla vs. Mechagodzilla* (1993). The 14th "Godzilla" feature. Followed by *The Terror of Godzilla* (1975). 84 minutes. MPAA rating: "G." Released March 1977.

Godzilla vs. the Smog Monster / Gojira tai Hedora ("Godzilla Against Hedora"). Executive Producer, Tomoyuki Tanaka; Director, Yoshimitsu Banno; Screenplay, Yoshimitsu Banno and Kaoru Mabuchi (Takeshi Kimura); Director of Photography, Yoichi Manoda; Music, Riichiro Manabe; Editor, Yoshitami Kuroiwa; Art Director, Yasuyuki Inoue; Sound Effects, Toho Sound Effects Group; Sound, Toho Recording Centre; Assistant Director, Hirayoshi Tsushima. *Toho Special Effects Group*: Director, Teruyoshi Nakano; Optical Photography, Yukio Manoda; Mechanical Effects, Takesaburo Watanabe; Assistant Director, Koichi Kawakita.

CAST: Akira Yamauchi (Dr. Yano), Hiroyuki Kawase (Ken Yano), Toshie Kimura (Mrs. Yano), Toshio Shibaki (Yukio Keuchi), Keiko Mari (Miki Fujiyama), Haruo Nakajima (Godzilla), Kenpachiro Satsuma (Hedora).

A Toho Co., Ltd. Production. Color (processed by Tokyo Laboratory, Ltd.). Panavision. 85 minutes. Released July 24, 1971.

U.S. VERSION: Released by American International Pictures. English-dubbed. A Samuel Z. Arkoff Presentation. English-dubbed. Producer, Samuel Z. Arkoff; Director, Lee Kresel; Postproduction Supervisor, Salvatore Billiteri; (Dialog Replacement) Editor, Eli Haviv; Rerecording, Titan Productions, Inc.; Song, "Save The Earth," English lyrics and

Vocal, Adryan Russ. Guy Hemric is credited with music for the song, but the number appears in the Japanese cut (in Japanese, of course). Wide screen process advertised as Colorscope in the United States. Satsuma is billed as "Kengo Nakayama." The 11th "Godzilla" feature. Followed by *Godzilla on Monster Island* (1972). 85 minutes. MPAA Rating: "G." Released February 1972.

Godzilla vs. the Thing / Mosura tai Gojira ("Mothra Against Godzilla"). Producers, Tomoyuki Tanaka and Sanezumi Fujimoto; Director, Ishiro Honda; Screenplay, Shinichi Sekizawa; Director of Photography, Hajime Koizumi; Music, Akira Ifukube; Editor, Ryohei Fujii; Sound Recording Director Fumio Yanoguchi; In Charge of Production, Boku Morimoto; Art Director, Takeo Kita; Lighting, Shoshichi Kojima; Sound Technician, Hisashi Shimonaga; Assistant Director, Koji Kajita; Sound Effects, Toho Sound Effects Group; Sound, Toho Recording Centre. *Toho Special Effects Group*: Director, Eiji Tsuburaya; Cameraman, Teisho Arikawa and Mototaka Tomioka; Lighting, Kuichiro Kishida; Art Director, Akira Watanabe; Suit Design, Teizo Toshimitsu; Optical Photography, Yukio Manoda, Mototaka Tomioka, Yoshiyuki Tokumasa; Matte Process, Hiroshi Mukoyama; Optical Effects Animation, Minoru Nakano; Assistant to Tsuburaya, Teruyoshi Nakano.

CAST: Akira Takarada (News Reporter Ichiro Sakai), Yuriko Hoshi (News Photographer Junko Nakanishi), Hiroshi Koizumi (Professor Murai), Yu Fujiki (Reporter Jiro Nakamura), Kenji Sahara (Banzo [Jiro in the US version] Torahata), Emi Ito and Yumi Ito [The Peanuts] (Mothra's priestesses), Jun Tazaki (newspaper editor), Yoshifumi Tajima (Kumayama), Kenzo Tabu (mayor), Yutaka Sada (old man), Akira Tani (village leader who sells the egg), Susumu Fujita (public relations officer), Ikio Sawamura (priest), Ren Yamamoto (sailor), Yoshio Kosugi (native chief), Senkichi Omura, Yutaka Nakayama, Hiroshi Iwamoto and Joji Uno (fishermen), Yasuhisa Tsutsumi (longshoreman), Haruo Nakajima (Godzilla), Kozo Nomura, Shin Otomo, Kazuo Suzuki, Katsumi Tezuka.

A Toho Co., Ltd. Production. Eastman Color (color by Tokyo Laboratory Ltd.). Toho Scope. Copyright 1964 by Toho Co., Ltd. 89 minutes. Released April 29, 1964.

U.S. VERSION: Released by American International Pictures. A James H. Nicholson & Samuel Z. Arkoff Presentation. English-dubbed. Produced by Titra Productions, Inc.; Rerecording, Titra Sound Corp.; Prints by Pathé. Copyright August 26, 1964 by American International Productions. Includes footage prepared by Toho especially for the English-language version. Wide screen process advertised as Colorscope in the United States. Double-billed with *Voyage to the End of the Universe* (AIP, 1964). Initially released to television by AIP-TV as above; reissued to television by UPA Productions of America and on video as *Godzilla vs. Mothra*. Reissued in Japan in 1970 (re-edited by Ishiro Honda to 74 minutes), 1980 and 1983. The 4th "Godzilla" feature. Followed by *Ghidrah—The Three-Headed Monster* (1964). More or less remade as *Godzilla vs. Mothra* (1992). 88 minutes. No MPAA Rating. Released September 17, 1964.

Godzilla's Revenge / Oru kaiju daishingeki ("All Monsters Big Attack"). Producer, Tomoyuki Tanaka; Director, Ishiro Honda; Screenplay, Shinichi Sekizawa; Director of Photography, Mototaka Tomioka; Music, Kunio Miyauchi; Editor, Masahima Miyauchi; Art Direction, Takeo Kita; Assistant Director, Masaaki Hisumatsu; Sound Effects, Toho Sound Effects Group; Recording, Toho Recording Centre. *Toho Special Effects Group*: Supervisor, Eiji Tsuburaya; Director, (uncredited) Ishiro Honda; Photography, Teisho Arikawa, Mototaka Tomioka; Optical Photography, Yukio Manoda, Sadao Iizuda; Art Director, Akira Watanabe; Lighting, Kuichiro Kishida; Wire Manipulation, Fumio Nakadai, Assistant Director, Teruyoshi Nakano.

CAST: Tomonori Yazaki (Ichiro), Kenji Sahara (Ichiro's father), Sachio Sakai, Kazuo Suzuki (bank robbers), Eisei Amamoto (Toy Consultant Inami), Yoshifumi Tajima and Chotaro Togin (detectives), Haruo Nakajima (Godzilla), Little Man Machan (Minira), Hiroshi Sekita (Gaborah), Machiko Naka (Ichiro's mother), Ikio Sawamura (street vendor), Shigeki Ishida (effeminate man), Yutaka Sada (the father's co-worker), Yutaka Nakayama.

A Toho Co., Ltd. Production. Color (processed by Tokyo Laboratory, Ltd.). Toho Scope. 70 minutes. Released December 20, 1969.

U.S. VERSION: Released by Maron Films, Ltd. A United Productions of America presentation. English-dubbed. Producer, Henry G. Saperstein; Postproduction, Riley Jackson; Theme Song, "March of the Monsters," Crown Records; Sound Recording, Ryder Sound Services, Inc.; Titles and Prints, Consolidated Film Industries. Copyright 1971 by UPA. According to *The Japanese Fantasy Film Journal,* this was originally released as *Minya, Son of Godzilla,* possibly by Toho International, in an English-dubbed version and minus screen credits. Picture was pulled, reedited to present length and released by Maron as *Godzilla's Revenge*. Double-billed with *Island of the Burning Damned* (Maron, 1971), also the film's television title. Includes extensive stock footage from *Ebirah, Horror of the Deep* (1966) and *Son of Godzilla,* as well as footage from *King Kong Escapes* (1967) and *Destroy All Monsters* (1968). No effects director is credited; the Japanese titles credit only "Toho Special Effects Group." The 10th "Godzilla" feature. Followed by *Godzilla vs. the Smog Monster* (1971). 69 minutes. No MPAA rating. Released December 8, 1971.

Goke, Bodysnatcher from Hell / Kyuketsuki Gokemidoro ("Vampire Gokemidoro"). Producer, Takashi Inomata; Director, Hajime Sato; Screenplay, Susumu Takaku and Kyuzo Kobayashi; Production Manager, Masayuki Fukuyama; Assistant Director, Keiji Shiraki; Art Director, Tadataka Yoshino; Set Decoration, Shin-ei Bijutsu Kogei Co., Ltd.; Director of Photography, Shizuo Hirase; Editor, Akimitsu Terada; Sound, Hiroshi Nakamura; Sound Effects, Takashi Matsumoto; Music, Shunsuke Kikuchi.

CAST: Teruo Yoshida (Ei Sugisaka), Tomomi Sato (Kazumi Asakura), Hideo Ko (Hirobumi Teraoka), Eizo Kitamura (Gozo Mano), Masaya Takahashi (Toshiyuki Saga), Cathy Horlan (Mrs. Neal), Kazuo Kato (Momotake), Yuko Kunsunoki (Noriko Tokumatsu), Norihiko Kaneko (Matsumiya), Hiroyuki Nishimoto (Airplane Captain), Harold S. Conway (Ambassador in flashback stills).

A Shochiku Co., Ltd. Production. Fujicolor (processed by Shochiku Laboratory). Shochiku GrandScope. 84 minutes. Released August 14, 1968.

U.S. VERSION: Released by Shochiku Films of America, Inc. in subtitled format, and possibly released dubbed at this same time. Alternate title: *Goke the Vampire*. Television and home video title: *Body Snatcher from Hell*, listed as a TFC and Pacemaker Films, Inc. Presentation (who may also have distributed the film theatrically), and running 82 minutes. 84 minutes. No MPAA rating. Released 1969.

The Golden Demon / Konjiki yasha ("The Golden Demon"). Executive Producer, Kiichi Satake; Producer, Masaichi Nagata; Director, Koji Shima; Screenplay, Koji Shima and Matsutaro Kawaguchi, based on the novel by Koyo Ozaki; Director of Photography, Michio Takahashi; Art Director, Mikio Naka; Music, Ichiro Saito; Sound Recording, Kenichi Nishii; Lighting, Koichi Kubota; Editor, Masanori Tsujii; Assistant Director, Koji Sugano.

CAST: Jun Negami (Kanichi), Fujiko Yamamoto (Miya), Kenji Sugawara (Akao), Mitsuko Mito (Akagashi), Kazuko Fushimi (Aiko), Eiji Funakoshi (Tomiyama), Shizue Natsukawa (Madam Miwa), Kumeko Urabe (Tose), Kinzo Shin (Shikazawa), Chikako Hosokawa (wife of Shikazawa), Shiko Saito (Wanibushi), Teppei Endo (Miwa), Jun Miyazake (Kamoda), Yoshio Takemi (Yusa), Sachiko Meguro (wife of Yusa).

A Daiei Motion Picture Co., Ltd. Production. Western Electric Mirrophonic Recording. Eastman Color. Academy ratio. 91 minutes. Released 1954.

U.S. VERSION: Distributor undetermined. Reissued by Janus Films. English subtitles. 91 minutes. No MPAA rating. Release date undetermined.

Gone with Love, Come with Memory / Tsugaru zessho ("Best Song of Tsugaru"). Director, Yoshihiko Okamoto; Screenplay, Ryuzo Kikushima; Director of Photography, Hiroshi Murai; Art Director, Yukio Higuchi; Music, Yasushi Miyagawa.

CAST: Kinya Kitaoji (Keiichi Natsukawa), Yuriko Hoshi (Kuniko Honda), Michiko Araki (Aunt Toyo), Shiro Otsuji.

A Toho Co., Ltd. Production. Eastman Color. Panavision (?). 96 minutes. Released April 12, 1969.

U.S. VERSION: Released by Toho International Co., Ltd. English subtitles. 96 minutes. No MPAA rating. Release date undetermined.

Gonza the Spearman / Yari no Gonza ("Spear of Gonza"). Producers, Kiyoshi Iwashita, Masayuki Motomochi, and Masatake Wakita; Director, Masahiro Shinoda; Screenplay, Taeko Tomioka, based on the play by Monzaemon Chikamatsu; Director of Photography, Kazuo Miyagawa; Music, Toru Takemitsu.

CAST: Hiromi Go, Shima Iwashita, Choichiro Kawarazaki, Shohei Hino, Haruko Kato.

A Shochiku Co., Ltd./Hyogensha Co., Ltd. Production. Color. Panavision (?). 126 minutes. Released 1986.

U.S. VERSION: Released by Kino International. English subtitles. 126 minutes. No MPAA rating. Released May 3, 1986.

The Good Little Bad Girl / Denki kurage, kawaii akuma ("Electric Jellyfish, Pretty Pearl"). Director, Reijiro Usuzaka; Screenplay, Ishio Shirosaka and Kanji Yasumoto; Director, Akira Uehara; Art Director, Shigeo Mano.

CAST: Mari Atsumi (Yumi), Reiko Kasahara (Nobuko), Kenzo Kaneko (Goro), Hiroko Kai (Hisako), Daigo Kusano (Koizumi), Yuji Moriya, Mitsuyo Inomata.

A Daiei Motion Picture Co., Ltd. Production. Fujicolor. DaieiScope. 83 minutes. Released August 22, 1970.

U.S. VERSION: Released undetermined, possibly by Daiei International Films. English subtitled version available.

Goodbye, Hello / Sayonara, Konichiwa ("Goodbye, Good Afternoon"). Producer, Kazuyoshi Takeda; Director, Kon Ichikawa; Screenplay, Kon Ichikawa and Kazuo Funabashi; Director of Photography, Setsuo Kobayashi; Music, Tetsuo Tsukahara; Art Director, Tomo Shimogawara; Lighting, Isamu Yoneyama; Sound Recording, Mitsuo Hasegawa.

CAST: Machiko Kyo (Umeko Ichige), Hitomi Nozoe (Michiko Aota), Fumiko Wakao (Kazuko Aota), Kenji Sugawara (Hanjiro Watanabe), Hiroshi Kawaguchi (Tetsu Kataoka), Eiji Funakoshi (Torao Ichige).

A Daiei Motion Picture Co., Ltd. Production. Eastman Color. DaieiScope. Running time undetermined. Released January 3, 1959.

U.S. VERSION: Distributor, if any, is undetermined, though likely Daiei International Films, Inc. No MPAA rating.

Goodbye Mama / Gubbai Mama ("Goodbye, Mama"). Producer, Kazuyoshi Okuyama; Director, Yasushi Akimoto; Screenplay, Yasushi Akimoto and Toshio Terada; Director of Photography, Tatsuo Suzuki; Music, Kazuo Otani.

CAST: Keiko Matsuzaka, Ken Ogata, Yuta Yamazaki.

A Shochiku Dai-Ichi Kogyo Co., Ltd./KSS, Inc. Production. Color. Panavision (?). 109 minutes. Released 1991.

U.S. VERSION: Distributor, if any, is undetermined.

Goodbye, Moscow / Saraba Mosukuwa gurentai ("Goodbye, Moscow Gangsters"). Producer, Sanezumi

Colorful paste-up from *Gorath* (1962), an underrated sci-fi epic.

Fujimoto; Director, Hiromichi Horikawa; Screenplay, Takeshi Tamura, based on the story "Saraba Mosukuwa gurentai," appearing in *Saraba Mosukuwa gurentai* (1967) by Hiroyuki Itsuki; Director of Photography, Yasumichi Fukuzawa; Art Director, Shinobu Muraki; Music, Toshiro Mayuzumi and Masao Yagi.

CAST: Yuzo Kayama (The Promoter), Toshiko Morita, Shigeru Koyama, Toshio Kurosawa.

A Toho Co., Ltd. Production. Eastman Color. Toho Scope (?). Filmed on location in Moscow and Tokyo. 97 minutes. Released May 1968.

U.S. VERSION: Released by Toho International Co., Ltd. English subtitles. 97 minutes. No MPAA rating. Released November 1968.

A Goodbye to the Girls / Sayonara no onnatachi ("Goodbye to the Girls"). Producers, Koichi Ishii and Choichi Ichimura; Director, Kazuki Omori; Screenplay, Kazuki Omori, based on an original story by Saeko Himuro; Director of Photography, Nobumasa Mizuno; Music, Tetsuro Kashibuchi.

CAST: Yuki Saito, Hiro Komura, Izumi Yukimura.

A Toho Co., Ltd. Production. Color. Spherical wide screen. 92 minutes. Released 1987.

U.S. VERSION: Distributor, if any, is undetermined, possibly by Toho International Co., Ltd. in subtitled format. Alternate title: *Women Who Say Goodbye*. No MPAA rating.

Gorath / Yosei Gorasu ("Ominous Star Gorath"). Executive Producer, Tomoyuki Tanaka; Director, Ishiro Honda; Screenplay, Takeshi Kimura, based on an original story by Jojiro Okami; Director of Photography, Hajime Koizumi; Production Manager, Yasuaki Sakamoto; Assistant Directors, Koji Kajita, Masashi Matsumoto, Katsumune Ishida, and Shoji Kuroda; Art Directors, Takeo Kita and Teruaki Abe; Music, Kan Ishii; Sound Recording Engineer, Toshiya Ban; Sound Effects, Hisashi Shimonaga,

Toho Sound Effects Group; Sound, Toho Recording Centre; Lighting, Toshio Takashima; Editor, Reiko Kaneko; Still Photographer, Issei Tanaka. *Toho Special Effects Group*: Director, Eiji Tsuburaya; Director of Photography, Teisho Arikawa and Mototaka Tomioka; Art Director, Akira Watanabe; Lighting, Kuichiro Kishida; Matte Work, Hiroshi Mukoyama; Optical Effects, Taka Yuki and Yukio Manoda; Assistant Optical Effects, Koichi Kawakita; Production Manager, Kan Narita; Assistant Director, Teruyoshi Nakano.

CAST: Ryo Ikebe (Dr. Tazawa), Yumi Shirakawa (Kiyo Sonoda), Takashi Shimura (Keisuke Sonoda), Kumi Mizuno (Ari Sonoda), Ken Uehara (Dr. Konno), Akira Kubo (Cadet Astronaut Tatsuo Kanai), Akihiko Hirata (Spaceship Otori [J-X Eagle] Captain Endo), Jun Tazaki (J-X Hawk [Spaceship Hayabusa] Captain Sonoda), Fumio Sakamoto (Sumio Sonoda), Ross Benette (Gibson), George Furness (Huverman), Sachio Sakai (physician), Shinpei Mitsui (newspaper reporter), Ikio Sawamura (taxi driver), Eisei Amamoto (drunk). *J-X Hawk [Spaceship Hayabusa] Crew*: Nadao Kirino (Dr. Manabe), Koji Suzuki (pilot), Kazuo Imai (radio operator), Wataru Omae (mathematician), Yasuo Araki (navigator), Akira Yamada (chief engineer), Tomo Suzuki (fuel checkout). *J-X Eagle [Spaceship Otori] Crew*: Kenji Sahara (1st Officer Saiki), Hiroshi Tachikawa (Astronaut Wakabayashi), Masaya Nihei (Astronaut Ito), Koichi Sato (pilot), Yasuhiko Saijo (radio operator), Toshihiko Furuta (navigator), Rinsaku Ogata (chief engineer), Tadashi Okabe (mathematician), Kozo Nomura (fuel checkout), Ko Mishima (Engineer Sinda). *The Parliament*: Takamaru Sasaki (Prime Minister Seki), Eitaro Ozawa (Minister of Justice Kinami), Seizaburo Kawazu (Minister of Commerce Tada), Ko Nishimura (Secretary of the Space Agency Murata), Keiko Sata (Murata's Secretary), Haruo Nakajima (Magma, the Giant Walrus), Osman Yuseph (technician attacked by Magma), Ed Keane (U.N. representative), Saburo Iketani (news anchor), Yasushi Matsubara, Junichiro Mukai, Masayoshi Kawabe, Yoshiyuki Uemura, Koji Uno, Kenichi Maruyama, Yukihiko Gondo, Katsumi Tezuka, Takuya Yuki, Hiroshi Takaki, Ichiro Shioji, Koji Ishikawa, Jiro Kumagai.

A Toho Co., Ltd. Production. Western Electric Mirrophonic Recording (encoded with Perspecta Stereophonic sound). Eastman Color (processed by Tokyo Laboratory Ltd.). Toho Scope. 89 minutes. Released March 21, 1962.

U.S. VERSION: Released by Brenco Pictures Corp. English-dubbed. Executive Producer, Edward L. Alperson; Producer, Stanley Meyer; Production Coordinator (for Toho), Sanezumi Fujimoto; Sound Recording, Ryder Sound Services, Inc.; Editor, Kenneth Wannberg; Story, John Meredyth Lucas; Postsynchronization Supervisor, Paul Frees; Voices, Paul Frees, William Eidleson, and Virginia Craig; Opticals, Pathé. Westrex Recording System (possibly encoded with Perspecta Stereophonic Sound, but this is unconfirmed). Alternate or announced titles: *Gorath, The Mysterious Star* and *Astronaut 1980*. Double-billed with *The Human Vapor* (1960). 83 minutes. No MPAA rating. Released May 15, 1964.

Goyokin ("Government Funds"). Executive Producers, Sanezumi Fujimoto, Hideo Fukuda, Hideyuki Shino, and Masayuki Sato; Director, Hideo Gosha; Screenplay, Hideo Gosha and Kei Tasaka; Director of Photography, Kozo Okazaki; Art Director, Motoji Kojima; Music, Masaru Sato.

CAST: Tatsuya Nakadai (Magobei Wakizaka), Tetsuro Tamba (Rokugo Tatewaki), Kinnosuke Nakamura (Samon Fujimaki), Isao Natsuyagi (Kunai), Yoko Tsukasa (Shino), Kunie Tanaka (Hyosuke), Ruriko Asaoka (Oriha).

A Fuji Telecasting Co., Ltd./Tokyo Eiga Co., Ltd. Production. A Toho Co., Ltd. Release. Eastman Color. Panavision. 124 minutes. Released May 17, 1969.

U.S. VERSION: Released by Toho International Co., Ltd. English subtitles. 124 minutes. No MPAA rating. Released September 1969. Reissued English-dubbed as *The Steel Edge of Revenge* by Kelly-Jordan in September 1974, running 85 minutes, with an MPAA rating of "PG."

Shintaro Katsu (right) in Daiei's epic *The Great Wall* (1962).

One source suggests that this was the first Japanese production filmed in Panavision; this is unconfirmed.

Gray Sunset/Hana Ichimonme

("The Little Petal"). Producer, Shigeru Okada; Director, Shunya Ito; Screenplay, Hiro Masuda; Director of Photography, Isamu Iguchi; Music, Shinichiro Ikeda.

CAST: Minoru Chiaki (Fuyukichi), Yukiyo Toake, Teruhiko Saigo, Haruko Kato.

A Toei Co., Ltd. Production. Color. Wide screen. 125 minutes. Released October 10, 1985.

U.S. VERSION: Distributor, if any, is undetermined. No MPAA rating.

The Great Shogunate Battle / Edo-jo Tairan

("Great Battle at Edo Castle"). Producers, Tan Takiwa and Koichi Murakami; Director, Toshio Masuda; Screenplay, Koji Takada; Director of Photography, Kiyoshi Kitasaka; Music, Shinichiro Ikebe.

CAST: Hiroki Matsukata, Yukio Towake, Tomokazu Miura.

A Toei Co., Ltd. Production. Color. Anamorphic wide screen (?). 113 minutes. Released 1991.

U.S. VERSION: Distributor, if any, is undetermined.

The Great Wall / Shin no shikotei

("The First Emperor of Chin"). Producer, Masaichi Nagata; Director, Shigeo Tanaka; Screenplay, Fuji Yahiro; Director of Photography, Michio Takahashi; Editor, Tatsuji Nakashizu; Music, Akira Ifukube.

CAST: Shintaro Katsu (Emperor Shih Huang Ti), Fujiko Yamamoto (Princess Chu), Ken Utsui (Crown Prince Tan), Hiroshi Kawaguchi (Hsi Liang), Ayako Wakao (Chiang-nu), Kojiro Hongo (Li Hei), Raizo Ichikawa (Ching Ko), Ganjiro Nakamura (Hsu Fu), Eijiro Tono (Li Tang), Isuzu Yamada (dowager empress), Ken Mitsuda (Mencius), Junko Kano, Kazuo Hasegawa, Machiko Kyo.

A Daiei Motion Picture Co., Ltd. Production. Technicolor. Super Technirama 70. Six-track magnetic stereo sound. Filmed on location in Taiwan. 200 minutes. Later released at 160 minutes. Released November 1, 1962.

Sid and Marty Krofft-esque thrills in Kinji Fukasaku's nutty *The Green Slime* (1968).

U.S. VERSION: Released by Magna Pictures. English-dubbed. A Marshall Naify Presentation. Dubbing Director, Brett Morrison. Some footage may have been filmed in DaieiScope and blown up to 70mm. 120 minutes. No MPAA rating. Released September 1965. Reissued running 104 minutes.

The Green Horizon / Afurika monogatari ("Africa Story"). Executive Producer, Shintaro Tsuji; Producers, Terry Ogisu and Yoichi Matsue; Directors, Susumu Hani and Simon Trevor; Screenplay, Shintaro Tsuji, based on an original story by Shuji Terayama; Director of Photography, Simon Trevor; Sound Recording, Jim Lynch; Editor, Nobuhiko Hosaka; Animal Trainers, Jill Woodley and John Seago; Assistant Director, Harry Hook; Music, Naozumi Yamamoto.

CAST: James Stewart (The Old Man), Phillip Sayer (The Man), Kathy [Cathleen Karen McOsker] (The Girl), Eleanora Vallone (The Woman), Heekura Simba (The Elder).

A Sanrio Production. A Toho Co., Ltd. Release. Filmed in Kenya. A Japanese production in English. Color. Spherical wide screen. 114 minutes. Released 1980.

U.S. VERSION: Apparently never released theatrically in the United States. International titles: *Afurika monogatari* and *A Tale of Africa*. Released to home video in 1981 as *The Green Horizon*. 120 minutes. No MPAA rating.

Green Light to Joy / Chichiko gusa ("Weed of Father and Son"). Director, Seiji Muruyama.

CAST: Kiyoshi Atsumi, Tetsuo Ishidate, Keiko Awaji, Yuriko Hoshi, Jun Hamamura.

A Toho Co., Ltd. Production. Black and white. Toho Scope. Released 1966.

U.S. VERSION: Released by Toho International Co., Ltd. English subtitles. 85 minutes. No MPAA rating. Released January 1967.

The Green Slime / Gamma sango uchu dai sakusen ("Gamma

III Space Big Military Operation"). Producers Ivan Reiner, Walter H. Manley, Kaname Ohgisawa, Koji Ohta; Director, Kinji Fukasaku; Screenplay, Charles Sinclair, William Finger, Tom Rowe, Takeo Kaneko; Story, Ivan Reiner; Script Assistants (Script Supervisors), Jacqueline Vaanice, Yasuyo Yamanouchi; Story, Ivan Reiner; Associate Producer, William Ross; Music, Toshiaki Tsushima; Title Song and Additional Music, Charles Fox; Director of Photography, Yoshikazu Yamasawa; Sound Recordist, Yoshio Watanabe; Editor, Osama Tanaka; Assistant to the Producer, Michie Ross; Art Director, Shinichi Eno; Costumes, Mami; Lighting, Shigeru Umetani; Set Decoration, Tasaburo Matsumo; Assistant Director, Kazuhiko Yamaguchi; Makeup, Takeshi Ugai; Special Effects, Nihon Special Effects Co., Ltd.; Special Effects Director and Art Director, Akira Watanabe; Special Effects Cameraman, Yukio Manoda.

CAST: Robert Horton (Commander Jack Rankin), Richard Jaeckel (Commander Vince Elliot), Luciana Paluzzi (Dr. Lisa Benson), Bud Widom (Chief of Staff General Jonathan Thompson), Ted Gunther (Station Space Consultant [sic] Dr. Hans Halversen), Robert Dunham (Captain Martin), David Yorston (Lieutenant Curtis), William Ross (Ferguson), Gary Randolf (Cordier), Richard Hylland (Assistant Station Space Consultant Michaels), Jack Morris (Lieutenant Morris), Carl Bengs (rocket pilot), Tom Scott (Sergeant Scott), Eugene Vince, Dan Plante (technicians), Enver Altenby, Gunther Greve, George Uruf (USNC technicians), Linda Hardisty, Cathy Horlan, Ann Ault, Susan Skersick, Helen Kirkpatrick, Linda Miller, Patricia Elliot (nurses), Linda Malson (USNC technician). Strong Ilimaiti (USNC doctor), Tom Conrad (sergeant) Arthur Stark (Barnett), David Sentman (officer), Clarence Howard (patient), Lynne Frederickson (Thompson's secretary), Hans Jorgseeberger (soldier #1), Bob Morris (soldier #2).

A Ram Films, Inc. and Southern Cross Films Production, in association with Toei Co., Ltd., and Lum Film. A Japanese/U.S./Italian co-production. Filmed at Toei-Tokyo Studios. Westrex Recording System. Fujicolor (processed by Toei Chemistry Co., Ltd.). ToeiScope. 77 minutes. Released December 1968.

U.S. VERSION: Released by Metro-Goldwyn-Mayer, Inc. English-dubbed. Prints by Metrocolor. Widescreen process advertised as Panavision, and in fact Panavision lenses may have used. Working and international title: *Battle Beyond the Stars*. U.K. Title (?): *Death and the Green Slime*. The fourth in Ivan Reiner's space series, preceded by *Space Devils* (1966), *The Wild, Wild, Planet* (1966), and *War Between the Planets* (1967), all U.S./Italian co-productions. 90 minutes. MPAA Rating: "G." U.S. premiere date: December 1, 1968. General release, May 21, 1969.

Gulliver's Travels Beyond the Moon / Gulliver no uchu ryoko ("Gulliver's Space Travels") **[animated]**. Producer, Hiroshi Okawa; Director, Yoshio Kuroda; Screenplay, Shinichi Sekizawa, based characters created in the novel *Gulliver's Travels* by Jonathan Swift; Animation Director, Hideo Furusawa.

VOICE CHARACTERIZATIONS: (unavailable).

A Toei Co., Ltd. Production. Color. Spherical wide screen. Released 1965.

U.S. VERSION: Released by Continental Distributing, Inc. English-dubbed. Music, Milton DeLugg and Anne DeLugg. SONGS: "I Wanna Be Like Gulliver!" "The Earth Song," "That's the Way It Goes," "Keep Your Hopes High," Music and Lyrics by Milton DeLugg and Anne DeLugg. 85 minutes. No MPAA rating. Released August 1966. Reissued in 1975.

Gunhed / Ganhedo ("Gunhed"). Executive Producers, Tomoyuki Tanaka, Eiji Yamamura, and Tetsuhisa Yamada; Director, Masato Harada; Screenplay, Masato Harada and James Bannon; Director of Photography, Junichi Fujisawa; Editor, Fumio Ogawa; Music, Toshiyuki Honda; Sound Effects, Toho Sound Effects Group. *Toho Special Effects Group*: Producer, Yasuo Nishi; Director, Koichi Kawakita; Director of Photography, Kenichi Eguchi; Optical Photography,

Does anyone out there still have a miniature H-man? And just what *is* a miniature H-Man anyway? From *The H-Man* (1958).

Masanori Nakamura; Art Directors, Naoyuki Yoshimura and Tetsuzo Ozawa; Lighting, Kaoru Saito; Wire Manipulation, Koji Matsumoto; Pyrotechnics, Tadaaki Watanabe; Assistant Director, Kiyotaka Matsumoto; Mechanical Design, Shoji Kawamori, Masaharu Ogawa and the Ogawa Modeling Group. Special Mechanical Effects, Noburo Watanabe; Animation, Keita Amamiya; Computer Graphics, Fumio Ohi and Yu Tsuchiya; Matte Paintings, Nobuaki Koga; Production Coordinators, Hiroshi Yamaguchi and Koji Ishihashi.

CAST: Masahiro Takashima (Brooklyn), Brenda Bakke (Sergeant Nim), Yujin Harada (Seven), Kaori Mizushima (Eleven), Aya Enjoji (Bebe), Mickey Curtis (Bancho), James B. Thompson (Balba [Barabbas]), Doll Nguyen (Boomerang), Jay Kabira (Bombay), Randy Reyes (voice of Gunhed), Michael Yancy (narrator).

A Toho Co., Ltd./Sunrise Co., Ltd. Production. A Toho Co., Ltd. Release. Color (processed by Tokyo Laboratory, Ltd.). Spherical wide screen. Dolby Stereo/TKL Stereo. 100 minutes. Released July 22, 1989.

U.S. VERSION: Unreleased in the United States as this book went to press. Released in Great Britain in 1994.

The H-Man / Bijo To Ekitai-Ningen ("Beauty and the Liquid People"). Producer, Tomoyuki Tanaka; Director, Ishiro Honda; Screenplay, Takeshi Kimura; Story, Hideo Kaijo; Art Director, Takeo Kita; Director of Photography, Hajime Koizumi; Editor, Ichiji Taira; Music, Masaru Sato; Sound, Choshichiro Mikami, Masanobu Mikami; Sound Recording, Toho Dubbing Theatre; Sound Effects, Toho Sound Effects Group; Production Manager, Teruo Maki; Assistant Directors, Koji Kajita and Yoshio Nakamura; Lighting, Tsuruzo Nishikawa. *Toho Special Effects Group:* Director, Eiji Tsuburaya; Photography, Hidesaburo Araki and Teisho Arikawa; Art Director, Akira Wanatabe; Lighting, Kuichiro Kishida; Optical Printing, Hiroshi Mukoyama.

CAST: Yumi Shirakawa (Chikako Arai), Kenji Sahara (Dr. Masada), Akihiko Hirata (Inspector Tominaga), Makoto Sato (Uchida), Koreya Senda (Dr. Maki), Yoshio Tsuchiya (Detective Taguchi), Yoshifumi Tajima (Detective Sakata), Eitaro Ozawa (Inspector Miyashita), Ayumi Sonoda (Emi), Toshiko Nakano (Okami, *the landlady*), Yosuke Natsuki (man who witnesses auto accident), Kamayuki Tsubouchi (Detective Ogawa), Minosuke Yamada (Officer Wakasugi), Jun Fujiro (Nishiyama), Akira Sera (Yasukichi), Naomi Shiraishi (Mineko), Nadao Kirino (Shimazaki), Hisaya Ito (Misaki), Shin Otomo (Hamano), Machiko Kitagawa (Hanae), Tetsu Nakamura (Chinese gentleman), Yutaka Nakayama (An-chan), Senkichi Omura (Oh-chan), Haruya Kato (Matsu-chan), Ko Mishima (Kishi), Kan Hayashi, Mitsuo Tsuda, Akio Kuama (Police Officers), Yutaka Sada (driver who strikes Misaki), Ren Yamamoto (gangster), Tadao Nakamaru (detective), Haruo Nakajima (sailor).

A Toho Co., Ltd. Production. Western Electric Mirrophonic recording (encoded with Perspecta Stereophonic Sound). Eastman Color (processed by Far East Laboratories, Ltd.). Toho Scope. 87 minutes. Released June 24, 1958.

U.S. VERSION: Released by Columbia Pictures Corp. English-dubbed. Dubbing Cast, Paul Frees, and others unidentified. Perspecta Stereophonic Sound (Westrex Recording System). Prints by Pathé. Double-billed with *Womaneater* (Columbia, 1959). 79 minutes. No MPAA rating. Released May 28, 1959.

Hachi-ko / Hachi-ko monogatari ("The Hachi-ko Story"). Producer, Kazuyoshi Okuyama; Director, Seijiro Koyama; Screenplay, Kaneto Shindo; Director of Photography, Masahisa Himeda; Music, Tetsuji Hayashi.

CAST: Tatsuya Nakadai (Professor Ueno), Kaoru Yachigusa (Shizuko), Mako Ishino (Chizuko), Toshiro Yanagiba (Moriyama), Toshinori Obi (Saikichi), Hiroyuki Nagato (Kiku), Hisashi Igawa.

A Tokyu Group/Mitsui Co., Ltd./ Shochiku Group Production. A Shochiku Co., Ltd. Release. Spherical wide screen. 107 minutes. Released 1987.

U.S. VERSION: Released by Shochiku Films of America, Inc. English subtitles. 107 minutes. No MPAA rating. Released 1988 (?).

Half a Loaf... / Yoku ("Desire"). Director, Heinosuke Gosho.

CAST: Junzaburo Ban, Yukiko Todoroki.

A Shochiku Co., Ltd. Production. Black and white (processed by Shochiku Laboratory). Shochiku GrandScope. 106 minutes. Released 1958.

U.S. VERSION: Released by Shochiku Films of America, Inc. English subtitles. No MPAA rating. 106 minutes. Released 1958.

Half Human: The Story of the Abominable Snowman / Jujin Yukiotako ("Abominable Snowman"). Producer, Tomoyuki Tanaka; Associate Producer, Minoru Sakamoto; Director, Ishiro Honda; Screenplay, Takeo Murata; Original Story, Shigeru Kayama; Director of Photography, Tadashi Iimura; Art Director, Takeo Kita; Lighting, Soichi Yokoi; Assistant Director, Kihachi Okamoto; Music, Masaru Sato; Sound, Yoshio Nishikawa; Sound Effects, Toho Sound Effects Group; Recording, Toho Dubbing Theatre. *Toho Special Effects Group*: Director, Eiji Tsuburaya; Optical

Lurid ad for *Half Human* (1955). Note the spelling of the producer's name. (Ad mat courtesy Ted Okuda.)

Photography, Hiroshi Mukoyama; Art Director, Akira Watanabe; Lighting, Masao Shirota.

CAST: Akira Takarada (Takeshi Ijima [The Boy]), Akemi Negishi (Chika [The Mountain Girl]), Momoko Kochi (Machiko Takeno [The Girl]), Kenji Kasahara (Shinsuke Takeno), Nobuo Nakamura (Professor Tanaka), Yoshio Kosugi (Oba), Kokuten Kodo (old man), Yasuhisa Tsutsumi (Kodama), Sachio Sakai (Norikata), Ren Yamamoto (Shinagawa), Koji Suzuki (Kurehara), Akira Sera (Matsui), Senkichi Omura (peasant).

A Toho Co., Ltd. Production. Western Electric Mirrophonic soundtrack. Black and white. Academy ratio. 95 minutes. Released August 14, 1955.

U.S. VERSION: Released by Distributors Corporation of America. English narration (for Japanese footage). Associate Producer, Robert B. Homel; Director/Editor, Kenneth G. Crane; Assistant Director, Hal Klein; Director of Photography, Lucien Andriot; Sound, Jack Wiler; Casting Supervisor, Lynn Stalmaster; Art Director, Nicholai Remisoff; Master of Properties, Sam Heiligman; Script Supervisor, Frances Steene; Wardrobe, Morrie Friedman. "The segments of this this picture depicting Japanese peoples and locales were written and filmed in Japan. Special credit is due the artists and technicians there who contributed much to the authenticity of this production." (!) New footage shot for 1.85 x 1 cropping, and cut with 1.33:1 Japanese footage. Double-billed with *Monster from Green Hell* (DCA, 1958). International title: *Monster Snowman*. 63 minutes (despite some sources' claims the picture runs 70 and even 78 minutes). No MPAA rating. Released December 1958 (though possibly released on a limited basis in 1957). Additional Cast for U.S. Version: John Carradine (Dr. John Rayburn), Russell Thorsen (Professor Phillip Osborne), Robert Karnes (Professor Alan Templeton), Morris Ankrum (Dr. Carl Jordan).

Happiness of Us Alone / Namonaku mazushiku utsukushiku

("Unknown, Poor, and Beautiful"). Producers, Sanezumi Fujimoto and Kenichiro Tsunoda; Director/Screenplay, Zenzo Matsuyama; Director of Photography, Masao Tamai; Art Directors, Satoru Nakakao and Takeshi Kano; Editor, Y. Sabura; Music, Hikaru Hayashi; Sound Recording, Kenji Nakaoka.

CAST: Hideko Takamine (Akiko Katayama), Keiju Kobayashi (Michio Katayama), Izumi Hara (Akiko's mother), Yoichi Numata (Akiko's brother), Mitsuko Kusabue (Akiko's sister), Yuzo

Kayama (Akira), Kamatari Fujiwara, Chieko Nakakita, Jun Tatara, Takeshi Kato, Momoko Kochi.

A Tokyo Eiga Co., Ltd. Production. A Toho Co., Ltd. Release. Black and white. Toho Scope. 130 minutes. Released January 15, 1961.

U.S. VERSION: Released by Toho International Co., Ltd. English subtitles. Alternate Title: *Nameless, Poor, Beautiful.* 114 minutes. No MPAA rating. Released August 14, 1962.

The Happy Pilgrimage II / Yajikita dochu sugoroku ("The Happy Pilgrimage"). Producers, Masumi Fujimoto and Shiro Yamamoto; Director, Yasuki Chiba; Screenplay, Ryozo Kasahara, based on the story by Ikku Juppensha; Director of Photography, Rokuro Nishigaki; Art Directors, Takeo Kita and Kiyoshi Shimizu; Music, Yuji Koseki.

CAST: Daisuke Kato (Yaji-san), Keiju Kobayashi (Kita-san), Musei Tokugawa (Ikku Juppensha), Nobuko Otowa (Yaji-san's wife), Keiko Awaji (Kita-san's wife), Koji Tsuruta (Tsuru-san).

A Toho Co., Ltd. Production. Eastman Color. Toho Scope. 117 minutes. Released December 7, 1958.

U.S. VERSION: Release undetermined, possibly by Toho International Co., Ltd. in subtitled format. Information on *The Happy Pigrimage* (1958) [?] was unavailable.

Happy Wedding / Oishii Kekkon ("Delicious Wedding"). Producer, Sadatoshi Fujimine; Director/Screenplay, Yoshimitsu Morita, based on an original story by Yo Matsumoto; Director of Photography, Yonezo Maeda; Music, Soichi Noriki.

CAST: Yoshiko Mita, Yuki Saito, Toshiaki Karasawa.

A Toho Co., Ltd. Production. Color. Spherical wide screen. 110 minutes. Released 1991.

U.S. VERSION: Distributor, if any, is undetermined.

Harakiri / Seppuku ("Harakiri"). Producer, Tatsuo Hosoya; Assistant Producer, Ginichi Kishimoto; Director Masaki Kobayashi; Screenplay, Shinobu Hashimoto, based on the story "Ibunronin ki," in *Sandi mainichi* (August 24, 1958) by Yasuhiko Takiguchi; Director of Photography, Yoshio Miyajima; Lighting, Shojiro Kambara; Art Directors, Junichi Ozumi and Shigemasa Toda; Editor, Hisashi Sagara; Music, Toru Takemitsu; Sound Recording, Hideo Nishizaki; Fencing Master, Seiji Iho.

CAST: Tatsuya Nakadai (Hanshiro Tsugumo), Shima Iwashita (Miho Tsugumo), Akira Ishihama (Motome Chijiiwa), Yoshio Inaba (Jinai Chijiiwa), Rentaro Mikuni (Kageyu Saito), Masao Mishima (Tango Inaba), Tetsuro Tamba (Hikokuro Omodaka), Ichiro Nakaya (Hayato Yazaki), Yoshio Aoki (Umenosuke Kawabe), Jo Azumi (Ichiro Shimmen), Hisashi Igawa, Shoji Kobayashi, and Ryo Takeuchi (young samurai), Shichisaburo Amatsu (page), Kei Sato (Masakazu Fukushima).

A Shochiku Co., Ltd. Production. Black and white. Shochiku GrandScope. 134 minutes. Released 1962.

U.S. VERSION: Released by Shochiku Films of America, Inc. English subtitles. 130 minutes. No MPAA rating. Released December 1963.

Harbor Light Yokohama / Kiri ni musebu yoru ("Foggy Night"). Associate Producers, Hideo Sasai and Kon Hirata; Director, Meijiro Umezu; Screenplay, Isao Mori and Hisashi Aku; Director of Photography, Kazumi Hamazaki; Editor, Teruo Nakajima; Music, Jun Suzuki; Sound Recording, Meguro Studio, Ltd.

CAST: Asahi Kurizuka (Akira Taki), Yuki Jono (Reiko Machida), Hiroshi Yamanami (Joji), Ken Kuroki (Ken), Ryohei Uchida (Shuhei Isshiki), Ichiro Sugai (Otaguro), Toru Abe (Ichizo Uchiyama), Eriko Sono (Naomi), Michiko Yajima (Mina), Nakajiro Tomita, Hiroshi Wada, Kuniko Ogata, Akiko Nakamura, Ken Yamanouchi.

A Shochiku Co., Ltd. Production. Color. Shochiku GrandScope (?). Released December 1968.

U.S. VERSION: Released by Shochiku

Films of America, Inc. English subtitles. 91 minutes. No MPAA rating. Released February 1970.

Harp of Burma see *The Burmese Harp*

Haru kuru oni ("The Demon Comes in Spring"). Producer, Kazuo Inoue; Director, Akira Kobayashi; Screenplay, Ryuzo Kikushima, based on an original story by Tokuhei Suji; Director of Photography, Yoshikatsu Suzuki; Music, Masaru Sato.

CAST: Toshiro Mifune, Masaru Matsuda, Sakae Takita, Hajime Hana.

An Arrow Enterprises, Inc. Production. A Shochiku Co., Ltd. Release. Color. Panavision (?). 137 minutes. Released 1989.

U.S. VERSION: Release undetermined, possibly by Shochiku Films of America, Inc. in subtitled format. No MPAA rating.

The Haunted Castle / Hiroku kaibyoden ("Secret Memoir: The Legend of the Monster Cat"). Executive Producer, Akihiko Murai; Producer, Masaiachi Nagata; Director Tokuzo Tanaka; Screenplay, Shozaburo Asai; Director of Photography, Hiroshi Imai; Assistant Director, Rikio Endo; Art Director, Seiichi Ota; Editor, Hiroshi Yamada; Music, Chumei Watanabe; Sound Recording, Yukio Kaibara; Sound, Daiei Recording Studio.

CAST: Kojiro Hongo (Hanzaemon), Naomi Kobayashi (Lady Toyo Nabeshima), Mitsuyo Kamei (Sayo), Mutsuhiro Toura (chamberlain), Koichi Uenoyama (Lord Nabeshima), Akihisa Toda (Monk Matashichiro), Akane Kawasaki, Natsuko Oka, Ikuko Mori, Yusaku Terajima, Shozo Nanbu, Shintaro Nanjo, Kazue Tamaki, Shosaku Sugiyama, Seishiro Hara.

A Daiei Motion Picture Co., Ltd. Production. A Masaichi Nagata Presentation. Westrex recording system. Fujicolor (processed by Daiei Laboratory). DaieiScope. 83 minutes. Released 1969.

U.S. VERSION: Released by Daiei International Films, Inc. English subtitles. International title: *Mystery of the Cat-Woman*. No MPAA rating. 83 minutes. Released December 20, 1969.

Haunted Gold / Goyo kiba—Oni no Hanzo yawa koban ("Gold Coins, Soft Flesh and Hanzo's Ghost"). Director, Yoshio Inoue; Screenplay, Yasuzo Masumura.

CAST: Shintaro Katsu (Hanzo), Mako Midori, Ko Nishimura, Mikio Narita, Asao Koike.

A Toho Co., Ltd. Production. Color (processed by Tokyo Laboratory Ltd.). Panavision (?). 84 minutes. Released 1974.

U.S. VERSION: Distributor, if any, is undetermined.

He Had to Die / Onryo sakura dai-sodo ("Ghost Sakura's Big Strife"). Producer, Mitsugu Okura; Director, Kunio Watanabe; Screenplay, Kunio Watanabe, based on an original story by Yoshihiro Takenaka; Director of Photography, Takashi Watanabe.

CAST: Kanjuro Arashi, Shoji Nakayama, Joji Oka, Minoru Takada, Ranko Hanai.

A Shintoho Co., Ltd. Production. Western Electric Mirrophonic recording. Black and white. Shintoho-Scope (?). 103 minutes. Released 1957.

U.S. Version:. Distributor, if any, is undetermined.

The Heart / Kokoro ("Heart"). Producer, Masayuki Takagi; Director, Kon Ichikawa; Screenplay, Masato Inomata and Keiji Hasebe, based on a story by Soseki Natsume; Director of Photography, Takeo Ito; Music, Yasushi Akutagawa; Art Director, Kazumi Koike; Lighting, Ko Fujibayashi; Sound Recording, Fumio Hashimoto.

CAST: Masayuki Mori (Nobuchi), Michiyo Aratama (his wife), Tatsuya Mihashi (Kaji), Shoji Yasui (Hioki).

A Nikkatsu Corp. Production. Black and white. Academy ratio. Running time undetermined. Released August 31, 1955.

U.S. VERSION: Distributor, if any, is undetermined.

The Heart of Hiroshima / Ai to shi no kiroku ("Record of Love and Death"). Director, Koreyoshi Kurahara.

CAST: Tetsuya Watari, Sayuri Yoshinaga, Tomoko Hamakawa, Asao Sano.

A Nikkatsu Corporation Production. Color (?). NikkatsuScope (?). Released 1966.

U.S. VERSION: Released by Toho International Co., Ltd. English subtitles. Running time undetermined. No MPAA rating. Released May 1967.

Hearts and Flowers for Tora-san / Otoko wa tsuraiyo—Torajiro ajisai no koi ("It's Tough to Be a Man—Heart and Flowers for Torajiro"). Producer, Kiyoshi Shimazu; Director, Yoji Yamada; Screenplay, Yoji Yamada and Yoshitaka Asama, based on characters created by Yoji Yamada; Director of Photography, Tetsuo Takaba; Music, Naozumi Yamamoto.

CAST: Kiyoshi Atsumi (Torajiro "Tora-san" Kuruma), Chieko Baisho (Sakura Suwa, *his sister*), Nizaemon Kataoka (a famous ceramist), Ayumi Ishida (his maid).

A Shochiku Co., Ltd. Production. Color. Shochiku GrandScope. 110 minutes. Released 1982.

U.S. VERSION: Released by Shochiku Films of America, Inc. English subtitles. The 29th "Tora-san" feature. Followed by *Tora-san, the Expert* (1982). 110 minutes. No MPAA rating. Released December 24, 1982.

Heat and Mud / Netsudeichi ("Heated Mud"). Producer, Tomoyuki Tanaka; Director, Kon Ichikawa; Screenplay, Kon Ichikawa and Ryoichi Itaya, based on the novel by Soju Kimura; Director of Photography, Minoru Yokoyama.

CAST: Susumu Fujita (Kurita), Harue Tone (Katsumi), Yuji Hori (Ogoshiba), Eijiro Tono (Chiba).

A Shintoho Co., Ltd. Production. Black and white. Academy ratio. 90 minutes. Released May 1, 1950.

U.S. VERSION: Distributor, if any, is undetermined. Running time of current Japanese version: 62 minutes. Alternate title: *The Hot Marshland.*

Heat-Haze Theatre / Kagero-za ("Heat Haze Theatre"). Producer, Genjiro Arato; Director, Seijun Suzuki; Screenplay, Yozo Tanaka, based on the novel by Kyoka Izumi; Director of Photography, Kazue Nagatsuka; Art Director, Noriyoshi Ikeya; Editor, Akira Suzuki; Music, Kaname Kawachi; Assistant Director, Koichi Shiraishi.

CAST: Yusaku Matsuda (Shunko Matsuzaki), Michiyo Okusu (Shinako), Katsuo Nakamura (Tamawaki), Yoshio Harada (Wada), Eriko Kusuda (Ine), Mariko Kaga (Miyo), Guytaro Otommo (Shisho).

A Cinema Placet Production. Color. Spherical wide screen (1.66:1). 139 minutes. Released 1981.

U.S. VERSION: Released by Genjiro Arato Pictures. English subtitles. The second in Suzuki's "Taisho Trilogy," and followed by *Yumeji* (1991). 139 minutes. No MPAA rating. Released 1993.

Heat Wave Island / Kagero ("Heat Haze"). Director, Kaneto Shindo; Screenplay, Kaneto Shindo and Isao Seki; Director of Photography, Kiyomi Kuroda; Art Director, Tokumichi Igawa; Music, Hikaru Hayashi.

CAST: Nobuko Otowa (Otoyo), Masako Tomiyama (Michiko), Mutsuhiro Toura (Chief Detective Oishi), Kozo Yamamura (Nakanishi), Takeshi Yoshizawa (Hori), Juzo Itami.

A Kindai Eiga Kyokai Production. A Shochiku Co., Ltd. Production. Black and white. Shochiku GrandScope. 102 minutes. Released October 29, 1969.

U.S. VERSION: Distributor undetermined, likely Shochiku Films of America, Inc. English subtitles. 102 minutes. No MPAA rating. Release date undetermined.

Heaven and Earth / Ten to chi to ("Heaven and Earth"). Executive Producer/Director, Haruki Kadokawa; Producer, Yutaka Okada; Line Producer, Yitaka Shingura; Associate Producer, Hisao Maru; Screenplay, Haruki Kadokawa, Toshio Kamata, and Isao Yoshihara;

Story, Chogoro Kaionji; Director of Photography, Yonezo Maeda; Production Designer, Hiroshi Tokuda; Editors, Akira Suzuki and Robert C. Jones; Costume Designer, Yono Tashibo; Sound, Tetsuo Segawa; Music, Tetsuya Segawa; Music Producers, Haruki Kadokawa and Ko Ishikawa; Production Consultants, Takashi Ohashi and Hiroshi Sugawara; Gaffer, Kazuo Yabe; Property Master, Yuki Sato; Script Supervisor, Nikkio Koyama; First Assistant Director, Mitsuyuki Yakishiji; Second Assistant Directors, Yasuhide Kidota, Fumio Inoue, Shinichi Higashida, and Masahieo Sakurai; First Assistant Camera, Hiroshi Takase; Second Assistant Camera, Shuji Kuriyama, Shogo Ueno, and Minoru Ishiyama; Best Boys, Seichi Takayanegi, Mitsuro Ogawa, Junichi Akatsu, Akihido Nemoto, and Noriyuki Obara; Grip, Tabaharu Hasezawa; Sound Assistants, Yutaka Tsurumaki, Atashi Nakamura, and Fusao Yuwaki; Art Director, Kazuhido Fujiwara; Art Department Assistants, Takeo Tanaka, Kunihido Yahimi, Hisao Inagaki, and Yukiharu Seshimo; Assistant Editor, Shizuo Arakawa; Production Managers, Junichi Sakai, Kenji Miyagawa; Wardrobe, Yoshio Ninomiya; Makeup, Shigeo Tamura; Fight Coordinator, Hiroshi Kuze; Horse Wranglers, Yoshihiko Kawamura and Shigemitsu Tanaka; Titles, Sekio Kaneda. *Canada*: Production Supervisor, Douglas MacLeod; Production Manager, Tom Dent-Duc; Assistant Director, Bill Bannerman; Stunt and Horse Coordinator, John Scott; Wardrobe Supervisor, Wendy Partridge; Assistant Production Manager, Anisa Lalani; Unit Manager, Murray Ord; Third Assistant Directors, Andy Nikita, Greg Zenon, Miles Gobovitch, Collin Leadlay, and Enid Sagurjonsson; Fight Coordinator, Jean-Pierre Rournier; Production Coordinator, Cathy Yost; Production Assistant, Heather Meehan; Production Accountant, Marilyn Moyer; Camera Operators, Roger Vernon and Ian Matheson; First Assistant Camera, Martin McNally and Rock Whitney; Second Assistant Camera, Jim Stacey and Dale Jahraus; Gaffer, Robert "Bruno" Bittner; Key Grip, Ivan Hawkes; Special Effects Supervisor, Stewart Bradley; Stunt Coordinator, Brent Woolsey; Propmaster, Marc Green; Assistant Propmaster, Dean Goodine; Samurai Costumes, Momentum Manufacturing, Ltd.; Assistant Wardrobe Supervisor, D. Lynne MacKay; Sets and Props Construction, P & D Scene Changes, Ltd.; Construction Coordinator, Bruce Robinson; Construction Supervisor, Dave Stevens; Head Carpenter, Warren Sims; Caterer, Filmworks Catering, Inc.; Catering Coordinator, David McLeod; Unit Publicists, Lawrence Weinburg and Tom Gray; Interpreters, Maree Strachan, Mike Nichoson (Nicholson?), Heger White, and Keiko Yagi; Medical Services Coordinator, Jane Thompson Vielleux; Assistant to John Scott, Jody Scott; Wrangler Coordinator, Tom Bews; Assistants to Tom Bews: George Cunningham, Ray Breckenridge, and T.J. Lewis; Transportation Coordinator, Coleman Robinson; Transportation Captain, Dennis Fugh; Camera Equipment, Panavision Canada, Inc.; Lighting/Grip Equipment, Canadian Prolite, Inc.; Special Thanks, W.O. Marsden (director, Film Industry Development, Province of Alberta, Canada), Laura Forsythe, David Parker, Chief John Snow, Jr., Lloyd Phillips, and the people of Goldnary, Okotoks, Whiskey Gap, Indian Bands of Hoadley (all Alberta, Canada).

CAST: Takaaki Enoki (Kenshin Uefugi), Masahiko Tsugawa (Takeda), Tsunehiko Watase (Usami), Atsuko Asano (Nami), Naomi Zaizen (Yae), Binpachi Ito (Katizaki), Isao Natsuyagi (Kansuke), Akira Hamada (Nabe), Masataka Naruse (Okuma), Osamu Yayama (Irobe), Takeshi Obayashi (Murakami), Masayuki Sudo (Onikojima), Kaitaro Nozaki (Naya), Tatsuhiro Tomoi (Sone), Takuya Goto (Tokura), Satoshi Sadanaga (Akiyama), Hiranogui Nomura (Taro), Hideo Murota (Obu), Taro Ishida (Tenkyu), Hiroyuki Onita (Kosaka), Akisayo Yamada (Hajikano), Morio Kazama (Imperial Messenger), Masato Ibu (Shoda), Yuki Kazamatsuri (Shoda's Wife), Kyoko Nishida (Servant), Hideo Ozaki (Musket Merchant), Guy Bews, Jerry Bremmer, Ryan Byrne, Yves Cameron, Dean Choe, Mike Crestejo, Norm Cuthbertson, Joe Dodds, John Dodds, Jim Dunn, Tom Eirikson (Erikson?), Jim Finkreiner, Michael Langlois, Mike Mitchell, Lyle

Lee Marvin and Toshiro Mifune in the interesting (if not entirely successful) *Hell in the Pacific* (1968).

Pambrun, Greg Schlosser, John Scott, Jim Shields, Dawn Stoffer-Rupp, Mike Vezina, Brent Woolsey (Stunts).

A Haruki Kadokawa Films, Inc. Production. A Haruki Kadokawa Presentation. Filmed on location in Alberta Canada (see above). Color (processed by Alpha Cine Laboratories, Inc.). Spherical Panavision. 119 minutes. Released 1990.

U.S. VERSION: Released by Triton. English subtitles. Additional Cast for U.S. Version: Stuart Whitman (narrator). 104 minutes. MPAA rating: "PG-13." Released February 1991.

Hell in the Pacific. Executive Producers, Selig J. Seligman and Henry G. Saperstein; Producer, Reuben Bercovitch; Director, John Boorman; Screenplay, Alexander Jacobs and Eric Bercovici; Story, Eric Bercovici; Director of Photography, Conrad Hall; Music, Lalo Schifrin; Editor, Thomas Stanford; Production Managers, Lloyd E. Anderson, Harry F. Hogan, and Isao Zeniya; Art Directors, Anthony D.G. Pratt and Masao Yamazaki; Assistant Director, Yoichi Matsue; Script Supervisor, John Franco; Production Assistant, B.C. "Doc" Wylie; Property Masters, Frank A. Wade and Kesataka Sato; Set Decorator, Makoto Kikuchi; Technical Adviser, Masaki Asukai; Technical Assistance, Trissen Enterprise S.A. (Tokyo); Camera Operator, Jordan Cronenweth; Key Grip, Arthur Brooker; Lighting, Harry Sundby; Communications, Bertil Hallberg; Special Effects, Joseph Zomar and Kunishige Tanaka; Sound Recording, Toru Sakata; Makeup, Shigeo Kobayashi; Recording Supervisors, Gordon E. Sawyer and Clem Portman; Assistant Editor, Neil Travis; Sound Effects, Frank E. Warner; Music Editor, James Henrikson; Sound, Samuel Goldwyn Studios (Hollywood).

CAST: Lee Marvin (The American Soldier), Toshiro Mifune (The Japanese Soldier).

A Selmur Pictures Corporation/Henry G. Saperstein Enterprises, Inc. Production. A U.S./Japanese co-production in English and Japanese. Filmed on location on Koror and other Palau Islands, Micronesia, and completed at Samuel Goldwyn Studios (Hollywood). Eastman Color. Panavision. Stereophonic sound. Westrex Recording System. Japanese title, running time and release date undetermined.

U.S. VERSION: Released by Cinerama Releasing Corporation. Prints by Technicolor. The Japanese ending is available on the letterboxed laserdisc version. Working titles: *Two Soldiers—East and West, Pacific War* and *The Enemy*. 103 minutes. MPAA rating: "G." Released December 18, 1968.

Hello, Kids! / Haro kidz ("Hello, Kids") **[documentary]**. Producer/Director/Screenplay/Music, Mariko Miyagi; Director of Photography, Kozo Okazaki.

WITH: Mariko Miyagi, Sadao Watanabe, Children of the Nemunoki School.

A Mariko Miyagi Production. Filmed on location in Harlem, New York City, and in Japan. Color. Academy ratio (?). 97 minutes. Released July 12, 1986.

U.S. VERSION: Distributor undetermined. 97 minutes. No MPAA rating. Released June 1986.

Hell's Tattooers / Tokugawa Irezumishi—Semejigoku ("Hell's Tattooers in the Tokugawa Period"). Director, Teruo Ishii; Screenplay, Teruo Ishii and Masahiro Kakefuda; Director of Photography, Motoya Washio; Art Director, Yoshimitsu Amamori; Music, Masao Yagi.

CAST: Teruo Yoshida (Horihide), Asao Koike (Horitatsu), Masumi Tachibana (Osuzu), Yumiko Katayama (Yumi), Mieko Fujimoto (Oryu), Haruo Tanaka (Samejima).

Toei Co., Ltd. Production. Eastman Color. ToeiScope. 95 minutes. Released May 3, 1969.

U.S. VERSION: Distributor, if any, is undetermined. English subtitled version available. No MPAA rating.

A Hen in the Wind / Kaze no naka no mendori ("A Hen in the Wind"). Director, Yasujiro Ozu; Screenplay, Yasujiro Ozu and Ryosuke Saito; Director of Photography, Yuharu Atsuta.

CAST: Kinuyo Tanaka, Shuji Sano, Kuniko Miyake, Chishu Ryu, Chieko Murata, Eijiro Tono, Koji Mitsuo.

A Shochiku Co., Ltd. Production. Filmed at Shochiku-Ofuna Studios. Black and white. Academy ratio. 90 minutes. Released September 20, 1948.

U.S. VERSION: Released by Shochiku Films of America, Inc. English subtitles. 90 minutes. No MPAA rating. Released 1975(?).

Hentai / Hentai ("Pervert"). Producer, Hidemaru Wushio; Director, Takashi Shiga.

CAST: Sayuri Sakurai, Masayoshi Nagami.

Production company undetermined. Black and white. Anamorphic wide screen. Released 1965 (?).

U.S. VERSION: Released by Olympic International Films. English subtitles (?). Producer, Felix Lomax. Wide screen process advertised as Centralscope in the United States. Alternate title: *Abnormal*. 71 minutes. No MPAA rating. Released September 2, 1966.

Her Brother / Ototo ("Brother"). Producer, Masaichi Nagata; Planning, Hiroaki Fujii; Director, Kon Ichikawa; Screenplay, Yoko Mizuki, based on a novel by Aya Koda; Director of Photography, Kazuo Miyagawa; Music, Yasushi Akutagawa; Sound Recording, Mitsuo Hasegawa; Art Director, Tomo Shimogawara; Lighting, Yukio Ito.

CAST: Keiko Kishi (Gen), Hiroshi Kawaguchi (Hekiro), Kinuyo Tanaka (mother), Masayuki Mori (father), Kyoko Kishida (Mrs. Tamura), Jun Hamamura (doctor), Noboru Nakaya (Patrolman Rokoru Shimizu).

A Daiei Motion Picture Co., Ltd. Production. Agfacolor. DaieiScope. 98 minutes. November 1, 1960.

U.S. VERSION: Distributor undetermined, though likely Daiei International Films, Inc. English subtitles. Alternate titles: *Little Brother* and *Younger Brother*. 98 minutes. No MPAA rating. Released 1960 (?).

The Hidden Fortress / Kakushi toride no san-akunin ("Three Bad Men in a Hidden Fortress"). Executive Producer, Tomoyuki Tanaka; Producers, Masumi Fujimoto and Akira Kurosawa; Director/Editor, Akira Kurosawa; Screenplay by Ryuzo Kikushima, Hideo Oguni, Shinobu Hashimoto, and Akira Kurosawa; Director of Photography, Kazuo Yamasaki; Lighting, Ichiro Inohara; Art Directors/Costumes, Yoshiro Muraki and Kohei Ezaki; Music, Masaru Sato; Sound Recording, Fumio Yanoguchi; Sound, Toho Dubbing Theatre; Sound Effects, Toho Sound Effects Group; Special Effects, Toho Special Effects Group.

CAST: Toshiro Mifune (General Rokurota Makabe), Misa Uehara (Princess Yukihime), Minoru Chiaki (Tahei), Kamatari Fujiwara (Matakishi), Takashi Shimura (General Izumi Nagakura), Susumu Fujita (General Hyoe Tadokoro), Eiko Miyoshi (lady-in-waiting), Toshiko Higuchi (girl), Kichijiro Ueda (slaver), Koji Mitsui (soldier), Rinsaku Ogata and Tadao Nakamaru (young men), Ikio Sawamura (gambling man), Shiten Ohashi (samurai buying horse), Kokuten Kodo (man at signboard), Takeshi Kato and Etsuro Saijo (stray soldiers), Yoshio Kosugi, Haruo Nakajima, Senkichi Omura (Akisuki soldiers waiting for fog), Shoichi Hirose (Yamana soldier), Toranosuke Ogawa (warrior), Yutaka Sada (guard at barrier gate), Shin Otomo (mounted samurai), Yutaka Nakayama, Makoto Sato, and Jiro Kumagai (foot soldiers), Akira Tani, Sachio Sakai (foot soldiers catching Rokurota), Takeo Oikawa, Yu Fujiki (soldiers at checking station), Yoshio Tsuchiya (mounted samurai of Hayakawa).

A Toho Co., Ltd. Production. Black and white (processed by Tokyo Laboratory, Ltd.). Toho Scope. Western Electric Mirrophonic recording (encoded with Perspecta Stereophonic Sound). 139 minutes. Released December 28, 1958.

U.S. VERSION: Released by Toho International Co., Ltd. English subtitles. 126 minutes. No MPAA rating. Released January 1962. Theatrical reissue and home video version restored (though monophonic). Video version letterboxed. Alternate title: *Three Bad Men in a Hidden Fortress*. The characters and story were the basis for *Star Wars* (1977).

High and Low / Tengoku to jigoku ("Heaven and Hell"). Executive Producers, Tomoyuki Tanaka and Ryuzo Kikushima; Producer/Director and Editor, Akira Kurosawa; Screenplay, Ryuzo Kikushima, Hideo Oguni, Eijiro Hisaita, and Akira Kurosawa, based on the novel *King's Ransom* (1959) by Ed McBain (i.e. Evan Hunter); Production Supervisor, Hiroshi Nezu; Directors of Photography, Asakazu Nakai and Takao Saito; Art Director, Yoshiro Muraki; Lighting, Ichiro Inohara; Music, Masaru Sato; Sound Recording, Hisashi Shimonaga; Sound, Toho Recording Centre; Sound Effects, Toho Sound Effects Group; Special Effects, Toho Special Effects Group; Assistant Director, Shiro Moritani.

CAST: Toshiro Mifune (Kingo Gondo), Kyoko Kagawa (Reiko Gondo), Tatsuya Mihashi (Kawanishi), Yutaka Sada (Aoki, *the chauffer*), Tatsuya Nakadai (Chief Inspector Tokuro), Takashi Shimura (police commisioner #1), Susumu Fujita (police commisioner #2), Kenjiro Ishiyama (Detective "Bos'n" Taguchi), Ko Kimura (Detective Arai), Takeshi Kato (Detective Nakao), Yoshio Tsuchiya (Detective Murata), Hiroshi Unayama (Detective Shimada), Koji Mitsui (reporter), Tsutomu Yamazaki (Ginjiro Takeuchi, *the kidnapper*), Jun Tazaki (Kamiya, *National Shoes publicity director*), Nobuo Nakamura (Ishimaru, *National Shoes design department director*), Yunosuke Ito (National Shoes director), Eijiro Tono (National Shoes factory worker), Ikio Sawamura (trolley man), Yoshifumi Tajima (prison guard), Kamatari Fujiwara (junk man), Senkichi Omura (man who gives kidnapper faked message), Minoru Chiaki (reporter).

A Kurosawa Films/Toho Co., Ltd. Production. A Toho Co., Ltd. Release. Black and white, with tinted insert. TohoScope. Western Electric Mirrophonic Recording (encoded with Perspecta Stereophonic Sound). Filmed at Toho Studios, Ltd., on location in Yokohama. 143 minutes. Released March 1, 1963.

U.S. VERSION: Released by Toho International Co., Ltd. English subtitles.

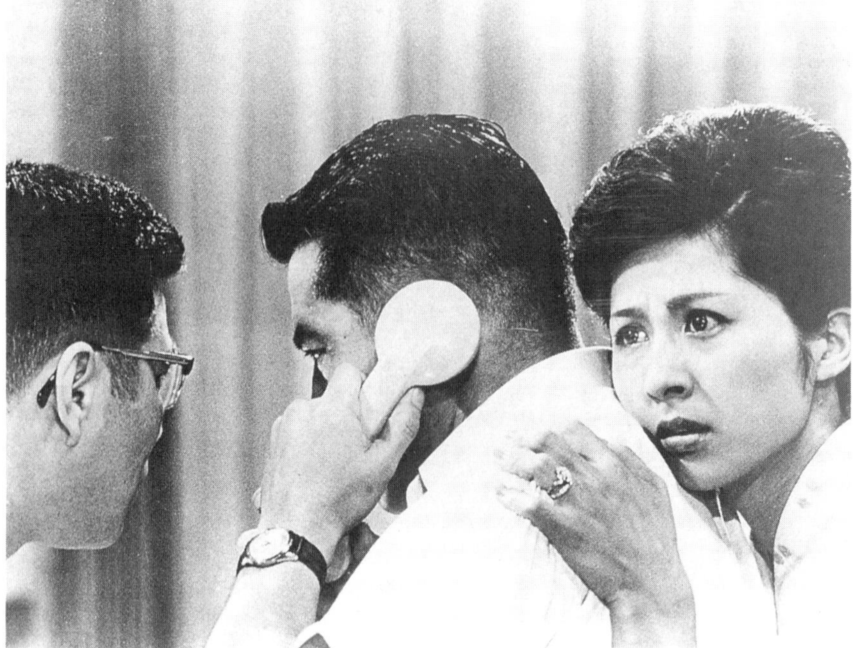

Tatsuya Mihashi, Toshiro Mifune, and Kyoko Kagawa listen to a kidnappers's demands in Kurosawa's *High and Low* (1963). (Photo courtesy Darrell Davis.)

subtitles, Herman G. Weinberg. Alternate titles: *Heaven and Hell* and *The Ransom*. 142 minutes. No MPAA rating. Released November 26, 1963. The AFI Catalog lists Continental as an additional distributor, possibly for reissue. Letterboxed laser-disc version available. Subtitles for reissue version, Audie Bock. Includes stock music from *The H-Man* (1958). An English-language remake has been announced.

High-School Outcasts / Koko sasuraiha ("High School Outcasts"). Director/Screenplay, Azuma Morisaki; Director of Photography, Kenichi Yoshikawa; Art Director, Kiminobu Sato; Music, Tomohiro Koyama.

CAST: Kensaku Morita (Tsutomu), Hideko Takehara (Kazuko), Norihiko Yamamoto (Yusuke), Chishu Ryu, Takashi Kanda.

A Shochiku Co., Ltd. Production. Eastman Color. Shochiku GrandScope. 86 minutes. December 16, 1971.

U.S. VERSION: Release undetermined, possibly by Shochiku Films of America, Inc. English subtitles. 86 minutes. No MPAA rating. Release date undetermined.

Hikarigoke ("Shiny Moss"). Producers, Taketoshi Naito, Toru Aizawa; Director, Kei Kumai; Screenplay, Taro Ikeda and Kei Kumai, based on the novel by Taijun Takeda; Production Designer, Takeo Kimura; Director of Photography, Masao Tochizawa; Editor, Osamu Inoue; Music, Teizo Matsumura; Sound, Kenichi Benitani.

CAST: Rentaro Mikuni (Captain/Headmaster), Eiji Okada (Nishikawa), Kunie Tanaka (Hachizo), Tetsuta Sugimoto (Gosuke), Taketoshi Naito (novelist), Hisashi Igawa (prosecutor), Masane Tsukayama (defense attorney), Chishu Ryu (presiding judge).

A Film Crescent/Neo-Life Production. Color. Widescreen. 118 minutes. Released 1991.

U.S. VERSION: Released by Herald Ace, Inc. English subtitles. 118 minutes. No MPAA rating. Released 1992.

Himatsuri ("Fire Festival"). Executive Producer, Kazuo Shimizu; Director, Mitsuo Yanagimachi; Screenplay, Kenji Nakagami; Director of Photography, Masaki Tamura; Art Director, Takeo Kimura; Lighting, Hitoshi Takaya; Music, Toru Takemitsu; Sound Recording, Yukio Kubota; Editor, Sachiko Yamaji; Assistant Director, Yusuke Narita.

CAST: Kinya Kitaoji (Tatsuo), Kiwako Taichi (Kimiko), Ryota Nakamoto (Ryota), Norihei Miki (Yamakawa), Rikiya Yasuoka (Toshio), Junko Miyashita (Sachiko, *Tatsuo's wife*), Kin Sugai (Tatsuo's mother), Sachiko Matsushita (Tatsuo's sister), Aoi Nakajima (Kimiko's sister), Kenzo Kaneko (her husband), Aiko Morishita (nursery school teacher).

A Production Gunro/Seibu Saison Group/Cine Saison Co., Ltd. Production. A Shibata Co., Ltd. Release. Color. Spherical wide screen. 120 minutes. Released 1985.

U.S. VERSION: Released by Kino International. English subtitles. 120 minutes. No MPAA rating. Released October 6, 1985.

Himiko ("Himiko"). Director, Masahiro Shinoda; Screenplay, Taeko Tomioka and Masahiro Shinoda; Director of Photography, Tatsuo Suzuki; Music, Toru Takemitsu.

CAST: Shima Iwashita, Masao Kusakari, Rentaro Mikuni, Rie Yokoyama, Yoshi Kato, Choichiro Kawarazaki.

A Hyogen-sha/Japan Art Theatre Guild, Ltd. Production. Eastman Color. Panavision (?). 100 minutes. Released 1974.

U.S. VERSION: Released by Toho International Co., Ltd. English subtitles. 100 minutes. No MPAA rating. Released February 23, 1979.

Hinotori ("Firebird"). Executive Producers, Kiichi Ichikawa, Kunihiko Murai; Director, Kon Ichikawa; Screenplay, Shuntaro Tanikawa; Story, Osamu Tezuka; Director of Photography, Kiyoshi Hasegawa; Special Effects Director, Teruyoshi Nakano; Animation Director, Osamu Tezuka; Animation, Tezuko Productions; Music, Michel Legrand and Jun Fukamachi; Sound, Toho Recording Centre; Sound Effects, Toho Sound Effects Group.

CAST: Tomisaburo Wakayama (Sarutohiko), Toshinori Omi (Nagi), Mieko Takamine (Himiko), Reiko Ohara (Hinaku), Ryuzo Hayashi (Guzuri), Masao Kusakari (Yumihiko), Kaoru Yumi (Uzume), Tatsuya Nakadai (Jingi).

A Toho Co., Ltd. Production. Color (processed by Tokyo Laboratory, Ltd.). Panavision. 137 minutes. Released August 19, 1978.

U.S. VERSION: Released by Toho International Co., Ltd. English subtitles. Advertised as *The Phoenix*. Alternate title: *The Firebird*. Sequel: *Hinotori-2772* (1980). 137 minutes. No MPAA rating. Released March 30, 1979.

Hinotori-2772 / Hinotori 2772 ai no Kosumozon ("Firebird 2772—Love of the Cosmos") **[animated]**. Producers, Kiichi Ichikawa and Susumu Akitagawa; Directors, Osamu Tezuka and Suguru Sugiyama; Screenplay, Osamu Tezuka and Suguru Sugiyama, based on an original story by Osamu Tezuka; Director of Photography, Iwao Yamaki; Art Directors, Tsuyoshi Matsumoto and Shinji Ito; Music, Yasuo Higuchi.

VOICE CHARACTERIZATIONS: (undetermined).

A Tezuka Production Co., Ltd. Production. A Toho Co., Ltd. Release. 94 minutes. Released 1980.

U.S. VERSION: Released by Toho International Co., Ltd. English subtitles. Alternate title: *Space Firebird 2772*. 94 minutes. No MPAA rating. Released July 13, 1982.

Hiroku onna ro ("Secret Record of a Woman's Prison"). Producer, Masaichi Nagata; Director, Akira Inoue; Screenplay, Shozaburo Asai; Art Director, Akira Naito; Director of Photography, Yasukazu Takemura; Editor, Hiroshi Yamada; Music, Takeo Watanabe; Sound Recording Supervisor, Masahiro Okumura; Sound, Daiei Recording Studio.

CAST: Michiyo Yasuda (Oshino), Sanae Nakahara (Otaki), Shigako Shimegi (Myonen), Mayumi Nigisa (Osaki), Machiko Hasegawa (Omatsu), Sei Hiraizumi

(Shinpachi Murase), Fumio Watanabe (Tatewaki Ishizu), Jotaro Sennami (Inokichi), Akifumi Inoue (Masugoro), Saburo Date (Kishino), Jun Hamamura (Gihei), Masako Mizuki (Otane), Naomi Kobayashi (Namie), Yusaku Terashima (old man in gambling den), Kazue Tamaki (Echizen-ya), Jun Katsumura (Tagawa), Ikuko Mori (Okane), Teruko Konoe (inn proprietess), Gen Kuroki (detective), Sumao Ishihara (stall owner).

A Daiei Motion Picture Co., Ltd. Production. A Masaichi Nagata Presentation. Filmed at Daiei-Kyoto Studios. Westrex recording system. Black and white (processed by Daiei Laboratory). DaieiScope. 96 minutes. Released 1968.

U.S. VERSION: Possibly released by Daiei International Films, Inc. English subtitles. International title: *Women's Prison*. Sequel: *Zoku hiroku onna ro* (1968).

Hiroshima / Hiroshima. Director, Hideo Sekigawa; Screenplay, Yasutaro Yagi, based on his story.

CAST: Yoshi Kato (Endo, *the father*), Eiji Ikada (Kitagawa, *the teacher*), Isuzu Yamada (Mine, *the mother*), Yasuaki Takano (Yukio Endo, *as a young boy*), Masayuki Tsukida (Yukio Endo, *as a young man*), Isako Machida (Michiko Oba), Hiromi Murase (Michiko, *as a child*), Yumeji Tsukioka (Miss Yonehara).

An East-West Films Production. Black and white. Academy ratio. 100 minutes. Released 1953.

U.S. VERSION: Released by Continental Distributing. English subtitles. 100 minutes. No MPAA rating. Released May 16, 1955.

Hiroshima mon amour / 24–Jikan no joji ("Hiroshima, My Love"). Director, Alain Resnais; Screenplay, Marguerite Duras; Directors of Photography, Sacha Vierny [France] and Michio Takahashi [Japan]; Cameramen, Goupil, Watanabe, and Ioda [no other names given]; Design, Esaka, Mayo, and Petri [no other name given]; Music, Giovanni Fusco, Georges Delerue, "and Japanese music; Sound Recording, P. Calvert, Yamamoto [no other name given], and R. Renault; Editor, Henri Colpi, Jasmine Chasney, Anne Sarraute.

CAST: Emmanuelle Riva (Elle), Eiji Okada (Lui), Bernard Fresson (L'Allemand), Stella Dassas (La Mere), Pierre Barbaud (Le Pere).

An Argos Films/Como Films/Daiei Motion Picture Co., Ltd./Pathe Overseas Production. A French/Japanese coproduction. Filmed at the Daiei-Tokyo Studios, and on location in Hiroshima (Japan), Paris and Nevers (France). Black and white. Academy ratio. 91 minutes. Released June 17, 1959.

U.S. VERSION: Released by Zenith International Film Corp. English subtitles. 88 minutes. No MPAA rating. Released May 1960. Reissued by Pathé Contemporary and, later still, by New Yorker Films. A dubbed version was also released. Credits for dubbed version: Producers, Dan Frankel and Noelle Gillmor. Dubbed at Titra Studios. Voices: Paulette Girard (Elle), Sho Anodera (Lui).

History of Postwar Japan as Told by a Bar Hostess / Nippon Sengoshi–Madam onboro no Seikatsu ("History of Postwar Japan as Told by a Bar Hostess"). Director/Screenplay, Shohei Imamura; Director of Photography, Masao Tochizawa; Editors, Mutsuo Tanji and Moriaki Matsumoto; Music, Harumi Ibe.

CAST: Etsuko Akaza (the bar hostess).

A Shinsei Horiba and Moto Ogasahara Production. A Nichie Shinsha Release. Black and white. Academy ratio (?). 105 minutes. Released 1970.

U.S. VERSION: Distributor undetermined. English subtitles. 105 minutes. No MPAA rating. Released 1983(?).

Holiday in Tokyo / Tokyo no kyujitsu ("Tokyo Holiday"). Producer, Shiro Horie; Director, Kajiro Yamamoto; Screenplay, Toshiro Ide and Kajiro Yamamoto; Director of Photography, Ichio Yamasaki; Art Director, Hyoe Hamagami; Music, Hachiro Matsui.

CAST: Yoshiko "Shirley" Yamaguchi (Mary Kawaguchi), Kaoru Yachigusa, Asami Kuji, Yoko Tsukasa, Akira Takarada, Keiju Kobayashi, Hiroshi Koizumi, Ken Uehara, Tessie Quintana, Bimbo Danao, Chen Hui-chu.

A Toho Co., Ltd. Production. Eastman

Color. Toho Scope. Running time undetermined. Released 1958.

U.S. VERSION: Release undetermined, possibly by Toho International Co., Ltd. in subtitled format. No MPAA rating.

Hometown / Furusato ("Hometown"). Director, Kenji Mizoguchi; Screenplay, Shuichi Iwao, based on his story; Director of Photography, Tatsuyuki Yokota; Sound Recording, Hoshikatsu Urashima and Toshio Naryu.

CAST: Yoshie Fujiwara (Yoshio Fujimura), Shizue Natsukawa (Natsuko), Fujiko Hamaguchi (Natsue Omura), Isamu Kosugi (Higuchi).

A Nikkatsu Corporation Production. Minatakie (part-sound). Black and white. Academy ratio. 107 minutes. Released 1930.

U.S. VERSION: Released by the Film Center of the National Museum of Modern Art (Tokyo). In Japanese with no English subtitles. 107 minutes. No MPAA rating. Released 1981.

Honolulu — Tokyo — Hong Kong. Executive Producers, Sanezumi Fujimoto and Lin Yung-tai; Director, Yasuki Chiba; Screenplay, Zenzo Matsuyama; Director of Photography, Rokuro Nishigaki; Music, Hachiro Matsui.

CAST: Akira Takarada (Yuichi Okamoto), Yu Ming (Wu Ai-ling), Yuzo Kayama (Jiro Okamoto), Yuriko Hoshi (Teruko), Wang Ing (Cheng Hao), Ken Uehara (father), Haruko Togo (mother), Choko Iida (Granny), Mitsuko Kusabue.

A Toho Co., Ltd./The Cathay Organization Co., Ltd. Production. A Japanese/Hong Kong co-production. A Toho Co., Ltd. Release. Eastman Color. Toho Scope. Released 1963.

U.S. VERSION: Released by Toho International Co., Ltd. English subtitles. 102 minutes. No MPAA rating. Released December 1963.

The Hoodlum Priest / Yakuza bozu ("The Yakuza Priest"). Director, Kimiyoshi Yasuda.

CAST: Shintaro Katsu, Mayumi Ogawa, Kayo Sanbongi, Naoko Kubo, Mikio Narita.

A Daiei Motion Picture Co., Ltd. Production. Color. DaieiScope (?). 84 minutes. Released November 1967.

U.S. VERSION: Released by Daiei International Films, Inc. English subtitles. Sequel: *The Hoodlum Priest, Part II* (1968). 84 minutes. No MPAA rating. Released June 1969.

Hoodlum Soldier / Heitai Yakuza ("Yakuza Soldier"). Director, Yasuzo Masumura; Screenplay, Ryuzo Kikushima, based on a story by Yoriyoshi Arima; Director of Photography, Setsuo Kobayashi; Music, Naozumi Yamamoto.

CAST: Shintaro Katsu, Takahiro Tamura, Keiko Awaji, Eiko Taki, Mikio Narita.

A Daiei Motion Picture Co., Ltd. Production. Black and white. DaieiScope. 103 minutes. Released 1965.

U.S. VERSION: Released by Daiei International Films, Inc. English subtitles. The first "Hoodlum Soldier" feature. The series ran nine films (1965–72). Followed by *Hoodlum Soldier, Part II* (1965). 103 minutes. No MPAA rating. Released December 4, 1979.

Hope and Pain / Dauntaun Hirozu ("Downtown Heroes"). Producer, Shizuo Yamanouchi; Associate Producer, Kogi Tanaka; Director, Yoji Yamada; Screenplay, Yoji Yamada and Yoshitaka Asama, based on the novel by Akira Hayasaka; Director of Photography, Tetsuo Takaba; Art Directors, Mitsuo Dekawa and Kyohei Morita; Music, Teizo Matsumura.

CAST: Hiroko Yakushimaru (Fusako), Hashinosuke Nakamura (Kosuke), Toshiro Yanagiba (Onkel), Toshinori Obi (Arles), Tetsuta Sugimoto (Gan *and* Holtan), Shinobu Sakagami (Chopinski), Eri Ishida (prostitute), Chieko Baisho (Kosuke's mother), Kiyoshi Atsumi (Havaosuke, *the dormitory cook*), Shikan Nakamura (Kosuke today).

A Shochiku Co., Ltd. Production. Color. Spherical Panavision. 120 minutes. Released August 6, 1988.

U.S. VERSION: Released by Shochiku Films of America, Inc. in subtitled format. No MPAA rating. Released September 23, 1988.

The Horizon / Chiheisen ("The Horizon"). Producer, Geshiro Kawamoto; Director, Kaneto Shindo; Screenplay, Kaneto Shindo; Director of Photography, Keiji Maruyama; Music, Hikaru Hayashi.

CAST: Toshiyuki Nagashima, Kumiko Akiyoshi, Miwako Fujitani, Misako Tanaka, Maiko Kawakami, Hisashi Igawa, Nobuko Otowa.

A Marugen Co., Ltd. Production. A Shochiku Co., Ltd. Release. Filmed on location in California. Color. Panavision (?). 136 minutes. Released 1984.

U.S. VERSION: Released by Shochiku Films of America, Inc. in subtitled format. No MPAA rating. Released September 1985.

Horror of a Deformed Man / Kyofu kikei ningen ("Horror of a Deformed Man"). Producer, Hiroshi Okawa; Director, Teruo Ishii; Screenplay, Teruo Ishii and Masahiro Kakefuda, based on the story, "Kyofo nikei ningen" by Rampo Edogawa; Director of Photography, Shigeru Akatsuka; Art Director, Akira Yoshimura; Music, Masao Yagi.

CAST: Teruo Yoshida (young Kamoda), Minoru Oki (old Kamoda), Asao Koike (Retainer), Yuki Kagawa (relative), Mitsuko Aoi (Mrs. Kamoda), Teruko Yumi, Michiko Obata, Tatsumi Hijikata.

A Toei Co., Ltd. Production. Toeicolor. ToeiScope. 99 minutes. Released 1969.

U.S. VERSION: Distributor undetermined. Alternate title: *Horror of Malformed Men.*

Horse / Uma ("Horse"). Producer, Nobuyoshi Morita; Director, Kajiro Yamamoto; Screenplay, Kajiro Yamamoto and Akira Kurosawa; Directors of Photography, Hiromitsu Karasawa (*Spring*), Akira Mimura (*Summer and Sets*), Hiroshi Suzuki (*Autumn*), and Takeo Ito (*Winter*); Art Director, Takashi Matsuyama; Music, Shigeaki Kitamura; Production Coordinator/Editor, Akira Kurosawa; Equestrian Supervisors, Jun Maki and Shoichiro Ozaki; Sound Effects, Toho Sound Effects Group; Sound, Toho Dubbing Theatre.

CAST: Hideko Takamine (Ine Onoda), Kamatari "Keita" Fujiwara (Jinjiro Onoda, *her father*), Chieko Takehisa (Saku Onoda), Kaoru Futaba (Grandma Ei), Takeshi Hirata (Toyokazu Onoda, *Ine's brother*), Toshio Hosoi (Kinjiro Onoda, *her youngest brother*), Setsuko Ichikawa (Tsuru Onoda, *her little sister*), Sadao Maruyama (Master Yamashita), Yoshio Kosugi (Zenzo Sakuma), Sadako Sawamura (Kikudo Yamashita), Tsuruko Mano (Madame Sakuma), Shoji Kiyokawa (Mr. Sakamoto).

A Toho Co., Ltd. Production. Black and white. Academy ratio. Filmed at Toho Studios, Ltd. (Tokyo). 129 minutes. Released 1941.

U.S. VERSION: Released by R5/S8. English subtitles. 129 minutes. No MPAA rating. Released May 1986.

The Hospital: The Last Place to Consult—A Home Care Network That Sustains the Elderly / Byouin wa kiraida, rojin no zaitaku-kea wo sasaeru netowaku ("I Don't Like the Hospital—A Home Care Network That Sustains the Elderly") [**documentary**]. Producers, Teizo Oguchi, Atsushi Suwa, Hirohisa Kawakami; Director/Screenplay, Toshie Tokieda; Director of Photography, Yoshinori Yagi; Music, Shinji Ishihara.

An Iwanami Productions, Inc. Production. Filmed in 16mm (?). Color. Academy ratio (?). 137 minutes. Released 1991 (?).

U.S. VERSION: Distributor, if any, is undetermined.

The Hot Little Girl / Shibirekurage ("Electric Jellyfish"). Director/Screenplay, Yasuzo Masumura; Director of Photography, Setsuo Kobayashi; Art Director, Taijiro Goto; Music, Tadashi Yamauchi.

CAST: Mari Atsumi (Midori), Ryo Tamura (Kenji), Yusuke Kawazu (Yamazaki), Ryoichi Tamagawa (Shosuke), Tomo Uchida.

A Daiei Motion Picture Co., Ltd. Production. Fujicolor. DaieiScope. 92 minutes. Released October 3, 1970.

U.S. VERSION: Release undetermined, possibly by Daiei International Films. English subtitles. 92 minutes. No MPAA rating.

Hotsprings Holiday / Onsen Gerira dai shogeki ("Hotsprings Guerilla: Big Laugh Attack"). Producer,

Kunio Sawamura; Director, Hirokazu Ichimura; Screenplay, Yasuo Tanami and Toshiro Hasebe; Original Story, Yasuo Tanami; Director of Photography, Masao Kosugi; Art Director, Chiyoo Umeda; Music, Hiroki Ogawa.

CAST: Hiroshi Inuzuka (Daisuke Yamato), Osami Nabe (Kosuke Yamato), Yoshiko Kayama (Emiko Kano), Hajime Hana (chief of police), Kingoro Yanagiya (Yamanouchi boss), Chosuke Ikariya, Chu Arai, Bo Takaki, Koji Nakamoto, Cha Kato, Michiyo Kogure, Etsuko Ikuta, Masumi Harukawa, Kumi Hayase, Norihei Miki, Akiyoshi Kitaura, Yoshijiro Uyeda, Hachiro Misumi, Koree Nakamura, Ryusuke Kita, Mitsuru Ooya, Tosen Hidari, Fukuoka Shogo, Michiko Saga, Tonpei Hidari, Taisuke Kobayashi.

A Geiei Productions, Ltd. Production. A Shochiku Co., Ltd. Release. Black and white. Shochiku GrandScope (?). Alternate title: *Kigeki dai shogeki.* Released 1968.

U.S. VERSION: Released by Shochiku Films of America, Inc. English subtitles. 90 minutes. No MPAA rating. Released February 1970.

House / Hausu ("House"). Executive Producer, Tomoyuki Tanaka; Producer/Director/Special Effects Director, Nobuhiko Obayashi; Screenplay, Chiho Katsura, Nobuhiko Obayashi; Director of Photography, Yoshihisa Sakamoto; Music, Asei Kobayashi and Miki Yoshino, performed by Godiego; Art Director, Kazuo Satsuya; Editor, Nobuo Ogawa; Assistant Director, Yasuhira Oguri; Sound, Toho Recording Centre; Sound Effects, Toho Sound Effects Group.

CAST: Kimiko Ikegami, Kumiko Oda, Ai Matsubara, Miki Jinbo, Mieko Sato, Masayo Miyako, Enko Tanaka, Saho Sasazawa, Haruko Wanibuchi, Kiyoko Ozaki.

A Toho Co., Ltd. Production. Color (processed by Tokyo Laboratory, Ltd.). Panavision. 100 minutes (possibly 87 minutes, sources vary). Released August 26, 1977.

U.S. VERSION: Released by Toho International Co., Ltd. English subtitles. Also known as *Ie* (or is that *Ei*?). 87 minutes. No MPAA rating. Released September 1977.

House of Bamboo Executive Producer, Darryl F. Zanuck; Producer, Buddy Adler; Director, Samuel Fuller; Screenplay, Harry Kleiner; Additional Dialogue, Samuel Fuller; Director of Photography, Joe MacDonald; Editor, James B. Clark; Music, Lionel Newman.

CAST: Robert Ryan (Sandy Dawson), Robert Stack (Eddie Spanier), Shirley Yamaguchi (Mariko), Cameron Mitchell (Griff), Brad Dexter (Captain Hanson), Sessue Hayakawa (Inspector Kita), Biff Elliot (Webber), Sandro Giglio (Ceram), Eiko Hanabusa (screaming woman), Harry Carey, Jr. (John), Peter Gray (Willy), Robert Quarry (Phil), DeForest Kelly (Charlie), John Doucette (Skipper), Teru Shimada (Nagaya), Robert Hosoi (doctor), May Takasugi (bath attendant), Robert Okazaki (Mr. Hommaru).

A Buddy Adler Production. A Twentieth Century–Fox Release. A U.S. production in English filmed in Japan. De Luxe Color. CinemaScope. Stereophonic Sound. 102 minutes. Released July 1956.

House of Hanging / Byoinzaka no Kubikukuri no ie ("House of Hanging at Byoinzaka"). Producers, Kon Ichikawa, Kazuo Baba, and Hideo Kurosawa; Planning, Haruki Kadokawa Office; Screenplay, Shinya Hidaka and Kon Ichikawa, based on an original story by Seishi Yokomizo; Director of Photography, Kiyoshi Hasegawa; Music, Shinichi Tanabe; Art Director, Iwao Akune; Sound Recording, Fumio Yanoguchi; Lighting, Kojiro Sato.

CAST: Koji Ishizaka (Kosuke Kindaichi), Yoshiko Sakuma (Yayoi Hogan), Junko Sakurada (Yukari Hogan), Koreharu Hisatomi (Takezo Igarashi), Takako Irie (Chizuru Igarashi), Hiromasa Kawahara (Shigeru Igarashi, *Takezo's grandchild*), Miki Sanjo (Mitsue Tanabe, *Shigeru's mother*), Midori Hagio (Fuyuko Yamauchi), Teruhiko Aoi (Toshio Yamauchi, *Fuyuko's stepson*), Junko Sakurada (Koyuki Yamauchi, *Fuyuko's daughter*), Takeshi Kato (Police Inspector Todoroki), Eitaro Ozawa (Tokubei Honjo, *the photographer*), Koji Shimizu (Naokichi Honjo, *his son*), Masao Kusakari (Mokutaro Hinatsu, *the assistant*).

A Toho Co., Ltd. Production, in association with Kadokawa Publishing Co., Ltd. (?). Color. Anamorphic wide screen (?). 139 minutes. Released May 26, 1979.

U.S. VERSION: Released by Toho International Co., Ltd. English subtitles. Preceded by *Queen Bee* (1978), and the final film of the series. 139 minutes. No MPAA rating. Released September 21, 1979.

The House of Strange Loves / Onna ukiyoburo ("World of Bathing Women Floating"). Producer, Eisei Koe; Director, Tan Ida; Screenplay, Iwao Yamazaki; Director of Photography, Hidematsu Iwahashi; Art Director, Haruyashi Kurosawa; Music, Seitaro Omori.

CAST: Ryoji Hayama (Shinzo), Jiro Okazaki (Takichi), Toshie Nihonyanagi (Hatsue), Miki Hayashi (Shun), Kaoru Miya (Toyo), Takako Uchida (Hatsuse).

A Nikkatsu Corporation Production. Fujicolor. NikkatsuScope. Released July 1968.

U.S. VERSION: Released by United Producers Releasing Organization. English subtitles (?). 83 minutes. No MPAA rating. Released September 19, 1969.

House of Terrors / Kaidan semushi otoko ("Ghost Story of a Hunchbacked Man"). Producer, Hiroshi Okawa; Director, Hajime Sato; Screenplay, Hajime Takaiwa; Director of Photography, Shoei Nishikawa.

CAST: Ko Nishimura, Yuko Kusunoki, Yoko Hayama, Masumi Harakawa, Shinjiro Ebara.

A Toei Co., Ltd. Production. Black and white (processed by Toei Chemistry Co. Ltd.). Toeiscope. 81 minutes. Released 1965.

U.S. VERSION: U.S. distributor, if any, undetermined. Also known as *The Ghost of a Hunchback*.

The House of the Sleeping Virgins / Nemureru bijo ("Sleeping Beauty"). Director, Kozaburo Yoshimura; Screenplay, Kaneto Shindo, based on the story "Nemureru bijo" in *Nemureru bijo* (1960) by Yasunari Kawabata; Director of Photography, Masamichi Sato; Art Director, Hisatake Satsumoto; Music, Shigeru Ikeno.

CAST: Takahiro Tamura (Eguchi), Yoshiko Kayama (Yoshiko), Kikko Matsuoka (first sweetheart), Sanae Nakahara (woman in Kobe), Satoshi Oide (Higuchi), Tetsuo Ishikawa (Yoshida).

A Kindai Eiga Kyokai Co., Ltd. Production. A Shochiku Co., Ltd. Release. Black and white. Shochiku GrandScope. Released February 1968.

U.S. VERSION: Released by Shochiku Films of America, Inc. English subtitles (?). 95 minutes. No MPAA rating. Released March 1969.

House on Fire / Kataku no hito ("House on Fire"). Producer, Shigero Okada; Director, Kinji Fukasaku; Screenplay, Fumio Konami, based on the novel by Kazuo Dan; Director of Photography, Daisaku Kimura; Music, Takayuki Inoue.

CAST: Ken Ogata (Kazuo Katsura), Ayumi Ishida (Yoriko), Keiko Matsuzaka (Yoko), Mieko Harada (Keiko).

A Toei Co., Ltd. Production. Color. ToeiScope (?). 132 minutes. Released 1986.

U.S. VERSION: Distributor, if any, is undetermined.

The House Where Evil Dwells. Producer, Martin B. Cohen; Director, Kevin Connor; Screenplay, Robert A. Suhosky, based on the novel by James W. Hardiman; Director of Photography, Jacques Haitkin; Second Unit Director of Photography, Anne Coffey; Editor, Barry Peters; Art Director, Yoshikazu Sano; Wardrobe, Shannon; Music, Kenneth Thorne; Music Director, Richard Kaufman; Sword Choreographer, Ikuo Hiyoshi; Production Manager, Tadashi Noguchi; Special Visual Effects, Cruse & Co.; Visual Effects Supervisor, William Cruse; Lighting, Haruo Nakayama; Sound Recording, Teruhiko Arakawa; Sound Editor, Graham Harris.

CAST: Edward Albert (Ted Fletcher), Susan George (Laura Fletcher), Doug McClure (Alex Curtis), Amy Barrett (Amy Fletcher), Mako Hattori (Otami), Toshiyuki Sasaki (Shugoro), Toshiya

Maruyama (Masanori), Tsyako Okajima (Mayjo witch), Henry Omitowa (Zen monk), Mayama Umeda (Noriko), Hiroko Takano (Wakado), Shuren Sakura (Noh mask maker), Shoji Ohara (assistant Noh mask maker), Jiro Shiraki (Tadashi), Kazuo Yoshida (editor), Kunihiko Shinjo (assistant editor), Gentaro Mori (Yoshio), Tomoko Shimizu (Aiko), Misao Aria (Hayashi), Chiyoko Hardiman (Mama-San), Hideo Shimado (policeman).

A Martin B. Cohen Productions, Inc. Production in association with Toei Co., Ltd. A Japanese/U.S. co-production in English. Filmed at Toei-Kyoto Studios. Color (processed by Toei Chemistry Co., Ltd.). Spherical wide screen. 88 minutes. Released 1982.

U.S. VERSION: Released by MGM/UA Entertainment Co. Prints by Technicolor. 88 minutes. MPAA rating: "R." Released May 13, 1982.

How to Care for the Senile / Caihosei Rojin no Sekai ("How to Care for the Senile") [**documentary**]. Producers, Takeji Takamura and Hirohisa Kawakami; Director/Screenplay, Sumiko Haneda; Director of Photography, Kiyoshi Nishio; Music, Yoshiyuki Totaka.

An Iwanami Productions, Inc. Production. Color. Academy ratio. 84 minutes. Released 1986.

U.S. VERSION: Distributor, if any, is undetermined. No MPAA rating.

The Human Condition / Ningen no joken ("The Human Condition"). Producer, Shigeru Wakatsuki; Director, Masaki Kobayashi; Screenplay, Masaki Kobayashi and Zenzo Matsuyama, based on the novel *Ningen no joken, vol. 1 & 2* (1958) by Jumpei Gomikawa; Director of Photography, Yoshio Miyajima; Art Director, Kazue Hirataka; Editor, Keiichi Uraoka; Music, Chuji Kinoshita; Sound Recording, Hideo Nishizaki.

CAST: Tatsuya Nakadai (Kaji), Michiyo Aratama (Michiko), So Yamamura (Okishima), Eitaro Ozawa (Okazaki), Akira Ishihama (Chen), Shinji Nambara (Kao), Ineko Arima (Yang Chun Lan), Chikage Awashima (Jin Tung Fu), Keiji Sada (Kageyama), Toru Abe (Watai), Masao Mishima (Kuroki), Koji Mitsui (Furya), Kyu Sazanka (Cho Meisan), Seiji Miyaguchi (Wang Heng Li), Nobuo Nakamura (chief of head office).

A Ninjin Club Production. A Shochiku Co., Ltd. Release. Black and white. Shochiku GrandScope. 208 minutes. Released January 9, 1959.

U.S. VERSION: Released by Brandon Films. English subtitles. 138 minutes. No MPAA rating. Released December 14, 1959. Reissued 1970 by Shochiku Films of America, Inc., and Beverly Pictures (running 200 minutes) with an MPAA rating of "R." VHS home video version letterboxed but recorded in EP mode. Video version title: *The Human Condition (Part I: No Greater Love).* First part of a trilogy, and followed by *The Human Condition (Part II: Road to Eternity)* (1959).

The Human Condition (Part II: Road to Eternity) / Ningen no joken II ("The Human Condition II"). Executive Producer, Shigeru Wakatsuki; Producer, Tatsuya Hosoya; Director, Masaki Kobayashi; Screenplay, Masaki Kobayashi and Zenzo Matsuyama, based on the novel *Ningen no joken, vol. 3 & 4* (1958) by Jumpei Gomikawa; Director of Photography, Yoshio Miyajima; Art Director, Chikara Hiraoka; Music, Chuji Kinoshita; Sound Recording, Hideo Nishizaki.

CAST: Tatsuya Nakadai (Pvt. 2nd Class Kaji), Michiyo Aratama (Michiko), Kokinji Katsura (Sasa), Jun Tatara (W.O. Hino), Michio Minami (Superior Pvt. Yoshida), Ryohei Uchida (Sgt. Hashitani), Kan Yanagidani (Pvt. 1st Class Tanoue), Kenjiro Uemura (Superior Pvt. Bannai), Keiji Sada (2nd Lieut. Kageyama), Yusuke Tsugawa (Pvt. Terada), Susumu Fujita (Pvt. Naruto), Minoru Chiaki (Corporal Onodera).

A Shochiku Co., Ltd. Production. Black and white. Shochiku GrandScope. 176 minutes. Released 1959.

U.S. VERSION: Released by Shochiku Films of America, Inc. and Beverly Pictures. English subtitles. 176 minutes. No

Gas Human Being #1 – Yoshio Tsuchiya as *The Human Vapor* (1960).

MPAA rating. Released February 1961. Reissued in 1970; MPAA rating: "GP." Home video version: A Janus Films Presentation. Picture divided into two parts: Part Three runs 101 minutes; Part Four runs 75 minutes. VHS home video version letterboxed but recorded at EP mode. Second part of a trilogy. Followed by *The Human Condition (Part III: A Soldier's Prayer)* (1961).

The Human Condition (Part III: A Soldier's Prayer) / Ningen no joken III ("The Human Condition III"). Producers, Shigeru Wakatsuki and Masaki Kobayashi; Director Masaki Kobayashi; Screenplay, Masaki Kobayashi, Zenzo Matsuyama and Koichi Inagaki, based on the novel *Ningen no joken, vol. 5 & 6* (1958) by Jumpei Gomikawa; Director of Photography, Yoshio Miyajima; Art Director, Kazue Hirataka; Editor, Keiichi Uraoka; Music, Chuji Kinoshita.

CAST: Tatsuya Nakadai (Kaji), Michiyo Aratama (Michiko), Taketoshi Naito (Private Tange), Keijiro Morozumi (Corporal Hironaka), Yusuke Kawazu (Private Terada), Kyoko Kishida (Ryuko), Reiko Hitomi (Umeko), Fijio Suga (Captain Nagata), Nobuo Kaneko (Corporal Kirahara), Tamao Nakamura (female refugee), Hideko Takamine (woman in settlers' village), Chishu Ryu (village elder).

A Ninjin Club/Shochiku Co., Ltd. Production. A Shochiku Co., Ltd. Release. Black and white. Shochiku GrandScope. 190 minutes. Released January 29, 1961.

U.S. VERSION: Released by Shochiku Films of America, Inc. English subtitles. 190 minutes. MPAA rating: "GP." Released August 5, 1970. VHS home video version is letterboxed but recorded in inferior EP mode. Third part of a trilogy, preceded by *The Human Condition (Part II: Road to Eternity)* (1959).

Human Patterns / Ningen moyo ("Human Patterns"). Producer, Hideo Koi; Director, Kon Ichikawa; Screenplay, Yoshikazu Yamashita and Natto Wada, based on a story by Fumio Niwa; Director of Photography, Kenji Ohara; Lighting, Ko Fujibayashi; Sound Recording, Hisao Negishi; Art Director, Takashi Kono; Assistant Director, Goro Kadono.

CAST: Ken Uehara (Kinuhiko Daiwa), Yoshiko Yamaguchi (Ginko Yoshino), Chiaki Tsukioka (Sayoko Arai), Goro Hoyama (Atsushi Komatsubara).

A Shintoho Co., Ltd. Production. Black and white. Academy ratio. 89 minutes. Released June 14, 1949.

U.S. VERSION: Distributor, if any, is undetermined. Alternate title: *Design of a Human Being.*

The Human Vapor / Gasu ningen dai ichigo ("Gas Human Being No. 1"). Executive Producer, Tomoyuki Tanaka; Director Ishiro Honda; Screenplay, Takeshi Kimura; Director of Photography, Hajime Koizumi; Music, Kunio Miyauchi; Art Director, Takeo Kita; Production Manager, Yasuaki Sakamoto; Assistant Director, Koji Kahita; Sound Effects, Hisashi Shimonaga, Toho Sound Effects Group; Sound, Toho Dubbing Theatre. *Toho Special Effects Group*: Director, Eiji Tsuburaya; Art Direction, Teisho Arikawa; Lighting, Kuichiro Kishida; Matte Process, Hiroshi Mukoyama; Optical Photography, Kinsaburo Araki.

CAST: Tatsuya Mihashi (Detective Okamoto), Keiko Sata (Reporter Kyoko), Kaoru Yachigusa (Fujichiyo, the dancer), Yoshio Tsuchiya (Mizuno, *the vapor man*), Bokuzen Hidari (Fujichiyo's guardian), Hisaya Ito, Takamaru Sasaki, Kozo Nomura, Yoshifumi Tajima, Yoshio Kosugi, Yutaka Oka, Tetsu Nakamura, Fuyuki Murakami, Ren Yamamoto, Tatsuo Matsumura.

A Toho Co. Ltd. Production. Western Electric Mirrophonic recording (encoded with Perspecta Stereophonic Sound). Eastman Color (processed by Far East Laboratories, Ltd.). Toho Scope. 92 minutes. Released December 11, 1960.

U.S. VERSION: Released by Brenco Pictures English-dubbed. An Edward L. Alperson and Stanley D. Meyer Presentation. Executive Producer, Edward L. Alperson; Producer, Stanley D. Meyer; Executive Director in Charge of Production (i.e. coordinator in the United States for Toho), Sanezumi Fujimoto; English Dialog, John Meredyth Lucas; Editor, Kenneth Wannberg; Dubbing Cast: James Hong (Mizuno), Paul Frees, William Eidleson (?), Virginia Craig (?); Sound, Ryder Sound Services, Inc.; Prints by Pathe; Westrex Recording System. Advertised as being "In Wide Screen and Stereophonic Sound," but may have been released mono in the United States. Double billed with *Gorath* (q.v.). 79 minutes. No MPAA rating. Released May 20, 1964.

Humanity and Paper Balloons / Ninjo kami fusen ("Humanity and Paper Balloons"). Director, Sadao Yamanaka; Screenplay, Shintaro Mimura; Director of Photography, Akira Mimura; Music, Chu Ota; Assistant Director, Ishiro Honda.

CAST: Kanemon Nakamura (Shinza, *the barber*), Chojuro Kawarazaki (Matajuro Unno, *a ronin samurai*), Shizue Yamagishi (Otaki, *Matajuro's wife*), Sukezo Suketayaka (Chobei, *the landlord*), Tsuruzo Nakamura (Genko), Hisako Hara (Otetsu), Choemon Bando (Yabuchi), Noboru Kiritachi (Okoma).

A Toho Co., Ltd. Production. Black and white. Academy ratio. 86 minutes. Released 1937.

U.S. VERSION: Distributor undetermined. English subtitles. 86 minutes. No MPAA rating. Released August 1982.

The Hunter's Diary / Ryojin nikki ("The Hunter's Diary"). Director, Ko Nakahira; Screenplay, Tatsuo Asano; Director of Photography, Yoshihiro Yamazaki.

CAST: Noboru Nakaya, Masako Togawa, Yukiyo Toake, Kazuo Kitamura, Yoko Ozono.

A Nikkatsu Corporation Production. Black and white. NikkatsuScope. Released 1964.

U.S. VERSION: Distributor undetermined,

possibly Toho International Co., Ltd. English subtitles (?). 123 minutes. No MPAA rating. Released December 11, 1964.

The Hurricane Drummer (production credits unavailable).

CAST: Tetsuya Watari.

A Toho Co., Ltd. Production. Color (?). Toho Scope (?). Released 1966 (?).

U.S. VERSION: Released by Toho International Co., Ltd. English subtitles (?). Running time undetermined. No MPAA rating. Released October 4, 1967.

Hymn to a Tired Man / Nippon no seishun ("Youth of Japan"). Director, Masaki Kobayashi; Screenplay, Sakae Hirosawa, based on an original story by Shusaku Endo; Director of Photography, Kozo Okazaki; Art Director, Motoji Kojima; Music, Toru Takemitsu.

CAST: Makoto Fujita (Zensaku Kosaka), Tomoko Naraoka (his wife), Toshio Kurosawa (his son), Michiyo Aratama (Yoshiko), Kei Sato (Suzuki), Wakako Sakai (his daughter).

A Toho Co., Ltd. Production. Black and white. Toho Scope. 130 minutes. Released June 8, 1968.

U.S. VERSION: Released by Toho International Co., Ltd. English subtitles. 130 minutes. No MPAA rating. Released 1981 (?).

I Am a Cat / Wagahai wa neko de aru ("I Am a Cat"). Producers, Ichiro Sato, Kiichi Ichikawa, and Michio Morioka; Director, Kon Ichikawa; Screenplay, Toshio Yasumi, based on the novel by Soseki Natsume; Director of Photography, Kozo Okazaki; Music Supervisor and Performer, Mitsuo Miyamoto; Art Director, Yoshinobu Nishioka; Sound Recording, Tetsuya Ohashi; Lighting, Yosuke Sakakibara; Editor, Chizuko Osada; Assistant Director, Tetsuro Kato.

CAST: Tatsuya Nakadai (Kusaya), Kuriko Hano (his wife), Juzo Itami (Meitei), Nobuto Okamoto (Kangetsu), Yoko Shimada (Yukie), Mariko Okada (Hanako), Hiroko Shino (Tomiko), Tonpei Hidari (Sampei Tatara), Shinsuke Minami (Kaneda), Teimu (Wagahai, *a four-year-old male cat*), Miiko (Mike, *one-year-old female cat*), Kuro (twelve-year-old male cat).

A Geiensha Co., Ltd. Production. A Toho Co., Ltd. Release. Color. Spherical wide screen. 116 minutes. Released May 31, 1975.

U.S. VERSION: Released by Toho International Co., Ltd. English subtitles. 116 minutes. No MPAA rating. Released June 25, 1982.

I Bombed Pearl Harbor / Taiheiyo no arashi ("Storm in the Pacific Ocean"). Executive Producer, Tomoyuki Tanaka; Director, Shue Matsubayashi; Screenplay, Shinobu Hashimoto, Takeo Kunihiro; Director of Photography, Kazuo Yamada; Art Director, Takeo Kita; Music, Ikuma Dan; Sound, Toho Dubbing Theatre; Sound Effects, Toho Sound Effects Group. *Toho Special Effects Group*: Director, Eiji Tsuburaya; Photography, Teisho Arikawa; Lighting, Kuichiro Kishida; Art Director, Akira Watanabe; Matte Processing, Hiroshi Mukoyama; Optical Photography, Kinsaburo Araki.

CAST: Yosuke Natsuki (Lt. Koji Kitami), Toshiro Mifune (Admiral Isoroku Yamamoto), Koji Tsuruta (Lt. Tomonari), Misa Uehara (Keiko), Aiko Mimasu (Sato), Jun Tazaki (captain), Makoto Sato (Lt. Matsura), Takashi Shimura (Tosaku), Daisuke Kato, Akira Takarada, Hiroshi Koizumi, Ryo Ikebe, Keiju Kobayashi, Tatsuya Mihashi, Seizaburo Kawazu, Ken Uehara, Yoshio Tsuchiya, Akihiko Hirata, Kenichi Enomoto, Tadao Nakamaru, Ko Mishima, Hisaya Ito, Jun Tazaki, Hiroshi Tachikawa, Yoshio Kosugi, Sachio Sakai, Ren Yamamoto, Yutaka Sada, Tetsu Nakamura, Senkichi Omura, Shin Otomo, Fuyuki Murakami, Yoshifumi Tajima, Yutaka Oka, Nadao Kirino, Hiroshi Sekita.

A Toho Co., Ltd. Production. Eastman Color (processed by Far East Laboratories, Ltd.). Toho Scope. Western Electric

***Opposite: I Bombed Pearl Harbor* (1960). (Left to right) Nadao Kirino, Hisaya Ito, So Yamamura, Yoshio Tsuchiya, Akihiko Hirata, Yoshifumi Tajima, Jun Tazaki, Toshiro Mifune, Ryo Ikebe, and unidentified.**

Mirrophonic Recording (encoded with Perspecta Stereophonic Sound). 118 minutes. Released April 26, 1960.

U.S. Version: Simultaneously released by Parade Releasing Organization (English-dubbed) and by Toho International (English subtitles), the latter as *The Storm Over the Pacific*. A Hugo Grimaldi Production. A Riley Jackson and Robert Patrick Presentation. Executive Producers, Riley Jackson and Robert Patrick; Producer/Director/Editor, Hugo Grimaldi; Music and Sound Supervisor, Gordon Zahler; Music, Walter Greene; Sound, Ryder Sound Services, Inc. Voice Characterizations, Paul Frees, others unidentified. Prints by Technicolor. Westrex Recording System. Mifune's role was erroneously billed as "Admiral Yamaguchi" (!). Mifune also played Yamamoto in *Admiral Yamamoto* (1968), *The Militarists* (1973) and *Midway* (1976). 98 [91] minutes. No MPAA rating. Released November 29, 1961.

I Flunked But... / Rakudai wa shita keredo ("I Flunked But..."). Director, Yasujiro Ozu; Screenplay, Akira Fushimi, based on an idea by Yasujiro Ozu; Director of Photography, Hideo Shigehara.

Cast: Tatsuo Saito, Ichiro Sukida, Kinuyo Tanaka, Tomiyo Yoko, Chishu Ryu.

A Shochiku Co., Ltd. Production. Filmed at Shochiku-Kamata Studios. Silent with benshi. Black and white. Academy ratio. 95 minutes. Released April 11, 1930.

U.S. Version: Released by Shochiku Films of America, Inc. A semi-sequel to *I Graduated But...* (1929). 65 minutes. No MPAA rating. Released 1972 (?).

I Graduated But... / Daigaku wa deta keredo ("I Graduated from College but..."). Director, Yasujiro Ozu; Screenplay, Yoshiro Aramaki, based on an idea by Hiroshi Shimizu; Director of Photography, Hideo Shigehara.

Cast: Minoru Takada, Kinuyo Tanaka, Utako Suzuki, Kenji Oyama, Shinichi Himori, Takeshi Sakamoto, Chishu Ryu.

A Shochiku Co., Ltd. Production. Filmed at Shochiku-Kamata Studios. Silent with benshi. Black and white. Academy ratio. 100 minutes. Released September 6, 1929.

U.S. Version: Distributor undetermined. Followed by *I Flunked But...* (1930). Released 1972 (?).

I Live in Fear / Ikimono no kiroku ("Record of Living"). Executive Producer, Tomoyuki Tanaka; Producer, Shojiro Motoki; Director/Editor, Akira Kurosawa; Screenplay, Shinobu Hashimoto, Hideo Oguni, and Akira Kurosawa; Director of Photography, Asakazu Nakai; Lighting, Kuichiro Kishida; Art Director, Yoshiro Muraki; Music, Fumio Hayasaka and Masaru Sato; Sound Recording, Fumio Yanoguchi; Sound, Toho Dubbing Theatre; Sound Effects, Toho Sound Effects Group.

Cast: Toshiro Mifune (Kiichi Nakajima), Eiko Miyoshi (Toyo Nakajima, *his wife*), Yutaka Sada (Ichiro Nakajima, *his first son*), Minoru Chiaki (Jiro Nakajima, *his second son*), Haruko Togo (Yoshi Nakajima, *his first daughter*), Kyoko Aoyama (Sue Nakajima, *his second daughter*), Kiyomi Mizunoya (Kiichi's first mistress), Saoko Yonemura (Taeko, *her daughter*), Akemi Negishi (Asako Kuribayashi, *his present mistress*), Kichijiro Ueda (Mr. Kuribayashi, *Asako's father*), Masao Shimizu (Takao Yamazaki, *Yoshie's husband*), Noriko Sengoku (Kimie Nakajima, *Ichiro's Wife*), Yoichi Tachikawa (Ryoichi Sayama, *Nakajima's son by a former mistress*), Takashi Shimura (Dr. Harada), Kazuo Kato (Susumu), Eijiro Tono (the old man from Brazil), Ken Mitsuda (Judge Araki), Toranosuke Ogawa (Hori), Kamatari Fujiwara (Okamoto), Nobuo Nakamura (psychiatrist), Yoshio Tsuchiya (foundry worker), Akira Tani and Senkichi Omura (Kiichi's cellmates), Bokuzen Hidari, Kokuten Kodo, Fumiko Homma.

A Toho Co., Ltd. Production. Black and white. Academy ratio. 113 minutes. Released November 22, 1955.

U.S. Version: Released by Brandon Films. English subtitles. Also known as *Record of a Living Being*. Alternate title: *What the Birds Knew*. Sato completed

Hayasaka's score following the latter's death. 104 minutes. No MPAA rating. Released January 25, 1967.

I, the Executioner / Minagoroshi no reika ("Ghost Song—Everyone Dies"). Director, Yasushi Kato; Screenplay, Haruhiko Mimura; Director of Photography, Keiji Maruyama; Art Director, Kyohei Morita; Music, Hajime Kaburagi.

CAST: Makoto Sato (Tadashi), Chieko Baisho (Haruko, *the girl*), Ying Lan-Fang, Sanae Nakahara, Toshiko Sawa, Kin Sugai, Yuki Kawamura (five women).

A Shochiku Co., Ltd. Production. Black and white. Shochiku GrandScope. 90 minutes. Released April 13, 1968.

U.S. VERSION: Release undetermined, possibly by Shochiku Films of America, Inc. English subtitled version avaialble. 90 minutes. No MPAA rating.

I Want to Be a Shellfish. Director, Shinobu Hashimoto; Screenplay, Shinobu Hashimoto, based on the writings of Tetsutaro Kato; Director of Photography, Asaichi Nakai; Music, Masuru Sato.

CAST: Frankie Sakai (Toyomatsu), Michiyo Aratama (his wife), Akio Suano (their son), Kumi Mizuno (Toshiko), Daisuke Kato (Takeuchi), Susumu Fujita (General Yano), Kamatari Fujiwara (Adachi), Chishu Ryu (Komiya).

A Toho Co., Ltd. Production. Toho Scope. Black and white. 113 minutes. Released 1959.

U.S. VERSION: Released by Toho International Co., Ltd. English subtitles. Japanese sources list running time at 89 minutes, possibly a reissue length. 113 minutes. No MPAA rating. Released March 17, 1971.

I Was Born But... / Umarete wa mita keredo ("I Was Born But..."). Director, Yasujiro Ozu; Screenplay, Akira Fushimi and Geibei Ibushiya; Story, James Maki (Yasujiro Ozu); Director of Photography/Editor, Hideo Shigehara; Set Design, Takejiro Tsunoda and Yoshio Kimura.

CAST: Hideo Sugawara (Ryoichi, *the elder son*), Tomio "Tokkankozo" Aoki (Keiji, *the younger son*), Tatsuo Saito (Yoshi, *their father*), Mitsuko Yoshikawa (their mother), Takeshi Sakamoto (boss), Seiichi Kato (Taro, *the boss' son*), Shoichi Kofujita (delivery boy), Seiji Nishimura (schoolmaster), Chishu Ryu.

A Shochiku Co., Ltd. Production. Filmed at Shochiku-Kamata Studios. Silent. Black and white. Academy ratio. 100 minutes. Released June 3, 1932.

U.S. VERSION: Released by New Yorker Films, Inc. English inter-subtitles. Immediately followed by the quasi-sequel *Where Now Are the Dreams of Youth?* (1932). 89 minutes. No MPAA rating. Released 1972 (?).

The Idiot / Hakuchi ("The Idiot"). Producer, Takashi Koide; Director, Akira Kurosawa; Screenplay, Eijiro Hisaita and Akira Kurosawa, based on the novel *Idiot* (1868-69) by Fedor Mikhailovich Dostoevski; Director of Photography, Toshio Ubukata; Camera Operator, Cheichi [Asakazu] Nakai; Lighting, Akio Tamura; Art Director, So Matsuyama; Settings [i.e. Construction?], Shohei Sekine; Set Decorator, Ushitaro Shimada; Editors, T. [Takao] Saito and Akira Kurosawa; Music, Fumio Hayasaka; Sound Recording, Yoshisaburo Imo.

CAST: Masayuki Mori (Kameda), Toshiro Mifune (Denkichi Akama), Setsuko Hara (Taeko Nasu), Takashi Shimura (Ono, *her father*), Chieko Higashiyama (Satoko, *her mother*), Chiyoko Fumiya (Noriko), Eijiro Yanagi (Tohata), Yoshiko Kuga (Ayako), Minoru Chiaki (Mutsao Kayama), Kokuten Kodo (Jyunpei), Eiko Miyoshi (Madame Kayama), Noriko Sengoku (Takako), Daisuke Inoue (Kaoru), Eijiro Yanagi (Tohata), Bokuzen Hidari (Karube), Mitsuyo Akashi (Madame Akama).

A Shochiku Co., Ltd. Production. Black and white. Academy ratio. Filmed at Shochiku Studios. 166 minutes, cut from prepared but unreleased 265-minute version. Released May 23, 1951.

U.S. VERSION: Released by Shochiku Films of America, Inc. English subtitles. 166 minutes. It is undetermined whether co-editor Saito is the same as the camerman Takao Saito. No MPAA rating. Released April 30, 1963.

Ikiru / Ikiru ("Living"). Producer, Shojiro Motoki; Director/Editor, Akira Kurosawa; Screenplay, Shinobu Hashimoto, Hideo Oguni, and Akira Kurosawa; Director of Photography, Asakazu Nakai; Art Director, So Matsuyama; Lighting, Shigeru Mori; Sound Recording, Fumio Yanoguchi; Music, Fumio Hayasaka.

CAST: Takashi Shimura (Kanji Watanabe), Nobuko Kaneko (Mitsu Watanabe), Kyoko Seki (Kazue Watanabe), Makoto Kobori (Kiichi Watanabe), Kumeko Urabe (Tatsu Watanabe), Yoshie Minami (the maid), Miki Odagiri (Toyo Odagiri), Kamatari Fujiwara (Sub Section Chief Ono), Minosuke Yamada (Saito), Haruo Tanaka (Sakai), Bokuzen Hidari (Ohara), Shinichi Himori (Kimura), Nobuo Nakamura (deputy mayor), Kazuo Abe (city assemblyman), Masao Shimizu (doctor), Ko Kimura (intern), Atsushi Watanabe (patient), Yunosuke Ito (novelist), Yatsuko Tanami (hostess), Fuyuki Murakami (newspaperman), Seiji Miyaguchi (gang-boss), Daisuke Kato (gang-member), Kin Sugai, Eiko Miyoshi, Fumiko Homma (housewives), Ichiro Chiba (policeman).

The unforgettable Takashi Shimura in Akira Kurosawa's *Ikiru* (1952).

A Toho Co., Ltd. Production. Black and white. Academy ratio. 143 minutes. Released October 9, 1952.

U.S. VERSION: Released by Brandon Films, Inc. English subtitles. Alternate titles: *To Live* and *Doomed*. 143 minutes. No MPAA rating. Released January 1960.

Illusion of Blood / Yotsuya kaidan ("The Yotsuya Ghost Story"). Producer, Ichiro Sato; Director, Shiro Toyoda; Screenplay, Toshio Yasumi, based on the Kabuki play *Tokaido Yotsuya kaidan*, by Namboku Tsuruya; Director of Photography, Hiroshi Murai; Music, Toru Takemitsu.

CAST: Tatsuya Nakadai (Iuemon Tamiya), Mariko Okada (Oiwa), Junko Ikeuchi (Osode), Kanzaburo Nakamura (Gonbei Naosuke), Mayumi Ozora (Oume), Keiko Awaji (Omaki), Yasushi Nagata (Samon Yotsuya), Eitaro Ozawa (Kihei Ito), Masao Mishima (Takuetsu), Kanjiro Taira.

A Tokyo Eiga (Tokyo Movie Co., Ltd.) Production, in association with Toho Co., Ltd. A Toho Co., Ltd. Release. Eastman Color. Toho Scope. 105 minutes. Released 1965.

U.S. VERSION: Released by Frank Lee International. English subtitles. 105 minutes. No MPAA rating. Released March 1966.

Image Wife / Riko na oyomesan ("Smart Wife"). Producer, Hiroshi Okawa; Director, Kenjyu Imaizumi; Screenplay, Koreya Senda; Art Director, Seigo Shindo; Director of Photography,

Nenji Oyama; Editor, Yoshiki Nagasawa; Music, Hiraku Hayashi.

CAST: Etsudo Ichihara, Kanjiro Taira, Chieko Higashiyama, Sue Mitobe, Kappei Matsumoto, Koreya Senda.

A Toei Co., Ltd. Production. Film processed by Toei Chemistry Co., Ltd. Academy ratio (?). Running time undetermined. Released 1958.

U.S. VERSION: Distributor undetermined. English subtitles. No MPAA rating. Released 1958.

Immortal Love / Eien no hito ("Immortal Love"). Producer, Sennosuke Tsukimori and Keisuke Kinoshita; Director/Screenplay, Keisuke Kinoshita; Director of Photography, Hiroyuki Kusuda; Art Director, Chiyo Umeda; Music, Chuji Kinoshita.

CAST: Hideko Takamine (Sadako), Yoshi Kato (Sojiro, *her father*), Keiji Sada (Takashi Kawanami), Kiyoshi Nonomura (Rikizo, *his eldest brother*), Tatsuya Nakadai (Heibei Koshimizu), Yasushi Nagata (Heizaemon, *his father*), Nobuko Otowa (Tomoko Kawanami, *Takashi's wife*), Masakazu Tamura (Eiichi, *Heibei's eldest son*), Masaya Tokuza (Morito, *Heibei's second son*), Yukiko Fuji (Naoko, *Heibei's daughter*), Akira Ishihama (Yutaka, *Takashi's only son*), Eijiro Tono (the policeman).

A Shochiku Co., Ltd. Production. Black and white. Shochiku GrandScope. Filmed on location at Mt. Aso. 107 minutes. Released 1961.

U.S. VERSION: Released by Shochiku Films of America, Inc. English subtitles.

Imperial Navy / Rengo kantai ("The Grand Fleet"). Executive Producer, Tomoyuki Tanaka; Director, Shue Matsubayashi; Screenplay, Katsuya Suzaki; Director of Photography, Katsuhiro Kato; Art Director, Iwao Akune; Lighting, Shinji Kojima; Sound Recording, Fumio Yanoguchi; Music, Shinji Tanimura and Katsuhisa Hattori; Song: "Gunjo," Music, Lyrics and Performer, Shinji Tanimura. *Toho Special Effects Group*: Director, Teruyoshi Nakano; Photography, Takao Tsurumi; Art Director, Yasuyuki Inoue; Lighting, Masakuni Morimoto.

CAST: Keiju Kobayashi (Admiral Yamamoto), Toshiyuki Nagashima, Kenichi Kaneda, Yuko Kotegawa, Takaichi Nakai, Yoshitaka Tamba, Tatsuya Mihashi, Koji Takahashi, Ichiro Zaitsu, Hiroyuki Nagato, Ichiro Nakaya, Takuya Fujioka, Kei Sato, Shigeru Koyama, Eitaro Ozawa, Nobuo Kaneko, Makoto Sato, Toru Abe, Jun Tazaki, Tetsuro Tamba, Susumu Fujita, Tomoko Naraoka, Kayo Matsuo, Chikako Yuri, Koji Tsuruta, Hisaya Morishige.

A Toho Co., Ltd. Production. Color. Spherical Panavision. 145 minutes. Released August 8, 1981.

U.S. VERSION: Released by Toho International Co., Ltd. in subtitled format. 145 minutes. No MPAA rating. Released November 28, 1983. Released to video by Sony. English-dubbed.

The Imposter. Producers, Shigeki Sugiyama and Koichi Takagi; Director, Tatsuo Osone; Screenplay, Hyogo Suzuki, based on an original story by Mitsuzo Sasaki.

CAST: Utaemon Ichikawa (Baron Mondosuke Sotome), Chikako Mitagi (Kyoya), Keiko Kishi (Kikuji), Koichi Takata (Jokai), Fijiro Yanagi (Naisen), Kodayu Ichikawa (Matsudaira), Kuniko Ikawa (Hagino), Minoru Oki (Kojiro), Ayuko Saijo (Nanae), Jogi Kaieda (Tokugawa).

A Shochiku Co., Ltd. Production. Black and white. Academy ratio. Running time and release date undetermined.

U.S. VERSION: Released by Brandon Films, Inc. English subtitles. Running time undetermined. No MPAA rating. Released March 22, 1955.

In the Realm of the Senses / Ai no korrida ("Bullfight of Love"). Producer, Anatole Dauman; Director, Nagisa Oshima; Screenplay, Nagisa Oshima, based on the life of Sada Abe; Director of Photography, Hideo Ito; Art Director, Jusho Toda; Music, Minoru Miki.

CAST: Eiko Matsuda (Sada Abe); Tatsuya Fuji (Kichi Zo), Aoi Nakajima (Toku), Taiji Tonoyama (old begger), Kanae Kobayashi (Kikuryu, *the old geisha*), Akiko Koyama.

An Oshima Productions/Anatole Dauman Production. A Japanese/French coproduction. Color. Spherical wide screen. 105 minutes. Released 1976.

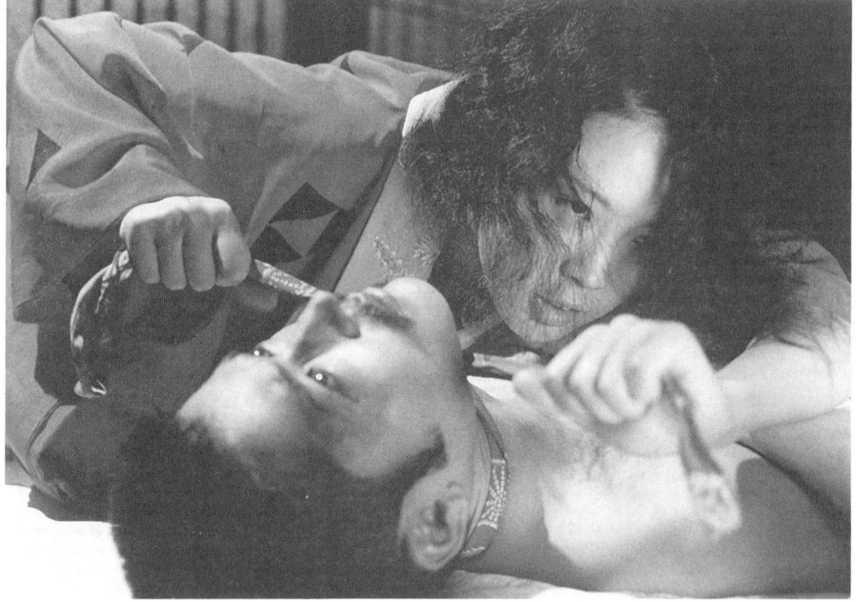

Eiko Matsuda and Tatsuya Fuji in *In the Realm of the Senses* (1976).

U.S. VERSION: Released by Cinema 5. English subtitles. The same story had been filmed before, as *A Woman Named Sada Abe* (1975). One source lists Argos Films and Oceanique as co-producers. 105 minutes. No MPAA rating. Released April 1, 1977. *Note:* The film was scheduled to make its U.S. premiere at the New York Film Festival on October 4, 1976, but the print was withheld by U.S. customs officials.

The Incident / Jiken ("Incident"). Producers, Yoshitaro Nomura and Akira Oda; Director, Yoshitaro Nomura; Screenplay, Kaneto Shindo, based on an original story by Shohei Oka; Director of Photography, Takashi Kawamata; Art Director, Kyohei Morita; Music, Yasushi Akutagawa.

CAST: Toshiyuki Nagashima, Keiko Matsuzaka, Shinobu Otake.

A Shochiku Co., Ltd. Production. Color. Panavision (?). 138 minutes. Released 1978.

U.S. VERSION: Released by Shochiku Films of America, Inc. in subtitled format. 138 minutes. No MPAA rating. Released December 15, 1978.

Industrial Spy Free-for-All / Kureji dayo tenkamuteki ("It's Crazy—There's No Enemy"). Executive Producer, Shin Watanabe; Director, Takashi Tsuboshima; Screenplay, Yasuo Tanami; Director of Photography, Fukuzo Koizumi; Music, Tessho Hagiwara.

CAST: Hajime Hana, Hitoshi Ueki, Kei Tani, Hiroshi Inuzaka, Senri Sakurai, Shin Yasuda, Eitaro Ishibashi [The Crazy Cats], Yumiko Nogawa.

A Watanabe Productions/Toho Co., Ltd. Production. Color. Toho Scope. 95 minutes. Released 1967.

U.S. VERSION: Release undetermined, possibly by Toho International Co., Ltd. in subtitled format. No MPAA rating. The 8th "Crazy" feature. Followed by *Las Vegas Free-for-All* (1967).

The Inheritance / Karami-ai ("Intertwinement"). Director, Masaki Kobayashi; Screenplay, Koichi Inagaki; Director of Photography, Ko Kawamata; Editor, S. Miyaki; Music, Toru Takemitsu.

CAST: Keiko Kishi (Yasuko), Misako Watanabe (Senzo), So Yamamura (clerk),

Minoru Chiaki (Marie), Tatsuya Nakadai, Yusuke Kawazu, Mari Yoshimura.

A Shochiku Co., Ltd. Production. Shochikucolor (?). Shochiku Grand-Scope. 118 minutes. Released 1961.

U.S. VERSION: Released by Shochiku Films of America, Inc. English subtitles. Note: Given that actor Chiaki is male, the role billed seems questionable. 107 minutes. No MPAA rating. Released February 24, 1964.

An Inn in Tokyo / Tokyo no yado ("An Inn in Tokyo"). Director, Yasujiro Ozu; Screenplay, Tadao Ikeda and Masao Arata; Director of Photography, Hideo Shigehara.

CAST: Takeshi Sakamoto, Yoshiko Okada, Choko Iida, Tomio Aoki, Chishu Ryu.

A Shochiku Co., Ltd. Production. Filmed at Shochiku-Kamata Studios. Silent with music track. Black and white. Academy ratio. 82 minutes. Released November 21, 1935.

U.S. VERSION: Distributor undetermined, possibly Shochiku Films of America, Inc. 82 minutes. No MPAA rating. Released 1972 (?).

Inn of Evil / Inochi bonifuro ("Let's Waste Our Lives"). Executive Producers, Masayuki Sato, Ginichi Kishimoto and Hideyuki Shino; Director, Masaki Kobayashi; Screenplay, Tomoe Ryu (i.e. Kyoko Miyazaki), based on the novel *Fukagawa anrakutei* by Sugoror Yamamoto; Art Director, Hiroshi Mizutani; Director of Photography, Hideo Nishizaki; Music, Toru Takemitsu; Sound, Toho Recording Centre; Sound Effects, Toho Sound Effects Group.

CAST: Ganemon Nakamura (Ikuzo), Komaki Kurihara (Omitsu), Kei Sato (Yohei), Tatsuya Nakadai (Sadahichi), Shintaro Katsu (nameless wanderer), Wakako Sakai (Okiwa), Shigeru Koyama (Officer Kanedo), Ichido Nakaya (Officer Okajima), Kei Yamamoto (Tomijiro), Yusuke Takida (Nadaya Kohei), Yosuke Kondo (Masaji), Daido Kusano (Yunosuke), Hatsuo Yamatani (Suke), Jun Makita (Senkichi), Shin Kishida (Genzo), Masao Mishima (Funayado Tokubei).

A Haiyuza/Toho Co., Ltd. Production. Westrex recording system. Color [?] (processed by Tokyo Laboratory Ltd.).

Toho Scope. 121 minutes. Released March 1, 1971.

U.S. VERSION: Released by Toho International Co., Ltd. English subtitles. 121 minutes. No MPAA rating. Released March 1972.

An Innocent Maid / Hakoiri musume ("An Innocent Girl"). Director, Yasujiro Ozu; Screenplay, Kogo Noda and Tadao Ikeda, based on a story by Sanu Shikitei; Director of Photography, Hideo Shigehara.

CAST: Kinuyo Tanaka, Choko Iida, Takeshi Sakamoto, Tomio Aoki, Kenji Oyama, Chishu Ryu.

A Shochiku Co., Ltd. Production. Filmed at Shochiku-Kamata Studios. Silent. Black and white. Academy ratio. 87 minutes. Released January 12, 1935.

U.S. VERSION: Never released theatrically in the United States. A lost film. Intended as the first film of a series of which this was, ultimately, the only entry.

Innocent Sinner / Yoru no Isoginchaku ("Night of the Starfish"). Director, Taro Yuge; Screenplay, Kazuo Funabashi; Director of Photography, Akira Uehara; Art Director, Taijiro Goto; Music, Sei Ikeno.

CAST: Mari Atsumi (Yoko Hamaguchi), Minoru Chiaki (Minister Wada), Michiko Otsuka (his wife), Kenzo Kaneko (Igawa), Osamu Sakai (Shibazaki), Emiko Iida.

A Daiei Motion Picture Co., Ltd. Production. Fujicolor. DaieiScope. 85 minutes. Released July 1, 1970.

U.S. VERSION: Release undetermined, possibly by Daiei International Films. English subtitled version available. 85 minutes. No MPAA rating.

The Insect Woman / Nippon konchuki ("Record of the Insect in Japan"). Producers, Kano Otsuka and Jiro Tomoda; Director, Shohei Imamura; Screenplay, Keiji Hasebe and Shohei Imamura; Director of Photography, Shinsaku Himeda; Art Director, Kimihiko Nakamura; Editor, Mitsuo Tanji; Music, Toshiro Mayuzumi; Sound Recording, Tsuneo Furuyama; Assistant Director,

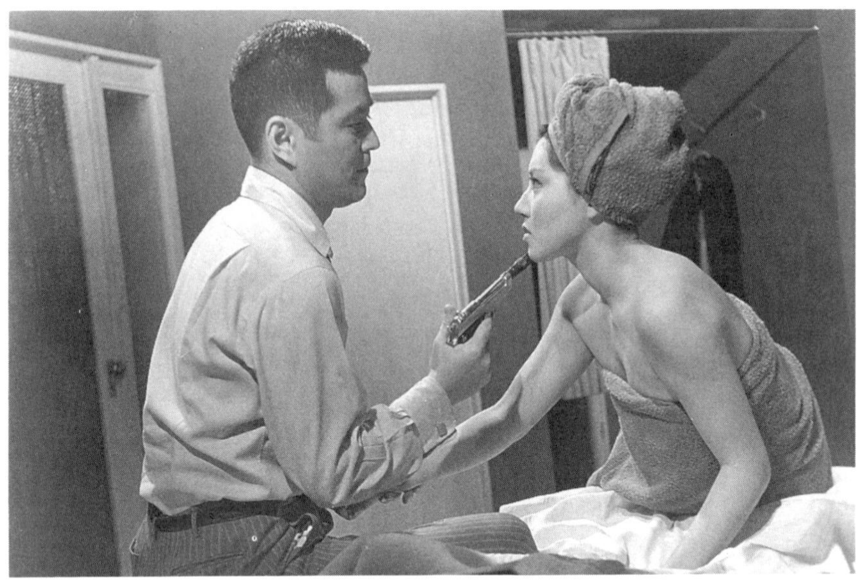

Tatsuya Mihashi and cult star Kumi Mizuno in *Interpol Code 8* (1963).

Tadahiko Isomi; Production Manager, Masanori Yamanoi.

CAST: Sachiko Hidari (Tome), Jitsuko Yoshimura (Nobuko), Hiroyuki Nagato (Matsunami), Seizaburo Kawazu (Karasawa), Kazuo Kitamura (Chuji), Sumie Sasaki (En), Shoichi Kuwayama (Owagawa), Daizaburo Hirata (Kamibayashi), Shoichi Ozawa (Ken), Taiji Tonoyama (foreman), Shoichi Tsuyuguchi (Honda), Tanie Kitabayashi (midwife), Emiko Higashi (Kane), Masumi Harukawa (Midori), Teruko Kishi (Rin), Asao Koike (Sawakichi), Emiko Aizawa (Rui).

A Nikkatsu Corporation Production. Westrex Recording System. Black and white. NikkatsuScope. 123 minutes. Released 1963.

U.S. VERSION: Released by Shochiku Films of America, Inc. English subtitles. Alternate title: *The Insect.* Reissued in 1989 by East-West Classics. Subtitles, Audie Bock. Letterboxed laserdisc version available. 123 minutes. No MPAA rating. Released June 30, 1964.

International Military Tribunal for the Far East: The Tokyo Trial / Tokyo Saiban ("Tokyo Trial") [**documentary**]. Producer, Hiroshi Suto; Director, Masaki Kobayashi; Screenplay, Ryu Yasutake, Masaki Kobayashi, and Kiyoshi Ogasawara; Director of Photography, Keiichi Uraoka; Music, Toru Takemitsu.

WITH: Kei Sato (narrator).

A Kodasha Ltd. Production. Black and white. Academy ratio (?). 277 minutes. Released 1983.

U.S. VERSION: Distributor, if any, is undetermined. English narrated version available. Narrators, Stuart Atkin and Frank Rogers. No MPAA rating. 277 minutes.

Interpol Code 8 / Kokusai himitsu keisatsu shirei hachigo ("International Secret Police—Interpol Code 8"). Executive Producers, Tomoyuki Tanaka and Reiji Miwa; Director, Toshio Sugie; Screenplay, Ei Ogawa; Music, Yoshiyuki Kozu.

CAST: Tatsuya Mihashi, Makoto Sato, Yosuke Natsuki, Kumi Mizuno, Jerry Ito.

A Toho Co., Ltd. Production. Eastman Color. Toho Scope. 94 minutes. Released 1963.

U.S. VERSION: Possibly released by Toho International Co., Ltd. English subtitles. English-dubbed version available. First feature of the 5-film "International Secret Police" film series. Some footage may have been incorporated into *What's Up, Tiger Lily?* (q.v.). 94 minutes. No MPAA rating.

An Introduction to Marriage / Kekkon gaku nyumon ("An Introduction to Marriage Study"). Director, Yasujiro Ozu; Screenplay, Kogo Noda, based on an idea by Toshio Okuma; Director of Photography, Hideo Shigehara.

CAST: Tatsuo Saito, Sumiko Kurishima, Minoru Takada, Mitsuko Yoshikawa, Chishu Ryu.

A Shochiku Co., Ltd. Production. Filmed at Shochiku-Kamata Studios. Silent with benshi. Black and white. Academy ratio. 107 minutes. Released January 5, 1930.

U.S. VERSION: Never released theatrically in the United States. A lost film.

The Inugami Family / Inugamike no ichizoku ("The Inugami Family"). Producers, Haruki Kadokawa and Kon Ichikawa; Director, Kon Ichikawa; Screenplay, Nario Nagata, Shinya Hidaka, and Kon Ichikawa, based on the novel *Inugamike no ichizoku* by Seishi Yokomizo, as published by Kadokawa Publishing Co., Ltd.; Director of Photography, Kiyoshi Hasegawa; Music, Yuji Ono; Art Director, Iwao Akune; Sound Recording, Tetsuya Ohashi; Lighting, Kenichi Okamoto.

CAST: Koji Ishizaka (Detective Kosuke Kindaichi), Yoko Shimada (Nonomiya), Mieko Takamine (Matsuko Inugami, *the first daughter*), Teruhiko Aoi (Sukekiyo Inugami, *Matsuko's son*), Miki Sanjo (Takeko Inugami, *the second daughter*), Mitsuke Kusabue (Umeko Inugami, *the third daughter*), Takeo Jii (Suketake Inugami, *Takeko's son*), Akira Kawaguchi (Sayako Inugami, *Takeko's daughte*r), Hisashi Kawaguchi (Suketomo Inugami, *Umeko's son*), Ryunosuke Kaneda (Toranosuke Inugami, *Takeko's husband*), Shoji Kobayashi (Kokichi Inugami, *Umeko's husband*), Yoko Shimada (Tamayo Nonomiya), Minoru Terada (Saruzo, *the servant*), Yuko Ozeki (Kikuno Aonuma), Teruhiko Aoi (Shizuma Aonuma, *Kikuno's son*), Rentaro Mikuni (Sayoe Inugami), Eitaro Ozawa (Kyozo Furukata, *the attorney*), Takeshi Kato (Police Inspector Todoroki).

A Haruki Kadokawa Films, Inc. Production. A Kon Ichikawa Film. A Toho Co., Ltd. Release. Color. Panavision (?). 146 minutes. Released November 13, 1976.

U.S. VERSION: Distributor, if any, is undetermined, likely Toho International Co., Ltd. English subtitles. First feature of a 5-film series (1976-79); all of the sequels were produced by Toho. Followed by *The Devil's Bouncing Ball Song* (1977).

Invasion of the Neptune Men / Uchu kaizoku-sen ("Space Pirate Ship"). Producer, Hiroshi Okawa; Director, Koji Ota; Screenplay, Shin Morita; Director of Photography, Shizuka Fuji.

CAST: Shinichi "Sonny" Chiba (Mr. Tabana/Space Chief [Iron Sharp]), Kappei Matsumoto, Mitsue Komiya, Shinjiro Ebara, Ryuko Minakami.

A Toei Co., Ltd. Production. Black and white (processed by Toei Chemistry Co., Ltd.). 1.33:1. 74 minutes. Released July 19, 1961.

U.S. VERSION: U.S. release undetermined, but sources indicate it was, in 1961, as *Space Greyhound*, possibly subtitled. Alternate titles (?): *Space Chief, Invasion from a Planet*. Released to television by Medallion TV, a division of Medallion Pictures, Inc. (and known today as Walter H. Manley Enterprises, Inc.). English-dubbed. Producer, ProPix, Inc. The possible inclusion of stock footage from *The Last War* (Toei, 1960) may account for the longer running time of the U.S. version. 82 minutes. No MPAA rating.

The Invisible Swordsman / Tomei Kenshi ("The Invisible Swordsman"). Producer, Hidemasa Nagata;

Director, Yoshiyuki Kuroda; Sound, Daiei Recording Studio.

CAST: (not available).

A Daiei Motion Picture Co., Ltd. Production. Daieicolor. DaieiScope. 79 minutes. Released 1970.

U.S. VERSION: Released by Daiei International Films. English subtitles. 79 minutes. No MPAA rating. Released September 30, 1970.

Irezumi–Spirit of the Tattoo / Sekatomu rai gishi Producers, Yasuyoshi Tokuma and Masumi Kanamaru; Planner, Yoichi Yamamoto; Assistant Producers, Yoshiaki Saito and Masayuki Motomochi; Director, Yoichi Takabayashi; Screenplay, Chiho Katsura, based on the novel by Baku Akae; Director of Photography, Hideo Fujii; Art Director, Seiten Shimoishizaka; Music, Masaru Sato.

CAST: Masayo Utsunomiya (Akane), Tomisaburo Wakayama (Kyogoro), Yusuke Takita (Fujieda), Masaki Kyomoto (Harutsune), Harue Kato (Katsuko), Naomi Shiraishi (Haruna), Taiji Tonoyama (Horiatsu).

A Daiei Co., Ltd. Production. Color. Spherical wide screen. 109 minutes. Released 1982.

U.S. VERSION: Released by Almi Classics. English subtitles. 109 minutes. No MPAA rating. Released May 9, 1984.

The Island / Hadaka no shima ("The Naked Island"). Producers, Kaneto Shindo and Eisaku Matsura; Director/Screenplay, Kaneto Shindo; Director of Photography, Kiyoshi Kuroda; Editor, Toshio Enoki; Music, Hikaru Hayashi; Sound Recording, Kunie Maruyama.

CAST: Nobuko Otowa (Toyo, *the mother*), Taiji Tonoyama (Senta, *the father*), Shinji Tanaka (Taro, *the elder son*), Masanori Horimoto (Jiro, *the younger son*).

A Kindai Eiga Kyoki Co., Ltd. Production. A Toho Co., Ltd. Release (?). Black and white. Toho Scope (?). 96 minutes. Released 1960.

U.S. VERSION: Released by Zenith International Film Corporation. English subtitles (?). Alternate title: *The Naked Island*. 96 minutes. No MPAA rating. Released September 10, 1962.

Island of Horrors / Gokumonto ("Island of Prison Gate"). Producers, Kon Ichikawa and Osamu Tanaka; Planning, Haruki Kadokawa Office; Director, Kon Ichikawa; Screenplay, Kon Ichikawa, based on a story by Seishi Yokomizo; Director of Photography, Kiyoshi Hasegawa; Music, Shinichi Tanabe; Art Director, Shinobu Muraki; Sound Recording, Fumio Yanoguchi; Lighting, Kojiro Sato.

CAST: Koji Ishizaka (Kosuke Kindaichi), Reiko Ohara (Sanae), Mitsuko Kusabue (Osayo, *Yosamatsu's second wife*), Kiwako Taichi (Tomoe, *Gihei's second wife*), Yoko Tsukasa (Katsuno), Eijiro Tono (Kaemon Kito), Taketoshi Naito (Yosamatsu Kito, *Kaemon's son*), Hirokazu Takeda (Chimata Kito, *Yosamatsu's son*), Shin Saburi (Priest Ryonen), Takeshi Kato (Police Inspector Todoroki).

A Toho Co., Ltd. Production. Color. Spherical wide screen. 141 minutes. Released August 27, 1977.

U.S. VERSION: Released by Toho International Co., Ltd. English subtitles. A sequel to *The Devil's Bouncing Ball Song* (1977), and followed by *Queen Bee* (1978). 141 minutes. No MPAA rating. Released January 27, 1978.

It Started in the Alps / Arupusu no wakadaisho ("Young Boss in the Alps"). Producer, Sanezumi Fujimoto; Director, Kengo Furusawa; Screenplay, Yasuo Tanami; Director of Photography, Tadashi Iimura; Music, Kenjiro Hirose.

CAST: Yuzo Kayama (Yuichi Tanuma), Yuriko Hoshi (Sumiko), Kunie Tanaka (Shinjiro), Ichiro Arishima (Yuichi's father), Choko Iida (Yuichi's grandmother), Edith Hanson (Lucienne), Akiko Wakabayashi, Tatsuyoshi Ebara, Machiko Naka, Osman Yusef.

A Toho Co., Ltd. Production. Color. Toho Scope. 94 minutes. Released 1966.

U.S. VERSION: Released by Toho International Co., Ltd. English subtitles. The 7th "Young Guy" feature. 94 minutes. No MPAA rating. Released December 21, 1966.

It's a Woman's World / Shin onna onna onna monogatari ("New Woman, Woman, Woman Story") [**documentary**]. Producer, Yukio Taniguchi; Director, Taijiro Tamura; Screenplay,

Saburo Nita; Director of Photography, Kazutoshi Akutagawa; Cameraman, Takeo Kurata; Editor, Hanzaburo Kaneko; Music, Shoichi Makino; Assistant Director, Satoru Kobayashi; Production Manager, Toshiyuki Ike.

WITH: Ayuro Miki (narrator).

A Phoenix Film Production. A Shochiku Co., Ltd. Release. Eastman Color. Shochiku GrandScope. Released October 1964.

U.S. VERSION: Released by Shochiku Films of America, Inc. English subtitles. 80 minutes. No MPAA rating. Released January 8, 1965.

The Ivory Ape. Executive Producer, Jules Bass; Producer, Arthur Rankin, Jr.; Associate Producers, Benni Korzen, Masaki Iizuka; Director, Tom Kotani; Screenplay, William Overgard; Story, William Overgard, Arthur Rankin, Jr.; Director of Photography, Yozo Inagaki; Music, Maury Laws, Bernard Hoffer; Conductor, Bernard Hoffer; Supervising Editor, Barry Walter, Editor, Wendy Mank; Assistant Director, Kaz Kazui; Second Assistant Director, James Bigham; First Assistant Cameraman, Takayoshi Oneda; Second Assistant Cameraman, Akio Inoue; Camera Loader, Peter Spera Production Designer, Kazuo Satsuya; Art Director and Property Master, Peter Politanoff; Lighting Director, Gengon Nakaoka; Lighting Assistants, Sadao Hasegawa, Koichi Kamada; Key Grip, Zeev Willy Neumann; Sound, Yuji Hiyoshi; Sound Assistant, Osamu Kukuoka; Sound Mixer, Robert Elder; Stunt Designer, Henry Schrady; Production Coordinator, Lee Dannacher; Sound Effects Editor, Jim Tatum, Jr.; Makeup Artist, Nick Crimi; Wardrobe, Alexandra Layman; Wardrobe Assistants, Sheila Dempster, Elizabeth Wingate; Assistant to the Producer, Barbara Adams; Production Coordinator, Lee Dannacher; Production Assistants, Todd Rankin, Sheena Tucker, Davina Tucker, Sandra Pedro; Still Photographer, Peter Moran; Property Assistants, Beverly Welch, Andrew Outerbridge, Layton Outerbridge, Michael Correia; Location Manager, J.A.D. Froud; Assistant Editor, Gena Hegleman; Dialog Director, David Man; Dialog Supervisor, Frances Herman; Second Unit Photography, Mike Spera, Jeri Sopranen; Transportation. Richard Floyd; Casting, Joy-Todd, Inc.; Location Casting, Richard Morbey; "Rangi" Technicians, Shunichi Mizuno, Masahito Sesaki; Stunt Designer, Henry Schrady; Special Effects, Tsuburaya Enterprises, Inc.

CAST: Jack Palance (Marc Kazarian), Cindy Pickett (Lil Tyler), Celine Lomez (Valerie Lamont Kazarian), Derek Partridge (Aubrey Range), Steven Keats (U.S. Department of Interior Special Agent Baxter Mapes), Earle Hayman (Chief Police Inspector Saint George), Lou David (Roomie Pope), Tricia Sembera (Vita Havermyer), William Horrigan (Ship's Captain), David Man (Dr. Cole), Leonard Daniels (Police Constable Smith), George Rushe (Police Constable Johnny Wilkinson), Daniel Thomas (Taxi Driver), Irving Wilkinson (Kazarian's Butler), Courtney Floyd (Courtney), John Truscott (Police Constable Collins), John Lough (Trot Toomer), Jane Bainbridge (Courtney's Mother), Charles Jeffers (Congo Father), Kevin Dill (Congo Son), Grace Rawlins (Congo Mother), Easton Rawlins (Congo Son), Marlene Butterfield (ZFB-TV Reporter), Barbara Adams (Baxter's Secretary), Duke Soares (Stuntman).

A Rankin/Bass Productions, Inc. Production, in association with Tsuburaya Enterprises, Inc. An Arthur Rankin, Jr./ Jules Bass presentation. A U.S./Japanese co-production in English. Distributed by Worldvision Enterprises, Inc. "The producer gratefully acknowledges the valuable cooperation of the Government of Bermuda and its Ministries." Filmed at Tsuburaya Studios, Tokyo, and on location in Bermuda and Japan. Color by Movielab. Wide screen (1.66:1 projected screen aspect ratio). 100 minutes. Released 1980 (?).

U.S. VERSION: Never released theatrically in the United States. Released directly to television, and was first broadcast on the American Broadcasting Companies, Inc. (ABC) network April 18, 1980. 96 minutes. Distributed by Worldwide Enterprises, Inc.

Jack and the Witch / Shonen Jack to Mahotsukai ("Jack the Boy and the Witch") [**animated**]. Director, Taiji Yabushita; Screenplay, Shinichi

Sekizawa and Susumu Takahisa; Director of Photography, Hideaki Sugawara.

VOICE CHARACTERIZATIONS: (undetermined).

A Toei Animation Co., Ltd. Production. A Toei Co., Ltd. Release. Eastman Color. ToeiScope. 80 minutes. Released 1967.

U.S. VERSION: Distributor, if any, is undetermined. Available with subtitles.

A Japanese Tragedy / Nihon no higeki ("Tragedy of Japan"). Producers, Takashi Koide and Tyotaro Kuwata; Director/Screenplay, Keisuke Kinoshita; Assistant Director, Yoshio Kawazu; Director of Photography, Hiroyuki Kusuda; Art Director, Kimihiko Nakamura; Music, Chuji Kinoshita.

CAST: Yuko Mochizuki (Haruko Inoue), Yoko Katsuragi (Utako, *Haruko's daughter*), Masami Taura (Seiichi, *Haruko's son*), Keiji Sada (Tatsuya), Ken Uehara (Masayuki Akazawa, *the English teacher*), Sanae Takasugi (Mrs. Akazaka), Keiko Awaji (Wakamaru).

A Shochiku Co., Ltd. Production. Black and white. Academy ratio. 116 minutes. Released 1953.

U.S. VERSION: Released by Shochiku Films of America, Inc. English subtitles. 116 minutes. No MPAA rating. Released May 30, 1979.

Jasei no in (title undetermined). Director, Thomas Kurihara; Based on the story by Akinari [Shusei] Ueda.

CAST: Tokihiko Okada, Yoko Benizawa.

A Taikatsu Production. Silent. Black and white. Academy ratio. Running time undetermined. Released 1920.

U.S. VERSION: Distributor, if any, is undetermined. International titles: *Obscenity of the Viper, Lasciviousness of the Viper* and *The Maliciousness of the Snake's Evil*. Remade as *Tales of Ugetsu* (Daiei, 1953).

Jigoku ("Hell"). Director, Tatsumi Kumashiro; Screenplay Yozo Tanaka, based on the screenplay by Ichiro Miyagawa and Nobuo Nakagawa for the 1960 production *The Sinners of Hell* (q.v.); Director of Photography, Shigeru Akatsuka; Special Effects Director, Nobuo Yajima; Music, Riichiro Manabe.

CAST: Mieko Harada, Kyoko Kishida, Ryuzo Hayashi, Renji Ishibashi.

A Toei Co., Ltd. Production. Toeicolor. Panavision. 122 minutes. Released 1979.

U.S. VERSION: Distributor undetermined. International title: *The Inferno*. Released 1981 (?).

Jotai johatsu ("A Woman's Body Vanishes"). Director, Seiichi Fukuda.

CAST: Midori Enoki (bar hostess), Hachiro Tsuruoka (Ejiri), Hiroko Fuji (Ejiri's ex-wife), Yuri Izumi, Machiko Sakyo, Kemi Ichiboshi.

A Nihon Cinema Production. Black and white. Academy ratio. 83 minutes. Released 1967.

U.S. VERSION: Distributor, if any, is undetermined. International title: *Woman's Body Vanishes*.

Journey of Honor. Executive Producers, Hiroshi Tsuchiya and Toshiaki Hayashi; Producer, Sho Kosugi; Director, Gordon Hessler; Screenplay, Nelson Gidding; Story, Sho Kosugi and Nelson Gidding; Yugoslavian Line Producer, Milos Antic; Associate Producer, Gene Kraft; Line Producer, Benni Korzen; Director of Photography, John Connor; Production Design, Adrian Gorton; Editor, Bill Butler; Music Composer and Conductor, John Scott, performed by the Hungarian State Opera Orchestra; Casting, Caro Jones; Second Unit Director/Unit Production Manager, Gene Kraft; Casting (U.K.), Hubbard Casting; Production Coordinator, Suzanne Kraft; Still Photographer, Peter Kernot; Assistant Film Editors, Lynne Butler and Les Butler; Supervising Sound Editor, Mike Le-Mare; Dialogue and ADR Editor, Anthony Palk; Sound Effects Editor, David Lewis Yewdall; Supervising Foley Editor, Karola Storr; Foley Editors, Paul Heslin, Donlee Jorgensen, John Post; Assistant Sound Editors, Uri Katoni, Janelle Showalter, Armond Ghzanian; Apprentice Sound Editor, Britton E. Taylor; Foley Artists, John Post and Paul Heslin; Rerecording Mixers, Douglas E. Turner, Frank Montano, and Grover Helsley;

Recordist, Leon Citarella; Foley Mixer, Troy Porter; ADR Mixers, Richard Rogers and Ron Bedrosian; Sound, Ryder Sound Services, Inc.; Music Editor, Richard Allen; Music Scoring Mixer, Keith Grant; Music Mixer, John Richards; Music Recorded at Malfilm Studios (Budapest), in cooperation with Intercom, Ltd., and Malfilm Audio, Ltd.; Music Mixed at Evergreen Recording Studios; Negative Cutter, Gary Burritt; Color Timer, Bill Pine; Production Assistants, Edrolfo L. Summoang, Daniel H. Holland, Allison Bell, Shlomo Eizencott; Studio Teacher, Nancy Flint; Kane's Acting Coach, Lilyan Chauvin; Stunt Coordinator, John Stewart; Unit Publicist, Bill Hersey; Production Accountants, Koo, Chow & Company, Patrick Fung, Chris Huang; Legal Services, Susan G. Schaefer; Accounting Services, Price Waterhouse. *Japan*: Associate Producers, Susumu Mishima and Kenichiro Fujiyama; Production Manager, Kunio Niwa; Asst. Production Managers, Akira Yamamoto and Ryo Yoshioka; Asst. to Sho Kosugi, Jimmy Obikawa; Production Secretary, Kuniko Kikuchi; 1st Asst. Director, Yoshihiro Hagiwara; 2nd Asst. Director, Naomasa Obata; 3rd Asst. Director, Takashi Takahata; 4th Asst. Director, Taku Harada; Art Director, Hiroyuki Kashiwa; 1st Asst. Art Director, Masuo Tsutsui; Asst. Art Directors, Akio Ito, Isao Akatsuka, Tetsuji Tatsuda; Prop Master, Koichi Hamamura; Props, Atsushi Ando, Yuzuru Sakai, Katsutaka Utena, and Reito Kurokawa; Hair and Makeup, Seiji Arai; Best Boy, Fumiaki Ozawa; Gaffer, Yiroyuki Nakazawa; Wardrobe, Haruo Hayashida, Yoshio Ninoyama, Yoshinao Inui; Camera Operator, Yukio Yata; 2nd Unit Camera Operator, Michio Iwamoto; 1st Camera Asst., Hisatake Watanabe; 2nd Camera Asst., Hiroshi Aoki; 3rd Camera Asst., Takahide Mashio; Still Photographers, Terutaka Hashimoto, Morikawa Masaru, Nagaishi Hidehiko; Script Supervsior, Jan Rudolph; Script Person, Yuka Honcho; Sound Mixers, David Kelson and Minoru Nobuoka; Boom Person, Yuka Honcho; Rerecording, Atsushi Kono; Production Assistants, Akihiko Iyama, Hiroshi Obikawa, Setsuo Sato, Ayumi Sato, and Kiemi Iwai; Choreographer, Hiroshi Kuze; Asst. Choreographers, Fumio Sasaki and Yuji Sawayama; Special Effects, Satoshi Narumi; Carpenters, Kazu haru Tsboi and Koetsu Nonaka; Lamp Operators, Masahiko Uchida, Tamihito Suzuki, Minoru Watanabe, Gen Hirai; Publicity, Akio Kitazawa (Shinto-Mirai Kikaku); Interpreters, Manami Mitami, S. Takae, and Tamura Kazuyoshi; Attorneys, Tokyo Aoyama Law Office, Shinichi Saito and Nobuko Narita; Auditor, Aoyama Kansa Co., Ltd (Price Waterhouse). *Yugoslavia*: Production Supervisor, Petar Jankovic; Unit Managers, Dragan Jovanovic, Dejan Sijakovic, Savo Radunovic, Savo Popovic, Nedjo Lecic; 1st Asst. Director, Petar Cvejic; 2nd Asst. Directors, Radenko Tomcic and Nikola Zivanovic; Camera, Djordje Nikolic; Focus Puller, Slavko Veljic; Assistant Camera, Milija Zivotic, Zoran Tosic, Miroslav Radoicic, Rajko Klimecki; 2nd Asst. Camera, Paja Todorovic; Script Supervisor, Bijana Mirkovic; Art Directors, Vlastimir Gavrik, Nemanja Petrovic, Dragoljub Ivkov, Bane Babic; Asst. Art Director, Aleksandar Stankovic; Prop Master, Velislav Glavas; Prop Buyer, Dragisa Maricic; Props, Zivan Vlajic; Chief Grip, Drago Zivotic; Grip I, Dragan Trpcevski; Grip II, Zika Jovanovic; Clapper Grip, Rajko Ognjanovic; Constructors, Kosta Kiskinov and Jovan Stankovic; Generator Man, Milovan Miletic; Electricians, Grada Novakovic, Dragan Josovic, Koja Mojsilovic; Gaffer, Stanko Bajalica; Makup, Stanislava Zaric, Rade Jeremic; Asst. Makeup, Aleksandra Kiskinov; Hairdresser, Vesna Popovic; Asst. Hairdresser, Suzana Djuric; Costume Designer, Emilija Kovacevic; Asst. Costume Designer, Snezana Stankovic; Wardrobe, Biljanka Mihailovic; Wardrobe Assts., Aleksandra Kiskinov and Snezana Yukcevic; Dressmaker, Sanja Jovanovic; Sound Mixer, Marko Rodic; Boom Operator, Milan Davidovic; Sound Operator, Jankov Marton; Asst. Editors, Nebojsa Popovic and Srdjan Pop-Konstatinovic; Stunts, Dragomir Bata Stanojevic-Kameni; Production Secretary, Milja Kolarevic; Special Effects, Boban Zivkovic and Srba Kabadajic; Brokers, Mile Pejovic and Pavle Petrici;

Doctor, Adam Cabric; Accountant, Zdenka Hrgovic; Cashier, Desanka Djordjevic; Interpreters, Mirjana Andric, Toni Sosic, Slobodan Arandjelovic; Manual Labor, Ljubomir Radevic; Property Labor, Dusko Todorovic; Hydralics, Ljuba Ziajic; Buffet, Dragan Mihailovic; Drivers, Dragan Prvanovic, Miroslav Stamenkovic, Goran Jokovic, Mladen Romic, Petar Nesic, Milorad Lukic, Mile Stanojevic, Sasa Gavran, Misa Petrovic, Vlada Pavlovic, Tahir Osmanovic, Maksimovic Mihailo, Tilomir Suletic, Miodrag Stanojevic, Milenko Gacevic, Jugoslav Bobera; Naval Constructor, Franjo Fles; Still Photographer, Sinisa Visnjic; Titles, Pacific Title, Opticals Cruse and Company; Thanks, Victoria Co., Ltd., H.T. Publisher, Inc., Ltd., Sanyo Securities Co., Ltd., Starrtts Corporation, Seiyu International Co., Ltd., General Lease Co., Ltd., Nippon Kowa Co., Ltd., Friends of Freesia Co., Ltd., Manshon Co., Ltd.

CAST: Sho Kosugi (Mayeda), David Essex (Don Pedro), Kane Kosugi (Yorimune), Christopher Lee (King Philip), Norman Lloyd (Father Vasco), Ronald Pickup (Captain Crawford), John Rhys-Davies (El Zaidan), Polly Walker (Cecilia), Dylan Kussman (Smitty), Toshiro Mifune (Lord Takugawa Ieyasu), Miwa Takada (Yadogimi), Nijiko Kiyokawa (counselor), Yuki Sugimura (Chiyo Mayeda), Ken Sekiguchi (Ishikawa), Naoto Shigemizu (Nakamura), Yuji Sawayama (East Army general), Toni Sosic (Dutch), Savic Milutin (1st pistoleer), Radevic Miomir (2nd pistoleer), Shinsuke Shirakura (Daisuke Mayeda, age 13-14), Masashi Muta (Daisuke Mayeda as an infant), Dusko Yujnnovic (Ibrahim), Stevan Minja (Salim), Ljubomir Skiljevic (taskmaster), John Stewart (sailor #1), Dragomir Stanojevic-Kameni (sailor #2), Bora Stojanovic (royal chamberlin), Tadashi Ogiwara (Mayeda's double), Yuji Sawayama (Yorimune stand-in), Osamu Yayama (Samurai in Edo Castle), Kenji Miura (interpreter for Ieyasu), Manami Mitani (interpreter for Yodogimi), Hidekazu Utsumi (page #1), Tadashi Ogasawara (page #2), Akira Hoshino, Kenji Yasunaga, Shogo Ikegami, Junichiro Hayama, Yoshiaki Iguchi (retainers for Ieyasu), Toshimi Yamaguchi, Tadashi Ogiwara, Satoru Fukasaku, Yuki Nasaka, Kazuhiro Taketoshi, Takashi Odajima (samurai guards for Ieyasu), John Stewart, Dale Gibson, Bob Ivy, Tadashi Ogiwara, Yuji Sawayama (stunts), Don Pedro Colley (narrator), John Dantona, Annie Korzen, Steve Kramer, Lisa Michelson, Ronnie Sperling, Suzanne Stanford (ADR performers).

A Sanyo Finance Co., Ltd./Sho Kosugi Corp./Sho Productions, Inc. Presentation. A Mayeda Productions, Inc. Film. A Japanese production in English and Japanese. Filmed on location in Japan and Yugoslavia. Dolby Stereo SR. De Luxe Color (processing by Technicolor [Rome]). Panavision. 107 minutes. Released 1991.

U.S. VERSION: Apparently never released theatrically in the United States. Released to television and home video by MCA Home Video, Inc. In English and Japanese with English subtitles. Alternate title: *Shogun Mayeda*. 107 minutes. Letterboxed laserdisc version available. MPAA rating: "PG-13." Released 1992.

Journey of Love / Kaze no bojo ("Yearning Wind"). Director, Noboru Nakamura; Screenplay, Sugako Hashida, based on his story; Director of Photography, Hiroshi Takemura; Art Director, Yutaka Yokoyama; Music, Taku Izumi.

CAST: Sayuri Yoshinaga (Yuko), Koji Ishizaka (Naoki), Yoshiko Kayama (Yuki).

A Shochiku Co., Ltd, Production. Eastman Color. Shochiku GrandScope. 93 minutes. Released July 1, 1970.

U.S. VERSION: Released by Shochiku Films of America, Inc. English subtitles. 93 minutes. No MPAA rating. Released April 2, 1971.

Ju Dou ("Ju Dou"). Executive Producers, Zhao Hangao, Shigeru Mori, and Hiroyuki Kato; Producers, Zhang Wenze, Yasuyoshi Tokuma, and Hu Jian; Production Directors, Fen Yitin and Michio Yokoo; Directors, Zhang Yimou and Yang Fengliang; Story, Liu Heng; Camera, Gu Chanwei and Yang Lun; Art Directors, Coa Jiuping and Xia Rujin;

Sound Recording, Li Lanhua; Music, Zhao Jipin; Editor, Du Yuan; Assistant Director, Zhou Youzhao; Lighting, Ji Jianmin; Assistant Cameramen, Tao Shiwei and Feng Yan; Assistant Art Director, Zhang Jiancun; Assistant Sound Recording, Dang Wans; Lighting Assistants, I. Yanzhong and Zeng Junwei (Hong Kong); Makeup, Sun Wei; Costumes, Zhang Zhian; Prop Masters, Ye Yaozhong and Cao Jiankong; Sceneries, Guo Zhengyi and Huang Minxian; Services, Salong Films (H.K.), Ltd.; Dolby Stereo Consultant, Mikio Mori, Continental Far East, Inc. (Tokyo); Cameras, Panavision.

CAST: Gong Li (Ju Dou), Li Baotian (Tianqing), Li Wei (Jinshan Yang), Zhang Yi (Tianbei Yang as an infant), Zheng Jian (Tianbei Yang as a youth).

A China Film Co-Production Corp./ China Film Export and Import Corp./ Tokuma Shoten Publishing Co., Ltd./Tokuma Communications Co., Ltd. Production. A Daiei Motion Picture Co., Ltd. Release. A Chinese/Japanese co-production in Mandarin with Japanese subtitles. Color. Academy ratio. Dolby stereo. Filmed in China and completed in Tokyo. Copyright 1990. 95 minutes.

U.S. VERSION: Released by Miramax Films. English subtitles. Spherical Panavision. Subtitles, Helen Eisenman, WJJ Opticals (New York). "For Renee Furst who expanded the boundries of cinema in America." *Note:* Despite the credit stating otherwise, this was not filmed in (anamorphic) Panavision. 95 minutes. No MPAA rating. Released March 1991.

Judo Champion / Minamitaheiyo no wakadaisho ("Young Boss of the South Pacific"). Executive Producers, Sanezumi Fujimoto and Kazuo Kamiya; Director, Kengo Furusawa; Screenplay, Yasuo Tanami; Director of Photography, Senkichi Nagai; Music, Kosaku Dan and Kenichiro Morioka.

CAST: Yuzo Kayama (Yuichi Tanuma), Yuriko Hoshi (Sumiko), Kunie Tanaka (Ishiyama), Beverly Maeda, Ichiro Arishima.

A Toho Co., Ltd. Production. Eastman Color. Toho Scope. Filmed on location in Honolulu, Hawaii, and at Toho Studios (Tokyo). 106 minutes. Released 1967.

U.S. VERSION: Released by Toho International Co., Ltd. English subtitles. The 10th "Young Guy" feature. Followed by *Go! Go! Young Guy* (1967). 106 minutes. No MPAA rating. Released 1967 (?).

Judo Saga / Sugata Sanshiro ("Sanshiro Sugata"). Executive Producers, Akira Kurosawa and Tomoyuki Tanaka; Director, Seiichiro Uchikawa; Screenplay, Akira Kurosawa, based on the novel(s) *Sugata Sanshiro* (1942-4) by Tsuneo Tomita, and the screenplays *Sugata Sanshiro* (1943) and *Sanshiro Sugata—Part 2* (1945) by Akira Kurosawa; Production Supervisor, Hiroshi Nezu; Music, Masaru Sato; Sound, Toho Recording Centre; Sound Effects, Toho Sound Effects Group.

CAST: Yuzo Kayama (Sanshiro Sugata), Toshiro Mifune (Shogoro Yano), Eiji Okada, Tsutomu Yamazaki, Yumiko Kokonoe, Yunosuke Ito, Daisuke Kato.

A Takarazuka Motion Picture Co., Ltd./Kurosawa Films, Ltd./Toho Co., Ltd. Production. A Toho Co., Ltd. Release. Black and white. Toho Scope (?). Western Electric Mirrophonic Recording (?). 159 minutes. Released 1965.

U.S. VERSION: Released by Toho International Co., Ltd. English subtitles. A remake of *Sanshiro Sugata* (1943) and *Sanshiro Sugata—Part 2* (1945). One source also credits Kurosawa as editor. Another version of the same story, *Judo Showdown* (1965?) followed. 159 minutes. No MPAA rating. Released August 27, 1965.

Judo Showdown / Yawara sempu doto no taiketsu ("Judo Cyclone: Raging Duel"). Director, Masateru Nishiyama; Screenplay, Daisei Motoyama and Narahiro Matsumura, based on the novel *Sugata Sanshiro* (1942-44) by Tsuneo Tomita; Director of Photography, Shozo Honda; Music, Eiichi Yamada.

CAST: Toshiya Wazaki (Sanshiro Sugata), Ryohei Uchida (Daizaburo Himon), Shoichi Hirai (Shogoro Yano), Seizaburo Kawazu (Okakura), Maki Katsura (Kaori, his daughter), Sanae Nakahara (Tone), Shinsuke Mikimoto (Gondo), Keiko Sajita, Yoko Matsuyama, Keiji Yano, Shintaro Kuraoka.

A Shochiku Co., Ltd. Production. Eastman Color. Shochiku GrandScope. Released 1965 (?).

U.S. VERSION: Released by Howard C. Brown and Shochiku Films of America, Inc. English subtitles (?). 87 minutes. No MPAA rating. Released April 1966.

Just for You / Iimono ageru. ("This Is for You"). Director, Yoshio Inoue; Screenplay, Kanji Yasumoto and Yoshio Inoue; Director of Photography, Setsuo Kobayashi; Art Director, Shigeo Mano.

CAST: Mari Atsumi (Yumi Ishikawa), Ryo Tamura (Keiichi), Keiko Sekine (Setsuko), Toyoshi Fukuda, Masaya Takahashi, Yoshi Kato.

A Daiei Motion Picture Co., Ltd. Production. Fujicolor. DaieiScope. 83 minutes. Released December 25, 1971.

U.S. VERSION: Release undetermined. English subtitled version available. 83 minutes. No MPAA rating.

Kagemusha / Kagemusha ("A General's Double"). Producers, Akira Kurosawa and Tomoyuki Tanaka; Director/Editor, Akira Kurosawa; Assistant Producer, Teruyo Nogami; Production Coordinator and 2nd Unit Director, Ishiro Honda; Production Advisers, Shinobu Hashimoto and Takao Saito; Screenplay, Akira Kurosawa and Masato Ide; Directors of Photography, Takao Saito and Masaharu Ueda; Photography Supervisors [Associate Photographers], Kazuo Miyagawa and Asakazu Nakai; Art Director, Yoshiro Muraki; Music, Shinichiro Ikebe, conducted by Kotaro Saito and performed by the New Japan Philharmonic Orchestra; Sound Recording, Fumio Yanoguchi; Lighting, Takeji Sano; Unit Production Manager, Toshiaki Hashimoto; Special Effects, Toho Special Effects Group.

CAST: Tatsuya Nakadai (Shingen Takeda *and* his double, *the Kagemusha*), Tsutomu Yamazaki (Nobukado Takeda, *Shingen's brother*), Kenichi Hagiwara (Katsuyori Suwa [Takeda], *Shingen's son*), Kota Yui (Takemaru Takeda, *Shingen's grandson*), Shuji Otaki (Masakage Yamagata, *Takeda Clan general, Fire Battalion leader*), Hideo Murata (Nobuharu Baba), Takayuki Shiho (Masatoyo Naito), Shuhei Sugimori (Masanobu Kosaka), Noboru Shimizu (Masatane Hara), Koji Shimizu (Katsusuke Atobe), Sen [Ren?] Yamamoto (Nobushige Oyamada), Daisuke Ryu (Nobunaga Oda, *Shingen's enemy*), Masayuki Yui (Ieyasu Tokugawa, *Shingen's enemy*), Yasuhito Yamanaka (Ranmaru Mori), Takashi Shimura (Gyobu Taguchi), Jinpachi Nezu (Sohachiro Tsuchiya, *Shingen's bodyguard*), Mitsuko Baisho (Oyunokata, *Shingen's concubine*), Kaori Momoi (Otsuyanokata, *Shingen's concubine*), Akihiko Sugizaki (Noda Castle soldier), Toshiaki Tanabe (Kugutsushi), Yoshimitsu Yamaguchi (salt vendor), Takashi Ebata (monk), Kumeko Otowa (Takemaru's nurse), Kamatari Fujiwara (doctor), Senkichi Omura (Takeda's stable boy), Tetsuo Yamashita, Kai Ato, Yutaka Shimaka, Eiichi Kanakubo, Yugo Miyazaki, Norio Matsu, Yasushi Doshita, Eihachi Ito, Noboru Sone, Masatsugu Kuriyama, Takashi Watanabe.

A Kurosawa Films, Ltd./Toho Co., Ltd. Production. A Toho Co., Ltd. Release. Eastman Color. Spherical Panavision (1.85:1). Dolby Stereo. Copyright 1980 by Toho Co., Ltd. 179 minutes. Released April 23, 1980.

U.S. VERSION: Released by Twentieth Century-Fox Film Corporation. English subtitles. Producers, Francis Ford Coppola and George Lucas; Assistant Producer, Audie Bock; Subtitle Supervsior, Donald Richie. Prints by DeLuxe. Available matted on laserdisc. Nakadai replaced Shintaro Katsu, who left over artistic differences with Kurosawa during the first week of filming. Shimura's role was cut from the American version. Advertised as *Kagemusha: The Shadow Warrior*. 162 minutes. MPAA rating: "PG." Released October 17, 1980.

Kai ("Oar"). Producer, Shigeru Okada; Director, Hideo Gosha; Screenplay, Koji Takada, based on an original story by Tomiko Miyao; Director of Photography, Fujio Morita; Music, Masaru Sato.

CAST: Ken Ogata, Yukiyo Toake, Yuko Naotori.

A Toei Co., Ltd. Production. Color. Panavision (?). 135 minutes. Released 1985.

U.S. VERSION: Distributor, if any, is undetermined. No MPAA rating.

Kaibyo Arima goten ("Ghost Cat of Arima Palace"). Executive Producer, Masaichi Nagata; Director, Ryohei Arai; Sound, Daiei Recording Studio.

CAST: Takako Irie, Kotaro Bando.

A Daiei Motion Picture Co., Ltd. Production. A Masaichi Nagata Presentation. Western Electric Mirrophonic recording. Black and white (processed by Daiei Laboratory). Academy ratio. Running time undetermined. Released 1953.

U.S. VERSION: Distributor, if any, is undetermined. International title: *Ghost-Cat of Arima Palace.*

Kaibyo Gojusan-tsugi ("Ghost-Cat of Gojusan-Tsugi"). Executive Producer, Masaichi Nagata; Director, Bin Kado; Sound, Daiei Recording Studio.

CAST: Shintaro Katsu, Tokiko Mita.

A Daiei Motion Picture Co., Ltd. Production. A Masaichi Nagata Presentation. Western Electric Mirrophonic recording. Black and white (processed by Daiei Laboratory). Academy ratio. Running time undetermined. Released 1956.

U.S. VERSION: Distributor, if any, is undetermined. International title: *Ghost-Cat of Gojusan-Tsugi.*

Kaibyo Karakuri Tenjo ("Ghost-Cat of Karakuri Tenjo"). Director, Kinnosuke Fukuda.

CAST: Ryunosuke Tsukigata, Kyonosuke Nango.

A Toei Co., Ltd. Production. Black and white (processed by Toei Chemistry Co., Ltd.). Academy ratio. Running time undetermined. Released 1958.

U.S. VERSION: Distributor, if any, is undetermined. International title: *Ghost-Cat of Karakuri Tenjo.*

Kaibyo koshinuke daisodo ("Weak-kneed from Fear of Ghost-Cat"). Director, Torajiro Saito.

CAST: Achako Hanabishi, Michiko Hoshi.

A Toei Co., Ltd. Production. Black and white (processed by Toei Chemistry Co., Ltd.). Academy ratio. Running time undetermined. Released 1954.

U.S. VERSION: Distributor, if any, is undetermined. International title: *Weak-kneed from Fear of Ghost-Cat.*

Kaibyo noroi no kabe ("The Ghost-Cat Cursed Wall"). Executive Producer, Sadao Zaisaki; Producer, Shin Sakai; Director, Kenji Misumi; Screenplay, Toshio Tamikado and Shigeo Okamoto; Director of Photography, Shoichi Aisaka; Art Director, Seiichi Ota; Lighting, Motoyoshi Nakaoka; Music, Ban Takahashi; Sound Recording, Masahiro Okumura; Sound, Daiei Recording Studio.

CAST: Shintaro Katsu (Kyonosuke Takeuchi), Chieko Murata (Satsuki), Meiko Kondo (Shino), Yoko Uraji (Kozue), Shosaku Sugiyama (Tenzen Tadokoro), Shinobu Araki (Shume), Ichiro Izawa (Lord Maeda), Akio Kobori (Priest Gendo), Yoichi Funaki (Ikujiro Atsumi), Michiyo Midori (Natsue), Sumire [no other name given] (Fujino), Keiko Makaze (Kaede), Yusaku Terashima (Dr. Chikusai), Hiroyuki Ota (Nobuchiyo).

A Daiei Motion Picture Co., Ltd. Production. Western Electric Mirrophonic recording. Black and white (processed by Daiei Laboratory). DaieiScope. 78 minutes. Released June 15, 1958.

U.S. VERSION: Distributor, if any, is undetermined. International Title: *Ghost-Cat Wall of Hatred.* Alternate title: *The Cursed Wall.*

Kaibyo noroi numa ("The Ghost-Cat Cursed Pond"). Producers, Shigeru Okada and Norimichi Matsudaira; Director/Screenplay, Yoshihiro Ishikawa; Director of Photography, Shigeru Aketsuke; Art Director, Tobumichi Igawa; Editor, Kozo Horiike; Music, Isao Tomita; Sound Recording, Yoshibumi Watanabe.

CAST: Ryohei Uchida (Nashige Nabeshima), Kotaro Satomi (Jonosuke Yuki), Kyoko Mikage (Yukiji), Hiroshi Nawa (Shuzen Kuroiwa), Yuriko Mishima (Yuri), Machiko Yashiro (Hyuga no Tsubone), Tatsuo Matsumura (Mataemon Tsuyama), Ryuko Azuma (Sei), Mitsuko Yoshikawa (Kumi), Bunta Sugahara (Ukon Shibayama), Kenji Kusumoto (Hayato Sasaki), Yoichi Numata (Torakichi), Masumi Numata (Torakichi), Masumi Tachibana (Orin no Kata), Hideo Kagawa (Chiyomaru), Misa Toki (Sayo), Yasuko Ogura (Satsuki), Keiko Kojima (Matsushima), Tokuko Miura (Fujimoto),

Keichiro Shimada (Takafusa Ryuzoji), Chiyo Okada (Princess Kiyo), Mie Hayashi (Tsuyama family maid), Ichitaro Kuni (Ukon follower), Kinji Nakamura (doctor at castle), Kinya Suzuki (priest at Zuimiyoji), Takayuki Akutagawa (narrator).

A Toei Co., Ltd. Production. Black and white (processed by Toei Chemistry Co., Ltd.). ToeiScope. 87 minutes. Released 1968.

U.S. VERSION: Distributor, if any, is undetermined. International title: *The Cursed Pond.*

Kaibyo Okazaki sodo ("Ghost-Cat of the Okazaki Upheaval"). Executive Producer, Masaichi Nagata; Director, Bin Kado; Sound, Daiei Recording Studio.

CAST: Takako Irie, Kotaro Bando.

A Daiei Motion Picture Co., Ltd. Production. A Masaichi Nagata Presentation. Western Electric Mirrophonic recording. Black and white (processed by Daiei Laboratory). Academy ratio. Running time undetermined. Released 1954.

U.S. VERSION: Distributor, if any, is undetermined. International title: *Terrible Ghost-Cat of Okazaki.*

Kaibyo Oma-ga-tsuji ("Ghost-Cat of Oma-ga-tsuji"). Executive Producer, Masaichi Nagata; Director, Bin Kado; Sound, Daiei Recording Studio.

CAST: Takako Irie, Shintaro Katsu.

A Daiei Motion Picture Co., Ltd. Production. A Masaichi Nagata Presentation. Western Electric Mirrophonic recording. Black and white (processed by Daiei Laboratory). Academy ratio. Running time undetermined. Released 1954.

U.S. VERSION: Distributor, if any, is undetermined. International title: *Ghost-Cat of Oma-Ga-Tsuji.*

Kaidan Bancho sara yashiki ("Ghost Story: Dishes at Bancho Mansion"). Director, Juichi Kono; Based on the play *Yotsuya kaidan* by Nanboku Tsuruya.

CAST: Chiyonosuke Azuma, Hibari Misora.

A Toei Co., Ltd. Production. Black and white (processed by Toei Chemistry Co., Ltd.). Academy ratio. Running time undetermined. Released 1957.

U.S. VERSION: Distributor, if any, is undetermined. International title: *Ghost Story of Broken Dishes at Bancho Mansion.* Alternate title: *The Ghost of Yotsuya.*

Kaidan botandoro ("Ghost Story: Peony Lantern"). Executive Producer, Masaichi Nagata; Director, Satsuo Yamamoto; Screenplay, Yoshitaka Yoda; Director of Photography, Chishi Makiura; Art Director, Yoshinobu Nishioka; Editor, Kanji Suganume; Music, Shigeru Ikeno; Sound Recording Supervisor, Tsuchitaro Hayashi; Sound, Daiei Recording Studio.

CAST: Kojiro Hongo (Shinzaburo), Miyoko Akaza (Otsuyu), Michiko Otsuka (Oyone), Mayumi Ogawa (Omine), Ko Nishimura (Banzo), Takashi Shimura (Hakuodo), Atsumi Uda (Kiku), Takamaru Sasaki (Zenzaemon), Koichi Mizahara (1st relative), Saburo Date (Rokusuke), Norio Shiozaki (elder brother), Kazuo Tamamoto (1st man), Gen Kimura (priest), Shinobu Araki (Priest Ryoseki), Shozo Nanbu (old man), Kimiko Tachibana (Mother Nao), Teruko Omi (1st wife), Yuko Mori (2nd wife).

A Daiei Motion Picture Co., Ltd. Production. A Masaichi Nagata Presentation. Filmed at Daiei-Kyoto Studios. Westrex recording system. Fujicolor (processed by Daiei Laboratory). DaieiScope. 89 minutes. Released June 15, 1968.

U.S. VERSION: Released by Daiei International Films, Inc. English subtitles. International titles: *The Bride from Hades* and *A Tale of Peonies and Lanterns.* Also known as *Bride from Hell*, *Ghost Beauty* and *My Bride Is a Ghost.* Daiei currently lists title as *Botandoro.* 89 minutes. No MPAA rating.

Kaidan Chibusa Enoki ("Ghost of Chibusa Enoki"). Director, Goro Katano.

CAST: Katsuko Wakasugi, Keiko Hasegawa.

A Shintoho Co., Ltd. Production. Western Electric Mirrophonic recording. Black and white. Academy ratio. Running time undetermined. Released 1958.

U.S. VERSION: Distributor, if any, is undetermined. International title: *Ghost of Chibusa Enoki.*

Kaidan Fukagawa jowa ("Ghost Story: Passion in Fukagawa"). Executive Producer, Masaichi Nagata; Director, Minoru Imuzuka; Sound, Daiei Recording Studio.

CAST: Mitsuko Mito; Yuji Hori.

A Daiei Motion Picture Co., Ltd. Production. A Masaichi Nagata Presentation. Western Electric Mirrophonic recording. Black and white (processed by Daiei Laboratory). Academy ratio. Running time undetermined. Released 1952.

U.S. VERSION: Distributor, if any, is undetermined. International title *Tragic Ghost Story of Fukagawa.*

Kaidan Gojusan-tsugi ("Ghost of Gojusan-Tsugi"). Director, Kokichi Uchide.

CAST: Kokichi Takada, Hiromi Hanazono.

Production company undetermined, though likely either Daiei or Toei. Black and white. Running time undetermined. Released 1960.

U.S. VERSION: Distributor, if any, is undetermined. International title: *Ghost of Gojusan-Tsugi.*

Kaidan hebionna ("Ghost of the Snake Woman"). Producers, Kaname Ogisawa and Tadayuki Okubo; Director, Nobuo Nakagawa; Director of Photography, Yoshikazu Yamasawa; Editor, Yoshiki Nagasawa; Sound Recording, Masanobu Otani; Music, Shunsuke Kikuchi.

CAST: Seizaburo Kawazu (Chobei Ohnuma), Shingo Yamashiro (Takeo), Akemi Negishi (Masae), Yukie Kagawa (Kinu), Chiaki Tsukioka (Sue), Yukiko Kuwabara (Asa), Ko Nishimura (Yasuke), Mariko Ko (Saki), Kunio Murai (Sutematsu), Akikane Sawa (Matsugoro), Junzaburo Ban (Fusataro), Hideo Murota (Saiji), Tamae Kiyokawa (Tami), Midori Yamamoto (Yoshi), Hideko Oda (Iku), Asako Hiraga (Mino), Keiko Ito (Fuku), Kayo Tauchi (Tome), Shunji Sayama (Kameshichi), Ozo Soma (1st man), Koichi Yamada (2nd man), Nobuo Hara (3rd man), Noboru Aihara (policeman), Sayoko Tanimoto (1st virgin in serivce of shrine), Michiyo Kozuki (2nd virgin in service of shrine), Toshio Ogo (male servant), Tetsuro Tamba (head of police).

A Toei Co., Ltd. Production. Filmed at Toei-Kyoto Studios. Fujicolor (processed by Toei Chemistry Co., Ltd.). ToeiScope. 83 minutes. Released 1968.

U.S. VERSION: Distributor, if any, is undetermined. International title: *Fear of the Snake Woman.* Alternate title: *Ghost of the Snake.*

Kaidan hitotsu-me Jizo ("Ghost Story: One-Eyed Jizo"). Director, Kinnosuke Fukuda.

CAST: Tomisaburo Wakayama, S. Chihara.

A Toei Co., Ltd. Production. Black and white (processed by Toei Chemistry Co., Ltd.). Academy ratio. Running time undetermined. Released 1959.

U.S. VERSION: Distributor, if any, is undetermined. International title: *Ghost from the Pond.*

Kaidan ijin yurei ("Ghost Story: Foreign Ghost"). Director, Satoru Kobayashi.

CAST: Miyako Ishijo, Kyoko Ogimachi.

An Okura Eiga Production. Black and white. Academy ratio. Running time undetermined. Released 1963.

U.S. VERSION: Distributor, if any, is undetermined. International title: *Caucasian Ghost.*

Kaidan Kagami-ga-fuchi ("Ghost Story: Depth of Kagami"). Director, Masaki Mori.

CAST: Noriko Kitazawa, Fumiko Miyata.

A Shintoho Co., Ltd. Production. Western Electric Mirrophonic recording. Black and white. Academy ratio. Running time undetermined. Released 1959.

U.S. VERSION: Distributor, if any, is undetermined. International title: *Ghost of Kagami-Ga-Fuchi.*

Kaidan Kakuidori ("Ghost Story of Kakui Street"). Executive Producer, Masaichi Nagata; Director, Issei Mori; Sound, Daiei Recording Studio.

CAST: Eiji Funakoshi, Katsuhiko Kobayashi.

A Daiei Motion Picture Co., Ltd. Production. A Masaichi Nagata Presentation. Western Electric Mirrophonic recording. Black and white (processed by Daiei Laboratory). Academy ratio (?). Running time undetermined. Released 1961.

U.S. VERSION: Distributor, if any, is undetermined. International title: *Ghost Story of Kakui Street.*

Kaidan Kasanegafuchi ("Ghost Story: Depth of Kasane"). Executive Producer, Masaichi Nagata; Director, Kimiyoshi Yasuda, based on the story "Shinkei Kasanegufuchi" by Encho Sanyutei; Sound Recording Supervisor, Masao Osumi; Sound, Daiei Recording Studio; Special Effects, Daiei Special Effects Department.

CAST: Ganjiro Nakamura, Yataro Kitagami.

A Daiei Motion Picture Co., Ltd. Production. A Masaichi Nagata Presentation. Western Electric Mirrophonic recording. Black and white (processed by Daiei Laboratory). Academy ratio (?). Running time undetermined. Released 1960.

U.S. VERSION: Never released theatrically in the United States. A remake of *The Depths* (Shintoho, 1957), and remade as *The Masseur's Curse* (Daiei, 1970).

Kaidan Oiwa no Borei ("The Ghost Story of Oiwa's Spirit"). Director, Tai Kato; Based on the play *Yotsuya kaidan* by Nanboku Tsuruya.

CAST: Tomisaburo Wakayama, Hiroko Sakuramachi.

A Toei Co., Ltd. Production. Black and white (processed by Toei Chemistry Co., Ltd.). Academy ratio. Running time undetermined. Released 1961.

U.S. VERSION: Distributor, if any, is undetermined. International title: *Ghost of Oiwa.* Alternate title: *Ghost of Yotsuya.*

Kaidan onibi no numa ("Ghost Story of Devil's Fire Swamp"). Executive Producer, Masaichi Nagata; Director, Bin Kado; Sound, Daiei Recording Studio.

CAST: Kenzaburo Jo, Mieko Kondo.

A Daiei Motion Picture Co., Ltd. Production. A Masaichi Nagata Presentation. Western Electric Mirrophonic recording. Black and white (processed by Daiei Laboratory). Academy ratio (?). Running time undetermined. Released 1963.

U.S. VERSION: Distributor, if any, is undetermined. International title: *Ghost Story of Devil's Fire Swamp.*

Kaidan ryoko ("Ghostly Trip"). Executive Producer, Kiyoshi Shimazu; Director, Shoji Segawa; Screenplay, Kazuo Funabashi; Director of Photography, Keiji Maruyama; Art Director, Masao Kumagi; Music, Seitaro Ohmori.

CAST: Frankie Sakai (Shinpei Owada), Tomoe Hiiro (Umeko and Satoe), Kensaku Morita (Daisuke Sakaguchi), Yumiko Nogawa (Yumi Okamura), Akane Kawasaki (Chizu), Casey Takamine (Conductor), Norihei Miki (Shosaku Sakaguchi).

A Shochiku Co., Ltd. Production. Color. Panavision (?). 91 minutes. Released June 10, 1972.

U.S. VERSION: Distributor, if any, is undertermined. International title (?): *Weird Trip.* The 10th of 11 "Train Station" features (1968-72), all of which starred Frankie Sakai.

Kaidan Saga yashiki ("Ghost of Saga Mansion"). Executive Producer, Masaichi Nagata; Director, Ryohei Arai; Sound, Daiei Recording Studio.

CAST: Takako Irie, Kotaro Bando.

A Daiei Motion Picture Co., Ltd. Production. A Masaichi Nagata Presentation. Western Electric Mirrophonic recording. Black and white (processed by Daiei Laboratory). Academy ratio (?). Running time undetermined. Released 1953.

U.S. VERSION: Distributor, if any, is undetermined. International title: *Ghost of Saga Mansion.*

Kaidan shamisen-bori ("Ghost Music of Shamisen"). Director, Kokichi Uchide.

CAST: Ryuji Shinagawa, Noriko Kitazawa.

A Toei Co., Ltd. Production. Black and white (processed by Toei Chemistry Co., Ltd.). Academy ratio. Running time undetermined. Released 1962.

U.S. VERSION: Distributor, if any, is

undetermined. International title: *Ghost Music of Shamisen.*

Kaidan yonaki-doro ("Ghost Story: Crying in the Night Lantern"). Executive Producer, Masaichi Nagata; Director, Katuhiko Tasaka; Sound, Daiei Recording Studio.

CAST: Ganjiro Nakamura, Katsuhiro [no other name given].

A Daiei Motion Picture Co., Ltd. Production. A Masaichi Nagata Presentation. Western Electric Mirrophonic recording. Black and white (processed by Daiei Laboratory). Academy ratio (?). Running time undetermined. Released 1962.

U.S. VERSION: Distributor, if any, is undetermined. International title: *Ghost Story of Stone Lanterns* and *Crying in the Night.*

Kaii Utsunomiya tsuritenjo ("Ghost of Hanging in Utsunomiya"). Director, Nobuo Nakagawa.

CAST: Ryuzaburo Ogasawara, Akemi Tsukuchi.

A Shintoho Co., Ltd. Production. Western Electric Mirrophonic recording. Black and white. Academy ratio. Running time undetermined. Released 1956.

U.S. VERSION: Distributor, if any, is undetermined.

Kamigata Kugaizoshi / Kamigata Kugaizoshi ("Kamigata Kugaizoshi"). Producers, Yasuhiko Kawano and Tetsutaro Murano; Director, Tetsutaro Murano; Screenplay, Yukiko Takayama; Director of Photography, Yasuhiro Yoshioka; Music, Hidetaro Honjo.

CAST: Hisashi Igawa, Mayumi Ogawa, Kazumi Harada.

A Production Eureka, Inc./Tetsu Production, Inc. Production. Color. Spherical wide screen. 98 minutes. Released 1991.

U.S. VERSION: Distributor, if any, is undetermined.

A Kamikaze Cop / Yakuza deka ("Yakuza Cop"). Director/Screenplay, Yukio Noda; Director of Photography, Yoshio Nakajima; Art Director, Hiroshi Kitagawa; Music, Masao Yagi.

CAST: Shinichi "Sonny" Chiba (Agent Shiro Hayata), Ryoji Hayama (Muira), Machiko Yashiro (Noriko), Bin Amatsu (Akutsu), Yoko Nogiwa.

A Toei Co., Ltd. Production. Eastman Color. ToeiScope. 89 minutes. Released May 23, 1970.

U.S. VERSION: Release undetermined. English subtitled version available. The 1st feature of a 4-film series (1970-71). Followed by *Kamikaze Cop, Marihuana Syndicate* (1970). 89 minutes. No MPAA rating.

Kamikaze Cop, Marihuana Syndicate / Yakuza deka, Marihuana mitsubai soshiki ("Yakuza Cop, Marihuana Syndicate"). Director, Yukio Noda; Screenplay, Norio Konami and Yukio Noda; Director of Photography, Kiichi Inada; Art Director, Shinichi Eno; Music, Masao Yagi.

CAST: Shinichi "Sonny" Chiba (Agent Shiro Hayata), Ryohei Uchida (Ishiguro), Koji Sekiyama (Mano), Fumio Watanabe (Natsui), Tomo Uchida (Shima), Toshiaki Minami, Kaoru Hama.

A Toei Co., Ltd. Production. Eastman Color. ToeiScope. 87 minutes. Released October 17, 1970.

U.S. VERSION: Released undetermined. English subtitled version available. The 2nd feature of a 4-film series (see above). 87 minutes. No MPAA rating.

Kanto Wanderer / Kanto mushuku ("Kanto Wanderer"). Producer, Kenzo Asada; Director, Seijun Suzuki; Screenplay, Yasutaro Yagi, based on the novel by Taiko Hirabayashi; Director of Photography, Shigeyoshi Mine; Art Director, Takeo Kimura; Editor, Akira Suzuki; Music, Masayoshi Ikeda; Assistant Director, Masami Kuzu.

CAST: Akira Kobayashi (Mitsuo Kabuta), Daizaburo Hirata ("Diamond" Fuyu), Chieko Matsubara (Tokiko Izu), Sanae Nakahara (Hanako Yamada), Chikako Shin (Matsue Ichikawa), Taiji Tonoyama (Sota Izu), Toru Abe (Dairyu Yoshida), Keisuke Noro (Tetsuo Bikkuri), Yunosuke Ito (Hachi Okaru).

A Nikkatsu Corp. Production. Color. NikkatsuScope. 93 minutes. Released 1963.

U.S. VERSION: Released by Nikkatsu Corp. English subtitles. 93 minutes. No MPAA rating. Released 1993.

Kappa: A River Goblin and Sampei / Kappa no Sanpei ("A Sampei River Goblin") [**animated**]. Producer, Toyoji Nishimura; Director, Toshio Hirata; Screenplay, Shunichi Yukimuro, based on a cartoon by Shigeru Mizuki; Animation Director, Takeo Kitahara; Director of Photography, Hazime Hasegawa; Art Director, Noboru Tatuike; Music, Kazuki Kuriyama.

VOICE CHARACTERIZATIONS: Mayumi Tanaka, Junko Hori, Yuri Amano, Jo Shishido, Chieko Matsubara, Norihei Miki.

A Nikkatsu Corp. Production. Color. Academy ratio. 90 minutes. Released 1993.

U.S. VERSION: Distributor, if any, is undetermined.

Kaseki ("Fossil"). Producer, Masayuki Sata; Director, Masaki Kobayashi; Screenplay, Shun Inagaki and Takeshi Yoshida, based on an original story by Yasushi Inoue; Director of Photography, Kozo Okazaki; Music, Toru Takemitsu.

CAST: Shin Saburi (Tajihei Itsuki), Keiko Kishi (Mme. Marcelin), Hisashi Igawa (Funazu), Kei Yamamoto (Kishi), Orie Sato (Mrs. Kishi), Komaki Kurihara and Mayumi Ogawa (Itsuki's daughters), Shigeru Koyama (Kihera), Haruko Sugimura (Itsuki's stepmother), Ichiro Nakatani (Itsuki's brother), Jukichi Uno (Itsuki's friend), Yusuke Takita (Sakagami), Go Kato (narrator).

A Haiyuza Film Production Co., Ltd./ Yonki-no-Kai Production. Color. Academy ratio. 200 minutes. Released 1975.

U.S. VERSION: Released by New Yorker Films. English subtitles. Running time also given at 213 minutes. Alternate title: *Fossil*. 200 minutes. No MPAA rating. Released September 1976.

Kenji Mizoguchi: The Life of a Film Director / Aru eiga kantoku no shogai ("The Life of a Film Director"). Producer/Director/Screenplay, Kaneto Shindo; Directors of Photography, Yoshiyuki Miyake, Kiyomi Kuroda and Hisashi Shimoda; Sound Recording, Shinpei Kikuchi.

WITH: Kinuyo Tanaka, Machiko Kyo, Isuzu Yamada, Ayako Wakao, Michiyo Kogure, Kyoko Kagawa, Nobuko Otowa, Ganjro Nakamura, Eitaro Ozawa, Eitaro Shindo, Kazuo Miyagawa, Yoshikata Yoda.

A Kindai Eiga Kyokai Co., Ltd. Production. Color. Academy ratio (?). 150 minutes. Released 1975.

U.S. VERSION: Distributor undetermined. English subtitles. 132 minutes. No MPAA rating. Released August 14, 1981.

The Kid Brother. Executive Producers, Matsuo Takahashi, Makoto Yamashima; Producers, Kiyoshi Fujimoto and Hirohiko Sueyoshi; Director/ Screenplay, Claude Gagnon; Director of Photography, Yudai Kato; Editor, Andre Corriveau; Music, Francois Dompierre; Art Director, Bill Bilowit; Costume Design, Maureen Hogan; Sound Recording, Russell Fager; Production Manager, Kathleen Caton; Line Producer, Dennis Bishop; Assistant Director, Eduardo Rossoff.

CAST: Kenny Easterday (Kenny), Caitlin Clarke (Sharon), Liane Curtis (Kay), Zack Grenier (Jesse), Jesse Easterday, Jr. (Eddy), Tom Reddy (Billy), Alain St. Alix (Philippe), John Carpenter (grandfather).

A Kinema Amerika/Yoshimura/Gagnon/Toho Co., Ltd. Production. A U.S./ Canadian/Japanese co-production in English and French (?). Fujicolor. Spherical wide screen (1.85:1). 95 minutes. Released 1987.

U.S. VERSION: Distributor undetermined. 95 minutes. No MPAA rating. Released November 18, 1988.

Kigeki ekiame kaidan ("Ghost Story of a Funny Act in Front of a Train Station"). Executive Producer, Tomoyuki Tanaka; Director, Kozo Saeki; Sound, Toho Recording Centre; Sound Effects, Toho Sound Effects Group.

CAST: Frankie Sakai, Hisaya Morishige.

A Toho Co., Ltd. Production. Western Electric Mirrophonic recording. Black and white (processed by Tokyo Laboratory Ltd.). TohoScope. 92 minutes. Released 1964.

U.S. VERSION: Distributor, if any, is undetermined. International title: *Ghost*

Story of Funny Act in Front of Train Station. The 8th of 24 "Train Station" features (1958-69).

Kiki's Delivery Service / Majo no Takkyubin ("The Witch's Delivery Service") **[animated]**. Producer/ Director, Hayao Miyazaki; Screenplay, Hayao Miyazaki, based on an original story by Eiko Kadono; Music, Joe Hisaishi.

VOICE CHARACTERIZATIONS: Minami Takayama.

A Tokuma Shoten Publishing Co., Ltd. Production. Color. Spherical wide screen. 103 minutes. Released 1989.

U.S. VERSION: Distributor, if any, is undetermined. No MPAA rating.

Kill! / Kiru ("Kill" [see below]). Producer, Tomoyuki Tanaka; Director, Kihachi Okamoto; Screenplay, Akira Murao and Kihachi Okamoto, based on the story "Torideyama no jushichinichi," in *Yamamoto Shugoro zenshu* (1964) by Shugoro Yamamoto; Director of Photography, Rokuro Nishigaki; Art Director, Iwao Akune; Editors, Kihachi Okamoto and Yoshitami Kuroiwa; Music, Masaru Sato.

CAST: Tatsuya Nakadai (Genta), Etsushi Takahashi (Hanjiro Tabata), Shigeru Kamiyama (Ayuzawa Tamiya), Eijiro Tono (Moriuchi Hyogo), Yuriko Hoshi (Chino), Yoshio Tsuchiya (Matsuo Shiroko), Tadao Nakamaru (Shoda Magobei), Eisei Amamoto (Shimada Gendaiu), Nami Tamura, Ko Hashimoto, Akira Kubo.

A Toho Co., Ltd. Production. Black and white. Toho Scope. 114 minutes. Released June 22, 1968.

U.S. VERSION: Released by Frank Lee International. English subtitles. Title also translates to "Cut." 114 minutes. No MPAA rating. Released August 1968.

Kill the Killer! / Dangai no ketto ("Duel at the Cliff"). Executive Producer, Sadao Sugihara; Director, Kozo Saeki; Screenplay, Fumio Shibano; Director of Photography, Kozo Okazaki; Music, Riichiro Manabe.

CAST: Yosuke Natsuki, Tatsuya Mihashi, Tetsuro Tamba, Keiko Awaji, Akihiko Hirata, Kumi Mizuno.

A Toho Co., Ltd. Production. Agfa color. Toho Scope. 85 minutes. Released 1961 (?).

U.S. VERSION: Released by Toho International Co., Ltd. English subtitles. 85 minutes. No MPAA rating. Release date undetermined.

Kill the Killers (production credits unavailable).

CAST: Ryunosuke Minegishi, Osamu Sakai, Hiroko Masuda.

A Daiei Motion Picture Co., Ltd. Production. Color (?). DaieiScope. Released 1969 (?).

U.S. VERSION: Released by Daiei International Films, Inc. English subtitles. Running time and Japanese title undetermined. No MPAA rating. Released March 11, 1970.

Killer's Mission / Shokin kasegi ("Hit Man"). Director, Shigehiro Ozawa; Screenplay, Koji Takada and Masaru Igami; Director of Photography, Nagaki Yamagishi; Art Director, Seiji Yada; Music, Masao Yagi.

CAST: Tomisaburo Wakayama (Ichibei), Yumiko Nogawa (Kagero), Tomoko Mayama (Akane), Chiezo Kataoka (Ukyo), Bin Amatsu (Nikaido), Masaya Takahashi (Shigetoshi), Koji Tsuruta.

A Toei Co., Ltd. Production. Eastman Color. ToeiScope. 90 minutes. Released August 13, 1969.

U.S. VERSION: Distributor, if any, is undetermined. English subtitled version available. 90 minutes. No MPAA rating.

The Killing Bottle / Kokusai Himitsu Keisatsu: Zettai zetsumei ("International Secret Police: Catch 22"). Producer, Tomoyuki Tanaka; Director, Senkichi Taniguchi; Screenplay, Shinichi Sekizawa; Story, Michio Tsuzuki; Art Director, Hiroshi Ueda; Director of Photography, Takao Saito; Editor, Yoshitami Kuroiwa; Music, Sadao Bekku; Recording, Yoshio Nishikawa; Sound, Toho Recording Centre; Sound Effects, Toho Sound Effects Group.

CAST: Tatsuya Mihashi (Jiro Kitami), Kumi Mizuno (a girl), Nick Adams (John Carter), Anne Mari (Ayako), Makoto Sato (Ken Hayata), Jun Tazaki (President of Buddabal), Akihiko Hirata (man with

Turkish hat), Yoshio Tsuchiya (General Rubesa), Tetsu Nakamura (head of ZZZ Hong Kong branch office), Ryuji Kita (head of secret police), Eisei Amamoto (1st murderer), Masaji Oshita (2nd murderer), Kazuo Kawakami (3rd murderer), Sachio Sakai (Shimada), Yasushi Yokoyama, Kiyoshi Yoshikawa, Jiro Makino (gang comedians), Mari Takeno (dancer), Tatsuo Hasegawa (man with rifle).

A Takarazuka Eiga Production for Toho Co., Ltd., in association with Nick Adams Enterprises, Inc. Westrex recording system. Eastman Color (processed by Tokyo Laboratory Ltd.). Toho Scope. 93 minutes. Released 1967.

U.S. Version: Distributor, if any, is undetermined. The 5th and final "International Secret Police" feature. Preceded by *International Secret Police: Key of Keys* (1965).

King Kong Escapes / King Kong no gyakushu ("King Kong's Counterattack"). Producers, Tomoyuki Tanaka and Arthur Rankin, Jr.; Director, Ishiro Honda; Screenplay, Kaoru Mabuchi (Takeshi Kimura), based on the Rankin/Bass Productions animated television series, "King Kong"; The character, "King Kong," from the motion picture, *King Kong*, used by permission of RKO General, Inc.; English Language Dialogue, William J. Keenan; Director of Photography, Hajime Koizumi; Music, Akira Ifukube; Art Director, Takeo Kita; Lighting, Shoshichi Kojima; Sound Recordist, Shoichi Yoshizawa; Sound, Toho Recording Centre; Sound Effects, Toho Sound Effects Group; Editor, Ryohei Fujii. *Toho Special Effects Group*: Director, Eiji Tsuburaya; Photography, Teisho Arikawa, Mototaka Tomioka; Art Director, Akira Wanatabe; Optical Photography, Yukio Manoda, Sadao Iizuda; Scene Manipulation, Fumio Nakadai.

Cast: Akira Takarada (Lt. Commander Jiro Nomura), Mie Hama (Madame X [Piranha]), Rhodes Reason (Commander Carl Nelson), Linda Miller (Lt. Susan Watson), Eisei Amamoto (Dr. Who); Yoshifumi Tajima, Susumu Kurobe, Sachio Sakai, Kazuo Suzuki, Nadao Kirino, Naoya Kusakawa (Who's henchmen) Ikio Sawamura (old native on Mondo Island); Andrew Hughes, Cathy Horlan (reporters), Haruo Nakajima (King Kong), Hiroshi Sekita (Mechani-Kong and Gorosaurus).

A Toho Co., Ltd./Rankin-Bass Production. A Toho Co., Ltd. Release. Westrex Recording System. Eastman Color (processed by Tokyo Laboratory, Ltd.). Toho Scope. 104 minutes. Released July 22, 1967.

U.S. Version: Released by Universal Pictures. English dubbed. An Ernest L. Scanlon Presentation. Produced by Rankin/Bass Productions, Inc. at Glen Glenn Sound. Executive Producer, Jules Bass; Producer/Director, Arthur Rankin, Jr.; Screenplay, William J. Keenan; Post-production Supervisor, Riley Jackson; Dubbing Director, Paul Frees; Dubbing Cast: Paul Frees (Dr. Who, misc. characters), others unknown; Titles, National Screen Service; Sound, Glen Glenn; Prints by Technicolor. Double-billed with *The Shakiest Gun in the West* (Universal, 1968). U.K. Title: *The Revenge of King Kong* (some U.S. prints may have carried this title). Reason and Miller are dubbed in the Japanese edition. Includes brief stock footage from *War of the Gargantuas* (1966). Reissued in Japan in 1973. 96 minutes. MPAA Rating: "G." Released June 19, 1968.

King Kong vs. Godzilla / King Kong tai Gojira ("King Kong against Godzilla"). Producer, Tomoyuki Tanaka; Director, Ishiro Honda; Screenplay, Shinichi Sekizawa, based on a screenplay by George Worthing Yates, from "King Kong versus Prometheus," a story by Willis O'Brien, and characters created by Merian C. Cooper and Shigeru Kayama; Director of Photography, Hajime Koizumi; Music, Akira Ifukube; Art Director, Takeo Kita; Lighting, Shoshichi Kojima; Editor, Ichiji Taira; Sound Effects, Hisashi Shimonaga, Toho Sound Effects Group; "King Kong" character and name used by permission of RKO General, Inc. *Toho Special Effects Group*: Director, Eiji Tsuburaya; Assistant Director, Teruyoshi Nakano; Photography, Teisho Arikawa, Mototaka Tomioka; Assistant Photography, Koichi Kawakita; Lighting, Kuichiro Kishida; Matte Process, Hiroshi Mukoyama; Optical Effects,

Akira Takarada, Linda Miller, Mie Hama, and Eisei Amamoto in *King Kong Escapes* (1967). Haruo Nakajima is in the Kong suit.

Taka Yuki, Yukio Manoda; Art Director (including Gojira and King Kong suit designs), Akira Watanabe; Suit Construction, Teizo Toshimitsu; Stop-motion Animation, Minoru Nakano.

CAST: Tadao Takashima (O. Sakurai), Mie Hama (Fumiko Sakurai), Kenji Sahara (Kazuo Fujita), Yu Fujiki (Kinsaburo Furue), Ichiro Arishima (Tako), Jun Tazaki (General Masami Shinzo), Akiko Wakabayshi (Tamiye), Tatsuo Matsumura (Dr. Makino), Akihiko Hirata (Premier Shigezawa), Senkichi Omura (TTV Translator Konno), Yoshio Kosugi (Farou Island chief), Ikio Sawamura (witch doctor), Akemi Negishi (dancing girl), Yoshifumi Tajima (man aboard ship), Somesho Matsumoto (official), Ren Yamamoto (helicopter pilot), Haruo Nakajima (Godzilla), Shoichi "Solomon" Hirose (King Kong).

A Toho Co., Ltd. Production. Western Electric Mirrophonic recording (encoded with Perspecta Stereophonic Sound). Eastman Color (processed by Tokyo Laboratory, Ltd.). Toho Scope. 98 minutes. Released August 11, 1962.

U.S. VERSION: Released by Universal Pictures Co., Inc., bearing the Universal-International logo. A John Beck Presentation. English-dubbed. Producer, John Beck; Director, Thomas Montgomery; Producer, John Beck; Screenwriters, Paul Mason and Bruce Howard; Editor and Music Supervisor, Peter Zinner; stock music from *Creature from the Black Lagoon* and other Universal titles by Henry Mancini, Herman Stein, Milton Rosen, Robert Emmett Dolan, and conducted by Joseph Gershenson; Sound Effects Editor, William Stevenson; prints by Technicolor; Westrex Recording System. Copyright July 2, 1963 by RKO General, Inc. RKO's role is uncertain, though it is likely Toho purchased the Far East rights to the picture and use of the Kong character in exchange for the English-language (or Western Hemisphere) rights and all production costs. RKO then took the finished film to

Universal, who produced the English-language version, the profits of which were then divided between Universal and RKO. Tajima's role was cut for U.S. version. U.S. version includes stock footage from *The Mysterians* (M-G-M, 1957). Double-billed with *The Traitors* (Universal, 1963). International Title: *King Kong vs. Godzilla* (sic). Reissued in Japan in 1964, 1970 (re-edited to 73 minutes), 1977, 1979 and 1983. The Japanese laserdisc reissue is in stereo; all other versions released mono only. 91 minutes. No MPAA Rating. Released June 3, 1963.

Additional Cast for U.S. Version: Michael Keith (Eric Carter), Harry Holcombe (Dr. Arnold Johnson), James Yagi (Yataka Omura), Les Tremayne (narrator, voice of general, etc.).

Knockout Drops / Tokyo no Tekisasu-jin ("A Texan in Tokyo"). Executive Producer, Tomoyuki Tanaka; Director, Motoyoshi Oda; Screenplay, Shinichi Sekizawa; Director of Photography, Isamu Ashida; Sound, Toho Recording Centre; Sound Effects, Toho Sound Effects Group.

CAST: M. Minami, E.H. Eric.

A Toho Co., Ltd. Production. Western Electric Mirrophonic recording (encoded with Perspecta Stereophonic Sound?). Black and white. Toho Scope (?). 59 minutes. Released 1957.

U.S. VERSION: Released by Toho International Co., Ltd., format undetermined. 59 minutes. No MPAA rating. Released 1957.

Kojiro / Sasaki Kojiro ("Kojiro Sasaki"). Associate Producer, Kenichiro Kakuta [Tsunoda]; Director, Hiroshi Inagaki; Screenplay, Yoshio Shirasaka, Takeo Matsura, and Hiroshi Inagaki; Story, Genzo Murakami; Director of Photography, Takao Saito; Art Director, Hiroshi Ueda; Editor, Hirokazu Iwashita; Music, Goichi Sakide [Sakaide]; Sound Recording, Yoshio Nishikawa; Production Manager, Hirotosu Tsutsumi; Special Effects, Toho Special Effects Group; Sound Effects, Toho Sound Effects Group; Sound, Toho Recording Centre.

CAST: Kikunosuke Onoe (Kojiro Sasaki), Yuriko Hoshi (Princess Ione [Tone]), Yoshio Tsuchiya (Heisuke Ichinami), Tadao Nakamaru (Toma Inose), Isamu Nagato (Shimabei), Yoko Tsukasa (Princess Nami), Tatsuya Mihashi (Jubei Minamiya), Mayumi Ozora (Hanasode), Keiko Sawai (Kabuki Man), Aiko Mimasu (Izumo no Okuni), Chusha Ichikawa (Bannai Sorori), Jotaro Togami (Nachimaru), Akihiko Hirata (Tadaoki Hosokawa), Tatsuya Nakadai (Musashi Miyamoto), Junichiro Mukoi (Jinbei Aizawa), Kenjiro Ishiyama (Tonda Echigonokami [Lord Tomita]), Susumu Fujita (Sakonshogen Yamasaki), Masao Shimizu (Sado Nagaoka), Ryosuke Kagawa (Naizen Ariyoshi), Minoru Takada (Seizaemon Yonezu), Yoshio Yoshida (Tenma Anabuki), Akira Kiuhoji (Nanadayu Agishi), Kiyoko Tsuji (old woman of Akaneya), Shoji Ikeda (Tamibe Ichikawa), Hiroshi Tanaka (Fuminoshin Takabe), Eisei Amamoto (ronin).

A Toho Co., Ltd. Production. Eastman Color (processed by Tokyo Laboratory, Ltd.). Toho Scope. Westrex Recording System. 151 minutes. Released April 1, 1967.

U.S. VERSION: Released by Toho International Co., Ltd. English subtitles. The AFI Catalog gives the running time of the Japanese version as 165 minutes, but Toho's credits lists this as above. However, it is possible that the extra 13 minutes may have included an overture, intermission, etc. Credits are Toho's; those in brackets come from the AFI Catalog. Filmed previously by Inagaki in 1950-51 as a trilogy. 151 minutes. No MPAA rating. Released August 1967.

Koshoku tomei ningen ("Lusty Transparent Man"). Director, Shinya Yamamoto.

CAST: (not available).

A Nikkatsu Corp. Production. Nikkatsucolor. NikkatsuScope. Running time undetermined. Released 1979.

U.S. VERSION: Distributor, if any, is undetermined. A sequel to *Lusty Transparent Man* (Nikkatsu, 1979).

Koya: Memorial Notes of Choken / Koya ("Koya"). Executive Producers, Tetsutaro Murano, Yukiko

Godzilla as seen in *King Kong vs. Godzilla* (1962).

Takayama and Hirohiko Sueyosi; Producer, Masanobu Suzuki; Director, Tetsutaro Murano; Screenplay, Yukiko Takayama, based on the original novel by Yasushi Inoue; Director of Photography, Ikuo Yada; Lighting, Hirokazu Oishi; Art Director, Akiyoshi Kanda; Editor, Hirohide Abe; Sound, Mituru Seya; Music, Kimio Nomura.

CAST: Yoko Natori (Yoko Akituki/Oren), Daisuke Ryu (Choken), Satoshi Sadanaga (Shoei).

A Tetsu Productions Production. Color. Spherical wide screen. 100 minutes. Released 1993.

U.S. VERSION: Distributor, if any, is undetermined.

Kuragejima—Legends from a Southern Island / Kamigami no fukaki yokubo ("Deep Desire of the Gods"). Producer, Masanori Yamanoi; Director, Shohei Imamura; Screenplay,

"Hoichi-the-Earless," from Masaki Kobayashi's *Kwaidan* (1964).

Shohei Imamura and Keiji Hasebe; Story, Shohei Imamura; Director of Photography, Masao Tochizawa; Music, Toshiro Mayuzumi.

CAST: Rentaro Mikuni (brother), Hideko Okiyama (retarded sister), Kanjuro Arashi (patriarch), Yasuko Matsui (sister), Kazuo Kitamura (engineer), Jun Hamamura, Yoshi Kato, Choichiro Kawarazaki, Hosei Lomatsu [Romatsu?], Taiji Tonoyama, Chikako Hosokawa, Chikage Ogi.

A Nikkatsu Corporation Production. Color. NikkatsuScope (?). 175 minutes. Released 1968.

U.S. VERSION: Released by Toho International Co., Ltd. English subtitles. Alternate title: *The Profound Desire of the Gods*. 150 minutes. MPAA rating: "GP." Released July 22, 1970.

Kuroneko / Yabu no naka no kuroneko ("Black Cat in the Bush"). Executive Producers, Nobuyo Horiba, Setsuo Noto and Kazuo Kuwahara; Director/Screenplay, Kaneto Shindo; Director of photography, Kiyomi Kuroda; Lighting Director, Shoichi Tabata; Music, Hikaru Hayashi; Editor, Hisao [Toshio] Enoki; Art Director, Takashi Marumo; Production Manager, Yasuhiro Kato; Assistant Directors, Hiroshi Matsumoto, Takase Usui, Seijiro Kamiyama, Katsuji Hoshi, Takashi Marumo; Sound Recording, Tetsuo Ohashi; Sound, Toho Recording Centre; Sound Effects, Toho Sound Effects Group; Make-up, Shigeo Kobayashi.

CAST: Kichiemon Nakamura (Gintoki [Ginji] Yabuno), Nobuko Otowa (the mother), Kiwako Taichi (the wife), Kei Sato (Raiko), Taiji Tonoyama (the farmer), Hideo Kanze (the Mikado), Yoshinobu Ogawa (Raiko follower), Mutsuhiro [Rokko] Toura (a warlord), Hidsaki Ezumi (first follower), Masaji Oki (second follower), Kentaro Kaji (third follower), Eiju Kaneda (Kumasunehiko), Ikuko Kosai, Kayoko Sebata, Chiyo Okada (beautiful girls), Noriyuki

Nishiuchi (first police and judicial chief), Masaru Miyata (second police and judicial chief).

A Nippon Eiga Shinsha and Kindai Eiga Kyokai Production. A Toho Co., Ltd. Release. Westrex recording system. Black and white (processed by Tokyo Laboratory, Ltd). Toho Scope. 99 minutes. Released February 24, 1968.

U.S. VERSION: Released by Toho International Co., Ltd. English subtitles. Advertised as *The Black Cat*. 99 minutes. No MPAA rating. Released July 1968.

Kuso tengoku ("Imaginary Paradise"). Producer, Shin Watanabe; Director, Takeshi "Ken" Matsumori; Screenplay, Yasuo Tanami; Art Director, Yoshifumi Honda; Director of Photography, Rokuro Nishigaki; Editor, Ume Takeda; Music, Tetsuaki Hagiwara; Recording, Fumio Yanoguchi; Sound, Toho Recording Centre; Sound Effects, Toho Sound Effects Group.

CAST: Kei Tani (Keitaro Tamaru), Masako Kyozuka (Hisako), Hideo Naka (Gamera), Wakako Sakai (Hiroko Yamamura), Akira Takarada (Takashi Maeno), Akemi Kita (Michiko Akiyama), Takuya Fujioka (Kondo), Yu Fujiki (Kuroda), Yutaka Sada (Chief Guard Yamamura), Yukihiko Gondo, Hiroshi Tanaka, Hirohito Kimura (followers), Keiko Nishioka, Sakayu Nakagawa, Yuko Yano (geishas), Keiji Yanoma (counter jumper), Ikio Sawamura (driver), Makoto Fujita (marathon runner), Yutaka Nakayama (policeman), Hajime Hana (1st detective), Senri Sakurai (2nd detective), Jun Tazaki (boss), Yasuo Araki (1st man), Hans Horneff (2nd man), Ultra Trio (thieves), Masao Komatsu (jailer), Yoshiko Toyoura (young lady with president), Wakako Tanabe (nurse).

A Toho Co., Ltd. Production. Westrex recording system. Fujicolor (processed by Tokyo Laboratory Ltd.). Toho Scope. 84 minutes. Released 1968.

U.S. VERSION: Distributor, if any, is undetermined. Alternate titles: *Imagery Paradise* and *Fancy Paradise*.

Kwaidan / Kaidan ("Ghost Story"). Executive Producer, Shigeru Wakatsuki; Director, Masaki Kobayashi; Screenplay, Yoko Mizuki, based on the stories "The Reconciliation," "Yuki-onna," "The Story of Mimi-nashi-Hoichi," and "In a Cup of Tea," from the collection *Kwaidan: Stories and Studies of Strange Things* (1900) by Lafcadio Hearn; Director of Photography, Yoshio Miyajima; Art Director, Shigemasa Toda; Lighting, Akira Aomatsu; Color Consultant, Michio Midorikawa; Picture of the Battle of Dan-no-ura, Masayoshi Nakamura; Editor, Hisashi Sagara; Main Title writer, Sofu Teshigawara; Title Design, Kiyoshi Kuritsh; Music, Toru Takemitsu; Sound Recording, Hideo Nishizaki; Sound, Toho Recording Centre; Sound Effects, Toru Takemitsu, Kuniharu Akiyama, Junosuke Okuyama, and Akira Suzuki.

CAST: *The Black Hair* ("Kurokami"): Rentaro Mikuni (samurai), Michiyo Aratama (1st wife), Misako Watanabe (2nd wife), Kenjiro Ishiyama, Ranko Akagi, Fumie Kitehara, Katsuhei Matsumoto, Yoshiko Ieda, Otome Tsukimiya, Kenzo Taneka, Kiyoshi Nakano. *The Woman of the Snow* ("Yuki-onna"): Keiko Kishi (Yuki, *The Snow Woman*), Tatsuya Nakadai (Minokichi), Mariko Okada (Minokichi's mother), Yuko Mochizuki, Kin Sugai, Noriko Sengoku, Akiko Momura, Torahiko Hamada, Jun Hamamura. *Hoichi-the-Earless* ("Mimi-nashi-Hoichi"): Kazuo Nakamura (Hoichi), Rentaro Mikuni (samurai spirit), Ganjiro Nakamura (priest), Takashi Shimura (head priest), Joichi [Yoichi] Hayashi (attendant), Tetsuro Tamba (Yoshitsune), Hideko Muramatsu, Kunie Tanaka, Kazuo Kitamura, Ichiro Nakatani, Masanori Tomotake, Tokue Hanazawa, Shin Ryuoka, Makiko Hojo, Shoichi Kuwayama, Mutsuhiko Tsurumaru, Akira Tani. *In a Cup of Tea* ("Chawan no naka"): Ganemon Nakamura (Kannai), Noboru Nakaya (Shikibu Heinai), Jun Tazaki (commander of the guards), Osamu Takizawa, Haruko Sugimura, Ganjiro Nakamura, Seiji Miyaguchi, Kei Sato, Tomoko Naraoka, Shigeru Kemiyama.

A Ninjin Club/Bungei Production for Toho Co., Ltd, in association with Toyo Kogyo Kabushiki Kaisha. A Toho Co.,

Ltd. Release. Western Electric Mirrophonic recording (possibly encoded with Perspecta Stereophonic Sound). Eastman Color (processed by Tokyo Laboratory, Ltd.). Prints by Toyo Co., Ltd. Toho Scope. 164 minutes. Released 1964.

U.S. VERSION: Released by Continental Distributing, Inc. English subtitles. A Walter Reade-Sterling Presentation. Reedited to 125 minutes (eliminating "The Woman of the Snow") after the film's Los Angeles premiere. Most current home video versions have restored the missing episode, run 164 minutes, and are letterboxed. Running time of Japanese version also given at 183 minutes (a roadshow version?). International Title: *Ghost Stories*. Alternate title: *Weird Tales*. Other Versions include: *Kaidan Yukigoro* (1968) and *Aido* (1969) No MPAA rating. Released July 15, 1965.

Kyofu no daiuzumaki ("Horror of the Giant Vortex"). Director, Buichi Saito.

CAST: Keiko Natsuo, Toshio Kurosawa.

A Kindai Eiga Kyokai Production. Color. Academy ratio. Running time undetermined. Released 1978.

U.S. VERSION: Distributor, if any, is undetermined. A Japanese telefeature released theatrically outside Japan. International title: *Horror of the Giant Vortex*.

Kyokanoko musume Dojoji ("Sweet Cake Young Girls at Dojo Temple"). [production credits unavailable].

CAST: Utaemon Nakamura.

A Shochiku Co., Ltd. Production. Shochikucolor. Academy ratio. 80 minutes. Released 1956.

U.S. VERSION: Distributor, if any, is undetermined. International title: *Dojoji Temple*.

Kyoren no onna shisho ("Passion of a Woman Teacher"). Director, Kenji Mizoguchi; Screenplay, Matsutaro Kawaguchi; Director of Photography, Tatsuyuki Yokota.

CAST: Yoneko Sakai (daughter), Eiji Nakano (lover), Yoshiko Okada (student).

A Nikkatsu Shingekibu Production. Silent. Black and white. Academy ratio. 85 minutes. Released 1926.

U.S. VERSION: Distributor, if any, is undetermined. International title: *Passion of a Woman Teacher*.

The Lady and the Beard / Shukujo to hige ("The Lady and the Beard"). Director, Yasujiro Ozu; Screenplay, Komatsu Kitamura; Director of Photography, Hideo Shigehara.

CAST: Tokihito Okada, Ichiro Tsukita, Toshiko Iizuka, Hiroko Kawasaki, Choko Iida, Tatsuo Saito, Satoko Date, Chishu Ryu.

A Shochiku Co., Ltd. Production. Filmed at Shochiku-Kamata Studios. Silent. Black and white. Academy ratio. 97 minutes. Released February 7, 1931.

U.S. VERSION: Released by Shochiku Films of America, Inc. English intertitles. Alternate title: *The Lady and the Moustache*. 75 minutes. No MPAA rating. Released 1972 (?).

The Lady from Musashino / Musashino fujin ("The Lady from Musashino"). Producer, Hideo Koi; Director, Kenji Mizoguchi; Screenplay, Yoshikata Yoda, based on the novel by Shohei Oka, and a story adaptation by Tsuneari Fukuda; Director of Photography, Masao Tamai; Art Director, Takashi Matsuyama; Music, Fumio Hayasaka.

CAST: Kinuyo Tanaka (Michiko Akiyama), Masayuki Mori (Tadao Akiyama, *her husband*), Akihiko Katayama (Tsutomu Miyaji, *her cousin*), Yukiko Todoroki (Tomiko Ono), So Yamamura (Eiji Ono, *another cousin*), Minako Nakamura (Yukiko Ono), Eitaro Shindo (Shinzaburo Miyaji), Satoshi Nishida (Narita), Toyoji Shiosawa (Harue Narita), Reiko Otani (Takako Sasamoto), Yasuzo Fukami (Tomozuka), Noriko Sengoku (maid in the Ono House), Michiko Tsuyama (Eiko), Mie Aso (Yoshiko).

A Toho Co., Ltd. Production. Black and white. Academy ratio. 88 minutes. Released September 14, 1951.

U.S. Version: Distributor undetermined. English subtitles. Alternate title: *Lady Musashino*. 87 minutes. No MPAA rating. Released 1981 (?).

The Lake / Onna no mizuumi ("The Lake of Women"). Associate Producer, Keinosuke Kubo; Director, Yoshishige Yoshida; Screenplay, Yoshio Ishido, Yasuko Ono, and Yoshishige Yoshida, based on the story "Mizumi" in *Shincho* (1954) by Yasunari Kawabata; Director of Photography, Tatsuo Suzuki; Editor, Sachiko Shimizu; Music, Shigeru Ikeno.

Cast: Mariko Okada (Miyako Mizuki), Shinsuke Ashida (Yuzo), Shigeru Tsuyuguchi (Ginpei Momoi), Tamotsu Hayakawa (Kintano), Keiko Natsu (Machie), K. Ichikawa, Aiko Masuda, Sakae Umezu, Keisuke Nakai, Kazumi Higuchi, Mitsuyo Omata.

A Gendai Eiga Production. A Shochiku Co., Ltd. Release. Black and white. Shochiku GrandScope (?). 98 minutes. Released 1966.

U.S. Version: Released by Shochiku Films of America, Inc. English subtitles. 98 minutes. No MPAA rating. Released April 1970.

Lake of Dracula / Chi o suu me—noroi no yakata ("Cursed House—Blood-sucking Eyes"). Executive Producer, Fumio Tanaka; Director, Michio Yamamoto; Screenplay, Ei Ogawa, Masaru Takesue, suggested by the novel *Dracula*, by Abraham Stoker; Director of Photography, Rokuro Nishigaki; Music, Riichiro Manabe; Editor, Hisashi Kondo; Art Director, Shigichi Ikuno; Lighting, Kojiro Sato; Assistant to the Director, Yoshisuke Kawasaki; Sound, Toho Recording Centre; Sound Effects, Toho Sound Effects Group. Special Effects Director, Teruyoshi Nakano; Special Effects, Toho Special Effects Group.

Cast: Midori Fujita (Akiko), Choei Takahashi (Dr. Takashi Saki), Sanae Emi (Natsuoke), Shin Kishida (The Stranger), Kaku Takashina, Shuji Otaki, Tadao Fumi, Mika Katsuragi, Tatsuo Matsushita, Fusako Tachibana, Yasuzo Ogawa, Wataru Omae, Mika Katsuragi, Tadao Futami.

A Toho Co., Ltd. Production. Color (processed by Tokyo Laboratory, Ltd.). Panavision. 82 minutes. Released June 16, 1971.

U.S. Version: Released by Toho International Co., Ltd. English subtitles. 82 minutes. No MPAA rating. Released August 1973. Dubbed into English and released to television by United Productions of America in 1980. A UPA Productions of America presentation. Executive Producer, Henry G. Saperstein. Television title: *The Lake of Dracula*. The television version was edited to 79 minutes, with the ending substantially cut. Alternate titles include: *Japula*, *Dracula's Lust for Blood*, *The Bloodthirsty Eyes* and *Lake of Death*.

Laputa: Castle in the Sky / Tenku no Shiro Laputa ("Laputa: Castle in the Sky") **[animated]**. Executive Producer, Yasuyoshi Tokuma; Producers, Tatsumi Yamashita, Hideo Ogata and Isao Takahata; Associate Producer, Toru Hata; Director/Editor, Hayao Miyazaki; Screenplay, Hayao Miyazaki, based on an extract from *Gulliver's Travels* by Jonathan Swift; Photography, Hirokata Takahashi; Production Design, Toshiro Nozaki and Nizo Yamamoto; Sound, Shigeharu Shiba; Animation Director, Yoshinori Kanada. Music, Joe Hisaishi.

Voice Characterizations: (undetermined).

A Tokuma Shoten Publishing Co., Ltd. Production. Color. Spherical wide screen. 124 minutes. Released 1986.

U.S. Version: Released by Streamline Pictures. English-dubbed. 124 minutes (?). No MPAA rating. Released August 11, 1989.

Las Vegas Free-for-All / Kureizi ogon sakusen ("Crazy: Golden Operation"). Executive Producer, Shin Watanabe; Director, Takashi Tsuboshima; Screenplay, Ryozo Kasahara and Yasuo Tanami; Director of Photography, Masaharu Utsumi; Music, Yasushi Miyagawa, Tessho Hagiwara.

CAST: Hitoshi Ueki (Shinran Machida, *the gambler*), Hajime Hana (Shigekane Itagaki, *the politician*), Ken Tani (Kaneo Nashimoto, *the doctor*), Mie Hama (Tsukiko), Mari Sono (Yuriko), Hiroshi Inuzuka (native American), Eitaro Ishibashi, Shin Yasuda (henchmen in love with Mary), Senri Sakurai (government official), Ichiro Arishima (Machida's boss), Peggy Neal (Mary), Andrew Hughes (Kid Gold), Yu Fujiki (Dr. Waniguchi), Shigeki Ishida, Nadao Kirino (Machida's co-workers), Kenjiro Ishida (government official), George Furness (executor of Kid Gold's estate), Ikio Sawamura (chip maker), Eric Nielsen (Al), Harold S. Conway (H. Conway, *President of the Riviera Casino*), Bob Whitley (cop in Santa Monica), Ed Keane (cop at jail), Masumi Okada (priest), Yuzo Kayama (singer in Hawaii), Emi Ito and Yumi Ito [The Peanuts], The Drifters, Choko Iida, Yutaka Sada, Kazuo Suzuki.

A Toho Co., Ltd./Watanabe Productions, Ltd. Production. Filmed on location in Hawaii; Los Angeles, California; and in Las Vegas, Nevada. Eastman Color. Toho Scope. 157 minutes. Released April 1967.

U.S. VERSION: Released by Toho International Co., Ltd. English subtitles. The 9th "Crazy" feature. Followed by *Monsieur Zivaco* (1967). The Drifters listed above are not to be confused with the American group of the 1950s. 157 minutes. No MPAA rating. Released January 25, 1968.

The Last Challenge / Aoi yogiri no chosenjo ("Cutting the Night"). Producers, Tomoyuki Tanaka and Reiji Miwa; Director, Kengo Furusawa; Screenplay, Motosada Nishigane; Director of Photography, Masaharu Utsumi; Music, Kenjiro Hirose.

CAST: Yosuke Natsuki (Ryuji), Yuriko Hoshi (Yukiko Sengoku), Makoto Sato, Jun Tazaki, Kumi Mizuno.

A Toho Co., Ltd. Production. Black and white. Toho Scope. 84 minutes. Released 1961.

U.S. VERSION: Released by Toho International Co., Ltd. English subtitles. 84 minutes. No MPAA rating. Release date undetermined.

Last Day of Samurai / Koto no Tsume ("Plucking the Koto"). Producer, Shiro Horie; Director, Hiromichi Horikawa; Screenplay, Ryuzo Kikushima and Tokuhei Wakao, based on *Genroku Chushingura, Oishi Saigo no Ichihichi*, by Seika Mayama; Assistant Director, Mimaji Naganose.

CAST: Senjaku Nakamura, Chikage Ogi, Koshiro Matsumoto, Ganjiro Nakamura.

A Toho Co., Ltd. Production. Black and white (?). Academy ratio (?). 54 minutes. Released July 1957.

U.S. VERSION: Released by Toho International Co., Ltd. English subtitles. 54 minutes. No MPAA rating. Released January 1962.

The Last Death of the Devil / Gekko kamen: Akuma no saigo ("Moonlight Mask: End of the Devil"). Director, Shoichi Shimazu.

CAST: Fumitake Omura, Harold S. Conway, Osman Yusef.

A Toei Co., Ltd. Production. Black and white (processed by Toei Chemistry Co., Ltd.). ToeiScope. 60 minutes. Released August 4, 1959.

U.S. VERSION: Reportedly released in the United States, distributor undetermined. The 6th and final film in the series (see *The Man in the Moonlight Mask*).

The Last Dinosaur / Kyokutei tankensen Pora-Bora ("Polar Probe Ship Polar-Borer"). Producers Arthur Rankin, Jr., Jules Bass; Co-producer (for Tsuburaya Productions), Noboru Tsuburaya; Associate Producers, Benni Korzen, Kineshiro Okubo, Masaki Iizuka, Kazuyoshi Kasai; Directors, Alex Grasshoff, Tsugunobu "Tom" Kotani; Screenplay, William Overgard; Director of Photography, Shoji [Masaji] Ueda; Supervising Editor, Barry Walter; Editors, Tatsuji Nakashizu, Minoru Kozono; Art Designer, Kazuhiko Fujiwara; Production Coordinators, Tsuburaya Enterprises, Inc.; Coordinator, Kiyokama Ugama; Lighting, Masaaki Yoneyama; Music, Maury Laws, Arranged and Conducted by Kenjiro Hirose; Song, "He's the Last

Dinosaur," Music by Maury Laws, Lyrics by Jules Bass, Arranged and Conducted by Bernard Hoffer, and performed by Nancy Wilson; Assistant Director, Shohei Tojo; Production Manager, Minoru Kurita; Sound Mixer, Yuji Hiyoshi; Sound Studio, Kaino Kai; Still Photographer, Isao Katsumura. Special Effects Unit: Director, Kazuo Sagawa; Director of Photography, Sadao Sato; Lighting, Yasuo Kitayama [Kitazawa]; Art Designer, Tetsuzo Osawa; Specialist, Moriaki Uematsu; Optical Photography, Michihisa Miyashige and Minoru Nakano; Assistant Director, Yoshiyuki Yoshimura; Production Manager, Kazuo Onashi; Production Coordinators, Kiyotaka "Jimmy" Okubo and Kazumi Kasai.

CAST: Richard Boone (Masten Thrust), Joan Van Ark (Francesca "Frankie" Banks), Steven Keats (Dr. Charles "Chuck" Wade), Luther Rackley (Bunta), Carl Hansen (Barney), Masumi Sekiya (prehistoric girl), Tetsu Nakamura (Dr, Kawamoto), William Ross (Expedition Captain), Tasso Kamamuda, Nancy Magsig, Don Maloney, Vanessa Cristina, James Dale, Mie Enoki, Smunsake Karita, Gary Gundersen.

A Rankin/Bass Productions, Inc./ Tsuburaya Productions, Ltd. Production. An Arthur Rankin, Jr./Jules Bass Film. A Towa Co., Ltd. Release. A Japanese/ U.S. co-production in English. Filmed at Tsuburaya Studios. Color (processed by Tokyo Laboratory Ltd.). Spherical wide screen. 105 minutes. Released September 15, 1977.

U.S. VERSION: Slated for theatrical release in New York City on February 11, 1977, but pulled by the American Broadcasting Companies, Inc. network (ABC), who owned the TV rights; ABC elected to telecast it on that date. Syndicated by Viacom International, Inc. 95 minutes. Japanese title also given as *Saigo no Kyoru*. No MPAA rating.

The Last Game / Eirei-tachi no Oenka ("Cheering for the Spirits of the College Baseball Players"). Producers, Tokumaru Kuniyasu, Juichi Tanaka, and Yo Higashi; Director, Kihachi Okamoto; Screenplay, Nobuo Yamada and Kihachi Okamoto, based on an original story by Keisuke Kamiyama; Director of Photography, Hiroshi Murai; Art Director, Kazuo Takenaka; Music, Masaru Sato.

CAST: Toshiyuki Nagashima, Hidekazu Nakamura, Hiroshi Katsuno.

A Tokyo Channel 12 TV, Ltd. Production. Color. Spherical wide screen (?). 124 minutes. Released 1979.

U.S. VERSION: Distributor, if any, is undetermined. Running time also given at 144 minutes. No MPAA rating.

The Last Lady. Director, Mitsumasa Saito.

CAST: Michiyo Aratama, Sanae Takasugi, Sayuri Yoshinaga.

A Toho Co., Ltd. Production (?). Color (?). Toho Scope (?). Released 1967 (?).

U.S. VERSION: Released by Toho International Co., Ltd. English subtitles. Running time and Japanese title undetermined. No MPAA rating. Released May 8, 1968.

The Last Samurai / Okami yo rakujitsu o kire ("Last Day of the Wolf Cat"). Director, Kenji Misumi; Screenplay, Takeo Kunihiro, based on an original story by Shotaro Ikenami; Director of Photography, Masao Kosugi.

CAST: Hideki Takahashi (Toranosuke Sugi), Ken Ogata (Hanjiro Hito Kiro), Tajaguri Shimura (Ikemototo Shigehei), Teruhiko Saigo (Okita Soshi), Keiko Matsuzaka (Reiko), Kiwako Taiji (nun).

A Shochiku Co., Ltd. Production. Color. Panavision (?). 159 minutes. Released 1974.

U.S. VERSION: Released by Shochiku Films of America, Inc. English subtitles. 159 minutes. No MPAA rating. Released June 1977.

The Last Voyage. Producers, Andrew L. Stone and Virginia L. Stone; Director/Screenplay, Andrew L. Stone; Director of Photography, Hal Mohr; Editor, Virginia L. Stone; Music Arranger and Conductor, Rudy Schrager; Assistant Director and Production Manager, Harrold A. Weinberger; Special Effects, A.J. Lohman; Sound Mixer, Philip N. Mitchell; Sound, Ryder Sound Services, Inc.

George Furness (right) and Joel Marsten try to help their dying captain (George Sanders) in *The Last Voyage*.

CAST: Robert Stack (Cliff Henderson), Dorothy Malone (Laurie Henderson, *his wife*), George Sanders (Captain Robert Adams), Edmond O'Brien (2nd Engineer Walsh), Tammy Marihugh (Jill Henderson, *Cliff and Laurie's daughter*), Woody Strode (Lawson), Jack Kruschen (Chief Engineer Pringle), Joel Marston (3rd Officer Ragland), George Furness (1st Officer Osborne and narrator), Richard Norris (Engineer Cole), Andrew Hughes (radio operator), Robert Martin (2nd Mate Mace), Bill Wilson (youth), Marshall Kent, Esther Malone.

An Andrew and Virginia Stone Production. A Metro-Goldwyn-Mayer Presentation. A Loew's, Inc. Release. A U.S. production in English. Filmed aboard the *S.S. Claridon* in Osaka, Japan. Eastman Color. Spherical wide screen. 91 minutes. No MPAA rating. Released 1960.

The Last War / Sekai daisenso ("The Great World War"). Producers, Sanezumi Fujimoto and Tomoyuki Tanaka; Director, Shue Matsubayashi; Screenplay, Toshio Yasumi and Takeshi Kimura; Director of Photography, Rokuro Nishigaki; Sound, Toho Recording Centre; Music, Ikuma Dan; Sound Effects, Toho Sound Effects Group. *Toho Special Effects Group*: Director, Eiji Tsuburaya; Photography, Teisho Arikawa, Mototaka Tomioka; Lighting, Kuichiro Kishida; Art Director, Akira Watanabe; Matte Process, Hiroshi Mukoyama; Optical Photography, Taka Yuki, Yukio Manoda; Assistant Director, Teruyoshi Nakano.

CAST: Frankie Sakai (Mokichi), Nobuko Otowa (Oyoshi), Akira Takarada (Takano), Yuriko Hoshi (Saeko), Harold S. Conway (missile silo officer), Jerry Ito (government official), Chishu Ryu (ship's cook), Chieko Nakakita (single mother), Eijiro Tono (ship's captain), Yumi Shirakawa, So Yamamura, Seizaburo Kawazu, Nobuo Nakamura, Minoru Takada, Saburo Iketani, Shigeki Ishida, Yutaka Sada, Nadao Kirino, Koji Uno, Toshiko Furuta, Jiro Kumagai, Wataru Omae, Osman Yusuf, Kozo Nomura, Ed Keane.

A Toho Co., Ltd. Production. Western Electric Mirrophonic recording (encoded with Perspecta Stereophonic Sound). Eastman Color (processed by Tokyo Laboratory, Ltd.) Toho Scope. 108 minutes plus 90-second overture. Released October 8, 1961.

U.S. VERSION: Release uncertain, possibly subtitled by Toho International, released dubbed by Brenco Pictures Corp., in association with Toho International Co., Ltd., or released directly to U.S. television. Television version, probably issued in 1964-65, is missing all production credits, but does include the song, "It's A Small World," music and lyrics by Richard M. Sherman and Robert B. Sherman. Brenco Version: Executive Producer, Edward L. Alperson; Producer, Stanley Meyer; Story, John Meredyth Lucas (?); Editor, Kenneth Wannberg; Sound, Ryder Sound Services, Inc.; prints by Pathé; Dubbing Cast: Paul Frees, other unknown. 73 minutes. No MPAA rating.

Late Autumn / Akibiyori ("Autumn Weather"). Producer, Shizuo Yamanouchi; Director, Yasujiro Ozu; Screenplay, Yasujiro Ozu and Kogo Noda, based on the novel by Ton Satomi; Director of Photography, Yushun Atsuta; Art Director, Tatsuo Hameda; Music, Takanobu Saito.

CAST: Setsuko Hara (Akiko Miwa), Yoko Tsukasa (Ayako), Chishu Ryu (Shukichi Miwa), Mariko Okada (Yuriko Sasaki), Keiji Sada (Shotaro Goto), Shin Saburi (Soichi Mamiya), Miyuki Kuwano (Michiko), Nobuo Nakamura (Shuzo Taguchi), Kuniko Miyake (Nobu), Yariko Tashiro (Yoko), Ryuji Kita (Seiichiro Hirayama), Shinichiro Mikami (Koichi), Shima Iwashita.

A Shochiku Co., Ltd. Production. Eastman Color. Academy ratio. 125 minutes. Released November 13, 1960.

U.S. VERSION: Released by New Yorker Films. English subtitles. 125 minutes. No MPAA rating. Released November 1973.

Late Spring / Banshun ("Late Spring"). Director, Yasujiro Ozu; Screenplay, Yasujiro Ozu and Kogo Noda, based on the novel *Father and Daughter*, by Kazuo Hirotsu; Director of Photography, Yuharu Atsuta; Editor, Yoshiyasu Hamamura; Art Director, Tatsuo Hamada; Lighting, Haruo Isono; Music, Senji Ito.

CAST: Chishu Ryu (Professor Shukichi Somiya), Setsuko Hara (Noriko, *his daughter*), Haruko Sugimura (Masa Taguchi, *Somiya's sister*), Hohi Aoki (Katsuyoshi, *her son*), Jun Usami (Shoichi Hattori), Yumeji Tsukioka (Ayako Kitagawa), Kuniko Miyake (Akiko Miwa), Masao Mishima (Professor Onodera), Yoshiko Tsubouchi (Kiku Onodera), Yoko Katsuragi (Misae Onodera).

A Shochiku Co., Ltd. Production. Filmed at Shochiku-Ofuna Studios. Black and white. Academy ratio. 108 minutes. Released September 19, 1949.

U.S. VERSION: Released by New Yorker Films. English subtitles. 108 minutes. No MPAA rating. Released August 1972.

Chishu Ryu (right) in Yasujiro Ozu's *Late Spring* (1949).

Richard Jaechel, Linda Haynes, Masumi Okada, Joseph Cotten, Akira Takarada and unidenintifid in *Latitude Zero* (1969). Cotten was gravely ill during filming and looks it.

Latitude Zero / Ido zero dai sakusen ("Latitide Zero: Great Military Operation"). Executive Producer, Tomoyuki Tanaka; Producer, Don Sharp; Director, Ishiro Honda; Screenplay, Ted Sherdeman (based on his "Latitude Zero" stories); Screenplay Advisor (i.e., Japanese Version), Shinichi Sekizawa; Director of Photography, Taiichi Kankura; Music, Akira Ifukube; Editor, Ume Takeda; Lighting, Kiichi Onda; Art Director, Takeo Kita; Costume Designer, Kiichi Ichida, Linda Glazman; Sound Recording Director, Masao Fujiyoshi; Sound Effects, Sadamasa Nishimoto, Toho Sound Effects Group; Mixing, Hisashi Shimonaga; Sound, Toho Recording Centre; Assistant Director, Seiji Tani; Production Manager, Yasuaki Sakamoto; Creative Advisor (additional dialog?), Warren Lewis; *Toho Special Effects Group*: Director, Eiji Tsuburaya; Photography, Teisho Arikawa; Lighting, Kuichiro [Kyuighiro] Kishida; Set Decoration, Akira Watanabe; Optical Photography, Yukio Manoda, Sadao Iizuda; Scene Manipulation, Fumio Nakadai; Assistant Director, Teruyoshi Nakano.

CAST: Joseph Cotten (Capt. Craig McKenzie), Cesar Romero (Dr. Malic), Richard Jaeckel (Perry Lawton), Patricia Medina (Lucretia), Linda Haynes (Dr. Anne Barton), Akira Takarada (Dr. Ken Tashiro), Masumi Okada (Dr. Jules Masson), Hikaru Kuroki (Kroiga), Mari Nakayama (Tsuruko Okada), Tetsu Nakamura (Dr. Okada), Akihiko Hirata (Dr. Sugata), Susumu Kurobe (Chin), Haruo Nakajima (winged lion), Wataru Omae.

A Toho Co., Ltd. Production, in association with Ambassador Productions. A Don Sharp Productions Presentation. A Japanese/U.S. co-production in English (and dubbed for Japanese release). Westrex Recording system. Eastman Color (processed by Tokyo Laboratory, Ltd.). Panavision. 108 minutes. Released July 26, 1969.

U.S. VERSION: Released by National General Pictures (a division of National General Corp.). English-dubbed. Prints by Technicolor. Reissued in Japan in 1974, doubled-billed with *Mothra* (q.v.). 95 minutes (possibly 99 minutes; copyright length 106 minutes). Takarada, Hirata, etc. speak English in the U.S. edition and are not dubbed. MPAA rating: "G." Test-screen in Dallas in July 1969. Released December 1970.

The Legacy of the 500,000 / Gojuman-nin no isan ("The Legacy of the 500,000"). Executive Producers, Sanezumi Fujimoto and Tomoyuki Tanaka; Producer/Director, Toshiro Mifune; Screenplay, Ryuzo Kikushima; Director of Photography, Takao Saito; Music, Masaru Sato; Assistant Director, Shigekichi Takemae.

CAST: Toshiro Mifune (Matsuo), Tatsuya Mihashi, Tatsuya Nakadai, Tsutomu Yamazaki.

A Mifune Productions, Ltd./Toho Co., Ltd. Production. A Toho Co., Ltd. Release. Black and white. Toho Scope. Released 1963.

U.S. VERSION: Released by Toho International Co., Ltd. English subtitles. 98 minutes. No MPAA rating. Released June 12, 1964.

The "Legend of the Dinosaurs" / Kyoryu – kaicho no densetsu ("Legend of the Dinosaur and Monster Bird"). Executive Producer, Keiichi Hashimoto; Director, Junji Kurata; Screenplay, Masaru Igami, Isao Matsumoto, Ichiro Otsu; Directors of Photography, Sakuji Shiomi and Shigeru Akazuka; Art Director, Yoshimitsu Amamori; Editor, Isamu Ichida; Music, Masao Yagi; Lighting, Koji Inoue; Sound Recording, Teruhiko Arakawa; Assistant Director, Kazuo Noda; Still Photographer, Takeshi Kimura; Publicity, Takeshi Fujimoto; Special Technical Adviser/Special Effects Director, Fuminori Obayashi.

CAST: Tsunehiko Watase (Setsu Serizawa), Nobiko Sawa (Akiko Osano), Shotaro Hayashi (Akira Taniki), Tomoko [Satoko] Kyoshima (Junko Sonoda), Fuyukichi Maki (Masahira Muku), Hiroshi Nawa (Masahiko Miyawaki), Kinji Nakamura (Hideyuki Sakai), Yusuke Tsukasa (Susumu Hirano), So Takizawa (Jiro Shimamoto), Goro Nawata [Oki?] (Hiroshi Sugiyama), Yukari Miyazen (Hiroko Takami), Masahiro Arikawa (Seitaro Shintaku), Tamikashi Karazawa (Uemura), Sachio Miyashiro (Kobayashi),

David Freedman, Maureen Peacock, Catherine Laub, Masaraka Iwao, Yukio Miyagi, Akira Moroguchi.

A Toei Co., Ltd. Production. Toeicolor. Panavision (advertised as ToeiScope). 94 minutes. Filmed at Toei Studios and on location at Mt. Fuji. Released April 29, 1977.

U.S. Version: Never released theatrically in the United States. Released to television by King Features Entertainment, a subsidiary of the Hearst Corp., in 1987. English-dubbed. Onscreen title is as it appears above. English-dubbed version produced by Frontier Enterprises; Dubbing Supervisor, William Ross. International title: *Legend of Dinosaurs and Monster Birds*. 94 minutes. No MPAA Rating.

Legend of the Eight Samurai / Satomi hakkenden ("Legend of Satomi Eight Dogs"). Executive Producer, Haruki Kadokawa; Producers, Masao Sato, Izumi Toyoshima, and Hiroshi Sugawara; Director, Kinji Fukasaku; Screenplay, Toshio Kamata and Kinji Fukasaku, based on the novel by Hutaro Yamada, published by Kadokawa Publishing Co., Ltd.; Director of Photography, Seizo Sengen; Art Directors, Chikara Imamura and Akira Takahashi; Music, Masahide Sakuma and Hiroyuki Namba; Singer, John O'Banion; Special Effects, Nobuo Yajima; Lighting, Mitsuo Watanabe; Action Coordinator, Shinichi "Sonny" Chiba.

Cast: Hiroko Takushimaru (Princess Shizu Satomi), Hiroyuki "Henry" Sanada (Shinbei), Sue Shihomi (Keno), Shinichi "Sonny" Chiba (Dosetsu), Keiko Matsuzaka (narrator), Mickey Narita.

A Haruki Kadokawa Films, Inc./Toei Co., Ltd. Production. A Haruki Kadokawa Presentation. A Toei Co., Ltd. Release. Toeicolor. Panavision. 133 minutes. Released 1983.

U.S. Version: Apparently never released theatrically in the United States. Released to home video in 1990 by Star-Maker Entertainment, Inc. English-dubbed. No MPAA rating. 133 minutes.

Let's Go, Grand' Ma! / Oreno yuku michi. Producer, Kunio Sawamura; Director, Shigeyuki Yamane; Screenplay, Shigeyuki Yamane and Eiji Hikari; Director of Photography, Hiroshi Takemura; Art Director, Masao Kumagai; Editor, Riichi Tomiya; Sound, Tokio Hiramatsu; Music, Shinichi Tanabe.

Cast: Kinuyo Tanaka (Grandmother Kiku), Choichiro Kawarazaki, Junko Natsu, Akiko Nomura, Hideki Saijo.

A Shochiku Co., Ltd. Production. Color. Panavision (?) 86 minutes. Released 1975.

U.S. Version: Released by Shochiku Films of America, Inc. English subtitles. 86 minutes. No MPAA rating. Released May 12, 1976.

Let's Go, Young Guy! / Retsu Go! wakadaisho ("Let's Go! Young Guy"). Executive Producer, Sanezumi Fujimoto; Director, Katsumi Iwauchi; Screenplay, Yasuo Tanami; Director of Photography, Yuzuru Aizawa; Music, Kenjiro Hirose.

Cast: Yuzo Kayama (Yuichi Tanuma), Yuriko Hoshi, Bibari Maeda, Akira Takarada, Chen Man Ling, Kunie Tanaka, To Man Rei, Choko Iida, Ichiro Arishima.

A Toho Co., Ltd. Production. Eastman Color. Toho Scope. Filmed on location in Hong Kong. 90 minutes. Released January 1967.

U.S. Version: Released by Toho International Co., Ltd. English subtitles. The 9th "Young Guy" feature. Followed by *Judo Champion* (1967). 90 minutes. No MPAA rating. Released November 8, 1967.

The Life and Opinion of Masseur Ichi / Zato Ichi monogatari ("The Story of Zatoichi"). Executive Producer, Ikuo Kubodera; Director, Kenji Misumi; Screenplay, Minoru Inuzuka, based on the novel by Kan Shimosawa; Director of Photography, Chishi Makiura; Art Director, Akira Naito; Editor, Kanji Suganuma; Music, Akira Ifukube; Sound Recording, Iwao Otani; Lighting, Hironari Kato; Assistant Director, Toshiaki Kunihiro; Martial Arts Director, Shohei Miyauchi; Natural Music Director, Toshio Nakamoto.

Cast: Shintaro Katsu (Zatoichi), Masayo Banri (Otane), Shigeru Amachi (Koshu Hirate), Ryuzo Shimada, Gen Mitamura, Michio Minami, Eijiro Yanagi, Toshiro Chiba, Manabu Morita, Yoshito Yamaji,

Yoichi Funaki, Eigoro Onoe, Ikuko Mori, Chitose Maki, Kinya Ichikawa.

A Daiei Motion Picture Co., Ltd. Production. Filmed at Daiei-Kyoto Studios. Black and white. DaieiScope. 96 minutes. Released April 12, 1962.

U.S. VERSION: Released by Daiei International Films, Inc. English subtitles. Reissued in Japan in 1976. First feature in the 26-film (to date) "Zatoichi" series, all of which starred Katsu, who also essayed the role in a television series. Followed by *The Return of Zatoichi* (1962). No MPAA rating. Release date undetermined.

Life of a Country Doctor / Fundoshi isha ("Loincloth Doctor"). Producer, Tomoyuki Tanaka; Director, Hiroshi Inagaki; Screenplay, Ryuzo Kikushima; Director of Photography, Kazuo Yamada; Music, Ikuma Dan.

CAST: Hisaya Morishige (Keisai Koyama), Setsuko Hara (Iku, *his wife*), Yosuke Natsuki (Hangoro), Chiemi Eri (Osaki), So Yamamura (Dr. Meikai Ikeda).

A Toho Co., Ltd. Production. Black and white. Toho Scope. 116 minutes. Released August 14, 1960.

U.S. VERSION: Released by Toho International Co., Ltd. English subtitles. English adaptation, Victor Suzuki. Alternate titles: *Life of the Country Doctor* and *The Country Doctor*. 116 minutes, later cut to 104 minutes. No MPAA rating. Released May 1961.

The Life of an Actor / Geido ichidai otoko ("The Life of a Man Devoted to the Art"). Director, Kenji Mizoguchi; Screenplay, Yoshikata Yoda, based on a story by Matsutaro Kawaguchi, and the life of Ganjiro Nakamura; Director of Photography, Kohei Sugiyama; Music, Senji Ito.

CAST: Senjaku Nakamura (Tamataro), Yoshiko Nakamura (Onami), Minosuke Bando (Uzo), Yoko Umemura (Otae), Kichisaburo Arashi (Enjaku), Kokichi Takada, Komako Hara, Narutoshi Hayashi, Seizaburo Kawazu.

A Shochiku Co., Ltd. Production. Filmed at Shochiku-Shimokamo Studios. Black and white. Academy ratio. Running time undetermined. Released February 9, 1941.

U.S. VERSION: Distributor, if any, is undetermined. Senjaku Nakamura was the son of Ganjiro Nakamura. The 3rd film in a trilogy.

The Life of an Office Worker / Kaishain seikatsu ("The Life of an Office Worker"). Director, Yasujiro Ozu; Screenplay, Kogo Noda; Director of Photography, Hideo Shigehara.

CAST: Tatsuo Saito, Mitsuko Yoshikawa, Takeshi Sakamoto, Tomio Aoki, Chishu Ryu.

A Shochiku Co., Ltd. Production. Filmed at Shochiku-Kamata Studios. Silent with benshi. Black and white. Academy ratio. 85 minutes. Released October 25, 1929.

U.S. VERSION: Never released in the United States. A lost film.

The Life of Chikuzan, Tsugaru Shamisen Player / Chikuzan Hitoritabi ("Hitoritabi Chikuzan"). Producers, Susumu Takashima, Sadaki Sato, Setsuo Noto, and Manabu Akashi; Director/Screenplay, Kaneto Shindo; Director of Photography, Kiyomi Kuroda; Art Director, Kazumasa Otani; Music, Hikaru Hayashi.

CAST: Ryuzo Hayashi, Nobuko Otowa, Chikuzan Takahashi.

A Kindai Eiga Kyokai Co., Ltd./Jean Jean Co., Ltd. Production. Color. Panavision (?). 125 minutes. Released 1977.

U.S. VERSION: Disitrbutor, if any, is undetermined.

Life of Oharu / Saikaku ichidai onna ("Saikaku, Life of Woman"). Executive Producer, Isamu Yoshii; Producer, Hideo Koi; Director, Kenji Mizoguchi; Screenplay, Yoshikata Yoda and Kenji Mizoguchi, based on the novel *Koshoku ichidai onna* ("The Woman Who Loved Love," 1686) by Saikaku Ihara; Director of Photography, Yoshimi Hirano; Art Director, Hiroshi Mizutani; Music, Ichiro Saito; Historical Consultant, Isamu Yoshi.

CAST: Kinuyo Tanaka (Oharu), Tsukue Matsura (Tomo, *Oharu's mother*), Ichiro Sugai (Shinzaemon, *Oharu's father*), Toshiro Mifune (Katsunosuke), Toshiake

Konoe (Lord Harutaka Matsudaira), Hisako Yamane (Lady Matsudaira), Jukichi Uno (Yakichi Ogiya), Eitaro Shindo (Kahee Sasaya), Akira Oizumi (Fumikichi, Sasaya's friend), Masao Shimizu (Kikuoji), Daisuke Kato (Tasaburo Hishiya), Toranosuke Ogawa (Yoshioka), Hiroshi Oizumi (Manager Bunkichi), Haruyo Ichikawa (Lady-in-Waiting Iwabashi), Kikue More (Myokai), Kyoko Tsuji (landlady at the inn), Yuriko Hamada (Otsubone Yoshioka), Kyoko Kusajima (lady-in-waiting Sodegaki), Noriko Sengoku (lady-in-waiting Sakurai), Sadako Sawamura (Owasa), Masao Mishima (Taisaburo Hishiya), Eijiro Yanagi (counterfeiter), Chieko Higashiyama (Myokai, the old nun), Bokuzen Hidari (clothes rental shop owner), Takashi Shimura (old man), Benkei Shiganoya (Jihei).

A Shintoho Co., Ltd./Koi Productions Production. Filmed at Shintoho's open-air studios in Hirakata. Black and white. Academy ratio. 148 minutes (later edited to 137 minutes). Released April 3, 1952.

U.S. VERSION: Released by Toho International Co., Ltd. English subtitles. Alternate title: *Koshoku ichidai onna*. 133 minutes. No MPAA rating. Released April 20, 1964.

Little Nemo: Adventures in Slumberland **[animated]**. Producer, Yutaka Fujioka; Co-Producers, Barry Glasser, Shunzo Kato, and Eiji Katayama; Associate Producers, Koji Takeuchi and Kaoru Nishiyama; Directors, Masami Hata and William Hurtz; Screenplay, Chris Columbus and Richard Outten; Story, Jean Moebius Giraud and Yutaka Fujioka, based on the comic strip by Winsor McCay, and an idea by Ray Bradbury; Story Consultants, Frank Thomas, Oliver Johnston, David Hilberman, Koji Shimizu, and Robert Towne; Music, Thomas Chase and Steve Rucker, performed by the London Symphony Orchestra; Songs, Richard M. Sherman and Robert B. Sherman; Title Song Singer, Melissa Manchester; Animation Directors, Kazuhide Tomonaga and Nobuo Tomizawa; Conceptual Design, Jean Moebius Giraud; Design Development, Brian Froud, Kazuhide Tomonaga, Corny Cole, Paul Julian, Ken Mundie, Nobuo Tomizawa; Visual Image Development, John Canemaker; Voice Director, David Swift; Casting Director, Zita Campisi; Additional Dialogue, Bruce Reid Schaefer; Editor, Takeshi Seyama; Director of Post-production, Susumu Aketagawa; Sound Mixer, Kunio Ando; Sound Effects Editor, Shizuo Kurahashi; Choregraphy, Michael Peters; Dancers, Peggy Holmes, Natham Prevost, Francis Morgan, David Robertson; Singers, Peggy Abernathy, Brian Cummings, Diana Harris, Kathy Levin, Sherwood Ball, Mitch Gordon, Rainy Haynes, Jack Lynch, Gary Stockdale, Ken Chandler, Jami Lynne Grenham, Mark Lennon, Gene Morford; Story Sketch, Ken Anderson, Boyd Kirkland, Nobuo Tomizawa, Bob Taylor, Yasuo Otsuka, Marty Murphy, Lee Mishkin, Roy Wilson, Leo Salkin, Kazuhide Tomonaga, Milt Schaefer; Storyboard, Masami Hata, Kazuhide Tomonaga, Nobuo Tomizawa, Yasuo Otsuka; Slugging, Sam Weiss, Sam Nicholson, Gwen Wetzler, Ruth Kissane; Exposure Sheets, Robert Alvarez, Karen Peterson, Steven Clark, Robert Shellhorn, Alfred Kouzel, Richard Trueblood; Mouth Code, Eric Peterson; Track Reading, Laurie Wetzler, Mike Truba, George Craig, Cecil Broughton, Mark McNally; Assistant Directors, Hiroaki Sato and Keiko Oyamada; 2nd Asst. Director, Hiroyuki Ishido; Asst. Editor, Hiroshi Adachi; Directing Animators, Yoshinobu Michihata, Kenji Hachizaki, and Toshihiko Masuda; Key Animation, Hiroyuki Aoyama, Hiroaki Noguchi, Atsuko Tanaka, Masaaki Kudo, Kuniyuki Ishii, Fumio Iida, Joji Yanase, Kazuyoshi Takeuchi, Hiroshi Shimizu, Masahiro Neriki, Kitaro Kosaka, Teichi Takiguchi, Yuichiro Yano, Masanori Ono, Tomomi Mizuta, Osamu Okubo, Keiko Tomizawa, Noboru Takano, Hiroyuki Horiuchi, Osamu Nabeshima, Shunji Saida, Toshio Kaneko, Yutaka Oka, Satoshi Sasaki, Makoto Tanaka, Toshio Mori, Sadahiko Sakamaki; Color Design, Hiroko Kondo; Air-Brush Artist, Tomoji Hashizume; Matte Artist, Masahito Aoki; Art Director, Nizo Yamamoto; Background Sketch, Ray Aragon, Dean Gordon, Carol Police,

Fred Water; Asst. Art Director, Seiji Sugawara; Asst. to Layout, Toshiya Washida; Director of Photogrphy, Hajime Hasegawa; Camera, Kenichi Kobayashi, Moriyuki Tershita, Takahisa Ogawa, Kazushige Ichinozuka, Atsuko Ito, Koji Asai, Takashi Nomura, Jin Nishiyama, Kiyoshi Kobayashi, Atsushi Yoshino, Kyoko Osaki, Askio Saito, Hiroshi Kanai, Hitoshi Shirao, Hironori Yoshino, Mika Sakai, Rie Takeuchi, Kazushi Torigoe; Executives in Charge of Production, Katsuro Tanaka and Sander Schwartz; Production Executive, Robert Eatman; Production Managers, Tat Ikeguchi, Sachiko Tsuneda, and Chuck Shiota; Translator, Miyoko Miura; Dialogue Recording Engineer, Larry Miller; Studio, The Recording Place/HLC; Dialogue Track Editor, Jeffrey Patch; ADR Recording Engineers, Vic Radulich and Cat Le Baigue; ADR Studio, Wally Burr Recording; Vocal Recording Engineer, Sheridan Eldridge; Music Recording Engineer, Michael Jarratt; Asst. Music Recording Engineers, Gareth Cousins and Dave Forty; Music Studio, Abbey Road Studios; Music Editor, Roy Pendergast (Music Design Group); Music Mixer, Akihiko Ono; Sound Effects, Sound Box; Dubbing Studio, Aoi Studio; Sound Editors, Masafumi Mima, Magic Capsule; Asst. Sound Mixer, Nobuyoshi Kanbayashi; Titles, Cinema Research Corp.; Additional Postproduction (Los Angeles), Heather Probert and Gregory Hicks; Dolby Stereo Consultant, Mikio Mori, Continental Far East Inc. (Tokyo); 32-Track Digital Recording Machine (X-880), Mitsubishi; Supporter, Lake.

A Tokyo Movie Shinsha Co., Ltd. Production. A Hemdale Pictures Corporation Release. A Japanese/U.S. coproduction in English. Dolby Stereo. Color (processed by Tokyo Laboratory, Ltd.). Spherical wide screen. 85 minutes. Released 1990.

VOICE CHARACTERIZATIONS: Gabriel Damon (Nemo), Mickey Rooney (Flip), Rene Auberjonois (Professor Genius), Danny Mann (Icarus), Laura Mooney (Princess Camille), Bernard Erhard (King Morpheus), William E. Martin (Nightmare King), Alan Oppenheimer (Oomp), Michael Bell (Oompy), Sidney Miller (Oompe), Neil Ross (Oompa), John Stephenson (Oompo), Jennifer Darling (Nemo's mother), Sherry Lynn (Bon Bon), John Stephenson (dirigible captain), Guy Christopher (courtier and cop), Nancy Cartwright, Ellen Gerstell (page), Tress MacNeille (elevator creature), Michael McConnohie (etiquette master), Beau Weaver (teacher #1 and cop), Michael Gough (teacher #2), Kathleen Freeman (dance teacher), Michael Sheehan (fencing master), June Foray (librarian), Gregg Barger (equestarian master), Bert Kramer (goblin general), Bever-Leigh Banfield (woman).

U.S. VERSION: Released by Hemdale Pictures. 85 minutes. MPAA rating: "G." Released 1992.

Little Norse Prince Valiant / Taiyo no Oji, Horusu no daiboken

("Prince of the Sun – A Horse's Great Adventure") **[animated]**. Director, Isao Takahata; Screenplay, Kazuo Fukasawa; Director of Photography, Jiro Yoshimura; Art Director, Mataji Urata; Music, Yoshio Mamiya.

VOICE CHARACTERIZATIONS: (undetermined).

A Toei Animation Studio (Tokyo) Production. A Toei Co., Ltd. Release. Eastman Color. ToeiScope. 82 minutes. Released July 21, 1968.

U.S. VERSION: Distributor, if any, is undetermined. English subtitled version available. 82 minutes. No MPAA rating.

The Little Prince and the Eight-Headed Dragon / Wanpaku ojo no daija taiji

("Brat Prince's Conquest of the Big Snake") **[animated]**. Executive Producer, Hiroshi Okawa; Associate Producers, Shin Yoshida, Isamu Takahashi, and Takashi Ijima; Director, Yugo Serikawa; Animaton Director, Yasuji Mori; Supervisors, Sanae Yamamoto and Koji Fukiya; Screenplay, Ichiro Ikeda and Takashi Ijima; Music, Akira Ifukube; Art Director, Reiji Koyama; Color Design, Saburo Yokoi; Backgrounds, Tomo Fukumoto; Animation, Hideo Furusawa, Masao Kumagawa, Yasuo Otsuka,

Daikichiro Kusube, Makoto Nagasawa, Reiko Okuyama, Masamu Kita, Chikao Katsui, Sadao Tsukioka, Yoichi Kotabe, Tomekichi Takeuchi, Norio Kikone.

VOICE CHARACTERIZATIONS: (undetermined).

A Toei Animation Studio (Tokyo) Production. A Toei Co., Ltd. Release. Eastman Color. ToeiScope. 86 minutes. Released 1963.

U.S. VERSION: Theatrical release uncertain. Released to television by Columbia Pictures Television. English-dubbed. A Columbia Pictures Corp. Release. English language version produced by United Services, Inc. (Tokyo). Director/Screenplay, William Ross. 86 minutes. No MPAA rating.

Live and Learn / Suppon onna-bancho ("School Boss – Miss Snapping Turtle"). Director, Taro Yuge; Screenplay, Fumi Takahashi; Director of Photography, Akira Uehara; Art Director, Taijiro Goto; Music, Sei Ikeno.

CAST: Eiko Yanami (Tetsuko), Yoshihiko Aoyama (Sankichi), Reiko Kasahara (Omatsu), Shin Minatsu (Masa), Junzaburo Ban, Keiko Matsuzaka.

A Daiei Motion Picture Co., Ltd. Fujicolor. DaieiScope. 83 minutes. Released January 27, 1971.

U.S. VERSION: Distributor undetermined. English subtitled version available. 83 minutes. No MPAA rating.

Live My Share, Mother / Mama Istumademo ikitene ("Live Forever, Mama"). Director, Kazuo Ikehiro; Screenplay, Aiko Ishimatsu, based on an original story by Yokichi Sugimoto; Director of Photography, Senkichiro Takeda; Music, Takeo Watanabe.

CAST: Mitsuteru Nakamura (Fumio), Munenori Oyamada, Chiaki Tsukioka (his parents), Taketoshi Naito (doctor), Yoko Atsuta, Michi Azusa, Chiho Yuki.

A Daiei Motion Picture Co., Ltd. Production. Fujicolor. DaieiScope. 86 minutes. Released September 23, 1970.

U.S. VERSION: Released by Daiei International Films. English subtitles. 86 minutes. No MPAA rating. Released March 17, 1971.

Live Today; Die Tomorrow! / Hadaka no jukyusai ("Naked 19-Year-Old"). Director, Kaneto Shindo; Screenplay, Kaneto Shindo, Shozo Matsuda and Isao Seki; Director of Photography, Kiyomi Kuroda; Art Director, Akira Haruki; Editor, Hisao Enoki; Sound, Tetsuo Ohashi; Music, Hikaru Hayashi.

CAST: Daijiro Harada (Michio), Nobuko Otowa (Michio's mother), Kiwako Taichi (whore), Daigo Kusano (Michio's father), Keiko Tori, Kei Sato, Taiji Tonoyama.

A Kindai Eiga Kyokai Production. A Toho Co., Ltd. Release. Black and white. Panavision (?). 120 minutes. Released October 31, 1970.

U.S. VERSION: Released by Toho International Co., Ltd. English subtitles. 120 minutes. No MPAA rating. Released September 29, 1971.

Live Your Own Way / Wakamono tachi ("Young People"). Director, Tokihisa Morikawa; Screenplay, Hisashi Yamanouchi; Director of Photography, Yoshio Miyajima; Art Director, Totetsu Hirakawa; Music, Masaru Sato.

CAST: Kunie Tanaka (Taro), Isao Hashimoto (Jiro), Kei Yamamoto (Saburo), Orie Sato (Orie), Shoji Matsuyama (Suekichi), Yasushi Nagata, Mie Minami, Michiko Otsuda.

A Gekidan Haiyuza Shinsei Eigasha Production. A Shochiku Co., Ltd. Release. Black and white. Academy ratio (?). Released May 1969.

U.S. VERSION: Released by Shochiku Films of America, Inc. English subtitles. 98 minutes. No MPAA rating. Released August 1970.

Living on the River Agano / Agano ni ikiru ("Living on Agano") [**documentary**]. Director, Makoto Sato; Director of Photography, Shigeru Kobayashi; Sound Recording, Shoji Suzuki; Music, Kyomaro [no other name given].

WITH: Shyouzi Suzuki (narrator), Yoshio Hasegawa, Miyae Hasegawa, Shuya Hokari, and others living along the Agano.

A Committee for *Living on the River*

Agano Production. 16mm. Black and white. 115 minutes. Released 1992.

U.S. VERSION: Released by Jay Film Co. English subtitles. *Note:* Director Sato is not the same as the famous actor. 115 minutes. No MPAA rating. Released May 17, 1993.

Living Skeleton / Kyuketsu dokuro sen ("Bloodsucking Skeleton Ship"). Executive Producer, Shiro Kido; Producer, Takashi Inomata; Director, Hiroki [Hiroshi] Matsuno; Screenplay, Kikuma Shimoizaka, Kyuzo Kobayashi; Production Manager, Yoshinori Ikeda; Assistant Director, Masami Tatesen; Art Director, Kyohei Morita; Director of Photography, Masayuki Kato; Editor, Kazuo Ota; Music, Noburo Nishiyama; Sound Hideo Kobayashi; Sound Effects, Hirofumi Sato.

CAST: Kikko Matsuoka (Saeko/Yoriko), Ko Nishimura (Nishizato), Masumi Okada (Tanuma), Nobuo Kaneko (Suetsuga), Yasunori Irikawa (Mochizuki), Asao Koike (Tsuji), Tomo Uchida (Ejiri), Noriyaki Yamamoto (Ono), Kaoru Yamamoto (Mayumi), Keiko Yanazawa (Sanae Suetsugu), Kaishu Uchida (Uchida), Keijiro Kikyo (first policeman), Minoru Hirano (second policeman).

A Shochiku Co., Ltd. Production. Black and white (processed by Shochiku Laboratory). Shochiku GrandScope. 81 minutes. Released November 9, 1968.

U.S. VERSION: Released by Shochiku Films of America. English subtitles. No MPAA rating. 81 minutes. Released 1969 (?).

Lonely Heart / Kofuku ("Happiness"). Producers, Yutaka Goto, Kazuo Baba, Kazuo Kuroi, Toshio Sakamoto, and Hitoshi Ogura; Director, Kon Ichikawa; Screenplay, Shinya Hidaka, Ikuko Oyabu, and Kon Ichikawa, based on the novel *Lady, Lady, I Did It!* by Ed McBain; Director of Photography, Kiyoshi Hasegawa; Art Director, Shinobu Muraki; Music, Toru Okada and Takahiko Ishikawa.

CAST: Yutaka Mizutani, Toshiyuki Nagashima, Rie Nakahara, Kei Tani.

A For Life Records, Inc. Production. A Toho Co., Ltd. Release. Color. Panavision (?). 105 minutes. Released 1981.

U.S. VERSION: Released by Toho International. English subtitles. No MPAA rating. Alternate title: *Happiness*. Released September 14, 1982.

Lonely Lane / Horoki ("Lonely Lane"). Executive Producers, Sanezumi Fujimoto, Mikio Naruse, and Tadahiro Teramoto; Director, Mikio Naruse; Screenplay, Toshiro Ide and Sumie Tanaka, based on the biography *Horoki* (1928) by Fumiko Hayashi; Director of Photography, Jun Yasumoto; Music, Yuji Koseki.

CAST: Hideko Takamine (Fumiko Hayashi), Kinuyo Tanaka, Daisuke Kato, Akira Takarada, Mitsuko Kusabue, Noboru Nakaya, Yoko Tsukasa, Keiju Kobayashi.

A Toho Co., Ltd. Production. Black and white. Toho Scope. 123 minutes. Released 1962.

U.S. VERSION: Released by Toho International Co., Ltd. English subtitles. 123 minutes. No MPAA rating. Released September 18, 1963.

Long Journey Into Love / Shinobu-Ito ("Shinobu-Ito"). Director, Masanobu Deme; Screenplay, Zenzo Matsuyama, based on an original story by Yuko Kitaizumi; Director of Photography, Kazutani Hara; Music, Masaru Sato.

CAST: Komaki Kurihara, Go Kato, Kyoko Mano.

A Toho Co., Ltd./Haiyuza Film Production Co., Ltd. Production. Color. Panavision (?). 168 minutes. Released 1973.

U.S. VERSION: Released undetermined, possibly by Toho International Co., Ltd. in subtitled format. 168 minutes. No MPAA rating. Released April 24, 1974.

Long Way to Okinawa. Director, Hideo Suzuki; Screenplay, Toshio Ide.

CAST: Akira Takarada, Yuriko Hoshi, Nobuko Otawa, Keiko Awaji, Takashi Shimura.

A Toho Co., Ltd. Production. Color. Toho Scope. Released 1962 (?).

U.S. VERSION: Released by Toho International Co., Ltd. English subtitles. 90 minutes. No MPAA rating. Released April 26, 1963.

Longing for Love / Ai no kawaki ("Thirst for Love"). Producer, Kanou Otsuka; Director, Koreyoshi Kurahara; Screenplay, Shigeya Fujita and Koreyoshi Kurahara, based on *Ai no kawaki* (1950) by Yukio Mishima; Director of Photography, Yoshio Mamiya; Music, Toshiro Mayuzumi.

CAST: Ruriko Asaoka (Etsuko), Nobuo Nakamura (father-in-law), Tetsuo Ishitachi (gardener), Akira Yamanouchi (second son), Chitose Kurenai (servant girl), Yuko Kusunoki, Yoko Ozono.

A Nikkatsu Corporation Production. Black and white with color inserts. NikkatsuScope. 99 minutes. Released March 1967.

U.S. VERSION: Distributor undetermined, possibly Toho International Co., Ltd. 99 minutes. No MPAA rating. Released October 7, 1966.

Lost in the Wilderness / Uemura Naomi monogatari ("The Naomi Uemura Story"). Producers, Juichi Tanaka, Haruyuki Takahashi, Hiroshi Takayama; Director, Junya Sato; Screenplay, Yoshiki Iwama and Junya Sato, based on the autobiography by Naomi Uemura; Directors of Photography, Hiroyuki Namiki, Etsuo Akutsu; Music, William Ackerman.

CAST: Toshiyuki Nishida, Chieko Baisho, Masato Furuoya, Ryo Ikebe, Go Wakabayashi, Muga Takewaki.

A Dentsu/Mainichi Hoso Production. Color. A Toho Co., Ltd. Release. Panavision (?). 140 minutes. Released 1986.

U.S. VERSION: Released by Toho International Co., Ltd. English subtitles. 140 minutes. No MPAA rating. Released October 1986.

Lost Luck / Ashi ni sawatta koun ("The Luck Which Touched the Legs"). Director, Yasujiro Ozu; Screenplay, Kogo Noda; Director of Photography, Hideo Shigehara.

CAST: Tatsuo Saito, Mitsuko Yoshikawa, Takeshi Sakamoto, Tomio Aoki, Ichiro Tsukita, Chishu Ryu.

A Shochiku Co., Ltd. Production. Filmed at Shochiku-Kamata Studios. Silent. Academy ratio. Black and white. 60 minutes. Released October 3, 1930.

U.S. VERSION: Never released in the United States. A lost film.

Lost Sex / Honno ("Instinct"). Producer/Director/Screenplay, Kaneto Shindo; Director of Photography, Kiyomi Kuroda; Lighting, Shiroaki Fujiyama; Music, Hikaru Hayashi; Sound Recording, Tetsuo Ohashi.

CAST: Hideo Kanze (the master), Nobuko Otowa (the housemaid), Eijiro Tono (neighbor [writer]), Yoshinobu Ogawa (neighbor [son]), Kaori Shima (neighbor [son's wife]).

A Kindai Eiga Kyokai Co., Ltd. Production. A Toho Co., Ltd. Release (?). Black and white. Anamorphic wide screen (?). 103 minutes. Released August 1966.

U.S. VERSION: Released by Chevron Pictures. English subtitles (?). 97 minutes. No MPAA rating. Released July 22, 1968.

The Lost World of Sinbad / Dai tozoku ("The Great Thief"). Producers, Tomoyuki Tanaka and Kenichiro Tsunoda; Director, Senkichi Taniguchi; Screenplay, Takeshi Kimura and Shinichi Sekizawa; Director of Photography, Takao Saito; Music, Masaru Sato; Sound Toho Recording Centre; Sound Effects, Hisashi Shimonaga, Toho Sound Effects Group; *Toho Special Effects Group*: Director, Eiji Tsuburaya; Art Director, Akira Watanabe; Photography, Sadamasa Arikawa, Mototaka Tomioka; Lighting, Kuichiro Kishida; Matte Process, Hiroshi Mukoyama; Optical Photography, Taka Yuki, Yukio Manoda; Assistant Director, Teruyoshi Nakano.

CAST: Toshiro Mifune (Sukezaemon, alias "Luzon" [Sinbad]), Makoto Sato (the Black Pirate), Jun Funato (Ming, *the Prince of Thailand*), Ichiro Arishima (Sennin the Wizard), Mie Hama (Princess Yaya), Kumi Mizuno (Miwa), Akiko Wakabayashi (Yaya's maid), Mitsuko Kusabue (Sobei), Tadao Nakamaru (the Premier), Jun Tazaki (Itaka Tsuzuka of the Royal Guards), Takashi Shimura (King Raksha), Eisei Amamoto (Granny the Witch), Little Man Machan (dwarf), Hideo Sunazuka, Masaya Nihei (bandits), Tetsu Nakamura (chief archer), Jerry Fujio (the princess' giant guard), Yoshio Kosugi (captain of Thai ship), Nadao

Kirino (member of Luzon's crew), Masashi Oki, Yutaka Nakayama, Nakajiro Tomita, Tadanori Kusagawa, Junichiro Mukai, Yasuhisa Tsutsumi, Kozo Nomura, Hiroshi Hasegawa, Hidezu Kane, Haruo Suzuki, Masako Shibaki, Akira Shimada, Rokumaru Furukawa, Chiyoko Tanabe, Toru Ibuki, Shoji Ikeda.

A Toho Co., Ltd. Production. Western Electric Mirrophonic Recording (encoded with Perspecta Stereophonic Sound). Eastman Color (processed by Tokyo Laboratory, Ltd.). Toho Scope. 97 minutes. Released October 26, 1963.

U.S. VERSION: Released by American International Pictures. English-dubbed. A James H. Nicholson & Samuel Z. Arkoff Presentation. English language version, Titra Sound Studios; Prints by Pathé. Wide screen process billed as Colorscope. Onscreen credits mis-identify co-screenwriter Sekizawa as director of photography. Retitled *Samurai Pirate* after initial engagements, then switched back to *The Lost World of Sinbad.* Announced by AIP as *7th Wonder of Sinbad* (!). Double-billed with *War of the Zombies* (AIP, 1965). No MPAA Rating. 95 minutes. Released March 17, 1965.

Love and Crime / Meiji-Taisho-Showa, Ryoki onna Hanzaishi ("Meiji-Taisho-Showa Periods, Crimes of the Woman"). Director, Teruo Ishii; Screenplay, Teruo Ishii, Masahiro Kakefuda, and Shizuo Nonami; Director of Photography, Motoya Washio; Art Director, Jiro Tomita; Music, Masao Yagi.

CAST: Rika Fujie (Kinue Munakata), Yukie Kagawa (Sada Abe), Eiji Wakasugi (Kichizo Ishida), Asao Loike (Yoshio Kodaira), Teruko Yumi (Oden Takahashi), Kenjiro Ishiyama (Kosuke Saito), Takashi Fujiki (Shibuya), Shinichiro Hayashi (Naminosuke), Teruo Yoshida.

A Toei Co., Ltd. Production. Eastman Color. ToeiScope. 92 minutes. Released August 27, 1969.

U.S. VERSION: Distributor, if any, is undetermined. English subtitled version available. 92 minutes. No MPAA rating.

Love and Faith / Oginsama ("Lady Ogin"). Producers, Tsuneyasu Matsumoto, Kyoko Oshima and Muneo Shimojo; Director, Kei Kumai; Screenplay, Yoshitaka Yoda, based on an original story by Toko Kon; Director of Photography, Kozo Okazaki; Music, Akira Ifukube; Art Director, Takeo Kimura; Editor, Tatsuji Nakashizu; Costumes, Mitsukoshi Department Store; Tea Ceremony Supervisor, Urasenke [no other name given].

CAST: Takashi Shimura (Sen Rikyu), Ryoko Nakano (Ogin), Toshiro Mifune (Taiko Hideyoshi), Daijiro Harada (Mozuya), Atsuo Nakamura (Soji Yamagami), Kichiemon Nakamura (Takayama Ukon), Eiji Okada (Ankokuji), Ko Nishimura (Sojin Kamiya).

A Takurazuka Eiga Production. A Toho Co., Ltd. Release. Color. Panavision (?). 154 minutes. Released 1978.

U.S. VERSION: Released by Toho International Co., Ltd. English subtitles. Alternate titles: *Love and Faith of Ogin, Ogin Her Love and Faith*, *Oginsaga*, *Love and Faith: Lady Ogin*. 150 minutes. No MPAA rating. Released March 1979. Later reissued at 115 minutes.

Love at Twenty / Hatachi no koi ("Love at Twenty"). Producer, Pierre Roustang; Editor, Claudine Bouche; Linking Music, Georges Delerue; Linking Music Singers, Yvon Samuel and Xavier Despras; Production Manager, Philippe Dussart; Artistic Adviser, Jean de Baroncelli; Linking Still Photographer, Henri Cartier-Bresson; Linking Sequences Director of Photography, Jean Aurel. *France*: Director/Screenplay, François Truffaut; Dialogue, Yvon Samuel; Director of Photography, Raoul Coutard; Camera Operator, Claude Beausoleil; Assistant Director, Georges Pellegrin. *Italy*: Director/Screenplay, Renzo Rossellini; Director of Photography, Mario Montuori; Assistant Director, Francesco Cinieri. *Japan*: Director/Screenplay, Shintaro Ishihara; Director of Photography, Shigeo Hayashida; Music, Toru Takemitsu. *West Germany*: Director/Screenplay, Marcel Ophuls; Director of Photography, Wolf Wirth. *Poland:* Director, Andrzej Wajda; Screenplay, Jerzy Stefen Stawinski; Director of Photography, Jerzy Lipman; Music, Jerzy Matuszkiewicz; Assistant Director, Andrzej Zulawski.

CAST: Henri Serre (narrator). *France*: Jean-Pierre Leaud (Antoine Doinel), Marie-France Pisier (Colette), Francois Darbon (Colette's father), Rosy Varte (Colette's mother), Patrick Auffay (Rene), Jean-Francois Adam (Albert Tazzi). *Italy*: Elenora Rossie-Drago (Valentina), Christina Gajoni (Christina), Geronimo Meynier (Leonardo). *Japan*: Koji Furuhata (Hiroshi), Nami Tamura (Fumiko). *West Germany*: Christian Doermer (Tonio), Barbara Frey (Ursula), Vera Tschechowa, Werner Finck. *Poland*: Barbara Lass (Basia), Zbiginew Cybulski (Sbyssek), Wladyslaw Kowalski (Wladek).

A Ulysse Productions/Unitec France/ Cinesecolo/Toho Co., Ltd./Towa Films/ Kamera Film Unit/Film Polski/Beta Film Production. A French/Italian/Japanese/ West German/Polish co-production with appropriate subtitles. A Toho Co., Ltd. Release (n Japan). Black and white. Totalscope and Toho Scope. 123 minutes. Released 1962.

U.S. VERSION: Released by Embassy Pictures. English subtitles. A Joseph E. Levine Presentation. Released in France in June 1962 as *L'Amour a vingt ans*, running 118 minutes; in Italy in June 1962 as *Amore a vent'anni*; in West Germany in 1962 as *Liebe mit zwanzig*; and in Poland in 1962 as *Milosc dwudziestolatkow*. The French episode, also known as *Antoine et Colette*, was part of director Truffaut's "Antoine Doinel" series, which was preceded by *The 400 Blows* (1959), and continued with *Stolen Kisses* (1968), *Bed and Breakfast* (1970), and *Love on the Run* (1979). Also released at 110 minutes. 113 minutes. No MPAA rating. Released February 6, 1963.

Love Betrayed / Kokoro ("Heart"). Director, Kaneto Shindo; Screenplay, Kaneto Shindo, based on the story by Soseki Natsume; Director of Photography, Kiyomi Kuroda; Music, Hikaru Hayashi.

CAST: Noboru Matsuhashi, Annri [no other name given], Kazunaga Tsuji.

A Kindai Eiga Kyokai Co., Ltd./Japan Art Theatre Guild Co., Ltd. Production. A Toho Co., Ltd. Release. Color. Panavision (?). 90 minutes. Released 1973.

U.S. VERSION: Distributor, if any, is undetermined, possibly by Toho International Co., Ltd. in subtitled format. No MPAA rating.

Love Letter / Rabu Reta ("Love Letter"). Producer, Kenzo Asada; Director, Seijun Suzuki; Screenplay, Kiichi Ishii, based on the novel by Takeo Matsuura; Director of Photography, Isamu Kakita; Art Director, Kazuo Yagyu; Music, Yoshio Mamiya.

CAST: Kyosuke Machida (Ryuji "Masao" Murakami), Frank Nagai (Ryota Fukui), Hisako Tsukuba (Kozue), Keisuke Yukioka (Shukichi).

A Nikkatsu Corp. Production. Black and white. NikkatsuScope. 40 minutes. Released 1959.

U.S. VERSION: Released by Nikkatsu Corp. English subtitles. 40 minutes. No MPAA rating. Released 1993.

Love Me, Love Me / Aishite aishite ("Love Me, Love, Me"). Executive Producers, Kajiro Yamamoto and Hisao Ichikawa; Director, Katsumi Iwauchi; Screenplay, Yasuo Tanami, based on an original story by Saho Sasazawa; Music, Ikuma Dan.

CAST: Kenji Mine, Yuki Nakagawa, Masao Shimizu, Keiko Awaji, Tadao Takashima.

A Toho Co., Ltd. Production. Black and white. Toho Scope. 83 minutes. Released 1962.

U.S. VERSION: Release undetermined, possibly by Toho International Co., Ltd. in subtitled format. 83 minutes. No MPAA rating.

The Love of Sumako the Actress / Joyu Sumako no koi ("The Love of Sumako the Actress"). Director, Kenji Mizoguchi; Screenplay, Yoshikata Yoda, based on the biographical play *Kurumen Yukinu* by Hideo Nagata; Director of Photography, Shigeto Miki; Art Director, Isamu Motoki; Music, Hisato Osawa.

CAST: Kinuyo Tanaka (Sumako Matsui), So Yamamura (Hogetsu Shimamura); Eijiro Tono (Shoyo Tsubouchi), Kikue Mori (Ichiko), Chieko Higashiyama, Koreya Senda, Sugisaku Aoyama, Zeya Chida, Teruko Kishi, Eitaro Ozawa, Shin Tokudaiji, Tomo Nagai.

A Shochiku Co., Ltd. Production. Filmed at Shochiku-Kyoto Studios. Black and white. Academy ratio. 96 minutes. Released August 16, 1947.

U.S. VERSION: Distributor undetermined. English subtitles. Teinosuke Kinugasa filmed the same story as *Actress*, also 1947.

The Love Robots. Director, Koji Wakamatsu.

CAST: Hidekatsu Shibata, Hideo Sakei, Tamami Wakahara.

Production company and Japanese title undetermined. Black and white. Anamorphic wide screen. Released 1965.

U.S. VERSION: Released by Olympic International Films. English-dubbed. Wide screen process advertised as CinemaScope in the United States. 63 minutes. No MPAA rating. Released 1965.

The Love Suicides at Sonezaki / Sonezaki shinju ("Sonezaki Double Suicide") **[puppet film]**. Producer/Director, Midori Kurisaki; Screenplay, Monzaemon Chikamatsu; Director of Photography, Kazuo Miyagawa; Editor, Toshio Taniguchi; Music, "Gidayu," a traditional piece; Production Coordinator, Kurisaki Productions; Lighting, Takeharu Sano; Art Director, Akira Naito; Set Decorators, Toshiharu Kozu and Masaru Arakawa; Sound Recording, Shotaro Yoshida.

CAST: Oridayu Takemoto, Rodayu Tayotake (Gidayu chanters), Seiji Tsuruzawa (Samisen).

Production company undetermined. Color. Academy ratio. 87 minutes. Released 1981.

U.S. VERSION: Released with English subtitles. Not to be confused with *Love Suicide at Sonezaki* (Toho, 1978). 87 minutes. No MPAA rating. Released March 20, 1982.

Love, Thy Name Be Sorrow / Koiya koi nasuna koi ("Love Love Love"). Director, Tomu Uchida; Screenplay, Yoshitaka Yoda; Director of Photography, Keiji Yoshida.

CAST: Hashizo Okawa, Michiko Saga, Sumiko Hidaka.

A Toei Co., Ltd. Production. Toeicolor (processed by Toei Chemistry Co., Ltd.). ToeiScope (?). 109 minutes. Released 1962.

U.S. VERSION: Distributor undetermined. Alternate titles: *Love Not Again* and *The Mad Fox*. No MPAA rating. Released 1962 (?).

Love Under the Crucifix / Oginsama ("Lady Ogin"). Producers, Sennosuke Tsukimori and Shigeru Wakatsuki; Director, Kinuyo Tanaka; Screenplay, Masashige Narusawa, based on the story *O-gin Sama* (1927) by Toko Kon; Director of Photography, Yoshio Miyajima; Art Director, Junichi Osumi; Music, Hikaru Hayashi.

CAST: Ineko Arima (Ogin), Ganjiro Nakamura (Rikyu Senno), Mieko Takamine (Riki), Tatsuya Nakadai (Ukon Takayama), Osamu Takizawa (Hideyoshi Toyotomi), Yumeji Tsukioka (Yodo Gimi), Koji Nanbara (Mitsunari Ishida), Keiko Kishi, Manami Fuji.

A Shochiku Co., Ltd. Production. Eastman Color. Shochiku GrandScope. Released 1960.

U.S. VERSION: Released by Shochiku Films of America, Inc. English subtitles. Remade in 1978 as *Love and Faith*. 102 minutes. No MPAA rating. Released April 1965.

The Lover / Koibito ("The Lover"). Producer, Nobuo Aoyagi; Director, Kon Ichikawa; Screenplay, Natto Wada and Kon Ichikawa, based on a story by Haruo Umeda; Director of Photography, Minoru Yokoyama; Art Director, Hiroshi Fujita; Music, Tadashi Hattori.

CAST: Ryo Ikebe (Seiichi Endo), Asami Hisaji (Kyoko Odagiri), Koreya Senda (Keisuke, *Kyoko's father*), Sachiko Murase (Setsuko, *Kyoko's mother*).

A Shintoho Co., Ltd. Production. Black and white. Academy ratio. 70 minutes. Released 1951.

U.S. VERSION: Distributor, if any, is undetermined. Not to be confused with Ichikawa's *The Lover* (1953).

The Lover / Aijin ("The Lover"). Producer, Masumi Fujimoto; Director, Kon Ichikawa; Screenplay, Natto Wada and Toshiro Ide, based on a story by

Kaoru Morimoto; Director of Photography, Masao Tamai; Music, Toshiro Mayuzumi; Art Director, Shinobu Muraki; Lighting, Choshiro Ishii; Sound Recording, Hisashi Shimonaga.

CAST: Ichiro Sugai (Teppu), Fubuki Koshiji (Shuwa), Kazuhiro Osao (Masamitsu), Mariko Okada (Miyo), Ineko Arima (Mao), Rentaro Mikuni (Kasuga).

A Toho Co., Ltd. Production. Black and white. Academy ratio. Running time undetermined. Released November 10, 1953.

U.S. VERSION: Distributor, if any, is undetermined. Not to be confused with Ichikawa's *The Lover* (1951). Alternate title: *The Sweetheart*.

Lovers of Ginza / Ginza no koibitotachi ("Lovers of Ginza"). Executive Producer, Masumi Fujimoto; Producer, Hidehisa Suga; Director, Yasuki Chiba; Screenplay, Toshiro Ide; Assistant Director, Mikio Komatsu.

CAST: Reiko Dan, Akira Takarada, Mitsuko Kusabue, Tatsuya Mihashi, Akemi Kita, Yukiko Shimazaki, Hiroshi Mizuhara, Hiroshi Koizumi, Yuzo Kayama, Haruko Togo, Choko Iida, Chisako Hara.

A Toho Co., Ltd. Production. Color. Toho Scope. 101 minutes. Released January 13, 1961.

U.S. VERSION: Released by Toho International Co., Ltd. English subtitles (?). 101 minutes. No MPAA rating. Released July 21, 1961.

The Lower Depths / Donzoko ("The Lower Depths"). Executive Producer, Tomoyuki Tanaka; Producers, Sojiro Motoki and Akira Kurosawa; Director/Editor, Akira Kurosawa; Screenplay, Hideo Oguni, Shinobu Hashimoto, and Akira Kurosawa, based on the play *Na dne* (1902) by Maxim Gorky; Director of Photography, Kazuo Yamasaki; Art Director, Yoshiro Muraki; Music, Masaru Sato; Sound, Toho Dubbing Theatre; Sound Effects, Toho Sound Effects Group.

CAST: Toshiro Mifune (Sutekichi), Isuzu Yamada (Osugi, *the landlady*), Ganjiro Nakamura (Rokubei, *her husband*), Kyoko Kagawa (Okayo, *her sister*), Bokuzen Hidari (Kahei, *the priest*), Minoru Chiaki (the ex-samurai), Kamatari Fujiwara (the actor), Eijiro Tono (Tomekichi, *the tinker*), Eiko Miyoshi (Asa, *his wife*), Akemi Negishi (Osen, *the prostitute*), Koji Mitsui (Yoshisaburo, *the gambler*), Nijiko Kiyokawa (Otaki), Haruo Tanaka (Tatsu), Kichijiro Ueda (police agent), Yu Fujiki.

A Toho Co., Ltd. Production. Black and white. Academy ratio. 137 minutes. Released September 17, 1957.

U.S. VERSION: Released by Brandon Films. English subtitles. The *AFI Catalog* credits Ichiro Yamazaki as DP. Other versions include Jean Renoir's *The Lower Depths* (1936). 125 minutes. No MPAA rating. Released February 9, 1962.

The Loyal 47 Ronin I / Genroku Chushingura I ("Genroku Period Chushingura"). Executive Producer, Shintaro Shirai; Director, Kenji Mizoguchi; Screenplay, Kenichiro Hara and Yoshikata Yoda, based on the play by Seika Mayama, and the popular legend, itself based upon historical events; Director of Photography, Kohei Sugiyama; Art Directors, Hiroshi Mizutani and Kaneto Shindo; Set Decoration, Matsuji Ono; Music, Shiro Fukai.

CAST: Chojuro Kawarazaki (Kuranosuke Oishi), Yoshizaburo Arashi (Takuminokami Asano), Mantoyo Mimasu (Kozunosuke Kira), Kanemon Nakamura (Sukeimon Tomimori), Utaemon Ichikawa (Tsunatoyo Tokugawa), Isamu Kosugi (Denpachiro), Mitusko Mimura (Yosenin), Seizaburo Kawazu (Etchumori Hosokawa), Tsuruzo Nakamura (Denuemon Horiuchi), Kunitaro Kawarazaki (Jurozaemon Isogai), Mieko Takamine (Omino), and members of the Zenshinza theater troupe.

A Koa Production, in association with Shochiku Co., Ltd. Black and white. Academy ratio. 111 minutes. Released December 1, 1941.

U.S. VERSION: Released by Shochiku Films of America, Inc. (?). English subtitles. Followed by *The Loyal 47 Ronin II* (1942). Alternate titles: *The Loyal 47 Ronin* and *The 47 Ronin of the Genroku Era*. One of many versions of the same story, which include Daiei's *Chushingura* (1958) and Hiroshi Inagaki's *Chushingura* (1962). 111 minutes. No MPAA rating. Released March 1979.

The attack on Kira (Mantoyo Mimasu) by Lord Asano (Yoshizaburo Arashi) sets the classic Chushingura tale in motion in this, the Mizoguchi version of *The Loyal 47 Ronin* (1941). (Photo courtesy Darrell Davis.)

The Loyal 47 Ronin II / Genroku Chushingura II ("Genroku Period Chushingura II"). Executive Producer, Shintaro Shirai; Director, Kenji Mizoguchi; Screenplay, Kenichiro Hara and Yoshikata Yoda, based on the play by Seika Mayama, and the popular legend, itself based upon historical events; Director of Photography, Kohei Sugiyama; Art Directors, Hiroshi Mizutani and Kaneto Shindo; Set Decorator, Matsuji Ono; Music, Shiro Fukai.

CAST: Chojuro Kawarazaki (Kuranosuke Oishi), Mantoyo Mimasu (Kozunosuke Kira), Kanemon Nakamura (Sukeimon Tominori), Utaemon Ichikawa (Tsunatoyo Tokugawa), Isamu Kosugi (Denpachiro), Mitsuko Miura (Yosenin), Seizaburo Kawazu (Etchumori Hosokawa), Tsuruzo Nakamura (Denuemon Horiuchi), Kunitaro Kawarazaki (Jurozaemon Isogai), Mieko Takamine (Omino), Daisuke Kato (ronin), and members of the Zenshinza theater troupe.

A Shochiku Co., Ltd. Production. Filmed at Shochiku-Kyoto Studios. Black and white. Academy ratio. 108 minutes. Released February 11, 1942.

U.S. VERSION: Released by Shochiku Films of America, Inc. (?). English subtitles. Preceded by *The Loyal 47 Ronin I* (1941). 108 minutes. No MPAA rating. Released March 1979.

Lusty Transparent Man / Tomei ningen-okase ("Lusty Transparent Man—Okase"). Producer, Akihiko Yameki; Director, Isao Hayashi; Screenplay, Chieko Katsura.

CAST: Izumi Shima, Maria Mari.

A Nikkatsu Corp. Production. Nikkatsucolor. Panavision (?). Running time undetermined. Released 1979.

U.S. VERSION: Distributor undetermined. A sequel to *Lusty Transparent Human* (1979). Released 1979.

MacArthur's Children / Setouchi shonen yakyu dan ("Setouchi Boys' Basball Team"). Producers, You-No-Kai and Masato Hara; Director, Masahiro Shinoda; Screenplay, Tsutome

Tamara, based on the novel by Yu Aku; Director of Photography, Kazuo Miyagawa; Music, Shinichiro Ikebe; Editor, Sachiko Yamaji.

CAST: Takaya Yamauchi (Ryuta), Yoshiyuki Omori (Saburo), Shiori Sakura (Mume), Masako Natsume (Komako), Juzo Itami (the captain), Shima Iwashita (Tome), Hiromi Go (Masao Nahai), Shuji Otaki (Tadao Ashigara), Haruko Kato (Haru Ashigara), Ken Watanabe (Tetsuo Nakai).

A Shochiku Co., Ltd. Production. Fuji Color and black and white. Spherical wide screen (1.75:1). 117 minutes. Released June 23, 1984.

U.S. VERSION: Released by Orion Classics. English subtitles. Followed by *MacArthur's Children—Part II* (1987). English subtitles. 115 minutes. MPAA rating: "PG." Released May 17, 1985.

MacArthur's Children—Part II / Setouchi shonen yakyu dan seishunhen Saigo no Rakuen ("Setouchi Boys' Baseball Team—Youth Chapter, The Last Paradise"). Producers, Yu Aku and Masato Hara; Director, Haruhiko Mimura; Screenplay, Mizuki Kawamoto and Haruhiko Mimura, based on the novel by Yu Aku; Director of Photography, Yoshimasa Hagata; Music, Morihisa Shibuya.

CAST: Toshihiko Tahara, Isako Waisio, Hikaru Kurosaki.

A Herald Ace, Inc. Production. Color. Spherical wide screen. 112 minutes. Released 1987.

U.S. VERSION: Distributor, if any, is undetermined. No MPAA rating.

The Mad Atlantic / Doto ichiman kairi ("Angry Waves 10,000 Sea-Miles"). Executive Producers, Tomoyuki Tanaka and Koichi Sekizawa; Director, Jun Fukuda; Screenplay, Ei Ogawa and Shinichi Sekizawa; Director of Photography, Takao Saito; Music, Masaru Sato; Assistant Director, Julio Sempere.

CAST: Toshiro Mifune, Makoto Sato, Mie Hama, Ryo Tamura, Tatsuya Mihashi, Tadao Nakamaru, Ikio Sawamura, Sachio Sukai, Akihiko Hirata.

A Mifune Productions Production. A Toho Co., Ltd. Release. Black and white. Toho Scope. 103 minutes. Released 1966.

U.S. VERSION: Released by Toho International Co., Ltd. English subtitles. 103 minutes. No MPAA rating. Released November 22, 1967.

Madadayo ("Not Yet"). Executive Producers, Yo Yamamoto and Yuzo Irie; General Producers, Yasuyoshi Tokuma and Gohei Kogure; Associate Producer, Seikichi Iizumi; Producer, Hisao Kurosawa; Director/Editor, Akira Kurosawa; Screenplay, Akira Kurosawa and Ishiro Honda, based on the literary works of Hyakken Uchida (published by Fukutake Publishing Co., Ltd.); Directorial Adviser, Ishiro Honda; Production Coordinator, Izuhiko Suehiro; Production Manager, Teruyo Nogami; Directors of Photography, Takao Saito and Masaharu Ueda; Art Director, Yoshiro Muraki; Lighting, Takeji Sano; Music, Shinichiro Ikebe; Sound Recording, Hideo Nishizaki; Costume Design, Kazuko Kurosawa; Assistant Director, Takashi Koizumi.

CAST: Tatsuo Matsumura (the Professor), Kyoko Kagawa (his wife). *His Students*: Hisashi Igawa (Takayama), George Tokoro (Amaki), Masayuki Yui (Kiriyama), Akira Terao (Sawamura), Asei Kobayashi (Kameyama), Takeshi Kusaka (Kobayashi).

A Daiei Co., Ltd./Dentsu, Inc./Kurosawa Production, Inc. Production, in association with Tokuma Shoten Publishing Co., Ltd. A Toho Co., Ltd. Release. Color. Spherical wide screen (1.85:1). Dolby stereo. 134 minutes. Released April 17, 1993.

U.S. VERSION: Unreleased in the United States as this book went to press. Honda's participation as co-screenwriter is unconfirmed. Title also given as *Madadayo: Not Yet*.

Madame Aki / Yushu heiya ("The Melancholy Plain"). Executive Producers, Ichiro Sato and Fumio Kinbara; Director, Shiro Toyoda; Screenplay, Toshio Yasumi; Story, Yasushi Inouye; Director of Photography, Kozo Okazaki; Music, Ikuma Dan.

CAST: Hisaya Morishige (Katayuki), Fujiko Yamamoto (Aki), Michiyo Aratama (Misako), Tatsuya Nakadai (Tatsumi), Chieko Naniwa, Hiroyuki Nagato, Mayumi Ozora.

A Tokyo Eiga Co., Ltd. Production. A

Toho Co., Ltd. Release. Eastman Color. Toho Scope. 114 minutes. Released 1963.

U.S. VERSION: Released by Toho International Co., Ltd. English subtitles. 114 minutes. No MPAA rating. Released November 21, 1963.

Madame O. Producer, Minoru Chiba; Director, Seichi Fukada.

CAST: Michiko Sakyo.

Production company undetermined. Black and white with Eastman Color insert. Anamorphic wide screen. 84 minutes.

U.S. VERSION: Released by Audubon Films. English subtitles (?). 84 minutes. No MPAA rating. Released 1970.

Madame Whitesnake / Byaku fugin no yoren ("The Bewitching Love of Madame White"). Executive Producers, Tomoyuki Tanaka and Run Run Shaw; Director, Shiro Toyoda; Screenplay, Toshio Yasumi, based on the Chinese fairy tale "Pai-she Chuan"; Art Director, R. Mitsubayashi; Director of Photography, Mitsuo Miura; Music, Ikuma Dan; Sound, Toho Recording Center; Sound Effects, Toho Sound Effects Group. *Toho Special Effects Group:* Director, Eiji Tsuburaya.

CAST: Shirley Yamaguchi (Pai Su-Chen), Ryo Ikebe (Hsui Hsien), Kaoru Yachigusa (Buddhist monk).

A Toho Co., Ltd./Shaw Brothers (H.K.) Ltd. Production. A Japanese/Hong Kong co-production. Filmed at Toho Studios. Western Electric Mirrophonic recording. Eastman Color (processed by Tokyo Laboratory Ltd.). Academy ratio. 103 minutes. Released 1956.

U.S. VERSION: Released by Toho International Co., Ltd. English subtitles. Released in Hong Kong as *Pai-she Chuan* in 1956. Released internationally by Toho in 1960 as *The Bewitched Love of Madame Pai.* Remade as *Pai-she Chuan* (Shaw Brothers; U.S. release, 1963), and is not to be confused with this production. Considering that actress Yachigusa is female, above billing is highly questionable. 103 minutes. No MPAA rating. Released 1965.

Magic Boy / Shonen Sarutobi Sasuke ("The Boy Sasuke Sarutobi") **[animated]**. Executive Producer, Hiroshi Okawa; Associate Producer, Hideyuki Takahashi; Director, Akira Daikubara; Screenplay, Dohei Muramatsu; Original Story, Kazuo Dan; Animation Director, Sanae Yamamoto; Character Animation, Akira Daikubara, Hideo Furusawa, Yasuji Mori, Masao Kumagawa, and Yasuo Otsuka; Animation, Chikao Tera, Kazuko Nakamura, Shuji Konno, Masatake Kita, Daikichiro Kusube, Taku Sugiyama, and Reiko Okuyama; Art Supervisor, Reiji Koyama; Photography, Seigo Otsuka and Mitsuaki Ishikawa; Art Director, Seigo Shindo; Editor, Shintaro Miyamoto; Music Director, Toru Funamura; Sound Engineer, Hisashi Kase; Assistant to the Producer, Teiji Yabushita.

VOICE CHARACTERIZATIONS: (undetermined).

A Toei Animation Studio Co., Ltd. Production. A Toei Co., Ltd. Release. Magicolor. ToeiScope. 83 minutes. Released 1960.

U.S. VERSION: Released by Metro-Goldwyn-Mayer, Inc. English-dubbed. 73 minutes. No MPAA rating. Released September 13, 1961.

The Magic Serpent / Kai tatsu daikessen ("Decisive Battle of the Giant Magic Dragons"). Producer, Shigeru Okawa; Director, Tetsuya Yamauchi; Screenplay, Masaru Igami, based on an original story by Mokuami Kawatake; Director of Photography, Mononari [Motonari] Washio; Art Director, Seiji Yada; Music, Toshiaki Tsushima.

CAST: Hiroki Matsukata (Ikazuchimaru), Tomoko Ogawa (Tsunate), Ryutaro Otomo (Orochimaru), Bin Amatsu (Yuki), Nobuo Kaneko.

A Toei Co., Ltd. Production. Eastman Color (processed by Toei Chemistry Co., Ltd.). ToeiScope. 86 minutes. Released 1966.

U.S. VERSION: Never released theatrically in the United States. Released directly to television by American International Television, Inc. in 1968. English-dubbed. A James H. Nicholson and Samuel Z. Arkoff Presentation. English-dubbed version produced by Titra Productions, Inc.; Director, Bret Morrison; Editors, Emil Haviv, Eli Haviv. Prints by Perfect. International title: *Grand Duel in Magic.*

Alternate title: *Froggo and Draggo*. The sloppily done American titles list producer Okawa twice. 86 minutes. No MPAA rating.

The Magic Sword of Watari

(no credits available).

CAST: Yoshinobu Kaneko (Watari), Pin-Pin Wong.

A Toei Co., Ltd. Production. A Japanese/Taiwanese co-production. Toeicolor. ToeiScope. 100 minutes. Released 1970.

U.S. VERSION: Released by Transocean, format undetermined. International title: *Watari and the Seven Monsters*. A sequel to *Watari, Ninja Boy* (Toei, 1966), and based on the popular comic strip "Watari."

The Magnificent Seven / Shichinin no samurai

("Seven Samurai"). Producer, Shojiro Motoki; Director/Editor, Akira Kurosawa; Screenplay, Shinobu Hashimoto, Hideo Oguni, and Akira Kurosawa; Director of Photography, Asakazu Nakai; Lighting, Shigeru Mori; Art Director, Takashi "So" Matsuyama; Historical Research, Kohei Ezaki (folklore), Yoshio Sugino (fencing), Ienori Kaneko (archery), Shigeru Endo (archery); Art Consultants, Seison Maeda and Kohei [Konei] Ezaki; Costumes, Kohei [Konei] Ezaki; Hair and Makeup, Junjiro Yamada; Fencing Choreography, Yoshio Sugino; Archery Director, Ienori Kaneko and Shigeru Endo; Sound Recording, Fumio Yanoguchi; Music, Fumio Hayasaka; Music Assistant, Masaru Sato; Assistant Director, Hiromichi Horikawa; Editing Manager, Hiroshi Nezu; Special Effects, Toho Special Effects Group; Sound Effects, Toho Sound Effects Group; Sound, Toho Dubbing Theatre.

CAST: *The Seven Samurai*: Takashi Shimura (Kambei Shimada, *leader of the Seven Samurai*), Toshiro Mifune (Kikuchiyo, *the would-be samurai*), Yoshio Inaba (Gorobei, *the wise warrior*), Seiji Miyaguchi (Kyuzo, *the master swordsman*), Minoru Chiaki (Heihachi, *the cheerful samurai*), Daisuke Kato (Shichiroji, *Kambei's old friend*), Ko Kimura (Katsushiro Okamoto, *Kambei's young desciple*). *The Peasants*: Kamatari Fujiwara (Manzo), Kokuten Kodo (Gisaku), Bokuzen Hidari (Yohei), Yoshio Kosugi (Mosuke), Yoshio Tsuchiya (Rikichi), Keiji Sakakida (Gisaku), Haruko Toyama (Gisaku's daughter-in-law), Jiro Kumagai, Tsuneo Katagiri, Yasuhisa Tsutsumi (peasants), Keiko Tsushima (Shino, *Manzo's daughter*), Yukiko Shimazaki (Rikichi's wife), Toranosuke Ogawa (grandfather), Yu Akitsu (husband), Noriko Sengoku (wife), Fumiko Homma (peasant woman), Ichiro Chiba (town priest). *Also*: Gen Shimizu (masterless samurai), Jun Tatara (coolie), Atsushi Watanabe (bun vendor), Sojin Kamiyama (blind minstral), Eijiro Tono (robber), Isao Yamagata (samurai), Jun Tazaki (tall samurai), Kichijiro Ueda (captured bandit scout), Shimpei Takagi (bandit chieftain), Akira Tani, Haruo Nakajima, Takashi Narita, Senkichi Omura, Shuno Takahara, Masanobu Okubo, Kichijiro Ueda (bandits), Tatsuya Nakadai, Hisaya Ito (wandering samurai).

A Toho Co., Ltd. Production. Black and white (processed by Kinuta Laboratories, Ltd.). Academy ratio. Western Electric Mirrophonic Recording. Running time of roadshow version: 208 minutes, including a 5-minute intermission. Running time of general release version: 160 minutes. Released April 26, 1954.

U.S. VERSION: Released by Columbia Pictures Corporation. English subtitles. 141 minutes. No MPAA rating. Released November 1956. According to one source, an English-dubbed version was also available. Reissued by Toho International during the 1960s as *Seven Samurai* and running 160 minutes. Complete 200-minute version broadcast on PBS-TV in 1972. Theatrically reissued by Landmark Films (later acquired by Avco Embassy Pictures Corp.) in December 1982 running 203 minutes. Reissued post-1982 by Avco Embassey Pictures Corporation, Janus Films, Inc. and Films Incorporated, all running 208 minutes. Running time of home video version: 208 minutes. Reissued in Japan in 1975 (with stereophonic sound) and 1991. The acknowledged remake was *The Magnificent Seven* (United Artists, 1960) with Yul Brynner in the Shimura role. Other versions include *Battle Beyond the Stars* (New World, 1980), and *The Seven Magnificent Gladiators* (Cannon Releasing Corp., 1984). Sojin Kamiyama appeared in silent films made in the United States under the name "Sojin."

The Magoichi Saga / Shirikurae Mogoichi ("'Kiss My Ass, Magoichi"). Director, Kenji Misumi; Screenplay, Ryuzo Kikushima; Story, Ryotaro Shiba; Director of Photography, Kazuo Miyagawa; Art Director, Yoshinobu Nishioka; Music, Masaru Sato.

CAST: Kinnosuke Nakamura (Magoichi Saika), Komaki Kurihara (Komichi), Kojiro Hongo (Priest Shinso), Katsuo Nakamura (Tokichiro Kinoshita), Shintaro Katsu (Lord Nobunaga Oda), Yoko Namikawa (Princess Kano), Eiko Azusa.

A Daiei Motion Picture Co., Ltd. Production. Eastman Color. DaieiScope. 105 minutes. Released September 1969.

U.S. VERSION: Released by Daiei International Films, Inc. English subtitles. 95 minutes. No MPAA rating. Released April 1970.

The Maid Story / Daidokoro Taiheiki ("Peaceful Times in the Kitchen"). Producers, Ichiro Sato and Fumio Kanahara; Director, Shiro Toyoda; Screenplay, Toshio Yasumi, based on the story by Junichi Tanizaki; Assistant Director, Akio Hirayama.

CAST: Hisaya Morishige, Chikage Awashima, Nobuko Otowa, Keiko Awaji.

A Tokyo Eiga Co., Ltd. Production. A Toho Co., Ltd. Release. Color. Toho Scope. 110 minutes. Released 1963.

U.S. VERSION: Released by Toho International Co., Ltd. English subtitles. No MPAA rating. 110 minutes. Released May 29, 1964.

Majin / Dai Majin ("Great Majin"). Producer, Masaichi Nagata; Director, Kimiyoshi Yasuda; Screenplay, Tetsuro Yoshida; Director of Photography, Fujio Morita; Art Director, Hisashi Okuda; Editor, Hiroshi Yamada; Music, Akira Ifukube; Sound Recordist Supervisor, Masao Osumi; Sound, Daiei Recording Studio; Special Effects Director, Yoshiyuki Kuroda; Majin Design, Ryosaku Takayama; Special Effects, Daiei Special Effects Department; Special Effects Photography, Yoshiyuki Kuoda.

CAST: Miwa Takada (Kozasa Hanabusa), Yoshihiko Aoyama (Tadafumi Hanabusa), Jun Fujimaki (Kogenta), Ryutaro Gomi (Lord Samanosuke Odate), Tatsuo Endo (Gunjuro), Riki Hoshimoto (Majin).

A Daiei Motion Picture Co., Ltd. Production. Eastman Color (processed by Daiei Laboratory). DaieiScope. 84 minutes. Released April 17, 1966.

U.S. VERSION: Simultaneously released in English-subtitled version by Daiei International Films, Inc. and in English-dubbed version by Bernard Lewis. Prints by Pathé. Reissued as *Majin the Hideous Idol*. Alternate titles: *The Devil Got Angry* and *The Vengence of the Monster*. Released to television by American International Television (AIP-TV) as *Majin, The Monster of Terror*. A James H. Nicholson and Samuel Z. Arkoff Presentation. The 1st "Majin" feature. Followed by *The Return of the Giant Majin* (1966). 86 minutes. No MPAA Rating. Released August 9, 1968.

Majin Strikes Again / Dai Majin gyakushu ("The Great Majin's Counterattack"). Producer, Masaichi Nagata; Director, Issei Mori; Screenplay, Tetsuo Yoshida; Directors of Photography, Fujio Morita, Hiroshi Imai; Music, Akira Ifukube; Art Director, Hisashi Okuda; Editor, Hiroshi Yamada; Sound Recording Supervisor, Masao Osumi; Sound, Daiei Recording Studio; Special Effects Director, Yoshiyuki Kuroda; Majin Design, Ryosaku Takayama; Special Effects, Daiei Special Effects Department.

CAST: Riki Hoshimoto (Majin), Hideki Ninomiya, Masahide Kizuka, Shinji Hori, Shiei Iizuka, Muneyuki Nagatomo, Junichiro Yamashita.

A Daiei Motion Picture Co., Ltd. Production. Eastman Color (processed by Daiei Laboratory). Daieiscope. 80 minutes. Released December 10, 1966.

U.S. VERSION: Never released theatrically in the United States.The third and final (to date) Majin film. International title: *The Return of Majin*, but not to be confused with the film that had preceded it, released in English as *The Return of the Giant Majin* (1966).

Majin Strikes Again (1966).

Make-up / Kesho ("Make-up"). Producer, Masatake Wakita; Director, Kazuo Ikehiro; Screenplay, Yozo Tanaka and Keiji Nagao, based on an original story by Junichi Watanabe; Director of Photography, Noritaka Sakamoto; Music, Shigeru Ikeno.

CAST: Keiko Matsuzaka, Machiko Kyo, Kimiko Ikegami, Yuko Kazu, Akira Emoto, Kiichi Nakai, Juzo Itami, Muga Takewaki, Akira Nakao, Norihei Miki.

A Shochiku Co., Ltd. Production. Color. Panavision (?). 137 minutes. Released May 2, 1984.

U.S. VERSION: Released by Shochiku Films of America, Inc. English subtitles. 137 minutes. No MPAA rating. Released February 1985.

The Makioka Sisters / Sasameyuki ("Snowflake"). Executive Producers, Tomoyuki Tanaka and Kon Ichikawa; Planning, Kazuo Baba; Director, Kon Ichikawa; Screenplay, Kon Ichikawa and Shinya Hidaka, based on the novel by Junichiro Tanizaki; Dialogue Supervisor, Matsuko Tanizaki; Director of Photography, Kiyoshi Hasegawa; Art Director, Shinobu Muraki; Sound Recording, Tetsuya Ohashi; Lighting, Kojiro Sahashi; Music, Shinnosuke Okawa and Toshiyuki Watanabe; Assistant Director, Kensho Yamashita.

CAST: Yoshiko Sakuma (Sachiko), Sayuri Yoshinaga (Yukiko), Yuko Kotegawa (Taeko), Juzo Itami (Tatsuo), Toshiyuki Hosokawa (Hashidera), Koji Ishizaka (Teinosuke), Keiko Kishi (Tsuruko), Ittoku Kishibe (Itakura, *the photographer*), Kopaicho Katsura (Okubata, *the rich boy*), Motoshi Egi (Higashidani), Shoji Kobayashi (Mr. Jimba, *the matchmaker*), Kazunaga Tsuji (Miyoshi, *the bartender*), Fujio Tsuneda (Igarushi, *Nomura's uncle*), Jun Hamamura (Otokichi, *the caretaker*), Kazuyo Kozaka (Nomura, *the fish expert*), Michiyo Yokoyama (Itani, *the hairdresser*), Kuniko Miyake (Aunt Tominaga), Akemi Negishi (Mrs. Shimozuma, *matchmaker*).

A Toho-Eizo Co., Ltd. Production. A Toho Co., Ltd. Release. Color. Spherical wide screen. 140 minutes. Released 1983.

U.S. VERSION: Released by Toho International Co., Ltd. English subtitles. Subtitles, Audie Bock, Cinetype, Inc. (Hollywood). Matted laserdisc version available. 140 minutes. No MPAA rating. Released December 30, 1983. Reissued February 15, 1985 by R5/58.

Man Against Man / Otoko tai otoko ("Man Against Man"). Director, Senkichi Taniguchi; Screenplay, Ichiro Ikeda and Ei Ogawa; Director of Photography, Rokuro Nishigaki; Music, Masaru Sato.

CAST: Toshiro Mifune, Ryo Ikebe, Takashi Shimura, Yumi Shirakawa, Akemi Kita, Yuriko Hoshi, Yuzo Kayama, Jun Tazaki, Akihiko Hirata, Yutaka Sada.

A Toho Co., Ltd. Production. Eastman Color. Toho Scope. 116 minutes. Released 1960.

U.S. VERSION: Released by Toho International Co., Ltd. English subtitles. Apparently reissued in Japan at 90 minutes. No MPAA rating. 116 minutes. Released March 1961.

Man and War / Senso to ningen ("Man and War"). Director, Setsuo Yamamoto; Screenplay, Nobuo Yamada, based on an original story Jumpei Gomikawa; Director of Photography, Shinsuke Himeda; Art Director, Yoshinaga Yoko; Music, Masaru Sato.

CAST: Osamu Takizawa (Yusuke Godai), Shinsuke Ashida (Kyosuke), Etsushi Takahashi (Eisuke), Ruriko Asaoka (Yukiko), Kankuro Nakamura (Shunsuke), Yoshio Aoki (Major Sagawa), Hideki Takahashi (Lt. Tsuge), Hideaki Nitani (Yatsugi), Takeo Ito (Shimegi), Rentaro Mikuni, Koji Takahashi, Yujiro Ishihara.

A Nikkatsu Corp. Production. Fujicolor. NikkatsuScope. 198 minutes. Released August 14, 1970.

U.S. VERSION: Released by Shochiku Films of America, Inc. English subtitles. Title also given as *Men and War*. Followed by *Men and War—Part Two* (1971). 198 minutes. No MPAA rating. Released June 28, 1972.

The Man from the East / Higashi kara kita otoko ("The Man from the East"). Executive Producer, Sadao Sugihara; Director, Umeji Inoue; Screenplay, Katsuya Suzaki and Yoshio

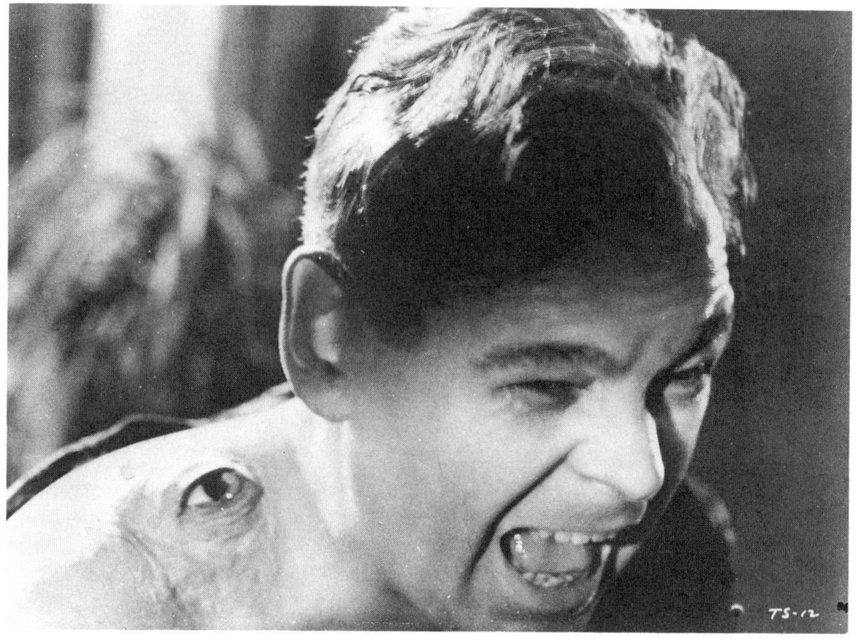

Peter Dyneley in a Dali-esque moment from *The Manster* (1961).

Hasuike; Director of Photography, Kozo Okazaki; Music, Hajime Kaburagi.

CAST: Yuzo Kayama, Yuriko Hoshi, Shiro Osaka, Makoto Sato, Jun Funato, Kazuo Yashiro, Kokinji Katsura, Shin Morikawa, Kenji Sahara, Toru Abe.

A Toho Co., Ltd. Production. Eastman Color. Toho Scope. 103 minutes. Released 1961.

U.S. VERSION: Released by Toho International Co., Ltd. English subtitles. 103 minutes. No MPAA rating. Released August 1961.

The Man in the Moonlight Mask / Gekko kamen ("Moonlight Mask"). Director, Tsuneo Kobayashi; Screenplay, Yarunori Kawauchi; Director of Photography, Ichiro Hoshijima.

CAST: Fumitake Omura, Junya Usami, Hiroko Mine, Mitsue Komiya, Yaeko Wakamizu, Yasushi Nagata.

A Toei Co., Ltd. Production. Black and white (processed by Toei Chemistry Co., Ltd.). ToeiScope. 102 minutes. Released April 1, 1959.

U.S. VERSION: U.S. distributor undetermined. Re-edited from *Gekko kamen: Dai ichibu* (51 minutes) and *Gekko kamen: Dai nibu* (52 minutes). First feature in the six-film Toei series. Followed by *The Claws of Satan* (1959). International title: *The Moonbeam Man*. Character was revived for the feature *Moonlight Mask* (1981). No MPAA rating.

The Man in the Storm / Arashi no naka otoko ("The Man in the Storm"). Executive Producer, Tomoyuki Tanaka; Director, Senkichi Taniguchi; Screenplay, Senkichi Taniguchi, Takero Matsuura, and Takeo Murata; Art Director, Yasuhide Kato; Music, Urato Watanabe.

CAST: Toshiro Mifune (Saburo Watari), Kyoko Kagawa (Akiko), Akio Kobori (Tsujido), Jun Tazaki (karate expert), Akemi Negishi (Okon).

A Toho Co., Ltd. Production. Black and white. Academy ratio (?). 95 minutes. Released 1957.

U.S. VERSION: Released by Toho International Co., Ltd. English subtitles. 95 minutes. No MPAA rating. Released August 1969.

A Man Vanishes / Ningen johatsu ("The Vaporated Man") [**documentary**]. Producer/Director/Screenplay, Shohei Imamura; Director of Photography, Kenji Ishiguro; Music, Toshiro Mayuzumi.

WITH: Yoshie Hayakawa, Shigeru Tsuyugushi.

An Imamura Production/Nippon Art Theatre Guild/Nichiei Shinsha Production. A Toho Co., Ltd. Release. Black and white. Academy ratio. 130 minutes. Released 1967.

U.S. VERSION: Released by Toho International Co., Ltd. English subtitles. 130 minutes. No MPAA rating. Released 1974.

The Man Who Stole the Sun / Taiyo o nusunda otoko ("The Man Who Stole the Sun"). Producer, Mataichiro Yamamoto; Director, Kazuhiko Hasegawa; Screenplay, Kazuhiko Hasegawa and Leonard Schrader, based on an original story by Leonard Schrader; Director of Photography, Tatsuo Suzuki; Art Director, Yoshinaga Yoko; Music, Takayuki Inoue.

CAST: Kenji Sawada (Makoto Kido), Bunta Sugawara (Yamashita), Kimiko Ikegemi, Yunosuke Ito, Toshiyuki Nishida, Yutaka Mizutani.

A Kitty Films Production. Color. 147 minutes. Released 1980.

U.S. VERSION: Released by Kitty Enterprises. English subtitles. 147 minutes. No MPAA rating. Released October 10, 1980.

The Man Without a Map / Moetsukita chizu ("Charred Map"). Director, Hiroshi Teshigahara; Screenplay, Kobo Abe, based on his story; Director of Photography, Akira Uehara; Art Director, Shigeo Mano; Music, Toru Takemitsu.

CAST: Shintaro Katsu (detective), Etsuko Ichihara (wife), Osamu Okawa (wife's brother), Kiyoshi Atsumi (Tashiro), Tamao Nakamura (detective's wife), Kinzo Shin (coffee shop owner).

A Katsu Production. A Daiei Motion Picture Co., Ltd. Release. Eastman Color. DaieiScope. 118 minutes. Released June 1, 1968.

U.S. VERSION: Release undetermined, possibly by Daiei International Films. English subtitled version available. 118 minutes. No MPAA rating.

The Man Without a Nationality / Mukokuseki ("Non-nationality"). Producers, Mitsuo Makino and Jiro Takagi; Director, Kon Ichikawa; Screenplay, Toshio Yasumi, based on a story by Jun Takami; Director of Photography, Minoru Yokoyama; Art Director, Seigo Shindo; Music, Akira Ifukube.

CAST: Ken Uehara (Tobari), Ichiro Sugai (Sakurai), Chikako Miyagi (Yoko), Michiko Tsuyama (Chiyoko), Harue Toshine (Harue), Jun Mihara (Shimosaka).

A Toyoko Eiga Film Co., Ltd. Production. Black and white. Academy ratio. Running time undetermined. Released April 14, 1951.

U.S. VERSION: Distributor, if any, is undetermined.

The Manster. Executive Producer, William Shelton; Producer, George P. Breakston; Associate Producers, Robert Perkins, Ryukichi Aimono; Directors, George P. Breakston, Kenneth G. Crane; Screenplay, Walter J. Sheldon, based on an original story by George P. Breakston; Production Supervisor, C.D. Sykes; Production Manager, Yuji Honda; Unit Manager, Richard Herbine; Assistant Director, Dan Takahashi; Continuity, Lynn Cariddi; Art Director, Noboru Miyakuni; Wardrobe, Kazuko Suzuki; Makeup, Fumiko Yamamoto; Director of Photography, David Mason; Special Effects, Shinpei Takagi; Recording Supervisor, Chisato Ota; Sound, Aoi Studio; Supervising Editor, Kenneth G. Crane; Music, Hiroki Ogawa.

CAST: Peter Dyneley (Larry Stanford), Jane Hylton (Linda Stanford), Tetsu Nakamura (Dr. Robert Suzuki), Terri Zimmern (Tara), Norman Van Hawley (Ian Matthews), Jerry Ito (Police Superintendent Aida), Toyoko Takechi (Emiko Suzuki), Alan Tarlton (Dr. H.B. Jennsen), Kenzo Kuroki, Shinpei Takagi, George Wyman.

A Shaw-Breakston Enterprises Production. A United Artists of Japan, Inc. Picture. A William Shelton Presentation. A Lopert Pictures Corp. Release. An American production filmed in Japan. RCA Photophone recording. Black and white. Prints by De Luxe. Spherical wide screen (1.66:1). 72 minutes. Released 1961.

U.S. VERSION: Released by Lopert Pictures Corp. (United Artists Corp.). Advertised as *The Manster—Half Man, Half Monster*. Working titles: *Nightmare* and *The Two-Headed Monster*. UK title: *The Split*. Double-billed with *The Horror Chamber of Dr. Faustus* (Lopert, 1962). 72 minutes. No MPAA rating. Released March 28, 1962.

Marco. Producers, Arthur Rankin, Jr. and Jules Bass; Director, Seymour Robbie; Screenplay/Lyrics, Romeo Muller; Music, Maury Laws; Songs: "By Damn," "Walls," "A Family Man," "Peaceberry"; Director of Photography, Richard R. Nishigaki; Art Director, Sinobu Muraki; Costumes, Emi Wada; Choreography, Ron Field.

CAST: Desi Arnaz, Jr. (Marco Polo), Zero Mostel (Kublai Khan), Jack Weston (Maffio Polo), Cie Cie Win (Aigiarm); Aimee Eccles (Kuklatoi), Fred Sadoff (Niccolo Polo), Mafumi Sakamoto (Letanpoing), Tetsu Nakamura (sea captain), Van Christie (Chontosai), Osamu Okawa (Ling Su), Masumi Okada (Ti Wai), Romeo Muller (Pitai Brahmas), Yuka Kamebuchi (Madama Tung), Ikio Sawamura (Lomar), Sachio Sakai.

An Arthur Raink, Jr./Jules Bass Production. A Cinerama Releasing Corporation (CRC) Release. A U.S./Japanese co-production in English. Filmed at Toho Studios (Tokyo). Eastman Color (prints by Technicolor). Spherical wide screen (with Animagic sequence). 109 minutes. MPAA rating: "G." Released December 1973.

Mariko—Mother / Nemunoki no uta ga Kikoeru ("Listen to the Song of Nemunoki") [**documentary**]. Producer/Director/Screenplay/Art Director/Music, Mariko Miyagi; Director of Photography, Kozo Okazaki.

A Nemunoki, Ltd. Production. Color. Academy ratio (?). 95 minutes. Released 1977.

U.S. VERSION: Disitrbutor, if any, is undetermined.

Marriage Counselor Tora-san / Otoka wa tsuraiyo—Yogiri ni Musebu, Torajiro ("It's Tough to Be a Man—Torajiro Cries in the Night"). Producer, Kiyoshi Shimazu; Director, Yoji Yamada; Screenplay, Yoji Yamada and Yoshitaka Asama, based on characters created by Yoji Yamada; Director of Photography, Tetsuo Takaba; Music, Naozumi Yamamoto.

CAST: Kiyoshi Atsumi (Torajiro "Tora-san" Kuruma), Chieko Baisho (Sakura Suwa, *his sister*).

A Shochiku Co., Ltd. Production. Color. Shochiku GrandScope. 102 minutes. Released 1984.

U.S. VERSION: Released by Shochiku Films of America, Inc. English subtitles. The 33rd "Tora-san" feature. Followed by *Tora-san's Forbidden Love* (1984). 102 minutes. No MPAA rating. Released December 21, 1984.

The Mask of Destiny / Shuzenji monogatari ("Shuzen Temple Story"). Producer, Kiyoshi Takamura; Director, Noboru Nakamura; Screenplay, Kido Okamato, based on his play; Art Director, Kisaku Ito; Director of Photography, Toshio Ubukata; Editor, Toshi Egata; Music, Toshiro Mayuzumi.

CAST: Teiji Takahashi, Chikage Awashima, Minosuke Bando, Keiko Kishi.

A Shochiku Co., Ltd. Production. Western Electric Mirrophonic recording. Eastman Color. Academy ratio. 105 minutes. Released 1955.

U.S. VERSION: Released by Stratford Pictures Corp., a subsidiary of Allied Artists Corp. Prints by De Luxe. International title: *The Mask and Destiny*. 105 minutes. No MPAA rating. Released 1957.

The Masseur's Curse / Kaidan kasane ga fuchi ("Ghost Story—Depth of Kasane"). Producer, Masaichi Nagata; Director, Kimiyoshi Yasuda; Screenplay, Shozaburo Asai, based on the story, "Shinkei Kasanegafuchi by Encho Sanyuti; Director of Photography, Tsuchimoto [Tsuchitaro] Hayashi (see note); Art Director, Akira Naito; Lighting, Motoyoshi Nakaoka; Editor, Kanji Suganuma; Assistant Director, Rikio Endo; Martial Arts Director, Eiichi Kusumoto; Music, Hajime Kaburagi; Sound Recording, Tsuchitaro Hayashi; Sound, Daiei Recording

Studio; Special Effects, Daiei Special Effects Department.

CAST: Kenjiro Ishiyama (Soetsu), Matsuko [Natsuko] Oka (Osono), Saburo Date (Fukami), Mitsuko Tanaka (Sawano), Ritsu Ishiyama, Maya Kitajima, Reiko Kasahara, Ryuko Minagami [Mizugami], Takumi Shinjo, Akane Kawasaki, Tsutomu Hashimoto, Ichiro Yamamoto, Teruko Omi, Kanae Kobayashi, Kazue Tamaki.

A Daiei Motion Picture Co., Ltd. Production. Westrex recording system. Daieicolor. DaieiScope. 82 minutes. Released June 20, 1970.

U.S. VERSION: Distributed by Daiei International Films, Inc. English subtitles. Also known as *Horror of an Ugly Woman*. Previously filmed as *The Depth* and *Kaidan Kasane ga fuchi*, the latter also by Yasuda. *Note:* One source lists the Director of Photography as Chishi Makimura. 82 minutes. No MPAA rating. Released 1970.

Max Mon Amour ("Max My Love"). Producer, Serge Silberman; Associate Producer, Ully Pickardt; Director, Nagisa Oshima; Screenplay, Nagisa Oshima and Jean-Claude Carriere, based on a story by Jean-Claude Carriere; Director of Photography, Raoul Coutard; Art Director, Pierre Guffroy; Editor, Helene Plemianikov; Costumes, Bernard Perris; Music, Michel Portal; Special Makeup Effects, Rick Baker; Special Effects, Ray Scott; Titles, Maurice Binder.

CAST: Charlotte Rampling, Anthony Higgins, Victoria Abril, Anne-Marie Besse, Nicole Calfan, Pierre Etaix, Bernard Haller, Sabine Haudepin, Christopher Hovik, Fabrice Luchini, Diana Quick, Milena Vukotic, Bernard Pierre Donnadieu.

A Greenwich Film Production S.A. (Paris)/Greenwich Film U.S.A., Inc. Production, in association with Oshima Films. A French/Japanese/U.S. co-production in French and English. Filmed on location in Paris. Color. Spherical Panavision. 93 minutes. Released 1986.

U.S. VERSION: Distributor undetermined. English subtitles. Video version matted. 93 minutes. No MPAA rating. Released April 17, 1988.

Melody in Gray / Hanare-Goze Orin ("Poor, Blind Orin, Shamisen Player"). Producers, Kiyoshi Iwashita and Seikichi Iizumi; Director, Masahiro Shinoda; Screenplay, Keiji Hasebe and Masahiro Shinoda, based on an original story by Tsutomu Minakami; Director of Photography, Kazuo Miyagawa; Art Director, Kiyoshi Awazu; Music, Toru Takemitsu.

CAST: Shima Iwashita, Yoshio Harada, Kirin Kiki.

A Hyogensha, Ltd. Production. Color. Panavision (?). 117 minutes. Released 1977.

U.S. VERSION: Distributor undetermined. 117 minutes. No MPAA rating. Released September 1978.

Memoir of Japanese Assassins / Nippon ansatsu hiroku ("Memoir of Japanese Assassins"). Director, Sadao Nakajima; Screenplay, Sadao Nakajima and Kazuo Kasahara, based on an original story by Tadashi Suzuki; Director of Photography, Sadatsugu Yoshida; Art Director, Takatoshi Suzuki; Music, Isao Tomita.

CAST: Shinichi "Sonny" Chiba (Tadashi Onuma), Chiezo Kataoka (Nissho Inoue), Yukie Kagawa (Tamiko), Jiro Tamiya (Lt. Fuji), Asao Koike (Ochiai), Koji Tsuruta, Ken Takakura, Tomisaburo Wakayama, Junko Fuji.

A Toei Co., Ltd. Production. Eastman Color. ToeiScope. 142 minutes. Released October 16, 1969.

U.S. VERSION: Release undetermined, possibly by Daiei International Films. English subtitled version available. 142 minutes. No MPAA rating.

Memories of You / Kaisha monogatari ("The Story of a Company"). Producer, Toshiaki Nakagawa; Director, Jun Ichikawa; Screenplay, Satoshi Suzuki and Jun Ichikawa; Director of Photography, Susumu Ono; Music, Fumi Itakura.

CAST: Hajime Hana, Yumi Nishiyama, Hitoshi Ueki, Akira Tani, Hiroshi Inuzuka.

A Shochiku Co., Ltd./Nippon Television Network Corp./Sedic Co., Ltd./ Office Sakamoto Production. A Shochiku

Co., Ltd. Release. Color. Panavision (?). 103 minutes. Released 1988.

U.S. Version: Distributor, if any, is undetermined, possibly Shochiku Films of America, Inc. in subtitled format. Alternate title: *The Story of a Company*. No MPAA rating.

Men and War—Part Two / Senso to ningen ("War and Men"). Director, Setsuo Yamamoto; Screenplay, Nobuo Yamada and Atsushi Takeda, based on the novel by Jumpei Gomikawa; Director of Photography, Shinsaku Himeda; Music, Masaru Sato.

Cast: Osamu Takizawa, Shinsuke Ashida, Hideki Takhashi.

A Nikkatsu Corp. Production. Color. NikkatsuScope. 182 minutes. Released 1971.

U.S. Version: Distributor, if any, is undetermined. Followed by *Men and War—Part Three* (1973). No MPAA rating.

Men and War—Part Three / Senso to ningen ("War and Men"). Director, Satsuo Yamamoto; Screenplay, Atsushi Takeda and Nobuo Yamada, based on the novel by Jumpei Gomikawa; Director of Photography, Shinsaku Himeda; Music, Masaru Sato.

Cast: Hideki Takahashi, Shinsuke Ashida, Sayuri Yoshinaga, Kei Yamamoto, Osamu Takizawa, Ruriko Asaoka, Kinya Kitaoji, Mitsuko Mito, Etsushi Takahashi, Mizusho Suzuki.

A Nikkatsu Corp. Production. Color. NikkatsuScope. 189 minutes. Released 1973.

U.S. Version: Released by Shochiku Films of America, Inc. English subtitles. 189 minutes. No MPAA rating. Released July 2, 1975.

The Men of Toho-ku / Tohoku no zummutachi ("The People of Toho-ku"). Producer, Masumi Fujimoto; Director, Kon Ichikawa; Screenplay, Kon Ichikawa, based on a story by Shiichiro Fukazawa; Director of Photography, Kazuo Yamada; Music, Ikuma Dan; Art Director, Tomo Nakafuru; Lighting, Choshichiro Ishii; Sound Recording, Masao Fujiyoshi.

Cast: Hiroshi Akutagawa (Risuke Zummu), Minoru Chiaki (Tasuke Zummu), Haruko Togo (Asa Zummu, *Tasuke's wife*), Kamatari Fujiwara (Hisakichi, *master of Sankaku Yashiki*), Chieko Naniwa (Oei), Eiko Miyoshi (old woman).

A Toho Co., Ltd. Production. Black and white. Toho Scope. Running time undetermined. Released October 1, 1957.

U.S. Version: Distributor, if any, is undetermined.

The Men Who Tread on the Tiger's Tail / Tora no O o Fumu Otokotachi ("Men Who Step on the Tiger's Tail"). Produced by Motohiko Ito; Director/Editor, Akira Kurosawa; Screenplay, Akira Kurosawa, based on the Kabuki play *Kanjincho*; Director of Photography, Takeo Ito; Art Director, Kazuo Kubo; Music, Tadashi Hattori.

Cast: Denjiro Okochi (Benkei), Susumu Fujita (Togashi), Masayuki Mori (Kamei), Takashi Shimura (Kataoka), Aritake Kono (Ise), Yoshio Kosugi (Suruga), Dekao Yoko (Hidachibo), Hanshiro Iwai (Yoshitsune), Kenichi "Enoken" Enomoto (porter), Yasuo Hisamatsu (Kajiwara's messenger), Shoji Kiyokawa (Togashi's messenger).

A Toho Co., Ltd. Production. Black and white. Academy ratio. 58 minutes. Produced in 1945 but release withheld by the American Occupation Forces. Released April 24, 1952.

U.S. Version: Released by Brandon Films, Inc. English subtitles. Alternate titles: *Those Who Tread on the Tiger's Tail, Walkers on the Tiger's Tail, They Who Step on the Tail of the Tiger*. The Noh Drama *Atake* and the Kabuki play *Kanjincho* are based on the same story. 58 minutes. No MPAA rating. Released January 1960.

The Merciless Trap/Nasake muyono wana ("The Merciless Trap"). Executive Producers, Tomoyuki Tanaka and Reiji Miwa; Director, Jun Fukuda;

Screenplay, Katsuya Suzaki; Director of Photography, Masaharu Utsumi; Music, Kenjiro Hirose.

CAST: Makoto Sato (Saburo Ninomiya), Akihiko Hirata (Morishima), Ichiro Nakatani (Detective Izaki), Kumi Mizuno (Masako).

A Toho Co., Ltd. Production. Black and white. Toho Scope. 82 minutes. Released 1961.

U.S. VERSION: Released by Toho International Co., Ltd. English subtitles. English-dubbed version also available. 82 minutes. No MPAA rating. Release date undetermined.

Merry Christmas, Mr. Lawrence / Senjo no Merii Kurisumasu ("Merry Christmas on the Battlefield"). Executive Producers, Masato Hara, Eiko Oshima, Geoffrey Nethercott, and Terry Glinwood; Producer, Jeremy Thomas; Director, Nagisa Oshima; Screenplay, Nagisa Oshima and Paul Mayersberg, based on the novel *The Seed and the Sower* (1951) by Sir Laurens van der Post; Director of Photography, Toichiro Naushima; Art Director, Andrew Sanders; Production Design, Jusho Toda; Music, Ryuichi Sakamoto; Sound Recording, Tetsuya Okashi and Mike Westgate; Editor, Tomoyo Oshima; Assistant Producer, Joyce Herlihy.

CAST: David Bowie (Major Jack Celliers), Tom Conti (John Lawrence), Ryuichi Sakamoto (Captain Yonoi), "Bent" Takeshi Kitano (Sergeant Hara), Jack Thompson (Hicksley), Johnny Okura (Kanemoto), Allistair Browning (De Jong), James Malcolm (Celliers' brother), Chris Brown (Celliers at age 12), Yuya Uchida (prison commandant), Ryunosuke Kaneda (president of the court), Takashi Naito (Lieutenant Iwata), Tamio Ishikura (prosecutor), Rokko Toura (interpreter), Kan Mikami (Lieutenant Ito).

A Recorded Picture Co., Ltd. Production. A Japanese/British/New Zealand co-production in English and Japanese. Filmed on location in New Zealand and Rartonga (Cook Islands). Dolby Stereo. Eastman Color (processed by Tokyo Laboratory). Spherical Panavision. 122 minutes. Released 1983.

U.S. VERSION: Released by Universal Pictures Corp. in English and Japanese with English subtitles. 122 minutes. MPAA rating: "R." Released August 26, 1983.

Message for the Future / Mirai eno dengon ("Message for the Future"). Producer, Seiji Matsuki; Director, Mitta Aleksandr Naumovich; Screenplay, Yoshiki Iwama and Cvetov Uldimir Iakovlevich; Director of Photography, Shuvalov Valerii Pavlovich; Music, Alfred Schnittke.

CAST: Komaki Kurihara, Akira Kume, Filatof Leonid Alekseevich.

A Shigato Film Production, Inc. Production. A Japanese-Russo co-production in Japanese and Russian (?). Color. Spherical wide screen (?). 111 minutes. Released 1991 (?).

U.S. VERSION: Distributor, if any, is undetermined.

Message from Space / Uchu kara no messeji ("Message From Space"). Producers, Banjiro Uemura, Yoshinori Watanabe, Tan Takaiwa; Co-Producers, Ryo Hirayama, Yusuke Okada, Simon Tse, Naoyuki Sugimoto, Akira Ito and Toru Hirayama; Director, Kinji Fukasaku; Screenplay, Hiro Matsuda; Director of Photography, Toru Nakajima; Music, Kenichiro Morioka, conducting the Columbia Symphony Orchestra of Japan. *Special Effects Unit*: Director, Nobuo Yajima; Director of Photography, Noboru Takanaski; Science Fiction Supervisory (?), Masahiro Noda; Space Flying Objects (design), Shotaro Ishimori; Optical Photography, Minoru Nakano; Art Director, Tetsuzo Osawa.

CAST: Vic Morrow (General Garuda), Shinichi "Sonny" Chiba (Hans), Philip Casnoff (Aaron), Peggy Lee Brennon (Meia), Sue Shiomi (Esmeralda), Tetsuro Tamba (Noguchi), Mikio Narita (Rockseia XII), Makoto Sato (Urocco), Hiroyuki Sanada (Shiro), Isamu Shimuzu (Robot Beba 2), Masazumi Okabe (Jack), Noburo Mitani (Kamesasa), Eisei Amamoto (Dark), Junkichi Orimoto (Kido), Harumi Sone (Lazari).

A Toei Co. Ltd./Tohokushinsha Film Co., Ltd. Production. Space Sound 4 (four-track magnetic stereophonic sound).

American ad art from Toei's *Message from Space* (1978).

Toeicolor (processed by Toei Chemistry Co., Ltd.). Spherical wide screen. 105 minutes. Released April 29, 1978.

U.S. VERSION: Released by United Artists Corp. English-dubbed. Prints by De Luxe. 105 minutes. MPAA Rating: "PG." Released October 30, 1978.

Mexican Free-for-All / Kureji Mekishiko dai sakusen ("Big Crazy Mexican Strategy"). Executive Producer, Shin Watanabe; Director, Takashi Tsuboshima; Screenplay, Yasuo Tanami; Director of Photography, Shoji Utsumi; Music, Yasushi Miyagawa and Tessho Hagiwara.

CAST: The Crazy Cats [Hitoshi Veki, Hajime Hara, Kei Tani, Hiroshi Inuzuka, Senri Sakurai, Shin Yasuda, Eitaro Ishibashi], Mie Hama, Mari Sono, Masumi Kagawa, Makoto Toda, The Drifters.

A Toho Co., Ltd./Watanabe Productions, Ltd. Production. Eastman Color. Toho Scope. 162 minutes. Released April 27, 1968.

U.S. VERSION: Released by Toho International Co., Ltd. in subtitled format. The 11th "Crazy" feature. Followed by *Computer Free-for-All* (1969). 162 minutes. No MPAA rating. Released October 25, 1968.

Midare karakuri ("Confusing Trick"). Director, Susumu Kodama; Sound, Toho Recording Centre; Sound Effects, Toho Sound Effects Group.

CAST: Yasaku Masuda, Hirako Shiro.

A Toho Co., Ltd. Production. Color (processed by Tokyo Laboratory Ltd.) Panavision (?). Running time undetermined. Released 1979.

U.S. VERSION: Distributor, if any, is undetermined.

Mighty Jack / Maitei Jiyaku ("Mighty Jack"). Producers, Eiji Tsuburaya, Yasuji Morita and Yasuhiro Ito; Director, Kazuho Mitsuta; Screenplay, Shinichi Sekizawa and Eizaburo; Editor, Akio Agura; Director of Photography, Yoshihiro Mori; Special Effects Director, Eiji Tsuburaya; Effects Photography, Kazuo Sagawa; Music, Isao Tomita, published by Tsuburaya Music Publishing Co., Ltd.

CAST: Hideaki Nitani, Naoko Kubo, Hiroshi Minami, Eisei Amamoto, Jerry Ito, Masaya Nihei, Wakako Ikeda, Akira Kasuga, Seiko Fukioka, Noriaki Inoue, Yoshitaka Tanaka, Mitsubu Oya, Eijiro Yanagi.

A Japanese teleseries re-edited to feature length for American television, and never released theatrically in Japan. A Tsuburaya Production Ltd. Production. 16mm. Color.

U.S. VERSION: Never released theatrically in the United States. Released directly to television in 1988 by King Features Entertainment, a subsidiary of the Hearst Corp. A Sandy Frank Enterprises Presentation. English-dubbed. Derived from the teleseries "Maitei Jiyaku," which ran 13 one-hour episodes in 1968. This feature was culled from episodes #1 ("The Man Who Vanished From Paris") and #13 ("The Mysterious Dirigible").

The Militarists / Gunbatsu ("The Militarists"). Executive Producer, Sanezumi Fujimoto; Producer, Hiroshi Hariu; Director, Hiromichi Horikawa; Screenplay, Ryozo Kasahara; Director of Photography, Kazuo Yamada; Art Directors, Iwao Akune and Shigekazu Ikuno; Music, Riichiro Manabe; Assistant Director, Masashi Matsumoto.

CAST: Keiju Kobayashi (General Hideki Tojo), Yuzo Kayama (Goro Arai), Toshio Kurosawa (Kamikaze pilot), Toshiro Mifune (Admiral Isoroku Yamamoto), Goro Tarumi (Takei), Matagoro Nakamura (Emperor Hirohito), Kenjiro Ishiyama (General Sugiyama), Tatsuya Mihashi (Takijiro Onishi), So Yamamura (Mitsumasa Yonai).

A Toho Co., Ltd. Production. Eastman Color. Panavision. 134 minutes. Released September 12, 1970.

U.S. VERSION: Released by Toho International Co., Ltd. English subtitles. 134 minutes. No MPAA rating. Released March 10, 1971.

Minamata / Minamata **[documentary]**. Director, Noriaki Tsuchimoto.

A Ryutaro Takagi Production. 16 mm. Black and white. Academy ratio. 167 minutes. Released 1972 (?).

U.S. VERSION: Released by Monument Films. English subtitles. 105 minutes. No MPAA rating. Released September 19, 1974.

Minbo—or the Gentle Art of Japanese Extortion / Minbo no onna ("Woman of Minbo"). Producer/Director/Screenplay, Juzo Itami; Director of Photography, Yonezo Maeda; Music, Toshiyuki Honda.

CAST: Nobuko Miyamoto (Mahiru Inoue), Akira Takarada (Kobayashi), Yasuo Daichi (Yuki Suzuki), Takehiro Murata (Taro Wagasuki), Shuji Otaki (hotel owner), Noboru Mitani (gang boss), Shiro Ito (Iriuchijima), Akira Nakao (Ibagi), Hosei Komatsu (Hanaoka), Tetsu Watanabe (Akechi).

An Itami Films Co., Ltd./Toho Co., Ltd. Production. Dolby Stereo. Color. Spherical Panavision (1.85:1). 123 minutes. Released May 16, 1992.

U.S. VERSION: Released by Northern Arts Entertainment. English subtitles. 123 minutes. No MPAA rating. Released October 19, 1994.

Mini-Skirt Lynchers / Zankoku onna rinchi ("Cruel Women Lynchers"). Director, Yuji Tanno; Screenplay, Iwao Yamazaki; Director of Photography, Yoshihiro Yamazaki; Art Director, Motozo Kawahara; Music, Mitsuhiko Sato.

CAST: Masako Ota (Toshie), Kiyomi Katena (Keiko), Teruko Hasegawa (Teruko), Setsuko Minami (Eri), Maya Maki (Akemi), Anne Mari (Rosa), Jiro Okazaki (Goro), Isao Sasaki (Okamoto), Eiji Go (Mukai).

A Nikkatsu Corp. Production. Black and white. NikkatsuScope. 82 minutes. Released June 28, 1969.

U.S. VERSION: Released undetermined. English subtitled version available. 82 minutes. No MPAA rating.

Mishima: A Life in Four Chapters. Executive Producers, George Lucas and Francis Ford Coppola; Producers, Mata Yamamoto and Tom Luddy; Director, Paul Schrader; Screenplay, Paul Schrader and Leonard Schrader, concieved in collaboration with Jun Shiragi, literary executor of the Mishima estate; Script Research, Akiko Hitomi; Japanese Script, Chieko Schrader; Associate Producers, Leonard Schrader, Chieko Schrader and Alan Mark Poul; Director of Photography, John Bailey; Executive Art Director, Jazuo Takenaka; Production Designer, Eiko Ishioka; Editor, Michael Chandler; Co-Editor (Tokyo), Tomoyo Oshima; Music, Philip Glass; Music Producer, Kurt Munkasci; Conductor, Michael Riesman; Line Producer, Yosuke Mizuno; Sound Design, Leslie Shatz; Casting, Nobuaki Muroka; Production Manager, Atsushi Takayama; First Assistant Director, Koichi Nakajima; Second Assistant Directors, Takayoshi Bunai, Yasuo Matsumoto, and Hisashi Toma; Executive Production Assistant, Akiko Hitomi; Costume Design, Etsuko Yagyu; Production Recordist, Shotaro Yoshida; Boompersons, Masashi Kikuchi and Soichi Inoue; Camera Operator, Toyomichi Kurita; Camera Assistants, Yuichi Tamura and Kazuhiro Nozaki; Key Grip, Jim Finnerty; Dolly Grip, George Schrader; Grip Assistants, Munetoshi Kamata and Kagari Yasuda; Gaffer, Kazuo Shimomura; Lighting Assistants, Tsutomu Kamata, Katsuji Watanabe, Chuji Sueyoshi, Kazuo Takano, Yuji Watanabe, Kazuhiko Tateishi, Masanobu Tomura, and Takamasa Nakamura; Script Supervisor, Chiyo Miyakoshi; Set Decorator, Kyoji Sasaki; Assistant Set Decorator, Kunio Okimura; Art Department, Yoshiyuki Ishida, Shunichiro Shoda, Kyoko Heya, Yasushi Ono, and Yasue Ito; Set Artist, Akiro Mizuno; Construction Coordinator, Kazuo Suzuki; Assistant to Eiko Ishioka, Shoichiro Takenoshita; Property Master, Yoichi Minagawa; Assistant Property Masters, Yuji Fukuzawa and Kyoko Machida; Prop Assistants, Toshihiko Higashimukai, Kazumi Koike, Masato Endo, Yoshikazu Furuya, and Norio Norisaki; First Assistant Editors, Jennifer Weyman-Cockle and Kathleen North; Assistant Editor, Wataru Takahashi; Apprentice Editor, Rick Finney; Rerecording Mixers, Leslie Shatz and Tom Johnson; Sound Editors, Tom Bellfort, Jerry Ross, and Giorgio Venturoli; Assistant Sound Editors, Lizabeth Gelber and Jennifer Hodgson Stein; Music Recording Engineer, Dan Dryden; Music Personal Manager, Earl Shendell; Solo Violin and Concertmaster, Elliot Rosoff; Historical Art Consultant, Kappei Uehara; Wardrobe Assistants, Toshiaki

Manki and Katsumi Harada; Bodybuilding Instructor, Mitsuo Endo; Ken Ogata's Hair, Jungi Ota; Makeup, Yasuhiro Kawaguchi, Masayuki Obuki and Noriyo Ida; Assistant Casting Directors, Yoshiro Yamaguchi and Kei Sugiura; Still Photographers, Yoshinori Ishizuki and Kitaro Miyazawa; Assistants to Mr. Schrader, Keiko Kawaguchi (Japan) and Linda Reisman (U.S.); Aide to Mr. Schrader, Makito Sugiyama; Location Coordinator, Susumu Ejima; Action Director, Kanzo Uni; Unit Publicist, Fusako Kawasaki; U.S. Production Manager, Whitney Green; Production Assistants, Kenichi Horii, Takao Shibaki, and Keiko Sakurai; Production Accountants, Kaname Hayase, Hiroko Uchida, Kazuko Nishikawa, Kuniko Sato, and Jean Autrey; Negative Cutting, D(onah) Bassett and Associates (U.S.) and Tome Minami (Japan); Title Design, Christopher Werner; Title Animation, Bruce Walters; Production Coordinator, Hiroki Tomohara; Title Calligraphy, Sharon Nakazato; Special Thanks, George Hayum, John [Jon?] Peters, Sidney Ganis; Opticals, Modern Film Effects; Postproduction Services provided by Sprocket Systems, a division of Lucasfilm, Ltd.; Additional Sound Postproduction, Russian Hill Recording (San Francisco); Music Recording, Greene St. Recording (New York).

CAST: *November 25, 1970*: Ken Ogata (Yukio Mishima), Masayuki Shionoya (Morita), Hiroshi Mikami (1st cadet), Junya Fukuda (2nd cadet), Shigeto Tachihara (3rd cadet), Junkichi Orimoto (General Mashita). *Flashbacks*: Naoko Otani (mother), Go Riju (Mishima, *age 18-19*), Masato Aizawa (Mishima, *age 9-14*), Yuki Nagahara (Mishima, *age 5*), Kyuzo Kobayashi (literary friend), Yuki Kitazume (dancing friend), Haruko Kato (grandmother). *The Temple of the Golden Pavilion*: Yaosuke Bando (Mizoguchi), Hisako Monda (Mariko), Naomi Oki (1st girl), Miki Takakura (2nd girl), Imari Tsuji (madame), Koichi Sato (Kashiwagi). *Kyoko's House*: Kenji Sawada (Osamu), Reisen Lee (Kiyomi), Setsuko Karasuma (Mitsuko), Tadanori Yoko (Natsuo), Yasuaki Kurata (Takei), Mitsuru Hirata (thug). *Runaway Horse*: Toshiyuki Nagashima (Isao), Hiroshi Katsumo (Lieutenant Hori), Naoya Makoto (Kendo instructor), Hiroki Ida (Izutsu), Jun Negami (Kurahara), Ryo Ikebe (interrogator). *Additional Cast*: Toshio Hosokawa ("Rokumeikan" producer), Hideo Fukuhara (military doctor), Yosuke Mizuno ("Yukoku" producer), Eimei Ezumi (Ichigaya aide-de-camp), Minoru Hodaka (Ichigaya colonel), Shoichiro Sakata (Isao's classmate), Alan Mark Poul (american reporter), Ren Ebata (first reporter), Yasuhiro Arai (second reporter), Fumio Mizushima (third reporter), Shinji Miura (Pavilion acolyte), Yuichi Saito (student), Sachiko Akagi (thug's girlfriend), Tsutomu Harada (Romeo), Mami Okamoto (Juliet), Atsushi Takayama (interrogation policeman), Kimiko Ito (grandmother's nurse), Kojiro Sato (first military policeman), Tatsuya Hiragaki (first actor), Shinichi Nosaka (policeman), Sachiko Hidari (Osamu's mother).

A Zoetrope Studios/Filmlink International/Lucasfilm, Ltd. Production. A Francis Ford Coppola and George Lucas Presentation. A Paul Schrader Film. From Zoetrope Studios. A Japanese/U.S. co-produciton in Japanese (see below). Filmed at Toho Studios, Ltd. (Tokyo). Dolby Stereo. Color (processed by Far East Laboratories, Ltd.). Spherical Panavision. Dolby Stereo. 122 minutes.

U.S. VERSION: Released by Warner Bros., Inc. (a Warner Communications Company) in Japanese with English subtitles and English narration. Additional cast for U.S. version: Roy Scheider (narrator). Prints by Technicolor. Program: (1) *Beauty "Temple of the Golden Pavilion"* (2) *Art "Kyoko's House"* (3) *Action "Runaway Horse"* (4) *Harmony of Pen and Sword*. 122 minutes. MPAA rating: "R." Released September 1986.

Miss Oyu / Oyu-sama ("Miss Oyu"). Producer, Masaichi Nagata; Director, Kenji Mizoguchi; Screenplay, Yoshikata Yoda, based on the novel *Ashikari* by Junichiro Tanizaki; Director of Photography, Kazuo Miyagawa; Art Director, Hiroshi Mizutani; Music, Fumio Hayasaka.

CAST: Kinuyo Tanaka (Oyu), Nobuko

Otowa (Shizu), Yuji Hori (Shinnosuke Seribashi), Eijiro Yanagi (Eitaro), Eitaro Shindo (Kusaemon), Kiyoko Hirai (Osumi), Reiko Kongo (Otsugi), Kanie Kobayashi (wet-nurse), Fumihiko Yokoyama, Jun Fujikawa, Soji Shibata (clerks), Inosuke Kuhara (shop boy), Ayuko Fujishiro (maid), Shozo Nanbu (doctor), Midori Komatsu (hostess), Sachiko Aima (teacher of flower arrangement), Sumao Ishihara (priest).

A Daiei Motion Picture Co., Ltd. Production. Filmed at Daiei-Kyoto Studios. Black and white. Academy ratio. 96 minutes. Released June 22, 1951.

U.S. VERSION: Released by Daiei International Films. English subtitles. 90 minutes. No MPAA rating. Released May 1981.

Mission Iron Castle / Shinobi no shu ("Silent Wanderers"). Director, Issei Mori; Screenplay, Takayuki Yamada, based on an original story by Ryotaro Shiba; Director of Photography, Fujio Morita; Art Director, Shigenori Shimoishizaka; Music, Hajime Kaburagi.

CAST: Hiroki Matsukata (Yoshiro), Ryunosuke Minegishi (Onikobu), Kojiro Hongo (Sukedayu), Michiyo Yasuda (Orin), Yoko Namikawa, Shiho Fujimura, Taketoshi Naito, Mutsuhiro Toura, Tomoo Uchida.

A Daiei Motion Picture Co., Ltd. Production. Black and white. DaieiScope. 79 minutes. Released February 7, 1970.

U.S. VERSION: Released by Daiei International Films. English subtitles. 79 minutes. No MPAA rating. Released June 28, 1972.

Mr. Baseball Executive Producers, John Kao, Jeffrey Silver and Susumu Kondo; Producers, Fred Schepisi, Doug Claybourne, and Robert Newmyer; Director, Fred Schepisi; Screenplay, Gary Ross, Kevin Wade, and Robert Newmyer, based on a story by Theo Pelletier and John Junkerman; Director of Photography, Ian Baker; Production Designer, Ted Haworth; Editor, Peter Honess; Costume Designer, Bruce Finlayson; Casting, Dianne Crittenden; Music, Jerry Goldsmith; Unit Production Manager, Tomo Ito; Assistant Producers, Hisao Maru and Hidekazu Uehara; 1st Asst. Director, Bruce Moriarty; 2nd Asst. Director, Cellin Gluck.

CAST: Tom Selleck (Jack Elliot), Ken Takakura (Uchiyama), Aya Takanashi (Hiroko Uchiyama), Dennis Haysbert (Max "Hammer" Dubois), Toshi Shioya (Yoji Nishimura), Kosuke Toyohara (Toshi Yamashita), Toshizo Fujiwara (Ryo Mukai), Mak Takano (Shinji Igarashi), Kenji Morinaga (Hiroshi Kurosawa), Jo Nishimura (Tomohiko Omae), Norihide Goto (Issei Itoi), Kensuke Toita (Akito Yagi), Naoki Fuji (Takuya Nishikawa), Takanobu Hozumi (Hiroshi Nakamura), Leon Lee (Lyle Massey), Bradley Jay "Animal" Lesley (Niven), Jun Hamamura (Hiroko's grandfather), Mineko Yorozuyo (Hiroko's grandmother), Shoji Ohoki (Coach Hori), Tomoko Fujita (Hiroko's assistant), Kinzo Sakura (Umpire #1), Ikuko Saito (Morita-san), Hikari Takano (commercial director), Tim McCarver (himself), Sean McDonough (himself), Art LaFleur (Skip), Greg Goosen (Trey), Nicholas Cascone (Doc), Larry Pennell (Howie Gold), Scott Plank (Ryan Ward), Charles Joseph Fick (Billy Stevens), Michael McGrady (Duane), Frank Thomas (rookie), Michael Papajohn (Rick), Roland Rodriquez (Manuel), Todd A. Provence (young ball player), Frank Mendoza (player—New York), Ken Medlock (umpire), Carrie Yazel (coed in bed), Mary Kohnert (player's wife), Makoto Kuno, Michiyo Washizukan (Japanese sportscasters), Shinsuke Aoki (Nikawa, *the Dragons' co-owner*), Rinzo Suzuki (Sato, *the Dragons' co-owner*). *The Dragons*: Shintaro Mizushima (Uchida), Nobuyuki Kariya (Uemoto), Satoshi Jinbo (Tsuboi), Masanao Matsuzaki (Sugita), Shotaro Kusumi (Takahashi), Katsushi Yamaguchi (Kobayshi), Hiro Nagae (Mutsui), Yoshimi Imai (Ishimaru), Cin Chi Cheng (Coach Itami), Makoto Kaketa (umpire #2), Shogo Nakajima (umpire #3).

An Outlaw Production, in association with Pacific Artists. A Universal Pictures Release. A U.S./Japanese co-production in English and Japanese. Dolby Stereo. De Luxe Color. Panavision. MPAA rating: "PG-13." Released October 2, 1992.

Mr. Lucky / Rakkii-san ("Mr. Lucky"). Producer, Masumi Fujimoto; Director, Kon Ichikawa; Screenplay, Masato Inomata, based on a story by Keita Genji; Director of Photography, Tadashi Iimura; Art Director, Teruaki Abe; Music, Yuji Koseki.

CAST: Keiju Kobayashi (Shumpei Wakahara), Hiroshi Koizumi (Yuzo Kondo), Yukiko Shimazaki (Yasuko), Reikichi Kawamura (President Akinawa), Yoko Sugi (Yukiko), Tatsuo Saito (Machida).

A Toho Co., Ltd. Production. Black and white. Academy ratio. Running time undetermined. Released February 21, 1952.

U.S. VERSION: Distributor, if any, is undetermined, though although almost certainly Toho International Co., Ltd.

Mr. Pu / Pu-san ("Mr. Pu"). Producers, Masumi Fujimoto and Masatada Kaneko; Director, Kon Ichikawa; Screenplay, Natto Wada, Shigeaki Nagaki, and Kon Ichikawa, based on a story by Taizo Yokoyama; Director of Photography, Asakazu Nakai; Music, Toshiro Mayuzumi; Art Director, Gen Akune; Sound Recording, Kan Shimonaga; Lighting, Choshiro Ishii.

CAST: Yunosuke Ito (Yonekichi Noro), Fubuki Koshiji (Kanko Kanamori), Kamatari Fujiwara (Fukichi), Eiko Miyoshi (Ran).

A Toho Co., Ltd. Production. Black and white. Academy ratio. 98 minutes. Released April 15, 1953.

U.S. VERSION: Released by Toho International Co., Ltd. English subtitles. Alternate title: *Pou-san*. 98 minutes. No MPAA rating. Release date undetermined.

Mistress / Gan ("Wild Geese"). Producers, Yuji Hirao and Kenji Kuroiwa; Director, Shiro Toyoda; Screenplay, Masashige Narusawa, based on the novel by Ogai Mori; Director of Photography, Mitsuo Miura; Supervising Art Director, Kisaku Ito; Art Director, Takeo Kimura; Lighting, Tsurekichi Shibata; Editor, Masanori Tsuji; Music, Ikuma Dan.

CAST: Hideko Takamine (Otama), Hiroshi Akutagawa (Okada), Eijiro Tono (Suezo, *the moneylender*), Jukichi Uno (Kimura, *Okada's friend*), Choko Iida (Osan), Eiza Tanaka (Zenso, *Otama's father*), Kumeko Urabe (Otsune, *Suezo's wife*), Miki Odagiri (Oume, *Otama's maid*), Kuniko Miutake (Osada, *the sewing mistress*).

A Daiei Motion Picture Co., Ltd. Production. Black and white. Academy ratio. 104 miknutes. Released 1953.

U.S. VERSION: Released by Edward Harrison. English subtitles. Alternate title: *Wild Geese*. Remade by Daiei in 1966. 104 minutes. No MPAA rating. Released February 2, 1959. Reissued by Kino International.

Moment of Terror / Hikinige ("Hit and Run"). Producer, Masumi Fujimoto; Director, Mikio Naruse; Screenplay, Zenzo Matsuyama; Director of Photography, Rokuro Nishigaki; Music, Masaru Sato.

CAST: Hideko Takamine (The Mother), Yoko Tsukasa, Eitaro Ozawa, Hisashi Nakayama, Toshio Kurosawa, Daisuke Kato, Natsuko Kahara, Yutaka Sada.

A Toho Co., Ltd. Production. Black and white. Toho Scope. 94 minutes. Released April 1966.

U.S. VERSION: Released by Toho International Co., Ltd. English subtitles. 94 minutes. No MPAA rating. Released February 1969.

Mondo Grottesco / Nippon '69 Sekkusu Ryoki chitai ("Strange Sex of Japan in '69") **[documentary]**. Director, Sadao Nakajima; Director of Photography, Shigeru Akatsuka; Music, Masao Yagi.

Narrator: Ko Nishimura.

A Toei Co., Ltd. Production. Eastman Color. Academy ratio. 93 minutes. Released January 19, 1969.

U.S. VERSION: Release undetermined. English subtitled version available. 93 minutes. No MPAA rating.

The Money Dance / Zeni no odori ("The Money Dance"). Producer, Masaichi Nagata; Planning, Hiroaki Fujii and Yonejiro Saito; Director, Kon Ichikawa; Screenplay, Shitei Kuri; Director of Photography, Kazuo Miyagawa; Special Effects, Yonesaburo Tsukuji; Music,

Hajime Hana; Art Director, Takesaburo Watanabe; Lighting, Sachio Ito; Sound Recording, Kimio Hida; Editor, Tatsuji Nakashizu.

CAST: Shintaro Katsu (Yamo Machida), Chiemi Eri (Tsukimi Jujo), Eiji Funakoshi (Kazue Hime), Jun Hamamura (Senzo Edo).

A Daiei Motion Picture Co., Ltd. Color. DaieiScope. 90 minutes. Released May 2, 1964.

U.S. VERSION: Released by Daiei International Films, Inc. (?). English subtitles (?). Alternate title: *Money Talks*. 90 minutes. No MPAA rating.

Monsieur Zivaco / Crazy Cats—Kaito Jibako ("Crazy Cats—Mysterious Thief Zivaco"). Producer, Shin Watanabe; Director, Takashi Tsuboshima; Screenplay, Yasuo Tanami; Director of Photography, Shoji Utsumi; Music Yasushi Miyagawa.

CAST: The Crazy Cats [Hitoshi Ueki, Hajime Hana, Kei Tani, Hiroshi Inuzuka, Senri Sakurai, Shin Yasuda, Eitaro Ishibashi], Mie Hama, Andrew Hughes, Eijiro Tono, Haruya Kato, Osman Yusef.

A Toho Co., Ltd./Watanabe Productions, Ltd. Production. Color. Toho Scope. 110 minutes. Released October 1967.

U.S. VERSION: Released by Toho International Co., Ltd. English subtitles. The 10th "Crazy" feature. Followed by *Mexican Free-for-All* (1968). 100 minutes. No MPAA rating. Released April 24, 1968.

Monster from a Prehistoric Planet / Dai kyoju Gappa ("Great Big Monster Gappa"). Producer, Hideo Koi; Director, Haruyasu Noguchi; Screenplay, Iwao Yamazaki, Ryuzo Nakanishi, based on a story by Akira Watanabe; Director of Photography, Muneo Ueda; Art Director, Kazumi Koike; Music, Seitaro Omori; Editor, Masanori Tsujii; Sound, Saburo Takahashi; Sound Recording, Nikkatsu Sound Studio. *Special Effects Unit:* Director, Akira Watanabe; Photography, Isamu Kakita, Kenji Kaneda, Yoshiyuki Nakano.

CAST: Tamio Kawaji (Hiroshi Kurosaki), Yoko Yamamoto (Itoko Koyanagi), Kokan Katsura (Sanburo Hayashi), Keisuke Yukioka (President Funazu), Saburo Hiromatsu (Hosoda), Shiro Oshimi (Oyama), Yuji Kotaka (Daizo Tonooka), Tatsuya Fuji (Dr. George Inoue), Koji Wada (Dr. Machida), Yuji Odaka [Oyagi] (Dr. Aihara), Bumon Kahara (a superior), Masanori Machida (Saki), Zenji Yamada (Kamomemaru shipmaster), Hiroshi Kawano (head of defense department), Toshinosuke Nahao (commander), Masaru Kamiyama (professor), Hiroshi Sugie (first reporter), Hiroshi Ito (second reporter), Takashi Koshiba (third reporter), Sanpei Mine (first islander), Kiyoshi Matsue (second islander), Kensuke Tamai (third islander), Mike Daning (sailor).

A Nikkatsu Corp. Production. Eastman Color (processed by Nikkatsu Laboratory). NikkatsuScope. 81 minutes. Released April 1967.

U.S. VERSION: Never released theatrically in the United States. Released to television by American International Television (AIP-TV) in 1968. English-dubbed. A James H. Nicholson and Samuel Z. Arkoff Presentation; Dialogue, William Ross; Postproduction Supervisor, Salvatore Billitteri; Prints by Pathé. International Title: *Gappa*. Also known as *Gappa—Triphibian Monster*. *Note:* This film is essentially an unauthorized remake of *Gorgo* (Metro-Goldwyn-Mayer, 1961). 81 minutes. No MPAA Rating.

The Monster Gorilla / Gekko kamen: Kaiju Kongu ("Moonlight Mask: Monster Kong"). Director, Satoru Ainoda.

CAST: Fumitake Omura, Yaeko Wakamizu.

A Toei Co., Ltd. Production. Black and white (processed by Toei Chemistry Co., Ltd.). ToeiScope. 60 minutes. Released April 1, 1959.

U.S. VERSION: Distributor undetermined. No MPAA rating. The 4th "Moonlight Mask" feature. Followed by *The Challenging Ghost* (1959). Released 1960 (?).

Monster Zero / Kaiju daisenso ("The Giant Monster War"). Producer, Tomoyuki Tanaka; Associate Producers, Henry G. Saperstein and Reuben Bercovitch; Director, Ishiro Honda; Screenplay, Shinichi Sekizawa; Director of

Photography, Hajime Koizumi; Music, Akira Ifukube; Editor, Ryohei Fujii; Art Director, Takeo Kita; Gaffer, Shoichi Kojima; Sound Recording, Ataru Konuma; Sound Mixing, Hiroshi Mukoyama; Sound Arrangement; Hisashi Shimonaga; Sound Effects, Sadamasa Nishimoto, Toho Sound Effects Group; Sound, Toho Recording Centre; Assistant Director, Koji Kajita; Production Managers, Masao Suzuki, Tadashi Koike. *Toho Special Effects Group*: Director, Eiji Tsuburaya; Photography, Teisho Arikawa, Mototaka Tomioka; Optical Photography, Yukio Manoda, Sadeo Iizuka; Assistant to Tsuburaya, Teruyoshi Nakano; Art Direction, Akira Watanabe; Lighting, Kuichiro Kishida; Wire Manipulation, Fumio Nakadai; Suit Design, Teizo Toshimitsu.

CAST: Akira Takarada (Astronaut K. Fuji), Nick Adams (Astronaut F. Glenn), Kumi Mizuno (Namikawa), Jun Tazaki (Dr. Sakurai), Akira Kubo (Tetsuo), Keiko Sawai (Haruno Fuji), Yoshio Tsuchiya (Controller of Planet X), Yoshifumi Tajima (army commander), Noriko Sengoku (Tetsuo's annoyed neighbor), Toru Ibuki, Kazuo Suzuki (X-ite henchmen), Nadao Kirino (soldier), Saburo Iketani (radio announcer), Somesho Matsumoto (priest), Kenzo Tabu (X-ite who burns Tetsuo's plans), Koji Uno (weak chin-type in glasses), Haruo Nakajima (Godzilla), Shoichi "Solomon" Hirose (King Ghidorah), Goro Naya (voice characterization for Nick Adams),Takamaru Sasaki, Fuyuki Murakami, Yasuhida Tsutsumi, Masaaki Tachibana, Kamayuki Tsubono, Takuzo Kumagaya, Yoshizo Tatake, Gen Shimizu, Mitzuo Tsuda, Hideki Furukawa, Ryoji Shimizu, Toki Shiozawa, Yutaka Oka, Minoru Ito, Rinsaku Ogata, Tadashi Okabe.

A Toho Co., Ltd. Production, in association with Henry G. Saperstein Enterprises. Westrex Recording system. Color (processed by Tokyo Developing Labs). Toho Scope. 94 minutes. Released December 19, 1965.

U.S. VERSION: Distributed by Maron Films Ltd. English-dubbed. A United Productions of America Presentation. Postproduction Supervisor, S. Richard Krown; Sound Recording, Glen Glenn Sound. Voice characterizations: Marvin Miller (Akira Takarada, many others), additional cast undetermined. Prints by Consolidated Film Industries. The 6th "Godzilla" feature. Followed by *Ebirah, Horror of the Deep* (a.k.a. *Godzilla versus the Sea Monster*, 1966). Includes stock footage from *Rodan* (1956), *Mothra* (1961) and *Ghidrah – The Three-Headed Monster* (1964). Double-billed with *The War of the Gargantuas* (q.v.). International Title: *Invasion of Astro-Monster*. Originally released sans any screen credits. Current television and home video title: *Godzilla vs. Monster Zero*, with new title credits via video supering. Reissued in Japan in 1971 (re-edited to 74 minutes), as *Kaiju daisenso Kingughidorah tai Gojira* ("The Giant Monster War: King Ghidorah against Godzilla"). 92 minutes. MPAA Rating: "G." Released July 29, 1970.

The Moon Mask Rider / Gekko kamen ("Moonlight Mask"). Executive Producer, Kohan Kawauchi; Producers, Hiromitsu Furukawa, Hisao Masuda; Director, Yukihiro Sawada; Screenplay, Kohan Kawauchi and Yukihiro Sawada, based on a novel by Kohan Kawauchi; Producer's Representative, Michiyo Yoshizaki; Music, Kohan Kawauchi; Motorcycle Design, Takuya Yura.

CAST: Daisuke Kuwabara, Etsuko "Sve" Shiomi, Takuya Fujioka, Takeo Chii, Hosei Komatsu.

A Nippon Herald Films, Inc. Production. Color. Panavision (?). 108 minutes. Released 1981.

U.S. VERSION: Distributor, if any, is undetermined. Nippon Herald also handled the international release. A remake of Toei's film series (1958-59).

Moonlight in the Rain / Onna kazoku ("Female Family"). Director, Seiji Hisamatsu.

CAST: Yoshiko Kuga, Akio Mimasu, Michiyo Aratama, Kazuyo Matsushita, Hikaru Mayuzumi, Tadao Takashima, Shoji Yasui, Jun Funato, Chieko Naniwa, Haruya Kato, Kenji Sahara, Michiyo Tamaki. A Takarazuka Motion Picture Co., Ltd. Production.

A Toho Co., Ltd. Release. Color (?). Toho Scope (?). 95 minutes. Released May 16, 1961.

U.S. VERSION: Released by Toho International Co., Ltd. English subtitles. 95 minutes. No MPAA rating. Released November 1961.

Mori no Ichimatsu yurei dochu ("Ishimatsu Travels with Ghosts"). Executive Producer, Tomoyuki Tanaka; Director, Kozo Saeki; Sound, Toho Recording Centre; Sound Effects, Toho Sound Effects Group.

CAST: Frankie Sakai, Kaoru Yachigusa.

A Toho Co., Ltd. Production. Western Electric Mirrophonic recording (encoded with Perspecta Stereophonic Sound). Black and white (?). Toho Scope. Running time undetermined. Released 1959.

U.S. VERSION: Distributor, if any, is undetermined. International title: *Ishimatsu Travels with Ghosts.*

The Most Beautiful / Ichiban Utsukushiku ("The Most Beautiful"). Producer, Motohiko Ito; Director/Screenplay/Editor, Akira Kurosawa; Director of Photography, Joji Ohara; Art Director, Teruaki Abe; Music, Seichi Suzuki.

CAST: Takashi Shimura (factory production head), Ichiro Sugai (his assistant), Yoko Yaguchi, Koyuri Tanima, Takako Irie, Toshiko Hattori (girls).

A Toho Co., Ltd. Production. Black and white. Academy ratio. 85 minutes. Released April 13, 1944.

U.S. VERSION: Released by Toho International Co., Ltd. English subtitles. Alternate title: *Most Beautifully.* 85 minutes. No MPAA rating. Release date undetermined.

The Most Terrible Time in My Life / Waga jinsei saiaku no toki ("The Most Terrible Time in My Life"). Producer, Yutaka Goto; Director, Kaizo Hayashi; Screenplay, Daisuke Tengan and Kaizo Hayashi; Director of Photography, Yuichi Nagata; Music, Meina, Co.

CAST: Masatoshi Nagase (Mike Hama), Yang Haitin, Kiyotaka Nanbara, Shiny Tsukamoto, Jo Shishido.

A For Life Records Production. Dolby Stereo. Black and white. Anamorphic wide screen. 92 minutes. Released 1992.

U.S. VERSION: Released by Herald Ace. English subtitles. 92 minutes. No MPAA rating. Released 1994.

Mother / Okasan ("Mother"). Producer, Ichiro Nagashima; Director, Mikio Naruse; Screenplay, Yoko Mizuki, based on the prize-winning girls' school essay, "My Mother"; Director of Photography, Hiroshi Suzuki; Editor, Hidetoshi Kasama; Art Director, Masatoshi Kato; Music, Ichiro Saito; Sound Recording, Kihachiro Nakai.

CAST: Kinuyo Tanaka (Masako Fukuhara), Kyoko Kagawa (Toshiko, *her daughter*), Eiji Okada (Shinjiro), Masao Mishima (Ryosuke Fukuhara, *Masako's husband*), Akihiko Katayama (Susumu Fukuhara, *Masako's eldest son*), Daisuke Kato (Uncle Kimura), Chieko Nakakita (Aunt Noriko), Keiko Enonami (Chako, *Masako's second daughter*).

A Shintoho Co., Ltd. Production. Black and white. Academy ratio. 98 minutes. Released 1952.

U.S. VERSION: Released by Concordia Pictures. English subtitles. 98 minutes. No MPAA rating. Released 1955. Reissued by Toho International Co., Ltd.

Mother / Haha ("Mother"). Producers, Nobuyoshi Otani, Junji Shizuma, and Matsuo Takahashi; Director, Zenzo Matsuyama; Screenplay, Zenzo Matsuyama, based on an original story by Keiko Tanaka; Director of Photography, Yoshihiro Yamazaki; Music, Masato Kai.

CAST: Takuzo Kawatani, Jitsuko Yoshimura, Teru Saito.

A Shochiku Co., Ltd./Big Bang Co., Ltd. Production. Color. Panavision (?). 75 minutes. Released 1988.

U.S. VERSION: Release undetermined, possibly by Shochiku Films of America, Inc. in subtitled format. No MPAA rating.

A Mother Should Be Loved / Haha o kawazuya ("A Mother Should Be Loved"). Director, Yasujiro Ozu; Screenplay, Tadao Ikeda and Masao Arata, based on an idea by Kogo Noda; Director of Photography, Isamu Aoki.

CAST: Den Ohinata, Hideo Mitsui, Mitsuko Yoshikawa, Yukichi Iwata, Shinyo Nara, Junko Matsui, Chishu Ryu.

A Shochiku Co., Ltd. Production. Filmed at Shochiku-Kamata Studios. Silent. Black and white. Academy ratio. 93 minutes. Released May 11, 1934.

One of the many elaborate miniatures constructed by Eiji Tsuburaya's effects crew for Ishiro Honda's *Mothra* (1961).

U.S. Version: Released by Shochiku Films of America, Inc. English subtitles. The first and last reels are lost. 71 minutes. No MPAA rating. Released 1973 (?).

Mothra / Mosura ("Mothra"). Producer, Tomoyuki Tanaka; Director, Ishiro Honda; Screenplay, Shinichi Sekizawa, based on an original story by Shinichiro Nakamura, Takehido Fukunaga, Yoshio Hotta, as published in *Asahi Shimbun*; Art Directors, Takeo Kita, Kimei Abe; Director of Photography, Hajime Koizumi; Editor, Ichiji Taira; Music, Yuji Koseki; Recording, Soichi Fujinawa, Masanobu Miyazaki; Lighting, Toshio Takashima; Production Manager, Shin Morita; Assistant Director, Masaji Nanagase; Sound, Toho Recording Centre; Sound Effects, Toho Sound Effects Group. *Toho Special Effects Group*: Director, Eiji Tsuburaya; Photography, Teisho Arikawa; Art Direction, Akira Watanabe; Optical Photography, Yukio Manoda; Production Manager, Kan Narita; Lighting, Kuichiro Kishida; Matte Work, Hiroshi Mukoyama.

Cast: Frankie Sakai ("Bulldog" Tsinchan [Junichiro Fukuda]), Hiroshi Koizumi (Dr. Shinichi Chujo), Kyoko Kagawa (Photographer Michi Hanamura), Emi Ito and Yumi Ito [The Peanuts] (Mothra's priestesses), Jerry Ito (Clark Nelson), Ken Uehara (Dr. Haradawa), Akihiko Hirata (doctor), Kenji Sahara (helicopter pilot), Seizaburo Kawazu (general), Takashi Shimura (news editor), Yoshio Kosugi (ship's captain), Yoshifumi Tajima (military advisor), Ren Yamamoto (rescued sailor), Haruya Kato (baby-faced rescued sailor), Tetsu Nakamura (Nelson's chief henchman), Akihiro Tayama (Shinji Chujo), Harold S. Conway (Rolisican official), Robert Dunham (well-dressed Rolisican), Ed Keane (Rolisican mayor), Osman Yusef (Nelson's Caucasian henchman), Haruo Nakajima (Mothra), Ko Mishima, Shoichi Hirose, Koro Sakurai, Hiroshi Iwamoto, Mitsuo Tsuda, Masamitsu Tayma, Toshio Miura, Tadashi Okabe, Akira Wakamatsu, Obel Wyatt, Akira Yamada, Koji Uno, Wataru Omae, Toshihiko Furuta, Keisuke Matsuyama, Yoshiyuki Kamimura, Katsumi Tezuka, Takeo Nagashima, Mitsuo Matsumoto, Shinpei Mitsu, Kazuo Higata, Shigeo Kato, Rinsaku Ogata, Yutaka Okada, Arai Hayamizu, Hiroyuki Satake, Kazuo Imai, Yoshio Hattori, Hiroshi Akitsu, Akio Kusama.

A Toho Co., Ltd. Production. Western Electric Mirrophonic recording (encoded with Perspecta Stereophonic Sound). Eastman Color (processed by Far East Laboratory, Ltd.). Toho Scope. 101 minutes. Released July 30, 1961.

U.S. Version: Released by Columbia Pictures Corporation. English-dubbed. Producer, David D. Horne; Director, Lee Kresel; English Dialog, Robert Myerson; Sound, Titra Sound Studios; prints by Pathé. Double-billed with *The Three Stooges in Orbit* (Columbia, 1962). Working title: *Daikaiju Mosura* (Giant Monster Mothra). Reissued in Japan in 1974 running 62 minutes, and double-billed with *Latitude Zero* (q.v.). 88 minutes. No MPAA rating. Released May 10, 1962.

Mt. Aso's Passion / Shikibu monogatari ("Shikibu Story"). Producer, Kazunobu Yamaguchi; Director, Kei Kumai; Screenplay, Kei Kumai, based on an original story by Matsuyo Akimoto; Director of Photography, Masao Tochizawa; Music, Teizo Matsumura.

Cast: Eiji Okuda, Keiko Kishi, Kyoko Kagawa, Mieko Harada, Taiko Shinbashi, Rika Abiko, Tetta Sugimoto.

The Seiyu, Ltd. Production. Color. Spherical wide screen (?). 112 minutes. Released 1990.

U.S. Version: Distributor, if any, is undetermined.

Mt. Hakkoda / Hakkodasan ("Mt. Hakkoda"). Producers, Shinobu Hashimoto, Yoshitaro Nomura, and Tomoyuki Tanaka; Director, Shiro Moritani; Screenplay, Shinobu Hashimoto, based on an original story by Jiro Nitta; Director of Photography, Daisaku Kimura; Art Director, Iwao Akune; Music, Yasushi Akutagawa.

Cast: Shogo Shimada (Maj. General Tomoda), Shuji Otaki (Col. Nakabayashi), Ken Takakura (Capt. Tokushima), Tetsuro Tamba (Col. Kojima), Takuya

Fujioka (Major Monma), Gin Maeda (Corp. Saito), Kinya Kitaoji (Capt. Kanda), Rentoro Mikuni (Major Yamada), Yuzo Kayama (Capt. Kurata), Keiju Kobayashi (Lt. Col. Tsumura), Shigeru Koyama (Major Kinomiya), Kensaku Morita (2nd Lt. Mikami), Ken Ogata (Corp. Murayama), Komaki Kurihara (Hatsuko Kanda), Mariko Kaga (Taeko Tokushima), Kumiko Akiyoshi (Sawa Takiguchi).

A Hashimoto Productions/Toho Co., Ltd./Shinano Kikaku Co., Ltd. Production. Color. Panavision (?). 169 minutes. Released June 13, 1977.

U.S. VERSION: Release undetermined, possibly by Toho International Co., Ltd. in subtitled format. No MPAA rating.

Muddy River / Doro no kawa ("Muddy River"). Producer, Motoyasu Kimura; Director, Kohei Oguri; Screenplay, Takako Shigemori, based on the novel by Teru Miyamoto; Director of Photography, Shohei Ando; Art Director, Akira Naito; Editor, Nobuo Ogawa; Music, Kuroudo Mori; Lighting, Tadaki Shimada; Sound Recording, Hideo Nishizaki and Hiroyuki Hirai.

CAST: Nobutaka Asahara (Nobuo), Takahiro Tamura (Shinpei), Yumiko Fujita (Sadako, *Nobuo's mother*), Minoru Sakurai (Kiichi), Mariko Shibata (Ginko), Mariko Kaga (Kiichi and Ginko's mother), Masako Yagi (Shinpei's first wife), Gannosuke Ashiya (Shinoda, the horse cart man), Reiko Hatsune (tobacco-shop woman), Keizo Kanie (policeman), Yoshitaka Nishiyama (warehouse guard), Taiji Tonoyama (man on festival boat).

A Kimura Productions Co., Ltd. Production. Black and white. Academy Ratio. 105 minutes. Released January 29, 1981.

U.S. VERSION: Released by Unifilm. English subtitles. 105 minutes. No MPAA rating. Released January 15, 1982.

The Munekata Sisters / Munekata shimai ("The Munekata Sisters"). Director, Yasujiro Ozu; Screenplay, Yasujiro Ozu and Kogo Noda, based on the novel by Jiro Osaragi; Director of Photography, Jyoji Ohara.

CAST: Kinuyo Tanaka, Hideko Takamine, Ken Uehara, So Yamamura, Chishu Ryu, Sanae Takasugi, Tatsu Saito.

A Shintoho Co., Ltd. Production. Academy ratio. Black and white. 112 minutes. Released August 25, 1950.

U.S. VERSION: Distributor undetermined, though possibly Toho International Co., Ltd. English subtitles. Toho Co., Ltd. currently controls this feature. 112 minutes. No MPAA rating.

Musashi Miyamoto / Miyamoto Musashi ("Musashi Miyamoto"). Director, Kenji Mizoguchi; Screenplay, Matsutaro Kawaguchi, based on a serial by Kan Kikuchi, appearing in *Mainichi Shinbun*; Director of Photography, Shigeto Miki; Fencing Sequences Supervisor, Hiromasa Kono; Music, Akira Ifukube.

CAST: Chojuro Kawarazaki (Musashi Miyamoto), Kanemon Nakamura (Kojiro Sasaki), Kinuyo Tanaka (Shinobu Nonomiya), Kigoro Ikushima (Genichiro Nonomiya).

A Shochiku Co., Ltd. Production. Filmed at Shochiku-Kyoto Studios. Black and white. Academy ratio. 53 minutes. Released December 28, 1944.

U.S. VERSION: Released by Shochiku Films of America, Inc. English subtitles. Other versions of the same story include Hiroshi Inagaki's *Samurai* trilogy (1954-56). 53 minutes. No MPAA rating. Released 1981.

Musashi Miyamoto / Miyamoto Mushashi ("Musashi Miyamoto"). Director, Tomu Uchida; Screenplay, Masashige Narisawa and Hisayuki Suzuki; Director of Photography, Makoto Tsuboi.

CAST: Kinnosuke Nakamura, Wakaba Irie, Isao Kimura, Chieko Naniwa, Rentaro Mikuni, Satomi Oka.

A Toei Co., Ltd. Production. Eastman Color. ToeiScope. 110 minutes. Released May 27, 1961.

U.S. VERSION: Distributor, if any, is undetermined. First part of Uchida's five-film "Musashi Miyamoto" series (1961–65). International title: *Zen and Sword*.

My Champion / Ritoru champion ("Little Champion"). Producer, Yasuhiko Kawano; Director, Gwen Arner; Production Supervisor, Jay W. Aubrey; Screenplay, Richard Matini, based on Michiko "Miki" Tsuwa-Gorman's autobiography; Director of Photography, Kimiaki Kimura; Music, David Campbell and Jun Sato.

CAST: Yoko Shimada (Michiko "Miki" Tsuwa-Gorman), Chris Mitchum (Mike Gorman), Andy Romero, Donald Moffat, Connie Sawyer.

A Shochiku Co., Ltd. Production in Japanese and English. Color. Panavision (?). 105 minutes. Released 1981.

U.S. VERSION: Released by Jaguar Distribution Corp. English subtitles. No MPAA rating (?). Released 1981 (?).

My Daughter and I / Musume to watashi ("My Daughter and I"). Producer, Ichiro Sato; Director, Hiromichi Horikawa; Screenplay, Sakae Hirosawa, based on the serial "Musume to watashi" by Bunroku Shishi, and published in *Shufu no tomo* (January 1953–May 1956).

CAST: Yuriko Hoshi (Mari), So Yamamura (Mari's father), Setsuko Hara (Mari's mother), Yoko Aonuma, Reiko Obashi (Mari as a child), Francoise Mollechand (French wife), Haruko Sugimura (aunt).

A Tokyo Eiga Co., Ltd. Production. A Toho Co., Ltd. Release. Black and white. Toho Scope (?). Running time undetermined. Released 1962.

U.S. VERSION: Released by Toho International Co., Ltd. English subtitles. Running time undetermined. No MPAA rating. Released February 1, 1963.

My Enemy, the Sea / Taiheiyo hitoribotchi ("Alone in the Pacific"). Producer, Akira Nakai; Associate Producer, Isao Zeniya; Director, Kon Ichikawa; Screenplay, Natto Wada, based on the log-book *Taiheiyo hitoribotchi* (1963) by Kenichi Horie; Director of Photography, Yoshihiro Yamazaki; Art Director, Takashi Matsuyama; Editor, Masanori Tsujii; Music, Yasushi Akutagawa and Toru Takemitsu; Sound Recording, Fumio Hashimoto; Production Manager, Isao Zeniya.

CAST: Yujiro Ishihara (Kenichi Horie, *the youth*), Masayuki Mori (his father), Kinuyo Tanaka (his mother), Ruriko Asaoka (his sister), Hajime Hana (his friend), Gannosuke Ashinoya (ship's carpenter), Shiro Osaka (shipyard master).

An Ishihara International Productions, Ltd. Production. A Nikkatsu Corp. Release. Filmed on location in San Francisco and Hawaii. Eastman Color. CinemaScope. 97 minutes. Released 1963.

U.S. VERSION: Exhibited at the San Francisco International Film Festival as *The Enemy, the Sea*, and at the New York Film Festival as *Alone in the Pacific*. Additional playdates unknown. 97 minutes. No MPAA rating. Released April 15, 1964.

My Friend Death / Yurei Hanjo-ki ("Flourishing Business Ghost Story"). Director, Kozo Saeki; Screenplay, Naoshi Izumo; Director of Photography, Hideo Ito; Music, H. Matsui; Sound, Toho Recording Centre; Sound Effects, Toho Sound Effects Group.

CAST: Frankie Sakai, Kyoko Kagawa, Ichiro Arishima, Kingaro Yanagiya.

A Toho Co., Ltd. Production. Western Electric Mirrophonic recording (encoded with Perspecta Stereophonic Sound?). Black and white (processed by Tokyo Laboratory Ltd.). Toho Scope. 95 minutes. Released July 26, 1960.

U.S. VERSION: Released by Toho International Co., Ltd. English subtitles. 95 minutes. No MPAA rating. Released 1961.

My Geisha. Producer, Steve Parker; Director, Jack Cardiff; Screenplay, Norman Krasna; Director of Photography, Shunichiro Nakao; 2nd Unit Photography, Stanley Sayer; Art Directors, Hal Pereira, Arthur Lonergan, and Makoto Kikuchi; Editor, Archie Marshek; Music, Franz Waxman (with selections from *Madama Butterfly* by Giacomo Puccini). Song: "You Are Sympathy to Me," by Hal David and Franz Waxman; Sound Recording, Harold

Lewis and Charles Grenzbach; Assistant Director, Harry Kratz; Production Manager, Harry Caplan; Costume Design, Edith Head; Makeup, Frank Westmore; Dialogue Director, George Tyne.

CAST: Shirley MacLaine (Lucy Dell/Yoko Mori), Yves Montand (Paul Robaix), Edward G. Robinson (Sam Lewis), Bob Cummings (Bob Moore), Yoko Tani (Kazumi Ito), Tatsuo Saito (Kenichi Takata), Alex Gerry (Leonard Lewis), Nobuo Chiba (Shig), Ichiro Hayakawa (Hisako Amatsu), George Furness (George, *the butler*), Marian Furness (Bob's girlfriend), Tamae Kiyokawa, Tsugundo Maki.

A Sachiko Productions Production, in association with Paramount Pictures. A Paramount Pictures Release. An American production in English and filmed in Japan. Eastman Color (prints by Technicolor). Technirama. 120 minutes. Released June 13, 1962.

My Hobo / Burari burabura monogatari

My Hobo / Burari burabura monogatari ("Wandering Story"). Executive Producer, Sanezumi Fujimoto and Hideyuki Shiino; Director/Screenplay, Zenzo Matsuyama; Director of Photography, Hiroshi Murai; Music, Hikaru Hayashi.

CAST: Keiju Kobayashi (Junpei), Hideko Takamine (Komako), Norihei Miki (Takeo), Reiko Dan (Mariko). A Tokyo Eiga Co., Ltd. Production. A Toho Co., Ltd. Release. Eastman Color. Toho Scope. 98 minutes. Released 1960.

U.S. VERSION: Released by Toho International Co., Ltd. English subtitles. 98 minutes. No MPAA rating. Released July 23, 1963.

My Love Has Been Burning / Waga koi wa moenu

My Love Has Been Burning / Waga koi wa moenu ("My Love Has Been Burning"). Producer, Hisao Itoya; Director, Kenji Mizoguchi; Screenplay, Yoshikata Yoda and Kaneto Shindo, loosely based on Hideko [Eiko] Kageyama's autobiography, *Warawa no hanshogai* ("My Half Life"); Director of Photography, Kohei Sugiyama; Art Director, Hiroshi Mizutani; Music, Senji Ito.

CAST: Kinuyo Tanaka (Hideko [Eiko] Hirayama), Ichiro Sugai (Kentaro Omoi), Mitsuko Mito (Chiyo), Eitaro Ozawa (Ryuzo Hayase), Kuniko Miyake (Toshiko Kishida), Koreya Senda (Prime Minister Inagaki), Eijiro Tono (State Councillor Ito), Sadako Sawamura (Masa), Zeya Chida.

A Shochiku Co., Ltd. Production. Filmed at Shochiku-Kyoto Studios. 84 minutes. Released February 13, 1949.

U.S. VERSION: Released by New Yorker Films. English subtitles. Alternate title: *My Love Burns*. 84 minutes. No MPAA rating. Released January 5, 1979.

My Neighbor Totoro / Tonari no Totoro

My Neighbor Totoro / Tonari no Totoro ("The Totoro Next Door") **[animated]**. Executive Producer, Yasuyoshi Tokuma; Producer, Toru Hara; Director/Story/Screenplay, Hayao Miyazaki; Production Planning Supervisors, Tatsumi Yamashita and Hideo Ogata; Production Designer, Yoshiharu Sato; Art Director, Kazuo Oga; Music, Jo Hisaishi; Songs: "Sanpo," Music, Jo Hisaishi; Lyrics, Reiko Nakagawa. "Tonari no Totoro," Music, Jo Hisaishi; Lyrics, Hayao Miyazaki. Original Art, Tsukasa Tannai, Masako Shinohara, Toshio Kawaguchi, Yoshinori Kanada, Makiko Futaki, Hideko Tagawa, Shinji Otsuka, Masaaki Endo, Katsuya Kondo, Hiromi Yamakawa; Background, Hajime Matsuoka, Kiyomi Ota, Yoji Takeshige, Toshiro Nozaki, Masaki Yoshizaki, Kiyoko Sugawara; Finishing, Michiyo Yasuda; Shooting, Hisao Shirai; Editor, Takeshi Seyama; Animation Checkers, Yasuko Tachiki, Hitomi Tateno; Color Design, Nobuko Mizuta; Finish Checker, Masae Motohashi; Recording Director, Shigeharu Shiba; Modulation, Shuji Inoue; Kazutoshi Sato; Production Manager, Eiko Tanaka; Production Coordinators, Hirokatsu Kihara and Toshiyuki Kawabata; Assistant Director, Tetsuya Endo; Original Art Cooperator, Mad House, Nobumasa Shinkawa, Masaaki Kudo and Yutaka Okamura; Finish Checkers, Teruyo Tateyama, Kenji Narita, and Miwako Nakamura; Special Effects, Kaoru Tanifuji; *Animation:* Masako Sakano, Kiyoko Makita, Kiyo Mizutani, Shinji Morohashi, Riwako Matsui, Yuka Endo, Akiko Teshima, Nagisa Miyazaki, Naoko Takenawa, Rie Niidome, Aki Yamagata, Keiko Watanabe, Komasa [no other name given], Ritsuko Tanaka, Ritsuko Shiina, Kumiko Otani, Keiichiro Hattori, Kazutka Ozaki, Emiko Iwayanagi, Yukari Maeda, Kazumi Okabe, Kyoko Higurashi, Kazuko Fukutomi; *Studio Fantasia*: Hajime Yoshida, Junichi Nagano, Masayuki Ota, Naoki Kitamura, Tsuyoshi Yamamoto; *Animation Totoro*: Yukari Yamaura, Koji Ito, Akiko Ishii, Tadateru Kawamura, Dragon Production. Checking, *Studio Killy*: Toshichika Iwakiri, Naomi Takahashi, Mayumi Watabe, Chiyomi Morisawa, Noriko Yamamura, Yuriko Kudo, Tokuko Harada, Fujino Komei, Toki Yanagi, Fumi Yamane, Michiko Ota, Yoko Fujino, Michiko Nishimaki, Nobuko Watanabe, Michiko Ode, Hisako Yoshida, Naoko Okawa, Yuki Takagi, Toyoko Kajita, Aiko Takahashi, Miyoko Oka, Hatsue Tanaka, Junko Adachi, Yoshiko Murata. *Studio Step*: Yuki Kyono, Hiromi Hanawa, Reiko Suzuki, Tomoko Asahi, Yorimi Sawauchi, Reiko Shibuya, Hiroe Takekura, Domesha, Studio Hibari, Group Joy, Studio Run Run, Studio Beam, Kyohei Production, Trans Arts Co. Background, *Kobayashi Production*: Shinji Kimura, Tsuyoshi Matsumoto, Sadahiko Tanaka, Makoto Shiraishi, Nobuhiko Otsuka. *Atelier BWCA*: Hidetoshi Kaneko, Keiko Tamura, Akira Yamakawa, Junko Ina, Yuko Matsuura. Shooting, *Studio Cosmos*: Yoichi Kuroda, Katsunori Maehara, Tetsuo Ofuji, Kazumi Iketani, Hiroshi Ito, Tomoko Sugiyama, Shinji Ikegami, Moto Ikegami, Noriko Suzuki, Kiyoshi Saeki, Hiroshi Noguchi, Mitsuko Nanba, Katsuji Suzuki; Production Coordinators, Hiroyuki Ito and Takaaki Suzuki; Assistant Editor, Hiroshi Adachi; Title, Takagu Atelier; Finish Technique Cooporate, Josai Duplo and Mamoru Murao; Cooperation, Animage Magazine Editorial Staff, Tokuma Shoten Publishing Co., Ltd.; Assistant Effect, Hironori Ono; Dialogue Editor, Akira Ida; Assistant Recording Director, Naoko Asari; Recording Staff, Makoto Sumiya, Koji Fukushima, Mutsuyoshi Otani; Recording Production Company, Omnibus Promotion, Inc.; Music Production, Mitsunori Miura, Takashi Watanabe, and Tokuma Japan Corp.; Recording Studio, Tokyo T.V. Center; Cooperation, Hakuhodo, Inc. *Tokuma Shoten Publishing Co., Ltd.* My Neighbor Totoro *Production Committee*: Hiroyuki Kato, Akira Kaneko, Masahiro Kasuya, Minoru Tadokoro, Tsutomu Otsuka, Takao Sasaki, Shigeru Aso, Yoshio Tsuboike, Toshio Suzuki, Osamu Kameyama, Hikogoro Shiraishi, Hisayoshi Odaka, Tomoko Kobayashi, Michio Yoko, Tetsuhiko Yoshida.

VOICE CHARACTERIZATIONS: (undetermined).

A Tokuma Shoten Publishing Co., Ltd./ Studio Ghibli Production. Dolby Stereo. Color (processed by Tokyo Laboratory, Ltd.). Spherical wide screen. 86 minutes. Released 1988.

U.S. VERSION: Released English-dubbed. Adapter, Carl Macek; ADR Dialogue Writer, Greg Snegoff; English Music Translation, Eugene H. Saburi and Kaiulani Kidani; English Lyrics, Severin Browne; English Music Coordinator, Yoshio Maki. 86 minutes. MPAA rating: "G." Released 1988. Voice Characterizations for U.S. version: Lisa Michaelson (Satsuki), Cheryl Chase (Mei), Greg Snegoff (Dad), Kenneth Hartman (Kanta), Alexandra Kenworthy (Mother), Natalie Core (nanny), Steve Kramer (farmer), Lara Cody (farm girl), Melenie McQueen (Kanta's mom).

My Son! My Son! / Shodo Satsujin—Musuko yo ("Impulsive Murder—My Son"). Producers, Toshihiro Iijima and Shigemi Sugizaki; Director, Keisuke Kinoshita; Screenplay, Keisuke Kinoshita, based on an original story by Hidero Sato; Director of Photography, Kozo Okazaki; Art Director, Shigemori Shigeta; Music, Chuji Kinoshita.

CAST: Tomisaburo Wakayama, Hideko Takamine, Ken Tanaka.

A Shochiku Co., Ltd./Tokyo Broadcasting System Co., Ltd. Production. Color. Panavision (?). 130 minutes. Released 1979.

U.S. VERSION: Release undetermined, possibly by Shochiku Films of America, Inc. in subtitled format. No MPAA rating.

My Sons / Musuko ("My Sons"). Producer, Nobuyoshi Otani; Director,

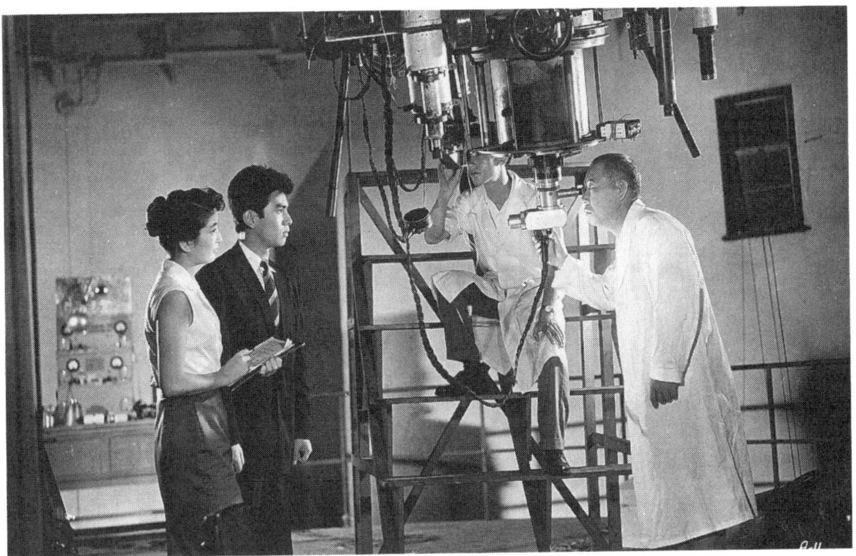

Momoko Kochi, Kenji Sahara and Takashi Shimura (far right) in Ishiro Honda's lively *The Mysterians* (1957).

Yoji Yamada; Screenplay, Yoshitaka Asama and Yoji Yamada, based on the book by Makoto Shiina; Director of Photography, Tetsuo Takaba; Editor, Iwao Ishii; Music, Teizo Matsumura.

CAST: Rentaro Mikuni (Akio), Masatoshi Nagase, Emi Wakui, Kunie Tanaka.

A Shochiku Co., Ltd. Production. Color. Panavision (?). 121 minutes. Released 1991.

U.S. VERSION: Released by Shochiku Films of America, Inc. English subtitles. 121 minutes. No MPAA rating. Released June 19, 1992.

My Way / Waga michi ("My Way"). Director/Screenplay, Kaneto Shindo; Director of Photography, Kiyomi Kuroda; Music, Hikaru Hayashi.

CAST: Nobuko Otowa, Taiji Tonoyama, Mutsuhiro Toura.

A Kindai Eiga Kyokai Co., Ltd. Production. Color. Panavision (?). 130 minutes. Released 1974.

U.S. VERSION: Distributor, if any, is undetermined.

The Mysterians / Chikyu Boeigun ("Earth Defense Force"). Producer, Tomoyuki Tanaka; Director, Ishiro Honda; Screenplay, Takeshi Kimura, based on an adaptation by Shigeru Kayama, from the original story by Jojiro Okami; Director of Photography, Hajime Koizumi; Lighting, Kuichiro Kishida; Art Director, Teruaki Abe; Editor, Hiroichi Iwashita; Music, Akira Ifukube; Sound Recording, Masanobu Miyazaki; Sound, Toho Dubbing Theatre; Sound Effects, Ichiro Minawa, Toho Sound Effects Group; Production Manager, Yasuaki Sakamoto; Assistant Director, Koji Kajita. *Toho Special Effects Group*: Director, Eiji Tsuburaya; Photography, Teisho Arikawa; Art Direction, Akira Watanabe; Optical Photography, Hidesaburo Araki; Matte Process, Hiroshi Mukoyama; Light Effects, Masao Shirota.

CAST: Kenji Sahara (Joji Atsumi), Yumi Shirakawa (Etsuko Shiraishi), Momoko Kochi (Hiroko), Akihiko Hirata (Ryoichi Shiraishi), Takashi Shimura (Dr. Adachi), Susumu Fujita (Commander Morita), Hisaya Ito (Captain Seki), Yoshio Kosugi (Commander Sugimoto), Fuyuki Murakami (Dr. Kawanami), Minnosuke Yamada (General Hamamoto), Yoshio Tsuchiya (leader of the Mysterians),

A flying saucer returns to its loudspeaker-like base in Daiei's *The Mysterious Satellite* (1956). Photo courtesy Ted Okuda.

Haruo Nakajima (Mogera, *the Mysterians' robot*), Harold S. Conway, George Furness (Western representatives), Tetsu Nakamura (scientist), Haruya Kato, Senkichi Omura (would-be firefighters), Heihachiro "Henry" Okawa, Takeo Okawa, Yutaka Sada, Hideo Mihara, Rikie Sanuo, Soji Oikata, Mitsuo Tsuda, Ken Imaizumi, Shin Otomo, Jiro Kumagi, Akio Kusuma, Shoichi Hirose, Tadao Nakamaru, Kaneyuki Tsubono, Rinsaku Ogata, Katsumi Tezuka.

A Toho Co., Ltd. Production. Western Electric Mirrophonic recording (encoded with Perspecta Stereophonic Sound). Eastman Color (processed by Toyo Development, possibly Tokyo Laboratory Ltd.). Toho Scope. 89 minutes. Released December 28, 1957.

U.S. Version: Released by Metro-Goldwyn-Mayer Pictures. English-dubbed. An RKO Radio Pictures, Inc. Presentation. A Loew's Inc. Release. English Language Supervisor, Jay Bonafield; English Dialog, Peter Riethof, Carlos Montalban; Prints by Metrocolor, or possibly Technicolor; Perspecta Stereophonic Sound. Originally purchased by RKO, who sold the picture to Loew's Inc. Wide screen process billed as Wide Screen and CinemaScope in the United States. Double-billed with *Watusi* (M-G-M, 1959). Reissued in Japan in 1978. 87 minutes. No MPAA rating. Released May 15, 1959.

The Mysterious Satellite / Uchujin Tokyo ni arawaru ("Spaceman Appears in Tokyo"). Producer, Masaichi Nagata; Director, Koji Shima; Screenplay, Hideo Oguni, based on the novel by Gentaro Nakajima; Director of Photography, Kimio Watanabe; Art Director, Shigeo Muno; Color Design, Taro Okamoto; Editor, Toyo Suzuki; Special Effects Director, Noriaki Yuasa; Sound Recording Supervisor, Masao Osumi; Music, Gentaro Nakajima; Special

Effects, Daiei Special Effects Department; Sound, Daiei Recording Studio.

CAST: Toyomi Karita (Hikari Aozora, Space-Man Ginko), Keizo Kawasaki (Toru), Isao Yamagata (Dr. Matsuda), Buntaro Miake (Dr. Komura), Shozo Nanbu (Dr. Isobe), Mieko Nagai (Taeko Komura), Kyoko Hirai (Mrs. Matusuda), Bin Yagasawa (No. 2 Pairan).

A Daiei Motion Picture Co., Ltd. Production. A Masaichi Nagata Presentation. DaieiScope. Eastman Color (processed by Daiei Laboratory). Western Electric Mirrophonic Recording. 87 minutes. Released January 29, 1956.

U.S. VERSION: Released in the United States by Daiei International Films, Inc. (?). Released to U.S. television as *Warning from Space* by American International Television. English-dubbed. Produced at Titra Sound Studios by Jay H. Cipes and Edward Palmer; Prints by Pathé. Released internationally as *Unknown Satellite Over Tokyo* by Daiei International in December 1956. Alternate titles: *The Cosmic Man Appears in Tokyo* and *Space Men [Spacemen] Appear Over [in] Tokyo*. Top-billed Karita portrays a female alien, though character's name is given as above. 81 minutes. No MPAA rating. Released 1960 (?).

The Naked General / Hadaka no taisho ("The Naked Champ"). Director, Hiromichi Horikawa; Screenplay, Yoko Mizuki, based on the life of Kiyoshi Yamashita; Director of Photography, Asakazu Nakai; Art Director, Yasuhide Kato; Music, Toshiro Mayuzumi.

CAST: Keiju Kobayashi (Kiyoshi Yamashita), Aiko Mimasu (his mother), Yasuko Nakada (girl in lunch shop), Daisuke Kato (master of eating house), Kyoko Aoyama (girl in eating house), Eijiro Tono (commander), Reiko Dan (bus conductor).

A Toho Co., Ltd. Production. Agfa-Color. Toho Scope. 92 minutes. Released October 28, 1958.

U.S. VERSION: Released by Toho International Co., Ltd. English subtitles. 92 minutes. No MPAA rating. Released December 15, 1964.

Naked Pursuit [production credits and Japanese title unavailable].

CAST: Masayoshi Nogami (student), Mari Oaki (girl), Ranko Mizukami (mother), Kyuzo Fuyuki.

Production company undetermined. Black and white with color sequence(s). Academy ratio (?). 73 minutes (?). Release date undetermined.

U.S. VERSION: Released by Boxoffice International Film Distributors. English subtitles (?). 73 minutes. No MPAA rating. Released November 1969.

Naked Youth / Seishun zankoku monogatari ("Cruel Story of Youth"). Producer, Tomio Ikeda; Director/Screenplay, Nagisa Oshima; Director of Photography, Takashi Kawatama; Art Director, Koji Uno; Music, Riichiro Manabe; Editor, Keiichi Uraoka.

CAST: Yusuke Kawazu (Kiyoshi Fujii), Miyuki Kuwano (Makoto Shinjo, *his girlfriend*), Yoshiko Kuga (Yuki Shinjii, *her sister*), Jun Hamamura (Masahiro Shingo, *their father*), Fumio Watanabe (Akimoto, *the doctor*), Kei Sato (Akira Matsuki, *the gangster*), Kan Nihonyanagi (Keizo Horio), Toshiko Kobayashi (Teruko Shimonishi, *the teacher*), Shinji Tanaka (Ito), Shinjiro Matsuzaki (Terada), Shinko Ujiie (Masae Sakaguchi), Aki Morishima (Yoko Ishikawa), Yuki Tominaga (Toshiko Nishioka), Asao Sano (the inspector).

A Shochiku Co., Ltd. Production. Eastman Color. Shochiku GrandScope. 96 minutes. Released 1960.

U.S. VERSION: Released by Shochiku Films of America, Inc. English subtitles. 96 minutes. No MPAA rating. Released July 1961. Released 1961 on West Coast only. Alternate titles: *Cruel Story of Youth* and *Story of Cruelty*. Reissued by New Yorker Films in 1984.

Namakubi jochi jiken ("Love Foolery Case for a Severed Head"). Director, Kinya Igawa.

CAST: Hachiro Tsuruoka (Goro Fujiyama), Kazue Hinotori (Reiko Fujiyama), Junko Kozuki (Junko Arishima), Yoshi Izumida (Dr. Mita), Yuri Izumi (Nurse Machiko).

An Okura Eiga Production. Black and

white. Academy ratio. Running time undetermined. Released 1967.

U.S. VERSION: Distributor, if any, is undetermined. International title: *Love Foolery Case for a Severed Head.*

Nanami: Inferno of First Love / Hatsukoi jigokuhen ("First Love: Hell Chapter"). Producer, Satoshi Fuji; Director, Susumu Hani; Screenplay, Susumu Hani and Shuji Terayama; Director of Photography, Yuji Okumura; Music, Akio Yashiro and Toru Takemitsu; Sound Recording, Yukio Kubota; Production Manager, Yoshimoto Tsutsumi.

CAST: Akio Takahashi (Shun), Kuniko Ishii (Nanami), Koji Mitsui (Otagaki, *Shun's stepfather*), Kazuko Fukuda (Mrs. Otagaki, *Shun's stepmother*), Haruo Asano (Algebra), Minoru Yuasa (Ankokuji, *the bearded man*), Ichiro Kimura (psychiatrist), Shinatora [no other name given] (gang leader).

A Hani Productions/Japan Art Theatre Guild Production. Black and white. Academy ratio (?). 108 minutes. Released 1968.

U.S. VERSION: Released by Golden Eagle Films, Inc., and RAF Industries. English subtitles. A color film according to one source. 87 minutes. MPAA rating: "X." Released June 11, 1969.

Nanmin Road / Nanmin Rodo ("Refugees Road"). Producer, Hisao Masuda; Director, Sho Igarashi; Screenplay, Yoichi Kitahara and Sho Igarashi, based on an original story by Yasuo Uchiyama; Director of Photography, Yoichi Shida; Music, Tamiya Terashima.

CAST: Le Manh Hung, Yu Hoang Pung, Trung Thi Thuy Trang.

A Premier International, Corp. Production. Color. Spherical wide screen (?). 101 minutes. Released 1992 (?).

U.S. VERSION: Distributor, if any, is undetermined.

Necromancy / Kaibyo Yonaki numa ("Ghost-Cat of Night Weeping Swamp"). Executive Producer, Masaichi Nagata; Director, Katsuhiko Tasaka; Screenplay, Toshio Tamikado; Director of Photography, Senkichiro Takada; Sound, Daiei Recording Studio.

CAST: Shintaro Katsu, Toshio Chiba, Toshio Hosokawa, Tokiko Mita, Michiko Ai.

A Daiei Motion Picture Co., Ltd. Production. A Masaichi Nagata Presentation. Western Electric Mirrophonic recording. Black and white (processed by Daiei Laboratory). Academy ratio. 89 minutes. Released 1957.

U.S. VERSION: Distributor undetermined. International title: *Ghost-Cat of Yonaki Swamp.*

Neo-Tokyo / Silent Mobius **[animation compilation]**. *Neo-Tokyo*: Executive Producer, Haruki Kadokawa. (*Labyrinth*) Director, Rin Taro; Screenplay, Rin Taro, based on the novel by Taku Mayumura; Character Design, Atsuko Fukushima; Art Director, Yamako Ishikawa. (*Running Man*) Director/Screenplay, Yoshiaki Kawajiri; Art Director, Katsushi Aoki; Backgrounds, Yuji Ikehata. (*The Order to Stop Construction*) Director/Screenplay, Katsuhiro Otomo; Art Director, Takamuro Mukuo. *Silent Mobius*: Producer, Haruki Kadokawa; Director/Character Design, Michitaka Kikuchi; Screenplay, Kei Shigema and Michitaka Kikuchi, based on the comics of Kia Asamiya; Music, Kaoru Wada; Art Director, Norihiko Hiraki.

VOICE CHARACTERIZATIONS: (undetermined).

Note: These are two featurettes, re-edited to feature length for U.S. release. *Neo-Tokyo* released 1986. *Silent Mobius* released 1991.

U.S. VERSION: Released by Streamline Pictures. English-dubbed. 103 minutes. No MPAA rating. Released April 24, 1993. Voice Characterizations for U.S. version: Robert Axelrod (Sugioka), Jeff Winkless (Robot 444-1/Lucifer Hawke), Michael McConnohie (reporter Bob Stone), Cheryl Chase (Sachi), Tom Wyner (Boss), Iona Morris (Katsumi), Alexandra Kenworthy (Miyuka), Joyce Kurtz (Kiddy), Wendy Lee (Nami), Malora Harte (Rally), Barbara Goodson (Lebia), Julie Donald (Yuki).

The New Earth / Atarashiki tsuchi ("The New Earth"). Producer/Director/Screenplay, Dr. Arnold Fanck;

Director of Photography, Richard Angst; Art Director, Kenkichi Yoshida; Music performed by the New Symphony Orchestra, conducted by Koscak Yamada.

CAST: Sessue Hayakawa (Iwao Yamato), Isamu Kosugi (Teruo Yamato), Setsuko Hara (Mitsuko Yamato), Yuriko Hanabusa (her maid), Ruth Eweller (Gelda), Eiji Takagi (Kosaku Kanda), Haruyo Ichikawa (Hideko Kanda).

An Arnold Fanck Production, in association with Towa Shoji Co., Ltd., the J.O. Studio, and Nikkatsu Corp. A Towa Shuji Release. A German/Japanese co-production in Japanese. Running time undetermined. Released February 1937.

U.S. VERSION: Apparently never released in the United States.

The New Japanese Cinema

[short film compilation]. Features the following award-winning short subjects originally exhibited at the 1968 Sogetsu Experimental Film Festival: *White City* (dir, Tatsuo Shimamura), *Folk Mythology* (dir, Fumio Ohi), *One, Two, Three, Four-shi-Death* (dir, Masataka Nakano), *Doctrine of Creation* (dir, Michio Okabe), *Won't You Have Some Milk?* (dir, Shoji Hosokawa), *Trap* (dir, Sanpei Kasu), and *Man Possessed of His Own Shadow* (dir, Teruo Okumura). Released by Film-Makers' Distribution Center. 16mm. Color and black and white. Running time undetermined. No MPAA rating. Released May 2, 1968.

New Tales of the Taira Clan / Shin Heike monogatari

("New Tales of the Taira Clan"). Producer, Masaichi Nagata; Planning, Matsutaro Kawaguchi and Hideo Matsuyama; Director, Kenji Mizoguchi; Screenplay, Yoshikata Yoda, Masashige Narusawa, and Hisakazu Tsuji, based on the novel by Eiji Yoshikawa, and the historical tale; Director of Photography, Kazuo Miyagawa; Color Consultant, Mitsuzo Wada; Art Director, Hiroshi Mizutani; Music, Fumio Hayasaka and Masaru Sato.

CAST: Raizo Ichikawa (Taira no Kiyomori), Yoshiko Kuga (Tokiko), Narutoshi Hayashi (Tokitada), Michiyo Kogure (Yasuko), Ichijiro Oya (Taira no Tadamori), Eitaro Shindo (Banboku), Ichiro Sugai (carpenter), Zeya Chida (Yorinaga), Eijiro Yanagi (Emperor Shirakawa), Tatsuya Ishiguro (Fujiwara no Tokinobu), Mitsusaburo Ramon (Ryokan), Kunitaro Sawamura (Joku), Akitake Kono (Heiroku), Shunji Natsume (Emperor Toba), Tamako Nakamura (Shigeko).

A Daiei Motion Picture Co., Ltd. Production. Filmed at Daiei-Kyoto Studios. Eastman Color. Academy ratio. 108 minutes. Released September 21, 1955.

U.S. VERSION: Released by Daiei International Films. English subtitles. Alternate title: *The Taira Clan*. Followed by *Yoshinaka's Three Women* and *The Dancer and the Warrior* (both 1956). 108 minutes. No MPAA rating. Released September 1964. Reissued by New Line Cinema in 1971.

Nichiren / Nichiren

("Nichiren"). Producer, Masaichi Nagata; Director, Noboru Nakamura; Screenplay, Noboru Nakamura, based on the novel by Matsutaro Kawaguchi; Director of Photography, Hiroshi Takemura; Music, Yasushi Akutagawa.

CAST: Kinnosuke Yorozuya (Nichiren), Keiko Matsuzaka (his sister), Takahiro Tamura, Kyoko Kishida, Sinjiro Ehara, Somegoro Ichikawa, Hiroaki Matsuhata, Katsuo Nakamura, Mitsuteru Nakamura, Toshiyuki Nagashima.

A Nagata Productions Production. A Shochiku Co., Ltd. Release. Color. Shochiku GrandScope (?). 143 minutes. Released 1979.

U.S. VERSION: Released by Shochiku Films of America, Inc. English subtitles. 140 minutes. No MPAA rating. Released November 1979.

Night Drum / Yoru no tsuzumi

("Night Drum"). Director, Tadashi Imai; Screenplay, Shinobu Hashimoto and Kaneto Shindo, based on a Bunraku play by Monzaemon Chikamatsu; Director of Photography, Shunichiro Nakao; Editor, Akikazu Kono; Music, Akira Ifukube.

CAST: Rentaro Mikuni (Hikokuro), Ineko Arima (Otane, *his wife*), Masayuki Mori (Miyaji, *the drum teacher*), Mannosuke Nakamura.

A Shochiku Co., Ltd. Production. Black and white. Shochiku GrandScope (?). 95 minutes. Released 1958.

U.S. Version: Distributor undetermined. English subtitles. Alternate titles: *The Adultress* and *The Adulterous Wife*. 95 minutes. No MPAA rating. Released to public television in 1974.

Night in Bangkok / Bankokku no yoru ("Night in Bangkok"). Producer, Sanezumi Fujimoto; Director, Yasuki Chiba; Screenplay, Ryozo Kasahara; Director of Photography, Taiichi Kankura; Music, Naozumi Yamamoto.

Cast: Chang Mei Yao (Meilan), Yuzo Kayama (Shuichi), Yuriko Hoshi (Masayo), Praprapon Pureem, Takashi Shimura.

A Toho Co., Ltd./Taiwan Films Studios/The Cathay Organization Production. A Toho Co., Ltd. Release. A Japanese/Taiwanese/Hong Kong co-production. Filmed in Kyoto, Nara, Tokyo (Japan), and Taipei, Bangkok (Taiwan). Eastman Color. Toho Scope. 105 minutes. Released 1966.

U.S. Version: Released by Toho International Co., Ltd. English subtitles. 105 minutes. No MPAA rating. Released June 17, 1966.

A Night in Hong Kong / Honkon no yoru ("Night in Hong Kong"). Executive Producers, Sanezumi Fujimoto and Robert Chung; Director, Yasuki Chiba; Screenplay, Toshiro Ide; Director of Photography, Rokuro Nishigaki; Music, Hachiro Matsui.

Cast: Akira Takarada (Hiroshi Tanaka), Yu Ming (Wu Li Hung), Yoko Tsukasa (Keiko Kimura), Mitsuko Kusabue, Ken Uehara, Daisuke Kato, Yu Fujiki, Won Inn, Ma Ree, Kang Pak King, Tetsu Nakamura, Hiroshi Koizumi, Michiyo Kogure, Mie Hama.

A Toho Co., Ltd./The Cathay Organization Production. A Toho Co., Ltd. Release. A Japanese/Hong Kong co-production. Eastman Color. Toho Scope. 119 minutes. Released July 8, 1961.

U.S. Version: Released by Toho International Co., Ltd. English subtitles. 119 minutes. No MPAA rating. Released December 22, 1961.

The Night of the Seagull / Suna no kaori ("Smell of the Sand"). Executive Producer, Yorihiko Yamada; Director, Katsumi Iwauchi; Screenplay, Mitsura Majima and Katsumi Iwauchi, based on the novel *Mermaid* by Matsutaro Kawaguchi; Director of Photography, Choichi Nakai; Music, Chumei Watanabe.

Cast: Mie Hama (woman), Jin Nakayama (young man), Megumi Matsumoto, Jitsuko Yoshimura, Natsuko Kahara.

A Toho Co., Ltd. Production. Eastman Color. Toho Scope (?). 90 minutes. Released October 1968.

U.S. Version: Released by Toho International Co., Ltd. English subtitles. 90 minutes. No MPAA rating. Released February 11, 1970.

Night on the Galactic Railroad / Ginga Tetsudo no yoru ("Night on the Galaxy Railway") **[animated]**. Producers, Masato Hara and Atsumi Tashiro; Director, Gizaburo Sugii; Screenplay, Minoru Betsuyaku, based on an original story by Kenji Miyazawa; Director of Photography, Yasuo Maeda; Music, Haruomi Hosono.

Voice Characterizations: (undetermined).

An Asahi Publishing Co., Ltd./Asahi National Broadcasting Co., Ltd. Production. Color. Spherical wide screen (?). 107 minutes. Released 1985.

U.S. Version: Released by Herald Ace. English-dubbed. No MPAA rating. 107 minutes. Released February 7, 1986.

Nightshade Flower / Ieraishan ("Nightshade Flower"). Producer, Toshio Mochizuki; Director, Kon Ichikawa; Screenplay, Takeo Matsuura and Kon Ichikawa; Director of Photography, Minoru Yokoyama; Art Director, Masatoshi Kato; Music, Ryoichi Hattori.

Cast: Ken Uehara (Saburo Seki), Asami Hisaji (Akiko Yabuki), Harue Tone (Gin), Shoroku Kawakita (Toshio Odagiri), Ryokichi Kawamura (Renkichi Kameyama), Chieko Tsukioka (Chiyo, *Seki's younger sister*).

A Shoei/Shintoho Co., Ltd. Production. Black and white. Academy ratio. 86 minutes. Released January 13, 1951.

U.S. Version: Distributor, if any, is undetermined.

Ninja Wars. Executive Producer, Haruki Kadokawa; Producers, Masao Sato, Izumi Toyoshima; Director, Mitsumasa Saito; Screenplay, Ei Ogawa, based on the novel by Hutaro Yamada, as published by Kadokawa Publishing Co., Ltd.; Director of Photography, Fujiro Morita; Art Directors, Norimichi Ikawa and Kazuyoshi Sonoda; Lighting, Yoshiaki Masuda; Editor, Isamu Ichida; Sound Recording, Fumio Hashimoto; Music, Toshiaki Yokota; Action Coordinator, Shinichi "Sonny" Chiba; Assistant Director, Isao Yoshihara; Continuity, Yukiko Morimura; Wardrobe Adviser, Junko Koshino; Choreographer, Toshio Sugawara; Special Effects Director, Hideo Suzuki.

CAST: Hiroyuki "Henry" Sanada, Noriko Watanabe, Jun Miko, Miho Kazamatsuri, Kongo Kobayashi, Ganjiro Sato, Noboru Matsuhashi, Akira Hamada, Seizo Fukomoto, Nodoka Kawai, Sanji Kojima, Hiroshi Tanaka, Shunji Sasamoto, Rentaro Mine, Yoshiji Nakahashi, Mieko Hoshino, Reiko Tamano, Yasunori Hikita, Yukio Miyagi, Kazuyuki Kosuga, Gentaro Mori.

A Haruki Kadokawa Films, Inc./Toei Co., Ltd. Production. Toeicolor. Panavision. 93 minutes. Released 1982.

U.S. VERSION: Released by American National Enterprises, Inc. A sequel (?) to *Samurai Reincarnation* (1981). Sequel: *Satomi Hakkenda* (1983) 93 minutes. MPAA rating: "R." Released 1984.

Nizaemon Kataoka: Kabuki Actor / Kabuki-yakushya: Kataoka Nizaemon ("Kabuki Actor: Nizaemon Kataoka") [**documentary**]. Producer, Mitsuru Kudo; Director, Sumiko Haneda; Director of Photography, Kiyoshi Nishio.

WITH: Nizaemon Kataoka.

A Jiyu Kobo Co., Ltd. Production. 16mm (?). Color. 488 minutes. Released 1991 (?).

U.S. VERSION: Distributor, if any, is undetermined.

No Greater Love Than This / Koto no taiyo ("Sun of the Old Capitol"). Director, Kenji Yoshida; Screenplay, Shigeki Chiba; Story, Keiichi Ito; Director of Photography, Kenji Hagiwara; Art Director, Motozo Kawahara; Music, Riichiro Manabe.

CAST: Fumie Kashiyama (Hatsuko Araki), Homare Suguro (Dr. Takaoka), Izumi Ashikawa, Junichi Uno, Gin Maeda, Terumi Niki, Jun Hamamura.

A Nikkatsu Corporation Production. Fuji Color. NikkatsuScope. 106 minutes. Released 1968.

U.S. VERSION: Released by Toho International Co., Ltd. English subtitles. 106 minutes. No MPAA rating. Released November 1969.

No Regrets for Our Youth / Waga seishun ni kuinashi ("No Regrets for Our Youth"). Producer, Keiji Matsuzaki; Director/Editor, Akira Kurosawa; Screenplay, Eijiro Hisaita and Akira Kurosawa; Director of Photography, Asakazu Nakai; Lighting, Chochiro Ishii; Art Director, Keiji Kitagawa; Music, Tadashi Hattori; Sound Recording, Isamu Suzuki; Sound, Toho Dubbing Theatre; Sound Effects, Toho Sound Effects Group.

CAST: Denjiro Okochi (Professor Yagihara), Eiko Miyoshi (Madame Yagihara, *his wife*), Setsuko Hara (Yukie Yagihara, *his daughter*), Susumu Fujita (Ryukichi Noge), Kokuten Kodo (Mr. Noge, *his father*), Haruko Sugimura (Madame Noge, *his mother*), Akitake Kono (Itokawa), Takashi Shimura (Police Commisioner Dokuichigo), Masao Shimizu (Hakozaki), Haruo Tanaka, Ichiro Chiba, Isamu Yonekura, Noboru Takagi, and Hiroshi Sano (students).

A Toho Co., Ltd. Production. Black and white. Academy ratio. Filmed at Toho Studios, Ltd. (Tokyo). 110 minutes. Released October 29, 1946.

U.S. VERSION: Released by Corinth Films. English subtitles. Alternate title: *No Regrets for My Youth*. 110 minutes. No MPAA rating. Released June 1980.

Nobody's Boy / Chibikko Remi to Meiken Kapi ("Small Remi and Smart Dog Kapi") [**animated**]. Director, Yugo Serikawa; Screenplay, Masaharu Segawa, based on an original story by

Hector H. Malot; Chief Animator, Akira Daikubara; Art Director, Tomo Fukumoto; Music, Chuji Kinoshita.

VOICE CHARACTERIZATIONS: (undetermined).

A Toei Animation Studio (Tokyo) Production. 3-D Eastman Color. ToeiScope. 81 minutes. Released March 17, 1970.

U.S. VERSION: Undetermined. English subtitled version available. 81 minutes. No MPAA rating.

Nogumi Pass / Nogumi toge ("Nogumi Pass"). Producers, Takero Ito and Tokuko Miyako; Director, Satsuo Yamamoto; Screenplay, Yoshi Hattori, based on an original story by Shigemi Yamamoto; Director of Photography, Setsuo Kobayashi; Art Director, Shigeo Kanno; Music, Masaru Sato.

CAST: Shinobu Otake, Mieko Harada, Chikako Yuri, Yuko Kotegawa, Takeo Jii, Ko Nishimura, Rentaro Mikuni.

A Shinnihon Eiga Production. Color. Spherical wide screen (?). 154 minutes. Released 1979.

U.S. VERSION: Distributor, if any, is undetermined. English subtitles. 154 minutes. No MPAA rating. Released December 28, 1979.

The Noh Mask Murders / Tenkawa densetsu satsujin jiken ("Tenkawa Legend Murders"). Producer, Haruki Kadokawa; Director, Kon Ichikawa; Screenplay, Kuri Shichi, Shiya Hidaka, and Shinichi Kabuki, based on the novel by Yasuo Uchida; Director of Photography, Yukio Isohata; Editor, Chizuko Osada; Music, Fumio Miyashita and Kensaku Tanigawa.

CAST: Takaaki Enoki, Keiko Kishi, Naomi Zaizen, Takeshi Kusaka.

A Kadokawa Shoten Co., Ltd. Production. Anamorphic wide screen (?). 110 minutes. Released 1991.

U.S. VERSION: Released by Toei Co., Ltd. English subtitles. 110 minutes. No MPAA rating. Released July 2, 1992.

None But the Brave / Yusha nomi ("None But the Brave"). Executive Producer, Howard W. Koch; Producer/Director, Frank Sinatra; Screenplay, John Twist and Katsuya Susaki; Story, Kikumaru Okuda; Associate Producer/Supervising Director of Photography, William H. Daniels; Director of Photography, Harold Lipstein; Music, Johnny [John] Williams; Music Supervisor and Conductor, Morris W. Stoloff; Japanese Music Consultant, Kenjiro Hirose; Art Director, Leroy Deane; Editor, Sam O'Steen; Assistant Director, David Salven; Set Decorator, George James Hopkins; Dialog Coach, Thom Conroy; Makeup Supervisor, Gordon Bau; Supervising Hair Stylist, Jean Burt Riley; Sound Supervisor, George R. Groves; Sound Recording, Stanley Jones; Aid and Cooperation, U.S. Department of Defense, U.S. Marine Corps, U.S. Navy, and the Hawaiian National Guard. *For Tokyo Eiga Co., Ltd.*: Producer, Kikumaru Okuda; Technical Adviser, Kazuo Inoue; Assistant Director, Mitsushige Tsurushima; Art Adviser, Haruyoshi Oshita; Dialog Coach, Tetsu Nakamura; Makeup, Shy Uemura; Interpreter, Masao Mera. *Toho Special Effects Group*: Director, Eiji Tsuburaya; Photography, Teisho Arikawa and Mototaka Tomioka; Art Director, Akira Watanabe; Assistant Director, Teruyoshi Nakano; Lighting, Kuichiro Kishida; Optical Effects, Hiroshi Mukoyama; Scene Manipulation, Fumio Nakadai.

CAST: Frank Sinatra (Chief Pharmacist's Mate Francis Maloney), Clint Walker (Capt. Dennis Bourke), Tommy Sands (2nd Lt. Blair), Brad Dexter (Sgt. Bleeker), Tony Bill (Air Crewman Keller), Tatsuya Mihashi (Lt. Kuroki), Takeshi Kato (Sgt. Tamura), Sammy Jackson (Cpl. Craddock), Homare Suguro (Lance Cpl. Hirano), Richard "Dick" Bakalyan (Cpl. Ruffino), Kenji Sahara (Cpl. Fujimoto), Rafer Johnson (Pvt. Johnson), Masahiko Tanimura (Lead Pvt. Ando), Jimmy Griffith (Pvt. J.D. Dexter), Hisao Dazai (Pvt. Tokumaru), Christopher Dark (Pvt. C.D. Searcy), Susumu Kurobe (Pvt. Goro), Don Dorrell (Pvt. Hoxey), Toru Ibuki (Pvt. Arikawa), Phil Crosby (Pvt. Magee), Takashi Inagaki (Pvt. Ishii), Ryuzo Shunputei (Pvt. Okuda), Kenichi Hata (Pvt. Sato), John Howard Long (Pvt. Waller), Roger Ewing (Pvt. Swensholm), Richard Sinatra (Pvt. Roth), Lorraine Stephens (Lori).

Brad Dexter, Clint Walker, Frank Sinatra, Tommy Sands, Hisao Dazai, Tatsuya Mihashi, Takeshi Kato, Kenji Sahara, and Susumu Kurobe in *None But the Brave* (1965).

A Tokyo Eiga Co., Ltd./Toho Co., Ltd./Artanis Productions, Inc. Production. A Toho Co., Ltd. Release. A Japanese/U.S. co-production in English and Japanese. Filmed at Toho Studios, Ltd. (Tokyo), and on location in Kauai (Hawaii), Japan, and completed at Warner Bros. Studios (Burbank). Eastman Color. Panavision. Western Electric Mirrophonic Recording (?) (possibly encoded with Perspecta Stereophonic Sound). 105 minutes (?). Released 1965.

U.S. VERSION: Released by Warner Bros. Pictures, Inc. Daniels' DP credit is unconfirmed. Artanis is Sinatra spelled backwards. RCA Photophone Recording. 105 minutes. No MPAA rating. Released February 1965.

Nowhere Man / Muno no hito

("Foolish Person"). Executive Producers, Toshiaki Nakazaw and Masaki Sekine; Producers, Kazuyoshi Okuyama, Shozo Ichiyama and Hirotsuyo Yoshida; Director, Naoto Takenaka; Screenplay, Toshiharu Maruchi, based on the comic strip "Muno no hito" by Yoshiharu Tsuge; Production Manager, Noriyuki Takahashi; Assistant Director, Yasu Matsumoto; Production Designer, Iwao Saito; Director of Photography, Yasushi Sasakibara; Editor, Yoshiyuki Okuhara; Music, Gontiti; Sound, Mineharu Kitamura.

CAST: Naoto Takenaka (Sukezo Sukegawa), Jun Fubuki (Momoko Sukegawa), Kotaro Santo (Sansuke Sukegawa).

A KSS/Shochiku Co., Ltd./Daiichi Kogyo Co., Ltd. Production. A Shochiku Co., Ltd. Release. Fujicolor. Spherical wide screen 107 minutes. Released 1991.

U.S. VERSION: Distributor, if any, is undetermined.

Nurses and Doctors / Fukkatsu no Asa ("Morning of Revival"). Producers, Toshio Kanda and Yoshitaro Nomura; Director, Tsuyoshi Yoshida; Screenplay, Motomu Furuta, based on an original story by Haru Egawa; Director of Photography, Takashi Kawamata; Music, Teizo Matsumura.

CAST: Shinobu Otake, Emi Wakui, Tsunehiko Watase.

A Production F. Co., Ltd. Production. Color. Spherical wide screen (?). 110 minutes. Released 1992.

U.S. VERSION: Distributor, if any, is undetermined.

A Nurse's Husband Fights On / Kangofu no Oyaji Ganbaru ("A Nurse's Husband Fights On"). Producers, Setsuo Noto and Manabu Akashi; Director, Seijiro Koyama; Screenplay, Isao Seki, based on an original story by Kenji Fujita; Director of Photography, Fuminori Minami; Art Director, Kazumasa Otani; Music, Masao Haryu.

CAST: Gin Maeda, Orie Sato, Nobuko Otowa.

A Kindai Eiga Kyokai Co., Ltd. Production. Color. Panavision (?). 115 minutes. Released 1980.

U.S. VERSION: Distributor, if any, is undetermined.

Nutcracker Fantasy **[animated]**. Executive Producer, Shintaro Tsuji; Producers, Walt deFaria, Mark L. Rosen, and Arthur Tomioka; Director, Takeo Nakamura; Screenplay, Shintaro Tsuji, based on *The Nutcracker and the Mouse King* by E.T.A. Hoffman, adapted by Shintaro Tsuji; Directors of Photography, Fumio Otani, Aguri Sugita, and Ryoji Takamori; Lighting, Toshikiyo Nakatani; Key Animation Directors, Fumiko Magari, Takeo Nakamura; Editors, Nobuo Ogawa and Takeo Nakamura; Set Design, Masaya Kaburagi, Hiroshi Yamashita; Puppet Design, Ichiro Komuro, Sadao Miyamoto, and Ricko Tazawa; Puppet Performers, Tadahito Mochinaga, Ichiro Komuro, Hosaka Puppet Factory, Shozo Tomonaga, Yuki Atai; Music Supervisors, Tsuneyoshi Nabeshima and Naozumi Yamamoto; Music, Peter Illych Tchaikovsky; Music Arranger, Akihito Wakatsuki and Kentaro Haneda, and performed by the New Japan Philharmonic Symphony Orchestra, conducted by Kazuhiro Koizumi; Choreography, Tetsutaro Shimizu; Matsuyama Ballet Company (featured performers: Yoko Morishita, Tetsutaro Shimizu); Production Manager, Tateo Haraya.

VOICE CHARACTERIZATIONS (U.S. VERSION): Michele Lee (narrator), Melissa Gilbert (Clara), Lurene Tuttle (Aunt Gerda), Christopher Lee (Uncle Drosselmeyer/Street Singer/Puppeteer/Watchmaker), Jo Anne Worley (Queen Morphia), Ken Sansom (Chamberlain/Poet/Wiseman), Dick Van Patten (King Goodwin), Roddy McDowall (Franz Fritz), Mitchel Gardner (Indian Wiseman/Viking Wiseman), Jack Angel (Chinese Wiseman/Executioner), Gene Moss (Otto von Atra/French Wiseman/Clovis), Eva Gabor (Queen of Time), Robin Haffner (Princess Mary), Joan Gerber, Maxine Fisher (miscellaneous voices).

A Sanrio Films Production. Color. Wide screen. 82 minutes. Released 1979.

U.S. VERSION: A Sanrio Films Release. English-dubbed. Screenplay, Thomas Joachim and Eugene Fournier; Dialogue Supervisor/Editor, Jack Woods; Music Supervisor, John Caper, Jr. U.S. prints by De Luxe. Songs: "Dance of the Dolls," "Empty Heart," Lyrics by Randy Bishop, Marty Gwinn, performed by Bishop and Gwinn; "In Your Heart of Hearts," "Click Clock Fantasy," Lyrics by Randy Bishop, performed by Christopher Lee; Opticals, Pacific Title; Sound Recording, Charlene Richards, T.E. Sadler; Rerecording, Robert Litt, Gregg Landaker, Howard Wollman, Samuel Goldwyn Studios; Sound Effects, Mag City, Hollywood; Production Assistant, Paula Marchese. 82 minutes. MPAA rating: "G." Released October 20, 1979.

Oban's Dipping Contest / Atomic no Obon, onna oyabuntaiketsu no maki ("Atomic Middle-Aged Women: Woman's Boss' Bottle, Volume One"). Director, Kozo Saeki.

CAST: Yoshie Mizutani, Sonomi Nakajima, Masumi Harukawa, Michiyo Yokoyama, Kiyoshi Atsumi, Ichiro Nakatani, Ichiro Arishima, Shizuko Kasagi.

A Tokyo Eiga Co., Ltd. Production. A Toho Co., Ltd. Release. Color (?). Toho Scope (?). 73 minutes. Released April 16, 1961.

U.S. VERSION: Released by Toho International Co., Ltd. English subtitles. No MPAA rating. Released November 1961.

An Ocean to Cross / Tenpyo no iraka ("An Ocean Roof"). Producers, Ichiro Sato and Fumio Kimbara; Director, Kei Kumai; Screenplay, Yoshitaka Yoda, based on an original story by Yasushi Inoue; Director of Photography, Masahisa Himeda; Art Director, Takeo Kimura; Music, Toru Takemitsu.

CAST: Katsuo Nakamura, Masaaki Daimon, Mitsuo Hamada, Takashi Shimura, Masaaki Daimon.

A "Tenpyo no iraka" Production Committee Production. A Toho Co., Ltd. Release. Color. Spherical wide screen (?). 152 minutes. Released 1980.

U.S. VERSION: Released by Toho International Co., Ltd. in subtitled format. 152 minutes. No MPAA rating. Released September 19, 1980.

Odd Obsession / Kagi ("Key"). Executive Producer, Hiroaki Fujii; Producer, Masaichi Nagata; Director, Kon Ichikawa; Screenplay, Natto Wada, Keiji Hasebe, and Kon Ichikawa, based on the novel by Junichiro Tanizaki; Director of Photography, Kazuo Miyagawa; Lighting, Tatsuo Ito; Color Consultant, Shozo Tanaka; Art Director, Tomo Shimogawara; Editors, Hiroaki Fujii and Kon Ichikawa; Music, Yasushi Akutagawa; Sound Recording, Kenichi Nishii; Production Manager, Asao Kumada; Assistant Director, Masunari Nakamura.

CAST: Machiko Kyo (Ikuko Kenmochi), Ganjiro Nakamura (Kenji Kenmochi), Junko Kano (Toshiko Kenmochi), Tatsuya Nakadai (Dr. Kimura), Tanie Kitabayashi (Hana, *the maid*), Ichiro Sugai (Mr. Ichizuka, *the masseur*), Jun Hamamura (Dr. Soma), Mantaro Ushio (Mr. Kodama), Kyu Sazanka (curio dealer), Mayumi Kurata (Ms. Koike, *the nurse*), Kenji Oyama (man at Haiku meeting), Saburo Date (1st policeman), Hikaru Hoshi (2nd policeman), Shizuo Nakajo (3rd policeman).

A Daiei Motion Picture Co., Ltd. Production. Agfa Color. DaieiScope. 107 minutes. Released June 24, 1959

U.S. VERSION: Released by Harrison Pictures. English subtitles. An Edward Harrison Presentation. English subtitles, Frederick Laing. 96 minutes. No MPAA rating. Released May 12, 1961.

The Ogre of Mount Oe / Oeyama shuten doji ("The Ogre of Mt. Oe"). Executive Producer, Masaichi Nagata; Director, Tokuzo Tanaka; Screenplay, Fuji Yahiro; Director of Photography, Hiroshi Imai; Sound Recording Supervisor, Masao Osumi; Sound, Daiei Recording Studio; Special Effects, Daiei Special Effects Department.

CAST: Kazuo Hasegawa, Raizo Ichikawa, Shintaro Katsu, Kojiro Hongo, Fujiko Yamamoto, Tamao Nakamura.

A Daiei Motion Picture Co., Ltd. Production. Western Electric Mirrophonic recording. Eastman Color (processed by Daiei Laboratory). Academy ratio. 114 minutes. Released 1960.

U.S. VERSION: Released by Daiei International Films English subtitles. No MPAA rating. 114 minutes. Released 1960.

Oh, My Comrade! / Kigeki aa gunka ("Comedy Military Song"). Director, Yoichi Maeda; Screenplay, Yoichi Maeda and Keiji Mitsutomo, based on an original story by Gyo Hayasaka; Director of Photography, Masayuki Kato; Art Director, Tadataka Yoshino; Music, Seitaro Omori.

CAST: Frankie Sakai (Fukuzo), Ichiro Zeitsu (Kato), Yuki Jono (Tsuneko), Tanie Kitabayashi (Harumi), Bokuzen Hidari, Chieko Baisho.

A Shochiku Co., Ltd. Production. Eastman Color. Shochiku GrandScope. 88 minutes. Released September 19, 1970.

U.S. VERSION: Release undetermined, possibly by Shochiku Films of America, Inc. English subtitled version available. 88 minutes. No MPAA rating.

Oh-te / Ote ("Checkmate"). Producer, Genjiro Arato; Director, Junji Sakamoto; Screenplay, Junji Sakamoto and Toshiaki Toyoda, based on an original story by Toshiaki Toyoda; Director of Photography, Akihiro Ito; Music, Shigeru Umebayashi.

CAST: Hidekazu Akai, Masaya Kato, Tomisaburo Wakayama.

A Genjiro Arato Pictures Production. Color. Spherical wide screen (?). 108 minutes. Released 1991.

U.S. VERSION: Distributor, if any, is undetermined.

Ohan ("Ohan"). Producers, Tomoyuki Tanaka and Kon Ichikawa; Director, Kon Ichikawa; Screenplay, Kon Ichikawa and Shinya Hidaka, based on the novel by Chiyo Uno; Director of Photography, Yukio Isohata; Music, Shinnosuke Okawa and Tomoyuki Asakawa.

CAST: Sayuri Yoshinaga (Ohan), Reiko Ohara (Okayo), Koji Ishizaka (Kokichi), Wataru Hasegawa (Satoru).

A Toho Co., Ltd. Production. Color. Spherical wide screen. 112 minutes. Released 1984.

U.S. VERSION: Released by Toho International Co., Ltd. English subtitles. 112 minutes. No MPAA rating. Released March 1985.

Ohayo ("Good Morning"). Producer, Shizuo Yamanouchi; Director, Yasujiro Ozu; Screenplay, Kogo Noda and Yasujiro Ozu; Director of Photography, Yushun Atsuta; Art Director, Tatsuo Hamada; Music, Toshiro Mayuzumi.

CAST: Koji Shidara (Minoru, *the elder brother*), Masahiko Shimazu (Isamu, *the younger brother*), Chishu Ryu (their father), Kuniko Miyake (their mother), Yoshiko Kuga (their aunt), Keiji Sada (their teacher), Haruo Tanaka (Tatsuko), Haruko Sugimura (Kikue, his wife), Teruko Nagaoka, Toyo Takahashi (neighbors), Eijiro Tono, Sadako Sawamura.

A Shochiku Co., Ltd. Production. Filmed at Shochiku-Ofuna Studios. Eastman Color. Academy ratio. 94 minutes. Released May 12, 1959.

U.S. VERSION: Released by Shochiku Films of America, Inc. English subtitles. Released in black and white in the United States. Alternate title: *Good Morning*. 93 minutes. No MPAA rating. Released February 1962.

Okasarete Byuakui ("Raped White Cloth"). Producer/Director, Koji Wakamatsu; Screenplay, Koji Wakamatsu, Masao Adachi and Juro Kara; Director of Photography, Hideo Ito; Production Manager, Masayuki Miyama; Special Effects, Fukushima Group; Editor, Fumio Tomita; Sound, Shin Kida; Music, Koji Takamura.

CAST: Juro Kara (The Boy), Michiko Sakamoto (The Girl), Reiko Koyanagi (The Head Nurse), Miki Hayashi, Shoko Kido, Makiko Saegusa, Kyoko Yayoi (nurses).

A Wakamatsu Productions Production. A Wakamatsu Release. Black and white, with color inserts. CinemaScope. 58 minutes. Released 1967.

U.S. VERSION: Distributor, if any, is undetermined. International title: *Violated Angels*. Alternate title: *Violated Women*.

Okoge ("Gay Men"). Producer/Director/Screenplay, Takehiro Nakajima; Project Adviser, Kenichiro Yamashita; Director of Photography, Yoshimasa Hakata; Lighting, Yasushi Watanabe; Art Director, Kunihiro Inomata; Editor, Kenji Goto; Sound Recording, Makio Ika and Ryuji Matsumoto; Music, EDISON; Music Producer, Hiroshi Ariyoshi; Casting, Tomo Kimura; Assistant Director, Tsutomu Takasaka; Production Managers, Makoto Obori and Hitoshi Numao.

CAST: Misa Shimuzu (Sayoko), Takehiro Murata (Go), Takeo Nakahara (Tochi), Atsushi Fukuwara (Tamio, *the singer*), Takatoshi Takeda (Tsuyoki, *the bartender*, Masayuki Shionoya (Kurihara), Kyozo Nagatsuka (Touichi, *Go's brother*), Noriko Sengoku (Kineo, *Go's mother*), Toshie Negishi (Yayoi, *Tochi's wife*), Mitsuko Oka, Michiko Yokoyama, Midori Kiuchi, Hairi Katagiri, Dump Matsumoto, Toshimori Omi, Casey Takamine, Guts Ishimatsu, Eriko Watanabe, Yoshiko Kuga.

An I.N.T./Group Film Production Committee Production. Color. Spherical wide screen (1.85:1). 120 minutes. Released 1992.

U.S. VERSION: Released by Cinevista. English subtitles. Video version matted. Subtitles, Donald Richie. 120 minutes. No MPAA rating. Released March 1993.

The Old Bear Hunter / Matagi ("Matagi"). Producer, Yoshichika Kojima; Director, Toshio Goto; Screenplay, Atsushi Yamatoya, based on an original story by Toshio Goto; Director of Photography, Takaya Yamazaki; Art Director, Kazumasa Otani; Music, Kentaro Hanada.

CAST: Ko Nishimura, Yoshito Ambo, Goichi Yamada, Ichiro Izawa, Yoshio Inaba.

A Seido Productions Production. A Toho Co., Ltd. Release. Color. Spherical wide screen (1.85:1). 103 minutes. Released 1982.

U.S. VERSION: Distributor, if any, is undetermined, possibly by Toho International Co., Ltd. in subtitled format. No MPAA rating.

Once a Rainy Day / Akogare ("Longing"). Director, Hideo Onchi; Screenplay, Taichi Yamada; Story, Keisuke Kinoshita; Director of Photography, Yuzuru Aizawa; Music, Toru Takemitsu.

CAST: Michiyo Aratama, Yoko Naito, Ryo Tamura, Daisuke Kato, Nobuko Otowa, Fukuko Sayo, Shoichi Ozawa.

A Toho Co., Ltd. Production. Eastman Color. Toho Scope. 85 minutes. Released 1966.

U.S. VERSION: Released by Toho International Co., Ltd. English subtitles. 85 minutes. No MPAA rating. Released February 1968.

One Generation of Tattoos / Irezumi Ichidai ("One Generation of Tattoos"). Producer, Nobutaka; Planner, Masayuki Takagi; Director, Seijun Suzuki; Screenplay, Kinya Naoi and Yoshi Hattori; Director of Photography, Kurataro Takamura; Editor, Akira Suzuki; Art Director, Takeo Kimura; Music, Masayoshi Ikeda; Assistant Director, Masami Kuzu.

CAST: Hideki Takahashi (Tetsutaro Murakami, *"White Tiger Tetsu"*), Kotobuki Hananomoto (Kenji Murakami), Akira Yamauchi (Yuzo Kinoshita), Hiroko Ito (Masayo Kinoshita), Masako Izumi (Midori Kinoshita), Kayo Matsuo (Oyuki), Yuji Odaka (Osamu Ezaki), Tadashi Takashina (Tsunekichi).

A Nikkatsu Corp. Production. Color. NikkatsuScope. 87 minutes. Released November 1965.

U.S. VERSION: Released by Toho International Co., Ltd. English subtitles. Alternate title: *White Tiger Tattoo*. 87 minutes. No MPAA rating. Released October 7, 1966.

One Hundred Gamblers / Bakuto hyakunin ("One Hundred Gamblers"). Director, Takashi Nomura; Screenplay, Iwao Yamazaki and Hisanori Kai, based on an original story by Kyo Shimamura; Director of Photography, Shigeyoshi Mine; Art Director, Toshiyuki Matsui; Music, Saburo Matsuura.

CAST: Hideki Takahashi (Satoru), Shinjiro Ebara (Boss Akieda), Joe Shishido (Killer Masa), Akira Kobayashi (Boss Mukoyama), Masako Izumi (Kayo), Kanjuro Arashi (Boss Murai), Takamaru Sasaki (Eto), Toru Abe (Goda), Hideaki Nitani.

A Nikkatsu Corp. Production. Fujicolor. NikkatsuScope. 89 minutes. Released May 14, 1969.

U.S. VERSION: Release undetermined. English subtitled version available. 89 minutes. No MPAA rating.

100 Monsters / Yokai hyaku monogatari ("100 Monster Stories"). Executive Producer, Eisa Nishizawa; Producer, Yamato Yatsuhiro; Director, Kimiyoshi Yasuda; Screenplay, Tetsuro Yoshida; Director of Photography, Yasukazu Takemura; Art Directors, Yoshinobu Nishioka and Shigeru Kato; Lighting Teiichi Ito; Editor, Kanji Suganuma; Music, Chumei Watanabe; Sound Recording Supervisor, Masao Osumi; Sound Daiei Recording Studio; Special Effects, Daiei Special Effects Department; Assistant Director, Akikazu Ota; Martial Arts Director, Eiichi Kusumoto.

CAST: Jun Fujimaki (Yasutaro), Miwa Takada (Okiku), Mikiko Tsubouchi (Osen), Takashi Kanda (Riemon Tajimaya [Tanbaya]), Ryutaro Gomi (Lord Hotta of Buzen), Yoshio Yoshida (Jusuke), Masaru [Sho] Hiraizumi (Takichi), Rookie Shinichi (Shinkichi), Shozo Hayashiya (storyteller), Koichi Ogura [Mizuhara] (Tobei), Jun Hamamura (Gohei), Shosaku Sugiyama (Bannai Ibaragi), Tatsuo Hanabu (Jinbei), Saburo Date (1st jobless samurai), Kazuo Yamamoto (2nd jobless samurai), Shozo Nanbu (old town counsellor), Shinobu Araki (old priest), Kazue Tamachi (village headman), Teruko Omi (Otora), Ikuko Mori (Ronin's wife), Yasuko Kankura (Oriku).

A Daiei Motion Picture Co., Ltd. Production. A Masaichi Nagata Presentation. Eastman Color (processed by Daiei Laboratory). DaieiScope. Westrex recording system. 79 minutes. Released March 20, 1968.

U.S. VERSION: Released by Daiei International Films, Inc. English subtitles. International title: *The Hundred Monsters*. Also known as *The Hundred Ghost Stories*. 79 minutes. No MPAA rating. Released 1968.

1001 Nights with Toho / Toho senichiya ("1,001 Nights With Toho"). Planning, Fuku Nakamura; Director of Photography, Akira Mimura.

CAST: Hisako Yamane, Susumu Fujita, Hideko Takamine, Tataro Kurokawa.

A Shintoho Co., Ltd. Production. Black and white. Academy ratio. Running time undetermined. Released 1947.

U.S. VERSION: Distributor, if any, is undetermined. Kon Ichikawa directed portions of this promotional film, which featured footage from the studio's product.

One Wonderful Sunday / Subarashiki nichiyobi ("One Wonderful Sunday"). Producer, Sojiro Motoki; Director/Editor, Akira Kurosawa; Screenplay, Keinosuke Uegusa and Akira Kurosawa; Director of Photography, Asakazu Nakai; Lighting, Kuichiro Kishida; Art Director, Kazuo Kubo; Music, Tadashi Hattori; Sound Recording, Jun Yasue; Sound, Toho Dubbing Theatre; Sound Effects, Toho Sound Effects Group.

CAST: Isao Numasaki (Yuzo), Chieko Nakakita (Masako), Ichiro Sugai (Yamiya, *the black-marketeer*), Midori Ariyama (Sono, *his mistress*), Masao Shimizu (bar owner), Sachio Sakai (ticket man), Toshi Mori (apartment superintendent), Tokuji Kobayashi (overweight man), Shiro Mizutani (waif), Zeko Nakamura (shop owner), Atsushi Watanabe (man), Aguri Hidaka (dancer), Katao Numazaki (bakery owner), Ichiro Namiki and Toppa Utsumi (street photographers).

A Toho Co., Ltd. Production. Black and white. Academy ratio. Filmed at Toho Studios, Ltd. (Tokyo). 108 minutes. Released June 25, 1947.

U.S. VERSION: Released by FDM. English subtitles. Alternate title: *Wonderful Sunday*. 95 minutes. No MPAA rating. Released June 1982.

Onibaba ("Witch"). Executive Producers, Hisao Itoya, Setsuo Noto and Tamotsu Minato; Producer, Toshio Konya; Director/Screenplay/Art Director, Kaneto Shindo; Director of Photography, Kiyomi Kuroda; Music, Hikaru Hayashi; Editor, Toshio Enoki.

CAST: Nobuko Otowa (the mother), Jitsuko Yoshimura (the daughter-in-law), Kei Sato (Hachi), Jukichi Uno (the warrior), Taiji Tonomura (Ushi, *the merchant*), Tatsuya Nakadai (Onimasa).

A Kindai Eiga Kyokai (Kindai Movie Co., Ltd.)/Tokyo Eiga Co., Ltd. Production. A Toho Co., Ltd. Release. Possibly encoded with Perspecta Stereophonic Sound. Black and white. Toho Scope. 104 minutes. Released 1964.

U.S. VERSION: Released by Toho International Co., Ltd. English subtitles. Also known as *The Hole*, *The Demon* and *Devil Woman*. The home video version is letterboxed (and slightly squeezed as well). 104 minutes. No MPAA rating. Released February 4, 1965.

The Only Son / Hitori musuko ("The Only Son"). Director, Yasujiro Ozu; Screenplay, Tadao Ikeda and Masao Arata, based on a screenplay by James Maki [Yasujiro Ozu]; Director of Photography, Shojiro Sugimoto.

CAST: Chishu Ryu, Choko Iida, Shinichi Himori, Masao Hayama, Yoshiko Tsubouchi, Mitsuko Yoshikawa, Tokkankozo.

A Shochiku Co., Ltd. Production. Filmed at Shochiku-Kamata Studios. Black and white. Academy ratio. 87 minutes. Released September 15, 1936.

U.S. VERSION: Released by Films, Inc. English subtitles. The last feature made at the Shochiku-Kamata Studios. 87 minutes. No MPAA rating. Released April 1, 1987.

Only Yesterday / Omoide poroporo ("Memory") **[animated]**. Producer, Yasuyoshi Tokuma; Director, Isao Takahata; Screenplay, Isao Takahata, based on an original story by Hotalu

Okamoto and Yuko Tone; Music, Katsu Hoshi.

VOICE CHARACTERIZATIONS: Miki Imai, Toshiro Yanagiba, Yoko Honda.

A Tokuma Shoten Publishing Co., Ltd. Production. Color. Spherical wide screen (?). 119 minutes. Released 1991.

U.S. VERSION: Distributor, if any, is undetermined.

Operation Enemy Fort / Yamaneko sakusen ("Wildcat Operation"). Executive Producer, Tomoyuki Tanaka; Director, Senkichi Taniguchi; Screenplay, Shinichi Sekizawa; Director of Photography, Fukuzo Koizumi; Music, Masaru Sato.

CAST: Makoto Sato (Lt. Isshiki), Yosuke Natsuki (Lt. Wakana), Toru Ibuki (Lt. Taira), Yuriko Hoshi, Kumi Mizuno, Jun Tazaki, Akihiko Hirata, Ren Yamamoto, Tadao Nakamaru.

A Toho Co., Ltd. Production. Eastman Color. Toho Scope. 95 minutes. Released 1962.

U.S. VERSION: Released by Toho International Co., Ltd. English subtitles. Third feature in Toho's 7-film war series. Followed by *Outpost of Hell* (1963). 95 minutes. No MPAA rating. Released August 28, 1964.

Operation Mad Dog / Norainu sakusen ("Operation Homeless Dog"). Executive Producer, Tomoyuki Tanaka; Director, Jun Fukuda.

CAST: Tatsuya Mihashi, Makoto Sato, Yosuke Natsuki, Reiko Dan.

A Toho Co., Ltd. Production. Black and white. Toho Scope. 98 minutes. Released 1963 (?).

U.S. VERSION: Released by Toho International Co., Ltd. English subtitles. English-dubbed version also available. 98 minutes. No MPAA rating. Release date undetermined.

Operation Neglige / Tsuyomushi onna to yowamushi otoko ("Woman Insect and Weaker Man"). Director/Screenplay, Kaneto Shindo; Director of Photography, Kiyomi Kuroda; Art Director, Tokumichi Igawa; Music, Hikaru Hayashi.

CAST: Nobuko Otowa (Fumiko, *the mother*), Eiko Yamagishi (Kimiko, *the daughter*), Taiji Tonoyama (Zenzo, *Fumiko's husband*), Hideo Kanze (Gonbei), Yoshiko Nakamura (Gonbei's mother).

A Kindai Eiga Kyokai Production. A Shochiku Co., Ltd. Release. Black and white. Shochiku GrandScope. 98 minutes. Released June 30, 1968.

U.S. VERSION: Release undetermined, possibly by Shochiku Films of America, Inc. English subtitled version available. 98 minutes. No MPAA rating.

Operation Room / Gekashitsu ("Operation Room"). Producers, Kyuemon Oda, Kazuyoshi Okuyama, and Genjiro Arato; Director, Tamasaburo Bando; Screenplay, Hiroshi Hashimoto, Genki Yoshimura, and Tamasaburo Bando, based on an original story by Kyoka Izumi; Director of Photography, Noritaka Sakamoto; Music, Sergei Rachmaninoff.

CAST: Sayuri Yoshinaga, Masaya Kato, Kiichi Nakai.

A Shochiku Co., Ltd./Aashi National Broadcasting Co., Ltd./Genjiro Arato Pictures Production. Color. Spherical wide screen (?). 50 minutes. Released 1991.

U.S. VERSION: Distributor, if any, is undetermined.

Operation X / Dobunezumi sakusen ("Sewer Rat Operation"). Executive Producers, Tomoyuki Tanaka and Kenichiro Tsunoda; Director/Screenplay, Kihachi Okamoto; Director of Photography, Yuzuru Aizawa; Music, Masaru Sato.

CAST: Yuzo Kayama, Yosuke Natsuki, Makoto Sato, Kumi Mizuno, Ichiro Nakatani, Tadao Nakamura, Kunie Tanaka, Mickey Curtis, Nami Tamura.

A Toho Co., Ltd. Production. Black and white. Toho Scope. 102 minutes. Released 1962.

U.S. VERSION: Released by Toho International Co., Ltd. English subtitles. 102 minutes. No MPAA rating. Released January 11, 1963.

Oracion / Yushun ("Great Horse"). Producers, Shigeaki Hazama, Hisashi Hieda, Yasushi Mitsui and Masayuki

Sato; Director, Shigemichi Sugita; Screenplay, Shunsaku Ikehata, based on an original story by Teru Miyamoto; Directors of Photography, Takao Saito and Kazutami Hara; Music, Shigeaki Saegusa.

CAST: Ken Ogata, Naoto Ogata, Tatsuya Nakadai, Yuki Saito, Hidetaka Yoshioka, Mariko Kaga.

A Fuji Television Network, Inc. Production. Color. Spherical wide screen (?). 128 minutes. Released 1988.

U.S. VERSION: Distributor undetermined. 128 minutes. No MPAA rating. Released December 1988.

Orgies of Edo / Genroku onna keizu ("Genroku Family Tree of Women"). Director, Teruo Ishii; Screenplay, Teruo Ishii and Masahiro Kakefuda; Director of Photography, Sadatsugu Yoshida; Art Director, Takatoshi Suzuki; Music, Masao Yagi.

CAST: Toyozo Yamamoto (Hanji), Mitsuko Aoi (Ochise), Akira Ishihama (Chokichi), Tetsuro Tamba, Masumi Tachibana, Yukie Kagawa, Asao Koike.

A Toei Co., Ltd. Production. Eastman Color. ToeiScope. 94 minutes. Released January 9, 1969.

U.S. VERSION: Release undetermined. English subtitled version available. 94 minutes. No MPAA rating.

The Orphan Brother / Anju to Zushio-maru ("Anjo and Zushio-maru") **[animated]**. Director, Taiji Yabushita; Screenplay, Sumie Tanaka, based on the story "Sansho the Bailiff"; Original Drawing, Akira Daikubara and Yasuji Mori; Director of Photography, Shinkichi Otsuka.

VOICE CHARACTERIZATIONS: Yoshiko Sakuma, Kinya Kitaoji.

A Toei Animation Studio Co., Ltd. Production. A Toei Co., Ltd. Release. Eastman Color. ToeiScope. 83 minutes. Released July 19, 1961.

U.S. VERSION: Distributor, if any, is undetermined.

Osaka Elegy / Naniwa hika ("Osaka Elegy"). Director, Kenji Mizoguchi; Screenplay, Kenji Mizoguchi and Yoshikata Yoda, based on the magazine serial "*Mieko*" by Saburo Okada, as published in *Shincho* Magazine; Director of Photography, Minoru Miki; Music, Koichi Takagi; Sound Recording, Hisashi Kase and Yasumi Mizuguchi.

CAST: Isuzu Yamada (Ayako), Seiichi Takegawa (Junzo, *her father*), Chiyoko Okura (Sachiko, *her younger sister*), Shinpachiro Asaka (Hiroshi, *her elder brother*), Benkei Shiganoya (Sonosuke Asai), Yoko Umemura (Sumiko), Kensaku Hara (Susumu Nishimura), Eitaro Shindo (Fujino), Kunio Tamura (doctor), Shizuko Takizawa (maid), Takashi Shimura (inspector).

A Daiichi Film Co., Ltd. Production. Filmed at Daiichi-Sagano Studios (Kyoto). Black and white. Academy ratio. 89 minutes. Released May 28, 1936.

U.S. VERSION: Distributor undetermined. English subtitles. Alternate title: *Naniwa Elegy*. 68 minutes. No MPAA rating. Released January 31, 1979.

Osorezan no onna ("Woman of Osore Mansion"). Director, Heinosuke Gosho; Screenplay, Hideo Horie; Director of Photography, Shozaburo Shinomura.

CAST: Jitsuko Yoshimura, Kin Sugai, Taiji Tonoyama, Keizo Kawasaki.

A Shochiku Co., Ltd. Production. Black and white (processed by Shochiku Laboratory). Shochiku GrandScope. 98 minutes. Released 1966.

U.S. VERSION: Distributor, if any, is unknown. International title: *An Innocent Witch*.

Our Dear Buddies / Kimi ga wakamono nara ("If You Are Young"). Director, Kinji Fukasaku; Screenplay, Takehiro Nakajima, Koji Matsumoto and Kinji Fukasaku; Director of Photography, Takamoto Ezure; Art Director, Totestu Hirakawa; Music, Taku Izumi.

CAST: Tetsuo Ishidate (Kikuo), Gin Maeda (Asao), Choichiro Kawarazaki (Kiyoshi), Hideki Hayashi (Ichiro), Ryunosuke Minegishi (Ryuji), Michie Terada (Yukiko), Michiko Araki (Kiyoshi's mother).

A Shinsei Eigasha-Bungakuza Production. A Shochiku Co., Ltd. Release. Eastman Color. Shochiku GrandScope. 89 minutes. Released May 27, 1970.

U.S. VERSION: Release undetermined, possibly by Shochiku Films of America, Inc. English subtitled version available. 89 minutes. No MPAA rating.

Our Earth: A Message to Our Children / Chikyu-kko inochi to ai no messeji ("Children of Earth: A Message of Life and Love"). Producer/ Director, Takuzo Makitsubo; Screenplay, Mieko Shimojima; Director of Photography, Aiko Kanenaka; Music, Hitoshi Komuro.

CAST: Ami Shitamoto, Michael Ken, Tokuko Sugiyama.

A The PAO Production Co. Production. Color. Spherical wide screen (?). 55 minutes. Released 1993.

U.S. VERSION: Distributor, if any, is undetermined. Running time also given at 83 minutes.

Our Silent Love / Chichi to ko ("Father and Son"). Executive Producers, Sanezumi Fujimoto and Hideyuki Shiino; Director/Screenplay, Zenzo Matsuyama; Director of Photography, Kozo Okazaki; Music, Toru Fuyuki.

CAST: Kinya Kitaoji, Keiju Kobayashi, Yoko Naito, Mayumi Ozora, Hideko Takamine, Izumi Hara, Daisuke Kato, Nobuko Otawa, Ryo Tamura.

A Tokyo Eiga Co., Ltd. Production. A Toho Co., Ltd. Release. Black and white. Toho Scope. 114 minutes. Released May 1967.

U.S. VERSION: Released by Toho International Co., Ltd. English subtitles. 114 minutes. No MPAA rating. Released June 1969.

The Outcast / Hakai ("Transgression"). Executive Producer, Masatsugu Hashimoto; Producer, Masaichi Nagata; Planning, Hiroaki Fujii; Director, Kon Ichikawa; Screenplay, Natto Wada, based on the novel by Toson Shimazaki; Director of Photography, Kazuo Miyagawa; Art Director, Yoshinobu Nishioka; Music, Yasushi Akutagawa; Sound, Masao Osumi; Lighting, Kenichi Okamoto; Editor, Shigeo Nishida.

CAST: Raizo Ichikawa (Ushimatsu Segawa), Hiroyuki Nagato (Ginnosuke Tsuchiya), Eiji Funakoshi (Keinoshin Kazama), Shio Fujimura (Oshio), Rentaro Mikuni (Inoko), Kyoko Kishida (Inoko's wife), Ganjuro Nakamura (priest of Rengeji Temple), Haruko Sugimura (madam), Yoshi Kato (uncle), Jun Hamamura (father), Sanemon Arashi (lord), Seiji Miyaguchi (principal), Kumeko Urabe (madam), Mantaro Ushio (Takayanagi), Bontaro Miyake (farmer).

A Daiei Motion Picture Co., Ltd. Production. Black and white. DaieiScope. 118 minutes. Released April 6, 1962.

U.S. VERSION: Distributor undetermined. Alternate titles: *Apostasy, The Broken Commandment, The Sin*. 118 minutes. No MPAA rating. Released July 1988.

The Outlaw Sword / Daikanbu—Burai ("High-Ranking Risk Taker"). Director, Keiichi Ozawa; Screenplay, Kaneo Ikegami and Keiji Kubota, based on a story by Goro Fujita; Director of Photography, Kurataro Takamura; Art Directors, Takeo Kimura and Motozo Kawahara; Music, Harumi Ibe.

CAST: Tetsuya Watari (Goro Fujikawa), Chieko Matsubara (Yukiko), Hideaki Nitani (Kosuke Asami), Junko Maya (Setsuko, *his wife*), Masako Ota (Keiko, *his sister*), Kayo Matsuo (Yumeko), Ryohei Uchida (Kiuchi), Akira Yamauchi (Izumi).

A Nikkatsu Corp. Production. Fujicolor. NikkatsuScope. 97 minutes. Released April 28, 1968.

U.S. VERSION: Release undetermined. English subtitled version available. 97 minutes. No MPAA rating.

Outpost of Hell / Dokuritsu kikanjutai imada shagekichu ("Independent Machine Gun Corps Are Still Shooting"). Executive Producers, Tomoyuki Tanaka and Kenjiro Tsunoda; Director, Senkichi Taniguchi; Screenplay, Masato Ide; Photography, Kazuo Yamada; Music, Ikuma Dan.

CAST: Tatsuya Mihashi (Sgt. Yamano), Makoto Sato (Corp. Watanabe), Makoto Terada (Private Shirai), Hiroshi Tachikawa (Private Hara), Sachio Sakai (Private Kaneko, *the coward*), Yosuke Natsuki.

A Toho Co., Ltd. Production. Black and white. Toho Scope. 92 minutes. Released 1963.

A scene from *Panda and the Magic Serpent* (1958), the first of a seemingly endless stream of animated features from Toei.

U.S. VERSION: Released by Toho International Co., Ltd. English subtitles. The 4th "Independent Gangsters" feature. Preceded by *Operation Enemy Fort* (1962). 92 minutes. No MPAA rating. Released April 29, 1966.

Oyuki the Madonna / Maria no Oyuki ("Oyuki the Madonna"). Director, Kenji Mizoguchi; Screenplay, Tatsunosuke Takashima, based on the story "Boule de Suif" by Guy de Maupassant, and adapted by Matsutaro Kawaguchi; Director of Photography, Shigeto Miki; Editor, Tokichi Ishimoto; Sound Recording, Junichi Murota.

CAST: Isuzu Yamada (Oyuki), Komako Hara (Okin), Daijiro Natsukawa (Shingo Asakura), Eiji Nakano (Kensuke Sadowara), Kinue Utagawa (Ochie Kurachi), Shin Shibata (Keishiro Yokoi), Yoko Umemura (Michiko Yokoi), Keiji Oizumi (Yoemon Kurachi), Toichiro Negishi (Sobe Gonda), Yoshisuke Koizumi (Gisuke), Tadashi Tori (army colonel).

A Daiichi Film Co., Ltd. Production. Filmed at Daiichi-Sagano Studio (Kyoto). Black and white. Academy ratio. 78 minutes. Released May 30, 1935.

U.S. VERSION: Distributor undetermined. Released with no English subtitles. 78 minutes. No MPAA rating. Released 1981 (?).

A Page of Madness / Kurutta ippeiji ("A Page of Madness"). Producer/Director, Teinosuke Kinugasa; Screenplay, Yasunari Kawabata and Teinosuke Kinugasa; Directors of Photography, Kohei Sugiyama and Eiji Tsuburaya; Music (for reissue version), Minoru Muraoka and Toru Kurashima.

CAST: Masao Inoue (custodian), Yoshi Nakagawa (his wife), Ayako Iijima (daughter), Hiroshi Nemoto (young man), Misao Seki (doctor), Minoru Takase (1st madman), Kyosuke Takamatsu (2nd madman), Tetsu Tsuboi (3rd madman), Eiko Minami (dancing girl).

A Kinugasa Productions/Shin Kankaka-ha Eiga Renami Production. Silent with Benshi (with musical score for reissue version, replacing Benshi performance). Black and white. Academy ratio. 60 minutes. Released 1926.

U.S. VERSION: Released by New Line Cinema Corp. Reissued in Japan with musical score in 1973. 60 minutes. No MPAA rating. Released January 1975.

The Pale Hand / Shiroi te ("The White Hand"). Producer, Shichiro Murakami; Director, Seijiro Koyama; Screenplay, Shigeto Sato, based on an original story by Makoto Shiina; Director of Photography, Masahiko Iimura; Music, Ryoichi Kuniyoshi.

CAST: Yoko Minamino, Katsuma Nakagaki, Manabu Fukuhara.

A Kansai Telecasting Corp. Production. Color. Spherical wide screen. 100 minutes. Released 1990.

U.S. VERSION: Distributor, if any, is undetermined.

Panda and the Magic Serpent / Hakuja den ("The Legend of the White Serpent") [**animated**]. Executive Producer, Hiroshi Okawa; Associate Producers, Hideyuki Takahashi, Koichi Akagawa, and Sanae Yamamoto; Directors, Kazuhiko Okabe and Teiji Yabushita; Screenplay, Teiji Yabushita and Shin Uehara, based on the Chinese fairy tale, *Pai she chaun*; Original Dialog, Seiichi Yashiro; Animation, Yasuo Otsuka and Yusaku Sakamoto; Original Drawings, Akira Daikubara and Yasuji Mori; Backgrounds, Kazuo Kusano; Director of Photography, Takamitsu Tsukahara; Art Directors, Kazuhiko Okabe and Kiyoshi Hashimoto; Editor, Shintaro Miyamoto; Music, Chuji Kinoshita; Sound Recording, Takeshi Mori.

VOICE CHARACTERIZATIONS: Hisaya Morishige, Kinya Kitaoji.

A Toei Animation Studio Co., Ltd. Production. A Toei Co., Ltd. Release. Eastman Color. ToeiScope (?). 78 minutes. Released October 22, 1958.

U.S. VERSION: Released by Globe Pictures. English dubbed. Narrator: Marvin Miller. International title: *The White Snake Enchantress*. Generally regarded as the first animated feature from Japan, even though one such film, *Momotaro umi no shinpei*, was released in 1945. 76 minutes. No MPAA rating. Released July 8, 1961.

The Passage to Japan / Fukuzawa Yukichi ("Yukichi Fukuzawa"). Producer, Shigeru Okada; Director, Shinichiro Sawai; Screenplay, Kazuo Kasahara; Director of Photography, Seizo Sengen; Music, Jo Hisaishi.

CAST: Kyohei Shibata, Toru Nakamura, Yoko Minamino.

A Toei Co., Ltd. Production. Color. Anamorphic wide screen (?). 123 minutes. Released 1991.

U.S. VERSION: Distributor, if any, is undetermined.

Passing Fancy / Dekigokoro ("Passing Fancy"). Director, Yasujiro Ozu; Screenplay, Tadao Ikeda, based on an idea by James Maki [Yasujiro Ozu]; Director of Photography, Shojiro Sugimoto.

CAST: Takeshi Sakamoto, Tokkankozo [no other name given], Den Ohinata, Nobuko Fushimi, Choko Iida, Chishu Ryu.

A Shochiku Co., Ltd. Production. Filmed at Shochiku-Kamata Studios. Silent. Black and white. Academy ratio. 101 minutes. Released September 17, 1933.

U.S. VERSION: Distributor undetermined.

Passion / Manji ("Fylfot"). Producer, Yonejiro Saito; Director, Yasuzo Masamura; Screenplay, Kaneto Shindo, based on the story "Manji," by Junichiro Tanizaki, in *Kaizo* (March 1928–April 1930); Director of Photography, Setsuo Kobayashi; Music, Tadashi Yamauchi.

CAST: Ayako Wakao (Mitsuko Tokumitsu), Kyoko Kishida (Sonoko Kaiuchi), Yusuke Kawazu (Eijiro Watanuki), Eiji Funakoshi (Kotaro Kakiuchi).

A Daiei Motion Picture Co., Ltd. Production. Eastman Color. DaieiScope. 91 minutes. Released August 1964.

U.S. VERSION: Released by Daiei International Films. English subtitles. 90 minutes. No MPAA rating. Released 1968.

Passion Without End / Hateshinaki jonetsu ("Passion Without End"). Producer, Hisashi Iuchi; Director,

Kon Ichikawa; Screenplay, Natto Wada; Director of Photography, Joji Ohara; Lighting, Ko Fujibayashi; Sound Recording, Toshio Negishi; Art Director, Kazuo Ogawa; Music, Ryoichi Hattori.

CAST: Yuji Hori (Taro Miki), Chiaki Tsukioka (Shin Ishikari), Shizuko Kasagi (Fukuko Amamiya), Yumeji Tsukioka (Yuko Odagiri).

A Shintoho Co., Ltd. Production. Black and white. Academy ratio. 91 minutes. Released September 27, 1949.

U.S. VERSION: Distributor, if any, is undetermined. Alternate title: *The Endless Passion.*

The Path Under the Platanes / Suzukake no Sanpomichi ("The Path under the Platanes"). Producers, Masumi Fujimoto and Masanori Kaneko; Director, Hiromichi Horikawa; Screenplay, Toshiro Ide and Tatsukado Okada, based on the drama by Yojiro Ishizaka; Director of Photography, Hajime Koizumi; Art Director, Shinobu Muraki; Music, Ryoichi Hattori.

CAST: Yoko Tsukasa (Kumiko), Keiko Tsushima (Nobuko), Kyoko Aoyama (Ayako), Masayuki Mori (Noro), Chishu Ryu (Ishimaru), Shinji Yamada (Murase).

A Toho Co., Ltd. Production. Agfacolor. Toho Scope. 71 minutes. Released January 9, 1959.

U.S. VERSION: Release undetermined, possibly by Toho International Co., Ltd. in subtitled format. No MPAA rating.

The Performers / Hana to namida to honoo ("Flower and Tear and Flame"). Director/Screenplay, Umeji Inoue; Director of Photography, Keiji Maruyama; Art Director, Gohei Morita; Music, Seitaro Omori.

CAST: Hibari Misora (Kasumi Fujihara), Shinichi Mori (Ryusuke), Shogo Shimada (Seijuro Fujihana), Yoichi Hayashi (Hiroshi), Yataro Kitagami (Kisaburo), Nana Ozaki (Hamako), Takamaru Sasaki, Osami Nabe, Shinichi Yanagizawa, Fujio Murakami, Ryusuke Kita, Kentaro Imai, Kyoko Mizuki, Natsuko Shiga, Michiko Yashima, Yoshisaburo Owa, Nobuko Suzuki, Fusako Maki.

A Shochiku Co., Ltd. Production. Eastman Color. Shochiku GrandScope. 94 minutes. Released January 1970.

U.S. VERSION: Released by Shochiku Films of America, Inc. English subtitles. 94 minutes. No MPAA rating. Released August 1970.

Perils of Bangaku Executive Producer, Sanezumi Fujimoto; Producer, Hisao Ichikawa; Director, Shue Matsubayashi; Screenplay, Matsuo Kishi and Kenjin Shindo, based on an original story by Kyoji Shirai; Assistant Director, Hirozo Yamamoto.

CAST: Keiju Kobayashi, Reiko Dan, Takashi Shimura, Manami Fuji, Hiroshi Koizumi, Yukiko Shimazaki, Kyu Sazanka, Toru Abe, Chishu Ryu, Toru Yuri, Mutsohi Happa, Michiyo Tamaki, Ikio Sawamura.

A Takarazuka Motion Picture Co., Ltd. Production. A Toho Co., Ltd. Release. Color (?). Toho Scope (?). 95 minutes. Released 1960.

U.S. VERSION: Released by Toho International Co., Ltd. English subtitles. No MPAA rating. 95 minutes. Released April 7, 1961.

The Phantom Cat. Director, Masamitsu Igayama.

CAST: Ryunosuke Tsukigata, Shinobu Chihara, H. Tomiya.

A Toei Co., Ltd. Production. Black and white (processed by Toei Chemistry Co., Ltd.). Academy ratio. 73 minutes. Released 1956.

U.S. VERSION: Distributor undetermined. International title: *Many Ghost-Cats.*

The Phantom Horse. Producer, Masaichi Nagata; Director, Koji Shima; Screenplay, Kimiyuki Hasegawa and Koji Shima, based on an original story by Hiroaki Fujii; Director of Photography, Michio Takahashi.

CAST: Ayako Wakao (Yuki Shiraishi), Yukokiko Iwatare (Jiro Shiraishi), Akihiko Yusa (Ichiro Shiraishi), Yoshiro Kitahara (Toki Onishi), Bontaro Miyake (Yasuke Shiraishi), Koreya Senda (Hamamura), Eijiro Yanagi (Hyogoro Onishi).

A Daiei Motion Picture Co., Ltd. Production. Filmed on location in Hokkaido and Tokyo. Eastman Color. Academy ratio. Running time undetermined. Released 1955.

U.S. VERSION: Released by Edward Harrison. English subtitles. Running time undetermined. No MPAA rating. Released July 23, 1956.

Pilgrimage to Japanese Baths / Nippon Yokujo monogatari ("Japanese Baths Story"). Director, Sadao Nakajima; Screenplay, Takeo Kaneko and Sadao Nakajima; Director of Photography, Shigeru Akatsuka; Music, Ichiro Araki.

CAST: Ikuko Kawamura, Fujio Tokita (narrators), Shoji Oki, Miwako Onaya.

A Toei Co., Ltd. Production. Eastman Color. ToeiScope. 89 minutes. Released January 12, 1971.

U.S. VERSION: Release undetermined. English subtitled version available. 89 minutes. No MPAA rating.

Pinku Redei no Katsudoshashin ("The Pink Ladies Motion Picture"). Director, Tsugunobu "Tom" Kotani.

CAST: Mitsuyo Nemoto, Keiko Masuda.

A Toho Co., Ltd. Production. Westrex recording system. Color (processed by Tokyo Laboratory Ltd.). Panavision. Running time undetermined. Released 1978.

U.S. VERSION: Distributor, if any, is undetermined. Also known as *The Pink Ladies Motion Picture*. The characters were later adapted for the U.S. teleseries "The Pink Ladies and Jeff," co-starring Jeff Altman.

The Pit / Ana ("The Pit"). Producer, Hidemasa Nagata; Planning, Hiroaki Fujii; Director/Screenplay, Kon Ichikawa; Director of Photography, Setsuo Kobayashi; Music, Yasushi Akutagawa; Art Director, Tomo Shimagawara; Lighting, Ishamu Yoneyama; Sound Recording, Toshikazu Watanabe.

CAST: Machiko Kyo (Nagako Kita), Eiji Funakoshi (Koisuke Chigi), So Yamamura (Keikichi Hakushu), Kenji Sugawara (Police Inspector Sarumaru), Ryoichi Ishii (Torigai Akita), Tanie Kitabayashi (Suga Akaba), Yasuko Kawakami (Fukiko Rokui), Mantaro Ushio (Sengi Kampaku), Fujio Harumoto (Gaiji Rokui), Sumiko Hidaka (Takeko Nakamura).

A Daiei Motion Picture Co., Ltd. Production. Black and white. Academy ratio. Running time undetermined. Released October 15, 1957.

U.S. VERSION: Distributor undetermined. English subtitles. No MPAA rating.

The Pitfall / Kashi to kodomo ("Sweet and Child"). Executive Producer, Hiroshi Teshigahara; Producers, Kiichi Ichikawa and Tadashi Ohono; Director, Hiroshi Teshigahara; Screenplay, Kobo Abe; Director of Photography, Hiroshi Segawa; Production Supervisor, Hiroshi Kawazo; Production Design, Kiyoshi Awazu; Lighting, Mitsuo Kume; Sound Recording, Keiji Mori; Music, Toru Takemitsu; Editor, Fusako Shuzui; Assistant Director, Masao Ogawa; Production Manager, Iwao Yashida.

CAST: Hisashi Igawa; K. Miyahara.

A Teshigahara Productions Production, in association with Toho Co., Ltd. A Toho Co., Ltd. Release. Westrex Recording System. Black and white. Toho Scope (?). 97 minutes. Released 1962.

U.S. VERSION: Distributor undetermined, possibly Toho International Co., Ltd. English subtitles. 97 minutes. No MPAA rating. Released 1964 (?).

Plants from the Dunes. Director, Ko Nakahira; Screenplay, Ichiro Ikeda and Akira Kato, based on an original story by Junnosuke Yoshiyuki; Director of Photography, Yoshihiro Yamazaki; Music, Toshiro Mayuzumi.

CAST: Noboru Nakaya (Ichiro Iki, *a salesman*), Kazuko Ineno (bar girl), Mieko Nisho (her sister), Yukiko Shimazaki (salesman's wife).

A Toho Co., Ltd. Production. Black and white with color inserts. Toho Scope (?). Running time and release date undetermined.

U.S. VERSION: Released by Toho International Co., Ltd. English subtitles. Running time undetermined. No MPAA rating. Released March 25, 1966.

Play It Cool / Denki kurage ("Electric Jellyfish"). Director, Yasuzo Masumura; Screenplay, Yasuzo Masumura, based on an original story by Masayuki

Toyama; Director of Photography, Setsuo Kobayashi; Art Director, Takesaburo Watanabe; Music, Hikaru Hayashi.

CAST: Mari Atsumi (Yumi), Yusuke Kawazu (Nozawa), Akemi Negishi (Tomi), Ko Nishimura (Kada), Ryoichi Tamagawa (Yoshimura), Sanae Nakahara (madam).

A Daiei Motion Picture Co., Ltd. Production. Fuji Color. DaieiScope. 93 minutes. Released May 1970.

U.S. VERSION: Released by Daiei Films International. English subtitles. 93 minutes. No MPAA rating. Released November 1970.

Playboy President / Shacho dochuki ("President's Travel Journal"). Director, Shue Matsubayashi.

CAST: Hisaya Morishige, Keiju Kobayashi, Tatsuya Mihashi, Daisuke Kato.

A Toho Co., Ltd. Production. Eastman Color. Toho Scope. 91 minutes. Released April 25, 1961.

U.S. VERSION: Released by Toho International Co., Ltd. English subtitles. The 15th "Company President" feature. Followed by *Playboy President Part II*, released May 30, 1961. 91 minutes. No MPAA rating. Released March 2, 1962.

The Pleasures of the Flesh / Etsuraku ("The Pleasures"). Producer, Masayuki Nakajima; Director/Screenplay, Nagisa Oshima; Director of Photography, Akira Takada; Art Director, Yasutaro Kon; Music Compilations, Joji Yuasa.

CAST: Katsuo Nakamura (Wakizaka), Mariko Kaga (Shoko), Yumiko Nogawa (Hitomi), Masako Yagi (Shizuko), Toshiko Higuchi (Keiko), Hiroko Shimizu (Mari), Shoji Kobayashi, Mitsuhiro Toura, Akira Hamada, Fumio Watanabe, Naramasa Komatsu, Mamoru Hirata, Daigo Kusano, Kei Sato.

A Sozo-sha Production. A Shochiku Co., Ltd. Release. Eastman Color. Shochiku GrandScope. 104 minutes. Released 1965.

U.S. VERSION: Released by Shochiku Films of America, Inc. English subtitles. 104 minutes. No MPAA rating. Released December 1965.

The Poem of the Blue Star. Producer, Sadao Sugihara; Director, Umeji Inoue; Screenplay, Tokuhei Wakao and Umeji Inoue; Assistant Director, Shoji Takano.

CAST: Akira Takarada, Tadao Takashima, Izumi Yukimura, Yukiji Asaoka, Ichiro Kanabe, Hiroshi Mizuhara, Shinichi Yanagisawa, Tatsuji Ebara, Michiyo Yamaki, Mitsuko Mito, Toru Abe, Kingoro Yanagiya, Shin Morikawa, Kyu Sazanka.

A Takarazuka Motion Picture Co., Ltd. Production. A Toho Co., Ltd. Release. Eastman Color. Toho Scope (?). 108 minutes. Released January 1960.

U.S. VERSION: Released by Toho International Co., Ltd. English subtitles. 108 minutes. No MPAA rating. Released October 25, 1961.

Poignant Story / Tsuma Toshite onna Toshite. Producers, Sanezumi Fujimoto and Hidehisa Suga; Director, Mikio Naruse; Screenplay, Toshiro Ide and Zenzo Matsuyama; Director of Photography, Atsushi Yasumoto.

CAST: Masayuki Mori, Hideko Takamine, Chikage Awashima, Yuriko Hoshi, Tatsuya Nakadai, Keiko Awaji, Kumi Mizuno, Choko Iida, Chieko Nakakita.

A Toho Co., Ltd. Production. Eastman Color. Toho Scope. 106 minutes. Released May 1961.

U.S. VERSION: Released by Toho International Co., Ltd. English subtitles. 106 minutes. No MPAA rating. Released March 23, 1962.

Poppy / Gubijinso ("Poppy"). Director, Kenji Mizoguchi; Screenplay, Haruo Takayanagi, based on the 1908 novel *Gubijinso*, by Soseki Natsume, and an adaptation by Daisuke Ito; Director of Photography, Minoru Miki; Costumes, Daizaburo Nakamura; Editor, Tsuruko Sakaneda.

CAST: Kuniko Miyake (Fujio), Ichiro Tsukida (Seizo Ono), Daijiro Natsukawa (Hajime Munechika), Yukichi Iwata (Tomotaka Inoue), Chiyoko Okura (Sayoko Inoue), Kazuyoshi Takeda (Kono), Ayako Nijo (Itoko), Mitsugu Terajima (Munechika's father), Toichiro Negishi (Asai), Yoko Umemura (Fujio's father), Kuniko Miyake (Fujio's mother).

A Daiichi Film Co., Ltd. Production. Filmed at Daiichi-Sagano Studios (Kyoto). Black and white. Academy ratio. 72 minutes. Released October 31, 1935.

U.S. VERSION: Distributor undetermined. English subtitles. 72 minutes. No MPAA rating. Released 1981 (?).

Porco Rosso / Kurenai no buta ("Pig of Deep Red") **[animated]**. Producer, Yasuyoshi Tokuma; Director/ Screenplay, Hayao Miyazaki; Music, Joe Hisaishi.

VOICE CHARACTERIZATIONS: Shuichiro Moriyama, Tokiko Kato.

A Tokuma Shoten Publishing Co., Ltd. Production. Color. Spherical wide screen (?). 93 minutes. Released 1992.

U.S. VERSION: Distributor, if any, is undetermined.

Port Arthur / Nihyakusankochi ("203 Plateaus"). Producer, Shigeru Okada; Director, Toshio Masuda; Screenplay, Kazuo Kasahara; Director of Photography, Masahiko Iimura; Art Director, Hiroshi Kitagawa; Music, Naozumi Yamamoto and Masashi Sada; Editor, Kiyoaki Saito; Sound, Hiroyoshi Munakata.

CAST: Tatsuya Nakadai, Teruhiko Aoi, Toshiro Mifune, Hisaya Morishige, Shigero Koyama, Teruhiko Aoi, Masako Natsume, Masayuki Yuhara, Kentaro Kaneko.

A Toei Co., Ltd. Production. Color. Panavision (?). 185 minutes. Released 1980.

U.S. VERSION: Released by Shochiku Films of America, Inc. English subtitles. 155 minutes. No MPAA rating.

Portrait of Chieko / Chieko-sho ("Portrait of Chieko"). Director, Noboru Nakamura; Screenplay, Minoru Hirose and Noboru Nakamura; Director of Photography, Hiroshi Takemura; Art Director, Tatsuo Hamada; Music, Masaru Sato.

CAST: Tetsuro Tamba (Kotaro Takamura), Shima Iwashita (Chieko), Eiji Okada (Tsubaki), Takamaru Sasaki (Koun Takamura), Jin Nakayama (Hoshu), Yoko Minamida (Kazuko).

A Shochiku Co., Ltd. Production. Eastman Color. Shochiku GrandScope (?). 125 minutes. Released 1967.

U.S. VERSION: Released by Shochiku Films of America, Inc. English subtitles. 125 minutes. No MPAA rating. Released March 13, 1968.

Trade ad for *Portrait of Hell* (1969)

Portrait of Hell / Jigokuhen ("Portrait of Hell"). Executive Producer, Tomoyuki Tanaka; Producer, Tatsuo Matsuoko; Director, Shiro Toyoda; Screenplay, Toshio Yasumi, based on the "Tokyo nichi nichi" serial, *Jigokuhen*, by Ryunosuke Akutagawa; Director of Photography, Kazuo Yamada; Music, Yasushi Akutagawa; Art Director, Shinobu Muraki; Sound, Toho Recording Centre; Sound Effects, Toho Sound Effects Group.

CAST: Kinnosuke Nakamura (Lord Hosokawa), Tatsuya Nakadai (Yoshihide, *the artist*), Yoko Naito (Yoshika, *his daughter*), Jun Oide, Kichiro Nakamura, Masanobu Okubo, Eisei Amamoto, Masao Yamafuki, Ikio Sawamara, Kumeko Otoba, Kazuo Suzuki.

A Toho Co., Ltd. Production. Westrex Recording system. Eastman Color (processed by Tokyo Laboratory, Ltd.). Panavision. 95 minutes. Released September 1969.

U.S. VERSION: Released by Toho International Co., Ltd. English subtitles. Reissued in April 1972 by Toho International. Alternate titles: *A Story of Hell* and *The Hell Screen*. 91 minutes. No MPAA rating. Released November 18, 1969.

Portrait of Madame Yuki / Yuki fujin ezu ("Portrait of Madame Yuki"). Producer, Kazuo Takimura; Director, Kenji Mizoguchi; Screenplay, Yoshikata Yoda and Kazuro Funabashi, based on the serialized novel by Seiichi Funabashi; Director of Photography, Joji Obara; Art Director, Hiroshi Mizutani; Music, Fumio Hayasaka; Sound Recording, Masakazu Kamiya.

CAST: Michiyo Kogure (Yuki Shinano), Ken Uehara (Masaya Kikunaka), Eijiro Yanagi (Naoyuki Shinano), Yuriko Hamada (Ayako), So Yamamura (Tateoka), Yoshiko Kuga (Hamako Abe), Haruya Kato (Seitaro), Kumeko Urabe (San), Shizue Natsukawa (Osumi), So Yamamura (Tateoka), Satoshi Komori and Rei Ishikawa (sushi bartenders at Utsubokan Inn), Ichiro Sawai (bellboy), Shiro Mizuki (driver).

A Takimura Productions/Shin Toho Co., Ltd. Production. Black and white. Academy ratio. 88 minutes. Released October 14, 1950.

U.S. VERSION: Distributor undetermined. English subtitles. Also known as *A Picture of Madame Yuki*. 86 minutes. No MPAA rating. Released 1978 (?).

Preparations for the Festival / Matsuri no junbi ("Preparations for the Festival"). Director, Kazuo Kuroki; Screenplay, Takehiro Nakajima, based on his original story; Director of Photography, Tatsuo Suzuki; Music, Teizo Matsumura; Art Directors, Takeo Kimura and Yugi Maruyama.

CAST: Jun Ito (Tateo), Keiko Takeshita (Ryoko), Yoshio Harada (Toshihiro).

A Japan Art Theatre Guild Co., Ltd./Soeisha Co, Ltd. Production. A Toho Co, Ltd. Release. Color. Panavision (?). 117 minutes. Released 1975.

U.S. VERSION: Released by ATG in subtitled format. 117 minutes. No MPAA rating. Released October 5, 1978.

Pressure of Guilt / Shiro to kuro ("White and Black"). Producer, Ichiro Sato; Director, Hiromichi Horikawa; Screenplay, Shinobu Hashimoto; Director of Photography, Hiroshi Murai; Art Director, Hiroshi Mizutani; Music, Toru Takemitsu; Sound Recording, Toshio Harashima.

CAST: Keiju Kobayashi (Ochiai), Tatsuya Nakadai (Hamano), Hisashi Igawa (Wakida), Koreya Senda (Munakata), Ko Nishimura (Hirao), Mayumi Ozora (Marumatsu), Chikage Awashima (Munakata's wife), Nobuko Otoba (Ochiai's wife).

A Toho Co., Ltd. Production. Black and white. Toho Scope. 113 minutes. Released 1963.

U.S. VERSION: Released by Toho International Co., Ltd. English subtitles. 113 minutes. No MPAA rating. Released January 1964.

Pride of the Campus / Ginza no wakadaisho ("Young Guy of Ginza"). Producer, Sanezumi Fujimoto; Director, Toshio Sugie; Screenplay, Ryozo Kasahara and Yasuo Tanami.

CAST: Yuzo Kayama, Yuriko Hoshi, Reiko Dan, Yoko Fujiyama, Tatsuyoshi Ehara, Machiko Naka, Akemi Kita, Ken Uehara, Ichiro Arishima, Kunie Tanaka, Asami Kuji, Choko Iida, Bokuzen Hidari.

A Toho Co., Ltd. Production. Eastman Color. Toho Scope. 94 minutes. Released February 1962.

U.S. VERSION: Released by Toho International Co., Ltd. English subtitles. The 2nd "Young Guy" feature. Followed by *Japan's No. 1 Young Guy* (1962). No MPAA rating. 94 minutes. Released December 14, 1962.

The Priest Killer Comes Back / Gokuaku Bozu, Nenbutsu Sandangiri ("Bad Priest – Invocation of the Three Stabbings"). Director, Takashi Harada; Screenplay, Akira Murao and Koji Takada; Director of Photography, Nagaki Yamagishi; Art Director, Akira Yoshimura; Music, Toshiaki Tsushima.

CAST: Tomisaburo Wakayama (Priest Shinkai), Yuriko Mishima (Hakuyo), Ichiro Nakatani (Takegoro Aizu), Shozo Arikawa (Inosuke), Shinichiro Mikami (Hideji), Eizo Kitamura (Torazo), Bunta Sugawara, Yuki Jono.

A Toei Co., Ltd. Production. Eastman Color. ToeiScope. 94 minutes. Released February 21, 1970.

U.S. VERSION: Release undetermined. English subtitled version available. A sequel to *The Priest Killer* (1969). 94 minutes. No MPAA rating.

Prince of Space / Yusei oji ("Planet Prince"). Director, Eijiro Wakabayashi; Screenplay, Shin Morita, based on an original story by Masaru Ito and an idea by Sanehiko Sonoda; Director of Photography, Masahiko Iimura; Special Effects, Shozo Muroki; Lighting, Kenzo Ginya; Art Director, Shuichiro Nakamura; Music, Katsuhisa Hattori; Theme Song, Toshiba Records; Lyrics, Shu Igami; Vocalist, Yoichi Ohe; Editor, Ko Nichii; Assistant Director, Hajime Sato; Sound Recording, Shozo Hirokami.

CAST: Tatsuya Umemiya (Prince Planet), Joji Oda, Hiroko Mine, Takashi Kanda, Nobu Yatsuna, Ken Sudo.

A Toei Co., Ltd. Production. A two-chapter serial. Black and white (processed by Toei Chemistry Co., Ltd.). ToeiScope. Chapter 1, 57 minutes; released March 19, 1959. Chapter 2, 64 minutes; released May 26, 1959.

U.S. VERSION: Released by Walter H. Manley Enterprises, Inc. English-dubbed. Advertised as *Invaders from Space*. Theatrical release in the United States uncertain. English language version produced by Bellucci Productions, Inc.; English Dialogue, Joseph Bellucci. Alternate titles: *Invaders from the Spaceship*, *The Star Prince*, *Prince Planet*, *Planet Prince*. 83 minutes. No MPAA rating. Released 1962 (?).

Princess from the Moon / Taketori monogatari ("The Story of Taketori"). Executive Producers, Tomoyuki Tanaka, Shigeaki Hazama; Producers, Masaru Kakutani, Hiroaki Fujii, and Junichi Shinsaka; Director, Kon Ichikawa; Screenplay, Ryuzo Kikushima, Mistuyoshi Ishigami, Kon Ichikawa, and Shinya Hidaka; Director of Photography, Setsuo Kobayashi; Costume Design, Emi Wada; Music, Kensaku Tanigawa. *Toho Special Effects Group:* Director, Teruyoshi Nakano.

CAST: Toshiro Mifune (Taketori), Ayako Wakao (Tayoshime, *his wife*), Yasuko Sawaguchi (Kaya, *Princess Kaguya*), Koji Ishizaka (Mikado), Kiichi Nakai (Minister of the Military), Koasa Shumputei (Minister of Culture), Takatoshi Takeda (Minister of Finance), Megumi Odaka (Akeno), Katsuo Nakamura, Shiro Ito, Fujio Tokita, Takeshi Kato, Kyoko Kishida, Hirokazu Yamaguchi, Jun Hamamura, Pen Idemitsu, Michiyo Yokoyama, Hirokazu Inoue, Miho Nakano.

A Toho Co., Ltd. Production. Dolby Stereo. Color. Spherical wide screen. 121 minutes. Released September 25, 1987.

U.S. VERSION: Released by Toho International Co., Ltd. English subtitles. 121 minutes. No MPAA rating. Released September 14, 1987.

The Princess of Badger Palace / Oatari Tanukigoken ("Racoon Palace Tanukigoken"). Producer, Sadao Sugihara; Director, Kozo Saeki; Screenplay, Tatsuo Nakata, based on the story by Keigo Kimura; Director of Photography, Kozo Okazaki; Music, Hachiro Matsui; Choreography, Keiji Hanayagi and Yoji Agata.

CAST: Hibari Misora (Tanukichiro), Izumi Yukimura (Princess Kinuta/Okuro, *the maid*), Shinji Yamada (Tanuchiyo), Yumi Shirakawa (Spirit of the Butterfly), Ichiro Arishima (Tanuzaemon), Kenji Sahara.

A Takarazuka Eiga Co., Ltd. Production, in association with Toho Co., Ltd. A Toho Co., Ltd. Release. Eastman Color. Toho Scope. 97 minutes. Released 1958.

U.S. VERSION: Release undetermined, possibly by Toho International Co., Ltd. in subtitled format. No MPAA rating.

Princess Yang Kwei Fei / Yokihi ("Princess"). Producers, Masaichi Nagata and Sir Run Run Shaw; Director, Kenji Mizoguchi; Screenplay, T'ao Chin, Matsutaro Kawaguchi, Yoshitaka Yoda, and Masashige Narusawa, loosely based on historical events, and the poem *Ch'ang hen Ko* by Pai Lo T'ien; Director of Photography, Kohei Sugiyama; Color Consultant, Tatsuyuki Yokota; Art Director, Hiroshi Mizutani; Period Authenticity, Lu Shih-hou; Lighting, Yukikazu Kubota; Music, Fumio Hayasaka; Sound Recording, Kunio Hashimoto.

CAST: Machiko Kyo (Yang Kwei Fei), Masayuki Mori (Emperor Hsuan-tsung),

So Yamamura (An Lu-shan), Eitaro Ozawa (Yang Kuo-chung), Isao Yamagata (Yang Hsien), Yoko Minamida (Hung-t'ao), Noboru Kiritachi (Ts'ui-hua), Chieko Murata (Lu-hua), Michiko Ai (Hung-hua), Eitaro Shindo (Kao Li-hsi), Tatsuya Ichiguro (Li Lin-fu), Bontaro Miake (Ch'en Hsuan-li), Haruko Sugimura (Princess Yen-ch'un), Osamu Maruyama (Li Kuei-nien), Sachiko Murase (Ch'eng-fei), Reiko Himeji, Yoshiko Kusunoki (Ch'eng-fei's attendants), Kinzo Shin (chamberlain), Fujio Harumoto (chamberlain).

A Daiei Motion Picture Co., Ltd./Sir Run Run Shaw Production. A Japanese/Hong Kong co-production in Japanese. Filmed at Daiei-Tokyo Studios. Eastman Color. Academy ratio. 98 minutes. Released May 3, 1955.

U.S. VERSION: Released by Buena Vista. English subtitles. Alternate title: *Yang Kwei Fei.* 85 minutes. No MPAA rating. Released September 10, 1956. Reissued in 1973 by New Yorker Films.

The Private Police / Soshiki Boryoku—kyodai sakazuki ("Society of Violent Brother's Sake Cup"). Director, Junya Sato; Screenplay, Yoshihiro Ishimatsu, based on an original story by Yoshito Iwasa; Director of Photography, Masahiko Iimura; Art Director, Hiroshi Kitagawa; Music, Shunsuke Kikuchi.

CAST: Noboru Ando (Oba), Bunta Sugawara (Kijima), Hitomi Nozue (Hiroko), Tomo Uchida (Kano), Tetsuro Tamba, Kyosuke Machida, Kanjuro Arashi.

A Toei Co., Ltd. Production. Eastman Color. ToeiScope. 93 minutes. Released September 6, 1969.

U.S. VERSION: Release undetermined. English subtitled version available. The 3rd and last feature of a series (1967-69). 93 minutes. No MPAA rating.

Procurers of Hell / Jigoku no utage ("Banquet of Hell"). Executive Producer, Ichiro Nagashima; Director, Kihachi Okamoto; Screenplay, Ichiro Ikeda and Ei Ogawa; Director of Photography, Tokuzo Kuroda; Music, Masaru Sato.

CAST: Tatsuya Mihashi (Tobe), Reiko Dan (Saeko), Jun Tazaki, Chieko Nakakita, Makoto Sato.

A Tokyo Eiga Co., Ltd. Production, in association with Toho Co., Ltd. A Toho Co., Ltd. Release. Black and white. Toho Scope. 95 minutes. Released 1961.

U.S. VERSION: Release undetermined, possibly by Toho International Co., Ltd. in subtitled format. No MPAA rating. Japanese title also given as *Jigoku no Kyoen.*

The Prodigal Son / Onna goroshi abura jigoku ("Murderess, Hell of Oil"). Associate Producers, Shiro Horie and Koji Toita; Director, Hiromichi Horikawa; Screenplay, Shinobu Hashimoto; Director of Photography, Asakazu Nakai; Art Director, Yasuhide Kato; Music, Koji Taku.

CAST: Senjaku Nakamura (Yohei), Ganjiro Nakamura (his father), Eiko Miyoshi (his mother), Kyoko Kagawa (his sister), Michiyo Aratama (Okichi), Takako Fujino (Kogiku).

A Toho Co., Ltd. Production. Eastman Color. Toho Scope. 99 minutes. Released 1958.

U.S. VERSION: Released by Toho International Co., Ltd. English subtitles. 99 minutes. No MPAA rating. Released January 29, 1964.

The Professional—Golgo 13 **[animated]**. Producer, Yutaka Fujioka, Mataichiro Yamamoto, and Nobuo Inada; Director, Osamu Dezaki; Based on the graphic novel by Takao Saito; Director of Photography, Hirokata Takahashi; Editor, Mitsuo Tsurubuchi; Music, Toshiyuki Omori.

VOICE CHARACTERIZATIONS: (undetermined).

A Tokyo Eiga Shinsha Production. Color. Spherical wide screen. 95 minutes. Release date undetermined.

U.S. VERSION: Released by Streamline Pictures. English-dubbed. Producer, Carl Macek; English Director/Dialogue Director, Greg Snegoff. Alternate title: *The Professional.* 95 minutes. No MPAA rating. Released October 1992. Voice characterizations for U.S. version: Greg Snegoff (Duke Togo, *aka Golgo 13*), Michael McConnohie (Leonard Dawson), Mike Reynolds (Bragan), Edie Mirman (Cindy), Joyce Kurtz (Cindy), Diane Michelle (Rita), Kerrigan Mahan (Pablo), David Povall (Garvin), Ed Mannix (Jefferson).

Project A-ko / Purojukuto A-ko ("Project A-ko") **[animated]**. Executive Producer, Naotaka Yoshida; Producer, Kazufumi Nomura; Director, Katsuhiko Nishijima; Screenplay, Yuji Moriyama, Katsuhiko Nishijima, and Tomoko Kawasaki, based on an original story by Katsuhiko Nishijima and Kazumi Shirasaka; Character Design/Animation Director, Yuji Moriyama; Art Director, Shinji Kimura (Kobayashi Productions); "Mecha" Animation Director, Shoichi Masuo; Music Director, Yasunori Honda; Music, Richie Zito, Joey Carbone, and Toji Akasaka. *Songs:* Producer/Composers, Joey Carbone and Richie Zito; "Dance Away" (A-ko's theme) Performer, Annie Livingston; "In Your Eyes" (B-ko's theme) Performer, Samantha Newark; "Follow Your Dreams" (C-ko's theme) Performer, Valerie Stevenson; Director of Photography, Takafumi Arai; "Mecha" Design, Graviton; Assistant Director, Shigeru Morikawa.

VOICE CHARACTERIZATIONS: Miki Ito (Eiko Magama, *A-ko*), Emi Shinohara (Biko Daitokuji, *B-ko*), Michie Tomisawa (Shiko Kotobuki, *C-ko*), Tetsuaki Genada (Mysterious Creature "D"), Shuichi Ikeda (captain), Asami Mukodono (Miss Ayumi), Daisuke Gori/Sayuri Ikemoto (Mari), Yoko Kogayu (Asa), Yoshino Takamori (Ine), Megumi Hayashibara (Ume).

A Soeishinsha Co., Ltd./A.P.P.P. Co., Ltd. Production. Dolby Stereo. Color. Spherical wide screen (1.66:1). 84 minutes. Released 1986.

U.S. VERSION: Released by Central Park Media Corporation. A U.S. Manga Corps. Release. English subtitles. Executive Producer, John McDonnell; Translator, Matt Thorn; Technical Supervisor, Neil Nadelman; Production Coordinator, Cliff Rosen. 84 minutes. No MPAA rating. Released 1991.

A Promise / Ningen no yakusoku ("A Man's Promise"). Producers, Kazunobu Yamaguchi, Chokichi Nakamichi, and Kiyoshi Fujimoto; Director, Yoshishige Yoshida; Screenplay, Yoshishige Yoshida and Fukiko Miyauchi, based on an original story by Shuichi Sae; Director of Photography, Yoshihiro Yamazaki; Music, Haruomi Hosono.

CAST: Rentaro Mikuni (Ryosaku Morimoto, *the father), Sachiko Murase (Tatsu, his wife*), Choichiro Kawarazaki (Yoshio, *their son*), Orie Sato (Ritsuko, *his wife*), Tetsuta Sugimoto (Takao, *Yoshio's son*), Kumiko Takeda (Naoko, *Yoshio's daughter*), Reiko Tajima (Saeko Nogawa, *Yoshio's mistress*), Tomisaburo Wakayama (Inspector Tagami), Sakatoshi Yonekura (Sgt. Miora), Choei Takahashi (Takeya Nakamura), Meiko Yuri (Noriko Nakamura).

A Seiyu Co., Ltd./TV Asahi/Kinema Tokyo Production. Color. Spherical wide screen (?). 124 minutes. Released 1986.

U.S. VERSION: Distributor undetermined. English subtitles. 124 minutes. No MPAA rating. Released March 17, 1987.

Prophecies of Nostradamus / Nostradamus no dai yogen Catastrophe—1999 ("Great Prophecies of Nostradamus: Catastrophe—1999"). Executive Producers, Tomoyuki Tanaka and Osamu Tanaka; Director, Toshio Masuda; Screenplay, Toshio Masuda, Yoshimitsu Banno, and Toshio Yasumi, based on an original story by Tsutomu Goto, and loosely based on the writings of Michel de Notredame; Director of Photography, Rokuro Nishigaki; Music, Isao Tomita; 2nd Unit Director, Yoshimitsu Banno; Sound, Toho Recording Centre; Sound Effects, Toho Sound Effects Group. *Toho Special Effects Group*: Director, Teruyoshi Nakano; Photography, Mototaka Tomioka; Lighting, Masakuni Morimoto; Art Director, Yasuyuki Inoue; Matte Process, Kazunobu Sanpei; Optical Photography, Takeshi Miyanishi; Assistant Director, Koichi Kawakita.

CAST: Tetsuro Tamba (Dr. Nishiyama), Takashi Shimura (worried doctor), Akihiko Hirata, Hiroshi Koizumi (scientists), Toshio Kurosawa, So Yamamura, Kaoru Yumi, Yoko Tsukasa, Osman Yusef.

A Toho Co., Ltd. Production. Color

(processed by Tokyo Laboratory, Ltd.). Panavision. 114 minutes. Released August 3, 1974.

U.S. VERSION: Released by Toho International Co., Ltd. English subtitles. 92 minutes. No MPAA rating. Released July 13, 1979. Released to television by United Productions of America, Inc. as *The Last Days of Planet Earth*. English-dubbed. A UPA Productions of America Release. Executive Producer, Henry G. Saperstein. Also released to television as *Catastrophe: 1999*, which is also the U.K. title. Includes stock footage from *The Last War* (1961). 72 minutes.

Pumpkin / Kabocha ("Pumpkin"). Director, Yasujiro Ozu; Screenplay, Komatsu Kitamura, based on an idea by Yasujiro Ozu; Director of Photography, Hideo Shigehara.

CAST: Tatsuo Saito, Yurie Hinatsu, Takeshi Sakamoto, Yoko Kozakura, Chishu Ryu.

A Shochiku Co., Ltd. Production. Filmed at Shochiku-Kamata Studios. Silent with benshi. Black and white. Academy ratio. 60 minutes. Released August 31, 1928.

U.S. VERSION: Never released in the United States. A lost film.

Punishment Room / Shokei no heya ("Punishment Room"). Producer, Hidemasa Nagata; Planning, Itsuo Doi; Director, Kon Ichikawa; Screenplay, Natto Wada and Keiji Hasebe, based on a story by Shintaro Ishihara; Director of Photography, Yoshihisa Nakagawa; Music, Koji Taku; Art Director, Tomo Shimogawara; Lighting, Masayoshi Izumi; Sound Recording, Takeo Suda.

CAST: Hiroshi Kawaguchi (Katsumi), Ayako Wakao (Akiko Aochi), Masayoshi Umewaka (Ito), Mamoru Kodaka (Ryoji), Keizo Kawasaki (Takejima).

A Daiei Motion Picture Co., Ltd. Production. Black and white. Academy ratio. 96 minutes. Released June 28, 1956.

U.S. VERSION: Distributor undetermined. English subtitles. No MPAA rating. Release date undetermined.

Pursuit at Dawn / Akasuki no tsuiseki ("Pursuit at Dawn"). Producer, Tomoyuki Tanaka; Director, Kon Ichikawa; Screenplay, Kaneto Shindo; Director of Photography, Minoru Yokoyama; Lighting, Choshiro Ishii; Sound Recording, Hisao Negishi; Art Director, Tomo Nakofuru; Music, Nobuo Iida.

CAST: Ryo Ikebe (Patrolman Ishikawa), Michitaro Mizushima (Patrolman Yamaguchi), Yunosuke Ito (Patrolman Hinoki), Jun Tazaki (Patrolman Date), Yoko Sugi (Tomoko), Chizuko Nogami (Yukie), Hiroshi Yanagiya (Patrolman Tabe), Fujio Nagahama (Funaki).

A Tanaka Company Production. A Shintoho Co., Ltd. Release. Black and white. Academy ratio. 94 minutes. Released October 3, 1950.

U.S. VERSION: Distributor undetermined. English subtitles. No MPAA rating. Release date undetermined.

Puss'n Boots / Nagagutsu o haita neko ("Puss'n Boots") [**animated**]. Director, Kimio Yabuki; Screenplay, Hisashi Inoue and Morihisa Yamamoto, based on the story by Charles Perrault; Chief Animator, Koji Mori; Art Director, Mataji Urata; Music, Seiichiro Uno.

VOICE CHARACTERIZATIONS: (undetermined).

A Toei Animation Studio (Tokyo) Production. Eastman Color. ToeiScope. 80 minutes. Released March 18, 1969.

U.S. VERSION: Release undetermined. English subtitled version available. 80 minutes. No MPAA rating.

Queen Bee / Jobachi ("Queen Bee"). Executive Producer, Haruki Kadokawa; Producers, Kazuo Baba and Osamu Tanaka; Director, Kon Ichikawa; Screenplay, Shinya Hidaka, Chiho Katsura, and Kon Ichikawa, based on a story by Seishi Yokomizo; Director of Photography, Kiyoshi Hasegawa; Music, Shinichi Tanabe; Art Director, Iwao Akune; Sound Recording, Fumio Yanoguchi; Lighting, Kojiro Sato.

CAST: Koji Ishizaka (Kosuke Kindaichi), Mieko Takamine (Takako Higashikoji),

Yoko Tsukasa (Tsutayo), Keiko Kishi (Hideko Kamio, *the governess*), Tatsuya Nakadai (Ginzo Daidoji), Midori Hagio (Kotoe Daidoji, *his wife*), Kie Nakai (Tomoko Daidoji, *her daughter*), Masaya Oki (Rentaro Tamon), Takeshi Kato (Todoroki, *the police inspector*).

A Toho Co., Ltd. Production, in association with Kadokawa Publishing Co., Ltd. Color. Spherical wide screen. 139 minutes. Released February 11, 1978.

U.S. VERSION: Released by Toho International Co., Ltd. English subtitles. 139 minutes. No MPAA rating. Released June 30, 1978.

Quick-Draw Okatsu / Hitokiri Okatsu ("Killer Okatsu"). Director, Nobuo Nakagawa; Screenplay, Koji Takada; Director of Photography, Masahiko Iimura; Art Director, Shinichi Eno; Music, Masahiko Takeda.

CAST: Junko Miyazono (Katsu), Reiko Oshida (Rui), Kenji Imai (Shiozaki), Yukie Kagawa (Saki), Chujiro Tomita (Torazo), Tetsuya Yamaoka (Samonji), Ko Nishimura

A Toei Co., Ltd. Production. Eastman Color. ToeiScope. 89 minutes. Released April 10, 1969.

U.S. VERSION: Release undetermined. English subtitled version available. The 2nd feature in a three-film series (1968-69). 89 minutes. No MPAA rating.

The Quiet Duel / Shizukanaru ketto ("A Silent Duel"). Producers, Sojiro Motoki and Hisao Ichikawa; Director, Akira Kurosawa; Screenplay, Senkichi Taniguchi and Akira Kurosawa, based on the play by Kazuo Kikuta; Director of Photography, Shoichi Aisaka; Editor, Masanori Tsuji; Lighting, Tsunekichi Shibata; Art Director, Koichi Imai; Music, Akira Ifukube; Still Photographer, Isamu Shiina; Sound Recording, Mitsuo Hasegawa.

CAST: Toshiro Mifune (Kyoji Fujisaki), Takashi Shimura (Konosue Fujisaki), Miki Sanjo (Misao Matsumoto), Kenjiro Uemura (Susumu Nakada), Chieko Nakakita (Takiko Nakada), Noriko Sengoku (Nurse Rui Minegishi), Jyunnosuke Miyazaki (Corporal Horiguchi), Isamu Yamaguchi (Patrolman Nosaka), Shigeru Matsumoto (appendicitis boy), Hiroko Machida (Imai), Kan Takami (laborer), Kisao Tobita (typhoid boy), Shigeyuki Miyajima (officer), Tadashi Date (father of appendicitis boy), Etsuko Sudo (mother of appendicitis boy), Seiji Izumi (policeman), Masateru Sasaki (old soldier), Kenichi Miyajima (dealer), Yosuke Kudo (boy), Yakuko Ikegami (gaudy female), Wakayo Matsumura (student nurse), Hatsuko Wakahara (Mii-chan).

A Daiei Motion Picture Co., Ltd. Production. Black and white. Academy ratio. 95 minutes. Released March 13, 1949.

U.S. VERSION: Released by Daiei International Films, Inc. English subtitles. Alternate title: *A Silent Duel*. 95 minutes. No MPAA rating. Released November 1983.

The Rabble / Garakuta ("The Rabble"). Producer, Tomoyuki Tanaka; Director, Hiroshi Inagaki; Screenplay, Shintaro Mimura, Masato Ide, and Hiroshi Inagaki; Director of Photography, Kazuo Yamada; Music, Ikuma Dan.

CAST: Somegoro Ichikawa (Kanzaburo), Yuriko Hoshi (Midori), Mayumi Ozora (Makie), Tadao Nakamaru, Ichiro Arishima.

A Toho Co., Ltd. Production. Eastman Color. Toho Scope. 120 minutes. Released 1964.

U.S. VERSION: Released by Frank Lee International. English subtitles. 116 minutes. No MPAA rating. Released March 22, 1964.

Rainbow Bridge / Niji no hashi ("Rainbow Bridge"). Producer, Yasuzo Ogawa; Director, Zenzo Matsuyama; Screenplay, Zenzo Matsuyama, based on the novel by Fujiko Sawada; Director of Photography, Takao Saito; Art Director, Yoshiro Muraki; Music, Masato Kai.

CAST: Emi Wakui (Chiyo), Atsuro Watabe (Sokichi), Masanobu Takashima (Fujita).

An Ogawa Kikaku, Inc. Production. Color. Spherical wide screen (1.85:1). 115 minutes. Released 1993.

U.S. VERSION: Distributor, if any, is undetermined.

Rainbow Brite and the Star Stealer **[animated]**. Producers, Jean Chalopin, Andy Heyward, and Tetsuo Katayama; Directors, Bernard Deyries and Kimio Yabuki; Screenplay, Howard R. Cohen, based on a story by Jean Chalopin, Howard R. Cohen, and characters developed by Hallmark Properties; Music, Haim Saban and Shuki Levy; Animation, Kaoru Hirata, Satoe Nishiyama, Fukuo Yamamoto, Mitsuru Aoyama, Masaki Kajishima, Nobuyuki Haga, Yasunopri Miyazawa, Kazuhiko Miyake, Yasushi Tanizawa, Kinichiroi Suzuki, Masami Shimada, Shinichi Imakuma, Yasuyuki Tada, Makoto Shinjou, Junzo Ono, Toshio Kaneko, Tado Katsu Yoshida, Michio Ikeda, Hitomi Kakubari, Atsumi Hashimoto, Kiyomi Masuda, Katsuo Takasaki, Yoshio Mukainakano, Hiroshi Oikawa, Shigetaka Kiyoyama, Katsuko Kanazawa, Takashi Hyodo, Akinobia Takahashi, Takenori Mihara.

VOICE CHARACTERIZATIONS (U.S. VERSION): Bettina (Rainbow Brite), Patrick Farley (Lurky, On-X, Buddy Blue, Dog Guard, Spectran, Slurthie, Glitterbot), Peter Cullen (Murky, Castle Monster, Glitterbot, guard, Skydancer, Slurthie), Robbie Lee (Twin, Shy Violet, Indigo, La La Orange, Spectran, Sprites), Andre Stojka (Starlite, Wizard, Spectran), David Mendenhall (Krys), Rhonda Aldrich (The Princess, The Creature), Les Tremayne (Orin, Bombo, TV announcer), Mona Marshall (Red Butler, witch, castle creature, Spectran, Patty O'Green, Canary Yellow), Jonathan Harris (Count Blogg), Marissa Mendenhall (Stormy), Scott Menville (Brian), Charles Adler (Popo), David Workman (Sergeant Zombo).

A DIC Enterprises Production. A U.S./Japanese co-production. Color. Spherical wide screen (1.85:1). 97 minutes. Released 1985.

U.S. VERSION: Released by Warner Bros. English-dubbed. Songs: "Brand New Day," "Rainbow Brite and Me." Prints by Technicolor. 97 minutes. MPAA rating: "G." Released November 16, 1985.

Rainbow Kids / Dai yukai ("Great Kidnapping"). Producers, Kishu Morichi and Yosuke Mizuno; Director, Kihachi Okamoto; Screenplay, Kihachi Okamoto, based on an original story by Makoto Tendo; Director of Photography, Masahiro Kishimoto; Music, Masaru Sato.

CAST: Ken Ogata, Tanie Kitabayashi, Toru Kazama, Hiroshi Nishikawa.

A Kihachi Production Company Production. Color. Anamorphic wide screen (?). 120 minutes. Released 1991.

U.S. VERSION: Released by Fujisankei. English subtitles. 120 minutes. No MPAA rating. Released July 1, 1992.

Ran ("Chaos"). Executive Producer, Katsumi Furukawa; Producers, Serge Silberman and Masato Hara; Director/Editor, Akira Kurosawa; Screenplay, Akira Kurosawa, Hideo Oguni, and Masato Ide, loosely based on the play *King Lear*, by William Shakespeare; Director of Photography, Takao Saito; Art Directors, Yoshiro Muraki and Shinobu Muraki; Associate Director, Ishiro Honda; Costumes, Emi Wada; Music, Toru Takemitsu, performed by the Sapporo Symphony Orchestra, and conducted by Hiroyuki Iwaki; Sound Recording, Fumio Yanoguchi and Shotaro Yoshida; Sound, Toho Recording Centre and Paris Studio Billancourt (Paris); General Production Manager, Ully Pickardt; Production Managers, Teruyo Nogami, Seikichi Iizumi, Satoro Izeki, and Takashi Ohashi; Production Coordinator, Hisao Kurosawa; 1st Assistant Directors, Fumiaki Okada and Bernard Cohn; 2nd Assistant Directors, Takashi Koizumi, Ichiro Yamamoto, Okihiro Yoneda, Kyoko Watanabe, Vittorio Dare Ole, and Kunio Nozaki; Camera Assistants, Yoshinori Sekiguchi, Noboru Asono, Kiyoshi Anzai, Satoru Suzuki, Shigeo Suzuki, Mazakazu Oka, Kosuke Matsushima, Hidehiro Igarashi, and Nobuyuki Kito; Gaffer, Takeharu Sato; Electricians, Koji Choya, Koichi Kamata, Tetsuo Sawada, Yoshio Iyama, Makoto Sano, Yuichi Oyama, Shintaro Tazaki, and Mutsuo Komine; Sound Assistants, Takenori Misawa, Hideo Takeichi, Takayuki Goto, and Soichi Inoue; Final Mixing, Claude Villand; Editing Assistants, Ryusuke Otsubo, Hideto Aga, and Hajime Ishihara; Set Decorators, Tsuneo Shimura, Osami Tonsho, Mitsuyuki Kimura, Jiro Hirai, and Yasuyoshi Ototake; Makeup,

Masayuki Mori and Machiko Kyo in Akira Kurosawa's landmark *Rashomon* (1950).

Shoichiro Ueda, Tameyuki Aimi, Chihako Naito, and Noriko Takamizawa; Visoria Professional Makeup by Christian Dior; Hair Dressers, Yoshiko Matsumoto and Noriko Sato; Wardrobe Assistants, Akira Fukuda, Noriko Taguchi, and Kazuko Numata; Still Photographers, Daisaburo Harada and Yoshio Sato; Still Photograph Processing, Central Color (Paris); Unit Managers, Masayuki Motomochi and Tsutomu Sakurai; Production Assistants, Masahiko Kumada and Ko Nanri; Accountant, Takeo Suga; Titles, Den Film Effect (Tokyo) and Les Films Michel Francois (Paris); Panaflex Cameras and equipment, Panavision and Sanwa Cine Equipment (Tokyo).

CAST: Tatsuya Nakadai (Lord Hidetora Ichimonji), Akira Terao (Taro, *the eldest son* [yellow army]), Jinpachi Nezu (Jiro, *the second son* [red army]), Daisuke Ryu (Saburo, *the youngest son* [blue army]), Mieko Harada (Lady Kaede, *Taro's wife*), Yoshiko Miyazaki (Lady Sue, *Jiro's wife*), Masayuki Yui (Tango), Kazuo Kato (Ikoma), Peter (Kyoami, *the jester*), Hitoshi Ueki (Fujimaki, *Saburo's father-in-law* [white army]), Jun Tazaki (Lord Ayabe [black army]), Norio Matsui (Ogura), Hisashi Igawa (Kurogane), Kenji Kodama (Shirane), Toshiya Ito (Naganuma), Takeshi Kato (Hatakeyama), Takeshi Nomura (Tsurumaru).

A Serge Silberman Production for Greenwich Film Production, S.A. (Paris)/Herald Ace, Inc. (Tokyo)/Nippon Herald Films, Inc. A Serge Silberman and Katsumi Furukawa Presentation. A Toho Co., Ltd. Release. A Japanese/French co-production. Filmed at Kurosawa Film Studio (Yokohama), Toho Studios (Tokyo), and on location at Himeji Castle (Himeji), Kumamoto Castle (Kumamoto), Nagoya Castle (Nagoya), and the cities of Gotemba, Kokonoe, Aso, and Shonai. Dolby Stereo. Color (processed by Far East Laboratories and Eclair). Spherical Panavision. 162 minutes. Released 1985.

U.S. VERSION: Released by Twentieth Century-Fox Film Corp. English subtitles. Subtitles, Anne Brav, Cinetitres—L.T.C. Sound recordist Yanoguchi died during filming. Laserdisc reissue version is matted. 161 minutes. MPAA rating: "R." Released December 25, 1985.

Rashomon ("Rashomon"). Executive Producer, Masaichi Nagata;

Producer, Minoru Jingo; Director, Akira Kurosawa; Screenplay, Shinobu Hashimoto and Akira Kurosawa, based on the stories "Rashomon" and "Yabu no naka" ("In a Grove") by Ryunosuke Akutagawa; Director of Photography, Kazuo Miyagawa; Art Director, So Matsuyama; Set Decorator, H. Motsumoto; Lighting, Kenichi Okamoto; Editor, Akira Kurosawa; Music, Fumio Hayasaka; Sound, Daiei Recording Studio.

CAST: Toshiro Mifune (Tajomaru, *the bandit*), Masayuki Mori (Takehiro, *the samurai*), Machiko Kyo (Masago, *the samurai's wife*), Takashi Shimura (woodcutter), Minoru Chiaki (priest), Kichijiro Ueda (commoner), Daisuke Kato (policeman), Fumiko Homma (medium).

A Daiei Motion Picture Co., Ltd. Production. Black-and-white (processed by Daiei Laboratory). Academy ratio. Western Electric Mirrophonic recording. 88 minutes. Released August 25, 1950.

U.S. VERSION: Released by RKO Radio Pictures Inc. English subtitles. Prints by Pathé. 88 minutes. Remade as *The Outrage* (Metro-Goldwyn-Mayer, 1964). No MPAA rating. Released December 26, 1951.

Rat Kid on Journey / Tabisugata nezumikozo ("Thief on Journey"). Producer, Tomoyuki Tanaka; Director, Hiroshi Inagaki; Screenplay, Hiroshi Inagaki and Takashi Takagi; Director of Photography, Asaichi Nakai; Art Director, Kan Ueda; Music, Shiro Fukai.

CAST: Koji Tsuruta (Rat Kid), Mitsuko Kusabue (Oyone), Hisaya Ito (Naojiro), Kaoru Yachigusa (prostitute), Choko Iida (old woman), Shosaku Sugiyama (Kamezo).

A Toho Co., Ltd. Production. Black and white. Toho Scope. 87 minutes. Released 1958.

U.S. VERSION: Release undetermined, possibly by Toho International Co., Ltd. in subtitled format. No MPAA rating.

Rebellion / Joi-uchi. Producers, Tomoyuki Tanaka and Toshiro Mifune; Director, Masaki Kobayashi; Screenplay, Shinobu Hashimoto, based on the story *Haiyo zuma shimatsu yori* by Yasuhiko Takiguchi; Director of Photography, Kazuo Yamada; Art Director, Yoshiro Muraki; Music, Toru Takemitsu.

CAST: Toshiro Mifune (Isaburo Sasahara), Takeshi Kato (Yogoro), Yoko Tsukasa (Ichi), Tatsuya Nakadai (Tatewaki Asano), Tatsuyoshi Ebara (Bunzo), Michiko Otsuka (Suga), Tatsuo Matsumura (Lord Matsudaira), Shigeru Koyama (Steward Takahashi), Masao Mishima (Chamberlain Yanase), Isao Yamagata (Kotani), Etsuko Ichihara.

A Toho Co., Ltd./Mifune Productions, Ltd. Production. A Toho Co., Ltd. Release. Black and white. Toho Scope. 128 minutes. Released June 3, 1967.

U.S. VERSION: Released by Toho International Co., Ltd. English subtitles. 120 minutes. No MPAA rating. Released December 1967.

Record of a Tenement Gentleman / Nagaya Shinshi Roku ("Record of a Tenement Gentleman"). Director, Yasujiro Ozu; Screenplay, Yasujiro Ozu and Tadao Ikeda; Director of Photography, Yuharu Atsuta.

CAST: Chishu Ryu (Tashiro, *the fortune teller*), Choko Iida (Otane), Takeshi Sakamoto (Kihachi), Eitaro Ozawa (Kohei's father), Mitsuko Yoshikawa (Kiku), Reikichi Kawamura, Tomihiro Aoki.

A Shochiku Co., Ltd. Production. Filmed at Shochiku-Ofuna Studios. Black and white. Academy ratio. 72 minutes. Released May 20, 1947.

U.S. VERSION: Released by Shochiku Films of America, Inc. English subtitles. 72 minutes. No MPAA rating. Released April 22, 1979.

Red Angel. Director, Yasuzo Masumura; Screenplay, Ryozo Kasahara, based on an original story by Yoriyoshi Arima; Director of Photography, Setsuo Kobayashi.

CAST: Ayako Wakao (Nurse Nishi), Sinsuke Ashida (Doctor Okabe), Yusuke Kawazu (Private Ohara), Jotaro Senba (Private Sakamoto).

A Daiei Motion Picture Co., Ltd. Production. Black and white. DaieiScope. 95 minutes. Released 1963.

U.S. VERSION: Released by Daiei International Films. English subtitles. 95 minutes. No MPAA rating. Released July 1971.

Red Beard / Akahige ("Red Beard"). Executive Producers, Tomoyuki Tanaka and Ryuzo Kikushima; Producer/Director and Editor, Akira Kurosawa; Screenplay, Ryuzo Kikushima, Hideo Oguni, Masato Ide, and Akira Kurosawa, based on the novel *Akahige Shinryotan* by Shugoro Yamamoto; Production Supervisor, Hiroshi Nezu; Directors of Photography, Asakazu Nakai and Takao Saito; Art Director, Yoshiro Muraki; Lighting, Hiromitsu Mori; Sound Recording, Shin Watari; Music, Masaru Sato; Assistant Director, Shiro Moritani; Sound, Toho Recording Centre; Sound Effects, Toho Sound Effects Group.

CAST: Toshiro Mifune (Dr. Kyojo "Akahige" ["Red Beard"] Niide), Yuzo Kayama (Dr. Noboru Yasumoto), Yoshio Tsuchiya (Dr. Handayu Mori), Tatsuyoshi Ehara (Genzo Tsugawa), Reiko Dan (Osugi), Kyoko Kagawa (mad woman), Kamatari Fujiwara (Rokusuke), Akemi Negishi (Okuni), Tsutomu Yamazaki (Sahachi), Miyuki Kuwano (Onaka), Eijiro Tono (Goheiji), Takashi Shimura (Tokubei Izumiya), Terumi Niki (Otoyo), Haruko Sugimura (Kin, *the madam*), Yoko Naito (Masae), Ken Mitsuda (Masae's father), Kinuyo Tanaka (Madame Yasumoto, *Noboru's mother*), Chishu Ryu (Mr. Yasumoto, *Noboru's father*), Yoshitaka Zushi (Chobo), Atsushi Watanabe (complaining patient), Bokuzen Hidari (wistful patient), Ko Nishimura (chamberlain), Yutaka Sada, Ikio Sawamura (Goheiji tenents), Reiko Nanao, Koji Mitsui, Yoko Fujiyama, Akira Nomura, Kin Sugai, Fumiko Homma.

A Kurosawa Films/Toho Co., Ltd. Production. A Toho Co., Ltd. Release. Black and white (processed by Tokyo Laboratory, Ltd.). Toho Scope. Perspecta Stereophonic Sound. 185 minutes. Released April 3, 1965.

U.S. VERSION: Released by Toho International Co., Ltd. English subtitles. Subtitled home video version is letterboxed, but monophonic. The last film of record in Perspecta Stereophonic Sound. 185 minutes. No MPAA rating. Released January 19, 1966. Reissued by Frank Lee International in December 1968.

Red Lion / Akage ("Red Hair"). Producers, Toshiro Mifune and Yoshio Nishikawa; Director, Kihachi Okamoto; Screenplay, Kihachi Okamoto and Sakae Hirosawa; Director of Photography, Takao Saito; Art Director, Hiroshi Ueda; Music, Masaru Sato.

CAST: Toshiro Mifune (Gonzo), Etsushi Takahashi (Hanzo), Shigeru Koyama (Staff Chief Aragaki), No Terada (Sanji), Shima Iwashita (Tomi), Yunosuke Ito (magistrate), Tokue Hanazawa (Komotora), Takahiro Tamura (Sozo Sagara), Jitsuko Yoshimura (Oyo), Yuko Mochizuki (Oharu), Tokue Hanazawa (Komatora), Kaai Okada, Nobuko Otowa.

A Mifune Productions Production. A Toho Co., Ltd. Release. Eastman Color. Panavision. 106 minutes. Released October 10, 1969.

U.S. VERSION: Released by Toho International Co., Ltd. English subtitles. Running time also given at 116 minutes. 106 minutes. No MPAA rating. Released December 17, 1969.

Renegade Ninjas. Director, Sadao Nakajima; Producers, Tan Takaiwa, Goro Kusabe, Norimichi Matsudaira, and Keizo Mimura; Director of Photography, Shigeru Akatsuka; Editor, Isao Ichida; Assistant Director, Toshiyuki Fujiwara; Art Director, Tokumichi Igawa; Set Construction, Genbei Inaba; 2nd Unit Director, Akira Shimizu; Dialogue Supervisor, Misae Tanaka; Lighting, Etsuaki Masuda; Sound, Teruhiko Arakawa; Costumes, Ken Toyonaka; Makeup, Towa Bisho; Choregrapher, Monzo Fujima; Fight Instructor, Toshio Sugawara. *Special Effects Unit*: Directors, Nobuo Yajima and Kazuo Sagawa; Photography, Kiyoshi Kitazawa; Art Director, Tetsuzo Osawa.

CAST: Hiroski Matsukata, Kinnosuke Yorozuya, Chiezo Kataoka, Tetsuro Tamba, Mieko Takamine, Tatsuo Umemiya, Mikio Narita, Shigeyo Shirai, Seiji Endo, Minori Terada, Shohei Hino, Masataka Iwao, Guts Ishimatsu, Takashi Noguchi, Teruhiko Aoi, Hiroyuki "Henry" Sanada, Kensaku Morita, Fujita Okamoto, Yoko Akino, Midori Hagiyo, Shoji

Kobayashi, Ichiro Ogura, Sakae Umezu, Kunioni Kitani, Jun Hamamura, Eizo Kitamura, Sachiko Kozuki, Kyoko Enami, Yasuyo Matsumura, Miyuki Tanigawa, Maki Tachibana, Nobuyo Keneko, Sengoro Hideyama, Ryosuke Kagawa.

A Toei Co., Ltd. Production. Eastman Color. ToeiScope. 148 minutes (?). Released 1979.

U.S. VERSION: Never released theatrically in the United States. Released directly to home video in 1985 by Prisim Entertainment. An American National Enterprizes, Inc. Presentation. English-dubbed. 107 minutes. No MPAA rating.

Repast / Meshi ("Repast"). Director, Mikio Naruse; Screenplay, Sumie Tanaka and Toshiro Ide, based on the novel by Fumiko Hayashi; Director of Photography, Masao Tamai; Art Director, Satoshi Chuko; Music, Fumio Hayasaka.

CAST: Ken Uehara (Hatsunosuke Okamoto), Setsuko Hara (Michiyo, *his wife*), Yukiko Shimazaki (Satoko Okamoto), Kan Nihonyanagi (Kazuo Takenaka), Hisako Takibana (Sumi Takenaka), Eitaro Shindo (Yuzo Takenaka), Haruko Sugimura (Matsu Murata, *Michiyo's mother*), Yoko Sugi (Mitsuko Murata, *Michiyo's sister-in-law*), Keiju Kobayashi (Shinzo Murata, *Michiyo's brother*), Ranko Hanai (Koyoshi Dohya), Akiko Kazami (Seiko Tomiyasu), Mitsue Tachibana (Katsuko Suzuki), Ceiko Nakakita (Keiko Yamakita).

A Toho Co., Ltd. Production. Black and white. Academy ratio. 97 minutes. Released 1951.

U.S. VERSION: Distributor undetermined. English subtitles. 97 minutes. No MPAA rating. Released September 21, 1984.

Resurrection of the Beast / Yaju no fukkatsu ("Resurrection of the Beast"). Producer, Fumio Tanaka; Director, Michio Yamamoto; Screenplay, Ei Ogawa; Director of Photography, Masaharu Utsumi; Art Director, Yoshibumi Honda; Music, Taicho Kosugi.

CAST: Tatsuya Mihashi (Ibuki), Toshio Kurosawa (Jiro), Yoshiko Mita (Miki), Mika Kitagawa (Emi), Goro Mutsumi (Sone).

A Toho Co., Ltd. Production. Eastman Color. Panavision. 86 minutes. Released December 6, 1969.

U.S. VERSION: Release undetermined, likely by Toho International Co., Ltd. English subtitles. No MPAA rating. Release date undetermined.

The Return of Masseur Ichi / Zoku Zato Ichi monogatari ("The Story of Zatoichi, Part 2"). Executive Producer, Ikuo Kubodera; Director, Issei Mori; Screenplay, Minoru Inuzuka, based on an original story by Kan Shimosawa; Director of Photography, Shozo Honda; Art Director, Seiichi Ota; Editor, Koji Taniguchi; Music, Ichiro Saito; Sound Recording, Tsuchitaro Hayashi; Lighting, Sadaichi Ito; Martial Arts Director, Shohei Miyauchi.

CAST: Shintaro Katsu (Zatoichi), Yoshie Mizutani (Osetsu), Masayo Mari (Otane), Kenzaburo Jo [Tomisaburo Wakayama] (Nagisa no Yoshiro), Yutaka Nakamura (Kagami no Sanzo), Sonosuke Sawamura (Seki no Kanbei), Shosaku Sugiyama (Tamigoro), Tamiemon Arashi (Kai Yoshida), Yoshito Yamaji (Yahei), Eijiro Yanagi (Sukegoro Hanoka), Fujio Harumoto (Lord Kuroda of Echizen), Koichi Mizuhara (Kanzo), Saburo Date (Mirosuke), Shintaro Nanjo (Samon Shiraishi), Shozo Nanbu (Gouemon Kashiya).

A Daiei Motion Picture Co., Ltd. Production. Black and white. DaieiScope. 72 minutes. Released 1962.

U.S. VERSION: Released by Daiei International Films, Inc. English subtitles. The 2nd "Zatoichi" feature. Followed by *Zatoichi Enters Again* (1963). 72 minutes. No MPAA rating. Released October 16, 1979.

The Return of the Giant Majin / Dai Majin ikaru ("The Great Devil Grows Angry"). Producer, Masaichi Nagata; Director, Kenji Misumi; Screenplay, Tetsuro Yoshida; Director of Photography, Fujio Morita; Art Director, Hisashi Okuda; Editor, Hiroshi Yamada; Sound, Daiei Recording Studio; Special Effects Director, Yoshiyuki Kuroda; Majin Design, Ryosaku Takayama; Special Effects, Daiei Special Effects Department.

CAST: Kojiro Hongo (Juro Chigusa), Shiho Fujimura (Sayuri), Taro Murui (Todohei), Takashi Kanda (Danjo Mikoshiba),

Riki Hoshimoto (Majin), Tara Fujimura, Jutaro Hojo, Koji Fujiyama.

A Daiei Motion Picture Co., Ltd. Production. Eastman Color (processed by Daiei Laboratory). DaieiScope. 79 minutes. Released August 13, 1966.

U.S. VERSION: Never released theatrically in the United States. Released directly to television by American International Television (AIP-TV) in 1968. English-dubbed. A James H. Nicholson & Samuel Z. Arkoff Presentation. Director, Lee Kressel; Postproduction Supervisor, Salvatore Billiteri; Editors, Eli Haviv and Emil Haviv; Lip Sync, Film-Rite, Inc.; Rerecording, Titan Productions, Inc.; Prints by Perfect. The second film in the "Majin" trilogy. Followed by *Majin Strikes Again* (1966). 79 minutes. No MPAA rating.

The Return of the Giant Monsters / Daikaiju kuchesen Gamera tai Gaos ("Giant Monster Air Battle: Gamera against Gaos"). Executive Producer, Masaichi Nagata; Producer, Hidemasa Nagata; Director, Noriyaki Yuasa; Planning, Kazutada Nakano; Screenplay, Nizo Takahashi; Director of Photography, Akira Uehara; Music, Tadashi Yamauchi; Editor, Tatsuji Nakashizu; Sound Recording Supervisor, Yukio Okumura; Sound, Daiei Recording Studio; Special Effects, Kazufumi Fujii and Yuzo Kaneko; Monster Design, Ryosaku Takayama.

CAST: Naoyuki Abe (Eiichi Kanamura), Kojiro Hongo (Shiro Tsutsumi), Kichijiro Ueda (Tatsuemon Kanamura), Reiko Kasahara (Sumiko Kanamura), Taro Marui (Mite no Kuma), Yukitaro Hotaru (Hachiko), Yoshiro Kitahara (Dr. Aoki), Shin Minatsu (Okabe), Jun Osanai (stock farm owner), Osamu Maruyama (Chief of Seismological Observatory), Yuju Moriya (announcer), Akira Natsuki (commander-in-chief), Kenji Oyama (chief of police headquarters), Koichi Ito (chief of road development section), Teppei Endo (local chief of road development section), Joe Ohara (hotel manager), Fujio Murakami (scholar), Takashi Nakamura (reporter), Naomasa Kawahima (cowboy), Daigo Inoue (assistant at defense headquarters), Kisao Hida (policeman), Eiko Yanami, Isamu Saeki, Mikio Tsubouchi, Yasushi Sakagami, Koji Fugiyama.

A Daiei Motion Picture Co., Ltd. Production. Eastman Color (processed by Daiei Laboratory). DaieiScope. Filmed at Daiei-Tokyo Studios. 86 minutes. Released March 15, 1967.

U.S. VERSION: Never released theatrically in the United States. Released directly to television by American International Television (AIP-TV) in 1967. English-dubbed. A James H. Nicholson & Samuel Z. Arkoff Presentation. Postproduction Supervisor, Salvatore Billitteri; Dubbing cast, Mel Wells, others undetermined. Prints by Perfect. Released to home video and reissued to television in 1987 as *Gamera vs. Gaos*, a Sandy Frank Film Syndication, Inc. Presentation, and distributed by King Features Entertainment, a subsidiary of the Hearst Corporation. Current version is minus AIP's credits and was not dubbed by Billitteri. Alternate titles: *Dai kaiju kuchusen* and *Boyichi and the Supermonster*. The third "Gamera" feature. Followed by *Destroy All Planets* (1968). More or less remade as *Gamera – The Guardian of the Universe* (1995). 86 minutes. No MPAA rating.

Return of the Streetfighter. Director, Shigehiro Ozawa; Screenplay, Koji Takada and Toshiaki Tsushima; Martial Arts Directors, Masafumi Suzuki, Ken Kamaza, and Reginald Jones; Director of Photography, Teiji Yoshida; Art Director, Tokumichi Igawa; Music, Toshiaki Tsushima.

CAST: Shinichi "Sonny" Chiba, Yoko Ichiji, Masafumi Suzuki, Donald Nakajima, Milton Ishibashi, Zulu Yachi, Claud Gannyon.

A Toei Co., Ltd. Production. Color. ToeiScope. Running time and release date undetermined.

U.S. VERSION: Released by New Line Cinema. English-dubbed. English Dialogue, Steve Autry. Wide screen process billed as "ActionScope" in the United States. Includes stock footage from *The Street Fighter* (1974), an apparently unrelated Japanese feature (as far as the Japanese were concerned) also starring

Chiba. 75 minutes. MPAA rating: "R." Released December 3, 1975.

Return to Manhood / Nanbanji no Semushi-Otoko ("Hunchbacked Man at Nanban Temple"). Executive Producer, Masaichi Nagata; Producer, Atsushi Sakai; Director, Torajiro Sato; Screenplay, Akira Fushimi; Story, Katsumi Mizoguchi, based on the novel *Notre Dame de Paris* by Victor Hugo; Director of Photography, Hiroshi Imai; Sound, Daiei Recording Studio.

CAST: Achako Hanabishi, Naitoshi Hayashi, Shunji Sakai, Kyu Sazanka, Tamao Nakamura.

A Daiei Motion Picture Co., Ltd. Production. Western Electric Mirrophonic recording. Black and white (processed by Daiei Laboratory). Academy ratio. 78 minutes. Released 1957.

U.S. VERSION: Released by Daiei International Films, Inc. English subtitles. No MPAA rating. 78 minutes. Released 1957.

The Revenge of Yukinojo: Revenge of a Kabuki Actor / Yukinojo henge ("Yukinojo Incarnation"). Producer, Masaichi Nagata; Director, Kon Ichikawa; Screenplay, Daisuke Kato, Teinosuke Kinugasa, and Natto Wada, based on a story by Otokichi Mikami; Director of Photography, Setsuo Kobayashi; Music, Yasushi Akutagawa; Art Director, Yoshinobu Nishioka; Lighting, Kenichi Okamoto; Sound Recording, Gen Otani.

CAST: Kazuo Hasegawa (Yukinojo Nakamura *and* Yamitaro), Fujiko Yamamoto (Ohatsu), Ayako Wakao (Namiji), Raizo Ichikawa (Hirutaro), Chusha Ichikawa (Kikunoju Nakamura), Ganjiro Nakamura (Sansai Dobe), Eijiro Yanagi (Kokaiya), Saburo Data (Kawaguchiya), Eigoro Ogami (Shogun).

A Daiei Motion Picture Co., Ltd. Production. Eastman Color. DaieiScope. 113 minutes. Released January 13, 1963.

U.S. VERSION: Never released theatrically. Released directly to the non-theatrical market. 113 minutes. No MPAA rating. Released June 1971.

The Revengeful Spirit of Eros / Erogami no onryo ("The Revengeful Spirit of Eros"). Director, Yasujiro Ozu; Screenplay, Kogo Noda, based on an idea by Seizaburo Ishihara; Director of Photography, Hideo Shigehara.

CAST: Tatsuo Saito, Satoko Date, Ichiro Tsukita, Hikaru Hoshi, Chishu Ryu.

A Shochiku Co., Ltd. Production. Filmed at Shochiku-Kamata Studios. Silent with benshi. Black and white. Academy ratio. 41 minutes. Released July 27, 1930.

U.S. VERSION: Never released in the United States. A lost film.

Rhapsody in August / Hachigatsu no rapusodi. Executive Producer, Toru Okuyama; Producer, Hisao Kurosawa; Director/Editor, Akira Kurosawa; Associate Director, Ishiro Honda; Associate Producers, Mike Y. Inoue and Seikichi Iizumi; Screenplay, Akira Kurosawa and Ishiro Honda, based on the novel *Nabe-no-kaka* by Kiyoko Murata; Directors of Photography, Takao Saito, Masaharu Ueda; Art Director, Yoshiro Muraki; Lighting, Takeji Sano; Costumes, Kazuko Kurosawa; Music, from the works of Franz Schubert and Antonio Vivaldi, and by Shinichiro Ikebe; Sound Recording, Kenichi Banitani

CAST: Sachiko Murase (Grandmother Kane), Hisashi Igawa (Tadao, *Kane's son*), Narumi Kayashima (Machiko, *Tadao's wife*), Tomoko Otakara (Tami, *their daughter*), Mitsunori Isaki (Shinjiro, *their son*), Toshie Negishi (Yoshie, *Kane's daughter*), Choichiro Kawarasaki (Noboru, *Yoshie's husband*), Hidetaka Yoshioka (Tateo, *their son*), Mie Suzuki (Minako, *their daughter*), Richard Gere (Clark, *Kane's nephew*), Narumi Kayashima, Sachio Sakai, Haruya Kato, Fumiko Homma.

A Kurosawa Films/Shochiku Co., Ltd. Production. A Feature Film Enterprise 2 Presentation. A Shochiku Co., Ltd. Release. Filmed on location in Nagasaki. Color. Spherical Panavision. Dolby Stereo. 98 minutes. Released May 25, 1991.

U.S. VERSION: Released by Orion Classics. English subtitles. Honda's contribution as co-screenwriter is uncredited. 98 minutes. MPAA rating: "PG." Released December 16, 1991.

The Rickishaw Man / Muhomatsu no issho ("A Life of Muhomatsu"). Producer, Tomoyuki Tanaka;

Director, Hiroshi Inagaki; Screenplay, Mansaku Itami and Hiroshi Inagaki, based on the story by Shunsaku Iwashita; Director of Photography, Kazuo Yamada; Art Director, Kan Ueda; Lighting, Ichiro Ihara; Editor, Yoshitami Kuroiwa; Music, Ikuma Dan; Sound Recording, Yoshio Nishikawa and Hisashi Shimonaga; Assistant Director, Teruo Maru.

CAST: Toshiro Mifune (Muhomatsu), Hideko Takamine (Yoshiko Yoshioka), Hiroshi Akutagawa (Captain Yoshioka), Kenji Kasahara (Toshio), Kaoru Matsumoto (Toshio as a youth), Chishu Ryu (Shigezo Yuki), Choko Iida (innkeeper), Haruo Tanaka (Kumakichi), Jun Tatara (theater employee), Ichiro Arishima (medicine peddler), Senkichi Omura.

A Toho Co., Ltd. Production. Agfa Color. Toho Scope. 104 minutes. Released March 1958.

U.S. VERSION: Released by Cory Film Corp. and Toho International Co., Ltd. English subtitles. A remake of Inagaki's *The Life of Matsu the Untamed* (1943). Alternate title: *Muhomatsu, the Riksha-Man*. Remade by Kenji Misumi as *The Wild One* (1965), starring Shintaro Katsu. 98 minutes. No MPAA rating. Released May 3, 1960.

Rika / Kosodate-gokko. Producers, Enzaburo Honda, Seiji Matsuki, Daishiro Miura; Director, Tadashi Imai; Screenplay, Naoyuki Suzuki, based on an original story by Kyozo Miyoshi; Director of Photography, Kazutami Hara; Art Directors, Yoshiaki Toko and Saburo Abe; Music, Shinichiro Ikebe.

CAST: Go Kato, Komaki Kurihara, Chie Ushihara.

A Gogatsusha Co., Ltd./Haiyuza Film Production Co., Ltd. Production. Color. Spherical wide screen (?). 118 minutes. Released 1979.

U.S. VERSION: Distributor, if any, is undetermined. No MPAA rating.

Rikyu ("Rikyu"). Executive Producers, Shizo Yamanouchi, Hisao Minemura, and Kazuo Watanabe; Producers, Yoshisuke Mae and Hiroshi Morie; Associate Producers, Noriko Nomura and Tsutomu Kamimura; Director, Hiroshi Teshigahara; Screenplay, Genpei Akasegawa and Hiroshi Teshigahara, based on the novel by Yaeko Nogami; Music, Toru Takemitsu; Costumes, Emi Wada; Director of Photography, Fujio Morita; Art Directors, Yoshinobu Nishioka and Shigemori Shigeta; Lighting, Gengo Nakaoka; Sound Recording, Hideo Nishizaki; Editor, Toshio Taniguchi; Assistant Directors, Keiji Mitsutomo and Masaru Tsushima; Special Makeup Effects, Etsuko Egawa; Hair Stylist, Kosuke Tamiya; Script Girl, Saehiko Hasegawa; Production Managers, Mamoru Komatsu and Hisao Watanabe; Production Supervisor, Toru Okuyama; Consultants, Ryuji Matsui and Atsushi Okumoto; Supervisors, Masao Nakamura, Seizo Hayashiya, Sokaku Kurakazu, and Toshiharu Takatsu; With the Support of Omote Senke, Ura Senke, and Musyanokoji Senke.

CAST: Rentaro Mikuni (Rikyu), Yoshiko Mita (Riki, *his wife*), Tsutomu Yamazaki (Lord Hideyoshi), Kyoko Kishida (his wife), Tanie Kitabayashi (his mother), Sayoko Yamaguchi (Chacha, *his mistress*), Ryo Tamura (Lord Hidenaga, *his brother*), Koshiro Matsumoto (Lord Oda), Kichiemon Nakamura (Lord Ieyasu), Yasosuke Bando (Mitsunari), Akira Kubo (Geni), Keishi Arashi (Oribe, *Rikyu's friend*), Hisashi Igawa (Soji), Ichiro Zaitsu (Abbott Kokei), Hideo Kanze (Rikyu's brother-in-law), Masao Imafuku (ceramist), Ruis Marques (Stefano), Donald Richie (priest).

A Teshigahara Production, Inc./Shochiku Co., Ltd./C. Ito & Co., Ltd./ Hakuhodo, Inc. Production. A Shochiku Co., Ltd. Release. Dolby Stereo. Color. Spherical wide screen. 135 minutes. Released September 15, 1989.

U.S. VERSION: Released by Capitol Entertainment. English subtitles. Released to home video as A Ted Goldberg Presentation through Capitol Entertainment. "Dedicated to Sofu Teshigahara and Isamu Noguchi." 116 minutes. No MPAA rating. Released January 18, 1991.

Rise Against the Sword / Abare Goemon ("Wild Goemon"). Executive Producer, Tomoyuki Tanaka; Director, Hiroshi Inagaki; Screenplay, Hiroshi Inagaki and Masato Ide; Director of Photography, Kazuo Yamada.

CAST: Toshiro Mifune (Abare Goemon),

Makoto Sato, Ryo Tamura, Yuriko Hoshi, Mayumi Ozora, Nobuko Otowa, Daisuke Kato.

A Toho Co., Ltd. Production. Black and white. Toho Scope. 101 minutes. Released January 15, 1966.

U.S. VERSION: Released by Toho International Co., Ltd. English subtitles. 101 minutes. No MPAA rating. Released November 1966.

Rise, Fair Sun / Asayake no uta ("Song of Asayake"). Director, Kei Kumai; Screenplay, Hisashi Yamauchi, Akiko Katsura, and Kei Kumai; Director of Photography, Kozo Okazaki; Music, Teizo Matsumura.

CAST: Tatsuya Nakadai (Sakuzo), Keiko Sekine (Haruko), Kinya Kitaoji (Asao), Shin Saburi (Inagi), Yoshio Inaba (Toraheita).

A Toho Co., Ltd./Haiyuza Film Production Co., Ltd. Production. A Toho Co., Ltd. Release. Eastman Color. Panavision (?). 130 minutes. Released 1973.

U.S. VERSION: Released by Toho International Co., Ltd. in subtitled format. 130 minutes. No MPAA rating. Released May 28, 1975.

River of Fireflies / Hotarugawa ("River of Fireflies"). Executive Producers, Matsuo Takahashi and Hiroaki Kato; Producer, Kiyoshi Fujimoto; Director, Eizo Sugawa; Screenplay, Eizo Sugawa and Kyohei Nakaoka, based on the novel by Teru Miyamoto; Director of Photography, Masahisa Himeda; Art Director, Iwao Akune; Editor, Jun Nabeshima; Music, Masatsugu Shinozaki; Sound Recording, Fujio Sato; Costume Design, Satoyoshi Kubo and Tomio Okubo; Special Effects, Koichi Kawakita.

CAST: Takayuki Sakazume (Tatsuo), Rentaro Mikuni (Shigetatsu), Yukiyo Toake (Chiyo), Tamae Sawada (Eiko), Tomoko Naraoka (Harue), Taiji Tonoyama (Ginzo).

A Kinema Tokyo/Nichiei Production. A Shochiku Co., Ltd. Release. Color. Academy ratio. 114 minutes. Released 1987.

U.S. VERSION: Released by Shochiku Films of America. English subtitles. 114 minutes. No MPAA rating. Released November 4, 1988.

River of Forever / Chikumagawa zessho ("A Superb Song of Chikuma River"). Executive Producers, Ichiro Sato and Hideyuki Shiino; Director, Shiro Toyoda; Screenplay, Zenzo Matsuyama; Director of Photography, Kozo Okazaki; Music, Masaru Sato.

CAST: Kinya Kitaoji, Yuriko Hoshi, Mikijiro Hira, Ayumi Ishida, Kunie Tanaka.

A Tokyo Eiga Co., Ltd. Production, in association with Toho Co., Ltd. A Toho Co., Ltd. Release. Black and white. Toho Scope. 102 minutes. Released February 1966.

U.S. VERSION: Released by Toho International Co., Ltd. English subtitles. 102 minutes. No MPAA rating. Released October 1967.

River Solo Flows / Bungawan Solo ("Bungawansolo"). Producer, Ichiro Sato; Director, Kon Ichikawa; Screenplay, Natto Wada and Kon Ichikawa, based on a story by Shozo Kanegai; Director of Photography, Minoru Yokoyama; Art Director, Takao Kono; Music, Nobuo Iida.

CAST: Ryo Ikebe (Superior Private Fukami), Hisaya Morishige (Private 1st Class Take), Yunosuke Ito (Field Soldier Noro), Susumu Fujita (Sergeant Odagiri), Asami Hisaji (Saria), Setsuko Wakayama (Karutie), Eijiro Tono (the father), Toyoko Takahashi (the mother).

A Shintoho Co., Ltd Production. Black and white. Academy ratio. 92 minutes. Released October 19, 1951.

U.S. VERSION: Distributor undetermined. English subtitles. 92 minutes. No MPAA rating.

The River with No Bridge / Hashi no nai kawa ("The River with No Bridge"). Producers, Shoji Iwaguchi and Suaki Takaoka; Director, Yoichi Higashi; Screenplay, Yoichi Higashi and Soo-Kil Kim, based on the novel by Sue Sumi; Director of Photography, Koichi Kawakami; Music, Ernesto Cavour.

CAST: Naoko Otani, Tamao Nakamura, Tetsuta Sugimoto.

A Seiyu, Ltd./Galeria Production. A Toho Co., Ltd. Release. Color. Wide screen (?). 139 minutes. Released 1992.

U.S. VERSION: Released by The Seiyu, Ltd. English subtitles. 139 minutes. No MPAA rating. Released October 1994.

Roar of the Crowd / Harukanaru koshien ("Faraway Koshien"). Producer, Yasuyoshi Tokuma; Director, Yutaka Osawa; Screenplay, Takeo Kunihiro, based on an original story by Takuji Ono, Osamu Yamamoto, and Yoshinari Tobe; Director of Photography, Shun Yamamoto; Music, Kensaku Tanigawa.

CAST: Tomokazu Miura, Yasufumi Hayashi, Tomoko Otakara, Hitoshi Ueki, Misako Tanaka, Mayumi Ogawa.

A Daiei Co., Ltd. Production. A Toho Co., Ltd. Release (?). Color. Spherical wide screen. 103 minutes. Released 1990.

U.S. VERSION: Distributor, if any, is undetermined.

Robot Carnival / Robot Carnival **[animation compilation]**. Producer, Kazufumi Nomura; Project Directors, Yuko Suzuki and Hideki Tonokatsu; Music, Joe Hisashi, Isaku Fujita, and Yasunori Honda; Assistant Director, Tetsu Kimura; Color Modelers, Kazuko Murakami and Yukiko Mayehara; Animation Checker, Kakiguichi Katsuko; Special Effects, Kashiwabara Toyohiko, Go Abe, and Shinji Teraoka. *Opening/Ending*: Designer/Directors/Screenplay, Katsuhiro Otomo and Atsuko Fukushima; Art Director, Fumi Yamamoto; Special Effects, Kazutoshi Sato. *Franken's Gear*: Designer/Directors/Screenplay, Kouji Morimoto; Art Director, Yuji Ikehata; Special Effects, Kazutoshi Sato. *Starlight Angel*: Designer/Director/Screenplay, Hiroyuki Kitazume; Art Director, Tada Shimazaki; Special Effects, Kenji Mori. *Cloud*: Designer/Director/Screenplay, Mao Lamdo; Original Animation, Manabu Ohashi, H. Ohashi, S. Ohashi; Art Director, Mao Lamdo; Special Effects, Suwara Productions. *Deprive*: Designer/Director/Screenplay, Hidetoshi Omori; Art Director, Kenji Matsumoto; Special Effects, Junichi Sasaki. *Presence*: Designer/Director/Screenplay, Yasuomi Umetsu; Production Coordinators, Nobusuke Terazawa and Hideki Nimura; Art Director, Akira Yamakawa; Special Effects, Kenji Mori. *A Tale of Two Robots—Chapter 3: Foreign Invasion*: Director/Screenplay, Hiroyuki Kitakubo; Character Design, Yoshiyuki Sadamoto; Mechanical Design, Mahiro Mayeda; Production Cooperation, Kazuaki Mori, Kumiko Kawana, and Juji Moriyama; Art Director, Hiro Sasaki; Special Effects, Junichi Sasaki. *Nightmare*: Designer/Director/Screenplay, Takashi Nakamura; Art Director, Yuji Sawai; Special Effects, Junichi Sasaki. Recording Studios, Acaco Creative Studio; Recording Engineers, Noriaki Kamimura, Yukio Abe; Sound Effects, Arts Pro.; Production Supervisor, Toshiharu Umetsu; Cooperating Studios, Ashi Production, West Cape Corp., Studio O.M., Kawaguchi Color, Sunshine Corp., Shinsei Pro., Domu-sha, Kurosasu, Studio Mac, Miyazaki Animation, Wa-A-Bu, Studio A.D.D., A.I.C., Gainax, Ginga Teikoku, Studio City, Studio Z-5, N.V.C., Kurebasu, Maki Pro., Studio Look, Wave, Only for a Laugh, Kaname Production, Sunrise, Star Production, Studio Dub, Studio Noah, Kinsei Pro., Magic Bus, Studio Road; Special Thanks, Asahi Production, Shindosha, Tomoko Kawasaki, Yuko Mitsumori, Akinori Nakashima, Mushi Production, Uni-Ace, Yoshiye Aizawa, Mayumi Sekiguchi, Tomoko Sato, Studio Goods, Shoko Oyama, Tanemori Hiromi.

An A.P.P.P. Co., Ltd. Production. Dolby Stereo. Color (processed by Tokyo Film Development Center). Spherical wide screen. 91 minutes. Released 1990.

U.S. VERSION: Released by Streamline Pictures. English-dubbed. Producer/Adaptation, Carl Macek; Associates, Michael Haller, Jerry Beck; ADR Script Polish, Tom Wyner; Recording Studio, Wally Burr Recording; Recording Engineer, Thomas Chan; Production Supervisor, Jerry Beck; Publicity, Svea Macek, Fred Patten. Some material rearranged for the U.S. release, and restored for the home video and television version. Dedicated to voice artist Lisa Michelson, who died in 1991. 91 minutes. No MPAA rating. Released 1991.

VOICE CHARACTERIZATIONS: *Presence*: Michael McConnohie (the man), Lisa Michelson (the girl), Barbara Goodman (old lady), Tom Wyner (the gent). *A Tale of Two Robots—Chapter 3: Foreign Invasion*: Bob Bergen (Sankichi), Lisa Michelson (Yayoi), Eddie Frierson (Kukusuke), Kerrigan Mahan (Danjiro), Tom Wyner (Daimaru), Steve Kramer (Volkeson).

The Rocking Horsemen / Seishun Dendeke, deke, deke ("The Youth Dendeke, deke, deke, deke"). Producers, Kuniyoshi Kawashima, Kyoko Obayashi, and Hideo Sasai; Director, Nobuhiko Obayashi; Screenplay, Shiro Ishimari, based on an original story by Sunao Ashihara; Directors of Photography, Kenji Hagiwara and Shigeru Iwamatsu; Music, Joe Hisashi.

CAST: Yasufumi Hayashi, Tadanobu Asano, Yoshiyuki Omori.

A Galuk Premium/PSC/Liberty Fox Production. Color. Spherical wide screen (?). 135 minutes. Released 1992.

U.S. VERSION: Distributor, if any, is undetermined.

Rodan / Sora no daikaiju Radon ("The Sky's Giant Monsters: Rodan"). Producer, Tomoyuki Tanaka; Director, Ishiro Honda; Screenplay, Takeshi Kimura and Takeo Murata; Story, Takashi Kuronuma; Director of Photography, Isamu Ashida; Art Direction, Takeo Kita; Sound, Masanobu Miyazaki, Toho Dubbing Theatre; Sound Effects, Toho Sound Effects Group; Lighting Shigeru Mori; Music, Akira Ifukube; *Toho Special Effects Group*: Director, Eiji Tsuburaya; Art Direction, Akira Watanabe; Lighting Masao Shirota; Optical Photography, Hiroshi Mukoyama.

CAST: Kenji Sahara (Shigeru), Yumi Shirakawa (Kiyo), Akihiko Hirata (Dr. Kashiwagi), Yasuko Nakata (young woman), Akio Kobori (Nishimura), Minosuke Yamada (Ohsaki), Yoshifumi Tajima (Izeki), Mike Daning (teletype operator), Kiyoharu Onaka, Fuyuki Murakami.

A Toho Co., Ltd. Production. Western Electric Mirrophonic recording. Eastman Color (processed by Far East Laboratories, Ltd.). Academy ratio. 82 minutes. Released December 26, 1956.

U.S. VERSION: Released by Distributors Corporation of America. English-dubbed. A King Brothers Productions, Inc. Presentation. Producers, Frank King, Maurice King; Narration (i.e. English Dialog), David Duncan; Dubbing Cast: Paul Frees, Keye Luke, George Takei, others unknown. Editor, Robert S. Eisen; Sound Effects Editor, Anthony Carras; Looping Editor, Frank O'Neill; Editorial Assistant, Joyce Sage; Administration, Maurice King; Public Relations, Herman King. Prints by Technicolor. Advertised as *Rodan the Flying Monster*, though film's onscreen title is as listed above. Much of Ifukube's score was replaced by library stock. Monster footage from *Rodan* appeared in the U.S. production *Valley of the Dragons* (Columbia, 1961). Released cropped to 1.85:1 in the United States. Reissued to television and home video by UPA Productions of America. 79 minutes. No MPAA Rating. Released August 1957.

Romance and Rhythm / Romansu matsuri ("Romance Festival"). Producer, Sadao Sugihara; Director, Toshio Sugie; Screenplay, Katsuya Suzaki; Director of Photography, Taiichi Kankura; Art Director, Tatsuo [Takeo?] Kita; Music, Yoshiyuki Kozu; Choreography, Yoji Agata.

CAST: Chimei Eri (Hisami Yagi), Izumi Yukimura (Mutsumi Hanamura), Achako Hanabishi (her father), Akira Takarada (Tajima), Ichiro Arishima (Matsui), Kyoko Mine (Reiko), Frankie Sakai, Frank Nagai.

A Takarazuka Eiga Co., Ltd. Production, in association with Toho Co., Ltd. A Toho Co., Ltd. Release. Eastman Color. Toho Scope. 103 minutes. Released 1958.

U.S. VERSION: Release undetermined, possibly by Toho Co., Ltd. in subtitled format. No MPAA rating.

Romance Express / Tokkyu Nippon ("Express Japan"). Director, Yuzo Kawashima.

CAST: Frankie Sakai, Reiko Dan, Yumi Shirakawa, Eitaro Ozawa, Sonomi Nakajima, Sadako Sawamura, Yusuke Takida, Kan Tachikawa, Shin Morikawa, Keiko Yanagawa, Michiyo Yokoyama, Keiko

Sata, Sachio Sakai, Akihiko Tanimura, Bontaro Hei.

A Toho Co., Ltd. Production. Eastman Color (?). Toho Scope. Not to be confused with *The Romance Express* (Shochiku, 1970), also starring Sakai. 86 minutes. Released April 4, 1961.

U.S. VERSION: Released by Toho International Co., Ltd. English subtitles. 86 minutes. No MPAA rating. Released August 18, 1961.

The Saga of Anatahan / Anatahan ("Hey, You!"). Producers, Yoshio Osawa, Nagamasa Kawakita, and Josef von Sternberg; Associate Producer, Takimura [no other name given]; Director, Josef von Sternberg; Screenplay, Josef von Sternberg, based on the story *Anatahan*, by Michiro Maruyama, and an article in *Life* magazine; Directors of Photography, Josef von Sternberg and Kozo Okazaki; Art Director, Asano [no other name given]; Artist, Watanabe [no other name given]; Music, Akira Ifukube; Special Assistant, Okawa [no other name given]; Assistant Director, Taguchi [no other name given]; Editor, Miyata [no other name given].

CAST: Akemi Negishi (Queen Bee), Tadashi Suganuma (husband), Kisaburo Sawamura, Shoji Nakayama, Jun Fujikawa, Hiroshi Kondo, Shozo Miyashita (the drones), Tsuruemon Bando, Kikuji Onoe (the skippers), Rokuriro Kineya (Maruyama, *the samisen-player*), Daijiro Tamura, Takashi Kitagawa, Takeshi Suzuki (the homesick ones), Shiro Amikura (the patriot).

A Daiwa Productions-Towa/Pathé-Contemporary Production. Black and white. Academy ratio. 92 minutes. Released 1953.

U.S. VERSION: Released by Arias Quality Pictures. English narration. Narrator, Josef von Sternberg. 92 minutes. No MPAA rating. Released May 1954. Reissued by Twyman in 1976 with material not included on the original release.

The Saga of Tanegashima / Teppo denraiki. Director, Issei Mori; Screenplay, Kimiyuki Hasegawa, based on an original story by Etsuko Takano; Director of Photography, Fujio Morita; Art Director, Yoshinobu Nishioka; Music, Hikaru Hayashi.

CAST: Ayako Wakao (Wakasa), Rick Jason (Pinto), Shiho Fujimura (Otane), Jun Fujimaki (Nobunaga Oda), Eijiro Tono (Kinbei Yaita), Taketoshi Naito (Tokiaki Tanegashima).

A Daiei Motion Picture Co., Ltd. Production. Eastman Color. DaieiScope. 109 minutes. Released May 18, 1968.

U.S. VERSION: Release undetermined, possibly by Daiei International Films. English subtitles. 109 minutes. No MPAA rating.

Saga of the Vagabonds / Sengoku gunto-den ("Saga of the Robbers in Warlike Ages"). Executive Producer, Tomoyuki Tanaka; Producers, Sanezumi Fujimoto and Kazuo Nishino; Director, Toshio Sugie; Screenplay, Sadao Yamanaka and Akira Kurosawa; Original Story, Juro Miyoshi; Director of Photography, Akira Suzuki; Music, Ikuma Dan; Sound, Toho Dubbing Theatre; Sound Effects, Toho Sound Effects Group; Special Effects, Toho Special Effects Group.

CAST: Toshiro Mifune (Rokuro Kai), Koji Tsuruta (Taro Tarao), Yoko Tsukasa (Tazu), Misa Uehara (Princess Koyuki), Takashi Shimura (Toki Saemon no Jo), Akihiko Hirata (Jiro Hidekuni), Seizaburo Kawazu (Hyoe Yamano), Yoshio Kosugi, Kenzo Tabu, Akira Tani, Ren Yamamoto, Sachio Sakai, Yoshifumi Tajima, Shin Otomo, Tadao Nakamaru.

A Toho Co., Ltd. Production. Agfacolor (processed by Tokyo Laboratory, Ltd.). Toho Scope. Western Electric Mirrophonic Recording (encoded with Perspecta Stereophonic Sound). 115 minutes. Released August 9, 1959.

U.S. VERSION: Released by Toho International Co., Ltd. English subtitles. 115 minutes. No MPAA rating. Released October 6, 1964. Released to home video as a Video Action Presentation, also with English subtitles. The home video version is from an anamorphic print, and retains the anamorphic compression.

Sakuratai 8.6 / Sakuratai Chiru ("Scattered Cherry Blossoms") [**documentary**]. Producers, Munetoshi Hidaka and

Michiyoshi Takashima; Director, Kaneto Shindo; Screenplay, Kaneto Shindo, based on an original story by Hagie Ezu; Director of Photography, Yoshiyuki Miyake; Music, Hikaru Hayashi.

WITH: Nobuko Otowa (narrator).

A Kindai Eiga Kyokai Co., Ltd./Tennozan Gohyakurakanji Production. Academy ratio. Color and Black and white. 110 minutes. Released 1988.

U.S. VERSION: Distributor, if any, is undetermined.

Samurai / Miyamoto Musashi ("Musashi Miyamoto"). Producer, Kazuo Takimura; Director, Hiroshi Inagaki; Screenplay, Tokuhei Wakao and Hiroshi Inagaki, based on the novel *Miyamoto Musashi* (1937-39) by Eiji Yoshikawa; Adaptation, Hideji Hojo; Director of Photography, Jun Yasumoto; Art Director, Makoto Sono and Kisaku Ito; Lighting, Shoji Kameyama and Shigeru Mori; Music, Ikuma Dan; Sound Recording, Choshichiro Mikami; Assistant Director, Jun Fukuda; *Toho Special Effects Group*: Director, Eiji Tsuburaya.

CAST: Toshiro Mifune (Musashi Miyamoto *nee* Takezo), Kaoru Yachigusa (Otsu), Rentaro Mikuni (Matahachi Honiden), Mariko Okada (Akemi), Kuroemon Onoe (Priest Takuan), Mitsuko Mito (Oko, *Matahachi's mother*), Eiko Miyoshi (Osugi), Akihiko Hirata (Seijiro Yoshioka), Daisuke Kato (Toji Gion), Kusuo Abe, Yoshio Kosugi, Sojin Kamiyama, Kanta Kisaragi.

A Toho Co., Ltd. Production. Eastman Color. Academy Ratio. 92 minutes. Released 1954.

U.S. VERSION: Released by Fine Art Films. English subtitles with English narration. Narration, William Holden. Inagaki filmed the same story previously, in 1942. Other versions include *Musashi Miyamoto* (Shochiku, 1944); *Musashi Miyamoto* (Toei, 1954), directed by Yasuo Kohata and starring Rentaro Mikuni; and Tomu Uchida's five-part *Zen and Sword* (1961-65), and *Musashi Miyamoto* (Shochiku, 1973). Reissued and released to home video restored and minus narration by Janus Films, alternately as *Samurai I, Samurai I: Musashi Miyamoto* and *Musashi Miyamoto*. Followed by *Samurai (Part II)* (1955). 92 minutes. No MPAA rating. Released January 9, 1956.

Samurai (Part II) / Miyamoto Musashi: Ichijoji no ketto ("Musashi Miyamoto: Duel at Ichijoji Temple"). Producer, Kazuo Takimura; Director, Hiroshi Inagaki; Screenplay, Hiroshi Inagaki and Tokuhei Wakao, based on the novel, *Miyamoto Musashi* (1937-39) by Eiji Yoshikawa; Directors of Photography, Jun Yasumoto and Asushi Atsumoto; Art Director, Makoto Sono; Lighting, Shigeru Mori; Music, Ikuma Dan; Sound Recording, Choshichiro Mikami; Assistant Director, Jun Fukuda.

CAST: Toshiro Mifune (Musashi Miyamoto), Koji Tsuruta (Kojiro Sasaki), Sachio Sakai (Matahachi Honiden), Akihiko Hirata (Seijuro Yoshioka), Yu Fujiki (Denshichiro Yoshioka), Daisuke Kato (Toji Gion), Eijiro Tono (Baiken Shishido), Kokuten Kodo (Old Priest Nikkan), Kenjim Iida (Jotaro), Kaoru Yachigusa (Otsu), Mariko Okada (Akemi), Ko Mihashi (Koetsu), Mitsuko Mito (Oko), Michiyo Kogure (Yoshino), Kuroemon Onoe (Priest Takuan).

A Toho Co., Ltd. Production. Eastman Color. Academy Ratio. 104 minutes. Released 1955.

U.S. VERSION: Released by Toho International Co., Ltd. English subtitles. Second part of "Samurai" trilogy. Preceded by *Samurai*, and followed by *Samurai III* (1956). Home video title: *Samurai II: Duel at Ichijoji Temple*. 104 minutes. No MPAA rating. Released October 20, 1967.

Samurai (Part III) / Miyamoto Musashi: Ketto Ganryujima ("Musashi Miyamoto: Ganryu Island Duel"). Producer, Kazuo Takimura; Director, Hiroshi Inagaki; Screenplay, Hiroshi Inagaki and Tokuhei Wakao, based on the novel *Miyamoto Musashi* (1937-39) by Eiji Yoshikawa; Director of Photography, Kazuo Yamada; Art Directors, Hiroshi Ueda and Kisaku Ito; Lighting, Tsuruzo Nishikawa; Music, Ikuma Dan; Sound Recording, Masanobu Miyazaki; Assistant Director, Jun Fukuda.

CAST: Toshiro Mifune (Musashi Miyamoto), Koji Tsuruta (Kojiro Sasaki), Sachio Sakai (Matahachi), Kaoru Yachigusa

Toshiro Mifune and Rentaro Mikuni learn the horrors of war in Hiroshi Inagaki's *Samurai* (1954).

(Otsu), Mariko Okada (Akemi), Takashi Shimura (Sado Nagaoka), Michiko Saga (Omitsu), Kyo Shimura.

A Toho Co., Ltd. Production. Eastman Color. Academy ratio. 105 minutes. Released 1956.

U.S. VERSION: Alternate title: *Musashi and Kojiro*. Part of the "Samurai" trilogy. Home video title: *Samurai III: Duel on Ganryu Island*. Released 1967.

Samurai Assassin / Samurai ("Samurai"). Producers, Tomoyuki Tanaka and Reiji Miwa; Associate Producer, Toshiro Mifune; Director, Kihachi Okamoto; Screenplay, Shinobu Hashimoto, based on the story *Samurai Nippon* ("Samurai Japan") by Jiromasa Gunji; Director of Photography, Hiroshi Murai; Music, Masaru Sato.

CAST: Toshiro Mifune (Niino), Keiju Kobayashi (Kurihara), Michiyo Aratama (Okiko Kukuhime), Yunosuke Ito (Hoshino), Koshiro Matsumoto (Lord Naosuke Ii), Nami Tamura, Kaoru Yachigusa, Haruko Sugimura, Takashi Shimura, Chusha Ichikawa, Susumu Fujita.

A Toho Co., Ltd./Toshiro Mifune Production. A Toho Co., Ltd. Release. Black and white. Toho Scope. 122 minutes. Released 1965.

U.S. VERSION: Released by Toho International Co., Ltd. English subtitles. 122 minutes. No MPAA rating. Released March 5, 1965.

Samurai from Nowhere / Dojo yaburi ("A Challenge Visit to a Fencing Hall"). Producer, Ginichi Kishimoto; Director, Seiichiro Uchikawa; Screenplay, Hideo Oguni; Story, Shoguro Yamamoto; Director of Photography, Yoshiharu Ota; Art Director, Junichi Osumi; Music, Masaru Sato.

CAST: Isamu Nagato (Ihei Misawa), Tetsuro Tamba (Gunjuro Ohba), Shima Iwashita (Tae), Chieko Baisho (Chigusa), Seiji Miyaguchi (Tatewaki Komuro).

A Shochiku Co., Ltd. Production. Black and white. Shochiku GrandScope. 93 minutes. Released 1964.

U.S. VERSION: Released by Shochiku Films of America, Inc. English subtitles. 93 minutes. No MPAA rating. Released May 20, 1964.

Samurai Reincarnation / Makai tensho ("Reincarnation of the Devil's World"). Executive Producer, Haruki Kadokawa; Director, Kinji Fukasaku; Screenplay, Tatsuo Nogami, Takako Ishikawa and Kinji Fukasaku, based on the novel by Hutaro Yamada, as published by Kadokawa Publishing Co., Ltd.; Directors of Photography, Kiyoshi Hasegawa and Shozo Sakane; Assistant Producers, Masao Sato, Tatsuo Honda, and Seiji Inaba; Action Coordinator, Shinichi "Sonny" Chiba; Lighting, Etsuaki Masuda; Sound Recording, Shigeji Nakayama; Editor, Isamu Ichida; Art Directors, Tokumichi Igawa and Yoshikazu Sano; Music, Hoza Yamamoto and Mitsunori Sugano; Script Girl, Misae Tanaka; Wardrobe, Takashi Matsuda; Assistant Director, Toru Dobashi.

CAST: Shinichi "Sonny" Chiba, Kenji Sawada, Akiko Kana, Tetsuro Tamba, Ken Ogata, Tomisaburo Wakayama, Julie Sawada, Hiroyuki "Henry" Sanada, Mikio Narita, Asao Uchida, Yuko Asuka, Masataka Iwao, Genji Kawai, Masaharu Arikawa, Katsutoshi Akiyama, Noboru Umezawa, Kojiro Shirakawa, Ryuko Azuma, Saburo Hayashi, Kinji Nakamura, Kaoru Beni, Fumio Takeda, Kyoko Furukawa, Tomoko Taguchi, Osamu Yamazaki, Mayumi Tokunaga, Mieko Hoshino, Tatsuo Inada, Shoji Sawada, Takaaki Yoshizwa, Makoto Kenmochi, Kayoko Shiraishi, Hitoshi Sakitsu.

A Haruki Kadokawa Films, Inc./Toei Co., Ltd. Production. Toeicolor. Panavision. 122 minutes. Released 1981.

U.S. VERSION: Distributor, if any, is undetermined. Released to home video in 1981 as *Samurai Reincarnation* (also the international title) by Marquis Video Corporation. English dubbed. Video version letterboxed. Sawada is not billed on the dubbed version, and story is credited to Futaro Yamada. Sequels (?): *Ninja Wars* (1982), *Satomi Hakkenda* (1983) and *Shogun's Ninja* (1984).

Samurai Saga / Aru kengo no shogai ("Life of an Expert Swordsman"). Producer, Tomoyuki Tanaka; Director/Screenplay, Hiroshi Inagaki; Director of Photography, Kazuo Yamada; Art Director, Yoshiaki Ito; Lighting, Masaichi Kojima; Music, Akira Ifukube; Sound, Yoshio Nishikawa.

CAST: Toshiro Mifune (Heihachiro Komaki), Yoko Tsukasa (Princess Chiyohime), Akira Takarada (Jurota), Seizaburo Kawazu, Kamatari Fujiwara, Akihiko Hirata, Keiko Awaji, Eiko Miyoshi.

A Toho Co., Ltd. Production. Eastman Color. Toho Scope. 111 minutes. Released April 28, 1959.

U.S. VERSION: Released by Toho International Co., Ltd. in subtitled format. 111 minutes. No MPAA rating. Released April 18, 1973.

Sandakan 8 / Sandakan hachiban shokan: Bokyo ("Sandakan No. 8 Whore House"). Producers, Masayuki Sato and Hideyuki Shiino; Director, Kei Kumai; Screenplay, Kei Kumai and Ei Hirosawa, based on the story by Tomoko Yamasaki; Director of Photography, Mitsuji Kaneo; Music, Akira Ifukube.

CAST: Kinuyo Tanaka (Osaki Yamakawa as an old woman), Yoko Takahashi (Osaki Yamakawa as a young woman), Komaki Kurihara (Keiko Mitani), Eitaro Ozawa (Tarozo), Mitsuo Hamada, Ichiro Nakatani, Takiko Mizunoe.

A Toho Co., Ltd./Haiyuza Film Production Co., Ltd. Production. Color. Academy ratio. 121 minutes. Released 1975.

U.S. VERSION: Released by Toho International Co., Ltd. English subtitles. 120 minutes. No MPAA rating. Released July 23, 1975. Alternate title: *Brothel #8*. Reissued by Peppercorn-Wormser August 7, 1977.

The Sandal Keeper / Horafuki Taikoki ("Story of Bragging Taiko"). Producer, Shin Morita; Director, Kengo Furusawa; Screenplay, Ryozo Kasahara; Director of Photography, Rokuro Nishigaki; Music, Yasushi Miyagawa.

CAST: Hitoshi Ueki (Tokichiro), Hajime Hana, Kei Tani, Mie Hama, Mitsuko Kusabue, Ichiro Arishima, Yu Fujiki, Eijiro Tono, Susumu Fujita.

A Toho Co., Ltd. Production. Eastman Color. Toho Scope. 98 minutes. Released October 31, 1964.

U.S. VERSION: Released by Toho International Co., Ltd. English subtitles. 96 minutes. No MPAA rating. Released October 22, 1965.

Sanjuro / Tsubaki Sanjuro ("Sanjuro Tsubaki"). Executive Producers, Tomoyuki Tanaka and Ryuzo Kikushima; Producer/Director and Editor, Akira Kurosawa; Screenplay, Ryuzo Kikushima, Hideo Oguni, and Akira Kurosawa, based on a *Tsubaki Sanjuro* story by Shugoro Yamamoto; Production Supervisor, Hiroshi Nezu; Director of Photography, Fukuzo Koizumi; Assistant Camera, Takao Saito; Art Director/Costumes, Yoshiro Muraki; Lighting, Ichiro Inohara; Sound Recording, Wataru Konuma and Hisashi Shimonaga; Music, Masaru Sato; Assistant Director, Shiro Moritani; Swordplay Advisor, Ryu Kuze; Special Effects, Toho Special Effects Group; Sound, Toho Recording Centre; Sound Effects, Toho Sound Effects Group.

CAST: Toshiro Mifune (Sanjuro "Tsubaki"), Tatsuya Nakadai (Hanbei Muroto), Yuzo Kayama (Iiro Izaka, *leader of the Samurai*), Akihiko Hirata, Kunie Tanaka, Hiroshi Tachikawa, Tatsuhiko Hari, Tatsuya Ehara, Yoshio Tsuchiya, Akira Kubo, Kenzo Matsui (samurai), Keiju Kobayashi (captured samurai in closet), Takashi Shimura (Kurofuji), Kamatari Fujiwara (Takebayashi), Masao Shimizu (Inspector Kikui), Yunosuke Ito (Chamberlain Mutsuta), Takako Irie (Mutsata's wife), Reiko Dan (Chidori), Sachio Sakai (guard at gate), Toranosuke Ogawa, Yutaka Sada, Shin Otomo.

A Toho Co., Ltd./Kurosawa Films, Ltd. Production. Black and white (processed by Tokyo Laboratory, Ltd.). Toho Scope. Western Electric Mirrophonic Recording (encoded with Perspecta Stereophonic Sound). 96 minutes. Released January 1, 1962.

U.S. VERSION: Released by Toho International Co., Ltd. English subtitles. Monophonic but letterboxed home video version available. 96 minutes. No MPAA rating. Released 14, 1962.

Sanshiro of Ginza / Ginza Sanshiro ("Sanshiro of Ginza"). Producer, Nobuo Aoyagi; Director, Kon Ichikawa; Screenplay, Naoyuki Hatta, based on a story by Tsuneo Tomita; Director of Photography, Jun Yasumoto; Lighting, Kaiyo Sato; Sound Recording, Kihachiro Nakai; Art Director, Kazuo Ogawa; Music, Nobuo Iida.

CAST: Susumu Fujita (Kumasuke Arai), Takashi Shimura (Daizo Matsubara), Sokichi Kawamura (Jimpei), Choko Iida (Taneko, *his wife*), Hisako Yamane (Kinue, *his daughter*), Akiko Kazami (Mariye Tachibana).

A Shintoho Co., Ltd. Production. Black and white. Academy ratio. 75 minutes. Released April 9, 1950.

U.S. VERSION: Distributor, if any, is undetermined.

Sanshiro Sugata / Sugata Sanshiro ("Sanshiro Sugata"). Producer, Keiji Matsuzaki; Director, Akira Kurosawa; Screenplay, Akira Kurosawa, based on the novel *Sugata Sanshiro* by Tsuneo Tomita; Director of Photography, Akira Mimura; Editors, Akira Kurosawa and Toshio Goro; Lighting, Masaki Onuma; Art Director, Masao Totsuka; Music, Seichi Suzuki; Editors, Toshio Goto and Akira Kurosawa; Assistant Director, Toshio Sugia; Sound Recording, Tomohisa Higuchi; Sound, Toho Dubbing Theatre; Sound Effects, Toho Sound Effects Group.

CAST: Susumu Fujita (Sanshiro Sugata), Denjiro Okochi (Shogoro Yano), Takashi Shimura (Hansuke Murai), Yukiko Todoroki (Sayo, *his daughter*), Yoshio Kosugi (Master Saburo Momma, *the jujitsu teacher*), Ranko Hanai (Osumi Mamma, *his daughter*), Ryunosuke Tsukigata (Gennosuke Higaki), Akitake Kono (Yoshima Dan), Soshi Kiyokawa (Yujiro Toda), Kunio Mita (Kohei Tsuzaki), Akira Nakamura (Toranosuke Niiseki), Sugisaku Aoyama (Tsunetami Iimura), Kokuten Kodo (priest), Ichiro Sugai (chief of police), Michisaburo Segawa (Hatta), Eisaburo Sakauchi (Nemeto), Hajime Hikari (Torakichi).

A Toho Co., Ltd Production. Filmed at Toho Studios, Ltd. (Kyoto). Black and white. Academy ratio. Running time undetermined (see below). Released March 25, 1943.

U.S. VERSION: Released by Toho International Co., Ltd. English subtitles. 80 minutes. No MPAA rating. Released April 1974. *Note:* The original Japanese cut was reconstructed and reissued in Japan in 1952; all current prints are taken from this reissue version, not the original release. Running time of reconstructed version: 80 minutes. Remade in 1955 and 1965, the latter version edited by Kurosawa. Title also given as *Judo Saga*. Followed by *Sanshiro Sugata—Part Two* (1945).

Sanshiro Sugata—Part Two / Zoku Sugata Sanshiro ("Sanshiro Sugata, Part Two"). Producer, Motohiko Ito; Director/Editor, Akira Kurosawa; Screenplay, Akira Kurosawa, based on the novel *Sugata Sanshiro* by Tsuneo Tomita; Director of Photography, Hiroshi Suzuki; Art Director, Kazuo Kubo; Music, Seichi Suzuki; Sound, Toho Dubbing Theatre; Sound Effects, Toho Sound Effects Group.

CAST: Susumu Fujita (Sanshiro Sugata), Denjiro Okochi (Shogoro Yano), Akitake [Aritake] Kono (Yoshima Dan), Ryunosuke Tsukigata (Gennosuke Higaki), Yukiko Todoroki (Sayo), Soshi Kiyokawa (Yujiro Toda).

A Toho Co., Ltd. Production. Filmed at Toho Studios, Ltd. (Tokyo). Black and white. Academy ratio. 83 minutes. Released May 3, 1945.

U.S. VERSION: Distributor undetermined, but theatrical release is confirmed, likely through Toho International Co., Ltd. in 1974. English subtitles. Records show this was usually exhibited with *Sanshiro Sugata*, so it may have become available at the same time, and possibly, in some cases, the two films were combined into a single feature running 183 minutes. Alternate title: *Judo Saga—II*.

Sansho the Bailiff / Sansho Dayu ("Sansho the Bailiff"). Producer, Masaichi Nagata; Director, Kenji Mizoguchi; Planning, Hisakazu Tsuji; Screenplay, Fuji Yahiro and Yoshitaka Yoda, based on the short story "Sansho the Steward" (1915) by Mori Ogai, itself based on the Buddhist parable "Sansho Dayu," and the popular legend; Director of Photography, Kazuo Miyagawa; Art Director, Kisaku Ito; Lighting, Kenichi Okamoto; Editor, Mitsuji Miyata; Music, Fumio Hayasaka; Sound Recording, Iwao Otani.

CAST: Yoshiaki Hanayagi (Zushio), Kyoko Kagawa (Anju), Kinuyo Tanaka (Tamaki, *their mother*), Eitaro Shindo (Sansho Dayu), Akitake Kono (Taro), Masao Shimizu (Taira no Masauji, *their father*), Ryosuke Kagawa (Donmo), Kikue Mori (Shinto priestess), Ken Mitsuda (Prime Minister Fujiwara no Mitsuzane), Chieko Naniwa (Ubatake), Kasuhito Okuni (Norimiura), Kimiko Tachibana (Namiji), Ichiro Sugai (Nio), Masahiko Kato (Zushio as an adolescent), Naoki Fujima (Zushio as a boy), Keiko Enami (young Anju), Keiko [Kanji] Koshiba (Kuranosuke Koto), Shinobu Araki (Satao), Reiko Kongo (Shiono, *the maidservant*), Shozo Nanbu (Taira no Masatomo), Ryonosuke Higashi (brothel manager), Bontaro Miake (Yoshitsugu), Saburo Date (Kanahira), Sachiko Aima (Sugano), Sachio Horikita (Jiro Sado), Hachiro Okuni (Saburo Miyazaki), Ikkei Tamaki (peace-keeping officer), Masayoshi Kikuno (jailer), Sumao Ishihara (old graveyard keeper), Tominosuke Hayama (old priest).

A Daiei Motion Picture Co., Ltd. Production. Filmed at Daiei-Kyoto Studios. Black and white. Academy ratio. 124 minutes. Released March 31, 1954.

U.S. VERSION: Released by Brandon Films. English subtitles. Alternate title: *The Bailiff*. Running time also given at 88 minutes. 124 minutes. No MPAA rating. Released September 1969.

Savage Wolf Pack / Yaju o kese ("Kill the Beast"). Director, Yasuharu Hasebe; Screenplay, Hidekazu Nagahara and Ryuzo Nakanishi; Director of Photography, Masahisa Himeda; Art Director, Takeo Kimura; Music, Koichi Sakata.

CAST: Tetsuya Watari (Asai), Meiko Fujimoto (Kyoko), Tatsuya Fuji (Yada), Toshiya Yamano (Bill), Yuri Yoshioka, Isao Bito, Meiko Tsudoi.

A Nikkatsu Corp. Production. Fujicolor. ToeiScope. 84 minutes. February 22, 1969.

U.S. VERSION: Release undetermined. English subtitled version available. 84 minutes. No MPAA rating.

Sayonara. Executive Producer, Marlon Brando; Producer, William Goetz; Director, Joshua Logan; Screenplay, Paul Osborn, based on the novel, *Sayonara*, by James A. Michener; Director of Photography, Ellsworth Fredericks; Music, Franz Waxman; Editors, Arthur P. Schmidt and Philip W. Anderson; Art Director, Edward S. "Ted" Haworth; Set Decorator, Robert Priestly; Costume Designer, Norma Koch; Revue Numbers Supervisor, LeRoy Prinz; Assistant Director, Ad Schaumer; Dialog Supervisor, Joseph Curtis; Script Supervisor, Marshall J. Wolins; Sound Supervisor, George R. Groves; Sound, McCluer A. Merrick; Song, "Sayonara—Goodbye," Music and Lyrics by Irving Berlin; Assistant Cameraman, Charles Termini; Key Grip, Weldon Gilbert; 2nd Unit Photography, Hans F. Keonekamp; Orchestration, Leonid Raab; Assistant Film Editor, Sam O'Steen; Casting, Hoyt Bowers; Makeup Supervisor, Gordon Bau; Production Associate, Walter Thompson; Technical Adviser for Kagekidan sequences, Masaya Tajiona.

CAST: Marlon Brando (Maj. Lloyd "Ace" Gruver), Red Buttons (Joe Kelly), Ricardo Montalban (Nakamura), Miiko Taka (Hana-ogi), Miyoshi Umeki (Katsumi), Patricia Owens (Eileen Webster), James Garner (Capt. Mike Bailey), Martha Scott (Mrs. Webster), Kent Smith (General Webster), Douglas Watson (Colonel Crawford), Reiko Kuba (Fumiko-san), Soo Yong (Teruko-san), Harlan Warde (Consul), and the Shochuku Kagekidan Girls Revue.

A Goetz Pictures, Inc./Pennebaker, Inc. Production. A Warner Bros. Pictures, Inc. Release. English language. An American production filmed in Kobe (Japan) and completed at Warner Bros. Studios (Burbank, California). RCA Photophone Recording. Perspecta Stereophonic Sound. Technicolor. Technirama. No MPAA rating. 147 minutes. Released December 1957.

Sayonara Jiyupeta ("Goodbye Jupiter"). Executive Producer, Tomoyuki Tanaka and Sakyo Komatsu; Associate Producers, Fumio Tanaka, Shiro Fujiwara; Director, Koji Hashimoto; Screenplay/Chief Director [Associate Producer], Sakyo Komatsu, based on his novel; Director of Photography, Kazutani Hara; Production Designer, Heio Takanaka; Continuity, Nubuo Ogawa; Editor, Masaji Ohima; Music, Kentaro Haneda; Songs—"Voyager/The Blue Ship" by Yumi Matsutoya; Incidental Songs—"Sayonara Jupiter/Four Seasons of the Earth" by Jiro Sugita; Soundtrack album available on Toshiba/EMI Records, licensed through Toho Music Publishing Co., Ltd.; Sound, Toho Recording Centre; Sound Effects, Toho Sound Effects Group; Production Manager, Kishu Morichi. *Toho Special Effects Group*: Director, Koichi Kawakita; Assistant Director, Kyotaka Matsumoto; Assistant to the Director, Kenji Suzuki; Director of Photography, Kenichi Eguchi; Lighting, Kaoru Saito; Wire Works, Koji Matsumoto; Miniature Pyrotechniques, Tadaaki Watanabe, Mamoru Kume; Production Design, Studio Nue.

CAST: Tomokazu Miura (Eiji Honda), Rachel Hugget (Millicent Wilem), Diane Dangely (Maria Basehart), Miyuki Ono (Anita), Akihiko Hirata (Ryutaro Inoue), Hisaya Morishige (President of Earth Federation), Masumi Okada (Mohamed Manshur), Paul Taiga (Peter), Kim Bass (Hooker), Marc Pinonnat (Carlos Arnez), Ron Irwin (Hoger Kinn), William H. Tapier (Edward Webb).

A Toho Co., Ltd./Kabushiki-kaisha Io Production. Dolby Stereo. Color (processed by Tokyo Laboratory Ltd.). Spherical Panavision. 129 minutes. Released March 17, 1984.

U.S. VERSION: Unreleased in the United States as of this writing. International Title: *Bye Bye Jupiter*.

Scandal / Shubun ("Scandal"). Producer, Takashi Koide; Director/Editor, Akira Kurosawa; Screenplay, Ryuzo Kikushima and Akira Kurosawa; Director of Photography, Toshio Ubukata; Art Director, Tatsuo Hamada; Music, Fumio Hayasaka.

CAST: Toshiro Mifune (Ichiro Aoye), Yoshiko Yamaguchi (Miyako Saigo), Takashi Shimura (Attorney Hiruta), Yoko Katsuragi (Masako Hiruta), Noriko Sengoku (Sumie), Eitaro Ozawa (Hori), Bokuzen Hidari (drunk), Kokuten Kodo and Kichijiro Ueda (farmers), Fumiko Okamura (Miyako's mother), Tanie Kitabayashi, Masao Shimizu.

A Shochiku Co., Ltd. Production. Filmed at Shochiku Studios. Black and white. Academy ratio. 105 minutes. Released April 30, 1950.

U.S. VERSION: Released by Shochiku Films of America, Inc. English subtitles. 105 minutes. No MPAA rating. Released June 1964. Reissued by Entertainment Marketing in August 1980.

The Scandalous Adventures of Buraikan / Buraikan ("Hooligan"). Producer, Yasushige Wakatsuki; Director, Masahiro Shinoda; Screenplay, Shuji Terayama, based on the story by Mokuami Kawatabe; Director of Photography, Kozo Okazaki; Art Director, Shigemasa Toda; Music, Masaru Sato.

CAST: Tetsuro Tamba (Soshun),Tatsuya Nakadai (Naojiro), Suisen Ichikawa (his mother), Shima Iwashita (Michitose), Shoichi Ozawa (Ushimatsu), Masakane Yonekura (Ichinojo Kaneko), Kiwako Taichi (Namiji), Fumio Watanabe (Seizo Moritaya), Hiroshi Akutagawa.

A Ninjin Club/Toho Co., Ltd. Production. A Toho Co., Ltd. Release. Eastman Color. Panavision. 105 minutes. Released April 18, 1970.

U.S. VERSION: Released by Toho International Co., Ltd. English subtitles. 105 minutes. No MPAA rating. Released November 1970.

The Scarlet Camellia / Goben no tsubaki ("Five Petalled Camellia"). Producer, Shiro Kido; Director, Yoshitaro Nomura; Screenplay, Masato Ide, based on the novel, *Goben no tsubaki* (1959) by Shugoro Yamamoto; Director of Photography, Ko Kawamata; Art Directors, Takashi Matsuyama and Chiyo Umeda; Music, Yasushi Akutagawa.

CAST: Shima Iwashita (Oshino), Yoshi Kato (Kihei Musashiya), Sachiko Hidari (Osono), Takahiro Tamura (Chodayu), Yunosuke Ita (Unno), Shoichi Ozawa (Seiichi), Ko Nishimura (Sakichi), Eiji Okada (Gen Maruu), Go Kato (Aoki).

A Shochiku Co., Ltd. Production. Eastman Color. Shochiku GrandScope. 163 minutes. Released 1964.

U.S. VERSION: Released by Shochiku Films of America, Inc. English subtitles. 117 minutes. No MPAA rating. Released February 26, 1965.

The School / Sensei ("Teacher"). Producer, Shinichi "Sonny" Chiba; Director, Shingo Yamashiro; Screenplay, Takako Shigemori; Director of Photography, Koichi Suzuki; Music, Toshiaki Tsushima.

CAST: Hiroki Matsukata, Tsunehiko Watase, Shinichi "Sonny" Chiba.

A Tom Sawyer Planning Co., Ltd. Production. Color. Panavision (?). 119 minutes. Released 1989.

U.S. VERSION: Distributor undetermined. 119 minutes. No MPAA rating. Released June 1989.

School of Love / Nikutai ("The Flesh"). Producer, Masakatsu Kaneko; Director, Ryo Kinoshita; Screenplay, Toshiro Ide, based on *Nikutai no gakko* (1964) by Yukio Mishima; Director of Photography, Yuzuru Aizawa; Music, Shigeru Ikeno.

CAST: Kyoko Kishida (Taeko), Tsutomu Yamazaki (Senkichi), Yuki Nakagawa, So Yamamura.

A Toho Co., Ltd. Production. Black and white. Toho Scope. 95 minutes. Released 1965.

U.S. VERSION: Released by Toho International Co., Ltd. English subtitles. Alternate title: *School for Sex*. 95 minutes. No MPAA rating. Released May 1966.

The Sea and Poison / Umi to dokuyaku ("Sea and Poison"). Producer, Kano Otsuka; Director, Kei Kumai; Screenplay, Kei Kumai, based on an original story by Shusaku Endo; Director of Photography, Masao Tochizawa; Music, Teizo Matsumura.

CAST: Eiji Okada, Ken Watanabe, Mikio Narita, Ken Nishida, Shigeru Kamiyama, Kyoko Kishida.

A *The Sea and Poison* Production Committee Production. Black and white. Spherical wide screen (?). 123 minutes. Released 1986.

U.S. VERSION: Released by Gades Films. English subtitles. 123 minutes. No MPAA rating. Released July 22, 1987.

The Sea Prince and the Fire Child / Shiriusu no densetsu ("Legend of Shiriusu") **[animated]**. Producer, Shintaro Tsuji; Director, Masami Hata; Screenplay, Chiho Katsura and Masami Hata, based on an original story by Shintaro Tsuji; Director of Photography, Iwao Yamaki; Art Director, Yukio Abe; Music, Koichi Sugiyama.

VOICE CHARACTERIZATIONS: (undetermined).

A Sanrio Co., Ltd. Production. Color. Spherical wide screen. 108 minutes. Released 1981.

U.S. VERSION: Distributor, if any, is undetermined. No MPAA rating.

Secret Information / Tarekomi ("Secret Information"). Director, Masaharu Segawa; Screenplay, Masaharu Segawa and Moto Nagai; Director of Photography, Masahiko Iimura; Art Director, Hiroshi Kitagawa; Music, Chuji Kinoshita.

CAST: Noboru Ando (Mamoru Sagara), Isao Kimura (Goro Izawa), Toru Abe (Yasaburo Oba), Eiji Okada (Toru Kijima), Hideo Takamatsu (Tetsuki Miki), Tamaki Sawa (Miyako).

A Toei Co., Ltd. Production. Eastman Color. ToeiScope. 90 minutes. Released May 14, 1969.

U.S. VERSION: Release undetermined. English subtitled version available. 90 minutes. No MPAA rating.

The Secret of the Fylfot / Shinobi no manji. Producer, Kanji Amao; Director, Norifumi Suzuki; Screenplay, Kan Saji and Ryunosuke Ono, based on the story "Shinobi no manji" by Futaro Yamada; Art Director, Yoshimitsu Amamori; Director of Photography, Juhei Suzuki; Sound Recording, Hiroo Nozu; Editor, Kozo Horiike; Music, Harumi Ibe.

CAST: Isao Natsuyagi (Shiinoba), Hiroko Sakuramachi (Kagiroi), Tatsuo Endo (Ujin), Kenji Ushio (Senjuro Momo), Yukiko Kuwabara (Yu), Akami Mari (Oei), Shingo Yamashiro (Tadanaga), Kiichi Yamamoto (Uemon Saori), Anne Maroi (Osai), Tomoko Mayama (Obuni), Kantaro Suga (Iemitsu), Akecho Sogamawariya (Doi Ohtanokami), Hosei Komatsu (Torii Tosanokami), Minoru Ohki (Yagui Tajimanokami), Eijiro Sekine (Kiiko), Masao Hori (Owariko), Kinji Nakamura (Mitoko), Kogiku Hanayagi (Lady Kasuga), Yuriko Mishima (Okuni Nokata), Harumi Kiritake (Ofune Nokata), Mariko Ogawa (Okuru), Hitoshi Omae (big warehouse keeper), Mitsukazu Kawamura (Goro Udai), Takeshi Kumagai (doctor at palace), Masaru Shiga (1st ninja), Daisuke Awaji (2nd ninja), Tokuko Miura (woman in boat house).

A Toei Co., Ltd. Production. Filmed at Toei-Kyoto Studios. Fujicolor (processed by Toei Chemistry Co., Ltd.). ToeiScope. 89 minutes. Released 1968.

U.S. VERSION: Never released theatrically in the United States.

The Secret of the Telegian / Denso ningen ("The Teleported Man"). Executive Producer, Tomoyuki Tanaka; Director, Jun Fukuda; Screenplay, Shinichi Sekizawa; Director of Photography, Kazuo Yamada; Art Director, Kyoe Hamagami and Takeo Kita; Lighting, Tsuruzo Nishikawa; Editor, Ichiji Taira; Assistant Producer, Boku Morimoto; Assistant Director, Taku Nagano; Music, Shigeru Ikeno; Sound Recording, Yoshio Nishikawa and Masanobu Miyazaki; Sound, Toho Recording Centre; Sound Effects, Toho Sound Effects Group. *Toho Special Effects Group*: Director, Eiji Tsuburaya; Art Director, Akira Watanabe; Photography, Hidezaburo Araki; Lighting Kuichiro Kishida; Matte Process, Hiroshi Mukoyama; Optical Photography, Hidesaburo Araki.

CAST: Koji Tsuruta (Kirioka), Yumi Shirakawa (Akiko), Yoshio Tsuchiya (detective), Tadao Nakamaru (former Corporal Sudo, *alias Goro Nakamoto*), Akihiko Hirata (Detective Kobayashi), Seizaburo Kawazu (Onishi), Yoshifumi Tajima (Takashi), Senkichi Omura (fisherman), Eisei Amamoto (bodyguard), Sachio Sakai, Takamaru Sasaki, Fuyuki Murakami, Ikio Sawamura, Shin Otomo, Ren Yamamoto, Fumio Matsuo, Kiyomi Mizunoya, Tsuruko Mano, Yutaka Sada, Nadao Kirino, Shiro Tsuchiya, Tatsuo Matsumura, Kyoro Sakurai, Akira Sera.

A Toho Co., Ltd. Production; Western Electric Mirrophonic recording (encoded with Perspecta Stereophonic Sound). Eastman Color (processed by Far East

Laboratories, Ltd.). Toho Scope. 85 minutes. Released April 10, 1960.

U.S. VERSION: Released by Toho International Co., Ltd. English subtitles. North American theatrical rights purchased by Herts-Lion International Corp., who released the picture directly to American television instead (with TV prints in black and white). English-dubbed. A color and English-dubbed version is also available. Announced as *The Telegians* and *Secret File of the Telegian*. 75 minutes (some English-language prints run 85 minutes). No MPAA rating. Tradescreened in Los Angeles July 21, 1961.

Secret Scrolls (Part I) / Yagyu Bugeicho ("Yagyu Military Scrolls"). Producer, Tomoyuki Tanaka; Director, Hiroshi Inagaki; Screenplay, Hiroshi Inagaki, Tomoyuki Tanaka, and Takeshi Kimura, based on the serialized novel *Yagyu Bugeicho* (1956-59) by Kosuke Gomi; Art Directors, Takeo Kita and Hiroshi Ueda; Director of Photography, Tadashi Iimura; Music, Akira Ifukube; Recording, Yoshio Nishikawa; Sound, Toho Dubbing Theatre; Sound Effects, Toho Sound Effects Group.

CAST: Toshiro Mifune (Tasaburo), Koji Tsuruta (Senshiro), Yoshiko Kuga (Yuhime), Kyoko Kagawa (Oki), Mariko Okada (Rika), Denjiro Okochi (Lord Yagyu), Jotaro Togami (Jubei), Akihiko Hirata (Tomonori), Senjaku Namamura (Matajuro), Hanshiro Iwai (Iyemitsu), Eijiro Tono (Fugetsusai).

A Toho Co., Ltd. Production. Western Electric Mirrophonic recording (encoded with Perspecta Stereophonic Sound). Agfacolor (processed by Tokyo Laboratory Ltd.). Academy ratio. 109 minutes. Released 1957.

U.S. VERSION: Released by Toho International Co., Ltd. English subtitles. Sequel: *Secret Scrolls (Part II)* (1958). Also known as *Yagyu Secret Scrolls*. 109 minutes. No MPAA rating. Released October 11, 1967.

Secret Scrolls (Part II) / Yagyu Bugeicho – Soryu hiken ("Yagyu Military Schools: The Art of Ninja"). Producer, Tomoyuki Tanaka; Director, Hiroshi Inagaki; Screenplay, Hiroshi Inagaki, Tomoyuki Tanaka, Takeshi Kimura, and Takuhei Wakao, based on the serialized novel, *Yagyu Bugeicho* (1956-59) by Kosuke Gomi; Art Directors, Takeo Kita and Hiroshi Ueda; Director of Photography, Asakazu Nakai; Music, Akira Ifukube; Recording, Yoshio Nishikawa; Sound, Toho Dubbing Theatre; Sound Effects, Toho Sound Effects Group.

CAST: Toshiro Mifune (Tasaburo), Koji Tsuruta (Senshiro), Nobuko Otawa (princess), Jotaro Togami (Jubei), Senjaku Namamura (Matajuro), Hanshiro Iwai (Iyemitsu), Yoshiko Kuga (Yuhime), Mariko Okada (Rika), Denjiro Okochi (Lord Yagyu), Kyoko Kagawa (Oki), Akihiko Hirata (Tomonori).

A Toho Co., Ltd. Production. Western Electric Mirrophonic recording (encoded with Perspecta Stereophonic Sound). Agfacolor (processed by Tokyo Laboratory Ltd.). Toho Scope. 106 minutes. Released 1958.

U.S. VERSION: Released by Toho International Co., Ltd. English subtitles. Also released in Japan as *Ninjitsu*. A sequel to *Secret Scrolls (Part I)* (1957). 106 minutes. No MPAA rating. Released May 22, 1968.

Secret Turkish Bath / Maruhi Torukoburo ("Secret Turkish Bath"). Director, Shinji Murayama; Screenplay, Kikuma Shimoizaka and Koji Harima; Director of Photography, Kiichi Inada; Art Director, Shuichiro Nakamura; Music, Masao Yagi.

CAST: Tatsuo Umemiya (Tatsu), Reiko Ohara (Ranko), Sanae Nakahara (Nami), Toyozo Yamamoto (Bungo), Yukiko Kuwahara (Keiko).

A Toei Co., Ltd. Production. Black and white. ToeiScope. 86 minutes. Released August 27, 1968.

U.S. VERSION: Release undetermined. English subtitled version available. 86 minutes. No MPAA rating.

Secret Zone of Tokyo / Tokyo maruhi chitai ("Secret Zone of Tokyo"). Director, Tan Ida; Screenplay, Ei Ogawa and Iwao Yamazaki; Director of Photography, Izumi Hagiwara; Art Director, Atsuji Shibata; Music, Yutaka Makino.

CAST: Jiro Okazaki (Ginichi), Eiji Go (Saburo), Yaeko Wakamizu (Utako), Masami Maki (Rumi), Sachiko Kuwabara (Yoko), Keiko Aikawa (Michiko), Shoki Fukae (Makino).

A Nikkatsu Corp. Production. Fujicolor. NikkatsuScope. 83 minutes. Released February 6, 1971.

U.S. VERSION: Distributor, if any, is undetermined. English subtitled version available. 83 minutes. No MPAA rating.

Secrets of a Woman's Temple / Hiroku Onnadera ("Secret Record of a Woman's Temple"). Director, Tokuzo Tanaka; Screenplay, Shozaburo Asai; Director of Photography, Chishi Makiura; Art Director, Yoshinobu Nishioka; Music, Hajime Kaburagi.

CAST: Michiyo Yasuda (Oharu), Shigako Shimegi (Shigetsuin), Sanae Nakahara, Machiko Hasegawa, Naomi Kobayashi, Yasuyo Matsumura.

A Daiei Motion Picture Co., Ltd. Production. Black and white. DaieiScope. 79 minutes. Released January 1969.

U.S. VERSION: Released by Daiei Films International. English subtitles. 79 minutes. No MPAA rating. Released July 23, 1969.

See You / Umi e shi yu ("Ocean to See You"). Producers, Masaru Otaki and Hiroshi Fujikura; Director, Koreyoshi Kurahara; Screenplay, So Kuramoto, based on an original story by Jose Jiobani; Director of Photography, Toshiaki Sato.

CAST: Ken Takakura, Ayumi Ishida, Junko Sakurada.

A Toho Co., Ltd. Production. Color. Spherical wide screen. 174 minutes. Released 1988.

U.S. VERSION: Release undetermined, possibly by Toho International Co., Ltd. in subtitled format. No MPAA rating.

Senbon Matsubara ("1,000 Pine Groves") **[animated]**. Producer, Yoshiaki Seto; Director, Satoshi Dezaki; Screenplay, Toshiaki Imaizumi, based on an original story by Takeo Kishi; Director of Photography, Hiroshi Isagawa; Music, Masumi Hiyoshi.

VOICE CHARACTERIZATIONS: Hisaya Morishige, Nozomu Sasaski, Taro Ishida.

A Space Ezo Production. Color. Spherical wide screen (?). 90 minutes. Released 1991 (?).

U.S. VERSION: Distributor, if any, is undetermined.

Sennin Buraku ("Village of 1,000 Persons"). Director, Shinpei Magutani; Screenplay, Isao Matsuki; Director of Photography, Shingenari Yoshida.

CAST: Yoichi Numata, Mayumi Ozora, Mako Sanjo, Akiro Hitomi.

A Shintoho Co., Ltd. Production. Western Electric Mirrophonic recording. Black and white. Shintoho-Scope. 82 minutes. Released 1960.

U.S. VERSION: Never released theatrically in the United States. International title: *Invitation to the Enchanted Town.*

Sensation Seekers / Nippon jitsuwa jidai ("True Story in Japan"). Executive Producers, Sanezumi Fujimoto and Masakatsu Kaneko; Director, Jun Fukuda.

CAST: Tadao Takashima, Mie Hama, Akiko Wakabayashi, Kunie Tanaka, Yu Fujiki.

A Toho Co., Ltd. Production. Eastman Color. Toho Scope. 83 minutes. Released 1966 (?).

U.S. VERSION: Released by Toho International Co., Ltd. English subtitles. 83 minutes. No MPAA rating. Release date undetermined.

Seven Mysteries / Kaidan Honjo nanfushigi ("Ghost Story: Honjo Seven Mysteries"). Director, Goro Katono; Screenplay, Otoya Hayashi and Nagayoshi Akasada; Story, Akira Sagawa; Director of Photography, Hiroshi Suzuki.

CAST: Juzaburo Akechi, Shigeru Amachi, Hiroshi Hayashi, Uraji Matsuura, Akiko Tamashita, Michiko Tachibana.

A Shintoho Co., Ltd. Production. Western Electric Mirrophonic recording. Black and white. Academy ratio. Running time undetermined. Released 1957.

U.S. VERSION: Distributor undetermined. Also known as *Ghost Story of Wanderer at Honjo.*

Sex and Life / Maruhi sei to seikatsu ("Secrets of Sex and Life"). Director, Tatsuichi Takamori; Screenplay, Ichiro Ikeda, based on an original story by Dr. Hsieh; Director of Photography, Masahiko Iimura; Art Director, Shinichi Eno; Music, Koichi Kawabe.

CAST: Kenjiro Ishiyama (gynecologist), Teruo Yoshida (gynecologist's son), Mariko Ko (young nurse), Yoko Mihara (patient), Shingo Yamashiro, Bokuzen Hidari.

A Toei Co., Ltd. Production. Eastman Color. ToeiScope. 88 minutes. Released February 11, 1969.

U.S. VERSION: Release, if any, is undetermined. English subtitled version available. 88 minutes. No MPAA rating.

The Sex Check / Daini no sei ("The Second Sex"). Director, Yasuzo Masamura; Screenplay, Ichiro Ikeda, based on an original story by Daikichi Terauchi; Director of Photography, Akira Kitazaki; Art Director, Tomo Shimogawara; Music, Tadashi Yamauchi.

CAST: Michiyo Yasuda (Hiroko Nagumo), Ken Ogata (Shiro Miyaji), Mayumi Ogawa (Akiko Mineshige), Yuzo Hayakawa (Sasanuma), Reiko Kasahara (Masako), Tazuko Niki (Reiko).

A Daiei Motion Picture Co., Ltd. Production. Fujicolor. DaieiScope. 89 minutes. Released June 1, 1968.

U.S. VERSION: Release undetermined, possibly by Daiei International Films. English subtitled version available. 89 minutes. No MPAA rating.

Sex Phobia / Maruhi sex kyofusho ("Secret Sex Phobia"). Director, Tatsuichi Takamori; Screenplay, Ichiro Ikeda; Director of Photography, Masahiko Iimura; Art Director, Shinichi Eno; Music, Toshiaki Tsushima.

CAST: Kentaro Kudo (Kosuke Izawa), Yukie Kagawa (Sawako), Hosei Komatsu (Junichi), Machiko Yashiro, Kunie Tanaka.

A Toei Co., Ltd. Production. Eastman Color. ToeiScope. 88 minutes. Released August 28, 1970.

U.S. VERSION: Distributor, if any, is undetermined. English subtitled version available. 88 minutes. No MPAA rating.

The Sexploiters / Kigeki hachurui ("Reptile Comedy"). Director, Yusuke Watanabe; Screenplay, Kei Tasaka; Director of Photography, Ryoichi Arano; Art Director, Kiminubo Sato; Music, Masao Yagi.

CAST: Kiyoshi Atsumi (Seki), Ko Nishimura (Yamaguchi), Shiro Osaka (Tsuyuki), Tetsuo Morishita (Sakura), Shoichi Ozawa (Kujo), Junzaburo Ban (Yoneda), Terry Angel (Mary Harlow).

A Shochiku Co., Ltd. Production. Eastman Color. Shochiku GrandScope. 90 minutes. Released May 15, 1968.

U.S. VERSION: Release undetermined. English subtitled version available. 90 minutes. No MPAA rating.

Shadow of Deception / Naikai no wa ("Circle Under the Sea"). Director, Koichi Saito; Screenplay, Nobuo Yamada and Fukiko Miyauchi, based on an original story by Seicho Matsumoto; Director of Photography, Hiroshi Takemura; Music, Katsuhisa Hattori.

CAST: Shima Iwashita (Minako), Akira Nakao (Sozo), Rentaro Mikuni, Miyoko Akaza, Yasunori Irikawa.

A Shochiku Co., Ltd. Production. Eastman Color. Shochiku GrandScope. 104 minutes. Released February 10, 1971.

U.S. VERSION: Release undetermined, possibly by Shochiku Films of America, Inc. English subtitled version available. 104 minutes. No MPAA rating.

The Shadow Within / Kage no kuruma ("Shadow of the Automobile"). Director, Yoshitaro Nomura; Screenplay, Shinobu Hashimoto, based on the novel *Senzai Kokei* by Seicho Matsumoto; Director of Photography, Takashi Kawamata; Art Director, Shigemori Shigeta; Editor, Yoshiyasu Yamamura; Music, Yasushi Akutagawa; Sound, Sojiro Kurita; Special Effects, Takashi Kawamata and Seitaro Nomura.

CAST: Go Kato (Yukio), Shima Iwashita (Yasuko), Mayumi Ogawa (Yukio's wife), Kaneko Iwasaki (widow mother), Yusuke Takita (uncle), Hisato Okamoto (Ken), Azusa Koyama (Yukio as a child), Shinsuke Ashida (detective).

A Shochiku Co., Ltd. Production. Eastman Color. Shochiku GrandScope. 97 minutes. Released June 6, 1970.

U.S. VERSION: Released by Shochiku Films of America, Inc. English subtitles. 97 minutes. No MPAA rating. Released January 23, 1971.

Shanghai Rhapsody / Shanhai bansukingu ("Shanghai Bons King"?). Producers, Akira Oda and Moritsune Saito; Director, Kinji Fukasaku; Screenplay, Yozo Tanaka and Kinji Fukasaku, based on an original story by Ren Saito; Director of Photography, Keishi Maruyama; Music, Nobuyoshi Koshibe.

CAST: Keiko Matsuzaka, Morio Kazama, Ryudo Uzaki.

A Shochiku Co., Ltd./Cine Saison Co., Ltd./Asahi National Broadcasting Co., Ltd. Production. A Shochiku Co., Ltd. Release. Color. Panavision (?). 132 minutes. Released 1988.

U.S. VERSION: Release undetermined, possibly by Shochiku Films of America, Inc. in subtitled format. No MPAA rating.

She and He / Kanojo to Kare ("She and He"). Director, Susumu Hani; Screenplay, Susumu Hani and Kunio Shimizu; Director of Photography, Juichi Nagano; Music, Toru Takemitsu; Sound Recording, Tetsuo Yasuda.

CAST: Sachiko Hidari (Naoko), Eiji Okada (Eiichi), Kikuji Yamashita (Ikona), Mariko Igarashi (Hanako), Akio Hasegawa (laundry boy), Takanobu Hobuzi (doctor), Kuma [a dog] (dog).

An Iwanami Productions/Eizo-Sha Co., Ltd. Production. Black and white. Academy ratio (?). 115 minutes. Released 1963.

U.S. VERSION: Released by Brandon Films. English subtitles. 110 minutes. No MPAA rating. Released June 1967.

She Was Like a Wild Chrysanthemum / Nogiku no gotoki kimi nariki ("She Was Like a Wild Chrysanthemum"). Producer, Kiyoshi Takamura; Director, Keisuke Kinoshita; Screenplay, Keisuke Kinoshita, based on the novel by Sachio Ito.

CAST: Shini Tanaka (Young Masao), Noriko Arita (Tamiko), Chishu Ryu (Old Masao), Haruko Sugimura (Masao's mother), Keiko Yukishiro (Tomi), Kumeko Urabe (grandmother).

A Shochiku Co., Ltd. Production. Black and white. Academy ratio. 92 minutes. Released 1955.

U.S. VERSION: Released by Brandon Films, Inc. English subtitles. 92 minutes (running time also given at 100 minutes). No MPAA rating. Released January 21, 1960.

Shimantogawa ("Shimanto River"). Producer, Hisao Nabeshima; Director, Hideo Onchi; Screenplay, Motomu Furuta, based on an original story by Kyuzo Sasayama; Director of Photography, Shohei Ando; Music, Kurodo Mori.

CAST: Kanako Higuchi, Kaori Takahashi, Teppei Yamada.

A Yamada Yoko Right Vision Co., Ltd. Production. Color. Spherical wide screen (?). 111 minutes. Released 1991.

U.S. VERSION: Distributor, if any, is undetermined.

Shinran: Path to Purity / Shinran: Shiroi michi ("Shinran: Path to Purity"). Producers, Nobuyoshi Otani, Hiroaki Kato, and Matsuo Takahashi; Director, Rentaro Mikuni; Screenplay, Den Fujita and Rentaro Mikuni, based on the book by Rentaro Mikuni; Director of Photography, Yoshihiro Yamazaki; Music, YAS-KAZ.

CAST: Junkyu Moriyama (Shinran), Michiyo Ogusu (Asa), Shigeru Izumiya (Ijika), Guto Ishimatsu (Atota), Hosei Komatsu (Utsuneymiya).

A Shochiku Co., Ltd./Nichiei Co., Ltd./KinemaTokyo Co., Ltd. Production. A Shochiku Co., Ltd. Release. Color. Panavision (?). 140 minutes. Released 1987.

U.S. VERSION: Released by Shochiku Films of America, Inc. English subtitles. 140 minutes. No MPAA rating. Released April 1988.

Shinshaku Yotsuya kaidan ("New Version of the Ghost of Yotsuya"). Producer, Koichiro Ogura; Director, Keisuke Kinoshita; Screenplay, Eijiro Hisaita, based on the play *Yotsuya kaidan* by

Nanboku Tsuruya; Director of Photography, Hiroshi Kusuda.

CAST: Ken Uehara (Iemon), Kinuyo Tanaka (Oiwa/Osode), Hisako Yamane (Oume), Haruko Sugimura, Choko Iida, Osamu Takizawa.

A Shochiku Co., Ltd. Production. Black and white. Academy ratio. 159 minutes (two parts running 86 and 73 minutes). Released 1949.

U.S. VERSION: Distributor, if any, is undetermined. International title: *New Version of the Ghost of Yotsuya*. Also known as *The Ghost of Yotsuya: New Version*.

(James Clavell's) *Shogun*. Executive Producer, James Clavell; Producer, Eric Bercovici; Associate Producers, Kerry Feltham and Ben Chapman; Director, Jerry London; Screenplay, Eric Bercovici, based on the novel *Shogun*, by James Clavell; Music, Maurice Jarre; Production Executive, Frank Cardea; Editors, James T. Heckert, William Luciano, Donald R. Rode, Benjamin H. Weissman, and Jerry Young; Production Designer, Joseph R. Jennings; Director of Photography, Andrew Laszlo; Unit Production Managers, Ben Chapman and Wallace Worsley; 1st Assistant Directors, Charles Ziarko and Phil Cook; Casting, Maude Spector and Tatsuhiko Kuroiwa; Set Decorator, Tom Pedigo; Foreign Production Coordinator, Chris Bartlett; Construction Coordinator, Al De Gaetano; Special Effects, Robert Dawson; Sound Editor, Howard Beals; Music Editor, John LaSalandra; Music Recordist, Gerry Ulmer; Camera Operator, Chuy Elizondo; Gaffer, Sal Orefice; Key Grips, Ken Johnson and Vern Matthews; Dialog Coach, Luca Bercovici; Script Supervisor, Larry K. Johnson; Special Consultant, Fred Ishimoto; Sound Mixer, John Glascock; Stunt Coordinator, Glenn R. Wilder; Production Accountant, Don Henry; Auditor, J. Steven Hollander; Property Master, Marty Wunderlich; Painter, Ed Charnock; Interpreter/Consultant, Chiho Adachi; Assistant to Eric Bercovici, Anna Mills; Assistant to James Clavell, Valerie Nelson; Title Design, Phill Norman; Title Opticals, Westheimer Co.; Recording Glen Glenn Sound. *Japanese Crew*: Art Director, Yoshinobu Nishioka; Costume Designer, Shin Nishida; Unit Production Managers, Shinji Nakagawa, Kazuo Shizukawa, and Keisuke Shinoda; Adviser to Jerry London, Umeo Minamino; Assistant Director, Masahiko Okumura; Set Decorator, Shoichi Yasuda; Makeup, Masato Abe; Wardrobe, Toshiaki Manki; Construction Department, Hideo Yoshioka; Script Supervisor, Chiyo Miyakoshi; Stunt Coordinator, Shinpachi Miyama; Production Services and Consultation, Tohokushinska Film Co., Ltd., and Banjuro Hemura. "We gratefully acknowledge the cooperation and assistance furnished by Himeji Castle (Himeji City, Japan).... The vessel 'The Golden Hinde' was photographed in this production."

CAST: Richard Chamberlan (John Blackthorne), Toshiro Mifune (Toranaga), Yoko Shimada (Mariko), Frankie Sakai (Yabu), Alan Badel (Father Dell'Aqua), Michael Hordern (Friar Domingo), Damien Thomas (Father Alvito), John Rhys-Davis (Vasco Rodrigues), Vladek Sheybal (Captain Ferriera), George Innes (Johann de Vinck), Leon Lissek (Father Sabastio), Hideo Takamatsu (Buntaro), Yuki Meguro (Omi), Nobuo Kaneko (Ishido), Edward Peel (Pieterzoon), Eric Richard (Maetsukker), Steven Ubels (Roper), Stewart MacKenzie (Croocq), John Carney (Ginsel), Ian Jentle (Salamon), Neil McCarthy (Spillbergen), Morgan Sheppard (Specz), Seiji Miyaguchi (Muraji), Toru Abe (Hiromatsu), Mika Kitagawa (Kiku), Shin Takuma (Naga), Hiroshi Hasegawa (galley captain), Akira Sera (old gardener), Hyoei Enoki (Jirobei), Miiko Taka (Kiri), Midori Takei (Sono), Ai Matsubara (Rako), Yumiko Morishita (Asa), Hiromi Senno (Fujiko), Rinichi Yamamoto (Yoshinaka), Yuko Kada (Sazuko), Masumi Okada (Brother Michael), Yosuke Natsuki (Zataki), Takeshi Obayashi (Urano), Yoshio Kitsuda (Kyoko), Masashi Ebara (Suga), Setsuko Sekine (Genjiko), Atsuko Sano (Lady Ochiba), Orson Welles (narrator).

A Paramount Television Production, produced by Paramount Pictures Corp. and NBC Entertainment, in association with Toho Co., Ltd., Asaki National Broadcasting Co., Ltd., and Jardine

Frankie Sakai and Richard Chamberlain (right) starred in James Clavell's *Shogun* (1980). The mini-series was heavily cut and released as a feature outside the United States.

Matheson Co., Ltd. A U.S./Japanese co-production in English and Japanese. Filmed at Toho Studios, Ltd. (Tokyo), Daiei-Kyoto Studios, and Shochiku Studios (Kyoto), and on location in Himeji City (Japan), Hikkone Castle, and completed at Paramount Studios (Hollywood, California). Color. Spherical Panavision. A Toho Co., Ltd. Release. Running time of Japanese theatrical version undetermined. Released 1980.

U.S. VERSION: Never released theatrically in the United States. Broadcast over the National Broadcasting Company, Inc. Network (NBC), over five nights, September 15–19, 1980. 580 minutes (Parts 1 & 5 ran 150 minutes; 2-4 run 93 minutes each). Released as a feature elsewhere, with some sequences not in the television version. Additionally, a separate home video feature version was released in the United States, this one running 125 minutes.

Shogun Assassin / Kozure Okami—Sanzu no Kawa no Ubagurama ("Wolf with a Kid: Stroller in the River Styx"). Producers, Shintaro Katsu and Hisaharu Matsubara; Director, Kenji Misumi; Screenplay, Kazuo Koike; Story, Kazuo Koike and Goseki Kojima; Director of Photography, Chishi Makiura; Art Director, Akira Naito; Editor, Toshio Taniguchi; Sound, Tsuchitaro Hayashi; Lighting, Hiroshi Mima; Music, Hideaki Sakurai; Sound Recording, Tsuchitaro Hayashi; Special Effects, Toho Special Effects Group; Sound, Toho Recording Centre; Sound Effects, Toho Sound Effects Group; Special Effects, Toho Special Effects Group.

CAST: Tomisaburo Wakayama (Itto Ogami, *"Lone Wolf"*), Masahiro Tomikawa (Daigoro), Kayo Matsuo (Supreme Ninja Sayaka), Minoru Oki, Shoji Kobayashi (The Evil Shogun), Shin Kishida (The Master of Death), Shogen Arata, Reiko Kasahara, Yukari Wakayama, Yuriko Mishima.

A Katsu Production Co., Ltd./Toho Co., Ltd. Production. Fujicolor (processed by Tokyo Laboratory Ltd.). Panavision (billed as Toho Scope). 81 minutes. Released 1972.

U.S. VERSION: Released by New World Pictures. A David Weisman & Peter Shanaberg Presentation. Executive Producer, Peter Shanaberg; Producer, David Weisman; Director, Robert Houston; Screenplay, Robert Houston, David Weisman; Associate Producers, Larry Franciose, Michael Maiello, Albert Ellis, Jr., Joseph Ellis; Music, W. Michael Lewis and Mark Lindsay, performed by The Wonderland Philharmonic; Soloists, W. Michael Lewis, Mark Lindsay, Marc Singer, Laine Cook, Robert Houston; Overture Composer and Conductor, Robert Houston; Music Producer, Mark Lindsay; Recording, Mixing and Rerecording, Samuel Goldwyn Studios (Hollywood); 1st Engineer, Paul McKenny, 2nd Engineer, Richard Gibbons; Technical Consultant, Ed Romano; Musical Coordinator, Michael Maiello; Psycho-acoustics, Malcom Cecil, courtesy of Centaur Studios; Supervising Sound Editor, Joe Percy; Sound Editor, Steve Nelson; Sound, Tim Holland and Val Kuklowsky; Assistant Sound Editor, Becky Nauert; Dialog Editor, Michael Minkler; Editor, Lee Percy; Sound Effects Recording, Courtney-Courtney Goodin; Budget-Accounting Coordinators, Larry Franciose; Titles, Jim Evans, Bill Evans and Gregory Boone; Production Assistants, Bill Evans, Marguerite Lucas; Opticals, Consolidated Film Industries; Acknowledgements, Andy Kuehn, Tetsuzo Ueda, Steve Corning, Mata Yamamoto, Dan Davis, Kaleidoscope Films, Bob Brent, Masa Tazuki, Igor Dimont, Morrie Eisenmann, Nelson Lyon, David Geffen. Voice Characterizations: Lamont Johnson (Lone Wolf), Gibran Evans (Daigaro), Marshall Efron, Sandra Bernhard, Vic Davis, Lennie Weinrib, Lainie Cook, Sam Weisman, Mark Lindsay, Robert Houston, David Weisman. Prints by Metrocolor. Dolby Stereo. Includes 10–12 minutes of stock footage from *Sword of Vengeance* (Toho, 1972). The second in the "Itto" series. Title also given as *Kozure Ohkmi n. 2* and *Baby Cart at the River Styx*. 90 minutes. MPAA rating: "R." Released November 11, 1980.

The Shogun Assassins / Sanada Yukimura no Boryaku ("Yukimura Sanada's Conspiracy"). Producers, Tan Takaiwa and Goro Kusakabe; Director, Sadao Nakajima; Screenplay, Kazuo Kasahara and Isao Matsumoto; Director of Photography, Shigeru Akatsuka; Art Director, Tokuzo Igawa; Music, Masaru Sato.

CAST: Hiroki Matsukata, Kinnosuke Yorozuya, Tetsuro Tamba.

A Toei Co., Ltd. Production. Color. Panavision. 148 minutes. Released 1979.

U.S. VERSION: Distributor, if any, is undetermined. No MPAA rating.

Shogun's Ninja. Executive Producer, Haruki Kadokawa; Director, Noribumi Suzuki; Screenplay, Takahiti Ishikawa, Fumio Koyama and Ishiro Otsu;

Directors of Photography, Toro Nakajima and Shin Ogawahara; Associate Producers, Goro Kusakabe and Tatsuo Honda; Lighting, Sakae Kaishi, Sound Recording, Kiyoshige Hirai; Editor, Isamu Ichida; Art Directors, Yoshikazu Sano, Teruyasu Tawarazaka; Script Girl, Teru Ishida; Decoration, Genzo Watanabe; Wardrobe, Mamoru Mori and Masakatsu Suzuki; Music Producer, Masakatsu Suzuki (it is unlikely that Suzuki, also credited with co-wardrobe, did both); Shooting Coordinators, Sonny Chiba Enterprises, Japan Action Club.

CAST: Shinichi "Sonny" Chiba, Hiroyuki "Henry" Sanada, Yuki Ninagawa, Shohei Hino, Kazuma Hase, Go Awazu, Kumiko Hidaka, Maki Tachibana, Katsumasa Uchida, Issei Lee, Mitishi Sakitsu, Go Iba, Hirofumi Koga, Seiji Koga, Muaisi Sasaki, Iyokazu Nakamuda, Isamu Kaneda, Iamaki Miyagawa, Kenzo Katsuno, Satoru Nabi, Goro Oki, Iyota Minowada, Matsutoshi Akiyama, Aneko Maruhira, Tetsuro Tamba, Yoko Nogima, Masumi Harukawa, Asao Koike, Makoto Sato, Isao Natsuki.

A Toei Co., Ltd. Production. Toeicolor. Panavision. 108 minutes. Released 1983.

U.S. VERSION: Released by American National Enterprises, Inc. 108 minutes. MPAA rating: "R." Released 1984. Presumably a sequel to *Satomi Hakkenda* (1983).

Shogun's Shadow / Gekitotsu ("Violent Clash"). Producer, Shigeru Okada; Director, Yasuo Furuhata; Screenplay, Hiro Matsuda, based on an original story by Sadao Nakajima; Director of Photography, Kiyoshi Kitasaka; Music, Masaru Sato.

CAST: Ken Ogata (Igo Gyobu), Shinichi "Sonny" Chiba (Iba Shoemon), Tetsuro Tamba (Hotta Masamori), Hu Chien Chiang (Shishi Jingoemon), Hiroki Matsukata (Abe Shigeji).

A Toei Co., Ltd. Production. Color. Panavision (?). 110 minutes. Released 1989.

U.S. VERSION: Distributor, if any, is undetermined. No MPAA rating.

Shonen tanteidan ("Boy Detectives"). Director, Eijiro Wakabayashi.

CAST: (not available).

A Toei Co., Ltd. Production. Toeicolor. ToeiScope. 61 minutes. Released 1959.

U.S. VERSION: Distributor, if any, is undetermined. A sequel to *20 Faces* (?). International title: *The Boy Detectives.*

Showdown at Nagasaki / Showa yakuza keizu—Nagasaki no kao ("Showa Yakuza Family Tree—Face of Nagasaki"). Director, Takashi Nomura; Screenplay, Kaneo Ikegami, based on an original story by Sachiya Nakamura; Director of Photography, Shigeyoshi Mine; Art Director, Toshiyuki Matsui; Music, Saburo Matsuura.

CAST: Tetsuya Watari (Keiji Takama), Noboru Ando (Koiwa), Kanjuro Arashi (Shinkichi), Yoshiaki Aoki (Matsui), Hiroko Masuda, Michitaro Mizushima.

A Nikkatsu Corp. Production. Fujicolor. NikkatsuScope. 94 minutes. Released October 18, 1969.

U.S. VERSION: Distributor, if any, is undetermined. English subtitled version available. 94 minutes. No MPAA rating.

Showdown for Zatoichi / Zato ichi jigokutabi ("Zatoichi's Trip to Hell"). Executive Producer, Masaichi Nagata; Producer, Hisashi Okuda; Director, Kenji Misumi; Screenplay, Daisuke Ito, based on an original story by Kan Shimosawa; Director of Photography, Chishi Makiura; Editor, Kanji Suganuma; Music, Akira Ifukube.

CAST: Shintaro Katsu (Zatoichi), Mikio Narita (Tadasu Jumonji), Chizu Hayashi (Enoshimeya), Kaneko Iwasaki (Otane), Gaku Yamamoto (Tomonoshin Sagawa).

A Daiei Motion Picture Co., Ltd. Production. Eastman Color. DaieiScope. 87 minutes. Released 1965.

U.S. VERSION: Released by Daiei International Films, Inc. English subtitles. The 12th film in the "Zatoichi series. Followed by *Zatoichi: The Blind Swordsman's Vengeance* (1966). 87 minutes. No MPAA rating. Released October 4, 1968. Letterboxed home video version: *Zatoichi: The Blind Swordsman and the Chess Expert.* A Chambara Entertainment Release; A John Wada and Gregg Yokoyama Presentation; Subtitles, Multi-Media Translations International.

Siege of Fort Bismarck / Chintao Yosai bakugeki meirei ("Siege of Fort Chintao"). Executive Producer, Tomoyuki Tanaka; Director, Kengo Furusawa; Screenplay, Katsuya Suzaki; Director of Photography, Fukuzo Koizumi; Art Director, Takeo Kita; Music, Hachiro Matsui; Assistant Director, Koji Kajita. *Toho Special Effects Group*: Director, Eiji Tsuburaya; Photography, Teisho Arikawa and Mototaka Tomioka; Art Director, Akira Watanabe.

CAST: Makoto Sato, Yosuke Natsuki, Yuzo Kayama, Ryo Ikebe, Mie Hama, Toru Ibuki, Jun Tazaki, Susumu Fujita, Akihiko Hirata, Kozo Nomura, Yutaka Sada, Bokuzen Hidari, Wataru Omae, Yutaka Oka, Masaya Nihei, Hiroshi Sekita, Katsumi Tezuka.

A Toho Co., Ltd. Production. Eastman Color. Toho Scope. 98 minutes. Released 1963.

U.S. VERSION: Released by Toho International Co., Ltd. English subtitles. 98 minutes. No MPAA rating. Released March 12, 1968.

Sign of the Jack / Jack no Irezumi ("Jack's Tattoo"). Director, Kazunari Takeda; Screenplay, Atsushi Yamatoya and Yoshitada Sone; Director of Photography, Kurataro Takamura; Art Director, Hiroshi Fukatami; Music, Hajime Kaburagi.

CAST: Akira Kobayashi (Hanamura), Eiji Go (Kurahara), Yoshiro Aoki (Noda), Shoki Fukae (Tarao), Junko Natsu, Rikiya Yasuoka, Kojiro Kusanagi.

A Nikkatsu Corp. Production. Fujicolor. NikkatsuScope. 83 minutes. Released October 14, 1970.

U.S. VERSION: Distributor, if any, is undetermined. English subtitled version available. 83 minutes. No MPAA rating.

Silence Has No Wings / Tobenai Chinmoko ("Silence Has No Wings"). Producer, Yasuo Matsukawa; Director, Kazuo Kuroki; Screenplay, Kazuo Kuroki, Yasu Matsukawa and Hisaya Iwasa; Director of Photography, Tatsuo Suzuki; Music, Teizo Matsumura; Sound, Toho Recording Centre; Sound Effects, Toho Sound Effects Group.

CAST: Mariko Kaga, Fumio Watanabe, Hiroyuki Nagato, Toshie Kimura, Kunie Tanaka, Minoru Nakahira, Takeshi Kusaka, Yukio Shirukaya, Katamasa Komatsu, Shoichi Ozawa.

A Film Shinsha Production. A Toho Co., Ltd. Release. Black and white (processed by Tokyo Laboratory Ltd.). Toho Scope. Westrex Recording System. 110 minutes. Released 1966.

U.S. VERSION: Released by Toho International Co., Ltd. English subtitles. 100 minutes. No MPAA rating. Released January 1967.

The Silent Stranger. Executive Producers, Allen V. Klein and Roberto Infascelli; Producer, Tony Anthony; Director, Vance Lewis (Luigi Vanzi); Screenplay, Vincenzo Cerami and Giancarlo Ferrando; Story, Tony Anthony; Director of Photography, Mario Capriotti; Editor, Renzo Lucidi; Music, Stelvio Cipriani; Production Managers, John P. Graff, Jr. and Luciano Volpato; In Charge of Japanese Production, William Ross.

CAST: Tony Anthony (the Stranger), Lloyd Battista (the American), Kin Omae, Kenji Ohara [Sahara?], Kita Mura, Sato [no other name given], Yoshio Nakano (the Japanese), Raf Baldassare.

An Allen V. Klein/Abkco Industries, Inc. Production. A Primex Italiana/Reverse Productions Picture. An Italian/Japanese/U.S. co-production. Filmed in Japan and completed in Rome. Westex Recording System. Eastman Color. Widescreen. Running time undetermined.

U.S. VERSION: Released by Metro-Goldwyn-Mayer, Inc. through United Artists. Prints by Metrocolor. Announced as *The Stranger in Japan*. Working titles (?): *Horseman and the Samurai*. Filmed in 1967 as *Samurai on a Horse*. Released in Italy as *Lo Straniero di silenzio* in 1968. Japanese release and participation undetermined. Third in "The Stranger Saga," preceded by *A Stranger in Town* (U.S. release: 1968), *The Stranger Returns* (U.S.: 1968), and followed by *Get Mean* (U.S.: 1976). MPAA rating: "PG." Released June 1975.

The Silk Road / Ton Ko ("Ton Ko"). Executive Producers, Yasuyoshi

Tokuma, Gohei Kogure, and Kazuo Haruna; Associate Producers, Yoshihiro Yuki, Ma Wang Liang, and Masahiro Sato; Producers, Atsushi Takeda and Yuzo Irie; Director, Junya Sato; Assistant Producers, Yo Tamamoto, Shigeru Mori, and Shingo Kori; Screenplay, Tsuyoshi Yoshida and Junya Sato, based on an original story by Yasushi Inoue; Director of Photography, Akira Shiizuka; Music, Masaru Sato; Title Calligraphy, Shunkei Iijima; Representatives of Dun Huang Committee, Ichiro Takahashi, Toshimichi Tanaka, Tatsumi Yamashita, Hideo Ichikura, and Jitsuzo Horiuchi; Production Assistance, Imagica Co., Ltd. Tokuma Shoten Publishing Co., Ltd., Toko Tokuma Co., Ltd., Daiei Eizo Films, Inc., New Century Producers Co., Ltd.; Special Assistance, Matsushita Electric Industrial Co., Ltd., Matsushita Electric Tading Co., Ltd.; Cooperation, China Film Co-Production Corporation, Chinese National Liberation Army, August First Film Studio, China Film Export and Import Corp.

CAST: Koichi Sato (Zhao Xingde), Toshiyuki Nishida (Zhu Wangli), Tsunehiko Watase (Li Yuanhao), Daijiro Harada (Weichi Kuang), Takahiro Tamura (Tsao Yanhui), Anna Nakagawa (Tsurpia), Yoshiko Mita (woman of Xixia).

A Daiei Co., Ltd./Dentsu, Inc./Marubeni Corporation Production. A Japanese/Chinese co-production in Japanese. Color. Panavision (?). 143 minutes. Released 1988.

U.S. VERSION: Released by Trimark Pictures. English subtitles. International title: *Dun-Huang*. 126 minutes. MPAA rating: "PG-13." Released 1992.

The Silk Tree Ballad / Nemu-no-ki no uta ("Song of Nerumi") **[documentary]**. Director/Screenplay/Music, Mariko Miyagi; Director of Photography, Kozo Okazaki; Editor, Michio Suwa.

WITH: Mariko Miyagi, the children of the Nemunoki Gakuen, Teachers and Employees of the Nemunoki Gakuen.

A Mariko Miyagi Production. Color. Academy ratio (?). Running time undetermined. Released 1974.

U.S. VERSION: Distributor, if any, is undetermined. No MPAA rating.

The Sinners of Hell / Jigoku ("Hell"). Producer, Mitsugu Okura; Director, Nobuo Nakagawa; Screenplay, Ichiro Miyagawa and Nobuo Nakagawa; Director of Photography, Mamoru Morita; Art Director, Haruyasu Kurosawa.

CAST: Shigeru Amachi (Shiro), Yoichi Numata (Tamura), Ukato Mitsuya (Sachiko), Torahiko Nakamura, Fumiko Miyata, Hiroshi Hayashi, Kimie Tokudaiji, Akiko Yamashita, Jun Otomo.

A Shintoho Co., Ltd. Production. Western Electric Mirrophonic recording. Eastman Color. Shintoho-Scope. 100 minutes. Released July 30, 1960.

U.S. VERSION: Distributor, if any, is undetermined. Also known as *The Sinners to Hell* and *Hell*. Remade by Toei in 1979. No MPAA rating.

Sister Streetfighter. Production credits unavailable.

CAST: Sue Shiomi, Shinichi "Sonny" Chiba.

A Toei Co., Ltd. Production. Color. ToeiScope. Running time and release date undetermined.

U.S. VERSION: Released by New Line Cinema. English-dubbed. Running time undetermined. MPAA rating: "R" (?). Released February 1976.

Sisters of Gion / Gion no shimai ("Sisters of Gion"). Director, Kenji Mizoguchi; Screenplay, Yoshikata Yoda and Kenji Mizoguchi, based on the novel *Yama* ("The Pit") by Alexander Ivanovich Kuprin, and an idea by Yoshikata Yoda; Director of Photography, Minoru Miki; Sound Recording, Hisashi Kase.

CAST: Isuzu Yamada (Omocha), Yoko Umemura (Umekichi), Benkei Shiganoya (Shinbee Furusawa), Eitaro Shindo (Kudo, *the dry goods merchant*), Taizo Fukami (Kimura), Fumio Okura (Jurakudo, *the antique dealer*), Namiko Kawajima, Reiko Aoi.

A Daiichi Film Co., Ltd. Production. A Shochiku Co., Ltd. Release. Filmed at Daiichi-Sagano Studios (Kyoto). Black and white. Academy ratio. 69 minutes. Released October 15, 1936.

U.S. VERSION: Released by Shochiku Films of America, Inc. (?). English subtitles. Also known as *Sisters of the Gion*.

Benkei Shiganoya and Isuzu Yamada in *Sisters of Gion* (1936). (Photo courtesy Darrell Davis.)

Remade by Hiromasa Nomura at Daiei in 1956. 69 minutes. No MPAA rating. Released November 1979.

Six Suspects / Dairoku no yogisha ("The Sixth Suspect"). Director, Umeji Inoue.

CAST: Tatsuya Mihashi, Akira Takarada, Shin Morikawa, Minoru Takada, Yumi Shirakawa, Chiaki Tsukioka, Yasuko Nakada, Hisaya Ito, Hideo Takamatsu, Masumi Okada.

A Takarazuka Motion Picture Co., Ltd./Toho Co., Ltd. Production. A Toho Co., Ltd. Release. Eastman Color (?). Toho Scope. 107 minutes. Released November 1960.

U.S. VERSION: Released by Toho International Co., Ltd. English subtitles. 107 minutes. No MPAA rating. Released April 21, 1961.

Sky Scraper! / Chokoso no akebono ("Dawn of the Skyscraper"). Director, Hideo Sekigawa.

CAST: Ryo Ikebe, Yoshiko Sakuma, Michiyo Aratama, Koshiro Matsuomoro.

A Toho Co., Ltd. Production. Color. Panavision (?). Running time undetermined. Released 1969.

U.S. VERSION: Released by Toho International Co., Ltd. English subtitles. Running time undetermined. No MPAA rating. Released September 23, 1970.

Slums of Tokyo / Jujiro ("Crossroads"). Director/Screenplay, Teinosuke Kinugasa; Director of Photography, Kohei Sugiyama; Art Director, Bonji Taira.

CAST: Junosuke Bando (Rikiya), Akiko Chihaya (Okiku, *his sister*), Yukiko Ogawa (Oume), J. Soma (the fake policeman).

A Kinugasa Productions/Shochiku Co., Ltd. production. A Shochiku Co., Ltd. Release. Silent. Black and white. Academy ratio. 60 minutes. Released 1928.

U.S. VERSION: Distributor, if any, is undetermined.

The Snake Girl and the Silver-Haired Witch / Hebimusume to hakuhatsuki ("The Snake Girl and the Silver-Haired Witch"). Executive Producer, Masaichi Nagata; Producer, Kazumasa Nakano; Director, Noriaki Yuasa; Screenplay, Kimiyuki Hasegawa, based on the story "Hebimusune to hakuhatsuki" by Kazuo Kozu; Art Director, Tomohisa Yano; Director of Photography, Akira Uehara; Editor, Yoshiyuki Miyazaki; Music, Shunsuke Kikuchi;

Sound Recording Supervisor, Kimio Iida; Sound, Daiei Recording Studio; Special Effects, Daiei Special Effects Department.

CAST: Yachie Matsui (Sayuri Nanjo), Mayumi Takahashi (Tamami Nanjo), Yoshiro Kitahara (Goro Nanjo), Yuko Hamada (Yuko Nanjo), Sachiko Meguro (Shige Kito), Sei Hiraizumi (Tatsuya Hayashi), Kuniko Miyake (Jamakawa), Saburo Ishiguro (Teacher Sasaki), Tadashi Date (school servant), Osamu Maruyama (doctor), Mariko Fukuhara (doll).

A Daiei Motion Picture Co., Ltd. Production. A Masaichi Nagata Presentation. Westrex Recording System. Black and white (processed by Daiei Laboratory). Daiei-Scope. 82 minutes. Released December 14, 1968.

U.S. VERSION: Released by Daiei International Films, Inc. English subtitles. 82 minutes. No MPAA rating. Released 1969.

Snow Country / Yukiguni ("Snow Country"). Producer, Ichiro Sato; Director, Shiro Toyoda; Screenplay, Toshio Yasumi, based on the novel *Yukiguni* (1947) by Yasunari Kawabata; Director of Photography, Jun Yasumoto; Art Directors, Kisaku Ito and Makoto Sono; Music, Ikuma Dan; Sound Recording, Masao Fujiyoshi; Editor, Hiroichi Iwashita.

CAST: Keiko Kishi (Komako), Ryo Ikebe (Shimamura), Kaoru Yachigusa (Yoko), Hisaya Morishige (Yukio), Chieko Naniwa (head maid), Maruo Tanaka (porter).

A Toho Co., Ltd. Production. Black and white. Academy ratio. 120 minutes. Released 1957.

U.S. VERSION: Released by Toho International Co., Ltd. English subtitles. Remade in 1965. 120 minutes. No MPAA rating. Released May 15, 1966.

Snow Country / Yukiguni ("Snow Country"). Producer, Shizo Yamanouchi; Director, Hideo Oba; Screenplay, Ryosuke Saito and Hideo Oba, based on the novel *Yukiguni* (1947) by Yasunari Kawabata; Director of Photography, Toichiro Narushima; Art Director, Inko Yoshino; Production Design, Ryotaro Kuwata; Music, Naozumi Yamamoto.

CAST: Shima Iwashita (Komako), Isao Kimura (Shimamura), Mariko Kaga (Yoko), Tamotsu Narushima (Yukio), Chieko Naniwa (the masseuse), Sadako Sawamura (the dance teacher), Mineko Bandai (the landlady), Shinichi Yanagisawa (the banto), Mutsuko Sakura (the maid), Kakuko Chino (Kikuyu), Kyomi Sakura (Kintaro), Takanobu Hozumi (the drunk guest), Ushio Akashi (the stationmaster), Kaneko Iwasaki (Mrs. Shimamura), Taketoshi Naito (Koizumi), Michisumi Sugawara (Komako's patron), Nijiko Kiyokawa (mistress of geisha house).

A Shochiku Co., Ltd. Production. Fuji Color. Shochiku GrandScope. 113 minutes. Released 1965.

U.S. VERSION: Released by Shochiku Films of America, Inc. English subtitles. Previously filmed in 1957. 113 minutes. No MPAA rating. Released March 1969.

Snow Fairy / Yuki ("Snow") **[animated]**. Producers, Ei Ito, Takeo Nishiguchi, and Saburo Watanabe; Director, Tadashi Imai; Screenplay, Akira Miyazaki, based on an original story by Ryusuke Saito; Director of Photography, Hiroshi Isagawa; Art Director, Yoshiyuki Uchida; Music, Kawachi Chito.

VOICE CHARACTERIZATIONS: (undetermined).

A Nikkatsu Children's Film, Inc. Production. Color. Spherical wide screen (?). 89 minutes. Released 1981.

U.S. VERSION: Distributor, if any, is undetermined. No MPAA rating.

Snow in the South Seas / Minami no shima ni yuki ga fura ("It Snows in the South Seas"). Executive Producers, Ichiro Sato and Fumio Kinbara; Director, Seiji Hisamatsu; Screenplay, Ryozo Kasahara, based on Daisuke Kato's autobiography; Director of Photography, Tokuzo Kuroda; Music, Kenjiro Hirose.

CAST: Daisuke Kato, Hisaya Morishige, Tatsuya Mihashi, Frankie Sakai, Junzaburo Ban, Kenji Sahara.

A Toho Co., Ltd. Production. Eastman Color. Toho Scope. 103 minutes. Released 1961.

U.S. VERSION: Released by Toho International Co., Ltd. English subtitles. 103 minutes. No MPAA rating. Released April 26, 1963.

Snow Trail / Ginrei no hate ("Snow-Capped Mountain"). Producer, Tomoyuki Tanaka; Director, Senkichi Taniguchi; Screenplay, Akira Kurosawa; Director of Photography, Junichi Segawa; Art Director, Taiji Kawashima; Music, Akira Ifukube.

CAST: Takashi Shimura (Nojiro), Toshiro Mifune (Ejima), Yoshio Kosugi (Takasugi), Akitake Kono (Honda), Setsuko Wakayama (Haruko), Kokuten Kodo (hut keeper).

A Toho Co., Ltd. Production. Black and white. Academy ratio. 97 minutes. Released 1947.

U.S. VERSION: Release undetermined, possibly by Toho International Co., Ltd. in subtitled format. No MPAA rating.

The Snow Woman / Kaidan yuki joro ("Ghost Story: Snow Prostitute"). Executive Producer, Masanori Sanada; Producer, Ikuo Kubodera; Director, Tokuzo Tanaka; Screenplay, Fuji Yahiro, based on the story, "Yuki-onna" ("Snow Woman") by Lafcadio Hearn from his collection *Kwaidan: Stories and Studies of Strange Things*; Director of Photography, Chishi Makiura; Art Director, Akira Naito; Lighting, Shunji Kurokawa; Editor, Hiroshi Yamada; Music, Akira Ifukube; Sound Recording, Yukio Kaibara; Sound, Daiei Recording Studio; Assistant Director, Atsuhiko Suguro; Special Effects, Daiei Special Effects Department.

CAST: Shino Fujimura (Yuki, *the Snow Woman*), Akira Ishihama (Yosaku), Machiko Hasegawa (Lady Okugata Mino), Taketoshi Naito (Vice-Governor of Mino), Mizuho Susuki (Gyokei), Fujio Suga (Lord Jito), Sachiko Murase (Soyo), Yoshiro Kitahara (Seijin), Masao Shimizu (the abbot), Hisataro Hojo (Matsukawa), Izumi Hara (virgin in service of shrine), Tatsuo Hanabu (Shigetomo), Tokio Oki (1st doctor), Jun Fujikawa (2nd doctor), Yukio Horikita (servant), Hajime Koshikite (porter), Shinya Saito (Taro).

A Daiei Motion Picture Co., Ltd. Production. Filmed at Daiei-Tokyo Studios. Westrex Recording System. Eastman Color (processed by Daiei Laboratory). DaieiScope. 80 minutes. Released April 20, 1968.

U.S. VERSION: Released by Daiei International Films, Inc. English subtitles. Advertised as *Snow Ghost*. International title: *Yuki-oona*. Also known as *Woman of the Snow*, and *Ghost of the Snow Girl Prostitute*. Previously filmed as a segment in *Kwaidan* (1964), and later as *Aido*. No MPAA Rating. 80 minutes.

So Young, So Bright / Janken musume ("Rock Paper Scissors Daughter"). Director, Toshio Sugie.

CAST: Hibari Misora, Chiemi Eri, Izumi Yukimura.

A Toho Co., Ltd. Production. Eastman Color. Academy ratio. 92 minutes. Released November 1955.

U.S. VERSION: Released by Topaz Film Corporation. English subtitles. 91 minutes. No MPAA rating. Released March 1963.

Soft Touch of Night / Yoru no hada ("Skin of Night"). Producer, Ichiro Sato; Director, Yuzo Kawashima; Screenplay, Yuzo Kawashima, Ruiju Yanagisawa, and Toshio Yasumi, based on the novel by Shigeko Yuki; Director of Photography, Atsushi Yasumoto; Music, Riichiro Manabe; Assistant Director, Kosaburo Hata.

CAST: Chikage Awashima, Michiyo Aratama, Tomoko Kawaguchi, Yunosuke Ito, Jun Tazaki, Frankie Sakai, Tatsuya Mihashi, Asumi Kuji.

A Tokyo Eiga Co., Ltd. Production, in association with Toho Co., Ltd. A Toho Co., Ltd. Release. Eastman Color. Toho Scope. 110 minutes. Released November 20, 1960.

U.S. VERSION: Released by Toho International Co., Ltd. English subtitles. 106 minutes. No MPAA rating. Released August 4, 1961.

Solar Crisis / Kuraishisu nijugoju nen ("Crisis 2050"). Executive Producers, Takehito Sadamura and Takeshi Kawata; Producers, Richard Edlund, Tsuneyuki [Morris] Morishima and James Nelson; Associate Producer, Barbara Nelson; Director, Alan Smithee [Richard C. Sarafian]; Screenplay, Joe Gannon, Crispan Bolt and Ted Sarafian, based on the novel by Takeshi Kawata; Director of Photography, Russ Carpenter; Production Design, George Jenson; Art

Director, John Bruce; Technical Advisor, Richard J. Terrile; Costume Designer, Robert Turturice; Music, Maurice Jarre; Additional Music, Michael Baddicker; Songs: "Was A Time," Words and Music by Les Hooper, Sung by Sherwood Ball (published by Hooperman Music); "Freedom Sings," Words and Music by Les Hooper, Sung by Carmen Twillie (published by Hooperman Music); "Orlop Piano," Music by Les Hooper; "Travis Rides Again" and "Strip Star Chase," Music by Tedi Sarafian; Casting, Diane Dimeo, C.S.A.; Production Managers, Kim Kurumada, Ronald B. Colby and Robert Anderson; 1st Asst. Directors, Jerry Ziesmer and Leonid Zisman; 2nd Asst. Directors, Robert Roda and Michael-McCloud Thompson; Technical Advisor, Richard Terrile, PhD; Art Director, John P. Bruce; Set Decorator, Donna Stamps; Camera Operator, Steven Finestone; Property Masters, Sal Sommatino and Mark Alan Luine; Illustrator, Thomas A. Cranham; Robotruck/Vertol Designs, Simon Murton; Assistant Art Directors, Peter Samishi and Stephen Dane; SPFX Coodinator, Kelly Kerby; Electronic Effects Coodinator, William Klinger, Jr.; Chief Lighting Technician, Reginald F. Lake; Key Grip, Curtiss Bradford; Production Sound Mixer, Dennis W. Carr; Script Supervisor, Connie Barzaghi; Costume Supervisor, Jill M. Ohanneson; Key Makeup Artist, Paula Sutor; Key Hair Stylist, Larry Waggoner; Construction Coordinator, Andrew Hanlen; Transportation Coordinator, Paul Howes; Set Designers, Gina Cranham and Beverly Eagan; 1st Asst. Cameraman, Mark Jackson; 2nd Asst. Camerman, Scott Herring; Still Photographer, Ernest Garza; Asst SPFX Coordinator, Michael O'Connor; Asst. Chief Lighting Technician, Bob Neville; Best Boy Grip, Cobie Fair; Dolly Grip, Malcolm Doran II; Asst. Property Masters, Anthony DiSalvo and Duff Miller; Leadman, John J.C. Scherer; Set Decorator Production Buyer, Wilhelm G. Pfau; On-Set Dresser, Tim Van Wormer; Key Costumer, Meg Goodwin; Set Costumer, Scott Barr Tomlinson; Boom Operator, Walter Anderson; Construction Foremen, Jerry Etzler, Bryce Walmsley, Verna Bagby and James Eric; Model Makers, Roderick Schumaker and Phillip Hartman; Transportation Captain, Les Orrison; Picture Car Coordinator, Ken Plumlee; Production Coordinator, Susan Becton; Location Manager, Christopher Ursitti; Production Accountants, Lisa Howard, Ramona Waggoner; Asst. Production Coordinator, Leslie A Tokunaga; Asst. Production Accountant, Leslie Falkinburg; Accounting Clerk, Michael Vasquez; Art Dept. Coordinator, Dayle Dodge; Art Dept. Researcher, John Curtis; DGA Trainee, Robert Scott; Production Assistants, Andrew Flynn, Jonathan Wachtel, Mark Spencer and Patricia O'Reilly; Asst. to the Executive Producer, Christine Iso; Assts. to Mr. Morishima, Fuyo Arimoto and Rod Findley; Publicist, Ann Strick; 1st Asst. Camera-Plate, Daniel Dayton; Camera Production Assistants, Morgan Tanaka, Brett Harding, and Gary George; Construction, Lexington Scenery and Props, and Time and Space, Inc.; Environmental Control System , Solex Technologies, Inc. (Houston); Special Props Designer, Ed Eyth; Futuristic Props Creator, Neotek; Strip Star Corvette, Gene Winfield of Rod & Custom; Animals, Hollywood Animal Rentals, Jungle Exotics, and Myers and Willis; Catering, Michelson's Food Service; Movie Magic Software, Screenplay Systems; Production Services and Equipment, Keylite PSI; Cranes and Dollies, Chapman; Special Thanks, Titeflex, Inc., Massini, Inc., Mikohn, Inc., Atari Computers, International Game Technology, Inc., Bureau of Land Management, The Westin Bonaventure Hotel, John Wayne Airport (Santa Ana). *Additional Production*: Producer, Joan McCormick-Cooper; Director of Photography, Steve Finestone; Editor, Charles V. Coleman; Production Manager/1st AD, Jerry Sobul; 2nd AD, Carole Keligian; Set Decorator, Inter World; Set Design and Construction, Time & Space; Special Effects, Howard Jensen; Wardrobe Supervisor, Scott Tomlinson; Key Makeup, Bonita DeHaven; Key Hair Stylist, Susan Mills; Property Master, Tony DiSalvo; Stills, Patrick Bock; Sound Mixer, Bo Harewood; Gaffer Mike Laviolette; Key Grip, Dylan Shephard; Script Supervisor, Annie Welles; Production Coordinator, Mary

Ramirez; Production Accountant, Steve Lazo; Asst. to Arthur Marks, Laurie Foi; Production Secretary, Grace Cobiella; Location Manager, Ron Carr; Casting, Marvin Page Casting; Additional Re-Recording Mixing, William Caughey, CAS, and Bob Beemer; Additional Re-Recording Facilities, Skywalker Sound, a division of LucasArts Entertainment Group. *Post Production*: Editor, Richard Trevor; Earth Sounds Editor, David Baldwin; Space Sounds Editor, Scott Martin Gershwin; Assistant Editor, Hazel Trevor; 2nd Asst. Editor, Linda Schubell-Sundlin; Apprentice Editor, Dawn Michelle King; Supervising ADR Editor, Greg Baxter, MPSE; Dialogue/ Foley Editors, George Fredrick, Kevin Hearst (Raoul) and Dan Rich; ADR Editors, Tom Bellfort and J. Chris Jargo, MPSE; Asst. Sound Editors, Kelly Oxford, Victor Ennis and Michael Hoskinson; Additional Audio, Mark Lanza; Foley Supervisor, Sukey Fontelieu; Foley Artists, Dan O'Connell and Alicia Stevenson; Music Editor, Dan Carlin, Sr.; ADR Group Coordinator, Burton Sharp; Re-recording Mixers, John Reitz, CAS, David Campbell, CAS, and Gregg Rudloff, CAS; ADR Mixers, Wally Beardon and Chris Tucker; Foley Mixer, Doc Kane; Scoring Mixer, Shawn Murphy; Asst. to Mr. Jarre, Patrick Russ; Negative Cutting, Gary Burritt; Color Timers, Bill Pine and Mike Stanwick; Sound Effects, Soundelux; Re-recorded at Buena Vista Sound; Special Lenses, Meade Industries; Additional Opticals, Howard A. Anderson Company and The Chandler Group; Titles, Howard A. Anderson Company; Computer Generated Main Title Design, Charles McDonald. *Special Visual Effects*: Boss Film Corporation; Producer, Neil Krepela; Director, Richard Edlund; Conceptual Futurist, Syd Mead; Sound Effects Design and Supervisors, Wylie Stateman and Lon E. Bender; (On-Set?) Special Effects, Craig Smith; Chief Lighting Technician, Rob Eyslee; Key Grip, John Donnely; Grip, Pat Van Guken; Pyrotechnician, Joseph Viskocil; Stage Production Asst., Mark Hartman; Matte Painter, Michelle Moen; Matte Camera, Alan Harding; Storyboard Illustrator, John Jensen and Brent Boates; Art Dept./ Animation Supervsior, Mauro Maressa; Animator, Phil Cummings; Asst. Animator, William Knoll; Animation Production Assistant, Colin Campbell; Techincal Animation Supervisor, Holly Hudson; Technical Animator, Maura Alvarez; Asst. Visual Effects Editor, Jim May; Editorial Production Assistant, Julia Rivas; Post Production Coordinator, Joni Harding; Visual Effects Coordinator, Donna Langston; Computer Graphics Coordinator, Christine Sellin; Camera Equipment Coordinator, Duane Mieliwocki; Stage Coordinator, Donna Lipshin; Production Secretary, Mary Johnston; Production Assistants, Stephen Ehrensberger and John LaPage; Supervising Model Maker, Pat McClung; Chief Model Maker, Leslie Ekker; Model Makers, Larry De Unger, Kent Gebo, Adam Gelbart, Pete Gerard, Ken Larson, Bruce MacRae, Gerald McClung and Nicholas Seldon; Mechanisms Key Man, Robert Johnson; Mechanisms, Gary Bierend; Head Painter, Ron Gress; Model Shop Production Assistants, Christine Cowan, Roberto DePalma, John Hagen-Brenner, Erik Haraldsted, Doug Miller, Paul Ozzimo, Mike Possert, Scott Schneider, Andy Siegal, and Jon Warren; Model Shop Coordinator, Chris Bowler; Model Shop Illustrator, John Eaves; Model Shop Consultant, Ray Shenusay; Machine Shop Foreman, Ken Dudderar; Electronics Technicians, Jeff Platt and Douglass Calli; Controller, Maryjane Zelickovics; Purchasing Agent, Greg Wolff; Special Solar Imaging, Peter Parks of Oxford, Scientific Films, Ltd., Assisted by Suzi Parks and Peter Field; *Computer Animation*: Pacific Data Images, Inc., Carl Rosendahl, President; Executive Producer, Glenn Entis; Producer, David McCullough; Technial Support/Animator, Jamie Dixon; Software/Technical Support, Thad Beier; Animators, Theresa Ellis and Rex Grignon; Technical Assistance, Terry Emmons; Video and Graphic Displays, Video Image (Rhonda C. Gunner, Richard Hollander, Gregory McMurray and John Wash); Video Image Coordinator, Janet Earl; Video Image Crew, Monte Swann and Pete Martinez.

CAST: Tim Matheson (Captain Steve Kelso), Charlton Heston (Admiral "Skeet" Kelso), Annabel Schofield (Alex Noffe),

Peter Boyle (Arnold Teague), Tetsuya Bessho (Ken Minami), Corin "Corky" Nemec (Mike Kelso), Jack Palance (Travis James Richards), Paul Koslo (Dr. Haas), Sandy McPeak (Gurney), Scott Alan Campbell (McBride), Frantz Turner (Lamare), Silvana Gallardo (T.C.), Dan Shor (Harvard), Dorian Harewood (Borg), Brenda Blake (Dr. Claire Beeson), Paul Williams (voice of Freddy), David Ursin (Kovac), Richard S. Scott (Meeks), Eric James (Louisiana), Rhonda Dotson (waitress), William A. Wallace (Pohl), Michael Berryman (Matthew), Roy Jenson (bartender), Jimmie F. Skaggs (biker), Chris Nash ("Corvette" driver), H.M. Wynant (IXL executive #1), Paul Carr (IXL executive #2), Milt Kogan (IXL man #2 [Baldy]), Arnold Quinn (IXL man #3 [Ponytail]) Louis Elias (IXL man #4 [Action Louie]), John Barrymore (Avery), Carole Hemingway (Rhonda), Don Craig (TV anchorman), Jerry Hauck (Corporal Flynn), John Hugh (Dr. Dufait), Bob Meroff (camel rider), Steve Welles (prophet), Rick Dorio (bandit #1), Mindy Rickles (astronaut #2), Nick Gambella (astronaut #3), Lehua Reid (astronaut #4), Jimmy Austin (technician), Sherwood Ball (Little Al's singer), Carmen Twillie (army band singer), Richard Eden (medical technician), Roy T. Fukagaw (Little Al's cook), Robert Hawkins (security officer #1), Jon Tabler (security officer #2), Tammy Maples (Mrs. Steve Kelso), Ted Montue (bridge officer), Richard Terrile (hologram operator), Michael Stanhope (astronomer), Kathryn Spitz (IXL receptionist), Ann Fink (VidPhone operator), Saida Rodrigues Pagan (correspondent), Stephen R. Kujala (voice of Robotruck), Tracy Jones Stateman (voice of Helios Computer), Terrence Beasor (narrator), Mario Roberts, Vince Deadrick, Larry Duran, Stacy Elias, Eurlyne Epper, Bill Hart (Bandits), Andy Armstrong, David Burton, Steve Lambert, James Lew, Billy Lucas, George Sack, Jr. (stunts).

A Japan America Picture Company, Inc. Production, in association with Asahi Breweries, Ltd., Toppan Printing Co., Ltd., Yamaichi Securities Co., Ltd., Lotte Co., Inc., Nippon Steel Corp., Mitsui & Co., Ltd., and Nissho Iwai Corporation. A Gakken (Hideto and Hiroshi Furuoka)/NHK Enterprises (Shuji Tanuma) Presentation. A Japanese/U.S. co-production in English. Filmed at Hewitt Street Studios, Harbor Stage, Los Angeles, Baker (California), and Clark County (California). Dolby Stereo SR (Spectral Recording). Color by DeLuxe. Panavision. Released 1990 (?).

U.S. Version: Never released theatrically in the United States. Released directly to home video in 1993 by Vidmark Entertainment. A Trimark Pictures Release. International distributor, Inter-Ocean Film Sales, Ltd. International title: *Solar Crisis*. Alternate titles: *Starfire* and *Crisis 2050*. MPAA rating: "PG-13." 111 minutes.

Son of Godzilla / Kaiju shima no kessen: Gojira no musuko

("Monster Island's Decisive Battle: Son of Godzilla"). Executive Producer, Tomoyuki Tanaka; Director, Jun Fukuda; Screenplay, Shinichi Sekizawa and Kazue Shiba; Director of Photography, Kazuo Yamada; Music, Masaru Sato; Art Director, Takeo Kita; Editor, Ryohei Fujii; Lighting, Eiji Yamaguchi and Shoshichi Kojima; Assistant Director, Takashi Nagano; Production Manager, Yasuaki Sakamoto; Sound Recordists, Shin Tokei and Toshiya Ban; Sound, Toho Recording Centre; Sound Effects, Minoru Kanayama, Toho Sound Effects Group. *Toho Special Effects Group*: Supervisor, Eiji Tsuburaya; Director, Teisho Arikawa; Assistant Director, Teruyoshi Nakano; Photography, Teisho Arikawa, Mototaka Tomioka; Optical Photography, Yukio Manoda, Sadao Iizuda; Art Director, Akira Watanabe; Lighting, Kuichiro Kishida; Scene Manipulation, Fumio Nakadai.

Cast: Akira Kubo (Goro Maki), Tadao Takashima (Dr. Kosumi), Bibari "Beverly" Maeda (Reiko [Saeko] Matsumiya), Akihiko Hirata (Fujisaki), Yoshio Tsuchiya (Furukawa), Kenji Sahara (Morio), Kenichiro Maruyama (Ozawa), Seishiro Kuno (Tashiro), Yasuhiko Saijo (Suzuki), Susumu Kurobe (aircraft captain), Kazuo Suzuki (radio operator), Wataru Omae (co-pilot), Chotaro Togin (surveyor),

Osman Yusef (man on submarine), Kiyoharu Onaka and Haruo Nakajima (Godzilla), Little Man Machan (Minira), Hiroshi Sekita.

A Toho Co. Ltd. Production. Eastman Color (processed by Tokyo Laboratory, Ltd.). Toho Scope. 86 minutes. Released December 16, 1967.

U.S. VERSION: Never released theatrically in the United States. Released to U.S. television by AIP-TV in 1969. English-dubbed. A James H. Nicholson & Samuel Z. Arkoff Presentation. Voice characterizations, Jack Grimes (for Akira Kubo). Prints by Berkey-Pathé. Kurobe, Suzuki, Omae, and Togin's roles were cut for the American version. The 8th "Godzilla" feature. Followed by *Destroy All Monsters* (1968). Released theatrically in the U.K. running 71 minutes. Reissued in Japan in 1973 (re-edited by Ishiro Honda to 65 minutes). 82 minutes. No MPAA rating.

Sonatine / Sonatine ("Sonatine"). Producer, Kazuyoshi Okuyama; Director/Screenplay/Editor, "Beat" Takeshi Kitano; Director of Photography, Katsumi Yanagishima; Art Director, Osamu Sasaki; Lighting, Hitoshi Takaya; Assistant Director, Toshihiro Tenma; Sound, Senji Horiuchi; Music, Joe Hisaishi.

CAST: "Beat" Takeshi Kitano (Murakawa), Aya Kokumai (Miyuki), Tetsu Watanabe (Uechi), Masanobu Katsumura (Ryoji), Susumu Terashima (Ken), Ren Osugi (Katagiri), Tonbo Zushi (Kitajima), Kenichi Yajima (Takahashi), Eiji Minakata (hit man).

A Bandai Visual Co., Ltd./Shochiku Dai-Ichi Kogyo Co., Ltd. Production. Color. Dolby Stereo. Spherical wide screen. 94 minutes. Released 1993.

U.S. VERSION: Released by Shochiku Films of America, Inc. English subtitles. 94 minutes. No MPAA rating. Released May 26, 1994.

The Song from My Heart / Waga Koi waga uta ("My Love, My Song"). Associate Producers, Koichi Enatsu and Saburo Muto; Director, Noboru Nakamura; Screenplay, Sakae Hirosawa, Noboru Nakamura; Story, Hitomi Yamaguchi and Soji Yoshino; Director of Photography, Hiroshi Takemura; Art Director, Chiyoo Umeda; Music, Masaru Sato.

CAST: Kanzaburo Nakamura (Hideo Yoshino), Shima Iwashita (Tomiko), Kaoru Yachigusa (Hatsuko), Katsuo Nakamura (Koichi), Muga Takewaki (Kenji), Sanae Kitabayashi (Motoko), Ken Ogata (Hitomi Yamaguchi), Mitsuyo Kamei (Mitsuyo), Sadako Sawamura (Hitomi's mother), Norihei Miki (Kasui Wakabayashi), Anna Losen, Hideko Okiyama, Kankuro Nakamura, Seitaro Okamura, Ushio Akashi, Jun Kojima, Nobuo Takagi, Reijiro Osugi, Kosaku Mizuno, Keiko Sawai, Kosaku Yamayoshi, Yoji Toki, Hideaki Komori, Sanzaemon Nakamura, Koyu Tsuruta, Takashi Suga, Noriyuki Watanabe, Eriko Wada, Nobuko Suzuki, Naoki Izumi, Reiko Mizuki.

A Shochiku Co., Ltd. Production. Eastman Color. Shochiku GrandScope. 99 minutes. Released October 1969.

U.S. VERSION: Released by Shochiku Films of America, Inc. English subtitles. 99 minutes. No MPAA rating. Released January 1970.

Song of Home / Furusato no uta ("Song of Hometown"). Director, Kenji Mizoguchi; Screenplay, Ryunosuke Shimizu, based on the story by Choji Matsui; Director of Photography, Tatsuyuki Yokota.

CAST: Shigeru Kido (Naotaro Sakuda), Mineko Tsuji (Okinu, *his sister*), Kentaro Kawamata (Junichi Okamoto).

A Nikkatsu Kansai Education Division Production, in association with the Ministry of Education. Silent. Black and white. Academy ratio. 45 minutes. Released 1925.

U.S. VERSION: Released by the Film Center of the National Museum of Modern Art (Tokyo). No English inter-titles. 45 minutes. No MPAA rating. Released May 15, 1981.

Song of the Camp / Roei no uta ("Song of the Camp"). Director, Kenji Mizoguchi; Screenplay, Shuichi Hatamoto, based on a battle song; Director of Photography, Junichiro Aojima; Music, Senji Ito.

CAST: Seizaburo Kawazu (Hideo), Fumiko Yamaji (Nobuko), Ichiro Sugai (Hideo's father), Akira Matsudaira,

Masao Shimizu, Haruo Tanaka, Yaeko Utagawa, Koichi Toribashi.

A Shinko Kinema Oizumi Co., Ltd. Production. Filmed at Shinko Kinema Oizumi Studios (Tokyo). Black and white. Academy ratio. Running time undetermined. Released February 17, 1938.

U.S. VERSION: Distributor, if any, is undetermined.

SOS from the Earth / Esu o esu kochira chikyu ("SOS from the Earth") **[puppet animation film]**. Producer, Kaichiro Nohara; Director, Akikazu Kono; Screenplay, Mei Kato; Director of Photography, Kunihiko Itami; Music, Tachio Akano.

VOICE CHARACTERIZATIONS: (undetermined).

A Kyodo Eiga Co., Ltd. Production. Color. Academy ratio (?). 68 minutes. Release date undetermined.

U.S. VERSION: Distributor, if any, is undetermined. No MPAA rating.

Souls of the Road / Rojo no reikon ("Souls of the Road"). Producer, Kaoru Osanai; Director, Minoru Murata; Screenplay, Kiyohiko Ushihara, based on the novel *Children of the Night* by Wilhelm Schmidtbonn, and the play *The Lower Depths* by Maxim Gorky; Directors of Photography, Bunjiro Mizutani and Hamataro Oda.

CAST: Kaoru Osanai (Yasushi Sugino), Haruko Sawamura (Yoko, *his wife*), Koreya Togo (Koichiro, *their son*), Mikiko Hisamatsu (Fumiko, *their daughter*), Ryuko Date (Mitsuko, *Koichiro's fiancée*), Yuriko Hanabusa (peer's daughter), Sotaro Okada (caretaker of the villa), Kumahiko Mohara (steward), Minoru Murata (Taro), Komei Minami (Tsurikichi, *a released convict*), Shigeru Tsutamura (Kamezo, *a released convict*).

A Shochiku Co., Ltd. Production. Silent. Black and white. Academy ratio. 91 minutes. Released 1921.

U.S. VERSION: Distributor undetermined.

Space Cruiser Yamato / Uchu senkan Yamato ("Space Cruiser Yamato") **[animated]**. Producer/Director/Screenplay, Yoshinobu Nishizaki; Character Design, Leiji Matsumoto; Chief Animator, Noboru Ishiguro; Music, Hiroshi Miyagawa.

VOICE CHARACTERIZATION: (undetermined).

An Office Academy Production. Color. Spherical wide screen (?). 135 minutes. Released 1977.

U.S. VERSION: Distributor, if any, is undetermined. Released in Great Britain in 1977 by Enterprise Pictures, Ltd. in December 1977 running 107 minutes. The first feature of a 5-film series (1977–83). No MPAA rating.

Space Firebird / Hinotori 2772—Ai no kosumozon **[animated]**. Producer/Story, Osamu Tezuka; Directors, Osamu Tezuka and Suguru Sugiyama; Director of Photography, Iwao Yamaki; Art Director, Tsuyoshi Matsumoto and Shinji Ito; Music, Yasuo Higuchi.

VOICE CHARACTERIZATIONS: (undetermined).

A Tezuka Production Co., Ltd. Production. A Toho Co., Ltd. Release. Color. Spherical wide screen. 94 minutes (running time also given at 122 minutes). Released 1980.

U.S. VERSION: Released undetermined, likely by Toho International in subtitled format. 94 minutes. No MPAA rating.

Space Warriors 2000 / Urutora 6-Kyodai tai kaiju gundan ("The Six Ultra-Brothers Against the Monster Army"). Executive Producer, Noboru Tsuburaya; Director, Sompote Sands.

CAST: (undetermined).

A Fuji Eiga/Tsuburaya Productions, Ltd. Production. A Japanese/Thai coproduction. Color. Anamorphic wide screen. Running time undetermined. Released 1979.

U.S. VERSION: Never released theatrically in the United States. Released directly to television by Cinema Shares International Television, Ltd. English-dubbed. A Dick Randall and Steve Minasian Presentation. Director, Marc Smith; Director of Photography, Ion Knoller; Music, De Wolf; Dubbing Cast (?): Robert Sessions, Nicholas Curror, Sarah Taunton, Wendy Danvers. Mothra does not appear in the film, despite billing in the opening credits. Released in most of Asia in 1974, but not released in Japan until 1979 for reasons undetermined. Thai title undetermined. Both versions contain extensive stock footage from various Tsuburaya-produced "Ultra" teleseries. This footage, filmed in 16mm and 35mm full frame, was converted to anamorphic wide screen, resulting in an extremely uncomfortable image on the current panned-and-scanned television version. 91 minutes. No MPAA rating.

Spoils of the Night / Iro ("Lust"). Director, Shinji Murayama; Screenplay, Masashige Narusawa; Director of Photography, Hanjiro Nakazawa.

CAST: Tatsuo Umemiya (Toru Matoba), Mako Midori (Kazuko Uehara), Reiko Ohara (Hatsue Uehara), Akiyo Kubo (older woman).

A Toei Co., Ltd. Production. Black and white. ToeiScope (?). 84 minutes. Released 1966.

U.S. VERSION: Released by William Mishkin. English subtitles. Subtitles, Lewis Mishkin. 84 minutes. No MPAA rating. Released August 14, 1969.

Spring Comes to the Ladies / Hana wa Gofujin Kara ("Flowers Come to the Ladies"). Director, Yasujiro Ozu; Screenplay, Tadao Ikeda and Takao Yanai, based on an idea by James Maki [Yasujiro Ozu]; Director of Photography, Hideo Shigehara.

CAST: Jiro Shirota, Tatsuo Saito, Yukiko Inoue, Takeshi Sakamoto.

A Shochiku Co., Ltd. Production. Filmed at Shochiku-Kamata Studios. Silent with benshi. Black and white. Academy ratio. 94 minutes. Released January 29, 1932.

U.S. VERSION: Never released theatrically in the United States. A lost film.

Stage-Struck Tora-san / Otoko wa tsuraiyo—Torajiro waga Michi o yuku ("It's Tough to Be a Man—Going My Way"). Producer, Kiyoshi Shimazu; Director, Yoji Yamada; Screenplay, Yoji Yamada and Yoshitaka Asama, based on characters created by Yoji Yamada; Director of Photography, Tetsuo Takaba; Music, Naozumi Yamamoto.

CAST: Kiyoshi Atsumi (Torajiro "Tora-san" Kuruma), Chieko Baisho (Sakura Suwa, *his sister*).

A Shochiku Co., Ltd. Production. Color. Shochiku GrandScope. 103 minutes. Released 1978.

U.S. VERSION: Released by Shochiku Films of America, Inc. English subtitles. The 21st "Tora-san" feature. Followed by *Talk of the Town Tora-san* (1978). 103 minutes. No MPAA rating. Released 1979 (?).

Star Force: Fugitive Alien II. Producers, Noboru Tsuburaya, Jushichi Sano, and Akira Tsuburaya; Directors, Kiyosumi Kukazawa and Minoru Kanaya; Teleplay, Keiichi Abe, Bunko Wakatsuki, Yoshihisa Araki, Hiroyasu Tamaura, Hideyoshi Nagasaka, and Toyohiro Ando; Music, Norio Maeda.

CAST: Tatsuya Azuma, Miyuki Tanigawa, Jo Shishido, Choei Takahashi, Tsutomu Yukawa, Hiro Tateyama.

A Japanese teleseries re-edited to feature length for American release, and never released theatrically in Japan. A Tsuburaya Productions, Ltd. Production. 16mm. Color.

U.S. VERSION: Never released theatrically in the United States. Released directly to television in 1986 by King Features Entertainment, a subsidiary of the Hearst Corporation. English-dubbed. A Sandy Frank Enterprises Presentation. Concept Editor, William L. Cooper, Jr.; Creative Consultant, Jessie Vogel and Cinemedia, Ltd. Preceded by *Fugitive Alien*, and derived from the teleseries "Sutaurufu ("Star Wolf"), which aired in Japan in 1978. 75 minutes. No MPAA rating.

Star of Hong Kong / Honkon no hoshi ("Star of Hong Kong"). Executive Producers, Sanezumi Fujimoto and Robert Chung; Director, Yasuki Chiba; Screenplay, Ryozo Kasahara; Director of Photography, Rokuro Nishigaki; Music, Hachiro Matsui; Assistant Director, Mikio Komatsu.

CAST: Yu Ming, Wang Ing, Reiko Dan, Akira Takarada, Rin Tsuong, Mitsuko Kusabue, Wong Yen, So Yamamura, Sadako Sawamura, Lin Chong, Hiroshi Koizumi, Yu Fujiki, Daisuke Kato, Asami Kuji.

A Toho Co., Ltd./The Cathay Organization Production. A Toho Co., Ltd.

Release. A Japanese/Hong Kong co-production in Japanese and English. Eastman Color. Toho Scope. 109 minutes. Released 1962.

U.S. VERSION: Released by Toho International Co., Ltd. English subtitles. 109 minutes. No MPAA rating. Released December 14, 1962.

Station / Eki ("Railway Station"). Producer, Jurichi Tanaka; Director, Yasuo Kohata; Screenplay, So Kuramoto; Director of Photography, Daisaku Kimura; Art Director, Yukio Higuchi; Sound Recording, Nobuyuki Tanaka; Lighting, Nideki Mochizuki; Music, Ryudo Uzaki; Assistant Producer, Akira Ogura.

CAST: Ken Takakura (Eiji Mikami), Ayumi Ishida (Naoko Mikami), Ryo Ikebe (Detective Nakagawa), Setsuko Karasumaru (Suzuko Yoshimitsu), Jinpachi Nezu (Goro Yoshimatsu), Ryudo Uzaki (Yukio Kinoshita), Chieko Baisho (Kiriko), Tetsuya Takeda (passenger on train), Shuji Otaki (Aia), Yuko Kotegawa (Fujiko Mikami), Toshiyuki Nagashima (Michio Mikano), Kunie Tanaka (Sugawara).

A Toho Co., Ltd. Production. Color. Spherical wide screen. 132 minutes. Released November 1981.

U.S. VERSION: Released by Toho International Co., Ltd. English subtitles. 132 minutes. No MPAA rating. Released April 23, 1982.

Step on the Gas! / Shinjuku autoro, buttobase ("Shinjuku Auto, Speeding Off"). Director, Toshiya Fujita; Screenplay, Shuichi Nagahara, Michio Sotake, and Toshiya Fujita; Director of Photography, Kenji Hagiwara; Art Director, Kazuhiko Chiba; Music, Hiroki Tamaki.

CAST: Tetsuya Watari (Yuji Nishigami), Yoshio Harada (Tadashi Matsukata), Meiko Kaji (Emiko), Chieko Harada (Shinko, *Tadashi's sister*), Kenji Imai (President Yuasa), Mikio Narita, Masaya Oki, Aoi Nakajima.

A Nikkatsu Corp. Production. Fujicolor. NikkatsuScope. 86 minutes. Released October 24, 1970.

U.S. VERSION: Distributor, if any, is undetermined. English subtitled version available. 86 minutes. No MPAA rating.

The Sting of Death / Shi no toge ("The Sting of Death"). Producer, Toru Okuyama; Director, Kohei Oguri; Screenplay, Kohei Oguri, based on the novel by Toshio Shimao; Director of Photography, Shohei Ando; Music, Toshio Hosokawa.

CAST: Keiko Matsuzaka (Miho), Ittoku Kishibe (Toshio), Midori Kiuchi (Kuniko), Takenori Matsumura (Shinichi), Yuri Chikamori (Maya).

A Shochiku Co., Ltd./Shochiku Dai-Ichi Kogyo Co., Ltd./Araki Office Co., Ltd. Production. Color. Spherical wide screen (1.66:1). 115 minutes. Released April 28, 1990.

U.S. VERSION: Released by Shochiku Films of America, Inc. English subtitles. 115 minutes. No MPAA rating. Released September 28, 1990.

Stolen Love / Nusumareta koi ("Stolen Love"). Producers, Jiro Takagi and Yoshie Ogawa; Director, Kon Ichikawa; Screenplay, Natto Wada and Kon Ichikawa, based on a novel by Jiro Kagami; Director of Photography, Minoru Yokoyama; Art Director, Takashi Kono; Music, Akira Ifukube.

CAST: Asami Kuji (Ryoko Kani), Michiko Kato (Hanko Noto), Masayuki Mori (Takashi Akune), Koroku Kawakita (Monta Mito), Takashi Shimura (Sotaro Munakata, *the art critic*).

A Shintoho Co., Ltd. Production. Black and white. Academy ratio. 89 minutes. Release date June 8, 1951.

U.S. VERSION: Distributor undetermined. English subtitles. 89 minutes. No MPAA rating.

Stopover Tokyo. Producer, Walter Reisch; Director, Robert L. Breen; Screenplay, Robert L. Breen and Walter Reisch, based on the novel by John P. Marquard; Director of Photography, Charles G. Clarke; Editor, Marjorie Fowler; Art Directors, Lyle R. Wheeler and Eddie Imazu; Music, Paul Sawtell; Japanese Music Supervision, Tak Shindo.

CAST: Robert Wagner (Mark Fannon), Joan Collins (Tina), Edmond O'Brien (George Underwood), Ken Scott (Tony Barrett), Reiko Oyama (Koko), Larry Keating (high commissioner), Sarah Selby (wife of high commissioner), Solly Nakamura (Nobika), Haiichiro "Henry" Okawa (Lt. Afumi), K.J. Seijto (Katsura), Demmei Susuki (Capt. Masao), Yuki Kaneko, Michei Miura.

A Walter Reisch Production, in association with Twentieth Century-Fox Film Corporation. A Twentieth Century-Fox Release. A U.S. Production in English and filmed in Japan, and at Twentieth Century-Fox Studios (Century City, Califonia). Four-track magnetic stereophonic sound. DeLuxe Color. CinemaScope. 100 minutes. No MPAA rating. Released October 1957.

Stormy Era / Showa no inochi ("Life of Showa"). Director, Toshio Masuda.

CAST: Yujiro Ishihara, Ryutaro Tatsumi, Hideki Takahashi, Mie Hama, Katsuo Nakamura, Ruriko Asaoka, Mitsuo Hamada, Eiji Okada, Shogo Shimada.

A Nikkatsu Corporation Production. Nikkatsucolor. NikkatsuScope. 165 minutes. Released 1968.

U.S. VERSION: Released by Toho International Co., Ltd. English subtitles. 165 minutes. No MPAA rating. Released March 1969.

A Story from Chikamatsu / Chikamatsu monogatari ("Chikamatsu Story"). Executive Producer, Masatsugu Hashimoto; Producer, Masaichi Nagata; Planning, Hisakazu Tsuji; Director, Kenji Mizoguchi; Screenplay, Yoshikata Yoda, based on Matsutaro Kawaguchi's adaptation of the Bunraku play *Daikyoji Sekireki* ("The Almanac-Maker's Tale") by Monzaemon Chikamatsu; Director of Photography, Kazuo Miyagawa; Art Director, Hiroshi Mizutani; Lighting, Kenichi Okamoto; Music, Fumio Hayasaka; Natural Music Directors, Tamezo Mochizuki and Enjiro Toyozawa; Sound Recording, Iwao Otani; Editor, Kanji Sugawara; Assistant Director, Tokuzo Tanaka.

CAST: Kazuo Hasegawa (Mohei), Kyoko Kagawa (Osan), Yoko Minamida (Otama, *the servant*), Eitaro Shindo (Ishun), Eitaro Ozawa (Sukaemon), Ichiro Sugai (Genbee), Haruo Tanaka (Doki), Chieko Naniwa (Oko), Tatsuya Ishiguro (Isan), Kimiko Tachibana (Umetatsu Akamatsu), Hisao Toake (Chamberlain Morinokoji), Shinobu Araki (nobleman's major-domo), Koichi Katsuragi (priest), Hiroshi Mizuno (Kuroki, the chief state's counsilor), Ikkei Tamaki (Jushiro Umegaki), Keiko Koyanago (Okaya), Kanai Kobayashi (Otatsu), Shiro Miura (worker), Nobuko Tanei (little girl), Soji Shibata (worker), Tadashi Iwata (Chushichi), Ichiro Amano (blind musician), Shichiro Hara, Sachio Horikita (dock workers), Reiko Kongo (boat maidservant), Sumai Ishihara (innkeeper), Shiro Osaki (chesnut seller), Midori Komatsu (old lady of the teahouse), Jun Fujikawa (village official), Fumihiko Yokoyama (village chieftain).

A Daiei Motion Picture Co., Ltd. Production. Filmed at Daiei Studios (Tokyo). Black and white. Academy ratio. 102 minutes. Released November 23, 1954.

U.S. VERSION: Released by New Line Cinema. English subtitles. Also known as *Crucified Lovers: A Story from Chikamatsu* and *A Tale from Chikamatsu*. 102 minutes. No MPAA rating. Released November 1970.

Story of a Prostitute / Shunpuden ("Story of a Prostitute"). Producer, Kaneo Iwai; Director, Seijun Suzuki; Screenplay, Hajime Takaiwa, based on the novel by Taijiro Tamura; Director of Photography, Kazue Nagatsuka; Editor, Akira Suzuki; Art Director, Takeo Kimura; Music, Naozumi Yamamoto; Assistant Director, Masami Kuzu.

CAST: Tamio Kawachi (Shinkichi Mikami), Yumiko Nogawa (Harumi), Isao Tamagawa (Lt. Narita), Tomiko Ishikawa (Yuriko), Kazuko Imai (Sachiko), Megumi Wakaba (Sakae), Kayo Matsuo (Midori), Shoichi Ozawa (Sgt. Akiyama), Kentaro Kaji (Uno).

A Nikkatsu Corp. Production. Black and white. NikkatsuScope. 96 minutes. Released 1965.

U.S. VERSION: Released by Nikkatsu Corp. English subtitles. Previously filmed as *Pursuit at Dawn* (1950). 96 minutes. No MPAA rating. Released 1993.

A Story of Floating Weeds / Ukigusa monogatari ("A Story of Floating Weeds"). Director, Yasujiro Ozu; Screenplay, Tadao Ikeda, based on the American film *The Barker*; Director of Photography, Hideo Shigehara.

CAST: Takeshi Sakamoto, Choko Iida, Koji "Hideo" Mitsui, Emiko Yagumo, Yoshiko Tsubouchi, Reiko Tani, Chishu Ryu.

A Shochiku Co., Ltd. Production. Filmed at Shochiku-Kamata Studios. Silent. Black and white. Academy ratio. 89 minutes. Released November 23, 1934.

U.S. VERSION: Released by New Yorker Films. English intertitles. Cut by Japanese censors from 107 minutes. Remade by Ozu in 1959 as *Floating Weeds*. 89 minutes. No MPAA rating. Released January 1994.

The Story of Tank Commander Nishizumi / Nishizumi senshacho-den ("The Story of Tank Commander Nishizumi"). Director, Kozaburo Yoshimura; Screenplay, Kogo Noda, based on the story by Kan Kikuchi; Director of Photography, Toshio Ubukata; Art Directors, Yoneichi Wakita and Tatsuo Hamada; Music, Ki Maeda; Assistant Directors, Keisuke Kinoshita and Noboru Nakamura.

CAST: Ken Uehara (Nishizumi), Takashi Sakamoto (Goto), Shin Saburi (Hosoki), Chishu Ryu (Osumi), Tatsuo Saito (officer in the 18th battlion), Michiko Kuwano (Chinese woman), Ichiru Kodama (Hosokawa), Seiji Nishimura (Murayama), Katsumi Kubota (Yamabe), Toshiji Kawara (Okada), Akio Isono (Uematsu).

A Shochiku Co., Ltd. Production. Black and white. Academy ratio. 126 minutes. Released 1940.

U.S. VERSION: Distributor undetermined. English subtitles. Running time also given at 136 minutes. 126 minutes. No MPAA rating. Release date undetermined.

The Story of the Last Chrysanthemums / Zangiku monogatari ("The Story of the Last Chrysanthemums"). Producer, Nobutaro Shirai; Director, Kenji Mizoguchi; Screenplay, Yoshikata Yoda and Matsutaro Kawaguchi, based on the story by Shofu Muramatsu, and a theatrical adaptation by Sanichi Iwaya; Directors of Photography, Shigeto Miki and Yozo Fuji; Lighting, Matsujiro Nakajima; Editor, Koshi Kawahigashi; Art Director, Hiroshi Mizutani; Set Decorators, Tsunetaro Kikukawa and Dai Arakawa; Music, Shiro Fukai and Senji Ito; Shamisen Player, Katsujiro Kineya; Narimono Player, Tamezo Mochizuki; Joruri Player, Enjiro Toyosawa; Singer in the Nagauta style, Sempachi Sakata; Singers in the Tokiwazu style, Bunshi Tokiwazu, Bunnosuke Tokiwazu; Choreography, Kikuzo Otowa; Costumes, Seizo Yamaguchi and Yoshizaburo Okumura; Hairdresser, Rikizo Inoue, Ishitaro Takagi, and Yoshiko Kimura; Sound Recording, Ryuichi Shikata, Fumizo Sugimoto; Artistic Research, Sohachi Kimura, Nanboku Kema; Historic Research, Seikichi Terakado; Production Assistants, Tazuko Sakane, Shozo Tahara, Taichiro Hanaoka; Special Effects, Taichi Shimizu and Shun Rokugo.

CAST: Shotaro Hanayagi (Kikunosuke Onoe), Kakuko Mori (Otoku), Gonjuro Kawarazaki (Kikugoro Onoe V), Kokichi Takada (Fukusuke Nakamura), Yoko Umemura (Osato, *Kikugoro Onoe's wife*), Yoshiaki Hayanagi (Tamijiro Onoe), Tokusaburo Arashi (Shikan Nakamura), Kinnosuke Takamatsu (Matsusuke Onoe), Benkei Shiganoya (Genshun Motosuke, *the masseur*), Yoneko Mogami (Otsuru Motosuke, *his daughter*), Ryotaro Kawanami (Dayu Eijyu), Junnosuke Hayama (Kanya Morita), Nobuko Fushimi (Eiryu, the importunate geisha), Tamitaro Onoe (Tamizo Onoe), Hideo Nagakawa (Otaku's uncle), Hisayo Nishi (Otaku's aunt), Komei Minami (the Shinto-za boss), Ichiro Yuki (man in the geisha house), Soichi Amano (theater costumer), Samao Ishihara (manager of the itinerant geishas), Takashi Mirota (leader of the itinerant geishas), Minpei Tomimoto (2nd man in geisha house), Kikuko Manaoka, Fujiko Shirakawa, Yoneko Mogami, Atsuko Shirata, Tomiko Akimoto, and Mitsue Kunihara (geishas), Yoshie Nakagawa (old lady in the tea house), Junko Kagami, Hisano Owa (Kikugoro's servants), Haruko Tagawa (doctor), Kimiko Shiratae (woman lute-player), Akira Shima (director of the Sumi-ya), Kiyoshi Marumoto (Enzaburo), Kazuyoshi Tachibana (Kikunosuke's pupil), Akio Isobe (young man), Eijiro Hose, Hiroshi Hanada (itinerant players), Haruko Yanagido (keeper of the geisha house), Hakoto Matsushita (man with the monkeys).

A Shochiku Co., Ltd. Production. Filmed at Shochiku-Shimokamo Studios (Kyoto). Black and white. Academy ratio. 143 minutes. Released October 13, 1939.

U.S. Version: Released by Films Incorporated. English subtitles. The first film of a trilogy; the second and third films do not survive. Followed by *The Woman of Osaka* (1940). Remade by Koji Shima in 1956. Running time also given at 115 minutes. 143 minutes. No MPAA rating. Released January 15, 1979.

A Straightforward Boy / Tokkan Kozo ("A Straitforward Boy"). Director, Yasujiro Ozu; Screenplay, Tadao Ikeda, based on an idea by Chuji Nozu [Kogo Noda, Tadamoto Okubo, Tadao Ikeda, and Yasujiro Ozu]; Director of Photography, Ko Nomura.

Cast: Tatsuo Saito, Tomio Aoki, Takeshi Sakamoto.

A Shochiku Co., Ltd. Production. Filmed at Shochiku-Kamata Studios. Silent with benshi. 57 minutes. Released November 24, 1929.

U.S. Version: Never released in the United States. A lost film.

The Strange Tale of Oyuki / Bokuto kidan ("The Strange Tale in Bokuto"). Producers, Jiro Shindo and Manabu Akashi; Director, Kaneto Shindo; Screenplay, Kaneto Shindo, based on an original story by Kafu Nagai; Director of Photography, Yoshiyuki Miyake; Music, Hikaru Hayashi.

Cast: Masahiko Tsugawa (Kafu Nagai), Yuki Shimada (Oyuki), Nobuko Otowa, Yoshiko Miyazaki.

A Kindai Eiga Kyokai Production. A Toho Co., Ltd. Release. Color. Anamorphic wide screen (?). 116 minutes. Released 1992.

U.S. Version: Released by Toho International Co., Ltd. English subtitles. A remake of *The Twilight Story* [?] (1960). 116 minutes. No MPAA rating. Released May 8, 1993.

Strawberry Road / Sutoroberi Road ("Strawberry Road"). Producer, Shinjiro Kayama; Director, Koreyoshi Kuruhara; Screenplay, Nobuo Yamada, based on the novel by Yoshimi Ishikawa; Director of Photography, Katsuhiro Kato.

Cast: Ken Matsudaira, Noriyuki "Pat" Morita, Mako, Toshiro Mifune.

A Tokyo Hoei Television Co., Ltd. Production in English and Japanese. Color. Spherical wide screen (?). 117 minutes. Released April 1991.

U.S. Version: Distributor, if any, is undetermined.

Stray Dog / Nora inu ("Stray Dog"). Producer, Sojiro Motoki; Director, Akira Kurosawa; Screenplay, Ryuzo Kikushima and Akira Kurosawa; Director of Photography, Asakazu Nakai; Camera Operator, H. Kusada; Editor, Yoshi Sugihara; Lighting, Choshiro Ishii; Art Director, So Matsuyama; Music, Fumio Hayasaka; Sound Recording, Fumio Yanoguchi; Assistant Director, Ishiro Honda.

Cast: Toshiro Mifune (Detective Murakami), Takashi Shimura (Chief Detective Sato), Isao Kimura (Shinjuro "Yuro" Yusa), Keiko Awaji (Harumi Namaki), Reisaburo Yamamoto (Honda), Noriko Sengoku (girl), Gen Shimizu (Nakajima), Yasushi Nagata (Abe), Reikichi Kawamura (Officer Ichikawa), Eiko Miyoshi (Madame Namiki), Kazuo Motohashi (Madame Sato-Tomi), Teruko Kishi (Ogin), Eijiro Tono (old man of wooden tub shop), Fumiko Homma (woman of wooden tub shop), Yunosuke Ito (manager of Bluebird Theatre), Choko Iida (Kogetsu Hotel mengeress), Minoru Chiaki (girlie show art director), Masao Shimizu (Nakamura), Hajime Sugai (Yayoi Hotel manager), Eizo Tanaka (old doctor), Shiro Mizutani (punkster), Isao Ubukata (Sei-san), Fujio Nagahama (Sakura Hotel manager), Akira Ubukata (police doctor), Kokuten Kodo (old man at apartment building), Rikie Sanjyo (wife of manager), Aso Mie (woman at pinball parlor), Haruko Toyama (Kintaro-geisha), Haruko Toda (Azuma Hotel madam).

A Shintoho Co., Ltd. Production. Black and white. Academy ratio. Filmed at Shintoho Studios (Tokyo). 122 minutes. Released October 17, 1949.

U.S. Version: Released by Toho International Co., Ltd. English subtitles. Rights acquired by Toho Co., Ltd. in

Terry (Sonny Chiba) is a bodyguard for Sarai (Yutaka Nakajima) in *The Street Fighter* (Toei, 1974), the first film to earn an "X" rating for violent content.

1959. 122 minutes. No MPAA rating. Released August 1963.

The Street Fighter / Gekitotsu Satsujinken. Director, Shigehiro Ozawa; Planner, Norimichi Matsudaira; Screenplay, Koji Takada and Motohiro Torii; Director of Photography, Kenji Tsukakoshi; Art Director, Takatoshi Suzuki; Martial Arts Director, Masafumi Suzuki; Wrestling Directors, Y. Harada and Reggy Jones; Kick Boxing Director, Ken Kazama; Music, Tony Sushima

CAST: Shinichi "Sonny" Chiba (Terry Sugury [Ken Takuma]), Goichi "Gerald" Yamada (Camel Chang, aka Ratnose), Yutaka "Doris" Nakajima (Sarai), Tony Cetera (Jadot, aka Shad), Masashi Ishibashi (Teijo Shikehara), Osman Yusef (King Stone, aka Wang Weng), Angel Cordero.

A Toei Co., Ltd. Production. Eastman Color. ToeiScope. 94 minutes. Released 1974.

U.S. VERSION: Released by New Line Cinema. English-dubbed. Dubbing, Titan Productions; English Dialogue, Steve Autry; Title Sequence, Jack Sholder. Wide screen process billed as Actionscope in the United States. Alternate title: *The Karate.* The first feature to receive an MPAA "X" rating for violent content. 92 minutes. MPAA rating: "X." Released November 1974. Reissued at 74 minutes with an MPAA rating of "R." Sequel (U.S. version only): *Return of the Street Fighter.*

Street of Shame / Akasen chitai ("A Red-Light District"). Producer, Masaichi Nagata; Director, Kenji Mizoguchi; Screenplay, Masashige Narusawa, based on the short story, "Susaki no onna," by Yoshiko Shibaki; Director of Photography, Kazuo Miyagawa; Editor, Keiichi Sakane; Art Director, Hiroshi Mizutani; Set Decoration, Kiichi Ishizaki; Music, Toshiro Mayuzumi; Sound Recording, Mitsuo Hasegawa.

CAST: Machiko Kyo (Mickey), Aiko Mimasu (Yumeko), Ayako Wakao (Yasumi), Michiyo Kogure (Hanae), Kumeko Urabe (Otane), Yasuko Kawakami (Shizuko), Eitaro Shindo (Kurazo Taya), Kenji

Sugawara (Aoki), Bontaro Miake (policeman), Hiroko Machida (Yorie), Toranosuke Ogawa (Mickey's father), Daisuke Kato (Officer Miyazaki), Sadako Sawamura (Tatsuko).

A Daiei Motion Picture Co., Ltd. Production. Filmed at Daiei-Kyoto Studios. Black and white. Academy ratio. 94 minutes. Released March 18, 1956.

U.S. VERSION: Released by Edward Harrison. English subtitles. 84 minutes. No MPAA rating. Released June 4, 1959. Video version restored. Alternate title: *Red-Light District*.

The Streetfighter's Last Revenge. Director, Shigehiro Ozawa.

CAST: Shinichi "Sonny" Chiba, Sue Shiomi, Masafumi Suzuki, Frankie Black, Reiko Ike, Willy Dosey.

U.S. VERSION: Released by New Line Cinema. English-dubbed. Postproduction, August Films, Inc.; Producers, Joseph Ellison and Simon Nuchtern. 78 minutes (also given at 85 minutes). MPAA rating: "R." Released November 2, 1979.

Structure of Hate / Kanryu ("Current"). Executive Producer, Reiji Miwa; Director, Hideo Suzuki; Screenplay, Tokuhei Wakao, based on a story by Seicho Matsumoto; Director, Yuruzu Aizawa; Music, Ichiro Sato.

CAST: Ryo Ikebe, Michiyo Aratama, Akihiko Hirata.

A Toho Co., Ltd. Production. Black and white. Toho Scope. 96 minutes. Released 1961.

U.S. VERSION: Released by Toho International Co., Ltd. English subtitles. 96 minutes. No MPAA rating. Release date undetermined.

The Submersion of Japan / Tidal Wave / Nippon chiubotsu ("The Submersion of Japan"). Executive Producer, Tomoyuki Tanaka; Associate Producer, Osamu Tanaka; Director, Shiro Moritani; Screenplay, Shinobu Hashimoto, based on the novel by Sakyo Komatsu; Directors of Photography, Hiroshi Murai and Daisaku Kimura; Music, Masaru Sato; Art Director, Yoshiro Muraki; Sound, Toshiya Ban, Toho Recording Centre; Sound Effects, Toho Sound Effects Group; Lighting, Kojiro Sato; Assistant Director, Koji Hashimoto; Editor, Michiko Ikeda; Stillman Yoshinori Ishizuki; Production Manager, Takehide Morichi; Technical Advisers, Hiroshi Takeuchi, Yorihiko Osaki, Noriyuki Nasu, Akira Suwa. *Toho Special Effects Group:* Director, Teruyoshi Nakano; Director of Photography, Mototaka Tomioka; Set Designer, Yasuyuki Inoue; Lighting, Masakuni Morimoto; Optical Photography, Takeshi Miyanishi; Matte Processing, Kazunobu Sampei; Miniature Set Operation, Fumio Nakadai, Koji Matsumoto; Assistant Director, Yoshio Tabuchi, Tadaaki Watanabe; Stillman, Kazukiyo Tanaka; Unit Manager, Keisuke Shinoda.

CAST: Keiju Kobayashi (Dr. Tanaka), Hiroshi Fujioka (Toshio Onoda), Tetsuro Tamba (Prime Minister Yamoto), Ayumi Ishida (Reiko), Shogo Shimada (Prince Watari), Nobuo Nakamura (Australian Ambassador), Andrew Hughes (Australian Prime Minister), Tadao Nakamaru, Yusuke Takita, Isao Natsuyagi, Hideaki Nitiani.

A Toho Co., Ltd. Production. Westrex recording system. Color (processed by Tokyo Laboratory Ltd.). Panavision. 140 minutes. Released December 29, 1973.

U.S. VERSION: Released by New World Pictures as *Tidal Wave* (see below). English-dubbed. A New World Pictures and Max E. Youngstein Productions, in association with Toho International Co., Ltd Production. A Roger Corman/ Max E. Youngstein Presentation. Executive Producer, Roger Corman; Producer, Max E. Youngstein; Director and Dialogue, Andrew Meyer; Director of Photography, Eric Saarinen; Sound, Ryder Sound Services, Inc. (?); processing and prints by Metrocolor. Also simultaneously released in the United States by New World uncut and in subtitled format as *Submersion of Japan* (with no MPAA rating). An international version was also released by Toho International, running 113 minutes. Running time of recut American edition: 90 minutes. MPAA Rating: "PG." Released May 1975.

Grainy still from *The Submersion of Japan* (1973), butchered and released in this country in 1975 as *Tidal Wave*. (Photo courtesy Ted Okuda.)

Additional Cast for U.S. Version: Lorne Greene (U.S. Ambassador Warren Richards), Rhonda Leigh Hopkins (Fran), John Fukioka (Narita), Marvin Miller, Susan Sennett, Ralph James, Phil Roth, Cliff Pellow, Joseph J. [Joe] Dante (voice characterizations).

Summer Clouds / Iwasi-gumo. Producers, Masumi Fujimoto and Reiji Miwa; Director, Mikio Naruse; Screenplay, Shinobu Hashimoto, based on the novel by Den Wada; Director of Photography, Masao Tamai; Art Directors, Satoshi Chuko and Makoto Sano; Music, Ichiro Saito.

CAST: Chikage Awashima (Yae), Isao Kimura (Okawa), Ganjiro Nakamura (Wasuke), Keiju Kobayashi (Hatsuji, *his son*), Yoko Tsukasa (Michiko), Haruko Sugimura (her mother), Kumi Mizuno.

A Toho Co., Ltd. Production. Agfacolor. Toho Scope. 128 minutes. Released September 2, 1958.

U.S. VERSION: Distributor undetermined, likely Toho International Co., Ltd. in subtitled format. Alternate title: *The Summer Clouds*. No MPAA rating. Release date undetermined.

Summer of the Moonlight Sonata / Gekko no natsu ("Summer of the Moonlight"). Producer, Masayuki Sato; Director, Seijiro Koyama; Screenplay, [undetermined], based on an original story by Tsuneyuki Mori; Director of Photography, Fumimori Minami; Music, Masao Haryu.

CAST: Mayumi Wakamura, Minoru Tanaka, Misako Watanabe.

A Shigoto Film Production, Inc. Production. Color. Spherical wide screen. Released 1993.

U.S. VERSION: Distributor, if any, is undetermined.

Summer Vacation 1999 / Sen-kyuhyaku-kyuju-kyu-nen nantsu yasumi ("Summer Vacation 1999"). Executive Producers, Yutaka Okada and Eiji Kishi; Producers, Naoya Narita, Mitsuhisa Hida; Director, Shusuke Kaneko; Screenplay, Rio Kishida; Director of

Photography, Kenji Takama; Lighting, Hiroyuki Yasukochi; Underwater Photography, Makoto Shionoya, Akihiro Uemura, Michiko Honda; Photographic Effects, Kenichi Yoshioka; Editor, Isao Tomita; Art Director, Shu Yamaguchi; Set Decorator, Akira Yamazaki, Keiichi Hasegawa, and Satoru Suda; Special Effects, Masatoshi Saito; Music, Yuriko Nakamura; Music, Director, Hiro Yanagida; Makeup, Feng Qixiao, Motoko Watanabe; Sound Recording, Koshiro Jimbo; Production Manager, Hajime Seta; Assistant Director, Hiroaki Tochihara.

CAST: Eri Miyajima (Yu/Kaoru/Last New Boy), Tomoko Otakara (Kazuhiko), Miyuki Nakano (Naoto), Rie Mizuhara (Norio). *Voice Characterizations:* Eri Miyajima (Yu), Minami Takayama (Kaoru), Nozomu Sasaki (Kazuhiko), Hiromi Murata (Naoto), Rie Mizuhara (Norio), Masaaki Maeda (narrator).

A New Century Producers/CBS-Sony Group Production. Eastman Color. Spherical wide screen (?). 90 minutes. Released 1988.

U.S. VERSION: Released by New Yorker Films. English subtitles. Subtitles, Donald Richie and Tadashi Shishido. 90 minutes. No MPAA rating. Released July 1989.

Sumo Do, Sumo Don't / Shiko Funjatta ("I Stamped on the Ring"). Producers, Yo Yamamoto and Izuru Hiraoki; Director/Screenplay, Masayuki Suo; Original Story, Masayuki Suo; Director of Photography, Naoki Kayano; Music, Yoshikazu Suo.

CAST: Masahiro Motiki (Shushei), Misa Shimizu (Natsuko), Naoto Takenaka (Aoki), Akira Emoto, Robert Hoffman.

A Daiei Co., Ltd./Cabin Co., Ltd. Production. Color. Spherical wide screen (?). 105 minutes. Released 1992.

U.S. VERSION: Distributor undetermined. English subtitles. 105 minutes. No MPAA rating. Released November 6, 1992.

Sun Above, Death Below / Sogeki ("Shooting"). Director, Hiromichi Horikawa; Screenplay, Hidekazu Nagahara, based on his play; Director of Photography, Kiyoshi Hasegawa; Art Director, Shinobu Muraki; Music, Riichiro Manabe.

CAST: Yuzo Kayama (Toru Matsushita), Ruriko Asaoka (Akiko), Masayuki Mori (Katakura).

A Toho Co., Ltd. Production. Eastman Color. Toho Scope. 87 minutes. Released November 23, 1968.

U.S. VERSION: Released by Toho International Co., Ltd. English subtitles. 87 minutes. No MPAA rating. Released March 28, 1969.

Sun-Wu King / Songoku. Producers, Tomoyuki Tanaka; Director/Screenplay, Kajiro Yamamoto; Director of Photography, Hajime Koizumi; Music, Ikuma Dan. *Toho Special Effects Group:* Director, Eiji Tsuburaya.

CAST: Reiko Dan, Norihei Miki, Yasuko Nakata, Henry Ogawa, Eisei Amamoto, Yutaka Oka.

A Toho Co., Ltd. Production. Western Electric Mirrophonic Recording (encoded with Perspecta Stereophonic Sound). Agfacolor. Toho Scope. 97 minutes. Released April 19, 1959.

U.S. VERSION: Released undetermined, possibly by Toho International Co., Ltd. in subtitled format. No MPAA rating.

The Sun's Burial / Taiyo no hakaba ("Grave of the Sun"). Director, Nagisa Oshima; Screenplay, Nagisa Oshima and Toshiro Ishido; Director of Photography, Takashi [Ko] Kawamata; Art Director, Koji Uno; Lighting, Isamu Sato; Editor, Keiichi Kamata; Music, Riichiro Manabe.

CAST: Kayoko Hono (Hanako), Masahiko Tsugawa (Shin), Isao Sasaki (Takeshi), Yusuke Kawazu (Yasu), Fumio Watanabe, Kamatari Fujiwara, Eitaro Ozawa, Tanie Kitabayashi, Junzaburo Ban.

A Shochiku Co., Ltd. Production. Color. Shochiku GrandScope. 87 minutes. Released 1960.

U.S. VERSION: Released by New Yorker Films. English subtitles. 87 minutes. No MPAA rating. Released January 2, 1985.

Super Monster / Uchu kaiju Gamera ("Space Monster Gamera"). Producers, Masaya Tokuyama, Shigeru Shinohara, Hirokazu Oba; Director, Noriaki Yuasa; Planner, Masaya Tokuyama;

Screenplay, Nizo Takahashi; Director of Photography, Akira Kitazaki; Additional Photography, Michio Takahashi, Akira Uehara; Editors (stock footage), Shoji Sekiguchi, Tatsuji Nakashizu, Zenko Miyazaki; Lighting, Tadaaki Shimada; Art Directors, Tomohisa Yano, Akira Inoue; Set Decoration, Nobuhisa Iwata; Music, Shunsuke Kikuchi; Song, "Love for Future," sung by Mach Fumiake; Sound Recording, Kimio Tobita; Sound, Daiei Recording Studio; Assistant Director, Hiromi Munemoto; Make-up, Chie Tsuchiya; Script Girl, Midori Kobayashi; Animated scenes courtesy Office Academy, Toei Animation Studios. *Special Effects Unit*: Directors, Noriaki Yuasa, Kazufumi Fujii, Yuzo Kaneko; Original Monster Design, Ryosaku Takayama.

CAST: Mach Fumiake (Kilara), Yaeko Kojima (Marsha), Yoko Komatsu (Mitan), Keiko Dudo (Gilage), Koichi Maeda (Keiichi), Toshie Takada (Keiichi's mother), Osamu Kobayashi (voice of Zanon captain), Hiroji Hayashi, Tetsuaki Toyosumi, Hideaki Kobayashi, Makato Ikeda, Kisao Hida.

A Daiei Film Distribution Co., Ltd. Production. Distributed in Japan by New Daiei Co., Ltd. Distributed internationally by Shochiku Co., Ltd. Westrex recording system. Daieicolor. Spherical Panavision. 91 minutes. Released March 20, 1980.

U.S. VERSION: Released by Shochiku Films of America, Inc. English subtitles. Released to television English-dubbed. A Filmways Pictures Release. Alternate titles: *Gamera Supermonster* and *Super Monster Gamera*. Includes stock footage from *Gammera the Invincible* (1965), *War of the Monsters* (1966), *Return of the Giant Monsters* (1967), *Destroy All Planets* (1968), *Attack of the Monsters* (1969), *Gamera vs. Monster X* (1970) and *Gamera vs. Zigra* (1971). Also includes footage from the animated features, *Space Cruiser Yamato* (1977) and *Galaxy Express 999* (1979). Eighth feature in the "Gamera" film series. Followed by *Gamera—Guardian of the Universe* (1995). 91 minutes. No MPAA rating. Released May 7, 1980.

Supergiant / Supa Jyaiantsu

("Supergiant"). Producer, Mitsugi Okura; Directors, Teruo Ishii [Chapters 1-6], Akira Mitsuwa [co-director, Chapter 3], Koreyoshi Akasaka [co-director, Chapter 3], Akira Miwa [Chapter 7], Chogi Akasaka [Chapters 8-9]; Screenplay, Ichiro Miyagawa, Shinsuke Niegishi, Ishiro Miyagawa; Directors of Photography, Takashi Watanabe, Akira Watanabe, Hiroshi Suzuki, Nobu Boshi, Kiminobu Okada [Chapters 8-9]; Music, Chumei Watanabe, Sadao Nagase [Chapters 8-9].

CAST: Ken Utsui (Starman [Super Giant]), Junko Ikeuchi [Chapters 1-2 only], Minako Yamada [Chapters 3-4], Utako Mitsuya [Chapters 5-6], Chisako Tahara [Chapter 7], Reiko Seto [Chapter 8], Terumi Hoshi [Chapter 9], Minoru Takada, Ryo Iwashita, Kan Hayashi, Akira Tamura, Hiroshi Asami, Teruhisha Ikeda, Junko Ikeuchi, Shoji Nakayama, Sachihiro Osawa, Fumiko Miyata, Kami Ashita, Reiko Seto, Tomohiko Otani, Joji Ohara, Shinsuke Mikimoto.

A Fuji Eiga Co., Ltd. Production. A Shintoho Co., Ltd. Release. Western Electric Mirrorphonic Recording. Some chapters filmed in Shintoho-Scope (?). Black and white. A multi-chapter serial/series. Original films are as follows:

1. *Kotetso no kyojin—Supa Jyaiantsu* ("The Steel Giant—Super Giant"). 49 minutes. Released July 30, 1957.
2. *Zoku kotetsu no kyojin—Supa Jyaiantsu* ("Follow-up to the Adventures of the Steel Giant"). 52 minutes. Released August 16, 1957.
3. *Kotetsu no Kyojin—Supa Jyaiantsu: Kaiseijin no mayo* ("The Steel Giant—Super Giant: The Evil Castle of the Mysterious Planet People"). 48 minutes. Released October 1957.
4. *Kotetsu no kyojin—Supa Jyaiantsu: chikyu metsubo sunzen* ("The Steel Giant—Super Giant: The Earth Will Be Annihilated Soon"). 39 minutes. Released October 8, 1957.
5. *Supa Jyaiantsu: jinko eisei to jinrui no hametsu* ("Super Giant: Satellites and the Destruction of Mankind"). 39 minutes. Released December 28, 1957.
6. *Supa Jyaiantsu: uchusen to jinko eisei no gekitotsu* ("Super Giant: The Spaceships and Satellites Duel"). 39 minutes. Released January 3, 1958.

7. *Supa Jyaiantsu: uchu kaijin shutsugen* ("Super Giant: Mysterious Spacemen Appear"). 45 minutes. Released April 28, 1958.
8. *Zoku Supa Jyaiantsu (dai hachibu): akuma no keshin* (Further Adventures of Super Giant [Chapter 8]: Devil Incarnate"). 57 minutes. Released March 27, 1959.
9. *Zoku Supa Jyaiantsu (dai kyubu): dokunga ookoku* ("Further Adventures of Super Giant [Chapter 9]: Kingdom of the Venomous Moth"). 57 minutes. Released April 24, 1959.

U.S. VERSION: Never released theatrically in the United States. Selected chapters released directly to television by Medallion TV (i.e. Walter H. Manley Enterprises, Inc.). English-dubbed. Unlike American serials, these films did not form one continuous narrative. Chapters 1-2, 3-4 and 5-6 were two-part stories; 7, 8, & 9 were independent entities. Chapters were recut for U.S. television in 1964-65. Sources differ as to corresponding chapters; an approximation follows: chapters 1-2 were recut as *Atomic Rulers* (aka *Atomic Rulers of the World*), running 74 minutes; chapters 3-4 became *Invaders from Space*, running 79 minutes; chapters 5-6 became *Attack from Space*, running 74 minutes; chapter 7 was recut as *Evil Brain from Outer Space*, running 78 minutes. Chapters 8-9 were apparently never issued in the United States. Alternate titles: (Chapter 1) *The Steelman from Outer Space*, (2) *Rescue from Outer Space,* (3) *Invaders from the Planets*, (4) *The Earth in Danger*, (5) *The Sinister Space-Ships*, (6) *The Destruction of the Space-fleet*. No MPAA rating.

Superman on Gale / Kaze no tengu ("Wind of the Long-Nosed Goblin"). Director, Keiichi Ozawa; Screenplay, Seiji Hoshikawa, based on an original story by Goyu Kojima; Director of Photography, Minoru Yokoyama; Art Director, Toshiyuki Matsui; Music, Hajime Kaburagi.

CAST: Hideki Takahashi (Kusanagi-Roppeita), Masako Izumi (Toki), Isao Natsuyagi (Uzuki-Kyonosuke), Seiichiro Kameishi (Tarao-Matahei), Yoshiro Aoki (Aochi-Godayu), Shoki Fukae (Nachi-Hanbei).

A Nikkatsu Corp. Production. Fujicolor. NikkatsuScope. 83 minutes. Released November 14, 1970.

U.S. VERSION: Released by Toho International Co., Ltd. English subtitles. Alternate title: *The Haunted Samurai*. 83 minutes. No MPAA rating. Released July 12, 1971.

The Surf / Shiosai ("The Surf"). Producer, Tomoyuki Tanaka; Director, Senkichi Taniguchi; Screenplay, Senkichi Taniguchi and Shinichiro Nakamura, based on the novel by Yukio Mishima; Director of Photography, Taiichi Kankura; Art Director, Takashi Matsuyama; Music, Toshio Mayuzumi.

CAST: Akira Kubo (Shinji), Kyoko Aoyama (Hatsue, *his sweetheart*), Yoichi Tachikawa (Yasuo, *his rival*), Sadako Sawamura (Shinji's mother), Toshiro Mifune (captain), Minoru Takashima, Kichijiro Veda, Keiko Miya, Daisuke Kato, Yoshio Kosugi, Fumiko Homma.

A Toho Co., Ltd. Production. Black and white. Academy ratio. 94 minutes. Released 1954.

U.S. VERSION: Released by Topaz Film Co. English subtitles 94 minutes. Remade by Nikkatsu in 1969, Toho in 1971 (directed by Shiro Moritani) and 1975, and Hori Productions in 1985. No MPAA rating. Released May 3, 1957.

The Swamp / Kaidan Chidori-ga-fuchi ("Ghost Story: Depth of Chidori"). Director, Eiichi Koishi.

CAST: Kinnosuke Nakamura, Yoshio Wakamizu.

A Toei Co., Ltd. Production. Black and white (processed by Toei Chemistry Co., Ltd.). Academy ratio. 66 minutes. Released 1956.

U.S. VERSION: Distributor, if any, is undetermined. International title: *Ghost of Chidori-Ga-Fuchi*. Released 1957 (?).

Sweet Sweat / Amai ase ("Sweet Sweat"). Producers, Ichiro Sato and Hideyuki Shino; Director, Shiro Toyoda; Screenplay, Yoko Mizuki, based on her teleplay; Director of Photography, Kozo Okazaki; Music, Hikaru Hayashi.

CAST: Machiko Kyo (bar girl), Keiji Sada, Junko Ikeuchi, Miyuki Kuwano.

A Toho Co., Ltd. Production. Black and white. Toho Scope. 120 minutes. Released 1964.

U.S. VERSION: Released by Toho International Co., Ltd. English subtitles. 120 minutes. No MPAA rating. Released September 24, 1965.

Swirling Butterflies / Onna no keisatsu, midarecho ("Women's Police, Swirling Butterflies"). Director, Keiichi Ozawa; Screenplay, Ryuzo Nakanishi, based on the story by Sueyuki Kajiyama; Director of Photography, Minoru Yokoyama; Art Director, Takeo Kimura; Music, Hajime Kaburagi.

CAST: Akira Kobayashi (Masaaki Kagari), Kumi Mizuno (Yuko), Ryohei Uchida (Kuroki), Asao Uchida (Tahei Daigo), Megumi Matsumoto (Yoko, *Kuroki's blind sister*), Eiji Go (Shiro), Noriko Maki (Noriko), Junko Natsu (Reiko), Mina Aoe.

A Nikkatsu Corp. Production. Fujicolor. NikkatsuScope. 86 minutes. Released July 11, 1970.

U.S. VERSION: Distributor, if any, is undetermined. English subtitled version available. The 4th and final film of the "Women's Policeman" series (1969-70). 86 minutes. No MPAA rating.

The Sword of Doom / Daibosatsu toge ("A Pass of Great Buddha"). Executive Producers, Sanezumi Fujimoto and Masayuki Sato; Director, Kihachi Okamoto; Screenplay, Shinobu Hashimoto, based on the story by Kaizan Nakazato; Director of Photography, Hiroshi Murai; Editor, Yoshitami Kuroiwa; Music, Masaru Sato.

CAST: Tatsuya Nakadai (Ryunosuke Tsukue), Toshiro Mifune (Toranosuke Shimada), Yuzo Kayama (Hyoma Utsuki), Michiyo Aratama (Ohama), Ichiro Nakaya (Bunnojo Utsuki), Ko Nishimura (uncle), Eisei Amamoto (Lord Kamio), Kamatari Fujiwara (grandfather), Yoko Naito, Kei Sato, Tadao Nakamaru.

A Takarazuka Film Co., Ltd./Toho Co., Ltd. Production. A Toho Co., Ltd. Release. Black and white. Toho Scope. 120 minutes. Released February 1966.

U.S. VERSION: Released by Toho International Co., Ltd. English subtitles. Letterboxed home video version available. 120 minutes. No MPAA rating. Released July 1, 1966.

The Sword of Penitence / Zange no Yaiba ("Sword of Penitence"). Directors, Yasujiro Ozu and Torajiro Saito; Screenplay, Kogo Noda, based on an idea by Yasujiro Ozu and the film *Kick-In* by George Fitzmaurice; Director of Photography, Isamu Aoki.

CAST: Saburo Azuma, Kunimatsu Ogawa, Eiko Atsumi, Iida Choko.

A Shochiku Co., Ltd. Production. Filmed at Shochiku-Kamata Studios. Silent with Benshi. Black and white. Academy ratio. 70 minutes. Released October 14, 1927.

U.S. VERSION: Never released theatrically in the United States. A lost film.

Sword of Vengeance / Kosure ookami–ko wo kashi ude kashi tsukatsuru ("White Wolf with a Kid"). Executive Producer, Shintaro Katsu; Director, Kenji Misumi; Screenplay, Kazuo Koike; Story, Kazuo Koike and Goseki Kojima; Director of Photography, Chishi Makiura; Art Director, Yoshinobu Nishioka; Lighting, Hiroshi Mima; Editor, Toshio Taniguchi; Music, Eiken Sakurai; Sound Recordist, Tsuchitaro Hayashi; Sound, Toho Recording Centre; Sound Effects, Toho Sound Effects Group; Special Effects, Toho Special Effects Group.

CAST: Tomisaburo Wakayama (Itto Ogami), Akihiro Tomikawa (Daigaro), Go Kato, Yuko Hama, Isao Yamagatu, Michitaro Mizushima, Ichiro Nakaya, Sayoko Kato, Daigo Kusano, Tomoko Mayama, Fumio Watanabe, Shigeru Tsuyuguchi, Yunosuke Ito, Yomiso Kato, Asao Uchida, Keiko Fujita, Sanburo Date.

A Katsu Production Co., Ltd./Toho Co., Ltd. Production. Color (processed by Tokyo Laboratory, Ltd.). Panavision. 83 minutes. Released 1972.

U.S. VERSION: Released by Toho International Co., Ltd. English subtitles. Reissued in English-dubbed version in August 1983 by Columbia Pictures Industries, Inc. as *Lightning Swords of Death*, with prints by Metrocolor and an MPAA rating of "R." 10-12 minutes of footage was later incorporated into the next film in the series, *Shogun Assassin* (1972). 83 minutes. No MPAA rating. Released August 1973.

Swords of Death / Shinken Shobu ("Serious Game"). Producers, Hideyuki Shiino and Shunji Okij; Director, Tomu Uchida; Screenplay, Daisuke Ito, based on the story by Eiji Yoshikawa; Director of Photography, Tokuzo Kuroda; Art Director, Tomo Nakafuru; Music, Taichiro Kosugi.

CAST: Kinnosuke Nakamura (Musashi Miyamoto), Rentaro Mikuni (Baiken Shishido), Hideko Okiyama (Baiken's wife), Hiroshi Tanaka, Koji Iwamoto, Chotaro Togin.

A Toho Co., Ltd. Production. Black and white. Toho Scope. 76 minutes. Released February 20, 1971.

U.S. VERSION: Released by Toho International Co., Ltd. English subtitled version available. Home video title: *Musashi Miyamoto–Swords of Death*. Director Uchida and star Nakamura had previously filmed five Musashi Miyamoto features at Toei (1961-65); this entry is not officially part of the series. Other Musashi Miyamoto adaptations include *Musashi Miyamoto* (1944), and Hiroshi Inagaki's *Samurai* trilogy (1954-56). 76 minutes. No MPAA rating. Released February 17, 1976.

Swords of the Space Ark. Producers, Kanetake Ochiai, Keizo Shichijo, Akimasa Ito, Masahide Shinozuka; Director, Minoru Yamada; Teleplay, Masaru Igami; Music, Shunsuke Kikuchi; Special Effects, Nobuo Yajima; Creators, Shotaro Ishimori, Masahiro Noda, Hiro Matsuda, and Kinji Fukasaku.

CAST: Hiroyuki "Henry" Sanada, others unidentified.

A Japanese teleseries re-edited to feature length for American television, and never released theatrically in Japan. A Toei Co., Ltd. Production. 16mm. Toeicolor.

U.S. VERSION: Never released theatrically in the United States. Released directly to television by New Hope Entertainment in 1981. English-dubbed. Producer/Director/Screenplay, Bunker Jenkins; Supervising Editor and Associate Producer, Michael Part; Editor, Floyd Ingram, Additional Effects, George Budd; English Production, 3B Productions; Postproduction, Gomillion Sound, Inc., American Film Factory; Music, Douglas Lackey and Joseph Zappala; Sound Design, Joseph Zappala. Derived from the teleseries "Uchu-kara no messeji: ginga taisen" ("Message from Space: Galactic Battle"), which ran for 27 episodes in 1978-79 on the NET (TV Asahi) network. International title (?): *Message from Space: Galactic Battle*. Running time of feature version also given at 121 minutes (which seems highly unlikely) and 94 minutes. 70 minutes. No MPAA rating.

Takamaru and Kikumaru. Director, Santaro Marune; Screenplay, Ryuta Mine and Noburo Mizukami; Director of Photography, Kiyomi Kuroda.

CAST: Kinshiro Matsumoto, Kotobuki Hanemoto, Hiroshi Nawa, Kiku Hojo, Kyoko Izumi.

A Shochiku Co., Ltd. Production. Shochikucolor. Academy ratio (?). 144 minutes. Released 1959.

U.S. VERSION: Released by Shochiku Films of America, Inc. 139 minutes. No MPAA rating. Released 1959.

Takarajima Ensei ("Trip to Treasure Island") (credits unavailable).

CAST: Kenichi "Enoken" Enomoto, Akira Kishii, Kiiton Masuda, Hibari Misora, Takako Kawada.

A Toei Co., Ltd. Production. Toeicolor (?). Academy ratio (?) 87 minutes. Released 1956.

U.S. VERSION: Distributor, if any, is undetermined. International title: *Peach Boy*.

Take Care, Red Riding Hood / Akazukinchan kiotsukete ("Take Care, Red Riding Hood"). Director, Shiro Moritani; Screenplay, Shiro Moritani and Toshiro Ide, based on the story by Kaoru Shoji; Director of Photography, Choichi Nakai; Art Director, Iwao Akune; Music, Taku Izumi.

CAST: Yusuke Okada (Kaoru), Kazuyo Mori (Yumi), Tetsuo Tomikawa (Kobayashi), Akiko Mori.

A Toho Co., Ltd. Production. Fujicolor. Toho Scope. 90 minutes. Released August 29, 1970.

Kinuyo Tanaka (left) and Masayuki Mori (right) in Kenji Mizoguchi's haunting *Tales of Ugetsu* (aka *Ugetsu*, 1953).

U.S. VERSION: Released by Toho International Co., Ltd. English subtitles. 90 minutes. No MPAA rating. Released 1971 (?).

Takeshi—Childhood Days / Shonen Jidai ("Boyhood Period"). Executive Producer, Fujio Fujiko; Director, Masahiro Shinoda; Screenplay, Taichi Yamada, based on original stories "The Long Road" by Hyozo Kashiwabara, and "Shonen Jidai" by Fujio Fujiko; Director of Photography, Tatsuo Suzuki; Art Director, Takeo Kimura; Music, Shinichiro Ikebe.

CAST: Tetsuya Fujita (Shinji Kazama), Yuji Horioka (Takeshi Ohara), Katsuhisa Yamazaki (Futoshi Tanabe), Noritake Kohinata (Kensuke Sudo), Minako Saeki (Atsuko Koyama).

A Hyogensha Production. A Toho Co., Ltd. Release. Color. Spherical wide screen. 117 minutes. Released 1990.

U.S. VERSION: Released by Toho International Co., Ltd. English subtitles. 117 minutes. No MPAA rating. Released November 2, 1990.

Tale of a Carpenter / Daiku taiheiki ("Peaceful Tale of a Carpenter"). Director, Shiro Toyoda.

CAST: Hisaya Morishige, Hajime Hana, Makoto Fujita, Junko Ikeuchi.

A Toho Co., Ltd. Production. Eastman Color. Toho Scope. 101 minutes. Released 1965.

U.S. VERSION: Released by Toho International Co., Ltd. English subtitles. 101 minutes. No MPAA rating. Released May 1966.

A Tale of Genji / Genji monogatari ("Genji Story") **[animated]**. Producers, Atsumi Tashiro and Masato Hara; Director, Gisaburo Sugii; Screenplay, Tomomi Tsutsui, based on an original story by Murasaki Shikibu; Director of Photography, Shigeo Sugimura; Music, Haruomi Hosono.

VOICE CHARACTERIZATIONS: (undetermined).

A Herald Ace, Inc. Production. Color. Spherical wide screen (?). 105 minutes. Released 1987.

U.S. VERSION: Distributor, if any, is undetermined. No MPAA rating.

Tales of Ugetsu / Ugetsu monogatari ("Tales of Ugetsu"). Producer, Masaichi Nagata; Associate Producer Kyuichi Tsuji; Director, Kenji Mizoguchi; Screenplay, Matsutaro Kawaguchi and Yoshikata Yoda, adapted from the stories "Asaji ga yado" ("The Inn at Asaji; English title: "The House of Wild Gramineons"); and "Jasei no in" ("Serpent of Desire; English title, "The Maliciousness of the Snake's Evil") by Akinari [Shusei] Ueda, from the collection *Ugetsu monogatari*, and on the story, "Le decoration," by Guy de Maupassant; Director of Photography, Kazuo Miyagawa; Choreography, Kinshichi Kodera; Art Director, Kisaku Ito; Scenery, Tasaburo Ota; Settings, Uichiro Yamamoto; Costumes, Shima Yoshimi; Period Authenticity of the Costumes (Costume Design), Kusune Kainosho; Pottery Consultant, Zengoro Eiraku; Lighting, Kenichi Okamoto; Recording, Iwao Otani; Sound Daiei Recording Studio; Music, Fumio Hayasaka, Ichiro Saito; Musical Direction, Fumio Hayasaka; Editor, Mitsuji [Mitsuzo] Miyata; Makeup, Zenya Fukushima; Hair Stylist, Ritsu Hanai.

CAST: Masayuki Mori (Genjuro), Eitaro Ozawa (Tobei Nakanogo), Machiko Kyo (Lady Wakasa Kitsuki) Kinuyo Tanaka (Miyagi), Mitsuko Mito (Ohama), Sugisaku Aoyama (old priest), Ryosuke Kagawa (village master), Kichijiro Tsuchida (silk merchant), Mitsusaburo Ramon (*Tamba* captain), Ichisaburo Sawamura (Genichi), Kikue Mori (Ukan [Ukon]), Syozo Nambu (Shinto priest), Ichiro Amano (boatman).

A Daiei Motion Picture Company, Ltd. Production. Western Electric Mirrophonic recording. Black and white (processed by Daiei Laboratory). Academy ratio. 96 minutes. Released March 26, 1953.

U.S. VERSION: Released by Edward Harrison Releasing. English subtitles. A Harrison & Davidson Presentation. Originally advertised as above, but reissued by Janus Films as *Ugetsu*. International title: *Tales After the Rain*. 96 minutes. No MPAA Rating. Released September 20, 1954.

Talk of the Town Tora-san / Otoko wa tsuraiyo — Uwasa no Torajiro ("It's Tough to Be a Man — Torajiro's Rumor"). Producer, Kiyoshi Shimazu; Director, Yoji Yamada; Screenplay, Yoji Yamada and Yoshitaka Asama, based on characters created by Yoji Yamada; Director of Photography, Tetsuo Takaba; Art Director, Mitsuo Idegawa; Editor, Iwao Ishii; Music, Naozumi Yamamoto.

CAST: Kiyoshi Atsumi (Torajiro "Tora-san" Kuruma), Chieko Baisho (Sakura Suwa, *his sister*), Reiko Ohara (young woman), Pinko Izumi (jilted girl), Hideo Murata (the young woman's husband), Takashi Shimura (Professor Suwa, *Hiroshi's father*), Masami Shimojo (Ryuzo Kuruma, *Tora's uncle*), Chieko Misaki (Tsune Kuruma, *Tora's aunt*), Hisao Dazai (Umetaro, *the printing shop president*), Gajiro Sato (Genko), Gin Maeda (Hiroshi Suwa, *Sakura's husband*), Chishu Ryu (Gozen-sama, *the temple priest*), Hayato Nakamura (Mitsuo, *Tora's nephew*).

A Shochiku Co., Ltd. Production. Color. Shochiku GrandScope. 105 minutes. No MPAA rating. Released December 28, 1978.

U.S. VERSION: Released by Shochiku Films of America, Inc. English subtitles. The 22nd "Tora-san" feature. Followed by *Tora-san the Matchmaker* (1979). 105 minutes. No MPAA rating. Released September 28, 1979.

Tampopo ("Dandelion"). Producers, Juzo Itami, Yasushi Tamaoki, and Seigo Hosogoe; Director/Screenplay, Juzo Itami; Director of Photography, Masaki Tamura; Art Director, Takeo Kimura; Lighting, Yukio Inoue; Music, Kunihiko Murai, with selections from Gustav Mahler, performed by the Tokyo City Philharmonic Orchestra, and conducted by Hiroshi Koizumi; Synthesizer, Minoru Mukoya and Shikou Anzai; Sound Recording, Fumio Hashimoto; Sound Recording Assistants, Daisuke Hayashi, Makoto Katsuki, Nobuhiro Chibayama; Nikkatsu Studio; Sound Effects, Masatoshi Saito; Action Choreographer, Kanichi Uetake; Editor, Akira Suzuki; Costume Designer, Emiko Kogo; Wardrobe, Kunio Nakayama; Makeup, Kenji Zuga (design), Masaji Pakase; Food Designer, Izumi Ishimori; Woking Stylist,

Seiko Ogawa; Dialect Coach, Joko Onaru; Graphic Designs, Kenichi Samura; Casting, Kosaburo Sasaoka; Assistant Directors, Kazuki Shiroyama, Kubota Nobuhiro, Kenji Suzuki; Assistant Camermen, Norimichi Kasamatsu, Takashi Moro, Yoko Mimori, Hidemi Ito; Visual Effects, Yasuo Ochiai.

CAST: Tsutomu Yamazaki (Goro), Nouko Miyamoto (Tampopo), Koji Yakusho (gangster in the white suit), Ken Watanabe (Gun), Rikiya Yasuoka (Pisken), Kinzo Sakura (Shohei), Mampei Ikeuchi (Tabo, *Tampopo's son*), Yoshi Kato (master of ramen making), Shuji Otaki (rich old man), Fukumi Kuroda (gangster's mistress), Setsuko Shinoi (rich old man's mistress), Yoriko Doguchi (girl oyster-fisher), Masahiko Tsugawa (supermarket manager), Moto Noguchi, Yoshihei Saga, Tsuguho Narita, Akio Tanaka, Choei Takahashi (company executives), Toshimune Kato (office junior), Isao Hashizume (waiter), Akira Kubo (rude owner of competing ramen shop), Saburo Satoki (owner of efficient ramen shop), Mario Abe (ramen stand owner), Hitoshi Takagi (ramen shop owner in Chinatown), Tadao Futami (his neighbor), Akio Yokoyama (Chinese ramen chef), Masato Tsujimura (small vagrant), Ei Takami (thin vagrant), Gilliark Amagasaki (long-faced vagrant), Norio Matsui (fat vagrant), Noburo Sato (vagrant with red nose), Tadakazu Kitami (dentist), Kyoko Oguma (lady owner of soba shop), Toshiya Fujita (man with toothache), Izuma Hara (old lady who pinches everything), Hisashi Igawa (man who runs to see dying wife), Kazuyo Mita (dying wife), Nobuo Nakamura (intended victim of con man), Naritoshi Hayashi (con man being conned), Ryutaro Otomo (master of ramen eating), Mariko Okada (teacher of etiquette).

An Itami Productions/New Century Producers Production. Color. Spherical Panavision. 114 minutes. Released November 1985.

U.S. VERSION: Released by New Yorker Films. English subtitles. The Akira Kubo listed above is not the same as the Toho star of the 1950s and 1960s. 114 minutes. No MPAA rating. Released December 1986.

Tange-Sazen ("Tange-Sazen"). Director, Seiichiro Uchikawa; Screenplay, Seiichiro Uchikawa, based on the novel by Fubo Hayashi; Director of Photography, Yoshikawa Ototu.

CAST: Tetsuro Tamba (Tange-Sazen *and* Genzaburo Yagyu), Keisuke Sonoi (Genojo Yagyu), Haruko Wanibuchi (Hagino), Michiko Saga (Ofuji).

A Shochiku Co., Ltd. Production. Color. Panavision (?). 95 minutes. Released 1963.

U.S. VERSION: Released by Shochiku Films of America, Inc. English subtitles. 95 minutes. No MPAA rating. Released May 1977.

Taro, the Dragon Boy / Tatsunoko Taro ("Dragon Boy Taro") **[animated]**. Producer, Chiaki Imada; Director, Kiriro Urayama; Screenplay, Kiriro Urayama, based on the story by Miyoku Matsutani; Director of Photography, Yoshihiro Yamada and Yuichi Takanoshi; Art Director, Isamu Tsuchida; Music, Riichiro Manabe.

VOICE CHARACTERIZATIONS: (undetermined).

A Toei Animation Studio (Tokyo) Production. Eastman Color. ToeiScope (?). 75 minutes. Released 1979.

U.S. VERSION: Distributor, if any, is undetermined.

Tasmania Story / Tasumania monogatari ("Tasmania Story"). Producer, Hiroaki Shikanai; Director, Yasuo Furuhata; Screenplay, Narito Kaneko; Director of Photography, Junichiro Hayashi; Music, Joe Hisaishi.

CAST: Kunie Tanaka, Hiroko Yakushimaru, Naoto Ogata, Tomoshi Taga, Jinpachi Nezu.

A Fuji Television Network, Inc. Production. Filmed on location in Australia and Tasmania (?). Color. Spherical wide screen (?). 110 minutes. Released 1990.

U.S. VERSION: Distributor, if any, is undetermined.

Tatsu/Doburoku no Tatsu ("Tatsu of Local Sake"). Executive Producer, Tomoyuki Tanaka; Director, Hiroshi Inagaki; Screenplay, Masato Ide and Toshio Yasumi, based on the novel by

Yoshio Nakae; Director of Photography, Kazuo Yamada; Music, Kan Ishii; Assistant Director, Masahiro Takase.

CAST: Toshiro Mifune (Tatsu), Tatsuya Mihashi, Chikage Awashima, Junko Ikeuchi, Ichiro Arishima, Yoshio Tsuchiya, Sonomi Nakajima, Jun Tazaki, Soji Kiyokawa, Ryosuke Kagawa, Chieko Nakakita, Yoshio Kosugi, Sachio Sakai.

A Toho Co., Ltd. Production. Agfacolor. Toho Scope. 115 minutes. Released 1962.

U.S. VERSION: Released by Toho International Co., Ltd. English subtitles. 115 minutes. No MPAA rating. Released November 22, 1962.

The Tattered Banner / Ranru no hata ("The Tattered Banner"). Director, Kozaburo Yoshimura; Screenplay, Ken Miyamoto; Director of Photography, Yoshio Miyajima; Music, Kazuo Okada.

CAST: Rentaro Mikuni, Ryo Tamura, Atsuo Nakamura.

A "Ranru no hata" Production Committee Production. Color. Spherical wide screen (?). 112 minutes. Released 1974.

U.S. VERSION: Distributor, if any, is undetermined. No MPAA rating.

Tattooed Swordswoman / Kaidan noboriryu ("Ghost Story: Rising Dragon"). Producer, Hideo Koi and Shiro Sasaki; Director, Teruo Ishii; Screenplay, Teruo Ishii and Yoshida Sone; Director of Photography, Shigeru Kitazumi; Art Director, Akinori Satani; Editor, Osamu Ionue; Music, Hajime Kaburagi; Sound Recording, Nikkatsu Sound Studio.

CAST: Mieko Kaji (Akemi), Hoki Tokuda (Aiko), Makoto Sato (Masaichi), Yoko Tagaki, Hideo Sunazuka, Toru Abe, Yuzo Hanumi, Yoshi Kato, Bumon Kahara.

A Nikkatsu Corp. Production. Fujicolor. NikkatsuScope. 84 minutes. Released June 20, 1970.

U.S. VERSION: Released by Toho International Co., Ltd. English subtitles. Alternate titles: *The Blind Woman's Curse*, *The Haunted Life of a Dragon-Tattooed Lass*. 84 minutes. No MPAA rating. Released August 6, 1971.

Tattooed Temptress / Irezumi muzan ("Cruel Tattoo"). Director, Hideo Sekikawa; Screenplay, Kikuma Shimoiizaka and Toru Ichijo, based on an original story by Akimitsu Takagi; Director of Photography, Masao Kosugi; Art Director, Koji Uno; Music, Masao Yagi.

CAST: Chizuko Arai (Osayo), Toru Abe (Tonomura), Yusuke Kawazu (Shinnosuke), Kikko Matsuoka (Okimi), Eiji Okada (tattooer), Chikako Miyagi (his wife).

A Shochiku Co., Ltd. Production. Eastman Color. Shochiku GrandScope. 88 minutes. Released April 13, 1968.

U.S. VERSION: Released by Shochiku Films of America, Inc. English subtitles. 88 minutes. No MPAA rating. Released December 12, 1973.

A Taxing Woman / Marusa no onna ("Woman of Marusa"). Executive Producer, Juzo Itami; Producers, Yasushi Tamaoki and Seigo Hosogoe; Director/Screenplay, Juzo Itami; Director of Photography, Yonezo Maeda; Editor, Akira Suzuki; Art Director, Shuji Nakamura; Music, Toshiyuki Honda; Music Producer, Naoki Tachikawa; Choreography, Atsumi Miyazaki; Costumes, Emiko Koai; Wardrobe, Masami Saito; Makeup, Midori Konuma; Sound Recording, Osamu Onodera; Sound Transfers, Akira Udagawa; Sound Effects, Masatoshi Saito; Special Effects, Yasuo Ochiai, (illustration) Tetsu Uehara; Production Manager, Takashi Kawasaki; Casting, Kozaburo Sasaoka; Assistant Directors, Nobehiro Kubota, Ikki Shirayama, Hatashi Aida, Hiromitsu Tosaka, Sukehiro Sato; Assistant Cameramen, Hiroshi Takase, Akisato Ueno, Yasuhito Hironaka and Minoru Ishiyama; Lighting, Akio Katsura; VTR Operator, Nagao Yasutatsu; Graphics, Kenichi Samura.

CAST: Nobuko Miyamoto (Ryoko Itakura), Tsutomu Yamazaki (Hideki Gondo), Masahiko Tsugawa (Hanamura), Yasuo Daichi (Ijuin), Eitaro Ozawa (pinball parlor's tax accountant), Shiro Ito (pinball parlor owner), Shuji

Otaki (Tsuyuguchi), Mach Fumiake (Akiyama), Daisuke Yamashita (Taro Gondo), Michiyo Yokoyama (woman accountant at hotel), Shinsuke Ashida (Kihachiro Ninagawa), Keiju Kobayashi (Chief of Investigating Department), Mariko Okada (Mitsuko Sugino), Kinzo Sakura (Kaneko), Hajime Aso (Himeda), Kiriko Shimizu (Kazue Kenmochi), Kazuyo Matsui (Hisami Shimaoka), Hideo Takarada (Shigekichi Ishii), Machiko Watanabe (nurse), Shotaro Takeuchi (Riheibi Mochida), Mitsuhiko Kiyoshisa (Gondo's chauffeur), Akira Shiozi (realtor), Koichi Ueda (Ninagawa's lieutenant), Yusuke Nanu, Junbo Sugita, Minoru Shiga, Hideaki Mishishiba, Usaburo Oshima, Atsushi Yamamoto, and Sachikazu Kuno (Ninagawa's thugs), Toshio Tomogane and Yusuke Koike (detectives), Bengaru Hatakeyama and Akiko Hatakeyama (young couple), Masahiro Yokota (child), Yuzuko Kinoshita (old lady), Masato Tsujimura (Kikuchi), Eichi Kikuchi and Kojiro Nakamura (Kikuchi's bodyguards), Susumu Honda (politician's secretary), Makoto Kakeda and Sachiyuki Shiotani (shop assistants), Shigeo Ikeda (tailor), Giriyaku Amagasaki (man with lottery ticket), Hiroshi Yanagitani (food store owner), Tokuko Sugiyama (food store owner's wife), Bitsatu Sato (linen service president), Isao Hashizume (banker), Yoshihiro Kato (Yamada), Zenpei Saga (tax official), Tadashi Okuno (director), Hideaki Ezuno, Katsuhiko Kobayashi, Masahiro Ito, Yuzo Mikawa, and Ryo Akashi (chief investigating officials), Hanbe Kawai, Masaki Yonekura, Takashi Yagi, Takashi Kanematsu, Tetsuri Ito, Sadami Sakamoto, Takashi Sasaki, Ryuta Kashiwagi, Sosuke Kaji, Takuji Iwao, Kazumasa Takemoto, Kaizo Hori, Masaru Sakurai, So Saito, Retsu Kuraya, Mitsuki Arima, Kazushige Osawa, Buntaro Aoyanagi, and Kejiro Shiga (investigating officials), Masatoshi Kimura, Hiroyuki Yamada, Ryodai Arai, Yusuke Tozawa, Yoshiaki Sugitani, Satoshi Yoshida, Satohiro Sakai, Tsutomu Ichikawa, Shinji Nomura, Yasuo Shirasaka, Kaido Yamazaki, Mari Sakai, Junko Ishida, Miyako Chiba, Mitsuru Uchida, and Nobuyuki Suzuki (other officials), Yorie Yamashita (girl), Kazuya Kosaka (middle-aged man), Banju Takeda (woman who swallows a memo), Chigusa Takayama (woman on the roof), Shingo Uchida and Shigeya Maru (hotel employees), Norisachi Okisasaki (screaming man), Mami Takagi (screaming woman), Harumi Masachika and Tomomi Akimoto (another couple), Ryohei Takaoka, Teiko Hara, Masayuki Fusegi, and Teratasu Tengen (hotel owners), Shohei Matsumoto (man on bicycle), Hashiru Funada (2nd man on bicycle), Hiroshi Tanaka, Kaiko Shintani, Kyoko Hirata, Tomoko Sakuma, Sanae Tomita, and Chizuko Yamada (bank employees), Ryuji Dan, Hiroshi Suzuki, Tsuyoshi Sato, Mitsuhiro Uehara, Miho Tanaka, and Eiji Tomita (security police), Setsuko Shinoi (maid), Naomi Oka (beauty parlor proprietress), Akio Tanaka (bank manager), Tsukiho Narita (senior official), Nagahide Takahashi (official), Akiko Ezawa.

An Itami Productions/New Century Producers Production. A Toho Co., Ltd. Release. Dolby Stereo. Color. Spherical wide screen. 127 minutes. Released 1987.

U.S. VERSION: Released by Fox/Lorber. English subtitles. English subtitled version monophonic. Followed by *A Taxing Woman's Return* (1988). 127 minutes. No MPAA rating. Released 1989.

(Juzo Itami's) *A Taxing Woman's Return / Marusa no onna 2* ("Woman of Marusa 2"). Producers, Juzo Itami, Yasushi Tamaoki, and Seigo Hosogoe; Director/Screenplay, Juzo Itami; Director of Photography, Yonezo Maeda; Art Director, Shuji Nakamura; Editor, Akira Suzuki; Music, Toshiyuki Honda.

CAST: Nobuko Miyamoto (Ryoko Itakura), Rentaro Mikuni (Teppei Onizawa), Toru Masuoka (Inspector Mishima), Masahiko Tsugawa (Assistant Chief Inspector Hanamura), Tetsuro Tamba (Chief Inspector Sadohara), Koichi Ueda (Nekota), Mansaku Fuwa ("Shorty" Masa), Haruko Kato (Mrs. Onizawa, *the Holy Matriarch*), Chishu Ryu.

An Itami Productions Production. A

Toho Co., Ltd. Release. Dolby Stereo. Color. Spherical wide screen. 127 minutes. Released 1988.

U.S. VERSION: Released by New Yorker Films. English subtitles. English subtitled version monophonic. 127 minutes. No MPAA rating. Released June 1989.

Tea and Rice / Ochazuke no aji ("The Flavor of Green Tea Over Rice"). Director, Yasujiro Ozu; Screenplay, Yasujiro Ozu and Kogo Noda; Director of Photography, Yushun Atsuta; Assistant Director, Shohei Imamura.

CAST: Shin Saburi, Michiyo Kogure, Koji Tsuruta, Keiko Tsushima, Kuniko Miyake, Chikage Awashima, Chishu Ryu, Yuko Mochizuki.

A Shochiku Co., Ltd. Production. Filmed at Shochiku-Ofuna Studios. Black and white. Academy ratio. 115 minutes. Released October 1, 1952.

U.S. VERSION: Released by Shochiku Films of America, Inc. English subtitles. 115 minutes. No MPAA rating. Released November 20, 1964. Reissued by New Yorker films as *The Flavor of Green Tea Over Rice*.

Teahouse of the August Moon. Producer, Jack Cummings; Director, Daniel Mann; Screenplay, John Patrick, based on his play and the book by Vern J. Sneider; Director of Photography, John Alton; Editor, Harold F. Kress; Art Director, William A. Horning and Eddie Imazu; Music, Saul Chaplin, with Okinawan songs arranged by Kikuko Kanai.

CAST: Marlon Brando (Sakini), Glenn Ford (Captain Fisby), Machiko Kyo (Lotus Blossom), Eddie Albert (Captain McLean), Paul Ford (Colonel Purdy), Jun Negami (Mr. Seiko), Nijiko Kiyokawa (Miss Higa Jiga), Mitsuko Sawamura (little Japanese girl), Henry "Harry" Morgan (Sgt. Gregovich), Kichizaemon Sarumaru (Mr. Hokaida), Frank Tokunaga (Mr. Omura), Raynum K. Tsukamoto (Mr. Oshira).

A Jack Cummings Production, in association with Metro-Goldwyn-Mayer, Inc. A Loews Corp., Inc. Release. A U.S. production in English. Filmed at the M-G-M studios (Culver City, California), with second-unit footage filmed on location in Okinawa (?). Four-track magnetic stereophonic sound. Eastman Color (prints by Metrocolor). CinemaScope. 123 minutes. Released October 1956.

Tell It to the Dolls / Oneichan ni makashitoki ("Count on the Girls"). Director, Masanori.

CAST: Reiko Dan, Sonomi Nakajima.

A Toho Co., Ltd. Production. Eastman Color. Toho Scope. 90 minutes. Released July 31, 1960.

U.S. VERSION: Distributor undetermined, though almost certainly Toho International Co., Ltd. with English subtitles. The 5th "Three Dolls" feature. Followed by *Anything Goes Three Dolls' Way* (1960). 90 minutes. No MPAA rating.

Temple of the Golden Pavilion / Kinkakuji ("Kinkaku Temple"). Producers, Teruo Takabayashi and Yoshinobu Nishioka; Director, Yoichi Takabayashi; Screenplay, Yoichi Takabayashi, based on the story by Yukio Mishima; Director of Photography, Fujio Morita; Art Director, Yoshinobu Nishioka; Music, Toru Kurashima.

CAST: Saburo Shinoda, Yoshie Shimumura, Mariko Kaga.

A Kosho, Ltd./Art Theatre Guild Co., Ltd. Production. Color. Spherical wide screen (?). 197 minutes. Released 1976.

U.S. VERSION: Release uncertain. English subtitled version available. 109 minutes. No MPAA rating.

Temptation in Glamour Island / Gurama-to no yuwaku ("Temptation of Glamour Island"). Producers, Kazuo Takimura and Ichiro Sato; Director, Yuzo Kawashima; Screenplay, Yuzo Kawashima, based on the play by Tadashi Iizawa; Director of Photography, Kozo Okazaki; Art Director, Motoji Kojima; Music, Toshiro Mayuzumi.

CAST: Hisaya Morishige (Prince Tamehisa), Frankie Sakai (Prince Tamenaga), Kokinji Katsura (Heido), Yukiko Todoroki (prostitute), Kaoru Yachigusa (young woman reporter), Tatsuya Mihashi (native man).

A Tokyo Eiga Co., Ltd. Production, in association with Toho Co., Ltd. A Toho Co., Ltd. Release. Agfacolor. Toho Scope. 104 minutes. Released January 15, 1959.

U.S. VERSION: Release undetermined, possibly by Toho International Co., Ltd. in subtitled format. No MPAA rating.

The Temptress and the Monk / Byokuya no yojo ("Emotion in White Night"?). Producer, Masayuki Takaki; Director, Eisuke Takizawa; Screenplay, Toshio Yasumi and Kyoka Izumi, based on the novel *Koya hijiri* (1901) by Kyoka Izumi; Art Director, Takashi Matsuyama; Director of Photography, Minoru Yokoyama; Editor, Masanori Tsujii; Music, Yutaka Makino; Sound, Nikkatsu Sound Studio.

CAST: Yumeji Tsukioka (wife [the temptress]), Ryoji Hayama (Monk Socho), Tadashi Kobayashi (the dwarf husband), Ichijiro Oya (grandfather), Jun Hamamura (outlaw), Akitake Kono.

A Nikkatsu Corp. Production. Eastman Color (processed by Nikkatsu Laboratory). NikkatsuScope. 88 minutes. Released 1958.

U.S. VERSION: Released by Gaston Hakim Productions International. English subtitles. Initially advertised as *The Temptress*. Wide screen format advertised as CinemaScope. 88 minutes. No MPAA rating. Released May 27, 1963.

Ten Dark Women / Kuroi junin no onna ("Ten Dark Women"). Producer, Masaichi Nagata; Planning, Hiroaki Fujii; Director, Kon Ichikawa; Screenplay, Natto Wada; Director of Photography, Setsuo Kobayashi; Music, Yasushi Akutagawa; Lighting, Yukio Ito; Sound Recording, Kenichi Nishii: Art Director, Tomo Shimogawara; Editor, Tatsuji Nakashizu.

CAST: Keiko Kishi (Ichiko Ishinoshita), Fujiko Yamamoto (Futaba Kaze), Mariko Miyagi (Miwako of the Art Printing Company), Tamao Nakamura (Shio Shimura), Kyoko Kishida (Sayoko Goto), Eiji Funakoshi (Matsukichi Kaze).

A Daiei Motion Picture Co., Ltd. Production. Black and white. DaieiScope. 103 minutes. Released May 3, 1961.

U.S. VERSION: Distributor undetermined, likely Daiei International Films, Inc. English subtitles. 103 minutes. No MPAA rating.

Tenamonya yurei dochu ("Tenamonya: Ghost Story"). Producers, Shin Watanabe and Tadahito Gomyo; Director, Shue Matsubayashi; Screenplay, Ryozo Kasahara and Ryuji Sawada, based on the story by Toshio Kagawa; Art Director, Takashi Matsuyama; Director of Photography, Kiyoshi Hasegawa; Editor, Shuichi Ioihara; Music, Tetsuaki Hagiwara; Recording, Fumio Yanoguchi; Sound, Toho Recording Centre; Sound Effects, Toho Sound Effects Group.

CAST: Makoto Fujita (Anka-ke no Tokijiro), Minoru Shiraki (Chinnem), Yumiko Nogawa (Yuki), Tomoko Kei (Koharu Hakata), Hajime Hana (Shunen), Kei Tani (Masaie Kagami), Senri Sakurai (Jun-an), Ichiro Zaitsu (Takejuro Miki), Ryo Tamura (Seinoshim Kondo), Yu Fujiki (Hyobe Kuroiwa), Toshiaki Minami (Nezumikozo Jirokichi), Ryoichi Tamagawa (Tadanosuke Moriyama), Chosuke Ikariya (Doemon Togashi), Cha Kato (Chanosuke Kato), Bu Takagi (Butaro Takagi), Koji Nakamoto (Konin Nakamoto), Chu Arai (Chuzo Arai), Nock Yokoyama (Sukkara Kanbe), Fuck Yokoyama (Kinta), Panch Yokoyama (Hansuke), Tatsuo [no other name given] (Genzo Osugi), Sanpei Taira (Tobe), Ikio Sawamura (Hachirobe), Shozo Nanbu (Hanpeita Katsuragi), Takashi Akiyama (call man), Tetsuo Hara (pack horse driver), Kazuo Kuwabara (visitor to theatre).

A Takarazuka Eiga Production. A Toho Co., Ltd. Release. Westrex recording system. Eastman Color (processed by Tokyo Laboratory Ltd.). Toho Scope. 90 minutes. Released 1967.

U.S. VERSION: Distributor, if any, is undetermined. International title: *Tenamonya: Ghost Journey*. Alternate title: *Ghost of Two Travelers at Tenamonya*. Third of a series.

Tenchu! / Hitokiri ("Manslaughter"). Producers, Hideo Gosha and Shintaro Katsu; Director, Hideo Gosha;

Screenplay, Shinobu Hashimoto; Director of Photography, Fujio Morita; Art Director, Yoshinobu Nishioka; Music, Masaru Sato.

CAST: Shintaro Katsu (Izo Okada), Tatsuya Nakadai (Hampeita Takechi), Yukio Mishima (Shimpei Tanaka), Yujiro Ishihara (Ryoma Sakamoto), Mitsuko Baisho, Takumi Shinjo, Noboru Nakaya, Tsutomu Shimomoto, Kei Yamamoto.

A Katsu Productions/Fuji Telecasting Co., Ltd. Production. A Daiei Motion Picture Co., Ltd. Release. Eastman Color. DaieiScope. 140 minutes. Released August 1969.

U.S. VERSION: Released by Daiei International Films, Inc. English subtitles. 140 minutes. No MPAA rating. Released February 1970.

Terror Beneath the Sea / Kaitei dai senso ("Battle Beneath the Sea"). Executive Producer, Masafumi Soga and Tokyo First Film Co., Ltd.; Producers, Ivan Reiner, Walter Manley, Koji Kameda and Seiichi Yoshino; Associate Producer, William Ross; Director, Hajime Sato; Screenplay, Kohichi Ohtsu, based on an original story by Masami Fukushima; Director of Photography, Kazuo Shimomura; Assistant Director, Akira Tateno; Production Manager, Masatoshi Kohno; Art Director, Shinichi Eno; Lighting Technician, Toshiaki Morisawa; Sound Recording, Kohichi Iwata; Music, Shunsuke Kikuchi; Editor, Fumio Soda; Underwater Photography, Akira Tateishi; Director of Special Effects, Nobuo Yajima.

CAST: Shinichi "Sonny" Chiba (Ken Abe), Peggy Neal (Jennie), Andrew Hughes (Professor Howard), Eric Nielsen (Dr. Rufus Moore), Mike Daning (Dr. Joseph Heim), Franz Gruber, Gunther Braun, Beverly Kahler, Hideo Murata, Tsuneji Miemachi, Hans Hornef, John Kleine, Kohsaku Okano, Tadashi Suganuma.

A Toei Co., Ltd./K. Fujita Associates Inc./Ram Films, Inc. Production. A Japanese/Italian/U.S. co-production in Japanese. Filmed at Toei Studios. Eastman Color (processed by Toei Chemistry Co., Ltd.). ToeiScope (Academy ratio according to some sources). 87 minutes. Released July 1, 1966.

U.S. VERSION: Never released theatrically in the United States. Released directly to television by Teleworld. English-dubbed. Dialogue Continuity, Linda Davies. *Note:* Toei's involvement with this production is uncertain. They may have helped finance the picture, or they may have merely rented studio space. Given credits above, it is included here. The "Terence Ford" credited as director on U.S. prints is a pseudonym for director Sato. Running time is also given by some sources as 95 minutes. International title: *Water Cyborgs*. 78 minutes. No MPAA rating. Released 1967.

Terror of Mechagodzilla / Mekagojira no gyakushu ("Mechagodzilla's Counterattack"). Executive Producer, Tomoyuki Tanaka; Associate Producer, Henry G. Saperstein; Director, Ishiro Honda; Screenplay, Yukiko Takayama; Director of Photography, Mototaka Tomioka; Music, Akira Ifukube; Art Director, Yoshifumi Honda; Assistant Director, Kensho Yamashita; Production Manager, Keisuke Shinoda; Lighting, Toshio Takashima; Editor, Yoshitami Kuroiwa; Sound Effects, Toho Sound Effects Group; Sound, Toho Recording Centre. *Toho Special Effects Group*: Director, Teruyoshi Nakano; Photography, Mototaka Tomioka; Optical Photography, Yukio Manoda; Mechanical Effects, Takesaburo Watanabe; Art Director, Yasuyuki Inoue; Assistant Directors, Toshiro Aoki and Kan Komura; Optical Effects, Yoshiichi Manoda; Matte Process, Kazunobu Mikame.

CAST: Katsuhiko Sasaki (Akira Ichinose), Tomoko Ai (Katsura Mafune), Akihiko Hirata (Dr. Shinji Mafune), Katsumasa Uchida (Murakoshi), Goro Mutsumi (Mugaru), Kenji Sahara (army commander), Tomoe Mari (Yuri Yamamoto), Shin Roppongi (Wakayama), Tadao Nakamaru (Tagawa), Kotaro Tomita (Tada), Masaaki Daimon (Kusagai), Ikio Sawamura (Mafune's mute butler), Kazuo Suzuki and Yoshio Kirishima (aliens), Toru Kawane (Godzilla), Kazunari Mori (Mechagodzilla 2), Tatsumi Fuyamoto (Titanosaurus), Toru Ibuki, Yasuzo Ogawa, Hiraya Kamita, Taro Yamada, Masaichi H., Saburo Kadowagi, Shigeo Kato, Kazuo Imagi,

Jack-of-all-trades Shinya Tsukamoto as the Metals Fetishist in *Tetsuo: The Iron Man* (1988). Tsukamoto also directed the film.

Kiyoshi Yoshida, Toshio Hosoi, Masayoshi Kikuchi, H. Ishiya, Shizuko Higashi.

A Toho Co., Ltd. Production, in association with Henry G. Saperstein Enterprises. A Toho Co., Ltd. Release. Color (processed by Tokyo Laboratory, Ltd.). Panavision. 83 minutes. Released March 15, 1975.

U.S. VERSION: Released by Bob Conn. English-dubbed. Special Material (i.e. English language version), UPA Productions of America. Executive Producer, Henry G. Saperstein; Production Supervisor, S. Richard Krown; Opening Montage, Richard Bansbach, Michael McCann; Sound, Quality Sound Co.; Titles, Freeze Frame. Saperstein's involvement with the original Japanese production is unconfirmed. Also advertised in the United States as *The Terror of Godzilla*. U.K. Title: *Monster from the Unknown Planet*. Alternate title: *The Escape of Megagodzilla*. Television and home video title: *Terror of Mechagodzilla* (though no actual onscreen title appears on some prints). Released to television by the Mechagodzilla Releasing Company (i.e. United Productions of America). Includes footage from *Godzilla vs. the Cosmic Monster* (1974). Also released theatrically in an English-subtitled version by Toho International, release date uncertain. The 15th "Godzilla" feature. Followed by *Godzilla 1985* (1984). 82 minutes. MPAA rating: "G." Released 1978.

Tetsuo: The Iron Man / Tetsuo ("Tetsuo"). Producer/Director/Screenwriter/Editor/Art Director/Lighting/Special Effects, Shinya Tsukamoto; Directors of Photography, Shinya Tsukamoto and Kei Fujiwara; Wardrobe, Kei Fujiwara; Music, Chu Ishikawa; Music Operator, Mitsuhiro Ozaki; Insert Music, Akio Okosawa; Sound, Asashi Sound Studio; Assistant Director, Kei Fujiwara; Production Assistants, Nobu Kanaoka, Hiroyuki Kobato, Akiko Ishigami, Tomoko Kodaka.

CAST: Tomoro Taguchi (The Salaryman), Kei Fujiwara (his girlfriend), Nobu

Kanaoko (woman in glasses), Shinya Tsukamoto (metals fetishist), Naomasa Musaka (doctor), Renji Ishibashi (tramp).

A Kaiju Theatre Production, in association with Japan Home Video/K2 Spirit/SEN. 16mm. Black and white. 67 minutes. Released 1988.

U.S. VERSION: Released by Original Cinema. English subtitles. Subtitles, Kiyo Joo and Tony Rayns. Generally paired with the U.S.-made, 25-minute short *Drum Struck* (Original Cinema, 1991) Note: the name Tetsuo as spelled in the Kanji means "iron man." No MPAA rating. Released 1991.

Tetsuo II: Body Hammer. Producers, Fuminori Shishido, Fumio Kurokawa; Executive Producers, Hiroshi Koizumi, Shinya Tsukamoto; Director, Screenwriter, Editor, Art Director and Co-Director of Photography, Shinya Tsukamoto; Co-Directors of Photography, Fumikazu Oda, Katsunori Yokoyama; Music, Chu Ishikawa; Special Make-up Effects, Takashi Oda, Kan Takahama, Akira Fukaya.

CAST: Tomoro Taguchi (Taniguchi Tomo), Nobu Kanaoka (Kana), Shinya Tsukamoto (Yatsu, "*The Guy*"), Keinosuke Tomioka (Minori), Sujin Kim (Taniguchi's father), Min Tanaka (Taniguchi's mother), Hideaki Tezuka (big skinhead), Tomo Asada (young skinhead), Toraemon Utazawa (mad scientist).

A Kaiju Theatre Production/Toshiba/EMI Production. Color. Wide screen. 81 minutes. Released 1992.

U.S. VERSION: Unreleased in the United States as this book was going to press. A sequel (in name only) to *Tetsuo*, though this was filmed in 35mm. *Note:* the executive producer is apparently not the same as the Toho leading man of the 1950s and 1960s.

That Night's Wife / Sono yo no tsuma ("That Night's Wife"). Director, Yasujiro Ozu; Screenplay, Kogo Noda, based on a story by Osuka Shisugoru [possibly Yasujiro Ozu]; Director of Photography, Hideo Shigehara.

CAST: Tokihiko Okada, Togo Yamamoto, Emiko Yakumo, Tatsuo Saito, Mitsuko Ichimura.

A Shochiku Co., Ltd. Production. Filmed at Shochiku-Kamata Studios. Silent with benshi. Black and white. Academy ratio. 100 minutes. Released July 6, 1930.

U.S. VERSION: Released by Shochiku Films of America, Inc. English intertitles. 67 minutes. No MPAA rating. Released March 17, 1994.

Theater of Life (Japanese title undetermined). Producers, Yoshiji Mishima and Yoshitaro Nomura; Director, Tai Kato; Screenplay, Yoshitaro Nomura, Haruhiko Mimura and Tai Kato, based on an original story by Shiro Ozaki; Director of Photography, Keiji Maruyama; Editor, Shizu Osawa.

CAST: Muga Takewaki (Hyokichi Aonari), Jiro Tamiya (Kira Tsune), Hideki Takahashi (Hisakaku), Tetsuya Watari (Miyagawa), Hisaya Morishige (Hyotaro Aonari), Keiko Tsushima (Omine), Yoshiko Kayama (Osode), Mitsuko Baisho (Otoyo).

A Shochiku Co., Ltd. Production. Color. Panavision (?). 165 minutes. Released 1973.

U.S. VERSION: Released by Shochiku Films of America, Inc. English subtitles. 165 minutes. No MPAA rating. Released May 20, 1974.

There Was a Father / Chichi ariki ("There Was a Father"). Director, Yasujiro Ozu; Screenplay, Tadao Ikeda, Takao Yanai, and Yasujiro Ozu; Director of Photography, Yushun Atsuta.

CAST: Chishu Ryu, Shuji Sano, Mitsuko Mito, Takeshi Sakamoto, Shin Saburi, Haruhiko Tsuda, Shinichi Himori.

A Shochiku Co., Ltd. Production. Filmed at Shochiku-Ofuna Studios. Black and white. Academy ratio. 94 minutes. Released April 1, 1942.

U.S. VERSION: Distributor undetermined, possibly Shochiku Films of America, Inc. English subtitles. 94 minutes. No MPAA rating. Released November 1982.

The Thin Line / Onna no nakani iru tanin ("Stranger in the Woman"). Executive Producers, Sanezumi

Fujimoto and Masakatsu Kaneko; Director, Mikio Naruse; Screenplay, Toshiro Ide; Director of Photography, Yasumichi Fukuzawa; Music, Hikaru Hayashi.

CAST: Keiju Kobayashi, Michiyo Aratama, Tatsuya Mihashi, Akiko Wakabayashi, Daisuke Kato, Mitsuko Kusabue.

A Toho Co., Ltd. Production. Black and white. Toho Scope. 102 minutes. Released 1966.

U.S. VERSION: Released by Toho International Co., Ltd. English subtitles. 102 minutes. No MPAA rating. Released July 1967.

30,000 Miles Under the Sea / Kaitei 30,000 Mairu ("30,000 Miles Under the Sea") **[animated]**. Chief Animator, Sadahiro Okuda; Screenplay, Katsumi Okamoto, based on an original story by Shotaro Ishimori; Art Director, Makoto Yamazaki; Music, Takeo Watanabe.

VOICE CHARACTERIZATIONS: (undetermined).

A Toei Animation Studio (Japan) Production. A Toei Co., Ltd. Release. Eastman Color. ToeiScope. 60 minutes. Released July 17, 1970.

U.S. VERSION: Distributor, if any, is undetermined. English subtitled version available. 60 minutes. No MPAA rating.

This Greedy Old Skin / Gametsui yatsu ("Greedy Guy"). Director, Yasuki Chiba.

CAST: Aiko Mimasu, Chinatsu Nakayama, Tadao Takashima, Chisako Hara, Hisaya Morishige, Mitsuko Kusabue, Reiko Dan, Masayuki Mori, Kyoko Anzai, Yu Fujiki, Haruko Togo.

A Toho Co., Ltd. Production. Eastman Color. Toho Scope. 108 minutes. Released September 18, 1960.

U.S. VERSION: Released by Toho International Co., Ltd. English subtitles. 108 minutes. No MPAA rating. Released August 1961.

This Is Noriko / Noriko wa ima ("Noriko Now"). Producers, Matsuo Takahashi and Teruji Shibata; Director/Screenplay, Zenzo Matsuyama; Director of Photography, Ko Ishihara; Art Director, Toshiaki Kurahashi; Music, Kenichiro Morioka; Acting Coach for Tsuji, Hideko Takamine.

WITH: Noriko Tsuji (herself), Misako Watanabe (her mother), Fumie Kashiyama.

A Kinema Tokyo Co., Ltd./Shibata Film Promotion Production. Color. Panavision (?). 117 minutes. Released 1981.

U.S. VERSION: Distributor undetermined. English subtitles. 117 minutes. No MPAA rating. Released June 5, 1982.

This Madding Crowd / Aobeka monogatari ("Aobeka Story"). Producers, Ichiro Sato and Hideyuki Shiino; Director, Yuzo Kawashima; Screenplay, Kaneto Shindo, based on the novel by Shugoro Yamamoto; Director of Photography, Kozo Okazaki.

CAST: Hisaya Morishige (professor), Eijiro Tono (Grandpa Yoshi), Sachiko Hidari (Osei), Nobuko Otowa (Kimino), Frankie Sakai (Goro), Meiko Nakamura (1st bride), Junko Ikeuchi (2nd bride).

A Tokyo Eiga Co., Ltd. Production for Toho Co., Ltd. Eastman Color. Toho Scope. 101 minutes. Released 1962.

U.S. VERSION: Released by Toho International Co., Ltd. English subtitles. 101 minutes. No MPAA rating. Released June 16, 1964.

This Transient Life / Mujo ("Transparent Uncertainty"). Director, Akio Jissoji; Screenplay, Yashiro Ishida; Director of Photography, Yozo Inagaki; Music, Toru Fuyuki.

CAST: Ryo Tamura (the boy), Michiko Tsukasa (his sister), Eiji Okada (sculptor).

A Jissoji Productions/Art Theatre Guild Production. Black and white. Academy ratio (?). 146 minutes. Released 1970.

U.S. VERSION: Released by Toho International Co., Ltd. English subtitles. 140 minutes. Released March 1971.

This Way, That Way / Ano te kono te ("This Way, That Way"). Planning, Hisakazu Tsuji; Director, Kon Ichikawa; Screenplay, Natto Wada and

Kon Ichikawa, based on a story by Nobuo Kyoto; Director of Photography, Senkichiro Takeda; Music, Toshiro Mayuzumi; Art Director, Yoshinobu Nishioka; Sound Recording, Gen Otani; Lighting, Kenichi Okamoto.

CAST: Yoshiko Kuga (Ako), Mitsuko Mito (Mrs. Chikako), Yuji Hori (Tenpei), Masayuki Mori (Toba).

A Daiei Motion Picture Co., Ltd. Production. Filmed at Daiei-Kyoto Studios. Running time undetermined. Released December 23, 1952.

U.S. VERSION: Distributor, if any, is undetermined.

Those Who Make Tomorrow / Asu o Tsukuru Hitobito ("Those Who Make Tomorrow"). Producers, Ryo Takei, Sojiro Motoki, Keiji Matsuzaki, and Tomoyuki Tanaka; Directors, Kajiro Yamamoto, Hideo Sekigawa, and Akira Kurosawa; Screenplay, Yusaku Yamagata and Kajiro Yamamoto; Directors of Photography, Takeo Ito, Mitsui Miura, and Taiichi Kankura.

CAST: Kenji Susukida (father), Cheiko Takehisa (mother), Chieko Nakakita (elder sister), Mitsue Tachibana (younger sister), Masayuki Mori (chauffer), Sumie Tsubaki (chauffer's wife), Ichiro Chiba (lightman), Hyo Kitazawa (director), Itoko Kono (actress), Takashi Shimura (theater manager), Masao Shimizu (section chief), Yuriko Hamada and Sayuri Tanima (dancing girls).

A Toho Co., Ltd. Production. Black and white. Academy ratio. 81 minutes. Released May 2, 1946.

U.S. VERSION: Distributor, if any, is undetermined.

Thousand Cranes / Sembazuru ("Thousand Cranes"). Executive Producer, Hiroaki Fujii; Producer, Masaichi Nagata; Director, Yasuzo Masumura; Screenplay, Kaneto Shindo, based on the novel *Senbazuru*, by Yasunari Kawabata; Director of Photography, Setsuo Kobayashi; Art Director, Tomo Shimogawara; Music, Hikaru Hayashi; Sound Recording, Yukio Okumura, Lighting, Choji Watanabe; Editor, Tatsuji Nakashizu; Assistant Director, Chikashi Sakiyama; Technical Consultant (Tea Ceremony), Soshitsu Sen and Kaisen Iguchi.

CAST: Machiko Kyo (Chikako Kurimoto), Ayako Wakao (Mrs. Ota), Mikijiro Hira (Kikuji Mitani), Eiko Azusa (Fumiko, *Mrs. Ota's daughter*), Yoko Namikawa (Yukiko Inamura), Tanie Kitabayashi (Toyo, *Kikuji's maid*), Eiji Funakoshi (Kikuji's father), Sachiko Meguro, Wakayo Matsumura, Mariko Fukuhara, Sumie Mikasa, Yoshio Take, Yo Hanabu, Nobuo Niimiya.

A Daiei Motion Picture Co., Ltd. Production. Filmed at Daiei-Tokyo Studios. Eastman Color. DaieiScope. 97 minutes. Released April 1969.

U.S. VERSION: Released by Daiei International Films, Inc. (?). English subtitles. 97 minutes. No MPAA rating. Released October 1969.

Three Dolls and Three Guys / Samurai to oneichan ("Samurai and Girls"). Director, Toshio Sugie.

CAST: Reiko Dan (Punch), Tatsuya Mihashi.

A Toho Co., Ltd. Production. Eastman Color. Toho Scope. 88 minutes. Released January 9, 1960.

U.S. VERSION: Distributor undetermined, likely Toho International Co., Ltd., with English subtitles. The 4th "Three Dolls" feature. Followed by *Tell It to the Dolls* (1960). No MPAA rating.

Three Dolls from Hong Kong / Oneichan makai toru ("Girls Have Their Own Way"). Executive Producer, Sanezumi Fujimoto; Director, Toshio Sugie; Screenplay, Ryozo Kasahara; Director of Photography, Taiichi Kankura; Music, Yoshiyuki Kozu.

CAST: Reiko Dan (Punch), Sonomi Nakajima (Pinch), Noriko Shigeyama (Senti), Tatsuya Ebara (Tatsuo Maebara), Akira Kubo (Hiroshi Kubota), Shinji Yamada (Hideo Kiyokawa), Ryo Ikebe.

A Toho Co., Ltd. Production. Eastman Color. Toho Scope. 98 minutes. Released November 22, 1959.

U.S. VERSION: Released by Toho International Co., Ltd. English subtitles. Alternate title: *Three Dolls Go to Hong*

Kong (and as the "Three Dolls" of the title are Japanese, it makes much more sense). The 3rd "Three Dolls" feature. Followed by *Three Dolls and Three Guys* (1960). 98 minutes. No MPAA rating. Released March 10, 1966.

Three Dolls in College / Daigaku no oneichan ("Girls in College"). Producer, Masumi Fujimoto; Director, Toshio Sugie; Screenplay, Ryozo Kasahara; Director of Photography, Taiichi Kankura; Art Director, Yoshiro Muraki; Music, Yoshiyuki Kozu.

CAST: Reiko Dan (Toshiko, aka "Punch"), Sonomi Nakajima (Mitsuko, aka "Pinch"), Noriko Shigeyama (Senti, aka Shigeko), Akira Takarada (Takada), Akira Kubo (Okubo), Yoko Tsukasa (Michiko), Yosuke Natsuki.

A Toho Co., Ltd. Production. Eastman Color. Toho Scope. 92 minutes. Released March 3, 1959.

U.S. VERSION: Distributor, if any, is undetermined, though almost certainly Toho International Co., Ltd., with English subtitles. First feature in the 8-film "Three Dolls" series (1959-63). Followed by *Three Dolls of Ginza* (1959).

Three Dolls in Ginza / Ginza no oneichan ("Girls in Ginza"). Director, Toshio Sugie; Screenplay, Yoshio Shirasaka; Director of Photography, Taiichi Kankura; Music, Yoshiyuki Kozu.

CAST: Reiko Dan (Punch), Sonomi Nakajima (Pinch), Noriko Shigeyama (Senti), Shinji Yamada.

A Toho Co., Ltd. Production. Eastman Color. Toho Scope. 97 minutes. July 14, 1959.

U.S. VERSION: Distributor, if any, is undetermined, though almost certainly Toho International Co., Ltd., with English subtitles. The 2nd "Three Dolls" feature. Followed by *Three Dolls from Hong Kong* (1959). No MPAA rating.

365 Nights / Sambyaku-rokujugo ya ("365 Nights"). Producer, Hideo Koi; Director, Kon Ichikawa; Screenplay, Kennosuke Tateoka, based on the novel *Romance* by Seijiro Kojima; Director of Photography, Akira Mimura; Lighting, Masayoshi Omura; Sound Recording, Fumio Yanoguchi; Art Director, Seigo Shindo.

CAST: Ken Uehara (Koroku Kawakita), Hisako Yamane (Teruko Oye), Mitsuko Yoshikawa (Shizu Oye, *her mother*), Hideko Takamine (Ranko Komaki), Shunji Kubo (Yuzo Komaki, *her father*), Yuji Hari (Atsushi Tsugawa).

A Shintoho Co., Ltd. Production. Black and white. Academy ratio. 119 minutes. Released September 12, 1948.

U.S. VERSION: Distributor, if any, is undetermined.

Three Old Ladies / Sanbaba ("Three Old Women"). Director, Noboru Nakamura; Screenplay, Kinji Obata and Toshiro Ide, based on an original story by Sawako Ariyoshi; Director of Photography, Hiroshi Murai; Music, Naozumi Yamamoto.

CAST: Kinuyo Tanaka, Aiko Mimasu, Michiyo Kogure.

A Tokyo Eiga Co., Ltd. Production. A Toho Co., Ltd. Release. Color. Spherical wide screen (?). 101 minutes. Released 1974.

U.S. VERSION: Released by Toho International Co., Ltd. English subtitles. Alternate title: *Three Old Women*. 101 minutes. No MPAA rating. Released March 5, 1975.

Three Stripes in the Sun. Producer, Fred Kohlmar; Director, Richard Murphy; Screenplay, Richard Murphy, based on an adaptation by Albert Duffy of E.J. Kahn, Jr.'s magazine article "The Gentle Wolfhound," published in *The New Yorker*; Director of Photography, Burnett Guffey; Art Director, Carl Anderson; Editor, Charles Nelson; Music, George Duning, conducted by Morris Stoloff; Technical Adviser, Master Sgt. Hugh O'Reilly.

CAST: Aldo Ray (High O'Reilly), Phil Carey (Colonel), Dick York (Cpl. Neeby Muhlendorf), Mitsuko Kimura (Yuko), Chuck Connors (Idaho), Camille Janclaire (Sister Genevieve), Haiichiro "Henry" Okawa (Father Yoshida), Tatsuo Saito (Konoya), Chiyaki [no other name given], Sgt. Demetrios [no other name given], Sgt. Romaniello [no other name given] (themselves), I. Tamaki (Mr. Ota), Lt. Colonel Mike Davis (Major Rochelle), Lt. Thomas Brazil (Lt. Brazil), Takeshi Kamikubo (Kanno), Tamao Nakamura (Satsumi), Teruko Omi (Yuko's mother), Kamiko Tachibana (Yuko's sister).

A Fred Kohlmer Production, in association with Columbia Pictures Corporation. A Columbia Pictures Release. A U.S. production in English filmed in Japan. Black and white. Spherical wide screen (1.85:1). 93 minutes. No MPAA rating. Released October 1955.

The Three Treasures / Nippon tanjo ("The Birth of Japan"). Producers, Sanezumi Fujimoto and Tomoyuki Tanaka; Director, Hiroshi Inagaki; Screenplay, Toshio Yasumi and Ryuzu Kikushima, based on the legends "Kojiki" and "Nihon Shoki," and the origin of Shinto; Director of Photography, Kazuo Yamada; Sound, Toho Dubbing Theatre; Sound Effects, Toho Sound Effects Group. *Toho Special Effects Group:* Director, Eiji Tsuburaya; Art Director, Akira Watanabe; Director of Photography, Teisho Arikawa; Lighting, Kuichiro Kishida; Matte Process, Hiroshi Mukoyama; Optical Photography, Kinsaburo Araki.

CAST: Toshiro Mifune (Prince Yamato Takeru), Yoko Tsukasa (Princess Tachibana), Kyoko Kagawa (Princess Miyazu), Koji Tsuruta (younger Kumaso), Takashi Shimura (elder Kumaso), Misa Uehara, Kinyuo Tanaka, Nobuko Otowa, Akira Kubo, Ganjuro Nakamura, Akira Takarada, Yu Fujiki, Eijiro Tono, Akihiko Hirata, Jun Tazaki, Hisaya Ito, Yoshio Kosugi, Yoshifumi Tajima, Akira Tani, Ikio Sawamura, Senkichi Omura, Yutaka Sada, Eisei Amamoto, Keiju Kobayashi, Ichiro Arishima, Shin Otomo, Kenichi "Enoken" Okomoto.

A Toho Co., Ltd. Production. Western Electric Mirrophonic recording (encoded with Perspecta Stereophonic Sound). Agfacolor (processed by Far East Laboratories, Ltd.). Toho Scope. 182 minutes. Released November 1, 1959.

U.S. VERSION: Released by Toho International Company, Ltd. English subtitles. Some engagements advertised as *Age of the Gods*. 112 minutes. No MPAA rating. Released December 20, 1960.

The Three Undelivered Letters / Haitatsu Sarenai Santsu no Tegami ("The Three Undelivered Letters"). Producers, Yoshitaro Nomura, Akira Oda, and Yasuyoshi Tanaka; Director, Yoshitaro Nomura; Screenplay, Kaneto Shindo, based on the novel *Calamity Town* by Ellery Queen; Director of Photography, Takashi Kawamata; Music, Yasushi Akutagawa.

CAST: Komaki Kurihara, Takao Kataoka, Keiko Matsuzaka, Shin Saburi, Nobuko Otowa, Mayumi Ogawa, Eitaro Ozawa.

A Shochiku Co., Ltd. Production. Color. Panavision (?). 130 minutes. Released 1979.

U.S. VERSION: Released by Shochiku Films of America, Inc. in subtitled format. 130 minutes. No MPAA rating. Released December 5, 1980.

Throne of Blood / Kumosu-djo ("Cobweb Castle"). Producers Sojiro Motoki and Akira Kurosawa; Director/Editor, Akira Kurosawa; Screenplay, Shinobu Hashimoto, Ryuzo Kikushima, Hideo Oguni, and Akira Kurosawa, based on the play *Macbeth* by William Shakespeare; Director of Photography, Asakazu Nakai; Music Masaru Sato; Art and Costumes, Yoshiro Muraki, Kohei Ezaki; Sound Recordist, Fumio Yanoguchi; Sound, Toho Dubbing Theatre; Sound Effects, Toho Sound Effects Group; Special Effects, Toho Special Effects Group.

CAST: Toshiro Mifune (Taketori Washizu), Isuzu Yamada (Asaji Washizu, *his wife*), Minoru Chiaki (Yoshiaki Miki), Akira Kubo (Yoshiteru Miki), Takamaru Sasaki (Kuniharu Tsuzuki), Yoichi Tachikawa (Kunimaru Tsuzuki), Takashi Shimura (Noriyasu Odagura), Chieko Naniwa (witch), Yoshio Tsuchiya (samurai at North Castle who prepares room), Ikio Sawamura, Sachio Sakai, Senkichi Omura, Akira Tani (guards at gate), Isao Kimura, Seiji Miyaguchi, Shin Otomo, Yutaka Sada, Nobuo Nakamura, Kokuten Kodo, Yu Fujiki.

A Toho Co., Ltd. Production. Black and white. Academy ratio. Western Electric Mirrophonic Recording (encoded with Perspecta Stereophonic Sound). 110 minutes. Released January 15, 1957.

U.S. VERSION: Released by Brandon Films, Inc. English subtitles. English Adaptation, Donald Richie. Alternate titles include: *The Castle of the Spider's Web*, *Cobweb Castle* and *Macbeth*. 105 minutes. No MPAA rating. Released November 22, 1961.

Through Days and Months / Hi mo tsuki mo ("Days and Months"). Director, Noboru Nakamura; Screenplay, Yuzuru Hirose, based on the novel by Yasunari Kawabata; Director of Photography, Hiroshi Takemura; Art Director, Yutaka Yokoyama; Music, Masao Yagi.

CAST: Shima Iwashita (Matsuko), Masayuki Mori (her father), Yoshiko Kuga (her mother), Jin Nakayama (Munehiro), Koji Ishizaka (Koji), Mayumi Ozora.

A Shochiku Co., Ltd. Production. Eastman Color. Shochiku GrandScope. 98 minutes. Released January 1969.

U.S. VERSION: Released by Shochiku Films of America, Inc. English subtitles. 98 minutes. No MPAA rating. Released May 1969.

Thumbelina / Oyayubihime ("Thumb Princess") **[animated]**. Producer, Chiaki Imada; Director, Yugo Serikawa; Screenplay, Tatsuji Kino and Kazuko Nakamura, based on the story by Hans Christian Andersen; Character Design; Osamu Tezuka; Art Director, Tomo Fukumoto; Music, Shunsuke Kikuchi.

VOICE CHARACTERIZATIONS: (undetermined).

A Toei Animation Co., Ltd. Production. Color. ToeiScope (?). 65 minutes. Release date undetermined.

U.S. VERSION: Distributor, if any, is undetermined.

Tiger Flight / Kyomo ware ozorani ari ("Today I Am in the Sky Again"). Executive Producer, Tomoyuki Tanaka; Director, Kengo Furusawa; Screenplay, Katsuya Suzaki; Director of Photography, Fukuzo Koizumi; Music, Kenjiro Hirose. *Toho Special Effects Group*: Director, Eiji Tsuburaya.

CAST: Tatsuya Mihashi (Lt. Col. Yamasaki), Makoto Sato (Capt. Mikami), Yosuke Natsuki, Takashi Inagaki, Yuriko Hoshi, Chotaro Togin.

A Toho Co., Ltd. Production. Eastman Color. Toho Scope. 104 minutes. Released August 1, 1964.

U.S. VERSION: Released by Toho International Co., Ltd. English subtitles. 104 minutes. No MPAA rating. Released July 2, 1965.

Till Tomorrow Comes / Ashita aru kagiri ("As Long as There Is Tomorrow"). Executive Producers, Ichiro Sato and Kenichiro Tsunoda; Director, Shiro Toyoda; Screenplay, Toshio Yazumi; Director of Photography, Kozo Okazaki; Music, Hikaru Hayashi.

CAST: Kyoko Kagawa, Yuriko Hoshi, Shuji Sano, Junko Ikeuchi, Kumi Mizuno, Haruko Sugimura, Tsutomu Yamazaki, Nobuko Otowa, Takashi Inagaki.

A Toho Co., Ltd. Production. Black and white. Toho Scope. 113 minutes. Released 1962.

U.S. VERSION: Released by Toho International Co., Ltd. English subtitles. 113 minutes. No MPAA rating. Released May 1962.

Till We Meet Again / Mata au himade ("Till We Meet Again"). Producer, Seio Sakagami; Director, Tadashi Imai; Screenplay, Yoko Mizuki and Toshio Yasumi; Director of Photography, Shinichiro Nakano; Art Director, Yasuo Kato; Music, Masahi Oki.

CAST: Eiji Okada (Saburo Tajima), Osamu Takizawa (Eisaku Tajima), Akitake Kono (Jiro Tajima), Akiko Kazami (Masako Tajima), Yoshiko Kuga (Keiko Ono), Haruko Sugimura (Suga Ono).

A Toho Co., Ltd. Production. Black and white. Academy ratio. 111 minutes. Relesed 1950.

U.S. VERSION: Distributor, if any, is undetermined, likely Toho International Co., Ltd. in subtitled format.

The Time of Reckoning / Fushin no taki ("The Time of Distrust"). Director, Tadashi Imai; Director of Photography, Setuo Kobayashi.

CAST: Jiro Tamiya, Ayako Wakao,

Mariko Okada, Kyoko Kishida, Mariko Kaga, Masao Mishima.

A Daiei Motion Picture Co., Ltd. Production. Color. DaieiScope (?). 120 minutes. Released June 29, 1968.

U.S. VERSION: Released by Daiei International Films, Inc. English subtitles. 120 minutes. No MPAA rating. Released April 8, 1970.

Time of the Apes. Producers, Mataichi Takahashi, Masashi Tadakuma; Directors, Atsuo Okunaka, Kiyasumi Fukazawa; Teleplay, Keiichi Abe; Original Story, Sakyo Komatsu, Koji Tanaka, Aritsume Toyoda; Music, Toshiaki Tsushima; Director of Photography, Yoshihiro Mori.

CAST: Reiko Tokunaga, Hiroko Saito, Masaaki Kaji, Hitoshi Omae, Tetsuya Ushida, Baku Hatakeyama, Kazue Takita, Noboru Nakaya.

A Japanese teleseries re-edited to feature length for American television, and never released theatrically in Japan. A Tsuburaya Productions Ltd. Production. Color. 16mm.

U.S. VERSION: Never released theatrically in the United States. Released directly to television by Sandy Frank Productions in 1987. Feature Concept and Editing, William L. Cooper, Jr.; Creative Consultants, Jessie Vogel Cinemedia Ltd. 94 minutes. No MPAA rating.

Time Slip / Sengoku jieitai ("Self-Defense Forces in a Warring State"). Producer, Haruki Kadokawa; Director, Kosei Saito; Screenplay, Toshio Kaneda, based on the novel by Ryo Hanmura; Director of Photography, Iwao Isayama; Shooting Coordinators, Sonny Chiba Enterprises; Music, Kentaro Haneda; Sound Recording, Fumio Hashimoto; Special Effects Director, Hiyoshi Suzuki; Choreographer of Battle Scenes, Shinichi "Sonny" Chiba.

CAST: Shinichi "Sonny" Chiba (Lieutenant Iba), Isao Natsuki (samurai leader), Miyuki Ono (village girl), Jana Okada (modern girl).

A Haruki Kadokawa Films, Inc. and Toei Co., Ltd. Production. A Kadokawa Publishing Co., Ltd. Picture. A Toei Co., Ltd. Release. Toeicolor. Panavision. 139 minutes. Released January 30, 1981.

U.S. VERSION: Released by American National Enterprises, Inc. English subtitles (?). 94 minutes. No MPAA rating. Released January 1981.

To Love Again / Ai futatabi ("Love Again"). Producers, Sanezumi Fujimoto and Ryu Yasutake; Director, Kon Ichikawa; Screenplay, Shuntaro Tanikawa; Director of Photgraphy, Kiyoshi Hasegawa; Music, Shunichi Magaino.

CAST: Renaud Verley (Nicol), Ruriko Asaoka (Miya), Seiji Miyaguchi (Miya's father), Tsuyako Yuki (Miya's mother), Kaoru Momoi (Miya's sister), Tetsuo Ishidate (Kii-chan).

A Toho Co., Ltd. Production. Color. Toho Scope. 96 minutes. Released July 3, 1972.

U.S. VERSION: Released by Toho International Co., Ltd. English subtitles. 96 minutes. No MPAA rating. Released December 22, 1972.

To Sleep So as to Dream / Yume miruyoni memuritau ("I Want to Sleep as if I'm Dreaming"). Producer/Director/Screenplay, Kaizo Hayashi; Director of Photography, Yuichi Nagata; Art Director, Takeo Kimura; Music, Hidehiko Urayama, Yoko Kumagai, Moe Kamura, and Morio Agata; Sound Recording, Akihiko Suzuki; Lighting, Tatsuya Osada; Editor, Yuichi Nagata and Kaizo Hayashi; Makeup, Mika Yoshida and Hikaru Sikihata; Sword Fight Supervisor, Tsuneo Nakamoto and Tatsuo Nakamoto.

CAST: Moe Kamura (Bellflower), Shiro Sano (Uotsuka), Koji Otake (Kobayashi), Fujiko Fukamizu (Madame Cherryblossom), Yoshio Yoshida (Matsunosuke, *the director*), Akira Oizumi, Morio Agata, and Kazunari Ozasa (the three magicians), Shunsui Matsuda (Akagaki, *the benshi*), Tsuneo Nakamoto and Tatsuo Nakamoto (the white masks), Kyoko Kusajima (old lady in comb shop).

An Eizo Tanteisha Production. A Shibata Film Co., Ltd. Release (?). 16mm. Black and white. Academy ratio. Silent with music and sound effects. 81 minutes. Released 1986.

U.S. VERSION: Released by New Yorker Films. English intertitles and subtitles. No MPAA rating. Released September 28, 1986.

Toki o kakeru shojo ("The Little Girl Who Ran with Time"). Executive Producer, Haruki Kadokawa; Producers, Norihiko Yamada and Kyoko Obayashi; Director, Nobuhiko Obayashi; Screenplay, Wataru Kenmotsu, based on the novel by Yasutaka Tsutsui; Assistant Director, Shuji Natio; Art Director, Kazuko Satsuya; Director of Photography, Zenshi Sakamoto; Lighting, Akio Watanabe; Sound, Shohei Hayashi; Editor, Nobuhiko Obayashi; Music, Masataka Matsutoya.

CAST: Tomoyo Harada (Yoshiyama), Ryoichi Takayanagi (Fukamachi), Toshinori Omi (Houkawa), Yukari Tsuda (Mariko), Ittoku Kishibe (Fukushima).

A Haruki Kadokawa Films, Inc./Toei Co., Ltd. Production. A Kadokawa Publishing Co., Ltd. Picture. Toeicolor (processed by Toei Chemistry Co., Ltd.). Spherical Panavision. 104 minutes. Released July 15, 1983.

U.S. VERSION: Distributor, if any, is undetermined. International title: *The Little Girl Who Conquered Time.*

Tokkan ("Battle Cry"). Director/Screenplay, Kihachi Okamoto; Director of Photography, Daisuke Kimura.

CAST: Toshitaka Ito (Senta), Yusuke Okaka (Manjiro), Etsushi Takahashi (Judayo Hoseya), Emiko Senba (Teru), Tetsuya Nakadai.

A Kihachi Productions Production. An Art Theatre Guild (ATG) Release. Color. 93 minutes. Released 1975.

U.S. VERSION: Released by East-West Classics. English subtitles. 93 minutes. No MPAA rating. Released May 1977.

Tokugawa onna keibatsushi ("The History of Torture of Women in Tokugawa"). Producer, Shigeru Okada; Director, Teruo Ishii; Screenplay, Teruo Ishii and Misao Arai; Director of Photography, Motonari Washio; Art Director, Taketoshi Suzuki; Editor, Tadao Kanda; Sound Recording, Teruhiko Arakawa; Music, Masao Yagi.

CAST: Masumi Tachibana (Mitsu), Teruo Yoshida (Yorimo Yoshioka/Shinzo), Fumio Watanabe (Kazunochi Nanbara), Asao Koike (Horicho), Yukie Kagawa (Reiho), Kinji Nakamura (Yamano Awajinokami), Akikane Sawa (Gonzo), Kichijiro Ueda (Minosuke), Gannosuke Asiya (Bancho's teacher), Ryota Monowada (Kanta), Seiji Mori (Sinzo follower), Miki Obana (Myoshin), Naomi Shiraishi (Rintoku), Reiko Okajima (Shotoku), Keiko Kojima (Gyokei), Mie Hanabusa (Son-ei), Shinichiro Hayashi (Shunkai), Reiko Mikasa (Hana), Tamaki Sawa (Kimicho), Toru Yuri (Sanuke), Yuko Namikaze (restaurant manageress), Ai Minose (female prisoner).

A Toei Co., Ltd. Production. Fujicolor (processed by Toei Chemistry Co., Ltd.). Toeiscope. Filmed at Toei-Kyoto Studios. 96 minutes. Released 1968.

U.S. VERSION: U.S. distributor, if any, is undetermined. International title: *The Joys of Torture.* Also known as *Criminal Women.*

Tokyo Bad Girls / Zubeko bancho, yume wa yoru hiraku ("Slut Boss, Dreams Come at Night"). Director, Kazuhiko Yamaguchi; Screenplay, Norio Miyashita and Kazuhiko Yamaguchi; Director of Photography, Hanjiro Nakazawa; Art Director, Hiroshi Kitagawa; Music, Toshiaki Tsushima.

CAST: Junko Miyazono (Madame Umeko), Reiko Oshida (Rika), Yukie Kagawa (Mari), Tatsuo Umemiya (Shinjiro), Masumi Tachibana, Mieko Tsudoi, Hayato Tani.

A Toei Co., Ltd. Production. Eastman Color. ToeiScope. 87 minutes. Released September 22, 1970.

U.S. VERSION: Distributor, if any, is undetermined. English subtitled version available. The first feature in the 4-film "Zubeko bancho" film series (1970-71). 87 minutes. No MPAA rating.

Tokyo Bath Harem / Onna ukiyoburo ("Vain Bath Women"). Director, Tan Ida; Screenplay, Iwao Yamazaki; Director of Photography, Hidemitsu Iwahashi; Art Director, Haruyasu Kurosawa; Music, Seitaro Omori.

CAST: Ryoji Hayama (Shinzo), Jiro Okazaki (Takichi), Toshie Nihonyanagi (Hatue), Miki Hayashi (Shun), Kaoru Miya (Toyo), Takako Uchida (Hatsuse).

A Nikkatsu Corp. Production. Fujicolor. NikkatsuScope. 83 minutes. Released July 10, 1969.

U.S. VERSION: Distributor, if any, is undetermined. English subtitled version available. 83 minutes. No MPAA rating.

Tokyo Blackout / Shuto Shoshitsu ("Disappearance of the Capital"). Executive Producers, Yasuyoshi Takuma and Shichira Murakami; Producers, Katsumi Mizoguchi and Motoki Kasahara; Director, Toshio Masuda; Screenplay, Toshio Masuda and Hiroyasu Yamaura, based on the book by Sakyo Komatsu; Director of Photography, Masahiko Imura; Art Director, Juichi Ikuno; Editor, Toshio Taniguchi; Music, Maurice Jarre; Sound Recording, Tetsuo Segawa; Special Effects Director, Teruyoshi Nakano.

CAST: Tsunehiko Watase (Tatsuya Asakura), Yuko Naotori (Mariko Koide), Shinji Yamashita (Yosuke Tamiya), Yoko Ishino (Mieko Matsunaga), Shuji Otaki (Seiichiro Otawara).

A Daiei Co., Ltd./Kansai Telecasting/Tokuma Shoten Publishing Production. Dolby Stereo. Color. Spherical wide screen. 120 minutes. Released 1987.

U.S. VERSION: Released by Daiei International Films. English subtitles. Released in Canada; additional Western playdates undetermined. 120 minutes. No MPAA rating. Released August 29, 1987.

Tokyo Bordello / Yoshiwara enjo ("Yoshiwara Conflagration"). Producer, Shigeru Okada; Director, Hideo Gosha; Screenplay, Sadao Nakajima, based on the book by Shinichi Saito; Director of Photography, Fujio Morita; Art Director, Yoshinobu Nishioka; Editor, Isamu Ichida; Music, Masaru Sato; Sound Recording, Kiyoshige Hirai.

CAST: Yuko Natori, Jinpachi Nezu, Rino Katase, Sayoko Ninomiya, Mariko Fuji, Mineko Nishikawa.

A Toei Co., Ltd. Production. Color. Panavision (?). 133 minutes. Released 1987.

U.S. VERSION: Release uncertain. Released in Canada August 28, 1987.

Tokyo Chorus / Tokyo no gassho ("Tokyo Chorus"). Director, Yasujiro Ozu; Screenplay, Kogo Noda, based on the novel by Komatsu Kitamura; Director of Photography, Hideo Shigehara.

CAST: Tokihiko Okada, Hideo Sugawara, Emiko Yagumo, Mitsuo Ichimura, Takeshi Sakamoto, Tatsuo Saito, Choko Iida, Hideko Takamine, Chishu Ryu.

A Shochiku Co., Ltd. Production. Filmed at Shochiku-Kamata Studios. Silent with benshi. Black and white. Academy ratio. 91 minutes. Released August 15, 1931.

U.S. VERSION: Released by Shochiku Films of America. English intertitles. 91 minutes. No MPAA rating. Released December 1982 (?).

Tokyo Decadence / Topazu ("Topaz"). Executive Producer, Eiten Taga; Associate Producers, Naoya Narita and Chosei Funahara; Producers, Yoshitaka Suzuki, Tadanobu Hirao, and Yosuke Nagata; Director/Screenplay, Ryu Murakami, based on his novel; Director of Photography, Tadashi Aoki; Editor, Kazuki Katashima; Music, Ryuichi Sakamoto; Music Supervision, Ryu Murakami.

CAST: Miho Nikaido, Sayoko Amano, Tenmei Kano, Kan Mikami, Masahiko Shimada, Yayoi Kusama, Chie Sema.

A Melsat Inc./JVD Co., Ltd. Production. Dolby Stereo. Color. Spherical wide screen. 113 minutes. Released 1992.

U.S. VERSION: Released by Northern Arts Entertainment, Inc. English subtitles. Postproduction Supervisor, Allen Schulman, Campus Video Tours; Subtitles, Simon Nuchtern, Katina Productions (NY); Video Editor, Ed Strollo; Electronic Titles, Paul Donegan. Copyright 1991 Melsat Co., Ltd. 108 minutes. No MPAA rating. Released April 30, 1993.

Tokyo Drifter / Tokyo nagaremono ("Tokyo Drifter"). Producer, Tetsuro Nakagawa; Director, Seijun Suzuki; Screenplay, Yasunori Kawauchi, based on his novel; Director of Photography, Shigeyoshi Mine; Editor, Shinya

Inoue; Art Director, Takeo Kimura; Music, So Kaburagi; Assistant Director, Masami Kuzu.

CAST: Tetsuya Watari (Tetsuya "Phoenix Tetsu" Hondo), Chieko Matsubara (Chiharu), Hideaki Nitani (Kenji Aizawa), Ryuji Kita (Kurata), Tsuyoshi Yoshida (Keiichi), Hideaki Esumi (Otsuka), Tamio Kawachi (Tatsuzo), Hiroshi Cho (Kumamoto).

A Nikkatsu Corp. Production. Color. NikkatsuScope. 83 minutes. Released 1966.

U.S. VERSION: Released by Nikkatsu Corp. English subtitles. Alternate title: *The Man from Tokyo*. 83 minutes. No MPAA rating. Released 1993.

Tokyo File 212. Executive Producer, Melvin Belli; Producers, Dorrell McGowan, George Breakston, in association with Ikuzo Suzuki and Tonichi Kogio, K.K.; Associate Producer, C. Ray Stahl; Director/Screenplay, Dorrell McGowan and Stuart McGowan; Story, George Breakston; Director of Photography, Herman Schopp; Art Directors, Seigo Shindo; Editor, Martin G. Cohn; Music/Lyrics, Yasuo Shimizu and Shizuo Yoshikawa; Song: "Oyedo Boogie," performed by Ichimaru and the Tainosuke Mochizuke Band; Imperial Theater Number, Takarazuka Revue; Sound Recording, Charles L. King III; Production Manager, B.C. "Doc" Wylie; Unit Manager, Hiroji Oshiyama; Casting Director, Ichiro Yoda; Assistant Director, Tadashi Tanjo; Makeup, Shigeo Kobayashi; Optical Effects, Consolidated Film Industries; Cooperation, The United States Department of Defense, The United States Army Far East Command, The Japanese Government, and the Tokyo Metropolitan Police.

CAST: Robert Peyton (Jim Carter), Florence Marly (Steffi Novak), Katsuhiko Haida (Taro), Reiko Otani (Taro's girl), Tatsuo Saito (Taro's father), Tetsu Nakamura (Oyama), Suisei Matsui (Joe), Byron Michie (Jeffrey), Henry Ogawa, Jun Tazaki, Dekao Yoko, Hideto Hayabusa, Gen Shimizu, Major Richard W.N. Childs [USAR], Cpl. Stuart Zimmerly, MP [USA], and Pvt. James Lyons, MP [USA].

A Breakston-McGowan Production, in conjunction with Ikuzo Suzuki and Tonichi Kogio, K.K. (Tonichi Enterprises Co., Ltd.) and Mainichi Newspapers. A U.S./Japanese co-production in English and Japanese (see below). Filmed entirely on location in Japan. Black and white. Academy ratio. 83 minutes. Released December 1950.

U.S. VERSION: Released by RKO Radio Pictures, Inc. The first U.S./Japanese co-production of record. Filmed July-August 1950. Working title: *Tokyo File 291*. 83 minutes. No MPAA rating. Released June 1951.

Tokyo March / Tokyo koshinkyoku ("Tokyo March"). Director, Kenji Mizoguchi; Screenplay, Chieo Kimura, based on an original story by Kan Kikuchi; Director of Photography, Tatsuyuki Yokota.

CAST: Shizue Natsukawa (Orie), Takako Irie (Sayuriko), Isamu Kosugi (Yukichi Sakuma), Koji Shima (Yoshiki Fujimoto), Eiji Takagi (Fujimoto, *the father*).

A Nikkatsu Uzumasa Production. Silent. Black and white. Academy ratio. 80 minutes. Released 1929.

U.S. VERSION: Distributor undetermined. Released minus English intertitles. Only a 20-minute fragment of this feature survives. 20 minutes. No MPAA rating. Released 1981.

Tokyo 196X / Showa Genroku Tokyo 196X-nen ("Showa, Genroku, Tokyo 196X"). Director, Hideo Onchi; Screenplay, Satoshi Kuramoto; Director of Photography, Tokuzo Kuroda; Art Director, Yukio Higuchi; Music, Masao Yagi.

CAST: Miku Yoshida (Yuri), Joji Ide (Kato), Isao Hashimoto (Murai), Juzo Itami, Hajime Shoji.

A Toho Co., Ltd. Production. Black and white. Toho Scope. 84 minutes. Released October 19, 1968.

U.S. VERSION: Release undetermined, likely by Toho International Co., Ltd. English subtitled version available. 84 minutes. No MPAA rating.

Tokyo Olympiad / Tokyo Olrmpikku ("Tokyo Olympiad") **[documentary]**. Producer, Suketaro Taguchi

Tokyo Olympiad (1965).

for the 13th Olympic Organizing Committee; Director, Kon Ichikawa; Technical Director, Michio Midorikawa; Screenplay, Natto Wada, Ishio Shirasaka, Shuntaro Tanikawa, and Kon Ichikawa; Technical Director, Michio Aokawa; Art Director, Yusaku Kamekura; Editor, Yoshio Ebara; Directors of Photography, Shigeo Hayashida, Kazuo Miyagawa; Photography, Juichi Nagano, Kinji Nakamura, and Tadashi Tanaka; Music, Toshiro Mayuzumi; Sound Recording, Toshihiko Inoue; Production Assistants, Jun Kiyofuji, Asao Kumada, and Senkichi Taniguchi

CAST: The athletes, trainers, spectators and other witnesses to the Games of the XVIII Olympiad.

A Production of the Organizing Committee for the Games of the XVIII Olympiad. A Toho Co., Ltd. Release. Eastman Color. Toho Scope. 154 minutes (also released at 132 minutes; later reconstructed to approximate original director's cut, running 170 minutes). Released March 20, 1965.

U.S. VERSION: Released by American International Pictures, Pan-World Film Exchange and Jack Douglas Enterprises. English narration. A Jack Douglas Presentation. Executive Producer, Jack Douglas; Associate Producers, Roger Janis and Roderick Tichenor; Screenplay, Donald Richie; Supervising Film Editor, Richard L. Van Enger, Jr.; Production Coordinator, Dennis Payne; Narration, Jack Douglas. Wide screen process billed as CinemaScope in the United States. 93 minutes. No MPAA rating. Released October 20, 1965. Reissued in Japan in 1966 as *Seido no kando* ("Inspiration of the Century"), running time undetermined. Reissued in the United States minus narration and running 170 minutes in 1984. Letterboxed laserdisc edition runs 170 minutes.

Tokyo Pop. Executive Producers, Jonathan Olsberg and Kaz Kuzui; Producers, Kaz Kuzui and Joel Tuber; Associate Producers, Akira Morishige and Nancy Tuber; Director, Fran Rubel Kuzui; Screenplay, Fran Rubel Kuzui and Lynn Grossman, based on an original story by Fran Rubel Kuzui; Director of Photography, James Hayman; Editor, Camilla Toniolo; Original Score/Music Director, Alan Brewer; Costume Designer, Asako Kobayashi; Lighting, Toshiaki Yoneyama; Production Design, Terumi Hosoishi; Sound Mixer, Yutaka Tsurumaki; Production Executives, David Lubell, Hajime Yuki (for Shochiku Fuji); Casting, Ellen Lewis, Julie Alter, and Yoshikuni Matsunaga; Co-Production Executives, Com Planning Committee, Noriyaki Nakagawa; Asst. to the Director/Interpreter, Tacey Miller; 1st Asst. Director, Yoshikuni Matsunaga; 2nd Asst. Director, Shinichio Makata; Production Manager, Hiroshi Mukuju.

CAST: Carrie Hamilton (Wendy Reed), Yutaka Tadokoro (Hiro Yamaguchi), Taiji Tonoyama (grandfather), Tetsuro Tamba (Dota), Masumi Harukawa (mother), Toki Shiozawa (Mama-san), Hiroshi Mikami (Saki, *the club manager*), Michael Cerveris (Mike), Gina Belefonte (Holly). *The Be-Bops:* Daisuke Oyama (Yoji, the keyboardist), Hiroshi Kobayashi (Kaz, the drummer), Hiroshi Sugita (Taro, the bass player), Satoshi Kanai (Shun, the lead guitarist), Rikiya Yasuoka (Club Ume manager), Sneri Yamazaki (Ava, the dancer), Hirofumi Hamada (Misoru), Kazuo Ishigaki (chief waiter), Makoto Fukuda (Hiro's father), Yuko Kimoto (Hiro's sister), Shun Shioya (Michey House manager), Constantina Blianas (Alice), Tommy Bell (John), Michael Waters (Yogi), Catherine Bird (Riva), Junko Horita, Kaori Yokoe, Yasumi Yamazaki (club hostesses), Hiroyuki Yamada, Saburo Yoko, Ben Ichikawa, Buntaro Aoyagi, Masayuki Kawakatsu (customers), Bull Nakano (Mean Jumbo), Yachiyo Hirata, Miari Kamiya, Erika Shishido, Ilsuko Mila, Mimi Shimada (wrestlers), Kensho Kato, Jumbo Sugita (Dota's assistants), Kaori Kuroki (Dota's secretary), Danny Jones (Kitty), Hirofumi Kishi (TV show host), Takashi Yamazaki (trainman), Gen Nakajima (taxi driver), Yukitomo Tochino (noodle shop man), Toto Kitamura (pink motel maid), John Kisk (reggae club owner), Gary Allen (Curtis), Gen Murakami, Mashahiko Hirota (fishermen), Shake Kogura, Kiyoshi Ogawa, Tatsuya Konuma (sleazy rockers), Asaka Kobayashi, Megummi Sakurai, Yasuko Ono, Miwa Ona, Yuki Hara (crepe shop), Hide Sato (press), Shigeru Muroi (Japanese gaijin), Katsunobu Ito (plastic shop assistant), Takashi Inoue (audition M.C.).

A Kuzui Enterprises Production. A Spectrafilm Presentation, in association with Lorimar. A Lorimar Films Release. An American production filmed in Japan in English and Japanese. Dolby Stereo. Spherical wide screen. 99 minutes. MPAA rating: "R." Released 1988.

Tokyo Story / Tokyo monogatari ("Tokyo Story"). Producer, Takeshi Yamamoto Director, Yasujiro Ozu; Screenplay, Kogo Noda and Yasujiro Ozu; Director of Photography, Yuharu Atsuta; Editor, Yoshiyasu Hamamura; Art Director, Tatsuo Hamada; Lighting, Itsuo Takashita; Music, Kojun Saito; Assistant Director, Shohei Imamura.

CAST: Chishu Ryu (Shukichi Hirayama), Chieko Higashiyama (Tomi Hirayama), Setsuko Hara (Noriko), So Yamamura (Koichi), Haruko Sugimura (Shige Kaneko), Kyoko Kagawa (Kyoko Hirayama), Kuniko Miyake (Fumiko), Nobuo Nakamura (Kurzao Kaneko, *Shige's husband*), Eijiro Tono (Sanpei Numata), Hisao Toake (Hattori), Shiro Osaka (Keizo), Zen Murase (Minoru), Mitsushiro Mori (Isamu), Toru Abe (railway clerk).

A Shochiku Co., Ltd. Production. Filmed at Shochiku-Ofuna Studios, and on location. Black and white. Academy ratio. 139 minutes. Released November 3, 1953.

U.S. VERSION: Released by New Yorker Films. English subtitles. 139 minutes. No MPAA rating. Released March 1972.

Tokyo Twilight / Tokyo boshoku ("Tokyo Twilight"). Director, Yasujiro Ozu; Screenplay, Yasujiro Ozu and Kogo Noda; Director of Photography, Yuharu Atsuta.

CAST: Setsuko Hara, Isuzu Yamada, Ineko Arima, Chishu Ryu, Masami Taura, Kinzo Shin, Nobuo Nakamura, Haruko Sugiyama, Teiji Takahashi, Fujio Suga.

A Shochiku Co., Ltd., Production. Black and white. Academy ratio. 141 minutes. Released April 30, 1957.

U.S. VERSION: Released by Shochiku Films of America, Inc. English subtitles. 141 minutes. No MPAA rating. Released July 19, 1972.

Tombstone for Fireflies / Hotaru no haka ("Grave of the Fireflies") **[animated]**. Producer, Ryoichi Sato; Director, Isao Takahata; Screenplay, Isao Takahata, based on an original story by Akiyuki Nosaka; Director of Photography, Nobuo Koyama; Music, Michio Mamiya.

VOICE CHARACTERIZATIONS: Ayano Shiraishi, Tsutomu Tatsumi.

A Shinchosha Co., Ltd. Production. Color. Spherical wide screen. 90 minutes. Released 1988.

U.S. VERSION: Distributor, if any, is undetermined.

Tomei ningen ("Invisible Man"). Producer, Takeo Kita; Director, Motoyoshi Oda; Screenplay, Shigeki Hidaka, loosely based on the novel *The Invisible Man* by H.G. Wells; Director of Photography, Eiji Tsuburaya; Music, Kyosuke Kami; Sound, Toho Dubbing Theatre, Sound Effects, Toho Sound Effects Group. *Toho Special Effects Group*: Director, Eiji Tsuburaya.

CAST: Seizaburo Kawazu, Minoru Takada, Yoshio Tsuchiya, Yutaka Sada, Haruo Nakajima, Miki Sanjo, Kamatari Fujiwara.

A Toho Co., Ltd. Production. Western Electric Mirrophonic recording. Black and white (processed by Kinuta Laboratories Ltd.). Academy ratio. 70 minutes. Released December 29, 1954.

U.S. VERSION: Distributor, if any, is undetermined. International titles: *The Invisible Man* and *The Invisible Avenger*.

Tomei ningen arawaru ("Invisible Man Appears"). Executive Producer, Masaichi Nagata; Director/Screenplay, Shinsei Adachi; Special Effects Director, Eiji Tsuburaya; Sound, Daiei Recording Studio.

CAST: Chizuru Kitagawa, Takiko Mizunoe.

A Daiei Motion Picture Co., Ltd. Production. Western Electric Mirrophonic recording. Black and white (processed by Daiei Laboratory). Academy ratio. 87 minutes. Released 1949.

U.S. VERSION: Never released theatrically in the United States. International title: *The Transparent Man*. Sequel: *The Transparent Man vs. the Fly Man* (1957).

Tomei ningen erohakase ("Invisible Man—Dr. Eros"). Producer, Minoru Suzuki; Director, Koji Seki; Directors of Photography, Hayato Hori, Yuji Go.

CAST: Jun Kitamura (Dr. Ohgari), Lilie Kagawa (Julie), Kako Tachibana (Rila), Reiko Akikawa, Yumiko Matsumoto, Shin Nagaoka.

A Shin Nihon Eiga Production. A Kohuei Release. Black and white. Academy ratio. 67 minutes. Released 1968.

U.S. VERSION: Distributor, if any, is undetermined. International title: *Invisible Man — Dr. Eros*.

Tom's Adventures / Chibi neko Tomu no daiboken ("Great Adventures of Little Tom Cat") **[animated]**. Producers, Shakudo [no other name given] and S.U. Planning; Director, Ryutaro Nakamura; Screenplay, Ryutaro Nakamura, based on an original story by Masumi Iino; Director of Photography, Akihiko Takahashi; Music, Kenji Kawai.

VOICE CHARACTERIZATIONS: Ryoko Sano, Yoshiko Fujita, Minami Takayama.

An Urban Products Production. Color. Spherical wide screen (?). 82 minutes. Released 1992 (?).

U.S. VERSION: Distributor, if any, is undetermined.

Toppo Gigio and the Missile War / Toppo Jijo no botan senso ("Toppo Gigio's Missile War") **[puppet film]**. Producers, Yoshio Aoyama, Federico Kaldorla, and Kon Ichikawa; Director, Kon Ichikawa; Screenplay, Kon Ichikawa, Rokusuke Ei, Albert Ongaro, and Federico Kaldorla; Director of Photography, Shigekazu Nagano; Music, Hachidai Nakamura; Art Director, Mario Mirani; Lighting, Mitsuo Kume; Sound Recording, Tetsuya Ohashi; Editor, Ichiro Horiuchi.

VOICE CHARACTERIZATIONS: Mieko Nakamura (Toppo Gigio), Goro Tojo (man in green socks), Tadashi Negami (man in red socks), Yagumo Sono (man in yellow socks), Koichi Fuse (man in blue socks), Tsune Sunaga (man in purple socks), Toru Ohira (boss).

A Perego/Ichikawa Productions Production. A Japanese/Italian co-production. Color (?). Academy ratio (?). Running time undetermined. Released July 20, 1967.

U.S. VERSION: Distributor, if any, is undetermined. A sequel to the all-Italian *The Magic World of Toppo Gigio* (1965).

Topsy-Turvy Journey / Gyakuten ryoko ("A Reversal Is Going Well"). Producer, Kiyoshi Shimazu; Director, Shoji Segawa; Screenplay, Kazuo Funabashi; Director of Photography, T. Takaha; Art Director, Masao Kumagi; Music, Taku Izumi.

CAST: Frankie Sakai (Goichi Hasegawa), Chieko Baisho (Sakura), Kensaku Morita (Shinsaku), Kumi Hayase (Ayako), Tomomi Sato (Kaori), Arihiro Fujimura (Mitsui), Toru Yuri (Arao), Chocho Miyako (Mine), Junzaburo Ban (Daikichi Yashiro), Utako Kyo, Keisuke Ko, Zaizu Ichiro, Hiroshi Minami, Bonta Sesshi, Harumi Miyako.

A Shochiku Co., Ltd. Production. Color. Shochiku GrandScope (?). 93 minutes. Released August 1969.

U.S. VERSION: Released by Shochiku Films of America, Inc. English subtitles. The 3rd "Shochiku Comedy" feature. Followed by *Yosakoi Journey* (1969). 93 minutes. No MPAA rating. Released April 1, 1970.

Tora! Tora! Tora! ("Tiger! Tiger! Tiger!"). Executive Producer, Darryl F. Zanuck; Executive in Charge of Production, Richard D. Zanuck; Producer, Elmo Williams; Associate Producers of Japanese Episodes, Otto Lang, Masayuki Tagaki, and Keinosuke Kubo; Director (U.S.), Richard Fleischer; Directors (Japan), Toshio Masuda and Kinji Fukasaku; Second Unit Director, Ray Kellogg; Screenplay, Larry Forrester, Hideo Oguni, and Ryuzo Kikushima, based on the books *Tora! Tora! Tora!* (1969) by Gordon W. Prange and *The Broken Seal: Operation Magic and the Secret Road to Pearl Harbor* (1967) by Ladislas Farango; Music, Jerry Goldsmith; Director of Photography (U.S.) Charles F. Wheeler; Directors of Photography (Japan), Sinsaku Himeda, Masamichi Sato, Osami Furuya; Art Directors, Jack Martin Smith, Yoshiro Muraki, Richard Day, and Taizo Kawashima; Sound Recording, James Corcoran, Murray Spivack, Douglas O. Williams, Theodore Soderberg, Herman Lewis, and Shin Watari; Set Decorators, Walter M. Scott, Norman Rockett, and Carl Biddiscombe; Orchestration, Arthur Morton; Makeup supervision, Daniel J. Striepeke; Makeup, Layne "Shotgun" Britton; Wardrobe Supervision, Courtney Haslam; Wardrobe, Edward Wynigear; Editors, James E. Newcom, Pembroke J. Herring, and Inoue Chikaya; Assistant Directors, David Hall, Elliott Shick, and Hiroshi Nagai; Unit Production Managers, William Eckhardt, Jack Stubbs, Stanley H. Goldsmith, and Masao Namikawa; Special

Photographic Effects, L.B. Abbott, Art Cruickshank, and Howard Lydecker; Mechanical Effects, A.D. Flowers, Glen E. Robinson; Script Supervisor, Duane Toler; Air Operations, Lt. Col. Arthur P. Wildern, Jr., USAF (Retd.), Capt. George Watkins, USN, and Jack Canary; Department of Defense Project Officer and Naval Coordinator, Commander E.P. Stafford, USN; Production Coordinators, Maurice Unger and Theodore Taylor; Technical Advisers, Kameo Sonokawa, Kuranosuke Isoda, Shizu Takada, Tsuyoshi Saka, Konrad Schreier, Jr., Commander Minoru Genda, and Robert Buckhart; Aerial Photography, Vision Photography, Inc.; Titles, Pacific Title; Director of Photography (Second Unit), David Butler; Supervising Sound Editor, Don Hall, Jr.; Supervising Music Editor, Leonard A. Engel; Unit Publicists, Ted Taylor and Hal Sherman; Still Photographers, Sterling Smith, Malcolm Bullock, Doug Kirkland, and Tamotsu Yato; Camera Operator, Jack Whitman, Jr.; Assistant Cameraman, Tom Kerschner; Camera Operators (Second Unit), Michael Butler and Tony Butler; Assistant Cameraman (Second Unit), John Fleckstein; Gaffer, Bill Huffman III; Gaffer (Second Unit), Don Knight; Key Grip (Second Unit), Chuck Record; Chief Pilot, Dave Jones; Construction Supervisor, Ivan Martin; Miniature Construction Supervisor, Gail Brown; Army Affairs Coordinator, Col. B.H. Watson, USA; Story Consultants, Rear Admiral Yasuji Watanabe, Retd. and Rear Admiral Shigeru Fukutomi; Japanese Aircraft Consultant, Kanoe Sonokawa; Production Auditor, Gaines Johnston; Cooperation, US Department of Defense, US Navy, US Army, US Air Force, US Embassy in Japan, Japanese Imperial Navy, Japanese Imperial Government.

CAST: Martin Balsam (Admiral Husband E. Kimmel), Jason Robards (Lt. General Walter C. Short), So Yamamura (Admiral Isoroku Yamamoto), Joseph Cotten (Secretary of War Henry L. Stimson), Tatsuya Mihashi (Commander Minoru Genda), E.G. Marshall (Lt. Col. Rufus G. Bratton), Takahiro Tamura (Lt. Commander Mitsuo Fuchida), James Whitmore, Sr. (Admiral William F. "Bull" Halsey), Eijiro Tono (Vice Admiral Chuichi Nagumo), Wesley Addy (Lt. Commander Alvin D. Kramer), Shogo Shimada (Abassador Kichisaburo Nomura), Frank Aletter (Lt. Colonel Thomas), Koreya Senda (Crown Prince Fumimaro Konoye), Leon Ames (Secretary of the Navy Frank Knox), Junya Usami (Admiral Zengo Yoshida), Richard Anderson (Capt. John Earle), Kazuo Kitamura (Foreign Minister Yosuke Matsuoka), Keith Andes (General George S. Marshall), Edward Andrews (Admiral Harold R. Stark), Neville Brand (Lt. Kaminsky), Leora Dana (Mrs. Kramer), Asao Uchida (General Hideki Tojo), George Macready (Secretary of State Cordell Hull), Norman Alden (Major Truman Landon), Walter Brooke (Captain Theodore S Wilkinson), Rick Cooper (Lt. George Welch), Elven Havard (Doris Miller), June Dayton (Ray Cave), Jeff Donnell (Cornelia), Richard Erdman (Colonel Edward F. French), Jerry Fogel (Lt. Commander William W. Outerbridge), Shunichi Nakamura (Kameto Kuroshima), Carl Reindel (Lt. Kenneth M. Taylor), Edmon Ryan (Rear Admiral Patrick N.L. Bellinger), Hisao Toake (Ambassador Saburo Kuruso), Paul Frees (voice characterization for Saburo Kuruso), Susumu Fujita, Bontaro Miyake, Ichiro Reuzaki, Kazuko Ichikawa, Hank Jones, Karl Lukas, Ron Masak, Kan Nihonyanagi, Toshio Josokawa.

An Elmo Williams and Richard Fleischer Production. A Japanese/U.S. co-production in English and Japanese. Filmed at Twentieth Century-Fox Studios (Century City), Toei Studios (Kyoto), Shochiku Studios (Tokyo), and on location in Hawaii, Washington, D.C. (USA), and Ashiya, Kagoshima Bay, Kyusho and Tokyo (Japan). Stereophonic sound. Fujicolor. Prints by Toei Chemistry Co., Ltd. Panavision. Westrex Recording System. 143 minutes plus overture and intermission. Released 1970.

U.S. VERSION: Released by Twentieth Century-Fox Film Corporation. U.S. color and prints by De Luxe. Also exhibited in Panavision 70 (i.e. 2.05:1, 70mm blow-up) for some engagements. Akira Kurosawa was fired as director/co-screenwriter of the Japanese sequences after several weeks of shooting in December 1969; none of his footage appears in the final film and the Japanese sequences were extensively rewritten. Toshiro Mifune was replaced in the role of Admiral Yamamoto. Longtime special effects artist Howard Lydecker died during shooting. Footage incorporated into *Midway* (Universal, 1976), *Pearl* (Warner Bros. Television, 1978), *From Here to Eternity* (Columbia Television, 1979), and other features and television programs. This was not the first Japanese/U.S. co-production, as was widely reported at the time. 143 minutes plus overture and intermission. MPAA rating: "G." Released September 23, 1970.

Tora's Pure Love / Otoko wa tsuraiyo—Torajiro junjoshishu ("It's Tough to Be a Man—Torajiro's Pure Book of Poems"). Producer, Toru Najima; Director, Yoji Yamada; Screenplay, Yoji Yamada and Yoshitaka Asama, based on characters created by Yoji Yamada; Director of Photography, Tetsuo Takaba; Music, Naozumi Yamamoto.

CAST: Kiyoshi Atsumi (Torajiro "Tora-san" Kuruma), Chieko Baisho (Sakura Suwa, *his sister*), Machiko Kyo, Fumi Dan.

A Shochiku Co., Ltd. Production. Color. Shochiku GrandScope. 104 minutes. Released 1976.

U.S. VERSION: Released by Shochiku Films of America, Inc. English subtitles. The 18th "Tora-san" feature. Followed by *Tora-san Meets His Lordship* (1977). 104 minutes. No MPAA rating. Released 1977 (?).

Tora's Tropical Fever / Otoko wa tsuraiyo—Torajiro haibisukasu no hana ("It's Tough to Be a Man—Torajiro's Hibiscus Flower"). Producer, Kiyoshi Shimazu; Director, Yoji Yamada; Screenplay, Yoji Yamada and Yoshitaka Asama, based on characters created by Yoji Yamada; Director of Photography, Tetsuo Takaba; Art Director, Mitsuo Degawa; Music, Naozumi Yamamoto.

CAST: Kiyoshi Atsumi (Torajiro "Tora-san" Kuruma), Chieko Baisho (Sakura Suwa, *his sister*), Ruriko Asaoka (Lily), Masami Shimojo (Ryuzo Kuruma, *Tora's uncle*), Chieko Misaki (Tsune Kuruma, *Tora's aunt*), Gin Maeda (Hiroshi Suwa, *Sakura's husband*), Hayato Nakamura (Mitsuo, *Tora's nephew*), Hisao Dazai (Umetaro, *the printing shop president*).

A Shochiku Co., Ltd. Production. Color. Panavision (?). 104 minutes. Released 1980.

U.S. VERSION: Released by Shochiku Films of America, Inc. English subtitles. The 25th "Tora-san" feature. Followed by *Foster Daddy, Tora!* (1980). 104 minutes. No MPAA rating. Released December 26, 1980.

***Tora-san* Series** Immensely popular Shochiku film series written and directed by Yoji Yamada and starring **Kiyoshi Atsumi** as Torajiro Kuruma—Tora-san. An itinerant peddler, Tora-san is both wise and naive. He is seen as something of an irresponsible nuisance by his family, but his gentle good humor and non-conformity (in an extremely conformist society) make his appeal obvious. Part Tati's Mr. Hulot, part Chaplin's tramp, he is an enduring free-spirit. The series was preceded by a 26-episode teleseries in which Tora-san was killed off in the last episode. Outraged fans protested the killing of their beloved character, and so Yamada and Atsumi responded with a theatrical feature, *It's Tough to be a Man/ Tora-san, Our Lovable Tramp* (1969). This proved extremely popular, and a sequel was released later that same year. The series continued with 2–3 entries a year through the late-1980s, and now appears to have settled into an annual affair, with virtually the same cast of characters and players as in the initial entries. Several prominent film actors have appeared in one or more entries, including Chishu Ryu and Toshiro Mifune. One entry featured actress Kyoko Kagawa and American character actor Herb Edelman. The 47th Tora-san feature was released in 1994.

Films Include: Am I Trying/Tora-san Our Lovable Tramp, Tora-san Part 2/ Tora-san's Cherished Mother (1969); Tora-san—His Tender Love, Tora-san's Grand Scheme, Tora-san's Runaway (1970); Tora-san's Shattered Romance, Tora-san the Good Samaritan, Tora-san's Love Call (1971); Tora-san's Dear Old Home, Tora-san's Dream-Come-True (1972); Tora-san's Forget-Me-Not, Tora-san Loves an Artist (1973); Tora-san's

Lovesick (1974); Tora-san's Lullaby, Tora-san's Rise and Fall (1975); Tora-san's Sunrise and Sunset, Tora's Pure Love (1976); Tora-san Meets His Lordship (1977); Tora-san the Matchmaker, Tora's Dream of Spring (1979); Tora's Tropical Fever, Foster Daddy Tora! (1980); Tora-san's love in Osaka (1981); Hearts and Flowers for Tora-san, Tora-san the Expert (1982); Tora-san Goes Religious (1983); Tora-san's Forbidden Love (1984); Tora-san the Go-Between (1985); Tora-san's Bluebird Fantasy (1986); Tora-san Goes North, Tora-san Plays Daddy (1987); Tora-san Goes to Vienna, Tora-san My Uncle (1989); Tora-san Takes a Vacation (1990); Tora-san Confesses (1991); Tora-san Makes Excuses (1992).

Tora-san Confesses / Otoko wa tsuraiyo—Torajiro no kokuhaku ("It's Tough to Be a Man: Torajiro's Confession"). Executive Producer, Kiyoshi Shimazu; Producers, Kazuyoshi Okuyama and Yoji Yamada; Director, Yoji Yamada; Screenplay, Yoji Yamada and Yoshitaka Asama, based on characters created by Yoji Yamada; Directors of Photography, Tetsuo Takaba and Mitsufumi Hanada; Art Director, Mitsuo Degawa; Editor, Iwao Ishii; Music, Naozumi Yamamoto; Sound Recording, Isao Suzuki.

CAST: Kiyoshi Atsumi (Torajiro "Tora-san" Kuruma), Chieko Baisho (Sakura Suwa, *his sister*), Masami Shimojo (Ryuzo Kuruma, *his uncle*), Chieko Misaki (Tsune Kuruma, *his aunt*), Gin Maeda (Hiroshi Suwa, *his brother-in-law*), Hidetaka Yoshioka (Mitsuo, *his nephew*), Kumiko Goto (Izumi Oikawa, *his nephew's girlfriend*), Chishu Ryu (*Gozen-sama, the temple priest*), Hidetaka Yoshioka (Tora's nephew).

A Shochiku Co., Ltd. Production. Color. Panavision (?). 104 minutes. Released 1991.

U.S. VERSION: Distributor, if any, is undetermined, likely Shochiku Films of America, Inc. The 44th "Tora-san" feature. Followed by *Tora-san Makes Excuses* (1992). 104 minutes. No MPAA rating. Released March 1992.

Tora-san Goes North / Otoko wa tsuraiyo—Shiretako bojo ("It's Tough to Be a Man—Shiretako Longing"). Producer, Kiyoshi Shimazu; Director, Yoji Yamada; Screenplay, Yoji Yamada and Yoshitaka Asama, based on characters created by Yoji Yamada; Director of Photography, Tetsuo Takaba; Music, Naozumi Yamamoto.

CAST: Kiyoshi Atsumi (Torajiro "Tora-san" Kuruma), Toshiro Mifune (Junkichi), Keiko Awaji (Etsuko), Keiko Takeshita (Rinko), Chieko Baisho (Sakura Suwa, *his sister*), Gin Maeda (Hiroshi Suwa, *her husband*), Masami Shimojo (Ryuzo Kuruma, *Tora's uncle*), Cheiko Misaki (Tsune Kuruma, *Tora's aunt*), Hisao Dazai (Umetaro, *the printing shop president*), Chishu Ryu (Gozen-sama, *the temple priest*).

A Shochiku Co., Ltd. Production. Filmed on location in Hokkaido. Color. Panavision. 107 minutes. Released 1987.

U.S. VERSION: Released by Shochiku Films of America, Inc. English subtitles. The 38th "Tora-san" feature. Followed by *Tora-san Plays Daddy* (1987). 107 minutes. No MPAA rating. Released January 11, 1990.

Tora-san Goes Religious? / Otoko wa tsuraiyo—Kuchibue o fuku Torajiro ("It's Tough to Be a Man—Torajiro's Whistle"). Producer, Kiyoshi Shimazu and Shigehiro Nakagawa; Director, Yoji Yamada; Screenplay, Yoji Yamada and Yoshitaka Asama, based on characters created by Yoji Yamada; Director of Photography, Tatsuo Takaba; Art Director, Mitsuo Degawa; Editor, Gan [Iwao] Ishii; Sound Recording, Isao Suzuki; Sound Mixer, Takashi Matsumoto; Music, Naozumi Yamamoto.

CAST: Kiyoshi Atsumi (Torajiro "Tora-san" Kuruma), Chieko Baisho (Sakura Suwa, *his sister*), Keiko Takeshita (Tomoko), Gin Maeda (Hiroshi Suwa, *Tora's brother-in-law*), Masami Shimojo (Ryuzo Kuruma, *Tora's uncle*), Chieko Misaki (Tsune Kuruma, *Tora's aunt*), Hisao Dazai (Umetaro, *the printing shop president*), Chishu Ryu (Gozen-sama, *the temple priest*), Gajiro Sato (Genko), Hidetaka Yoshioka (Mitsuo, *Tora's nephew*), Kiji Nakai.

A Shochiku Co., Ltd. Production. Color. Panavision (?). 105 minutes. Released 1983.

U.S. VERSION: Released by Shochiku Films of America, Inc. English subtitles. The 32nd "Tora-san" feature. Followed by *Marriage Counselor Tora-san* (1984). 105 minutes. No MPAA rating. Released June 29, 1984.

Tora-san Goes to Vienna / Otoko wa tsuraiyo—Torajiro kokoro no Tabiji ("It's Tough to Be a Man—Torajiro's Troubled Trip"). Executive Producer, Makoto Naito; Producers, Kiyoshi Shimazu and Kiyotsugu Kurosu; Director, Yoji Yamada; Screenplay, Yoji Yamada and Yoshitaka Asama, based on characters created by Yoji Yamada; Director of Photography, Tetsuo Takaba; Editor, Iwao Ishii; Art Director, Mitsuo Degawa; Sound Recording, Isao Suzuki; Music, Naozumi Yamamoto.

CAST: Kiyoshi Atsumi (Torajiro "Torasan" Kuruma), Chieko Baisho (Sakura Suwa, *his sister*), Chieko Misaki (Tsune Kuruma, *his aunt*), Keiko Takeshita (Kumiko), Gin Maeda (Hiroshi Suwa, *Tora's brother-in-law*), Masami Shimojo (Ryuzo Kuruma, *Tora's uncle*), Hisao Dazai (Umetaro, *the printing shop president*), Chishu Ryu (Gozen-sama, *the temple priest*), Hayato Nakamura (Mitsuo, *Tora's nephew*), Keiko Awaji (the madam), Martin Loschberger (Hermann), Vivien Dybal (Therese).

A Shochiku Co., Ltd. Production. Filmed on location in Vienna. Color. Panavision. 109 minutes. Released 1989.

U.S. VERSION: Released by Kino International. English subtitles. The 41st "Tora-san" feature. Followed by *Torasan, My Uncle* (1989). 109 minutes. No MPAA rating. Released November 1989.

Tora-san, His Tender Love / Otoko wa tsuraiyo—Futen no Tora ("It's Tough to Be a Man—Restless Tora"). Producer, Director, Azuma Morisaki; Screenplay, Yoji Yamada, Akira Miyazaki, and Shunichi Kobayashi, based on characters created by Yoji Yamada; Director of Photography, Tetsuo Takaba; Music, Naozumi Yamamoto.

CAST: Kiyoshi Atsumi (Torajiro "Torasan Kuruma), Chieko Baisho (Sakura Suwa, *his sister*), Gin Maeda, (Hiroshi Suwa, *his brother-in-law*), Cheiko Misaki (Tsune Kuruma, *his aunt*), Shin Morikawa (Ryuzo Kuruma, *his uncle*), Michiyo Aratama, Yoshiko Kayama.

A Shochiku Co., Ltd. Production. Color. Shochiku GrandScope. 89 minutes. Released January 15, 1970.

U.S. VERSION: Released by Shochiku Films of America, Inc. English subtitles. The 3rd "Tora-san" feature. Followed by *Tora-san's Grand Scheme* (1970). 89 minutes. No MPAA rating. Released October 20, 1973.

Tora-san Loves an Artist / Otoko wa tsuraiyo—watashino Torajiro ("It's Tough to Be a Man—My Torajiro"). Producer, Kiyoshi Shimazu; Director, Yoji Yamada; Screenplay, Yoji Yamada and Yoshitaka Asama, based on characters created by Yoji Yamada; Director of Photography, Tetsuo Takaba; Art Director, Kiminobu Sato; Editor, Iwao Ishii; Sound Recording, Kan Nakamura; Sound Effects, Ryuji Matsumoto; Music, Naozumi Yamamoto.

CAST: Kiyoshi Atsumi (Torajiro "Torasan" Kuruma), Chieko Baisho (Sakura Suwa, *his sister*), Chieko Misaki (Tsune Kuruma, *Tora's aunt*), Gin Maeda (Hiroshi Suwa, *Sakura's husband*), Keiko Kishi, Tatsuo Matsumura, Takehiko Maeda.

A Shochiku Co., Ltd. Production. Color. Shochiku GrandScope. 107 minutes. Released 1973.

U.S. VERSION: Released by Shochiku Films of America, Inc. English subtitles. The 12th "Tora-san" feature. Alternate title: *Tora-san Goes French*. Followed by *Tora-san's Lovesick* (1974). 107 minutes. No MPAA rating. Released May 22, 1974.

Tora-san Makes Excuses / Otoko wa tsuraiyo—Torajiro no seishun ("It's Tough to Be a Man: Torajiro's Youth"). Producer, Shigehiro Nakagawa; Director, Yoji Yamada; Screenplay, Yoji Yamada and Yoshitaka Asama, based on characters created by Yoji Yamada; Directors of Photography, Tetsuo Takaba and Mitsufumi Hanada; Music, Naozumi Yamamoto.

CAST: Kiyoshi Atsumi (Torajiro "Torasan" Kuruma), Chieko Baisho (Sakura Suwa, *his sister*), Chieko Misaki (Tsune Kuruma, *his aunt*), Hidetaka Yoshioka

(Tora's nephew), Kumiko Goto (his nephew's girlfriend), Gin Maeda (Hiroshi Suwa, *Tora's brother-in-law*), Chishu Ryu (Gozen-sama, *the temple priest*), Hisao Dazai (Umetaro), Gajiro Sato (Genko), Masaki Shimojo (Ryuzo Kuroma, *Tora's uncle*), Jun Hubuki, Masatoshi Nagase, Mari Natsuki.

A Shochiku Co., Ltd. Production. Color. Panavision (?). 102 minutes. Released 1992.

U.S. VERSION: Distributor, if any, is undetermined, likely Shochiku Films of America, Inc. The 45th "Tora-san" feature. Followed by a sequel. 102 minutes. No MPAA rating.

Tora-san Meets His Lordship / Otoko wa tsuraiyo—Torajiro to tonosama ("It's Tough to Be a Man—Torajiro and His Lordship"). Producer, Kiyoshi Shimazu; Director, Yoji Yamada; Screenplay, Yoji Yamada and Yoshitaka Asama, based on characters created by Yoji Yamada; Director of Photography, Tetsuo Takaba; Art Director, Mitsuo Idegawa; Music, Naozumi Yamamoto.

CAST: Kiyoshi Atsumi (Torajiro "Tora-san" Kuruma), Chieko Baisho (Sakura Suwa, *his sister*), Kyoko Maya (widow), Kanjuro Arashi (his lordship), Chieko Misaki (Tsune Kuruma, *Tora's aunt*), Masami Shimojo (Ryuzo Kuruma, *Tora's uncle*), Gin Maeda (Hiroshi Suwa, *Sakura's husband*), Chishu Ryu (Gozen-sama, *the temple priest*), Hayato Nakamura (Mitsuo, *Tora's nephew*), Kyoko Maya, Nokihei Mei [Norihei Miki?].

A Shochiku Co., Ltd. Production. Color. Shochiku GrandScope. 99 minutes. Released 1977.

U.S. VERSION: Released by Shochiku Films of America, Inc. English subtitles. The 19th "Tora-san" feature. Alternate title: *Tora-san and a Lord*. Followed by *Tora-san Plays Cupid* (1977). 99 minutes. No MPAA rating. Released August 25, 1978.

Tora-san, My Uncle / Otoko wa tsuraiyo—boku no ojisan ("It's Tough to Be a Man: My Uncle"). Director, Yoji Yamada; Screenplay, Yoji Yamada and Yoshitaka Asama, based on characters created by Yoji Yamada; Director of Photography, Tetsuo Takaba; Music, Naozumi Yamamoto.

CAST: Kiyoshi Atsumi (Torajiro "Tora-san" Kuruma), Chieko Baisho (Sakura Suwa, *his sister*), Chieko Misaki (Tsune Kuruma, *his aunt*), Gin Maeda (Hiroshi Suwa, *his brother-in-law*), Hidetaka Yoshioka (Mitsuo, *his nephew*), Kumiko Goto (Izumi Oikawa, *his nephew's girlfriend*), Chishu Ryu (Gozen-sama, *the temple priest*), Fumi Dan.

A Shochiku Co., Ltd. Production. Color. Panavision. 101 minutes. Released 1989.

U.S. VERSION: Released by Shochiku Co., Ltd. English subtitles. The 42nd film in the "Tora-san" series. Followed by *Tora-san Takes a Vacation* (1990). 101 minutes. No MPAA rating. Released May 18, 1990.

Tora-san Pt. 2 / Zoku otokowa tsuraiyo ("It's Tough to Be a Man, Part 2"). Associate Producer, Tsuguo Saito; Director/Story, Yoji Yamada; Screenplay, Yoji Yamada, Shunichi Kobayashi, and Akira Miyazaki; Planning, Yukio Takashima; Director of Photography, Tetsuo Takaba; Editor, Iwao Ishii; Music, Naozumi Yamamoto.

CAST: Kiyoshi Atsumi (Torajiro "Tora-san" Kuruma), Chieko Baisho (Sakura Suwa, *his sister*), Shin Morikawa (Ryuzo Kuruma, *his uncle*), Chieko Misaki (Tsune Kuruma, *his aunt*), Gin Maeda (Hiroshi Suwa, *his brother-in-law*), Eijiro Tono (Sampo Tsubouchi), Orie Sato (Natsuko), Tsutomu Yamazaki (Dr. Fujimura), Chocho Miyako (Okiku), Hisao Dazai (Umetaro, *the printing shop president*), Gajiro Sato (Genko), Shoko Kazemi, Hiroaki Tsukasa, Keiroku Sato.

A Shochiku Co., Ltd. Production. Color. Shochiku GrandScope. 93 minutes. Released November 15, 1969.

U.S. VERSION: Released by Shochiku Films of America, Inc. English subtitles. The 2nd "Tora-san" feature. Followed by *Tora-san, His Tender Love* (1970). Alternate titles: *Tora-San's Cherished Mother* and *Am I Trying, Part II*. 93 minutes. No MPAA rating. Released July 1, 1970.

Tora-san Plays Cupid / Otoko wa tsuraiyo—Torajiro ganbare ("It's Tough to Be a Man—Hang in There, Torajiro"). Producer, Kiyoshi Shimazu;

Director, Yoji Yamada; Screenplay, Yoji Yamada and Yoshitaka Asama, based on characters created by Yoji Yamada; Director of Photography, Tetsuo Takaba; Music, Naozumi Yamamoto.

CAST: Kiyoshi Atsumi (Torajiro "Tora-san" Kuruma), Chieko Baisho (Sakura Suwa, *his sister*), Shinobu Otake, Masatoshi Nakamura, Shiho Fujimura.

A Shochiku Co., Ltd. Production. Color. Shochiku GrandScope. 95 minutes. Released 1977.

U.S. VERSION: Released by Shochiku Films of America, Inc. English subtitles. The 20th "Tora-san" feature. Followed by *Stage-Struck Tora-san* (1978). 95 minutes. No MPAA rating. Released 1978 (?).

Tora-san Plays Daddy / Otoko wa tsuraiyo — Torajiro monogatari ("It's Tough to Be a Man: Torajiro's Story"). Producer, Kiyoshi Shimazu; Director, Yoji Yamada; Screenplay, Yoji Yamada and Yoshitaka Asama, based on characters created by Yoji Yamada; Director of Photography, Tetsuo Takaba; Music, Naozumi Yamamoto.

CAST: Kiyoshi Atsumi (Torajiro "Tora-san" Atsumi), Chieko Baisho (Sakura Suwa, *his sister*), Kumiko Akiyoshi (Takako), Midori Satsuki (Hideyoshi's mother), Yuichiro Ito.

A Shochiku Co., Ltd. Production. Color. Panavision. 102 minutes. Released 1987.

U.S. VERSION: Released by Shochiku Films of America, Inc. English subtitles. The 39th "Tora-san" feature. Followed by *Tora-san's Salad-Day Memorial* (1988). 102 minutes. No MPAA rating. Released 1988 (?).

Tora-san Takes a Vacation / Otoko wa tsuraiyo — Torajiro no kyujitsu. ("It's Tough to Be a Man: Torajiro's Day Off"). Producer, Makoto Naito; Director, Yoji Yamada; Screenplay, Yoji Yamada and Yoshitaka Asama, based on characters created by Yoji Yamada; Director of Photography, Tetsuo Takaba; Music, Naozumi Yamamoto.

CAST: Kiyoshi Atsumi (Torajiro "Tora-san" Kuruma), Chieko Baisho (Sakura Suwa, *his sister*), Chishu Ryu (Gozen-sama, *the temple priest*), Hidetaka Yoshioka (Mitsuo, *his nephew*), Kumiko Goto (Izumi Oikawa, *his nephew's girlfriend*), Mari Natsuki, Masami Shimojo.

A Shochiku Co., Ltd. Production. Color. Panavision (?). 106 minutes. Released 1990.

U.S. VERSION: Released by Shochiku Films of America, Inc. English subtitles. The 43rd "Tora-san" feature. Followed by *Tora-san Confesses* (1991). 106 minutes. No MPAA rating. Released 1992 (?).

Tora-san, the Expert / Otoko wa tsuraiyo — hanamo arishmo Torajiro ("It's Tough to Be a Man — Flowers and Stream Torajiro"). Producers, Kiyoshi Shimazu and Tetsuo Sasho; Planner, Shunichi Kobayashi; Director, Yoji Yamada; Screenplay, Yoji Yamada and Yoshitaka Asama, based on characters created by Yoji Yamada; Director of Photography, Tetsuo Takaba; Art Director, Mitsuo Dekawa; Music, Naozumi Yamamoto.

CAST: Kiyoshi Atsumi (Torajiro "Tora-san" Kuruma), Chieko Baisho (Sakura Suwa, *his sister*), Yuko Tanaka (Keiko), Kenji Sawada (Saburo), Masami Shimojo (Ryuzo Kuruma, *Tora's uncle*), Chieko Misaki (Tsune Kuruma, *Tora's aunt*), Gin Maeda (Hiroshi Suwa, *Tora's brother-in-law*), Chishu Ryu (Gozen-sama, *the temple priest*), Hisao Dazai (Umetaro, *the printing shop president*).

A Shochiku Co., Ltd. Production. Color. Shochiku GrandScope. 106 minutes. Released 1982.

U.S. VERSION: Released by Shochiku Films of America, Inc. English subtitles. The 30th "Tora-san" feature. Followed by *Tora-san's Song of Love* (1983). 106 minutes. No MPAA rating. Released 1983 (?).

Tora-san, the Go-Between / Otoko wa tsuraiyo — Torajiro renaijuku ("It's Tough to Be a Man — Torajiro's Love School"). Producer, Kiyoshi Shimazu; Director, Yoji Yamada; Screenplay, Yoji Yamada and Yoshitaka Asama; Director of Photography, Tetsuo Takaba; Music, Naozumi Yamamoto.

CAST: Kiyoshi Atsumi (Torajiro "Tora-san" Kuruma), Chieko Baisho (Sakura Suwa, *his sister*), Kanako Higuchi, Mitsuru Hirata, Sugai Gin.

A Shochiku Co., Ltd. Production.

Color. Panavision (?). 108 minutes. Released 1985.

U.S. VERSION: Released by Shochiku Films of America, Inc. English subtitles. The 35th "Tora-san" feature. Followed by *Tora-san's Island Encounter* (1985). 108 minutes. No MPAA rating. Released 1986 (?).

Tora-san, the Good Samaritan / Otoko wa tsuraiyo – Funto-hen ("It's Tough to Be a Man – Struggle Chapter"). Producer, Tsuguo Saito; Associate Producer, Toru Najima; Director, Yoji Yamada; Screenplay, Yoji Yamada and Yoshitaka Asama, based on characters created by Yoji Yamada; Director of Photography, Tetsuo Takaba; Art Director, Kiminobu Sato; Music, Naozumi Yamamoto.

CAST: Kiyoshi Atsumi (Torajiro "Tora-san" Kuruma), Chieko Baisho (Sakura Suwa, *his sister*), Rumi Sakakibara (Hanako), Chyochyo Miyako (Okiku Kuruma, *Tora's mother*), Gin Maeda (Hiroshi Suwa, *Tora's brother-in-law*), Chieko Misaki (Tsune Kuruma, *his aunt*), Shin Morikawa (Ryuzo Kuruma, *his uncle*), Kunie Tanaka.

A Shochiku Co., Ltd. Production. Color. Shochiku GrandScope. 91 minutes. Released April 28, 1971.

U.S. VERSION: Released by Shochiku Films of America, Inc. English subtitles. The 7th "Tora-san" feature. Followed by *Tora-san's Love Call* (1971). 91 minutes. No MPAA rating. Released June 25, 1975.

Tora-san, the Intellectual / Otoko wa tsuraiyo – Katsushika risshi hen ("It's Tough to Be a Man – Katsushika Decision"). Producer, Kiyoshi Shimazu; Director, Yoji Yamada; Screenplay, Yoji Yamada and Yoshitaka Asama, based on characters created by Yoji Yamada; Director of Photography, Tetsuo Takaba; Editor, Iwao Ishii; Music, Naozumi Yamamoto.

CAST: Kiyoshi Atsumi (Torajiro "Tora-san" Kuruma), Chieko Baisho (Sakura Suwa, *his sister*), Fumie Kashiyama (Reiko Kakei, *the pretty boarder*), Keiju Kobayashi (Tadokoro, *her professor*), Masami Shimojo (Ryuzo Kuruma, *Tora's uncle*), Chieko Misaki (Tsune Kuruma, *Tora's aunt*), Gin Maeda (Hiroshi Suwa, *Sakura's husband*), Junko Sakurada (Junko Mogami), Hayato Nakamura (Mitsuo, *Tora's nephew*), Gajiro Sato (Genko), Chishu Ryu (Gozen-sama, *the temple priest*), Masakane Yonekura (policeman), Shuji Otaki (priest).

A Shochiku Co., Ltd. Production. Color. Shochiku GrandScope. 97 minutes. Released 1975.

U.S. VERSION: Released by Shochiku Films of America, Inc. English subtitles. The 16th "Tora-san" feature. Followed by *Tora-san's Sunrise and Sunset* (1976). 97 minutes. No MPAA rating. Released December 31, 1976.

Tora-san, the Matchmaker / Otoko wa tsuraiyo – tonderu Torajiro ("It's Tough to Be a Man – 'Hip' Torajiro"). Producer, Kiyoshi Shimazu; Director, Yoji Yamada; Screenplay, Yoji Yamada and Yoshitaka Asama, based on characters created by Yoji Yamada; Director of Photography, Tetsuo Takaba; Music, Naozumi Yamamoto.

CAST: Kiyoshi Atsumi (Torajiro "Tora-san" Kuruma), Chieko Baisho (Sakura Suwa, *his sister*), Kaori Momoi (wealthy young woman), Chieko Misaki (Tsune Kuruma, *Tora's aunt*), Masami Shimojo (Ryuzo Kuruma, *Tora's uncle*), Gin Maeda (Hiroshi Suwa, *Sakura's husband*), Hayato Nakamura (Mitsuo, *Tora's nephew*), Chishu Ryu (Gozen-sama, *the temple priest*), Akira Fuse.

A Shochiku Co., Ltd. Production. Color. Shochiku GrandScope. 107 minutes. Released 1979.

U.S. VERSION: Released by Shochiku Films of America, Inc. English subtitles. Alternate title: *Tora-san Riding High*. The 23rd "Tora-san" feature. Followed by *Tora-san's Dream of Spring* (1979). 107 minutes. No MPAA rating. Released May 1980.

Tora-san's Bluebird Fantasy / Otoko wa tsuraiyo – Shiawase no Aoitori ("It's Tough to Be a Man – Bluebird of Happiness"). Producers, Kiyoshi Shimazu and Shigehiro Nakagawa; Planning, Shunichi Kobayashi; Director, Yoji Yamada; Screenplay, Yoji Yamada and Yoshitaka Asama; Director of Photography, Tetsuo Takaba; Art Director, Mitsuo Degawa; Music, Naozumi Yamamoto.

CAST: Kiyoshi Atsumi (Torajiro "Tora-san" Kuruma), Chieko Baisho (Sakura Sawa, *his sister*), Etsuko Shiomi (Miho), Tsuyoshi Nagabuchi (Kenkichi), Masami Shimojo (Ryuzo Kuruma, *Tora's uncle*), Chieko Misaki (Tsune Kuruma, *Tora's aunt*), Gin Maeda (Hiroshi Suwa, *Tora's brother-in-law*), Chishu Ryu (Gozen-sama, *the temple priest*), Hisao Dazai (Umetaro, *the printing shop president*).

A Shochiku Co., Ltd. Production. Color. Panavision (?). 102 minutes. Released 1986.

U.S. VERSION: Released by Shochiku Films of America, Inc. English subtitles. The 37th "Tora-san" feature. Followed by *Tora-san Goes North* (1987). 103 minutes. No MPAA rating. Released June 1987.

Tora-san's Dear Old Home / Otoko wa tsuraiyo—Shibamata bojo ("It's Tough to Be a Man—Shibamata Longing"). Producer, Kiyoshi Shimazu; Director, Yoji Yamada; Screenplay, Yoji Yamada and Yoshitaka Asama, based on characters created by Yoji Yamada; Director of Photography, Tetsuo Takaba; Art Director, Kiminobu Sato; Editor, Gan [Iwao] Ishii; Sound Recording, Kan Nakamura; Music, Naozumi Yamamoto.

CAST: Kiyoshi Atsumi (Torajiro "Tora-san" Kuruma), Chieko Baisho (Sakura Suwa, *his sister*), Gin Maeda (Hiroshi Suwa, *his brother-in-law*), Chieko Misaki (Tsune Kuruma, *his aunt*), Sayuri Yoshinaga, Tatsuo Matsumura, Seiji Miyaguchi.

A Shochiku Co., Ltd. Production. Color. Shochiku GrandScope. 108 minutes. Released 1972.

U.S. VERSION: Released by Shochiku Films of America, Inc. English subtitles. Alternate title: *Tora-san's New Romance*. The 9th "Tora-san" feature. Followed by *Tora-san's Dream-Come-True* (1972). 108 minutes. No MPAA rating. Released March 10, 1974.

Tora-san's Dream-Come-True / Otoko wa tsuraiyo—Torajiro yumemakura ("It's Tough to Be a Man—Torajiro's Dream Pillow"). Producer, Kiyoshi Shimazu; Associate Producers, Yukio Takashima and Shunichi Kobayashi; Director, Yoji Yamada; Screenplay, Yoji Yamada and Yoshitaka Asama, based on characters created by Yoji Yamada; Director of Photography, Tetsuo Takaba; Art Director, Kiminobu Sato; Editor, Iwao Ishii; Sound Recording, Kan Nakamura; Music, Naozumi Yamamoto.

CAST: Kiyoshi Atsumi (Torajiro "Tora-san" Kuruma), Chieko Baisho (Sakura Suwa, *his sister*), Kaoru Yachigusa (Chiyo), Gin Maeda (Hiroshi Suwa, *his brother-in-law*), Chieko Misaki (Tsune Kuruma, *his aunt*), Hayato Nakamura (Mitsuo, *Tora's nephew*), Hisao Dazai (Umetaro, *the printing shop president*), Gajiro Sato (Genko), Chishu Ryu (Gozen-sama, *the temple priest*), Kinuyo Tanaka, Naritoshi Yonekura, Tatsuo Matsumura, Masaaki Tsusaka, Yoshio Yoshida.

A Shochiku Co., Ltd. Production. Color. Shochiku GrandScope. 98 minutes. Released December 1972.

U.S. VERSION: Released by Shochiku Films of America, Inc. English subtitles. The 10th "Tora-san" feature. Followed by *Tora-san's Forget Me Not* (1973). 98 minutes. No MPAA rating. Released May 1973.

Tora-san's Dream of Spring / Otoko wa tsuraiyo—Torajiro haru no yume ("It's Tough to Be a Man—Torajiro's Dream of Spring"). Producer, Kiyoshi Shimazu; Director, Yoji Yamada; Screenplay, Yoji Yamada, Yoshitaka Asama and Leonard Schrader, based on characters created by Yoji Yamada; Director of Photography, Tetsuo Takaba; Art Director, Mitsuo Idegawa; Music, Naozumi Yamamoto.

CAST: Kiyoshi Atsumi (Torajiro "Tora-san" Kuruma), Chieko Baisho (Sakura Suwa, *his sister*), Kyoko Kagawa (Keiko), Herb Edelman (Michael Jordan), Gin Maeda (Hiroshi Suwa, *Tora's brother-in-law*), Chieko Misaki (Tsune Kuruma, *Tora's aunt*), Masami Shimojo (Ryuzo Kuruma, *Tora's uncle*), Chishu Ryu (Gozen-sama, *the temple priest*), Hisao Dazai (Umetaro, *the printing shop president*), Hayato Nakamura (Mitsuo, *Tora's nephew*), Hiroko Hayashi.

A Shochiku Co., Ltd. Production. Filmed on location, in part, in the United States. Color. Shochiku GrandScope. 104 minutes. Released 1979.

U.S. VERSION: Released by Shochiku

Films of America, Inc. English subtitles. The 24th "Tora-san" feature. Followed by *Tora's Tropical Fever* (1980). Note the name of Edelman's character. 104 minutes. No MPAA rating. Released June 1, 1980.

Tora-san's Forbidden Love / Otoko wa tsuraiyo – Torajiro Shinjitsu Ichiro ("It's Tough to Be a Man – Torajiro's Road to the Truth"). Producers, Kiyoshi Shimazu and Shigehiro Nakagawa; Director, Yoji Yamada; Screenplay, Yoji Yamada and Yoshitaka Asama; Director of Photography, Tetsuo Takaba; Art Director, Mitsuo Degawa; Music, Naozumi Yamamoto.

CAST: Kiyoshi Atsumi (Torajiro "Tora-san" Kuruma), Chieko Baisho (Sakura Suwa, *his sister*), Reiko Ohara (Fujiko), Masakane Yonekura (Kojima, *her husband*), Jun Miho (the young wife), Chishu Ryu (Gozen-sama, *the temple priest*), Masami Shimojo (Ryuzo Kuruma, *Tora's uncle*), Chieko Misaki (Tsune Kuruma, *Tora's aunt*), Gin Maeda (Hiroshi Suwa, *Sakura's husband*), Hisao Dazai (Umetaro, *the printing shop president*).

A Shochiku Co., Ltd. Production. Color. Panavision. 107 minutes. Released 1984.

U.S. VERSION: Released by Shochiku Films of America, Inc. English subtitles. Includes stock footage from *The X from Outer Space* (1967). The 34th "Tora-san" feature. Followed by *Tora-san, the Go-Between* (1985). 107 minutes. No MPAA rating. Released May 1985.

Tora-san's Forget Me Not / Otoko wa tsuraiyo – Torajiro wasurenagusa ("It's Tough to Be a Man – Torajiro's Forget Me Not"). Producer, Kiyoshi Shimazu; Director, Yoji Yamada; Screenplay, Yoji Yamada, Akira Miyazaki and Yoshitaka Asama, based on characters created by Yoji Yamada; Director of Photography, Tetsuo Takaba; Art Director, Kiminobu Sato; Editor, Iwao Ishii; Sound Recording, Hiroshi Nakamura; Music, Naozumi Yamamoto.

CAST: Kiyoshi Atsumi (Torajiro "Tora-san" Kuruma), Chieko Baisho (Sakura Suwa, *his sister*), Ruriko Asaoka (Lily), Chieko Misaki (Tsune Kuruma, *Tora's aunt*), Gin Maeda (Hiroshi Suwa, *Sakura's husband*), Hayato Nakamura (Mitsuo, *Tora's nephew*), Hisao Dazai (Umetaro, *the printing shop president*), Gajiro Sato (Genko), Chishu Ryu (Gozen-sama, *the temple priest*), Yoshio Yoshida, Tatsuo Matsumura.

A Shochiku Co., Ltd. Production. Color. Shochiku GrandScope. 99 minutes. Released 1973.

U.S. VERSION: Released by Shochiku Films of America, Inc. English subtitles. The 11th "Tora-san" feature. Followed by *Tora-san Loves an Artist* (1973). 99 minutes. No MPAA rating. Released January 4, 1974.

Tora-san's Grand Scheme / Shin otoko wa tsuraiyo ("New It's Tough to Be a Man"). Director, Shunichi Kobayashi; Screenplay, Yoji Yamada and Azuma Morisaki, based on characters created by Yoji Yamada; Director of Photography, Tetsuo Takaba; Art Director, Koji Uno; Music, Naozumi Yamamoto.

CAST: Kiyoshi Atsumi (Torajiro "Tora-san" Kuruma), Chieko Baisho (Sakura Suwa, *his sister*), Gin Maeda (Hiroshi Suwa, *his brother-in-law*), Shin Morikawa (Ryuzo Kuruma, *his uncle*), Chieko Misaki (Tsune Kuruma, *his aunt*), Komaki Kurihara (Haruko), Chishu Ryu (Gozen-sama, *the temple priest*), Hisao Dazai (Umetaro, *the printing shop president*).

A Shochiku Co., Ltd. Production. Eastman Color. Shochiku GrandScope. 92 minutes. Released February 27, 1970.

U.S. VERSION: Released by Shochiku Films of America, Inc. English subtitles. The 4th "Tora-san" feature. Followed by *Tora-san's Runaway* (1970). 92 minutes. No MPAA rating. Released July 25, 1973.

Tora-san's Island Encounter / Otoko wa tsuraiyo – Shibamata yori ai o komete ("It's Tough to Be a Man – Best Wishes from Shibamata"). Producers, Kiyoshi Shimazu and Shigeru Nagawa; Director, Yoji Yamada; Screenplay, Yoji Yamada and Yoshitaka Asama, based on characters created by Yoji Yamada; Director of Photography, Tetsuo Takaba; Art Director, Mitsuo Degawa; Music, Naozumi Yamamoto.

CAST: Kiyoshi Atsumi (Torajiro "Tora-san" Kuruma), Chieko Baisho (Sakura

American Herb Edelman is given a less-than-friendly welcome by Tora-san (Kiyoshi Atsumi) as Chieko Baisho, Gin Maeda, Chieko Misaki, Masami Shimojo and Hisao Dazai look on. From *Tora-san's Dream of Spring* (1979). (Photo courtesy Darrell Davis.)

Suwa, *his sister*) Komaki Kurihara (Machiko, *the island schoolteacher*), Takuzo Kawatani (Harada), Masami Shimojo (Ryuzo Kuruma, *Tora's uncle*), Chieko Misaki (Tsune Kuruma, *Tora's aunt*), Hisao Dazai (Umetaro, *the printing shop president*), Gin Maeda (Hiroshi Suwa, *Sakura's husband*), Chishu Ryu (Gozen-sama, *the temple priest*), Jun Miho (Akemi, *Umetaro's daughter*).

A Shochiku Co., Ltd. Production. Color. Shochiku GrandScope. 105 minutes. Released 1985.

U.S. VERSION: Released by Shochiku Films of America, Inc. English subtitles. The 36th "Tora-san" feature. Followed by *Tora-san's Bluebird Fantasy* (1986). 105 minutes. No MPAA rating. Released 1986 (?).

Tora-san's Love Call / Otoko wa tsuraiyo – Torajiro koiuta ("It's Tough to Be a Man – Torajiro's Love Song"). Producer, Kiyoshi Shimazu; Associate Producers, Yukio Takashima and Shunichi Kobayashi; Director, Yoji Yamada; Screenplay, Yoji Yamada and Yoshitaka Asama, based on characters created by Yoji Yamada; Director of Photography, Tetsuo Takaba; Art Director, Kiminobu Sato; Editor, Iwao Ishii; Sound Recording, Hiroshi Nakamura; Music, Naozumi Yamamoto.

CAST: Kiyoshi Atsumi (Torajiro "Tora-san" Kuruma), Chieko Baisho (Sakura Suwa, *his sister*), Gin Maeda (Hiroshi Suwa, *his brother-in-law*), Chieko Misaki (Tsune Kuruma, *his aunt*), Shin Morikawa (Ryuzo Kuruma, *his uncle*), Takashi Shimura (Professor Suwa, *Hiroshi's father*), Junko Ikeuchi (Takako), Chishu Ryu (Gozen-sama, *the temple priest*).

A Shochiku Co., Ltd. Production. Color. Shochiku GrandScope. 113 minutes. Released December 1971.

U.S. VERSION: Released by Shochiku Films of America, Inc. English subtitles. The 8th "Tora-san" feature. Alternate title: *Tora-san's Love Song*. Followed by *Tora-san's Dear Old Home* (1972). 107 minutes. No MPAA rating. Released April 14, 1973.

Tora-san's Love in Osaka / Otoko wa tsuraiyo – Naniwa no koi no Torajiro (It's Tough to Be a Man – Torajiro's Love in Osaka"). Producers,

***Tora-san's Lovesick* (1974).**

Kiyoshi Shimazu and Tetsuo Sasho; Planning, Yukio Takashima and Shunichi Kobayashi; Director, Yoji Yamada; Screenplay, Yoji Yamada and Yoshitaka Asama; Director of Photography, Tetsuo Takaba; Art Director, Mitsuo Degawa; Music, Naozumi Yamamoto.

CAST: Kiyoshi Atsumi (Torajiro "Tora-san" Kuruma), Chieko Baisho (Sakura Suwa, *his sister*), Keiko Matsuzaka (Osaka geisha), Masami Shimojo (Ryuzo Kuruma, *Tora's uncle*), Chieko Misaki (Tsune Kuruma, *Tora's aunt*), Gin Maeda (Hiroshi Suwa, *Sakura's husband*), Hisao Dazai (Umetaro, *the printing shop president*), Chishu Ryu (Gozen-sama, *the temple priest*), Gonosuke Ashiya.

A Shochiku Co., Ltd. Production. Color. Shochiku GrandScope. 104 minutes. Released 1981.

U.S. VERSION: Released by Shochiku Films of America, Inc. English subtitles. Alternate title: *Tora's Many Splintered Love*. The 27th "Tora-san" feature. Followed by *Tora-san's Promise* (1981). 104 minutes. No MPAA rating. Released January 1, 1982.

Tora-san's Lovesick / Otokowa tsuraiyo—Koi yatsure ("It's Tough to Be a Man—Lovesick"). Producer, Kiyoshi Shimazu; Director, Yoji Yamada; Screenplay, Yoji Yamada and Yoshitaka Asama, based on characters created by Yoji Yamada; Director of Photography, Tetsuo Takaba; Art Director, Kiminobu Sato; Music, Naozumi Yamamoto.

CAST: Kiyoshi Atsumi (Torajiro "Tora-san" Kuruma), Chieko Baisho (Sakura Suwa, *his sister*), Sayuri Yoshinaga, Seiji Miyaguchi.

A Shochiku Co., Ltd. Production. Color. Shochiku GrandScope. 104 minutes. Released 1974.

U.S. VERSION: Released by Shochiku Films of America, Inc. English subtitles. Alternate title: *Tora-san's Lovesickness*. The 13th "Tora-san" feature. Followed by *Tora-san's Lullaby* (1974). 104 minutes. No MPAA rating. Released 1975 (?).

Tora-san's Lullaby / Otoko wa tsuraiyo – Torajiro komodiuta ("It's Tough to Be a Man – Torajiro's Lullaby"). Producer, Kiyoshi Shimazu; Associate Producers, Yukio Takashima and Shunichi Kobayashi; Director, Yoji Yamada; Screenplay, Yoji Yamada and Yoshitaka Asama, based on characters created by Yoji Yamada; Director of Photography, Tetsuo Takaba; Music, Naozumi Yamamoto.

CAST: Kiyoshi Atsumi (Torajiro "Torajiro" Kuruma), Chieko Baisho (Sakura Suwa, *his sister*), Yukiyo Toake (nurse), Gin Maeda (Hiroshi Suwa, *her husband*), Chieko Misaki (Tsune Kuruma, *Tora's aunt*), Masami Shimojo (Ryuzo Kuruma, *Tora's uncle*), Hisao Dazai (Umetaro, *the printing shop president*), Chishu Ryu (Gozen-sama, *the temple priest*), Hayato Nakamura (Mitsuo, *Tora's nephew*).

A Shochiku Co., Ltd. Production. Color. Shochiku GrandScope. 104 minutes. Released 1974.

U.S. VERSION: Released by Shochiku Films of America, Inc. English subtitles. The 14th "Tora-san" feature. Followed by *Tora-san's Rise and Fall* (1975). 104 minutes. No MPAA rating. Released December 1975.

Tora-san's Promise / Otoko wa tsuraiyo – Torajiro kamifusen ("It's Tough to Be a Man – Torajiro's Paper Balloon"). Producers, Kiyoshi Shimazu and Tetsuo Sasho; Director, Yoji Yamada; Screenplay, Yoji Yamada and Yoshitaka Asama, based on characters created by Yoji Yamada; Director of Photography, Tetsuo Takaba; Music, Naozumi Yamamoto.

CAST: Kiyoshi Atsumi (Torajiro "Tora-san" Kuruma), Chieko Baisho (Sakura Suwa, *his sister*), Kayoko Kishimoto (the runaway), Shoichi Ozawa (peddler), Mikiko Otonashi (his wife), Masami Shimojo (Ryuzo Kuruma, *Tora's uncle*), Chieko Misaki (Tsune Kuruma, *his aunt*), Gin Maeda (Hiroshi Suwa, *Sakura's husband*), Hisao Dazai (Umetaro, *the printing shop president*), Hidetaka Yoshioka (Mitsuo, *Tora's nephew*), Chishu Ryu (Gozen-sama, *the temple priest*), Gajiro Sato (Genko), Takeo Chii.

A Shochiku Co., Ltd. Production. Color. Shochiku GrandScope. 101 minutes. Released 1981.

U.S. VERSION: Released by Shochiku Films of America, Inc. English subtitles. The 28th "Tora-san" feature. Followed by *Hearts and Flowers for Tora-san* (1982). 101 minutes. No MPAA rating. Released June 1982.

Tora-san's Rise and Fall / Otoko wa tsuraiyo – Torajiro Aigasa ("It's Tough to Be a Man – Torajiro Shares an Umbrella"). Producer, Producer, Kiyoshi Shimazu; Director, Yoji Yamada; Screenplay, Yoji Yamada and Yoshitaka Asama, based on characters created by Yoji Yamada; Director of Photography, Tetsuo Takaba; Music, Naozumi Yamamoto.

CAST: Kiyoshi Atsumi (Torajiro "Tora-san" Kuruma), Chieko Baisho (Sakura Suwa, *his sister*), Gin Maeda (Hiroshi Suwa, *his brother-in-law*), Ruriko Asaoka (Lily), Eiji Funakoshi.

A Shochiku Co., Ltd. Production. Color. Shochiku GrandScope. 91 minutes. Released 1975.

U.S. VERSION: Released by Shochiku Films of America, Inc. English subtitles. The 15th "Tora-san" feature. Alternate titles: *Tora-san: Love Under the Umbrella*, *Tora-san Finds a Sweetheart*, and *Tora-san Meets the Songstress Again*. Followed by *Tora-san, the Intellectual* (1975). 91 minutes. No MPAA rating. Released June 12, 1977.

Tora-san's Runaway / Otoko wa tsuraiyo – Bokyo hen ("It's Tough to Be a Man – Homesick Chapter"). Producer, Tsuneo Ozumi; Associate Producers, Yukio Takashima and Toshikaza [Shunichi?] Kobayashi; Director, Yoji Yamada; Screenplay, Yoji Yamada and Akira Miyazaki, based on characters created by Yoji Yamada; Director of Photography, Tetsuo Takaba; Art Director, Kiminobu Sato; Editor, Iwao Ishii; Sound Recording, Sachio Obi; Sound Effects, Hiroji Matsumoto; Music, Naozumi Yamamoto.

CAST: Kiyoshi Atsumi (Torajiro "Tora-san" Kuruma), Chieko Baisho (Sakura

Suwa, *his sister*), Shin Morikawa (Ryuzo Kuruma, *his uncle*), Chieko Misaki (Tsune Kuruma, *his aunt*), Tatsuo Matsumura [Matsumoto] (doctor), Kida Michio (Tora's ex-boss), Shoji Matsuyama (his ex-boss' son), Aiko Nagayama (Setsuko), Gin Maeda (Hiroshi Suwa, *Sakura's husband*), Chishu Ryu (Gozen-sama, *the temple priest*), Gajiro Sato (Genko), Tadaaki Tsusaka, Tokuko Sugiyama, Hisashi Igawa, Masahiko Tanimura.

A Shochiku Co., Ltd. Production. Eastman Color. Shochiku GrandScope. 88 minutes. Released August 26, 1970.

U.S. VERSION: Released by Shochiku Films of America, Inc. English subtitles. The 5th "Tora-san" feature. Alternate title: *Tora-san Homebound*. Followed by *Tora-san's Shattered Romance* (1971). 88 minutes. No MPAA rating. Released May 28, 1971.

Tora-san's Salad-Day Memorial / Otoko wa tsuraiyo – Torajiro sarada kinenbi ("It's Tough to Be a Man – Torajiro's Salad-Day Memorial"). Producer, Kiyoshi Shimazu; Director, Yoji Yamada; Screenplay, Yoji Yamada and Yoshitaka Asama, based on characters created by Yoji Yamada and a collection of poems by Machi Tawara; Director of Photography, Tetsuo Takaba; Editor, Iwao Ishii; Art Director, Mitsuo Dekawa; Music, Naozumi Yamamoto.

CAST: Kiyoshi Atsumi (Torajiro "Tora-san" Kuruma), Chieko Baisho (Sakura Suwa, *his sister*), Yoshiko Mita (Machiko), Gin Maeda (Hiroshi Suwa, *Tora's brother-in-law*), Masami Shimojo (Ryuzo Kuruma, *Tora's uncle*), Chieko Misaki (Tsune Kuruma, *Tora's aunt*), Hisao Dazai (Umetaro, *the printing shop president*), Hidetaka Yoshioka (Tora's nephew), Chishu Ryu (Gozen-sama, *the temple priest*), Hiroko Mita, Tomoko Naraoka, Toshinori Obi.

A Shochiku Co., Ltd. Production. Color. Panavision (?). 100 minutes. Released 1988.

U.S. VERSION: Released by Shochiku Films of America, Inc. English subtitles. The 40th "Tora-san" feature. Followed by *Tora-san Goes to Vienna* (1989). 100 minutes. No MPAA rating. Released 1989 (?).

Tora-san's Shattered Romance / Otoko wa tsuraiyo – Junjo hen ("It's Tough to Be a Man – Pure Heart Chapter"). Producer, Takao Ozumi; Director, Yoji Yamada; Screenplay, Yoji Yamada and Akira Miyazaki, based on characters created by Yoji Yamada; Director of Photography, Tetsuo Takahane; Art Director, Kiminobu Sato; Editor, Iwao Ishii; Sound Recording, Kan Nakamura; Music, Naozumi Yamamoto.

CAST: Kiyoshi Atsumi (Torajiro "Tora-san" Kuruma), Ayako Wakao (Yuko), Shin Morikawa (Ryuzo Kuruma, *his uncle*), Chieko Misaki (Tsune Kuruma, *his aunt*), Chieko Baisho (Sakura Suwa, *his sister*), Gin Maeda (Hiroshi Suwa, *her husband*), Hisao Dazai (Umetaro,*the printing shop president*), Chishu Ryu (Gozen-sama, *the temple priest*), Gajiro Sato (Genko), Hisaya Morishige, Nobuko Miyamoto, Tatsuo Matsumura, Goro Tarumi.

A Shochiku Co., Ltd. Production. Eastman Color. Shochiku GrandScope. 89 minutes. Released January 15, 1971.

U.S. VERSION: Released by Shochiku Films of America, Inc. English subtitles. The 6th "Tora-san" feature. Alternate title: *Tora-san in Love*. Followed by *Tora-san, the Good Samaritan* (1971). 89 minutes. No MPAA rating. Released September 1, 1971.

Tora-san's Song of Love / Otoko wa tsuraiyo – Tabi to onna to Torajiro ("It's Tough to Be a Man – A Trip, a Woman, and Torajiro"). Producers, Kiyoshi Shimazu and Tetsuo Sasho; Director, Yoji Yamada; Screenplay, Yoji Yamada and Yoshitaka Asama, based on characters created by Yoji Yamada; Director of Photography, Tetsuo Takaba; Art Director, Mitsuo Degawa; Editor, Gan [Iwao] Ishii; Sound Recording, Isao Suzuki; Sound Mixer, Takashi Matsumoto; Music, Naozumi Yamamoto; Song: "It's Tough to Be a Man," Music, Naozumi Yamamoto; Lyrics, Yoji Yamada.

CAST: Kiyoshi Atsumi (Torajiro "Tora-san" Kuruma), Chieko Baisho (Sakura Suwa, *his sister*), Harumi Miyako (Harumi), Masami Shimojo (Ryuzo Kuruma, *Tora's uncle*), Chieko Misaki (Tsune Kuruma, *Tora's aunt*), Gin Maeda (Hiroshi Suwa, *Sakura's husband*), Hisao Dazai (Umetaro, *the printing shop president*), Gajiro Sato (Genko), Hidetaka Yoshioka

(Mitsuo, *Tora's nephew*), Chishu Ryu (Gozen-sama, *the temple priest*).

A Shochiku Co., Ltd. Production. Color. Shochiku GrandScope. 101 minutes. Released July 1983.

U.S. VERSION: Released by Shochiku Films of America, Inc. English subtitles. The 31st "Tora-san" feature. Followed by *Tora-san Goes Religious?* (1983). 101 minutes. No MPAA rating. Released January 20, 1984.

Tora-san's Sunrise and Sunset / Otoko wa tsuraiyo – Torajiro yuyake koyake ("It's Tough to Be a Man – Torajiro's 'Sunset Sunset'"). Producer, Toru Najima; Director, Yoji Yamada; Screenplay, Yoji Yamada and Yoshitaka Asama, based on characters created by Yoji Yamada; Director of Photography, Tetsuo Takaba; Editor, Iwao Ishii; Art Director, Mitsuo Takada; Music, Naozumi Yamamoto.

CAST: Kiyoshi Atsumi (Torajiro "Tora-san" Kuruma), Chieko Baisho (Sakura Suwa, *his sister*), Kiwako Taichi (geisha), Jukichi Uno (Ikenouchi Seikan, *the artist*), Yoshiko Okada (elderly lady), Masami Shimojo (Ryuzo Kuruma, *Tora's uncle*), Chieko Misaki (Tsune Kuruma, *Tora's aunt*), Gin Maeda (Hiroshi Suwa, *Tora's brother-in-law*), Chishu Ryu (Gozen-sama, *the temple priest*).

A Shochiku Co., Ltd. Production. Color. Shochiku GrandScope. 109 minutes. Released 1976.

U.S. VERSION: Released by Shochiku Films of America, Inc. English subtitles. The 17th "Tora-san" feature. Alternate title: *Tora-san's Sunset Glow*. Followed by *Tora's Pure Love* (1976). 109 minutes. No MPAA rating. Released May 6, 1977.

Tough Guy / Akumyo ("Tough Guy"). Director, Tokuzo Tanaka; Screenplay, Yoshikata Yoda; Director of Photography, Kazuo Miyagawa.

CAST: Shintaro Katsu, Jiro Tamiya, Tamao Nakamura, Yasuko Nakada, Yoshie Mizutani, Reiko Fujiwara.

A Daiei Motion Picture Co., Ltd. Production. Daiei Color. DaieiScope. 94 minutes. Released 1961.

U.S. VERSION: Released by Daiei International Films, Inc. English subtitles. 94 minutes. No MPAA rating. Released July 29, 1970.

Tracked / Usugesho ("Natural Makeup"). Producers, Nobutoshi Masumoto and Takeishi Endo; Director, Hideo Gosha; Screenplay, Motomu Furuta; Director of Photography, Fujiro Morita; Music, Masaru Sato.

CAST: Ken Ogata, Kazuyo Asari, Atsuko Asano.

A Shochiku Co., Ltd. Production. Color. Panavision (?). 124 minutes. Released 1985.

U.S. VERSION: Distributor, if any, is undetermined.

Traffic Jam / Jutai ("Traffic Jam"). Producer, Yutaka Okada; Director, Mitsuo Kurotsuchi; Screenplay, Mitsuo Kurotsuchi and Mineyo Sato; Director of Photography, Kenji Takama; Art Director, Yuji Maruyama; Editor, Akimasa Kawashima; Music, Kenny G.

CAST: Kenichi Hagiwara (father), Hitomi Kuroki (mother), Eiji Okada (grandfather), Emiko Azuma (grandmother), Ayako Takarada (daughter), Shingo Yazawa (son).

A Mitsubishi Corp./Suntory, Ltd./New Century Producers Co., Ltd. Production. An Argo Project, Inc. Release. Color. Spherical wide screen. 109 minutes. Released 1991.

U.S. VERSION: Released by Walter Bearer Films, Inc. English subtitles. 109 minutes. No MPAA rating. Released 1994 (?).

The Transparent Man vs. the Fly Man / Tomei ningen to Hai-Otoko ("The Transparent Man vs. the Fly Man"). Producer, Hidemasa Nagata; Executive Producer, Masaichi Nagata; Director, Mitsuo Murayama; Screenplay, Hajime Takaiwa; Director of Photography, Hiroshi Murai; Sound, Daiei Recording Studio; Special Effects, Daiei Special Effects Department.

CAST: Ryuji Shinagawa, Yoshiro Kitahara, Joji Tsurumi, Yoshihiro Hamaguchi, Junko Kano.

A Daiei Motion Picture Co., Ltd. Production. Western Electric Mirrophonic recording. Black and white (processed by

Daiei Laboratory). Academy ratio. 96 minutes. Released 1957.

U.S. VERSION: Released by Daiei International Films, Inc. English subtitles. Also advertised as *The Murdering Mite*. A sequel to *Tomei ningen arawaru* (1949).

Trapped, the Crimson Bat / Mekura no Oichi jigokuhada ("Blind Oichi—Hell Flesh"). Director, Teiji Matsuda; Screenplay, Hiro Matsuda and Ikuro Suzuki, based on characters created by Teruo Tanashita; Director of Photography, Shintaro Kawasaki; Art Director, Toshiaki Kurahashi; Music, Hajime Kaburagi.

CAST: Yoko Matsuyama (Oichi, *the Crimson Bat*), Yasunori Irikawa (Mosaku), Kikko Matsuoka (Oen), Toru Abe (Bunzo), Jushiro Konoe (Hanbei).

A Shochiku Co., Ltd. Production. Eastman Color. Shochiku GrandScope. 87 minutes. Released June 21, 1969.

U.S. VERSION: Released by Shochiku Films of America, Inc. English subtitles. The 2nd "Crimson Bat" feature. Followed by *Watch Out, Crimson Bat!* (1969). 87 minutes. No MPAA rating. Released June 16, 1972.

Treasure Mountain / Takara no yama ("Treasure Mountain"). Director, Yasujiro Ozu; Screenplay, Akira Fushimi, based on an idea by Yasujiro Ozu; Director of Photography, Hideo Shigehara.

CAST: Tokuji Kobayashi, Ayako Okamura, Choko Iida, Yurie Hinatsu, Tomoko Naniwa.

A Shochiku Co., Ltd. Production. Filmed at Shochiku-Kamata Studios. Silent with benshi. Black and white. Academy ratio. 100 minutes. Released February 22, 1929.

U.S. VERSION: Never released theatrically in the United States. A lost film.

Tree Without Leaves / Rakuyoju ("Tree Without Leaves"). Producer, Shosaku Imai; Director/Screenplay, Kaneto Shindo; Director of Photography, Yoshiyuki Miyake; Music, Hikaru Hayashi.

CAST: Nobuko Otowa, Ichiro Zaitsu, Kazuki Yamanaka.

A Marui Kobunsha Co., Ltd. Production. Black and white. Spherical wide screen (?). 105 minutes. Released 1986.

U.S. VERSION: Distributor, if any, is undetermined. No MPAA rating.

Tsuru / Tsuru ("Tsuru"). Producers, Hideyuki Takai and Hiroaki Fujii; Director, Kon Ichikawa; Screenplay, Natto Wada, Kon Ichikawa and Shinya Hidaka; Director of Photography, Yukio Isohata; Music, Kensaku Tanigawa.

CAST: Sayuri Yoshinaga, Hideki Noda, Kirin Kiki.

A Toho Co., Ltd. Production. Color. Spherical wide screen. 93 minutes. Released 1988.

U.S. VERSION: Distributor, if any, is undetermined.

Tunnel to the Sun / Kurobe no taiyo ("The Sun of Kurobe"). Producers, Toshiro Mifune, Akira Nakai, and Yujiro Ishihara; Director, Kei Kumai; Screenplay, Masato Ide and Kei Kumai; Story, Sojiro Motoki; Director of Photography, Mitsuji Kanau; Music, Toshiro Mayuzumi.

CAST: Toshiro Mifune (Kitagawa), Yujiro Ishihara (Iwaoka), Osamu Takizawa, Ryutaro Tatsumi, Jukichi Uno, Eijiro Yanagi, Eiji Okada, Shuji Sano, Mieko Mayuzumi, Akihiko Hirata, Takashi Shimura.

A Mifune/Ishihara Productions Production. A Toho Co., Ltd. Release. Eastman Color. Toho Scope. 196 minutes. Released March 1968.

U.S. VERSION: Released by Toho International Co., Ltd. English subtitles. 196 minutes (also released at 137 minutes). No MPAA rating. Released October 2, 1968.

Twelve Chapters About Women / Josei ni kansuru junisho ("Twelve Chapters About Women"). Producer, Masumi Fujimoto; Director, Kon Ichikawa; Screenplay, Natto Wada, based on a story by Sei Ito; Director of Photography, Mitsuo Miura; Music, Toshiro Mayuzumi; Art Director, Yasuhide Kato; Lighting, Masao Shirota; Sound Recording, Yoshio Nishikawa.

CAST: Keiko Tsushima (Minako Asuka),

Hiroshi Koizumi (Koheita Kure), Ken Uehara (Tatsuo Kurumada), Ineko Arima (Chieri Mie), Sumiko Koizumi (Hatsuko Otori).

A Toho Co., Ltd. Production. Black and white. Academy ratio. Running time undetermined. Released November 23, 1954.

U.S. VERSION: Distributor undetermined, possibly Toho International Co., Ltd. English subtitles. No MPAA rating.

20 Faces / Shonen tanteidan—Kabutomushi no Yoki ("Boy Detectives: A Weird Air of Beetles"). Director, Hideo Ogawa; Screenplay, Tadashi Edogawa; Story, Ranbo Edogawa, based on a work by Noboru Nezu; Director of Photography, Hiroshi Fukushima.

CAST: Eiji Okada, Jun Usami, Takashi Nakamura, Mitsue Komiya.

A Toei Co., Ltd. Production. Black and white (processed by Toei Chemistry Co., Ltd.). Academy ratio (?). 43 minutes. Released 1957.

U.S. VERSION: Distributor undetermined. Also known as *Tetto no kaijin*.

Twenty-Four Eyes / Nijushi no hitome ("Twenty-Four Eyes"). Director, Keisuke Kinoshita; Screenplay, Keisuke Kinoshita, based on the novel by Sakae Tsuboi; Director of Photography, Hiroyuki Kusuda; Art Director, Kimihiko Nakamura; Music, Chuji Kinoshita.

CAST: Hideko Takamine (Hisako Oishi), Eisei Amamoto (Hisako's husband), Shizue Natsukawa (Hisako's mother), Chishu Ryu (teacher), Toyo Takahashi (woman teacher), Ushio Akashi (schoolmaster), Takahiro Tamura (Isokichi Isoda), Hideki Goro (Isokichi in lower class), Hitobumi Goko (Isokichi in upper class), Rei Miura (Takeichi Takeshita), Yukio Watanabe (Takeichi in lower class), Shiro Watanabe (Takeichi in upper class), Yasukuni Toida (Yoshitsugu Tokuda), Makoto Miyagawa (Yoshitsugu in lower class), Junichi Miyagawa (Yoshitsugu in upper class), Giichi Otsuki (Tadashi Morioika), Takeo Terashita (Tadashi in lower class), Takaaki Terashita (Tadashi in upper class), Tatsuo Shimizu (Jinta Aizawa), Kunio Sato (Jinta in lower class), Takeshi Sato (Jinta in upper class), Yumeji Tsukioka (Masuno Kagawa), Hiroko Ishii (Masuno in lower class), Shisako Ishii (Masuno in upper class), Toyoko Shinohara (Misako Nishiguchi), Yasuyo Koike (Misako in upper class), Yasuyo Koike (Misako in lower class), Kuniko Ikawa (Matsue Kawamoto), Setsuko Kusano (Matsue in lower class), Sadako Kusano (Matsue in upper class), Toshiko Kobayashi (Sanae Yamaishi), Kaoko Kase (Sanae in lower class), Kayoko Kase (Sanae in upper class), Yumiko Tanabe (Kotsuru Kabe in lower class), Naoko Tanabe (Kotsuru Kabe in upper class), Ikuko Kambara (Fujiko Yamashita in lower class), Toyoko Ozu (Fujiko Yamashita in upper class), Yoshiko Nagai (Kotoe Katagiri), Hiroko Uehara (Kotoe in lower class), Masako Uehara (Kotoe in upper class).

A Shochiku Co., Ltd. Production. Black and white. Academy ratio. 154 minutes. Released 1954.

U.S. VERSION: Released directly to PBS in November 1974. Reissued theatrically by Films, Inc. and Janus Films. English subtitles. No MPAA rating. 116 minutes. Remade as *Children on the Island* (1987).

Twilight of the Cockroaches / Gokiburi ("Cockroach") **[part-animated]**. Executive Producers, Taysumi Watanabe and Mayumi Izumi; Producers, Hiroaki Yoshida and Hidenori Taga; Director/Screenplay, Hiroaki Yoshida; Character Design, Hiroshi Kurogane; Music, Morgan Fisher; Sound, Susumu Aketagawa; Director of Photography, Kenji Misumi; Art Director, Kiichi Ichida; Lighting, Masaki Uchida.

CAST: Kaoru Kobayashi, Setsuko Karsuma.

A TYO (Spirit of Tokyo) Productions, Inc./Kitty Films, Inc. Production. A Kitty Enterprises Release. Dolby Stereo. Spherical Panavision. 105 minutes. Released 1987.

U.S. VERSION: Released by Streamline Pictures, Ltd. English subtitles. No MPAA rating. 105 minutes. Released October 6, 1989. Reissued English-dubbed.

Twilight Path / Daikon to ninjin ("Radish and Carrot"). Director, Minoru Shibuya; Screenplay, Yoshiro

Shirasaka and Minoru Shibuya; Original Story, Yasujiro Ozu; Director of Photography, Hiroyuki Nagaoka; Art Director, Nobutaka Yoshino; Music, Toshiro Mayuzumi.

CAST: Chishu Ryu (Tokichi Yamaki), Nobuko Otowa (Nobuyo Yamaki), Mariko Kaga (Keiko Yamaki), Isao Yamagata (Gohei Suzuka), Shima Iwashita (Mie Kawano), Ryo Ikebe (Kotaki), Mariko Okada (Kyoko), Ineko Arima (Natsuko), Yoko Tsukasa (Haruko), Shinichiro Mikami (Saburo), Sinzo Shin (Akiyama), Hiroyuki Nagato (Kosuke), Daisuke Kato.

A Shochiku Co., Ltd. Production. Eastman Color. Shochiku GrandScope. 107 minutes. Released 1964.

U.S. VERSION: Released by Shochiku Films of America, Inc. English subtitles. Alternate titles: *Radishes and Carrots* and *Mr. Radish and Mr. Carrot*. 107 minutes. No MPAA rating. Released May 7, 1965.

The Twilight Story / Bokuto kidan ("Strange Tale of Bokuto"). Producer, Ichiro Sato; Director, Shiro Toyoda; Screenplay, Toshio Yasumi, based on the novel by Kafu Nagai; Director of Photography, Masao Tamai; Music, Ikuma Dan; Assistant Director, Akio Hirayama.

CAST: Hiroshi Akutagawa (The Teacher), Fujiko Yamamoto (The Prostitute), Masao Oda (The Uncle), Michiyo Aratama, Eijiro Tono, Nobuko Otowa, Keiko Awaji, Shikaku Nakamura.

A Tokyo Eiga Co., Ltd. Production for Toho Co., Ltd. A Toho Co., Ltd. Release. Black and white. Toho Scope. 120 minutes. Released August 1960.

U.S. VERSION: Released by Toho International Co., Ltd. English subtitles. 120 minutes. No MPAA rating. Released April 6, 1962.

Twin Sisters of Kyoto / Koto ("Old Capital"). Producer, Ryotaro Kuwata; Director, Noboru Nakamura; Screenplay, Toshihide Gondo, based on the novel by Yasunari Kawabata; Director of Photography, Toichiro Narushima; Art Director, Junichi Ozumi; Editor, Hisashi Sagara; Music, Toru Takemitsu.

CAST: Shima Iwashita (Chieko/Naeko), Seiji Miyaguchi (Takichiro Sada), Teruo Yoshida (Ryusuke Mizuki), Tamotsu Hayakawa (Shinichi Mizuki), Hiroyuki Nagato, Michiyo Tamaki.

A Shochiku Co., Ltd. Production. Eastman Color. Shochiku GrandScope. 105 minutes. No MPAA rating. Released 1963.

U.S. VERSION: Released by Shochiku Films of America, Inc. English subtitles. 105 minutes. No MPAA rating. Released March 1964.

Twinkle / Kira kira hikaru ("Twinkle"). Producer, Koichi Murakami; Director, Joji "George" Matsuoka; Screenplay, Joji Matsuoka, based on an original story by Kaori Ekuni; Director of Photography, Norimichi Kasamatsu; Editor, Mari Kishi; Music, Masamichi Shigeno; Sound, Shimpei Kikuchi.

CAST: Hiroko Yakushimaru (Shoko), Etsushi Toyokawa (Mutsuki), Michitaka Tsutsui (Kon).

A Fuji Television Network, Inc./Space Bond Production. Stereophonic Sound. Color. Spherical wide screen. 103 minutes. Released 1992.

U.S. VERSION: Distributor undetermined. English subtitles. 103 minutes. No MPAA rating. Released July 11, 1993.

Two Hearts in the Rain / Meguri-ai ("Meeting"). Producer, Masakazu Kaneko; Director, Hideo Onchi; Screenplay, Hideo Onchi and Nobuo Yamada; Director of Photography, Fumio Tajima; Art Director, Yoshifumi Honda; Music, Toru Takemitsu and Kazuo Okada.

CAST: Toshio Kurosawa (Tsutomu Eto), Wakako Sakai (Noriko Imai), Shoichi Kuwayama (Tsutomu's father), Mitsuko Mori (Noriko's mother).

A Toho Co., Ltd. Production. Eastman Color. Toho Scope. 91 minutes. Released March 27, 1968.

U.S. VERSION: Release undetermined, possibly by Toho International Co., Ltd. English subtitled version available. 91 minutes. No MPAA rating.

Two Iida / Futari no Iida ("Two Iida"). Producers, Itsuro Yamaguchi and Akira Akai; Director, Zenzo Matsuyama; Screenplay, Zenzo Matsuyama and Yoji Yamada, based on an original story by Miyoko Matsutani; Director of

Photography, Yoshihisa Nakagawa; Art Director, Shinobu Muraki; Music, Chuji Kinoshita.

CAST: Chieko Baisho, Kenichi Kamiya, Yuko Haraguchi.

A *Two Iida* Production. Color. Panavision (?) 110 minutes. Released 1976.

U.S. VERSION: Distributor, if any, is undetermined.

Two in the Shadow / Midaregumo ("Scattered Clouds"). Executive Producers, Sanezumi Fujimoto and Masakatsu Kaneko; Director, Mikio Naruse; Screenplay, Nobuo Yamada; Director of Photography, Yuzuru Aizawa; Art Director, Satoru Nakano; Music, Toru Takemitsu.

CAST: Yuzo Kayama (Shiro Mishima), Yoko Tsukasa (Yumiko), Mitsuko Mori (Katsuko), Mitsuko Kusabue (Ayako Ishikawa), Daisuke Kato (Yuzo), Yoshio Tsuchiya (Hiroshi), Yumiko Iida, Naoya Kusakawa, Mie Hama.

A Toho Co., Ltd. Production. Eastman Color. Toho Scope. 108 minutes. Released January 3, 1968.

U.S. VERSION: Released by Toho International Co., Ltd. English subtitles. Alternate title: *Scattered Clouds*. 108 minutes. No MPAA rating. Released April 24, 1968.

Ukiyoe / Ukiyoe zangoku monogatri ("Cruel Picture Story"). Director, Tetsuji Takechi; Screenplay, Tetsuji Takechi, based on an original story by Dosuke Haguro; Director of Photography, Seishiro Fukami; Art Director, Shigeru Nagakura; Music, Sukehisa Shiba.

CAST: Tamawa Karina (Okyo Miyagawa), Genki Koyama (Choshun Miyagawa, *her father*), Jushiro Kobayashi (Shunga Kano), Junya Usami, Ryuji Inazuma, Ken Yatabe.

A Takechi Production. A Daiei Motion Picture Co., Ltd. Release. Fujicolor. DaieiScope. 86 minutes. Released September 7, 1968.

U.S. VERSION: Release undetermined, possibly by Daiei International Films. English subtitled version available. 86 minutes. No MPAA rating.

Uminchu—The Old Man and the East China Sea / Rojin to Umi ("The Old Man and the Sea"). Producer, Tetsujiro Yamagami; Director, John Junkerman; Loosely based on the novel *The Old Man and the Sea* by Ernest Hemingway; Director of Photography, Shimizu Yoshio; Music, Komuro Hitoshi.

CAST: Shigeru Itokazu.

A Shiglo, Ltd. Production. Color. Spherical wide screen (?). 101 minutes. Released 1990 (?).

U.S. VERSION: Distributor, if any, is undetermined.

Under the Banner of Samurai / Furin kazan ("Wind, Forest, Fire, and Mountain"). Executive Producer, Tomoyuki Tanaka; Producers, Hiroshi Inagaki and Toshiro Mifune; Director, Hiroshi Inagaki; Screenplay, Shinobu Hashimoto, based on the novel by Yasushi Inoue; Director of Photography, Kazuo Yamada; Art Director, Hiroshi Ueda; Music, Masaru Sato.

CAST: Toshiro Mifune (Kansuke Yamamoto), Kinnosuke Nakamura (Shingen Takeda), Yoshiko Sakuma (Princess Yufu), Kankuro Nakamura (Katsuyori Takeda), Mayumi Ozora (Princess Okoto), Ganemon Nakamura (Mobukata Itagaki), Katsuo Nakamura (Nobusato Itagaki), Masakazu Tamura (Nobushige Takeda), Yujiro Ishihara (Kenshin Uesugi), Ken Ogata.

A Mifune Productions Production for Toho Co., Ltd. A Toho Co., Ltd. Release. Eastman Color. Toho Scope. 166 minutes. Released March 1, 1969.

U.S. VERSION: Released by Toho International Co., Ltd. English subtitles. Alternate title: *Samurai Banners*. 166 minutes. No MPAA rating. Released June 25, 1969.

Under the Blossoming Cherry Trees / Sakura no Mori no Mankai no shita ("Under the Blossoming Cherry Trees"). Director, Masahiro Shinoda; Screenplay, Taeko Tomioka and Masahiro Shinoda, based on an original story by Ango Sakaguchi; Director of Photography, Tatsuo Suzuki; Music, Toru Takemitsu.

CAST: Tomisaburo Wakayama, Shima Iwashita, Ko Nishimura.

A Geiensha Co., Ltd. Production. A Toho Co., Ltd. Release. Color. Panavision (?). 95 minutes. Released 1975.

U.S. VERSION: Release uncertain, possibly by Toho International Co., Ltd. in subtitled format. No MPAA rating.

The Underground Syndicate / Sengo hiwa, hoseki ryakudatsu ("Secret Postwar Story, Jury Plunder"). Director, Sadao Nakajima; Screenplay, Sadao Nakajima and Takeo Kaneko, based on an original story by Tsusai Sugawara; Director of Photography, Giich Yamazawa; Art Director, Syuichiro Nakamura; Music, Isao Tomita.

CAST: Bunta Sugawara (Yamada), Hosei Komatsu (Ohara), Asao Koike (Parliment Member Seki), Tetsuro Tamba (Kuroki), Chiezo Kataoka (Okamura), Junichi Takagi (Nakamura, *Okamura's former secretary*), Tomisaburo Wakayama (Sung), Tsusai Sugawara (Dosai), Yasuko Matsui, Masumi Tachibana.

A Toei Co., Ltd. Production. Eastman Color. ToeiScope. 100 minutes. Released June 4, 1970.

U.S. VERSION: Distributor, if any, is undetermined. English subtitled version available. 100 minutes. No MPAA rating.

Unholy Desire / Akai satsui ("Red Murderous Intent"). Director, Shohei Imamura; Screenplay, Keiji Hasebe and Shohei Imamura; Original Story, Shinji Fujiwara; Director of Photography, Masahisa Himeda; Music, Toshiro Mayuzumi.

CAST: Masumi Harukawa (Sadako Takahashi), Ko Nishimura (Koichi Takahashi), Shigeru Tsuyuguchi (Hiraoko), Yuko Kusonoki (Yoshiko Masuda), Haruo Itoga (Yasuo Tamura).

A Nikkatsu Corp. Production. Black and white. NikkatsuScope. 150 minutes. Released 1964.

U.S. VERSION: Released by Toho International Co., Ltd. English subtitles. 150 minutes. No MPAA rating. Released November 17, 1964.

Unico in the Island of Magic / Unico maho no shima e ("Unico in the Island of Magic") **[animated]**. Producer, Shintaro Tsuji; Director, Morimi Murano; Screenplay, Morimi Murano, based on an original story by Osamu Tezuka; Directors of Photography, Iwao Yamaki and Kinichi Ishikawa; Music, Ryo Kitayama.

VOICE CHARACTERIZATIONS: (undetermined).

A Sanrio Co., Ltd. Production. Color. Spherical wide screen (?). 91 minutes. Released 1984.

U.S. VERSION: Distributor, if any, is undetermined.

Universal Laws / Uchu no hosoku ("Universal Laws"). Producer, Toshihiro Kojima; Director, Kazuyuki Izutsu; Screenplay, Akira Asai and Kazuyuki Izutsu; Director of Photography, Noboru Shinoda; Music, Stardust Review.

CAST: Masato Furuoya (Yoshiaki), Kyozo Nagastuka (Kazuya), Megumi Yokoyama (Miki), Mari Torigoe (Reiko), Haruko Mabuchi, Yoshimi Ashikawa.

A Daiei Co., Ltd. Production. A Toho Co., Ltd. Release (?). Color. Spherical wide screen (?). 119 minutes. Released 1990.

U.S. VERSION: Distributor, if any, is undetermined.

Until the Day We Meet Again / Mata au hi made ("Until the Day We Meet Again"). Director, Yasujiro Ozu; Screenplay, Kogo Noda; Director of Photography, Hideo Shigehara.

CAST: Joji Oka, Yoshiko Okada, Hiroko Kawasaki, Satoko Date, Shinyo Nara, Chishu Ryu.

A Shochiku Co., Ltd. Production. Filmed at Shochiku-Kamata Studios. Silent with synchronized music and sound effects. Black and white. Academy ratio. 110 minutes. Released November 24, 1932.

U.S. VERSION: Apparently never released in the Unted States. A lost film.

An Urban Affair / Kigeki: Ekimae danchi ("Comedy: Apartment in Front of the Station"). Director, Seiji Hisamatsu.

CAST: Hisaya Morishige, Junzaburo Ban, Frankie Sakai.

A Tokyo Eiga Co., Ltd. Production for Toho Co., Ltd. A Toho Co., Ltd. Release. Black and white. Toho Scope. 88 minutes. Released August 1961.

U.S. VERSION: Released by Toho International Co., Ltd. English subtitles. The second film in the 24-feature "Train Station" series (1958–69). 88 minutes. No MPAA rating. Released April 6, 1962.

Urutoraman ("Ultraman"). Executive Producer, Eiji Tsuburaya; Producers, Toshiaki Ichikawa, Masayoshi Sueyasu; Director, Hajime Tsuburaya; Screenplay, Shinichi Sekizawa, Tetsuo Kinjo, Shozo Uehara, Bunzo Wakatsuki, based on characters created by Eiji Tsuburaya; Director of Photography, Masaharu Utsumi; Art Director, Chikyu Iwasaki; Music, Kunio Miyauchi; Sound, Kinuta Laboratory, Ltd.; Optical Photography, Minoru Nakano.

CAST: Susumu Kurobe (Hayata), Shoji Kobayashi (Captain Muramatsu), Ikichi Ishii (Arashi), Hiroko Sakurai (Akiko Fuji), Masanori Nihei (Ide), Toshi Furuya (Ultraman), Koji Ishizaka, Mitsu Urano (narrators).

A Tsuburaya Productions, Ltd. Production. A Toho Co., Ltd. Presentation. Blown up to 35mm from 16mm original. Eastman Color (prints by Tokyo Laboratory, Ltd.). 1.37:1 projected screen aspect ratio. Double-billed with *King Kong Escapes* (1967). 79 minutes. Released 1967.

U.S. VERSION: Never released in the United States. This theatrical feature was derived from the popular 1966-67 Japanese television series, "Urutoraman," originally broadcast on the TBS network in Japan. This feature was compiled from several episodes of the series (and possibly including newly shot linking footage). International title: *The Ultra Man*. Alternate title: *Ultra Man*. Note: Several episodes from the various "Ultra" series ("Ultraman," "Ultra Seven," "Ultraman Taro," "Ultraman Leo," "Ultraman 80," etc.) have been re-edited and shown theatrically in Japan, usually shorts, but occasionally as features as well. They include *Urotoruman* (1979), *Urotoruman—Kaiju Daikessen* (1979; released internationally as *Ultraman—Monster Big Battle*) and *The Six Ultra Brothers vs. the Monster Army* (1979), the latter a Japanese/Thai co-production feature filmed in 1974 Tsuburaya.

Urutoraman sutori ("The Ultraman Story"). Executive Producers, Noburo Tsuburaya and Kiyotaka Ugawa; Director, Koichi Takano; Creator/Planner, Noburo Tsuburaya; Screenplay, Yasushi Hirano; Director of Photography, Takeshi Yamamoto; Lighting, Kenji Ushiba; Art Director, Jun Yamaguchi and Tsuneo Kantake; Assistant Director, Kenichi Uraoka; Research, Koichiro Fujishima and Masumi Kaneda; Music, Toru Fuyuki and Shunsuke Kikuchi, Tsuburaya Music Publishing, Inc.; Music Producers, Shizuka Tamagawa and Kunio Miyauchi.

CAST: (not available).

A Tsuburaya Productions Picture. A Shochiku/Fuji Co., Ltd. Release. Color. Academy ratio (?). Running time undetermined. Released July 14, 1984.

U.S. VERSION: Distributor, if any, is undetermined. Includes stock footage from the various "Ultra" series.

Utamaro and His Five Women / Utamaro o meguru gonin no onna ("Utamaru and His Five Women"). Director, Kenij Mizoguchi; Screenplay, Yoshikata Yoda, based on the biographical story by Kanji Kunieda; Director of Photography, Shigeto Miki; Art Director, Isamu Motoki; Music, Hisato Osawa and Tamezo Mochizuki.

CAST: Minosuke Bando (Utamaro), Kinuyo Tanaka (Okita), Kotaro Bando (Seinosuke), Hiroko Kawasaki (Oran), Toshiko Iizuka (Takasode), Kyoko Kusajima (Oman), Eiko Ohara (Yukie), Shotaro Nakamura (Shozaburo), Kinnosuke Takamatsu, Minpei Tomimoto (Takemaro), Mitsuaki Minami (Kano), Masao Hori, Kinnosuke Takamatsu.

A Shochiku Co., Ltd. Production. Filmed at Shochiku-Kyoto Studios. 93 minutes. Released December 17, 1946.

U.S. VERSION: Released by Shochiku Films of America, Inc. (?). English subtitles. Running time also given at 106 minutes. 93 minutes. No MPAA rating. Released 1972. Reissued by New Yorker Films.

Utamaro, Painter of Women. Producer, Masaichi Nagata; Director/Screenplay, Keigo Kimura.

CAST: Kazuo Hasegawa (Utamaro), Chikage Awashima (Otami), Hitomi Nozoe (Oyuki), Fujiko Yamamoto (Kohan), Yasuko Nakada (Tamaki), Keiko Awaji (Otose), Masumi Harukawa (Ocho), Yuko Mori (Ogurama), Seizaburo Kawazu (Eisen Kano), Kyu Sazanka (landlord), Tamae Kiyokawa (Okaku), Bontaro Miyake (Jinpachi), Sonosuke Sawamura (Lord Matsudara).

A Daiei Motion Picture Co., Ltd. Production. Color. DaieiScope. Running time undetermined. Released 1959.

U.S. VERSION: Released by Harrison Pictures Corp. English subtitles. Running time undetermined. No MPAA rating. Released October 16, 1960.

Vacuum Zone / Shinku chitai ("Vacuum Zone"). Director, Satsuo Yamamoto; Screenplay, Yusaku Yamagata, based on the novel by Hiroshi Noma; Director of Photography, Minoru Maeda; Art Director, Yasuzo Kawashima; Music, Ikuma Dan.

CAST: Isao Kimura (Kitani), Takashi Kanda (Troop Commander Mine), Yoshi Kato (Lt. Hayashi), Eiji Okada (Okamoto), Yoichi Numata (Duty Officer of the Week), Koichi Nishimura (Sergeant Osumi), Asao Sano (Ikeno), Isao Numazaki (Hikoza), Tsuyomu Shimomura (Soda), Toshio Takahara (Some), Kiyoshi Nonomura (Uchimura), Kenji Susukita (Uchimura's father), Harue Tone (Hanayei).

A Shinsei Film Co., Ltd. Production. Black and white. Academy ratio. 129 minutes. Released 1952.

U.S. VERSION: Distributor undetermined. English subtitles. 129 minutes. No MPAA rating.

The Vampire Doll / Yureiyashiki no kyofu: chi o su ningyo ("Fear of the Ghost House: Blood-Sucking Doll"). Executive Producers, Tomoyuki Tanaka, Fumio Tanaka; Director, Michio Yamamoto; Screenplay, Ei Ogawa, Hiroshi Nagano; Director of Photography, Kazutami Hara; Art Director, Yoshifumi Honda; Music, Riichiro Manabe; Sound, Toho Recording Centre; Sound Effects, Toho Sound Effects Group. *Toho Special Effects Group*: Director, Teruyoshi Nakano.

CAST: Kayo Matsuo (Keiko), Yukiko Kobayashi (Yuko), Yoko Minazake (the mother), Atsuo Nakamura (Kazuhiko), Junya Usami (Dr. Yamaguchi), Akira Nakao (the friend), Sachio Sakai (taxi driver), Itaru Takashima, Jun Hamamura, Kinzo Sekiguchi.

A Toho Co., Ltd. Production. Color (processed by Tokyo Laboratory, Ltd.). Panavision. 93 minutes. Released July 4, 1970

U.S. VERSION: Released by Toho International Co., Ltd. English subtitles. International title: *The Night of the Vampire.* 71 minutes. No MPAA rating. Released August 6, 1971.

Vampire Hunter D / Vampire Hunter D **[animated]**. Executive Producers, Shigeo Maruyama and Yutaka Takahashi; Producers, Hiroshi Kato, Mitsuhisa Koeda, and Yukio Nagasaki; Director/Art Director, Toyo Ashida; Screenplay, Yasushi Hirano; Character Design, Yoshitaka Amano; Music, Noriyoshi Matsuura.

VOICE CHARACTERIZATIONS: (undetermined).

An Epic/Sony, Inc., Movie, Inc. and CBS Sony Group, Inc./Ashi Production. A Toho Co., Ltd. Release. Stereophonic Sound. Color. Spherical wide screen (?). 81 minutes. Released 1985.

U.S. VERSION: Released by Streamline Pictures. English-dubbed. Producer/Director/Screenplay, Carl Macek; Dialogue Director, Tom Wyner; Sound, Deb Adair. 76 minutes. No MPAA rating. Released August 1992.

Voice Characterizations for U.S. VERSION: Michael McConnohie, Barbara Goodson, Jeff Winkless, Edie Mirman, Kerrigan Mahan, Steve Kramer, Steve Bulen, Joyce Kurtz, Lara Cody, Tom Wyner, Kirk Thornton.

The Vanity of the Shogun's Mistress / Ooku emaki ("Scroll of the Shogun's Mistress"). Director, Kosaku Yamashita; Screenplay, Masashige Narusawa; Director of Photography, Juhei Suzuki; Art Director, Seiji Yada; Music, Ichiro Saito.

CAST: Yoshiko Sakuma (Aki), Chikage Awashima (Asaoka), Reiko Ohara (Machi,

Appropriately inept ad for *Varan the Unbelievable* (1958). Less than 15 minutes of the original film survived the American cut (ad mat courtesy Ted Okuda).

Aki's younger sister), Aiko Mimasu (Lady Matsushima), Takahiro Tamura (Ienari Tokugawa), Junko Miyazono.

A Toei Co., Ltd. Production. Eastman Color. ToeiScope. 96 minutes. Released November 16, 1968.

U.S. Version: Distributor, if any, is undetermined. English subtitled version available. 96 minutes. No MPAA rating.

Varan the Unbelievable / Dai kaiju Baran ("The Great Monster Baran"). Producer, Tomoyuki Tanaka; Director, Ishiro Honda; Screenplay, Shinichi Sekizawa; Original Story, Takeshi "Ken" Kuronuma; Director of Photography, Hajime Koizumi; Lighting, Mitsuo Kaneko; Editor, Ichiji Taira; Art Director, Kiyoshi Suzuki; Music, Akira Ifukube; Sound, Toho Dubbing Theatre; Sound Effects, Toho Sound Effects Group; Production Manager, Shotaro Kawakami; Assistant Director, Koji Kajita. *Toho Special Effects Group*: Director, Eiji

Tsuburaya; Photography, Teisho Arikawa; Art Director, Akira Watanabe; Lighting, Kuichiro Kishida and Masao Shiroda; Optical Photography, Hiroshi Mukoyama; Monster Suit, Teizo Toshimitsu.

CAST: Kozo Nomura (Dr. Kenji Uozaki), Ayumi Sonoda (Yuriko Shinjo), Fumio Matsuo (Motohiko Horiguchi), Koreya Senda (Dr. Sugimoto), Akihiko Hirata (Dr. Fujimura), Fuyuki Murakami (Dr. Umajima), Akira Sera (priest), Akio Kusama (1st Officer Kusama), Yoshio Tsuchiya (3rd Officer Katsumoto), Minosuke Yamada (Secretary of Defense), Hisaya Ito (Ichiro Shinjo), Yoshifumi Tajima (captain), Nadao Kirino (Yutaka Wada), Akira Yamada (Issaku), Yoshikazu Kawamata (Jiro), Yasuhiro Kasanobu (Sankichi), Takashi Ito (Ken, *the village boy*), Toku Ihara (village youth), Fumiko Homma (mother), Haruo Nakajima and Katsumi Tezuka (Varan), Soji Oikata, Jiro Kumagai, Masaichi Hirose, Keisuke Yamada, Hideo Shibuya, Koji Suzuki, Masaki Shinohara, Toshiko Nomura, Hiroshi Angeizu, Mitsuo Matsumoto, Yasuo Onishi, Rinsuke Ogata, Junichiro Mukai, Kakue Ichibanji, Mitoko Taira, Eisuke Nakanishi, Ko Narita, Keiichiro Katsumoto, Anzai Sakamoto, Ryuichi Hosokawa, Sen Hayamizu, Tokio Okawa, Hiroko Terazawa, Toriko Takahara.

A Toho Co., Ltd. Production. Western Electric Mirrophonic recording (encoded with Perspecta Stereophonic Sound). Black and white (processed by Tokyo Laboratory, Ltd.). Toho Scope (billed as Toho Pan Scope; some footage converted from Academy ratio). 87 minutes. Released October 14, 1958.

U.S. VERSION: Released by Crown International Pictures, Inc. English-dubbed. A Dallas Productions/Cory Productions Picture. Producer/Director, Jerry A Baerwitz; Screenplay, Sid Harris; Director of Photography, Jacques "Jack" Marquette; Special Photographic Effects, Howard A. Anderson Company; Supervising Film Editor, Jack Ruggiero; Assistant Editor, Ralph Cushman; Music Editor, Peter Zinner; Sound Mixer, Victor Appel; Wardrobe, Robert O'Dell; Makeup, Robert Cowan; Assistant Director, Leonard Kunody; Property Master, Sam Harris; Script Supervisor, Margaret Lawrence; Sound Effects Editor, Kurt Hernfeld; Music, Albert Glasser (from his score of *The Amazing Colossal Man*, 1957, and possibly other Glasser music and/or library music); Sound (mono), Glen Glenn Sound. The new version makes no mention of Toho or any of its production crew in the credits. New Footage filmed in Totalscope (2.35 x 1 anamorphic wide screen), using the Westrex Recording System. Began as a Japanese/U.S. coproduction for U.S. television and possible theatrical release. Double-billed with *First Spaceship on Venus* (Crown, 1962). 70 minutes. No MPAA rating. Released December 12, 1962. Additional Cast for U.S. VERSION: Myron Healey (Commander James Bradley), Tsuruko Kobayashi (Anna Bradley), Clifford Kawada (Captain Kishi), Derick Shimazu (Matsu), Hideo Imamura, George Sasaki, Hiroshi Hisamune, Yoneo Iguchi, Michael Sung, Roy T. Ogata.

Vengeance Is Mine / Fukusho suruwa ware ni ari ("Vengeance Is Mine"). Executive Producer, Shohei Imamura; Producer, Kazuo Inoue; Director, Shohei Imamura; Screenplay, Masaru Baba, based on the novel by Ryuzo Saki; Director of Photography, Masahisa Himeda; Editor, Keiichi Uraoka; Music, Shinichiro Ikebe.

CAST: Ken Ogata (Iwao Enokizu), Rentaro Mikuni (Shizuo Enokizu), Chocho Mikayo (Kayo Enokizu), Mitsuko Baisho (Kazuko Enokizu), Mayumi Ogawa (Haro Asano), Nijiko Kiyokawa (Hisano Asano).

An Imamura Productions Picture for Shochiku Co., Ltd. ShochikuColor. Spherical wide screen. 140 minutes. Released October 17, 1979.

U.S. VERSION: Released by Shochiku Films of America, Inc. English subtitles. Reissued June 1985 in the United States by Kino International. 128 minutes. No MPAA rating. Released October 17, 1979.

Victory of Women / Josei no shori ("Victory of Women"). Producer, Sennosuke Tsukimori; Director, Kenji Mizoguchi; Screenplay, Kogo Noda and

Kaneto Shindo; Director of Photography, Toshio Ubukata; Music, Kyoka Asai.

CAST: Kinuyo Tanaka (Hiroko Hosokawa), Michiko Kuwano (Michiko), Toyoko Takahashi (their mother), Eiko Uchimura (Yukiko), Mitsuko Miura (Moto [Tomo] Asakura), Shin Tokudaiji (Keita Yamaoka), Yoshihira [Katsuhira] Matsumoto (Prosecutor Kono), Akiko Kazami, Shinyo Nara.

A Shochiku Co., Ltd. Production. Filmed at Shochiku-Ofuna Studios (Tokyo). Black and white. Academy ratio. 80 minutes. Released April 18, 1946.

U.S. VERSION: Distributor undetermined. English subtitles. Actress Kuwano died shortly after shooting was completed. 80 minutes. No MPAA rating. Release date undetermined.

Victory Song / Hisshoka ("Victory Song"). Directors, Kenji Mizoguchi, Masahiro Makino, Hiroshi Shimizu, and Tomotaka Tasaka; Screenplay, Matsuo Kishi and Hiroshi Shimizu, based on the novel by Kei Moriyama, and an adaptation by Tomotaka Tasaka; Directors of Photography, Shigeto Miki, Haruo Takeno, Koichi Yukiyama, and Takeshi Saito.

CAST: "The Shochiku All-Stars."

A Shochiku Co., Ltd. Production, in association with the Information Bureau. Black and white. Academy ratio. Running time undetermined. Released February 22, 1945.

U.S. VERSION: Never released theatrically in the United States.

Vietnam in Turmoil / Doran no Betonamu ("Vietnam in Turmoil") **[documentary]**. Director, Masaharu Akasa; Photography, Shinichi Ogawa, Masao Mizukami, Masayori Fukazawa, and Isamu Nagayama.

A Shin Riken Eiga Co., Ltd. Production for Mainichi (?). A Daiei Motion Picture Co., Ltd. Release. Eastman Color. Anamorphic wide screen. 83 minutes. Released 1965.

U.S. VERSION: Released by Harrison Pictures, Inc. English subtitles. An Edward Harrison Presentation. Wide screen process billed as CinemaScope in the United States. 83 minutes. No MPAA rating. Released March 25, 1966.

The Village / Harakara ("Brothers and Sisters"). Director, Yoji Yamada; Screenplay, Yoji Yamada and Yoshitaka Asama, based on an original story by Yoji Yamada; Director of Photography, Tetsuo Takaba; Art Director, Kiminobu Sato; Music, Kyoko Okada.

CAST: Akira Terao (Takashi Saito), Hisashi Igawa (Hiroshi Saito, *his older brother*), Chieko Baisho (Hideko Kono), Mari Okamoto (Aiko), Mahito Akazuka (Chuji), Toru Tsuchiya (Shigeru), Kazuhiko Kasai (Kikuchi), Shuji Otaki (principal), Kiyoshi Atsumi.

A Shochiku Co., Ltd. Production. Eastman Color. Shochiku GrandScope. 127 minutes. Released 1975.

U.S. VERSION: Released by Shochiku Films of America, Inc. English subtitles. Running time also given at 124 minutes. 127 minutes. No MPAA rating. Released May 12, 1976.

Village of Eight Gravestones / Yatsu hukamura ("Village of the Eight Gravestones"). Producers, Yoshitaro Nomura, Shigemi Sugesiaki and Akira Oda; Director, Yoshitaro Nomura; Screenplay, Shinobu Hashimoto, based on the novel by Seishi Yokomizo; Director of Photography, Takashi Kawamata; Art Director, Kyohei Morita; Music, Yasushi Akutagawa.

CAST: Kiyoshi Atsumi (Detective Kosuke Kindaichi), Kenichi Hagiwara (Tatsuya Terada), Mayumi Ogawa (Miyako Mori), Ryoko Nakano (Tsuruko, *Tatsuya's mother*), Yoshi Kato (Ushimatsu, *Tatsuya's maternal grandfather*), Tsutomu Yamazaki (Hisaya, *Tatsuya's brother* and Yozo, *Tatsuya's father*), Yoko Yamamoto (Haruyo, *Tatsuya's half-sister*), Masami Shimojo (Kudo, *the primary school principal*), Ninako Yamaguchi (Koume, *Tatsuya's grand-aunt*), Etsuko Ichihara (Kotake, *Tatsuya's 2nd grand-aunt*), Junko Toda (the exorcist), Takuya Fujioka (Dr. Kuno).

A Shochiku Co., Ltd. Production. ShochikuColor. Panavision. 151 minutes. Released October 29, 1977.

U.S. VERSION: Released by Shochiku

***The Village* (1975). Stars Chieko Baisho and Akira Terao are center.**

Films of America, Inc. English subtitles. International title: *Village of the Eight Tombs*. 151 minutes. No MPAA rating. Released March 17, 1978.

Violated Paradise. Producer/Director, Marion Gering; Based on the books *Ore giapponesi* (1958) and *L'isola delle pescatrici* (1960) by Fosco Maraini; Directors of Photography, Fosco Maraini and Roy M. Yaginuma; Music Supervision, Marcello Abbado; Original Score, Sergio Pagoni.

CAST: Kazuko Mine (Tomako), Paulette Girard (narrator).

Production companies undetermined. An Italian/Japanese co-production. Eastman Color. Academy ratio (?). 68 minutes. Release date undetermined.

U.S. VERSION: Released by Victoria Films and Times Films Corporation. English narration. English narration writer, Tome Rowe. Robert De Leonardis is billed in some sources as co-director. Announced as *Diving Girls of Japan* and *The Diving Girls' Island*. Alternate titles: *Scintilating Sin* and *Sea Nympths*. 68 minutes. No MPAA rating. Released June 7, 1963.

Virus / Fukkatsu no hi ("Resurrection Day"). Producer, Haruki Kadokawa; Associate Producers Yutaka Okada and Takashi Ohashi; Director, Kinji Fukasaku; Screenplay, Koji Takada Gregory Knapp, and Kinji Fukasaku, based on the novel by Sakyo Komatsu; Director of Photography, Daisaku Kimura; Art Director, Yoko Yoshinaga; Editor, Akira Suzuki; Music, Teo Macero; Song, "Tourjours Gai Mon Cher," Lyrics and Performance, Janis Ian; Music Producer, Teo Macero; Executive Music Producers, PMC International, George Braun, President; Sound Mixer, Kenichi Benitani; Gaffer, Hideki Mochizuki; 1st Assistant Directors, Junnosuke and J. Anthony Robinow; Script Clerk, Mikiko Koyama; Production Managers, Isao Nagaoka, Susan A. Lewis, Katsumas Amano; Assistant Directors, Kenichiro Fujiyama, Kazuo Yoshida; 2nd Assistant Director, Jesse Nishihata; Camera Assistants, Masahiro Kishimoto; Toshifumi Nobusaka, Tsutomu Takada; Gaffer, Bob Gallant; Sound Man, Minoru Nobuoka; Boom Man, Brian Richmond; Lighting Technicians, Isao Koyama, Shohei Iriguchi; Key Grip, Jim Craig; Best Boy, Frieder Hochheim; Assistant Grip, Daniel Narduzzi; Assistant Art Directors, Fumio Ogawa, Masumi Suzuki, Lindsay Goddard; Set Dresser, Patricia Gruben; Assistant Set Dresser, Jackie Fields; Set Props, Don Miloyevich; Assistant Set Props, Dawn Tanaka; Special Props, Fernand Durand; Make-up, Kathleen Mifsud; Costumers, Minoru Yamada, Kat Moyer; Wardrobe, Arthur Rowselle; Casting Directors, Shinichi Nakata, Howard Ryshpan, Masayoshi Omodaka; Assistant Casting Director, Arden Ryshpan; Hair Dresser, Tom Booth; Assistant Editor, Akimasa Kawashima; Script Assistant, Nancy Eagles; Director's Interpreter, Toshiko Adilman; Interpreters, Shizuko Kumada, Kazumi Takeshita, Maya Koizumi, John Wales; Special Effects Assistant Director, Ichiro Higa; Special Miniature Consultant, Gregory Jein; Sky Spy Model Design and Matte Paintings, Michael Minor; Special Visual Effects, Coast Productions; Special Visual Effects Supervisor, Phillip Kellison; Still Photographer, Takashi Ikeda; Production Assistant, John Roberts; Production Secretary, Francoise McNeil; Unit Location Manager, Jason Paikowsky; Accountant, Molly Tharyan; Transport Manager, Robert Bartman. *International Version*: Music Post-Production and Creative Sound, Neiman-Tillar Associates, Inc.; Editor, Pieter Hubbard; Associate Editor, Elodie Keene; Music Editors, Jack Tillar and Marty Wereski; Publicity, Guttman and Pam, Ltd.; Assistant Producer, Yoshiaki Tokutome; Supervisors, William R. Kowalchuk, Jr., Kosaku Wada; Special Thanks, Armada de Chile, National Film Board of Canada, Embassy of Canada in Japan, Canadian Armed Forces, Officers and Crew of HMCS Okanagan, Cities of Toronto and Halifax, Charles F. Chaplin, I.F.D., Sony of Canada, Ltd., Zodiac, University of Chile (Tsuyoshi Nishimura), Japanese Society of Peru (Eiichi Amamiya), Filmed in Alaska (Toshio Hishimura), Kenwood; Construction, Scenic Productions (Toronto), International Film Studio (Toronto); Canadian

Production Services, Marlow Pictures, Inc.; Titles and Opticals, Pacific Title (Hollywood); Rerecording Studios, Nikkatsu Studio (Tokyo), Producers Sound Services (Hollywood); Lenses and Panaflex Cameras, Panavision.

CAST: *U.S. Antarctic Wintering Team*: George Kennedy (Admiral Conway), Bo Svenson (Major Carter), Stephanie Faulkner (Sarah), Nicholas Campbell (radio operator). *Japanese Antarctic Wintering Team*: Masao Kusakari (Yoshizumi), Isao Natsuki (Dr. Nakanishi), Tsunchiko Watase (Tatsuno), Shinichi "Sonny" Chiba (Dr. Yamaguchi), Kensaku Morita (Mazawa). *Soviet Antarctic Wintering Team*: Chris Wiggins (Dr. Borodinov), John Evans (Captain Nevsky). *Norwegian Antarctic Wintering Team*: Olivia Hussey (Marit). *Other Countries' Antarctic Winter Teams*: Cec Linder (Dr. Latour), Edward James Olmos (Captain Lopez), Eve Crawford (Irma Ollich), John Granik (Dr. Turowicz), John Bayliss (Major King), Ara Hovanessian (Major Giron), Ted Follows (Major Barnes), Danielle Schneider, Diane Lasko, Laura Pennington, Julie Khaner (secretaries). *United States of America*: Glenn Ford (President Richardson), Stuart Gillard (Dr. Meyer), Henry Silva (Chief of Staff Garland), Robert Vaughn (Senator Barkley), George Touliatos (Colonel Rankin), Larry Reynolds (Morrison), David Gardner (Watt), J. Roger Periard (orderly), Dan Kippy (Reed), William Binney (Simmons), Ron Hartman (Dr. Rogers). *East Germany*: Ken Pogue (Krause), Wally Bundarenko (guard), Jim Bearden (officer). *British Nuclear Submarine "Neried" Crew Members*: Chuck Conners (Captain McCloud), Ken Camroux (Officer Jones), Gordon Thompson (radio operator and sonar man), John Rutter (sailor #1), Alfred Humphreys (sailor #2), Peter Heppleston (periscope operator), Matt Hawthorne (navigator), Lt. Commander David Griffiths (first officer), Michael Tough (young sailor). *Soviet Nuclear Submarine "T232" Crew Members*: Jan Muszynski (Ensign Smirnov), Charles Northcote (sonar man). *Tokyo, Japan*: Yumi Takigawa (Noriko), Ken Ogata (Tsuchiya), Ichiro Kijima (Tadokoro), Takashi Noguchi (intern #1), Nenji Kobayashi (intern #2), Tayori Hinatsu, Keiko Ito, Tomoko Igarashi, Sachiko Sato (nurses), Sanae Nakahara (young mother), Yukiko Watanabe (daughter). Also: Colin Fox (Spy Z), Richard Ayres (little man), Jefferson Mappin (big man), Dick Grant (pilot), Tyler Miller (boy cossack), Charles L. Campbell (TV narrator), Terry Martin, George Wilber (stunts).

A Haruki Kadokawa Films Production, in association with the Tokyo Broadcasting System (TBS). A Toho Co., Ltd. Release. A Japanese Production in English, Japanese, German, French, etc., with Japanese subtitles. Eastman Color (processed by Film House [Toronto], Far East Laboratories, Ltd. [Tokyo] and Consolidated Film Industries [Hollywood]). Spherical Panavision. 156 minutes. Released 1980.

U.S. VERSION: Never released theatrically. Sold directly to cable television. A Broadwood Productions, Inc. Presentation. The non-English-language footage was dubbed for U.S. release. Reviewed at Cannes in May 1980 as "a work-in-progress," running 155 minutes. Current versions are minus footage of Takigawa. Video version: 108 minutes. Current television version: 93 minutes.

Vixen / Jotai ("A Woman's Body"). Executive Producers, Yoshiro Kaga and Harutada Kawasaki; Director, Yasuzo Masumura; Screenplay, Yasuzo Masumura and Ichiro Ikeda; Director of Photography, Setsuo Kobayashi; Art Director, Takesaburo Watanabe; Music, Hikaru Hayashi; Sound Recording, Takeo Suda; Lighting, Choji Watanabe; Editor, Tatsuji Nakashizu; Assistant Director, Chikashi Sakiyama.

CAST: Ruriko Asaoka (Michi Hama), Eiji Okada (Nobuyuki Ishido), Kyoko Kishida (Akie Ishido, *Nobuyuki's wife*), Eiko Azusa (Yukiko, *Ishido's sister*), Takao Ito (Akizuki, *Yukiko's fiancé*), Yusuke Kawazu (Goro, *Michi's old boyfriend*), Eitaro Ozawa (Chancellor Ishido, *Akie's father*), Kazuo Kitamura, Yoshihiko Aoyama, Shizuo Nakajo, Takashi Nakamura, Koichi Ito, Yuzo Hayakawa, Jun Osanai, Tsutomu Nakada.

A Daiei Motion Picture Co., Ltd. Production. Filmed at Daiei-Tokyo Studios.

Fuji Color. DaieiScope. 95 minutes. Released October 1969.

U.S. VERSION: Released by Daiei International Films, Inc. English subtitles. 95 minutes. No MPAA rating. Released May 1970.

Voyage Into Space. Producer, Mitsuru Yokoyama; Director, Minoru Yamada; Head Writer, Masaru Igami; Music, Takeo Yamashita.

CAST: Mitsunobu Kaneko (Johnny Sokko, *Unicorn Agent U-7*), Akio Ito (Jerry Mono, *Unicorn Agent U-3*).

A Japanese teleseries re-edited to feature length for American television and never released theatrically in Japan. A Toei Co., Ltd. Production. 16mm. Color (processed by Toei Chemistry Co., Ltd.).

U.S. VERSION: Never released theatrically in the United States. Released directly to television in 1970 by American International Television, Inc. (AIP-TV). Derived from episodes of "Jiyaianto Robo" ("Giant Robot"), originally broadcast on the NET (TV Asahi) network, which ran 26 thirty-minute episodes in 1967–68. The series was also syndicated in the United States as "Johnny Sokko and His Flying Robot." Producer, Salvatore Billitteri. 88 minutes. No MPAA rating.

Waiting for the Flood / Aitsu ("That Guy"). Producer, Kei Ijichi; Director, Atsushi Kimura; Screenplay, Atsushi Kimura and Ichiro Fujita, based on their original story; Director of Photography, Akihiro Ito; Music, Seigen Ono.

CAST: Kenichi Okamoto (Hikaru), Hikari Ishida (Yuki), Frankie Sakai (grandfather), Tadanobu Asano, Ittoku Kishibe.

A Kitty Film, Inc. Production. Color. Spherical wide screen (?). 118 minutes. Released 1991.

U.S. VERSION: Distributor, if any, is undetermined.

Walk Cheerfully / Hogaraka ni ayume ("Walk Cheerfully"). Director, Yasujiro Ozu; Screenplay, Tadao Ikeda, based on an idea by Hiroshi Shimizu; Director of Photography, Hideo Shigehara.

CAST: Minoru Takada, Hiroko Kawasaki, Satoko Date, Takeshi Sakamoto, Chishu Ryu, Nobuko Matsuzono, Hisao Yoshitani.

A Shochiku Co., Ltd. Production. Filmed at Shochiku-Kamata Studios. Silent. Black and white. Academy ratio. 95 minutes. Released April 11, 1930.

U.S. VERSION: Released by Shochiku Films of America, Inc. English intertitles. 95 minutes. No MPAA rating. Released March 1, 1991.

Wall-Eyed Nippon / Yabunirami Nippon ("Squint-Eyed Japan"). Producer, Seitan Kaneko; Director, Hideo Suzuki; Screenplay, Nagaharu Okuyama; Director of Photography, Taiichi Kankura.

CAST: Akira Takarada (Shin Moriyama), Yumi Shirakawa (Momoko), Jerry Ito (John Machihei), Muza Kemanai (Meery Sweet), E.H. Eric (Lafcadio Yearn), Akiko Wakabayashi (Nashiko).

A Toho Co., Ltd. Production. Eastman Color. Toho Scope. 97 minutes. Released 1964.

U.S. VERSION: Released by Toho International Co., Ltd. English subtitles. 90 minutes. No MPAA rating. Released September 2, 1963.

The Wanderers / Matatabi ("The Wanderers"). Producers, Kinshiro Kuzui, Sachio Tomizawa, and Hiromitsu Oka; Associate Producer/Director, Kon Ichikawa; Screenplay, Shuntaro Tanigawa and Kon Ichikawa; Director of Photography, Setsuo Kobayashi; Music, Shitei Kuri; Art Directors, Yoshinobu Nishioka and Ryoichi Kamon; Sound Recording, Tetsuya Ohashi; Lighting, Masahiro Shiono; Assistant Producer, Osamu Yasumuro; Editor, Saburobe Hirano.

CAST: Ichiro Ogura (Genta), Isao Bito (Shinta), Kenichi Hagiwara (Mokutaro), Reiko Inoue (Okuni), Tadao Futami (Bangame), Akiko Nomura (Oharu), Shinpachi Miyama (Hambei), Toshimitsu Omiya (Yasukichi).

An Ichikawa Productions/Art Theatre Guild Production. Color. Spherical wide screen (?). 96 minutes. Released April 7, 1973.

U.S. VERSION: Distributor undetermined. English subtitles. 96 minutes. No MPAA rating. Released July 10, 1974.

Wanton Journey / Shin Santo Juyaku: Teishu kyo iku no maki. Producer, Sanezumi Fujimoto; Director, Shue Matsubayashi; Screenplay, Ryozo Kasahara, based on the novel *Zuiko-san* by Keita Genji.

CAST: Hisaya Morishige, Asami Kuji, Keiju Kobayashi, Daisuke Kato, Michiyo Aratama, Keiko Awaji, Norihei Miki, Reiko Dan, Kyu Sazanka, Tatsuya Mihashi, Mie Hama, Choko Iida.

A Toho Co., Ltd. Production. Black and white. Toho Scope. 90 minutes. Released 1961.

U.S. VERSION: Released by Toho International Co., Ltd. English subtitles. 90 minutes. The 12th "Company President" feature. No MPAA rating. Released December 22, 1961.

The War in Space / Wakusei Daisenso ("Great Planet War"). Executive Producers, Tomoyuki Tanaka and Fumio Tanaka; Director, Jun Fukuda; Screenplay, Ryuzo Nakanishi, Shuichi Nagahara, based on an idea by Hachiro Jinguji; Director of Photography, Yuzuru Aizawa; Art Director, Kazuo Satsuya; Lighting, Shinji Kojima; Music, Toshiaki Tsushima; Sound Recordist, Toshiya Ban; Sound, Toho Recording Centre; Sound Effects, Toho Sound Effects Group. *Toho Special Effects Group*: Director, Teruyoshi Nakano; Photography, Takashi Yamamoto, Toshimitsu Oneda; Art Director, Yasuyuki Inoue; Mechanical Effects, Takesaburo Watanabe; Optical Photography, Yukio Manoda; Assistant Director, Koichi Kawakita.

CAST: Kensaku Morita (Miyoshi), Ryo Ikebe (Professor Takigawa), William Ross (Dr. Schmidt/alien), Akihiko Hirata (Defense Countermeasure Supreme Commander Oshi), David Perin (Jimmy), Yuko Asano (June?), Hiroshi Miyauchi (Morrei?), Goro Mutsumi (alien commander), Masaya Oki, Shuji Otaki, Katsutoshi Atarashi, Isao Hashimoto, Shoji Nakayama, Masao Kusakari.

A Toho-Eizo Production. A Toho Co., Ltd. Release. Color (processed by Tokyo Laboratory, Ltd.). Panavision. 90 minutes. Released December 17, 1977.

U.S. VERSION: Never released theatrically. Released to television by Gold Key Entertainment, Inc. English-dubbed. International Title: *War of the Planets.* Includes stock footage from *The Last War* (1961), *Submersion of Japan* (1973) and *Prophecies of Nostradamus* (1974). 90 minutes. No MPAA Rating.

War of the Gargantuas / Furankenshutain no kaiju–Sanda tai Gairah ("Frankenstein Monsters–Sanda against Gaira"). Producers, Tomoyuki Tanaka and Kenichiro Tsunoda; Associate Producers, Henry G. Saperstein and Reuben Bercovitch; Director, Ishiro Honda; Screenplay, Ishiro Honda and Kaoru Mabuchi (Takeshi Kimura); English Dialogue, Reuben Bercovitch; Director of Photography, Hajime Koizumi; Music, Akira Ifukube; Art Director, Takeo Kita; Lighting, Toshio Takashima; Chief Assistant Director, Kohi Kajita; Production Manager, Shoichi Koga; Production Manager, Kenichiro Tsunoda; Sound Effects, Hisashi Shimonaga, Toho Sound Effects Group; Sound, Toho Recording Centre. *Toho Special Effects Group*: Director, Eiji Tsuburaya; Photography, Teisho Arikawa, Mototaka Tomioka; Production Manager, Yasuaki Sakamoto; Art Director, Akira Wanatabe; Editor, Ryohei Fujii; Assistant to Tsuburaya, Teruyoshi Nakano; Optical Photography; Yukio Manoda, Sadao Iizuka; Scene Manipulation, Fumio Nakadai.

CAST: Russ Tamblyn (Dr. Paul Stewart), Kumi Mizuno (Akemi, *his assistant*), Kenji Sahara (Yuzo), Jun Tazaki (army commander), Kipp Hamilton (singer), Yoshifumi Tajima (policeman), Nobuo Nakamura (gray-haired biochemist), Hisaya Ito (Police Chief Izumida), Nadao Kirino, Kozo Nomura (military aides), Tadashi Okabe (reporter), Yutaka Oka (reporter in bow tie), Haruo Nakajima (Gaira), Hiroshi Sekita (Sanda), Ikio Sawamura (frightened fisherman), Ren Yamamoto (terrified sailor), Goro Mutsumi (voice characterization for Russ Tamblyn), Shoichi Hirose, Henry Okawa.

A Toho Co., Ltd. Production. Westrex Recording System. Eastman Color (processed by Tokyo Laboratory, Ltd.). Toho Scope. 93 minutes. Released July 31, 1966.

U.S. VERSION: Released by Maron Films Ltd. English-dubbed. A United Productions of America Release. A Henry G. Saperstein Presentation. Executive Producers, Henry G. Saperstein and Reuben Bercovitch; Editor, Fredric Knudtson; Dialog Supervisor, Riley Jackson; Sound Recording, Glen Glenn Sound Co.; Production Supervisor, S. Richard Krown; Song: "Feel in My Throat"; prints by Consolidated Film Industries. Double-billed with *Monster Zero* (q.v.). U.K. title: *Duel of the Gargantuas*. Working titles: *The Frankenstein Brothers* and *Adventure of the Gargantuas*. A quasi-sequel to *Frankenstein Conquers the World* (1965). A proposed match-up between a gargantua and Godzilla was scripted but never made. 93 minutes. MPAA rating: "G." Released July 29, 1970.

War of the Monsters / Daikaiju ketto Gamera tai Barugon

("Great Monster Duel: Gamera Against Barugon"). Executive Producer, Masaichi Nagata; Producer, Hidemasa Nagata; Director, Shigeo Tanaka; Planning, Yonejiro [Yonehiro] Saito; Screenplay, Nizo Takahashi; Director of Photography, Michio Takahashi; Music, Chuji Kinoshita; Special Effects Directors, Noriaki Yuasa, Kazufumi Fujii; Monster Design, Ryosaku Takayama; Special Effects, Daiei Special Effects Department; Sound, Daiei Recording Studio.

CAST: Kyoko Enami (Karen), Kojiro Hongo, Akira Natsuki, Koji Fujiyama, Yuzo Hayakawa, Ichiro Sugai.

A Daiei Motion Picture Co., Ltd. Production. Eastman Color (processed by Daiei Laboratory). DaieiScope. 100 minutes. Released April 17, 1966.

U.S. VERSION: Never released theatrically in the United States. Released directly to television by American International Television (AIP-TV). English-dubbed. Postproduction Supervisor, Salvatore Billitteri; Prints by Pathé. Reissued to television and released to home video by King Features Entertainment, a division of the Hearst Corporation in 1987, as *Gamera vs. Barugon*; A Sandy Frank Frank Syndication Inc. Presentation. Second feature in the "Gamera" film series. Followed by *The Return of the Giant Monsters* (1967). Includes footage from *Gammera the Invincible* (1965). 100 minutes. No MPAA rating.

Warring Clans / Sengoku yaro

("The Guy in a Warring State"). Executive Producer, Tomoyuki Tanaka; Director, Kihachi Okamoto; Screenplay, Kihachi Okamoto and Shinichi Sekizawa; Director of Photography, Yuzuru Aizawa; Music, Masaru Sato.

CAST: Yuzo Kayama (Ochikitsutan), Yuriko Hoshi (Sagiri), Ichiro Nakatani (Dokoharima), Makoto Sato (Tokichiro Kinoshita), Kumi Mizuno, Tadao Nakamaru, Jun Tazaki.

A Toho Co., Ltd. Production. Black and white. Toho Scope. 97 minutes. Released 1963.

U.S. VERSION: Released by Toho International Co., Ltd. English subtitles. No MPAA rating. Released July 3, 1963.

Warriors of the Wind / Kaze no tani Naushika

("Naushita, Valley of the Wind") **[animated]**. Producer, Isao Takahata; Director/Screenplay, Hayao Miyazaki; Director of Photography, Koji Shirakami; Music, Joe Hisaishi.

VOICE CHARACTERIZATIONS: (undetermined).

A Tokuma Shoten Co., Ltd./Hakuhodo Co., Ltd. Production. Color. Spherical wide screen. 116 minutes. Released 1984.

U.S. VERSION: Released by New World Pictures. English-dubbed. 95 minutes. No MPAA rating. Released April 1986.

Watari, Ninja Boy.

Producer, Hiroshi Okawa; Director, Sadao Nakajima; Screenplay, Masaru Igami and

Shunichi Nishimura, based on the comic strip "Watari"; Directors of Photography, Kunio Kunishida, Shigeru Akatsuka; Special Effects Director, Junji Kurata.

CAST: Yoshinobu Kaneko (Watari), Ryutaro Otomo, Chiyoko Honma, Toshitaka Ito.

A Toei Co., Ltd. Production. Toeicolor. ToeiScope. 83 minutes. Released 1966.

U.S. VERSION: Released by Toei Co., Ltd., format undetermined. Alternate title: *Ninja Boy*. Sequel: *The Magic World of Watari* (1970).

Watch Out, Crimson Bat! / Mekura no Oichi midaregasa ("Blind Oichi's Disordered Umbrella"). Director, Hirokazu Ichimura; Screenplay, Kinya Naoi and Yoshi Hattori, based on characters created by Teruo Tanashita; Director of Photography, Masao Kosugi; Art Director, Koji Uno; Music, Takeo Watanabe.

CAST: Yoko Matsuyama (Oichi), Goro Ibuki (Gennosuke), Asahi Kurizuka (Sakon), Jun Hamamura (Tessai), Kiyoko Inoue (Kotoe).

A Shochiku Co., Ltd. Production. Eastman Color. Shochiku GrandScope. 87 minutes. Released October 1, 1969.

U.S. VERSION: Released undetermined, possibly by Shochiku Films of America, Inc. English subtitled version available. The 3rd "Crimson Bat" feature. Followed by *Crimson Bat Oichi: Wanted, Dead or Alive* (1970). 87 minutes No MPAA rating.

The Water Magician / Taki no Shiraito ("White Strings of the Waterfall"). Director, Kenji Mizoguchi; Screenplay, Yasunaga Higashibojo, based on the novel by Kyoka Izumi; Director of Photography, Shigeru Miki.

CAST: Takako Irie (Taki no Shiraito), Tokihiko Okada (Kinya Murakoshi), Suzuko Taki (Nadeshiko), Ichiro Sugai (Iwabuchi), Koji Murata (Nankin), Bontaro Miake (Shinzo), Kumiko Urabe (Ogin).

An Irie Productions Production. Silent with benshi. Black and white. Academy ratio. 110 minutes. Released 1933.

U.S. VERSION: Distributor undetermined. English intertitles, Donald Richie. Irie is the sister if screenwriter Higashibojo. Some prints run 98 minutes. 110 minutes. No MPAA rating. Released 1981 (?).

Waterfront Blues / Hatoba onna no burusu ("Waterfront Women Blues"). Director, Koichi Saito; Screenplay, Kikuma Shimoiizaka; Director of Photography, Hiroshi Takemura; Art Director, Tadataka Yoshino; Music, Seitaro Omori.

CAST: Mariko Okada (Maki), Koji Moritsugu (Kazumasa), Meiko Nishio (Takako), Ko Nishimura, Shinichi Mori.

A Shochiku Co., Ltd. Production. Eastman Color. Shochiku GrandScope. 87 minutes. Released October 3, 1970.

U.S. VERSION: Released by Shochiku Films of America, Inc. English subtitles. Alternate title: *Harbor Light Blues*. 87 minutes. No MPAA rating. Released April 28, 1971.

The Way-Out Shrine (Production credits and original title undetermined).

CAST: Hisaya Morishige.

A Toho Co., Ltd. Production. Eastman Color (?). Toho Scope (?). Running time and release date undetermined.

U.S. VERSION: Released by Toho International Co. Ltd. English subtitles. Running time undetermined. No MPAA rating. Released October 11, 1967.

Way Out, Way In / Kokosei bancho ("A Juvenile Gang Leader in High School"). Director, Michihiko Obimori; Screenplay, Katsuya Suzaki; Director of Photography, Yoshihisa Nakagawa; Art Director, Shigeo Mano; Music, Harumi Ibe.

CAST: Yoko Namikawa (Miho Sakai), Ichiro Ogura (Hiroto Miyagawa), Saburo Shinoda (Yuji Shibata), Kozaburo Onogawa (Kenta Namiki), Akiko Naruse (Yuki Nohara), Eiko Yanami (Taeko), Sumie Mikaja.

A Daiei Motion Picture Co., Ltd. Production. Fuji Color. DaieiScope. 84

minutes. No MPAA rating. Released May 1970.

U.S. VERSION: Released by Daiei International Films. English subtitles. 84 minutes. No MPAA rating. Released November 1970.

The Wayside Pebble / Robo no ishi ("The Wayside Pebble"). Director, Seiji Hisamatsu; Screenplay, Kaneto Shindo; Director of Photography, Shojiro Sugimoto; Music, Ichiro Saito.

CAST: Hiroyuki Ota (Goichi Aikawa), Setsuko Hara (Oren Aikawa), Hisaya Morishige (Shogo Aikawa), Tatsuya Mihashi (Tsugino), Kyu Sazanka (Chusuke), Yusuke Takita, Masao Oda.

A Tokyo Eiga Co., Ltd. Production, in association with Toho Co., Ltd. A Toho Co., Ltd. Release. Black and white. Toho Scope. 104 minutes. Released May 15, 1960.

U.S. VERSION: Released by Toho International Co., Ltd. English subtitles. 104 minutes. No MPAA rating. Released October 1962.

We Are Not Alone / Bokura wa minna ikiteiru ("We Are All Alive"). Producer, Toshio Kobayashi; Director, Yojiro Takita; Screenplay, Nobuyuki Ishiki, based on his novel; Director of Photography, Takeshi Hamada; Music, Yasuaki Shimizu.

CAST: Hiroyuki "Henry" Sanada (Keichi Takahashi), Ittoku Kishibe (Kenzo Tomita), Tsutomu Yamazaki (Hiroshi Nakaido), Kyusaku Shimada (Tatsuya Masumoto).

A Shochiku Co., Ltd. Production. Color. Spherical wide screen. 115 minutes. Released 1993.

U.S. VERSION: Released by Shochiku Films of America, Inc. English subtitles. 115 minutes. No MPAA rating. Released May 24, 1994.

We Will Remember / Senjo ni nagareru uta ("The Song Running in the Battlefield"). Producer, Sanezumi Fujimoto; Director/Screenplay, Zenzo Matsuyama; Story and music, Ikuma Dan; Director of Photography, Asakazu Nakai; Sound Recording, Akira Saito.

CAST: Hisaya Morishige, Kiyoshi Kodama, Chang Mei Yao, Yoichi Mashino, Keiju Kobayashi, Masaya Nihei, Daisuke Kato, Akira Kubo, Kon Omura, Yuzo Kayama, Yukihiko Gondo, Kazuo Suzuki, Chotaro Togin, Yoko Fujiyama.

A Toho Co., Ltd, Production. Eastman Color. Toho Scope. 134 minutes. Released 1965.

U.S. VERSION: Released by Toho International Co., Ltd. English subtitles. 134 minutes. No MPAA rating. Released April 15, 1966.

Weaker Sex / Ah jonan ("Ah, Trouble through Women"). Director, Toshio Sugie; Screenplay, Ryosuke Saito, based on the novel by Shotaro Yasuoka; Assistant Director, Susumu Kodama.

CAST: Frankie Sakai, Hajime Hana, Yoshie Mizutani, Michiyo Yokoyama, Ichiro Arishima, Mitsuko Kusabue, Sadako Sawamura, Kuji Asami, Chisako Hara, Kiyoshi Kodama.

A Toho Co., Ltd. Production. Black and white. Toho Scope. 87 minutes. Released December 1960.

U.S. VERSION: Released by Toho International Co., Ltd. English subtitles. 87 minutes. No MPAA rating. Released August 4, 1961.

Wedding March / Kekkon koshinkyoku ("Wedding March"). Producer, Masumi Fujimoto; Director, Kon Ichikawa; Screenplay, Toshiro Ide, Natto Wada, and Kon Ichikawa; Director of Photography, Tadashi Iimura; Art Director, Yasuhide Kato; Music, Takio Niki.

CAST: Ken Uehara (Nakahara), Hisako Yamane (Toriko), Yoko Sugi (Kanako), Hagime Izu (Ino).

A Toho Co., Ltd. Production. Black and white. Academy ratio. 83 minutes. Released December 28, 1951.

U.S. VERSION: Distributor undetermined. English subtitles. 83 minutes. No MPAA rating.

The Weed of Crime / Ankokugai no kiba ("Fangs of the Underworld"). Executive Producers, Tomoyuki Tanaka and Reiji Miwa; Director, Jun Fukuda; Screenplay, Ei Ogawa, Jun Fukuda and Takashi Tsuboshima; Director of Photography, Masaharu Utsumi;

Music, Kenjiro Hirose; Special Effects Director, Eiji Tsuburaya.

CAST: Tatsuya Mihashi (Natsuo Kizaki, *alias Ken*), Yosuke Natsuki (Yuji Kizaki), Makoto Sato (Tsuda), Mie Hama (Yuji's girlfriend), Akiko Wakabayashi (Jiro's girl), Jun Tazaki (Hariya), Kumi Mizuno (Iwama's girlfriend, *the unhappy moll*), Toru Ibuki (Jiro), Sachio Sakai (Iwama), Akihiko Hirata (chief narcotics investigator), Eisei Amamoto (Tsuda's whipping boy), Tadao Nakamaru (Tsuda's chief henchman), Nadao Kirino, Kazuo Suzuki, Masaya Nihei (henchmen).

A Toho Co., Ltd. Production. Filmed in Takatsu City, and at Toho Studios (Tokyo). Eastman Color. Toho Scope. 90 minutes. Released 1964.

U.S. VERSION: Released undetermined, possibly by Toho International Co., Ltd. in subtitled format. No MPAA rating.

The Weird Love Makers / Kyonetsu no kisetsu ("Season of Crazy Heat"). Director, Koreyoshi Kurahara; Screenplay, Nobuo Yamada; Director of Photography, Yoshio Mamiya; Editor, Akira Suzuki; Music, Toshiro Mayuzumi.

CAST: Tamio Kawaji (Al), Noriko Matsumoto (Fumiko), Yuko Chiyo (Yuki), Hiroyuki Nagato (Kashi).

A Nikkatsu Corporation Production. Black and white. NikkatsuScope. 75 minutes. Released 1960.

U.S. VERSION: Released by Audubon Films. English subtitles. A Radley H. Metzger Presentation. Wide screen process billed as CinemaScope in the United States. Alternate titles: *Wild Love-Makers* and *The Weird Lovemakers*.

Westward Desperado / Dokuritsu gurentai nishi-e ("Independent Gangsters Go West"). Director, Kihachi Okamoto; Screenplay, Shinichi Sekizawa and Kihachi Okamoto; Director of Photography, Yuzuru Aizawa; Music, Masaru Sato; Assistant Director, Susumu Takebayashi.

CAST: Yuzo Kayama, Makoto Sato, Kumi Mizuno, Frankie Sakai, Ichiro Nakaya, Akihiko Hirata, Sachio Sakai, Shoji Oki, Tatsuji Ebara, Yasushi Yamamoto, Akira Kubo, Tadao Nakamaru, Mayumi Tamura, Michiyo Yokoyama, Ichiro Nakatani.

A Toho Co., Ltd. Production. Black and white. Toho Scope. 107 minutes. Released October 20, 1960.

U.S. VERSION: Released by Toho International Co., Ltd. English subtitles. The 2nd "Independent Gangsters" feature. Followed by *Operation Enemy Fort* (1962). 107 minutes. No MPAA rating. Released June 1961.

The Whale God / Kujira-gami ("Whale God"). Producer, Masaichi Nagata; Director, Tokuzo Tanaka; Screenplay, Kaneto Shindo, based on an original story by Koichiro Uno; Director of Photography, Setsuo Kobayashi; Art Director, Shigeo Mano; Music, Akira Ifukube; Editor, Tatsuji Nakashizu; Lighting, Choji Watanabe; Sound Recording Supervisor, Masao Osumi; Sound Recording, Kenichi Nishii; Sound, Daiei Recording Studio; Assistant Director, Otoya Nakamura; Special Effects, Daiei Special Effects Department.

CAST: Shintaro Katsu (Kishu), Kojiro Hongo (Shaki), Shiho Fujimura (Ei), Kyoko Enami (Toyo), Reiko Fujiwara (Okoma), Michiko Takano (Yuki), Takashi Shimura (whale priest), Yosuke Takemura (Kasuke), Kichijiro Ueda (Tochizame), Jutaro Hojo (Katame), Chieko Murata (Shaki's mother), Yasushi Sugita (Shaki's father), Tsutomu Hashimoto (Higezura, *beard man*), Koji Fujiyama (Shaki's brother).

A Daiei Motion Picture Co., Ltd. Production. Black and white. DaieiScope. Western Electric Mirrophonic recording. 100 minutes. Released July 15, 1962.

U.S. VERSION: Released by Daiei International Films, Inc. English subtitles. Also released as *Killer Whale*. No MPAA rating. Released 1962.

What Did the Lady Forget? / Shukujo wa nami o wasuretaka ("What Did the Lady Forget?"). Director, Yasujiro Ozu; Screenplay, Akira Fushimi and James Maki [Yasujiro Ozu]; Director of Photography, Hideo Shigehara.

CAST: Sumiko Kurishima, Tatsuo Saito, Michiko Kuwano, Shuji Sano, Takeshi Sakamoto, Choko Iida, Mitsuko Yoshikawa, Masao Hayama.

A Shochiku Co., Ltd. Production. Filmed at Shochiku-Ofuna Studios. Black and white. Academy ratio. 73 minutes. Released March 3, 1937.

U.S. VERSION: Released by Shochiku Films of America. English subtitles. 73 minutes. No MPAA rating. Released May 4, 1990.

(Woody Allen's) ***What's Up, Tiger Lily? / Kokusei himitsu keisatsu: Kagi no kagi*** ("International Secret Police: Key of Keys"). Executive Producers, Tomoyuki Tanaka and Makoto Morita; Director, Senkichi Taniguchi; Director of Photography, Kazuo Yamada; Music, Sadao Bekku; *Toho Special Effects Group*: Director, Eiji Tsuburaya.

CAST [Character names are for U.S. version only]: Tatsuya Mihashi (Phil Moskowitz), Mie Hama (Terri Yaki), Akiko Wakabayashi (Suki Yaki), Tadao Nakamaru (Shepherd Wong), Susumu Kurobe (Wing Fat), Kumi Mizuno (woman who has fling with Moscowitz), Eisei Amamoto (Wing Fat henchman with Peter Lorre voice), Sachio Sakai (2nd Wing Fat henchman), Makoto Sato (agent with Moscowitz at club), Tetsu Nakamura (man who explains egg salad recipe).

A Toho Co., Ltd. Production. Eastman Color. Toho Scope. 94 minutes. Released 1965.

U.S. VERSION: Released by American International Pictures. English-dubbed. A Henry G. Saperstein/Reuben Bercovitch Production. A James H. Nicholson and Samuel Z. Arkoff Presentation. Executive Producer, Henry G. Saperstein; Associate Producer/Director, Woody Allen; Screenplay/Dubbing Cast, Woody Allen, Frank Buxton, Len Maxwell, Louise Lasser, Mickey Rose, Bryna Wilson, Julie Bennett; Title Sequence, Murakami-Wolf, Phil Norman; Title Conception, UPA Pictures, Inc.; Editor, Richard Krown; Production Manager, Jerry Goldstein; Production Conception, Ben Shapiro; Script Supervisor, Sue Kelly; Music, Jack Lewis; Theme Songs: "Pow," "Pow Revisited," Music, Lyrics and Performance by The Lovin' Spoonful. Songs: "Gray Prison Blues," "Unconscious Minuet," "A Cool Million," "Lookin' to Spy," "Phil's Love Theme," Music, Lyrics and Performance by The Lovin' Spoonful; "Fishin' Blues," Arranged and Adapted by John Sebastian, and performed by The Lovin' Spoonful; "Respoken," Music/Lyrics and Performance by John Sebastian; "Speakin' of Spoken," Music and Lyrics by John Sebastian, and performed by The Lovin' Spoonful. Derived from the 4th "International Secret Police" feature and relooped as a comedy. Additional footage filmed in anamorphic wide screen. Bekku's music was deleted for the American version. The prologue and possibly other footage was culled from another Toho production, title undetermined. 80 minutes. No MPAA rating. Released November 2, 1966. Reissued in 1978 with an MPAA rating of "PG." Additional Cast for U.S. VERSION: Woody Allen (himself), China Lee (herself), The Lovin' Spoonful [John Sebastian, Steve Boone, Zal Yanovsky, Joe Butler] (themselves).

When a Woman Ascends the Stairs / Onna ga kaidan o agaru toki ("When a Woman Ascends the Stairs"). Producer, Ryuzo Kikushima; Director, Mikio Naruse; Screenplay, Ryuzo Kikushima; Director of Photography, Masao Tamai; Editor, H. Ito; Art Director, Satoshi Chuko; Music, Toshiro Mayuzumi.

CAST: Hideko Takamine (Keiko Yashiro), Masayuki Mori (Nobuhiko Fujisaki), Daisuke Kato (Matsukichi Sekine), Tatsuya Nakadai (Kenichi Komatsu), Reiko Dan (Junko Ichihashi), Keiko Awaji (Yuri), Ganjiro Nakamura (Goda, *the old patron from Osaka*) Yu Fujiki (patron), Yoshifumi Tajima (electronics company president), Eitaro Ozawa (Minobe).

A Toho Co., Ltd. Production. Black and white. Toho Scope. Western Electric Mirrophonic Recording (encoded with Perspecta Stereophonic Sound). 111 minutes. Released 1960.

U.S. VERSION: Released by Toho International Co., Ltd. English subtitles. Home video version letterboxed with subtitles by Joseph L. Anderson. One source claims actress Takemine also served as costume designer; this is unconfirmed. 111 minutes. No MPAA rating. Released June 25, 1963.

When Chimneys Are Seen / Entotsu no mieru basho ("Place

Where You Can See Chimneys"). Producer, Yoshishige Uchiyama; Director, Heinosuke Gosho; Screenplay, Hideo Oguni, based on the novel, *The Good People* by Rinzo Shiina; Director of Photography, Mitsuo Miura; Editor, Nobu Nagata; Art Director, Tomo Shimogawara; Music, Yasushi Akutagawa; Sound Recording, Yuji Dogen.

CAST: Ken Uehara (Ryukichi Ogata), Kinuyo Tanaka (Hiroko), Hiroshi Akutagawa (Kenzo Kubo), Hideko Takamine (Senko Azuma), Chieko Seki (Yukiko Ikeda), Ranki Hanai (Katsuko Ishibashi), Haruo Tanaka (Chuji Tsukahara).

A Studio Eight/Shintoho Co., Ltd. Production. Black and white. Academy ratio. Production. 108 minutes. Released 1953.

U.S. VERSION: Distributor undetermined. English subtitles. Alternate titles: *Four Chimneys* and *Chimney Scene*. 108 minutes. No MPAA rating. Release date undetermined.

Where Now Are the Dreams of Youth? / Seishun no yume ima izuko ("Where Now Are the Dreams of Youth"). Director, Yasujiro Ozu; Screenplay, Kogo Noda; Director of Photography, Hideo Shigehara.

CAST: Ureo Egawa, Haruo Takeda, Kinuyo Tanaka, Tatsuo Saito, Choko Iida, Kenji Oyama, Chishu Ryu.

A Shochiku Co., Ltd. Production. Filmed at Shochiku-Kamata Studios. Silent. Black and white. Academy ratio. 90 minutes. Released October 13, 1932.

U.S. VERSION: Released by Shochiku Films of America, Inc. English intertitles. 90 minutes. No MPAA rating. Released 1991 (?).

Where Spring Comes Late / Kazoku ("Family"). Director, Yoji Yamada; Screenplay, Yoji Yamada and Akira Miyazaki, based on an original story by Yoji Yamada; Director of Photography, Tetsuo Takahane; Art Director, Kiminobu Sato; Music, Masaru Sato.

CAST: Chieko Baisho (Tamiko), Hisashi Igawa (Seiichi, *her husband*), Chishu Ryu (Genzo, *his father*), Gin Maeda (Tsutomu, *Seiichi's brother*), Shin Morikawa, Hajime Hana, Kiyoshi Atsumi, Hisao Dazai.

A Shochiku Co., Ltd. Production. Eastman Color. Shochiku GrandScope. 106 minutes. Released November 11, 1970.

U.S. VERSION: Released by Shochiku Films of America, Inc. English subtitles. 106 minutes. No MPAA rating. Released May 8, 1971.

Whirlpool of Women / Onna no uzu to fuchi to nagare ("Vortex, Abyss, and a Stream of Women"). Director, Ko Nakahira; Screenplay, Masashige Narusawa; Director of Photography, Yoshihiro Yamazaki.

CAST: Kazuko Inano (Sugako), Noboru Nakaya (husband), Sadako Sawamura, Tamio Kawaji.

A Nikkatsu Corporation Production. Black and white. NikkatsuScope. 116 minutes. Released 1964.

U.S. VERSION: Released by Toho International Co., Ltd. English subtitles. Alternate title: *Whirlpool of Flesh*. 116 minutes. No MPAA rating. Released December 14, 1966.

Whirlwind / Dai tatsumaki ("Big Tornado"). Executive Producer, Tomoyuki Tanaka; Director, Hiroshi Inagaki; Screenplay, Hiroshi Inagaki and Takeshi Kimura, based on the novel *Shikonmado* by Norio Nanjo; Director of Photography, Kazuo Yamada; Music, Akira Ifukube; Sound, Toho Recording Centre; Sound Effects, Toho Sound Effects Group; Assistant Director, Akihiro Takase. *Toho Special Effects Group*: Director, Eiji Tsuburaya.

CAST: Toshiro Mifune (Lord Akashi), Somegoro Ichikawa (Jubei), Yuriko Hoshi (Kozato), Kumi Mizuno (the witch), Yosuke Natsuki (Kyunosuke), Yoshiko Kuga, Makoto Sato, Akira Kubo, Akihiko Hirata, Sachio Sakai, Yoshio Kosugi, Akira Tani, Ren Yamamoto, Somesho Matsumoto, Yoshio Inaba, Jotaro Togami.

A Toho Co., Ltd./Takarazuka Eiga Production. Western Electric Mirrophonic recording (possibly encoded with Perspecta Stereophonic Sound). Eastman Color (processed by Tokyo Laboratory,

Ltd.). Toho Scope. 107 minutes. Released January 3, 1964.

U.S. VERSION: Released by Toho International Co., Ltd. English subtitles. 107 minutes. No MPAA rating. Released December 25, 1964.

Whispering Joe / Sasayaski no Joe ("Whispering Joe"). Producer/ Director/Screenplay/ Director of Photography/Music, Koichi Saito; Art Director, Kuninobu Yasuda.

CAST: Jin Nakayama (Joe), Reiko Aso (Kanako), Manami Fuji (woman), Ko Nishimura (her husband), Kinzo Shin (tramp).

A Saito Productions Co., Ltd. Production. A Shochiku Co., Ltd. Release. Black and white. Shochiku GrandScope. 90 minutes. Released December 1967.

U.S. VERSION: Released by Shochiku Films of America, Inc. English subtitles. 90 minutes. No MPAA rating. Released April 4, 1969.

A Whistle in My Heart / Kotan no kuchibue ("Kotan's Whistle"). Producer, Tomoyuki Tanaka; Director, Mikio Naruse; Screenplay, Shinobu Hashimoto, based on an original story by Nobuo Ishimori; Director of Photography, Masao Tamai; Art Director, Satoshi Chuko; Music, Akira Ifukube.

CAST: Satoshi Kubo (Yutaka), Yoshiko Koda (Masa, *his sister*), Masayuki Mori (father), Eiko Miyoshi (old woman), Kumi Mizuno (Fue, *her granddaughter*), Akira Takarada (Teacher Taniguchi), Takashi Shimura (Teacher Tazawa), Akira Kubo (Kiyoshi).

A Toho Co., Ltd. Production. Agfacolor. Toho Scope. 125 minutes. Released March 29, 1959.

U.S. VERSION: Distributor undetermined, likely Toho International Co., Ltd. in subtitled format. No MPAA rating.

White Rose of Hong Kong / Honkon no shiroibara ("White Rose of Hong Kong"). Producer, Sanezumi Fujimoto; Director, Jun Fukuda; Screenplay, Ichiro Okeda; Story, Shinobu Hashimoto; Director of Photography, Shinsaku Uno; Music, Sadao Bekku.

CAST: Chang Mei Yao (Yuli Rin), Tsutomu Yamazaki (Shiro Matsumoto), Akira Takarada (Susumu Uzuki), Kumi Mizuno (Yoshiko Nakao), Kenjiro Ishiyama (Syozo Tabe), Mar Chi (Eidatsu Ki), Yu Fujiki (Chief of Police Jin), Eijiro Yanagi (Kiyoaki Hayashi).

A Toho Co., Ltd. Production. Eastman Color. Toho Scope. 110 minutes. Released 1965.

U.S. VERSION: Released by Toho International Co., Ltd. English subtitles. 110 minutes. No MPAA rating. Released December 21, 1965.

White Wolf / Hashire Shiroi Okami ("Run! White Wolf") **[animated]**. Producer, Shigeji Tsuiki; Director, Yosei Maeda; Screenplay, Wataru Kenmochi, based on an original story by Mel Ellis; Directors of Photography, Isamu Kumata and Shinsuke Eguchi; Music, Atsumi Tashiro.

VOICE CHARACTERIZATIONS: Katsumi Torimi, Hiroshi Arikawa.

A Group Tac Production. Color. Spherical wide screen (?). 83 minutes. Released 1990.

U.S. VERSION: Distributor, if any, is undetermined.

Wife! Be Like a Rose! / Tsuma yo bara no yi ni ("Wife! Be Like a Rose"). Director, Mikio Naruse; Screenplay, Mikio Naruse, based on the play by Minoru Nakano; Director of Photography, Hiroshi Suzuki; Music, Noboru Ito.

CAST: Sadao Maruyama (Shunsaku Yamamoto), Tomoko Ito (Etsuko Yamamoto, *his wife*), Sachiko Chiba (Kimiko Yamamoto, *his daughter*), Yuriko Hanabusa (Oyuki, *his mistress*), Setsuko Horikoshi (Shizuko, *Oyuki's daughter*), Kaoru Ito (Kenichi, *Oyuki's son*), Kamatari Fujiwara (Shingo, *Etsuko's brother*).

A P.C.L. Production. Black and white. Academy ratio. 74 minutes. Released 1935.

U.S. VERSION: Released by George Eastman House. English subtitles. Exhibited in New York in April 1937 by the International Film Bureau as *Kimiko*.

Wife Lost / Nyobo funshitsu ("Wife Lost"). Director, Yasujiro Ozu; Screenplay, Momosuke Yoshida, based on an idea by Ononosuke Takano, and a prize-winning magazine story; Director of Photography, Hideo Shigehara.

CAST: Tatsuo Saito, Ayako Okamura, Takeshi Sakamoto, Junko Matsui, Ogura Shigeru, Kano Shichiro, Chishu Ryu.

A Shochiku Co., Ltd. Production. Filmed at Shochiku-Kamata Studios. Silent with benshi. Black and white. Academy ratio. 50 minutes. Released June 16, 1928.

U.S. VERSION: Never released theatrically in the United States. A lost film.

The Wife of Seishu Hanaoka / Hanaoka Seishu no tsuma ("The Wife of Seishu Hanaoka"). Director, Yasuzo Masamura; Director of Photography, Setsuo Kobayashi.

CAST: Raizo Ichikawa, Ayako Wakao, Hideko Takamine, Yunosuke Ito, Misako Watanabe, Chisako Hara.

A Daiei Motion Picture Co., Ltd. Production. Black and white. DaieiScope. 100 minutes. Released 1967.

U.S. VERSION: Released by Daiei International Films. English subtitles. 100 minutes. No MPAA rating. Released October 1970.

The Wild Sea / Arai umi ("The Wild Sea"). Director, Tokujiro Yamazaki; Screenplay, Kinya Naoi, Tokujiro Yamazaki and Yoshi Hattori; Director of Photography, Tomoki Kasuga; Art Director, Shigematsu Abiko; Music, Shigeru Ikeno.

CAST: Tetsuya Watari (Yoji Kitami), Hideki Takahashi (Katsuyuki Shinoda), Tomo Nagai (Ogaki), Hatsuo Ito (Taichiro), Masako Izumi, Ko Nishimura.

A Nikkatsu Corp. Production. Eastman Color. NikkatsuScope. 123 minutes. Released November 1, 1969.

U.S. VERSION: Distributor, if any, is undetermined. English subtitled version available. 123 minutes. No MPAA rating.

Wildcat Rock / Noraneko rokku ("Homeless Rock"). Director, Yasuharu Hasebe; Screenplay, Shuichi Nagahara and Yasuharu Hasebe; Director of Photography, Muneo Ueda; Art Director, Yoshio Saito; Music, Kunihiko Suzuki.

CAST: Akiko Wada (Ako), Meiko Kaji (Mei), Koji Wada (Michio), Ken Sanders (Kerry), Goro Mutsumi (Hanada), Bunjaku Han, Mari Koiso.

A Nikkatsu Corp. Production. Fujicolor. NikkatsuScope. 81 minutes. Released May 2, 1970.

U.S. VERSION: Distributor, if any, is undetermined. English subtitled version available. The 1st feature in the 5-film "Wildcat Rock" film series (1970-71). 81 minutes. No MPAA rating.

Will to Conquer / Tenka no Abarenbo ("Wild Person Under the Heavens"). Producers, Tomoyuki Tanaka and Masayuki Sato; Director, Seiji Maruayama; Screenplay, Toshio Yasumi; Director of Photography, Rokoru Nishigaki; Art Director, Tomo Nakafuru; Music, Akira Ifukube.

CAST: Kinnosuke Nakamura (Yataro Iwasaki), Yoshiko Sakuma (Ritsu), Tatsuya Nakadai (Toyo Yoshida), Isao Kimura (Hanpeita Takechi), Eijiro Tono (Sezaemon, *Ritsu's father*), Tamao Nakamura, Kinya Kitaoji, Takahiro Tamura, Nisashi Igawa, Wataru Omae.

A Toho Co., Ltd. Production. Fujicolor. Toho Scope. 113 minutes. Released October 17, 1970.

U.S. VERSION: Released by Toho International Co., Ltd. English subtitles. 113 minutes. No MPAA rating. Released April 21, 1971.

Willful Murder / Bosatsu Shimoyama jiken ("Bosatsu Shimoyama Murder Case"). Producers, Masayuki Sato and Nohito Abe; Director, Kei Kumai; Screenplay, Ryuzo Kikushima, based on an original story by Kimio Yada; Director of Photography, Shunichiro Nakao; Art Director, Takeo Kimura; Music, Masaru Sato.

CAST: Tatsuya Nakadai (Yashiro), Kei Yamamoto (Oshima), Mikijiro Hira (Okuno), Yoko Asaji (Kawada).

A Haiyuza Eiga Hoso Co., Ltd. Production. Black and white. Spherical wide screen. 131 minutes. Released 1981.

U.S. VERSION: Released by Shochiku Films of America, Inc. English subtitles. 131 minutes. No MPAA rating. Released May 1982.

Willy McBean and His Magic Machine **[animated]**. Executive Producer, Marshall Naify; Producer/Director/Screenplay, Arthur Rankin, Jr.; Associate Producers, Larry Roemer and Jules Bass; Music and Lyrics, Edward Thomas, Gene Forrell, and James Polack.

VOICE CHARACTERIZATIONS: Larry D. Mann, Billie Richards, Alfred Scopp, Paul Kligman, Bunn Cowan, Paul Soles, Peggi Loder.

A Videocraft International Productions Production, in association with Dentsu Motion Picture Co., Ltd. A Marshall Naify Presentation. A U.S./Japanese co-production in English. Eastman Color. Spherical wide screen. A puppet animation feature filmed in Anamagic. 94 minutes. Released June 23, 1965.

The Wiser Age / Onna no za ("Position of Women"). Executive Producers, Sanezumi Fujimoto and Hidehisa Suga; Director, Mikio Naruse; Screenplay, Toshiro Ide and Zenzo Matsuyama; Director of Photography, Atsushi Yasumoto.

CAST: Hideko Takamine, Tatsuya Mihashi, Akira Takarada, Yoko Tsukasa, Reiko Dan, Yuriko Hoshi, Chishu Ryu, Haruko Sugimura, Keiju Kobayashi, Yosuke Natsuki, Mitsuko Kusabue, Keiko Awaji, Aiko Mimasu, Daisuke Kato.

A Toho Co., Ltd. Production. Black and white. Toho Scope. 111 minutes. Released 1962.

U.S. VERSION: Released by Toho International Co., Ltd. English subtitles. 111 minutes. No MPAA rating. Released November 9, 1962.

Witness Killed / Ankokugai gekimetsu meirei ("Underworld Destruction Order"). Executive Producers, Reiji Miwa and Tomoyuki Tanaka; Director, Jun Fukuda; Screenplay, Ei Ogawa; Director of Photography, Shoji Utsumi; Music, Shungo Sawada.

CAST: Tatsuya Mihashi (Harada), Makoto Sato (Hiroshi), Yuriko Hoshi (hatcheck girl), Jun Tazaki (Yasaka), Kumi Mizuno (dancer), Seizaburo Kawazu.

A Toho Co., Ltd. Production. Eastman Color. Toho Scope. 87 minutes. Released 1962.

U.S. VERSION: Released by Toho International Co., Ltd. English subtitles. No MPAA rating. Release date undetermined.

The Wolves / Shussho iwai ("Celebration of the Release"). Executive Producers, Sanezumi Fujimoto, Eiji Shiino, and Masayuki Sato; Director, Hideo Gosha; Screenplay, Kei Tazaka and Hideo Gosha; Director of Photography, Kozo Okazaki; Art Director, Motoji Kojima; Music, Masaru Sato; Editor, Michio Suwa.

CAST: Tatsuya Nakadai (Seiji Iwahashi), Noboru Ando (Gunjiro Ozeki), Komaki Kunihara (Aya), Kyoko Enami (Oyu), Toshio Kurosawa (Tsutomu Onodera), Kunie Tanaka (Matsuzo Tsumura), Tetsuro Tamba (Genryu Asakura), Hisashi Igawa (narrator), Eisei Amamoto.

A Tokyo Eiga Co., Ltd. Production. A Toho Co., Ltd. Release. Color. Panavision. 131 minutes. Released 1971.

U.S. VERSION: Released by Toho International Co., Ltd. English subtitles. Letterboxed laserdisc version available. 131 minutes. No MPAA rating. Released June 7, 1972.

Wolves of the City / Furyo bancho ("Delinquent Boss"). Director, Yukio Noda; Screenplay, Isao Matsumoto and Hideaki Yamamoto; Director of Photography, Yoshikazu Yamazawa; Art Director, Hiroshi Fujita; Music, Masao Yagi.

CAST: Tatsuo Umemiya (Kosaka), Tanami Natsu (Ryuko), Ying Lan-Fang (Yukiko), Hayato Tani (Tani), Koji Nambara, Kenjiro Ishiyama.

A Toei Co., Ltd. Production. Eastman Color. ToeiScope. 89 minutes. Released October 1, 1968.

U.S. VERSION: Distributor, if any, is undetermined. English subtitled version available. The 1st feature in the 16-film "Furyo bancho" film series (1968-72). 89 minutes. No MPAA rating.

Wolves of the City, Check Mate / Furyo bancho otebisha ("Delinquent Boss, Checkmate"). Director, Makoto Naito; Screenplay, Isao Matsumoto and Hideaki Yamamoto; Director of Photography, Ichiro Hoshijima; Art Director, Shinichi Eno; Music, Masao Yagi.

CAST: Tatsuo Umemiya (Kosaka), Hayato Tani (Tani), Fumio Watanabe (Daimon), Bunta Sugawara (Takigawa), Toru Abe (Osaki), Noriko Sakakibara (Akiko).

A Toei Co., Ltd. Production. Eastman Color. ToeiScope. 87 minutes. Released January 9, 1970.

U.S. VERSION: Distributor, if any, is undetermined. English subtitled version available. The 6th feature in the "Wolves of the City" film series. 87 minutes. No MPAA rating.

The Woman Gambler / Onna tobakushi ("The Woman Gambler"). Director, Taro Yuge.

CAST: Kyoko Enami, Sae Kawaguchi, Goichi Yamada, Kojiro Hongo, Ryohei Uchida.

A Daiei Motion Picture Co., Ltd. Production. Eastman Color. DaieiScope. The 2nd "Woman Gambler" feature. The series ran 17 features (1966–71). 85 minutes. Released July 1967.

U.S. VERSION: Released by Daiei International Films. English subtitles. The 2nd "Woman Gambler" feature. The series ran 17 features (1966–71). 85 minutes. No MPAA rating. Released June 1969.

Woman in the Dunes / Suna no onna ("Women in the Dunes"). Producers, Kiichi Ichikawa and Tadashi Ohono; Director, Hiroshi Teshigahara; Screenwriter, Kobo Abe, based on his novel; Director of Photography, Hiroshi Segawa; Editor, F. Susui; Music, Toru Takemitsu; Production Supervisor, Hiroshi Kawazoe; Production Manager, Iuao Yoshida; Art Directors, Totetsu Hirakawa and Masao Yamazaki; Lighting, Mitsuo Kume; Still Photographer, Yasuhiro Yoshioka; Sound Recording, Ichiro Kato and Shigenosuke Okuyama; Sound, Keiji Mori; Assistant Director, Masuo Ogawa; Script Supervisor, Eiko Yoshida; Editor, Fusako Shuzui; Design, Kiyoshi Auazu.

CAST: Eiji Okada (the man), Kyoko Kishida (the woman), Koji Mitsui, Hiroko Ito, Sen Yano, Ginzo Sekigushi, Kiyohiko Ichihara, Tamotsu Tamura, Hiroyuki Nishimoto (villagers).

A Teshigahara Productions Production. Westrex Recording System. Black and white. Academy ratio. 123 minutes. Released 1964.

U.S. VERSION: Released by Pathé Contemporary Films. English subtitles. 123 minutes. No MPAA rating. Released October 25, 1964.

The Woman of Osaka / Naniwa onna ("The Woman of Osaka"). Director, Kenji Mizoguchi; Screenplay, Yoshikata Yoda, based on the life and art of Danpei Toyozawa; Director of Photography, Shigeto Miki; Art Director, Hiroshi Mizutani; Music, Senji Ito.

CAST: Kotaro Bando (Danpei Toyozawa), Kinuyo Tanaka (Ochika), Shinpachiro Asaka (Koshiji Dayu), Ryotaro Kawanami (Osumi Dayu), Yoko Umemura (Otaka), Kokichi Takada (Fumikichi), Yoshiko Nakamura (Okuni), Soroku Kazama (Sayuri Dayu).

A Shochiku Co., Ltd. Production. Filmed at Shochiku-Shimokamo Studios (Kyoto). Black and white. Academy ratio. Running time undetermined. Released September 19, 1940.

U.S. VERSION: Never released in the United States. A lost film.

A Woman of Rumor / Uwasa no onna ("Woman of Rumor"). Producer, Masaichi Nagata; Planning, Hisakazu Tsuji; Director, Kenji Mizoguchi; Screenplay, Yoshikata Yoda and Masashige Narusawa; Director of Photography, Kazuo Miyagawa; Art Director, Hiroshi Mizutani; Lighting, Kenichi Okamoto; Music, Toshiro Mayuzumi; Sound Recording, Iwao Otani; Noh Sequences, Kyuemon Katayama; Kyogen Sequences, Chuzaburo Shigeyama and Sengoro Shigeyama.

CAST: Kinuyo Tanaka (Hatsuko Umabuchi), Tomoemon Otani (Kenji Matoba), Yoshiko Kuga (Yukiko Umabuchi), Eitaro Shindo (Yasuichi Harada), Bontaro Miake (Kobayashi), Chieko Naniwa (Osaki), Haruo Tanaka (Kawamoto),

Hisao Toake (Yamada), Michiko Ai (Aioi Dayu), Sachiko Mine (Chiyo), Teruko Daimi (Onoue Dayu), Teruko Kusugi (Tamakoto Dayu), Kimiko Tachibana (Usugumo Dayu), Teruyo Hasegawa (Kisaragi Dayu), Keiko Koyanagi (Bisha Dayu), Kan Ueda (Takeshita), Saburo Date (Nakauchi), Sumao Ishihara (store owner), Kotaro Kawada (Takejiro), Midori Komatsu (Okanu), Kanae Kobayashi (Oharu), Koyako Nakagami (Oteru), Kyoko Hisamatsu (Oume).

A Daiei Motion Picture Co., Ltd. Production. Filmed at Daiei-Kyoto Studios. Black and white. Academy ratio. 83 minutes. Released June 20, 1954.

U.S. VERSION: Distributor undetermined. English subtitles. 83 minutes. No MPAA rating. Release date undetermined.

A Woman of Tokyo / Tokyo no onna ("Woman of Tokyo"). Director, Yasujiro Ozu; Screenplay, Kogo Noda and Tadao Ikeda, based on a story by Ernst Schwartz [Yasujiro Ozu]; Director of Photography, Hideo Shigehara.

CAST: Yoshiko Okada, Ureo Egawa, Kinuyo Tanaka, Shinyo Nara, Chishu Ryu.

A Shochiku Co., Ltd. Production. Filmed at Shochiku-Kamata Studios. Silent with music and sound effects. Black and white. Academy ratio. 70 minutes. Released February 9, 1933.

U.S. VERSION: Released by Shochiku Films of America, Inc. English intertitles. 47 minutes. No MPAA rating. Released December 1982.

The Woman Vampire / Onna kyuketsuki ("The Woman Vampire"). Producer, Mitsuga Okura; Director, Nobuo Nakagawa; Screenplay, Shin Nakazawa and Katsuyoshi Nakatsu; Director of Photography, Yoshimi Hirano.

CAST: Shigeru Amachi (Vampire), Yoko Mihara (Niwako), Keinosuke Wada, Junko Ikeuchi.

A Shintoho Co., Ltd. Production. Western Electric Mirrophonic recording. Black and white. Shintoho-Scope. 78 minutes. Released 1959.

U.S. VERSION: Distributor, if any, is undetermined. Above is international title: Alternate titles: *The Male Vampire* and *Vampire Man*. No MPAA rating.

The Woman Who Touched the Legs / Ashi ni sawatta onna ("The Woman Who Touched the Legs"). Producer, Masumi Fujimoto; Director, Kon Ichikawa; Screenplay, Natto Wada and Kon Ichikawa, based on a story by Bumatsu Sawada; Director of Photography, Jun Yasumoto; Art Director, Yasuhide Kato; Music, Toshiro Mayuzumi.

CAST: Fubuki Koshiji (woman), Ryo Ikebe (detective), So Yamamura (novelist), Sadako Sawamura (woman shoplifter).

A Toho Co., Ltd. Production. Black and white. Academy ratio. 84 minutes. Released November 6, 1952.

U.S. VERSION: Distributor undetermined. English subtitles. 84 minutes. No MPAA rating. Remade in 1960.

A Woman's Life / Onna no rekishi ("A History of Woman"). Producers, Sanezumi Fujimoto and Masakazu Kaneko; Director, Mikio Naruse; Screenplay, Ryozo Kasahara; Director of Photography, Asakazu Nakai; Music, Ichiro Sato.

CAST: Hideko Takemine (Nobuko), Tatsuya Nakadai (Akimoto), Akira Takarada (Koichi), Yuriko Hoshi (hostess), Tsutomu Yamazaki.

A Toho Co., Ltd. Production. Black and white. Toho Scope. 126 minutes. Released 1963.

U.S. VERSION: Released by Toho International Co., Ltd. English subtitles. 120 minutes. No MPAA rating. Released June 1964.

A Woman's Testament / Jokyo ("Going to Tokyo"). Directors, Yasuzo Masumura (Part I), Kon Ichikawa (Part II), Kimasaburo Yoshimura (Part III); Screenplay, Toshio Yasumi, based on the novel by Shofu Muramatsu; Directors of Photography, Hiroshi Murai (Part I), Setsuo Kobayashi (Part II), Kazuo Miyagawa (Part III); Music, Yasushi Akutagawa.

CAST: *Part I*—Ayako Wakao (Kimi), Hiroshi Kawaguchi (Tabata), Sachiko Hidari (Satsuki). *Part II*—Fujiko Yamamoto (Tsuneko), Eiji Funakoshi (Yasushi), Kenji Sugahara (Oishi), Hitomi Nozoe (girl). *Part III*—Machiko Kyo (Omitsu), Ganjiro Nakamura (Gosuke), Junko Kano (Yumiko), Jun Negishi (Kanemitsu).

A Daiei Motion Picture Co., Ltd.

Production. Eastman Color. DaieiScope. 103 minutes. Released 1960.

U.S. VERSION: Distributor, if any, is undetermined, though likely Daiei International Films, Inc. English subtitles. No MPAA rating.

Women of Design / Sono bashoni onna arite ("There Is a Woman There"). Executive Producer, Masakatsu Kaneko; Director, Hideo Suzuki; Screenplay, Shoji Masuda; Music, Joe Aizawa.

CAST: Yoko Tsukasa, Akira Takarada, Jun Hamamura, Chisako Hara, Tsutomu Yamazaki.

A Toho Co., Ltd. Production. Eastman Color. Toho Scope. 95 minutes. Released 1962.

U.S. VERSION: Release undetermined, possibly by Toho International Co., Ltd. in subtitled format. No MPAA rating. Release date undetermined.

Women of the Night / Yoru no onnatachi ("Women of the Night"). Director, Kenji Mizoguchi; Screenplay, Yoshikata Yoda, based on the novel *Joseimatsuri* ("Girls' Holiday") by Eijiro Hisaita; Director of Photography, Kohei Sugiyama; Art Director, Hiroshi Mizutani; Music, Hisato Osawa.

CAST: Kinuyo Tanaka (Fusako Owada), Sanae Takasugi (Natsuko), Mitsuo Nagata (Kuriyama), Tomie Tsunoda (Kumiko), Kumeko Urabe, Minpei Tomimoto, Mitsugu Fujii, Fusako Maki, Sadako Sawamura.

A Shochiku Co., Ltd. Production. Filmed at Shochiku-Kyoto Studios, and on location in Osaka. Black and white. Academy ratio. 73 minutes. Released May 28, 1948.

U.S. VERSION: Released by Shochiku Films of America, Inc. English subtitles. 73 minutes. No MPAA rating. Released February 28, 1979.

Women ... Oh, Women! / Onna onna onna monogatari ("Women Women Women Story") [**documentary**]. Director, Tetsuji Takechi; Screenplay, Tatsuji Tsuta; Director of Photography, Kazutoshi Akutagawa.

A Sano Art Productions Production for Shochiku Co., Ltd. A Shochiku Co., Ltd. Release. Eastman Color. Shochiku GrandScope. 80 minutes. Released 1963.

U.S. VERSION: Released by Shochiku Films of America, Inc. English narration (?). 80 minutes. No MPAA rating. Released September 18, 1964.

Women Smell of Night / Onna wa yoru no nioi ("Woman Smell of Night"). Director, Takashi Nomura; Screenplay, Ei Ogawa; Director of Photography, Shigeyoshi Mine; Art Director, Toshiyuki Matsui; Music, Taichiro Kosugi.

CAST: Akira Kobayashi (Hanamura), Ryohei Uchida (Yuki), Noriko Maki (Keiko), Gen Mitamura (Numaken), Fujio Suga (Boss Matsumura), Hosei Komatsu (Nakai), Masaya Oki, Nobuko Aoki.

A Nikkatsu Corp. Production. Fujicolor. NikkatsuScope. 82 minutes. Released December 5, 1970.

U.S. VERSION: Distributor, if any, is undetermined. English subtitled version available. 82 minutes. No MPAA rating.

Women's Police / Onna no Keisatsu ("Women's Police"). Director, Mio Ezaki; Screenplay, Ryuzo Nakanishi, based on an original story by Toshiyuki Kajiyama; Director of Photography, Minoru Yokoyama; Art Director, Akiyoshi Satani; Music, Makoto Sato.

CAST: Akira Kobayashi (Masaaki Kagari), Yukiyo Toake (Chiyoko), Yuji Kodaka, Noriko Maki, Kyoko Maki, Masako Ota, Mina Aoe.

A Nikkatsu Corp. Production. Fujicolor. NikkatsuScope. 82 minutes. Released February 8, 1969.

U.S. VERSION: Distributor, if any, is undetermined. English subtitled version available. The 1st feature in the 4-film "Women's Police" film series (1969-70). Followed by *Women's Police, Part II* (1969). 82 minutes. No MPAA rating.

Women's Police, Part II / Zoku onna no keisatsu ("Women's Police, Part II"). Director, Mio Ezaki; Screenplay, Ryuzo Nakanishi; Director of

Photography, Minoru Yokoyama; Art Director, Akinori Saya; Music, Mitsuhiko Sato.

CAST: Akira Kobayashi (Masaaki Kagari), Tatsuya Fuji (Hayazaki), Akiko Koyama (Hisayo), Mitsuko Oka (Kumi), Rumi Koyama (Chie), Eiji Go (Jiro).

A Nikkatsu Corp. Production. Fujicolor. NikkatsuScope. 83 minutes. Released May 28, 1969.

U.S. VERSION: Distributor, if any, is undetermined. English subtitled version available. The 2nd feature in the "Women's Police" film series. 83 minutes. No MPAA rating.

The Wonderful World of Song! / Ore-tachi no Kokyogaku ("Our Symphony"). Producer, Toru Najima; Director, Yoshitaka Asama; Screenplay, Yoshitaka Asama and Masao Kajiura, based on a story by Yoji Yamada; Director of Photography, Kenichi Yoshikawa; Art Director, Mitsuo Idegawa; Music, Yuzo Kayama.

CAST: Tetsuya Takeda, Takahiro Tamura, Mami Kumagi, Chikako Yuri, Toshiyoki Nagashima.

A Shochiku Co., Ltd. Production. Color. Panavision (?). 113 minutes. Released 1979.

U.S. VERSION: Released by Shochiku Films of America, Inc. in subtitled format. Alternate title: *Wonderful World of Music*. 112 minutes. No MPAA rating. Released August 10, 1979.

The Worship of the Flesh / Meiji Jakyoden ("Maiji's False Religion"). Director, Michiyoshi Doi; Screenplay, Kozo Uchida; Director of Photography, Makoto Tsuboi; Art Director, Haruyasu Kurosawa; Music, Hiroki Ogawa.

CAST: Masaya Takahashi (Takejiro), Takako Uchida (Okin), Mitsuko Aoi (Ogin), Yumi Kanai (Okei), Nobuo Kaneko (Denbei), Ryohei Uchida (Toshiichi).

A Nikkatsu Corp. Production. Black and white. NikkatsuScope. 85 minutes. Released July 10, 1968.

U.S. VERSION: Distributor, if any, is undetermined. English subtitled version available. 85 minutes. No MPAA rating.

The X from Outer Space / Uchu daikaiju Girara ("Great Space Monster Girara"). Producer, Akihiko Shimada; Director, Kazui Nihonmatsu; Screenplay, Kazui Nihonmatsu, Hidemi Motomochi and Moriyoshi Ishida; Art Director, Shigemori Shigeta; Director of Photography, Shizuo Hirase; Editor, Yoshi Sugihara; Sound, Hiroshi Nakamura; Music, Taku Izumi; Special Effects Director, Hiroshi Ikeda.

CAST: Eiji Okada (Kato), Toshiya Wazaki [Toshinari Kazusaki] (Captian Sano), Peggy Neal (Lisa), Itoko Harada (Michiko), Shinichi Yanagisawa (Miyamoto), Franz Gruber (Dr. Berman), Keisuke Sonoi (Dr. Shioda), Mike Daning (Dr. Stein), Torahiko Hamada (Kimura), Ryuji Kita (Chief of Staff), Takanobu Hozumi (Member of FAFC), Chuji Sato (guard), Hiroshi Fujioka, Kusanosuke Oda (moon station correspondents), Kamon Kawamura (substation clerk), Wataru Nakajima (President of Defense Headquarters), Masaji Hashimoto (Manager of Secretariat), Koji Nakada (President of Police Headquarters), Cathy Horlan (nurse).

A Shochiku Co., Ltd. Production. Eastman Color (processed by Shochiku Laboratory). Shochiku GrandScope. 89 minutes. Released March 25, 1967.

U.S. VERSION: Never released theatrically in the United States. Released directly to television by American International Television (AIP-TV) in 1968. English-dubbed. A James H. Nicholson and Samuel Z. Arkoff Presentation. Post-production Supervisor, Salvatore Billitteri; Prints by Perfect. 88 minutes. No MPAA rating.

Yearning / Midareru ("Be Confused"). Producers, Sanezumi Fujimoto and Mikio Naruse; Director, Mikio Naruse; Screenplay, Zenzo Matsuyama; Director of Photography, Jun Yasumoto; Music, Ichiro Saito.

CAST: Hideko Takamine (Reiko), Yuzo Kayama (Koji), Yumi Shirakawa, Mie Hama.

A Toho Co., Ltd. Production. Black and white. Toho Scope. 98 minutes. Released 1964.

U.S. VERSION: Released by Toho International Co., Ltd. English subtitles. 98

minutes. No MPAA rating. Released October 23, 1964.

The Yellow Handkerchief / Shiawase no Kiiroi hankachi ("Happy Yellow Handkerchief"). Producer, Toru Najima; Director, Yoji Yamada; Screenplay, Yoji Yamada and Yoshitaka Asama, based on the story by Pete Hamill; Director of Photography, Tetsuo Takaba; Art Director, Mitsuo Idegawa; Music, Masaru Sato.

CAST: Ken Takakura (Yusaku Shima), Tetsuya Takeda (Kinya), Kaori Momoi (Akemi), Chieko Baisho (Mrs. Shima), Kiyoshi Atsumi (police chief).

A Shochiku Co., Ltd. Production. Color. Panavision. 108 minutes. Released 1977.

U.S. VERSION: Released by Shochiku Films of America, Inc. English subtitles. A remake—a coproduction between Universal and Shochiku—has been announced. 108 minutes. No MPAA rating. Released April 28, 1978.

The Yen Family / Kimurake no hitobito ("Members of the Kimura Family"). Executive Producer, Koichi Murakami; Producers Shuji Miyajima and Shinya Kawai; Assistant Producers, Toshio Kobayashi and Noriko Murao; Director, Yojiro Takita; Screenplay, Nobuyuki Ishiki, based on the story "The Kimura Family," by Toshihiko Tani; Director of Photography, Yoichi Shiga; Art Director, Katsumi Nakazawa; Lighting, Kazuo Abe; Editor, Isao Tomita; Music, Katsuo Ono; Sound, Hisayuki Miyamoto; Hair/Makeup, Seiko Igawa; Theme Song, Bakafu Slump.

CAST: *The Kimura Family*: Takeshi Kaga (Hajime Kimura), Kaori Momoi (Noriko Hajime), Hiromi Iwasaki (Terumi Kimura), Mitsunori Isaki (Taro Kimura). *The Amamiya Family*: Akira Emoto (Shinichi Amamiya), Midori Kiuchi (Sayuri Amamiya), Akiko Kazami (Mitsu Amamiya). *The Takakura Family*: Hiroyuki Konishi (Masashi Takakura), Michiko Shimizu (Sayaka Takakura), Makoto Nakano (Ken Takakura). *The Old Folks*: Yoshi Kato (Tokijiro), Michio Kida (Matsukichi), Koen Okumura (Takekichi), Jun Tatara (Umekichi), Chigusa Tsuyuhara (Fujie), Imari Tsuji (Takae), Kazuko Imai (Nasue). *Kimura's Coworkers*: Toshinari Sakai (Hirono), Mari Torigoe (Yasuyo), Yutaka Ikejima (supervisor), Koichi Ueda (section chief). *At School*: Yoko Emori (Kamikochi), Takashi Tsumura (principal). Townspeople: Naoto Takenaka (hidden rubbishman), Yukijiro Hotaru (dancing teacher), Rupan Suzuki (newspaper depot chief), Koji Yamaguchi (poor student), Mikiko Miki (secretary), Kenji Kobayashi (noodle vendor #1), Kiichi Nozaka (noodle vendor #2), Kazuyo Esaki (amorous housewife), Yukiko Tachibana (indifferent housewife). Bengal (middle-aged man).

Production company undetermined. Color. Spherical wide screen (?). 113 minutes. Released 1988.

U.S. VERSION: English subtitles. 113 minutes. No MPAA rating. Released January 18, 1989.

Yoba ("Witch"). Executive Producer, Masaichi Nagata; Producer, Yasuyoshi Tokuma; Director, Tadashi Imai; Planning, Masumi Kanamaru; Screenplay Yoko Mizuki, based on the short story by Ryunosuke Akutagawa; Director of Photography, Kazuo Miyagawa; Music, Riichiro Manabe.

CAST: Machiko Kyo (Oshima), Kazuko Inano (Sawa), Shinjiro Ebara (Shinzo, Oshima's Husband), Rentaro Mikuni (Unryu), Kiyoshi Kodama (Ihara), Tanie Kitabayashi (Midwife), Miki Jinbo (Otoshi), Taro Shigaki (Shinzo, *Otoshi's fiancé*).

A Nagata Productions and Daiei Motion Picture Co., Ltd. Production. A Shochiku Co., Ltd. Release. Fujicolor. Panavision. 96 minutes. Released October 16, 1976

U.S. VERSION: Distributor, if any, is undetermined. International title (?): *The Possessed*. Alternate title (?): *The Witch*.

Yog—Monster from Space / Kessen! nankai no daikaiju Gezora Ganime Kameba ("Decisive Battle! Giant Monsters of the South Seas: Gezora, Ganime, Kameba"). Producers, Tomoyuki Tanaka and Fumio Tanaka; Director, Ishiro Honda; Screenplay, Ei Ogawa; Director of Photography, Taiichi Kankura; Music, Akira Ifukube; Editor,

Ad for *Yog—Monster from Space* (1970), the first of Toho's special effects features made without the guiding hand of Eiji Tsuburaya.

Masahisa Himi; Art Director, Takeo Kita; Sound Recording, Kanae Masuo; Assistant Director, Seiji Tani; Sound, Toho Recording Centre; Sound Effects, Toho Sound Effects Group; *Toho Special Effects Group*: Director and Photography, Teisho Arikawa; Assistant Director, Teruyoshi Nakano; Optical Photography, Yoichi Manoda and Yoshiyuki Tokumasa.

CAST: Akira Kubo (Taro Kudo), Atsuko Takahashi (Ayako Hoshino), Yoshio Tsuchiya (Dr. Kyoichi Miya), Kenji Sahara

(Makoto Obata), Noritake Saito (Rico), Yukiko Kobayashi (Saki), Tetsu Nakamura (Native Chief Ombo), Chotaro Togin (Engineer Yokoyama), Wataru Omae (Sakura), Sachio Sakai (magazine editor), Yu Fujiki (promotion division manager), Yuko Sugihara (stewardess), Haruo Nakajima (Gezora).

A Toho Co., Ltd. Production. Color (processed by Tokyo Laboratory, Ltd.). Panavision. 84 minutes. Released August 1, 1970.

U.S. VERSION: Released by American International Pictures. English-dubbed. A Samuel Z. Arkoff Presentation. Postproduction Supervisor, Salvatore Billitteri; prints by Movielab. Wide screen process billed as ColorScope in the United States. International Title: *The Space Amoeba.* 81 minutes. MPAA Rating: "G." Released 1971.

Yojimbo the Bodyguard [sic] / ***Yojimbo*** ("The Bodyguard"). Executive Producers, Tomoyuki Tanaka and Ryuzo Kikushima; Producer/Director/Editor, Akira Kurosawa; Screenplay, Ryuzo Kikushima, Hideo Oguni, and Akira Kurosawa; Director of Photography, Kazuo Miyagawa; Art Director/Costumes, Yoshiro Muraki; Lighting, Choshiro Ishii; Swordplay Choreography, Ruy Kuze; Music, Masaru Sato; Sound Recording, Hisashi Shimonaga and Choshichiro Mikami; Sound Effects, Toho Sound Effects Group; Sound, Toho Dubbing Theatre; Special Effects, Toho Special Effects Group; Production Supervisor, Hiroshi Nezu; Assistant Director, Shiro Moritani.

CAST: Toshiro Mifune (Sanjuro "Kuwabatake"), Eijiro Tono (Gonji, *the sake-seller*), Kamatari Fujiwara (Tazaemon, *the silk merchant*), Takashi Shimura (Tokuemon, *the sake merchant*), Seizaburo Kawazu (Seibei), Isuzu Yamada (Orin, *his wife*), Hiroshi Tachikawa (Yoichiro), Kyu Sazanka (Ushitora), Tatsuya Nakadai (Unosuke), Daisuke Kato (Inokichi, *his ugly brother*), Ikio Sawamura (Hansuke, *the corrupt official*), Ko Nishimura (Kuma), Yoshio Tsuchiya (Kohei, *the unlucky gambler*), Yoko Tsukasa (Nui, *his wife*), Susumu Fujita (Homma, *the cowardly but wise samurai*), Atsushi Watanabe (coffin maker), Yosuke Natsuki (the rebellious son, *who longs for a short and exciting life*), Jerry Fujio (Roku, *the giant*), Eisei Amamoto (thug).

A Toho Co., Ltd. Production, in association with Kurosawa Films, Ltd. Filmed at Toho Studios, Ltd (Tokyo). Western Electric Mirrophonic Recording (encoded with Perspecta Stereophonic Sound). Black and white (processed by Tokyo Laboratory, Ltd.). Toho Scope. 110 minutes. Released April 25, 1961.

U.S. VERSION: Released by Seneca International, Ltd. Released in both English subtitled and English-dubbed format. Alternate title: *The Bodyguard.* Home video versions are subtitled. Letterboxed laserdisc version available. 1964's *Per un pugno di dollari* ("For a Fistful of Dollars"; U.S. title: *Fistful of Dollars*) was an unauthorized remake over which Kurosawa sued. *Zatoichi Against Yojimbo* (1970) featured Mifune in a similar role. Released September 1961.

Yokohama Girl Director, Hideo Onchi; Screenplay, Yoshiro Shirasaka, based on a story by Shintaro Ishihara.

CAST: Reiko Dan, Akira Kubo, Nami Tamura, Takashi Shimura, Taro Sekimoto.

A Toho Co., Ltd. Production. Eastman Color (?). Toho Scope (?). Running time and release date undetermined.

U.S. VERSION: Released by Toho International Co., Ltd. English subtitles. Running time undetermined. Billed as a sequel to *Ayako* (q.v.). Possibly the same film as *La fée diabolique* (q.v.). No MPAA rating. Released August 14, 1964.

Yongary, Monster from the Deep / Dai koesu Yongkari. Director, Kiduck Kim; Screenplay, Yunsung Suh; Director of Photography, Kenichi Nakagawa; Special Effects, Inchib Byon.

CAST: Yungil Oh, Chungim Nam, Soonjai Lee, Moon Kang, Kwang Ho Lee.

A Kuk Dong Film Co., Ltd. Production, in association with Toei Co., Ltd. A South Korean/Japanese co-production. Filmed in South Korea. Color.

Anamorphic wide screen. 100 minutes. Released 1967.

U.S. Version: Never released theatrically. Released directly to television by American International Productions/ AIP-TV. English-dubbed. Executive Producers, James H. Nicholson and Samuel Z. Arkoff; Post-production supervisor, Salvatore Billitteri; Rerecording, Titra Sound Studios; Prints by Pathé. Alternate titles: *Monster Yongkari* and *Great Monster Yongkari.* 79 minutes. No MPAA Rating.

Yosakoi Journey / Yosakoi ryoko ("Yosakoi Journey"). Producer, Kiyoshi Shimazu; Director, Shoji Segawa; Screenplay, Kazuo Funabashi; Director of Photography, Sozaburo Shinomura; Art Director, Masao Kumagi; Music, Taku Izumi.

Cast: Frankie Sakai (Goichi Hasegawa), Chieko Baisho (Machiko), Chocho Miyako (Sei Ueda), Junzaburo Ban (Kichigoro Yamashita), Aiko Nagayama (Takako), Shinichi Yanagizawa (Rikizo), Takuya Fujioka (Ryotei Katsurai), Kensaku Morita (Shinsuke), Yasushi Koga (Sanpei Koga), Yasushi Suzuki, Toshie Kusunoki, Chiharu Kuri, Hiroshi Tatehara, Pinky and the Killers.

A Shochiku Co., Ltd. Production. Color. Shochiku GrandScope (?). 91 minutes. Released November 1969.

U.S. Version: Released by Shochiku Films of America, Inc. English subtitles. The 4th "Shochiku Comedy" feature. Followed by *Romance Express* (1970). 91 minutes. No MPAA rating. Released July 1970.

Yotsuya kaidan ("Yotsuya Ghost Story"). Executive Producer, Kuichi Tsuji; Producer, Nobuo Miura; Director, Kenji Misumi; Screenplay, Fuji Yahiro, based on the Kabuki play *Tokaido yotsuya kaidan*, by Nanboku Tsuruya; Director of Photography, Yukimasa Makita; Art Director, Seiichi Ota; Lighting, Teiichi Ito; Editor, Kanji Suganuma; Assistant Director, Sensho Nishizawa; Music, Seiichi Suzuki; Natural Music Director, Toshio Nakamoto; Sound Recording, Iwao Otani; Martial Arts Director, Shohei Miyauchi.

Cast: Kazuo Hasegawa (Iemon Tamiya), Yasuko Nakada (Oiwa), Yoko Uraji (Oume), Meiko (Osode), Joji Tsurumi (Kohei), Naritoshi [no other name given] (Yomoshichi), Hideo Takamatsu (Gonbei Naosuke), Chieko Murata (Omaki), Shosaku Sugiyama (Akiyama), Shinobu Araki (Uncle Hikoroku), Ryonosuke Azuma (Takuetsu), Fujio Suga, Sanemon Arashi, Yasuhiko Shima, Saburo Date.

A Daiei Motion Picture Co., Ltd. Production. Filmed at Daiei-Kyoto Studios. Fujicolor. DaieiScope. 84 minutes. Released July 1, 1959.

U.S. Version: Distrubutor, if any, is undetermined. Available with English subtitles. International title: *Thou Shalt Not Be Jealous.* Not to be confused with *The Ghost of Yotsuya* (Shintoho, also 1959).

You Can Succeed, Too / Kimimo shussega dekiru ("You Can Succeed, Too"). Producer, Sanezumi Fujimoto; Director, Eizo Sugawa; Screenplay, Toshiro Ide and Ryozo Kasahara; Music, Toshiro Mayuzumi; Assistant Director, Ken Sano; Choreographer, Yukio Sekiya.

Cast: Frankie Sakai, Tadao Takashima, Izumi Yukimura, Keaton Masuda, Mie Hama, Ichiro Arishima.

A Toho Co., Ltd. Production. Eastman Color. Toho Scope. 102 minutes. Released May 1964.

U.S. Version: Released by Toho International Co., Ltd. English subtitles. 102 minutes. No MPAA rating. Released December 1964.

The Young Beast / Wakai kemono ("The Young Beast"). Producers, Masumi Fujimoto and Masanori Kaneko; Director/Screenplay, Shintaro Ishihara, based on his novel; Director of Photography, Minoru Kuribayashi; Art Director, Hyoe Hamagami; Music, Toshiro Mayuzumi.

Cast: Akira Kubo (Susumu Miyaguchi), Reiko Dan (Yumi), Seizaburo Kawazu (Okazaki), Michiyo Aratama (Tokiko), Kenji Sahara (reporter), Eijiro Tono (Susumu's father).

A Toho Co., Ltd. Production. Black and white. Academy ratio. 99 minutes. Released 1958 (?).

U.S. VERSION: Release undetermined, possibly by Toho International Co., Ltd. in subtitled format. No MPAA rating.

Young Guy Graduates / Furesshumen wakadaisho ("Freshman Young Boss"). Director, Jun Fukuda; Screenplay, Yasuo Tanami; Director of Photography, Yuzuru Aizawa; Art Director, Yoshifumi Honda; Music, Kenjiro Hirose.

CAST: Yuzo Kayama (Yuichi Tanuma), Wakako Sakai (Setsuko), Kunie Tanaka (Ishiyama), Keiko Cho (Midori), Choko Iida, Ichiro Arishima, Machiko Naka, Tatsuyoshi Ebara.

A Toho Co., Ltd. Production. Eastman Color. Toho Scope. 90 minutes. Released January 1, 1969.

U.S. VERSION: Released by Toho International Co., Ltd. English subtitles. The 13th "Young Guy" feature. Followed by *Young Guy on Mt. Cook* (1969). 90 minutes. No MPAA rating. Released May 28, 1969.

Young Guy on Mt. Cook / Nyujirando no wakadaisho ("Young Boss in New Zealand"). Director, Jun Fukuda; Screenplay, Yasuo Tanami; Director of Photography, Shinsaku Uno; Art Director, Juichi Ikuno; Music, Kenjiro Hirose.

CAST: Yuzo Kayama (Yuichi Tanami), Wakako Sakai (Setsuko), Kunie Tanaka (Ishiyama), Tatsuyoshi Ebara (Enguchi), Jessica Peters (Elizabeth), Choko Iida (Riki), Ichiro Arishima (Kyutaro), Midori Utsumi (Saeko), Machiko Naka (Teruko), Mari Nakayama.

A Toho Co., Ltd. Production. Eastman Color. Toho Scope 86 minutes. Released July 12, 1969.

U.S. VERSION: Released by Toho International Co., Ltd. English subtitles. The 14th "Young Guy" feature. Followed by *Bravo! Young Guy* (1970). 86 minutes. No MPAA rating. Released October 8, 1969.

A Young Man's Stronghold / Wakamono no toride ("A Young Man's Stronghold"). Director, Toshiya Fujita; Screenplay, Toshiya Fujita and Saburo Kurusu, based on an original story by Masaaki Tatehara; Director of Photography, Kenji Hagiwara; Art Director, Kazuo Yagyu; Music, Hiroki Tamaki and Jiro Inagaki.

CAST: Takeo Chii (Jiro), Shoji Ishibashi (Yuichi), Yoko Minamida (Fuse), Chieko Matsubara (Seiko), Shinjiro Ebara (Takahiko), Meiko Kaji (Ryoko), Kazuyo Sumida (Sanae).

A Nikkatsu Corp. Production. Fujicolor. NikkatsuScope. 89 minutes. Released April 4, 1970.

U.S. VERSION: Distributor, if any, is undetermined. English subtitled version available. 89 minutes. No MPAA rating.

Young People / Wakai hito ("Young People"). Producer, Masumi Fujimoto; Director, Kon Ichikawa; Screenplay, Naoya Uchimura, Natto Wada and Kon Ichikawa, based on a story by Yojiro Ishizaka; Director of Photography, Kazuo Yamada; Art Director, Yasuhide Kato; Music, Yasushi Akutagawa.

CAST: Ryo Ikebe (Shintaro Kanzaki), Asami Hisaji (Sumi Hashimoto), Kumoko Shimazaki (Keiko Enami), Haruko Sugimura (Hatsu Enami).

A Toho Co., Ltd. Production. Black and white. Academy ratio. 113 minutes. Released July 8, 1952.

U.S. VERSION: Distributor, if any, is undetermined.

Young Swordsman / Hiken ("Secret Sword"). Producer, Tomoyuki Tanaka; Director, Hiroshi Inagaki; Screenplay, Hiroshi Inagaki and Takeshi Kimura; Special Effects, Toho Special Effects Group.

CAST: Somegoro Ichikawa (Tenzen Hayakawa), Hiroyuki Nagato (Chojuro), Nami Tamura (fiancée), Junko Ikeuchi (hill woman), Ryunosuke Tsukigata.

A Toho Co., Ltd. Production. Black and white. Toho Scope. 108 minutes. Released 1963.

U.S. VERSION: Released by Toho International Co., Ltd. English subtitles. 108 minutes. No MPAA rating. Released May 1964.

Youth / Seishun ("Youth") [**documentary**]. Executive Producer, Tomo Hiroka; Producers, Takeo Ina, and Chokichi Sugano; Director, Kon Ichikawa;

Screenplay, Masato Ide, Ishio Shirasaka, Shuntaro Tanigawa, and Kiyoshi Ito; Director of Photography, Eikichi Uematsu; Music, Naozumi Yamamoto; Sound Recording, Tetsuya Ohashi; Editor, Masao Takagi.

Narrator: Hiroshi Akutagawa.

An Asahi/Toho Co., Ltd. Production. A Toho Co., Ltd. Release. Black and white (?). Academy ratio (?). Running time undetermined. Released September 21, 1968.

U.S. VERSION: Distributor, if any, is undetermined.

The Youth and His Amulet / Gen to Fudo-Myoh ("Gen and Fudo-Myoh"). Executive Producer/Director, Hiroshi Inagaki; Screenplay, Toshiro Ide and Zenzo Matsuyama, based on the story by Shizue Miyaguchi; Director of Photography, Kazuo Yamada; Music, Ikuma Dan; Sound, Toho Recording Centre; Sound Effects, Toho Sound Effects Group. *Toho Special Effects Group*: Director, Eiji Tsuburaya; Photography, Teisho Arikawa, Motonari Tomioka; Matte Photography, Yukio Manoda, Taka Yuki; Matte Process, Hiroshi Mukoyama; Art Director, Akira Watanabe; Lighting, Kuichiro Kishida; Assistant Director, Teruyoshi Nakano.

CAST: Toru Koyanagi (Gen), Hisako Sakabe (his sister), Toshiro Mifune (Fudo-Myoh), Chishu Ryu, Yosuke Natsuki, Minoru Chiaki, Nobuko Otowa, Mie Hama, Yoshio Kosugi, Bokuzen Hidari, Kenzo Tabu, Akira Tani, Yutaka Sada, Ikio Sawamura, Noriko Sengoku, Kin Sugai.

A Toho Co., Ltd. Production. Western Electric Mirrophonic recording (possibly encoded with Perspecta Stereophonic Sound). Black and white with color insert (processed by Tokyo Laboratory Ltd.). Toho Scope. 102 minutes. Released 1961.

U.S. VERSION: Released by Toho International Co., Ltd. English subtitles. 102 minutes. No MPAA rating. Released March 29, 1963.

Youth in Fury / Kawaita mizuumi ("The Dried-Up Lake"). Director, Masahiro Shinoda; Screenplay, Shuji Terayama; Story, Eiji Shimba; Director of Photography, Masao Kosugi; Art Director, Kiminobu Sato; Editor, Keiichi Uraoka; Music, Toru Takemitsu; Production Supervisor, Tetsuo Ueno.

CAST: Shinichiro Mikami (Takuya Shimojo), Shima Iwashita (Yoko Katsura), Hizuru Takachiho (Fumie Sono), Kayoko Honoo (Setsuko Kitamura), Junichiro Yamashita (Michihiko Kihara), Kazuya Kosaka (Seiichi Mizushima), Yunosuke Ito (Oseto), Yachiyo Otori (Shizue), Shinji Takano (Fujimori), Eiko Kujo (Miyako Edamura), Yuki Tominaga (Sakiko Ota), Keiko Kuni (Takako Shinoyama), Teiko Sawamura.

A Shochiku Co., Ltd. Production. Eastman Color. Shochiku GrandScope. 89 minutes. Released 1960.

U.S. VERSION: Released by Shochiku Films of America, Inc. English subtitles. 89 minutes. No MPAA rating. Released July 25, 1961.

The Youth of Heiji Zenigata / Seishun Zenigata Heiji ("The Youth of Heiji Zenigata"). Producer, Tomoyuki Tanaka; Director, Kon Ichikawa; Screenplay, Natto Wada, based on a story by Kodo Nomura; Director of Photography, Seiichi Endo; Music, Toshiro Mayuzumi; Art Director, Takeo Kita; Lighting, Soichi Yokoi; Sound Recording, Masanobu Miyazaki.

CAST: Tomoemon Otani (Heiji Zenigata), Yunosuke Ito (Hachigoro), Yoko Sugi (Oshizu).

A Toho Co., Ltd. Production. Black and white. Academy ratio. Running time undetermined. Released August 19, 1953.

U.S. VERSION: Distributor, if any, is undetermined.

Youth of the Beast / Yaju no seishun ("Youth of the Beast"). Producer, Keinosuke Kubo; Director, Seijun Suzuki; Screenplay, Ichiro Ikeda and Tadaaki Yamazaki, based on the novel by Haruhiko Oyabu; Director of Photography, Kazue Nagatsuka; Art Director, Yoshinaga Yoko; music, Hajime Okumura; Assistant Director, Noboru Watanabe.

CAST: Jo Shishido (Joji Mizuno), Ichiro

Kijima (Koichi Takeshita), Misako Suzuki (Hirokawa), Shoji Kobayashi (Tatsuo Nomoto), Kinzo Shin (Shinsuke Onodera), Eiji Go (Shigeru Takechi).

A Nikkatsu Corp. Production. Color. NikkatsuScope. 91 minutes. Released 1963.

U.S. Version: Released by Nikkatsu Corp. English subtitles. 91 minutes. No MPAA rating. Released 1993.

Yumeji / Yumeji ("Yumeji"). Producer, Genjiro Arato; Director, Seijun Suzuki; Screenplay, Yozo Tanaka; Director of Photography, Junichi Fujisawa; Editor, Akira Suzuki; Art Director, Noriyoshi Ikeya; Music, Kaname Kawachi and Shigeru Umebayashi; Assistant Director, Yasushi Saisha.

Cast: Kenji Sawada (Yumeji Takehisa), Tomoko Mariya (Tomoyo), Yoshio Harada (Sokichi Wakiya), Masumi Miyazaki (Hikono), Tamasaburo Bando (Gyoshu Inamura), Reona Hirota (O-Yo), Chikako Miyagi (wet-nurse), Kazuhiko Hasegawa (Onimatsu), Michiyo Okusu (landlady).

A Genjiro Arato Picture Production. Color. Spherical wide screen (1.66:1). 128 minutes. Released 1991.

U.S. Version: Released by Genjiro Arato Pictures. English subtitles. The third film of a trilogy. 128 minutes. No MPAA rating. Released 1993.

***Zatoichi* Series** Long-running Daiei series of feature films starring Shintaro Katsu as Zatoichi ("Masseur Ichi"), a wandering, bumbling blind masseur who is, in fact, a gambler and expert swordsman, despite his affliction. Films typically revolve around Zatoichi's efforts to help a family or young woman in trouble with local Bosses (corrupt officials). A Japanese counterpart to Peter Falk's "Columbo" character, Katsu became a huge and powerful star with this series, and has directed and/or produced several entries. A television series, also starring Katsu, followed *Zatoichi's Conspiracy* (1973), and the series was revived with the theatrical release of *Zatoichi* in 1989. (An American-made, updated adaptation of the series, *Blind Fury*, was released the following year.) As nearly every entry in the series has at least one alternate title, they are listed according to their earliest known moniker. It should also be noted that the main character's name (and thus the title of the films) is alternately given as "Zatoichi," "Zato Ichi," "Masseur Ichi," and "The Blind Swordsman." "Zatoichi" is the preferred name here, unless the use of one of the alternates has been confirmed.

Films Include: The Life and Opinion of Zatoichi, The Return of Zatoichi (1962); Zatoichi Enters Again (1963); Zatoichi the Fugitive, Zatoichi, Zatoichi and a Chest of Gold, Zatoichi's Flashing Sword, Fight Zatoichi Fight (1964); Adventures of a Blind Man, The Blind Swordsman's Revenge, Zatoichi and the Doomed Men, Showdown for Zatoichi (1965); Zatoichi—The Blind Swordsman's Vengeance, Zatoichi—The Blind Swordsman's Pilgrimage (1966); Zatoichi's Cane-Sword, Zatoichi—The Blind Swordsman's Rescue, Zatoichi Challenged (1967); Zatoichi—The Blind Swordsman and the Fugitives, Zatoichi—The Blind Swordsman Samaritan (1968); Zatoichi Meets Yojimbo (1970); Zatoichi Meets His Equal [Jap/HK] (1971); Zatoichi at Large (1972); Zatoichi in Desperation, Zatoichi's Conspiracy (1973); Zatoichi (1989).

Zatoichi / Zato Ichi kenkatabi ("Zatoichi: Fighting Journey"). Producer, Ikuro Kubokawa; Director, Kimiyoshi Yasuda; Screenplay, Minoru Inuzuka, based on the story by Kan Shimozawa; Director of Photography, Shozo Honda; Art Director, Yoshinobu Nishioka; Fight Sequences Choreographer, Shohei Miyachi; Music, Akira Ifukube.

Cast: Shintaro Katsu (Zatoichi), Shiho Fujimura (Omitsu), Ryuzo Shimada (Jingoro), Reiko Fujiwara (Ohisa), Matasaburo Niwa (Yamada), Yoshio Yoshida (Tomegoro), Sonosuke Sawamura (Tobei), Shosaku Sugiyama (Hikozo), Yutaka Nakamura (Matsu).

A Daiei Motion Picture Co., Ltd. Production. Eastman Color. DaieiScope. 87 minutes. Released 1963.

U.S. Version: Released by Daiei International Films, Inc. English subtitles. Alternate title: *Zatoichi and the Scoundrels.*

The 5th feature (and not the 1st, as the title suggests) in the "Zatoichi" series. Followed by *Zatoichi: Masseur Ichi and a Chest of Gold* (1964). This apparently was the first film in the series to be exhibited in the United States. 87 minutes. No MPAA rating. Released June 27, 1968. Released to home video as *Zatoichi on the Road* by Chambara Entertainment. A John Wada and Gregg Yokoyama Presentation. Subtitles, Multi-Media Translations International. Video version letterboxed.

Zatoichi / Zato Ichi ("Zatoichi"). Producer/Director, Shintaro Katsu; Co-Screenplay, Shintaro Katsu, based on a story by Kan Shimosawa.

CAST: Shintaro Katsu (Zatoichi), Ken Ogata, Yusaka Matsuda.

A Katsu Production Co., Ltd. Production. Color. Spherical wide screen. 124 minutes. Released 1989.

U.S. VERSION: Unreleased in the United States and final "Zatoichi" film as this book went to press. The 26th feature in the "Zatoichi" film series, and the first theatrical feature in 16 years.

Zatoichi and the Doomed Men / Zato Ichi sakata giri ("Zatoichi: Backhand Grip Cut"). Executive Producer, Masaichi Nagata; Director, Issei Mori; Screenplay, Shozaburo Asai, based on an original story by Kan Shimosawa; Director of Photography, Hiroshi Imai; Music, Hajime Kaburagi.

CAST: Shintaro Katsu (Zatoichi), Kanbei Fujiyama, Eiko Taki, Masako Myojo, Koichi Mizuhara.

A Daiei Motion Picture Co., Ltd. Production. Eastman Color. DaieiScope. 88 minutes. Released 1965.

U.S. VERSION: Distributor, if any, is undetermined. The 11th "Zatoichi" feature. Followed by *Showdown for Zatoichi* (1965).

Zatoichi at Large / Zato Ichi goyotabi ("Zatoichi: An Arrest Journey"). Producer, Shintaro Katsu; Director, Issei Mori; Screenplay, Kinya Naoi, based on the story by Kan Shimosawa; Director of Photography, Fujio Morita; Art Director, Seiichi Ota; Music, Hideaki Sakurai.

CAST: Shintaro Katsu (Zatoichi), Hisaya Morishige (Tobei), Naoko Otani (Oyae), Etsushi Takahachi (Sataro), Rentaro Mikuni (Tetsugoro), Osamu Sakai (Seiji).

A Katsu Production Co., Ltd./Toho Co., Ltd. Production. A Toho Co., Ltd. Release. Filmed at Toho Studios, Ltd. (Tokyo). Fuji Color. Panavision. 90 minutes. Released January 15, 1972.

U.S. VERSION: Released by Toho International Co., Ltd. English subtitles. The 23rd "Zatoichi" feature. Followed by *Zatoichi in Desperation* (1972). 88 minutes. No MPAA rating. Released September 1973.

Zatoichi Challenged / Zato Ichi chikemuri kaido ("Zatoichi Bloodly Smoke Road"). Executive Producers, Eiji Nishizawa and Masaichi Nagata; Producer, Ikuo Kubodera; Director, Kenji Misumi; Screenplay, Ryozo Kasahara, based on an original story by Kan Shimosawa; Director of Photography, Chishi Makiura; Art Director, Narinori Shimoshizaka; Music, Akira Ifukube; Sound, Iwao Otani; Lighting, Reijiro Yamashita; Editor, Toshio Taniguchi; Assistant Director, Toshikata Tomoeda; Martial Arts Director, Shohei Miyauchi.

CAST: Shintaro Katsu (Zatoichi), Jushiro [Tushiro] Konoe (Tajuro Akazuka), Miwa Takada (Omitsu), Yukiji Asaoka (Tomoe), Mikiko Tsubouchi (Osen), Miei Nakao (Miyuki); Takao Ito (Shokichi), Asao Koike (Maebara of Gonzo), Midori Isomura (Omine), Tatsuo Matsumura (Tahe), Eitaro Ozawa (Torikoshi), Jotaro Chinami [Sennami] (Chokichi), Kojiro Kusanada (Kurisu), Kenzo Tabu [Tatake] (Kanai of Manzo), Osamu Nabei [Nabe] (Dicer Hanzo), Hirohisa Toda (Shinnosuke Emi), Koji Fujiyama (Gokishi), Koichi Mizuhara (Minowa of Sobe), Shosaku Sugiyama (Naruyama), Ikuko Mori (waitress at Fukube).

A Daiei Motion Picture Co., Ltd. Production. Filmed at Daiei-Kyoto Studios. Eastman Color. DaieiScope. 86 minutes, Released 1967.

U.S. VERSION: Released by Daiei International Films, Inc. English subtitles. The 17th "Zatoichi" feature. Followed by

Zatoichi: The Blind Swordsman and the Fugitives (1968). 86 minutes. No MPAA rating. Released April 1970.

Zatoichi Enters Again / Shin Zato Ichi monogatari ("New Zatoichi Story"). Executive Producer, Masaichi Nagata; Director, Tokuzo Tanaka; Screenplay, Minoru Inuzuka, based on an original Story, Kan Shimosawa; Director of Photography, Chishi Makiura; Music, Akira Ifukube.

CAST: Shintaro Katsu (Zatoichi).

A Daiei Motion Picture Co., Ltd. Production. Daieicolor. DaieiScope. 91 minutes. Released 1963.

U.S. VERSION: Distributor, if any, is undetermined. Possibly released as Masseur Ichi Enters Again. The 3rd "Zatoichi" feature. Followed by *Zatoichi, the Fugitive* (1963).

Zatoichi in Desperation / Shin Zatoichi monogatari: Oretatsue ("New Zatoichi Story: A Broken Stick"). Producer/Director, Shintaro Katsu; Screenplay, Minoru Inuzuka, based on an original story by Kan Shimosawa; Director of Photography, Fujio Morita; Lighting, Gengo Miyamoto; Art Director, Seiichi Ota; Music, Mitsuo Miyamoto and Kunio Murai; Sound Recording, Masao Osumi.

CAST: Shintaro Katsu (Zatoichi), Kiwako Taichi (Nishikigi), Kyoko Yoshizawa (Kaede), Yasuhiro Koune (Shinkichi), Katsuo Nakamura (Ushimatsu), Asao Koicke (Kagiyu Mangoro), Joji Takagi (Shijo Tokiwa), Masumi Harukawa (Ohama).

A Katsu Production Co., Ltd./Toho Co., Ltd. Production. A Toho Co., Ltd. Release. Filmed at Toho Studios, Ltd. (Tokyo). Eastman Color. Panavision. 92 minutes. Released February 21, 1972.

U.S. VERSION: Released by Toho International Co., Ltd. English subtitles. The 24th "Zatoichi" feature. Followed by *Zatoichi's Conspiracy* (1973). 92 minutes. No MPAA rating. Released February 17, 1973.

Zatoichi: Masseur Ichi and a Chest of Gold / Zato Ichi senryokubi ("Zatoichi: A Wanted Criminal for Stealing 1,000 Ryo"). Executive Producer, [Planning], Hiroshi Ozawa; Director, Kazuo Ikehiro; Screenplay, Shozaburo Asai and Akikazu Ota, based on an original story Kan Shimosawa; Director of Photography, Kazuo Miyagawa; Art Director, Yoshinobu Nishioka; Music, Ichiro Saito; Fighting Sequences Director, Shoei Miyauchi; Color Consultant, Shozo Tanaka.

CAST: Shintaro Katsu (Zatoichi), Shogo Shimada, Mikiko Tsubouchi, Machiko Hasgawa, Kenzaburo Jo [Tomisaburo Wakayama] (Jushiro), Tatsuya Ishiguro, Shinjiro Asano, Saburo Date, Hikosaburo Kataoka, Matasaburo Tanba, Toranosuke Tennoji, Koichi Mizuhara, Hiroshi Hayashi, Yusaku Terashima, Ichiro Takakura.

A Daiei Motion Picture Co., Ltd. Production. Eastman Color. DaieiScope. 83 minutes. Released 1964.

U.S. VERSION: Distributor, if any, is undetermined. Released to home video in 1992 by Chambara Entertainment. English subtitles. A John Wada and Gregg Yokoyama Presentation. Subtitles, Multi-Media Translations International. Jo is Katsu's real-life brother. Video version letterboxed. The 6th "Zatoichi" feature. Followed by *Zatoichi's Flashing Sword* (1964). 83 minutes. No MPAA rating.

Zatoichi Meets His Equal / Zato Ichi "Yabure! Tojin-ken" ("Zatoichi, Beat the Chinese Sword!"). Producer, Shintaro Katsu; Co-producer, Sir Run Run Shaw; Director, Kimiyoshi Yasuda; Screenplay, Kimiyoshi Yasuda, based on an original story by Kan Shimosawa, and a character created by Shaw Brothers, Ltd. Productions; Director of Photography, Fujio Morita.

CAST: Shintaro Katsu (Zatoichi), Wang Yu Chu [Jimmy Wang] (Wang Kong, *the One-Armed Swordsman*), Yuko Hamada (Osen), Michie Terada (Oyone), Koji Nambara (Kakuzen).

A Katsu Production Co., Ltd./Daiei Motion Picture Co., Ltd./Shaw Brothers (H.K.) Ltd. Production. A Japanese/Hong Kong co-production. Daieicolor. DaieiScope. 95 minutes. Released 1971.

U.S. VERSION: Released by Toho International Co., Ltd. English subtitles. Advertised as *Zatoichi Meets the One-Armed Swordsman*. The 22nd "Zatoichi" feature, as well as a sequel to the Shaw Brothers' *The One-Armed Swordsman*. The last Daiei-produced "Zatoichi" feature. Followed by *Zatoichi at Large* (1972). 95 minutes. No MPAA rating. Released 1973.

Zatoichi Meets Yojimbo / Zato Ichi to Yojimbo

("Zato Ichi and Yojimbo"). Executive Producer, Masaichi Nagata; Producer, Shintaro Katsu; Director, Kihachi Okamoto; Screenplay, Kihachi Okamoto and Tetsuro Yoshida, based on an original story by Kan Shimozawa, and a character created by Ryuzo Kikushima, Akira Kurosawa, and Hideo Oguni; Director of Photography, Kazuo Miyagawa; Art Director, Yoshinobu Nishioka; Editor, Toshio Taniguchi; Music, Akira Ifukube; Sound Recording, Tsuchitaro Hayashi.

CAST: Shintaro Katsu (Zatoichi), Toshiro Mifune (Sassa, *the yojimbo*), Shin Kishida (Kuzuryu), Yonekura Masakene (Masagoro), Toshiyuki Hosokawa (Sanaemon Goto), Kanjuro Arashi [Arachi] (Hyoroku), Osamu Takizawa (Yasuke Eboshiya), Ayako Wakao (Umeno), Shigeru Kamiyama (Jinzaburo Wakiya), Masakane Yonekura (Boss Masagoro).

A Katsu Production Co., Ltd./Daiei Motion Picture Co., Ltd. Production. Westrex Recording System. Eastman Color. DaieiScope. Filmed at Daiei-Kyoto Studios. 116 minutes. Released January 1970.

U.S. VERSION: Released by Daiei International Films, Inc. English subtitles. Advertised as *Zatoichi vs. Yojimbo*. 116 minutes. No MPAA rating. Released July 17, 1970. Reissued November 22, 1971 by Bijou of Japan, Inc. Reissued by R5/S8, date undetermined. Eastern hemisphere rights currently controlled by Toho Co., Ltd. Curiously advertised as "Not Seen in Ten Years!" when first released in the United States. Mifune's character is technically *not* his character from Kurosawa's *Yojimbo* (1961), though the similarity between the two characters was certainly deliberate. The 20th feature in the "Zatoichi" film series. Followed by *Zatoichi's Fire Festival* (1970). *Note:* Current video version is not letterboxed.

Zatoichi: The Blind Swordsman and the Fugitives / Zato Ichi hatashijo

("Zatoichi: A Letter of Challenge"). Executive Producer, Masaichi Nagata; Producer, Ikuo Kubodera; Director, Kimiyoshi Yasuda; Screenplay, Kinya Naoi, based on an original story by Kan Shimosawa; Director of Photography, Kazuo Miyagawa; Art Director, Shigeru [no other name given]; Editor, Kanji Suganuma; Music, Hajime Kaburagi; Sound Recording, Iwao Otani.

CAST: Shintaro Katsu (Zatoichi), Yumiko Mikimoto (Oshizu), Kyosuke Machida (Ogano Genpachiro), Takashi Shimura (Junan), Akifumi Inoue (Kumeji), Jotaro Sennami (Minokichi), Hisataro Hojo (Genta), Hosei Komatsu (Matsugoro), Koichi Mizuhara (Sennosuke), Kazuo Yamamoto (Isuke), Ryuji Funabashi (Ushimatsu), Shozo Nanbu (Tokuzaemon), Yukio Horikita (Inokichi), Seishiro Hara (Sakata), Rieko Oda (Osei), Yukari Mizumachi (Yoshida-ya's maid), Teruko Oumi (Osato).

A Daiei Motion Picture Co., Ltd. Production. Filmed at Daiei-Kyoto Studios. Eastman Color. DaieiScope. 82 minutes. Released August 10, 1968.

U.S. VERSION: Released by Daiei International Films, Inc. English subtitles. Possibly released as *The Blind Swordsman and the Fugitives*. The 18th "Zatoichi" feature. Followed by *Zatoichi: The Blind Swordsman Samaritan* (1968). 82 minutes. No MPAA rating. Release date undetermined.

Zatoichi: The Blind Swordsman Samaritan / Zato Ichi kenka daiko

("Zatoichi – Fighting Drums"). Executive Producers, Akihiko Murai and Masaichi Nagata; Producer, Hisakazu Tsuji; Director, Kenji Misumi; Screenplay, Hisashi Sugiura, Tetsuro Yoshida, and Kiyokata Saruwaka, based on an original story by Kan Shimosawa; Director of Photography, Fujio Morita; Art Director, Akira Naito; Editor, Toshio Taniguchi; Assistant Director, Mitsuaki Tsuji; Music, Shigeru Ikeno; Sound Recording, Yukio Kaibara; Lighting, Shunji Kurokawa.

CAST: Shintaro Katsu (Zatoichi), Yoshiko Mita (Osode), Makoto Sato (Yasaburo Kashiwazaki), Ko Nishimura (Sosuke Saruya), Takuya Fujioka (Shinkichi), Chocho Miyako (Ohaya), Akira Shimizu (Kumakichi), Ryoichi Tamagawa (Chohachi), Machiko Soga (Osen), Ryutaro Gomi (Sashichi), Osamu Okawa (Tokuji), Mutsuhiro Toura (Choji), Kazue Tamaki [Tamachi] (Aburaya no Banto, *the oil shop clerk*), Yukio Horikita (Isokichi), Takeshi Date (Kinzo), Yasuhiro Minakami (Unokichi), Moto Kimura (Daisaku Igawa), Shosaku Sugiyama (Kinsuke), Kazuo Yamamoto (dice player), Akira Moroguchi (Shota), Takeshi Hamada (Hyoma Muraki), Jun Katsumura (Rokusuke), Takeshi Yabuchi (Jakujiro), Teruko Omi (Okatsu).

A Daiei Motion Picture Co., Ltd. Production. Filmed at Daiei-Kyoto Studios. Fujicolor. Daieiscope. 82 minutes. Released 1968.

U.S. VERSION: Released by Daiei International Films, Inc., possibly as *The Blind Swordsman Samaritan*. English subtitles. Also known as *The Blind Swordsman and the Drums* and *Zatoichi Fighting Drums*. 82 minutes. No MPAA rating. Release date undetermined. The 19th "Zatoichi" feature. Followed by *Zatoichi Meets Yojimbo* (1970). Released to home video by Chambara Entertainment as *Zatoichi: The Blind Swordsman Samaritan*. A John Wada and Gregg Yokoyama Presentation. Subtitles, Multi-Media Translations International. Video version letterboxed.

Zatoichi: The Blind Swordsman's Fire Festival / Zato Ichi abare himatsuri ("Zatoichi: A Violent Fire Festival"). Executive Producer, Masaichi Nagata; Producer, Shintaro Katsu; Director, Kenji Misumi; Based on an original story by Kan Shimosawa; Director of Photography, Kazuo Miyagawa.

CAST: Shintaro Katsu (Zatoichi), Tatsuya Nakadai (Ronin), Reiko Ohara (Okiya), Masayuki Mori (Yamikubo), Peter (Umeji).

A Katsu Production Co., Ltd./Daiei Motion Picture Co., Ltd. Production. Daieicolor. DaieiScope. 95 minutes. Released August 12, 1970.

U.S. VERSION: Distributor, if any, is undetermined. Possibly released as *Masseur Ichi's Fire Festival* and *The Blind Swordsman's Fire Festival*. The 21st "Zatoichi" feature. Followed by *Zatoichi Meets His Equal* (1971).

Zatoichi: The Blind Swordsman's Pilgrimage / Zato Ichi umi o wataru ("Zatoichi Goes Across the Sea"). Executive Producer, Hiroshi Ozawa; Director, Kazuo Ikehiro; Screenplay, Kaneto Shindo, based on an original story by Kan Shimosawa; Director of Photography, Senkichiro Takeda; Art Director, Yoshinobu Nishioka; Editor, Toshio Taniguchi; Music, Ichiro Saito; Sound Recording, Iwao Otawa; Lighting, Reihiro Yamashita; Assistant Director, Hachizo Miyajima; Martial Arts Director, Eiichi Kusumoto.

CAST: Shintaro Katsu (Zatoichi), Michiyo Yasuda (Okichi), Takahiko Tono (Yasuzo), Isao Yamagata (Tohachi), Ryutaro Gomi (Jonenbo), Jotaro Chinami (Pickpocket), Hisashi Igawa (Eigoro), Kunie Tanaka (Talkative Man), Masao Mishima (Gonbei), Manabu Morita (Shinzo), Saburo Date (Kagimatsu), Yukio Horikita (Heita), Shosaku Sugiyama (Gorobei), Yusaku Terajima (Boss C), Seishiro Hara (Yosaemon).

A Daiei Motion Picture Co., Ltd. Production. Eastman Color. DaieiScope. 81 minutes. Released August 13, 1966.

U.S. VERSION: Released by Daiei International Films, Inc. English subtitles. Title also given as *Masseur Ichi Goes Abroad*, *Zatoichi Goes Abroad*, *Zatoichi's Pilgrimage* and *The Blind Swordsman's Pilgrimage*. The 14th "Zatoichi" feature. Followed by *Zatoichi: The Blind Swordsman's Cane-Sword* (1967). 81 minutes. No MPAA rating. Release date undetermined.

Zatoichi: The Blind Swordsman's Rescue / Zato Ichi royaburi ("Zatoichi Breaking jail"). Executive Producer, Masaichi Nagata; Producer, Shintaro Katsu; Director, Satsuo Yamamoto; Screenplay, Takehiro Nakajima, Koji Matsumoto, and Kiyokata Saruwaka, based on an original story by Kan Shimosawa; Director of Photography, Kazuo Miyagawa; Production Manager, Genichiro Adachi; Assistant Directors, Shigeru Inoue, Umeo Nanno, and Toshiaki Kuniatsu; Art Director, Yoshinobu Nishioka; Editor, Kanji Suganuma; Music, Shigeru Ikeno; Sound Recording, Tsuchitaro Hayashi.

CAST: Shintaro Katsu (Zatoichi), Rentaro Mikuni (Kiyotaki of Asagoro), Ko Nishimura (Seshiro Suga), Yuko Hamada (Shino), Takuya Fujioka (Zatosanji), Kenjiro Ishiyama (Tatsugoro), Mizuho Suzuki (Shuho Ohara), Tatsuo Endo (Iwai no Tomizo), Toshiyuki Hosokawa (Sunosaki of Jinzaburo), Tatsuo Matsushita (Yamagen), Osamu Sakai (Sadamatsu), Kayo Mikimoto (Yuki), Yuzo Hayakawa (Hyogo Saito), Ryoichi Tamagawa (Senemon), Rokku Furukawa (Zatokinsuku), Keisuke Otori (Jinsuke), Utako Kyo (woman), Manabu Morita (Hatono Tetsu), Sen Yano (Farmer Zenpachi), Naoya Mizushima (Farmer Matashichi), Koichi Mizuhara (Farmer Gohei), Saburo Date (Yamagen's clerk), Gen Kimura (Farmer Fusajiro), Ikuko Mori (Sei).

A Katsu Production Co., Ltd./Daiei Motion Picture Co., Ltd. Production. A Daiei Motion Picture Co., Ltd. Release. Filmed at Daiei-Kyoto Studios. Eastman Color. DaieiScope. 95 minutes. Released August 12, 1967.

U.S. VERSION: Released by Daiei International Films, Inc. English subtitles. The 16th "Zatoichi" feature. Followed by *Zatoichi Challenged* (1967). 95 minutes. No MPAA rating. Release date undetermined.

Zatoichi: The Blind Swordsman's Revenge / Zato Ichi nidan giri ("Zatoichi: Double Cut"). Director, Akira Inoue; Screenplay, Minoru Inuzuka, based on an original story by Kan Shimosawa; Director of Photography, Fujio Morita; Music, Akira Ifukube.

CAST: Shintaro Katsu (Zatoichi), Norihei Miki, Mikiko Tsubouchi, Takeshi Kato, Fujio Harumoto.

A Daiei Motion Picture Co., Ltd. Production. Daieicolor. DaieiScope. 83 minutes. Released 1965.

U.S. VERSION: Distributor, if any, is undetermined. Possibly released as *The Blind Swordsman's Revenge*. The 10th "Zatoichi" feature. Followed by *Zatoichi and the Doomed Men* (1965).

Zatoichi: The Blind Swordsman's Vengeance / Zato Ichi no uta ga kikoeru ("I Hear Zatoichi Singing"). Executive Producer, Masaichi Nagata; Director, Tokuzo Tanaka; Screenplay, Hajime Takaiwa, based on an original story by Kan Shimosawa; Planning, Ikuo Kubodera; Director of Photography, Kazuo Miyagawa; Editor, Kanji Suganuma; Music, Akira Ifukube.

CAST: Shintaro Katsu (Zatoichi), Shigeru Amachi, Mayumi Ogawa, Kei Sato, Jun Hamamura.

A Daiei Motion Picture Co., Ltd. Production. Eastman Color. DaieiScope. 83 minutes. Released May 1966.

U.S. VERSION: Theatrical release uncertain. Possibly distributed by Daiei International Films, Inc., as *The Blind Swordsman's Vengeance*. English subtitles. 83 minutes. No MPAA rating. Release date undetermined. Released to home video by Chambara Entertainment in 1992 as *Zatoichi: The Blind Swordsman's Vengeance*. A John Wada and Gregg Yokoyama Presentation. Subtitles, Multi-Media Translations International. Video version letterboxed. The 13th "Zatoichi" feature. Followed by *Zatoichi: The Blind Swordsman's Pilgrimage* (1966).

Zatoichi, the Fugitive / Zatoichi kyojotabi ("Zatoichi: A Criminal Journey"). Executive Producer, Masaichi Nagata; Director, Tokuzo Tanaka; Screenplay, Seiji Hoshikawa, based on an original story by Kan Shimosawa; Director of Photography, Chishi Makimura; Music, Akira Ifukube.

CAST: Shintaro Katsu (Zatoichi), Miwa Takada, Misayo Banri, Junichiro Narita, Katsuhiko Kobayashi.

A Daiei Motion Picture Co., Ltd. Production. Daieicolor. DaieiScope. 86 minutes. Released 1963.

U.S. VERSION: Distributor, if any, is undetermined. Possibly released as *Masseur Ichi, the Fugitive*. Not to be confused with *The Blind Swordsman and the Fugitives* (1968). The 4th "Zatoichi" feature. Followed by *Zatoichi* (1963).

Zatoichi's Cane-Sword / Zato Ichi tekkatabi ("Zatoichi's Gambling Travels"). Executive Producer, Masaichi Nagata; Producer, Ikuo Kobodera; Director, Kimiyoshi Yasuda; Screenplay, Ryozo Kasahara, based on an original story by Kan Shimosawa; Director of Photography, Senkichiro Takeda; Art Director, Yoshinobu Nishioka; Editor, Toshio Taniguchi; Music, Ichiro Saito; Sound Recording, Masao Osumi.

CAST: Shintaro Katsu (Zatoichi), Shiho Fujimura (Oshizu), Yoshihiko Aoyama (Seikichi), Makoto Fujita (Umazo), Kiyoko Suizenji (Oharu), Eijiro Tono (Sanzo the swordmaker), Masumi Harikawa (Oryu), Masako Aboshi (Omatsu the maid), Junichiro Yamashita (Shinnosuke), Ryutaro Gomi (Ronin), Fujio Suga (Seisuke Kuwayama), Tatsuo Endo (Iwagoro), Ryuji Kita (Genbei Shimotsukeya), Eigoro Onoe (Zato), Yusaku Terashima (owner of noodle shop), Gen Kimura (Hanzo the dice player), Sachio Horikita (Mosuke), Kimiko Tachibana (Otane).

A Daiei Motion Picture Co., Ltd. Production. Filmed at Daiei-Kyoto Studios. Eastman Color. DaieiScope. 93 minutes. Released January 3, 1967.

U.S. VERSION: Released by Daiei International Films, Inc. English subtitles. Possibly released as *The Blind Swordsman's Cane Sword*. Japanese title also given as *Zato Ichi tekka tasi*. The 15th "Zatoichi" feature. Followed by *Zatoichi: The Blind Swordsman's Rescue* (1967). 93 minutes. No MPAA rating. Released August 16, 1971.

Zatoichi's Conspiracy / Shi Zatoichi monogatari: Kasama no chimatsuri ("Zatoichi: A Blood Offering in Kasama"). Producers, Shintaro Katsu and Nishioika Kozen; Director, Kimiyoshi Yasuda; Original Story, Kan Shimosawa; Director of Photography, Chishi Makiura; Music, Akira Ifukube.

CAST: Shintaro Katsu (Zatoichi), Eiji Okada (Shinbei), Kei Sato (bailiff), Takashi Shimura (Sakubei), Yukie Toake (Omiyo).

A Katsu Production Co., Ltd./Toho Co., Ltd. Production. A Toho Co., Ltd. Release. Filmed at Toho Studios, Ltd. (Tokyo). Color. Panavision. 88 minutes. Released 1973.

U.S. VERSION: Released by Toho International Co., Ltd. English subtitles. One source lists Shozo Honda as Director of Photography. The 25th "Zatoichi" feature. Followed by a teleseries and, 16 years later, the theatrical series was revived with *Zatoichi* (1989). 88 minutes. No MPAA rating. Released April 1974.

Zatoichi's Flashing Sword / Zato ichi abaredako ("Zatoichi: A Tough Kite"). Executive Producer, Masaichi Nagata; Director, Kazuo Ikehiro; Screenplay, Minoru Inuzuka and Shozaburo Asai, based on the original story by Kan Shimozawa; Director of Photography, Yasukaza Takemura.

CAST: Shintaro Katsu (Zatoichi), Bokuzen Hidari (Kyubei, *the fireworks maker*), Naoko Kubo, Mayumi Nagisa, Ryutaro Gomi, Tatsuo Endo, Ko Sugita, Takashi Etajima, Yutake Nakamura.

A Daiei Motion Picture Co., Ltd. Production. Eastman Color. DaieiScope. 82 minutes. Released 1964.

U.S. VERSION: Theatrical release uncertain. Possibly released by Daiei International Films, Inc. as *The Blind Swordsman's Flashing Sword*. English subtitles. The 7th "Zatoichi" feature. Followed by *Fight, Zatoichi, Fight* (1964). 82 minutes. No MPAA rating. Release date undetermined. Released to home video as *Zatoichi's Flashing Sword* by Chambara Entertainment. A John Wada and Gregg Yokoyama Presentation. Subtitles,

Multi-Media Translations International. Video version letterboxed.

Zegen ("Zegen"). Producer, Shigeru Okada; Director/Screenplay, Shohei Imamura; Director of Photography, Masao Tochizawa; Music, Shinichiro Ikebe.

CAST: Ken Ogata (Iheiji Muraoka, aka *Zegen*, Mitsuko Baisho (Shiho), Ko Chun-Hsiung ("Boss" Wang), Norihei Miki (Tomenaga).

A Toei Co., Ltd. Production. Agfa Color. Spherical wide screen. 124 minutes. Released September 5, 1987.

U.S. VERSION: Distributor, if any, is undetermined.

Zeram / Zeiramu ("Zeram"). Executive Producers, Shigeki Takeuchi and Hiroshi Uchida; Producers, Yoshinori Chiba and Koichi Sugisawa; Director, Keita Amamiya; Screenplay, Keita Amamiya and Hajime Matsumoto; Director of Photography, Hiroshi Kidokoro; Lighting, Yoshimi Hosaka.

CAST: Yuko Moriyama (Ilya), Yukijiro Hotaru (Kamiya), Kunihiko Iida (Teppei), Mizuho Yoshida, Sachi Kashino, Satoko Kurenai.

A Gaga Communications, Inc./Growd, Inc. Production. A Toho Co., Ltd. Release (?). Eastman Color. Spherical wide screen. 96 minutes. Released August 1991.

U.S. VERSION: Released by Fox Lorber. English subtitles. Alternate title: *Zeiram*. Video version English-dubbed. English-dubbed credits: Producer/Director, Carl Macek; ADR Dialogue Script, Steve Kramer; Additional Dialogue, Carl Macek; Studio, Screen Music Studios (Studio City, Califonia); Recording Engineers, Deb Adair, David Walsh; Final Mix, Ernie Sheesley; Production Manager, Scott Narrie. Followed by a sequel. 96 minutes. No MPAA rating. Released May 1994.

VOICE CHARACTERIZATIONS FOR DUBBED VERSION: Robert Axelrod, Steve Bulen, Edie Mirman, Jeff Winkless, Juliana Donald, Steve Kramer.

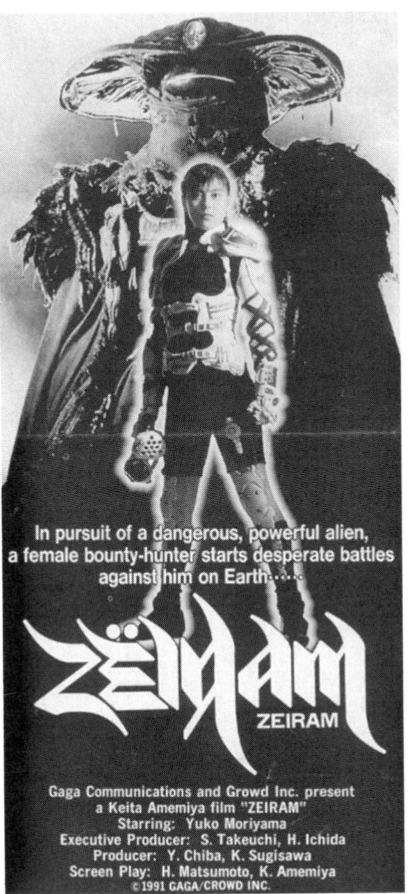

Trade ad for *Zeram* (1991).

Zero Fighters / A, zerosen ("Oh, Zero Fighters"). Executive Producer, Yoshizo Numata; Director, Mitsuo Murayama; Screenplay, Katsuya Suzaki, based on his original story; Director of Photography, Hiroshi Ishida; Art Director, Koichi Takahashi; Lighting, Choji Watanabe; Editor, Toyo Suzuki; Assistant Director, Sugano Koji; Music, Chuji Kinoshita; Sound, Yasayuki Saegusa.

CAST: Kojiro Hongo (Captain Kaji), Akeo Hasegawa (1st Lt. Natsubori), Yoshihiko Aoyama (Sgt. Yamagata), Jun Negami (Lt. Colonel Takada), Toru Koyanagi (Sgt. Minegishi), Kazumoto Ohashi (Captain Koseki), Terumi Miki (Tomoko Hidaka), Yuji Hayakawa (Tokunaga), Mikio Narita (Lt. Colonel Yagi), Bontaro Miake (Commander), Koji Fujiyama (Sgt. Morigami), Yoshihiro Hamaguchi (Mechanic), Yukitaro Hotaru (Soldier A), Osamu Okawa, Osamu Maruyama.

A Daiei Motion Picture Co., Ltd. Production. Black and white. Daieiscope. 86 minutes. Released September 4, 1975.

U.S. VERSION: Distributor, if any, is undetermined.

Zigeunerwisen / Zigeunerweisen ("Zigeunerweisen"). Producer, Genjiro Arato; Director, Seijun Suzuki; Screenplay, Yozo Tanaka; Director of Photography, Kazue Nagatsuka; Editor, Nobutake Kamiya; Art Directors, Takeo Kimura and Yoshito Tada; Music, Kaname Kawachi; Assistant Director, Sumio Yamada.

CAST: Yoshio Harada (Nakasago), Naoko Otani (Koine/Sono), Toshiya Fujita (Aochi), Michiyo Okusu (Shuko), Kisako Makishi (Taeko), Kirin Kiki (Kimi), Akaji Maro (blind man).

A Cinema Placet Production. A Genjiro Arato Release (later a Toho Co., Ltd. Release). Color. Spherical wide screen (1.66:1). 145 minutes. Released 1980.

U.S. VERSION: Released by Genjiro Arato Pictures. English subtitles. The title is derived from a recording of gypsy violin music by Pablo de Sarasate. The first film of Suzuki's "Taisho Trilogy," and followed by *Heat-Haze Theatre* (1981). 145 minutes. No MPAA rating. Released 1993.

Zoku hiroku onna ro ("A Secret Memoir of Women's Jail, Part Two"). Executive Producer, Masaichi Nagata; Producer, Sadao Zaizen; Director, Kimiyoshi Yasuda; Screenplay, Shozaburo Asai; Art Director, Yoshinobu Nishioka; Director of Photography, Chishi Makiura; Editor, Hiroshi Yamada; Music, Takeo Watanabe; Sound Recording Supervisor, Masao Osumi; Sound, Daiei Recording Studio.

CAST: Michiyo Yasuda (Onami), Sanae Nakahara (Okuma), Kayo Mikimoto (Oseki), Mutsuhiro Toura (Senzo Takeuchi), Mayumi Katsuyama (Otama), Yasuyo Matsumura (Okichi), Gen Kimura (Saeki), Tomo Nagai (Tatewaki Ishide), Saburo Date (officer of the law), Kazue Tamachi (Yomin Chiga), Keiko Koyanagi (Otaka), Junko Toyama (Oroku), Hiroko Yashiro (Otoshi), Hiromi Inoue (newcomer), Hajime Koshikawa (jailer), Chikara Hashimoto (superintendent officer in the feudal age).

A Daiei Motion Picture Co., Ltd. Production. A Masaichi Nagata Presentation. Westrex Recording System. Black and white (processed by Daiei Laboratory). DaieiScope. 84 minutes. Released 1968.

U.S. VERSION: Distributor, if any, is undetermined. International title: *Women's Cell*. A sequel to *Hiroku onna ro* (1968).

Appendices

The following appendices are provided to aid researchers in gaining a better understanding of the Japanese film industry that produced and consumed the works appearing in this book. A brief chronological history and statistical analysis of the motion picture industry in Japan are included, as well as a listing of awards received by Japanese filmmakers and films.

Appendix I. A Chronology

1896 Edison's Kinetoscope first exhibited
Vitascope and Cinematograph imported

1897 Vitascope and Cinematograph exhibited
First film shot in Japan (Tokyo street scenes)

1899 Japanese-made shorts exhibited

1900 Japanese cameras produced
First newsreels

1903 First permanent motion picture theatre opens (Asakusa, Tokyo)

1908 First motion picture studio built (in Meguro, Tokyo)

1909 First film magazine published
First actors' training school

1911 First feature-length documentary
First motion picture exhibition company established

1912 Japan Motion Picture Co., Ltd., the predecessor to Nikkatsu Corp., established

1914 Natural Motion Picture Co., Ltd., begins making color films in Kinema Colour process
Experimental talking pictures produced by Nippon Kinetophone Co., Ltd.

1917 First animated cartoon shorts

1918 Movement to replace female impersonators with actresses
Artificial lighting employed at the Nikkatsu-Mukojima Studio

1919 First educational films produced

1920 Shochiku Kinema Gomeisha, the predecessor to Shochiku Co., Ltd., established

1923 Shochiku-Kamata and Nikkatsu-Mukojima Studios destroyed in the Great Kanto Earthquake

1925 Home Ministry assumes control of film censorship
De Forest Phonofilm imported

1927 First recording studio for talking pictures established
First part-talking feature, *Daybreak/Reimei*, produced by record and film system

1929 First all-talking U.S. production released
First exhibition of a Japanese film overseas, in Moscow
1931 First all-talking Japanese feature released, Shochiku's *The Neighbor's Wife and Mine/Madamu to nyobo*
1932 Beshi (narrators) and musicians resist talking pictures, go on strike
PCL (Photo Chemical Laboratory), the predecessor to Toho Co., Ltd., established
1934 Fuji Photo Film Co., Ltd., established and begins to manufacture motion picture film
The Motion Picture Control Commission established by the Home Ministry
1935 Great Japan Motion Picture Association, a semigovernmental advisory body, established
1937 First co-production, *The New Earth/Atarashiki tsuchi*, produced (with Germany)
Import restrictions on foreign films enforced
1938 Admission tax enforced
License system on imported foreign films introduced
First film entered at Venice Film Festival, *Five Scouts/Gonin no sekkohei*
1939 Film industry completely controlled by government
1941 Production companies integrated into three majors
1942 Great Japan Motion Picture Production Co., Ltd., the predecessor to Daiei Motion Picture Co., Ltd., established
Distribution circuits unified
1943 Japan Motion Picture School established
1945 Occupation begins
Total government control of industry ends
1946 Import of American films resumes (February)
All Japan Motion Picture and Drama Employees Union formed
"Flag of Ten" strike at Toho (October–December)
1947 Shintoho Co., Ltd., established
Japan Motion Picture Association, the predecessor to the Motion Picture Producers Association of Japan, Inc., established
Export of Japanese films resumes (December)
1948 Strike at Toho (April–October)
1949 Administration Commission of Motion Picture Code of Ethics established
1950 "Leftists" purged by Occupation Forces
Motion Picture Industry Promotion Council, the predecessor to the Federation of Japanese Film Industry, established
First Japanese/U.S. co-production: *Tokyo File 212*
1951 First color feature, Shochiku's *Carmen Comes Home/Karumen Kokyo ni kaeru*, released (March)

Toei Co., Ltd., established
Daiei's *Rashomon* wins grand prize at the Venice Film Festival and a special Academy Award as "the most outstanding foreign language film released in the United States during 1951"

1953 NHK begins television broadcasting (February)
Commercial broadcasts begin (August)
Nikkatsu Corp. resumes production
Federation of Motion Picture Producers in Asia formed
First imported CinemaScope feature, *The Robe*, is released (December)

1954 First Film Festival in Asia held in Tokyo
Daiei's Gate of Hell wins grand prize at the Cannes Film Festival, Academy Award for Costume Design (Color), and a special award as the "best foreign language film first released in the United States during 1954"

1955 First imported Cinerama film released in Japan (January)
Motion Picture Council established within the cabinet
Annual film production exceeds 400/year, leads world production
Toho's *Samurai I* wins a special Academy Award as "the best foreign language film released in the United States during 1955"
Fujicolor introduced

1956 First Japanese Film Week held, in Rome
Inauguration of Motion Picture Day (December)
First imported 70mm film, *Oklahoma!*, is released
Nikkatsu's *The Burmese Harp* nominated for an Academy Award as Best Foreign Language Film

1957 First (anamorphic) wide screen film, Toei's *The Lord Takes a Bride/ Otori-jo no Hanayome*, released (April)
UniJapan Film—Association for the Diffusion of Japanese Films Abroad, Inc., established

1958 Toho's *The Rickshaw Man* wins grand prize at the Venice Film Festival
First feature-length animated cartoon, Toei's *White Snake Enchantress*, released (September)

1960 Color television broadcasting begins
Toho LaBrea opens in Los Angeles (August)

1961 Shintoho ceases production (May)
First 70mm film, *Buddha*, released
Shochiku's *Immortal Love* nominated for an Academy Award as Best Foreign Language Film
Art Theatre Guild (ATG) established

1962 Admission tax reduced by 10 percent

1963 The five majors decide to show their features on television (June)
Toei's *Bushido—Samurai Saga* wins grand prize at the Berlin Film Festival

Shochiku's *Twin Sisters of Kyoto* nominated for an Academy Award as Best Foreign Language Film

1964 Import of foreign films liberalized (June)

Woman in the Dunes nominated for an Academy Award as Best Foreign Language Film

1965 Special Showing System for Japanese Films, corresponding to screen quota, begins

Toho's *Kwaidan* nominated for an Academy Award as Best Foreign Language Film

1966 The Japanese Film Export Council established to finance export-market films made by the production companies

The National Theatre opens

1967 Shochiku's *Portrait of Chieko* nominated for an Academy Award as Best Foreign Language Film

1970 Daiei ceases operations (December)

1971 Toho's *Dodes'ka-den* nominated for an Academy Award as Best Foreign Language Film

1973 Daiei reorganized as a production company

1975 Kurosawa's *Dersu Uzala* wins the Academy Award for Best Foreign Language Film

1976 Revenue from imported films exceeds domestic product

1980 Toho's *Kagemusha* nominated for an Academy Award as Best Foreign Language Film

1981 Kimura Production's *Muddy River* nominated for an Academy Award as Best Foreign Language Film

1985 Akira Kurosawa nominated for an Academy Award as Best Director (for *Ran*)

1987 Attendance reaches lowest level since World War II

Appendix II. Japanese Home Market Statistics

Number of Motion Picture Theaters in Japan

Year	*Showing Only Domestic Films*	*Showing Only Imported Films*	*Showing Both Imported and Domestic*	*Total Number of Theaters*
1992	560	697	487	1744
1991	579	718	507	1804
1990	600	735	501	1836
1989	630	755	527	1912
1988	715	747	543	2005
1987	759	721	573	2053
1986	817	720	572	2109
1985	877	718	542	2137
1984	914	703	574	2191
1983	981	680	578	2239
1982	1002	677	588	2267
1981	1041	689	568	2298
1980	1085	701	578	2364
1979	1079	707	588	2374
1978	1136	691	565	2392
1977	1182	672	566	2420
1976	1214	658	581	2453
1975	1238	622	583	2443
1974	1297	618	553	2468
1973	1332	632	556	2530
1972	1382	694	597	2673
1971	1595	766	613	2974
1970	1758	755	733	3246
1969	2047	710	845	3602
1968	2174	719	921	3814
1967	2469	735	915	4119
1966	2633	711	952	4296

Number of Theaters, continued

Year	*Showing Only Domestic Films*	*Showing Only Imported Films*	*Showing Both Imported and Domestic*	*Total Number of Theaters*
1965	2831	754	1064	4649
1964	3299	824	804	4927
1963	4035	879	1250	6164
1962	4505	864	1373	6742
1961	4991	772	1468	7231
1960	5132	794	1531	7457
1959	4880	850	1670	7400

Number of Features Released in Japan

Year	*Indepen-dents*	*Majors*	*Total Japanese*	*Imported Features*	*Total: All Features*	*% of Color Features*
1992	180	60	240	377	617	
1991	156	74	230	467	697	
1990	181	58	239	465	704	
1989	185	70	255	520	775	
1988	163	102	265	485	750	
1987	150	136	286	361	647	
1986	176	135	311	289	600	
1985	191	128	319	264	583	
1984	210	123	333	232	565	
1983	201	116	317	181	498	
1982	206	116	322	198	520	
1981	209	123	332	223	555	
1980	201	119	320	208	528	
1979	211	120	331	196	527	
1978	213	113	326	179	505	
1977	199	138	337	221	558	
1976	187	169	356	245	601	
1975	177	156	333	225	558	
1974	170	163	333	241	574	
1973	197	208	405	252	657	
1972	214	186	400	283	683	
1971	241	180	421	243	664	
1970	202	221	423	236	659	
1969	256	238	494	253	747	
1968	245	249	494	249	743	41%/196
1967	169	241	410	239	649	46%/189
1966	179	263	442	250	692	40%/176
1965	219	268	487	264	751	31%/153
1964	69	277	346	259	605	44%/151

Year	Independents	Majors	Total Japanese	Imported Features	Total: All Features	% of Color Features
1963	28	335	363	267	630	50%/182
1962	11	367	375	228	606	53%/200
1961	4	533	535	229	766	47%/251
1960	3	552	547	216	771	44%/239
1959	1	499	493	210	710	34%/167
1958			504	169		30%/150
1957			443	194		19%/85
1956			514			6%/32
1955			423			3%/11
1954			370			1%/5
1953			302			1%/3
1952			278			0%/1
1951			208			0%/1
1950			215			
1949			156			
1948			123			
1947			97			
1946			67			

Revenue Distribution (in Million Yen)

Year	Domestic Films	Imported Films	Total Revnue
1993	25,692	46,119	71,811
1992	28,134	34,227	62,361
1991	27,847	38,687	66,534
1990	29,407	41,675	71,082
1989	31,272	35,883	67,155
1988	32,532	32,993	65,525
1987	30,638	33,098	63,736
1986	36,182	36,454	72,636
1985	35,295	34,080	69,375
1984	33,120	35,086	68,206
1983	41,442	37,331	78,773
1982	33,368	31,900	65,268
1981	33,690	28,130	61,820
1980	34,897	28,557	63,454
1979	32,943	28,670	61,613
1978	32,144	33,969	66,113
1977	30,841	29,928	60,769
1976	27,533	29,274	56,807
1975	22,871	28,665	51,536
1974	22,832	21,652	44,484
1973	19,458	15,010	34,468
1972	14,900	13,800	28,700

Revenue Distribution, continued

Year	*Domestic Films*	*Imported Films*	*Total Revnue*
1971	15,613	14,912	30,525
1970	18,496	12,616	31,112
1969	21,400	12,030	33,439
1968	21,232	11,731	32,963
1967	19,817	12,500	32,317
1966	20,221	11,771	31,992
1965	22,528	11,230	33,758
1964	22,284	11,538	33,822
1963	24,825	11,687	36,512
1962	27,126	10,296	37,422
1961	29,445	8,849	38,304
1960	31,065	8,512	39,577
1959	30,858	8,865	39,723
1958	29,971	9,435	39,406
1957	25,988	11,600	37,588

Attendance

Year	*Attendance in Thousand Persons*	*Total Admission in Million Yen*	*Admission Fee in Yen*
1993	130,720	163,700	1252
1992	125,600	152,000	1210
1991	138,330	163,378	1181
1990	146,000	171,910	1177
1989	143,573	166,681	1161
1988	144,825	161,921	1118
1987	143,935	161,155	1120
1986	160,758	179,428	1116
1985	155,130	173,438	1118
1984	150,527	172,202	1144
1983	170,430	186,300	1093
1982	155,280	169,522	1092
1981	149,450	163,259	1093
1980	164,422	165,918	1009
1979	165,088	158,177	958
1978	166,042	160,509	967
1977	165,171	152,373	923
1976	171,020	145,709	852
1975	174,020	130,750	751
1974	185,738	117,107	631
1973	185,324	92,689	500
1972	188,642	77,441	411

Year	*Attendance in Thousand Persons*	*Total Admission in Million Yen*	*Admission Fee in Yen*
1971	216,754	79,971	366
1970	254,799	82,488	324
1969	283,980	83,805	295
1968	313,398	82,026	262
1967	335,067	78,943	236
1966	345,811	75,750	219
1965	372,676	75,506	203
1964	431,454	76,937	178
1963	511,121	77,734	152
1962	662,279	not available	not available
1961	863,430	57,321	103
1960	1,014,364	59,003	85
1959	1,088,111	56,679	79
1958	1,127,452	56,528	78
1957	1,098,882	53,597	75

Television in Japan

Year	*Number of Television Sets*	*Percent of Households with Television Sets*
1962	11,799,869	57.2
1961	9,248,949	44.8
1960	5,770,408	28.0
1959	3,463,447	19.3
1958	1,566,801	8.7
1957	747,603	4.2

The Silent-to-Sound Transition Period

Year	*Talkie*	*Sound*	*Silent*	*Imported Films*	*Movie Theaters*	*Theaters/ Domestic*	*Theaters/ Imported*	*Theaters/ Both*	*Theaters Equipped*	*Attendance*
1926	0	0	n/a	n/a	n/a	414	39	604		117,805,932
1927	0	0	n/a	n/a	n/a	577	39	556		127,184,332
1928	0	0	n/a	n/a	n/a	714	46	509		140,263,001
1929	0	0	n/a	n/a	n/a	807	53	410		152,439,679
1930	n/a	n/a	n/a	270	n/a	925	53	410	0	158,368,142
1931	n/a	n/a	n/a	251	1485	1029	53	367	92	164,717,249
1932	n/a	n/a	n/a	293	1496	1025	49	386	339	177,343,933
1933	n/a	n/a	n/a	287	1664	1065	47	386	576	178,245,443
1934	61	40	298	320	1718	1076	46	416	806	198,927,124
1935	133	133	178	311	1774	1117	59	410	1207	184,922,485
1936	300	121	137	341	1997	1130	64	433	1368	n/a
1937	365	50	159	287	2097	n/a	n/a	n/a	n/a	n/a
1938	513	16	25	n/a						

Appendix III. Awards

Japanese Academy Awards

1977

Film: The Yellow Handkerchief
Director: Yoji Yamada (The Yellow Handkerchief, Tora-san series)
Actor: Ken Takakura (The Yellow Handkerchief)
Actress: Shima Iwashita (Banished Orin)
Supporting Actor: Takuya Takeda (The Yellow Handkerchief) and Tomisaburo Wakayama (Sanshiro)
Cinematography: Kazuo Miyagawa (Banished Orin)

1978

Film: The Accident
Director: Yoshitaro Nomura (The Accident, Possessed)
Actor: Ken Ogata (Possessed)
Actress: Shinobu Otake (The Accident)
Supporting Actor: Tsunehiko Watase (The Accident)
Supporting Actress: Shinobu Otake (The Clergy's Gravestone)

1979

Film: Vengeance Is Mine
Director: Shohei Imamura (Vengeance Is Mine)
Actor: Tomisaburo Wakayama (The Impulse Murder of My Son)
Actress: Kaori Momoi (No More Easy Going, A Baby Given to God, Tora-san the Matchmaker)
Supporting Actor: Bunta Sagawara (The Man Who Stole the Sun)
Supporting Actress: Mayumi Ogawa (Vengeance Is Mine, Three Undelivered Letters)

1980

Film: Zigeunerweisen
Director: Seijun Suzuki (Zigeunerweisen)
Actor: Ken Takakura (Upheaval, A Distant Cry from Spring)
Actress: Chieko Baisho (A Distant Cry from Spring, Tora-san's Dream of Spring)
Supporting Actor: Tetsuro Tamba (Port Arthur)
Supporting Actress: Michiyo Okusu (Zigeunerweisen)

1981

Film: Station
Foreign Film: The Tin Drum
Director: Kohei Oguri (Muddy River)
Actor: Ken Takakura (Station)
Actress: Keiko Matsuzaka (Gateway to Youth, Tora-san's Love in Osaka)
Supporting Actor: Katsuo Nakamura (Theatre of Shimmering Light, Tin Medal)
Supporting Actress: Yuko Tanaka (The Works of Hokusai, Eijinaika)
Screenplay: So Kuramoto (Station)
Cinematography: Shohei Ando (Muddy River)
Lighting: Tadashi Shimada (Muddy River)
Music: Ryudo Uzaki (Station)

1982

Film: Kamata March
Foreign Film: E.T., the Extra-Terrestrial
Director: Kenji Fukasaku (Kamata March)
Actor: Mitsuru Hirata (Kamata March)
Actress: Keiko Matsuzaka (Kamata March, Dotonbori River)
Supporting Actor: Morio Kazama (Kamata March)

Supporting Actress: Rumiko Koyanagi (Kidnap News)
Screenplay: Kohei Tsuka (Kamata March)
Cinematography: Shinsaku Himeda (Kidnap News)
Lighting: Toshio Yamaguchi (Kidnap News)
Music: Masato Kai (Kamata March)

1983

Film: The Ballad of Narayama
Foreign Film: An Officer and a Gentleman
Director: Hideo Gosha (Yokiro)
Actor: Ken Ogata (The Ballad of Narayama)
Actress: Rumiko Koyanagi (Legend of the White Snake)
Supporting Actor: Morio Kazama (Yokiro, Human Theatre)
Supporting Actress: Atsuko Asano (Yokiro, Last Hero)
Screenplay: Koji Takada (Yokiro)
Cinematography: Fuji Morita (Yokiro)
Art Direction: Yoshinobu Nishioka and Kenji Yamashita (Yokiro)
Lighting: Yoshiaki Masuda (Yokiro)
Music: Masaru Sato (Yokiro, Kairei)

1984

Film: The Funeral
Foreign Film: Once Upon a Time in America
Director: Juzo Itami (The Funeral)
Actor: Tsutomu Yamazaki (The Funeral, A Farewell to the Ark)
Actress: Sayuri Yoshinaga (Ohan, Heaven Station)
Supporting Actor: Kaku Takeshima (Mahjong Gamblers)
Supporting Actress: Kin Sugai (The Funeral)
Screenplay: Juzo Itami (The Funeral)
Cinematography: Kazuo Miyagawa (MacArthur's Children)

1985

Film: Grey Sunset
Foreign Film: Amadeus
Director: Shinichiro Sawai (Tale of Early Spring)
Actor: Minoru Chiaki (Grey Sunset)
Actress: Mitsuko Baisho (Love Letter, Friend Sleep Quietly, The Nuclear Gypsies)
Supporting Actor: Kaoru Kobayashi (And Then)
Supporting Actress: Yoshiko Mita (The Tragedy of W)
Screenplay: Hiro Matsuda (Grey Sunset)
Art Direction: Yoshiro Muraki and Shinobu Murai (Ran)
Music: Toru Takemitsu (Ran)

1986

Film: House on Fire
Foreign Film: Back to the Future
Director: Kinji Fukasaku (House on Fire)
Actor: Ken Ogata (House on Fire)
Actress: Ayumi Ishida (House on Fire, Adieu l'hiver)
Supporting Actor: Hitoshi Ueki (Congratulatory Speech, Big Joys Small Sorrows)
Supporting Actress: Meiko Harada (House on Fire, Matchless Country, Portrait of Persian Blue)

1987

Film: A Taxing Woman
Foreign Film: Platoon
Director: Juzo Itami (A Taxing Woman)
Actor: Tsutomu Yamazaki (A Taxing Woman)
Actress: Nobuko Miyamoto (A Taxing Woman)
Supporting Actor: Masahiko Tsugawa (A Taxing Woman)
Supporting Actress: Nashi Katse (Wicked Wives II)
Screenplay: Juzo Itami (A Taxing Woman)
Cinematography: Shinsaku Himeda (River of Fireflies)
Editing: Akira Suzuki (A Taxing Woman)
Art Direction: Shinobu Muraki (Princess from the Moon)
Lighting: Tadaki Shimada (River of Fireflies)
Sound: Osamu Onodera (A Taxing Woman)

1988

Film: Tonko
Foreign Film: The Last Emperor
Director: Junya Sato (Tonko)
Actor: Toshiyuki Nishida (Tonko)
Actress: Sayuri Yoshinaga (Flower of Confusion)
Supporting Actor: Tsurutaro Kataoka (The Discarnates)
Supporting Actress: Eri Ishida (Flower of Confusion)
Screenplay: Shinichi Ichikawa (The Discarnates)
Cinematography: Akira Shizuka (Tonka)
Editing: Ako Suzuki (The Woman Who Bites)
Art Direction: Hiroshi Tokuda (Tonko)
Lighting: Shigeru Umitami (Tonko)
Sound: Tonko

Kinema Jumpo Awards

1955
Film: Floating Clouds
Foreign Film: East of Eden
Director: Mikio Naruse (Floating Clouds)
Foreign Director: Elia Kazan (East of Eden)
Actor: Masayuki Mori (Floating Clouds)
Actress: Hideko Takamine (Floating Clouds)

1956
Film: Darkness at Noon
Foreign Film: Gervaise
Director: Tadashi Imai (Darkness at Noon)
Foreign Director: Rene Clement (Gervaise)
Actor: Keiji Sada (I'll Buy You)
Actress: Isuzu Yamada (Shozo a Cat and Two Women & Flowing)

1957
Film: Rice
Foreign Film: La Strada
Director: Tadashi Imai (Rice)
Foreign Director: Federico Fellini (La Strada)
Actor: Frankie Sakai (Sun Legend of the Shogunate's Last Days)
Actress: Isuzu Yamada (Throne of Blood, The Lower Depths, and Downtown)
Screenplay: Toshio Ha (Roar and Earth, Snow Country, and The Story of Chieko)

1958
Film: The Ballad of Narayama
Foreign Film: The Big Country
Director: Keisuke Kinoshita (The Ballad of Narayama)
Foreign Director: William Wyler (The Big Country)
Actor: Raizo Ichikawa (Conflagration)
Actress: Kinuyo Tanaka (The Ballad of Narayama)
Screenplay: Shinobu Hashimoto (The Hidden Fortress, Night Drum, Chase)

1959
Film: Kiku and Isamu
Foreign Film: Twelve Angry Men
Director: Tadashi Imai (Kiku and Isamu)
Foreign Director: Sidney Lumet (Twelve Angry Men)
Actor: Eiji Funakoshi (Fires on the Plain)
Actress: Michiyo Aratama (The Human Condition I)
Screenplay: Natto Wada (Fires on the Plain, Odd Obsession)

1960
Film: Her Brother
Foreign Film: The Great Dictator
Director: Kon Ichikawa (Her Brother)
Foreign Director: Charles Chaplin (The Great Dictator)
Actor: Keiju Kobayashi (Black Book)
Actress: Fujiko Yamamoto (A Woman's Testament, Twilight Story)
Screenplay: Shinobu Hashimoto (Black Book, The Bad Sleep Well)

1961
Film: Bad Boys
Foreign Film: The Virgin Spring
Director: Susumu Hani
Foreign Director: Ingmar Bergman (The Virgin Spring)
Actor: Toshiro Mifune (Yojimbo, Daredevil in the Castle)
Actress: Ayako Wakao (A Geisha's Diary, A Wife Confesses)
Screenplay: Yoko Mizuki (Pan Chopoli, Marriageable Age, The Shrikes)

1962
Film: Being Two Isn't Easy
Foreign Film: Wild Strawberries
Director: Kon Ichikawa (Being Two Isn't Easy)
Foreign Director: Ingmar Bergman (Wild Strawberries)
Actor: Tatsuya Nakadai (Harakiri, Sanjuro)
Actress: Mariko Okada (This Year's Love, Fate of a Child in the Mist)
Screenplay: Kaneto Shindo (Aobe ga monogatari, Shitoyakana)

1963
Film: The Insect Woman
Foreign Film: Lawrence of Arabia
Director: Shohei Imamura (The Insect Woman)
Foreign Director: David Lean (Lawrence of Arabia)
Actor: Shintaro Katsu (Zatoichi series, Wicked Name series)
Actress: Sachiko Hidari (The Insect Woman, The Young Samurai)
Screenplay: Shohei Imamura (The Insect Woman, The Young Samurai)

1964
Film: Woman in the Dunes
Foreign Film: The Long Absence

Director: Hiroshi Teshigahara
Foreign Director: Henri Colpi (The Long Absence)
Actor: So Yamamura (A Public Benefactor)
Actress: Machiko Kyo (Sweet Sweat)
Screenplay: Yoko Mizuki (Sweet Sweat, Kwaidan)

1965

Film: Red Beard
Foreign Film: 8½
Director: Akira Kurosawa (Red Beard)
Foreign Director: Federico Fellini (8½)
Actor: Rentaro Mikuni (A Burglar Story)
Actress: Ayako Wakao (The Wife of Seisaku, The Moment of Glory, The Shadow of Waves)
Screenplay: Kei Kumai (The Japanese Archipelago)

1966

Film: The Ivory Tower
Foreign Film: Panther Panchali
Director: Satsuo Yamamoto (The Ivory Tower)
Foreign Director: Satyajit Ray (Panther Panchali)
Actor: Shoichi Ozawa (The Pornographers)
Actress: Yoko Tsukasa (The River Kii, Moment of Terror, The Daphne)
Screenplay: Shinobu Hashimoto (The Ivory Tower)

1967

Film: Rebellion
Foreign Film: The Battle of Algiers
Director: Masaki Kobayashi (Rebellion)
Foreign Director: Gillo Pontecorvo (The Battle of Algiers)
Actor: Raizo Ichikawa (The Wife of Seishu Hanaoka, A Certain Killer)
Actress: Shima Iwashita (Portrait of Chieko, Clouds at Sunset, Life of a Woman)
Screenplay: Shinobu Hashimoto (Rebellion, The Emperor and a General)

1968

Film: Kuragejima—Legends from a Southern Island
Foreign Film: Bonnie and Clyde
Director: Shohei Imamura (Kuragejima . . .)
Foreign Director: Arthur Penn (Bonnie and Clyde)
Actor: Toshiro Mifune (Admiral Yamamoto, Tunnel to the Sun, The Day the Sun Rose)
Actress: Ayako Wakao (The Time of Reckoning, One Day at Summer's End, The House of Wooden Blocks)
Screenplay: Tsutomu Tamura, Mamaru Sasaki, Michinori Fukao, and Nagisa Oshima (Death by Hanging)

1969

Film: Double Suicide
Foreign Film: Oedipus Rex
Director: Masahiro Shinoda (Double Suicide)
Foreign Director: Pier Paolo Pasolini (Oedipus Rex)
Actor: Kiyoshi Atsumi (Am I Trying)
Actress: Shima Iwashita (Double Suicide)
Screenplay: Tsutomu Tamura (Boy)

1970

Film: Where Spring Comes Late/The Family
Foreign Film: Easy Rider
Director: Yoji Yamada (Where Spring Comes Late)
Foreign Director: Dennis Hopper (Easy Rider)
Actor: Hisashi Igawa (Dodes'ka-den, Where Spring Comes Late)
Actress: Chieko Baisho (Where Spring Comes Late, Tora-san's Runaway)
Screenplay: Yoji Yamada and Noboru Miyazaki (Where Spring Comes Late, Tora-san's Runaway)

1971

Film: The Ceremony
Foreign Film: Death in Venice
Director: Nagisa Oshima (The Ceremony)
Foreign Director: Luchino Visconti (Death in Venice)
Actor: Kei Sato (The Ceremony)
Actress: Junko Fuji (Red Peony Gambler: Death for the Wicked)
Screenplay: Nagisa Oshima, Tsutomu Tamura, and Mamoru Sasaki (The Ceremony)

1972

Film: The Long Darkness
Foreign Film: The Last Picture Show
Director: Kei Kumai (The Long Darkness)
Foreign Director: Peter Bogdanovich (The Last Picture Show)
Actor: Hisashi Igawa (The Long Darkness, Home from the Sea)
Actress: Hiroko Isayama (Drenched Passion, Shirayubi's Joking)
Screenplay: Tatsumi Kumashiro (Drenched Passion, Shirayubi's Joking); and Kei Kumai and Keiji Hasebe (The Long Darkness)

1973

Film: Tsugaru Folksong
Foreign Film: Scarecrow
Director: Koichi Saito (Tsugaru Folksong)
Foreign Director: Jerry Schatzberg (Scarecrow)
Actor: Bunta Sagawara (The Yakuza Papers)
Actress: Kyoko Enami (Tsugaru Folksong)
Screenplay: Kazuo Kasahara (The Yakuza Papers)
Readers' Choice: The Yakuza Papers, Johnny Got His Gun

1974

Film: Sandakan 8
Foreign Film: Amarcord
Director: Kei Kumai (Sandakan 8)
Foreign Director: Federico Fellini (Amarcord)
Actor: Kenichi Hagiwara (Youth's Fiasco)
Actress: Kinuyo Tanaka (Sandakan 8)
Screenplay: Yoji Yamada (The Sand Castle)
Readers' Choice: The Sand Castle, The Sting

1975

Film: Kenji Mizoguchi: The Life of a Film Director
Foreign Film: Harry and Tonto
Director: Kaneto Shindo (Kenji Mizoguchi...)
Foreign Director: Paul Mazursky (Harry and Tonto)
Actor: Shin Saburi (Fossils)
Actress: Ruriko Asaoka (Tora-san Finds a Sweetheart)
Supporting Actor: Yoshio Harada (Preparation for the Festival)
Supporting Actress: Shinobu Otake (Gateway to Youth)
Screenplay: Takehiro Nagashima (Preparation for the Festival)
Readers' Choice: Bullet Train

1976

Film: The Youth Killer
Foreign Film: Taxi Driver
Director: Kazuhiko Hasegawa (The Youth Killer)
Foreign Director: Martin Scorsese (Taxi Driver)
Actor: Yutaka Mizutani (The Youth Killer)
Actress: Mieko Harada (The Youth Killer, A Cradle Song from the Earth)
Supporting Actor: Shuji Otaki (The Marginal Land, His Younger Sister)
Supporting Actress: Kiwako Taichi (Tora-san's Sunrise and Sunset)
Screenplay: Tsutomu Tamura (The Youth Killer)
Readers' Choice: The Inugami Family, One Flew Over the Cukoo's Nest

1977

Film: The Yellow Handkerchief
Foreign Film: Rocky
Director: Yoji Yamada (The Yellow Handkerchief)
Foreign Director: John G. Avildsen (Rocky)
Actor: Ken Takakura (The Yellow Handkerchief, Mt. Hakkoda)
Actress: Shima Iwashita (Banished Orin)
Supporting Actor: Takuya Takeda (The Yellow Handkerchief)
Supporting Actress: Kaori Momoi (The Yellow Handkerchief)
Screenplay: Yoji Yamada (The Yellow Handkerchief)
Readers' Choice: The Yellow Handkerchief, Rocky

1978

Film: Third Base
Foreign Film: Conversation Piece
Director: Yoichi Higashi (Third Base)
Foreign Director: Luchino Visconti (Conversation Piece)
Actor: Ken Ogata (Possessed)
Actress: Meiko Kaji (Love Suicide at Sonezaki)
Supporting Actor: Tsunehiko Watase (The Accident, The Fall of Akojo)
Supporting Actress: Shinobu Otake (The Accident, The Clergy's Gravestone)
Screenplay: Kaneto Shindo (The Accident)
Readers' Choice: Bitter Sweet, Star Wars

1979

Film: Vengeance Is Mine
Foreign Film: The Travelling Players
Director: Shohei Imamura (Vengeance Is Mine)
Foreign Director: Theo Angelopoulos (The Travelling Papers)
Actor: Tomisaburo Wakayama (The Impulse Murder of My Son)
Actress: Kaori Momoi (No More Easy Going)
Supporting Actor: Rentaro Mikuni (Vengeance Is Mine)
Supporting Actress: Mayumi Ogawa (Vengeance Is Mine)
Screenplay: Ataru Baba (Vengeance Is Mine)
Readers' Choice: The Man Who Stole the Sun, The Deer Hunter

1980

Film: Zigeunerweisen
Foreign Film: Kramer vs. Kramer

Director: Seijun Suzuki (Zigeunerweisen)
Foreign Director: Robert Benton (Kramer vs. Kramer)
Actor: Tsunehiko Watase (A Baby Given by God, Writhing Tongue)
Actress: Naoko Otani (Zigeunerweisen)
Supporting Actor: Tsutomu Yamazaki (Kagemusha)
Supporting Actress: Michiyo Okusu (Zigeunerweisen)
Screenplay: Yoko Tanaka (Zigeunerweisen, Wet Channels)
Readers' Choice: Port Arthur, Kramer vs. Kramer

1981

Film: Muddy River
Foreign Film: The Tin Drum
Director: Kohei Oguri (Muddy River)
Foreign Director: Volker Schlondorff (The Tin Drum)
Actor: Toshiyuki Nagashima (Distant Thunder, Happiness)
Actress: Chieko Baisho (Station)
Supporting Actor: Katsuo Nakamura (Theatre of Shimmering Light, Love Letter)
Supporting Actress: Mariko Koga (Muddy River, Theatre of Shimmering Light)
Screenplay: So Kuramoto (Station)
Readers' Choice: Station, Raiders of the Lost Ark

1982

Film: Kamata March
Foreign Film: E.T., the Extra-Terrestrial
Director: Kinji Fukasaku (Kamata March)
Foreign Director: Steven Spielberg (E.T.)
Actor: Jinpachi Nezu (A Farewell to the Land)
Actress: Keiko Matsuzaka (Kamata March, Dotonbori River)
Supporting Actor: Mitsuru Hirata (Kamata March)
Supporting Actress: Rumiko Koyanagi (Kamata March)
Screenplay: Kohei Tsuka (Kamata March)
Readers' Choice: Kamata March, E.T., the Extra-Terrestrial

1983

Film: The Family Game
Foreign Film: Sophie's Choice
Director: Yoshimitsu Morita (The Family Game)
Foreign Director: Alan J. Pakula (Sophie's Choice)
Actor: Yusaka Matsuda (The Family Game, Antarctica)
Actress: Yuko Tanaka (Amagi Pass)
Supporting Actor: Juzo Itami (The Family Game, The Makioka Sisters)
Supporting Actress: Eiko Nagashima (Ryuji)
Screenplay: Yoshimitsu Morita (The Family Game)
Readers' Choice: Merry Christmas Mr. Lawrence, Tootsie

1984

Film: The Funeral
Foreign Film: Once Upon a Time in America
Director: Juzo Itami (The Funeral)
Foreign Director: Sergio Leone (Once Upon a Time in America)
Actor: Tsutomu Yamazaki (The Funeral, Farewell to the Ark)
Actress: Sayuri Yoshinaga (Ohan, Heaven Station)
Supporting Actor: Kaku Takeshima (Mahjong Gamblers)
Supporting Actress: Yoshiko Mita (The Tragedy of W)
Screenplay: Shinichiro Sawai and Hidehiko Arai (The Tragedy of W)
Readers' Choice: Warriors of the Wind, Streets of Fire

1985

Film: And Then
Foreign Film: Amadeus
Director: Yoshimitsu Morita (And Then)
Foreign Director: Milos Forman (Amadeus)
Actor: Kinya Kitaoji (Spring Bell, Himatsuri)
Actress: Mitsuko Baisho (Love Letter, The Nuclear Gypsies)
Supporting Actor: Kaoru Kobayashi (And Then)
Supporting Actress: Yumiko Fujita (The Lonely and Cute)
Screenplay: Tomomi Tsutsui (And Then)
Readers' Choice: The Lonely and Cute, Witness

1986

Film: The Sea and Poison
Foreign Film: Stranger Than Paradise
Director: Kei Kumai (The Sea and Poison)
Foreign Director: Jim Jarmusch (Stranger Than Paradise)
Actor: Yuya Uchida (Comic Magazine)
Actress: Yoko Akino (Angel's Love)
Supporting Actor: Hitoshi Ueki (Big Joys Small Sorrows)
Supporting Actress: Ayumi Ishida (House on Fire)

Screenplay: Yoshimitsu Morita (The House of Wedlock)
Readers' Choice: House on Fire, Aliens

1987

Film: A Taxing Woman
Foreign Film: Good Morning, Babylon
Director: Juzo Itami (A Taxing Woman)
Foreign Director: Paolo Taviani and Vittorio Taviani (Good Morning Babylon)
Actor: Sanguro Tokito (Eternal Half)
Actress: Nobuko Miyamoto (A Taxing Woman)
Supporting Actor: Masahiko Tsugawa (A Taxing Woman, Reason for Not Divorcing)
Supporting Actress: Junko Sakurada (Itazu)
Screenplay: Juzo Itami (A Taxing Woman)
Readers' Choice: The Emperor's Naked Army Marches On, Stand by Me

1988

Film: My Neighbor Totoro
Foreign Film: The Last Emperor
Director: Kazuo Kuroki (Tomorrow)
Foreign Director: Stanley Kubrick (Full Metal Jacket)
Actor: Hiroyuki Henry Sanada (Kaito Ruby)
Actress: Kaori Momoi (Tomorrow, The Yen Family)
Supporting Actor: Tsurutaro Kataoka (The Discarnates)
Supporting Actress: Kumiko Akiyoshi (The Discarnates)
Screenplay: Haruhiko Arai (Revolver)

1989

Film: Black Rain
Foreign Film: Die Hard
Director: Shohei Imamura (Black Rain)
Foreign Director: Barry Levinson (Rain Man)
Actor: Rentaro Mikuni (Rikyu)
Actress: Yoshiko Tanaka (Black Rain)

Kinema Jumpo's Award Winners

Note: The director's name follows the film title.

1926

1. The Woman Who Touched the Legs (Abe)
2. The Sun (Murata)
3. Mermaid of the Land (Abe)
4. A Page of Madness (Kinugasa)
5. Collar Button (Nomura)
6. Jyunange (Ushihara)
7. A Paper Doll's Whisper of Spring (Mizoguchi)
8. Downfall (Inoue)
9. Lord Mito (Ikeda)
10. Spider (undetermined)

1927

1. Diary of Chuji's Travels I-II (Ito)
2. The Five Women Around Him (Abe)
3. Emperor Restoration (Ikeda)
4. Diary of Chuji's Travels III (Ito)
5. Brave Men of the Sea (Shimizu)
6. Tricky Girl (Gosho)
7. The Cuckoo (Mizoguchi)
8. Under the Evil Star (Nikawa)
9. The Servant (Ito)
10. Sad Song of the Road (Inoue)

1928

1. The Street of Masterless Samurai/Beautiful Conquest (Makino)
2. King of the Land (Ushihara)
3. Ooka Trial (Ito)
4. Shuzen Temple Riding Ground (Makino)
5. He and Life (Ushihara)
6. The Village Bride (Gosho)
7. Cockfight (Makino)
8. Wedding Duet (Murata, Tasaka, and Abe)

10\. Crossroads (Kinugasa)
10\. Chikemuri Takada no Baba (Ito)

1929

1. Beheading Place (Makino)
2. Ashes (Murata)
3. The Streets of Masterless Samurai Part III: Obsessed People (Makino)
4. A Living Doll (Uchida)
5. Skyscrapers: Battle Episode (Murata)
6. Man-Slashing, Horse-Piercing Sword (Ito)
7. Three Pipes (Takizawa)
8. Muriyari Sanzengoku (Matsuda)
9. The Great City: Chapter on Labor (Ushihara)
10. Metropolitan Symphony (Mizoguchi)

1930

(modern films)

1. What Made Her Do It? (Suzuki)

2. Why Do You Cry, Young People? (Ushihara)
2. Young Miss (Ozu)

(historical films)
1. Ooka's Trial (Ito)
2. Time of the Cyclone (Shinami)
3. Suronin Chuya (Ito)

1931
1. The Neighbor's Wife and Mine (Gosho)
2. Heart of Reality (Tasaka)
3. Tokyo Chorus (Ozu)
4. A Sword and the Sumo Ring (Inagaki)
5. Street of Foreign Civilization (Fuyushi)
6. The Revenge Champion (Uchida)
7. What Did She Kill? (Suzuki)
8. Prison Bride (Okihiro)
9. Ooka's Trial II (Ito)
10. The ABC's of Life (Shimazu)

1932
1. I Was Born But... (Ozu)
2. Maiden in the Storm (Shimazu)
3. The Loyal 47 Ronin (Kinugasa)
4. Oatsurae Jirokichi Goshi (Ito)
4. Yataro's Sedge Hat (Inagaki)
6. Peerless Patriot (Itami)
6. Motheaten Spring (Naruse)
8. Banquet of the White Night (Makino)
8. Spring and a Girl (Tasaka)
8. Sleeping With a Long Sword (Yamanaka)
8. First Steps Ashore (Shimazu)

1933
1. Passing Fancy (Ozu)
2. The Water Magician (Mizoguchi)
3. Everynight Dreams (Naruse)
4. Apart from You (Naruse)
4. Two Stone Lanterns (Kinugasa)
6. Sazen Tange (Ito)
7. The Life of Bangoku (Yamanaka)
8. Nezumi Kozo Jirokichi (Yamanaka)
9. Hotta Hayato (Ito)
9. Gimpei from Koina (Kinugasa)

1934
1. The Story of Floating Weeds (Ozu)
2. Our Neighbor, Miss Yae (Shimazu)
3. Everything that Lives (Gosho)
4. Warship of the Samurai Way (Itami)
5. The Elegant Swordsman (Yamanaka)
6. "Japan, Go Northward!" (a documentary, director undetermined)
7. Women of the Night of Death (Shimazu)
8. A Sword and the Sumo Ring (Kinugasa)
9. Mist Flute (Murata)
10. Taro Kaido (Yamanaka)

1935
1. Wife! Be Like a Rose! (Naruse)
2. The Village Tattooed Man (Yamanaka)
3. Okoto Sasuke (Shimazu)
4. Chuji Uridasu (Itami)
5. Chuji Kunidasa (Yamanaka)
6. Burden of Life (Gosho)
7. If We Desert the Child (Saito)
8. The Girl in the Rumor (Naruse)
9. An Inn at Tokyo (Ozu)
10. An Actor's Revenge (Kinugasa)

1936
1. Sisters of the Gion (Mizoguchi)
2. Theatre of Life (Uchida)
3. Osaka Elegy (Mizoguchi)
4. The Only Son (Ozu)
5. Kakita Akanishi (Itami)
6. Family Reunion (Shimazu)
7. Older Brother, Younger Sister (Kimura)
8. Hikoroku Laughs Heartily (Kimura)
9. Takuboku, Poet of Passion (Kumagai)
10. "Forbidden Jehol" (Kozo Akutagawa)

1937
1. Endless Advance (Uchida)
2. Many People/These People (Kumagai)
3. The Straits of Love and Hate (Mizoguchi)
4. Children in the Wind (Shimazu)
5. The Naked Town (Uchida)
6. Young People (Toyoda)
7. Humanity and Paper Balloons (Yamanaka)
8. What Did the Lady Forget? (Ozu)
9. The Summer Battle of Osaka (Kinugasa)
10. Lights of Asakusa (Shimazu)

1938
1. Five Scouts (Tasaka)
2. A Pebble by the Wayside (Tasaka)
3. Mother and Child (Shibuya)
4. "Shanghai" (Miki)
5. Composition Class (K. Yamamoto)
6. Nightingale (Toyoda)
7. Crybaby Apprentice (Toyoda)
7. The Abe Clan (Kumagai)
9. Ah, My Home Town (Mizoguchi)
10. Toward the Light (Abe)

1939
1. Earth (Uchida)
2. The Story of the Last Chrysanthemum (Mizoguchi)
3. Mud and Soldiers (Tasaka)
4. A Brother and his Younger Sister (Shimazu)
5. Shanghai Landing Party (Kumagai)

6. Four Seasons of Children (Shimizu)
7. Warm Current (Tsuji)
8. Airplane Drone (Tasaka)
9. Weeds with Flowers (Shimizu)
10. Sea Corps (Tsuji)

1940

1. Spring on Leper's Island (Toyoda)
2. The Story of Tank Commander Nishizumi (Yoshimura)
3. Kaze no Matsaburo (Shima)
4. The Woman of Osaka (Mizoguchi)
5. Thousands of Miles of Good Soil (Kurata)
6. Ioko Okamura (Toyoda)
7. History (Uchida)
8. The Burning Sky (Abe)
9. The Second Husband and Wife (Nobuchi)
10. Wooden Head (Gosho)

1941

1. The Brothers and Sisters of the Toda Family (Ozu)
2. Horse (K. Yamamoto)
3. The Tower of Mikaeri/The Introspection Tower (Shimizu)
4. The Life of an Actor (Mizoguchi)
5. The Last Days of Edo (Inagaki)
6. The Story of Jiro (Shima)
7. House of Love (Haruhata)
8. Festival Across the Sea (Inagaki)
9. Soaring Passion (Koishi)
10. Tales of Leaders (Kumagai)

1942

1. The War at Sea from Hawaii to Malaysia (K. Yamamoto)
2. There Was a Father (Ozu)
3. Generals and Soldiers (Taguchi)
4. Mother-and-Child Grass (Tasaka)
5. Bouquets of the Southern Sea (Abe)
6. New Snow (Gosho)
7. The Loyal 47 Ronin II (Mizoguchi)
8. One-Eyed Dragon (Inagaki)
9. Omura Masujiro (Mori)
10. The Day England Fell (S. Tanaka)

1943–1945

(no awards given)

1946

1. Morning for the Osone Family
2. No Regrets for Our Youth (Kurosawa)
3. Lord for a Night (Kinugasa)
4. Chijoyuke no onna (Makino)
5. The Girl I Loved (Kinoshita)

1947

1. A Ball at the Anjo House (Yoshimura)
2. War and Peace (Kamei and S. Yamamoto)
3. Once More (Gosho)
4. Record of a Tenement Gentleman (Ozu)
5. Actress (Kinugasa)
6. One Wonderful Sunday (Kurosawa)
7. Snow Trail (Taniguchi)
8. Four Love Stories (Toyoda, Naruse, K. Yamamoto, Kinugasa)
9. Flowering Family (Chiba)
10. Invitation to Happiness (Chiba)

1948

1. Drunken Angel (Kurosawa)
2. Children Hand in Hand (Inagaki)
3. Women of the Night (Mizoguchi)
4. Children of the Beehive (Shimizu)
5. The Day Our Lives Shine (Yoshimura)
6. Apostasy (Kinoshita)
7. A Hen in the Wind (Ozu)
8. The Chess King (Ito)
9. A Living Portrait (Chiba)
10. A Second Life (Sekigawa)

1949

1. Late Spring (Ozu)
2. Blue Mountains (Imai)
3. Stray Dog (Kurosawa)
4. Broken Drum (Kinoshita)
5. Forgotten Children (Inagaki)
6. Here's to the Girls/A Toast to the Young Miss (Kinoshita)
7. A Woman's Life (Kamei)
8. The Quiet Duel (Kurosawa)
9. Ishimatsu of the Forest (Yoshimura)
10. Mr. Shosuke Ohara (Shimizu)

1950

1. Until the Day We Meet Again (Imai)
2. Return to the Capitol (Oba)
3. Escape at Dawn (Taniguchi)
4. Execution Reprieve/The Deferment (Saburi)
5. Rashomon (Kurosawa)
6. Scandal (Kurosawa)
7. The Munekata Sisters (Ozu)
8. Street of Violence (S. Yamamoto)
9. The Makioka Sisters (Abe)
10. The Rainbow-Colored Flower (Haruhata)

1951

1. Early Summer (Ozu)
2. Repast (Naruse)
3. Clothes of Deception (Yoshimura)
4. Carmen Comes Home (Kinoshita)

5. And Yet We Live (Imai)
6. Twenty Years in a Storm (Saburi)
7. A Tale of Genji (Yoshimura)
8. Ah, Youth (Saburi)
9. Beautiful Life (Oba)
10. The Story of a Beloved Wife (Shindo)

1952
1. Ikiru (Kurosawa)
2. Lightning (Naruse)
3. No Consultation Today/Doctor's Day Off (Shibuya)
4. The Moderns (Shibuya)
5. Carmen's Pure Lobe (Kinoshita)
6. Vacuum Zone (S. Yamamoto)
7. Mother (Naruse)
8. Echo School (Imai)
9. The Life of Oharu (Mizoguchi)
10. Lamentation (Saburi)

1953
1. Muddy Waters (Imai)
2. Tokyo Story (Ozu)
3. Tales of Ugetsu/Ugetsu (Ozu)
4. Where Chimneys Are Seen/Four Chimneys (Gosho)
5. Older Brother, Younger Sister (Naruse)
6. A Japanese Tragedy (Kinoshita)
7. The Tower of Lilies (Imai)
8. The Mistress/Wild Geese (Toyoda)
9. A Geisha (Mizoguchi)
10. Epitome/A Geisha Girl (Shindo)

1954
1. Twenty-Four Eyes (Kinoshita)
2. The Garden of Women (Kinoshita)
3. Seven Samurai (Kurosawa)
4. Black Tide (Yamamura)
5. A Story from Chikamatsu/The Crucified Lovers (Mizoguchi)
6. Sounds of the Mountains (Naruse)
7. Late Chrysanthemums (Naruse)
8. Medals (Shibuya)
9. Sansho the Bailiff (Mizoguchi)
10. An Inn at Osaka (Gosho)

1955
1. Floating Clouds (Naruse)
2. Marital Relations (Toyoda)
3. She Was Like a Wild Chrysanthemum (Kinoshita)
4. I Live in Fear/Record of a Living Being (Kurosawa)
5. Here Is a Spring (Imai)
6. Police Diary (Hisamatsu)
7. The Maid's Kid (Tasaka)
8. A Bloody Spear on Mt. Fuji (Uchida)
9. Duckweed Story (S. Yamamoto)
10. Beauty and the Dragon (Yoshimura)

1956
1. Darkness at Noon (Imai)
2. Undercurrent/Night River (Yoshimura)
3. Karakorum (Hayashida)
4. Shozo, a Cat and Two Women (Toyoda)
5. The Burmese Harp (Ichikawa)
6. Early Spring (Ozu)
7. Typhoon #13 (S. Yamamoto)
8. Flowing (Naruse)
9. The Rose in His Arm (Kinoshita)
10. I'll Buy You (Kobayashi)

1957
1. Rice (Imai)
2. A Story of Pure Love (Imai)
3. Times of Joy and Sorrow (Kinoshita)
4. Throne of Blood (Kurosawa)
4. Saheiji Finds a Way/Sun Legend of the Shogunate's Last Days (Kawashima)
6. The Unbalanced Wheel (Shibuya)
7. The Eleventh Hour (Uchida)
8. Roar and Earth (Sekigawa)
9. Stepbrothers (Ieki)
10. The Lower Depths (Kurosawa)

1958
1. The Ballad of Narayama (Kinoshita)
2. The Hidden Fortress (Kurosawa)
3. Equinox Flower (Ozu)
4. Conflagration (Ichikawa)
5. The Naked Sun (Ieki)
6. Night Drum/The Adultress (Imai)
7. The Rickshaw Man (Inagaki)
8. Chase (Nomura)
9. The Naked General (Horikawa)
10. The Build-Ups/Giants and Toys (Masamura)

1959
1. Kiku and Isamu (Imai)
2. Fires on the Plain (Ichikawa)
3. My Second Brother/Diary of Sueko (Imamura)
4. The Song of the Cart (S. Yamamoto)
5. The Human Condition I (Kobayashi)
6. The Human Wall (S. Yamamoto)
7. Their Own World (Uchida)
8. Lucky Dragon #5 (Shindo)
9. The Key/Odd Obsession (Ichikawa)
10. The Human Condition II

1960
1. Her Brother (Ichikawa)
2. Black Book (Horikawa)
3. The Bad Sleep Well (Kurosawa)

4. The River Fuefuki (Kinoshita)
5. Late Autumn (Ozu)
6. The Island (Shindo)
7. Pigs and Battleships/The Flesh Is Hot (Imamura)
8. The Battle Without Arms (S. Yamamoto)
9. Secret of the Himalayas (director undetermined)
10. Night and Fog in Japan (Oshima)

1961
1. Bad Boys (Hani)
2. Yojimbo (Kurosawa)
3. Immortal Love (Kinoshita)
4. The Human Condition III (Kobayashi)
5. Happiness of Us Alone (Matsuyama)
6. The Conspirator (Ito)
7. Pan Chopali (Imai)
8. Run Genta Run (Tasaka)
9. The Catch (Oshima)
10. Ten Dark Women (Ichikawa)

1962
1. Being Two Isn't Easy (Ichikawa)
2. The Foundry Town/A Cupola Where Furnaces Glow (Urayama)
3. Harakiri (Kobayashi)
4. The Outcast (Ichikawa)
5. Sanjuro (Kurosawa)
6. A Man/A Human Being (Shindo)
7. The Pitfall (Teshigahara)
8. An Autumn Afternoon (Ozu)
9. The Old Women of Japan (Imai)
10. Akizu Hot Springs (Yoshida)

1963
1. The Insect Woman (Imamura)
2. High and Low (Kurosawa)
3. House of Shame (Tasaka)
4. My Enemy, the Sea/Alone in the Pacific (Ichikawa)
5. Bushido (Imai)
6. Elegant Beast (Kawashima)
7. She and He
8. Mother (Shindo)
9. Pressure of Guilt (Horikawa)
10. Each Day I Cry (Urayama)

1964
1. Woman in the Dunes (Teshigahara)
2. Kwaidan (Kobayashi)
3. The Scent of Incense (Kinoshita)
4. Unholy Desire (Imamura)
5. Hunger Straits/A Fugitive from the Past (Uchida)
6. A Story from Echigo (Imai)
7. A Public Benefactor/Tycoon (S. Yamamoto)
8. Sweet Sweat (Toyoda)
9. Revenge (Imai)
10. Could I But Live (Matsuyama)

1965
1. Red Beard (Kurosawa)
2. Tokyo Olympiad (Ichikawa)
3. The Japanese Archipeglago/A Chain of Islands (Kumai)
4. A Burglar Story (S. Yamamoto)
5. The Witness Seat (S. Yamamoto)
6. Osan (Tasaka)
7. The Woman from Osorezan/An Innocent Witch (Gosho)
8. Bwana Toshi (Hani)
9. Conquest (Shindo)
10. Forbidden Love/The Story Written by Water (Yoshida)

1966
1. The Ivory Tower/The Great White Tower (S. Yamamoto)
2. The Amorists/The Pornographers (Imamura)
3. The Kii River (Nakamura)
4. Koto: Lake of Tears (Tasaka)
5. The Face of Another (Teshigahara)
6. Bride of the Andes (Hani)
7. Lost Sex (Shindo)
8. Heart of the Mountains (Yoshimura)
9. Violence at Noon (Oshima)
10. The Thin Line (Naruse)

1967
1. Rebellion (Kobayashi)
2. A Man Vanishes (Imamura)
3. The Emperor and the General (Okamoto)
4. Two in the Shadow (Naruse)
5. The Wife of Seishu Hanaoka (Masamura)
6. Portrait of Chieko (Nakamura)
7. Longing for Love (Kobayashi)
8. Clouds at Sunset (Shinoda)
9. Eyes, the Sea and a Ball (Kinoshita)
10. Band of Ninja (Oshima)

1968
1. Kuragashima—Legends from a Southern Island (Imamura)
2. Human Bullet (Okamoto)
3. Death by Hanging (Oshima)
4. Tunnel to the Sun (Kumai)
5. Head (Moritani)
6. Nanami: Inferno of First Love (Hani)
7. Hymn to a Tired Man (Kobayashi)
8. The Man Without a Map (Teshigahara)
9. Kaku and Tsune (Uchida)
10. The Shy Deceiver (Yamada)

1969
1. Double Suicide (Shinoda)
2. The Girl I Abandoned (Urayama)
3. Boy (Oshima)
4. Heat Wave Island (Shindo)
5. The River with No Bridge (Imai)
6. Am I Trying (Yamada)
7. Vietnam (S. Yamamoto)
8. Diary of a Shinjuku Thief (Oshima)
9. Tora-san Pt. 2 (Yamada)
10. Under the Banner of Samurai (Inagaki)

1970
1. Where Spring Comes Late (Yamada)
2. Man and War (S. Yamamoto)
3. Dodes'ka-den (Kurosawa)
4. Eros + Massacre (Yoshida)
5. The Swarming Earth/Apart from Life (Kumai)
6. This Transient Life/All Is Vanity (Jissoji)
7. The Shadow Within (Nomura)
8. Tora-san's Runaway (Yamada)
9. The River with No Bridge II (Imai)
10. The 19-Year-Old Misfit (Shindo)

1971
1. The Ceremony (Oshima)
2. Silence (Shinoda)
3. A Girl Named En (Imai)
4. Human Being and War: Mountains and Rivers of Love and Sadness (S. Yamamoto)
5. Inn of Evil (Kobayashi)
6. Musashi Miyamoto—Swords of Death (Uchida)
7. Those Quiet Japanese (Higashi)
8. Tora-san's Love Call (Yamada)
9. Throw Away Your Books, Let's Go Into the Streets (Terayama)
10. Wet Sand in August (Fujita)

1972
1. The Long Darkness (Kumai)
2. Under the Flag of the Rising Sun (Fukasaku)
3. Home from the Sea (Yamada)
4. Journey of Solitude (Saito)
5. The Rendezvous (Saito)
6. Tora-san's Dear Old Home (Yamada)
7. Eternal Cause (Imai)
8. Sayuri Ichijo: Most Desired/Drenched Passion (Kumashiro)
9. Summer Soldiers (Teshigahara)
10. Shirayubi's Joking (Muragawa)

1973
1. Tsugaru Folk Song (Saito)
2. The Yakuza Papers (Fukasaku)
3. Time Within Memory (Narushima)
4. The Wanderers (Ichikawa)
5. Man in Rapture (Toyoda)
6. Paper Doors of a Secret Room (Kumashiro)
7. Coup d'etat (Yoshida)
8. The Yakuza Papers II (Fukasaku)
9. Tora-san's Forget-Me-Not (Yamada)
10. Men and War III (S. Yamamoto)

1974
1. Sandakan 8 (Kumai)
2. The Castle of Sand (Nomura)
3. Elaborate Family (S. Yamamoto)
4. Youth's Fiasco (Kumashiro)
5. Ryoma Assassination (Kuroki)
6. My Way (Shindo)
7. Operation Summit (Fukasaku)
8. A Tattered Flag (Yoshimura)
9. Red Paper Lantern (Fujita)
10. My Sister (Fujita)

1975
1. Kenji Mizoguchi: The Life of a Film Director (Shindo)
2. Preparation for the Festival (Kuroki)
3. Annular Eclipse (S. Yamamoto)
4. Fossil (Kobayashi)
5. Tora-san's Rise and Fall (Yamada)
6. Pastoral Hide and Seek (Terayama)
7. Bullet Train (Sato)
8. The Graveyard of Honor and Humanity (Fukasaku)
9. Brethren (Yamada)
10. The True Story of Sada Abe (N. Tanaka)

1976
1. The Youth Killer (Hasegawa)
2. Tora-san's Sunrise and Sunset (Yamada)
3. A Cradle Song from the Earth (Masamura)
4. The Marginal Land (S. Yamamoto)
5. The Inugami Family (Ichikawa)
6. His Younger Sister (Imai)
7. Ah! Flower Cheerleaders (Sone)
8. The Graveyard of Yakuza: Gardenia (Fukasaku)
9. Goodbye, Summer Sun (Yamane)
10. Stroller in the Attic (N. Tanaka)

1977
1. The Yellow Handkerchief (Yamada)
2. The Solitary Travels of Chikuzan (Shindo)
3. Banished Orin (Shinoda)
4. Mt. Hakkoda (Moritani)
5. Gateway to Youth—Independence (Urayama)

6. The Devil's Bouncing Ball (Ichikawa)
7. The Silk Tree Ballad (Miyagi)
8. Boxer (Terayama)
9. Suddenly, Like a Storm (Yamane)
10. The Far Road/The Long Single Road Ahead (Hidari)

1978

1. Third Base (Higashi)
2. Love Suicide at Sonezaki (Masamura)
3. Empire of Passion (Oshima)
4. The Incident (Nomura)
5. Bitter Sweet (Fujita)
6. Possessed (Nomura)
7. Dynamite Don Don (Okamoto)
8. Flower in Winter (Furahata)
9. Event of an Assault (N. Tanaka)
10. Hakataite's Pure Love (Sone)

1979

1. Vengeance Is Mine (Imamura)
2. The Man Who Stole the Sun (Hasegawa)
3. Keiko (Claude Gagnon)
4. [title undetermined] (Kumashiro)
5. My Son (Kinoshita)
6. Mt. Gassan (Murano)
7. A 19-Year-Old's Plan (Yanagimachi)
8. No More Going Easy/I'm Not Resting My Chin on My Fist Anymore (Higashi)
9. Nogumi Pass (S. Yamamoto)
10. [title undetermined]

1980

1. Zigeunerweisen (Suzuki)
2. Kagemusha (Kurosawa)
3. Disciples of Hippocrates (Omori)
4. A Baby Given by God (Maeda)
5. A Distant Cry from Spring (Yamada)
6. Parents, Awake! (Kinoshita)
7. Natsuko (Higashi)
8. The Sound of the Tide (Hashiura)
9. Crazy Thunder Road (Ishii)
10. Child of the Sun (Urayama)

1981

1. Muddy River (Oguri)
2. Distant Thunder (Negishi)
3. Theatre of Shimmering Light/Theatre Troupe Kagero (Suzuki)
4. Station (Furuhata)
5. Woman's Obscene Song (Kumashiro)
6. Happiness (Ichikawa)
7. Empire of Punks (Izutsu)
8. Edo Porn (Shindo)
9. Eijanaika (Imamura)
10. At This Late Date, the Charleston (Okamoto)

1982

1. Kamata March (Fukasaku)
2. A Farewell to the Land (Yanagimachi)
3. I Am You, You Are Me (Obayashi)
4. A Japanese Village: Furuyashikimura (Ogawa)
5. Suspicion (Nomura)
6. Man with a Tattoo (Takahashi)
7. A Pool Without Water (Wakamatsu)
8. The Legend of Sayo (Murano)
9. Kidnap News (T. Ito)
10. The Living Koheiji (Nakagawa)

1983

1. The Family Game (Morita)
2. The Makioka Sisters (Ichikawa)
3. Merry Christmas, Mr. Lawrence (Oshima)
4. Military Tribunal for the Far East: The Tokyo Trials (Kobayashi)
5. The Ballad of Narayama (Imamura)
6. Ryuji (Kawashima)
7. Search for Fish/The Catch (Somai)
8. Amagi Pass (Mimura)
9. Mosquito on the 10th Floor (Sai)
10. Home Village (Koyama)

1984

1. The Funeral (Itami)
2. The Tragedy of W (Sawai)
3. MacArthur's Children (Shinoda)
4. Mahjong Gamblers (Wada)
5. A Farewell to the Ark (Terayama)
6. Ohan (Ichikawa)
7. Warriors of the Wind (Miyazaki)
8. For Kayako (Oguri)
9. [title undetermined] (Obayashi)
10. The Hoods (Kawashima)

1985

1. And Then (Morita)
2. Ran (Kurosawa)
3. Himatsuri (Yanagimachi)
4. Typhoon Club (Somai)
5. The Lonely and Cute/Miss Lonely (Obayashi)
6. Love Letter (Kumashiro)
7. The Nuclear Gypsies (Morisaki)
8. The Burmese Harp (Ichikawa)
9. Tale of Early Spring (Sawai)
10. Grey Sunset (T. Ito)

1986

1. The Sea and Poison (Kumai)
2. Comic Magazine (Takita)
3. The House of Wedlock/An Unstable Family (Negishi)
4. A Promise (Yoshida)

5. House of Fire/Man in a Hurry (Fukasaku)
6. Gonza the Spearman (Shinoda)
7. Loving Girls (Omori)
8. Laputa: Castle in the Sky (Miyazaki)
9. Final Take (Yamada)
10. Dixieland Daimyo (Okamoto)

1987

1. A Taxing Woman (Itami)
2. The Emperor's Naked Army Marches On (Hara)
3. Tales from the Magino Village (Ogawa)
4. Half Forever (Negishi)
5. Actress (Ichikawa)
6. Tora-san Goes North (Yamada)
7. The Pimp (Imamura)
8. Ugly (J. Ichikawa)
9. Luminous Woman (Somai)
10. Paper Lanterns (Kajimeshi)

1988

1. My Neighbor Totoro (Miyazaki)
2. Tomorrow (Kuroki)
3. The Discarnates (Obayashi)
4. Rock, Flow Smoothly (Nagasaki)
5. Homesickness (Nakajima)
6. Graveyard of the Fireflies (Takahata)
7. Sakura Theatre Group Has Gone (Shindo)
8. The Yen Family (Takita)
9. Revolver (Fujita)
10. Ruby, the Thief (Wada)

1989

1. Black Rain (Imamura)
2. Knockout
3. The Death of a Tea Master
4. Untamagiru
5. The Witch Express
6. Beijing Watermelon (Obayashi)
7. Rikyu (Teshigahara)
8. Violent Cop
9. Company Executives
10. Buddies

1990

1. The Cherry Orchard
2. Takeshi—Childhood Days
3. The Sting of Death
4. Akira Kurosawa's Dreams (Kurosawa)
5. Bataashi Goldfish
6. Ready to Shoot
7. Boiling Point
8. Ronin City
9. Tsugumi
10. The Pale Hand

1991

1. My Sons
2. Rainbow Kids/The Great Kidnapping
3. Rhapsody in August
4. Nowhere Man
5. Chizuko's Younger Sister
6. A Scene from the Sea
7. The Gentle Twelve
8. Ote
9. Only Yesterday
10. 40,000 Ten River

1992

1. Stamping on the Sumo Ring
2. The Rocking Horsemen
3. Living in Aga
4. Porco Rosso
5. I Can Die
6. The River with No Bridge
7. The Day That Glitters Someday
8. Screwed Souske
9. The Strange Tale of Oyuki
10. Twinkle

1993

1. All Under the Moon
2. Moving
3. Dying at the Hospital
4. Sonatine
5. We Are Not Alone
6. A Class to Remember
7. About Love, Tokyo
8. Bloom in the Moonlight
9. The Night of Nude
10. Madadayo

1994

1. The Whole Body Novelist
2. Chushingura Version Yotsuya Ghost Story
3. Bar Ghost
4. Sorrows of a Stick
5. The Friends
6. 119
7. 800 Two Lap Runners
8. Heisei tanuki Raccoon Battle, Ponpoco
9. New World of Love
10. Permanent Vacation

Appendix IV. Animated Features

Panda and the Magic Serpent (Toei, 1958)
The Adventures of Little Samurai (Toei, 1959)
Alakazam the Great (Toei, 1960)
Magic Boy (Toei, 1960)
The Orphan Brother (Toei, 1961)
Doggie March (Toei, 1963)
The Little Prince and the Eight-Headed Dragon (Toei, 1963)
Cyborg 009 (Toei, 1965)
Gulliver's Travels Beyond the Moon (Toei, 1965)
Willy McBean and His Magic Machine (Videocraft International, 1965)
Cybord 009 – Underground Duel (Toei, 1967)
Jack and the Witch (Toei, 1967)
Fables from Hans Christian Andersen (Toei, 1968)
Little Norse Prince Valiant (Toei, 1968)
The Fox with Nine Tails (Japan Animated Film/Daiei, 1969)
Flying Phantom Ship (Toei, 1969)
Puss'n Boots (Toei, 1969)
Nobody's Boy (Toei, 1970)
30,000 Miles Under the Sea (Toei, 1970)
Adventures of the Polar Bear Cubs (Nikkatsu, 1979)
Nutcracker Fantasy (Sanrio, 1979)
Taro, the Dragon Boy (Toei, 1979)
Hinotori-2772 (Tezuka/Toho, 1980)
Alladin and the Wonderful Lamp (Toei, 1981)
The Sea Prince and the Fire Child (Sanrio, 1981)
Snow Fairy (Nikkatsu, 1981)
Aesop's Fables (Toei, 1983)
Barefoot Gen (Gen, 1983)
Unico in the Island of Magic (Sanrio, 1984)
Warriors of the Wind (Tokuma Shoten, 1984)
Rainbow Brite (DIC, 1985)
Vampire Hunter D (Epic/Sony/Ashi, 1985)
The Adventures of an American Rabbit (Toei, 1986)
Fist of the North Star (Toei, 1986)
Laputa (Tokuma Shoten, 1986)
Neo-Tokyo (Kadokawa, 1986)
A Tale of Genji (Herald Ace, 1987)
Twilight of the Cockroaches [part-animae] (TYO/Kitty, 1987)
Akira (Akira Committee, 1988)
My Neighbor Totoro (Tokuma Shoten, 1988)
Tombstone for Fireflies (Shinchosha, 1988)
Kiki's Delivery Service (Tokuma Shoten, 1989)
Little Nemo: Adventures in Slumberland (Tokyo Movie Shinsha, 1990)
Robot Carnival (APPP, 1990)
The Castle of Cagliostro (TMS, 1991)
Senbon Matsubara (Space Ezo, 1991)
Silent Mobius (Kadokawa, 1991)
The Professional – Golgo 13 (undetermined, 1992)
Tom's Adventures (Urban Products, 1992)

Selected Bibliography

In addition to the material listed below, there were two especially important sources used for this book. The clippings file at the Margaret Herrick Library of the Academy of Motion Picture Arts and Sciences, and the personal archives of Moto Yokoyama proved invaluable; each provided an endless array of original programs, newspaper clippings, exhibitor booklets, film festival information, magazine articles, etc. To the ever-patient staff at the Margaret Herrick Library and the very generous Mr. Yokoyama, my deepest thanks.

Allyn, John. *Kon Ichikawa: A Guide to References and Resources*. Boston: G.K. Hall, 1985.

Andrew, Dudley, and Paul Andrew. *Kenji Mizoguchi: A Guide to References and Resources*. Boston: G.K. Hall, 1981.

Barrett, Gregory. *Archetypes in Japanese Film: The Religious Significance of the Principal Heroes and Heroines*. Selinsgrove, Pa.: Susquehanna University Press, 1985.

Bock, Audie. *Japanese Film Directors*. Tokyo, New York and San Francisco: Kodansha International, 1978.

Buehrer, Beverley Bare. *Japanese Films: A Filmography and Commentary, 1921–1989*. Jefferson, N.C.: McFarland, 1990.

Carr, Robert E. and R.M. Hayes. *Wide Screen Movies: A History and Filmography of Wide Gauge Filmmaking*. Jefferson, N.C.: McFarland, 1988.

Cowie, Peter, gen. ed. *World Filmography*. London: Tantivy Press, 1977. Two volumes.

Film Literature Index (volumes 1-19). Albany: State University of New York at Albany, 1973-1991.

Galbraith, Stuart, IV. *Japanese Science Fiction, Fantasy and Horror Films: A Critical Analysis and Filmography of 103 Features Released in the United States, 1950–1992*. Jefferson, N.C.: McFarland, 1993.

Goble, Alan, ed. *The International Film Index, 1895–1990*. London: Bowker-Saur, 1991.

Hammer, Tad Bentley. *International Film Prizes—An Encyclopedia*. New York: Garland, 1991.

Hanson, Patricia King, and Stephen L., eds. *The Film Review Index* (volume 2). Phoenix, Ariz.: Oryx, 1987.

Isemura, Yoshifumi and Hiroshi Nakamitsu, ed. *Cinema Club 1994*. Tokyo: Pia Corp., 1993.

Katz, Ephraim. *The Film Encyclopedia*. New York: Cromwell, 1979.

Krafsur, Richard P., ex. ed. *The American Film Institute Catalog of Motion Pictures: Feature Films, 1961–1970*. New York: Bowker, 1976.

Kuroda, Toyoji, ed. *UniJapan Film* and *Japanese Film*. Tokyo: UniJapan Film, 1960 (?)-1992.

Kurosawa, Akira. *Something Like an Autobiography*. New York: Random House, 1982.

Larson, Randall D. "The Film Music of Akira Ifukube." *CinemaScore*, no. 15 (1987): x38–44.

________. "Masaru Sato." *CinemaScore*, no. 15 (1987): x35–37.

Lee, Walt, comp. *Reference Guide to Fantastic Films: Science Fiction, Fantasy and Horror*. Los Angeles: Chelsea-Lee Books, 1972–1974. Three volumes.

Lenburg, Jeff. *The Encyclopedia of Animated Cartoons*. New York: Facts on File, 1991.

Lent, John A. *The Asian Film Industry*. London: Christopher Helm, Publishers, 1990.

Mellen, Joan. *Voices from the Japanese Cinema*. New York: Liveright, 1979.

New York Times Film Reviews: 1913–1968. The New York Times and Arno Press, 1970.

Nolletti, Anthony Jr., and David Desser, eds. *Reframing Japanese Cinema: Authorship, Genre, History*. Bloomington and Indianapolis, IN: Indiana University Press., 1992.

Owens, David. *Mizoguchi the Master: A Series of Films by Kenji Mizoguchi*. (brochure) New York: Japan Film Center, 1981.

Re-Thinking the Emergence of Wide-Screen in Japan. unpublished essay. No date given and author undetermined.

Richie, Donald. *Ozu*. Berkeley, CA: University of California Press, 1974.

________. *The Films of Akira Kurosawa*. Berkeley and Los Angeles: University of California Press, 1985.

Sato, Tadao. *Currents in Japanese Cinema*. Trans. Gregory Barrett. New York: Harper & Row, 1982.

Silver, Alain. *The Samurai Film*. Woodstock, New York: Overlook Press, 1977.

Slide, Anthony. *The American Film Industry*. Westport, CT: Greenwood, 1986.

________. *The International Film Industry*. Westport, CT: Greenwood, 1989.

Svensson, Arne. *Screen Series: Japan*. New York: A.S. Barnes & Co., 1971.

Thomas, Nicholas, ed. *International Dictionary of Films and Filmmakers: Actors and Actresses*. Chicago and Lond: St. James Press, 1990. Second Edition.

________, ed. *International Dictionary of Films and Filmmakers: Directors*. Chicago and London: St. James Press, 1990. Second Edition.

Tsushinsha, Jiji, ed. *Japanese Motion Picture Almanac 1957*. Tokyo: Promotion Council of the Motion Picture Industry of Japan, Inc., 1957.

Variety Film Reviews, 1905–1992. New York and London: Garland, 1989–1994.

Variety Obituaries, 1905–1986. New York and London: Garland, 1989.

Selected Periodicals:

Boxoffice
Cult Movies
The Hollywood Reporter
Kinema Jumpo
The Los Angeles Times
Monthly Film Bulletin
The New York Times
Sight and Sound
UniJapan Film Quarterly
Variety

Index of Titles and Alternate Titles

Numbers in **boldface** refer to pages with photographs.

Abandoned 92
Abnormal *see* Hentai
About Love, Tokyo 92
An Actor's Revenge *see* The Revenge of Ukeno-ho: Revenge of a Kabuki Actor
Actress 92
Admiral Yamamoto 92–93
The Adolescent 93
The Adulteress *see* Night Drum
The Adulterous Wife *see* Night Drum
Adventure in Takla Makan *see* Adventures of Takla Makan
Adventure in the Strange Castle *see* Adventures of Takla Makan
Adventure of the Strange Stone Castle *see* Adventures of Takla Makan
The Adventures of an American Rabbit 93
The Adventures of Little Samurai 93–94
The Adventures of Milo and Otis 94
Adventures of Takla Makan 94
Adventures of the Polar Cubs 94
Aesop's Fables 94
The Affair 95
Afurika monogatari *see* The Green Horizon
The Age of Assassins 95
Age of the Gods *see* The Three Treasures
Ah, My Home Town 95
AIDO—Slave of Love 95
A.K. 92
AKIKO—Portrait of a Dancer 95–96
Akira 96–97
Akira Kurosawa's Dreams 97–99
Alakazam the Great 99–100, **100**
The Alaska Story 100
All of Myself 100–1
The All-Out Game 101
All Right, My Friend *see* Daijou, mai furendo
All Under the Moon 101
Alladin and the Wonderful Lamp [sic] 101
Alone in the Pacific *see* My Enemy, the Sea
Along with Ghosts 101, **102**
Am I Trying 101–3
Am I Trying, Pt. 2 *see* Tora-san Pt. 2
The Ambitious 103
The Ambush *see* The Ambush: Incident at Blood Pass
The Ambush: Incident at Blood Pass 103
The Amorists 103
Ancient City 103
The Angry Sea 103–4
Antarctica 104
Anything Goes Three Dolls' Way 104
Apostasy *see* The Outcast
Appointment with Danger 104
Aru mitsu "Bi to shu" 104
Asiapol Secret Service 104–5
The Assassin 105
At This Late Date, the Charleston 105
Atomic Rulers *see* Supergiant
Atomic Rulers of the World *see* Supergiant

Atoragon the Flying Supersub *see* Atragon
Atragon 105–6, **105**
Attack from Space *see* Supergiant
Attack of the Marching Monsters *see* Destroy All Monsters
Attack of the Monsters 106
Attack of the Mushroom People 106–7
Attack of the Super Monsters 107
Attack Squadron! 107
Aurora 107
An Autumn Afternoon 107–8
Ayako 108

Bad Boys 108
The Bad News Bears Go to Japan 108–9
The Bad Sleep Well 109, **110**
The Bailiff *see* Sansho the Bailiff
Ballad of Death 109
Ballad of Narayama (1958) 109
The Ballad of Narayama (1983) 111
Band of Assassins 111
Bandits on the Wind 111
Bang! 111–12
The Barbarian and the Geisha 112
Barefoot Gen 112
The Bastard 112
Battle Beyond the Stars *see* The Green Slime
Battle in Outer Space 112–14
The Battle of Okinawa 114
Battle of the Japan Sea 114
Beast Alley 114
The Beast and the Magic Sword 114–15
The Beasts' Carnival 115
Beat '71 115
The Beautiful Swindlers 115
Beauty's Sorrows 115–16
Before Dawn 116
Being Two Isn't Easy 116
The Bell 117
The Bermuda Depths 117
Between Women and Wives 117–18
The Bewitched Love of Madame Pai *see* Madame Whitesnake
BGS of Ginza 118
The Big Boss 118
Big Duel in the North Sea *see* Ebirah, Horror of the Deep
Big Joys, Small Sorrows 118
Big Shots Die at Dawn 118
The Big Wave 118–19
Big Wind from Tokyo 119
A Billionaire 119
The Birth of Judo 119
The Bite 119–20
The Black Cat *see* Kuroneko
Black Cat Mansion 120
Black-Jet Family *see* The Crazy Family
Black Lizard 120
Black Rain (1988) 120–21
Black Rain (1989) 121
Black Rose 122
Blazing Continent 122
The Blind Beast 122
The Blind Woman's Curse *see* Tattooed Swordswoman
Blood 122
Blood on the Sea 123
Blood Sword of the 99th Virgin *see* The Bloody Sword of the 99th Virgin
Blood Type: Blue *see* Buru kurismasu
The Bloodthirsty Eyes *see* Lake of Dracula
Bloodthirsty Roses *see* Evil of Dracula
The Bloody Sword of the 99th Virgin 123
Bloom in the Moonlight 123
The Blue Beast 123
The Blue Revolution 123
The Body 123
Body Beautiful 124
Body Snatcher from Hell *see* Goke, Bodysnatcher from Hell
The Bodyguard 124
Bonchi 124
Booted Babe, Busted Boss 124
The Born Fighter *see* Fighting Elegy
Born in Sin 124
The Boss of Pick-Pocket Bay 125
A Boss with the Samurai Spirit 125
Botandoro (1955) 125
Botandoro (1968) *see* Kaidan botandoro
Boy 125
A Boy and Three Mothers 125
Brand of Evil 126
Branded to Kill 126
Bravo, Young Guy 126
The Bride from Hades *see* Kaidan botandoro
Bride from Hell *see* Kaidan botandoro
Bride of the Andes 126
The Bridge Between 126
Bridge of Japan 126–27
Bridge to the Sun 127
The Broken Commandment *see* The Outcast
Broken Swords 127
Brothel #8 *see* Sandakan 8

Brother and Sister 127
The Brothers and Sisters of the Toda Family 127
Buddha 127-29, **128**
Bull of the Campus 129
Bullet Wound 129
The Burmese Harp (1956) 129
The Burmese Harp (1985) 129-30
Buru kurisumasu 130
Bushido 130
Bwana Toshi 130

The Call of the Flesh 130
Campus A-Go-Go 130
Carmen Comes Home 130-31
Carmen from Kawachi 131
Carmen 1945 131
Carmen's Pure Love 131
The Castle of Cagliostro 131
The Castle of Sand 131
The Castle of the Spider's Web *see* Throne of Blood
Catastrophe: 1999 *see* Prophecies of Nostradamus
Caucasian Ghost *see* Kaidan ijin yurei
The Ceremony 131-32
A Certain Adultery *see* Aru mitsu "Bi to shu"
The Challenge 132-33
Challenge to Live 133
The Challenging Ghost 133
Cherry Blossoms in the Air—The Suicide Raiders—Oh, Buddies! 133
The Cherry Orchard 133
The Child Writers 133
Children Drawing Rainbows 133-34
Children of Nagasaki 135
Children on the Island 135
Chimney Scene *see* When Chimneys Are Seen
Chizuko's Younger Sister 135
Chushingura **134**, 135-36
Chushingura: 47 Samurai *see* Chushingura
City of Beasts 136
A Class to Remember 136
The Claws of Satan 136
The Cleanup 136
Cobweb Castle *see* Throne of Blood
The College Hero 136-37
College Is a Nice Place 137
Come Marry Me 137
Comic Magazine 137
Company Executives 137
Computer Free-for-All 137-38
The Concubines 138
Conflagration 138
Conquest 138
The Cosmic Man Appears in Tokyo *see* The Mysterious Satellite
Could I But Live 138-39
Counterstroke 139
The Country Doctor *see* Life of a Country Doctor
A Couple on the Move 139
The Crab-Canning Ship 139
The Crazy Family 139
The Creature Called Man 139-40
The Crescent Moon 140
The Crest of Man 140
Criminal Women *see* Tokugawa onna keibatsushi
Crimson Bat Oichi: Wanted, Dead or Alive 140
Crimson Bat, the Blind Swordswoman 140
Crisis 2050 *see* Solar Crisis
Crossroads *see* Slums of Tokyo
The Crowded Streetcar 140
Crucified Lovers: A Story from Chikamatsu *see* A Story from Chikamatsu
Cruel Ghost Legend *see* Curse of the Blood
Cruel Story of Youth *see* Naked Youth
Cry for Happy 141
Cry of the Mountain 141
Crying in the Night *see* Kaidan yonakidoro
Curse of the Blood 141
The Curse of the Ghost 141
Curse of the One-Eyed Corpse *see* Ghost of the One-Eyed Man
The Cursed Pond *see* Kaibyo noroi numa
The Cursed Wall (1958) *see* Kaibyo noroi no kabe
Cyborg 009 142
Cyborg 009—Underground Duel 142

Dagora, the Space Monster 142
Daijou, mai furendo 142-43
The Dancer 143
Dancing Mistress 143
The Dangerous Kiss 143
The Daphne 143
Daredevil in the Castle 143-44
The Daring Nun 144
Dark the Mountain Snow 144

Dawn of Judo 144
Day-Dream 144–45
The Day the Sun Rose 145
Days of Youth 145
Death and the Green Slime *see* The Green Slime
Death by Hanging 145
Death of a Tea Master 145
Death on the Mountain 145
Deathquake 146
The Deep Desire of the Gods *see* Kuregejima – Legends from a Southern Island
Deer Friend 146
The Demon 146
The Demon (1964) *see* Onibaba
Demon Pond 146–47
Demons 147
The Depths 147
Dersu Uzala 147–48
Desperado Outpost 149
Destroy All Monsters **148**, 149–50
Destroy All Planets 150
Detective Bureau 2-3: Go to Hell, Bastards! 150
Devil in the Castle *see* Daredevil in the Castle
Devil Woman *see* Onibaba
The Devil's Bouncing Ball Song 150–51
Devil's Temple 151
Diamonds in the Andes 151
Diary of a Shinjuku Burglar *see* Diary of a Shinjuku Thief
Diary of a Shinjuku Thief 151
Different Sons 151–52
The Diplomat's Mansion 152
The Dirty Girls *see* The Flesh Is Hot
Disciples of Hippocrates 152
Dismembered Ghost 152
A Distant Cry from Spring 152
The Distant Setting Sun *see* Faraway Sunset
Dixieland Daimyo 152
Dodes'ka-den 152–53
Doggie March 153
Dojoji Temple *see* Kyokanoko musume Dojoji
Don't Call Me a Con Man 153
Don't Call Me a Crime Man *see* Don't Call Me a Con Man
Doomed *see* Ikiru
Double Suicide 153–154
Double Suicide at Sonezaki 154
Double Trouble 154
The Downfall of Osen 154
Downtown 154
Dracula's Lust for Blood *see* Lake of Dracula
Dragnet Girl 154–55
The Dragon's Fangs 155
Dream of Love 155
Dreams *see* Akira Kurosawa's Dreams
The Dreams of Youth 155
Drifting Avenger 155
Drunken Angel 155
Duel at Ezo 155–56
Duel at Ichijoji Temple *see* Samurai II
Duel in the Storm 156
Duel of the Gargantuas *see* War of the Gargantuas
Duel on Ganryu Island *see* Samurai III
Dun-Huang *see* The Silk Road
Dying at a Hospital 156

Eagle of the Pacific 156
Early Autumn 156
Early Spring 156–57
Early Summer 157
Earth 157
The Earth 157
East China Sea 157
Ebirah, Horror of the Deep 157–58
Edo Porn 158
Eijanaika 158
Elegy for a Quarrel *see* Fighting Elegy
Elegy to Violence *see* Fighting Elegy
The Emperor and a General 158–59
The Emperor's Naked Army Marches On 159
Empire of Passion 159
The Empty Table 159–60
Enchanted Princess 160
The Enchantment 160
The End of Summer *see* Early Autumn
The Endless Passion *see* Passion Without End
The Enemy, the Sea *see* My Enemy, the Sea
Epoch of Murder Madness *see* The Age of Assassins
Equinox Flower 160
Eriko 161
Erogami no onryo 161
Escapade in Japan 161
E.S.P./SPY *see* ESPY
ESPY 161
Eternal Love 161–62
Eternity of Love 162

Evil Brain from Outer Space *see* Supergiant
Evil of Dracula 162
Eyes, the Sea and a Ball 162

Fables from Hans Christian Andersen 162
The Face of Another 162–63
The Face of War 163
The Falcon Fighters 163
The Family Game 163, **164**
The Famous Sword 163–64
The Famous Sword of Bijomaru *see* The Famous Sword
Fancy Paradise *see* Kuso tengoku
Faraway Sunset 164
Farewell, My Beloved 164
Farewell to the Ark 164–65
Father 165
Fear of the Snake Woman *see* Kaidan hebionna
La Fée Diabolique 165
Fight for the Glory 165
Fighting Elegy 165
Fighting Friends – Japanese Style 165
Final Take 165–66
The Final War 166
Fire Festival *see* Himatsuri
The Firebird *see* Hinotori
Fireflies in the North 166
Fires on the Plain 166
Fist of the North Star 166
5 Gents on the Spot 167
Five Gents' Trick Book 167
Five Scouts 167
The Flesh Is Hot 167
Flight from Ashiya 167–68
Floating Clouds 168
Floating Weeds 168
The Flower 168
A Flower Blooms 169
Flying Phantom Ship 169
Forbidden Affair 169
The Forbidden Fruit 169
Fort Graveyard 169
The Fort of Death 169–70
The 47 Ronin of the Genroku Era *see* The Loyal 47 Ronin I
Forward, Ever Forward 171
Fossil *see* Kaseki
Foster Daddy, Tora! 171
Four Chimney's *see* When Chimneys Are Seen
Four Days of Snow and Blood 171
The Fox with Nine Tails 171
Frankenstein Conquers the World **170**, 171–72
Free and Easy 172
Free and Easy II 172
The Friendly Killer 172–73
Froggo and the Draggo *see* The Magic Serpent
Fugitive Alien 173
The Funeral 173–74
Funeral Parade of Roses 174

Gambler's Code 174
Gamblers in Okinawa 174
The Gambling Samurai 174
Gamera *see* Gammera the Invincible
Gamera – The Guardian of the Universe 175
Gamera Super Monster *see* Super Monster
Gamera vs. Barugon *see* War of the Monsters
Gamera vs. Guiron *see* Attack of the Monsters
Gamera vs. Gyaos *see* Return of the Giant Monsters
Gamera vs. Monster X 175
Gamera vs. Zigra 175–76
Gammera the Invincible **176**, 177
The Gangster VIP 177
Gappa *see* Monster from a Prehistoric Planet
Gappa: Triphibian Monster *see* Monster from a Prehistoric Planet
Gate of Flesh 177–78
Gate of Hell 178, **179**
The Gate of Youth (1976) 178
The Gate of Youth (1982) 178
The Gate of Youth – Part II 178–79
Gateway to Glory 179–80
The Gay Braggart 180
A Geisha 180
The Geisha 180
Genocide 180
The Gentle Twelve 180–81
Get 'Em All 181
Getting Old with a Sense of Security 181
Ghidrah – The Three-Headed Monster 181–82
Ghost Beauty *see* Kaidan botandoro
Ghost-Cat of Arima Palace *see* Kaibyo Arima goten
Ghost-Cat of Chidori-Ga-Fuchi *see* The Swamp

Ghost-Cat of Gojusan-Tsugi *see* Kaibyo Gojusan-tsugi
Ghost-Cat of Karakuri Tenjo *see* Kaibyo Karakuri Tenjo
Ghost-Cat of Oma-Ga-Tsuji *see* Kaibyo Oma-ga-tsuji
Ghost-Cat of Otam-ag-Ike *see* Ghost of Otamaga-Ike
Ghost-Cat of Yonkai Swamp *see* Necromancy
Ghost-Cat Wall of Hatred *see* Kaibyo noroi no kabe
Ghost from the Pond *see* Kaidan hitotsu-me Jizo
Ghost Music of Shamisen *see* Kaidan shamisen-bori
The Ghost of a Hunchback *see* House of Terrors
Ghost of Chibusa Enoki *see* Kaidan Chibusa Enoki
Ghost of Gojusan-Tsugi *see* Kaidan Gojusan-tsugi
Ghost of Kagami-Ga-Fuchi *see* Kaidan Kagami-ga-fuchi
The Ghost of Kasane *see* The Depths
Ghost of Oiwa *see* Kaidan Oiwa no Borei
Ghost of Otamaga-Ike 182
Ghost of Saga Mansion *see* Kaidan Saga yashiki
Ghost of the One-Eyed Man 182
Ghost of the Snake *see* Kaidan hebionna
Ghost of Two Travelers at Tenamonya *see* Tenamonya yurei dochu
The Ghost of Yotsuya (1957) *see* Kaidan Bancho sara yashiki
The Ghost of Yotsuya (1959) 182
The Ghost of Yotsuya (1961) *see* Kaidan Oiwa no Borei
The Ghost of Yotsuya—New Version *see* Shinshaku Yotsuya kaidan
Ghost Ship 182
Ghost Stories *see* Kwaidan
A Ghost Story—Barabara Phantom *see* Dismembered Ghost
Ghost Story of Booby Trap *see* The Ghostly Trap
Ghost Story of Broken Dishes at Bancho Mansion *see* Kaidan Bancho sara yashiki
Ghost Story of Devil's Fire Swamp *see* Kaidan onibi no numa
Ghost Story of Funny Act in Front of Train Station *see* Kigeki ekiame kaidan
Ghost Story of Kakui Street *see* Kaidan Kakuidori
A Ghost Story of Passage *see* The Lady Was a Ghost
Ghost Story of Stone Lanterns *see* Kaidan yonaki-doro
Ghost Story of Two Travelers *see* The Lady Was a Ghost
Ghost Story of Yotsuya in Tokaido *see* The Ghost of Yotsuya
Ghost Story of Youth 182–83
Ghost Story—The Kasane Swamp *see* The Depths
The Ghostly Trap 183
Ghosts on Parade 183
Gigantis the Fire Monster 183–85, **184**
Gion Festival Music *see* A Geisha
Gion Matsuri *see* The Day the Sun Rose
Girl Diver of Spook Mansion 185
The Girl I Abandoned 185
Girl in the Mist 185
Girl of Dark 185
Girl with Bamboo Leaves 185–86
Go and Get It 186
The Go Masters 186
Godzilla *see* Godzilla, King of the Monsters!
Godzilla Against Mechagodzilla *see* Godzilla vs. the Cosmic Monster
Godzilla, King of the Monsters! 187–88
Godzilla 1985 188–90
Godzilla on Monster Island 190–91, **190**
Godzilla Raids Again *see* Gigantis the Fire Monster
Godzilla vs. Biollante 191–92
Godzilla vs. Gigan *see* Godzilla on Monster Island
Godzilla vs. King Ghidorah 192–93
Godzilla vs. Mechagodzilla (1974) 193
Godzilla vs. Megalon 193
Godzilla vs. Monster Zero *see* Monster Zero
Godzilla vs. Mothra (1964) *see* Godzilla vs. the Thing
Godzilla vs. Mothra (1992) 193–94
Godzilla vs. Space Godzilla 194
Godzilla vs. the Bionic Monster *see* Godzilla vs. the Cosmic Monster
Godzilla vs. the Cosmic Monster 194–95
Godzilla versus the Sea Monster *see* Ebirah, Horror of the Deep
Godzilla vs. the Smog Monster 195–96
Godzilla vs. the Thing **195**, 196
Godzilla's Revenge 196–97

Goke, Bodysnatcher from Hell 197
Goke the Vampire *see* Goke, Bodysnatcher from Hell
The Golden Demon 197–98
Gone with Love, Come with Memory 198
Gonza the Spearman 198
The Good Little Bad Girl 198
Good Morning *see* Ohayo
Goodbye, Hello 198
Goodbye Mama 198
Goodbye, Moscow 198–99
A Goodbye to the Girls 199
Gorath 199–200
Goyokin 200
Grand Duel in Magic *see* The Magic Serpent
Gray Sunset 201
The Great Kidnapping *see* Rainbow Kids
The Great Shogunate Battle 201
The Great Wall 201–2
The Green Horizon 202
Green Light to Joy 202
The Green Slime 202–3
Gulliver's Travels Beyond the Moon 203
Gunhed 203–4

The H-Man 204–5
Hachi-ko 205
Half a Loaf... 205
Half Human: The Story of the Abominable Snowman 205–6, **206**
Happiness *see* Lonely Heart
Happiness of Us Alone 206–7
The Happy Pilgrimage II 207
Happy Wedding 207
Harakiri 207
Harbor Light Blues *see* Waterfront Blues
Harbor Light Yokohama 207
Harp of Burma *see* The Burmese Harp
Haru kuru oni 208
The Haunted Castle 208
The Haunted Cave *see* Girl Diver of Spook Mansion
Haunted Gold 208
Haunted Life of a Dragon-Tattooed Lass *see* Tattooed Swordswoman
The Haunted Samurai *see* Superman on Gale
He Had to Die 208
The Heart 208–9
The Heart of Hiroshima 209
Hearts and Flowers for Tora-san 209
Heat and Mud 209
Heat-Haze Theatre 209
Heat Wave Island 209
Heaven and Earth 209–10
Heaven and Hell *see* High and Low
Hell *see* The Sinners of Hell
Hell in the Pacific 211–12
Hello, Kids! 212
Hell's Tattooers 212
A Hen in the Wind 212
Hentai 212
Her Brother 212
The Hidden Fortress 213
High and Low 213–14, **214**
High-School Outcasts 214
Hikarigoke 214–15
Himatsuri 215
Himiko 215
Hinotori 215
Hinotori-2772 215
Hiroku onna ro 215–16
Hiroshima 216
Hiroshima mon amour 216
History of Postwar Japan as Told by a Bar Hostess 216
Hogs and Warships *see* The Flesh Is Hot
The Hole *see* Onibaba
Holiday in Tokyo 216–17
Hometown 217
Honolulu-Tokyo-Hong Kong 217
The Hoodlum Priest 217
The Hoodlum Soldier 217
Hope and Pain 217
The Horizon 218
Horror of a Deformed Man 218
Horror of a Malformed Man *see* Horror of a Deformed Man
Horror of an Ugly Woman *see* The Masseur's Curse
Horror of the Giant Vortex *see* Kyofu no daiuzumaki
Horse 218
The Hospital: The Last Place to Consult—A Home Care Network That Sustains the Elderly 218
The Hot Little Girl 218
The Hot Marshland *see* Heat and Mud
Hotsprings Holiday 218–19
House 219
House of Bamboo 219
House of Hanging 219–20
The House of Strange Loves 220
House of Terrors 220
The House of the Sleeping Virgins 220

House on Fire 220
The House Where Evil Dwells 220–21
House with No Dining Table *see* The Empty Table
How to Care for the Senile 221
The Human Condition 221
The Human Condition (Part I: No Greater Love) *see* The Human Condition
Human Condition (Part II: Road to Eternity) 221–22
Human Condition (Part III: A Soldier's Prayer) 222
Human Patterns 223
The Human Vapor **222**, 223
Humanity and Paper Balloons 223
Hunter's Diary 223–24
The Hurricane Drummer 225
Hymn to a Tired Man 225

I Am a Cat 225
I Am Two Years Old *see* Being Two Isn't Easy
I Bombed Pearl Harbor **224**, 225–26
I Flunked, But... 226
I Graduated, But... 226
I Live in Fear 226–27
I, the Executioner 227
I Want to Be a Shellfish 227
I Was Born But... 227
The Idiot 227
Ikiru 228, **228**
Illusion of Blood 228
Image Wife 228–29
Imagery Paradise [sic] *see* Kuso tengoku
Immortal Love 229
Imperial Navy 229
The Imposter 229
In the Realm of Passion *see* Empire of Passion
In the Realm of the Senses 229–30
The Incident 230
The Incorrigible One *see* The Bastard
Industrial Spy Free-for-All 230
The Inferno *see* Jigoku
The Inheritance 230–31
An Inn in Tokyo 231
Inn of Evil 231
An Innocent Maid 231
Innocent Sinner 231
The Insect *see* The Insect Woman
The Insect Woman 231–32
International Military Tribunal for the Far East: The Tokyo Trial 232
Interpol Code 8 232–33
An Introduction to Marriage 233
The Inugami Family 233
The Inugamis *see* The Inugami Family
Invaders from Space (1957) *see* Supergiant
Invaders from Space (1959) *see* Prince of Space
Invaders from the Spaceship *see* Prince of Space
Invasion of Astro-Monster *see* Monster Zero
Invasion of the Neptune Men 233
The Invisible Avenger *see* Tomei ningen
The Invisible Man – Dr. Eros *see* Tomei ningen erohakase
The Invisible Swordsman 233–34
Invitation to an Enchanted Town *see* Sennin Buraku
Irezumi – Spirit of the Tattoo 234
Ishimatsu Travels with Ghosts *see* Mori no Ichimatsuu yurei dochu
The Island 234
Island of Horrors 234
It Started in the Alps 234
It's a Woman's World 234–35
The Ivory Ape 235

Jack and the Witch 235–36
A Japanese Tragedy 236
Japan's Longest Day *see* The Emperor and a General
Japula *see* Lake of Dracula
Jasei no in 236
Jigoku (1979) 236
Jotai johatsu 236
Journey Along Tokaido Road *see* Along with Ghosts
Journey of Honor 236–38
Journey of Love 238
The Joys of Torture *see* Tokugawa onna keibatsushi
Ju Dou 238–39
Judo Champion 239
Judo Saga 239
Judo Saga (1943) *see* Sanshiro Sugata
Judo Saga – II *see* Sanshiro Sugata – Part Two
Judo Showdown 239–40
Just for You 240

Kagemusha 240
Kagemusha: The Shadow Warrior *see* Kagemusha

Kai 240–41
Kaibyo Arima goten 241
Kaibyo Gojusan-tsugi 241
Kaibyo Karakuri Tenjo 241
Kaibyo koshinuke daisodo 241
Kaibyo noroi no Kabe 241
Kaibyo noroi numa 241–42
Kaibyo Okazaki sodo 242
Kaibyo Oma-ga-tsuji 242
Kaidan Bancho sara yashiki 242
Kaidan botandoro 242
Kaidan Chibusa Enoki 242–43
Kaidan Fukagawa jowa 243
Kaidan Gojusan-tsugi 243
Kaidan hebionna 243
Kaidan hitotsu-me Jizo 243
Kaidan ijin yurei 243
Kaidan Kagami-ga-fuchi 243
Kaidan Kakuidori 243–44
Kaidan Kasanegafuchi 244
Kaidan Oiwa no Borei 244
Kaidan onibi no numa 244
Kaidan ryoko 244
Kaidan Saga yashiki 244
Kaidan Shamisen-bori 244–45
Kaidan yonaki-doro 245
Kaii Utsunomiya tsuritenjo 245
Kamigata Kugaizoshi 245
Kamikaze *see* Attack Squadron!
A Kamikaze Cop 245
Kamikaze Cop, Marihuana Syndicate 245
Kanto Wanderer 245–46
Kappa: A River Goblin and Sampei 246
The Karate *see* The Street Fighter
Kaseki 246
Kenji Mizoguchi: The Life of a Film Director 246
The Key *see* Odd Obsession
The Kid Brother 246
Kigeki ekiame kaidan 246–47
Kiki's Delivery Service 247
Kill! 247
Kill the Killer! 247
Kill the Killers 247
Killer Whale *see* The Whale God
Killer's Mission 247
The Killing Bottle 247–48
Kimiko *see* Wife!Be Like a Rose!
King Kong Escapes 248, **249**
King Kong vs. Godzilla 248–50, **251**
Knockout Drops 250
Kojiro 250
Koshoku tomei ningen 250
Koya: Memorial Notes of Choken 250–51
Kuregejima—Legends from a Southern Island 251–52
Kuroneko 252–53
Kuso tengoku 253
Kwaidan **252**, 253–54
Kyofu no daiuzumaki 254
Kyoren no onna shisho 254

The Lady and the Beard 254
The Lady and the Moustache *see* The Lady and the Beard
The Lady from Musashino 254–55
Lady Musashino *see* The Lady from Musashino
The Lady Was a Ghost 255
The Lake 255
Lake of Death *see* Lake of Dracula
Lake of Dracula 255
The Lake of Dracula *see* Lake of Dracula
Laputa: Castle in the Sky 255–56
Las Vegas Free-for-All 256
Lasciviousness of the Viper *see* Jasei no in
The Last Challenge 256
Last Day of the Samurai 256
The Last Days of Planet Earth *see* Prophecies of Nostradamus
The Last Death of the Devil 256
The Last Dinosaur 256–57
The Last Game 257
The Last Lady 257
The Last of Summer *see* Early Autumn
The Last Samurai 257
The Last Voyage 257–59
The Last War 259
Late Autumn 259
Late Spring 259–61
Latitude Zero **260**, 261
The Legacy of the 500,000 261
Legend of Dinosaurs and Monster Birds *see* The "Legend of the Dinosaurs"
The "Legend of the Dinosaurs" 261–62
Let's Go, Grand' Ma! 262
Let's Go, Young Guy! 262
The Life and Opinion of Masseur Ichi 262–63
Life of a Country Doctor 263
The Life of a Film Director *see* Kenji Mizoguchi: The Life of a Film Director
The Life of an Actor 263
The Life of an Office Worker 263
Life of Chikuzan, Tsugaru Shamisen Player 263
Life of Oharu 263–64

Life of the Country Doctor *see* Life of a Country Doctor
Lightning Swords of Death *see* Sword of Vengeance
Little Brother *see* Her Brother
The Little Girl Who Conquered Time *see* Toki o kakeru shojo
Little Nemo: Adventures in Slumberland 264-65
Little Norse Prince Valiant 265
The Little Prince and the Eight-Headed Dragon 265-66
Live and Learn 266
Live My Share, Mother 266
Live Today; Die Tomorrow! 266
Live Your Own Way 266
Living on the River Agano 266-67
Living Skeleton 267
Lonely Heart 267
Lonely Lane 267
Long Journey Into Love 267
Long Way to Okinawa 267
Longing for Love 268
Lost in the Wilderness 268
Lost Luck 268
Lost Sex 268
The Lost World of Sinbad 268-69
Love and Crime 269
Love and Faith 269
Love and Faith: Lady Ogin *see* Love and Faith
Love and Faith of Ogin *see* Love and Faith
Love at Twenty 269-70
Love Betrayed 270
Love Foolery Case for a Severed Head *see* Namakubi jochi jiken
Love Letter 270
Love Me, Love Me 270
Love Not Again *see* Love, Thy Name Be Sorrow
The Love of Sumako the Actress 270-71
The Love Robots 271
The Love Suicides at Sonezaki 271
Love, Thy Name Be Sorrow 271
Love Under the Crucifix 271
The Lover (1951) 271
The Lover (1953) 271-72
Lovers of Ginza 272
The Lower Depths 272
The Loyal 47 Ronin I 272, **273**
The Loyal 47 Ronin II 273
Lusty Transparent Man 273
MacArthur's Children 273-74
MacArthur's Children—Part II 274
Macbeth *see* Throne of Blood
The Mad Atlantic 274
The Mad Fox *see* Love, Thy Name Be Sorrow
Madadayo 274
Madadayo: Not Yet *see* Madadayo
Madame Aki 274-75
Madame O 275
Madame Whitesnake 275
Magic Boy 275
The Magic Serpent 275-76
The Magic Sword of Watari 276
The Magnificent Seven 276
Magnitude 7.9 *see* Deathquake
The Magoichi Saga 277
The Maid Story 277
Majin 277
Majin Strikes Again 277, **278**
Majin the Hideous Idol *see* Majin
Make-up 279
The Makioka Sisters 279
The Male Vampire *see* The Woman Vampire
The Maliciousness of the Snake's Evil *see* Jasei no in
Man Against Man 279
Man and War 279
The Man from the East 279-80
The Man from Tokyo *see* Tokyo Drifter
The Man in the Moonlight Mask 280
The Man in the Storm 280
A Man Vanishes 281
The Man Who Stole the Sun 281
The Man Without a Map 281
The Man Without a Nationality 281
The Manster **280**, 281-82
The Manster—Half Man, Half Monster *see* The Manster
Many Ghost-Cats *see* The Phantom Cat
March of the Monsters *see* Destroy All Monsters
Marco 282
Mariko—Mother 282
Marriage Counselor Tora-san 282
The Mask and Destiny *see* The Mask of Destiny
The Mask of Destiny 282
Masked Terror *see* Dokuro kyojo
The Masseur's Curse 282-83
Matango, Fungus of Terror *see* Attack of the Mushroom People
Max Mon Amour 283
Melody in Gray 283

Memoir of Japanese Assassins 283
Memories of You 283–84
Men and War *see* Man and War
Men and War—Part Two 284
Men and War—Part Three 284
The Men of Toho-ku 284
The Men Who Tread on the Tiger's Tail 284
The Merciless Trap 284–85
Merry Christmas, Mr. Lawrence 285
Message for the Future 285
Message from Space 285–87, **286**
Message from Space: Galactic Battle *see* Swords of the Space Ark
Mexican Free-for-All 287
Midare karakuri 287
Mighty Jack 287
The Militarists 287
Minamata 287
Minbo—or the Gentle Art of Japanese Extortion 288
Mini-Skirt Lynchers 288
Mishima *see* Mishima: A Life in Four Chapters
Mishima: A Life in Four Chapters 288–89
Miss Oyu 289–90
Mission Iron Castle 290
Mr. Baseball 290
Mr. Lucky 291
Mr. Pu 291
Mr. Radish and Mr. Carrot *see* Twilight Path
Mistress 291
Moment of Terror 291
Mondo Grottesco 291
The Money Dance 291–92
Money Talks *see* The Money Dance
Monsieur Zivaco 292
Monster from a Prehistoric Planet 292
The Monster Gorilla 292
Monster Snowman *see* Half Human: The Story of the Abominable Snowman
Monster Zero 292–93
The Moon Mask Rider 293
Moonlight in the Rain 293–94
Mori no Ichimatsu yurei dochu 294
The Most Beautiful 294
Most Beautifully *see* The Most Beautiful
The Most Terrible Time in My Life 294
Mother (1952) 294
Mother (1988) 294
A Mother Should Be Loved 294–95
Mothra **295**, 296
Mt. Aso's Passion 296
Mt. Hakkoda 296
Muddy River 297
Muhomatsu, the Rickshaw Man *see* The Rickshaw Man
The Munekata Sisters 297
Musashi and Kojiro *see* Samurai (Part III)
Musashi Miyamoto (1944) 297
Musashi Miyamoto (1954) *see* Samurai
Musashi Miyamoto (1961) 297–98
Musashi Miyamoto—Swords of Death *see* Swords of Death
My Blood Belongs to Someone Else *see* Blood
My Bride Is a Ghost *see* Kaidan botan-doro
My Champion 298
My Daughter and I 298
My Enemy, the Sea 298
My Friend Death 298
My Geisha 298–99
My Hobo 299
My Love Burns *see* My Love Has Been Burning
My Love Has Been Burning 299
My Neighbor Totoro 299–300
My Son! My Son! 300
My Sons 300–1
My Way 301
The Mysterians 301–2, **301**
The Mysterious Satellite 302–3
Mystery of the Cat-Woman *see* The Haunted Castle

The Naked General 303
The Naked Island *see* The Island
Naked Pursuit 303
Naked Youth 303
Namakubi jochi jiken 303–4
Nanami: Inferno of First Love 304
Naniwa Elegy *see* Osaka Elegy
Nanmin Road 304
Necromancy 304
Neo Tokyo 304
The New Earth 304–5
The New Japanese Cinema 305
New Tales of the Taira Clan 305
New Version of the Ghost of Yotsuya *see* Shinshaku Yotsuya kaidan
Nichiren 305
Night Drum 305–6
Night in Bangkok 306
A Night in Hong Kong 306
The Night of the Seagull 306
Night on the Galactic Railroad 306

Nightshade Flower 306
Ninja Boy *see* Watari, Ninja Boy
Ninja Wars 307
Ninjitsu *see* Secret Scrolls (Part II)
Nizaemon Kataoka: Kabuki Actor 307
No Greater Love *see* The Human Condition (Part I)
No Greater Love Than This 307
No Regrets for My Youth *see* No Regrets for Our Youth
No Regrets for Our Youth 307
Nobody's Boy 307
Nogumi Pass 308
The Noh Mask Murders 308
None But the Brave 308–9, **309**
Not Yet *see* Madadayo
The Notorious Concubines *see* The Concubines
Nowhere Man 309
Nurses and Doctors 310
A Nurse's Husband Fights On 310
Nutcracker Fantasy 310

Oban's Dipping Contest 310–11
Obscenity of the Viper *see* Jasei no in
An Ocean to Cross 311
Odd Obsession 311
Ogin Her Love and Faith *see* Love and Faith
Oginsaga *see* Love and Faith
The Ogre of Mount Oe 311
Oh, My Comrade! 311
Oh-te 311–12
Ohan 312
Ohayo 312
Okasarete Byuakui 312
Okoge 312
The Old Bear Hunter 313
Older Brother, Younger Sister *see* Brother and Sister
Once a Rainy Day 313
One Generation of Tattoos 313
One Hundred Gamblers 313
100 Monsters 313–14
1001 Nights with Toho 314
One Wonderful Sunday 314
Onibaba 314
The Only Son 314
Only Yesterday 314–15
Operation Enemy Fort 315
Operation Mad Dog 315
Operation Monsterland *see* Destroy All Monsters
Operation Neglige 315
Operation Room 315
Operation X 315
Oracion 315–16
Orgies of Edo 316
The Orphan Brother 316
Osaka Elegy 316
Osorezan no onna 316
Our Dear Buddies 316–17
Our Earth: A Message to Our Children 317
Our Silent Love 317
The Outcast 317
The Outlaw Sword 317
Outpost of Hell 317–18
Oyuki the Madonna 318

A Page of Madness 318–19
The Pale Hand 319
Panda and the Magic Serpent **318**, 319
The Passage to Japan 319
Passing Fancy 319
Passion 319
Passion Without End 319–20
The Path Under the Platanes 320
Peach Boy *see* Takarajima Ensei
Peonies and Stone Lanterns *see* Botan-doro (1955)
The Performers 320
Perils of Bangaku 320
The Phantom Cat 320
The Phantom Horse 320–21
The Pheonix *see* Hinotori
A Picture of Madame Yuki *see* Portrait of Madame Yuki
Pigs and Battleships *see* The Flesh Is Hot
Pilgrimage to Japanese Baths 321
The Pink Ladies Motion Picture *see* Pinku Redei no Katsudoshashin
Pinku Redei no Katsudoshashin 321
The Pit 321
The Pit of Death *see* The Ghostly Trap
The Pitfall 321
Planet Prince *see* Prince of Space
Plants from the Dunes 321
Play It Cool 321–22
Playboy President 322
The Pleasures of the Flesh 322
The Poem of the Blue Star 322
Poignant Story 322
Poppy 322–23
Porco Rosso 323
The Pornographers *see* The Amorists
The Pornographers: An Introduction to Anthropology *see* The Amorists

Portrait of Madame Yuki 324
Port Arthur 323
Portrait of Chieko 323
Portrait of Hell 323, **323**
Pou-san *see* Mr. Pu
Preparations for the Festival 324
Pressure of Guilt 324
Pride of the Campus 324
The Priest Killer Comes Back 324-25
Prince of Space 325
Prince Planet *see* Prince of Space
Princess from the Moon 325
Princess of Badger Palace 325
Princess Yang Kwei Fei 325-26
The Private Police 326
Procurers of Hell 326
The Prodigal Son 326
The Professional *see* The Professional–Golgo 13
The Professional–Golgo 13 326
The Profound Desire of the Gods *see* Kuregejima–Legends from a Southern Island
Project A-ko 327
A Promise 327
Prophecies of Nostradamus 327-28
Pumpkin 328
Punishment Room 328
Pursuit at Dawn 328
Puss'n Boots 328

Queen Bee 328-29
Quick-Draw Okatsu 329
The Quiet Duel 329

The Rabble 329
Radishes and Carrots *see* Twilight Path
Rainbow Bridge 329
Rainbow Brite and the Star Stealer 330
Rainbow Kids 330
Ran 330-31
The Ransom *see* High and Low
Rashomon 331-32, **331**
Rat Kid on Journey 332
Rebellion 332
Record of a Living Being *see* I Live in Fear
Record of a Tenement Gentleman 332
Red Angel 332-33
Red Beard 333
Red-Light District *see* Street of Shame
Red Lion 333
Renegade Ninjas 333-34
Repast 334
Resurrection of the Beast 334
The Return of Masseur Ichi 334
The Return of the Giant Majin 334-35
The Return of the Giant Monsters 335
Return of the Streetfighter 335-36
Return to Manhood 336
The Revenge of King Kong *see* King Kong Escapes
The Revenge of Yukinojo: Revenge of a Kabuki Actor 336
The Revengeful Spirit of Eros 336
Rhapsody in August 336
The Rickishaw [sic] Man 336-37
The Rickshaw Man *see* The Rickishaw Man
Rika 337
Rikyu 337
Rise Against the Sword 337-38
Rise, Fair Sun 338
River of Fireflies 338
River of Forever 338
River Solo Flows 338
The River with No Bridge 338-39
Road to Eternity *see* The Human Condition (Part II: Road to Eternity)
Roar of the Crowd 339
Robot Carnival 339-40
The Rocking Horsemen 340
Rodan 340
Rodan the Flying Monster *see* Rodan
Romance and Rhythm 340
Romance Express 340-41
The Rose in the Mud *see* The Bad Sleep Well

The Saga of Anatahan 341
The Saga of Tanegashima 341
Saga of the Vagabonds 341
Sakuratai 8.6 341-42
Samurai 342, **343**
Samurai (Part II) 342
Samurai (Part III) 342-43
Samurai Assassin 343
Samurai Banners *see* Under the Banner of Samurai
Samurai from Nowhere 343-44
Samurai I *see* Samurai
Samurai I: Musashi Miyamoto *see* Samurai
Samurai Pirate *see* The Lost World of Sinbad
Samurai Reincarnation 344
Samurai Saga 344

Samurai II: Duel at Ichijoji Temple *see* Samurai (Part II)
Samurai III: Duel on Ganryu Island *see* Samurai (Part III)
Sandakan 8 344
The Sandal Keeper 344
Sanjuro 344–45
Sanshiro of Ginza 345
Sanshiro Sugata 345–46
Sanshiro Sugata—Part Two 346
Sansho the Bailiff 346
Savage Wolf Pack 346
Sayonara 347
Sayonara Jupiter 347
Scandal 347–48
The Scandalous Adventures of Buraikan 348
The Scarlet Camellia 348
The School 348
School of Love 348
Scuffle Elegy *see* Fighting Elegy
The Sea and Poison 348
The Sea Prince and the Fire Child 349
Secret Information 349
Secret of the Fylfot 349
The Secret of the Telegian 349–50
Secret Scrolls (Part I) 350
Secret Scrolls (Part II) 350
Secret Turkish Bath 350
Secret Zone of Tokyo 350–51
Secrets of a Woman's Temple 351
See You 351
Senbon Matsubara 351
Sennin Buraku 351
Sensation Seekers 351
Seven Mysteries 351
Seven Samurai *see* The Magnificent Seven
Sex and Life 352
The Sex Check 352
Sex Phobia 352
The Sexploiters 352
Shadow of Deception 352
The Shadow Within 352–53
Shanghai Rhapsody 353
She and He 353
She Was Like a Wild Chrysanthemum 353
Shimantogawa 353
Shinran: Path to Purity 353
Shinshaku Yotsuya kaidan 353–54
Shogun (James Clavell's) 354–56, **355**
Shogun Assassin 356
The Shogun Assassins 356
Shogun Mayeda *see* Journey of Honor
Shogun's Ninja 356–57
Shogun's Shadow 357
Shonen tanteidan 357
Showdown at Nagasaki 357
Showdown for Zatoichi 357
Siege of Fort Bismarck 357–58
Sign of the Jack 358
Silence Has No Wings 358
The Silent Duel *see* The Quiet Duel
Silent Mobius *see* Neo Tokyo
The Silent Stranger 358
The Silk Road 358–59
The Silk Tree Ballad 359
The Sin *see* The Outcast
The Sinners of Hell 359
The Sinners to Hell *see* The Sinners of Hell
Sir Galahad in Campus [sic] *see* Bull of the Campus
Sister Streetfighter 359
Sisters of Gion 359–60, **360**
Sisters of the Gion *see* Sisters of Gion
Six Suspects 360
Sky Scraper! 360
Slums of Tokyo 360
The Snake Girl and the Silver-Haired Witch 360–61
Snow Country (1957) 361
Snow Country (1965) 361
Snow Fairy 361
Snow in the South Seas 361
Snow Trail 362
The Snow Woman 362
So Young, So Bright 362
Soft Touch of Night 362
Solar Crisis 362–65
A Soldier's Prayer *see* The Human Condition (Part III)
Son of Godzilla 365–66
Sonatine 366
The Song from My Heart 366
Song of Home 366
Song of the Camp 366–67
SOS from the Earth 367
Souls of the Road 367
The Sound of the Waves *see* The Surf
Space Cruiser Yamato 367
Space Firebird 367
Space Greyhound *see* Invasion of the Neptune Men
Space Men Appear Over Tokyo *see* The Mysterious Satellite

Space Monster Dogora *see* Dagora, the Space Monster
Space Warriors 2000 367–68
Spoils of the Night 368
Spook Warfare *see* Ghosts on Parade
Spring Comes to the Ladies 368
Stage-Struck Tora-san 368
Star Force: Fugitive Alien II 368
Star of Hong Kong 368–69
Starfire *see* Solar Crisis
Station 369
Step on the Gas! 369
The Sting of Death 369
Stolen Love 369
Stopover Tokyo 369–70
Stormy Era 370
A Story from Chikamatsu 370
Story of a Prostitute 370
Story of Cruelty *see* Naked Youth
A Story of Floating Weeds 370–71
The Story of Tank Commander Nishizumi 371
The Story of the Last Chrysanthemums 371–72
A Straightforward Boy 372
The Strange Tale of Oyuki 372
Strawberry Road 372
Stray Dog 372
The Street Fighter 373, **373**
Street of Shame 373–74
The Streetfighter's Last Revenge 374
Structure of Hate 374
Submersion of Japan 374, **375**
Summer Clouds 375
The Summer Clouds *see* Summer Clouds
Summer of the Moonlight 375
Summer Vacation 1999 375–76
Sumo Do, Sumo Don't 376
Sun Above, Death Below 376
Sun-Wu King 376
The Sun's Burial 376
Super Monster 376–77
Super Monster Gamera *see* Super Monster
Supergiant 377–78
Superman on Gale 378
The Surf 378
The Swamp 378
Sweet Sweat 378–79
The Sweetheart *see* The Lover (1953)
Swirling Butterflies 379
The Sword of Doom 379
The Sword of Penitence 379
Sword of Vengeance 379–80
Swords of Death 380
Swords of the Space Ark 380

The Taira Clan *see* New Tales of the Taira Clan
Takamaru and Kikumaru 380
Takarajima Ensei 380
Take Care, Red Riding Hood 380–81
Takeshi—Childhood Days 381
Takeshi—Childhood Days *see* Takashi—Childhood Days
A Tale from Chikamatsu *see* A Story from Chikamatsu
Tale of a Carpenter 381
A Tale of Africa *see* The Green Horizon
A Tale of Genji 381
A Tale of Peonies and Lanterns *see* Kaidan botandoro
Tales After the Rain *see* Tales of Ugetsu
Tales of Ugetsu 381–82, **381**
Talk of the Town Tora-san 382
Tampopo 382–83
Tange-Sazen 383
Taro, the Dragon Boy 383
Tasmania Story 383
Tatsu 383–84
The Tattered Banner 384
Tattooed Swordswoman 384
Tattooed Temptress 384
A Taxing Woman 384–85
A Taxing Woman's Return (Juzo Itami's) 385
Tea and Rice 386
Teahouse of the August Moon 386
Tell It to the Dolls 386
Temple of the Golden Pavilion 386
Temptation in Glamour Island 386–87
The Temptress *see* The Temptress and the Monk
The Temptress and the Monk 387
Ten Dark Women 387
Tenamonya: Ghost Journey *see* Tenamonya yurei dochu
Tenamonya yurei dochu 387
Tenchu! 387–88
Terrible Ghost-Cat of Okazaki *see* Kaibyo Okazaki sodo
Terror Beneath the Sea 388
The Terror of Godzilla *see* Terror of Mechagodzilla
Terror of Mechagodzilla 388–89
Tetsuo: The Iron Man 389–90, **389**

Tetsuo II: Body Hammer 390
That Night's Wife 390
Theater of Life 390
There Was a Father 390
They Who Step on the Tail of the Tiger *see* The Men Who Tread on the Tiger's Tail
The Thin Line 390–91
30,000 Miles Under the Sea 391
This Greedy Old Skin 391
This Is Noriko 391
This Madding Crowd 391
This Transient Life 391
This Way, That Way 391–92
Those Who Make Tomorrow 392
Those Who Tread on the Tiger's Tail *see* The Men Who Tread on the Tiger's Tail
Thou Shalt Not Be Jealous *see* Yotsuya kaidan
Thousand Cranes 392
Three Bad Men in a Hidden Fortress *see* The Hidden Fortress
Three Dolls and Three Guys 392
Three Dolls from Hong Kong 392–93
Three Dolls Go to Hong Kong *see* Three Dolls from Hong Kong
Three Dolls in College 393
Three Dolls in Ginza 393
365 Nights 393
Three Old Ladies 393
Three Old Women *see* Three Old Ladies
Three Stripes in the Sun 393–94
The Three Treasures 394
The Three Undelivered Letters 394
Throne of Blood 394–95
Through Days and Months 395
Thumbelina 395
Tidal Wave *see* The Submersion of Japan
Tiger Flight 395
Till Tomorrow Comes 395
Till We Meet Again 395
The Time of Reckoning 395–96
Time of the Apes 396
Time Slip 396
To Live *see* Ikiru
To Love Again 396
To Sleep So as to Dream 396–97
Toki o kakeru shojo 397
Tokkan 397
Tokugawa onna keibatsushi 397
Tokyo Bad Girls 397
Tokyo Bath Harem 397–98
Tokyo Blackout 398
Tokyo Bordello 398
Tokyo Chorus 398
Tokyo Decadence 398
Tokyo Drifter 398–99
Tokyo File 212 399
Tokyo March 399
Tokyo 196X 399
Tokyo Olympiad 399–401, **400**
Tokyo Pop 401
Tokyo Story 401–2
Tokyo Twilight 402
Tombstone for Fireflies 402
Tomei ningen 402
Tomei ningen arawaru 402
Tomei ningen erohakase 402
Tom's Adventures 403
Toppo Gigio and the Missile War 403
Topsy-Turvy Journey 403
Tora! Tora! Tora! 403–5
Tora's Pure Love 405
Tora's Tropical Fever 405
Tora-san: Love Under the Umbrella *see* Tora-san's Rise and Fall
Tora-san and a Lord *see* Tora-san Meets His Lordship
Tora-san Confesses 406
Tora-san Finds a Sweetheart *see* Tora-san's Rise and Fall
Tora-san Goes French *see* Tora-san Loves an Artist
Tora-san Goes North 406
Tora-san Goes Religious? 406–7
Tora-san Goes to Vienna 407
Tora-san, His Tender Love 407
Tora-san Homebound *see* Tora-san's Runaway
Tora-san in Love *see* Tora-san's Shattered Romance
Tora-san Loves an Artist 407
Tora-san Makes Excuses 407–8
Tora-san Meets His Lordship 408
Tora-san Meets the Songstress Again *see* Tora-san's Rise and Fall
Tora-san, My Uncle 408
Tora-san, Our Lovable Tramp *see* Am I Trying
Tora-san, Pt. 2 408
Tora-san Plays Cupid 408–9
Tora-san Plays Daddy 409
Tora-san Riding High *see* Tora-san, the Matchmaker
Tora-san Takes a Vacation 409
Tora-san, the Expert 409
Tora-san, the Go-Between 409–10
Tora-san, the Good Samaritan 410

Tora-san, the Intellectual 410
Tora-san, the Matchmaker 410
Tora-san's Bluebird Fantasy 410-11
Tora-san's Cherished Mother *see* Tora-san Pt. 2
Tora-san's Dear Old Home 411
Tora-san's Dream-Come-True 411
Tora-san's Dream of Spring 411-12, **413**
Tora-san's Forbidden Love 412
Tora-san's Forget Me Not 412
Tora-san's Grand Scheme 412
Tora-san's Island Encounter 412-13
Tora-san's Love Call 413
Tora-san's Love in Osaka 413-14
Tora-san's Love Song *see* Tora-san's Love Call
Tora-san's Lovesick 414, **414**
Tora-san's Lovesickness *see* Tora-san's Lovesick
Tora-san's Lullaby 415
Tora-san's Many-Splintered Love *see* Tora-san's Love in Osaka
Tora-san's New Romance *see* Tora-san's Dear Old Home
Tora-san's Promise 415
Tora-san's Rise and Fall 415
Tora-san's Runaway 415-16
Tora-san's Salad Day Memorial 416
Tora-san's Shattered Romance 416
Tora-san's Song of Love 416-17
Tora-san's Sunrise and Sunset 417
Tora-san's Sunset Glow *see* Tora-san's Sunrise and Sunset
Tough Guy 417
Tracked 417
Traffic Jam 417
Tragic Ghost Story of Fukagawa *see* Kaidan Fukagawa jowa
The Transparent Man *see* Tomei ningen arawaru
The Transparent Man vs. the Fly Man 417
Trapped, the Crimson Bat 418
Treasure Mountain 418
Tree Without Leaves 418
Tsuru 418
Tunnel to the Sun 418
Twelve Chapters About Women 418-19
20 Faces 419
Twenty-Four Eyes 419
Twilight of the Cockroaches 419
Twilight Path 419-20
The Twilight Story 420
Twin Sisters of Kyoto 420
Twinkle 420
Two Hearts in the Rain 420
Two Iida 420-21
Two in the Shadow 421
226 *see* Four Days of Snow and Blood

Ugetsu *see* Tales of Ugetsu
Ugetsu monogatari *see* Tales of Ugetsu
Ukiyoe 421
Ultraman *see* Urutoraman
The Ultraman *see* Urutoraman
Uminchu—The Old Man and the East China Sea 421
Under the Banner of Samurai 421
Under the Blossoming Cherry Trees 421-22
The Underground Syndicate 422
Unholy Desire 422
Unico in the Island of Magic 422
Universal Laws 422
Unknown Satellite Over Tokyo *see* The Mysterious Satellite
Until the Day We Meet Again 422
An Urban Affair 422-23
Urutoraman 423
Urutoraman sutori 423
Utamaro and His Five Women 423
Utamaro, Painter of Women 423-24

Vacuum Zone 424
The Vampire Doll 424
Vampire Hunter D 424
Vampire Man *see* The Woman Vampire
Vanity of the Shogun's Mistress 424-25
Varan the Unbelievable 425-26, **425**
Vengeance Is Mine 426
Victory of Women 426-27
Victory Song 427
Vietnam in Turmoil 427
The Village 427, **428**
Village of Eight Gravestones 427-29
Violated Angels *see* Okasarete Byuakui
Violated Paradise 429
Violated Women *see* Okasarete Byuakui
Virus 429-30
Vixen 430-31
Voyage Into Space 31

Waiting for the Flood 431
Walk Cheerfully 431
Walkers on the Tiger's Tail *see* The Men Who Tread on the Tiger's Tail
Wall-Eyed Nippon 431

The Wanderers 431-32
Wanton Journey 432
War and Youth 432
The War in Space 432
War of the Gargantuas 432-33
War of the Monsters (1966) 433
War of the Monsters (1972) *see* Godzilla on Monster Island
War of the Planets *see* The War in Space
Warehouse *see* The Blind Beast
Warning from Space *see* The Mysterious Satellite
Warring Clans 433
Warriors of the Wind 433
Watari and the Seven Monsters *see* The Magic Sword of Watari
Watari, Ninja Boy 434
Watch Out, Crimson Bat! 434
The Water Magician 434
Waterfront Blues 434
The Way-Out Shrine 434
Way Out, Way In 434-35
The Wayside Pebble 435
We Are Not Alone 435
We Will Remember 435
Weak-kneed from Fear of Ghost-Cat *see* Kaibyo koshinuke daisodo
Weaker Sex 435
Wedding March 435
The Weed of Crime 435-36
The Weird Love Makers 436
The Weird Lovemakers *see* The Weird Love Makers
Weird Tales *see* Kwaidan
Weird Trip *see* Kaidan ryoko
Westward Deperado 436
The Whale God 436
What Did the Lady Forget? 436-37
What the Birds Knew *see* I Live in Fear
What's Up, Tiger Lily? (Woody Allen's) 437
When a Woman Ascends the Stairs 437
When Chimneys Are Seen 437-38
Where Now Are the Dreams of Youth? 438
Where Spring Comes Late 438
Whirlpool of Flesh *see* Whirlpool of Women
Whirlpool of Women 438
Whirlwind 438-39
Whispering Joe 439
A Whistle in My Heart 439
White Rose of Hong Kong 439
The White Snake Enchantress *see* Panda and the Magic Serpent
White Wolf 439
The Widower *see* An Autumn Afternoon
Wife! Be Like a Rose! 439-40
Wife Lost 440
The Wife of Seishu Hanaoka 440
Wild Geese *see* Mistress
Wild Love-Makers *see* The Weird Love Makers
The Wild Sea 440
Wildcat Rock 440
Will to Conquer 440
Willful Murder 440-41
Willy McBean and His Magic Machine 441
The Wiser Age 441
Witness Killed 441
The Wolves 441
Wolves of the City 441
Wolves of the City, Check Mate 442
The Woman Gambler 442
Woman in the Dunes 442
The Woman of Osaka 442
A Woman of Rumor 442-43
A Woman of Tokyo 443
The Woman Vampire 443
The Woman Who Touched the Legs 443
Woman's Body Vanishes *see* Jotai johatsu
A Woman's Life 443
A Woman's Testament 443-44
Women of Design 444
Women of the Night 444
Women. . . Oh, Women! 444
Women Smell of Night 444
Women's Police 444
Women's Police, Part II 444-45
Women's Prison *see* Hiroku onna ro
Wonderful Sunday *see* One Wonderful Sunday
Wonderful World of Music *see* The Wonder World of Song!
The Wonderful World of Song! 445
World War Three Breaks Out *see* The Final War
The Worse You Are the Better Your Sleep *see* The Bad Sleep Well
The Worship of the Flesh 445

The X from Outer Space 445

Yagyu Secret Scrolls *see* Secret Scrolls (Part I)

Yang Kwei Fei *see* Princess Yang Kwei Fei
Yearning 445–46
The Yellow Handkerchief 446
The Yen Family 446
Yoba 446
Yog—Monster from Space 446–48, **447**
Yojimbo *see* Yojimbo the Bodyguard
Yojimbo the Bodyguard 448
Yokohama Girl 448
Yongary, Monster from the Deep 448–49
Yosakoi Journey 449
Yotsuya kaidan 449
You Can Succeed, Too 449
The Young Beast 449–50
Young Guy Graduates 450
Young Guy on Mt. Cook 450
A Young Man's Stronghold 450
Young People 450
The Young Rebel *see* The Bastard
Young Swordsman 450
Younger Brother *see* Her Brother
Youth 450–51
The Youth and His Amulet 451
Youth in Fury 451
The Youth of Heiji Zenigata 451
Youth of the Beast 451–52
Yumeji 452

Zatoichi (1963) 452–53
Zatoichi (1989) 453
Zatoichi and the Doomed Men 453
Zatoichi and the Scoundrels *see* Zatoichi (1963)
Zatoichi at Large 453
Zatoichi Challenged 453–54
Zatoichi Enters Again 454
Zatoichi Fighting Drums *see* Zatoichi: The Blind Swordsman Samaritan
Zatoichi Goes Abroad *see* Zatoichi: The Blind Swordsman's Pilgrimage
Zatoichi in Desperation 453–54
Zatoichi: Masseur Ichi and a Chest of Gold 454
Zatoichi Meets His Equal 454–55
Zatoichi Meets the One-Armed Swordsman *see* Zatoichi Meets His Equal
Zatoichi Meets Yojimbo 455
Zatoichi on the Road *see* Zatoichi (1963)
Zatoichi: The Blind Swordsman and the Fugitives 455
Zatoichi: The Blind Swordsman Samaritan 455–56
Zatoichi: The Blind Swordsman's Cane-Sword *see* Zatoichi's Cane-Sword
Zatoichi: The Blind Swordsman's Fire Festival 456
Zatoichi: The Blind Swordsman's Pilgrimage 456–57
Zatoichi: The Blind Swordsman's Rescue 457
Zatoichi: The Blind Swordsman's Revenge 457
Zatoichi: The Blind Swordsman's Vengeance 457
Zatoichi, the Fugitive 457
Zatoichi vs. Yojimbo *see* Zatoichi Meets Yojimbo
Zatoichi's Cane-Sword 458
Zatoichi's Conspiracy 458
Zatoichi's Flashing Sword 458–59
Zatoichi's Pilgrimage *see* Zatoichi: The Blind Swordsman's Pilgrimage
Zegen 459
Zeram 459, **459**
Zero Fighters 459–60
Zigeunerwisen 460
Zoku hiroku onna ro 460